01   2010

Encyclopedic Dictionary of

Cults, Sects, and World Religions

Encyclopedic Dictionary of

Cults, Sects, and World Religions

REVISED AND UPDATED EDITION

LARRY A. NICHOLS • GEORGE A. MATHER • ALVIN J. SCHMIDT
KURT VAN GORDEN, CONSULTING EDITOR

FORMERLY PUBLISHED AS DICTIONARY OF
CULTS, SECTS, RELIGIONS, AND THE OCCULT

ZONDERVAN ®

GRAND RAPIDS, MICHIGAN 49530

ZONDERVAN.COM/
AUTHORTRACKER

We want to hear from you. Please send your comments about this book to us in care of zreview@zondervan.com. Thank you.

ZONDERVAN ®

Encyclopedic Dictionary of Cults, Sects, and World Religions
Copyright © 2006 by George A. Mather, Larry A. Nichols, and Alvin J. Schmidt

Formerly published as *Dictionary of Cults, Sects, Religions, and the Occult*

Requests for information should be addressed to:

Zondervan, *Grand Rapids, Michigan 49530*

Library of Congress Cataloging-in-Publication Data
    Mather, George A.
      Dictionary of cults, sects, and world religions / George A. Mather, Larry A. Nichols, Alvin J. Schmidt.— Rev. and updated ed.
         p. cm.
      Rev. ed. of: Dictionary of cults, sects, religions, and the occult. 1993.
      Summary: "This updated dictionary explores a variety of religious beliefs"—Provided by publisher.
      Includes bibliographical references and index.
      ISBN-10: 0-310-23954-0 (alk. paper)
      ISBN-13: 978-0-310-23954-3
      1. Religions—Dictionaries. 2. Cults—Dictionaries. 3. Sects—Dictionaries. I. Nichols, Larry A. II. Schmidt, Alvin J. III. Mather, George A. Dictionary of cults, sects, religions, and the occult. IV. Title.
    BL31.M295 2005
    200'.3—dc22
                                      2005000820
                                          CIP

This edition printed on acid-free paper.

Interior design by Nancy Wilson

Printed in the United States of America

06 07 08 09 10 • 10 9 8 7 6 5 4 3 2 1

George Mather would like to dedicate this book to those friends and family who have been a continued source of encouragement during the writing of this book.

Larry Nichols would like to dedicate this book in loving memory of his mother, Joyce Nichols, and his father-in-law, Alfred Medeiros, along with all of the members of Our Redeemer Evangelical Lutheran Church, Smithfield, Rhode Island.

Alvin Schmidt would like to dedicate this book to his two sons, Timothy and Mark, to help them see that religious diversity does not conform to what Christ said, "Not everyone who says to me, 'Lord, Lord,' will enter into the kingdom of heaven."

Table of Contents

Acknowledgments   9

Introduction 11

World Religions 15

Dictionary Entries 353

Appendixes 467

Bibliography 477

Indexes. 523

Acknowledgments

The authors would like to acknowledge various individuals for their support and contributions to this project.

George and Larry extend thanks to Alvin Schmidt, who has come aboard as one of the authors. In the first edition he served as consulting editor. It has been good to have him contribute his scholarship.

We thank Kurt van Gorden, our present consulting editor, for his very careful reading of the entire manuscript and his many helpful suggestions, comments, and constructive criticisms along the way. Kurt has done a yeoman's work and is a true servant of the cross of Christ.

We wish to thank Arthur Pena for his critical review of the article on The Baha'i Faith. We thank Keith MacGregor and MacGregor Ministries, Kurt van Gorden, Jill Rische, Paul Carden, Arthur Varnick, and Dale Broadhurst for their review and remarks on Mormonism. Concerning the Jehovah's Witnesses, we thank David Reed, Watchman Fellowship, and Christian Research Institute. We thank Verle and Orie Streifling for their contributions to the article on Seventh-day Adventism. We offer thanks to Gary Zeolla for providing helpful information on several parts of the book. The authors acknowledge and thank Robert Pardon, the director of the New England Institute for Religious Research.

Special thanks goes to Lois Smith for her tireless work in xeroxing the entire hard copy used in the editing process. We also thank Melissa Nichols for her work on the appendixes.

Larry Nichols would like to note that during the final months of writing, his mother was afflicted with a terminal illness. The dedication of this book is for her along with his late father-in-law and grandparents. At the same time, Larry's father was diagnosed with cancer. By the grace of God, he has had successful surgery and has recovered. He wants to thank both of his parents (as was done in the first edition) for their love, prayers, and support through the years.

Larry would like to acknowledge and thank professors who have taught him throughout the years:

John Calvin Holsinger, history professor at Evangel University, who has kept in touch and has been a constant source of encouragement for continuing to pursue graduate studies

John Stroup, professor of church history at Yale University Divinity School (now at Rice University), who taught his students to think and write critically and at times skeptically

Paul Holmer, George Lindbeck, (the late) Hans Frei, and Brevard Childs of Yale University

Arthur Just, who taught him to understand Luke and the sacraments

the late Robert Preus, who manifested a breadth of knowledge of Post-Lutheran systematic theology and a deep understanding of the doctrine of "justification by grace through faith"

Timothy Quill, who, because of the first edition to this encyclopedic dictionary, invited him to participate in the "Russian Project"—that is, to teach at the Siberian Lutheran Seminary in Russia and at the Luther Academy in Latvia

David Scaer ("All theology is Christology"), for teaching all of his students to *never* take ourselves too seriously, but to take Christ most seriously

William Weinrich, a great patristics scholar whose writings and personal conversations through the years have proved most enlightening

Dean Wenthe, for his outstanding scholarship, exceptional leadership, and deep insights into the ongoing narrative of the Old/New Testament church and the response of the church to today's postmodern world.

Finally, we would together reserve our deepest appreciation for our wives and children, who certainly sacrificed the most. Larry Nichols would acknowledge his wife, Zelia, for her constant love and devotion and patience for putting up with his many hours at the computer. His daughters—Melissa, Charissa, Alicia, and

Faythe—are the wonderful gifts of God for whom he is deeply thankful.

George Mather would like to thank his wife, Sharon, for her patience during the writing of this work, and acknowledge his daughter, Jennnifer, and his sons, Khristian, Joshua and wife, Shannon, and Andrew and wife, Berenice. He would also like to acknowledge his grandchildren: Grace, Priscilla, Benjamin, Ethan, Emma, and Vasty, along with his sister Charlotte, and her husband, Paul, and his brother Jack, and his wife, Mary, his mother-in-law, Phyllis, and her husband, Bob.

Alvin Schmidt would like to thank and acknowledge his wife, Carol, fort her support and patience.

Introduction

When the First Amendment to the Constitution of the United States of America was added, it was agreed that Congress and government in general would not be actively supporting or participating in the *establishment* of religion, nor would it be in the business of *prohibiting the free exercise thereof.* Religious life in our newly formed country would never be the same thereafter. The religious milieu and the historical context in which the First Amendment was first applied were to the so-called "Judeo-Christian" (mostly Christian) heritage. Had this and many other books whose theme addresses American religious cults, sects, and new religions been written in the late 1700s, they would be considerably thinner volumes.

Changes over the centuries of this nation's comparatively short history, however, have been voluminous. The nineteenth and twentieth centuries witnessed a veritable explosion of growth into the many denominations of Christendom. Adherents to the world religions and the cults have found a welcome home under the protection of the First Amendment. In just the thirteen years since the first edition of this volume (1993), the authors have labored to keep up with the rapid evolution of multifarious new religious groups that are constantly springing up.

In recent decades, words like "multiculturalism," "diversity," and "postmodernism" have become household nomenclature in religious dialogue or conversation. Many people today distinguish between religion and spirituality. The former is (negatively) associated with organized objective and structured forms of religious expression while many understand the latter as a mystical and liberating opportunity to tap into the inner soul in the quest for religious meaning independent of the extraneous discipline of objective religion.

In the words of Ronald Enroth, the writer of the foreword to our first volume, "religious freedom has allowed for and in fact encouraged, religious pluralism." Multiculturalism is a word that not only describes the cultural diversity of America, but the complete and total tolerance of *religious* diversity as well. All religions are considered equally valid or equally invalid—that is, if we press the meaning of postmodernism. In the postmodern outlook on life, truth (religious truth or otherwise) is not believed to lie in objective propositions contained in a sacred or even in a scientific text. Truth is simply not there to be encountered, apprehended, or discovered. Truth in a postmodern world is manufactured and contextualized, rendering a meaning for the moment to propositions and utterances.

The authors of this volume are committed to the belief that there is, in fact, objective truth that can be discovered or encountered. We know that Christianity's claim that the Bible is God's inspired Word, providentially preserved in the sacred texts of both the Old and New Testaments, is the truth. We know that there is an answer to Pilate's question, "What is truth?" (John 18:38), and Thomas's confusion (John 14:5) and his doubt (John 20:24–29). The answer we moderns of the early twenty-first century give is that Jesus Christ is "the way, the truth and the life" (John 14:6). Our volume attempts to present this central truth to those who believe a host of other competing claims, whether it be the vague spirituality of the New Age Movement, the various "enlightenments" of Hindu and Buddhist gurus, the utopia of Mormonism, or the dark world of magic, neopaganism, satanism, and witchcraft.

Concerning this volume, we believe that in the spirit of St. Peter, we are engaging in the task of rendering "an answer to everyone who asks [us] to give the reason for the hope [we] have" (1 Peter 3:15). And in the spirit of St. Paul in his encounter with the worldly philosophers on the Areopagus (Acts 17), we are offering a challenge to the religious pluralism of our own day. This volume rests on the foundation of "Christ and him crucified" (1 Cor. 2:2); thus, all competing claims that challenge that Christ is the truth or suggest that there are other ways to salvation are therefore false. We also believe that "those who oppose us [we] must gently instruct, in the hope that God will grant them repentance leading … to a knowledge of the truth" (2 Tim. 2:25).

This is the second edition to our first volume *Dictionary of Cults, Sects, Religions, and the Occult*. This new edition has taken on the threefold task of updating, adding/including, and excluding/deleting.

In terms of *updating*, much has happened in the last thirteen years in the histories of the groups originally covered in the first edition. One need only think for a moment about Islam, the attacks of terrorists on 9/11/01, and the subsequent wars with Afghanistan and Iraq. Much has also happened in the world of the cults and the occult.

It has also been a task of *including* new religious developments that have transpired since then. On the week when the first edition was published, we were getting calls from the media and other interested parties as to our knowledge of David Koresh and the burning of the Branch Davidian compound in Waco, Texas. The fact of the matter is that we did not include, nor did we know much of anything about, the Waco group when we turned in our manuscript to our publisher in 1992, several months before the country and the world would know about the Branch Davidians's standoff with the U.S. government.

This new edition has included the Branch Davidians, along with the other new groups that have come into existence. We have included numerous new articles including Native American religion, the Masonic Lodge, Aum Supreme Truth, Heaven's Gate, the Boston Movement, and so on, along with numerous new terms and personalities to the dictionary portion of this work.

Several articles of the original volume that that have been *excluded* from this new edition were not necessarily eliminated because they ceased to exist or no longer exerted significant influence on contemporary America society, but because there was simply nothing new to say. Readers would be equally served by reading our first edition.

This volume's arrangement has also changed from the first edition. The first volume was entirely arranged alphabetically. This second edition has separated the encyclopedic articles on religions, cults, and sects from the dictionary terms and personalities associated with the groups included in the encyclopedic section. Whenever a major religious group included in a longer encyclopedic entry appears, the group is put into small capital letters (e.g., MORMONISM).

When a dictionary term or a person associated with a particular group included in the encyclopedic section appears, it is noted with this symbol ⸿. For example, the term ⸿Aaronic priesthood informs the reader that this term is in the dictionary portion of the volume. Personal names appear in the dictionary portion, such as Joseph ⸿Smith (the last named being noted). The reader will seek information under "S" for ⸿Smith, not "J" for Joseph.

As far as overall structure of the entries is concerned, the encyclopedic articles include the following general outline:

Name of the group
Brief introduction
History of the group
Organization
Teachings, beliefs. (accompanied by a Christian evaluation of the religion)
Conclusion
Address
Website
Sacred Text(s)
Literature
Statistics
Notes

Regarding the shorter dictionary entries, the group that each term is associated with appears in parentheses at the head of each entry. To follow our Mormon example, the *name* "Joseph Smith" appears as follows:

Smith, Joseph (MORMONISM). *Then follows a description who Joseph Smith was.*

The Mormon *term* "Aaronic Priesthood" in the dictionary portion appears similarly as:

Aaronic Priesthood (MORMONISM). *The definition of this term.*

There are also several appendixes (see the Table of Contents).

The authors have each contributed to this volume in the following way:

George Mather was responsible for the gathering of data, sources, some of the photos, writing some of the definitions, and editing.

Larry Nichols sifted through the data, provided additional research, and wrote most of the articles. He also updated the bibliography and the appendices in the first volume, including the new one on claims of exclusivity of cult leaders.

Alvin Schmidt, the consulting editor in the first edition, authored and edited a number of the articles in this second edition.

Kurt van Gorden, our consulting editor, read each of the articles and dictionary terms carefully and edited the entire manuscript.

Recognizing that an attempt to be encyclopedic and at the same time current with regard to telling the story of religions and their respective developments is only successful if it remains an ongoing project. Books, like photographs, capture isolated moments in time that exclude the future. One must continue to write as one must continue to snap photos as the future progresses. We therefore look forward to the possibility of a third edition someday in order that the narrative may remain up to date.

We relate our work in the name of him who is "the Alpha and the Omega . . . who is, and who was, and who is to come, the Almighty" (Rev. 1:8).

—*Larry Nichols*

World Religions

ABAKUA

Abakua dance and music have been popularized by dance companies as a harmless cultural heritage. Abakua, however, is much more than music and dance troupes. Also called Naniguismo, it is an all-male secret religious society in Cuba. It is one of many religions blending together West African, Cuban, and Christian elements. The slave trade of the seventeenth and eighteenth centuries saw the transport of native Africans to the West Indies, and when they arrived at their new homes, they brought along with them their culture, music, and religion.

HISTORY

In Cuba, Abakua is considered to be the most African of all the West Indies ᵇcults. Abakua began as a secret society in 1834 in the village of La Regla, Cuba. The group was named after its leader, Abakua. His strategy was to form a number of independent societies in order to make it difficult for the secrets of the cult to be revealed or exposed. Originally, whites and mulattoes were barred so as to retain a strictly African influence.

Four major ethnic groups from Africa were taken to Cuba: the ᵇBantu, ᵇYoruba, and Ibibio, and the ᵇDahomey (present-day Benin) people, called *Ewe/Fon*. Today, the Abakua cult consists of two large groups: the ᵇEfo group, which still excludes whites from membership; and the ᵇEfi group, which has relaxed its reins a bit, allowing nonblacks to become members. Despite ambitious proselytizing efforts on the part of Roman Catholic missionaries, both Portuguese and Spanish, these West Africans and the natives indigenous to the regions of the West Indies and South America have consistently refused to allow CHRISTIANITY an exclusive place in their considerable pantheon of deities. Any attempt on the part of the Christian church to replace the cultic rituals of these peoples has steadily been resisted.

ORGANIZATION

It varies from group to group. Because of the secret nature of the societies, no accurate organizational model can be presented. The lavish ceremonies are described below.

BELIEFS AND PRACTICES

The priests of the Abakua cult, called ᵇokobio, are all male, with the exception of one priestess called a ᵇca-sican. The worship centers around the temple, called the ᵇfamba. Candles, plants, bowls, and other instruments adorn the altars of the *famba*. Christian influence is evidenced by the presence of crucifixes and pictures of the Christ child and the Virgin.

Music is extremely important in Abakua ceremonies. The drums, called by various names (*see* ᵇerikunde, ᵇekon, ᵇmaracas, and ᵇifon), play rhythms that are strictly African. The dance, the music, and the sacrifices all center around the goal of conjuring up a supernatural spirit popularly known as the ᵇdiablito. The name used by members of the cult for this spirit is ᵇIreme. The shaking action of the *maracas* is instrumental in causing *Ireme* to appear. In his left hand he holds an *ifan*, and in his right, the *iton*. The presence of *Ireme* is announced by the ringing of metal bells known as ᵇenkanika. *Ireme* is adorned in a decorative mask and his presence wards off evil spirits. The whole concept of the *diablito* is West African. There is no syncretism with indigenous cultic practices of Cuban Indians.

Much of the Abakua ritual is derived from religious rites of the Yoruba. The ᵇdivination practices are parallel. Initiates undergo ceremonies wherein they are baptized by soil contained in a bowl made from a skull. The alternate method of initiation, used by the *Efi* group, is to pour water on the initiate and cover or sprinkle him with ᵇalbahaca. The new member becomes servant to a specific ᵇorisha, and he is then referred to as ᵇomo-orisha. Often the new member comes to the group with a Christian name. Upon initiation, he or she is assigned an African name that is forever to remain their secret identity.

As stated above, Christian missionaries have met with much disappointment and a sense of failure in their many attempts to bring the gospel of Christ to the devotees of Abakua. It is not that Christianity is out and out rejected, but it is adapted and incorporated into the pantheon of deities already worshiped by its adherents. Religious syncretism has had a long history dating back to Israel in the Old Testament. The judges, prophets, and righteous kings of Israel and Judah were often raised up by Yahweh to extirpate all idols and false gods as these were forbidden in the Israel's law (Ex. 20:1–6). This tradition was carried over into the New Testament as the early church taught that the center of faith is exclusively in the person and work of the

Lord Jesus Christ as described in Scripture and the ecumenical creeds (*see* Appendix 1).[1]

CONCLUSION

Abakua continues to flourish alongside numerous other cults in this unique area of the world. Many of the South American and Caribbean groups are making inroads into the United States, chiefly through migrations into the larger metropolitan areas of the country, particularly Miami and New York City.[2]

ADDITIONAL INFORMATION_____

Websites

www.rhythmweb.com/bongo/history.htm; www.folkcuba.com

Statistics

There are roughly six million people in Cuba who practice Afro-Cuban religions of various forms. Precisely how many of these are adherents of Abakua is indeterminate.

Notes

[1] See SOUTH AMERICAN, CENTRAL AMERICAN, and CARIBBEAN CULTS for a further evaluation of Christianity as a religious phenomenon in its encounter with West African cults.

[2] See SANTERIA and VOODOO for more specific observations of the growing links between South American and Caribbean cults.

AETHERIUS SOCIETY, THE (TAS)

"Service is the jewel in the rock of attainment!" Other phrases like "cosmic evolution of man," "read and evolve," and the claim, "For the first time the connection between the science of Yoga, the theology of all major religions and the mystery of UFOs is explained," greet those who happen upon the website of the Aetherius Society (TAS). There are a host of NEW AGE MOVEMENT ▶cults that are specifically classified as UFO groups. Several are covered in this present volume. Among the more popular is TAS.

HISTORY

The Aetherius Society, founded in 1955 in London, traces its beginnings back to George ▶King (1919–1997). King spent ten years mastering Yoga while residing in London. On May 8, 1954, he heard a loud, audible voice that he attributed to an extraterrestrial being, who told him, "Prepare yourself! You are to become the voice of Interplanetary Parliament." Eight days following this prophetic message, King was visited by a "world-renowned Yoga master" who entered the apartment while the door was locked and gave King certain instructions in advanced Yoga. From this, he was able to establish rapport with Master Aetherius, who resided on the planet Venus. King was selected as the "primary terrestrial channel" for communications between "space masters" and earthlings. King then founded the Aetherius Society.

King began to lecture in London, charging a small fee, but met with little or no success. During Operation Starlight, begun in 1958, King allegedly made contact with one Master Jesus who, like Aetherius, was residing on the planet Venus. Master Jesus gave King the first chapter of his ▶Aquarian Age Bible. King also

This ten-foot alien display was brought in for a Milwaukee fantasy convention. The UFO phenomenon is growing with such Hollywood TV events as *Roswell*.
Courtesy Jack M. Roper/CARIS

began to receive "transmissions" from Master Aetherius, which were subsequently published in a magazine titled *Aetherius Speaks*. In another revelation about Jesus, King attacked the virgin birth of Christ by claiming that Jesus was dropped to Earth by a spaceship, the "star of Bethlehem," and he denied Christ's divinity as the Son of God.

King gained a small audience in California who were open to his ideas. He claimed he was able to receive frequent transmissions from other voices of the cosmos, which he published. *Aetherius Speaks* was changed to the more descriptive title *Cosmic Voice*. At the bidding of the space masters, King was instructed to go to Los Angeles in 1959. The following year, TAS was incorporated in California. Amid his travels to the United States, Mr. King began calling himself "Dr. George King," although no record exists for an earned doctorate in any legitimate American institution.

Any transmissions from "cosmic masters" are recorded on tape. Three tapes of the received transmissions are made and stored in underground vaults in Los Angeles and other areas in California. Thus, all of the cosmic messages are preserved for the future. "In years to come, these tapes will be an impeachable [*sic*] reference source as to the exact words of the Cosmic Masters," says King.

ORGANIZATION

TAS is organized around its various centers. The American headquarters is located in Los Angeles and the European headquarters in London. There are various societies located in Canada, Africa, Australia, and New Zealand. One may seek membership by filling out an application that is available online. Membership is offered on three levels. A "Friend of the Aetherius Society" pays a small fee, receives the periodical and newsletter, and generally is considered a seeker who wishes to learn more. An "Associate Member" pays a higher annual fee, receives the periodicals, has read King's *The Nine Freedoms,* his treatise on evolution, and *The Cosmic Plan.* A *"*Full Member" supports the "cosmic missions" of the society. Full members pay the same fee as Associate Members. They make pilgrimages to holy mountains, attend prayer services in various locations around the world, visit hospitals, and administer "spiritual healing" to patients.

TEACHINGS

The essential mission of TAS is to serve. Aetherian minister Alex Moseley puts the matter bluntly: "We are not really popular. It's because our message is work and service. People don't want work and service." Numbered among the various service projects was Operation Bluewater. A glass pyramid filled with coils was maneuvered in a boat over the "psychic center" of the earth. According to King, Operation Bluewater prevented "the worst earthquake America would have ever known." "Operation Bluewater was completely successful," announced King to his followers at its conclusion. "The fact that the West Coast of America is intact proves its success."

Ascended Masters

The Ascended Masters are the long line of spiritual leaders who have ascended to the higher order of the cosmos and whose wisdom and powers are available to those are willing to seek and serve. They include Jesus, St. Germaine, El Morya, and the ▸Buddha. In 1954, King claims that he was to take up his place as the next of the next Cosmic Master.

Like a host of other religious personalities, King claimed to have been contacted by Master Jesus, who visited from Venus and gave him a new Aquarian Age Bible. Traditional orthodox CHRISTIANITY maintains the uniqueness of Jesus Christ (John 14:6), who "sits at the right hand of the Father" (Nicene Creed; see Appendix 1). Jesus, that is, is in heaven, at the right hand of the glory of God (Acts 7:55), not on Venus. He indeed was virgin-born (Matt. 1:23, a verse that also testifies to his deity as "God with us").

Extraterrestrial Life

King and members of TAS assumed the existence of energy planes in outer space. These beings are superior to those on Earth and can be evasive to the telescope and space travel. They make contact with select people on Earth when they choose to.

Humanity and Prayer

Each person exists within his or her consciousness. This means that after death, the soul survives the body, when it ascends to the ▸astral plane. Here it remains until the time comes for it to be reincarnated (see ▸reincarnation) in another body. Once born to another body, it is subjected to the law of Karma, only to be reincarnated again.

Traditional Christian doctrine also affirms the soul's distinction from the body. But at death, the Christian is brought into the presence of God in heaven (2 Cor. 5:6, 8) and will not be returned to the earth for another lifetime in another body (Heb. 9:26–28).

Christianity has little or nothing to say concerning

the existence of life in other regions of the universe. The Bible speaks concerning the existence of invisible beings such as ▸angels, ▸demons, and the like. But heaven is not described in terms of "energy planes" or a specific location in outer space. The word "eternal" (timeless) as distinguished from "temporal" (time) is used to describe the difference between heaven and earth (2 Cor. 4:18).

TAS believes that it forestalls world disaster through "Operation Prayer Power." The end of the world has been imminent for several decades. To respond to this threat, King constructed what is known as the "prayer battery." This device resembles a pale blue box and is designed to be "capable of receiving the highest frequencies of Spiritual Energies and putting them in a physical container." It is loaded on Thursday evenings at a "charging session." Here the prayer leader approaches the battery and begins to pray. His prayers are then graded by onlookers. Good prayers increase the power in the prayer battery; poor prayers decrease the charge. Prayer power stored up in the battery is reserved for crisis periods such as famines, earthquakes, wars, and other related phenomena. TAS members believe that the end of the world will come as a result of advanced technological developments and crass materialism.

TAS places much deal of emphasis on the study of extraterrestrial visits to earth by the Cosmic Masters. These visits prove the validity of Aetherian doctrines. TAS investigates UFO reports and claims worldwide governmental cover-up conspiracies to answer critics.

King had been a disciplined student of Yoga. Eastern rites are evident during the group's ceremonies. Part of the *cultus* of charging the prayer battery involves the intonation of a ▸mantra taken from a Tibetan chant—*mani padme om*. As a result of praying this chant, it is believed that "spiritual energies" are stored up and subsequently released for the benefit of humankind when needed. The power of the prayer battery is coveted by "evil powers" as well as good.

In order to join TAS, one is carefully screened. Only "members," "associate members," and "sympathizers" are allowed to attend meetings. To become a sympathizer, one must perform mantra exercises for fifteen minutes on a daily basis. King rewrote the Lord's Prayer, which he claimed as a revelation from the Venusian Jesus in 1961. In conformance with TAS doctrine, the prayer was converted to a longer mantra to channel "inner vision" and "energy" to our "higher selves." At the end of some meetings the group energetically chants this prayer.

Certainly the mission of the Christian church is to "serve," as is the mission of TAS: "The Son of Man did not come to be served but to serve, and to give his life as a ransom for many" (Mark 10:45). The purpose for Christ's coming into the world was to atone for sin. This constitutes, for the church, the ultimate form of service. Service, for TAS, has more to do with utilization of cosmic powers to benefit humanity and humanitarian concerns.

Christianity, like TAS, believes ardently in the power of prayer. But unlike the society, Christianity has no concept of classifying prayer as being "good" and "bad" except in connection with whether a prayer is offered up to God in faith or unbelief. If a prayer is prayed in faith and is according to God's will, God hears it, and it is a good prayer (Mark 11:24). God does not hear prayers that are not offered up in faith (James 1:6–7).

A second contrast concerning prayer is the differing roles it plays for the group. In TAS, prayer and the accompanying emotional fervor is measured by a physical object (the prayer battery). The prayer's success or failure depends on the power left in the battery after the negative forces have been subtracted. We should note that the creeds of the church are silent on the subject of prayer, for they concern themselves with who God is—Father, Son, and Holy Spirit—and with what he does as Creator, Redeemer, and Sanctifier. Prayer is not alluded to because it does not change in any way who God *is* and what he *does*. God is still Creator, Redeemer, and Sanctifier, with or without prayer. In short, the creeds of Christendom speak of God's grace to the Christian; prayer is the *response* of the Christian to God. Prayer is not to be substituted for grace or be used as a means of grace, as it is in TAS.

Third, the Bible represents a closed canon. God does not grant new revelation or revelation that will alter, contrast, or add to what he gives in the Bible. When King altered the Matthean text for the Lord's Prayer (6:9–13), he violated Proverbs 30:6 and proves himself a liar.

Fourth, the goal of Christianity is to spread the message of God's kingdom; this kingdom is "not of this world" (John 18:36). The thrust of TAS lies in establishing peace in the present with the aid of the cosmic master.

Both TAS and Christianity predict the end of the world. While the former seeks to delay it through charging up the prayer battery, the latter confesses, "from thence he will come to judge the living and the dead" (Apostles' Creed; see Appendix 1). This anticipated day is the "blessed hope" of the church.

CONCLUSION

TAS continues to exist into the twenty-first century. Operation Prayer Power meetings are regularly held along with spiritual healing services. Classes and lectures are frequently held at all of the TAS centers. Members continue to believe that contact with extraterrestrial intelligence will bring enlightenment to the inhabitants of the earth. The official website provides current information on the various activities, seminars, products, and services offered.

ADDITIONAL INFORMATION

Headquarters

(American) The Aetherius Society, 6202 Afton Place, Hollywood, CA 90028.

(Europe) The Aetherius Society, 757 Fulham Road, London, England SW6 5UU.

Website

www.aetherius.org

Sacred Texts

The Twelve Blessings; The Nine Freedoms; Cosmic Masters Speak to Earth. Other writings by King include *You Are Responsible* (1961); *The Day the Gods Came* (1965); *The Five Temples of God* (1967); *You Too Can Heal* (1976); *Operation Space Magic—The Cosmic Connection* (1982); *The Three Saviours Are Here* (1982).

Periodicals

Cosmic Voice; The Aetherius Society Newsletter.

Membership

The latest figures for membership are unavailable but in all likelihood, it is under 1000 members. The organization itself will not give out exact figures but claim that there are several thousand members. Most members of TAS reside in England.[1]

Note

[1] J. Gordon Melton, *The Encyclopedia of American Religions,* 2 vols. (Wilmington, N.C.: McGrath, 1978), 2:119.

ALAMO CHRISTIAN MINISTRIES; ALAMO CHRISTIAN FOUNDATION (ACF)

The Alamo Christian Foundation was one of many popular groups that proliferated in the heyday of the countercultural "Jesus people" revolution of the 1960s and 1970s.

HISTORY

Established in 1969 by Susan *Alamo (d. 1982) in the Los Angeles area, the ACF began as a Pentecostal-style gathering of hippies and misfits evangelized off the streets by the charismatic personalities of Susan and her husband, Tony. Susan Alamo's real name was Edith Opal *Horn, and Tony's former name was Bernard Lazar *Hoffman. According to a feature article in *People Weekly*, June 13, 1983,

> Susan was the foundation's spark, the divinely chosen "handmaiden of God," who would make a miracle, curing herself, thus focusing attention on the foundation. Then she and Tony would lead a glorious world crusade.... Susan's death shook the faith of her followers. This, says an insider, is why Tony preaches resurrection: "As long as Tony has Susan's body, he has her power."

The Alamos' method of evangelism (in the 1960s and 1970s) was to invite hippies wandering the streets

to come in for free food and music, after which Tony would come out and preach. An appeal to accept Christ as personal Savior was made, and many did so. Converts were then assigned to an "older" Christian, who would maintain constant supervision over them. Once absorbed into the foundation, they would work in one of the many business interests established by the group.[1] In 1977, the U.S. Department of Labor filed suit against the ACF for violation of fair-labor practices in thirty-two commercial enterprises run by the organization. The *Los Angeles Times*, April 24, 1985, reported:

> The foundation derives most of its income from service stations, clothing stores, groceries, hog farms and other commercial enterprises that are staffed by workers it calls "associates." The workers do not receive salaries but are compensated with meals, lodging, clothing, shelter, transportation and health care.
>
> Tony's response to the suit was: "The U.S. Department of Labor is a poison on the American system that needs to be yanked like a rotten tooth and thrown in the garbage."

Headquarters for the ACF shifted to Alma, Arkansas, in 1975, and large tracts of land were purchased in order to operate the diversified commercial interests in which the Alamos engaged. Arkansas social services found it necessary to investigate the foundation's day care center, which was reported to have an enrollment of seventy children. They found the conditions at the facility deplorable, and no children were enrolled at the time of the inspection.

Defections from the ACF were common in the later 1970s. Many who left reported such things as having been under constant supervision, poor nutrition, brainwashing, hard labor, and deprivation of sleep. The Alamos' own daughter, Chris Mick, testified against her mother before a Senate subcommittee after leaving the foundation.

Like so many groups that arose in the "era of protest," the ACF experienced widespread appeal within its sphere of influence. That sphere of influence, however, has rapidly declined in the mid-1970s to the present.

The year 1982 proved to be fateful for the ACF in that Susan Alamo died, marking the end of an era for the foundation. Add to this the extensive media coverage of the ▶Jonestown tragedy four years previous, which resulted in a mass public awareness of the goings-on in cultic circles, and the tide began to shift away from groups controlled by charismatic personalities. The ACF was no exception to this trend.

Trouble erupted for Tony Alamo in 1988 when he was sought by police for alleged child abuse, for which he was later acquitted. The December 21, 1989, *Los Angeles Times* reported that Alamo Designs, Inc., had filed a $250 million lawsuit against the Jewish Federation for libel and slander. Alamo claimed that the federation had been "persecuting" and maligning him, accusing him of child beating before he could defend himself by due process in a court of law.

Alamo's protest centered around the issue that the Jewish Federation was attempting to discourage sales of Alamo Designs clothing, claiming that profits went toward the financing of a cult. Alamo Designs attempted to distance itself from Alamo, as sales had drastically dropped in the Los Angeles area. The explanation for this was bad public relations, which Alamo attributed to the activities of several anticult groups. Alamo sued the several organizations but was unsuccessful in court.[2]

The *Los Angeles Times* makes a different claim, however. In a telephone interview with the *Times* in August 1989, Tony Alamo is quoted as saying (with respect to Alamo Designs), "I make all the decisions in the business, all of them. Wherever I am is the [company] headquarters. If you can find me, you've found the headquarters."[3]

In February 1993, Alamo was indicted by a grand jury in Memphis, Tennessee, on charges of falsely filing income tax returns from 1985 through 1988. He was arrested in April, and in June was convicted of all of the charges against him and sentenced to six years in prison. In 1995, further tax cases were heard against Alamo, who in July of that year filed a double jeopardy motion, claiming that he was punished twice because the amount of money and assets that the government seized was far in excess of his actual tax liability. Alamo was considered for parole as a model prisoner in June 1995 but was denied and later released in late 1998.

TEACHINGS

The Bible

The ACF claims that the ▶Bible is the Word of God and the ACF's authority in matters of faith. Tony Alamo, however, claimed to have received personal revelations from God, which he then passed on to the group.

God

The foundation maintains a belief in the theology of the ▶Trinity of traditional CHRISTIANITY.

Jesus Christ

Jesus is the Son of God and Redeemer of humankind. He was physically resurrected from the dead and is able, therefore, to impart forgiveness of sins to those who turn to him in faith. This simply stated ▶Christology is also in conformity with historical Christian ▶orthodoxy. The ACF has not developed its Christology beyond this.

Salvation

The following prayer and subsequent instructions, published in Tony Alamo's *The Pope's Secrets*, reveals the foundation's basic beliefs regarding how one may receive salvation:

My Lord and my God, have mercy upon my soul, a sinner. I believe that Jesus Christ is the Son of the living God. I believe that He died on the cross and shed His blood for the forgiveness of all my sins. I believe that God raised Jesus from the dead by the power of the Holy Ghost. I open up the door of my heart, and I invite you into my heart, Lord Jesus. Wash all of my sins away in the precious blood that you shed for me. You will not turn me away, Lord Jesus; you will save my soul. I know because your Word, the Bible, says so. Your Word says that you will turn no one away, and that includes me. Therefore, I know that you have heard me, and I know that you have answered me, and I know that I am saved, and I thank you, Lord Jesus, for saving my soul. . . . [To readers] Now that you are saved, raise your hands toward heaven and praise the Lord.

After you have said this prayer and know that you are saved, read *only* the King James Version of the Bible. And call or write us soon for instructions on how to receive power from God by receiving the baptism of the Holy Ghost, and for instructions on how to please the Lord fully.[4]

Insofar as the foundation preaches the *person* of Jesus Christ—that it is Christ as the Son of God who grants the forgiveness of sins, and that this forgiveness is imparted to the penitent—it is in conformity with the idea of salvation in the Christian church of the first four centuries. However, with respect to ⏵soteriology, there are two notable differences between the foundation and the traditional Christian ⏵orthodoxy and orthopraxies. First, baptism is treated differently than it was in the early church. The ACF regarded the sacramental washing to be an integral and essential part of the conversion process. Just as circumcision was a mark of the old covenant (Gen. 17:10–11), an act that incorporated the believer into the covenant community of faith, baptism was regarded as being the mark of the new covenant (Col. 2:11–12) that incorporated the believer into the body of Christ. Baptism was much more closely linked to the doctrine of justification in the early ACF communities than it is in contemporary Protestant groups that place more emphasis on the actual decision to receive Christ and less on the sacrament of incorporation and initiation into the church.[5]

This leads to a second observation. The New Testament reports the conversion of *individuals*, but the *households* of such individuals were also included in several instances (Acts 16:15, 30–32). In the social matrix of twentieth-century American society, particularly within the hippie counterculture of the 1960s and 1970s, the emphasis was on the *individual*, who more often than not was disenfranchised from his or her family. Furthermore, modern conversion is not so much a matter of salvation from pagan deities, as was the case in the early church, as it is conversion from a "dead" mainline Christian denomination to a more "alive" and "Spirit-filled" group of believers who are "true" Christians. Insofar as the ACF is concerned, this idea takes on a special significance with respect to its doctrine of the church.

Church

All other churches in the world are corrupt. The ACF is the only true church. For traditional orthodox Christianity, by contrast, all believers are a part of the "one holy catholic and apostolic church" (Nicene Creed). No one denomination or leader has sole claim to the truth to the exclusion of all others. The standard lies in the doctrines laid out in the Bible and expressed in the ecumenical creeds. which unite all of Christendom in matters of faith and doctrine (*see* Appendix 1). Other evidence of their exclusivity is that Tony Alamo is frequently called "World Pastor Tony Alamo," which elevates him to an unbiblical position.

Other beliefs taught by the ACF include the conviction that the Vatican is the tool of the ⏵devil and that the pope is the Antichrist. Alamo adamantly believes that the Vatican is on a conspiratorial mission to seize control of the world. In *The Pope's Secrets*, Alamo asserts:

> Because of her age-old desire to control the world government and church, the serpent-like Vatican has infested the world and the U.S. government with so many of her zealous, highly-trained and dedicated Jesuit devotees, that she now controls the **United Nations** (which she created); the **White House**; **Congress**; every state, federal, civic, and social government agency including the **U.S. Department of Labor**, the **IRS**, the ***FRO, Supreme Court, judicial systems, the armed forces; state, federal and other police; also the international banking and federal reserve systems (called the Illuminati and Agentur); labor unions, the Mafia** and most of the heavyweight news media.[6]

Alamo also argues that in addition to the corruptions resulting from Vatican infiltration, communism is an evil force threatening the welfare and safety of the United States. In this contention, he is in agreement with Sun Myung ⏵Moon and numerous conservative fundamentalist (see ⏵fundamentalism) groups.

CONCLUSION

Alamo continues to minister and lead the organization that bears his name. Followers call him "World Pastor." The negative media exposure, the attacks by (now defunct) CAN, and the government seizures of much of the assets of the organization took its toll on the organization.

ADDITIONAL INFORMATION_____

Headquarters
Holy Alamo Christian Church, P. O. Box 398, Alma, Arkansas 72921.

Website
www.alamoministries.com

Sacred Text
The Bible

Other Writings
Numerous pamphlets have been published by Alamo, including *The Pope's Secrets* (n.d.); *Guilt by Association* (n.d.);

and *Alamo's Answer to Rabbi Nuri* (n.d.). *World Newsletters* is available online with Alamo's monthly messages.

Notes
[1] Gregory Perrin, "Cult Begins Local Recruiting Drive" (Brooklyn, N.Y.: Prospect Press), vol. 21 (November 1982), 11–24.
[2] Eric W. Francke, "A Brief History of the Alamo Christian Foundation" (see *http://nierr.org/alamohist.htm*).
[3] Ibid.
[4] Ibid.
[5] Michael Green, *Evangelism in the Early Church* (Grand Rapids: Eerdmans, 1970), 152–65.
[6] Alamo, *Pope's Secret*, 1.

ANANDA MARGA YOGA SOCIETY

Ananda Marga is one of the numerous Hindu (see HINDUISM) family of ▸cults that proliferated in the United States during the 1960s and 70s.

HISTORY

This movement was founded by Prabhat Ranjan Sarkar (1921–1990). He was renamed Shrii Shrii ▸Anandamurti, which means "One upon seeing him turns to bliss." Sarkar achieved religious enlightenment at an early age. At four he began to propound his philosophy in India.

Ananda Marga came to the United States in 1969 under the leadership of Acharya ▸Vimalananda, who has since left the movement and founded the Yoga House Ashram. In America, Sarkar gained much more of a following than he had in India, where he was not without his problems. During the turbulent 1960s and early 1970s, when Indira Gandhi was becoming less and less popular, Sarkar ran for political office. Former members of his group, however, accused him of participating in a conspiracy to commit murder. He was arrested and remained in prison throughout the national emergency declared by Gandhi, which lasted from June 1975 to January 1977. Sarkar, along with many political opponents who had also been arrested, was subsequently set free. In the mid–1970s the Indian government considered the Society a terrorist organization that taught its members to carry out ritual murder. Sarkar continued to teach the values and ideals of the organization until the time of his death in 1990. As of May, 2004, 125 of Sarkar's books have been published in English, with more and more translations being made.

ORGANIZATION

The different centers of Ananda Marga activities around the world are called "sectors," and each of these are listed on the organization's website. Spiritual and social activity centers are found in over 160 countries in the world. By 1973 over one hundred centers had been established in the United States and abroad. Because it considered itself service-oriented, several organizations were formed for the purpose of helping disaster relief victims. These included Ananda Marga Universal Relief Team (AMURT) and Ananda Marga Universal Relief Team Ladies (AMURTEL). Other activities carried out by the Society include aid to refugees around the world, outreach to prisoners, the bringing of pure drinking water to areas of Africa, and disaster relief to the victims of the terrorist attacks on September 11, 2001.

TEACHINGS

Ananda Marga's teachings are based on HINDUISM with special emphasis on ▸Kundalini and ▸Tantra ▸Yoga techniques. Part of the meditation rituals include a dance known as ▸*Kiirtan*, accompanied by the ▸Mantra Baba Nam Kevalam ("the universal father is everywhere"). The world, according to the movement, is an expression of the personality and character of God. The individual achieves enlightenment when the "ego-bound mind" is broken down and the individual is displaced from dwelling on his or her own needs. Having accomplished this, the devotee is able to then dwell on the needs of others. As already noted, members of Ananda Marga expend considerable energy in public service. The concept is essentially that the more one devotes to others, the less bound one is to oneself, and the closer one is to enlightenment.

Ananda Marga uses what is called the ♦sixteen points created by Sarkar. Under the sixteen points comes the term *paincaseva*, which means "five services." "Whatever service is needed at a given time should be rendered." These include free food distribution, sale of cheap vegetarian food, clothing distribution, medical supplies distribution, and books and educational supplies distribution.

A striking comparison with ♦orthodox CHRISTIANITY lies in the biblical principle of God's love and concern for the poor (Isa. 1:17; Luke 4:18; James 2:5–6). For the Christian, the display of love and concern for others is motivated by God's love, already given to the Christian through the work of redemption accomplished by Jesus Christ. "A good tree cannot bear bad fruit" (Matt. 7:18).[1]

CONCLUSION

The society continues to grow and proliferate in many areas of the world.

ADDITIONAL INFORMATION

World Headquarters
Ananda Marga Global Headquarters, Eastern Metropolitan By-Pass, V.I.P. Nagar, Tiljala, Calcutta 700039, India.
New York Sector 97–38 42nd Ave 1-F, Corona, New York, 11368. Other North American sectors include locations in California, North Carolina, Missouri, and Mexico City.

Website
www.anandamarga.org

Sacred Texts
The numerous writings of Sarkar

Publications
The society produces several periodicals, including a monthly newsletter, *Sadvipra*, begun in 1973, and a magazine titled *Renaissance Universal*.

Membership
Exact figures are uncertain. The official website, however, claims that there are close to one million followers.

Note
[1] The implications of this point along with a further discussion of comparisons of and contrasts with Christianity are found in Hinduism.

ARICA (ARICA INSTITUTE)

Arica is a NEW AGE group that brings together a blend of Eastern religions and psychotherapy, which was eventually merged with a defensive martial arts school known as the T'ai Chi Foundation and the School of T'ai Chi Chuan (Supreme Ultimate Fist). It was invented and developed by Oscar ♦Ichazo and takes its name from the remote town of Arica, Chile.

HISTORY

In 1971 Ichazo came to the United States and founded the Arica Institute in New York City. Since that time, it has expanded rapidly, with centers in San Francisco, Los Angeles, London, and elsewhere.

TEACHINGS

The student of Arica learns to focus on the mind and through training is able to "awaken" it. Ichazo contends that the subconscious mind alone possesses the knowledge of salvation. One must tap this vast treasure lying within to arrive at one's "essence." Essence and ego lie in diametrically opposite poles in the human psyche. In the beginning, the conflict people encountered with their world resulted in a falling away from pure essence. As a result, they tumbled into ego.

Each individual is born of pure essence but begins to experience a dissonance because of societal demands to conformity. This begins between the ages of four and six. Conflict that the individual experiences results in the rise of the ego aspect of the mind. Ego is the fundamental problem of a "self" living in a world inhabited by millions of other egos.

The student of Arica is taught to think with all parts of the body. Different parts of the body are assigned to different planes, called "mentations"—twelve in all. Additionally, three specialized centers make up the individual: ♦*path,* ♦*oth,* and ♦*kath. Kath* is the most important, as it is in control, or at least one learns to allow it to be so. The idea is to learn to transfer mental energies and conscience from the mind (*path*) to the body center (*kath*). The goal of Arica is to expose and destroy the ego and usher the person into a state that Ichazo calls ♦Permanent 24, the state of total awareness and personal enlightenment.

In essence, Arica is a philosophy comprising a

potpourri of ancient Greek thought, HINDUISM, BUD-DHISM, and SUFISM, while T'ai chi discipline draws heavily on the dualistic philosophy found in TAOISM, whereby everything is connected to the bipolar opposites such as positive–negative, male–female, and the like. There is little that resembles traditional CHRISTIANITY in Arica. As one of the many therapeutic self-help groups that constitutes the New Age, Arica's basic assumption is that divinity resides within each individual. It remains for a trained specialist to "awaken" it. This is done for a fee, and the training lasts as long as three months in its initial stages, followed by "open path" workshops.

Ichazo contends that Arica is not a religion and that he is not a ▸guru. "When you are mature," he says, "you don't need a papa, you need a friend. A friend will advise you with goodwill. You can either take it or leave it."[1] One of the basic goals of the therapy is to liberate one from guilt and other psychological maladies. The methods used in accomplishing this closely resemble aspects of Eastern religions. "The mystical name of the radiant being" that is latent within every person is *toham kum rah*. The student learns breathing techniques, ▸mantras, and incantations, all for the purpose of reaching Permanent 24.

Arica has no concept of human malady having any relationship to sin and active rebellion against God, as in the case of Christianity. There is, therefore, no concept of atonement for sin. Christianity teaches that "all have sinned and fall short of the glory of God, and are justified freely by his grace through the redemption that came by Christ Jesus" (Rom. 3:23–24).

There is no concept of church, ▸sacraments, creeds, or any other aspect of Christianity in Arica. Ichazo contends that one may embrace the tenets of any religion and still utilize his techniques. Christianity, however, posits a view of the world, of life, of God, and of humanity that is diametrically opposite from Arica. Arica presupposes an existential philosophy in which the individual views himself or herself as being the center of existence, while the Christian places the triune God at the center of life, both in the present world and in the life to come.

The Christian outlook is one where the present life is a prelude to heaven. Permanent 24, the Arica equivalent to heaven, is a state of existence one never attains in this life, or at least no one yet has. It is a state not unlike that of ▸nirvana in Eastern thought.

ADDITIONAL INFORMATION

Website

www.taichifoundation.org/arica.shtml

Note

[1] "The Same Old Yen for Zen," *Newsweek* (November 9, 1981), 20.

ASSOCIATION FOR RESEARCH AND ENLIGHTENMENT (ARE)

This is an organization that gathers chiefly for the purpose of studying the writings and teachings of Edgar ▸Cayce and for the continued promotion of ▸psychic awareness, ▸clairvoyance, and other related phenomena.

HISTORY

Edgar Cayce was born March 18, 1877, on a farm outside of Hopkinsville, Kentucky. His father served as a Justice of the Peace. As a child, Cayce was interested in the ▸Bible and enjoyed attending church regularly. Several key events in his childhood shaped the direction his life would take. As an infant, he is reported to have cried incessantly throughout his first month. An elderly black woman whom the family knew suggested pricking his nipples with a pin. Milk was reported to have flowed from his breasts, after which the crying marathon stopped. At the age of either seven or eight, Cayce was one day

> off by himself in a secluded outdoor nook where he had been reading in the Bible of the vision of Manoah, for he loved dearly the story of Samson. Suddenly there was a humming sound, and a bright light filled the glade where he usually hid to read the wonderful stories. As he looked up, he saw a figure in white, bright as the noonday light, and heard a voice: "Your prayers have been heard. What would you ask of me that I may give it to you?" The boy was not startled. Even then it seemed natural to see visions. "Just that I may be helpful to others," he replied, "especially to children who are ill, and that I may love my fellow man."[1]

This vision began to affect Cayce's life almost immediately. Not a good student, he attempted to put his vision to work in improving his grades. Cayce recalls what happened shortly after his vision:

> In the evening I had the same hard time in preparing my spelling lesson. I studied it and each time felt that I knew it, yet when I handed the book to my father and he gave me the words to spell I couldn't spell them. After wrestling with it for two or three hours, receiving many rebuffs for my stupidity, something inside me seemed to say, "Rely on the promise." I asked my father to let me sleep on my lesson just five minutes. He finally consented. I closed the book, and leaning on the back of the chair went to sleep. At the end of five minutes I handed my father the book. I not only knew my lesson, but I could spell any word in the book; not only spell the words but could tell on what page and what line the word would be found. From that day on I had little trouble in school, for I would read my lesson, sleep on it a few minutes, and then be able to repeat every word of it.[2]

This method spelled out the way that Cayce would receive his ▸readings throughout the rest of his life. For this reason he became known as "the sleeping prophet." His family was familiar with ▸divination and the ▸occult; for example, his father was a practicing water dowser (see ▸dowsing) and claimed to have made a broom dance. The young Cayce was said to have seen apparitions of his grandfather after he died.

In 1900–1901, Cayce suffered from extreme headaches and, after one such attack, lost his voice. After several doctors failed to diagnose the problem, a friend succeeded in getting Cayce to speak (but only under hypnosis). While in this trance, Cayce diagnosed his own illness and prescribed a cure. By following the prescribed cure, his voice returned and his throat was healed. The hypnotist, A. C. Layne, then suggested that Cayce diagnose the conditions of others. In a self-induced sleep trance, Cayce successfully diagnosed the physical condition of Layne, using medical terminology totally unfamiliar to him.[3] Layne hired Cayce as a partner in his practice. For the next forty years, Cayce composed nearly 16,000 readings. He reportedly

> predicted the sex of unborn infants; diagnosed and prescribed successful cures for epilepsy, diabetes, cancer, nervous disorders, pyorrhea, tuberculosis, hemorrhoids, appendicitis, hernias, hay fever, arthritis, common colds, etc.; he predicted in April of 1929 the stock market crash of that year, the end-

ing of the Depression in 1933, and the future value of land at Cape Henry and Norfolk.... A photographer by trade, with only a grammar school education, his medical vocabulary (while under a self-induced trance) perplexed some Bostonian authorities. Cayce could also speak numerous foreign languages fluently while in his trance, a feat he was unable to accomplish in everyday life.[4]

In 1923, Cayce met Arthur Lammers, a printer from Dayton, Ohio, who was a student of THEOSOPHY and the ▸occult. Lammers persuaded Cayce to apply his clairvoyant gifts to more than the curing of physical ills, encouraging him to conduct "life readings" that transported him to the spiritual and theosophical realm. Cayce began to combine eastern philosophy with CHRISTIANITY, particularly the Hindu (see HINDUISM) ideas of ▸reincarnation and ▸karma. Initially Cayce struggled with what he perceived was a clash of worldviews between his Christian faith and the influences of Hinduism. However, he soon reconciled the two and assimilated them to his apparent satisfaction. Over a forty-year period, he gave a known total of 14,256 readings, consisting of more than 49,000 pages of material dealing with a wide range of topics.

In 1928, Cayce founded Atlantic University in Virginia Beach as a place where students could come and study. Out of this school arose the Association for Research and Enlightenment (ARE) in 1931. The purpose of his organization was "to preserve, study and present the Edgar Cayce readings" and to "carry on psychical research."[5] ARE ▸study groups gathered all around the world. Virginia Beach was selected as the location for headquarters because, according to Cayce, it was the safest place on earth in light of future geological catastrophes he had predicted.

On January 3, 1945, Cayce died at the age of sixty-seven. His popularity did not cease, however, as many millions of people, suffering from a variety of physical, emotional, and spiritual ailments, continue to seek the aid of the ARE. Cayce was succeeded as leader of the association by his son, Hugh L. ▸Cayce. The current president of ARE is Charles Thomas Cayce, PhD.

ORGANIZATION

The ARE has what are called "regional offices" in the United States and Canada. Edgar Cayce Centers are located in over eighty countries throughout the world.

TEACHINGS

As noted above, Cayce combined elements of orthodox Christianity with Eastern ideas. Basic to his thought was the doctrine of reincarnation. It was in 1923 in Dayton, when Cayce met Lammers, that he said he was awakened out of a trance "to be told that he had asserted the reality of reincarnation: that man is born in many different bodies."[6] Though he resisted the anti-Christian nature of reincarnation, even admitting the doctrine to be unbiblical, Cayce eventually "came to terms with it, and incorporated it into his orthodox Christian doctrine."[7] What follows are a number of his doctrinal views:

God

God is Spirit, everywhere, permeating everything. God is Creative Energy, the maker of all that is in the universe. When man creates, it is the God force within that is the thought, the plan, the execution. God is mind, force, life itself. . . . God is not a person but very personal to us as we manifest Him in our lives. To come to this realization activity is necessary, for the Lord our God is a living, active God. He is then personal to us only as we become like Him in word, thought and act.[8]

Cayce's doctrine of God, in this instance, is pantheistic (*see* pantheism). The locus of God's essence is relegated to the human manifestation of the god within.

The Christianity he embraced as a child and young adult is contrary to this Hindu-like conception.[9] It spelled out implications that affected his views on many other points of Christian theology.

Jesus Christ

Jesus was one in a long line of reincarnations. In one of his readings, Cayce states what he specifically believed about Jesus:

Q. When did Jesus become aware that he would be the Savior of the World?

A. When he fell in Eden.

Q. Does this mean that Jesus had been Adam?

A. Study the book which tells of Him, Jesus, born of the Virgin Mary; (Then) know this is the soul-entity (Jeshua) who reasoned with those who returned from captivity in those days when Nehemiah, Ezra, Zerubbabel were factors in the attempts to re-establish the worship of God; and that as Jeshua, the scribe, translated the rest of the books written up to that time. Then realize (also) that is the same entity who, as Joshua, was the mouthpiece of Moses, who gave the law; and was the same soul-entity who was born in Bethlehem. The same soul-entity who, in those peri-

ods of the strength and yet the weakness of Jacob in his love for Rachel, was their first-born, Joseph. As Zend (father of Zoroaster)—this was the same entity. And this entity was that one who had manifested . . . as Melchizedek . . . as Enoch . . . Or, as the first begotten of the Father, who came as Amilius in the Atlantean land and allowed himself to be led into the ways of self-ishness. And this was also the entity Adam—this was the Spirit of Light.[10]

During this same reading, Cayce stated that Jesus "possibly had some thirty incarnations during his development in becoming The Christ."

Cayce, like ROSICRUCIANISM, theosophical groups, and various Eastern religions, taught that Christ was one of history's great avatars. For Cayce the "Christ" exists in all ages, while Jesus lived only in one. The Christ-spirit accompanies the great religious figures of every age. But when the Christ-spirit united with Jesus, the combination resulted in a perfection, strength, and maturity unmatched in any other age by any other combination.

This was a serious departure from the Christianity of Cayce's childhood. Traditional Christianity teaches that Christ was the *eternal* Son of God and the second person of the Trinity (Apostles' and Nicene Creeds, Article 2, Appendix 1). For Cayce, Jesus only *became* the Son in the Trinity as a result of a process of moral and spiritual development.

Why did Jesus come into the world? For Christianity, the incarnate Son of God (John 1:1ff.) came in order to redeem the human race from sin. Cayce does not share this understanding of Christ's atonement (Rom. 3:21–26). He states quite succinctly in the following:

He sent His Son, that in His life and sacrifice we might get a physical manifestation of light through love. That as He in His service to His fellow man might show to us God; and that we might also manifest divine attributes. To understand our relationship to the Father we must be familiar with the attributes of his perfect manifestation, Jesus, the Christ. He chose the hard way of life. He loved His enemies. He bore temptations and endured persecution. He knew the laws of God yet never used them for His own glory. Thus He became the pattern for those who likewise would know the way . . . Jesus, the Christ, the perfect manifestation of God in the flesh, showed the world through service and unselfish love what God expected of His children if they would be one with Him. He made the sacrifice once and for all, that those who would be like Him might find the way easy through Him. We are in like manner to offer ourselves a living sacrifice for others. . . . God knows our personal needs in the same manner as life is manifested in a grain of wheat. Until we become a god, a savior to someone else in purpose, in activity, we do not take hold of that personality.[11]

Humanity

Cayce's teachings concerning God are paralleled by his view of humankind. Human beings were not created in a space-time continuum, as the biblical cosmology states in Genesis 1:1ff. Rather, all souls have preexisted from the beginning. At the time of the Fall, the unity with God was lost. This Fall "denotes not an ontological phenomenon—as though the fact of distinct consciousness, or creation itself, constituted evil—but a primarily ethical phenomenon."[12]

All of this occurred before Creation itself. In fact, Cayce taught that man fell "into matter" rather than into sin. Before this there was not yet a physical creation. Cayce simply believed there was no reason for such before the Fall. Genesis, for Cayce, represents "the second creation."

> Then [after the first fall] there became the necessity of the awareness of self's being out of accord with or out of the realm of blessedness . . . By becoming aware in a material world is—or was—the only manner or way through which spiritual forces might become aware of their separation from the spiritual surroundings, of the maker.[13]

And further,

> So in passing through our various experiences, even as He, the first Adam, our soul becomes aware of its separation from its Creator. As the nature of our relationship to our maker grows clearer, we begin to walk more and more in the Light in our physical experiences. We came here for this purpose. Through experience, through suffering, we come to know day and night, light and darkness, good and evil, even as the Son, the Adam. "Though he were a Son, yet learned he obedience by the things which He suffered." Finally, we recognize that we are on our way back to the source. This alone brings satisfaction to our souls.[14]

The human race therefore became alienated from God by two falls, one when humanity was soul, and the second while embodied during the physical creation in Eden (Gen. 1–2). Christianity, by contrast, maintains that both soul and body are created by God as a unity. Before this creation, the soul does not exist. Upon death, both soul and body are separated, the soul going to its eternal destiny (Phil. 3:21; John 5:29) and the body to the grave (Job 19:26; Eccl. 12:7). Christianity also teaches that the body will one day be joined with the soul to live eternally with God (Job 19:26; 1 Cor. 15:51–52; Apostles' and Nicene creeds—*see* Appendix 1).

Salvation

Reincarnation, as stated above, becomes the key to Cayce's ▸soteriology. As Jesus was one in a successive series of reincarnations, so too the human race moves through the cycles. By gaining knowledge, attaining higher consciousness, and realizing one's own divinity, a person eventually experiences salvation. Physical existence is part of the divine plan for the soul and its search for becoming one with God again. This is made possible through putting off old lives and bad ▸karma. Hell is not the place of eternal punishment, as taught in Christianity (Matt. 10:28); rather, it is a state of imperfection, which will eventually achieve perfection as the wheel of reincarnation unfolds itself.

Other

Cayce spoke on many more subjects than the Bible and Christianity. He believed, for example, in the lost civilization of ▸Atlantis, which for him existed over ten million years ago. Though he attempted throughout his life to remain on friendly terms with Christianity, the latter often did not return the favor, particularly those who called themselves orthodox and evangelical Christians. John Warwick Montgomery writes:

> With Cayce, there is little doubt that the negative axe should strike at the root of the tree: while alive, he employed his powers to bolster a mishmash of Eastern religiosity (karma and reincarnation) and out-of-context biblical teaching, and now this eclectic theosophizing is being promoted by his "Association for Research and Enlightenment." Here we have a classic case of a "seer" being in reality blind: the blind leading the blind.[15]

CONCLUSION

Most bookstores, including many health-food stores, stock books by or about Cayce and the ARE. Among his most celebrated works is his official biography, Thomas Sugrue's *There Is a River: The Story of Edgar Cayce* (Virginia Beach: ARE Press, 1973). The organization's website lists in detail the many activities and areas of service in which the organization was involved in the early part of the twentieth century.

ADDITIONAL INFORMATION_____

Headquarters
ARE Visitor Center, Virginia Beach, VA.

Website
www.are-cayce.com

Sacred Texts
The numerous writings of Edgar Cayce

Periodicals
A.R.E. Journal (quarterly); *A.R.E. News* (monthly).

Membership
Exact membership figures are unknown, but there are regional offices throughout Canada and the United States. Also there are a growing number of Edgar Cayce Centers throughout the world.

Notes
[1] Jess Stearn, *Edgar Cayce—The Sleeping Prophet* (New York: Doubleday, 1967), 26–27.
[2] Jeffrey Furst, *Edgar Cayce's Story of Jesus* (New York: Coward-McCann, 1969), 336.
[3] Bob Larson, *Larson's Book of Cults* (Wheaton, Ill.: Tyndale, 1986), 244.
[4] James Bjornstad, *Twentieth Century Prophecy—Jeane Dixon; Edgar Cayce* (Minneapolis: Bethany, 1969), 79–80.
[5] Furst, *Edgar Cayce's Story of Jesus*, 350.
[6] Colin Wilson, *The Occult: A History* (New York: Random, 1971), 168.
[7] Ibid.
[8] Bjornstad, *Twentieth Century Prophecy*, 79–80.
[9] See HINDUISM.
[10] Furst, *Edgar Cayce's Story of Jesus*, 23.
[11] Association for Research and Enlightenment, *A Search for God*, book 3 (Virginia Beach: A.R.E. Press, 1950), 14–15.
[12] Richard H. Drummond, *Unto the Churches—Jesus Christ, Christianity and the Edgar Cayce Readings* (Virginia Beach: A.R.E. Press, 1978), 197.
[13] Association for Research and Enlightenment, *A Search for God*, book 2 (Virginia Beach: A.R.E. Press, 1950), 13–14.
[14] Ibid., 14.
[15] John Warwick Montgomery, *Principalities and Powers* (Minneapolis: Bethany, 1973), 126.

AUM SHINRIKYO; AUM SUPREME TRUTH; AUM; ALEPH

A ᵇcult formed in Japan in the late 1980s that received international attention on March 25, 1995, when members released a chemical nerve gas called sarin on the Tokyo subway system. The plan was systematically executed on fifteen different subway stations, resulting in the deaths of twelve people and the injury of nearly 4,000. The organization was renamed Aleph in 2000 and maintains a presence in at least thirty-five municipalities of Japan. The former name, however, will be used in this article.

HISTORY

Aum Supreme Truth was formed in 1987 when partially blind Chizuo Matsumoto (b. 1955) changed his name to Asahara Shoko and named his group Aum Shinrikyo. *Aum* is a ᵇSanskrit word that means "powers of destruction and creation." *Shinrikyo* means "instruction in the supreme truth."

Shoko had attended a school for the blind since he was five years old and finally graduated in 1977. He applied to Tokyo University but failed the entrance exam. From there he turned to the study of acupuncture. In 1978, he married. His wife was also interested in herbal medicines and acupuncture.[1] He adopted a newfound and intense interest in religion and got involved with several religious groups that practiced ᵇmeditation and the belief in the possibility of liberation from bad ᵇkarma through suffering and afflicting pain on others.

A trip to the Himalayas in 1986 brought him ᵇenlightenment, and the following year he assumed his new name. In 1989, the group began to involve itself in politics, forming the Shinri Party. It was announced that *Shinrikyo* was the only means through which the world could be saved. Twenty five members of the organization attempted to gain seats in the election of 1990, which they failed to do. This failure led to the group becoming more reactionary and violent. They began to acquire weapons, a helicopter, and the chemical clostridium botulinum. A large plant was built in order to produce sarin, the chemical used in Tokyo. They also formed their own government at this time, declaring the state government corrupt.

Through a series of chemical attacks in the early 1990s, which included attacks on the Japanese Parliament in 1990, the wedding of the Japanese crown prince in 1993, and an anthrax attack also in 1993, Aum Supreme Truth began to receive press coverage and national attention. That same year, a group of doctors in the cult traveled to Africa. They claimed to be medical missionaries, but their real mission was to investigate the possibility of bringing the Ebola virus to Japan for use in terrorist warfare. In June 1994, sarin was used in an attack that killed seven people in Matsumoto (central Japan); Asahara was blamed for ordering the attack.

Possessing an intense hatred for America, he charged that the United States was evil, intending to proliferate materialism, imperialism, and support for Jewish causes. Admixtures of religious apocalyptic ideas pervade the group. For example, the United States was labeled as the beast in the book of Revelation in the ▸Bible. Also, Asahara regarded SOKA-GAKKAI as his chief religious/political rival and attempted to murder its honorary president. Hatred for the Jews was also paramount in the cult. The Jews aim, so Asahara claimed, to dominate the world. The Jews already controlled the economy of the United States.[2] Jews aim to destroy Japan, so it is believed by members of the group, and it is with the aid of the superpower America that such an attempt will be carried out.

On March 20, 1995, the cult carried out the subway attacks that brought them international notoriety. Today, the organization has lost its tax status as a religion and also its legal status. In 1997, the government attempted to disband the group altogether under the Antisubversive Activities Law. This effort met with failure when the government's Public Securities Examination Commission turned down the request on the grounds that the cult no longer presented a threat since its highest ranking leaders were in prison. One hundred five members of the group, including Asahara himself, were indicted on various charges, ranging from illegal drug production, lynching, kidnapping, and murder. In 2000, some Russian followers tried to free Asahara, but their efforts were thwarted, and many of the other members were condemned to die. Asahara was sentenced to death on February 27, 2004, but he has appealed his case.

ORGANIZATION

The groups has established a Tokyo Center and there are now at least twenty-six centers nationwide.

BELIEFS

Aum's theology is drawn from a variety of sources and concepts from world religions. These include HINDUISM,

apocalyptic concepts in CHRISTIANITY (drawn chiefly from the book of Revelation), BUDDHISM, NEW AGE beliefs, and ▸shamanism. From Hinduism, Aum borrows from the idea of ▸Shiva, the Hindu God of destruction. While the concept in Hinduism is to account for "change" in the universe, Aum adopted the idea that human initiative must be used to bring about such change. Thereby, destruction must arise to bring about good. One destroys in order to save. From Buddhism, Aum members adopt the idea of rebirth. Even when destruction and death come in the present order, one wakes up to a better world.[3]

Anti-Semitism, according to one source, is a central theme of Aum theology.[4] In January 1995, two months before the poison gas attacks, the group published a tract titled "Manual of Fear" (see note 2), in which it claimed that the ambition of the Jews was world domination and conquest. Apocalyptic themes from Revelation center around divine judgment that will be visited by God on the Jews. Before the terrorist attacks on the United States on September 11, 2001, Asahara, while in prison, had expressed surprise that there had never been any attacks on Americans,[5] and Aum's vitriol and outrage were focused on the Jews. Everything changed after September 11. Attacks on the United States are now a reality. There is little doubt that members of Aum interpret September 11 as a judgment on America for participating in the "Jewish lie."

CONCLUSION

Though no longer considered a dangerous threat or violence-prone, the Japanese government continues to keep a watchful eye on developments in the group.

ADDITIONAL INFORMATION_____

Headquarters
Tokyo Center

Website
aum-shrinkyo.members.easyspace.com/html/english

Sacred Texts
There are no specific sacred texts, but this is not to say that the sacred texts of the world religions are not referred to. As mentioned above, they frequently refer to Revelation in the Bible. Much of the group's inspiration comes directly from sermons, letters, and teachings of Asahara himself.

Membership
At the time of the gas attacks and before Asahara's imprisonment, there were over 9,000 members of Aum Supreme Truth in Japan and (perhaps) as many as 40,000 supporters of the cause worldwide. After 1995, followers and membership dropped considerably, yet strong support has continued for

nearly a decade. In 2004 the membership was estimated between 1,500 and 2,000 with presence in thirty-five Japanese communities. There are probably approximately 500 members of the group in existence today.

Notes

[1] From *http://religiousmovements.lib.virginia.edu/nrms/aums.html*, 1.

[2] A tract called "Manual of Fear," as cited in *Anti-Semitism Worldwide 1995/6* (Project for the Study of Anti-Semitism; Jerusalem: Tel Aviv University), 265.

[3] This idea is suggested by the title of Robert Lifton's *Destroying the World to Save It: Aum Shinrikyo; Apocalyyptic Violence and the New Global Terrorism* (New York: Metropolitan Books/Henry Holt, 1999).

[4] Ely Karmon, "The Anti-Semitism of Japan's Aum Shinrikyo: A Dangerous Rival," *Anti-Semitism Worldwide 1998/9* (The Stephen Roth Institute for the Study of Contemporary Anti-Semitism and Racism at Tel Aviv University; Lincoln: Nebraska Univ. Press).

[5] Ibid., 7.

BAHA'I FAITH, THE

A religious movement founded in the nineteenth century as an independent religious movement branching off from ISLAM. The Baha'i Faith has always been an ecumenical movement in that it sees as its goal the eventual unity of all of the world's different faiths into the Baha'i Faith. The Baha'i Faith has met with great resistance in Islamic countries, especially Iran. It sees itself as having the same relationship to Islam a CHRISTIANITY has to JUDAISM.

HISTORY

Islam was in need of reform in the nineteenth century, and Muslims had been long awaiting the coming of a prophet whom 'Allah would raise up to enact it. In 1844 Mirza Ali 'Muhammad (1819–50) claimed for himself the title *Bab* (meaning Glory of God), or the one who would herald the coming of the prophet. Mirza Ali gained a considerable group of followers, who were referred to as Babis. His heralding mission came to a sudden end, however, in 1850, when he was executed by religious zealots called *mujtahids*, who were unreceptive to his break from Islam.

One follower, Mirza Husayn 'Ali (1817–92), known also as Baha'u'llah, became convinced that he was the very prophet of whom Mirza Ali had spoken. However, it was not until 1863 that Baha'u'llah announced that he was the long-awaited *Mahdi,* or "him whom God should manifest." Immediately he began to teach openly from that point until his death in 1892. Since his death, the Baha'is believe that he continues to lead the Faith through a New World Order established by him.

Baha'u'llah's son, Abdu'l 'Baha (1844–1921), assumed leadership of the group after his father's death. During his reign the Baha'i Faith came to the United States (1893). Abdu'l proved to be an outstanding interpreter of his father's teachings, and Baha'i became solidified into an established movement under Abdu'l's tenure. He built a $2.5 million temple in the Chicago suburb of Wilmette, Illinois, the U.S. headquarters for the movement. The first Baha'i community was introduced in America by Ibrahim George Kheiralla and five American converts. The small community was known as the "First Assembly of Baba'ists in America–1895."

In 1899, a conflict between Kheiralla and Abdu'l Baha arose over leadership in the Baha'i organization in the United States. Kheiralla was a powerful and persuasive teacher who was recognized by members of the organization as the chief leader. Abdu'l Baha responded to this crisis in a letter in 1900 stating that "no one should expect to have themselves appointed a chief" because it was part of the original teachings of Baha'u'llah that no clergy would be recognized. Kheiralla disagreed and left the organization. This dispute, however, did not hurt the movement in America as it continued to grow.

After the death of Abdu'l Baha in 1921, Shoghi 'Effendi (1897–1957), Abdul Baha's grandson, through a series of written wills and testaments became the new leader. Effendi appointed the Hands of the Cause of God as an institution that advised and guided the movement. It is now almost extinct because the Universal House of Justice is unable to appoint hands. Only Baha'u'llah, Abdul Baha, and Shoghi Effendi were empowered to so designate individuals. When Effendi died, there were twenty-seven hands. In 1994, there were only three left and they were in their eighties. To carry forward their functions (though not their rank), the Universal House of Justice has appointed "counselors."[1]

One former close adherent to The Baha᾽i Faith, in a personal correspondence, relates:

> The conflict that came with the passing of the Guardian is the most significant one—the one that makes it virtually impossible for The Baha᾽i Faith to continue in any internally consistent or coherent way. The "Covenant" was written down explicitly, and it provides for a continuing line of Guardians (an inherited title and function), who were to interact with the Universal House of Justice as both head and voting member of that legislative body. But the blow came when Shogi Effendi died without leaving any will or any possible successor.

> The structure of the faith was defined by Shogi Effendi in his role as the first—and, as it turned out, the last—Guardian. And this structure was defined, in no uncertain terms, to represent the very meaning of Baha᾽u᾽llah's "New World Order." But when that structure is defined in terms of "twin pillars"—the Guardians and the Universal House of Justice—and both of these pillars are defined as "essential" and "inseparable" by the Guardian himself, what happend when one of those twin pillars is taken away?

> The Baha᾽i's world order with no Guardian defies the vision of the founders of that Faith.

In August 2000, a Millennium Peace Summit for Religious and Spiritual Leaders was held in the chamber of the United Nations General Assembly. The Summit was addressed by Dr. Albert Lincoln, the General Secretary of The Baha᾽i International Community. The focus of the Summit was to identify "core values" for peace. Dr. Lincoln defined the real problem in the world as the existence of a "moral vacuum" and the "pervasive materialism" of the modern world. The Summit was attended by more than a thousand spiritual leaders from a variety of faith traditions around the world. All world religions, including CHRISTIANITY, were represented.

A Baha᾽i temple.   Courtesy Jack Roper/CARIS

ORGANIZATION

The leader of The Baha᾽i Faith is called the secretary-general, who reports and is accountable to the supreme governing body of the organization. This governing body is called the Universal House of Justice. Only males can be members. This board acts as the legislative and executive governing bodies, seeking to promote and apply the laws of Baha᾽u᾽llah. Local groups, called spiritual assemblies, meet in major cities all over the world. These are governed in each nation by a National Spiritual Assembly comprised of nine members. Baha᾽i temples are situated in cities throughout the world. The most holy place is regarded as Bahji in Israel, where the remains of Baha᾽u᾽llah are kept.

The temple in Wilmette is constructed with the numeral nine as the central architectural motif. Nine is the Baha᾽i symbol of unity. There are nine sides to the building, nine pillars, nine arches, nine gates, and nine fountains.

There are fourteen individuals who are regarded as manifestations of God: Adam, Noah, Salih, Hud, Abraham, Moses, ᾽Confucius, Jesus, ᾽Muhammad, ᾽Zoroaster, ᾽Buddha, ᾽Krishna, Bab, and Baha᾽u᾽llah—whom God has raised up throughout the centuries

The Baha᾽i Faith uses a calendar revolving around the key dates in the lives of Mirza Ali Muhammad and Baha᾽u᾽llah. The year begins on March 21, which is considered to be a holy day. Other holy days include April 21, 29, and May 23—Baha᾽u᾽llah's declaration and mission; November 12—the birth of Baha᾽u᾽llah; October 20—the birth of Bab; May 29—the death of Baha᾽u᾽llah; and July 9—the martyrdom of Bab. Bab established a calendar of nineteen months of nineteen days each, allowing for four intercalary days (five in leap years).

To become a member of The Baha᾽i Faith one must profess a belief in the teachings of Baha᾽u᾽llah and sign a card to that effect. There are no ᾽sacraments or rituals and no professional clergy. Members are expected to pray daily; fast nineteen days per year; observe the holy days; make at least one pilgrimage during their lifetime to Haifa, Israel, the location of the world head-quarters for the movement; and abstain from alcohol and refrain from all substance abuse, fornication, and homosexuality.

TEACHINGS

The writings of Baha'u'llah have been translated into over eight hundred languages. Religious activities center around the calendar (*see* above), and the rising and setting of the sun begins and ends each day in The Baha'i Faith.

Many of the teachings and beliefs are contained in the more than one hundred literary contributions of Baha'u'llah, including such titles as *al-kitab al Aqdas* (*The Most Holy Book*), which contains the laws governing Baha'i; *ketab-e Iqan* (*The Book of Certitude*); *The Hidden Words*; and *The Seven Valleys*. All of the writings of Baha'u'llah are believed to be inspired sacred text by Baha'i devotees.

The main principle of The Baha'i Faith is the belief in a fundamental harmony to truth. The world's religions have all contained such truth, but to embrace The Baha'i Faith is to understand ultimate truth. "Ye are the fruits of one tree and the leaves of one Branch," stated Baha'i's founder. "The earth is but one country and mankind its citizens," is another oft-quoted slogan of the movement, capturing the essence of its basic thrust toward understanding The Baha'i Faith's goal of being the one, true unifying faith.

This ideal is contrary to traditional Christianity and, predictably, to The Baha'i Faith's parent religion, Islam. Traditional Christianity teaches that the sole means for unity and peace in the world lies in faith in Jesus Christ as "the way and the truth and the life" (John 14:6). In keeping with these words, the creeds of Christendom have always maintained that the one true faith to the exclusion of all others is Christianity: "Whoever will be saved shall, above all else, hold the catholic faith" (Athanasian Creed, Appendix 1). This is similarly true of Islam: "There is no God but Allah and Muhammad is his prophet," states the 'shahada. Traditional Muslims dismiss the Baha'i Faith's claim to being Muslim because of what Islam regards as heretical teachings chiefly because it has substituted a new prophet (Baha'u'llah) for Muhammad. At least among some of the world religions, therefore, Baha'i's tenet of unity among all faiths is considered an unrealizable goal.[3]

Other teachings include: independence in the search for truth, oneness of the human race, harmony between science and religion, compulsory education, the goal of attaining one universal language, equality between the sexes, the abolition of extreme wealth and poverty, universal peace, and the elimination of racism.

Another stark contrast to traditional Christianity is the belief that the great religious teachers in history are "manifestations" of God. For Christianity, Jesus is confessed as the 'incarnation of God. This "fleshing" of God in the person of Jesus is rejected by the proponents of The Baha'i Faith, who claim that God simply cannot be identified in the flesh of Jesus or exclusively in any other great religious leader.

Members of The Baha'i Faith observe and practice the Ten Commandments. Members are forbidden to use alcohol and drugs. Gambling and gossip are also not allowed.

CONCLUSION

Its mission into the twenty-first century continues to be the holding forth of a vision for a global community and an attainment of peace and harmony throughout the world through efforts to present The Baha'i Faith as the new religious paradigm, to replace all others, in the modern world. To date, this vision has not changed.

ADDITIONAL INFORMATION

Headquarters
The Baha'i Faith National Center, 112 Linden Ave., Wilmette, IL 60091.

Website
www.bahai.org

Sacred Texts
The highest and most revered text is the *Kitab-I-Aqbas* written by Baha' U'llah. Other of his writings that are regarded as authoritative are *Gleanings from the Writings of Baha'u'llah; Prayers and Meditations; The Seven Valleys and the Four Valleys; Epistle to the Son of Wolf.* The works of Shogi Effendi are also regarded as authoritative, as is also true of the writing of Abdul' Baha. Statements and letters are issued from the Universal House of Justice.

Membership
Five million members in 235 countries. There are close to 130,000 Baha'i members living in the United States.

Notes
[1] From a book review of the first edition of this volume. See *http://bahai-library.com/excerpts/mather/html*.
[2] Author's email correspondence with Arthur Peña, February 28, 2005.
[3] See HINDUISM for the greatest expression of Baha'i's central principle—the unity of all faiths.

BRANCH DAVIDIANS

The Branch Davidians were a relatively unknown and obscure group until April, 1993, when they dominated the news headlines for seven weeks concerning their gunpoint standoff against the United States government that tragically ended in a fire at their Waco, Texas, facility. In the end, several government employees and many of the Branch Davidians lost their lives—an event that sparked pro and con investigations. This incident also provoked a rethinking effort about cults, religious freedom, and the place of government oversight.

HISTORY

The story of the Branch Davidians begins at the close of the nineteenth century with the birth of its founder, Victor Houteff, on March 2, 1885, in Raikovo, Bulgaria. Houteff encountered the teachings of SEVENTH-DAY ADVENTISM (see also ᐳMillerite movement) in 1918. In 1929, he came to a decision that Adventist doctrine was incorrect. The Adventists distanced themselves from Houteff, but he did not completely break all ties with the SDA.

Houteff did form a new movement known as The Shepherds Rod. In keeping with Adventist theology, he was greatly interested in the end times. He read and studied Revelation with avid interest. He soon decided that he was included in its prophecies. It was his divinely appointed task to assemble the 144,000 (Rev. 7:4). He believed that it would one day be the mission of the group to go to Palestine, where the second coming of Christ would finally take place and the Davidic kingdom would be established.

Houteff chose Waco, Texas, as the place to begin. Mount Carmel Center was founded in 1935 just outside of the city limits. In 1942, Houteff did, in fact, finally break all ties with the SDA when the SDA would not grant him or members of the group "conscientious objection" status with the onset of America's involvement in World War II. The Shepherds Rod was then renamed Davidian Seventh-day Adventist Association. By 1955, the year of Houteff's death, the group had grown to 155 members.

The death of their leader sent members into somewhat of a panic. He had promised them that God had chosen him to lead them in ushering in the "reign of God." It thus appeared to the fledgling group of members that he was wrong. Houteff's wife, Florence, however, became the leader of the group. She predicted that the end of the world would come on April 22, 1959, because of the fulfillment of a prophecy in Revelation 11. About a week before this, members began to make preparations to travel to the Holy Land to await the arrival of the kingdom. Florence Houteff sold the compound to Ben Roden in 1961, and he renamed the group the Branch Davidian Seventh-Day Adventists.

Vernon ᐳHowell joined the group in 1981. He was a shy and unassuming personality. Roden's leadership in the group was unsuccessful. He lost most of his following and his debt was growing. He was imprisoned for a period of six months. This gave Howell the chance to take over leadership of the group, which he did by managing to pay off years of bad debts, which afforded him the title to Mount Carmel.

In 1989, Roden committed a vicious ax murder and was institutionalized. He managed a brief escape, during which time Howell armed his followers, believing that Roden would return to seek revenge for his demise. From here, Howell emerged as the dominant personality of the Branch Davidians. He changed his name in 1990 to David ᐳKoresh—the first name based on King David of the Old Testament and the last name the Old Testament word for Cyrus, king of Persia. Koresh's success was largely due to a charismatic side to his personality, combined with an impressive command of Scripture. Koresh also capitalized on an impulse that had always been a part of Adventist theology, namely, ᐳmillennialism and the imminent end of the world.

Informed by an almost exclusive millennial theology, Koresh taught his followers to interpret all current day events as having immediate fulfillment of various prophetic passages in the ᐳBible, especially Revelation. The U.S. government was referred to as "Babylonians" while the Davidians were the "elect" and Koresh the "Lamb" of Revelation 7:10. The Davidians viewed the government intervention and surrounding of the Waco compound as the beginning of the battle of Armageddon (Rev. 16:16).

Koresh had made frequent appearances in public in order to purchase weapons and supplies. In addition to guns, Koresh stockpiled chemicals that could be used to manufacture explosives and also purchased night-vision scopes. In May 1992, a UPS package broke open while being delivered to the compound. It contained hand grenades. Local authorities were contacted and the Bureau of Alcohol, Tobacco, and Firearms (ATF) was brought in. Koresh renamed Mount Carmel "Ranch Apocalypse."

On February 28, 1993, in the first raid on the compound, four ATF agents were killed and sixteen wounded. Six members of the Davidians were also believed to have been wounded, including Koresh's two-year-old daughter. Now a regular part of the nightly news the world over, the fifty-one-day siege from late February through April 19 was underway. This included a complete encirclement of the compound, a cutting off of all communications, the halting of any supplies coming in, and constant attempts to simply talk the Davidians into surrendering. These were met with what the federal agents referred to as Koresh's "Bible-babble," where he bewildered negotiators with his millennial musings. Twenty-three members of the compound were, in fact, allowed to come out—two women and twenty-one children.

The ATF attempted to aggravate the members of the compound by playing loud music. Koresh threatened not to allow any more members to leave if the music did not stop. Electricity was turned off, and floodlights, Buddhist chants, sounds of animals being slaughtered, and so on were all used to further intimidate the Davidians to come out. No negotiating techniques worked. On April 19, 1993, the FBI attacked the compound. A fire started and by the end of the day, with the thirty-mile-per-hour winds, the compound was reduced to ashes and rubble with most of the remaining members of the Davidians, including Koresh, killed. The total deceased were eighty-six, with nine survivors.

In the aftermath, eleven Davidians were prosecuted by the Clinton administration. Nine of them were convicted in the "murders" of federal agents, though in June 2000 their lengthy sentences were reversed.

Much controversy has surrounded the Waco disaster. Questions arose in the media as to the culpability of the FBI, the ATF, and in particular Attorney General Janet Reno. Many believed that the attack and the siege were unnecessary, especially in light of the fact that forty children lost their lives. Opponents of the government's actions argued that Koresh could have been apprehended peacefully, given time and patience. Others contend that Koresh was dangerous and that the stockpiling of weaponry posed a threat to the public that could not be ignored.

As recently as 1999, the FBI was still being accused of responsibility for the disaster at Waco. Some in the media claimed that the use of flammable tear gas and the presence of secret Delta forces were unnecessary

and in fact placed clear blame on the U.S. government. Reno denied any knowledge of these facts and vowed to conduct a full investigation. The investigation headed by Senator John Danforth concluded on July 21, 2000, that the government should not be held responsible for the firings on the compound since the Davidians initiated the attack. Yet the FBI's own FLIR (Forward Looking Infrared Red) technology demonstrated that the first shots were indeed fired on the compound.

ORGANIZATION

The Davidians lived together in a communal lifestyle, and David Koresh was the authority figure who made all the major decisions in the life of the group.

TEACHINGS

The basic theology of the Branch Davidians was shaped by Seventh-day Adventism. Fundamental beliefs that one would readily recognize in Protestant and evangelical circles parallel Davidian doctrine, including the literal existence of the Garden of Eden, the existence of Satan and evil, the Fall, the divinity of Christ, the Trinity, the belief that Christ's death atones for sin, and the Bible as the infallible and inerrant Word of God.

Koresh

David Koresh's theology also brought some innovations. He adopted a messianic role and derived much of his eschatological impulses from his reading of Revelation.

This included his belief that he had been given knowledge of the seven seals in Revelation. He had initially promised during the siege that he would write an interpretation to these seven seals and then surrender, but then he changed his mind. Koresh also decided that he was called to create a new lineage that would be derived from his seed. He ordained that he cohabitate with "pure" females and that these "spiritual wives" would bear him the offspring that would be the beginning of his new family line. Koresh arranged all marriages, and all monies earned were deposited with the group.

Koresh had a profound knowledge of the Bible, but he frequently broke the well-established rule in the discipline of ▶hermeneutics that one should first interpret passages within their *own* context before making a modern-day application. Koresh took passages from the Scripture and linked them with other passages anywhere else in the Bible to produce a theology of his own that pertained to the peculiarities of the Davidians.

CONCLUSION

The significance of the Branch Davidians today lies in the critical questions surrounding the extent to which the government intervened and set a precedent—namely, whether the Davidians fired first, how many of the members wanted to surrender peaceably, the fact and length of sentences imposed on the remaining members, and the degree to which anti-government individuals and groups found new reasons for blaming federal authorities for what they believe are the evils plaguing America. For example, Timothy McVeigh, the Oklahoma City bomber, claimed that his hatred for the government was inflamed by the Waco incident, which caused him to blow up the Alfred Murrah Federal Building on April 19, 1995, killing 168 people.

Today the few remaining members continue to wait for David Koresh's return to lead them to the Promised Land. These people gather on the Saturday Sabbath for prayer. "Our hopes are that God will intervene before the rest of us dying," said Clive Doyle, caretaker of the Mount Carmel site and keeper of the flickering Branch Davidian flame. "But we do have to face facts. Eventually, everyone gets old and dies. We worry that we will go the way of the Shakers and other groups who did not get new members or have children."[1]

ADDITIONAL INFORMATION

Websites

www.rense.com/general12/danfo.htm (the Danforth investigation and its critics). *www.ambs.edu/LJohns/waco.htm; www.waco93.com/* (the documentary "Rules of Engagement")

Sacred Text

The Bible

Membership

The group's membership more than likely never exceeded 150.

Note

[1] Howard Witt, "Branch Davidians Dwindle in Waco's Shadow," *Chicago Tribune* (June 25, 2004).

BRANHAMISM

A twentieth-century Pentecostal movement founded and spread by William Branham. Branham claimed to have received revelations that afforded this movement a uniqueness that inspired a significant following. Branham died in 1965. Inscribed on the pyramid-shaped tombstone in Jeffersonville, Indiana, are the words:

THE PROPHET WM. BRANHAM

ONE DAY I HEARD OF A PROPHET, WHOSE MESSAGE WENT STRAIGHT TO THE WORD

BACK TO THE BIBLE HE TOOK US: WITH HIS, "THUS SAITH THE LORD!"

I THOUGHT THAT THOSE DAYS WERE OVER, AND ALL OF GOD'S PROPHETS WERE DEAD; BUT GOD GAVE HIS VINDICATION, A PILLAR OF FIRE OVER HIS HEAD!

HE PREACHED PREDESTINATION, AND BAPTISM IN JESUS' NAME; DIVINE HEALING, THE SEED OF THE SERPENT, AND THAT GOD IS FOREVER THE SAME!

THE SICK, THE BLIND, AND THE CRIPPLED, THE POSSESSED, THE DEAF, AND THE LOST, CAME BY THE THOUSANDS TO SEE HIM, WHILE HE PREACHED THE WORD AT ANY COST!

MALACHI 4 TOLD US HE WAS COMING, AND GOD'S WORD WILL NEVER FAIL; AS HE LEFT US HE GAVE US A PROMISE, ONCE MORE I WILL RIDE THIS TRAIL!

WE DON'T KNOW WHAT'S FIXING TO HAPPEN, FOR GOD'S WAYS WE CAN'T UNDERSTAND; BUT WE'LL STAND ON HIS WORD TIL HE CALLS US, WITH THE BRIDE TO THAT HEAVENLY LAND!

A TENT AND COMPLETE TRANSFORMATION, IN A VISION OUR PROPHET DID SEE; THOUGH HE'S GONE, IT WILL BE COMPLETED, IT'S A PROMISE AND SO SHALL IT BE!

IT'S THUS SAITH THE LORD!!!

Branham's followers are convinced that he was a prophet invested with the power and spirit of Elijah, raised by God to minister to the church in modern times. Branhamites refer to such times as the "Laodicean Age," based on a dispensational interpretation of the seven churches in Revelation 2–3.

HISTORY

William Branham was born in Kentucky on April 6, 1909. His father was a bootlegger, and neither of his parents attended any Christian churches. However, when William was born, his parents and the midwife reported that they saw a halo resting above the baby's head. They were frightened and did not know how to interpret this phenomenon. Followers believe this was a sign that God had his hand on young William right from his birth. In 1950, the halo allegedly appeared again in Houston, Texas, when Branham was on a preaching tour. A photo of the phenomenon was taken to George Lacy, examiner of questioned documents, who on inspecting it, issued the following statement to Branham, his followers, and the press: "Rev. Branham, you will die like all other mortals but as long as there is a Christian civilization, your picture will live on."[1]

Branham reports that the first time God spoke to him was at age seven. While carrying water for his father's moonshine, he paused to rest under a tree. In the wind rustling through the leaves, a voice spoke, saying, "Never drink, smoke, or defile your body in any way, for I have a work for you to do when you get older."[2] Branham's father often called his son a sissy because he refused to drink. In a weak moment, young William decided to prove to his father that he could consume alcohol like all the other Branhams (his four brothers all drank with their father). Raising the bottle to his lips, he suddenly heard the voice in the wind and began to cry, to which his father promptly responded, "See, I told you he was a sissy."[3] The voice repeated this message on several occasions in Branham's life before his conversion.

Branham's conversion to CHRISTIANITY came through the preaching of a Baptist minister. Shortly thereafter he felt called to preach, and plans were made to conduct his first church service. In 1933, under a tent in Jeffersonville, Indiana, Branham preached to approximately three thousand people.

Branham considered the death of his wife, Hope Brumback, and his baby daughter, both in 1937, to be God's judgment for not heeding a call to minister to ONENESS PENTECOSTALS, with whom he had become acquainted during a revival near the Mishawaka River in Indiana.

In 1946 Branham claimed to have been visited by an angel in a secret cave, where he purportedly was granted the power to discern people's illnesses. Subsequently, thousands attended the mystic preacher's healing services and revivals in auditoriums and stadiums throughout the world. From October–December 1951, Branham traveled to South Africa and conducted what has been dubbed the "greatest religious meetings ever." All manner of miracles and healings were reported to have taken place at these meetings, attended by hundreds of thousands. Services were held in Cape Town, Johannesburg, and Durban. Julius Stadsklev documents the various healings in his book, *William Branham—A Prophet Visits South Africa* (1952). Walter Hollenwegger, who interpreted for Branham in Zurich, Switzerland, on one occasion writes that he "is not aware of any case in which he [Branham] was mistaken in the often detailed statements he made."[4]

D. J. Wilson summarizes the reasons for Branham's immense popularity and success:

> In contrast to the caricature of the image-minded evangelist, he lived modestly, dressed moderately, and boasted of his youthful poverty. This endeared him to the throngs who idealized him. He was self-conscious about his lack of education, but the simplicity of his messages had worldwide appeal.
>
> By emphasizing healing and prosperity and neglecting his Oneness theology Branham was able to minister in Trinitarian Pentecostal circles as well.[5]

Branham was killed by a drunk driver in 1965. Some of his followers awaited his resurrection, while others memorialized him by building a shrine in his honor at his grave in Jeffersonville. In addition to the hagiographic poem inscribed in the monument (*see* beginning of this essay), a second side of the shrine has inscribed the names of seven great Christian leaders throughout the history of the church, of which Branham is the final one: Paul, Irenaeus, Martin, Columba, Luther, Wesley, and Branham. Each one is seen as being the prophet God raised up in each of the seven church ages in the book of Revelation. A third side of the monument lists the seven churches—Ephesian, Smyrnaean, Pergamean, Thyatirean, Sardisean, Philadelphian, and Laodicean, the latter to which Branham was assigned.

ORGANIZATION

Independent groups claimed William Branham as their prophet or prophetic teacher following his death. They numbered in the tens of thousands. He was instrumental in the "Latter Rain Movement" among Pentecostals, which would separate over his denial of the Trinity. Early Branhamites often met in homes and listened to old recordings of Branham's sermons. Several thousand members left after his prediction failed, which said that 1977 would see American destroyed. Today's representative groups exist mainly in the United States and Canada. The internet has afforded the Branhamites worldwide access. The most prominent group is the Branham Tabernacle in Jefferson, Indiana, which also publishes 1,100 sermons, booklets, and audio messages. Other groups are called Bibleway, Bible Believers, and William Branham Evangelistic Association.

TEACHINGS

Essentially, Branham's theology is oneness in character, denying the ▸Trinity of traditional Christian theology. He states, "At the Nicene Council, the Apostles' teachings were traded for a much newer and more accepted doctrine called the Trinity."[6]

God

Oneness theology teaches that God is one person or one essence. The ancient church encountered this idea in ▸modalistic ▸monarchianism or ▸Sabellianism (named for one of its prominent advocates, Sabellius, who taught that God manifested himself in different "modes" at different times). At creation, God was the eternal Father. When Jesus was born, it was God himself (formerly the Father) who took on human form as the redeeming Son. After Jesus' ascension, God then manifested himself as Holy Spirit, wherein he now moves in and through the church. Modalism was originally the well-meant attempt to preserve the unity of the Godhead. But in so doing, the independent subsistence of the Father, Son, and Holy Spirit, of which the Bible refers to on ample occasions, was lost.

Modalism was challenged by leading theologians in the early church, such as Dionysius of Alexandria. The Trinitarian theology that emerged out of the Council of Nicea (A.D. 325) was a testimony to the fact that the church recognized the distinctive subsistence of the Father, Son, and Holy Spirit as being clearly attested to in the apostolic writings of the New Testament.[7]

Baptism

Branham reasoned that because God is one, the doctrine of the Trinity "is of the ▸devil." Therefore, anyone who has been baptized in the name of the triune God must be rebaptized "in the name of Jesus only." Branham understood the baptismal formula given by Jesus in Matthew 28:18–20 as being a summary of the modalistic idea discussed above: "Why don't you examine your baptism of Father, Son, and Holy Ghost, and that false 'trinity' it's so-called, which is nothing in the world but three offices of one God, titles. No name of Father. There's no such thing as name, Father, Son, and Holy Ghost."[8]

Humanity

Branham taught a doctrine he called "serpent's seed," in which he believed that Eve had sexual rela-

tions with the serpent in the Garden of Eden. Some human beings therefore are predestined to hell. Hell, however, is not a place of eternal torment as traditional Christianity maintains. Hell will be done away with by God. Others, however, are born of the "seed of God," not corrupted by Eve's faithless union; they are heirs of eternal life. Branham believed that those who follow his teachings are of the righteous seed.

Orthodox Christian doctrine does not teach that Eve had sexual relations with the devil and that the resultant offspring were the souls predestined for damnation. This is an idea embraced by some ▸occult and ▸satanist groups. Augustine believed that "original sin" is inherited by the human race through sexual lust or "concupiscence," but it was Adam who sinned, and together with sinful Eve they produced sinful progeny. Together they produced an offspring that inherited corruption. Branham's serpent's seed doctrine is clearly outside the boundaries of ▸orthodoxy.

Church

According to Branham, all denominations within Christendom are apostate and of the devil. People from different denominational churches may be saved, but they must undergo suffering in a future period of time known as the Great Tribulation. True Christians must be rebaptized "in the name of Jesus only" and follow the doctrines taught by God's apostle to the seventh and final age of church history—William Branham. To be part of a denominational church is to have the mark of the beast (Rev. 13:6–18).

For traditional orthodoxy, denominations are an unfortunate testimony to the fact that sinful human beings who are Christians cannot always agree on matters, whether they be doctrinal issues or personality clashes. There were divisions in the church almost from the beginning. Paul and Barnabas had a sharp disagreement between them over whether to take John Mark on Paul's second missionary journey (Acts 15:36–41). Paul encountered problems with division in the church at Corinth (1 Cor. 1:10–12 and elsewhere); yet the plurality and diversity within Christendom is compensated for in the unity that all Christians experience in the love and forgiveness extended through Jesus Christ (John 3:16). All who believe in Christ comprise the "holy, catholic, and apostolic Church" (Nicene Creed, Appendix 1). The Apostles' Creed speaks of all true believers who have received the "forgiveness of sins" as being members of the "communion of saints." Narrow sectarianism has always been denounced within the church and will continue to be denounced (Matt. 10:40; Luke 9:49–50).

Some of Branham's followers believed that he (Branham) was virgin-born. Christianity regards this notion as rank heresy. None other than the Founder of Christendom may claim such a unique entrance into the world.

End Times

Branham believed himself to be the promised Elijah of Malachi 4:5, sent as a herald to usher in the end times. Traditional Christian exegesis of Malachi 4:5 has rendered John the Baptist as being the herald spoken of (John 1:6–9). Even though John denied it (1:21), he perfectly fulfilled the role of the herald in Isaiah 40:3. Interestingly enough, it is only orthodox JUDAISM that maintains that the coming of Elijah is yet future.

CONCLUSION

Although Branham died in 1965, his followers avidly believe in the truth of his cause. His son, Billy Paul Branham, assumed the position of president of the William Branham Evangelistic Association (WBEA). Voice of God recordings is a website (*www.branham.org*) that followers maintain. Branham's sermons are published in many languages and are available on the website. Extremist followers continue to believe he will be resurrected by God to vindicate his mission. Still others believe he was God himself in human form. Most of his admirers, however, simply believe and follow one whom they consider to be a prophet for the modern world. Branham joins the ranks with many who preceded him—

and many who will follow—who believe themselves the chosen of God, singled out by a perceived voice or a vision.

ADDITIONAL INFORMATION_____

Headquarters
PO Box 950, Jeffersonville, IN 47131.

Website
www.biblebelievers.org; www.williambranham.com

Sacred Text
The Bible

Membership
unknown

Notes
[1] Julius Stadsklev, *William Branham—A Prophet Visits South Africa* (Minneapolis: Julius Stadsklev, 1952), 35.
[2] Ibid., 3.
[3] Ibid., 6.
[4] Walter J. Hollenwegger, *The Pentecostals* (Minneapolis: Augsburg, 1972), 354.
[5] D. J. Wilson, "Branham, William Marion," in *The New International Dictionary of Pentecostal and Charismatic Movements*, ed. by Stanley Burgess and Eduard M. van der Maas (Grand Rapids, Zondervan, 2002), 441.
[6] William Branham, *Thus Saith the Lord* 2 no. 5, 4–7 as quoted in "William Branham," *Christian Research Institute Fact Sheet,* ed. Cal Beisner (San Juan Capistrano, Calif.: Christian Research Institute, 1979), 2.
[7] See CHRISTADELPHIANISM and THE WAY INTERNATIONAL for a further discussion of the Trinity.
[8] William Branham, *The Lord God Hath Spoken*, a compendium of tape-recorded messages containing utterances of Branham on various subjects.

BUDDHISM

One of the great world religions found chiefly in Asia and the Far East, Buddhism has been growing in the West rapidly in the twentieth and early twenty-first centuries.

HISTORY

Buddhism was founded by Siddharta ʼGautama (563–483 B.C.; Siddharta means "Goal Achieved" and Gautama means "Best Cow"), who was born to a Hindu agricultural tribe in the Himalayan foothills of Nepal. Accounts of his life are filled with both facts and fancy. At the age of twenty-nine, he renounced a legitimate claim to political power. Leaving his wife and children behind, Gautama became a mendicant, wandering from

place to place in search of truth (*see* the ʼGreat Renunciation). He spent some time experimenting with ʼBrahmanism but became totally disillusioned with it. Soon afterward, he engaged in a period of intense meditation and received the long-awaited ʼenlightenment that afforded him the title ʼBuddha. Gautama spent the rest of his life in travel, teaching the religion—or better, the philosophy—that gained him millions of followers in the centuries ahead.

In 245 B.C. a council of five hundred Buddhist monks gathered together the oral traditions of over three centuries and assembled them into written form in the Pali language. These writings were called ʼTripitaka.

This Buddhist temple is found in Milwaukee, Wisconsin.

Courtesy Jack M. Roper/CARIS

Buddhism spread rapidly under ▸Asoka (274–236 B.C.), who sent missionaries to Syria, Egypt, Macedonia, and as far east as Burma and Ceylon. Buddhism was basically a unified movement at this time. As is often the case when a powerful military leader dies, however, the followers, previously united under him, split into their own factions. Asoka's empire was no exception. A geographical and philosophical split took place shortly after his death. Two systems of thought emerged as a result: THERAVADA to the south, which retained the Pali language, and MAHAYANA to the north, where the literature and language was Sanskrit. These two major parties further divided into the multiplicities of ▸sects that constitute Buddhism today.

In a real sense, Buddhism is not a religion at all, if religion is defined as being belief in a divine or supernatural deity, or if prayer, sacrifices, and concepts of a future life constitute vital components. Gautama did not deny the existence of deities, but he dismissed them as being useless in everyday life. Buddhism, therefore, has been called the religion of practical atheism. Nancy Wilson Ross correctly points out, however, that it is incorrect to label Buddhism as being atheistic in the deep sense of the term:

> Buddhist teaching in relation to the true nature of the soul, or self, probably accounts in part for the allegation that it is a form of atheism. Actually, Buddhism is no more atheistic than it is theistic or pantheistic. The charge of atheism can hardly be laid at the door of a teacher who declares of the universe, or cosmos, in its wholeness (or thusness): "There is an unborn, an originated, an unmade, an uncompounded. Were there not, O mendicants, there would be no escape from the world of the born, the originated, the made and the compounded."[1]

Buddhism has had a marked effect on the United States, particularly on the West Coast. The first Buddhist temple in America was built in 1898 in San Francisco. In 1942 the Buddhist Churches of America with

100,000 members was incorporated. There were approximately 300,000 Buddhists in America in 2000. A separate movement known as NICHIREN SHOSHU of America was formed, which proved to be attractive to many non-Asian Americans. Another modification of Buddhism that has had considerable influence in America and has received recognition as being a separate denomination is ZEN Buddhism. Branches of each of the movements exist in major cities across the United States.

The breakdown of the Soviet Union and subsequent relaxation of the persecution of religion has affected Buddhism. Buddhist temples have begun to be built in Moscow, St. Petersburg, and other cities of the former Soviet Union. In July 1991, Buddhism celebrated 250 years as a recognized Russian religion.

In November 1990, a thirty-three foot statue of the Buddha was unveiled in Baltimore, Maryland, as a token of desire on the part of Japanese diplomats and businessmen to improve relations between the two countries. On the same token, large Buddhist statues standing in the mountains of Afghanistan were blown up in 2001 by the Taliban government before its demise as a result of the war with the United States following the September 11 attack on the World Trade Center. Buddhists come together under the banner of the General Conference of the World Fellowship of Buddhists.

TEACHINGS

Like the Brahmans of Hinduism, Gautama embraced the idea of *reincarnation. Salvation is an ultimate escape from the cycle of rebirth. Other Hindu concepts such as the *caste system and the validity of the Vedic writings (*see* *Vedism) were rejected by Gautama.

A central idea in Eastern thought is the notion that *avidya (ignorance) is the root of all evil. Buddhism embraces this concept in full. Gautama worked out a way of liquidating ignorance that was unlike any of the approaches formulated up to his time. Having considered the rigors of *asceticism on the one hand and unbridled hedonism on the other as being workable means of gaining self-discipline and control, he rejected each as being a failure to destroy that which is fundamental to human nature, namely, passion and desire. His philosophy is contained in the *Four Noble Truths:

1. Suffering is universal.
2. Suffering is caused by desire.
3. To eliminate suffering is to eliminate desire.
4. A path must be followed in order to achieve this (to end rebirth).

The path that Gautama proposed is composed of eight steps, known popularly as the *Eightfold Path": (1) right belief; (2) right feelings; (3) right speech; (4) right conduct; (5) right livelihood; (6) right effort; (7) right memory; and (8) right meditation or concentration. If one follows these principles, one will become an *arhat. Ignorance now eliminated, the Buddhist is then free to enter *nirvana. *Karma is "blown out," and the cycle of rebirth is ended.

Buddhism distinguishes between five modes of being: (1) the "buddhas" or those who have become buddhas; (2) *bodhisattvas (future buddhas); (3) *pratyeka* buddhas—namely, those who have sought enlightenment personally but have yet to pass such great knowledge to others; (4) *aryas* (those already on the road leading to nirvana); and (5) *prithagjanas*—the majority of disciples who do not aspire to the lofty goals of the *arhat*.

In addition to fulfilling the requirements of the Eightfold Path, the Buddhist monk who aspires to be a true and faithful follower of Gautama follows ten commandments forbidding: (1) murder; (2) theft; (3) fornication; (4) lying; (5) drinking alcoholic beverages; (6) eating during times when abstinence is in force; (7) dancing, singing, and all forms of worldly entertainment; (8) using perfumes and/or ornamental attire; (9) sleeping on beds that are not on the floor; and (10) accepting alms of gold or silver.

The following compares and contrasts Buddhism and CHRISTIANITY, with respect to God, sin, salvation, the future, and morality:

God

In stark contrast to Christianity, Buddhism does not embrace the notion of a personal God who is at the same time *immanent and *transcendent. Rather than a God who is comprised of a threefold personality (Trinity), the Buddhist notion of God is devoid of personality, so that he is spoken of as a Void without emotion. In the end, the goal for each Buddhist is to divest oneself of personality and emotions to achieve absorption into the great Void (Nirvana), thus breaking the cycle of reincarnation. Buddhists have been traditionally classed as being atheistic by the Christian church (see above). Classical Christian apologetics has been tempered in modern times by a much more tolerant and liberal attitude. The brand of Christianity influenced by existentialism and speculative idealism has resulted in a major paradigm shift in the last 150 years. A modern scientific cosmology has caused many theologians, both Catholic and Protestant, to rethink the whole doctrine of the existence of God. The result has been an attitude of tolerance and openness. The liberal Roman Catholic theologian Hans Küng articulates this position clearly:

> Today the Christian view of Buddhism stresses information instead of denunciation, complementarity instead of antagonism, dialogue instead of proselytism, "speaking of Christ with people of different faiths" instead of "winning unbelievers for Christ."[2]

While more conservative Christians reject the modernist paradigms, they nevertheless wish also to be in active dialogue with Buddhists and those of other religions. However, for churches that embrace the ancient confessional symbols, the question of God's existence is simply not a question.

Sin

Sin for the Buddhist is a concept known as ▸*tanha*. The word is often translated "lust," and it means all lust or desire arising in one's life. Christianity does not teach that all desire is sinful; only desire that is self-serving violates the moral laws of God. Christianity maintains that sin is both "original" and "actual"; that is to say, sin is part of both one's nature and one's actions. Humans are now conceived in sin and actively rebel against the living God.

Four of the Ten Commandments accepted in JUDAISM and Christianity forbid stealing, killing, adultery, and lying. But breaking compulsory fasts, dancing, or sleeping on a suspended bed do not constitute a violation of God's moral law in the ▸Bible and are therefore not sins. For the Buddhist, any and all desire results in sin. In Christian thought, it is a sin not to desire that which is right (loving God, loving one's neighbor, etc.).

Salvation and the Future

Historically, Buddhism was a nonmissionary religion, meaning that proselytizing efforts were minimal. In more recent times, however, various schools have implemented missionary programs that rival Christianity. Salvation for Buddhism lies in two areas of emphasis. First, it is the liberation from the cycle of rebirth, or to "cease to exist." "By the destruction of thirst (*tanha*), Attachment is destroyed; by the destruction of Attachment, Existence is destroyed" (*Vinaya Pitaka*). Second, salvation is also considered to be the cultivation of character and ethical stature in the present life by the fulfillment of the law and diligent obedience to the Eightfold Path. Salvation must be attained by the

Buddhist himself or herself with no aid from any external source. "By one's self the evil is done; by one's self one suffers; by one's self evil is left undone; by one's self one is purified. Lo, no man can purify another."[3]

The contrast here between Buddhism and Christianity is readily apparent. In contrast to the Buddhist idea of the self-attainment of salvation, Christianity teaches that God sent his only Son, Jesus Christ, into the world to live a sinless life, to die on a cross, and to rise from the dead in order to complete the work of atonement and proclaim victory over death. The Christian does not look within himself or herself for salvation, but rather outward, in faith, toward Christ. The third article of the Apostles' Creed summarizes the Christian doctrine of salvation succinctly: "I believe in . . . the holy catholic Church, the communion of saints, the forgiveness of sins, the resurrection of the body, and the life everlasting. Amen." Ephesians 2:8–9 states, "For it is by grace you have been saved, through faith—and this not from yourselves, it is the gift of God—not by works, so that no one can boast." The church, then, is comprised of the "communion of saints"—that is, those who have become believers, who through faith have had their sins forgiven and who have been baptized. At the end of the world there will be the resurrection of the dead. The body will rise from the grave as an incorruptible body.

This doctrine stands in contrast with the Buddhist doctrine of salvation on several counts. First, as we have observed, for Christianity salvation lies in the person and work of Jesus Christ. For the Buddhist, one attains salvation through self-effort and diligently pursuing the Eightfold Path. Second, for the Christian death is a prelude to an immediate translation into the presence of God. Not so in Buddhist thought, where death is one part in a cycle or series of deaths and rebirths. Third, the idea of a bodily resurrection, an integral part of Christian doctrine, has no place in the Buddhist system. For Buddhists, the body is a vessel that merely contains that which is permanent and remains behind as one grows closer toward the denouement of the cycle of rebirth.

Mahayana and Theravada Buddhists differ in their ideas of salvation and the afterlife. Mahayana Buddhists believe that a buddha, called a *Bodhisat,* is presently alive in a heavenly realm and is yet to become incarnate in human form. This figure is the object of prayer and devotion. It is an interesting point that here Buddhism closely parallels Christianity on several counts. The *Bodhisat* is believed to have accumulated a treasury of merit that is to be used for those who direct their faith toward him. Similarly, it is Christ's merit and righteousness that justifies the sinner who turns to him in faith. Second, the *Bodhisat* comes to the earth incarnate, as did Jesus. Finally, the belief in a heavenly realm in the religion of so-called practical atheism may sound a bit paradoxical but is, nevertheless, a point at which both Buddhism and Christianity converge.[4]

Morality

Buddhist morality developed out of a reaction against Hinduism. Protesting the caste system and its ranking of society into superior and inferior classes, Buddhism propounded an ethic of egalitarianism. It concerns itself not so much with outward ceremony and ritual as with an emphasis on the inner state of affairs of the soul. Like Christianity, love becomes the overarching principle of ethical and moral conduct for the Buddhist. Missing from the latter, however, is an ethic of love for God. Love is the means of overcoming hatred and evil.

Another striking contrast between Buddhism and Christianity is the former's mingling of moral laws with ceremonial observances. The teaching that it is wrong to commit murder or to steal shares a place next to the commandment to refrain from sleeping on a bed suspended off the ground or to fast at designated periods of time. For the Christian, the ceremonial laws of the Old Testament have been abrogated in Christ (Col. 2:20–23). Christ has become the presupposition on which all of morality is built, and when the commandments are broken and sin is committed, the believer can repent and receive absolution by Christ, who atoned

One of the most celebrated contemporary Buddhists is the Dalai Lama, a Tibetan Buddhist seen here speaking in Madison, Wisconsin. His followers believe he is God incarnate.   Courtesy Jack M. Roper/CARIS

for sin (1 John 1:9). No such recourse is available to the Buddhist.

The Mahayana Buddhists, as stated above, believe in the existence of a heavenly Bodhisat to whom prayers are directed, but there is no concept of a blood atonement for sin. For the Buddhist who fails to observe the moral and ceremonial law, there are two alternatives. One is the desire to keep the laws and to follow the Eightfold Path. This becomes a contradiction because desire itself is forbidden. Therefore, the remaining resolve is to lapse into ethical indifference, which for the Buddhist is far more noble.

CONCLUSION

There are many systems of Buddhism. The two major groupings, the Mahayana and Theravada Buddhists, are divided geographically between northern and southern Asia. Buddhism has enjoyed a resurgence of popularity in recent years. For example, in 1989 the government of Kampuchea made Buddhism the official state religion. Simultaneously, Theravadan and Nichiren Shoshu Buddhists actively spread their teachings in Singapore. But in other countries Buddhist monks have not been so well received. Persecutions against Buddhists broke out in Sri Lanka because of antigovernment demonstrations staged by Buddhist monks. China continues to persecute Buddhism in an attempt to proliferate the Cultural Revolution.[5]

ADDITIONAL INFORMATION_____

Headquarters
The North American headquarters for Buddhist Churches of America is located at 1710 Octavia St., San Francisco, CA 94109.

Websites
www.buddha.net (a large amount of information on Buddhism); *www.buddhistchurchesofamerica.com*

Sacred Texts
The Sutra Pitaka; The Vinaya Pitaka; Abhidharma Pitaka

Periodicals
There are many periodicals of or about Buddhism. See the website *edharma.com* (above). A popular publication is *Trycycle: The Buddhist Review.*

Membership Statistics
Buddhism is ranked as the fourth largest of the world's religions, behind Christianity, ISLAM, and Hinduism, and claims over 329 million adherents. Mahayana Buddhists comprise 56 percent of the world's Buddhist population, with an estimated 185 million. Therevada Buddhism makes up 38 percent, with 124 million, and Vajrayana, or Tibetan Buddhists, comprise 6 percent, or 20 million Buddhists.

Notes

[1] Nancy Wilson Ross, *Buddhism: A Way of Life and Thought* (New York: Knopf, 1980), 29–30.

[2] Hans Küng, Josef van Ess, Heinrich von Stietencron, and Heinz Bechert, *Christianity and the World Religions: Paths to Dialogue with Islam, Hinduism, and Buddhism*, trans. Peter Heinegg (Garden City, N.Y.: Doubleday, 1986), 309.

[3] Dhammapada, *The Sayings of the Buddah*, ed. Thomas Byrom (New York: Knopf, 1976), 365.

[4] See further comparisons/contrasts between Christianity and Buddhism in MAHAYANA and THERAVADA Buddhism.

[5] *Britannica Book of the Year* (Chicago: Encyclopedia Britannica, 1990), 315.

CABILDO

A religion started in Africa and developed through slaves from the Congo transported to the Carribean. Cabildo is one of several religions that uniquely combines African folk religion with the various religions native to the islands of the West Indies.

HISTORY

The Cabildos arrived in Cuba from Africa during the heyday of slave trade in the West Indies. Originally, it was the Spanish who brought the inhabitants of western and southern Africa to work the plantations in Cuba. The Cabildo ᐤcult is to be sharply distinguished from the SANTERIA cult, as Cabildo adherents are, for the most part, Africans of ᐤBantu origin, while the Santeria cult is comprised largely of people of ᐤYoruba tribal origin. The influences that each cultic tradition has exerted on the other is readily apparent, however. For example, the deities worshiped by each group coincide in many instances. Though there are hundreds of ᐤorisha, names such as ᐤElegba and ᐤShango are common to both.

ORGANIZATION

Originally thought to be a secret society, the Cabildo are comprised of groups of people who meet regularly to celebrate the deep and rich cultural heritage of their past.

BELIEFS AND PRACTICES

Chief features of Cabildo rituals are processions and dances. The festival dance is known as the ᐤwemilere. The ceremony begins at the center of the town or village with the ringing of the *agogo*. As in Santeria, the ceremony then proceeds with the beating of drums of various sizes in precise rhythmic patterns. The dance is directed to the *orisha* and always concludes with a dance for Shango. Because the cult no longer practices its rituals secretly, it has, by and large, become syncretized and acculturated into the daily life of Cuban society.

CONCLUSION

For a better understanding of the basic beliefs contained in Cabildo lore and for more information concerning the pantheon of deities and other Caribbean cults, see SANTERIA and VOODOO.

The Cabildo traditions are a vital link to the identity and culture of its members. The Christian church has found it extremely difficult to penetrate these cultural barriers with any singular impact. More often than not, CHRISTIANITY has played an influential role, but certainly not an exclusive one.

CANDOMBLE

The largest and most important of the MACUMBA ᐤcults in Brazil is Candomble (see also ᐤUmbanda). Candomble flourishes in the rural areas of the country and is mostly concentrated in the state of Bahia.

HISTORY

Candomble is a syncretistic amalgamation of West African cult traditions, Brazilian cults, Roman Catholicism, and European culture. During the heyday of the slave trade between the sixteenth and nineteenth centuries, Portuguese, Dutch, and English merchants transported West African blacks to the West Indies and Brazil to work on the numerous sugar, tobacco, coffee, and rubber plantations, as well as in the mines. These Africans of ᐤYoruba, ᐤDahomean, and ᐤBantu cultures brought their religious practices to their new homelands, where they mixed traditions with the indigenous religions of the natives. Roman Catholicism, brought by Portuguese missionaries during the time of European expansion into the New World and the predominant religion of Brazil, also enters into the mix. Many profess to be Catholic but simultaneously practice the rites and ceremonies of Candomble.

BELIEFS AND RITUALS

The basic rituals of Candomble parallel in many ways the practices of the Cuban cults (*see* CABILDO). Candomble has been labeled, however, as being the most African of the Macumba groups. The ceremonial sites are outdoors, and the familiar elements of animal sacrifice, offerings, and rhythmic dance characterize the ritual.

A typical ceremony begins with prayers to the Yorubic deity *Eshu.* Then a host of other deities are evoked. Each god has its own songs, drumbeats, and a special animal to be used in the sacrifices. *Eshu* is considered to be the mediator or liaison between the various other gods and humans. He is also tied to black magic from the influence of the Bantu traditions.

Though held outdoors, the ceremony centers around the *terreiro,* or temple. Each *terreiro* is overseen by a priest or priestess called a babalao, who is considered to have absolute power over the lives of the devotees. In Candomble, the *babalao* operates only within the presence of a small number of people. The hierarchy of priests in the Candomble cult are the babalorisha, the *babalao,* the *balosaim,* and the babaoge.

When a priest or priestess dies, the funeral rites are conducted somberly without the beating of the drums. By contrast, in the funerals of the nonpriestly members of the cult drum beating does accompany the procession. During a Candomble funeral, known as asheshe, the souls of the eguns (dead) are warded off and lured into jars.

The use of shells, akoveo, adjikone, and opele often accompany most incantations and divination ceremonies. Candomble initiation rites are lengthy, ranging from several months to several years before a member is received into the cult. The neophyte must live in solitude and is not allowed to speak. The hair is completely shorn and then washed in the blood of an animal sacrificed for the occasion. Gradually the body is tattooed with various cultic symbols. The initiate receives a new name and learns the cult secrets. Betrayal of these secrets results in retribution from the spirits, and outsiders attempting to intrude into the mysteries could be killed.

Candomble and other animistic (*see* animism) cults of the West Indies and South America are in part able to embrace CHRISTIANITY and at the same time adapt it to their own religious traditions. It is a polytheistic religion rooted in the occult. The deities are spirit beings able to initiate blessings or curses, usually determined by the intensity of the ritualistic dances and accompanying rhythmic drumbeats.

As a missionary religion, Christianity receives its impulse to evangelize because it states to be the one true faith to the exclusion of all others. Christianity is monotheistic. God is one, yet comprised of three persons in the divine Trinity. God is transcendent and a separate entity with respect to the created world. Animistic religions do not distinguish between creature and Creator.

Initiation into the Candomble cult is accompanied by the blood sacrifice of an animal. Initiation into Christianity also involves an initiation rite, namely, baptism, predicated on the blood atonement provided by Jesus Christ, who offered up himself as a supreme sacrifice before God (Rom. 3:21–24)—no longer the blood of animals, but his own blood (Heb. 9:12); no longer once yearly, but now once for all time (Heb. 10:14).

Roman Catholic missionaries have certainly been faced with the perplexity of bringing an exclusive religion to a people all too willing to embrace it "along with," rather than "in place of," their own existing religious traditions.[1]

CONCLUSION

Today, Candomble and the many other Macumba sects continue to flourish. The Catholic church, as well as the Christian church in general, has attempted, sometimes through force, to stamp out the practices of these sects. On the whole, they have been unsuccessful.

ADDITIONAL INFORMATION_____
Websites
http://groups.yahoo.com/group/ASHE-DE-ORISHA
http://www.tulane.edu/~tuhulla/19970912/forum/VOODOO.html

Statistics
There are over 1000 Candomble temples in Salvador, Bahia.

Note
[1] For a more detailed analysis of this problem, see SOUTH AMERICAN, CENTRAL AMERICAN, AND CARIBBEAN CULTS.

CHRIST THE SAVIOR BROTHERHOOD (CSB)

CSB was formerly called the Holy Order of MANS. The term *MANS* is an acronym with each letter standing for a Greek word—*mysterion, agape, nous,* and *sophia,* or "mystery," "love," "mind," and "wisdom," respectively.

Before the Order was reorganized, it was comprised of a blend of traditions prevalent in CHRISTIANITY, particularly Roman Catholicism and the monastic orders. In fact, the label "Pauline Catholic" has been applied by the movement. The first edition to this volume reflected the theology prevalent in the older Holy Order of MANS. Here we reflect the changes that have taken place since that edition was published, with some qualifications.

HISTORY

The original order was founded by Father Earl Paul ▶Blighton (1900–1974) in the early 1960s in San Francisco, California, and was incorporated in 1968. Blighton claimed that the order was more a discipleship movement than a separate religion. He blended Eastern ▶Orthodox theology with ▶gnosticism, ▶mysticism, ROSICRUCIANISM, and THEOSOPHY, which brought it clearly outside the pale of orthodox Christianity. His *Book of Activity* became an important source of authority within the organization.

After his death in 1974, leadership of the movement was carried on by his widow Ruth Blighton, but not without a struggle for power between her and several others. She eventually broke away and formed a splinter group known as the Science of Man Church. Shortly thereafter, Father Andrew Rossi, along with his wife, Isjesian, assumed the mantle of ▶Director General.

Changes took place rather rapidly in the movement, particularly after the ▶Jonestown tragedy in 1978. Under public criticism and close scrutiny from critics, Rossi began leading the Order toward Christian ▶orthodoxy. He underwent a conversion to Eastern Orthodoxy in the early 1980s. Rossi did not wish to leave the order but rather sought to win as many members over as possible. In order to do this he invited Gleb Podmoshensky, an orthodox priest, to travel to the different Orders of MANS throughout the country and to speak to the members. This idea proved effective, given the strong charismatic leadership that Podmoshensky brought. In 1988, 750 members converted to orthodox Christianity, and the name of the Order was changed to Christ the Savior Brotherhood. Those loyal to the teachings of Blighton left to form splinter groups. These include the Gnostic Order of Christ formed in 1988, the Science of Man Church formed in 1987, the Foundation of Christ Church, and the American Temple.

ORGANIZATION

The head of the order is the Director General, and the priests who serve under the director (formerly called the ▶Esoteric Council) is the ▶Apostolic Brotherhood. Membership is now described in terms of baptismal initiation and faith in Christ as Savior rather than secret initiation rites based on mysticism.

TEACHINGS

The first edition of this volume described the original teachings of the Holy Order of MANS under Rossi's leadership. Since the Order has now aligned itself with Eastern Orthodoxy, it conforms to a much more traditional theology based on the historical creeds of Christianity, particularly the Nicene Creed (Appendix 1). Rossi also denounced the use of the *Book of Activity,* claiming that the ▶Bible is the one sacred religious authority. The CSB embraced the sacraments and liturgical rites of the Eastern Orthodox Church and renounced all the elements of mysticism, Rosicrucianism, theosophy, and other esoteric teachings. Women no longer serve as clergy.

CONCLUSION

The story of the Holy Order of MANS in its transformation to Christ the Savior Brotherhood is almost without precedent. While many individuals undergo conversions to or from cults, it is rare that an entire group undergoes such a transformation. One such occurrence is the WORLDWIDE CHURCH OF GOD.[1]

It must also be pointed out that some people have expressed concerns about the changes in the CSB. The official website, for example, still maintains a link to all of Blighton's books and revelations. These are the very teachings that the new leadership has claimed to have renounced. The site states that these pages were set up to "honor the memory of the Holy Order of MANS."[2] Moreover, the CSB is certainly open to scrutiny, as is the Worldwide Church of God. Any concerns that have been expressed are not intended to imply that genuine changes have not taken place in what was formerly a New Age cult.

ADDITIONAL INFORMATION_____

Headquarters

Former headquarters for the organization was in Cheyenne, Wyoming. World headquarters was located in San Francisco. The newly formed CSB presently maintains headquarters in Forestville, California. Many of its functions and activities are held in Portland, Oregon.

Website

www.holyorderofmans.org

Sacred Text

The Bible

Membership Statistics

The Holy Order of MANS grew to about 3000 members before the transformation to the new church. Christ the Savior Brotherhood is under 1000 members, the remaining leaving the organization altogether or joining one of the above-listed splinter groups.

Notes

[1] See Larry Nichols and George Mather, *Discovering the Plain Truth: How the Worldwide Church of God Encountered the Gospel of Grace* (Downers Grove, IL: InterVarsity Press, 1996).

[2] See *www.holyorderofmans.org/intropage.htm.*

CHRISTADELPHIANISM

A ᐅcult growing out of ᐅProtestant CHRISTIANITY that was heavily influenced by nineteenth-century revivalism, anti-Trinitarian impulses, and ᐅrestorationism.

HISTORY

This movement was founded by John ᐅThomas (1805–1871) in 1848 after he withdrew from the Disciples of Christ. Thomas grew up in London, England, where he studied medicine. After becoming a physician in 1832, he moved to the United States. The Disciples of Christ had been founded by Thomas Campbell (1763–1854) and his son, Alexander Campbell (1788–1866). Thomas was, himself, in disagreement with the Campbells early in his association with them and broke away from the Disciples in 1844.

The "Thomasites," as the Christadelphians were originally called, protested some of the basic tenets of the Christian church, chiefly the doctrine of the ᐅTrinity (see below). Thomas also contended that all existing denominations had apostatized from the truth as expressed in the simplicity and purity of the early church with its practices and primitive teachings.

It was during the Civil War (1864) that Thomas adopted the name Christadelphian, meaning "Brothers of Christ." As pacifists who wanted to remain exempt from military obligations, they were compelled to adopt a formal name.

After Thomas's death in 1871, changes took place within the movement. Controversy broke out in the 1890s when two members, Robert Roberts and J. J. Andrew, split over an issue called "resurrectional responsibility." The schism produced two separate movements: the "Amended" group, which insisted that only those who are "in Christ" will be resurrected to everlasting life; and the "Unamended" group, which maintained that at the Final Judgment, all, the wicked as well as the righteous, will be raised up. The two factions have existed side by side to the present. In the 1970s an attempt was made to reunite them, at which time the groups discovered that they agreed on far more than they disagreed on. They saw eye to eye on the doctrine of baptism, the nature of humanity, the inspiration of the ᐅBible, and the doctrine of "fellowship." The one bone of contention that prevented unity was the issue of resurrectional responsibility.

ORGANIZATION

A local congregation is called an ᐅ*ecclesia*. Given its loose, independent, congregational polity, there is much flexibility for each *ecclesia* to govern themselves without outside influence. *Ecclesias* are located in many countries. There are no colleges or seminaries sponsored by the Christadelphian church. Several Bible schools exist that hold sessions in the summer months. No functional or hierarchical distinctions are made between clergy and laity. Though there is no central organization that rules or governs the *ecclesia*, the church does hold an annual fraternal gathering. Those who serve in leadership capacities do so without compensation. *Ecclesia* meetings are usually held in rented halls or within the homes of its members.

TEACHINGS

The following represents a summary of the basic doctrines of the Christadelphian church in comparison of and contrast to the orthodox Christian church.

God

One of the goals of the Disciples of Christ was to purge Christianity of all nonbiblical terminology and any words deemed theologically abstract. It is not at all surprising, therefore, that the word ▸Trinity became the focus of Thomas's objections as well. The notable difference between the Campbells and Thomas was that while the former rejected the *term* "Trinity," the latter rejected both the term and the *concept* behind the term.[1] It should be noted that in the writings of both Campbell and Thomas, there is much more of an explicit protest leveled against Roman Catholicism than Trinitarianism.

The Christadelphian church understands God to be one in essence. He exists in and through himself. This point is emphasized in order to stress the aversion the Christadelphian church has to the doctrine of the Trinity as stated, for example, in the Athanasian Creed: "we worship one God in three persons and three persons in one God, neither confusing the persons nor dividing the substance" (Appendix 1). Christadelphianism, therefore, is ▸unitarian in its doctrines of God and ▸Christology. Additionally, the Christadelphian position is similar to the teachings of ▸Arianism and ▸dynamic monarchianism, both of which taught that God does not share his divinity with another substance or essence. Monarchianism was a theological position against which the universal church reacted in the third and fourth centuries, culminating in the confession that God is three persons but one in essence.

Jesus Christ

Jesus is the "Son of God" and Son of Man, who was born of a virgin mother by the operation of the Holy Spirit. It was through Christ, they say, that the Father was revealed. The *work* of Christ consisted in his dying to atone for sin and then in his rising from the dead in order to make such forgiveness both possible and complete. There is little to contrast here with Christian ▸orthodoxy, except for the Christadelphian doctrine of the *person* of Christ. In keeping with the rejection of the doctrine of the Trinity, the Christadelphians do not recognize Jesus as being God incarnate who possesses a nature coeternal with the Father in heaven, as understood traditionally in such biblical passages as John 1:1ff.; 8:58; 1 Timothy 3:16; Hebrews 13:8; and as confessed by the early church in its historical symbols.

Implicit in Christadelphian thought is the idea that the work of Christ to atone for sin included the need to atone for his own sin as well as for those of the world.

"We reject the doctrine that Christ's nature was immaculate" ("Doctrines to Be Rejected," no. 5). Though Christ possessed a divine nature through his being conceived by the Holy Spirit, he also possessed a human nature, born of the Virgin Mary. It was the human nature of Christ to which his atoning work applied. The Council of Chalcedon (A.D. 451) recognized that Christ indeed possesses two natures. Yet these two natures do not exist separately or independently of one another. The two natures of Christ exist "without confusion, without change, without division, and without separation." Furthermore, though Christ had two natures, he was not two separate persons, but one. This Chalcedonian Christology is the doctrinal expression of the Greek Orthodox church, the Roman Catholic church, and the Protestant churches of the Reformation. Christadelphianism stands outside the historic catholic faith in its Christology, as its own literature readily testifies.[2]

Holy Spirit

The Holy Spirit is the "power of God." The Spirit does not exercise a personal will but rather serves as the executor of the will of the Father. In fact, the Holy Spirit is not a separate person from the Father. As the "power of God," the Holy Spirit cannot be distinguished from the person of the Father. Denial of the Holy Spirit's place within the Trinity once again sets Christadelphians at odds with orthodoxy. The latter has historically recognized that although the Holy Spirit does indeed act as an agent to carry out the Father's will, the Holy Spirit also "proceeds from the Father and the Son, who with the Father and the Son together is worshiped and glorified" (Nicene Creed).

Humanity

The human being exists either as a "responsible" believer or as an unbeliever. The human race was created from the dust of the ground and, because of sin, was condemned to die, returning to the dust. After a future resurrection from the dead and final judgment, the responsibles will be granted immortality while the wicked are annihilated (*see* ▸annihilationism). The controversy concerning who will be resurrected at the Final Judgment divides the "Amended" and the "Unamended" (see above).

Immortality

The idea that the soul is immortal is, for Christadelphians, an unbiblical and pagan notion. Immortality is reserved for the future and will occur for the righteous only. It is a gift for those who obey what God has commanded in his law. Therefore, life is terminated at death and is restored only at the time of resurrection for the Final Judgment. Those granted immortality will live with God eternally, while unbelievers will remain eternally dead.

The Christian church has always taught that there will be a final judgment and that both the living and the dead will face that time of eternal reckoning with God. But at the same time, Christianity has commonly also maintained that the soul is indeed immortal, else Christ would not have "descended into hell" to preach deliverance to the captives and/or the spirits in prison (1 Peter 3:19; 4:6), or Paul would not have been able to say, "I desire to depart and be with Christ" (Phil. 1:23). At death, the body returns to the ground and becomes dust, and the soul separates from the body. The two are joined together at the time of the resurrection from the dead. At the time of judgment, both believers and unbelievers alike continue in an immortal state of existence. "They that have done good will go into life everlasting; and they that have done evil, into everlasting fire" (Athanasian Creed; cf. John 5:29).

The Devil

The 'devil is not a real living creature or being; rather, it is an evil principle that lies deep within human nature and predisposes humans toward sin and active rebellion against God.

The Scriptures and Jesus himself speak directly to the existence of 'Satan or the devil. His place within Christianity has always been maintained in orthodox circles and is substantiated by many biblical references. In our modern era, there have been varying interpretations of who and/or what Satan is. Among more liberal theologians, particularly those influenced by Friedrich Schleiermacher and, more recently, Rudolf Bultmann and Paul Tillich, the notion of a literal devil has been replaced by that of an evil principle that exists in the world and within the heart of sinful humanity, an idea not entirely unlike that espoused by Christadelphianism.

Hell

Christadelphianism teaches that the word "hell" in the Bible refers strictly to the grave. This teaching is identical to the position held by numerous religious groups, such as SEVENTH-DAY ADVENTISM, the WORLDWIDE CHURCH OF GOD, and THE WAY INTERNATIONAL. Because Christadelphians teach that there is no immortal soul that lives on after death, there is no need for a place of eternal torment for it to dwell in.

Salvation

The "saved" are those who believe the gospel and are obedient to Christ's command to be baptized. Baptism is strictly by immersion, a teaching similar to some Christian denominations and 'sects. The baptismal rite is conducted in the name of Christ, not in the name of the Father, the Son, and the Holy Spirit.

End Times

The place where the righteous will dwell throughout all eternity will be the earth. This teaching parallels the doctrine of the JEHOVAH'S WITNESSES, who maintain that the earth will be the paradise for all Jehovah's people, with the exception of 144,000, who will reign eternally with God in the heavens.

The Christadelphian church is strongly millennial in its eschatology. The faithful will reign with Christ for one thousand years and will be served by the mortal people of all nations. Israel will be restored to its former glory. When death itself is destroyed at the end of the Millennium, the earth will be populated by those who have received the gift of eternal life.

Many Christian groups hold a similar eschatology, particularly denominations influenced by 'dispensationalism. Though there are differences, several motifs appear common to all millenarians. Israel plays an important role during the time of the end; a period of one thousand years (a millennium) will ensue, culminating in a final judgment; the return is close at hand as all of the events prophesied to precede Christ's Second Advent have been or are now being fulfilled.

Many understandings of Christian eschatology are not as elaborate as dispensationalism. The Apostles' Creed confesses the simple formulation, "he ascended into heaven and sits at the right hand of God the Father Almighty. From thence he will come to judge the living and the dead."

Authority

The Christadelphians believe the Bible to be their final authority in matters of faith and practice.

Fellowship

Christadelphians are extremely dogmatic in their doctrinal orientation. Members generally do not attempt to fellowship with those who hold to doctrines considered to be apostate. Members are also forbidden to take part in public affairs or to run for public office.

CONCLUSION

Christadelphian literature is available on request by writing to the local assemblies. The website and various links contain a wealth of further information.

ADDITIONAL INFORMATION

Headquarters

The Christadelphians do not have a central headquarters. Each *ecclesia* is equal to all others. One particular address from which to obtain information is the Detroit Christadelphian Ecclesial Library, 14676 Berwick, Livonia, MI 48154.

Website

www.christadelphia.org

Sacred Text

The Bible

Periodicals

The Christadelphian (monthly mag.); *The Christadelphian Tidings of the Kingdom of God; The Bible Magazine; The Testimony Magazine; The Gospel News; Faith Alive; Lookout; The Christadelphian Advocate*

Membership

850 congregations worldwide. Total membership estimated at around 11,000.

Notes

[1] See JEHOVAH'S WITNESSES and UNITARIAN-UNIVERSALIST ASSOCIATION, both of which also reject the ▸Trinity and its attending concept.

[2] Christadelphianism's ▸Christology closely parallels that of nearly every non-Christian group that contains a doctrine of Jesus Christ.

CHRISTIAN FELLOWSHIP MINISTRIES; POTTER'S HOUSE; THE DOOR; VICTORY CHAPEL

A Pentecostal ▸sect that has invited considerable controversy because of what some have termed "bizarre" practices. Despite its sizable growth through the last three decades, a growing number of ex-members have published strong statements claiming that they were abused by a ▸cult that exercised extreme measures to control its constituents.

HISTORY

Also called Christian Center, Crossroads Chapel, The Door—*La Puerta*, Potter's House, and various other names, Christian Fellowship Ministries (CFM) was begun in Prescott, Arizona, in 1970 by Wayman Mitchell. Mitchell was originally a member of the Pentecostal denomination called International Church of the Foursquare Gospel. He broke from Foursquare in the 1960s. The name "Potter's House" was chosen to designate the idea that true believers are those who are willing to be submissively molded and shaped by God, the potter. In their beliefs (see below), CFM appear to be simply another Pentecostal ▸denomination. It has grown rapidly with over one thousand churches in nearly eighty countries. Mitchell was able to reach out successfully to many young people who were disenfranchised with traditional forms of Christian churches.

Other leaders in the movement include Paul Campo, a close associate of Mitchell who became leader for most of the CFM congregations in the Eastern United States and pastor of one of the largest and most successful CFM churches, Victory Chapel in South Dennis on Cape Cod, Massachusetts. Harold Warner became the leader of The Door Christian Fellowship Church in Tucson, Arizona.

Some of the noted incidents characterized as bizarre behavior include the following. In 1992 members of Potter's House Christian Center, a CFM church in Ballard, Washington, took part in an annual Norwegian Seventeenth of May parade. Members of the church entered a float in which a Roman soldier was whipping another member playing Jesus carrying a cross. The garment covering the figure of Jesus was blood-soaked. The parade committee received a considerable amount of protest from parents who said that their children were frightened by the crass display. The pastor, Rev. Kevin Hannston, explained that the float was designed to introduce the issue of Jesus so that parents could explain to their children who he was. Parade planners concluded that the purpose of the parade was to promote Norwegian culture. The pastor later made a public statement that they would conform to the community's guidelines for parades in the future.

Another instance included a pastor in an Indiana CFM church who dressed up as the ▸devil and, in an attempt to scare a four-year-old girl to fear God, had her place her hand in a bucket of blood with a cow's heart in it. The pastor yelled, "You will never get your hand out!" He later explained that "there is a certain amount of fear that is good!"

Organization

The Potter's House is governed by the pastor, who is surrounded by a group of elders. Together, this comprises the church council. The pastor in each congregation is responsible for the financial, spiritual, and moral leadership and for decision-making. Wayman Mitchell wrote by-laws that govern each church within the CFM organization.

TEACHINGS AND PRACTICES

The theology of Potter's House is both ▸fundamentalist and Pentecostal. They claim to hold to the same doctrines as the Assemblies of God. Their statement of faith is as follows:

> We Believe:
>
> That Jesus Christ is the Son of the Living God and the only Savior from sin.
>
> That Jesus Christ is the Great Physician and Healer of the body and soul through the blood atonement.
>
> That Jesus Christ is the baptizer with the Holy Ghost today, just as He was on the Day of Pentecost.
>
> That Jesus Christ is the soon-coming King, coming back to earth again as the only hope for our dying world.
>
> That Jesus Christ is the same yesterday, today, and forever.[1]

Concerning its specific Pentecostal theology, CFM believes that the gift of tongues is for today and the baptism in the Holy Spirit is the indication that a believer is filled with the Holy Spirit. CFM embraces ▸dispensationalism and a pretribulation rapture theory.

It is not so much the actual theology that has attracted so much controversy and subsequent media attention or even the conclusion reached by many that CFM is a cult. It is more the actual *practices* leaders and members engage in. It should also be pointed out that much of the criticism of the group has come from those who have left. There are ample statements from ex-members accusing CFM leaders of mind control, using fear tactics, cursing, and shunning. Members are constantly made to feel guilty, threatened, and condemned. They are separated from "unbelieving" family and friends.

The issue of accountability is also important. Ex-members have claimed that statements made in sermons are decisive and not subject to question. These include the private whims and opinions of the preacher rather than doctrinal statements supported by the Bible.

Also, long hours and slavish commitment to the cause of the group have resulted in "burn-out" among many who have left and among those who remain.

The usual response to these criticisms has been that the gospel calls for radical commitment to the life of discipleship. Mitchell used the words "disciple-making without apology." At a Bible conference in 1990, Mitchell said, "In the face of Jim ▸Jones, in the face of Bob Mumford, in the face of the whole world, I am a disciple-maker."

CONCLUSION

A glance at the websites of the various CFM churches quickly show that despite the exits, accusations, and criticisms, the movement continues to grow into the new century, particularly among young people. CFM is involved in numerous activities, and its objective remains to bring the gospel to the world and win souls through engaging the community in whatever means it takes to draw attention to itself and its message.

Based on conversations with some members and the doctrinal statement, CFM appears simply to be a Pentecostal organization that in some instances has perhaps gone too far, but it is not a cult.

ADDITIONAL INFORMATION_____

Address
The Potters House in Clifton: 204 N. Coronado Blvd. Clifton, AZ 85533 (one among many other CFM congregations).

Websites
http://macgregorministries.org/cult_groups/potters.html;
www.thepottershouse.faithweb.com/

Sacred Text
The Bible

Publications
Bulls' Eye (a periodical for youth), produced by "The Door" in Tucson, AZ.
Ron Simpkins, *An Open Door* (Prescott, AZ: Potter's Press, 1985). (A history of the Potter's House as told by a member).

Membership
Unknown and difficult to calculate accurately because of a high turnover rate.

Note
[1] *www.pottershouselubbock.com*

CHRISTIAN SCIENCE

Christian Science has been regarded as the most popular among the religious groups classified as ᵇmind sciences.

HISTORY

The story of Christian Science is largely the story of its founder, Mary Baker ᵇEddy (1821–1910). Mary Baker was raised in a Congregationalist home in Bow, New Hampshire. In 1838, at age seventeen, she joined a Congregational church in Tilton, New Hampshire, but never seemed content with its doctrines.

Eddy was plagued by illnesses throughout her life, including during her early childhood. In 1843 she married George Glover. The happy marriage was not to last, ending one and a half years later when Glover died in Charleston, South Carolina, leaving his wife behind pregnant with a son, who was born in September 1844. Her condition became worse than ever, and she grew extremely interested in the study of medicine and health.

Eddy married for the second time in 1853 to a dentist named Daniel Patterson. This marriage was not as happy as her first. Patterson appears to have been a womanizer. In 1866 they were separated, and in 1873 she secured a divorce.

Interest in medicine led her in 1862 to Phineas Parkhurst ᵇQuimby (1802–66), who resided in Portland, Maine. She gave herself over to his care, as he treated her for "spinal inflammation." Soon she claimed that Quimby's treatments had healed her. Quimby had been an early student of ᵇmesmerism and ᵇanimal magnetism and espoused a theory of mental healing that he called "The Science of Man." Many scholars believe that Quimby's work served as the basis for much of what Eddy later brought together in her *Science and Health with Key to the Scriptures,* published in 1875. Some sources maintain that she in fact plagiarized considerable portions from her mentor.[1]

A third and final marriage came in 1877, when Mary Baker met and married Asa G. Eddy, from whom she derived her present name. He died shortly afterward of coronary thrombosis.

In 1866, following Quimby's death, Mary retired and for nearly ten years worked on her *Science and Health with Key to the Scriptures.* Four years later, in 1879, she founded the Church of Christ, Scientist in Boston. In 1892, under a program of restructuring, it became known as the ᵇMother Church, the First Church of Christ, Scientist. It has been the headquarters of Christian Science ever since. Eddy remained the head of the church until her death on December 3, 1910. During the last twenty years of her life, Eddy had become a virtual recluse. She was not even present during the dedication of the Mother Church in 1895. Since her death, control of the church has been passed on to a board of trustees.

One historian notes that "Christian Science is one of at least five large and easily differentiated religious movements that bear the stamp 'made in America.' Mormonism, Seventh-Day Adventism, Jehovah's Witnesses, and Pentecostalism are the others."[2] Growth was rapid during the 1880s. Membership climbed until around 1930, when it leveled off. Since 1960, Christian

The Mother Church of the Christian Science movement, in Boston.
© Lee Snider/Photo Images/CORBIS

Science has been steadily losing members. Christian Science has always tended to attract those who seek an intellectual alternative to the Christian answers to the problem of suffering and pain.

In 1991 the church entered into a controversy by agreeing to publish Bliss Knapp's *The Destiny of the Mother Church*, a book that had been condemned in 1947 because it deified Eddy. *Encyclopedia Britannica 1992 Yearbook* reports that the Knapps had left some $90 million to the church on condition that the book be published and prominently displayed in Christian Science reading rooms.[3] Opponents of publication accused the church of heresy in order to fund the controversial expansion of its media enterprises.

ORGANIZATION

The headquarters for Christian Science is in Boston, Massachusetts. Eddy authored *The Manual of the Mother Church* in 1895, which was edited regularly throughout her life. The Church's board of directors is comprised of five members. Local congregations, called branches, are autonomous.

There are no ordained clergy. Readers serve for a three-year period as an aid in the study of healing and spirituality. However, individual participants in Christian Science Reading Rooms, as they are frequently called, pray for themselves for healing. But they may also call on a practitioner who has received training in spiritual council and prayer.

TEACHINGS

According to the Christian Science *Church Manual*, the whole basis for the church's existence is to "reinstate primitive Christianity and its lost element of healing." Basic to Eddy's (Quimby's) thought is the Greek dualistic concept that matter is evil. The material world is illusory. The only reality is mind.

> There is no life, truth, intelligence, nor substance in matter. All is infinite Mind and its infinite manifestation, for God is All-in-all. Spirit is immortal Truth; matter is mortal error. Spirit is the real and eternal; matter is the unreal and temporal.[4]

It had been Quimby's conviction that sickness was the result of ill-formed beliefs. Eddy apparently held to this idea as well. She also believed that sickness was caused by evil or malicious animal magnetism, another aspect of Quimby's thought.

All matter is opposed to spirit and/or mind—the substance of God. All sensory perceptions are deceitful. To believe that matter has or possesses reality is

evil and a lie. This led naturally to Eddy's convictions concerning sickness and disease. "The cause of all so-called disease is mental, a mortal fear, a mistaken belief or conviction of the necessity and power of ill-health; also a fear that Mind is helpless to defend the life of man and incompetent to control it."[5] Once a person realizes that sickness is nonexistent, for matter itself does not exist, then one will also realize that one is not, nor ever has been, sick in the first place. Death itself is illusory because it pertains to the physical body—which is not real. "Death is but another phase of the dream that existence can be material."[6] What makes the unreality of sickness, disease, and death, or for that matter any sensory experiences, seem real is wrong belief.

Fundamentally, the difference between Christian Science and traditional CHRISTIANITY is in the former's insistence on a ⁾dualism between flesh and spirit. Christianity encountered this philosophy early in its expansion into the Greek world surrounding the eastern Mediterranean. The gnostic (*see* ⁾gnosticism) insisted that matter, including the human body, was an evil substance that hindered one from the higher quest of attaining an exclusively "spiritual" existence. Gnostics, therefore, rejected a fundamental tenet of the Christian faith, namely, the incarnation of Christ. Christ only seemed to be human, the gnostics argued. The docetists (*see* ⁾docetism) also adopted this view, against which the church reacted early through Ignatius, who vehemently attacked it, saying a docetic view of Christ denied the fundamental necessity of a suffering Christ or an incarnational Christ. Some have seen docetism as being a type of dualism.

During the Enlightenment (1700s), this dualism took on a new twist in the philosophy of Descartes, who insisted that mind and body were totally separate substances. This Cartesian dualism had a profound impact on intellectual history. Rather than viewing the body and the mind as a whole, life was now seen as consisting of two spheres. Subsequent thinkers went on to emphasize either the significance of matter and the denial of spirit, or the reality of spirit and the denial of matter. Quimby, and then Eddy, was influenced by this latter view. All suffering, sickness, disease, or any aspect of fleshly existence was dismissed as being illusory.

Christianity, in it earliest form, knows of no such dualism. Paul reasoned that the spiritual warfare being conducted in his own person (Rom. 7) was a warfare between the flesh and the spirit, or between the old Adam and the new Adam. Nowhere, however, does he conclude that the Holy Spirit is battling an *evil flesh*. It is not the flesh that is evil, but rather, "it is sin living in me" (Rom. 7:17). Augustine later picked up Paul's view of himself and developed it, insisting that sin is a foreign substance that invaded the human race at the Fall. That which God created is good. Both body and soul are good. It is sin that has corrupted humanity. Adam and Eve passed on this corruption through the human sex act (according to Augustine).

Christian Science, therefore, bears little resemblance to historic Christianity. Each is built on a different foundation—the former on the fundamentals of Greek and Cartesian dualism, the latter on a Hebraistic worldview and a biblical ▶monotheism.

God

"God" in Christian Science is synonymous with other concepts like mind, spirit, goodness, health, and well-being. Fundamental to Christian Science are the four points:

1. God is All-in-all.
2. God is good. Good is Mind.
3. God, Spirit, being all, nothing is matter.
4. Life, God, omnipotent good, deny death, evil, sin, disease—Disease, sin, evil, death, deny good, omnipotent God, Life.[7]

Traditional ▶orthodox Christianity teaches that "God is a spirit" (John 4:24), that God is the Creator of the world and of matter (Gen. 1), and that the created world was "good." Eddy taught that the historical doctrine of the Trinity should be ranked with polytheism.[8]

Jesus Christ

He was a historical figure who lived nearly two thousand years ago. But as a man he was limited to a physical body and since matter is illusory, Jesus' mission on earth was to teach humankind that any and all sickness is also illusory. Jesus was not God incarnate in human flesh, a doctrine taught by Christianity, though he was born of a virgin. Eddy believed that Christ was an idea only.[9] Christian Science makes a sharp distinction between the "man" Jesus and the Christ, who envelops the "divine idea."

> Christ is the ideal Truth, that comes to heal sickness and sin through Christian Science, and attributes all power to God. Jesus is the name of the man who, more than all other men, has presented Christ, the true idea of God.... Jesus is the human man and Christ is the divine idea; hence the duality of Jesus the Christ.[10]

Traditional ▶Christology maintains that Jesus Christ is the incarnate Son of God, fully human and fully divine (Rom. 1:3–4; Apostles', Nicene, and Chalcedonian Creeds). Eddy eschewed the idea that Jesus' human blood was necessary to atone for sin (1 John 1:7). Jesus' humanity and divinity are so related that the human element (blood) is able to save because it is in complete relationship with his divine nature.

Holy Spirit

The Holy Spirit is defined as being "Divine Science" itself. It is also referred to as being eternal Life, Truth, and Love.[11] Jesus "proved that Christ is the divine idea of God—the Holy Ghost, or Comforter, revealing the divine Principle, Love, and leading into all truth."[12]

As understood in Christianity, the Holy Spirit is a person, not an idea or divine principle. The Holy Spirit is referred to as "Counselor" (John 14:16, 26), the "Lord and Giver of Life" (Nicene Creed), and Jesus referred to the Holy Spirit with the personal pronoun "he" (John 16:13).

Humanity

> What is man? Man is not matter; he is not made up of brain, blood, bones, and other material elements. The Scriptures inform us that man is made in the image and likeness of God. Matter is not that likeness. . . . Man is idea, the image of love; he is not physique. He is the compound idea of God, including all right ideas.[13]

According to traditional Christian teaching, man is indeed comprised of a physical body. The name "Adam" means "ground" or "dust." Man is comprised of a body and a soul, which are separated at death.

Sin

To Christian Science, sin is part of the illusory material world. It simply does not exist. "Man is incapable of sin, sickness, and death."[14] But sin is not an illusion for Christians. It was a real act committed first by Adam and Eve (Gen. 3) and is understood as a transgression of God's law (1 John 3:3–5), for which Jesus made atonement in his sacrificial death (1 Peter 2:24).

Hell

▶Hell is "mortal belief; error; lust; remorse; hatred; revenge; sin; sickness; death; sufferings and self destruction; self-imposed agony; effects of sin; that which worketh abomination or maketh a lie."[15] Hell, therefore, is a state of mind or conscience stricken by illusion or guilt.

Christian Science once again departs from traditional Christian teaching regarding hell. Although there are varying interpretations, hell is regarded as the place of eternal torment for the unbeliever and the wicked.

Salvation

Salvation is "life, Truth, and Love understood and demonstrated as being supreme over all; sin, sickness, and death destroyed."[16] When one is liberated from the illusion of believing in matter on the one hand and sinfulness on the other, one has obtained salvation.

Christianity teaches that because sin is real and not illusory, salvation is also real and is a finished work that Christ earns through his sacrificial death (Rom. 3:21–24). It is understood as forgiveness, not knowledge or enlightenment.

Church

The church for Christian Science is one structure on earth where truth and love dwell. Wherever such a structure is found, there lies the church. Furthermore:

> The church is that institution, which affords proof of its utility and is found elevating the race, rousing the dormant understanding from the material beliefs to the apprehension of spiritual ideas and the demonstration of divine Science, thereby casting out devils, or error, and healing the sick.[17]

Christianity understands the church in a rich variety of ways, including "bride of Christ" (Eph. 5:23ff.) and "the communion of saints" (Apostles' Creed). It is comprised of believers in Jesus Christ, those who have been buried with Christ in baptism (Rom. 6:1–3).

Sacraments

In orthodox Christian circles, the ‣sacraments convey grace or at least symbolize God's saving grace through physical means. Baptism uses water, and in holy communion, wine and bread accompany the ritual. Not so for Christian Science. There can be no physical or material means through which grace is conveyed or symbolized. Matter simply does not exist.

> The sacraments, however, are celebrated twice yearly. But no visible elements such as bread, wine, or in the case of baptism, water, may be present. The spiritual significance is sought. Baptism is "submergence in Spirit."[18]

End Times

Because the universe is comprised of God only, or Spirit only, there is no significance or direction in human history, nor is there anticipation that a transformation will occur in the future. Heaven is defined as being "Harmony, the reign of Spirit, government by divine Principle, spirituality, bliss, the atmosphere of Soul."[19]

For traditional Christianity, the end is that time when Jesus returns in glory (Mark 14:62; Acts 1:11) and, as the Apostles' Creed confesses, "He shall come again to judge the living and the dead." Heaven is the eternity of God's presence, where the Christian soul will reside in perfect union with God (John 14:1–6; 1 Cor. 2:9; Rev. 21:2–7).

In general, it is readily apparent that the heart of Christian Science lies in the dualism described above. All of its tenets are influenced by this overarching philosophy and worldview. This belief differs drastically from the Christian position as expressed in the second article of the Apostles' Creed, that Jesus Christ, the incarnate Word of God, was conceived and born, that he suffered, died, was buried, and was raised up from the dead. To traditional Christianity, herein lies the focal point of human history. For Christian Science, however, history itself is a nonentity insofar as it embodies the melodrama of a suffering humanity, which it concludes does not ultimately even exist.

CONCLUSION

Christian Science has been declining in membership in recent years. Nevertheless, it continues to exert an impact chiefly through the proliferation of its literature. Controversy within the organization continues to revolve around the issue of healing through prayer alone, without the help of medicine or doctors.

ADDITIONAL INFORMATION_____

Headquarters

First Church of Christ, Scientist, Christian Science Center, Boston, MA 02115.

Websites

www.christianscience.org; www.tfccs.com (headquarters)

Sacred Texts And Publications

Major works and publications in Christian Science include: *Science and Health with Key to the Scriptures*, first published in 1875 (other editions have followed); *Christian Science Journal*, 1883; *Christian Healing and Other Writings*, 1886; *Christian Science Sentinel*, 1898; *Christian Science Monitor*, 1908. Concerning the last-mentioned publication, the *Christian Science Monitor* was established by Eddy in 1908 in order to offer a journalistic alternative to the bias and sensationalism often appearing in conventional newspapers. Today the *Monitor* has become far more successful than the organization that first published it. It is highly respected in academic, political, and economic circles for its high-quality journalism and is widely read, featuring regional editions in major metropolitan areas.

A cable television program called *World Monitor* was launched in 1988. Just ten months later, however, the Monitor Channel was put up for sale because of growing financial pressures. In the April 27, 1992, edition of *Time*, it was reported that $235 million in losses forced layoffs and final shutdown of the Monitor Channel.

Membership

Christian Science has 400,000 members worldwide with app. 100,000 considered active participants. The church reports that there are readers of *Science and Health* in approximately 120 countries and about 2,200 congregations (branch churches) in over 70 countries worldwide.[20]

Notes

[1] *New York Times* (July 10, 1904).

[2] Sydney Ahlstrom, *A Religious History of the American People*, 2 vols. (Garden City, N.Y.: Image Books, 1975), 2:530.

[3] *Encyclopedia Britannica World Data*, "Religion" (Chicago: Encyclopedia Britannica, 1992), 262.

[4] Mary Baker Eddy, *Miscellaneous Writings* (1896), 21.

[5] Mary Baker Eddy, *Science and Health with Key to the Scriptures* (Boston: Trustees Under the Will of Mary Baker G. Eddy, 1875), 377.

[6] Ibid., 427.

[7] Ibid., 113.

[8] Ibid., 256.

[9] Ibid., 332.

[10] Ibid., 361.

[11] Ibid., 558.

[12] Ibid., 332.

[13] Ibid., 474.

[14] Ibid.

[15] Ibid., 588.

[16] Ibid., 593.

[17] Ibid., 583.

[18] Ibid., 581.

[19] Ibid., 587.

[20] *http://religiousmovements.lib.virginia.edu/nrms/chrissci.html*

CHRISTIANITY

One would certainly expect an essay on Christianity to be a lengthy treatise in a book of this nature. Christianity is the largest of the world's religions and has played a critical role in civilization and culture for the last two thousand years. Throughout this volume, the central doctrines of Christianity are presented. It has been the authors' express intent to offer a comparison/contrast between Christianity and the ▶cults, ▶sects, religions, and the ▶occult.

INTRODUCTION

With the exception of the doctrinal development of the first four centuries, particularly in ▶Christology, the extensive story of the Christian church will not be repeated here. After the first four centuries have been discussed, an abbreviated account of the major periods and divisions of Christendom will be presented, the chief aim being to demonstrate points of continuity/discontinuity and fragmentation/catholicity. Brief allusion will be made to Eastern Orthodoxy up to the eleventh century, though the prime focus is on the Western church.

Christianity, like its parent religion JUDAISM, contains two essential principles that, on the surface, have always appeared to be mutually exclusive: its claims to particularity and to universality. Christianity is particular in that it unabashedly claims to be the one true faith fully disclosed in the person and work of Jesus Christ (*see* Apostles' and Nicene Creeds in Appendix 1), outside of whom there is no salvation. Christianity claims universality in that it is God's full disclosure of himself to *all* of humanity through that particular work of Jesus Christ. All other religions, according to the principle of universality, are summarily ruled "out of court." Therefore, Christianity, by definition, claims to be the one true faith for all humankind.

Although there is truth contained in other religions, Christianity claims that the one and only way to attain eternal life, that is, eternal existence with God forever, is through faith in Jesus Christ. Because Christianity is not universally embraced, however, as evidenced from the existence of so many other competing religions, the very notion of an exclusive religion appears scandalous. Nevertheless, this "scandal of particularity" holds true within traditional orthodox circles on the basis of the fact that if Christianity were to forfeit its exclusivity, and, for that matter, its universality, it would by definition cease to be Christianity.

The Christianity referred to here and throughout this volume is "traditional" and/or ▶orthodox Christianity.

What this means is simply Christianity that adheres to the ecumenical creeds (Appendix 1) and all of the attendant doctrines confessed therein. This includes the broad spectrum of Eastern Orthodoxy, Roman Catholicism, and many Protestant denominations born out of the 'Reformation. The forms of Christianity *not* referred to under the umbrella "orthodox" are those that have departed from the ecumenical creeds and have either introduced alternate or competing doctrines (*see*, e.g., ONENESS PENTECOSTALISM) or have conformed to the paradigms of modernity and the philosophical presuppositions of the "Age of Reason" (more below). In these latter forms of Christianity, the notions of particularity and universality are no longer viable, nor is it possible to assign any one "essence" to the Christian faith.

ROOTS

Christianity grew out of its parent religion Judaism and was born in the Old Testament. The first followers of Jesus of Nazareth were Jewish, and indeed the first generation of Christians were almost exclusively Jewish. The reason for "converting" to Christianity (a concept not understood as Christianity yet) was because these followers of Jesus understood him to fill a vital historical role within the context of Judaism. That role was the long-awaited 'Messiah (lit., "anointed one"), promised throughout the Old Testament. Therefore, when Peter preached the first Christian sermon on the Day of Pentecost (Acts 2:14–36), the large mass of three thousand converts (v. 41) were Jewish, and they received Peter's words on the basis of the way in which he linked the story of Jesus with their own story.

Peter begins by saying that the miraculous visitation of the Holy Spirit (Acts 2:1–13) was a fulfillment of the prophecy of Joel (vv. 16–19), who wrote that the Messiah would initiate such miracles. Peter tells the crowd that Jesus of Nazareth is that very Messiah (v. 22) and that his arrest, death, crucifixion, and resurrection were no accidents but were all part of the predetermined council of God (vv. 23–24). Again Peter links the life of Jesus to the Old Testament context when he introduces King David as one who foreshadowed the coming Messiah (vv. 25–35). It is apparent that Luke, recording this message of Peter, is conveying in no uncertain terms that Jesus of Nazareth is not some new and novel religious phenomenon, but rather the very necessary extension of and conclusion to the story of Judaism. Therefore, the "scandal of particularity" (Israel as God's elect people) and the notion of universality (through the seed of Abraham all nations

will be blessed; see Gen. 17) extend to the church on the Day of Pentecost, insofar as the church begins to preach the message of Jesus Christ (particularity) to the entire world (universality).

This summarizes the activity of the early Christian community as it spread rapidly from Jerusalem. The serious issue that arose almost immediately, however, is what role, if any, the Law ('Torah) should play in the lives of non-Jewish (Gentile) converts, who were now part of the promise to Abraham. The Torah was one of the pillars of Judaism. As long as the Christian message was a message to Jews exclusively, the Torah remained a vital part of the new convert's religious life. Jesus came, not to abrogate the Law, but to fulfill it (Matt. 5:17). The real problem entered in when the Christian message came to be embraced by non-Jews. How did the Law apply to the Gentiles?

The apostle Paul faced that issue squarely. Paul was converted from being a zealous persecutor of the church to its most able apologist and a missionary to the Gentiles (Acts 9; 13–28). When news reached the apostles in Jerusalem that Paul was not insisting that Gentiles be circumcised or embrace the Torah, they called him to account at the Council of Jerusalem (Acts 15). The issue had previously come to a head when Paul confronted Peter (Gal. 2:9–15) over the issue of Jews eating with uncircumcised Gentiles. Peter had found no problem in eating with Gentile believers. But when "certain men . . . from James" (in Jerusalem) came into Peter's presence, Peter withdrew himself. Paul interpreted this as hypocrisy and upbraided Peter for it. It is interesting to note that at the Jerusalem Council, Peter himself advocated that Gentiles need not be burdened with circumcision or the rigid adherence to the Law of Moses (Acts 15:7–11). God has poured out his love on both Jew and Gentile alike and grants both grace (v. 11). The decision on the part of James and the apostles in Jerusalem to allow Paul's ministry to the Gentiles to continue without the necessity of circumcision and the Law spelled out the direction that the Christian church would ultimately take.

After A.D. 70, when the Roman general Titus marched into Jerusalem and leveled the temple, Jewish Christianity began to disappear, especially when Hellenized or Gentile Christians began to abandon their Jewish roots. The book of Acts presses in the direction of an all-out Gentile mission. Acts begins in Jerusalem and ends in Rome. It begins with an account of Jewish Christianity and ends in an almost exclusive ministry to Gentiles. The chief apostle of the Jews, Peter, occupies that first part of Acts, but soon yields to Paul, the great missionary to the Gentiles. Jerusalem, Jews, and Peter give way to Rome, Gentiles, and Paul.

What follows is a brief summary of the Patristic era (A.D. 100–170), the Ante-Nicene period (170–325), and the Post-Nicene period (325–590). As stated previously, these periods together will receive the most treatment. The Middle Ages, Reformation, and modernity will follow to summarize quickly changes springing off from the ancient church.

THE PATRISTIC ERA (A.D. 100–170)

This period is the time in which the Apostolic Fathers (i.e., the immediate successors to the apostles) lived and taught. As the church in every age has both champions and enemies, here are some of the great champions of the patristic era, along with enemies they fought.

Polycarp (ca. 69–156). Bishop of the church in Smyrna who was martyred; student of the apostle John. His famous writing is his *Letter to the Philippians*.

Irenaeus (d. ca. 202). He likely sat at the feet of Polycarp in Smyrna and became presbyter of Lyons, Gaul (France), in 177 and bishop of Lyons in 178. Irenaeus's great contribution to the church was his opposition to ⟩gnosticism, his ideas concerning apostolic succession, and his theory of recapitulation, wherein he believed that the Logos of God underwent human suffering in order to redeem humankind. Irenaeus's works include *Detection and Overthrow of the False Gnosis* (also known as *Against Heresies*) and his doctrinal work *Demonstration of the Apostles' Teaching.* He was martyred in 202.

Tertullian (ca. 155/160–ca. 220/230). Born in Carthage as the son of a Roman centurion, he studied law and practiced in Rome. After he converted to Christianity (ca. 190/195), he returned to Carthage, where he became presbyter. His legal mind, combined with his writing and communications skills, enabled him to expound Christian doctrines clearly. As an able apologist, he wrote vehemently against gnosticism, particularly the heretic Marcion. His works include *Apologetics, Baptism,* and *Against Marcion.*

Clement of Alexandria (ca. 150–ca. 215). Founder of the great theological school of Alexandria. After fleeing to Palestine to escape persecution, his pupil Origen (see below) succeeded him. His works include *Exhortation to the Heathen, Instructor,* and *Stromata.* His works were dedicated to the goal of demonstrating that Jesus Christ is the true focal point of all knowledge (*gnosis; see* ⟩gnosticism).

Origen (ca. 185–ca. 254). Greek church father of Alexandria, who taught school and instructed catechumens. Origen traveled widely and was ordained in 230 in Palestine. However, his ordination was not considered valid in Alexandria. Exiled, he taught in Caesarea in Palestine, where he experienced persecution under Decius. Origen was a deep and original thinker. His literary contributions were voluminous, the most famous of which was his *Against Celsus*. His ideas enabled the primitive church to advance greatly in its understanding of the person of Christ.

As the early church encountered gnosticism and met its challenges through the able defenders of the faith (above) in the Patristic and Ante-Nicene era, what emerged was a *creed* and a *canon.* The word *creed* comes from the Latin word *credo,* meaning "I believe." The creed became a primary tool for Christian catechesis and apologetics against the gnostics.[1] The *canon* or "list" of books that would eventually constitute the New Testament began to be assembled. Those writings, which were considered canonical, were those recognized as authoritative within the believing community over against many other writings of the day authored by Christians, gnostics, heretics, or otherwise.

The issue of authority also arose rather quickly after the apostolic era in matters concerning the doctrine, faith, and practice in the church. Both the heretical gnostics and the defenders of the orthodox church claimed support from the Old Testament and the writings of the apostles. Thus the question formed as to what would constitute a final authority in matters of faith. The solution was that the church itself would establish final authority through the bishops. In the apostolic era, the word "bishop" (*episkopos,* i.e., overseer) was synonymous with elder (*presbyteros* or presbyter) and pastor (*poimen* or shepherd; cf. Acts 20:17, 28; Titus 1:5, 7). What emerged, however, in the early part of the second century was a more hierarchical form of leadership, known as the monarchial episcopate, in which the bishop assumed a position of authority above the parish pastors in order to judge matters of doctrine and faith.

ANTE-NICENE ERA

For the first three hundred years, the church had experienced persecution, not in a prolonged or aggrandized fashion but in forms more or less intense—depending on the emperor and the particular province(s) of the Roman Empire in question.[2] Constantine (ca. 280–337) became emperor in 312 when he defeated Maxentius at the Mulvian Bridge outside of Rome. He claimed to have seen the sign of the cross in the sky with the accompanying words of exhortation: "In this sign, conquer." This he interpreted to mean that his battles and victories would come in the name of Christ, the "Son."[3]

However one chooses to interpret this event, the important point is that Constantine immediately issued the famous Edict of Milan in A.D. 313, granting freedom and toleration for all religions in the empire. Essentially, this spelled the end of persecution for Christians. Although some persecutions broke out again under Licinius, Constantine defeated him in 324, making himself sole emperor. This became one of the most important events in the history of the church, for Christianity now became the preferred religion. What began with a small band of apostles and the few converts who were mostly poor and uneducated, after three hundred years of struggle emerged victorious over heathenism and paganism.

The Edict of Milan proved to be a mixed blessing. While the era of persecution ended, the church entered an era in which the influences of the culture, religions, and philosophies of heathenism began to exert themselves on Christians. Christians even began to use force to compel others to enter the ranks of the faithful, an idea utterly foreign to the teachings of the founder of Christianity. Another issue that arose as a result of the Edict of Milan was that of the relationship between church and state. Before, the church existed and promulgated itself in spite of the hostility of the state, many times becoming a prophetic witness against the state. After 313, however, the state and the church began to cooperate. In exchange for allowing the church the freedom to conduct its affairs without persecution, Constantine insisted on having a voice in its affairs. The problem of church and state has occupied the Christian church to the present day, and different thinkers and (in the modern era) different denominations have developed different theological postures concerning how the church should relate to secular society and the state.

THE ECUMENICAL COUNCILS

The need for further organization and consolidation became necessary as the church began to grow and spread its wings on the mission fields. Further heresies continued to challenge the church's doctrines as well. The first council was, it will be recalled, the Council of Jerusalem (Acts 15). In the Ante-Nicene and Post-Nicene eras, the church had grown so large that the need arose for ecumenical councils that brought together all of the local churches for the sake of doctrinal unity and consolidation. The Great Ecumenical Councils that we will note here are four in number: The Council of Nicea (325), the Council of Constantinople (381), the Council of Ephesus (431), and the Council of Chalcedon (451).

The Council of Nicea. The question that had plagued the earliest opponents of Christianity, namely, the scribes and Pharisees, was that Jesus was not only claiming to be the chosen Messiah, but that he was also claiming to be God (John 10:33). The struggle that ensued for the next three hundred years over this issue culminated in the emergence of two outstanding personalities: Arius (250–ca. 336) and Athanasius (ca. 296–373). Arius, noted for his great preaching and pious life, could not fathom the notion of Jesus as God for the simple reason that this would imply the existence of two Gods. Arius believed that this would lead to disastrous consequences, especially if Christianity was going to set itself apart from the heathen who believed in the existence of many gods. He therefore concluded that Jesus was closer to God than any other being, but he had a beginning, whereas God is eternal. There was a time when Jesus was not; there was never a time when God was not. This constituted the essence of what became known as ▸Arianism in the ancient church.

Arius's able opponent was the much younger Athanasius. For the latter, the whole issue of Christ's divinity was not a detached debate about the person of Christ; rather, it was the question of Jesus' divinity, and it lay at the very root of salvation. Sin had left humankind in such a hopeless condition that it could never save itself. Only God could accomplish this. If Christ was not the divine God incarnate in human flesh, then he cannot be a Savior either.

Both parties locked horns in bitter opposition. The dispute was only brought to some resolution when Emperor Constantine intervened by calling a council to settle it. The Council, attended by about three hundred bishops in 325, was held in the town of Nicea (now Iznik). At this first ecumenical council, the church condemned Arianism and maintained, with Athanasius, that Christ is "very God." The statement of faith that emerged from this council was the Nicene Creed, the church's first written confession (Appendix 1). In it, the church boldly attested that Christ was of "one substance with the Father." The word *substance* (Gk. *ousia*) was a controversial term (not agreed to by Arians, of course) that was supplied to counter the Arian claim that Christ was not coeternal with the Father.

Arius, however, along with several bishops, refused to sign the Nicene Creed. He mounted a considerable following that caused Athanasius to spend the remainder of his life defending the orthodoxy established at Nicea. Henry Chadwick observes:

> It was the misfortune of the fourth century church that it became engrossed in a theological controversy at the same time it was working out its institutional organization. The doctrinal disagreements quickly became inextricably associated with matters of order, discipline, and authority. Above all they became bound up with the gradually growing tension between the Greek East and the Latin West.[4]

It was this growing rift between East and West, politically, ecclesiastically, and culturally, that Arianism was able to use to its considerable advantage in the East. During the reigns of Constantine, Constantius II, and Julian, Athanasius was forced into exile four times.[5] After the death of Julian (363), Athanasius returned to Alexandria, where he continued to support the orthodox cause of the Nicene Council.

The Council of Constantinople. When Athanasius died in 373, leadership for the orthodox cause fell into the hands of three intellectually gifted theologians known as the Cappadocian Fathers: Basil the Great (ca. 330–79), bishop of Caesarea in Cappadocia; Gregory (329–89), bishop of Constantinople; and Gregory of Nyssa (ca. 330–95), bishop of Nyssa. Like Athanasius, these latter three took a strong stand in the defense of the orthodox cause. But it was not until Emperor Theodosius I convened a council in 381 in Constantinople that the cause of orthodoxy was firmly established and Arianism was finally rejected by most of the churches.

Several key issues were addressed in this second ecumenical council. While the deity of Christ had been recognized, nothing had yet been said about the divinity of the Holy Spirit. The result was the emergence of a longer statement affirming that the Holy Spirit too was true God. The theologians present at Constantinople also had to reckon with another opponent of Arius, namely Apollinarius, bishop of Laodicea (ca. 310–ca. 390). A friend of Athanasius, this man taught that while Christ possessed full deity, he did not possess a truly human soul. In its place was the ▸Logos of God. While Christ was in full possession of deity, thereby countering Arius, Apollinarius did not keep Christ's human nature intact, thus countering the confession at Nicea that Jesus was both fully God and fully human. The Cappadocian fathers opposed ▸Appolinarianism, which was ultimately rejected at the Council of Constantinople. Arianism and Apollinarianism passed into the background as the church pressed on into the fifth century, only to meet head-on with new challenges.

Two schools of theology. Fertile minds within the church wrestled with the deep doctrinal issues. Two schools developed, each centering in a geographical region in the East—Antioch and Alexandria. The Antiochene school featured such theologians as Paul of Samosata, Lucian of Antioch, John Chrysostom, Theodore of Mopsuestia, and the famed Nestorius. Characteristics of this school included a rejection of allegorical interpretation of the ▸Bible and a desire to discover the intent of the biblical writers in arriving at the meaning of a given text. The most notable feature of this school was its Christology. The Antiochene tradition tended to emphasize the humanity of Christ and to allow a rather loose connection between Christ's two natures, both divine and human.

If the Antiochene school was more Aristotelian and "rationalist," the second tradition, the Alexandrian school, tended more toward Platonic ▸mysticism. This latter school featured such theologians as Clement of Alexandria, Origen, Athanasius, and Cyril of Alexandria. This school leaned more toward an allegorical interpretation of the Bible and emphasized the divinity of Christ, along with a much more unified view of the two natures of Christ. Because Jesus' humanity was less distinguishable from his divinity in this school than in the Antiochene tradition, the notion of "God suffering on the cross" met with ready acceptance among the Alexandrians.

In the Antiochene school, Nestorius espoused the view that Jesus' humanity was to be distinguished from his divinity to the point that Nestorius himself utterly rejected the notion that God suffered or that God died on the cross. It was merely the human Jesus who suffered and died. The reaction in the Alexandrian school to ▸Nestorianism produced a rival and extreme Christology known as ▸monophysitism, which overemphasized the divinity of Christ (Christ has only one (*mono*) nature (*physis*), and that nature was totally divine. The two theological traditions were bound to meet with the challenge of a third ecumenical council.[6]

The Council of Ephesus. Emperor Theodosius II (401–50) convened the Council of Ephesus in 431. The chief purpose for this council was to settle the question of Nestorianism. Cyril of Alexandria, Nestorius's chief opponent, opened the Council fifteen days after it was originally scheduled, because several bishops had not yet arrived. Refusing any further delay, on the very day that the Council was convened, Nestorianism was condemned and Nestorius himself was excommunicated. The term *theotokos* ("mother of God") and the logical implication that God was born, suffered, died, and resurrected were Christological resolutions upheld by the Council. In reality, however, the Council of Ephesus was much more than a personal war between Nestorius and Cyril. It was also the clash between the two rival schools of Antioch and Alexandria.

Another important decision of the Council of Ephesus was the decision to condemn ▶Pelagianism (discussed below). The Christological question itself, however, was not yet settled. There would still be more challenges to orthodoxy that called forth from within the church's rank and file the sharpest theological minds to probe the Holy Scriptures still further, in order to come up with clearer articulations of how the two natures of Christ were related.

The Council of Chalcedon. Emperor Marcian called a fourth Ecumenical Council to deal with another questionable Christology, that espoused by Eutyches (d. 454). Like Apollinarius, Eutyches taught that Jesus' divinity was of sole importance. He embraced monophysitism (see above). This thinking ran counter to the already established orthodox doctrine of Christ with two natures, human and divine.

Six hundred bishops attended the Council of Chalcedon. In coming to grips with ▶Eutychianism, the Council arrived at a confession of faith that reasserted the church's confession of the full deity of Christ and equally of his full humanity. The most important aspect of the Chalcedonian Council was its all-encompassing Christological formulation. The famous "four qualifying adjectives" asserted against Eutychianism that the two natures of Christ are "without confusion" and "without

change," and against Nestorianism that the two natures were "without division" or "without separation."

The Christology of Chalcedon has been the Christology of orthodox Christendom from the fifth century to the present. The personal union of the two natures of Christ were understood as being related to each other hypostatically (*see* ▶hypostatic union). The divine nature is so related to the human that each shares the qualities of the other. To speak of God dying is as compatible as saying that Jesus' human blood saves. God (divinity) shares in the human quality of dying. Blood (human) shares in the divine offer of salvation.

The Council of Chalcedon, as already stated, established a Christology that has never been altered in orthodox Christianity. Even the ▶Great Schism of A.D. 1054 between the East and the West, and the ▶(Protestant) Reformation, which has shattered the unity of the Western church to this very day, did not reject the Christology of these early creeds (Appendix 1). These ecumenical symbols stand as clear testimony to the true catholicity of the church regarding her chief doctrine, namely, that of her bridegroom, the Lord Jesus Christ. These four ancient symbols unite the Eastern Orthodox churches, Roman Catholic, and most churches falling under the Protestant umbrella, despite many other divergences.

THE LATIN FATHERS

Christian history cannot be told without reference to three of the greatest theologians in the Western church: Ambrose, Jerome, and Augustine.

Ambrose (340–97), born in Germany, was the son of a Roman statesman. He himself was appointed to the office of governor of a sizeable portion of northern Italy, known as Aemilia-Liguria. He lived in Milan. An Arian bishop, Auxentius, held the bishopric of Milan until his death in 374. The orthodox Catholics sought vigorously to fill the office with a non-Arian bishop. Ambrose was selected, even though he had not yet been baptized and was only a catechumen. He accepted the post, underwent baptism, and became one of the church's most influential advocates for orthodoxy; he was instrumental in the conversion of Augustine. Ambrose was a strong advocate for the church's independence from political and civil powers, and wrote and preached much on moral and ethical issues.

Jerome (ca. 342–420) was born in Dalmatia and was educated in Rome. He became a widely traveled monk and was known for his contributions as a biblical scholar. The last years of his life were spent in Bethlehem, where he lived for thirty-four years in a cave,

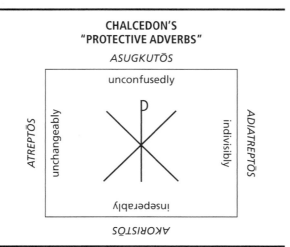

CHALCEDON'S "PROTECTIVE ADVERBS"

ASUGKUTŌS

unconfusedly

ATREPTŌS — unchangeably

ADIATREPTŌS — indivisibly

inseperably

AKORISTŌS

A chart depicting the four qualifying adverbs of the orthodox Christology defined at the Council of Chalcedon.

next to the cave where Christ was supposedly born. Jerome's greatest contribution as a Western churchman was that he translated the Bible, both the Old and New Testaments, into the Latin language. His translation became known as the *Vulgate*. Jerome had learned Hebrew while living in Palestine and was able to offer a translation of the Old Testament, not from the Greek ♦Septuagint, but from the Hebrew texts. The Vulgate became the sole Bible of the Western Church through the Middle Ages until Erasmus reintroduced the Greek and Hebrew texts in the sixteenth century.

Augustine. The greatest of the Latin Fathers was Augustine (354–430). Born in Tagaste, North Africa, Augustine's father was a pagan while his mother, Monica, was a Christian. Augustine's parents early recognized the literary gifts of their son. At sixteen, Augustine was sent to school in Carthage where he studied rhetoric, his intention being eventually to study law. Carthage, in addition to being a great center of learning, was also a city given to wickedness and paganism. Succumbing to these influences, Augustine soon abandoned the Christianity of his mother and even took on a mistress. All the while, Monica continually prayed for the conversion of her son.

Far from believing in Christianity at this time, Augustine was preoccupied with a newfound interest in philosophy; in 373 he embraced ♦Manichaeism. However, when the Manichaean philosopher Faustas failed to answer Augustine's probing questions, the latter became greatly disillusioned with Manichaeanism and abandoned it. Next came a migration to Rome against his mother's hopes and prayers. Monica was comforted by a friend who assured her, "A son of so many prayers cannot be lost."

Augustine's travels took him to Milan, where he was appointed a teacher of rhetoric. The bishop of Milan at this time was Ambrose (see above). Augustine listened to Ambrose's preaching quite often. At first, he was only interested in the rhetorical skills exhibited by the famous bishop, not the substance of what was being said. While in Milan, Monica joined her son, who was beginning to alter his views. Augustine now became interested in the philosophy of neo-Platonism and in the sermons of Ambrose. Reading the life of St. Antony and some key portions of the Bible, Augustine was converted in 386 and baptized on Easter Eve, 387.

Things happened quickly. In 388 Augustine returned to Africa and founded a small monastery in Tagaste. In 391 he became a priest, and in 396 he became bishop of Hippo, a post he held until his death in 430. Augustine's importance lay in his profound and deep percep-

tions of Christianity. His opposition to Manichaeanism and Pelagianism and his stand in the ♦Donatist controversy—all issues that were of paramount importance to the church in his day—not only refined his own theology, but were instrumental in the formulation of the church's theology, particularly that of the Western church, to this very day.

As noted above, Augustine was earlier a disciple of Manichaeanism, which posited a ♦dualism whereby evil and good were equal forces that continually struggled for preeminence. Augustine rather easily demonstrated that this philosophical system begged more questions than answers. In its place he advanced the neo-Platonic notion that good is the primary reality of the universe and that evil is a privation of the good. Theologically, this translated into the Bible's clear testimony that God alone is the source of all goodness and that the powers of darkness and evil arose as a result of the privation of good. All of this was under the permissive will of God.

The Donatist controversy, while originally a local dispute in Augustine's own territory of North Africa a century before his birth, became far-reaching in its implications. At the heart of the controversy lay the question of whether Christians who had denied their faith during the persecution under Decius (in 249) should be allowed back into the church. Large numbers of Christians had lapsed from their faith, but when the persecutions came to a halt under Constantine's edict (above), many wished to reenter the Catholic church. Those who had remained faithful through persecution were accepting these lapsed people back into the church under relatively easy terms. Cyprian (d. 258), bishop of Carthage, had strongly opposed this practice, arguing that a period of time for examination and repentance should take place before entrance back into the Catholic church. Bishops who had surrendered copies of the Holy Scriptures to the authorities during the persecution should never be permitted to administer the ♦sacraments again or ordain other priests.

During times of peace within the empire the Donatist controversy raged on. Donatists withdrew from the church and formed churches of their own. For the first time in the relatively short history of the church, there arose the concept of plurality. No longer was the church universal or catholic, but now Donatist and Catholic. This gave rise to serious questions such as: What is the church? How do Donatist Christians and Catholic Christians relate to each other? How does the church relate to society? Can Christians exist outside the church? Answers to these crucial questions would be left largely to the able bishop of Hippo, whose answers perhaps did more to shape the subsequent direction of the Western church than any other theologian in history.

The church, insisted Augustine, was the one true catholic church. "I should not have believed the Gospel except as moved by the authority of the Catholic Church." The church is holy and divine, not because her members are holy, but because the divine Christ has instituted it for the dissemination of the Gospel. The church was comprised of both evil people and good. As to the role of the state, Augustine believed that coercion was justified in bringing schismatics back into the Catholic faith. He opposed, however, the use of extreme force. Justice must remain the state's solitary motive. No one should be put to death for schism or heresy, a view the church in subsequent centuries sometimes ignored. Augustine believed that all who were baptized into the Christian faith, if not already members of the church, would become so before death.

Donatism itself was denounced in 411. While it continued to persist despite the ban and mounting pressure, it would not be destroyed until Islamic (see ISLAM) forces swept through North Africa during the seventh and eighth centuries.

A third controversy, one that occupied the latter part of Augustine's life, became the one that had the most impact on the Western church for centuries—the Pelagian controversy. In his celebrated *Confessions* (10.29.40), Augustine asserted: "And my whole hope is in thy exceeding great mercy. Give what thou commandest, and command what thou wilt." In the year 410, he learned that Pelagius had fiercely disagreed with this statement, asserting that humankind was free to take the first initiative by exercising free will to accept or reject God.

A fierce controversy ensued as Augustine began to preach and write against Pelagius's innovative ideas. Without getting bogged down with the controversy itself and all of its details, the significance was that it forced Augustine to spell out his thoughts on the Fall and its effects, original sin, and ultimately the doctrine of predestination. Centuries later, in the Reformation, particularly Luther and Calvin seized on these themes and advanced them to their fullest theological implications. Pelagius's views were condemned by the Second Council of Orange in 529. Pelagianism also was revived shortly after the Reformation began in the doctrines and teachings of the Dutch Reformed theologian Jacobus Arminius (1560–1609).

In response to Pelagius, Augustine asserted that Adam's sin had so affected the human race that sin was not merely an act or "habit" (Pelagius) but was now part of human nature. Free will was lost in Adam's fall in the Garden of Eden. The only freedom a sinful human being has is the freedom to choose sin continually. Only by an act of God's grace can one be delivered from sin. Thus, Augustine concluded, the saved are those on whom God has bestowed his divine grace.

Augustine's influence on the Catholic church is profound. His theology and overall thought spelled out a specific Christian philosophy of history that has been unmatched to this day. His theology laid the foundation for Christian thought throughout the Middle Ages and even during the Protestant Reformation.[7]

THE FIVE PATRIARCHS

In the first five centuries of Christianity, another important development took place. Five major cities became busy centers of Christian activity: Jerusalem, Antioch, Alexandria, Constantinople, and Rome. Each of these, as well as each diocese throughout the church, had its appointed bishops. Bishops of the larger churches gradually were recognized as being higher in rank than the bishops of less-populated Christian communities. The bishops of the churches in the five great metropolitan centers gradually were recognized as the five highest-ranking bishops. These were called patriarchs. Note that four out of the five cities were located in the eastern part of the empire; Rome was the sole patriarchal center of the west.

1. The church in Jerusalem was recognized by all as the mother church (at least up through the fourth century).
2. Gradually, however, Jerusalem was supplanted by Antioch, the city where the disciples of Jesus were first called Christians (Acts 11:26). From Antioch Christianity had begun to spread its wings throughout the Gentile world; many bishops were ordained there.
3. Alexandria's importance was due to mission work conducted there by Mark, even though it could not claim apostolic origin. Moreover, Alexandria boasted the greatest cultural center of the east and was noted for its great theologians, Origen and Athanasius.
4. Constantinople was the youngest of the patriarchal centers. It was important because Constantine lived there. The city, formerly called Byzantium, was renamed in his honor.
5. Rome was, of course, the center of the empire. From a Christian standpoint, more and more

Christian activity pointed to Rome. The book of Acts concludes with Paul laboring in that city. Tradition has it that Peter founded the church in Rome. The Roman bishop was continually looked to for leadership. Irenaeus had early on written that Rome set the standard of leadership for the church.

Gradually, after the barbarians invaded Rome in the fifth century and drove away the political institution that had governed the empire for centuries, a political vacuum was created. The only institution left that was able to fill the vacuum was the church. The head of the church in Rome was, of course, its bishop, who began to assume more and more political responsibilities; this culminated in the establishment of the Holy Roman Empire.

More and more of the bishops of the Western churches came to acknowledge the supremacy of the bishop of Rome. The Late Latin word for "father," *papa* (translated "pope"), was first applied to Siricius, the bishop of Rome from 384–99. Although Ambrose wrote that the bishop of Rome possessed a "primacy of confession, not office, a primacy of faith, not of rank," still the notion of the primacy of rank of the bishop of Rome as head of the church was ready to emerge as a result of a power struggle between the churches in the East and in the West.

Leo I (440–61) was the first to assert that Rome enjoyed full primacy over all of Christendom, basing his claim on that fact that Peter was the "prince of the apostles," who "rightly rules all who are ruled in the first instance by Christ."[8] This claim spelled the beginning of a new era in the church. The title "pope" was hereafter applied to each successor to the office of the bishop of Rome. Such a claim, however, has never been unchallenged. Some of the North African and Eastern churches opposed it from the outset.

Many church historians argue that when the Christian church passed from the stage of being a millenarian movement immediately conscious of the eschatological reality of the imminent return of Jesus Christ, to being a religion totally "absorbed" and acculturated into the Roman Empire, it ceased to represent the true character of Christianity. They further argue that this development led to the deterioration of the church. Just as Israel had become corrupted by the influences of heathen religions, so too the church. Pagan practices, the worship of "Christian" relics, the veneration of martyrs and saints, and all manner of superstition entered in. Rather than being an institution that stood as a prophetic witness over against the world, the church became an institution of the world, willing and able to adapt itself to the ways of the prevailing *polytheism and paganism within the collapsing Roman Empire.[9]

MONASTICISM

One reaction to the acculturation of the church to the world was monasticism. Anthony of Thebes (c. 251–356) is believed to be the first monk or hermit, withdrawing himself to the deserts of Egypt around 270, where he lived in a cave in order to escape the pollutions of the world and to pursue a holy life. He attracted a number of disciples. Occasionally, Anthony did come out of hiding, as when he openly supported Athanasius in the Arian controversy.

Monasticism soon developed in a number of regions, branching out from Egypt. Some individuals went to great extremes to express their distaste for the ways of the world. The most famous example was Simon Stylites, who spent thirty years of his life living at the top of pillars (*styles*) that he had erected. More pillar saints followed his example in Syria.

Specific monastic orders began to spring up. Benedict (480–550) introduced his "Rule," which was used by his and many other monastic orders throughout the Middle Ages. According to Benedict, monks were to live as a family, the head of which was the abbot. Each monk divided his time between domestic work (usually agricultural) and observances of the central act of the community, the *opus Dei* (or Divine Office). The *opus Dei* was structured around the seven canonical hours. They were (and are) approximately as follows:

1. 2:00 A.M. Vigils
2. 4:30 A.M. Lauds
3. 6:00 A.M. Prime
4. 9:00 A.M. Terce
5. 12:00 P.M. Sext
6. 4:30 P.M. Vespers
7. 6:00 P.M. Compline

Benedict founded his order at Monte Cassino in Italy. A much more exacting and severe form of monasticism was introduced by Columbanus (543–615) in Gaul (France). The Columban monks enjoyed less of a community spirit than the Benedictines and were enjoined to fast, work, pray, and read every day.[10]

Many additional monastic orders were founded during the Middle Ages, each of which was governed by different rules, principles, and priorities. Some were founded as "reform" movements against the corruptions either of the church itself or of another monastic order that had deteriorated morally. Several of the more famous orders included the Carmelites (1154), the Franciscans (1209), the Dominicans (1215), the Augustinians (1256), and the Jesuits (1540).

MISSIONS

The invasion of the Roman Empire by Germanic barbarians (Germans, Goths, Huns, Vandals, and Visigoths) was, in retrospect, a mixed blessing. In 410 Rome was sacked by the Visigoths, led by Alaric. This event shocked the world. Christians were blamed for bringing a curse on the mighty empire. In this context, Augustine wrote his *City of God*.

To fill the power vacuum created by the invasion of the barbarians, the church stepped in. This in turn opened doors for the church to go beyond the boundaries of the empire and bring its message to the peoples who had come to conquer. Although many in the empire were murdered at the hands of the barbarians, many of the learned were not. These included the monks, who were among the most literate and educated of society. Consequently, this exclusive group was able to provide capable and learned missionaries to bring the gospel to the heathen.

Significant to the history of the Christian church was the conversion of the Franks, led by their king, Clovis, who eventually extended his conquests throughout Gaul. From this time on, Gaul was called France. Clovis was baptized as a Christian in 496, and through his influence, a whole nation became Christian.

Christianity came to England through Christian soldiers of the Roman Empire. St. Patrick (c. 390–c. 460) brought the gospel to Ireland. Columba (c. 521–97), another Irish monk, founded the famous monastery on the island of Iona. His work resulted in the gospel's spread to Scotland. And from Scotland, missionaries set their sights back on the mainland, especially on Germany.

When the Anglo-Saxons invaded England, Christianity was dismantled. A century later, however, Pope Gregory the Great sent Augustine of Canterbury (d. 604 or 605) to *Angleland* (England) to recapture the country for Christendom. Augustine's success was multiplied because from England, many missionaries were trained and sent forth from England throughout the world. One of the greatest of these was Boniface (680–754), called the "Apostle of Germany." Willibrord (658–739), another English missionary, established Christianity at Utrecht in the Netherlands.

By the year 1000, Christianity had spread like wildfire throughout Europe and even into Russia. When Christianity came to the Americas, Roman Catholicism spread to the southern and southwestern regions of North America and almost all of the southern hemisphere. Protestantism occupied much of the future United States, from which the church's most ambitious missionary efforts would eventually be launched.[11]

THE MIDDLE AGES

Pope Gregory the Great (540–604) was the first monk to become a pope. He is known as the "father of the medieval papacy" and, in essence, bridged the gap between the ancient period and the so-called Middle Ages, a period marked by the marriage between church and state, by the accession of popes to the height of political power, and by the establishment of the Holy Roman Empire. This was not a period of great doctrinal development as compared to the first four centuries, but great thinkers did contribute to Christian theology nevertheless.

During the Middle Ages, the ▶Iconoclastic Controversy raged from 752–842. Islam was born and presented a great challenge and threat to the church. The Crusades were organized to surmount the onslaught of Islam. Another great split in the church took place (recall Donatism and Arianism) when in 1054, the Roman Catholic west and the Greek Orthodox east divided. Heretical sects arose, such as the Waldensians, Albigenses, Cathari, and Bogomils.

The late Middle Ages also saw the rise of a great revival in classical learning, and the great universities of France, Italy, Germany, and England became the hub of the new theological school known as scholasticism. The great schoolmen, Anselm (1033–1109), Abelard (1079–1142), Peter Lombard (1100–1160), Albertus Magnus (1200–1280), Duns Scotus (1265–1308), and Thomas Aquinas (1225–1274) all lived in this period. Scholasticism sought to distinguish faith from reason and at the same time to show how they could be compatible. The great saints Bernard of Clairvaux (1091–1153) and Francis of Assisi (1181/2–1226) also lived in the high Middle Ages. The devotional writings of the latter are still widely read to this day.

Just before the Reformation, the Catholic church experienced a decline, culminating in the Great Schism and the Babylonian Captivity. John Wycliffe (ca. 1325–84) in England translated the Bible from Jerome's Vulgate to English and advocated strong reform in the church. John Hus (1372–1415) taught many of Wycliffe's reform measures in Bohemia and was burned at the stake for heresy. Girolamo Savanarola (1452–98) preached against the wealth and luxury of the clergy; he was martyred in 1498. In the Netherlands, Gerhard Groote (1340–84) founded the Brethren of the Common Life. Desiderius Erasmus (1496–1536), a humanist ("man of letters") and scholar, was heavily influenced by the Brethren. One of the most widely read devotional works ever written, *The Imitation of Christ*, flowed from the pen of yet another student of the Brethren, Thomas à Kempis (1380–1471). Both Martin Luther and Ignatius Loyola held the *Imitation of Christ* in highest regard.[12]

THE REFORMATION

The next great period of theological activity in the West came at a time when the cry for reform in the church was at its height. Erasmus's pen poked fun at and criticized sharply the lives of the monks and clergy. But it remained for another man to attack the very core of the medieval church, her doctrine. This man was Martin Luther (1483–1546). In this limited space we cannot give Luther his due. It has been claimed that more books have been written on the life of Luther than any other person in the history of Christendom save Jesus Christ himself. This is probably true.[13] Luther challenged the church in 1517 by writing his Ninety-Five Theses, statements that attacked ▸indulgences and the authority of the pope. The Ninety-Five Theses precipitated a mass movement known as the Protestant Reformation.

Luther, an Augustinian monk, taught that salvation was by "grace alone," by "faith alone," and that the sole authority in matters of faith was the "Bible alone." By purchasing indulgences for the forgiveness of sins, one loses Christ. By trusting in "Christ alone," indulgences are rendered utterly unnecessary. So strong were Luther's convictions on these doctrines that at the Diet of Worms in 1521, in the presence of Emperor Charles V and various leaders of the Roman church, Luther, when asked if he would recant his doctrines, responded: "If any man can show me from Scripture where I am wrong, I will recant. Here I stand. I can do no other. May God help me. Amen." Luther also translated the Bible into German as Wycliffe had done for England, with one important difference. Luther used Erasmus's Greek text published in 1516, while Wycliffe had used the Vulgate.

Other great Reformers of the sixteenth century include the leader of the Swiss Reformation, Ulrich Zwingli (1484–1531); of the French Reformation, John Calvin (1509–64); and of the Reformation in Scotland, John Knox (c. 1505–72). The English Reformation arose as the result of a combination of influences, including the teaching of Luther, Calvin, and Thomas Cranmer (1489–1556), as well as the political intrigues of Henry VIII (1491–1547).[14]

The temperament of Calvinism differed somewhat from that of Lutheranism. While Luther's theological center was the ▸incarnation of Christ and the "theology of the cross," Calvin's focus was on the glory and sovereignty of God. While Luther emphasized that the church should operate independently from the state, Calvin, at least in principle, argued that while the church should be separate, the affairs of the church should be carried out by the civil authorities, who themselves should be Christians. While Luther argued in true Pauline/Augustinian fashion that the human will is bound in sin and that God has elected his church by grace, Calvin (while agreeing with Luther) argued further that not only does God predestine those called to salvation, but also he predestines others to damnation.

Both Reformers advocated the need for education and taught the doctrine of the "priesthood of all believers." These emphases resulted in the far-reaching consequence of granting dignity and honor to all Christians. During the Middle Ages, the clergy and monks had been afforded a higher status than the common people. The Reformation advocated that all vocations were honorable in God's kingdom and that the clergy differed not in rank but in call.

Another group, known as the Anabaptists, arose during the Reformation. These were Protestants who believed that the reforms wrought by Luther were good but did not go far enough. Luther remained too much the Catholic by continuing to teach infant baptism and a high view of the sacraments. Conrad Grebel (1498–1526), an ardent Zwinglian, soon departed from Zwingli's doctrines and rebaptized (hence the name Anabaptist) Christians who had been previously baptized as infants. Infant baptism was blamed for much of the worldliness and immorality in the church.

A second Anabaptist group tried to erect a "kingdom of God" in Münster, Germany. This group was led by Melchior Hoffman (1500–1543), Jan Mathys (d. 1534), and Jan von Leiden. The Anabaptists were massacred in 1535 after a prolonged siege by Protestant and Catholic armies.

A third Anabaptist group was founded by Menno Simons (1492–1559), who introduced a much milder form of Anabaptism in Holland. A fourth group were the Amish, followers of a stern disciplinarian, Jacob Amman (1644–1730); he arose from the ranks of the Swiss Mennonite movement. Many of these eventually settled in America. Later, Separatists in England and

Holland and Baptists in America were labeled Anabaptists, but because of the pejorative connotations of this title, these groups repudiated such a label.

The Reformation era, like the Patristic era, was a time of great creedal activity. The following major confessions were produced: the Sixty-Seven Articles (by Zwingli in 1523); the Augsburg Confession (by the Lutherans in 1530); the Helvetic Confession (by the Swiss in 1536); the Thirty-Nine Articles of Anglicanism (by Cranmer, final revision in 1571, heavily influenced by Lutheranism); the Heidelburg Catechism (by Calvinists in 1562); and the Westminster Confession (by Presbyterians in 1647).

The Roman Catholic church responded to the Reformation with a confession and council of its own, called the Council of Trent. The Council of Trent (often called the Counter Reformation) met from 1545–1563, though not continuously. Many of the abuses that had caused the Reformation were corrected, a catechism was written, and the clergy received much better education.

The hundred years from 1545–1648 were turbulent years, during which religious wars between Catholics and Protestants were vehemently fought. Rome launched the Spanish Inquisition, the Council of Trent produced an index of books to be banned, the Jesuits ambitiously sought to win back Protestants through teaching and preaching, and the Holy Roman Emperor Charles V launched a war "to root out heresy" in Europe. In France on August 24, 1572 (St. Bartholomew's Day), the king ordered the massacre of thousands of Calvinists (called Huguenots). In the Netherlands over 18,000 were massacred at the hands of the Spanish Inquisition. William the Silent (d. 1584) rose up to defend the Protestant cause in the Netherlands. In 1618, the Peace of Augsburg was broken and fighting erupted again. The Swedish king Gustavus Adolphus II (1594–1632) stepped in and saved Germany and Protestantism. Finally in 1648, the Thirty Years War was brought to a close with the signing of the Peace of Westphalia. The new treaty restored peace to Germany and also extended it to Calvinists. According to the terms of the treaty, the religion of each realm was to be determined by each principal ruler.

THE MODERN ERA

The church after the Reformation found itself divided not only into Greek East and Roman West, but now the Roman Church stood over against Lutheranism, Calvinism, Anglicanism, Anabaptism, Pietism, and a flurry of denominations and sects that would explode into existence once Christianity came to America.

When Separatists left England in 1620, they established autonomy in Plymouth Colony. Almost a decade later, the Puritans (i.e., those who stayed within the English church but wished to see it "purified") settled in Massachusetts Bay Colony. In 1635 Roger Williams (1603–1683) was banished from Massachusetts and founded a new colony called Providence; there he established America's first Baptist church. Rhode Island is significant for Christianity in the modern world because the constitution for that colony that Williams drew up was the first official document ever written in the history of the church in which a sovereign state granted complete religious toleration. The principle of religious freedom would become a pillar of America's future constitution.

Because of the climate of toleration in America, it soon became host to every denomination of Christendom, each settling in a certain geographical area. We cannot recount the history of the various denominations of Christianity here. The reader should consult Sydney Ahlstrom's *A Religious History of the American People* for an excellent survey of each group, the contributions of Jonathan Edwards (1703–1758), the ▶Great Awakening, ▶transcendentalism, and so on.

Also noteworthy in the modern period are the far-reaching changes brought to theology as a result of the Enlightenment. The French philosophers, English deists, and German idealists did much to change the complexion of Christianity. The nineteenth century saw the rise of Darwinism, which introduced a new and alternative "scientific" explanation for human origin, challenging the biblical account. Karl Marx (1818–83) extended Darwinism to the economic sphere, explaining human alienation as a result of class struggle. He argued that religion was an "opiate" that kept the masses fixated on an other-worldly utopia, thereby escaping the reality of the sufferings of alienation in this world. Marx believed that the need for religion would disappear when alienation and class-consciousness disappeared. His ideas proved wrong, however, as the collapse of Marxist communism has shown in recent years. Christians living in the Soviet Union suffered greatly through most of the twentieth century. Many thousands were martyred throughout the world under Marxist governments.

Sigmund Freud (1856–1939) also contributed to the intellectual current of nineteenth-century unbelief. If Darwinism explained human origin and Marxism human alienation, Freud's psychoanalytic method helped explain away God and sin as a neurosis of the mind. To Freud, the very concept of God is a "fictitious extension of the human father ideal as a refuge from fear."

The Germany that gave the church Martin Luther also produced some of the most destructive critics of the Bible during the nineteenth and twentieth centuries. David Strauss (1808–1874) wrote *Das Leben Jesu (The Life of Jesus)* in 1835, in which he separated the historical Jesus from the Jesus of the Bible. F. C. Baur (1792–1860) founded the Tübingen School in Germany and argued that the real essence of Christianity is its ethical content. Baur was among the first German critics to teach that only Romans, 1 and 2 Corinthians, and Galatians were genuinely Pauline while the other traditional Pauline epistles were spurious. Friedrich Schleiermacher (1768–1834) denied divine ▶revelation, insisting that the locus of religion is an aspect of inner consciousness and that true Christianity is a "feeling of absolute dependence." Schleiermacher had been influenced by the Halle tradition of pietism, and his theology is described in his monumental *Der Christliche Glaube (The Christian Faith)*. Schleiermacher was arguably the most noted theologian of the nineteenth century.

Søren Kierkegaard (1813–1855) sharply criticized the Lutheran church in Denmark for its corruption and worldly character. His writings articulated a theology that would later be labeled Christian existentialism. Kierkegaard believed that the genuine Christian life is a lonely desperate struggle and that authentic faith rests not in propositional truth statements or creeds, but in one's personal involvement and encounter with God. Kierkegaard's thought would have a profound influence a century later for ▶evangelicalism in America.

Albrecht Ritschl (1822–89), influenced by Baur, Kant, Hegel, and Schleiermacher, founded a school of his own. Ritschl argued that religion is apprehended by faith, not reason, and that the truth of religion is based on "value judgments." For example, Jesus' divinity should not be regarded as historical fact; rather, it possesses "revelational value" for the believing community (the church). The Ritschlian school stressed, as had Baur, the ethical nature of Christianity. One of Ritschl's disciples, Adolf von Harnack (1851–1930), was a brilliant historian and theologian. Harnack believed that the church's emphasis on dogma was the result of the Greek influence on the early church. He taught that it was necessary for early forms of Christianity to pass away in order that Christianity itself remain intact. For Harnack, the central core was Jesus' teachings, not about himself but about the kingdom of God, the fatherhood of God, and the infinite value of the human soul.

One of Harnack's students was Karl Barth (1886–1968). At the close of the nineteenth century, liberal theology was in its heyday. Karl Barth rebelled against his teachers, and in his 1919 commentary on the book of Romans, he received a wide hearing for a new orthodoxy. Barth's chief contribution lay in his desire to bring theology back to the Bible and the principles of the Reformation. Barth again emphasized the ▶transcendence of God and the reality of sin. He repudiated Schleiermacher's emphasis on feeling and experience, insisting that God revealed himself through the person of Christ. Barthian neo-orthodoxy received its widest acclaim from the 1930s through the 1950s in many American seminaries. Conservatives, however, tended to see Barthianism as still too compatible with Ritschl's liberalism.[15]

The Roman Catholic Church also reacted to the liberalizing tendencies of the nineteenth century. In 1869–1870, the First Vatican Council convened, in which the infallibility of the pope was upheld. In an age when the authority of the Bible was being steadily undermined, it was only logical that the authority of the church and the pope be reevaluated and reaffirmed. In England, the Oxford Movement began in 1833, a movement that sought to escape the liberal-rationalistic tendencies of the day through a "romantic" repristination to an earlier (seventeenth century) pre-Enlightenment era, when the Church of England possessed an authority it no longer enjoyed. Several of the leaders of the movement returned to the Roman Catholic Church, including J. H. Newman (1801–1890).

Paralleling the Oxford Movement (a largely intellectual endeavor) grew the various Nonconformist traditions that would be embraced enthusiastically by many of the laity of the Church of England. The first of these movements began when a Presbyterian minister, Edward Irving (1792–1834), founded the Catholic Apostolic Church. Irving taught that the gifts possessed by the apostles could be had in the present age. These included speaking in tongues, healings, prophesying, and all of the other gifts of the Holy Spirit.

Another Nonconformist group, known as the Plymouth Brethren, reacted against the Anglican church. John Nelson Darby (1800–1882), an Anglican priest in Plymouth, England, joined the movement in 1828. He taught that because all believers are priests, it is not necessary for the church to have ordained clergy. The "Darbyites" (as they were also called) repudiated all forms of "outward religion," including subscription to creeds and denominationalism. The unity of all believers was stressed along with the breaking of bread and prayer. Darby also popularized the theological tradition now known as ▸dispensationalism. Both the Irvingites and the Brethren greatly influenced the Holiness and Pentecostal traditions of the twentieth century (below).

While the Nonconformist tradition during the nineteenth century was raging in England and was soon to play a large role in twentieth-century America, German idealism and the higher critical method also had its profound effects in America—particularly in New England, which became the birthplace of transcendentalism and UNITARIAN-UNIVERSALISM. Harvard had long since traded its Puritan/Calvinist roots for the new Romanticism. Ministerial candidates educated at Harvard were more in tune with philosophy than theology, and New England became the seedbed for what would become mainline Protestant liberalism, which reached its zenith in the twentieth century.

A conservative voice that answered Darwinism arose at Princeton in the nineteenth century. While Romanticism was at its height at Harvard and in New England, Princeton became the citadel for the old orthodoxy. Charles Hodge (1797–1878) became a noted and able apologist against liberalism; B. B. Warfield (1851–1921) defended the verbal inerrancy of the Bible.[16]

The twentieth century opened with many theological crosscurrents in the churches and in the universities. As a direct result of the Enlightenment, the academy and the church were displaced from one another. Pastors filled pulpits while academic professors filled the podiums of various university divinity schools and seminaries. This was a wholly different phenomenon than in the previous eras of church history, when the church leaders (priests, monks, pastors) were also the church's theologians. This phenomenon led to the possibility of distinguishing between church dogma and an academic theology that found it necessary to adjust theology to the philosophies and "pop" cultures of the day.

The lines were drawn between mainline liberalism and conservative orthodoxy at the outset of the twentieth century with the advent of ▸fundamentalism.[17] The term *fundamentalism* was originally used to articulate five basic points of doctrine that one had to believe if one were to be a Christian. Soon, however, the term became a shibboleth for conservative churches and denominations that rejected liberalism and took the Bible literally. Because the term *fundamentalism* became such a pejorative label, a new term still in use today by conservatives is the word *evangelical*.

Paralleling the rise of fundamentalism was the birth and spread of the Holiness Movement. John Wesley (1701–93), the father of Methodism, had laid the foundation for Holiness theology in the eighteenth century when he taught that ▸sanctification (holiness) is a necessary experience in the life of the believer subsequent to ▸justification. For Wesley, the evidence of such holiness is the perfected or holy life that he believed could be attained by a Christian before death. During the twentieth century, the Holiness Movement was heavily influenced by Methodism, by fundamentalism, and by ▸premillenialism and dispensationalism. Many Holiness or Pentecostal denominations have sprung up in the twentieth century, the largest of which is the Assemblies of God.

Pentecostalism, like Methodism, taught the necessity of the new birth followed by the holy life. For Pentecostals, the believer may become empowered to live a holy life through "baptism in the Holy Spirit with the evidence of speaking in tongues" (*see* ▸glossolalia).[18] In the 1950s, a newer ▸charismatic movement was born. Like fundamentalism, the movement was interdenominational. Charismatics believe in glossolalia but emphasize the rich variety of spiritual gifts that the believer should possess and use.

German higher criticism continued to impact American Christianity. Rudolf Bultmann (1884–1976) argued that because the Bible was written in a prescientific era, it therefore needed to undergo reinterpretation to be heard in today's scientific world. The miracles of Jesus were really myths. Bultmann introduced a program to radically "demythologize" the Bible, interpreting such doctrines as the incarnation and resurrection existentially. For Bultmann, the significance of Jesus' resurrection was not in its historical authenticity but in its value to resurrect the conscience to authentic existence. Paul Tillich (1886–1965), like Bultmann, tried to bridge the gap between faith and modernity. He proposed a method of correlation whereby the content of revelation is determined by questions that are raised by a given culture.[19]

Mainline denominations produced pastors who were heavily influenced by Barth, Bultmann, Tillich, and various other theologians espousing social and political agendas as their mainstay. After the 1960s, which triggered the cult explosion, mainline churches experienced a mass exodus.[20] Many members became involved with the various cults and sects described in this volume. Others, tired of sermons focusing on social issues, joined the various fundamentalist, Holiness, and Pentecostal denominations; these are the main elements of evangelicalism, which continues to grow, and they have had a powerful influence on religious life in America. Evangelicals first attempted to cooperate with the formation of the Evangelical Alliance in 1846. Its influence was effective until the turn of the century. In 1942 the National Association of Evangelicals (NAE) and the American Council of Christian Churches were organized, both uniting evangelicals and attempting to oppose liberalism. The NAE continues to operate on local and statewide levels.

The most influential evangelical of the twentieth century has been the Rev. Billy Graham, who has preached to over 220,000,000 people all over the world. The Billy Graham crusades have been a mainstay in evangelical circles, but Graham himself has transcended them, appearing before world leaders and befriending American presidents. His "ecumenical evangelicalism" has proven to be a large factor in the success of his organization.

From the 1950s through the present, evangelicalism has successfully made its presence known through numerous other parachurch ministries as well. One of the most influential campus ministries has been Campus Crusade for Christ, founded by Bill Bright and his wife, Vonette, in 1951 at the UCLA. The Brights were assisted by Billy Graham. Intervarsity Christian Fellowship is likewise a popular presence on campuses in the United States and throughout the world.

Alliances continued to spring up in many denominations. The Lutheran World Federation (formed in 1947), the United Church of Christ (1957), the Methodist Church in the United States (1939), and the World Alliance of Reformed Churches are several examples.

Mainline denominations also sought alliance. The World Council of Churches was formed in 1948 and grew out of three earlier alliances: The International Missionary Council, The World Conference on Life and Work, and The World Conference on Faith and Order. In 1948 the World Council met in Amsterdam, and it continues to meet every six years. Members include most Protestant denominations and Eastern Orthodox churches. The Roman Catholic Church is not a member of the council and, before Vatican II (1962–1965), shied away from ecumenical dialogue.

At Vatican II, not only were Protestants no longer regarded as heretics, but the harshness of the word "heretic" was toned down to "separated brethren." Protestant leaders were invited to the Council, and ecumenical dialogue between Protestants and Catholics has been frequent in the last three decades.[21] Conservative and fundamentalist churches continue to decline in membership in the WCC for fear of compromising the Bible for the sake of unity. Ecumenical dialogue, however, has been a strong feature of church bodies and theologians in recent years. Near the end of the twentieth century, documents declaring unity and agreement have circulated among some Lutherans, Episcopalians, Roman Catholics, and other Reformed and Protestant traditions. This activity will no doubt continue into the new century.

Another development in the Protestant world in the last fifty years has been the growth of the evangelical "megachurch." In the postmodern world, a fear has arisen that the traditional "church" is unable to communicate the gospel to a culture that has become more and more secularized. Concern for growth has led to a downplaying of traditional worship and in its place more contemporary approaches. Praise bands together with drums, guitars, worship leaders, and so on are more popular now than traditional liturgy, organs, and the like. Buildings that look more like business enterprises and less like churches have been springing up everywhere. The harshest critics of the megachurch movement argue that this approach is entertainment-oriented and caters to the whims of a culture that is wholly given over to individualism, not to the call to discipleship and service that comprise an integral part of the gospel of Jesus Christ.

A popular evangelical movement that is of more recent origin is Promise Keepers. On March 20, 1990, the organization was founded. The first conference was held in-state at Boulder in July 1991. Over 4,000 men attended the event. The growth and popularity of this movement knew no bounds after that. 50,000 men attended a conference also in Boulder, Colorado, two years later. By 1994, the growing movement had filled seven stadiums around the country with numbers of 250,000 plus in attendance. During the mid 1990s, the numbers grew to over two million men gathering en masse to reaffirm commitments to God, Christ, family, and self. On October 4, 1997, over 700,000 men attended the nationwide "Standing in the Gap" rally in Washington, D.C. Promise Keeper rallies continue to be held on a regular basis throughout the United States and its effects are being felt internationally as well.

Another movement that has attracted much attention in the late twentieth century and on into the twenty-first century is the Vineyard movement. This ministry grew out of a fundamentalist group called Calvary Chapel, a group founded in the 1960s in California by Rev. Chuck Smith. Smith's ministry was a success amongst the hippies, and huge numbers were converted and baptized. However, several of the members of

Smith's church wanted to see more of a Pentecostal manifestation. Ken Gulliksen, a member of Calvary Chapel, became an associate pastor with Smith in 1974. He and his wife, Joanie, began pastoring a congregation in Los Angeles at that time. The Gulliksens were especially influenced by Pentecostalism and started to emphasize healing, the spiritual gifts, and the speaking in tongues (see ‣glossolalia).

This new emphasis was more than Smith and the leaders of Calvary Chapel were prepared to support. Consequently Gulliksen decided to call their congregation the Vineyard to distinguish them from Calvary Chapel. Another Calvary Chapel pastor named John Wimber became the most popular leader in the movement. During the 1980s a number of additional Calvary Chapel churches linked up with this new umbrella movement. Other evangelical and Pentecostal groups also joined. The diversity of the groups joining resulted in numerous names for the Vineyard. Another name is Power Evangelism, because of the reliance on the powers of the Holy Spirit to effect salvation. Another designation is the Signs and Wonders Movement, because many of the meetings featured the workings of miracles. The Third Wave is another title for the group as well. The idea here is that the move of the Holy Spirit that the Vineyard churches were experiencing was in its third large detectable manifestation. The name Vineyard itself was accepted as that of a denomination in 1988.

Controversy arose in the 1990s when the Vineyard church in Toronto, Canada, started manifesting what has become known as holy laughter. A South African evangelist by the name of Rodney Howard Brown had been teaching that the Holy Spirit is manifested in worship by the outbreak, not just of speaking in tongues, but in uncontrolled fits of laughter. The Toronto church went beyond even the laughter to animal noises. Wimber had his limits and decided that this new manifestation was not of God. In 1994, through much difficult deliberation, the Toronto Airport church was dismissed from association with the Vineyard Movement. As Wimber and Gulliksen had regarded Calvary Chapel as not being as open to the Holy Spirit, the Toronto Blessing, as it came to be called, moved on as a separate movement. The Vineyard Ministries has continued to spread to many countries in the last two decades.

One of the significant challenges to Christianity at the beginning of the twenty-first century is the paradigm shift of the general world culture away from Christianity. In essence, the gospel is increasingly finding its place in a context not altogether unlike that when it was put forth in the first several centuries—that is, to a world that is unfamiliar with its essential message. Its symbols, culture, music, and defining paradigm have largely been replaced by a new world order that increasingly seeks to define itself in terms of secular globalization, consumerism, individualism, multiculturalism, postmodernism, and generally speaking a culture of disbelief.

The terrorist actions of September 11, 2001, which saw the collapse of the World Trade Center in New York City, has been a defining moment in Christian history as well as secular. It has forced many thinking Christians to reflect on the Gospel in an era where the evils of human nature evidence themselves on a grand scale. It has also seen the huge response of many organizations and church bodies come forward to offer help where it is most needed.[22]

Nearly two thousand years of church history have elapsed. Kingdoms, empires, and governments have risen and fallen, yet the church continues in the postmodern era. The challenge of the Christian church today lies in the presentation of its gospel to a world that has, at the beginning of the twenty-first century, become secular and pluralistic. Yet, despite persecution, moral laxity, heresies challenging it both within and without, the church of Jesus Christ prevails, fulfilling Jesus' words that "the gates of Hades [hell] will not overcome it" (Matt. 16:18). It has experienced dark moments, but even as the darkness of the first Good Friday gave way to the brightness and splendor of the resurrection and the empty tomb, so too has the church experienced a glorious history with a future that will be brighter still when Jesus and the church—that is, when the bridegroom and the bride—unite forever.

ADDITIONAL INFORMATION_____

Notes

[1] See J. N. D. Kelly, *Early Christian Creeds* (London: Longman, 1960).

[2] A good summary of this era is Henry Chadwick, *The Early Church* (New York: Penguin, 1967).

[3] An outstanding, scholarly, yet brief account of the life of Constantine is *The Conversion of Constantine*, ed. John Eadie (Huntington, N.Y.: Robert E. Krieger, 1977).

[4] Chadwick, *The Early Church*, 133.

[5] Constantine himself was not an Arian, but because of Eusebius, who was an Arian and who accused Athanasius of calling a dock strike that halted the grain supply from Alexandria, Constantine was provoked to anger (ibid., 135).

[6] See Appendix 2.

[7] See Peter Brown, *Augustine of Hippo*, rev. ed. (Berkeley and Los Angeles: Univ. of California Press, 2000).

[8] A most excellent survey of the history of the papacy is Geoffrey Barraclough, *The Medieval Papacy* (New York: Norton, 1968).

[9] Robin Lane Fox, *Pagans and Christians* (New York: Alfred A. Knopf, 1987).

[10] See Margaret Deansley, *A History of the Medieval Church* (London: Methuen, 1925; repr. 1978).

[11] A classic history of missions is Kenneth Scott Latourette, *A History of the Expansion of Christianity*, 7 vols. (New York: Harper, 1937–1945).

[12] An outstanding survey of the Middle Ages in Norman F. Cantor, *Medieval History: The Life and Death of a Civilization*, 2nd ed. (London and New York: Macmillan, 1969). For excellent studies on the late Middle Ages, see Heiko Oberman, *The Harvest of Late Medieval Theology* (Durham, N.C.: Labyrinth, 1983), and *Forerunners of the Reformation: The Shape of Late Medieval Thought* (Philadelphia: Fortress, 1966).

[13] The books on Luther's life and theology are voluminous. Two excellent surveys of Luther's life are Roland Bainton, *Here I Stand: A Life of Martin Luther* (Nashville: Abingdon, 1950), and James Kittelson, *Luther the Reformer: The Story of the Man and His Career* (Minneapolis: Augsburg, 1986). An excellent treatment of Luther's theology is Paul Althaus, *The Theology of Martin Luther*, trans. Robert C. Schultz (Philadelphia: Fortress, 1966).

[14] See Steven Ozment, *The Age of Reform 1250–1550* (New Haven and London: Yale Univ. Press, 1980).

[15] See Cornelius Van Til, *Christianity and Barthianism* (Nutley, N.J.: Presbyterian and Reformed, 1977).

[16] Theodore P. Letis provides groundbreaking work on Warfield's introduction of the word "inerrancy" and what Warfield meant by the term. See his "B. B. Warfield: Common Sense Philosophy and Biblical Criticism," *American Presbyterians* 69 (Fall 1991).

[17] See J. I. Packer, *Fundamentalism and the Word of God* (Grand Rapids: Eerdmans, 1977). For a more critical survey, see James Barr, *Fundamentalism* (Philadelphia: Westminster, 1977).

[18] There are many fine surveys of the Pentecostal/charismatic movement. The most complete one-volume work is *The New International Dictionary of Pentecostal and Charismatic Movements*, ed. Stanley M. Burgess and Eduard M. van der Maas, rev. ed. (Grand Rapids: Zondervan, 2002).

[19] See James C. Livingstone, *Modern Christian Thought: From the Enlightenment to Vatican II* (New York: Macmillan, 1971).

[20] See Richard N. Ostling, "Those Mainline Blues," *Time* (May 22, 1989), 94–96.

[21] John Richard Neuhaus, *The Catholic Moment* (San Francisco: Harper & Row, 1987).

[22] See Alvin Schmidt, *How Christianity Changed the World* (Grand Rapids: Zondervan, 2001).

THE CHURCH OF BIBLE UNDERSTANDING; FOREVER FAMILY (COBU)

Stewart ʾTraill, founder of the Forever Family, or as it was renamed, The Church of Bible Understanding, writes:

> It is the older generation that is 100 percent responsible, humanly speaking, for the weirdness of their kids.... They don't realize that they are sick, and that you're (the younger generation) only half sick. Probably your parents are into money; getting ahead in the world; evil; pride; prejudice; looking down on people; materialism; caring for what the neighbors think; TV; etc.... They hate us because they're afraid you won't be like them—sick beyond measure.[1]

HISTORY

Traill was born in 1936 in Quebec, Canada. In his formative years he claimed to have been an atheist. In 1959 he married Shirley A. Rudy, and together they had five children. He worked as a used vacuum-cleaner salesman, purchasing old vacuum cleaners, reconditioning and then selling them.

In the years after the birth of his children, Traill began exploring different religions, his motive being to present religious training to his children in an informed and intelligent manner. In an open-minded way, he explored a wide range of world religions, including HINDUISM, ISLAM, and CHRISTIANITY. He concluded that Christianity was the least corrupt of all and affiliated himself with a Pentecostal church in the Allentown, Pennsylvania, area. Almost immediately, however, Traill reached the conclusion that most Christians had failed to interpret the ʾBible correctly. He began to question his church leaders and became a source of internal strife. Soon they asked him to leave, but not before he had gathered together a loyal group of followers, chiefly from among the young people whom he had influenced as a youth leader.

In Allentown, in 1971, Traill formed what he called the Forever Family. Throughout most of the 1970s, the group experienced rapid growth. By 1978 they boasted a total membership of two thousand. Some sources allege that worldwide membership totaled close to four thousand at its highest point. The numbers of members have varied (see below).

Financing of the church came in the form of various business enterprises, including Christian Brothers Cleaning Service, Inc., which proved to be extremely successful in the New York City area, mostly because of the free labor contributed by hundreds of Forever Family members.

In 1976 Traill and his wife divorced. Six weeks later, Stewart married his secretary, Gayle Gillespie. A prolonged custody battle for the children ensued and may have been one of the factors contributing to changing the group's name from Forever Family to the present-day name, Church of Bible Understanding (COBU).

Implicit in the new name is the suggestion that Traill alone understood the true message of the Bible. Traill insisted that God had hidden the true meaning of the Bible in secret codes to which only he could supply decoded interpretations in the form of an elaborate "figure system" and a ten-color coding scheme, whereby the Bible was marked by color groupings arranged by themes.

Young people, especially those under thirty years of age, were the most successful targets for Traill's evangelistic efforts. As noted in the quote at the beginning of this essay, he considered the "older generation" largely responsible for the problems of today. Such a message was timely in the 1960s, an age characterized by unrest and dissatisfaction with authority and institutional paradigms.

The method of evangelism Traill advocated was confrontational in style. Young people were attracted in large numbers because appeal was made to their integrity against the hypocrisy of their parents and those who were part of the "establishment." Group members wore large red buttons that stated, "Get Smart, Get Saved." An accompanying pamphlet titled *Get Smart— Get Saved* states:

> But a lot of people are jealous of Him (Jesus) and won't listen to Him for real and they make up their own way of life. We should love truth and stick up for Jesus because He is the only one that cares about us. These ordinary people just want your money and for you to join their religion so that they can look good and get off on you. They don't really love you and down deep in your heart, you know it.

Pamphleteering was an effective tool for attracting initial interest in the group. Potential converts were further drawn in because they perceived the COBU to be a caring community that met the basic needs lacking in the materialistic and worldly environments of their parents. Increased pressure was placed on the new converts to abandon their parents and live in one of the communal "family houses" run by the church. Growing pressure was then exerted on converts to conform to the expectations of the group. One former member confessed, "I was brainwashed into submission and paralyzed by fear of damnation."[2]

The church began missionary work in 1978 by sending a group to Haiti, which resulted in two orphanages that continue today. To ward off criticism and feign cooperation with other Christians, they invited well-known missionaries as speakers, such as Richard Wurmbrand, who was once imprisoned and tortured by communists for his Christian faith.

In 1989, Traill claimed to have become "born again" and that all of his teachings previously had been in error. Ex-members believe that this is because he was trying to cover up for sexual indiscretions with certain female members of the group a year earlier. During the 1990s, Traill kept a quiet profile. He shunned the media and photographers. Many people left the group, but in spite of his tarnished image, COBU congregations continued to spring up.

Today, although the membership is not what it used to be, Traill continues to teach and maintain a lavish lifestyle. He spends a good deal of time in Fort Lauderdale, where one of the newer fellowships sprang up in the late 1990s. According to Sabrina Erdaly, writer for *Philadelphia Magazine*, Traill owns four airplanes, spends much time working with the cult's younger women, and still maintains an ever-present control over the leadership of the group.[3]

ORGANIZATION

The church is organized into hierarchical groups. The *guardians* are the leaders, and they play an active role in the supervision and governing of those in the lower categories. The *sheep* are considered to be the "advanced believers," and *lambs* are new converts. Five members gather in organizational units known as *communal houses*.

TEACHINGS

Because the COBU does not believe in publishing doctrinal statements, it is difficult to assess the group's theology. A brief summary of what can be ascertained from both primary and secondary literature, along with some comparisons of and contrasts to traditional Christianity, follows.

God

Traill's early booklet, *Understanding the Colored Bible* (1975), referred to the Apostles' Creed as "valid." This creed affirms the historic doctrine of the ▸Trinity. Traill's book *The Gospel of John in Colors* (1976) states that "purple . . . is the color of royalty and it describes the nature of God in his three persons—Father, Son, and Holy Spirit." However, by 1979, during a taped interview with *Cornerstone Magazine* ("Jesus People U.S.A., Chicago"), Traill denied the Trinity. Older members claim that this interview is not binding and that they still hold to the Trinity doctrine.

Nevertheless, COBU is anti-Trinitarian. Traill contended that while the Christian concepts of Father, Son, and Spirit are biblical, the doctrine of the Trinity is not. Traill, like many other religious leaders outside traditional Christian ▸orthodoxy, rejects the Trinity as being unbiblical because neither the *word* Trinity nor the *concept* is found in the Bible. Orthodoxy, on the other hand, acknowledges that while the *term* is lacking, the *concept* is not. The Athanasian Creed (*see* Appendix 1) explains in detail the church's understanding of the three persons being one God.[4]

Jesus Christ

Christ is viewed as the "Savior." The language used by COBU members in witnessing bears a remarkable resemblance to the language and phraseology in vogue in conservative evangelical circles in the 1970s and 1980s ("born-again," "get saved," etc.). A common pin worn by members says, "Get Smart—Get Saved." But it is difficult to ascertain COBU's ▸Christology. What is certain is that, because the doctrine of the Trinity was rejected, the deity of Christ necessarily is rejected as well. Jesus is "Savior," but he is not God, the Savior.

Humanity

For the COBU, human beings are lost sinners in need of salvation. This teaching is similar to Christianity's position on the subject. In actuality, however, Traill portrays salvation not as reconciliation between God and humans through faith in the redemptive work of Christ, nor as the "forgiveness of sins," but more as freedom from a this-worldliness of an older and corrupt generation. Age thirty and under is considered to be the time when salvation is most attainable. After this age, people tend to become a part of, rather than apart from, the institutions of society.

Sin

Sin is the equivalent of "worldliness" and "hypocrisy" for the COBU. The older one gets, the more encumbered by worldliness one becomes. Young people are less burdened by the cares of this life and are therefore more productive and responsive in proselytizing efforts.

For true Christianity sin and worldliness affect all, young and old. Nowhere in the Bible or in the creeds is there an attempt to categorize the spiritual potential of people according to age. All are instructed to repent of sin, because "all have sinned" (Rom. 6:23). If anything, young people might be considered more susceptible to the problems and encumbrances of the flesh. Paul instructs the young pastor Timothy to "flee the evil desires of youth" (2 Tim. 2:22), implying, of course, that young people are quite capable of sinful affections.

Salvation

The essential message of salvation is to repent and receive the forgiveness of sins through Jesus. This is similar to the Christian doctrine of ▸soteriology insofar as it is stated. For Christendom, however, the presupposition for the confession "I believe in the . . . forgiveness of sins" (Apostles' Creed, Article 3), is the second article of the creed in its confession of the person and work of Jesus Christ. Because the COBU does not embrace the doctrine of the Trinity, that article cannot be included in the movement's concept of salvation. For the COBU, Jesus is *a* savior, but not God, *the* Savior.

Church

The true church is comprised of members of the COBU, with Stewart Traill as the leader. Like a host of other religious leaders, Traill concluded that the mainline Christian churches are all corrupted beyond hope. The COBU has been raised up by God to restore the purity of faith as it was depicted in the New Testament.

The Apostles' Creed states, "I believe in . . . the holy catholic church, the communion of saints. . . ." The "communion of saints" constitutes the essence of the church in Christendom. It is the one universal church that spans every age and takes in all believers in Jesus Christ.

End Times

The COBU will play a key role in ushering in the second coming of Christ. Traill hinted on a number of occasions that he knew the date that this momentous event will transpire. As with other *dispensationalist groups, Traill became obsessed with excitement of end-time "signs" or Christ's return.

Many religious groups have suggested that they alone will play vital roles in the events transpiring at the end of the world. Many have also set dates and predicted the time when Jesus will return. The traditional Christian view of last things is that Jesus is returning "to judge both the living and the dead" (Nicene Creed), though no one knows the day or the hour.

Some of the teachings of Traill have tended to change throughout the group's short history. This includes the doctrine concerning the end times. There has been a shift in focus away from the end of the world and the millennium toward more of a preoccupation with death. According to Erdely, "The group's newest mantras are 'Death in Christ is far more interesting than anything this life can offer' and 'You're gonna die anyway, why not die constructively.' "[5]

CONCLUSION

The 1980s saw a rapid decline in membership. The *Jonestown tragedy of 1978 in Guyana proved to be a watershed in the history of *cult awareness in general and resulted in a decline in the membership of many religious groups, particularly the personality cults. Other reasons given for the decline are Traill's marital problems, criticism of his lavish lifestyle, questions raised about finances, and the resignation of former insiders. Public awareness and a much more critical attitude in general have made it unlikely that the COBU will ever grow or expand again as it did during the 1970s.

ADDITIONAL INFORMATION_____

Headquarters

There are several addresses that can be contacted. The Church of Bible Understanding, P.O. Box 841, New York, New York, 10019; also–1300 South 58th Street, Philadelphia, PA, 19143; also–(Haiti)–L'Eglise de la Comprehesion de la Bible, P.O. B. 15518, Petionville, Haiti, WI.

Websites

A website is filled with helpful information by ex-members on the goings on of Traill and the Forever Family. It is *www.angelfire.com/nm/cobu.sum.htm*. Its organization's website is *www.cbuhaiti.org*.

Sacred Text

The Bible (as it is interpreted through Stewart Traill's "ten color" method, outlined in *Understanding the Colored Bible*, 1975).

Membership

The claims vary. One source lists as many as ten thousand members in the COBU's heyday. This is unlikely. Other figures range from two to four thousand members and currently, the membership is more than likely to be no more than a few hundred.

Notes

[1] Stewart Traill, as quoted by William Alnor and David Clark, "Other Gospels, New Religions: Church of Bible Understanding," *SCP Newsletter* (May/June 1980), 6.

[2] Joan Galler, "Inside a New York Cult: Ex-Followers Tell Why They Quit," *New York Daily News* (January 2, 1979), C9.

[3] See Sabrina Rubin Erdely, "I'll Be Damned," *Philadelphia Magazine*, June 1999; see *www.phillymag.com*.

[4] See a further analysis of Christianity and the Trinity in the articles on the JEHOVAH'S WITNESSES and CHRISTADELPHIANISM.

[5] Erdely, "I'll Be Damned."

THE CHURCH OF THE LIVING WORD; THE WALK (CTLW)

The Church of the Living Word grew out of the milieu of Pentecostalism in the latter half of the twentieth century. Its doctrines, however, shaped by its founder, took on NEW AGE themes to the extent that the movement was forced to leave the mainline Pentecostal traditions shaped early on in the twentieth century.

HISTORY

The Church of the Living Word was founded in 1954 by John Robert *Stevens (b. 1919). Stevens was raised in Washington, Iowa, in a Pentecostal home. He attended Life Bible College, a Foursquare Bible school in Los Angeles, during 1939–1940 but never graduated. He had previously been ordained by Full Gospel Temple in Moline, Illinois, however, and the Foursquare Movement recognized his ordination as legitimate. However, in 1949 his ordination was revoked because of his "aberrant" doctrines. The Assemblies of God, another Pentecostal denomination, had continued to recognize his ordination even though it had been revoked previously, but in April 1951 this church body also asked him to depart.

Stevens wasted no time in starting a church of his own in South Gate, California. This served as the base from which "The Walk" (a name Stevens chose) emerged. In 1954 Stevens experienced a vision that he compared to Paul's Damascus Road conversion (Acts 9).[1] This signaled the beginning. Congregations spread rapidly. California alone has twenty-six. Over seventy congregations were established throughout the United States and abroad.[2]

This expansion was due to the wide distribution of Stevens's seven thousand sermons in print and tape where believers were promised power as they "push Stevens higher." Observers became concerned over mind control when it was revealed that Stevens was a master hypnotist. The group was largely criticized for unfair business competition by church-owned businesses, using volunteer labor in product manufacturing. Their church was reported as saturated with loud, boisterous shouting and ecstatic utterances, often in tongues, while participants hit one another on the top of the head to open a hole for the Holy Spirit to enter.

Stevens died in 1983 of severe respiratory complications. His followers allegedly announced his future resurrection. Some members reportedly placed Stevens's body in a room and underwent a lengthy vigil awaiting their leader's resurrection before interment. Following his death, Stevens's wife, Marilyn, whom he had appointed to be his successor, began leading the movement. Gary Hargrave, the leader of the California churches, married Marilyn, and together they began leading under the title of "Apostolic Fathering Ministries."

Stevens referred to Washington, Iowa, as "the spiritual center of the world, the beginning of God's creation."[3] A statement of faith called "This We Believe and Know" (posted on the group's website) lists thirty-one doctrinal points. Some of these show a move toward a more traditional view of classical Christian doctrines than was held to by Stevens. These can hardly be reconciled with the teachings of Stevens himself as delineated below. The group continues to believe in open and continued revelation, ▸restorationism, the full use of the gifts listed in the New Testament, and ▸dispensationalism.

ORGANIZATION

The theology of restorationism has shaped the understanding that the CTLW has advanced in its organizational structure. Members believe that Stevens possessed apostolic authority. Churches are affiliated only in spiritual relationship to each other. Therefore, there is a large degree of autonomy between each congregation. Leaders in each group regard themselves as having command of the fivefold teaching office described in Ephesians 4:11.

TEACHINGS

Basic to Stevens's theology is a concept called ▸transference—a person lays aside all personal identity and allows himself or herself to become "a part of Christ."[4] There is a strong anti-intellectualism inherent in the movement. Members are encouraged to disparage reason so as to allow the Spirit free rein. Revelations and visions are encouraged and members actively seek them. It must be noted, however, that all revelations must be in conformity with Stevens's interpretation, for he is the one possessing the highest "apostolic" authority.

The basic doctrines of this group in comparison to CHRISTIANITY are as follows.

God

There is a ▸Trinity in the Godhead, but there is no infinite and qualitative distinction between God and creation as orthodox Christianity holds to. The church, as well as each individual, is to become a god. "God becoming man means nothing unless we become God, unless we become lost in Him."[5]

Jesus Christ

Christ possesses no unique role as the Son of God. Christ is not one man, one Person; rather, Christ is a many-membered body.[6] The church itself, composed of individual believers, becomes Christ. Each member shares in the very being of Christ.

Holy Spirit

The Holy Spirit functions in such a way as to enable believers to become God in the sense that each participates in the divine nature. The Spirit also bestows immediate supernatural gifts on believers.

The Holy Spirit's work in the Christian church is one of sanctification. The Holy Spirit is the third member of the Trinity and is therefore "worshiped and glorified" (Nicene Creed). The Holy Spirit does not enable Christians to become God, but rather, to become *more like* God.

Humanity

As already stated, the CTLW teaches that human beings can become God. Therefore, the highest calling that an individual has is to deny any sense of personal identity. Personality is an encumbrance to the Deity. When fully deified, human beings can then reach perfection in this life. God, after all, cannot sin.

The notion of "deified humanity" departs from traditional Christianity. The church has never considered the possibility of any person perfecting himself or herself. Even though some of the language used in Christendom might sound vaguely familiar to this notion— for example, Eastern Orthodoxy's doctrine of ᵖdeification, or John Wesley's doctrine of ᵖperfectionism—sinless perfectionism is never embraced outside the context of the uniqueness of the person and work of Jesus Christ in either of these traditions.

Sin

Given Stevens's view of humanity, his doctrine of sin logically follows. Sin is separation from God. A human being does not know God and is separate from God. This separation results in the human being becoming victim to his or her own individuality and a slave to self.

Salvation

While Christianity teaches that salvation comes through the person and work of Jesus Christ (see John 3:16; also the second article of the Apostles' Creed), Stevens taught that salvation, in addition to Christ, comes through membership in the CTLW. Salvation is accomplished when the transference from individuality to deity takes place.

Positions within the church are also of paramount importance in the CTLW's theology. The mediatory role of the priesthood is taught in such a way that the priest may touch the throne of God in order to bestow the sinless perfection of Christ onto the sinful.

Church

Because the CTLW is the "true church," all other churches are "false," "apostate," and "thoroughly corrupt." The Holy Spirit operates exclusively within the parameters of Stevens's ministry.

"I believe in one holy catholic and apostolic church"—so reads the Nicene Creed. The church is the "communion of saints." Stevens's dogmatism and exclusivity is characteristic of many of the ᵖcults and ᵖsects that fall outside the parameters of Christian orthodoxy.

The Bible

The ᵖBible as it stands is an authoritative document, but only for times past. Because it is outdated, the church needs new and supplementary revelation. Such new revelation is always channeled through and guided by Stevens's authority as apostle in the church. This belief is still maintained by the group.

By relegating the Bible's authority to the past, Stevens is, in essence, denying its authority altogether. This leads to the need for a supplemental authority. This authority is not located in the church or in the Bible, but within the person of Stevens himself as God's apostle. Christianity teaches that the true Christian faith as articulated in the Bible and summarized by the great creeds of the church needs no further supplementation by modern-day apostles.

End Times

The CTLW is the equivalent of the second coming of Jesus Christ. The organization becomes partaker of the divine nature. Therefore, to become deified is a coming of Jesus, namely, the Second Coming spoken of in the New Testament.

The Apostles' Creed confesses that Christ shall "come to judge the living and the dead." To Stevens and the CTLW there is no separation between Christ, the believer, and the church. Christ, of course, has already returned visibly through the visible appearance of the CTLW.

According to the orthodox heritage, the church, or "communion of saints," is Christ's bride, to be distinguished from Christ himself. The second advent of Christ is yet to come. It is the blessed hope for which the church still longs.

CONCLUSION

Stevens wrote numerous pamphlets and books. While the headquarters for the movement remains in Washington, Iowa, the greatest concentration of followers and congregations is in California.

ADDITIONAL INFORMATION_____

Headquarters
The Living Word Fellowship; Pastoral and Administrative Offices, PO Box 3429, Iowa City, IA, 52244; Living Word Publications, PO Box 958, North Hollywood, CA, 91603.

Website
www.thelivingword.org

Sacred Text
The Bible

Publications
Shiloh Newsletter; many tapes and books authored by John Robert Stevens.

Membership

There are congregations listed in seventeen cities in nine states, and also ministries in Canada, Mexico, Japan, and Brazil.

Notes

[1] Walter Martin, *The New Cults* (Ventura, Calif.: Regal, 1980), 269.

[2] Ibid., 270.

[3] John Robert Stevens, *Apostolic Directives* (North Hollywood, Calif.: Living Word, 1976).

[4] John Robert Stevens, *The Manchild* (n.d.), 7.

[5] John Robert Stevens, *Plumb Perfect* (North Hollywood, Calif.: Living Word, 1977), 13.

[6] Stevens, *The Manchild*, 6.

CHURCH OF THE NEW JERUSALEM; SWEDENBORGIANISM (CNJ)

Like so many religious movements, the Church of the New Jerusalem received its initial impulses from the inspirations of a single individual. Unlike many, however, it received its impetus from an extremely gifted and brilliant intellectual, Emmanuel Swedenborg (1688–1772).

HISTORY

Swedenborg was born as Emmanuel Swedberg in Stockholm, Sweden, in 1688, the son of a Lutheran pastor (Jasper Swedberg) and court chaplain. Young Emmanuel proved to be a precocious child, early proving his abilities in academic endeavor, particularly mathematics and science. Long before he developed an interest in theology, he distinguished himself as a geologist, mathematician, inventor, and engineer. His intellectual activity was expansive, and his contributions to his native country were so great that thirty-six years after his death his remains were removed from London and brought back to Uppsala Cathedral.

Educated at the University of Uppsala, Emmanuel also traveled to England and met with some of the world's leading scientists. He studied engineering and mechanics while traveling through England, Holland, and France. Returning to Sweden in 1715, he began to publish the country's first scientific journal, called *Daedalus Hyperboreus*. Charles XII recognized Swedenborg's genius and appointed him special assessor of the Royal Board of Mines. In 1718, his family was ennobled, and according to custom they were renamed Swedenborg. Among his inventions were a stove, "flying machine," dock design, a submarine, hearing aids, new methods of salt manufacture, and an air machine gun.

On a second trip abroad in 1721 Swedenborg published two Latin volumes in chemistry and philosophy. He was greatly influenced by the French philosopher René Descartes. In 1734 he published his three-volume *Opera Philosophica et Mineralis*, which contains his philosophy of nature, the influence of Descartes being readily evident in this work. During his life he operated in the highest intellectual circles of Europe.

The year 1743 proved to be a watershed in Swedenborg's life. He reports:

> But all that I have thus far related, I consider to be of little importance; for it is far transcended by the circumstance that I have been called to a holy office by the Lord himself, who most mercifully appeared before me, his servant, in the year 1743 when he opened my sight into the spiritual world, and enabled me to converse with spirits and angels; in which state I have continued up to the present day. From that time I began to print and publish the various arcana that were seen by me, or revealed to me, concerning heaven and hell, the state of man after death, the true worship of God, the spiritual sense of the Word, and many other important matters conducive to salvation and wisdom.[1]

For the remaining three decades of his life, Swedenborg wrote a tremendous volume of religious literature. He learned Hebrew and studied theology with as much energy and proficiency as he had the various sciences.

His works include titles such as *The Angelic Wisdom Respecting the Divine Love and Wisdom*, 1763; *The Angelic Wisdom Respecting the Divine Providence*, 1764; *Arcana Coelestia*, twelve volumes, 1749–56; and *Apocalypse Explained*, six volumes, 1785–89 (published posthumously). His religious ideas gained acceptance though celebrated personalities like Helen Keller, who wrote affectionately of Swedenborg in her 1927 book *My Religion*.

TEACHINGS

Swedenborg's entire theological project became a quest to interpret history in light of corresponding spiritual truths. The mundane and earthly elements of the ⸰Bible, for example, are to be understood as being prefixes to spiritual reality. He combined intuition with rare scientific genius. Swedenborg's theological ideas are summarized below.

God

The source of all creation and the power of all life in the universe is God. God, for Swedenborg, was one person, the Father. The Father became the Son. The Holy Spirit is not God but is the energy that proceeds from God to man. While the terms Father, Son, and Holy Spirit are often used, they have entirely different meanings from ⸰orthodox CHRISTIANITY.

In contrast to the doctrine of the ⸰Trinity, Swedenborg believed that Christianity falsely advocated the belief in three Gods. He blames this on the corrupting influences of the Apostles' and Nicene creeds. He argues that God cannot be God if he proceeds from another aspect of the Godhead. Here he is thinking of the Holy Spirit, confessed to be proceeding "from the Father and the Son" (Nicene Creed, Appendix 1).

The traditional orthodox response to this is that the church confesses with Israel that God is one (Deut. 6:4). Yet in the divine economy, the one essential God has manifested himself in three persons (Matt. 28:18–19; Mark 1:9–11). The Father is the Creator, the Son is the Redeemer, and the Holy Spirit is the Sanctifier. But this is not to say that each person of the Trinity possesses qualities or an essence unlike the other two. All three persons extend and share the Godhead one with another. According to the formulators of the Nicene and Athanasian creeds, the doctrine of the Trinity is a divine mystery that cannot be explained to complete human satisfaction. Swedenborg's concept of the Trinity is Sabellian and modalistic (see ⸰modalistic monarchianism) in nature when he assigns the one essence not as three distinct persons but as three aspects—love, wisdom, and activity—of that one essence. Ancient ⸰Sabellianism taught that God is one, yet exists as three separate and distinct manifestations. The Athanasian Creed represents the church's response to this idea.[2]

To Swedenborg, the divine Trinity has a corresponding finite Trinity with respect to humanity. The Lord Jesus Christ embodies this finite Trinity. God clothed himself in Jesus, as a human organization of divinity in order to save humans. The finite Trinity is composed of soul, body, and power. Orthodox Christianity maintains that Jesus was both human and divine. For that reason, there is an infinite and qualitative difference between Jesus and other human beings, who possess *only* a human

nature. Theologians have long debated whether or not humanity is in possession of a tripartite nature (body, soul, and spirit) or a bipartite nature (body and soul).

Jesus Christ

Jesus was born to Mary and lived a sinless life in full obedience to the Word of God. This enabled him to lay aside all of his human qualities and thereby become the embodiment of the divine soul. Swedenborg's most serious departure from orthodoxy in general, and his Lutheran roots in particular, was precisely in his ⸰Christology. Jesus was the Father, that aspect of the divine Being who came into the world, to establish contact with lost and fallen humankind. It was Jesus' victory over all temptation and sin that in the end caused him to lay aside all of his human qualities and once again assume his true Godhood.

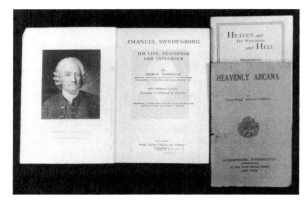

Books by and about Emmanuel Swedenborg.
Courtesy Jack M. Roper/CARIS

Salvation

Salvation is the result of Jesus' victory over the dominion of evil in the world. By not yielding to temptation, Jesus, in his person, broke the powers of the hells, or the communities of evil spirits. Humankind is able to achieve redemption by believing in Christ and trusting in the triumph and imposition he made on the evil powers of the hells. However, it must be coupled with learning heavenly secrets, which only the true mystic or spiritually enlightened can understand—a belief from early gnosticism.

As alluded to above, a central theme in Swedenborg's thought lies in the idea of correspondence. All that is earthly, material, and physical is invested with truth only in the spiritual plane. Therefore, much of his voluminous writings are devoted to private interpretive keys for unlocking the hidden truths of the Bible as revealed to Swedenborg.

It is precisely this alleged communication with the spirit world that has led not just a few to conclude that Swedenborg helped pave the way for a full-blown SPIRITUALISM. This inner communion with the noumenal also constitutes the heart of his departure from the historic Christian faith, embodied in the Lutheran church (to which he declared himself a member throughout his life). If it were not for his great accomplishments and sheer intellectual prowess, Swedenborg would differ only in degree from many other religious leaders who ultimately ended up placing visions and mystical *revelations above the revealed Word of God. The following represents his points of departure from traditional Christianity.

Swedenborg flatly rejected as foolishness the idea that Jesus came to effect vicarious atonement for sin or that the shedding of his blood was necessary to appease an angry God. In so doing, he constantly found himself in opposition to Paul (Rom. 3:21–26) and to Lutheranism itself. Martin Luther championed the doctrine of justification by grace through faith.

Swedenborg also protested vehemently against the Pauline/Lutheran idea of imputation. That is, he rejected the notion that Christ's righteousness is imparted to a believer in an instantaneous way, simply by virtue of faith.

> Instantaneous salvation, by an immediate act of mercy, is to this day a fiery, flying serpent in the church, and that thereby religion is abolished, security introduced and damnation imputed to the Lord.[3]

These remarks stand in marked contrast to Paul (Rom. 4:4–5, 8, 22–24).

Luther, following Paul's thoughts, wrote as follows:

> Let us, therefore, be on our guard against this hellish poison and not lose Christ, the consoling Savior. Above all things, Christ must be kept in this matter of salvation. It is certainly true that as David says (Ps. 32:2), and Paul (Rom. 4:8): "Blessed is the man to whom the Lord will not impute sin." But St. Paul introduces the thought in order to show that this divine imputation comes only to him who believes in Christ and not to the free will of man or human nature because of good works. . . . The gracious imputation of which the Psalm speaks had first to be bought and acquired for us from His righteousness.[4]

"Jesus," for Swedenborg, was separate and distinct from the "Christ." This idea is certainly not peculiar to Swedenborg. The idea that Christ existed only humanly for a time was called *Nestorianism and was rejected by the Council of Ephesus in A.D. 431. The separation of "Christ" from "Jesus" is also an idea that has been adopted by many of the NEW THOUGHT religions such as CHRISTIAN SCIENCE and THEOSOPHY.

Humanity

Swedenborg's penchant for dividing spirit and flesh (the influence of *gnosticism) also became the legacy of Theosophy. As he divided the earthly "Jesus" from the eternal and spiritual "Christ," in similar fashion he divided the human being into eternal spirit and temporal flesh.

Traditional Christianity, it is true, teaches the separation of body from "soul" or "spirit" at death. But the church also teaches that the body will one day be raised (John 6:40; 11:25; 1 Cor. 15:22) and the new body will be immortal and incorruptible (1 Cor. 15:50ff.). From these passages of Scripture, the early church formulated the confession, "I believe in the . . . resurrection of the body, and the life everlasting" (Apostles' Creed, Appendix 1).

Authority

Swedenborg placed his own authority over the authority of the Bible and the church. Wherever his theology differed from the Scriptures, Swedenborg rejected the Scriptures in light of his theology. Like Marcion (d. A.D. 160), Swedenborg selected the books of the Bible he deemed "authoritative" or canonical. Marcion rejected all of the Jewish writings and embraced the Pauline letters and the gospel of Luke. Swedenborg, by contrast, rejected the Pauline letters, especially Romans 1–8, and accepted the four Gospels and the book of Revelation. "I enjoy perfect inspiration," Swedenborg stated.[5]

In what brilliance Swedenborg acclaimed in scientific achievements, he utterly failed in his revelatory precepts concerning God and science. His revelations in *Earths in the Universe* (1758) limited his solar system to six planets. Saturn being the furthest, which theory is refuted by modern astronomy. Still, the volume contained supposed conversations that Swedenborg had with inhabitants on the moon and other planets, hence proving his revelations false by modern scientific investigations.

End Times

Swedenborg believed that the Bible had an outer and an inner sense. He also believed that he had been granted the gift of interpreting the latter, the inner sense of Scripture. Swedenborg believed, based on the book of Revelation, that Jesus Christ returned in the eighteenth century and that the new Jerusalem (Rev. 21:2) had descended and now exists, embodied in the teachings of Jesus Christ channeled through Swedenborg himself.

Contrariwise, the Christian church waits in hope for the return of Jesus Christ, which is yet future (1 Thess. 4:14–17). "From thence he will come to judge the living and the dead" (Apostles' Creed).

CONCLUSION

Swedenborg died in 1772, but his ideas certainly did not. A "Lutheran" throughout his life, he never founded a church. By the mid–1780s, however, various Swedenborgian societies had been formed. In 1788, the "New Church" was established by Robert Hindmarsh in London. Other societies formed rapidly and by 1789 a conference comprised of the various societies was held, also in London. Except for brief periods of time early in its history, the General Convention of the New Church has met yearly. In 1784 James Glen, an English church planter, came to America and lectured on Swedenborg's ideas. An American branch, called the Swedenborgian Society, was formed in 1792 in Baltimore. In 1817, the General Convention of the New Jerusalem was established in Philadelphia. Disagreement in teachings, however, led to the establishment of a splinter group known as the General Church of the New Jerusalem in 1897. The two American churches together with the General Convention in England constitute the three main bodies of Swedenborgian theology.

Education is an important facet of the Church of the New Jerusalem. A theological school is located in Newton, Massachusetts. A college in Bryth Athyn, Pennsylvania, a secondary school, and eight elementary schools are also run by the church. Present headquarters are in Bryth Athyn, where a beautiful cathedral has been built.

Worship in the Swedenborgian societies and churches is characteristically liturgical with the preaching centered around the writings of Swedenborg. Like Lutheranism, the two ᵇsacraments of baptism and holy communion are administered. Bishops, pastors, and ministers serve as ordained leaders in the church. Bishops are chosen by the General Assembly, a governing body that is itself appointed by the joint British General Conference and the U.S. General Convention. Ministerial candidates are normally expected to attend four years of school in one of the two American colleges or at the Woodford Green school located in Essex, England.

The church is governed by a general council. Support units oversee goals and areas of ministry focus. A cabinet is comprised of the chair of each support unit and the president of the Swedenborgian Church. A council of ministers consists of ordained ministers in the church. These meet annually. The president is usually ordained.

Women can join the Church of the New Jerusalem at the age of eighteen. Men are eligible to become members at twenty-one. A period of time, usually several months, studying the writings of Swedenborg is required preceding membership.

An aggressive missions program is carried out by the New Church societies, with chief focus on Africa. The writings of Swedenborg have been translated into many languages, including Italian, French, German, and Swedish. There are several weekly and monthly journals and one quarterly journal published by the church.

As Swedenborg's influence was due to his writings and his intellectual prowess and not through the founding of a church, it is also the case that his ideas and influence stretch far beyond the boundaries of the church(es) that exist in his honor.

ADDITIONAL INFORMATION

Headquarters
General Church of the New Jerusalem, Bryn Athyn, Pennsylvania.

Website
www.swedenborg.org

Sacred Texts
The numerous writings of Swedenborg and portions of the Bible.

Periodicals
Arcana

Membership
The United States has 2,600 members in approximately forty-five churches; international membership is approximately 50,000.

Notes
[1] Emmanuel Swedenborg, as quoted in *Schaff-Herzog Encyclopedia of Religious Knowledge*, 3 vols. (New York: Funk and Wagnalls, 1883), 3:2271.
[2] See also THEOSOPHY, CHRISTADELPHIANISM, CHRISTIAN SCIENCE, UNIFICATION CHURCH, and THE WAY INTERNATIONAL for further discussion of the two natures of Christ.
[3] Emmanuel Swedenborg, *Miscellaneous Theological Works* (New York: Philosophical Library, 1916), 204–5.
[4] Martin Luther, as quoted in *What Luther Says—An Anthology*, ed. E. M. Plass, 3 vols. (St. Louis: Concordia, 1959), 2:709.
[5] Sydney Ahlstrom, *A Religious History of the American People*, 2 vols. (New York: Image Books, 1975), 2:586.

CHURCH UNIVERSAL AND TRIUMPHANT (CUT); THE "I AM" ASCENDED MASTERS

There are numerous churches that grew out of the "I AM" movement, chief of which was the Church Universal and Triumphant (CUT). "I AM" has its roots in an eclecticism of ancient ▸gnosticism, Eastern ▸mysticism, ▸THEOSOPHY, and CHRISTIANITY. Borrowed from Exodus 3:14, the phrase "I AM" attempts to capture the locus and essence of deity that resides in a line of "Ascended Masters" throughout history.

HISTORY

The "I AM" movement proper began in the 1930s with Guy ▸Ballard (1878–1939) and his wife, Edna (1886–1971). Borrowing from the gnostic idea that God, as absolute spirit, is only accessible through human intermediaries, the Ballards taught that these "Masters" had been raised up at various times throughout history to reveal God's truth. The chiefs of the Ascended Masters were Jesus and a seventeenth-century ▸occultist, Saint Germain, with whom Ballard claimed to have had contact in 1930 on Mount Shasta in California.

The immediate precedent to the Ballards were the books and teachings of Baird T. Spalding. Spalding's *Life and Teachings of the Masters of the Far East* (1935) contained ideas parallel to those of Ballard and other "I AM" teachers. Spalding also believed that the essential "I AM presence" dwells within everyone.

Ballard recalled his encounter with Germain in his book *Unveiled Mysteries* (1934). Germain had related to Ballard that he (Germain) had gone through successive stages of ▸reincarnations and had finally achieved the status of an Ascended Master. Ballard himself, Germain revealed, had also been reincarnated many times throughout history. One of these reincarnations was George Washington.

Ballard's "I AM" movement flourished during the 1930s, and *Unveiled Mysteries* was in great demand. As many as 3.5 million people were reported to be a part of the movement, though statistics are difficult to verify. Headquarters is presently located in Schaumburg, Illinois.

Trouble erupted for the Ballards in 1939 when the movement received severe criticism from the media. Meetings were suspended for a time and when resumed were restricted to members only. This was because hecklers would come to the meetings and interrupt the serene atmosphere of the classes. Further complica-

tions arose with the death of Guy Ballard in December 1939. Edna claimed that her late husband was now an Ascended Master himself. Skepticism and disillusionment arose, however, and many left the movement because the Ballards had taught that physical death would not come in the process of becoming spiritually liberated and enlightened.[1] Edna, however, claimed that she had been in constant communication with her husband after his death.

Additional problems arose for Edna and her son Donald when they were accused of mail fraud and fraudulent solicitation of funds. They were convicted and subsequently released. She continued to provide leadership for the movement until her death in 1971. She was succeeded by Jerry and Ann Craig and Edna Ballard's former organist, Frederick Landwehr. Membership has steadily declined in the last two decades.

Before examining the teachings and theology of the "I AM" movement, we should examine the largest and most significant offshoot of "I AM," the Church Universal and Triumphant. Because the teachings are similar to those of Ballard and Spalding, they are singularly presented below, following historical consideration of the CUT.

The CUT was founded by Mark L. ▸Prophet (1918–1973). Prophet, a theosophist, claimed to have received revelations in 1958 from the Ascended Master El Morya, after which Prophet announced that he was the secretary or revealer of El Morya's thoughts and discourses.[2] A book titled *Leaves of Morya's Garden* (1923) by Nicolas Roerich served as a guide to many of Prophet's own ideas.

In 1975 the CUT, then known as the Summit Lighthouse, published an important document allegedly written by El Morya. In this work the movement attempted to show an intricate link between key leaders of theosophy, Ascended Masters throughout history, the Ballards, and finally, Mark Prophet.

> In 1876, Helena Petrovna ▸Blavatsky was ordered by the Master Kuthumi and me, then known as the Masters K. H. and M., to write Isis Unveiled.... Commissioned by Jesus the Christ, the Ascended Master Hilarion, and Mother Mary, Mary Baker Eddy was given certain revelations that she set forth in *Science and Health with Key to the Scriptures.*

Though at times beset with their own preconceptions and the burden of the mass consciousness, these witnesses codified the truth and the law of East and West as the culmination of thousands of years of their souls' distillations of the Spirit. . . .

In the 1930s came the twin flames Guy W. Ballard and Edna Ballard imparting the sacred mystery of the law of the I Am, further knowledge of hierarchy, the invocation of the sacred fire, and the path of the ascension. Representatives tried and true of Saint Germain, they were commissioned to remain the only messengers of the hierarchy of the Aquarian age until mankind should redeem a certain portion of their karma.

When that cycle was fulfilled, Saint Germain, together with the Darjeeling Council, sponsored Mark and Elizabeth Prophet to carry on the work not only of the Ballards and the I Am movement, but also of Nicholas and Helna Roerich. . . . And so the Mother flame of Russia and the Mother flame of America converge in the spirals of freedom and victory for the sons and daughters of God in both nations and in every nation upon earth.[3]

Elizabeth Clare Wolf attended some of Mark Prophet's early conferences. She was immediately attracted to him as they shared a common vision on the night of April 22, 1961, in Boston. They were soon married and found themselves in constant contact with the spirit world. According to one source, "eventually, Mark and Elizabeth began to proclaim themselves the divinely appointed messengers of the great white brotherhood and sought international outlets for their teachings."[4] The "messengers" alluded to above were understood to be the divinely appointed heralds spoken of in Revelation 11:3.

The Summit Lighthouse had been founded in 1958 in Washington, D.C. The Prophets moved to Colorado Springs, Colorado, in 1966 and there purchased a mansion to house their new headquarters.

By 1969 approximately one hundred followers had been amassed in the organization. They had been told of, and were waiting eagerly for, Prophet's ascension into oneness with God. Shock and disappointment came, however, when Mark died suddenly of a stroke on February 26, 1973. Greatly disillusioned, many of the disciples began to leave the movement, as had previously been the case when Ballard died in 1939. And like Edna Ballard, Elizabeth Clare Prophet declared that her husband had become an Ascended Master by the name of Lanello. Lanello then allegedly dictated the words to a book titled *Cosmic Consciousness As the Highest Expression of the Heart* (1976).

Far more important than the work written supposedly after Mark Prophet had died was the major book written by the Prophets while Mark was still alive— *Climb the Highest Mountain* (1972). This work is considered the organization's authoritative text, containing the collective revelations of the Ascended Masters (see below).

Shortly after Mark's death, Elizabeth married Randall King. Headquarters were relocated to a Roman Catholic monastery in California called Camelot. It was here that King and Prophet decided to rename the organization the Church Universal and Triumphant, retaining the name Summit Lighthouse for the publishing arm of the organization. The organization was not alone, however, in experiencing a name change. Through a series of dictations from the Ascended Masters, Elizabeth Prophet was granted the titles of "Guru Ma," "Mother of the Flame," and "Mother of the Universe."[5]

Shortly after the move to California, Elizabeth discovered King was having an affair. She divorced him both from the church and herself, and in 1981 married a third time to Edward Francis. This new marriage also precipitated a move. Also in 1981, the CUT purchased the Malcolm Forbes ranch in Corwin Springs, Montana. Five years later, Camelot was sold and headquarters were relocated to the new home. In 1987 headquarters were moved to a forty-thousand-acre Inner Retreat near Gardiner, Montana. Not unlike other end-times groups, the CUT came into considerable conflict with local residents. Clare Prophet attracted national attention when she predicted that the United States would come under missile attack by the (former) Soviet Union in April 1990. Many people flocked to the ranch, paying as much as $12,000 apiece to take cover in the underground bomb shelters that the group made available.

Other problems also came to haunt the CUT. The government attempted to remove the group's tax-exempt status and collect over $2,000,000 in back taxes. The government based its case when the group illegally purchased weapons and the group stockpiled them under the guise of a mass preparation for Armageddon. They eventually agreed to dispense with the weapons in exchange for continued tax-exempt status as a recognized and organized religion. Other problems for the group included petroleum leaks on the ranch, which brought government intervention and great opposition from hostile neighbors. Suits by ex-members were leveled, with charges that included accusations that the Prophets and other leaders in the group were benefiting from slave labor as members worked long hours. Prophet's own daughter went on public record calling her mother a "hypocrite." After Prophet's divorce from Francis, she remarried a fourth time, claiming that this marriage was divinely inspired, yet this one also quickly crumbled, ending in divorce.

In January 1999, Elizabeth Clare Prophet, suffering from Alzheimer's, announced that she was stepping down from CUT leadership. Her daughter Erin announced her intent to write a book speaking about her own disillusionments with the organization and her mother.

Despite all of this, the CUT has continued to hold its own. Receiving large donations by members who have left money to the church in their wills, it continues to maintain itself despite opposition. In August 2005, the Summit Lighthouse celebrated forty-seven years since its founding.

ORGANIZATION

The "I AM" movement is most clearly represented today in the CUT. Headquarters remain in Montana. The group's administration is comprised of a board of directors. The entry level of the group consists of men and women who make up the Keepers of the Flame Fraternity. ᵖCommunicants are members who have demonstrated the most earnest commitment to the organization.

TEACHINGS

The core of teachings embraced by the CUT are believed to have been handed down from the Great White Brotherhood. As alluded to above, the brotherhood is comprised of outstanding spiritual figures from history—such as ᵖConfucius, ᵖBuddha, Jesus Christ, Jesus' mother Mary, Saint Francis, Saint Germain, El Morya, and among present figures, Guy Ballard and Mark Prophet.

Climb the Highest Mountain is the most oft-quoted and highly regarded text among members of the CUT. From it, some of the group's major doctrines may be deciphered.

God

God does not exist apart from the created universe. The group embraces a ᵖpantheism similar to that of HINDUISM. Like many other groups, the CUT does not make the distinction between God and creation that Christianity does:[6]

> If man would learn to enjoy the bliss of being a drop in the ocean of God, he would forevermore rejoice

in that oneness. He would realize that he does not have a separate identity apart from God; nor would he desire separation from the great sea of God's Being.[7]

God is the source of all that is. The CUT understands this to mean that God is likened to the Great Central Sun at the center of the universe. The individual light rays emanating from the rays of this sun came forth and were "individualized in many individual sparks, each a replica of God, a personalized fragment of the Deity. The seeds of light are called the 'I Am' presence, the Lord, or godly part of each individual."[8]

God possesses both female and male characteristics and is thus called "Father-Mother." *Climb the Highest Mountain* contains numerous appellations for God. In addition to being called Father-Mother, God is also Son and Holy Spirit. As Father, God is "Wisdom-Power," who initiates the great plan of creation. As Mother, God is the "Power-Love" that actually gives birth to creation. In the realm of matter, Christ is the embodiment of the Wisdom-Power. This God-force is to be manipulated by human beings in order to achieve one's highest potential.

Orthodox Christianity also accepts both male and female metaphors for God, as recorded in the Bible. The God who created the world (Gen. 1:1) is also the God who, in motherly fashion, overshadows his people with protective wings like a mother hen (Ps. 36:7). Attributes of God also include wisdom (Rom. 11:33), power (Gen. 17:1), and love (1 John 4:8). But Christianity also carefully distinguishes God's incommunicable attributes from those that are communicable. There are incommunicable attributes that God alone possesses and thus cannot be shared (omnipotence, omnipresence, omniscience, etc.), as well as those that human beings may indeed share in to a lesser degree (love, wisdom, kindness, etc.). This distinction cannot be made in CUT because of its pantheistic orientation. God is not a ᵖTrinity but rather "His Being and Consciousness appear in the Persons of the Trinity according to the level or plane of individual awareness."[9]

Jesus Christ

For the CUT, "Jesus" and "Christ" are understood as two different concepts. Similar to CHRISTIAN SCIENCE and the numerous ᵖmind sciences, "Jesus" was the historical person who lived in Palestine two thousand years ago, while "Christ" embodies a principle of higher divine consciousness possessed by everyone. Jesus' outstanding *fait accompli* was his ability to achieve an unprecedented level of this consciousness, which in effect enabled him to achieve the status of "Christ." The CUT, like many other groups within the scope of this volume, does not embrace the Christian doctrine of the two natures of Christ in ▸hypostatic union.[10]

The orthodox or traditional articulation of the tri-une nature of the Godhead, by contrast, recognizes the divinity of Jesus. Jesus is distinct, not only in degree but also in kind, from all of humanity. Yet in his humanity, an insoluble link is formed between God and humankind. "Christ" is a title reserved for Jesus Christ alone and is not to be shared by any human being. For those who separate "Jesus" from "the Christ," 1 John 2:22 clearly states: "Who is the liar? It is the man who denies that Jesus is the Christ. Such a man is the antichrist—he denies the Father and the Son."

Concerning the work of Christ, for the CUT, Jesus was one of the Ascended Masters. Elizabeth Clare Prophet believed that Jesus' silent years were spent studying with the masters of the Far East in order to prepare him to achieve the status of an Ascended Master. Jesus' work would be to one day demonstrate Christhood for others.

That Jesus is to be worshiped as the second person of the divine Trinity is vehemently denied by the CUT:

> ... so that when the Christ should come to save their souls from perdition, they would no longer recognize him as the archetype of their own God-identity and the exemplar of that mission which they had failed to fulfill. They would either reject him totally or worship his personality as one who could do for them that which they had no right to do for themselves.[11]

For traditional Christianity, numerous passages from the Bible formulate the Christian understanding that Jesus is indeed to be worshiped (Isa. 45:23; John 20:28; Phil. 2:9–11). Furthermore, Jesus' ascension to the right hand of God relegates him to a place of the highest honor. This honor and glory are never to be shared by human beings, in this life or in the next. It is always the duty and privilege of the Christian to render to God a sacrifice of praise on earth and in heaven (Rev. 4:10–11).

Holy Spirit

The CUT's doctrine of the Holy Spirit also resembles the teachings of many of the mind sciences. The movement speaks of the Spirit as being a depersonalized "energy," a "germinal power in nature," or the "Fire of the Cosmos." The essential work of the Spirit is to charge all of life with the knowledge of God.

Historic Christianity advances the doctrine of the person of the Holy Spirit as being the third member of the divine Trinity. The Spirit is the Counselor (John 15:26), giver of life (John 6:63), teacher (John 16:13), divine guide (Acts 16:7), the discerner of truth (1 Cor. 2:14), and worker of numerous other activities. The Spirit was with God in the creation (Gen. 1:2) and in revelation, and he emanates from the Father and the Son (John 15:26). The Nicene Creed confesses the Holy Spirit as being "Lord and giver of life, who proceeds from the Father and the Son, who with the Father and the Son together is worshiped and glorified" (*see* Appendix 1).

Humanity

Man is a creature consisting of a "lower self" or body, and a "higher self" or spirit. The body is the part of a person that has been ill-affected by the wrong use of the latent energies within, resulting in bad ▸karma. Over a period of time, however, a person may be elevated to the state of ▸deification. When this happens, the "higher self" reigns supreme, unhindered and unencumbered by the body. Gnostic motifs are certainly inherent in these ideas.[12]

The Christian church teaches no such view of humanity. The Bible relegates the human race to a much humbler role. Declared a sinner (Ps. 51:5; Rom. 3:23), a human being is a hopeless and condemned creature to whom God pours out his infinite mercy, love, and grace. For the CUT, humankind's inherent goodness, or "higher self," is in no need of such grace from without. God dwells within, and the will of humanity is predisposed toward good.

Salvation

This anthropology implies a specific doctrine of salvation. Like HINDUISM and Eastern thought in general, the essence of salvation lies in self-realization. When one becomes aware of one's own divinity, salvation is accomplished. In the end, all people will eventually find enlightenment (salvation).

The CUT does, however, teach that there is a certain degree of atonement in the "work" of the "I AM" Ascended Masters. The atonement is not Jesus' substitutionary sacrifice for sin, as Christianity teaches (Rom. 3:21–26), but rather a certain substitution on the part of the Masters, for bad karma. "▸Avatars—souls of great Light and spiritual attainment, such as Jesus the Christ and ▸Gautama Buddha—were sent to take upon themselves a certain portion of mankind's planetary karma."[13]

Salvation is thereby regarded by the CUT as being both a divine and human act. The Masters absorb karma and point the way to ♭enlightenment, where each individual can choose to utilize the infinite potential within to ascend toward the "I AM." Elizabeth Clare Prophet made the following statement:

> The only way to get God or to get any portion of God as hierarchy is through the flame in your heart. I can't do it for you. They come to help you do it yourself. The ascended masters' teachings are a do-it-yourself kit. They give us the instruction, the formula: but nothing happens until we do it.[14]

Church

Mrs. Prophet believes and teaches that America embodies the new promised land for the lost ten tribes of Israel.[15] The "I AM" race comprises those following the teachings of the Ascended Masters, a limited number of people from every part of the world. Those who know they are part of this race constitute the church. Specifically, the CUT sees itself as being the true church. To become a member a person must become a "keeper of the Flame," subscribe to the "tenets" of the church, be formally baptized, and tithe his or her income.[16]

End Times

Members of the CUT are predicting the end of the world and are presently preparing for the coming ♭Armageddon by building bomb shelters at the world headquarters in Montana. Such preparation, it is believed, will enable the CUT to survive the holocaust. In the summer of 1989, Prophet predicted that the Soviet *glasnost* was a mere ruse to put "America the Vulnerable" off guard for a surprise attack.[17] Such fear tactics continue to provide CUT with sufficient impetus to continue the pursuit of "digging in" and preparing for the end. Prophet's latest eschatological extravaganza is a lengthy book titled *Astrology of the Four Horsemen* (1991).

CONCLUSION

The CUT has grown rapidly in the United States. Official membership figures are difficult to estimate. The movement has spread throughout the world, with heavy concentrations of members in Ghana and Sweden. Teaching centers and study groups are located across the United States. The most involved training takes place through Summit University, which conducts classes in twelve-week quarters. In addition to the many publications of the group, a weekly periodical titled *Pearls of Wisdom* is printed in order to disseminate the most recent revelations from the "I AM" Masters to the movement's members.

ADDITIONAL INFORMATION

Headquarters
The Summit Lighthouse, PO Box 5000, Gardiner, MT 59030–5000.

Website
www.tsl.org

Sacred Texts
Climb the Highest Mountain, numerous other writings of the Prophets.

Publications
Heart to Heart; Pearls of Wisdom

Membership
Estimated 3,000 members and approximately 237 congregations (study groups). Internationally, the group has a presence in at least twenty foreign countries and in almost fifty cities worldwide.

Notes
[1] *Encyclopaedia Britannica,* 15th ed., s.v. "I Am Movement."
[2] "Church Universal and Triumphant," *Spiritual Counterfeits Project Newsletter* (December–January 1977), n.p.
[3] El Morya, *The Chela and the Path* (Colorado Springs, Colo.: The Summit Lighthouse, 1975), 121–22, as quoted in Walter Martin, *The New Cults* (Santa Ana, Calif.: Vision House, 1980), 215.
[4] Ibid., 216.
[5] "Church Universal and Triumphant," *Spiritual Counterfeits Project*, n.p.
[6] See HINDUISM, CHRISTIAN SCIENCE, ANANDA MARGA YOGA SOCIETY.
[7] Mark and Elizabeth Prophet, *Climb the Highest Mountain* (Los Angeles: Summit Lighthouse, 1975), as quoted in James A. Baker, "The Church Universal and Triumphant, Its Teachers and Teachings" (M.Div. thesis, Concordia Theological Seminary [Fort Wayne, Ind.], 1982), 46.
[8] J. Gordon Melton, *Encyclopedic Handbook of Cults in America* (New York and London: Garland, 1986), 137.
[9] Prophet, *Climb the Highest Mountain*, 322.
[10] See THE WAY INTERNATIONAL, CHRISTIAN SCIENCE, UNIFICATION CHURCH, etc.
[11] Prophet, *Climb the Highest Mountain*, 71.
[12] See ♭Gnosticism.
[13] Prophet, *Climb the Highest Mountain*, 443.
[14] Elizabeth Clare Prophet, *The Great White Brotherhood in the Culture, History and Religion of the United States* (Los Angeles: Summit Univ. Press, 1980), 63.
[15] See WORLDWIDE CHURCH OF GOD, particularly ♭Anglo-Israeliism.
[16] Melton, *Handbook of Cults*, 137–38.
[17] William F. Allman, "Fatal Attraction: Why We Love Doomsday," *U.S. News and World Report* (April 30, 1990), 13.

CHURCH WITHOUT A NAME, THE; GO PREACHERS; NO NAME CHURCH, TWO BY TWOS, THE NAMELESS HOUSE SECT, COONEYITES

The movement derives its name, Two by Twos, from its practice of sending members out two by two to spread their message. They based this practice on Mark 6:7–12. They are best classified as a ▶fundamentalist ▶Protestant ▶denomination.

HISTORY

William ▶Irvine (1863–1947) was a "Pilgrim preacher" for the Faith Mission. In 1897, he began teaching that no preachers should receive a salary but should be homeless. Gathering several more ministers, including Edward Cooney, the message (also called "the experiment") began to spread.

In 1900, the Faith Mission and Irvine parted company. That same year, followers held a convention in Rathmolyn, Ireland, which lasted for three weeks. Irvine, a powerful orator, convinced his followers to call themselves "workers," to sell all of their possessions, and to take vows of poverty, celibacy, obedience, and self-denial. Irvine began to gather followers in the United States, Canada, Australia, and New Zealand. Members were organized into two classes. The "senior members" or "senior brothers" were the full-time missionaries. The general membership held secular jobs. Like the JEHOVAH'S WITNESSES, Irvine claimed that his followers were the 144,000 in Revelation and believed also that the end of the world was coming in 1914. After this date, no one else could be saved.

This met with much controversy in the group and a split resulted. Irvine was excommunicated by his own followers. Edward Cooney became the leader soon after, but because he proposed that the group return to its original teachings, he too met with opposition. In 1928, he was also removed from the "workers." Following Irvine's removal, he moved to Jerusalem and wrote hundreds of letters to four hundred or so other followers who had been excommunicated along with him. He called these, "Little Ones, "Message People," and "Friends." Irvine remained in Jerusalem for the rest of his life, dying there in 1947.

ORGANIZATION

The group has held annual conventions in numerous locations around the world. Although the movement insists on not possessing a name, they have been required by different nations to adopt a "title." These titles vary in different countries. In England they are registered under the name "The Testimony of Jesus." In the United States they are called "Christian Conventions," and in Canada, "Christian Assemblies." They do not enjoy a tax-exempt status, nor do they own buildings, schools, or any legal property.[1] Members lead a disciplined life. Ministers take vows of poverty, abstinence from sexual relations, and obedience. Although in former decades television was strictly forbidden, along with dancing, smoking, the use of alcoholic beverages, and so on, more and more members are purchasing televisions and using the computer.[2]

BELIEFS

Theologically, the Two by Twos are Unitarian, believing that God is one person, the Father. Therefore, they deny the ▶Trinity. Jesus Christ is called Savior, but only to the degree that he was a perfect man who vicariously atoned for humanity's sins. The Holy Spirit is a force that represents God in action. These theological tenets are denied in force by ample Scripture on the Godhead: God is one (Deut. 6:4; Isa. 43:10); the Father is God (Isa. 63:16); the Son is God (John 1:1; 20:28); the Holy Spirit is God (Acts 5:3–4; 1 Cor. 6:19–20). Since there is but one God and all three persons are exclusively called God, we accept this biblical testimony that the three are the one God, the Trinity.

Most of the beliefs of this group are fundamentalist in nature without much variation; a detailed list of these doctrines is available on the website listed below. An important distinction in the group is their belief on the way one is saved. One must hear the gospel by a member of the Two by Twos. This, however, is not what is generally told to outsiders, where the message conveyed is that salvation is based solely upon faith in Christ and a rigid adherence to a holy life. One can lose salvation at any given time; thus, the pressure to continue to pursue holiness diligently is a daily preoccupation of each member. They practice baptism by immersion, oppose infant baptism, and have communion each Sunday with grape juice. All previous baptisms are unrecognized, so that a new member of the group must be rebaptized. The Two by Twos are pacifists and forbid members to kill in wartime as soldiers.

They may serve but not bear arms. Weddings are civil ceremonies because the ministers do not have licenses to perform religious ceremonies.

CONCLUSION

Ex-members of the Two by Twos have formed discussion groups about their experiences. (See website below). One group, calling themselves the Veterans of Truth, expend much energy in attempting to prove to members of the group that they have been lied to and that there are things about the group that need to be exposed, particularly the truths concerning the founder, William Irvine.

ADDITIONAL INFORMATION_____

Headquarters
None; gatherings are held annually in various locations.

Websites
There is an email discussion list available and is comprised mostly of ex-members. It is found at *listserv@home.ease.lsoft.com*. An informative website is *http://home.earth link.net/~truth/* and an active website was founded by ex-members who call themselves Veterans of Truth: *http://ourworld.compuserve.com/homepages/*

Sacred Text
The King James Version of the ▸Bible only (in English).

Publications
Some writings and sermons.

Membership
Possibly 40,000 members, mostly in the Northwest United States and Canada. In 1987, the number of "workers" in the U.S.A and Canada were 1,071.

Notes
[1] *www.religioustolerance.org/chr_2x2.htm*
[2] Ibid.

COMMUNITY OF CHRIST; REORGANIZED CHURCH OF JESUS CHRIST OF LATTER DAY SAINTS

The new name for the smaller branch of MORMONISM historically known as the Reorganized Church of Jesus Christ of Latter Day Saints (hereafter, RLDS/COC).

HISTORY

The story of the largest splinter group of the Mormon church began in the year 1844 after Joseph ▸Smith Jr. and his brother Hyrum were arrested in Nauvoo, Illinois, on charges of treasonable act of destroying a free press newspaper office that published a series of unfavorable articles about Smith, called the *Nauvoo Expositor*. An angry mob stormed the prison and murdered both Joseph and his brother.[1] Smith's widow, Emma, firmly believed that leadership of the church rightfully belonged to his son, Joseph Smith III. Smith III, however, was very young and was usurped by Brigham ▸Young, who disagreed, convinced that the mantle of leadership had fallen on him. He led the much larger group of Mormons in 1847 westward to Utah, to the Salt Lake City area. Those who believed that Smith's son was the legitimate heir remained behind. In 1906 they settled in Independence, Missouri, which Smith had prophesied as Zion, where they believe Christ will one day return at his second coming.

The RLDS/COC even by 1852 (sometimes cited as its beginning date) had only the semblance of an organization. This changed when in 1860 it was formally organized in Amboy, Illinois, at which time Joseph Smith III accepted his post as leader and president of the church. In 1869 the word "Reorganized" was added to the name. The RLDS/COC has claimed to be the only legitimate Mormon church because of the rightful succession of Smith's sons. Recently, a letter was discovered dated January 17, 1844, reportedly written by Joseph Smith Jr. The letter discloses the fact that Joseph had indeed desired to hand the reins of leadership over to his son. The letter turned out to be a forgery. Brigham Young had led the largest group to the Salt Lake basin in Utah and there established the Mormon church, which today is a powerful religious, social, and political entity.

Both groups denounce each other. The Salt Lake Mormons do not recognize the Reorganized church because Joseph Fielding Smith (the sixth president) dismissed the RLDS/COC as being apostate (see ▸apostasy) for not practicing ▸baptism for the dead. Conversely, the Reorganized church does not recognize the Utah Mormons because they repudiated the leadership of Joseph Smith III and thus ignored the Mormon doctrine of ▸apostolic succession. Some other doctrines of the Salt Lake group from which the Reorganized church departs are discussed below.

Most recently the RLDS/COC is making strides to distance itself even further from the Utah Mormons and is actually moving closer to American Protestantism, albeit in a liberal form. In April 1992, Peggy Stack wrote in the *Salt Lake Tribune* that the Missouri Mormons are removing sections from *Doctrine and Covenants* that discuss baptism for the dead, challenging the belief that the *Inspired Version of the KJV is superior, rejecting the idea that the Reorganized Church is the only true church, questioning the *Book of Mormon* as history, and ordaining women to priesthood.[2]

ORGANIZATION

The polity and infrastructure of the RLDS/COC resemble those of the Salt Lake Mormons. There are two priesthoods, the *Aaronic and the *Melchizedek. Under the Melchizedek priesthood, there is a *president and two counselors, a *council of twelve apostles, *high priests, *bishops, *patriarchs, the *quorum of seventy, and the *elders. Under the Aaronic priesthood, there are three offices: *priests, *teachers, and *deacons. Ecclesiastical courts are divided into the Elder's Court, the Bishop's Court, and the Standing High Council, which itself consists of twelve high priests and a member of the high presidency. Local congregations, as is also the case with the Utah group, are divided into districts and *stakes.

Officers are elected to serve under the auspices of the various congregations. A world conference is held every two years where the supreme legislative governing body meets and decides on issues concerning the future of the church. The church has two colleges: Graceland College in Lamoni, Iowa, and Park College in Kansas City, Missouri. It also has a seminary called Temple School, located in Independence, Missouri.

TEACHINGS

Some of the doctrines of the RLDS/COC are identical to those of the larger Salt Lake church. However, there are some differences that set it apart from the Utah Mormons. Interestingly, the RLDS/COC does not use the name Mormon because of Mormonism's association with the doctrine of polygamous marriages. This doctrine, the RLDS/COC leaders say, was introduced by Brigham Young, not by Joseph Smith Jr.; it was not part of the original teachings of the church. Here, of course, the RLDS/COC is unequivocally wrong, for Joseph Smith Jr. had a number of wives before he was assassinated in 1844.[3] Secret rites, practiced by the

Utah Mormons, are repudiated by the RLDS/COC. Additionally, sealed marriages are not conducted as they are in the temples of the Utah group.

The *Bible is accepted as the Word of God by the RLDS/COC. The official text is The Inspired Version of the King James Version, once used by Joseph Smith Jr. The Salt Lake Mormons also use the King James Version "insofar as it is correctly translated," rather than the Inspired Version. Also, the *Book of Mormon* and *Doctrine and Covenants* are accepted as being authoritative for doctrine, faith, and practice. However, their *Book of Mormon* is slightly different from the Utah Mormon edition, since they hold to Smith's 1838 edition as the corrected edition, and their *Doctrine and Covenants* has 162 sections in contrast to 140 for the Utah Mormons. The RLDS/COC believe that Joseph Smith Jr. fell from grace and that his revelations stopped at Section 112, long before Smith claimed revelations on *polygamy and *polytheism. Since that time, the RLDS/COC has added numerous revelations, not least of which admitted women to the priesthood and church ordination (Section 156 in 1984).

Similar to the Mormons of Utah, the RLDS/COC teaches that the canon is open, meaning that God has not spoken only in the past to the men who wrote the authoritative books (the Bible, *Book of Mormon*, etc.), but God continues to grant his "true church" continued *revelation. The doctrine of an open canon is one of the many differences between the RLDS/COC and traditional CHRISTIANITY.

The RLDS/COC rejects the Utah Mormon view of polytheism, and they deny that God the Father is an exalted, resurrected man of flesh and bone. Although their official doctrine on God states, "The one eternal, living God is triune: one God in three persons," questions remain that fail to bring them into Christian union with the historic Christian creeds since Joseph Smith's first vision unequivocally rejected them as abominable. This remains an unresolved contradiction until the day they reject Smith's first vision. To their credit, they regard the appearance of the Father in that vision as a theophanic vision rather than literal flesh and bone. Their view of the Holy Spirit is similar to that of Christian doctrine.

The RLDS/COC teaches salvation by grace through faith and that works follow salvation as a testimony. The RLDS/COC does not regard the temple rituals rigorously required by the Salt Lake Mormons as necessary for salvation. Also, the Reorganized branch does not adhere to the doctrine of baptism by proxy for the dead (see below). The RLDS/COC, however, built a temple at their headquarters as a message to the world. It appears to reflect NEW AGE mysticism rather than Mormonism, since no rituals that Smith practiced at the Nauvoo, Illinois, temple are used here. A feature found in the RLDS/COC that is not found among the Utah Mormons is the use of the bare cross as a symbol of Christ's crucifixion and resurrection. Nearly all RLDS/COC buildings bear the cross while no Utah Mormon building does.

The RLDS/COC has never accepted either the Apostles' or the Nicene creeds. Thus, although it has made some notable changes, not unsimilar to the WORLDWIDE CHURCH OF GOD, it is not yet a bona fide Christian denomination.

CONCLUSION

The RLDS/COC has made some significant additional changes recently. In April of 2000 it changed its name to Community of Christ, although legally it is still known as the RLDS/COC. On its website it says: "We proclaim Jesus Christ. . . ." All church presidents were direct descendants of Joseph Smith Jr. until Wallace B. Smith appointed W. Grant McMurray as his successor in 1996. McMurray stepped down in 2004, opening the door for general election of all continuing presidents. The church presidents and general authorities have their offices at the Independence headquarters.

ADDITIONAL INFORMATION_____

Headquarters
Community of Christ World Headquarters, 1001 W. Walnut, Independence, MO 64050.

Website
www.cofchrist.org

Sacred Texts
The Inspired Version (King James Bible); *Book of Mormon*; *Doctrine and Covenants*

Publications
10 Minute News

Membership
Approximately 250,000 members

Notes
[1] See MORMONISM for a more detailed analysis of Mormon theology. Comparisons with Christianity are also reserved for the article treating regular Mormonism.
[2] Peggy Fletcher Stack, "Reorganized LDS Church Embarks on Move Away from Mormon Roots," *Salt Lake Tribune* (April 25, 1992); mentioned in "What Ís New in the Headlines?" *Christian Research Newsletter*, Vol. 5, No. 3 (May/June 1992), 2.
[3] A well-researched book by Todd Compton, *In Sacred Loneliness: The Plural Wives of Joseph Smith* (Salt Lake City: Signature, 1997), conclusively documents Smith's polygamous behavior.

CONFUCIANISM

Much like BUDDHISM and SHINTOISM, Confucianism began as a this-worldly philosophy rather than a transcendent religion. The concerns of its founder, 'K'ung Fu Tzu, were to address the moral laxity of the culture of his day and to inquire into ethical and moral behavior of individuals. Confucianism is often associated with wise sayings or 'analects written and spoken by its founder.

HISTORY

K'ung Fu Tsu ('Confucius) was born approximately 551 B.C. in Lu, the modern-day Shantung province of China. The moral slackness of the society in which he lived disturbed him greatly. He gathered students and taught them about the moral and ethical life. He was also concerned, as Plato and Aristotle were later, about the welfare of the citizenry of the state and how rulers may govern justly. In his later life, Confucius traveled much throughout China and spoke and taught before rulers. His students grew in number as he traveled more and more. He returned back to his home province of Lu in the last years of his life and taught and wrote right up to the time of his death in (ca. 479 B.C.).

Confucius' writings include five major works— *Ching*: *Book of History*, *Book of Songs*, *Book of Changes*, *Spring and Autumn Annals*, and *Book of Rites*.

TAOISM and Buddhism exerted much influence on the development of Confucianism, especially between 400 B.C. and 200 B.C. While Confucius had gained some followers during his lifetime, he remained relatively unknown by many outside his own teaching circles. However, in approximately 212 B.C., the writings of Confucius, which had been hidden by disciples, managed to escape a mass book burning ordered by Shi Huang Ti. A short time after this, those writings were copied and disseminated widely. State worship of Confucius began in the Han Dynasty in approximately 200 B.C. and lasted until as recently as 1912. Confucianism spread to other countries in the sixth century A.D. and following, including Japan and Korea.

The Communist Revolution in 1949 found cooperative advocacy amongst the adherents of Confucianism. For Confucius, loyalty to the state is a basic duty of the citizenry. This, of course, was a fundamental precept of communist doctrine, and it made for a unique form of socialism that developed quite differently in China from that in the former USSR and other countries influenced by Marxism. In Russia, for example, having been a Christian country since A.D. 987, loyalty to the state could only come when loyalty to God and his kingdom was not compromised. However, the religious aspects of Confucianism in communist China were dismissed outright.

Today, some six million people identify themselves as followers of Confucius. These are mostly in China.

BELIEFS AND TEACHINGS

As stated above, much of Confucius' writings deal with morality and ethics, including the ways in which the state should function to govern justly in society. Confucianism was heavily influenced by both Taoism and Buddhism. The Taoist teachings concerning the harmony of nature and the individual, along with the Buddhist development of beliefs about the afterlife, were both incorporated into Confucianism. The three religions have traditionally peacefully coexisted with one another in China.

From 200 B.C. to A.D. 900 Buddhism exerted its greatest influences on Confucianism, albeit through Taoist categories. Worship of the emperor, referred to as the Son of Heaven, was now popular. This was combined with a worship of heaven and earth, especially during key times of the year. Eventually, many different gods and spirits were added to the pantheon of deities. Spirits of famous individuals throughout history, ancestors, deities of harvest, corn, wind, the sun, moon, and stars, and so on were worshiped. Christianity strictly forbids the worship of any object or person except for the one true God (Ex. 20:3; Rom. 1:25).

Confucius' teachings revolved around the three great virtues of love, wisdom, and courage. These are sometimes referred to as his "universal virtues." The highly ethical nature of his thought and teachings revolved around *li*—beliefs concerning social etiquette, rituals, and personal property; *hsaio*—the mutual love and respect owed to all members of a family; *yi*—justice

and believing and doing what is right; *xin*—faithfulness and trustworthiness; *jen*—the highest virtue, that is, the showing of kindness and goodness toward all living things; and *chung*—loyalty to the government. Other world religions also strive toward these lofty goals.

Christianity certainly elevates all of these virtues as true, good, and noble. Beliefs about family property, love and mutual respect for family and all people, concerns for social justice, faithfulness, stewardship for all living things in creation, and honoring the government have been the consistent and ongoing teachings of Christianity.

But Confucius, as already stated, did not understand his teachings to be religious or transcendent in nature. Rather, he sought to proffer them as guidelines for daily living both as individuals, and at the same time as individuals living in the context of the state.

Examples of guidelines for ethical and moral living are replete in all world religions. Every state and accompanying government and/or religion has laws that, when breached, must be judged and punished. Christianity affirms this (Rom. 13:1–3). But for the latter, there is a higher power and a higher law that must be answered to, namely, the law of God. The violation of God's moral law is sin. Moreover, Christianity addresses what should ensue when ethical and moral guidelines are not followed. At the same time, Christianity addresses how immorality and all forms of sinful and unethical behaviors are atoned for in Christ (Rom. 3:21–24).

As all religions honor rites of passage in life, Confucianism honors four key life passages:

1. Birth—There are strict laws accompanying any threats to the health or well-being of the expecting mother.
2. Reaching adulthood and maturity—This one is now being essentially ignored by most followers of Confucius.
3. Marriage—Performed in six different stages: proposal, engagement, dowry, procession, marriage and reception, and the morning after.
4. Death—Belongings of the deceased are placed into the coffin (including food), family members mourn aloud, and rituals are performed by Taoist and/or Buddhist priests.

There are six different schools of Confucianism. These largely regard interpretation: Han Confucianism, Neo-Confucianism, Contemporary Neo-Confucianism, Korean Confucianism, Japanese Confucianism, and Singapore Confucianism.

CONCLUSION

Today, Confucianism as a religion in China is waning in the larger cities. The rural villages, however, do continue to hold fast to Confucius' teachings. Modernization has raised questions concerning traditional teachings about family, ancestry, paternalism, and cooperative loyalty. Modernism and westernization has introduced into the thinking of many modern Confucian thinkers the possibility of a new and reconstructed modern form of China's ancient philosophy and religion.

ADDITIONAL INFORMATION_____

Sacred Texts

Assembled by Chu Hsi (1130–1200). *Si Shu—Four Books*; *Lun Yu—The Analects of Confucius*; *Chung Yung—Doctrine of the Mean*; *Ta Hsueh—The Great Learning*; *Meng Tzu* (371–289 B.C.); *Wu Jing—Five Classics*; *Wu Jing—Classics of History*; *Shih Ching—Classic of Odes*; *I Ching—Book of Changes*; *Ch'un Ch'u—Spring and Autumn Annals*; *Li Ching*.

Statistics

Approximately six million Confucians (mostly in China). North America has approximately 26,000.

CONVINCE

An Afro-Jamaican ᵖcult comprised of members known as ᵖBongo men, the Bokongo immigrants of 1840 from the Bongo nation. Like MYAL and VOODOO, Convince advocates the worship of the sundry deities of the ᵖObeah cults.[1] The rhythm of Bongo songs are kept by beating sticks, accompanied by changes that bring acenstral or demonic spirit to inhabit the Bongo participants.

An important variation, distinguishing bongo men from the other SOUTH AMERICAN AND CARIBBEAN CULTS, lies in the belief that the devotee may be inhabited or possessed by more than one spirit at a time. Like the others in its family, Convince members practice dance rituals to initiate the attention of the deities. Unlike many of the others, however, Convince does not meet regularly. Meetings and ceremonies are held during a rite of passage, such as a memorial for the dead, the celebration of a particular occasion, or for carrying out an act of vengeance or some other deed more evil in nature.

The doctrine of ᵖdemon possession has been treated variously throughout the history of the church.[2] The ᵖBible records numerous instances where individuals were possessed by demons (e.g., Mark 1:21–28; 9:14–29) and at least one occasion in which an individual was possessed by more than one (Luke 8:26–39). Convince and others of the Obeah cults do not refer to these spirit beings as "demons," though they do embrace the concept of malicious deities.

Christian missionaries have continually attempted to bring the gospel to the Afro-Jamaican cults. The constitution of Jamaica allows for religious freedom, and nearly every Christian denomination is represented on this beautiful tropical island. Unlike most of the other Caribbean islands, which are heavily influenced by the Roman Catholic church, Jamaica's largest Christian denomination is the Anglican church. Missionary efforts have succeeded in "Christianizing" this English-speaking culture, but there are still many ᵖsects (e.g., the Pocomania and the Cumina sects) that, along with Convince, have not been seriously affected by the Christian gospel. Where these cults have embraced Christianity, they often adapt or incorporate Christian elements into their practices.

Membership in Convince is on the decline, but the cult shows no signs of extinction.

ADDITIONAL INFORMATION_____

Notes

[1] See also ABAKUA, CABILDO, CANDOMBLE, MYAL, SOUTH AMERICAN, CENTRAL AMERICAN, AND CARIBBEAN CULTS, and VOODOO.

[2] See SANTERIA for additional allusions to possession and religious syncretism, as well as current influences in the United States.

DIVINE LIFE SOCIETY; DLS; SATCHIDANANDA ASHRAM INTEGRAL YOGA INSTITUTE

"Be good, do good," counseled Sri ᵖSwami Sivananda ᵖMaharaj (1887–1963), the founder of Divine Life Society. This religious body is an offshoot of HINDUISM that became popular in the United States, particularly in the 1960s and 1970s when many related Eastern religious groups were gaining a following.

HISTORY

Sivananda had become a medical doctor after showing extraordinary intellectual prowess during his college years, rising to the top in his class. Sivananda grew disillusioned with worldly living and embarked on a spiritual pilgrimage during which he encountered Sri Swami Viswananda Saraswati. Saraswati was a member of the Sankaracharya tradition of Hindu thought. Sivananda became one of Saraswati's disciples and soon was initiated into the Sannyas Order. In conjunction with his spiritual training, Sivananda again began to practice medicine. His fame grew when he achieved ʼsamadhi and disciples began to gravitate to him. He subsequently founded the Divine Life Society in 1936.

Though Sivananda never left India, many of his disciples came to the West and founded numerous centers. The Integral Yoga Institute is one of numerous centers that have sprung up since the 1960s. These include the Sivananda ʼYoga VEDANTA Center, founded by one of the most successful of Sivananda's followers, Swami Vishnu Devananda (b. 1927); the Holy Shankaracharya Order, founded by Swami Lakshmy Devyashram (a female) and headquartered in the Pocono Mountains of Pennsylvania; the Integral School of Yoga and Vedanta, founded by Swami Jyotir Maya Nanda, which publishes *Vision of Eternity* and is headquartered in Miami, Florida; and the Yasodhara Ashram Society, founded by Sylvia Hellman, a former student of Self Realization Fellowship. This ʼsect is located in Canada, just north of the panhandle of Idaho. In 1979, folk-singer, Carole King donated 600 acres of woodland in Virginia. Here the society built LOTUS (Light of Truth Universal Shrine). It is also the location of the Satchinanda Ashram—Yogaville, founded by the Reverend Sri Swami Satchidananda, one of Sivananda's great disciples. Three Integral Yoga Institutes in San Francisco, New York, and New Jersey operate under his direction.

ORGANIZATION

As of 2001, there were seventeen centers in the United States, twenty-one international centers, and seven institutes, plus DLS centers located around the world. Two of these are located in the United States, in Maryland and Texas. The overarching leader of the DLS is called the secretary general. Each society is independent yet shares in the activities, conferences, and meetings of the other societies. A student or would/be disciple attaches himself/herself to a ʼguru.

Interest in the various forms of yoga is evidenced by the number of books written on the topic.
Courtesy George A. Mather

TEACHINGS

Sivananda believed in the essential unity of all religions. This is a basic principle of Hinduism. The goal of yoga is to bring perfection to a person's mental and physical well-being. Self-control, a keen intellect, a strong will, love, and mercy all number among the traits that are developed with yogic training. The different yogas are practiced in order to develop maturity in every aspect of the self. "Serve, love, meditate, and realize" is another of Sivananda's oft-repeated slogans. The disciple then embarks on a ʼsadhana. The yogas that Sivananda taught were ʼraja yoga, ʼjapa yoga, ʼhatha yoga, ʼkarma yoga, ʼbhakti yoga, and ʼjnana yoga.

An important divergence from Hinduism is that Sivananda rejected the ʼcaste system. This was a significant factor that led to the movement's somewhat respectable success in the West, particularly in the United States. Like CHRISTIANITY, Sivananda maintained that all people may seek truth; it is not confined to the privileged. Concern for social welfare is another prominent theme of the institute.

While Christianity also repudiates discrimination of the poor and the "lower castes" of society, it rejects the idea that all religions are paths that lead to God, or that all religions are harmonious in their essence and goals. Jesus Christ, the founder of Christianity, declared himself to be the only way to heaven (John 14:6), and through his person and work, as confessed in the second article of the Apostles' and Nicene creeds (Appendix 1), the forgiveness of sins is offered to the penitent.[1]

In keeping with the principle of harmony between faiths, members of the Integral Yoga Institute are noted for honoring major religious holidays of the religions of the world. These include Yom Kippur, Hanukkah, Thanksgiving, Christmas, and Easter.

CONCLUSION

Insofar as the goals of the Integral Yoga Institute are to generate peace, religious harmony, and physical well-being (see above), it may be properly classified as part of the network of the NEW AGE MOVEMENT. While interest in the personality ʼcults has waned in the 1980s, the West has continued to exhibit noteworthy interest in the ʼoccult and religions of the East, particularly the derivatives of Hinduism.

ADDITIONAL INFORMATION

Headquarters
The Divine Life Society, Shivanandanagar, Pin Code 249 192, District Terri Garwal Uttaranchal, India.

Website
www.swame-krishnananda.org

Sacred Texts
The *Upanishads*; the *Bhagavadgita*; the numerous writings of Sivananda, Swami Chidananda, and Swami Krishnananda

Periodicals, Journals
Divine Life Magazine; Attempt; Auroville News; Auroville Today, Collaboration, Invocation, Jyoti Matagiri Newsletter, Matrimandir Journal

Membership
Unknown

Note
[1] For a more detailed comparison/contrast between Christianity and the religious ideas of Sivananda, consult HINDUISM, ISKCON, NEW AGE MOVEMENT, and the VEDANTA SOCIETY.

DIVINE SCIENCE CHURCH

Divine Science Church is an offshoot of CHRISTIAN SCIENCE and may be classified, along with NEW THOUGHT, UNITY SCHOOL OF CHRISTIANITY, and RELIGIOUS SCIENCE as one of the ʼmind sciences.

HISTORY

The story of the Divine Science Church begins with Emma Curtis ʼHopkins, who was a student of Mary Baker ʼEddy, the originator of the Christian Science movement. Emma had served as general editor of Eddy's *Christian Science Journal.* Contention arose, however, and Eddy and Hopkins parted company, the former dismissing the latter as a "fraud." In 1887 Hopkins went on to found Christian Science Theological Seminary in Chicago. This school would soon become a hub of activity for New Thought.

Nona Brooks was introduced to Hopkins' teachings indirectly through a third woman, Mrs. Frank Bingham, to whom Hopkins had ministered healing. Brooks attended Bingham's lectures in Pueblo, Colorado. Having been healed of a throat condition, Nona began to treat others. Together with her two sisters, Fanny Brooks and Aletha Brooks Small, she began to study and teach what would soon become Divine Science.

Meanwhile, in Denver, another woman, Melinda Cramer, was also teaching ideas similar to those of Hopkins and Bingham. When Nona Brooks moved to Denver, she heard Cramer. Together in 1898, the two of them formed a Divine Science college, and in 1899 they organized the first Divine Science church with Sunday services held that same year.[1]

After Cramer died in 1907, the movement began to grow under the direction of the three Brooks sisters. The church never expanded into a major movement, however, as did Unity School of Christianity. By 1957 many Divine Science chapters were organized into the Divine Science Federation International. Headquarters for the movement have been in Washington, D.C., since 1956. There are Divine Science colleges in Denver and Washington, D.C., and satellite schools in Pueblo, Colorado, and Roanoke, Virginia. These schools educate practitioners.

TEACHINGS

The central tenet of Divine Science is a principle that could well be posited as the central teaching of all of the mind sciences—that is, since God is "perfect mind," since his presence in the universe is the only real and authentic presence there is, and, furthermore, since spirit is "the substance of all form," the reality of sin, sickness, or any tangible malady is both illusory and contradictory. Evil in the world and in people's lives is the result of a lack of knowledge of God's goodness. In fact, the very omnipotence, omnipresence, and unity of God prove that evil is not real in essence. It is relegated to the status of nonbeing.

The key to salvation is to know that spirit is reality. Atonement is the acceptance of unity; hency, Divine Science changes the biblical meaning of atonement to "at-one-ment." This signifies a "unity" or "being at one," not "atoning for."[2] Healing is possible physically when the mind is cured of all false concepts of evil and its unreality. The only real sin that exists, therefore, is ignorance.

The Christian ᴵTrinity takes on a new meaning in Divine Science. The "Father" is the "source" and "cause" of all goodness. But this source or cause is not necessarily external to the human, as it is in CHRISTIANITY.[3] The "Son" or "Christ" is also an all-pervasive, eternal, indwelling principle. Christ is a principle that all people have the potential to realize. He represents the "universal man." The Holy Spirit is that force that imparts divine illumination of the heavenly realm or realm of self-realization.

The goal of all life is to achieve oneness with the divine. When this is achieved, all evil will disappear and all illusions within the physical realm will vanish. The human being is not a sinful being in the Christian sense of sin as transgression against the will of God. The human being, rather, has the capacity to achieve perfection. It is only because one is not conscious of one's own perfection that the illusion of evil appears as reality.

CONCLUSION

Much of what Divine Science teaches has been influenced by the other mind sciences and is in most instances parallel. Nona Brooks wrote several key works read by members of the movement.

ADDITIONAL INFORMATION

Headquarters
There is no central headquarters. Divine Science churches are a federation. The St. Louis church serves in a loose way as a spearhead for the movement. Two other main churches exist in Washington and Denver.

Website
www.divinescience.org

Sacred Texts
The Bible; the writings of Nona Brooks, including *Mysteries, Short Lessons in Divine Science*, and *Why I Am a Divine Scientist*. Other important works include *The Divine Science Practitioner* by L. Frederick, *The Divine Science Way*, and *Divine Science; Its Principles and Faith: The Cardinal Points of the Teaching Program of Divine Science*, published by the Divine Science Federation International.

Publication
Aspire to Better Living

Membership
In 1974 Divine Science churches numbered approximately twenty with twenty-six ᴵpractitioners. Today there are approximately 5,000 members worldwide in thirty congregations.

Notes
[1] Unity School of Christianity was also founded in 1889. Like Nona Brooks, Charles and Myrtle ᴵFillmore also studied under Emma Curtis Hopkins.

[2] Murray, *New Thought on Old Doctrine* (Divine Science Library, 1918), 106.

[3] For an analysis and comparison of Christianity and some of the leading mind sciences, see Christian Science and Unity School of Christianity.

ECKANKAR

Eckankar is an eclectic blend of Eastern religions with ideas borrowed from HINDUISM, CHRISTIANITY, ᴵmysticism, the ᴵoccult, and ᴵpanpsychism.

HISTORY

The movement was founded in 1965 by John Paul ᴵTwitchell (d. 1971), a journalist and former staff member of the church of SCIENTOLOGY. His exact date of birth is uncertain, with claims ranging from 1908 to 1922. The United States Library of Congress claims that Twitchell was born in Paducah, Kentucky, in 1908. His marriage certificate claims 1912 as his date of birth. A third source, Twitchell's death certificate, lists 1922 as his birth year.

An apocryphal version of Twitchell's life appears in a monograph titled *In My Soul I Am Free* (1968), written by Brad Steiger. According to Steiger (a personal friend of Twitchell), Twitchell was raised by a half-Chickasaw Indian stepmother in a small town called China Point, only to discover later that he had been born out of wedlock in a Mississippi riverboat.[1] There are serious questions, however, about these claims. The names and locations in this account are largely fictitious. Note that Steiger's chief source of data was Twitchell himself.

There are other unsubstantiated claims in Steiger's "biography." His first spiritual instructor was Kay-Dee (actual name Katherine), who had learned ʼastral projection from her father. She had gone to Paris to study art and was later joined by Twitchell. It was there, writes Steiger, that both Kay-Dee and Paul met the living Eck Master, Sudar Singh. Together they followed the ʼguru back to India, where they studied for one year in Singh's ashram. Later Twitchell supposedly met a second Eck Master, Rebazar Tarzs, in the Himalaya mountains. Tarzs "commissioned" Twitchell to bring the teachings of Eckankar to the West.

In an independent research project titled "The Making of a Spiritual Movement: The Untold Story of Paul Twitchell and Eckankar" (1978), David Christopher Lane of California State University has provided a more trustworthy and accurate account of Eckankar and its founder. Lane contends that most of Steiger's account is false.

Twitchell was most likely born in Paducah, Kentucky, in 1908, to Jacob and Effie Twitchell. In Lane's account, Twitchell never visited Paris or India. but rather attended Western State Teacher's College at Western Kentucky University, wrote poetry as a hobby, and later joined the United States Navy. Sudar Singh is perhaps a fictitious name for a person who did have a degree of influence on Twitchell's life at some point. In August 1942, while still in the navy, he married Camille Ballowe in Providence, Rhode Island. After he resigned from the navy, he moved to New York City where he worked as a writer, editor, and later a correspondent for *Our Navy* magazine in Washington, D.C. It was in Washington that both Paul and his wife joined the Self Revelation Church of Absolute Monism (a group derived from SELF REALIZATION FELLOWSHIP). He became the editor of the movement's publication, *The Mystic Cross*.

The year 1955 proved to be a watershed in Twitchell's life, for he was asked to leave the Self Realization church, the stated reason being misconduct. Five years later he and his wife were separated and divorced. But the most significant change came when an Eastern guru, Kirpal Singh, came to the United States. According to Woodrow Nichols and David Alexander,

Kirpal Singh's teaching was derived from another amalgamated Eastern tradition—that of the Radha Soami Beas, led by Master Sawan Singh. When Sawan Singh died, he was succeeded by his disciple, Jagat Singh. At this point, Kirpal Singh left the Radha Soami ... and formed his own movement, which he called Ruhani Satsang, the "Divine Science of the Soul." This is crucial background knowledge for understanding the history of ECKANKAR. ... The teachings and practices of ECKANKAR are little more than rehashed Surat Shabd Yoga (the Yoga of Audible Sound Current) systematized by Sawan Singh, borrowed by Kirpal Singh, and popularized in America by Dr. Julian Johnson.[2]

In 1955 Kirpal Singh initiated Twitchell into *ruhani satsang*. For at least two years he attended the guru's ʼsatsangs, but he also availed himself of the teachings of other Eastern religions. In 1958 he came into contact with L. Ron ʼHubbard, the founder of Scientology, and even became a staff member, claiming to be a ʼclear.

Steiger's account of the years between 1955 and 1960 does not harmonize with Lane's findings. There is no mention of Kirpal Singh or L. Ron Hubbard. Rather, Twitchell is portrayed as being a romantic adventurer roaming the world in search of his fortune, while serving as a freelance writer of short stories, magazine articles, and so on.

By 1964 Twitchell had broken all ties with his spiritual mentors. That same year, he married Gail Atkinson. In one of his early books, *The Tiger's Fang* (1967), he even went so far as to change the name of Kirpal Singh to Rebazar Tarzs, a name that would find frequent mention in Twitchell's writings as his personal advisor during times when he was "out of the Body," and from whom, on October 22, 1965, he received the title of Eck Master.[3] In 1971, John-Roger Hinkins, a former member of Eckankar, formed a parallel yet separate movement called Movement of Spiritual Awareness (MSIA).

On September 17, 1971, Twitchell died of a heart attack in a hotel in Cincinnati, Ohio. Members of the movement reported his death as being his translation from the "Wheel of 84." The mantle of leadership passed on to the 972nd Eck Master, Darwin ʼGross. Gross married Twitchell's widow and led Eckankar for ten years. This marriage ended in divorce in 1978. After a tremendous struggle for power, Gross was removed in 1981 and replaced by Harold ʼKlemp, who became the newest living Eck Master. Gross subsequently began a new movement that he called Ancient Teachings of the Masters (ATOM). He is no longer considered an official Eck Master.

October 22, 1990, is the "most important date in spiritual history" for Eck leaders and members, for on that day the Temple of Eck was dedicated in Chanhassen, Minnesota. In 1999, the group's worldwide seminar made plans for a spiritual campus. In September 2000 they received approval for the construction of the campus that includes an outdoor Eck Celebrations of Life Chapel and a new Eckankar Spiritual Center.

ORGANIZATION

The Living Eck Master is the leader or *mahanta of Eckankar. There are Eck Centers is almost every state in the United States and in many countries (see the website listed below). Eck affiliates regularly conduct regional seminars.

TEACHINGS

Three basic principles make up the essence of Eckankar. First, the soul is an eternal substance with no beginning or ending. It lives independently of the material encumbrances of the body. Second, devotees to Eckankar will eventually inhabit the spiritual plane. Third, the soul is alleviated and exists only in the present. Astral projection is, therefore, the means through which the soul is able to exert its independence from the body.

As is the case with many *cults, members of Eckankar believe that they alone possess the one true path to God. Other religions only reflect fragments of divine truth, but all truth is expressed clearly in Eckankar.

The heart of Eckankar theology is that souls ascend the astral planes (god worlds of Eck) in pursuit of the kingdom of heaven where god (*Sugmad) resides. The chela (student) ascends through a series of twelve planes or realms. Each of these levels is identified by a peculiar sound heard on that plane alone. The first four planes are the lower, physical realms. The chela must clothe himself or herself in a number of bodies, or "sheaths," in order to travel through these layers. The traveler must seek out a guide to take him or her through the spiritual planes. These guides are the Eck Masters. For exam-

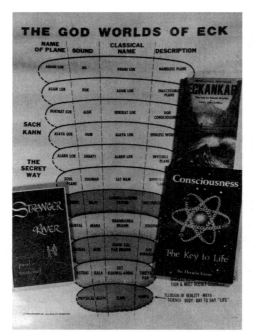

The God worlds of Eck, along with books written by Paul Twitchell and Sri Darwin Gross. Courtesy Jack M. Roper/CARIS

ple, Rebazar Tarzs was, according to Twitchell, his Eck Master.

It is in the physical planes that the chela is able to undergo *bilocation or astral projection. According to Twitchell, many of the great religious leaders were teachers of astral projection. He frequently alludes to Christ and other *Bible persons as having dabbled with soul travel. In his book *Eckankar, The Key to Secret Worlds*, Twitchell writes,

> According to the Gospels, Jesus said, "Come and follow me." But few knew what He was saying, that He wanted them to go with Him into the worlds beyond. They were not prepared to take the journey, so He turned away from them, leaving an eternal message: "I go to prepare a place for you."[4]

Others included in Twitchell's list of spiritual greats are Plato, Pythagoras, Lao Tan, *Buddha, *Hare Krishna, Homer, Dante, Shakespeare, and *Muhammad. Twitchell claimed to have been designated by Tarzs as the 971st Eck Master.

The remaining eight planes in Twitchell's scheme are spiritual. Before entering the first one, the chela dispenses with his or her physical body and resumes the journey in the *tuza, or soul. The highest plane, the region where God dwells, is called Sugmad. The greatest aspiration of the chela is to become one of the *silent ones who serve Sugmad by "running the universes, carrying out his laws and regulations."[5] Therefore, it is not the goal of the devotee to become god but to become god's "co-worker." This is the underlying meaning of the term Eckankar.

Eckankar guides teach many techniques to enable the chela to enter soul travel, such as meditation, chanting of *mantras, *hypnotism, *trancing, and *altered states of consciousness. The difficulties that most face in the pursuit of god-realization are the encumbrances of the physical body. The mind is a handicap because it engages the "five passions"—lust, anger, greed, materialism, and vanity. Giving in to the passions accrues "bad "karma," a debt that must be worked off through a series of reincarnations. Previous incarnations may have bad karma for which they have not been fully "atoned." Therefore, the spiritual traveler faces the possibility of endless cycles of rebirths if he or she is to achieve god-realization.

Genuine spiritual travelers are "supermen." Those who reject or do not engage in soul travel are like animals fighting against God. Those with abnormalities or physical deformities are unable to become spiritual travelers, according to Twitchell.

God

Eckankar has been considerably influenced by Hinduism, which is pantheistic in its concept of God. God is in all things, but one cannot know God. God, or Sugmad, resides on the highest astral plane and is a formless, all-embracing, impersonal, and infinite Ocean of love and mercy. All life flows from it and to it via the Eck current. The *knowledge* of God is not as important as the *fact* of God. God simply is. God is an impersonal "it" that is detached from the concerns of individuals. Perpetuation of "life" is the dominant concern of "it."

For Christianity, by contrast, God is not an impersonal monism but a God who possesses both transcendence and imminence in his relationship to creation. The personality of God exists in a divine Trinitarian (see Trinity) relationship of Father-Creator, Son-Redeemer, and Holy Spirit-Comforter/Sanctifier. No such concept exists for Eckankar.[6]

Jesus Christ

Christianity teaches that human beings may know God because Jesus Christ has brought them back to a right relationship with him through his death on the cross and subsequent resurrection. Once again, however, for Twitchell, God is not interested in the personal well-being of any one individual, and the idea of Jesus being the incarnate Son of God translates into an irrational absurdity. Jesus was merely one of the Eck Masters of yesteryear, not the crucified and risen God who "appeared in a body" (1 Tim. 3:16). Twitchell taught that Jesus was a son of Kal Nirajan (the "devil") and was a chela of two hundred years ago.

Sin

Sin in Eckankar is basically the Hindu concept of bad karma that prevents one from ascending the astral planes. Twitchell criticizes Christianity on the subject of sin: "All the doctrines of man born in sin, to be puri-fied by the appearance of a messiah who dies for man's sins, is that of a kalistic belief."[7]

Kal Nirajan is a lesser-evil deity who exists in the lower physical realm. If the analogy is possible, Kal Nirajan plays a similar role for the devotee as does Satan for the Christian. Satan's role is to keep human beings from repentance and faith in Christ. He does so through lies, deception, false teaching, and temptation. Kal Nirajan keeps the soul in ignorance so as to prevent it from leaving the physical realm.

Salvation

Salvation is essentially the realization of Sugmad through ascending the astral planes where "it" resides. Bad karma is punished by returning one to the physical realm of a lesser being such as a plant, rock, or mineral. The chela must work off bad karma in order to begin an ascent to a significant being (human) in the physical realm and then into the higher spiritual realms.

Christianity encountered a form of this thought early in its history in the Neo-Platonic cosmology of Plotinus. This thinking developed into gnosticism, which the Christian church denounced as being heretical, especially in its supposedly Christian forms advocated by Valentinus (A.D. 136–65) and Marcion (died ca. A.D. 160). The Greek gnostics and Neo-Platonic philosophers, long before Twitchell, had constructed an ontological schema in which the entire cosmos is situated on various levels, the physical material world being the lower and inferior, and the spiritual realm being the higher and superior. The god of the demiurge was the creator god. The supreme god was the divine being located in the ethereal, unknowable regions beyond the cosmos. Early Christian fathers—Tertullian, Irenaeus, and Hippolytus—wrote vehemently against gnosticism, denouncing it as heretical.

The terminology that Twitchell employed differs from the cryptic nomenclature of the ancient gnostics, but the concept is similar. Twitchell's designation for ultimate salvation was to escape from the wheel of 84.

In Eckankar beliefs, there are four basic ceremonies in the course of life, called "celebrations of life." These include a consecration ceremony (for children), the rite of passage (teens and younger adults), the wedding ceremony, and the memorial service.

CONCLUSION

Eckankar is truly an eclectic religion. It has borrowed heavily from gnosticism, mysticism, Hinduism, the occult, and a number of other sources. Sri Harold Klemp has and continues to author numerous books and articles. He presently travels throughout the world and lectures at seminars and gatherings. The general theme that Klemp emphasizes, which is a subheading at the Eckankar official website, is: "Religion of the light and sound of God." The website includes links to Eckankar websites in at least nineteen countries worldwide.

ADDITIONAL INFORMATION

Headquarters
Eckankar, PO Box 27300, Minneapolis, MN, 55427.

Website
www.ECKANKAR.org

Sacred Texts
These include *The Precepts of ECKANKAR* (n.d.); *The Shariyat-Ki-Sugmad* (San Diego: Illuminated Way Press, 1970–71); *Soul Travel: Illuminated Way* (Las Vegas: ECKANKAR ASOST, 1967); *The Tiger's Fang* (Las Vegas: ECKANKAR ASOST, 1967); *ECKANKAR, The Key To Secret Worlds* (San Diego: Illuminated Way, 1969); *The Far Country* (Menlo Park, Calif.: Illuminated Way, 1971); plus many more publications by Twitchell and Klemp.

Periodicals
A quarterly publication called *Mystic World* and a regular publication called *The Living ECK Master.*

Membership
Eckankar has 50,000 members in over 100 countries (from the official homepage) Membership is made through application, which can be expedited online. The public is recruited through a variety of techniques including lectures, magazine advertisements, books placed in libraries, and free literature. While attempting to draw people into membership, it claims to be a non-proselytizing religion.

Sri Darwin Gross, who for ten years was the Mahanta of ECKANKAR.
Courtesy Spiritual Counterfeit Project

Notes
[1] Brad Steiger, *In My Soul I Am Free* (San Diego: Illuminated Way, n.d.), 33–34.
[2] Woodrow Nichols and David Alexander, "Paul Twitchell and the Evolution of ECKANKAR," *SCP Journal* 3/1 (September 1979): 8.
[3] Ronald Enroth, *A Guide to Cults and New Religions* (Downers Grove, Ill.: InterVarsity Press, 1983), 61.
[4] Paul Twitchell, *ECKANKAR, The Key to Secret Worlds* (San Diego: Illuminated Way, 1969), 12.
[5] Ibid., 112.
[6] See Hinduism's concept of God compared to that of Christianity.
[7] Paul Twitchell, *The Shariyat-Ki-Sugmad* (San Diego: Illuminated Way, 1970–71), 1:72.

ELAN VITAL; EV; THE DIVINE LIGHT MISSION (DLM); DLM/EV

Elan Vital, as it is now called, is one of the numerous Eastern religions derived from HINDUISM that proliferated in the United States in the years following the turbulent 1960s.

HISTORY

The Divine Light Mission was founded in 1971 by ▸guru ▸Maharaj Ji, born in 1957 in Hardwar, India, as Balyogeshwar Param Hans Satgurudev Shri Sant J. Maharaj. Inheriting a substantial amount of wealth, Maharaj Ji was only thirteen years old when he received

the ▸revelation that he was to become the savior of humanity. Arriving in Los Angeles in 1971, he was greeted by only a few devoted followers. However, 1972 was a watershed in the career of this wonder child from India when he reached two thousand converts, called ▸premies, in Montrose, Colorado. From there on, the movement began to grow substantially. At the Houston Astrodome in the following year came the event called Millennium '73, attended by some twenty thousand devotees who worshiped Maharaj Ji as he sat on a throne suspended high above them.

The popularity did not last, not even with the guru's mother, Mata Ji. Besides mounting debts and accusations of smuggling, Maharaj Ji married an airline stewardess in 1974, pronouncing her a goddess. When Mata Ji arrived in Malibu to see her son, his new bride did not allow her to visit his estate. Enraged, Mata Ji publicly denounced her son as being a "drunken, carousing, meat eater." She then appointed Maharaj Ji's older brother, Shri Satyapal Ji, as the new ▸avatar of the movement, which she renamed the Spiritual Life Society.

Though his following continued for some months, gradually the numbers lessened because of the extravagant lifestyle that many observed the "incarnate" youthful god to be living in the United States. A passion for automobiles, real estate, and the best of foods convinced many that they had been duped. Followers in the United States dropped from an estimated fifty-two thousand to about seven thousand.

Maharaj Ji chose his most faithful followers to be his personal ▸mahatmas, later called ▸initiators. It was their assignment to recruit additional followers.

In 1979 the DLM moved its headquarters to Miami, but returned to Malibu in the early 1980s. Additionally, Maharaj Ji changed the name of the movement to Elan Vital. Maharaj has attempted to better adapt the DLM/EV to the ways of the West. He no longer wore traditional Indian clothing. In its place he wore Western-styled suits. Many of the cultural trappings have been eliminated to accommodate Western tastes.

ORGANIZATION

Many of the original followers of Maharaj Ji were hippies and were inimical to organizational infrastructure. Formality and rules were schewed. Life for a premie basically revolved around the spontaneous activities associated with "hanging around" an ashram, namely, participating in satsang services, meditating, and the like.

The organization today basically exists to promote the message of Maharaj Ji. Material sent around the world are provided by Visions International.

TEACHINGS

The theology of the Divine Light Mission/Elan Vital derives from Hinduism, as was the case with many of

In 1973 the Divine Light Mission held "Millennium '73" in the Astrodome, where Maharaj Ji announced that he was Savior of the world. He is seated on his throne.
Courtesy Spiritual Counterfeit Project

the personality cults of the late 1960s and early 1970s. Devotees "receive knowledge" directly from Maharaj Ji, who instructs them to reach into themselves in order to discover the "divine self" that every human being possesses. Devotees use a form of ʼyoga called ʼ*siddha* and sometimes use a T-shaped baragon to aid in meditation.

Followers must observe Maharaj Ji's five commandments: Refrain from postponing till tomorrow what can be done today; always meditate on the holy name; never doubt; never avoid attending ʼsatsang; always have faith in God.

As to the basic doctrines of DLM/EV, God is pantheistic (see ʼpantheism) and Hindu in orientation. God is an all-pervasive divine energy. Maharaj Ji is the ʼincarnation of the divine. The Holy Spirit is knowledge that flows from Maharaj Ji. Humanity is inherently divine. The key is to be given the proper knowledge to discover the "goodness within." One must relinquish one's rational capacities to allow the guru to provide knowledge that leads to ʼenlightenment.

Salvation is knowledge/enlightenment. Knowledge comes through the ʼfourfold path: ʼthird eye, ʼthird ear, ʼdivine nectar, and ʼprimordial vibration. When the premie has achieved these four states, he or she is ready to feel a sense of oneness and unity with the deity.

The Hindu scriptures serve as the basis for the DLM/EV's teaching canons, though the main source of authority for the movement is the teachings and revelations of guru Maharaj Ji.

Hinduism and CHRISTIANITY have little in common with each other. It cannot be expected, therefore, that the Divine Light Mission will have close parallels to Christianity. For Christianity, the fount of all wisdom and knowledge is Jesus Christ (Col. 2:3). For the DLM/EV, Maharaj Ji is the key personality. According to the ʼBible and the ancient creeds, the heart and soul of Christianity is in the concept of the incarnate ʼLogos, or "Word of God," crucified and resurrected on the third day in vicarious atonement for the sins of the world. The DLM/EV speaks of the incarnation of the Guru Maharaj Ji, who is himself the savior of the world.

As to the doctrine of humankind, Christianity teaches that human beings are conceived and born in sin and are, therefore, in a state of active rebellion against God. God, in mercy, love, and grace, extended an offer of forgiveness to the world by sending his Son to die for sin (see the second article of the Apostles' Creed, Appendix 1). DLM/EV, however, has no concept of sin or active rebellion against God and therefore, no concept of a separation between God and humankind. Salvation is not a matter of repentance from sin and faith in Jesus Christ; rather, it becomes a matter of personal enlightenment. One's salvation takes place when the divinity within is discovered. The guru serves to initiate this process and enable the premie to put aside that which impedes progress the most, that is, the mind. Total surrender of the mind to the guru results in an inner dynamic referred to by followers as being "blissed-out." This occurs during meditation and concentration on the fourfold path.

Finally, the five commandments of the Maharaj Ji are in reality a series of moralistic precepts. The Ten Commandments of JUDAISM and Christianity were summarized by Jesus Christ when he reduced the essence of the law to love—that is, love of God and love of neighbor (Matt. 22:36–40).

CONCLUSION

Maharaj Ji continues to speak and travel extensively. A quick look at the "enjoying life" website lists such trips.

ADDITIONAL INFORMATION_____

Headquarters
Elan Vital, P.O. Box 2220, Agoura Hills, CA, 91376

Websites
www.maharaji.org; www.elanvital.org; www.enjoyinglife.org (a website of Maharaji's followers); *www.ex-premie.org* (a website of Maharaji's ex-followers).

Sacred Text
"Knowledge," expounded by Maharaj Ji himself.

Publications
The title of the DLM/EV's periodical is *Divine Times*. There are numerous pamphlets and books available.

Membership
Maharaj Ji's messages have reached 80 countries and in 60 languages. He currently has only several hundred followers and approximately four thousand periodical supporters.

FAMILY, THE; THE CHILDREN OF GOD; THE FAMILY OF LOVE; COG/FOL; HEAVEN'S MAGIC

One of the most popular ᐅcults to come out of CHRISTI-ANITY in the final three decades of the twentieth century was The Children of God, as they were commonly known as in the 1970s. In 1972, their leader, Moses ᐅDavid, uttered the following:

> I'm Aquarius—I'm the Water Bearer—the Water Bearer of whom all the others were just types. I am Aquarius—this is my age! Jesus told me so, because I'm bringing the water of Life to this generation![1]

HISTORY

David, formerly David Brandt ᐅBerg (1919–1994), was born in Oakland, California. Berg was the son of Hjalmer Emmanuel David and Virginia Lee Brandt-Berg. His father was a pastor in the Disciples of Christ ᐅdenomination and subsequently an administrator at a Christian college in Santa Barbara, California. His mother was also involved directly in the ministry and served as a radio evangelist with the Christian and Missionary Alliance.

In 1941 Berg was discharged from the U.S. Army for medical reasons. He immediately joined the Christian and Missionary Alliance, where he met his wife, Jane, and was married in 1944. They had four children together.

During the next two decades, Berg worked diligently as an evangelist and preacher. In 1949 he was involved in the building of a church in Arizona. His radical ideas about sharing wealth met with much opposition, and he was eventually asked to leave. This proved to be a watershed in Berg's life, for it was at this time that he disenfranchised himself from all organized religion and insisted that true Christianity began by Christians breaking away from the church.

Berg aspired to become "educated" in theology and enrolled in a course titled "Soul Clinic Personal Witnessing Course," taught by popular radio evangelist Fred Jordan. After completing the three-month course, Berg went to work for Jordan, and the two combined their resources and shared in numerous projects together. He also worked as Jordan's publicity agent for the latter's radio and television ministries.

Another turning point came for Berg in 1968. In response to an invitation from his mother, he joined the Teen Challenge Coffeehouse in Huntington Beach,

California. It was here that he began to gain a following from disenfranchised hippies and antiestablishment "Jesus people," most of whom became his disciples in the later-formed Children of God (COG). He broke ties with his mother rather quickly, left the coffeehouse, and established "Teens-for-Christ." Though Berg was presumably one of the first to adopt the nomenclature "Jesus people," his theology proved to be too radical, even for many of the young people who, while seeking to move beyond the structures of organized religion, nevertheless had no intention of abandoning their churches.

With a core group of approximately seventy people who could be considered disciples, Berg had the options of "fight or flight." He chose the latter. Abandoning the Huntington Beach ministry, he led his faithful little band, now called "Revolutionaries for Jesus," into the wilderness and on into Tucson, Arizona. Here he met a church secretary named Maria, who subsequently joined the group. Shortly after this, she and Berg began a relationship together. Carole Hausmann and Gretchen Passantino relate the following:

> The first of the famous ᐅMo letters from Berg to his group was shortly published. Entitled Old Love, New Love, or The Old Church and the New Church, the pamphlet justified his relationship with Maria by using her as the symbol of the new church (COG), approved by God, and the old church (established Christianity), represented by his first wife, Jane. Berg did not entirely abandon Jane. According to the letter, she was still allowed to sleep with him every other night. The name "Children of God" was coined by a newsman in Camden, New Jersey, and was quickly picked up and used by Berg.[2]

This was just the beginning of the general decline in morality within the movement. Soon, more and more of the "Mo missives" were written espousing his hedonistic ethic. For example: "Flesh can satisfy flesh, but only Spirit can satisfy Spirit and we soon found that we had to give of *both* to satisfy *all* their needs according to His riches in glory."[3]

Berg and the COG began to move about extensively. At the 1967 World's Fair in Montreal, Berg changed his name to "Moses David." His followers still refer to him as "Father David." (Hereafter in this article we refer to Berg as "David"). He continued an association with Fred Jordan, but their relationship became strained, eventually resulting in David and the COG leaving Jordan's ranch.

Many transitions took place for the COG in the 1970s. Besieged by legal problems, including charges in 1973–1974 of tax evasion, kidnapping, assault, and immorality, the organization suffered a loss in credibility because of the failed prophecies against America.[4] David withdrew from the public eye and restricted his activities and influence to the COG. An investigation conducted by the attorney general of the state of New York resulted in a report in 1974 that listed the above charges in addition to the charge that the COG was using brainwashing techniques and was guilty of solicitation of funds in an illegal manner.

Continuing his "flight" pattern, David led many of his followers out of the United States and into Europe, where various and sundry colonies, numbering eight hundred by 1977, were formed under his leadership. Of the reportedly seventy-five hundred members in this year, only five hundred lived in America; the rest were among the colonies in over seventy countries.

In 1974 David introduced a form of evangelism called ▶*FFing*, short for "Flirty Fishing." He used the "fishers of men" (Matt. 5:19) passage in the Bible to justify sending female members of the cult out into the highways and byways to solicit sexual favors of men for money. This sanctified prostitution evidently paid off for the Family of Love, and David in particular reaped rewarding returns from this enterprise.

The Mo letters that flowed from David's pen by the hundreds were addressed to two different groups—the public at large and the COG. For example, when protest came from outside the group concerning flirty fishing, one Mo letter written in 1978 read as follows:

If they clamp down on *FFing* (Flirty Fishing) and call it *prostitution*, you may have to stop *that* too, or run the risk of small fines. . . . An "Escort Service" is one of the safest kinds of "Fronts" to have. Even a massage parlour is not that good a front—the police can bust in on you and catch you in the act! Whereas in an escort service, normally you go home with the man or to his hotel and he foots the bill.[5]

In 1978, the COG was formally dissolved, and a new organization, The Family of Love (soon shortened to The Family), was formed. A hierarchical structure maintained control in the group. At the top was the ▶Royal Family, headed by David himself. Below this were the leaders of the various colonies. At the lowest

level of the infrastructure were the ▶babes. This arrangement was sufficient for several years, but in 1981 it was abolished and the group was reorganized in such a way as to leave David in total command. At this time many members left. David fired many of the leaders, including members of his own family—his daughter, alias Queen Debbie, and son-in-law John Treadwell.

David dropped out of sight in 1980, relinquishing control over the group to his Royal Family. As early as 1976 he published a Mo letter titled "Death in Your Arms." He seemed to be anticipating his own death: "So I am never going to leave you nor forsake you either, if I can help it, even if I have to haunt you afterwards." He continued to exercise control over the group from behind the scenes and through his writings.

In 1984 David's disenfranchised daughter, Deborah Davis, published through Zondervan an exposé titled *The Children of God: The Inside Story*. The book brought to light many of the actual teachings and practices of the group that had previously not been known. Since then, other former members have related their experiences.

By 1988, the group had become highly organized, especially with regards to the education of its children. This became known as the Family School System.

Brazil became a safe haven for the group during the 1990s. Many members who found themselves unwelcome in other countries were readily received in South America. Dalva Lynch and Paul Carden relate the following concerning the South American connection:

Though the AIDS epidemic caused the cult to cut back on some of its extreme sexual practices elsewhere in the world, in Brazil things continued unabated. One example would be the famous GAFMs (Greater Area Family Meetings), which were nothing more than gigantic bacchanals, with three days of wine, group sex, erotic dances, stripteases, and every sort of debauchery, in which all COG disciples of all the greater area homes participated.

These orgies were prohibited in all other countries of the world around 1983, but in Brazil the practice was only recently abolished. Because of the AIDS epidemic, orgies are now held only in the privacy of one's home, but the videos of the GAFMs remain as a reminder of the "good times." In September, 1993, in Buenos Aires, the police raided five Family Homes in Argentina. 137 children were removed from these homes and 21 adults were imprisoned for over three months while the children were examined to see whether or not they had been abused. This resulted in worldwide media attention given to the Family and other cults as well, following the Waco debacle. Other raids during the early 1990's included Melbourne and Sydney, Australia; Lyon, France; and Barcelona, Spain.

Rio de Janeiro was the center for the cult's lucrative audio and video cassette recording and duplicating operation in Brazil. Tapes destined for Brazil and the rest of South America are produced in a music studio under the direction of Billy Blanco, Jr., the son of a famous Brazilian musician (who is himself well known, having even worked with Yoko Ono). The tapes were duplicated by professional studios like RCA and GEL and then sold as though they were legal, even though the cult pays no taxes and gives the materials fictitious numbering. The cult is currently enjoying great success in selling its literature, videos, and audio tapes to unsuspecting Christian churches and schools—at exorbitant prices—in many parts of Brazil.[6]

The South American connection was indeed an intricate one. Lavish cult mansions are scattered throughout several countries. David's letters continued to be published. The literature is translated into Spanish and Portuguese for the many members in this region.

The Philippines offered the Family the greatest receptivity of all the countries of the world. Several letters known as "The Jumbo Series" described the intricacies of the COG's operations there. Lynch and Carden report how the COG were so successful in that country.

One of the cult's most successful subversive operations is described in several letters known as "The Jumbo Series." Armed with music and inspirational tapes, very well-dressed young women from the group infiltrated military barracks and offices, presenting themselves to the secretaries and asking to speak with colonels and generals, saying: "Tell him that two pretty young girls want to talk to him about love." Not surprisingly, most of the time they were welcomed into the most closed of offices. When the official in question was known to be moral (and the girls would be careful to inquire about this beforehand), the approach was more circumspect.

In just a few months, the COG had thoroughly infiltrated the military, using their anti-Communist literature, their sexual favors, and their music to win the highest officials in the nation. Even the Philippine army's anthem, "We Give Our Lives," is said to be written by COG disciples! During the entire infiltration operation, Moses David and his wife, Maria, directed the work and counseled their teams through letters and phone calls, and nothing was done without their express permission.

The demise of the Marcos regime resulted in rapid spread of the COG's influence. This is attributable to the aid and protection given by the army. "The layer of military protection is so great that a round-the-clock military armed guard has been provided at "Jumbo"—the cult's mansion in Manila.[7]

In a recent study, Dr. Charlotte Hardman reported that the Family has successfully passed its teachings to the next generation. She writes, "The Family children have wholeheartedly adopted the meaning system of their parents and feel empowered thereby."[8]

In 1992, police and social workers in Melbourne and Sydney, Australia, raided six Family homes and brought 142 children into custody. The concern was whether children were being abused. After a week of intense examination, the children were released back to the homes, the conclusion being that there was no evidence to substantiate the accusations. In 1999, a generous settlement was reached in favor of the Family children. Other such raids took place in Barcelona, Spain, and in Lyon, France. The charges in those places were also dropped.

In 1994, the Family was struck by the momentous death of their leader. Moses David died at the age of 75, but not without preparing his successor, Maria. As the group's new prophet, she married Peter Amsterdam. The Family adopted a "Love Charter" in 1995. All members received this publication, which delineated the rights, responsibilities, and beliefs of the Family. The Charter became a working document for Family members worldwide.

ORGANIZATION

Before 1981, the COG was under a single overarching organizational structure. David decided to reorganize in order to generate more enthusiasm and involvement amongst the members. He called his new initiative a "fellowship revolution." The idea was to bring local homes together for area fellowship meetings. David, however, remained the sole leader of the movement. In the 1980s local homes comprising seven members were brought together to form "combos," which were two homes now made one with at least ten members. Some homes grew substantially, reaching as many as forty-member households. They practiced home-schooling, which eventually led to a highly organized family school system. The above-mentioned Love Charter introduced organizational changes to what they are today in The Family. The charter restricts houses to a maximum of thirty-five members.

TEACHINGS

In the first edition of this volume, the authors presented David's basic doctrines and theology. These will not be revisited here. The Family today has rewritten their statement of faith. They presently believe the basic fundamental doctrines that fall within the pale of ▶Protestant, ▶Pentecostal, and ▶fundamentalist beliefs. During his lifetime, David introduced numerous other ideas not characteristic of the simplified anti-structural Jesus people movements of the 1960s and 1970s. He had a lifelong involvement in the ▶occult and believed he could communicate with spirits of the dead. He was a follower of Jean ▶Dixon and embraced the doctrine of ▶reincarnation.

Still basic to The Family's teaching, as was the case in the formative years under David's leadership, was a radical revolutionary imperative against the so-called establishment. Any structure or order to the society and the church is the work of the ▶devil. Various catchwords, such as ▶systemites," "revolution," and "Jesus revolution" abounded in the Mo letters.

Anti-Semitism also loomed large within the doctrines of The Family. David visited Israel in 1970. After this time, he viciously attacked Jews in his Mo letters:

> So I asked the Lord to really curse those God-damned Jews and to do something to really teach them a lesson. . . . May God damn the God-damned Jews! My God, I think if I could get over there and had a gun I think I'd shoot 'em myself! My Lord, help us to help them somehow, Lord in Jesus' name! My Lord help us! . . . May God damn every Israeli! They are all robbers!—All terrorists! And all thieves! All oppressors! They're all guilty! There's no such thing as an innocent Israeli civilian![9]

Sexual immorality had abounded within The Family in the 1970s and 1980s, and sexual language permeated the Mo letters during these years. In addition to *FFing,* David's followers condoned all manner of perversions.

> We have a sexy God and a sexy religion with a very sexy leader with an extremely sexy young following! So if you don't like sex, you'd better get out while you can still save your bra! Salvation sets us free from the curse of clothing and the shame of nakedness![10]

In order to induce sexual behavior, David encouraged members to drink wine. He even suggested that Jesus Christ had sexual intercourse on a number of occasions with prostitutes. That Christ may have had

venereal disease was also a possibility for David. While David himself advocated sexual activity with minors, claiming that the Bible offered no injunctions against such a practice, present-day followers have repudiated this and offer it as grounds for excommunication from the Family. The current website reflects the fact that present members of The Family still strongly support David's rationale, even after his death, but they claim that today the group needs now to explore "other forms of outreach"! In 1995 a statement proclaimed that all sex with outsiders is officially banned. They began to use the phrase "▶DFing" instead. The Family does advocate open sex outside of marriage between consenting adult members of the group. Open sex coupled with fundamentalist beliefs is not without precedent in the history of cults and religions.

Prophecy still plays a large role in The Family. Members still evoke the name of "Father David" and earnestly await his predictions to come true.

The Family still believes in the practice of communal living, is still antistructural and anti-Roman Catholic, and follows a strong ▶dispensationalist ▶eschatology.

CONCLUSION

The Family's influence has dwindled significantly in the United States in the last decade. The group, however, does continue to reach out to those who are yearning for a legitimacy outside standard cultural norms. Now that there are second-generation members of The Family, there have been problems with incorporating the children in the group. This is done through involving them in leadership. Also, the new generation has brought with it a tendency for the Family to institutionalize and organize in ways that David would have never advocated in the former years.

ADDITIONAL INFORMATION_____

Headquarters
The world headquarters is in Zurich, Switzerland. The U.S. base is Chicago.

Website
www.thefamily.org

Sacred Texts
The Bible; the letters of Moses David. Also, the *Mama Letters* authored by Maria are considered authoritative.

Publications
Mo letters; Power Links (available through email upon request (see website); *Reader's Corner* (website).

Statistics

Total membership worldwide is estimated to be between twelve and thirteen thousand with 1,400 centers or communities in 100 countries.

Notes

[1] "A Psalm of David" (n.d.).

[2] Walter Martin, *The New Cults* (Ventura, CA: Regal, 1980), 146.

[3] "The Family of Love" (n.d.).

[4] In November 1973, David prophesied that the comet Kohoutek would arrive, bringing judgment on America for its sins and wickedness.

[5] "Going Underground" (n.d.).

[6] Dalva Lynch and Paul Carden, "Inside the Heavenly Elite: The Children of God Today," *Christian Research Journal* (Summer 1990), 19.

[7] Ibid., 20.

[8] Susan J. Palmer and Charlotte E. Hardman, *Children in New Religions* (Camden, NJ: Rutgers Univ. Press, 1999).

[9] "A Prayer for the Poor" (March 1978).

[10] "Come on Ma!—Burn Your Bra!" (December 1973).

FIVE PERCENTERS; GODS AND EARTHS

Five-Percenters are a small yet somewhat popular sect of the NATION OF ISLAM.

HISTORY

A man by the name of ClarenceX (d. 1969) began to teach that the Black Man was the god race of the universe and women are the earths of the universe. This splinter group claims that its origins were in Mecca. His teaching, considered much too radical, resulted in his suspension from the Nation of Islam. He then went on to found the Five Percent Nation of Islam in 1964. Followers called him Father Allah. He died in 1969, the causes of which were considered questionable.

TEACHINGS

The basic belief that ClarenceX taught his followers was that the black race is superior and was the original race. Eighty-five percent of the world's peoples are ignorant of divinity; 10 percent are the power-hungered corrupted rulers over the 85 percent, but they purposely hide the truth. The remaining 5 percent are the true and devoted followers of Allah; they know and live the truth. These teachings are called Supreme Mathematics.

The basic tenets of Five Percenters are as follows:

- Black people are the original people of this planet.
- Black people are the fathers and mothers of civilization.
- The science of Supreme Mathematics is the key to understanding humanity's relationship to the universe.
- Islam is a natural way of life, not a religion.
- Education should be fashioned to enable us to be self-sufficient as a people.
- Each one should teach one according to their knowledge.
- The black man is god and his proper name is ALLAH: Arm, Leg, Leg, Arm, Head.
- Our children are our link to the future and they must be nurtured, respected, loved, protected, and educated.
- The unified black family is the vital building block of the nation.[1]

CONCLUSION

Five Percenters' beliefs and propaganda are spread through various pop-culture modicums, including rap music. Popular groups include King Sun, The Supreme Team, Lakim Shabazz, Rakim Allah, Brand Nubian, and The Poor Righteous Teachers.[2]

ADDITIONAL INFORMATION

Notes

[1] http://www.apologeticsindex.org/f14.html

[2] http://www.answering-islam.org/ReachOut/emergence.html

FORUM; LANDMARK FORUM; LANDMARK EDUCATION; LEC; (FORMERLY – EST)

The NEW AGE MOVEMENT is not a specific organization but a general ideology that is manifest in various particular groups, institutions, and actual organizations.

An important aspect of the New Age is the human potential movement. The Forum is an organization characterized as New Age and specifically as human potential. Originally named after its founder Werner Erhard, it was formerly called EST, an acronym for Erhard Seminars Training. The name designation EST/Forum is used for most of the references to the group in this article.

HISTORY

The Forum began in 1971 by John Paul Rosenberg, alias Werner Erhard (b. 1935). The name change from Rosenberg to Erhard came in 1960 after he abandoned his wife and four children and moved from Philadelphia to St. Louis. He worked in various sales jobs, including automobiles, magazines, and encyclopedias. Erhard frequently involved himself with various groups such as SCIENTOLOGY and ZEN BUDDHISM, and at one point he was even a lecturer and instructor in mind dynamics.

Erhard's sales and managerial skills together with his ability to piece together fragments of religion, philosophy, and psychology combined to formulate the basics of EST/Forum. The group began with thirty-two people in attendance. Just eight years later, over 160,000 persons had enrolled in his courses, with over three hundred receiving the training at a time. In 1985, Erhard decided to abandon the name EST and renamed the organization "The Forum." The shift that Erhard was aiming at was to have *goal-oriented* training rather than *reprogramming* traditional ways of thinking, which had been the focus of EST.

In 1988, Erhard was awarded the Mahatma Gandhi Humanitarian Award. In 1991, followers and employees of Erhard purchased the organization and formed the new company called Landmark Educational Corporation (LEC). Erhard's brother, Harry Rosenberg, became CEO of the new company. He claimed that Landmark was begun in the midst of "chaos and uncertainty." The media had been in relentless pursuit of Erhard, but he was no longer part of the new organization. The organization pressed forward with the belief that they had undergone a complete paradigm shift. The new thinking, again, turned more toward human potential rather than human failings that needed radical "reprogramming."

Between 1991 and 1997, growth in The Forum/LEC was tremendous, increasing from 32,000 to 65,000. By 1997, revenues in the organization increased to nearly $50 million. Immediately, LEC decided on a new strategic plan, setting the year 2020 as the next date set to accomplish its future goals. The organization became sensitive to and dependent on defending itself against the negative public image that had been directed against it by the media, religious groups, and numerous publications. But more than a defensive posture, the organization presses toward making a positive difference in the world with its teachings. LEC thinks along a global and world-changing level. Erhard left the United States in 1991 and presently has no control over the organization. He continued to lecture widely.

TEACHINGS

In 1971, while driving across the Golden Gate Bridge, Erhard claimed to have received what he called "permanent enlightenment," an experience that he described as realizing "What is, is, and what isn't, isn't." Erhard asserted that "in one moment I knew nothing and came to knowing everything." This statement forms one of the basic underlying assumptions of EST/Forum, namely, that the way in which rational persons view the world is in exact opposition to the way the world really is. To be rational is to be illusory. Meaning cannot be imposed on the individual from outside the person. Rational thought must be halted, and in its place is substituted the "ever-present now." Erhard advances a monistic/solipsistic worldview in which each individual's mind determines and shapes reality. Therefore, there are no objective criteria for determining absolute truth. "Truth believed is a lie. If you go around telling the truth, you are lying."

To attain the point where one accepts this highly irrational and subjective worldview, EST/Forum offered sixty hours of intense seminar training. A person in the early days paid as much as $300 for a weekend of instruction, the goal of which was to enable the initiates to "get it." What "it" was was never determined or defined precisely. The training process, however, can be described.

As the seminar began, 250 to 300 people assembled together in a large room, usually in a hotel or motel. Immediately, house rules were established that all had to observe throughout the training session: no talking unless the trainer granted permission; no use of substances such as alcohol or cigarettes; no eating; no exiting to use the restrooms; no writing and/or note taking.

Any and all belief systems that a candidate had were subjected to intense ridicule.[1] The object was to subdue and destroy belief systems of all kinds because they stood in the way of the ultimate goal—"getting it." One author describes a particularly embarrassing scene:

> Mark Brewer reports one leader as saying to a group of trainees that they were "hopeless. They did not know what they were doing, did not know how to experience life, were struggling, desperate, confused. They were ASSHOLES!" In fact they were continually referred to as "assholes" throughout the

training. . . . Another great "revelation" of est is that our minds are like machines. One leader declared, "You're a machine. . . . A machine!" So for $300 you not only get to be called an "asshole," but a "mechanical asshole."[2]

After intense and repeated haranguing, shouting, and denial, coupled with physical deprivation, trainees began to lose all sense of resistance, became more pliable, and were easily manipulated. They were then informed that they were free to "create their own space." That is, the candidates became introspective and gave free vent to their inner emotions and feelings. At this point in the training, mass hysteria erupted. Crying, laughing, screaming—all took place at once.

The trainees were then ready to accept the fact that they were perfect as they were. If a person realized this, then descriptively speaking he or she "got it." To reach outside the self and cling to meaning or absolutes that transcend personal experience was to fail to "get it."

The world is like a giant game, trainees were told. We as humans are really like gods, because we know that the world is an illusion, while those who have not become EST/Forum graduates still believe that illusions are reality. The following is a conversation recorded in Walter Martin's *The New Cults* between a female trainee and a trainer who was attempting to convince her that the only reality in the universe was that which resides in the inner self. He insisted that she enjoys having her apartment robbed:

Trainer: Do you take responsibility for not having created friends who might have stayed in the apartment most of the time?
Trainee: Maybe, but—
Trainer: Whose idea is it that because you come home and find things missing from your apartment that you were robbed?
Trainee: My idea!
Trainer: Precisely.
Trainee: Damn it! [says Barbara irritably.] Precisely what?
Trainer: Precisely you created the idea that you were robbed.
Trainee: But I didn't cause the robbery.
Trainer: There was no robbery unless you created it. If your stereo was stolen, you did it.
Trainee: You're out of your mind!
Trainer: That's what est is all about. . . . GET OUT OF YOUR MIND, BARBARA! YOU'RE THINKING IN CLICHES AND LETTING OTHER PEOPLE DICTATE REALITY when you actually create it yourself.[3]

As alluded to above, in the latter stages of the Forum and after the formation of the LEC, the focus in the organization shifted away from reprogramming to goal-oriented training. Nevertheless, the basic underlying foundation of human potential still provides the foundation around which LEC defines itself. The concept of "getting it" is still LEC's main goal. Shifting to the potential one can achieve, LEC claims that the training one receives can deepen personal happiness, help one to become unloosed from the shackles and limitations of the past, aid one in creative problem solving, provide a means to clarify personal values, and tap into one's power and potential.

LEC has updated its vocabulary and in fact calls its new technology a "new language." Key terms and concepts in LEC are as follows:

Distinction: that which "opens a new way of relating to reality because reality is experienced differently for the person realizing the distinction."[4] A "distinction is the difference between a *fact* defined as actual things or events that have taken place, and an *interpretation*, or the story "about what happened." Breakdowns in communications come when "interpretations" of an event are put forth, not merely by the telling of the "facts" of the event. According to LEC, persons become locked in to their own interpretations, and it is therefore difficult to break out of them to other interpretations.

Winning formulas: cognitive constructs people form as habits to enable them to survive and cope with others and to appear confident and composed. But they present barriers to possible breakthroughs to new and higher levels of human potential.

Curriculum for Living: LEC's basic plan and educational agenda. It comes under four different programs.

The Landmark Forum—A three and one-half day course that is foundational in nature. A fundamental goal of this first phase is to help people understand their potential and to see that their past can be the greatest barrier to moving on.
The Landmark Forum in Action—Ten classes that develop the basic concepts learned in step 1.
The Landmark Advanced Course—A four and one-half day course designed to begin to help the student to abandon the strictures of the past and to start to creatively break forth to new definitions of the self based on one's future.
The Landmark Self-Expression and Leadership Program—meeting on three separate Saturdays and on twelve evenings. In this session, the new

trainee seeks the support of others who will reinforce their new roles rather than cast them back to the former paradigms from which they have broken free.

Graduate: When a person completes the four programs, he or she has graduated.

There is little to compare between CHRISTIANITY and the potpourri of ideas that constituted the original teachings of EST/Forum under Erhard's leadership. Many of the leaders claim that the organization is not even a religion. However, the basic claims made about human nature and human potential definitely cross the boundaries of what religious traditions have to say about the same issues.

- LEC continues to teach that human nature is essentially benign, hence the supposition that untapped potential is the goal of human strivings. Christianity teaches that human beings are conceived and born in sin (Ps. 51:5) and are therefore sinful by nature and that their intellect and reason are fallen (1 Cor. 2:14).
- Founded in the 1970s, a time characterized as the "me decade," Erhard capitalized on this seemingly intense focus on the self. Christianity's focus is on the communal and the sacramental life (Acts 2:41–44) and the importance of living as servants in order to love and benefit others and Jesus Christ (Mark 10:45; Luke 9:23; 1 Cor. 8).
- Erhard claimed that truth is discoverable through breaking out of old paradigms; LEC still teaches this. Christianity teaches that the old paradigm is the sin nature we are born with and we need a new nature that comes through a spiritual rebirth (John 3:1–16).
- EST/LEC attempts to bring an individual to a place where he or she is released from the strictures of the past. Traditional Christianity affirms the ultimate importance of our link with the past. The second article of the Apostles' and Nicene creeds reaffirms this by pointing to the reality of the historical events and deeds in the person and work of Jesus (*see* creeds, Appendix 1).
- Furthermore, while Erhard taught that humanity must learn to accept its perfection in order to "get it," Christianity maintains that humanity is sinful by nature and can only be made perfect in Jesus Christ.
- Salvation is "getting it." "It," as stated above, has not been defined in EST/Forum, but "it" may be achieved presently, if sought after. Salvation for

the Christian comes, not from membership in a training seminar but through membership in the body of Christ, the holy Catholic Church (Apostles' Creed). Getting "it" comes through repentance, faith, baptism, and grace—all summed up in the finished work of Jesus Christ.

Erhard himself once said, "How do I know that I'm not the reincarnation of Jesus Christ?" Jesus said that there would be many false prophets (bearing false messages) and many false Christs in the world (Mark 13).

There have been intense criticisms leveled against Erhard and LEC through the years. These include:

- Is EST a form of brainwashing? Are followers "Werner-worshipping robot esties?"[5] The term "brainwashing" has fallen into disuse in cult studies. It is in fact unfair to label adherents to the various programs in this manner. Trainees are permitted to speak and freely come or go of their own choosing.
- EST is characterized by authoritarian dogmatism. Under Erhard and his trainers, this charge was far more true than it is now. Again, the focus is not reprogramming as it had been through 1985, but it now works at achieving new goals.
- EST is dangerous. Certain people who are highly unstable can be severely harmed by undergoing this training. While there have been lawsuits and certainly the potential for danger exists, as it does in any organization that deals with the treatment of people, LEC insists that there are special efforts made to screen highly unstable people and not allow potential risks into the programs.
- EST was founded by a salesman, not a qualified scholar. His motivation was to make money. Erhard did in fact lack a background that would qualify him in being an expert in psychology. He did make a sizable amount of money, and the tuition for the various courses at LEC today are expensive. The official website contains an updated and detailed report on the current costs of all its courses.
- Allegations surrounding Erhard's personal life prove that EST was a fraudulent organization. Erhard encountered problems with the IRS, and sexual allegations were made against him. Appearing on television's *60 Minutes*, his own daughters claimed that he was an abusive father. Erhard, however, was cleared of all tax and abuse charges both in court and in the media.

CONCLUSION

Under the new directives of LEC, the idea of human potential continues. EST/Forum/LEC has been an alternate religious venture for those seeking to fulfill the New Age quest for the enhancement of self-image.

ADDITIONAL INFORMATION

Headquarters
Landmark Educational Corporation; 353 Sacramento St. Suite 200, San Francisco, CA, 94111. There are 43 sites worldwide and they are listed on the LEC website.

Official Website
www.landmarkeducation.com

Sacred texts
none

Total Membership
More than 700,000 participants as EST/The Forum and as many as 400,000 as LEC.

Notes
[1] Martin and Diedre Bobgan, *The Psychological Way/The Spiritual Way* (Minneapolis: Bethany, 1978), 100.
[2] Ibid., 101.
[3] Walter Martin, *The New Cults* (Ventura, CA.: Regal, 1980), 117–18.
[4] Wruck, Karen Hopper, and Mikelle Fisher Eastley, "Lanmark Education Corporation: Selling a Paradigm Shift," *Harvard Business School Paper 9-898-081* (Harvard Business School Pub., 1997), 8.
[5] Luke Rhinehart, *The Book of EST.* (New York: Holt, Rhinehart and Winston, 1976), 259.

FOUNDATION OF HUMAN UNDERSTANDING (FHU)

Ruben Obermeister, today known as Roy Masters (b. 1928), is the founder of the Foundation of Human Understanding. He claims to have hated his mother, has feelings of anger toward his father, and propounds that most social ills are instilled in children by the corrupting influences of parents. His followers have been at times referred to as "Roybots."

Of Masters's thinking, Lauren Kessler writes:

- "Women are the embodiment of evil and temptation."
- "There are no men in America. They're all wimps who've been killed by their mothers."
- "Less and less sex makes a person more of a human being."
- "Education is setting up children for a socialist society."
- "The more knowledge you have, the more problems you have."
- "The worst type of human being is the liberal. He sympathizes with the lowest of human nature."
- "Intellectuals are the most dangerous people, and most intellectuals are homosexuals."
- "I have the spirit on my side and you can't do me wrong without being tormented."
- "I could solve the world's problems in one week if I could get on TV."[1]

HISTORY

Roy Masters was born in London, the son of a Jewish diamond cutter. He learned the trade at his uncle's factory in England, and as a teenager began to develop an interest in the occult, specifically hypnotism. He went to South Africa to continue as an apprentice in the diamond industry. On the side, he learned hypnotic skills and techniques, which were greatly augmented through study with African witch doctors.

Many leaders of religions and teachers of philosophy came to the United States for the prime purpose of promulgation and proselytization. Apparently, Masters made his first trip to the United States in 1949 to lecture on diamonds. According to Todd Ehrenborg and Gretchen Passantino, Masters discovered that lecturing on hypnosis "became more personally rewarding in the fifties [1950s] in the wake of the Bridey Morphy hypnosis case."[2]

Masters founded the Institute for Hypnosis, but his work was interrupted when the American Medical Association charged that he had practiced medicine without a license; he was convicted and imprisoned for thirty days.

In 1961 Masters established the Foundation of Human Understanding (FHU) in Los Angeles. He also began to broadcast a live radio call-in show, which today is aired on stations across the country and the world.

In the late 1970s the FHU purchased a 373-acre boys' ranch in Selma, Oregon, and moved its headquarters from Los Angeles into a former Seventh-day Adventist church in Grants Pass, just twenty miles from Selma. Originally intended as a retreat for troubled teens, Masters' mecca, known as Tall Timber Ranch, has become a haven for all who want to make the pilgrimage.

Masters is a controversial radio personality, broadcasting out of Los Angeles, but the controversy is greatest in Grants Pass. His opponents consider him a ♦cult leader and in the 1980s feared that Grants Pass would become another Rajneeshpuram.[3] Masters may have many opponents, but he certainly has many advocates. His radio audience has been estimated to be at least three million. Sales of tapes, books, and records number in the thousands each year. He publishes a monthly magazine called *The Iconoclast*, which in the early 1980s had a circulation of over six thousand. Masters's book *How Your Mind Can Keep You Well* (1968) contains his basic meditation techniques; it is the most widely read of his books and is still being advertised on radio stations into the new century.

People from all walks of life come to Grants Pass for a sizeable fee (over $1,000.00) to sit in the gazebo and listen to Masters.[4] Some local residents continue to argue vehemently that the organization's activities do not qualify it as a religious nonprofit organization. In 1987, however, Masters won a lawsuit against the IRS when the latter refused to recognize the Foundation as a bona-fide religious organization.

ORGANIZATION

The Foundation declares itself a church. No one is ordained, however. Masters is the executive of the organization and people travel to Grants Pass, listen to the radio broadcasts, order tapes, attend Masters's lectures, and send in donations for the ongoing work of the FHU.

TEACHINGS

Religion plays an important role in the basic belief system of the Foundation and is mixed in with philosophy and psychology. The key ingredient in Masters' menu is his belief in the power of meditation. Passantino and Ehrenborg note:

> Rather than starting with a well-defined theology and moving to resulting religious practices, the Foundation has seemingly started with religious practices (meditation methods) and gradually evolved an inconsistent theology from the meditation.[5]

But Masters writes:

> Through meditation, you will begin to see that all of your troubles come from (1) doubting the truth, (2) being ambitious and (3) living out of the emotional upset which results from and perpetuates the

first two mistakes. Your futile attempts to deal with symptoms and to compensate for your guilt have only made matters worse.[6]

What follows in *How Your Mind Can Keep You Well* is an extended discourse on the power of meditation to free one's mind of the deep wounds incurred from past experiences. He describes a self-hypnosis technique, designed to help students to see their own mind's eye and be aware of their own thought patterns. The meditation exercise, intended to make the mind well, is described in a series of three steps: (1) "the preparation"—a primer to the reader on some preliminaries to the actual meditation process; (2) "the meditation exercise"—a descriptive section that delineates a meditation technique using the hand and fingers and the "mind's eye" to enable one to "dissolve unnecessary, unwanted thoughts simply by becoming aware of the present moment";[7] (3) principles that protect the meditative state—this is the prescriptive stage, where heightened awareness yields to one the ability to see and rid oneself of "silly ego-needs." This result-oriented stage brings out the virtues that one possesses, such as love, patience, faith, spontaneity, courage. When people are able to reach beyond themselves, they are able to cope with the inadequacies of others.

> Do not say, "Stupid idiot!" when you see someone who is acting foolish. Let your attitude say, "Here, let me help you." Observe their faults, but do not emotionally puff up or resent them for this. Make allowances right on the spot.[8]

Many such aphorisms dot the pages of *How Your Mind Can Keep You Well*. What stands out in contradistinction to CHRISTIANITY in Masters' meditation methods, however, is the focus on one's own well-being. In the Judeo-Christian tradition, the virtues are directed away from the self toward God and one's neighbor (Matt. 22:37–40).

One also notices that the mediator seeks ♦enlightenment and heightened awareness from within the subjective psyche. Christianity clearly teaches that human beings are not self-actualized but must look to God for identity, self-worth, and salvation; "I can do everything through him who gives me strength" (Phil. 4:13).

Meditation techniques are an important phase of Masters' thought, but he also discusses religion in general, and Christianity in particular, frequently on his radio program and in his literature. What are Masters' concepts of Christianity and religion? He professes to be a Christian (see below). His magazine, *The Iconoclast*, articulated its purpose in the following statement:

The primary purpose of this magazine is disclosed in its definition. "Iconoclast" ... comes from the Greek word "icon" meaning "image." "Iconoclast" means: 1) one who destroys religious images or opposes their veneration; 2) one who attacks established beliefs or institutions.[9]

On close examination, Masters does indeed attack established beliefs or institutions.

God

Masters refers to God as being an impersonal reality or principle. God is also "the Ultimate Stillness."[10] Part of the difficulty in ascertaining precisely Masters' ideas of God are the absence of any systematic statements about God and the abundance of "God-talk" in the midst of psychological and existential concepts. God seems to be at once both personal and impersonal.

For traditional Christianity, the God who has revealed himself through the prophets in the Old Testament and through Jesus Christ in the New Testament is an unequivocally personal God. Eastern conceptualizations of God, as advanced, for example, in HINDUISM, suggest a God who is highly impersonal—a concept or idea that proceeds from the mind. Philosophically, this reflects an existentialist worldview. Masters appears to be strongly influenced by an eclectic blend of Eastern religion, ▶existentialism, and psychology, but again, it is difficult to declare with any certainty the precise reference to the terminology he employs.

Jesus Christ

The Foundation of Human Understanding offers nothing in the way of a doctrine of ▶Christology. Masters, however, often speaks of Jesus. When he does mention Jesus on the radio or in his writings, Masters seems to imply that Jesus was a philosopher. However, in a letter to *Christian Research Journal*'s Fall 1991 exposé, entitled "Old Lies and Half-Truths," Masters responded by stating:

> For the record: I believe that Jesus Christ is the Son of God, born of the virgin Mary, that his physical life on earth provided the perfect guide for human behavior, that he gave his life as the payment for the sins of mankind, and that salvation comes through belief in him and acceptance of his gift of eternal life.
>
> I believe in Christ, and in the literal interpretation of the Bible as the inspired Word of God.... I utterly reject yoga, hypnotism, and New Age religion as being anything but false answers to mankind's problems.[11]

For Christians, Jesus' person and work are the central foci of all our religious thought. The Apostles' and Nicene creeds delineate this centrality with respect to Christ's person and work (*see* Appendix 1). The Christian recognizes his or her sinfulness before God and is commanded to repent and believe in Jesus Christ (John 3:16–18; Acts 16:30–32). Such contrition and repentance lead to forgiveness, as Christ promises (Mark 2:5).

Holy Spirit

There are no conclusive statements concerning the Holy Spirit in FHU literature. For the Christian church, the Holy Spirit is the third person of the ▶Trinity, who points to the centrality of the second person, Jesus Christ (John 15:26–27).[12]

Humanity

Masters clearly teaches that truth is latent within a person's own soul:

> Everything you "learn" as a result of the meditation exercise is what you already know; the only thing new about it is the way it enters the mind and feelings from within rather than having been pressured to accept it.
>
> If you do this exercise for the purpose of overcoming a problem through your own will, you are trying to remove symptoms and ignoring the cause.... Remember that it is your own meditation that will re-establish your connection with your true self and provide you with your own insight. Seek the kingdom of Heaven within yourself, for that is where you will find it.[13]

"You are the walking wounded," Masters tells his faithful flock as they come to hear him at Grants Pass. But the wounds he speaks of are not the result of the sin inherent within human nature (Rom. 3:23), but more the negative influence that one's family, particularly one's parents, inflict. Children are negatively influenced by the "toxic" teachings of fathers and mothers. The goal, achieved through meditation exercises, is to eliminate this poisonous past from the human psyche and to find solace and peace from within.

Salvation

Masters used to speak of salvation in a sense not dissimilar to Hinduism and Eastern thought. Because humankind is inherently good, the need for salvation as atonement from sin disappears. The kingdom of heaven lies within (see above). The key is to discover it for oneself. This comes through Masters's meditation process articulated in his radio program and various books and publications.

Masters offers frank counsel to those encumbered by residual influences from religious training.

> For the time being don't call upon a name that you have been educated to accept, or else you may revive a conditioned reflex response to words that connect you to the outer world. The God, Jesus, and Buddha that you may have accepted via brainwashing is not the real one. Many of us have accepted a "holy spirit" in a moment of excitement, but it turned out to be the unholy one instead, and by him you justified every sin while you got worse.[14]

In the end, the disciple of Roy Masters seeks salvation through the exercises and techniques of the FHU. He has recently stated, however, that some of his comments were irresponsible in the light of the media and that he has said things that were misguided. Masters now affirms, "I am a Christian and I have said so openly for many years now."[15]

CONCLUSION

Masters's voice is still heard, and his books, tapes, and lectures continue to be disseminated to many people on into the 2000s. It is difficult to ascertain precisely how many followers the Foundation of Human Understanding has amassed, but there can be little doubt that Masters has left his mark on the minds of many in the United States and abroad.

The FHU offers an abundance of materials both in books and lectures. Such books as *How to Control Your Emotions*, *How to Conquer Suffering Without Doctors*, *The Secret of Life and Death*, *The Satan Principle*, and *How to Survive Your Parents* articulate key facets of Masters' thought. Many cassettes containing his teachings are available by ordering from The Foundation of Human Understanding.

ADDITIONAL INFORMATION_____

Headquarters
The Foundation of Human Understanding, PO Box 1000, Grants Pass, OR 97528.

Official Website
www.fhu.com

Sacred Texts
Masters reads from a variety of sacred traditions and quotes the Bible frequently.

Periodicals
New Insights (monthly); *The Iconclast.*

Total Membership/Following
It is claimed that up to three million people listen to the radio broadcasts.

Notes
[1] Lauren Kessler, "Roy Masters: 'I Can Do No Wrong,'" *The Sunday Oregonian Magazine—Northwest* (September 4, 1983), 6.
[2] Walter Martin, *The New Cults* (Ventura, CA.: Regal, 1980), 298.
[3] See Bhagwan Shree ▸Rajneesh.
[4] Kessler, "Masters," 6.
[5] Martin, *The New Cults*, 299.
[6] Roy Masters, *How Your Mind Can Keep You Well* (Los Angeles: Foundation of Human Understanding, 1978), i–ii.
[7] Ibid., 9.
[8] Ibid., 17.
[9] *The Iconoclast* (Los Angeles: Foundation of Human Understanding). This statement is found on the inside cover of each issue.
[10] Roy Masters, *The Secret of Life and Death* (Los Angeles: Foundation Press, 1964), 79.
[11] Masters, in a letter to the editor of *Christian Research Journal* (Winter 1992), 4.
[12] See HINDUISM, CHRISTADELPHIANISM, JEHOVAH'S WITNESSES, etc. for a further examination of the Christian doctrine of the Trinity.
[13] Masters, *How Your Mind Can Keep You Well*, 47–49.
[14] Ibid., 192.
[15] Masters, letter in *Christian Research Journal* (Winter, 1992), 4.

FREEMASONRY (MASONIC LODGE)

In a volume of this nature, Freemasonry presents an anomaly. Does it qualify as a religion? Or is it a large fraternal organization that exists for the mutual benefit of all of its members and society as a whole? Is it as secretive as many claim? Or is its greatest secret the fact that there really are no secrets? If a person is a Mason, does this present a contradiction with being an orthodox Christian? These and other questions abound. What follows is an attempt to understand and answer inquiries such as these.

HISTORY

It is difficult to recount a distinctive history of Freemasonry.[1] Some Masons believe that the origin of their organization dates back to Genesis and the time of Adam and Eve. Because Adam sewed fig leaves, these were the first aprons that would later be used in formal Masonic ceremonies. Others date the origin of the Masonic Lodge to the time of Solomon, who employed the stone masons in the construction of the temple in Jerusalem. A third rendition links Masons to the construction of the Tower of Babel. Others claim that the Masons are the descendants of the Knights Templar. The ancient mystery religions are also thought to have influenced the beginnings of the Lodge.

Credible historians trace the real beginnings of Freemasonry back to the Goose and Gridiron Tavern in London, England, in 1717.[2] It immediately met with opposition from the Roman Catholic Church because of what was perceived to be the secretive nature of the organization. During the formative years of the development of the Masonry, James Anderson wrote his *Constitutions*, which revised a fourteenth-century stonemason's Christian guidebook entitled *Gothic Constitutions*. This primary document was instrumental in shaping and developing the infant organization. In 1717, Anderson, along with George Payne and John Theophilus Desaguliers, united their efforts to form the Grand Lodge. Lodges started to spring up all over Europe and America. Almost from the outset attempts were made to bring all of the lodges under one Supreme Grand Lodge, but it never succeeded. Although lodges work together, each one is governed by its own constitution and bylaws.

It was in the United States that the lodges experienced their greatest success. The London lodge granted a charter to the first official lodge in America in July, 1733, in Boston. A Jew by the name of Moses Michael Hays introduced the first Scottish Rite Freemasonry into the United States in the 1760s. The 1800s saw the establishment of several thousand lodges throughout North America. It became a powerful and significant institution in American society.

Freemasonry also met with some persecution. During the 1820s a man by the name of William Morgan began passing out secret Masonic literature. He disappeared in 1826, fueling the fires of suspicion that the Masons were responsible for his death. The Masons were denounced for being a malevolent society filled with secrets and rituals known only to Masons. This lent itself to vast conspiracy theories, which are held to this day. This strong so-called anti-Masonic period lasted from 1826 to 1840.

Those who seemed to be most attracted to Masonic membership and affiliation were immigrants who were largely only nominally religious, unaffiliated, or anti-clerical.[3]

Freemasonry soon spread to other parts of the Americas, including Canada and South America. Canada's first Masonic lodge was built in Cape Breton in 1745. Brazil, Mexico, the West Indies, and numerous other countries all became homes to Freemasonry.

The Lodge has attracted people from all walks of life. Many prominent people have been Masons, such as George Washington and thirteen other U.S. presidents; eighteen vice Presidents; five Chief Justices of the U.S. Supreme Court; astronauts Edwin Aldrin, Virgil Grissom, and Gordon Cooper; actors John Wayne and Clark Gable; comedian Red Skelton; composer John Philip Sousa; and General Douglas MacArthur.

RITES AND ORDERS

Freemasonry is comprised of several orders and rites.

▶Blue Lodge

All ▶Master Masons undergo initiation in the Blue Lodge. They go through the three degrees of ▶Entered Apprentice, ▶Fellow Craft, and Master Mason. Candidates for membership must be recommended by a present member. Fellow members then come together at a meeting and cast votes. If the candidate is ▶blackballed, a foul is announced and a second vote is taken. If a candidate is blackballed a second time, he is rejected. Otherwise, they begin to earn the Entered Apprentice degree. After participating in the required rituals for the degrees, the candidate must take an oath. The words of the oath are as follows:

> I promise and swear that I will not write, print, stamp, stain, hew, cut, carve, indent, paint, or engrave it [Masonic secrets] on anything movable or immovable . . . binding myself under no less penalty than to have my throat cut across, my tongue torn out by the roots, and my body buried in the rough sands of the sea at the lower water mark . . . where the tide ebbs and flows twice in twenty-four hours; so help me God, and keep me steadfast in the due performance of the same.[4]

Questions have arisen as to whether this oath has ever literally been carried out. Anti-Masons claim that this is precisely what happened to Captain Morgan in 1826, though there is no proof that this ever took place.

Some Blue Lodges today have stopped using this blood-curdling oath.

York and Scottish Rites

After completing the degrees in the Blue Lodge, Masons may choose to move on and earn additional degrees in one of two rites: the ▶York and ▶Scottish Rites. These various degrees and rites are perhaps best illustrated by a chart (see below).

Other Masonic Orders

There are numerous other allied orders within Freemasonry in the British tradition. These are:

Ancient Arabic Order of the Nobles of the Mystic Shrine (popularly known as *Shriners*). The Shrine was founded in 1872 in New York, where thirteen Masons met and discussed the idea of forming a fraternity for the purpose of socializing, apart from getting together for the normal ritual gatherings. Two men, Dr. Walter Fleming and actor William Florence, both Americans, played major roles in the development of the Shriners. In order to become a Shriner, one must have achieved the thirty-second degree of the Scottish Rite, or the Knights Templar degree of the York Rite. National leadership of the Shrine falls under the auspices of the Imperial Council. Since 1922, the Shrine has been very influential in working in children's hospitals and is also known for its three burn centers in Boston, Massachusetts, Galveston, Texas, and Cincinnati, Ohio.

The Order of the Eastern Star. Founded in 1850 by Dr. Robert Morris, the Eastern Star is a women's order. Membership is open to women who are related to Masons. Additional requirements include belief in a Supreme Being, being free from addictions to alcohol, and upstanding moral character. In 1855, Morris organized the first order and placed himself at the head with

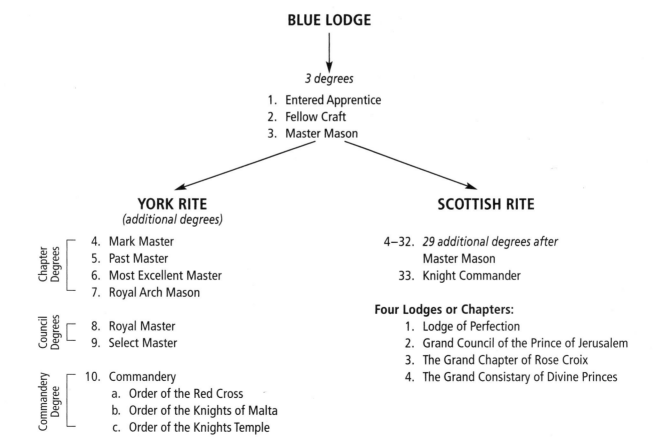

the title "Most Enlightened Grand Luminary." There are five degrees within the Eastern Star, based on five women in the Bible. These are Adah (first degree), stressing obedience; Ruth (second degree), devotion; Esther (third degree), fidelity; Martha (fourth degree), faith; Electa[5] (fifth degree), charity. Like the Shriners, the Order of the Eastern Star is involved in philanthropic organizations such as hospitals, orphanages, and shelters.

Daughters of the Eastern Star. Organized in 1925, this order is for the daughters of fathers who are Masons or mothers who are members of the Eastern Star. They must be between the ages of fourteen and twenty. The organization is found only in New York. Three degrees are conferred on members of this order. They include Initiatory, Honorary Majority, and Public.

The Order of the White Shrine of Jerusalem. Organized in Chicago in 1884 and headquartered in Romulus, Michigan, the presiding officer is called the Supreme Worthy High Priestess. The Order of the Eastern Star does not recognize the legitimacy of this organization.

Order of DeMolay. This order takes its name from Jacques DeMolay, fourteenth-century leader of the Knights Templar, who was burned at the stake. The order was founded in 1919 by Mr. Frank Land and nine high school students from Kansas City, Missouri. It is comprised of white males ages fourteen through twenty-one. DeMolay is not directly affiliated with any lodge. It enjoyed its greatest growth in the 1950s and 1960s. DeMolay chapters are located throughout the world. Its stress lies in emphasizing patriotism, citizenship, good morality, cleanliness, and faith in God.

International Order of Job's Daughters. Founded in 1920 by Ethel T. W. Mick in Omaha, Nebraska, the IOJD is a sister order sponsored by the Masonic Lodge and Eastern Star (above). Mick founded the order for the express purpose of helping girls between the ages of eleven and twenty to develop both morally and spiritually. Philanthropic deeds for the good of the community are a regular staple of the organization. The group has established a college fund for members, granted at no cost.

Rituals in the IOJD are based on the book of Job in the Bible. The text cited is Job 42:15—"Nowhere in all the land were there found women as beautiful as Job's daughters; and their father granted them an inheritance along with their brothers." Secret rituals are enacted and members swear not to divulge those secrets. Membership is limited to white females. There are excep-

tions to this today, but a majority of the organizations still adhere to this traditional practice. IOJD is an international order, and it operates on national, regional, and local levels.

International Order of Rainbow Girls. This order was founded in 1922 by Rev. Mark Sexson, chaplain of the Grand Lodge of Oklahoma. Its primary purpose is to prepare young white girls between the ages of twelve and twenty for membership in the Eastern Star. Faith, hope, and charity (love) serve as the basic theme of the Rainbow ritual. The covenant that God made never to destroy the earth again by flood and sealed with the sign of the rainbow is the defining biblical text of the organization.

The Order of Amaranth. This order's history predates Freemasonry. Historians trace its origins to 1653 where Christina, Queen of Sweden, desired to organize a group of fifteen knights and fifteen ladies. She adopted the name "amaranth" as the flower that symbolizes eternal life. In 1860, James B. Taylor, an American Mason from New Jersey, began writing a new order based on the Swedish model. Taylor's work served as a catalyst for two other men, Robert Macoy and Robert Taylor, to write rituals and a series of degrees that would become the Order of Amaranth.

This order was founded formally in 1873 in New York City with membership open to all Master Masons, their wives, daughters, granddaughters, sisters, widows, and so on. It is organized into local Courts, Grand Courts, and an International Supreme Council. Three degrees are conferred: the Order of the Eastern Star, Queen of the South, and Order of Amaranth. Its purpose as stated in its *Authorized Ritual* is to serve God, country, and fellow human beings.

Lesser Masonically related Orders. Other Orders include *Daughters of Makonna, Daughters of the Nile, Knights of the Red Cross, Ladies Oriental Shrine of North America, National Sojourners, Order of the Builder, Social Order of the Beauceant of the World, Tall Cedars of Lebanon of the USA,* and *True Kindred.*

Masonic College Fraternities. There are many fraternities that have no direct connection to the Masonic Lodge. These various organizations, however, have adopted the Lodge's rituals and practices, including its mystery, secrecy, oaths of loyalty, grips, signs, traditions, emblems, badges, and the like. There are several specifically Masonic-affiliated organizations, such as *Acacia, The Square and Compass, Sigma Mu Sigma, The Order of the Golden Key,* and *Tau Kappa Epsilon.*

Prince Hall Freemasonry. This order was formed as an alternative lodge for blacks since they have traditionally been barred from membership in the organizations. In the late 1700s Prince Hall, a black man from the West Indies, migrated to America. He pastored a congregation in Cambridge, Massachusetts. Hall became a Mason in the British Army Lodge in 1775. He petitioned for membership in the Lodge of Massachusetts but was denied because of his race. He then petitioned the Grand Lodge of England and was granted a charter in March of 1784.

Racism in Freemasonry was a peculiarly American phenomenon. The Prince Hall Lodge, along with other independent lodges, is called "clandestine," meaning that they are not recognized as legitimate by the various white Lodges. Some lodges have abandoned racism, but not all. It must be remembered that all lodges are independent. The actions of one do not affect the polity of the others in any way.

BELIEFS AND DOCTRINES

An important issue with respect to lodges is the question whether or not it is a religion. There are Masonic authors who claim that it is, but there are others who insist it is not. For example, one of the major authorities in Freemasonry, Albert Mackey, writes: "Freemasonry is . . . an eminently religious organization."[6] But Allan D. Large argues that the Lodge is not a religion but merely a fraternal organization.

> Religion, as the term is commonly used, implies several things: a plan of salvation or path by which one reaches the afterlife; a theology which attempts to describe the nature of God; and the description of the ways or practices by which a man or a woman may seek to communicate with God. Masonry does none of those things. We offer no plan of salvation. . . . Instead we tell him that he must find the answers to these great questions in his own faith, in his church or synagogue or other house of worship.[7]

Note that those who attempt to argue that Freemasonry is not a religion do so in order to attempt to make the case that there is no incompatibility between Freemasonry and religion. For example, in the early 1980s and 1990s, controversy broke out in the Southern Baptist Convention when the church body faced the fact that many of its clergy and laypersons were also members of the Lodge. The issue was assigned to the Denomination's Home Missions Board for study. The HMB later concluded that Freemasonry is not a religion.

In 1992, a Southern Baptist physician, Dr. James Holly charged the Southern Baptists as "the first Christian denomination that essentially blesses the Masonic Lodge."[8] The denomination then appointed an Interfaith Witness Department to study the compatibility of Southern Baptist and Masonic doctrine. In March, 1993, the HMB then published a new report thata contradicted the former report on Freemasonry. This report commended Masonry for its great works of charity, contributions to education, and its emphasis on high moral values. The report then outlined areas where compatibility with CHRISTIANITY is not possible. These differences include: Offensive titles such as Worshipful Master, bloody oaths and obligations, the pagan and occult nature of many of the past writings in Masonic literature, a salvation by works doctrine, the belief in universalism, and the refusal of most lodges to allow black membership. The report concluded with the recommendation that the autonomy of each congregation is such that "membership in a Masonic Order be a matter of personal conscience."

The classical Masonic authors generally argued that Freemasonry was and is a religion. More recent writers try to make the case that it is not. It is the position of the authors of this volume that Freemasonry does in fact meet all of the requirements of a religion. Webster's *Third New International Dictionary* says as one of the definitions given for the term *religion*: "A personal awareness or conviction of the existence of a supreme being or of supernatural powers or influences controlling one's own, humanity's, or all nature's destiny." Freemasonry in British and American lodges:

> Excludes atheists from membership. This suggests a fundamentally religious predisposition in the organization.
>
> The rituals of many of the lodges include prayers, pledges, and hymns.
>
> The various accoutrements of religion are present, such as altars, pulpits, readings, etc. Scottish Rite Freemasonry refers to its meeting places as "temples."
>
> Masonry has prescribed funeral rituals. During a funeral, the assurance is given to those Masons attending that the departed has now gone to "the Supreme Lodge Above."
>
> Part of the ritual of becoming a Mason involves being delivered from the pollution of the profane world and receiving "new birth."[9]

In the words of one Masonic author: "If the Lodge is not a religion, what would it have to do, that it is not now doing, in order to be rightly defined a religion?"

Masons have responded that the Boy Scouts require a belief in God and use the word "reverent" in one of their pledges, yet no one attempts to argue that they are a religion. But there is really little to compare here. The Boy Scouts do little more than include the name "God" in their oaths and motto. They do not have any accoutrements of religion in their meetings, nor do they attempt to define sin or salvation or to prescribe funeral rituals.

CHRISTIANITY AND FREEMASONRY

The following theological issues are the reasons for the incompatibility of traditional orthodox Christian doctrine and the Freemasonry.

God

In American and British Freemasonry, a member may not be an atheist, but at the same time, he may invoke the name of *any* god(s). Usually, God is invoked as "the All-Seeing Eye" or the "Great Architect." According to the Bible, Christians and Jews are forbidden to worship any other God (see Ex. 20:3). Christianity teaches that Jesus Christ along with the Father and the Holy Spirit is alone to be worshiped (Matt. 28:18; John 5:23; Acts 4:12). In short, Masonry has a form of deism in its conceptualization of God. For Christianity, the focus of faith and life is Jesus Christ (1 Cor. 2:2). Outside of Christ, God is not revealed (Heb. 1:1).

Initiation

When someone joins Freemasonry, he is asked to undergo an initiatory ritual that describes him as "in darkness, helpless, and ignorant." He is said to be covered with the pollutions of a profane world. He is to seek a "new birth" and to withdraw "the veil which conceals divine Truth from their [uninitiated] sight." The Bible says that through faith in Christ, Christians have already escaped the defilements of the world (1 Peter 1:22–23) and have already undergone the new birth (John 3:3).

Brotherhood

Freemasonry claims to uphold the "Fatherhood of God and the brotherhood of man." For Christianity, spiritual unity and solidarity are based solely in Christ (John 17:20–21).

Prayer

The specific name of Jesus Christ is omitted from prayers by Masons. But for Christians, Jesus' name is the basis of prayer (Acts 4:10–12), and one may never deny the name of Jesus (Mark 8:38; Luke 9:26).

The Bible

For Masons, the Bible is a guidebook for the promotion of good values and morals, though other sacred texts carry equal weight for those from various other religions who become Masons. For Christianity, the Bible is the only revealed and inspired Word of God (2 Tim. 3:16).

Human Nature and Sin

According to Masons, human beings can improve their moral condition and behavior through acts of charity, moral living, voluntary performance of civic duties, and so on. Mackey writes: "The ladder is a symbol of progress . . . its three principal rungs representing Faith, Hope, and Charity, present us with the means of advancing from earth to heaven, from death to life— from mortality to immortality."[10] Christianity teaches that human nature is not heading for perfection. Human nature is sinful (Rom. 3:23; 1 John 1:8) and in need not first of all of moral improvement, but of salvation (John 3:16; Rom. 3:21–24).

Oaths

Oaths and symbols are a vital part of Freemasonry and its various ceremonies and rites. They reason that because the oaths are symbolic, a Christian should be able to join and say the oaths without violating his conscience or Scripture. For Christianity, it is not taking an oath that is offensive. Oaths are a part of life, such as when a Christian takes the oath of office or when a witness holds up his or her right hand and swears to tell the truth. It is not the oath in itself; rather, it is the *content* of the oath. Christians may not make oaths that wish the harm of other people. One author writes:

> The dreadful oaths of Masonry are immoral from the Christian point of view not only because of the macabre punishments invoked ("your throat cut across, your tongue torn out by the root," etc.) in the name of God, but also because it is sinful to swear in UNCERTAIN matters. For the oaths are required BEFORE the candidate discovers the "secrets." . . . Either the oaths are taken seriously, but then they are blasphemous (cursing and swearing by God's name). Or else they are not taken seriously, but then they are also blasphemous (literally taking the name of the Lord in vain)! This reflects the general dilemma of Freemasonry: Either the oath is taken seriously, but then it is a sin against the First Commandment (Idolatry). Or else it is not taken seriously, but then it is a sin against the Second

Commandment (Blasphemy, taking the name of the Lord in vain).[11]

One commandment specifically states that the name of God may not be misused (Ex. 20:7; Lev. 19:12). As to cursing, the Bible states that Christians cannot and should not curse (Matt. 3:35–37; 14:6–9; 26:69–75; Acts 23:12; James 3:9–10). We should also remember that Jesus condemned divided loyalties in his followers (Matt 6:24; 10:37).

CONCLUSION

There are numerous reasons why Masonry attracts candidates for membership. It affords a sense of identity or belonging; opportunities for advancement in rank, titles, office, and achievement in general; and a chance to meet other people fraternally. Masonry affords individuals certain advantages, such as job promotions and business interactions. Freemasonry is also well known for its promotion of and commitment to charitable causes, fascination with secret oaths, a drawing of those who wish to participate in a form of religiosity expressed in moral precepts and ornate ritualism, and so on.

At the same time Freemasonry continues to be an anomaly. Christians who wish to take their faith and commitment to Christ seriously struggle with the issue of divided loyalties. There is perhaps less of a struggle on the issue of Freemasonry for those who understand Christianity more as a system of morality and works righteousness. But for Christians who understand that the gospel of grace is not about being justified by good works or a system of moral precepts, there can be no compatibility with an ideology that is based squarely on such an ideology.

Over the years, there have been some Christian churches or denominations that prohibited their members from joining Freemasonry and some other fraternal organizations as well. Here is a parital list that did so. The Congregational Church of New England in 1871; the General Association of the Congregational Church of Illinois in 1866; the General Synod of the Reformed Church of America in 1870; the Reformed Presbyterian Church of North America in 1897; the Presbyterian Church of Scotland in the 1920s; the Synod of the Dutch Reformed Church in the Cape,

South Africa, in 1940; the Orthodox Presbyterians of America in 1942. This list is clearly dated. Today, most Protestant denominations no longer bar lodge members from church membership. Only a few conservative denominations still oppose lodge membership.

ADDITIONAL INFORMATION

Headquarters
The numerous independent Lodges are located in nearly every state in the United States.[12]

Websites
Each Lodge has its own website.

Periodicals
See General Bibliography

Statistics
From 1960 through 2004 Freemasonry's membership in the United Sates has continuously declined. In 1990 there were 4,099,319 Masons, but in 2004 the organization's membership has dwindled to 1,617,032. Moreover, most of the members are in the upper-age brackets.

Notes
[1] This article is based largely on a book written by the authors of this volume. See George Mather and Larry Nichols, *Masonic Lodge* (Grand Rapids: Zondervan, 1995).

[2] See Alvin Schmidt, *The Greenwood Encyclopedia of American Institutions: Fraternal Organizations* (Westport, Conn.: Greenwood, 1980), 120.

[3] Sydney Ahlstrom, *A Religious History of the American People*, 2 vols. (Garden City, N.Y.: Image Books, 1975), 2:212.

[4] Schmidt, *Fraternal Organizations*, 123.

[5] The name "Electa" is a reference to "the elect lady" in 2 John 1.

[6] Albert G. Mackey, *Encyclopedia of Freemasonry*, 2 vols., rev. ed. (Chicago: Masonic History Co. 1946), 2:847.

[7] Allan D. Large, "Questions and Answers on Religion and Freemasonry," *Scottish Rite Journal* (February 1993), 14.

[8] "Masonry Is Anti-Christian," *Christian News*, 32 no. 21 (May 24, 1993), 1.

[9] See Albert Mackey, *Masonic Ritualist* (New York: Maynard & Merril, 1867).

[10] Mackey, *Encyclopedia of Freemasonry*, 2:361.

[11] Kurt Marquardt, "Christianity and Freemasonry," *Christian News* (March 19, 1968; reprinted May 24, 1993), 23.

[12] For a listing of these, see Mather and Nichols, *Masonic Lodge*, 68–69.

HANUMAN FOUNDATION

This is an organization of the NEW AGE MOVEMENT founded in the 1970s that blended Eastern 'mysticism, HINDUISM, psychology, liberal drug use, and various other elements to constitute one of the numerous 'cults characteristic of the late twentieth century.

HISTORY

Harvard psychology Professor Timothy 'Leary (1920–1996) made newspaper headlines when in 1963 he was fired for experimenting with LSD. A fellow professor, Dr. Richard 'Alpert (b. 1931), also began "dropping" LSD and met with the same fate as his colleague. After several years of experimenting with drugs, Alpert became dissatisfied with their seeming inability to provide any lasting states of higher consciousness. Discouraged, he decided to go to India in 1967. There he met his new teacher, 'guru 'Maharaj-Ji, who began to instruct him in the techniques of 'Raja yoga.

Alpert soon changed his name to Baba Ram 'Dass and, returning to the United States, wrote a book in 1971 titled *Be Here Now*. The thesis of the book was essentially that people are not living in the past or the future. They should therefore devote themselves to the art of living only in the present. In 1974 Ram Dass founded the Hanuman Foundation along with the Hanuman Temple. Hanuman is a Hindu god appearing in the form of a monkey, who, according to the Hindu epic 'Ramayana, carried a mountain of healing herbs to help the wounded in 'Rama's army.

Among the numerous activities that the foundation began to perform was a ministry to prisoners called the "Prison Ashram Project." Another was the "Living-Dying Project," which provided support for those who were both conscious and dying. In 1978, Ram Dass cofounded the Seva Foundation, dedicated to the relief of human suffering worldwide. In February 1997, Ram Dass suffered a stroke that left the right side of his body paralyzed and he was unable to speak. Thirteen months later, on March 11, 1998, he was able to again give a public lecture. He continues to travel, lecture, and write. The website lists his books, tapes, and videos.

TEACHINGS

The focus of Alpert's books and teachings revolves around the basic principles of the nature of human consciousness. One such principle is the teaching of Hinduism that all religious paths lead to 'enlightenment. One must seek the aid of a guru to attain such enlightenment. Because all people are at different levels of progression on their spiritual pilgrimage, the gurus each prescribe differing instructions and exercises. Melton summarizes:

> Some might need yoga, renunciation, mantras, sex, or even psychedelic drugs. For Baba Ram Dass, 'karma yoga—loving service, feeding all human beings in a way that manifests the spirit that pervades all—was the path to enlightenment.[1]

The Hanuman Foundation was formed to help proliferate karma yoga techniques. Additionally, the foundation provides counseling services in prisons and hospitals.

CONCLUSION

Interest in and study of Eastern religions has remained popular in the twenty-first century. Baba Ram Dass continues to travel and lecture widely as a spokesman for the New Age Movement, promoting the principles of inner peace and enlightenment, bringing the "Age of Aquarius" to the twentieth-first century.[2]

ADDITIONAL INFORMATION

Headquarters
Ram Dass, 524 San Anselmo Ave., San Anselmo, CA 94960.

Official Website
www.ramdasstapes.org

Writings
Many books, tapes, and lectures, most of which are listed on the website.

Notes
[1] J. Gordon Melton, *The Encyclopedia of American Religions*, 2 vols. (Wilmington, N.C.: McGrath, 1978), 2:382.
[2] See HINDUISM for an analysis and comparison of the teachings of Baba Ram Dass with those of historic orthodox CHRISTIANITY.

HEAVEN'S GATE

As a UFO cult that shocked the world in March, 1997, Heaven's Gate, with a following of only thirty-nine members, was perhaps even more unsettling than the news of the burning of the BRANCH DAVIDIAN compound in Waco, Texas, just four years earlier. Intelligent men who were well schooled in computer technology do not usually follow a leader who has visions of being caught up in a flying saucer and whisked away from earth. But this is in fact what they believed. And upon this belief, they acted.

HISTORY

The name Heaven's Gate had been adopted only recently. In 1994 they were known as Total Overcomers Anonymous. Before this, they members simply called themselves "The Group." In its early life in the mid-1970s, it was called the Bo and Peep UFO cult. At that time they began to gather followers. The media referred to them as HIM (Human Individual Metamorphosis).

Marshall Applewhite (1931–1997), called "Do" for short, was born in Spur, Texas. His wife, Bonnie Lu Nettles (1927–1997), was called "Ti." Her birthplace is unknown. Applewhite earned a BA at Austin College in 1952 and then briefly attended Union Theological Seminary in Richmond, Virginia. In addition to theological interests he began to study music and held the position of music director at a Presbyterian church in North Carolina. Shortly thereafter, he moved to Houston, Texas, and became a professor of music at St. Thomas University. Here Applewhite met his wife-to-be.

Nettles was a nurse and a member of a local THEOSOPHICAL society. Nettles awakened a heightened interest in Applewhite for things metaphysical. In 1972, Applewhite was expelled from his teaching post at the university. The charges centered around a sexual scandal involving a male student. Applewhite apparently wavered between homosexual and heterosexual tendencies. But his sexuality was not a factor in his relationship with Nettles. In fact, there is reason to believe that Applewhite found shelter from his confused sexual identity with Nettles. The couple delved deep into the world of the paranormal. They claimed to have come into contact with spirit beings from outer space, who prompted them to place all of their attention on pursuit of the spiritual life in the worlds beyond earth.

In 1973, in Oregon, Applewhite claimed he had had the vision that brought together all the fragments of the different experiences that he and Nettles were encountering. Here is the apparent inspiration for what the world witnessed in 1997. That "revelation" was that Applewhite and Nettles were the two prophets of Revelation 11. They would be given 1,260 days to preach the truth, and then they would be killed, followed by their ascension into heaven in a "cloud." Applewhite believed that this "cloud" was really a symbol for a spacecraft of some sort. The two-shepherd theme lay behind their early decision to call themselves "Bo and Peep," after having previously referred to themselves and "Guinea and Pig."

Traveling to California and lecturing in Los Angeles, "Bo and Peep" managed to convert two dozen students of metaphysics. After returning to Oregon, the couple gained a following of as many as 150 people. In 1975 in Walport, Oregon, the group attracted the attention of the national media when some thirty members of the group disappeared from a beach following a lecture on flying saucers.

The group then migrated to Denver, Colorado. Here Applewhite and Nettles announced that they were going to drop out of sight in order to prepare for what they termed "the demonstration." They believed that they would be assassinated and in order to "demonstrate" that they had the truth, they would then be resurrected and ascend to heaven. For the next six months, followers did not hear from them. The groups fragmented and members simply left. Bo and Peep next appeared in Gulfport, Mississippi, where some one hundred followers reassembled under their leadership. In typical cult fashion, Bo and Peep then determined that only those who were their faithful followers possessed the ultimate truth and were now ready to move up and be given more truth. "The demonstration" was canceled, or at the least postponed. More preparation was needed by the devotees of the two shepherds.

The next location was Wyoming, where in the vast wilderness Bo and Peep began instructing the members who accompanied them in the truths they had discovered while in exile. Included in this was a sophisticated space-age vocabulary. Further migrations included moves to Salt Lake City, back to Denver, Dallas-Fort Worth, and finally to the now famous home in Santa Fe, New Mexico. Additionally, in Albuquerque, New Mexico, the group began constructing a compound, which they named "Earthship." When the group became sudden news in 1997, they were prospering in the computer business and their expertise lay in website development. They called their business "Higher Source."

TEACHINGS AND BELIEFS

A combination of Christian (Presbyterian) roots, Nettles's membership in the Theosophical Society, and various other metaphysical ideas constituted the beliefs of Heaven's Gate. It is not surprising, therefore, that a blending of biblical themes and overtones and theosophical ideas and science fiction constitute their belief system.

Earth: Our planet is a garden once planted by extraterrestrials that visited several thousand years ago and decided that it had developed enough to merit the descent of a being from one level higher than that of earth. This (apparently) was Jesus. But earthlings killed him, not yet wishing to be liberated and illuminated to a higher plane of existence. Therefore the world continued to be ruled by evil as it still is.

Heaven: Heaven is the escape route for all who do not want to be under the dominion of the evil one. The group believed heaven was a place to which they could travel in the proper spacecraft.

Boarding Pass: The qualification for being included on the spacecraft to heaven included obedient adherence to the teachings of Applewhite.

HIM: Human Individual Metamorphosis that occurs when one is transported to the higher spiritual/evolutionary level.

Practices: Included the total renunciation of materialism and worldly desires. The consumption of alcohol and drugs, engaging in sexual activity, and contacts with the outside world (i.e., anyone outside of the group itself) were strictly prohibited.

The Demonstration: As noted above, "the demonstration" was the eventual assassination of Bo and Peep. They would then be resurrected and ascend by way of a flying saucer to heaven.

Science Fiction: As a literary genre the reading of science fiction was extremely influential in the ongoing evolutionary development of the group.

Beliefs are powerful. The members of Heaven's Gate believed that there actually was a flying saucer behind the Hale-Bopp comet that would transport them out of the darkness of this world to a much better place. Based on this belief, they committed suicide. To the thirty-nine who died, however, their deaths were not really suicide. As Christians we do believe that death is not really death but a translation into heaven, Applewhite and his faithful few, however, believed that they were ascending to a higher plane of existence on the evolutionary plane.

In one sense, the death of Heaven's Gates members was an event unlike Waco, Jonestown, or other cult suicides. In those instances, the followers were reacting to the attacks of the outside world. For Heaven's Gate, it was a private affair. There was no political pressures or direct involvement, as was the case in both Waco and Jonestown.

Applewhite had predicted that he would soon die from cancer. The group was perhaps motivated not just a little from the belief that he might not be with them too much longer. Cult members usually do not respond well in the absence of the dynamic leader who forms the cohesive glue that holds the group together in the first place.

CONCLUSION

When the news broke about the thirty-nine members found dead, the media scurried around for information that few cult experts had. Yet there are few cults that have left so much information behind. Robert Balch has researched Heaven's Gate and has provided much helpful information on this group; his research has been well published on the internet. Together with his extensive writings, there are sites and internet links that provide a voluminous amount of information.

ADDITIONAL INFORMATION

Websites

www.wave.net/upg/gate

www.clas.utl.edu/users'gthursby/rel/gate This website is operated by a surviving member of Heaven's Gate, who chose not to "leave his body" (suicide) with the other members. It contains the original Heaven's Gate website and publications as well as his personal updates.

HINDUISM

Among the oldest religions of the world, Hinduism provides an important theological background for many ᵇcults and ᵇsects that have arisen in the West in the recent past. These include the VEDANTA SOCIETY, ISKCON, TRANSCENDENTAL MEDITATION, the NEW AGE MOVEMENT, individual personality cults like Bhagwan Shree ᵇRajneesh, and so on.

HISTORY

Philosophically and foundationally, the essence of Hinduism is that all reality is one and that all of the diversity in the cosmos is ultimately reduced to a ʼmonism. Hinduism in present-day India and the diaspora is traced back to three influences. The first is the Indo-European, dating from c. 1500 B.C.–500 B.C. These Aryan peoples, coming from the steppes of Russia and Central Asia, swept the Indian peninsula, bringing with them their religion known as ʼVedism. The second influence came from neighboring Iranian tribes, whose native languages were mingled with the Sanskrit language of the Aryan invaders. The third influence came from the religious ideas endemic to India itself.

The literary source of Vedism is the hymns collectively known as the ʼ*Rigveda*. Vedism itself was a fire cult that embraced the notion that purity emerges from fire, an early idea that may have strongly influenced the practice of cremation of the dead and the later development of the doctrine of ʼreincarnation.

Hindu history is generally divided into four periods. A pre-Vedic period dating back as far as 3000 B.C.–1500 B.C. featured ʼanimism, practiced by the natives of the Indus Valley. Here, the Harappa culture developed the cult of the goddess and the bull. The greatest contribution of this period is the many artifacts left behind that have enabled archaeologists to piece together its basic history.

The second period, the Vedic, was marked, as already stated, by the Aryan invasions. But unlike the pre-Vedic period, the Vedic did not produce a vast storehouse of material artifacts. Its greatest treasure was its literary contribution, the *Rigveda*. Its 1,028 hymns were composed over several centuries. This period is the one in which the intense ʼpolytheism of Hinduism underwent its greatest development. Another important aspect of modern Hindu life, the ʼcaste system, emerged during this period. This system of classifying individuals into castes is vocational and related to skin color. The *Rigveda* speaks of five social castes: (1) the ʼbrahmins—the priestly-scholarly caste; (2) the ʼ*kshatriyas*—the warrior-soldier caste; (3) the ʼ*vaishyas*—the agricultural and merchant caste; (4) the ʼ*sudras*—the peasant and servant caste; (5) the ʼ*hariyan*—the outcasts or "untouchables." Over time these castes underwent thousands of subdivisions. The top of the social scale remains the brahmins, while the very bottom is still the "untouchables." Untouchables were regarded as less than human and were treated as such. Even though Mahatma ʼGandhi succeeded in enacting social reform to outlaw "untouchability" in 1949, psychologically and spiritually it is still embraced in many villages in India, especially in southern India.

The third period of Hindu history is called the Upanishad period, which began around 700 B.C. The word *upanishad* means literally "to sit at the feet of." It was during this phase that Hinduism underwent its greatest transformation toward what it is today. The "this-worldly" character of the Vedic period with its superhuman deities was transformed into an "other-worldly" orientation. Asceticism and the doctrine of reincarnation were developed in this period, as was the rise of the teacher/student or ʼguru/disciple relationship on an intensely spiritual level. Those released from the cycle of rebirth (ʼ*moksha*) instructed others in the disciplines necessary to undergo good ʼkarma in order to receive total ʼenlightenment themselves.

The Upanishad period was a time of rebellion against the rituals of the Vedic era. Devotees willingly forsook the authority of the brahmins to follow a guru who could show the way out of rebirth (ʼ*samsara*). ʼGautama Buddha is a prime example of a nonorthodox ascetic who could instruct one in the path of enlightenment. His path led to the major world religion of BUDDHISM. The third century B.C. saw the spread of BUDDHISM in India through the influence of the Mauryan ruler ʼAsoka, who also maintained a favorable attitude toward Hinduism.

The fourth era of Hindu history began approximately in the second century B.C. and went on through the second century A.D. During this time, the Vedantic texts underwent a revival. The god, Brahma, rose to a place of hegemony over the lesser gods. However, a more significant god, Lord ʼKrishna, one of the ten incarnations of Vishnu, becomes the dominant deity of Hinduism. Also, the god ʼSiva—the creator, preserver, and destroyer of the universe—became the third most important deity referred to in Hindu lore at this time.

The ʼ*Bhagavad Gita* is one of the most popular of all Hindu texts. The poem is a prolonged discourse between the warrior Arjuna and his charioteer, Krishna. Arjuna decides not to kill his own kinsmen in battle, whereon Krishna proceeds to exhort him to forsake personal feelings and do what is right (dharma). The overarching motif in the *Bhagavad Gita* is intense spiritual devotion, an idea most prevalent in Hinduism to this day.

Hinduism and its counterpart, Buddhism, went on to make a tremendous impact in Asia, while CHRISTIANITY transformed the West. In the fourth through the eighth centuries A.D., a popularization of Hinduism took place in the writings known as the *Puranas*. They comprise an anthology of Hindu literature, summarizing the three gods of the Hindu trinity, Brahma, Vishnu, and Siva, as well as all of the major ideas of the religion. The *Puranas* became the text of the common people.

The first centuries A.D. also saw the development of a multiplicity of cults and sects exalting various deities, including Shakti, the mother goddess; Skanda, the son

The *Bhagavad Gita* and other Hindu writings are widely available in English translation; many use these writings for religious guidance.

Courtesy George A. Mather

of Siva; Surya, the sun god; Lakshmi, goddess of fortune and consort of Vishnu; and hundreds of others. The paradox of Hinduism was its ability to adapt itself to a mass polytheism while simultaneously advancing ᵐmonotheistic tendencies.

During the latter part of the first millennium A.D., a time equivalent to the beginning of Europe's Middle Ages, a spirit of antagonism against Buddhism arose among prominent Hindu philosophers, particularly ᵖShankara and Kumarila. Reports of the destruction of Buddhist temples and the murder of monks were becoming more commonplace after the seventh century.

Hinduism found itself threatened by ᵖMuslim invasions beginning in the eleventh century (see ISLAM). Occupation of northern India resulted in the strengthening of Hinduism in the south. Islam failed to influence the theology of Hinduism but did have an effect on language and culture. Many Arabic and Persian words wove their way into Indian vocabulary.[1] The practice of secluding women from upper classes (*purdah*) was concomitant with Islamic doctrine. The greatest harmonization efforts between the two religions took place under the rule of the Muslim ᵖSultan Akbar (1556–1605). His efforts were influential but met with failure exacerbated by a Muslim revival in the eigh-

teenth century and the subsequent rule of Great Britain, which spread Christianity on the Indian peninsula.

Hinduism itself impacted the West with its ideas in the latter half of the nineteenth century and throughout the twentieth, particularly through its reform movements. SIKHISM represents the most significant of such movements, begun in the late fifteenth century by ᵖGuru Nanak. Nanak's reforms included the rejection of the caste system. Sikhism merits its own treatment elsewhere in this volume, but its ideas are important because they impacted America, particularly in the teachings of ᵖYogi ᵖBhajan.

The first introduction of an organized Hindu society to America came in the 1890s when ᵖSwami ᵖVivekananda, a disciple of yet another Hindu reformer, ᵖRamakrishna, established the Vedanta Society in New York City in 1895.

THEOSOPHY, ELAN VITAL, ISKCON, TRANCENDENTAL MEDITATION, RAJNEESHISM, and numerous other sects became extremely popular in the West in the twentieth century, all of which receive their primary impulse from Hinduism. The most significant non-Christian cultural shaping force, the New Age Movement, relies heavily on Hinduism to supply its religious foundation.

Hinduism also underwent a renaissance in the West through the influence of Mahatma Gandhi's successful social reform movement, stressing nonviolence and egalitarianism between the sexes. His ideas on nonviolent social reform inspired Martin Luther King Jr., a prominent leader of the American civil rights movement.

The historical tension between Sikhs and Hindus was exacerbated in the 1990s. Relationships between Muslims and Hindus have eroded as a result of a dispute in 1986 over a sacred shrine in the state of Uttar Pradesh, to which both religions have laid claim. Since the terrorist attacks of September 11, 2001, there is more of an awareness of world religions, as leaders from all of them seek to understand the impulses that drive terrorist organizations. Hindi leaders have addressed this issue as well as Christians and chiefly Muslims.

TEACHINGS

Much of what makes up Hindu theology has already been discussed in the historical survey. What follows is a brief examination of key facets of Hindu doctrine accompanied by comparisons to Christianity.

Hinduism is classically divided into six systems or schools of thought, called ᵖ*dharsana* (ᵖSankhya, ᵖYoga, ᵖNyaya ᵖVaisheshika, ᵖPurva Mimamsa, and ᵖUttara Mimamsa).[2] Heinrich von Stietencron notes that all these systems are concerned with explaining the world and with the highest goal of humanity—salvation—and they all strive to reach this goal through cognition. The older Mimamsa seeks to establish correct understanding of the Vedas and their injunctions . . . as the basis for right behavior. For all other systems and for the later stages of the Purva Mimamsa, what counts is knowledge as a means of salvation from the cycle of rebirth, with the final state conceived either as a complete coming to rest of the individual soul (Nyaya/Vaisheshika and the later Purva Mimamsa) or an overcoming of the distance between individual and absolute consciousness (Samkhya, Yoga) and parts of the Vedanta.[3]

Von Stietencron goes on to point out that although the systems have similar goals, each system has a different orientation through which to achieve them. These are summarized in the dictionary portion of this volume.

Although Hinduism has undergone tremendous development throughout its evolution, and although there are thousands of Hindu sects possessing peculiarities that differentiate them from each other, certain key components remain constant.

Texts

First are the Vedic texts, including the *Rigveda* and the *Upanishads*. The voluminous *Mahabharata* contains the universally adored *Bhagavad Gita*. Additional texts include the *Brahmanas*, the *Sutras*, the *Aranyakas*, and numerous other sacred writings.

God

The heart of Hinduism lies in its conception of God, reality, and humankind's relationship and affinity to that reality. Its fundamental conception is that *Brahman is the all-encompassing principle of ultimacy. It is a manifested in all creation, both animate and inanimate, as a lower vibration of the ultimate higher spirit Brahman. Hinduism adheres both to monotheism and monism in that all of reality proceeds from this one essence. Yet it is also polytheistic in that it advocates worshiping many lesser deities; this one essence is expressed pluralistically in the material universe. For this reason Hinduism also adheres to *pantheism. The individual self-expression of Brahman in each being is called *atman. The ultimate goal or quest of all of religion according to Hinduism is to identify atman with Brahman.

Hinduism differs greatly from Christianity, JUDAISM, and Islam with respect to its doctrine(s) of God. The

Indian expression *ekambrahman dvitiyanasti* ("Brahman is one and there is no second") resonates with the Hebrew *Shema*, "Hear, O Israel: The LORD our God, the LORD is one" (Deut. 6:4). On the surface it appears as if Hinduism is advancing a monotheism comparable to the other great religions of the world. But the similarity quickly disappears when one discovers what is actually meant by the expression "Brahman is one." It is not the case, as in Christianity where God is conceived in terms of both *immanence and *transcendence, that this is the Hindu conception. The Hindu conceives Brahman not as a separate metaphysical reality, but rather as a principle of life that comprises all that exists. That there may be lesser deities (whether hundreds or thousands) does not matter. Brahman is a neuter principle through which and by which all of reality is a part.

Paradoxically, Brahman is conceived as being nonpersonal, yet at the same time indistinct from humanity. For Christianity, God is personal insofar as he is immanent. God's transcendent nature makes him no less a personal God. It merely distinguishes God from his creation. The very notion of God as being distinct from creation, fundamental and essential to Christian thought, is inconceivable to the Hindu.

Comparisons have frequently been made between the Hindu and Christian conceptions of God as a divine *Trinity. The Christian God, revealed as Father, Son, and Holy Spirit, is often equated with the Hindu doctrine of God as being Brahman, Vishnu, and Siva (Creator, Preserver, Destroyer). But once again, this similarity is misleading. The mere fact that Christianity embraces the doctrine of God as being transcendent rules such a similarity null and void. For Hinduism, because God is a neuter principle of reality, the triad of deities is but a manifestation of that one reality. Christianity conceives of God as being one in essence and three in persons. The Father is the all-powerful Creator (*see* Apostles' and Nicene creeds, Appendix 1). God is all-powerful and yet as "Father" he is a personal and loving God. The Son is the *incarnation of God in the person of Jesus Christ, whose work is first and foremost redemption. The Holy Spirit is the "Lord and giver of life" (Nicene Creed) and is the sanctifier, comforter, and teacher.

In Hinduism, Brahman is conceived of as being a creator like God the Father in Christianity. But Brahman's work of creation consists of creating new manifestations of reality, which are continuously unfolding. For Christianity, God created the earth within the confines of time. According to Genesis, this time was six days (Gen. 1), after which God rested on the seventh day, concluding that the creation was "very good" (1:31) and complete (2:1).

Vishnu is referred to as the preserver. The creations of Brahman are thus preserved by Vishnu. Vishnu is worshiped in ten incarnations. These are described in the Vedic literature. When *dharma* (order) is threatened, Vishnu leaves the heavenly realm and becomes incarnate in one of ten forms to restore and preserve order.

The classical number of these incarnations is ten, ascending from theriomorphic (animal form) to fully anthropomorphic (human form) manifestations. These are: fish (Matsya), tortoise (Kurma), boar (Varaha), man-lion (Narasimha), dwarf (Vamana), rama-with-the-ax (Parasurama), King Rama, Krishna, Buddha, and the future incarnation, Kalkin.[4]

In Christianity, Jesus Christ is God's singular incarnation. As in Hinduism, this incarnation was necessary to restore order, but this order was essential to bring about reconciliation between God and creation through a specific act of atonement. Therefore, Jesus did not come to "preserve" the existing order of things. Rather, the work of the second person of the Trinity can be described as being a work of re-creation and restoration of the creation alienated from God by sin.

Siva, the third God of the Hindu triad, is called the destroyer. Siva is the most ambivalent of Hindu deities. He is a god who shows mercy, or on a moment's notice becomes the god who destroys. He represents unpredictability and caprice. The element of eroticism is introduced in Siva worship. Siva is often worshiped in the form of the 'linga or symbol of creation. Many have conceptualized the linga as a phallic symbol, but this is misleading. He is seduced by the goddess 'Parvati, who herself is personified as being various female deities (Devi, 'Kali), and she is Siva's very source of power.

Christianity offers no correspondence to Siva in its doctrine of the third person of the Trinity. The Holy Spirit, far from being a destroyer, is "Lord and giver of life" (Nicene Creed). Again, each of the persons of the Christian Godhead proceed from one single essence. Christianity remains strictly monotheistic, offering a sharp contrast to the pluralistic ideas endemic to Hindu thought.

Creation

Another important difference between these two great religions of the world is that Christianity teaches that God created the world *ex nihilo* ("out of nothing"). An oft-repeated aphorism from the Sanskrit captures the contrast of Hinduism: *navastuno vastusiddhih* ("out of nothing nothing can come"). A helpful illustration of how the Hindu views God's involvement in creation was provided by a Christian missionary to India, S. H. Kellogg.

> If I go into a dark room and see a rope which I mistake for a snake, the rope is the cause of the appearance of that snake; even so, when I see the world, which seems to everyone to be other than God, yet is really That One, I must say that God is the cause of what appears to me to be a world.[5]

Karma, Reincarnation, and Salvation

The central loci of Hindu thought are the doctrines of atman, Brahman, and karma. Karma is the law of retributive justice, whereby one's actions and deeds result in release (*moksha*) from a previous birth to a higher or lower rebirth in the cycle of reincarnation, depending on deeds done in a previous existence. The soul (atman) is caught up in this wandering process (*samsara*), the end of which results in atman and Brahman becoming identified. Continuous bad karma results in rebirth into lower life-forms. One of the reasons why the incredible poverty and social inequity that exist in lower castes do not elicit a sympathetic response from the more well-to-do is because an attempt to intervene is seen as an interruption in the cosmic process ('lila). For the Hindu, reality is spirit. All matter is an illusion ('maya).

The devout Hindu works toward the escape from rebirth through following the different paths of the six schools (see above). One may follow the path of 'jnana marga (way of knowledge), the path of 'karma marga (way of works), or the path of 'bhakti marga (the way of devotion). All lead to the same end. These three paths comprise the Hindu way of salvation. Ramakrishna and Vivekananda in the nineteenth century insisted that all religions were summarized under these three paths. Movements within the various religions have emphasized one or more of them.

The traditional Christian view of these matters differs greatly from that of Hinduism. First, the distinction between good and evil is denied by the Hindu because material reality is illusory. Illusion arises when the supreme Brahma as unconditioned ('nirgun) becomes conditioned in the world. Because all is Brahma (pantheism), sin becomes utter illusion. Karma is not sin in the sense of rebellion against God. Rather, it is merely a designated part of one's destiny. Although Hindu literature speaks frequently of the confessions of sins, responsibility toward God for such is denied.

Salvation in Hinduism, therefore, is not the forgiveness of sins committed against God. Contrariwise, salvation is a quest to end all earthly suffering, an escape from illusion, and the successful attainment of ᵖnirvana. An Indian folk song laments:

> How many births are past, I cannot tell.
> How many yet to come no man can say:
> But this alone I know, and know full well,
> That pain and grief embitter all the way.[6]

For Christianity, history is linear. Death for the Christian results in immediate translation to life eternal. In Hindu thought, history is cyclical, and death results in rebirth into another life-form. The rebirth is a necessary and natural consequence of karma, whether good or bad.

Incarnation

Along the lines of the incarnation of God, it has already been mentioned that Hinduism wholeheartedly acknowledges the divine intervention into history of the ten incarnations of Vishnu (see above). These god-men are known as ᵖavatars, who have descended from the sublime to the visible illusory realm throughout history. For Hinduism, all of creation is an aspect of the deity, and the creation plays an active role in incarnation. In Christianity, incarnation is the activity of God revealing himself in the person of Jesus Christ. This incarnation is different because it involves the infinite and qualitatively unique Son of God. Second, for Christianity the Christ's incarnation has as its purpose the activity of atonement and redemption from sin. It has already been shown that this idea is foreign to Hindu doctrine. Third, the Christian incarnation is a one-time event (Gal. 4:4). For Hinduism, there have been nine incarnations. Eight have manifested themselves, with one remaining. Finally, the unique Christian incarnation of God in Christ means that salvation is possible through Christ alone (Rom. 3:24; 6:23). The very antithesis of this is taught in Hinduism, namely, that salvation is a universal enterprise and that all paths lead to God.

In many of the Hindu sects it is believed that some of the great leaders in history were avatars. Jesus Christ is considered one of them.[7]

Other

Many folk myths remain an important ingredient in Hindu life and have adapted themselves most remarkably to modernity. Important cultural and political leaders have been quite easily identified as being incarnations. The philosopher Shankara and the social reformer Mahatma Gandhi are but two examples of this.

Of special importance is the sanctity of specific holy places. The ᵖGanges River of northern India is the most sacred of all. Believed to have been brought down from heaven by King Bhagiratha in order to purify the ashes of his departed ancestors, it has become a goddess in itself and the place where Hindus gather for worship, or to sprinkle the ashes of their own departed loved ones for purifying.

Devotion is a way of life in India. God is worshiped more domestically than publicly. Many rites, foreign to Christianity, are celebrated in Hindu homes. Notes von Stietencron:

> There is also a difference in the attitude of the individual toward God. Like Westerners, Indians have many ways of relating to God. But if we were to attempt to pick an especially characteristic attitude, we could say that in his dealings with God, the Christian is perhaps above all a repentant sinner and the Muslim an obedient slave, while the Hindu encounters his god primarily as a host.[8]

Von Stietencron goes on to identify sixteen domestic rituals or ᵖupacaras.

> (1) The deity is led in, (2) offered a seat . . . (3) offered water to wash his feet, (4) face and hands as well as (5) water to rinse his mouth. . . . Then the deity is (6) bathed, (7) dressed, (8) furnished with the sacred cord carefully decorated, and (9) rubbed with aromatic ointments—usually sandalwood paste, camphor, and saffron. The god receives (10) blossoms from his favorite flowers and trees, (11) incense, and (12) light from a lamp burning sesame oil or melted butter. Then a sacrificial meal (13) is set before the god and after that some betel nuts (14). Only when the guest has dined is he given a present (15), and the ritual ends (16) with a reverential circumambulation of the deity.[9]

The devotional life is comprised of four stages or ᵖashramas. The first stage is that of ᵖbrahmacarin, where one learns the piety of religion. Second is ᵖgrihastha, where one becomes domesticated (marriage accompanying) and enjoys the status of a householder. Third is ᵖvanaprastha, or the stage usually entered into on becoming grandparents, where religious devotion is intensified. The fourth stage, ᵖ sannyasin, is optional. The sannyasin renounces caste and becomes a homeless wandering ascetic, seeking only to become enlightened and one with God.

Meditation is an important component of devotional life. There are numerous forms and approaches. Yoga is most common.

The most distinguishing feature of Hindu thought is its all-embracing pluralism. It is tolerant of other systems of thought and non-Hindu religions for the same reason that other religions are intolerant toward it and each other. Each religion's truth is, from its own perspective, the highest of all truths. For Hinduism, the highest of all truths is the truth of all religions. Therefore by definition it adjusts itself to the most divergent thought forms.

CONCLUSION

Eighty percent of the Hindu population in the world are ᵇvaishnavites, while the remainder are members of Hindu reform movements or neo-Hindu sects, the most important of them being the *arya-samaj*. The influence of Hinduism in the West, particularly in America, was far-reaching during the twentieth century and on into the twenty-first. Americans continue to explore and embrace the ideals of this fascinating religion in a variety of expressions especially adapted to the West.

ADDITIONAL INFORMATION_____

Websites
www.hinduweb.org; www.hinduismtoday.com; www.hinduism.co.za

Sacred Texts
The *Vedas*, *Upanishads*, and numerous other scared writings.

Statistics
There are an estimated eight hundred million to one billion Hindus in the world. There are just under one million in the United States.

Notes
[1] *Encyclopaedia Britannica*, 15th ed., s.v. "Hinduism."
[2] See other entries for a more detailed definition of each of the six schools.
[3] Hans Küng, Josef van Ess, Heinrich von Stietencron, and Heinz Bechert, *Christianity and the World Religions: Paths to Dialogue with Islam, Hinduism, and Buddhism*, trans. Peter Heinegg (New York: Doubleday, 1986), 154–55.
[4] *Encyclopaedia Britannica*, 15th ed., s.v. "Hinduism."
[5] S. H. Kellogg, *A Handbook of Comparative Religions* (Philadelphia: Westminster, 1899), 30.
[6] Ibid., 70.
[7] Other such avatars include ᵇGautama Buddha, Guru ᵇNanak, Ramakrishna, etc. Reform movements and sects tend to consider their respective founders as avatars. For example, ᵇEckankar believes Paul ᵇTwitchell to be a modern-day avatar.
[8] Küng et al., *Christianity and the World Religions*, 244.
[9] Ibid., 245–46.

IDENTITY MOVEMENTS; CHRISTIAN IDENTITY; WHITE SUPREMACY

The events of September 11, 2001, brought the frightening realities of terrorism to the forefront of the world's stage. However, it was the bombing of the Alfred Murrah Federal Building in Oklahoma City in 1995 that previously brought the shocking realities of terrorism on the home front, an ominous precursor to the fall of the World Trade Center.

HISTORY

THE NATION OF ISLAM (Black Muslim Movement), RASTAFARIANISM, and names such as Marcus ᵇGarvey, Elijah ᵇMuhammad, ᵇMalcolm X, Wallace ᵇFard, and Louis ᵇFarrakhan are organizations or leaders bound, at least philosophically, to the conviction that the black race reigned supreme in the past and will one day rise to hegemony again. Christian Identity movements constitute the white version of the same melodrama, played out, not in temples, synagogues, or ᵇmosques dotted throughout the large urban areas of the country, but in the heartland of rural America, where "churches" and survival camps have been springing up in the past several decades. The hatred and racism that was so much a part of America's past, although no longer sanctioned legally, still lives on in the souls of extremists both white and black, an ever-ominous testimony to the fact that the human heart is as desperately wicked as Jeremiah said well over two millennia ago (Jer. 17:9).

Christian Identity is an umbrella concept embodying a plurality of movements championing a prowhite, fiercely anti-Semitic, antigovernment, and promilitia set of dogmas based on the conviction that the white race, or Aryan peoples, are the true descendants of Adam. The term *identity* denotes the belief that white Anglo-Saxon Protestants are the "true identity" of Israel, particularly the lost ten tribes of Israel, and that America is the new promised land where these chosen people of God have been predestined to reside.[1] Identity is inclusive of all organizations and movements loyal to these principles. What follows is a general discussion of some of the significant Identity groups and an analysis of their general theological precepts.

Ku Klux Klan

All discussion of white supremacy in America begins with the Ku Klux Klan, founded in Pulaski, Tennessee, in 1866 by six Confederate officers. Borrowing the name from a college fraternity, early Klansmen mendaciously sought to terrorize blacks by donning white sheets and posing as ghosts of dead Confederate soldiers. In essence, the Klan was part of the white resistance movement to radical post-Civil War reconstruction. Klan terror reached its zenith in the late 1860s when it was known also as the "Invisible Empire of the South." Its first ▶Grand Wizard, Nathan Bedford ▶Forrest, ordered the "Empire" to disband in 1869 because of the extreme violence, and in 1871 Congress passed the Ku Klux Act, imposing heavy penalties on any organization that inflicted violence on individuals or groups of citizens. Klan activities ceased though white supremacy in the South resurfaced in the decades following.

The twentieth century saw the rebirth of the Klan in 1915, when a preacher named William Simmons organized a new movement outside of Atlanta, Georgia. Simmons had been influenced by D. W. Griffith's film *The Birth of a Nation*, where Klansmen of the nineteenth century were romantically portrayed as heroes who had preserved the moral fiber and character of America. The new version of the Klan's crusading included warning America of the incipient dangers of communism following the Bolshevik Revolution in 1917. Roman Catholics, Jews, and labor unions were added to the list of evils threatening the well-being of white Christian Americans.

The popularity of the Klan surged between 1915 and 1930, with a total membership between four and six million. However, the onslaught of the Great Depression and the continued use of extreme violence again thinned the ranks in the 1930s. By 1944 the organization had become defunct. Ten years later, however, Klan activity sprang up again in response to the famous *Brown v. Board of Education* ruling that racial segregation in public schools was unconstitutional. But a far more significant resurgence in Klan activity arose as the Civil Rights Act (1964) produced violent reactions to forced compliance in the South. The civil rights movement of the turbulent 1960s resulted in extreme public protest against the Klan, especially concerning its role in the murder of several activists and other acts

of violence, and by 1970 membership had been reduced to a mere several thousand.

The Ku Klux Klan has become divided into smaller klaverns in the last several decades, and it is these splinter groups that have become aligned with the Identity movement and various neo-Nazi groups. Currently there are three major Klans that have influenced still smaller groups of Klansmen. According to Andy Oakley, who spent six years as an undercover reporter investigating white supremacist organizations, the three main groups are:

> The United Klans of America [which is] . . . threatened with extinction due to a 1987 court ruling awarding seven million dollars to the mother of a black teenager who was brutally murdered by the Klan in 1981. The Invisible Empire, Knights of the Ku Klux Klan, is strongest in Connecticut and virtually in every southern state, despite a declaration of bankruptcy by formal Imperial Wizard Bill Wilkinson in 1983. The Knights of the Ku Klux Klan has made inroads in the north as well as in Georgia and Alabama.[2]

According to Klanwatch Project of the Southern Poverty Law Center, there are many lesser klaverns located throughout the country, particularly in the South. Leadership for the movement as a whole, however, is provided by the three large groups.

Before examining the beliefs and practices of the Klan, we will analyze other significant white supremacist and Identity movements.

Neo-Nazism

Adolf Hitler's National Socialists, or Nazi party, with its violent and pernicious anti-Semitic agenda carried out in Germany between 1933 and 1945, elicited admiration from sympathetic white Americans, some of whom were Klansmen. Others became followers of George Lincoln ▶Rockwell, who formed the American Nazi Party in Arlington, Virginia, in 1958. In Hitler-like fashion, Rockwell succeeded in drawing attention to himself and his racist ideology through his charisma and speaking ability, though he did not gain enough support for his political party. Rockwell himself was murdered in August 1967 in Arlington. The party was renamed the National Socialist White People's Party and subsequently The New Order, today consisting of approximately four hundred members. Many neo-Nazi parties have formed since the time of Rockwell's assassination. According to Oakley, "Anywhere between five to twenty-five active Nazi groups can coexist in a given month, depending on how many cadres form anew, split, consolidate, or cease to exist."[3]

One of the significant differences between the Klan and the neo-Nazis is that most movements within the latter are inspired by a sociopolitical ideology much the same as Hitler's championing of the cultural and intellectual superiority of the Aryan people. The Klan, on the other hand, justifies its existence from a quasi-religious and pseudo-Christian belief system. The outstanding exception to this general rule is the Aryan Nations (see below), which eclectically combines elements of Nazism and Christianity.[4]

Other

A third category of white supremacists classified also as being members of the Identity movement are eclectic groups that do not necessarily claim allegiance to the Klan or to the National Socialists. Some denounce the extremism of the other two groups, while others would go to extremes far beyond the excesses of Klansmen and neo-Nazis. Oakley includes over one hundred groups in this latter category.[5]

Anecdotal stories break out regularly in the news concerning individuals and groups who go far enough in their extremism to attract attention. A few examples will suffice.

- In March 2000 in Branson, Missouri, a group gathered to celebrate white supremacy.

- August B. Kreis, a leader of Aryan Nations in the northeast United States, stated in August 2001, in the defense of another Identity friend, Christopher Slavin, on trial at the time for the murder of two Mexicans, that he (Kreis) does not support the killing of blacks and Jews because it will be God who will "eliminate all non-whites."

- Timothy McVeigh, before his bombing of the Federal Building, was known to be a devout follower of Identity principles. He had phoned an Identity community called Elohim City in Muskogee, Oklahoma.

- According to one recent source, "many Identity enthusiasts . . . argue vehemently that the Oklahoma bombing in 1995 was the work of the U.S. Government, as part of a plot to discredit the right."[6] Many within the movement have come to identify the government as ZOG (Zionist Occupation Government).

The most vocal spokesman for Identity theology has been Pastor Richard Butler of the Church of Jesus Christ Christian/Aryan Nations. Excerpts of his sermons appear in the "Teachings and Beliefs" section. Due to age, ill health, and a loss of power, Butler stepped down from control of the organization in 2001 after a lawsuit caused the loss of the Idaho compound. A dispute arose within Aryan Nations when it was alleged that the national director, Pastor Ray Redfeairn, was attempting to step into leadership over Butler. Refeairn denied this allegation. In its place, he announced the establishment of a high council comprised of three officers, including Butler and August Kreis. Butler died in September 2004. Kreis is completely convinced of the Anglo-Israeli theory and is motivated by extreme anti-Semitism, his goal being that all Jews eventually be removed from the United States.

TEACHINGS AND BELIEFS

There were over 530 groups at the beginning of the twenty-first century, so we cannot discuss all of the Identity movements in the United States and their various beliefs. What follows is an analysis of the doctrines of some of the

Publications typical of white supremacy groups: *Creed of the Klansmen*, along with copies of *Christian Vanguard* and *Racial Loyalty*.

Courtesy Jack M. Roper/CARIS

more popular groups (popular defined by media coverage). It is not inaccurate to say that the following analysis speaks broadly for all of the Identity movements, although each group may differ in some particulars.

> Adolf Hitler was not just another man. Into a world which had lost its sense of direction, He came to show the way. Into a world of decadence and false values, He came to proclaim the great eternal truths. Into a world grown cynical and materialistic, He came to bring a new birth of radiant idealism. Into a world standing at the abyss, He came to offer hope and salvation to an entire race.[7]

If Matthias Koehl, leader of the National Socialist White People's Party based in Arlington, Virginia, had not revealed from the outset that Hitler was the recipient of this generous kudo, the reader would no doubt be predisposed to conclude that this litany of praise is referring to Jesus Christ himself. If we shift scenes and move from Arlington to the panhandle of Idaho to the site of the Aryan Nations, Church of Jesus Christ Christian, we hear the words of Janet Hounsel, church secretary, who claimed in 1983, "We're not saluting Hitler—we're saluting God."[8]

Deeply embedded within Identity movements is the belief that the white race is the chosen race of God. Adam is the ancestor of whites only, while other races, predating Adam, are descended from *Satan or fallen angelic beings. White supremacists who pursue their beliefs from a religious and Christian perspective adhere to the notion that Israel is God's chosen people and comprises twelve tribes (Ex. 28:21; Rev. 21:12), all of which are descended from the twelve sons of Jacob (Gen. 48–49). Moreover, Israel, dispersed from Palestine in the first century, continues to exist through the white Anglo-Saxons of the British Isles. Migrating to America, the British entered the new promised land intended by God to be settled by whites alone. According to the statement of faith issued by Kingdom Bible Institute:

> We believe the time has come (Isaiah 27:12) when the lost Israel "nation and company of nations" (Gen. 35:11) is being found and positively identified. Only one race today answers in every detail to the Bible picture of Israel "in the latter days," and that is the Anglo-Saxon race—the British Empire and the United States of America. They possess what Israel was to possess and they are doing what Israel was to do. The "identities" of this race with Israel are so many and so pronounced that one who re-reads and carefully studies his Bible in the light

of this great truth will make discoveries that will cause him to give this subject more serious thought, especially in view of what is happening in literal fulfillment of the Bible prophecy in the world today. The Gentile kingdoms are being broken, the time of Israel's captivity is terminating, the old Gentile social order is being overthrown, and the world is being prepared for the coming reign, on the throne of David, of our Lord, the uniting of all the tribes (Ezek. 37) and the restoration of His Kingdom in the earth (Zech. 14:9ff.; Luke 1:32–33).[9]

Like Herbert W. *Armstrong, many Identity groups argue that even the etymology of the term *British* testifies to the truth of Anglo-Israeliism. The Rev. William P. Gale, an official of the survivalist and antitax group Posse Comitatus (meaning "power of the county"), leader of Committee of the States, and publisher of the quarterly *Identity* writes as follows on the similarity between English and Aramaic:

> Researchers of philology have written that the 19th Century establishes such affinity as can be accounted for, only by the fact that the nations who originally spoke them had a common origin. This common origin traces back to Adam and Eve and their progeny who spoke and wrote in the language with which Adam arrived on the earth: ancient Aramaic, otherwise known as Hebrew. This is not to be confused with the language spoken by Jews (Yiddish) and it should be understood that the Jews are NOT Hebrews. The Book to the Hebrews is in the NEW Testament. The languages mentioned above and the people who speak them can be traced back to the Aramaic or Hebrew origin. And it is interesting to note that the word Brit-Ain is actually two Hebrew words, Brith-Ain, meaning "Covenant Land." The word Brit-Ish is also two Hebrew words meaning "Covenant Man." Here again is the word "ish" for "man" (Adam).[10]

Based on the comments of "Brigadier General" Gordon "Jack" Mohr of Crusade for Christ and Country, the Anglo-Israeliism of Identity should not be mistaken for Armstrong's version of the same.[11] Aside from Identity's emphasis on white supremacy, most of the churches and organizations within its ranks teach orthodox Christian doctrine, particularly of a conservative *fundamentalist rendition.

Identity advances a theology of racism that includes all nonwhite races in addition to Jewish people. They use several theories to justify racism from a biblical/theological standpoint. One theory suggests that

Noah's son Ham became the descendant of the black race because Ham was cursed by Noah (Gen. 9:20–27). A second argument suggests that Cain was the progeny of a sexual encounter between Eve and Satan and therefore became the "seed of the serpent" in Genesis 3:15. Many who advocate this idea believe that the Jews were descended from Cain, while Cain's brother Abel was the pure descendant of Adam.[12] Some believe that Cain's murder of Abel brought on him a curse or a "mark" that resulted in eternal slavery, passed down not to Jews but to blacks, hence justifying why Christians can still serve God and own slaves. Whatever the various "theologies" advanced, the unifying principle within the Klan and all Identity movements is that the white race is the superior race descended from Adam.

The most vocal spokesman for Identity was Richard G. Butler of the Aryan Nations, Church of Jesus Christ Christian. He was arrested in 1987 on charges of conspiracy and sedition, though subsequently he was acquitted of these charges. The *Seattle Times* summarizes one of Butler's sermons as follows:

> Butler began with a vision of an Aryan race as "conquerors of the earth from Pole to Pole and from sea to sea." "White people must know who they are, where they came from and why they are here," Butler proclaimed. "The evolutionists try to tell you that you and your children evolved from an ape, that the ape evolved from a fish and that the fish evolved from scum.
>
> "But this is not so, because Aryan man is the son of God."
>
> In rapid order, Butler criticized sex education in schools, reminded his congregation that "herpes is a totally incurable disease," condemned the United States aid to Israel and proclaimed that "atomic energy is contrary to the law of God."
>
> He condemned communism and homosexuals, labeled a nationally renowned evangelist a "lying preacher and a fairy," warned that all the nation's industry soon will be relocated in foreign lands, contended that Jews control world finance, branded blacks as cultural and intellectual misfits and then ended his sermon with the bottom line: "You are the sons and daughters of the Most High God. The final battle was not Berlin. It is the United States, where we will fight to the end to preserve the purity of our race."[13]

Butler quoted Hitler regularly, keeping a copy of *Mein Kampf* right next to his ▶Bible. Despite Hitler's campaign against the Jews, Butler argues that the Holocaust of World War II is an "elaborate, Jew concocted hoax."

A violent offshoot of the Aryan Nations, the Klan, and the Missouri/Arkansas-based survivalist group, the Covenant, the Sword, and the Arm of the Lord, was a group called The Order. Many of its leaders have been arrested for acts of violence, including robbery and shootings. The *Oregonian* in 1985 reported that the emerging Order referred to itself as being the "Fifth Era." "In the past . . . Klan members had worked only to keep blacks and other minorities in their place." The Order proposes "the final solution" as was applied in Nazi Germany, the complete removal and/or extermination of all Jews.[14]

Another popular version of white supremacy finds expression in the Skinheads of America, a neo-Nazi subculture comprised of youthful punk-rockers.

> We are working class Aryan Youth. We oppose the capitalist and the communist scum that are destroying our Aryan race. We also realize that the parasitic Jewish race is at the heart of our problem, along with the traitors of our own race, who willingly do the Jews' bidding. Our heads are shaved for battle.[15]

The eschatology of Identity is expectant of a full-fledged race war culminating in the total victory of the white race. Survivalism is an important concept within their ranks. Many groups are storing food, water, and ammunition in survival camps dotted throughout the country in anticipation of the long-awaited Armageddon. Some extremists believe it is their place to initiate violence now in order to help usher in the Millennium (*see* ▶millennialism). Increasingly there are reports of violence and bloodshed linked to Identity movements.

Milder contemporary solutions to the "Jewish problem" are suggested by "Brigadier General" Jack Mohr:

> So we could easily start off, not with bullets, but by cutting off their supply of blood. Stop buying from the Jews; refuse to sell to them, to do business with them. "Oh," but you say, "that would ruin my business." But it might keep you alive and free! Advertisers on TV and in the daily newspapers are helping the Jews, so boycott them! Television preachers like Jerry Falwell, and Pat Robinson, and Billy Graham are Jewish stooges, so refuse to support them with the Lord's money. . . . Don't socialize with the Jews. Don't vote for those they support and who support them. . . . THE TIME HAS COME! IF WE CAN'T VOTE THEM OUT, THROW THEM OUT! BUT GET RID OF THE PARASITES.[16]

August Kreis more recently put it this way: "How much longer is it going to take for His True Chosen Race to awake to the menace of this blight of parasitic Satanic Jews sucking the blood from our very nation?"[17]

Traditional CHRISTIANITY stands in contradistinction to the racism and hatred espoused by "Christian" white supremacists. Nowhere does the Bible support the idea of a culturally, intellectually, and morally superior nation or race. "All have sinned and fall short of the glory of God" (Rom. 3:23). God's covenant promise to Abraham was that he would be the father of "many nations" (Gen. 17:5). According to long-held Christian belief, this promise remained unfulfilled until the Day of Pentecost, when the Holy Spirit was poured out and the Christian church was born (Acts 2:38–39; 3:25). At this point, Jews, Arabs, Greeks, Romans, and others began to embrace Christianity, but it must be remembered that the majority of early Christians were Jews. It was only after A.D. 70 when the Romans leveled the city of Jerusalem that Christianity became an increasingly Gentile movement. We must also remember that throughout the history of the church, many Jewish have become Christians.

Moreover, Jesus stated emphatically that "salvation is from the Jews" (John 4:22), and Paul always preached in the synagogues on his arrival in any town to establish a mission (Acts 13:14; 14:1; 17:1, 17; 18:4, 19, 26; 19:8). "For I am not ashamed of the gospel of Christ: for it is the power of God unto salvation to every one that believeth; to the Jew first, and also to the Greek" (Rom. 1:16 KJV).

Finally, we must remember that it is faith in Christ that saves, not adherence to the law (Gal. 2:21). This includes both Jews and Gentiles. Abraham was justified by faith long before Moses presented Israel with the Ten Commandments (Ex. 20; Rom. 4:9). Although scholars disagree on the correct interpretation of Romans 9–11, most conclude that Paul is arguing that God has not turned away from Israel or the Jews. What Paul does state emphatically is that Israel has always had a faithful remnant who were "justified by faith." And it is this faithful remnant, or "spiritual Israel," that must be distinguished sharply from those Israelites claiming to be God's elect simply because they were of the seed of Abraham (Rom. 9:7–8). Paul does concede that the majority of the Jews turned their backs on Jesus of Nazareth and lost the true righteousness of God as the result of unbelief. He calls them "disobedient" (10:21) and says that their unbelief is what cut them off from salvation (11:19). But in the same breath, Paul warns that unbelief causes both Jew and Gentile to stumble. If this is true, then the inverse is also true.

Faith in Christ justifies *both Jew and Gentile*. Throughout the history of the church, there have always been Jewish believers in Jesus Christ.

Even if every single Jewish person who ever lived rejected the Christian gospel, the Christian is still instructed to love all people, even enemies: "Love your enemies and pray for those who persecute you" (Matt. 5:44). Some white supremacists regard Jews as subhuman. Nowhere is this in the Bible, unless one deliberately misinterprets the Scriptures. "The Son of Man is going to be betrayed into the hands *of men*" (Mark 9:31), not subhumans (italics added).

To the argument that it was the Jews who crucified Jesus, the Christian response is clear. First, although the Jews instigated the crucifixion with the arrest and mock trial, it was the Romans who carried it out. Both Jew and Gentile alike played a role in the execution. Second, the crucifixion was necessary. Without it, there could never have been salvation. Jesus himself asked God to forgive his enemies on the grounds that they were ignorant of what they had done (Luke 23:34). Nowhere does Jesus curse them or advocate hatred and bigotry toward his adversaries. Furthermore, Peter, in his first sermon on the Day of Pentecost, bluntly tells the Jews that it was their wicked hands that crucified the Christ (Acts 2:23). But does he then advocate that all Jews be rounded up and exterminated, as extremists in the Identity movement do? No! He commands them to repent and be baptized (2:38), and Scripture declares that many (Jews) became believers (2:41–47).

Paul had been an avid persecutor of Christians, carrying out what he believed was a righteous holy-war theology for the cause of JUDAISM. Acts reports his dramatic conversion (Acts 9:1–9). If God had turned away from Jews because they were the Christ-slayers and enemies of the church, why was a loving hand of forgiveness extended to Paul? Why did Ananias, who was a believer, forgive Paul (9:10ff.)? Why did any Jews convert to Christianity?

Racial and intellectual superiority have no place within the Christian religion. The greatness of a person's character is measured by humility, as Jesus demonstrated by washing his disciples' feet (John 13:5), by holding up a child as an example of who will inhabit the kingdom of heaven (Mark 10:15), and by dying on the cross for the love of the world (John 3:16).

With regard to slavery, the argument has been raised that not only does the Bible not condemn slavery, it seems to at least permit it. Therefore, subsuming the black race to slavery was merely the continuation of a practice common in Jesus' time. Members of the Ku

Klux Klan advanced this argument to at least justify the past. While it is true that the Bible does not condemn slavery, the New Testament seems to do so *implicitly*. Paul's letter to Philemon is an entreaty to Philemon to receive back his runaway slave Onesimus, not as a servant, but as a brother (Philem. 16). The gospel rightly understood destroys slavery as it changes the status of a person in Jesus Christ from a slave to a brother or sister. "There is neither Jew nor Greek, slave nor free, male nor female, for you are all one in Christ Jesus" (Gal. 3:28).

CONCLUSION

"Aryan Nations won't remain inconspicuous," Reverend Butler once vowed. "Aryan Nations . . . has been kind of like the oak. It doesn't grow fast—but it grows big and it grows strong."[18] It is not certain just how big this "oak tree" has become. In the twenty-first century there has been a surge of growth, with new splinter groups arising from the ranks of Aryan Nations and other movements. Oakley, along with others who study and write about Identity theology, demonstrates that it is at least a tree with many branches. Though some of them are sawed off through public pressure and arrests, the tree itself remains an ever-present reminder of the fact that human beings cannot always be tempered by the outward constraints of law, culture, or civilization. If this tree of racism, bigotry, and hatred must remain among the many others in the eclectic garden of human philosophy and religious expression, then like the "tree of the knowledge of good and evil" (Gen. 2–3), may it stand alone, and may its forbidden fruit remain untouched and uneaten.

ADDITIONAL INFORMATION

Websites for the More Popular Identity Groups Include:
Ku Klux Klan: *www.kkk.com*

Aryan Nations: *www.christian-aryannations.com*
Posse Comitatus: *www.posse-comitatus.org*
Kingdom Identity Ministries: *www.kingidentity.com*
White Aryan Resistance: *www.resist.com*

Membership
537 groups (as of 2000); app. 200,000 members; militia groups estimated to be active in almost forty states

Notes
[1] See WORLDWIDE CHURCH OF GOD for a discussion of Anglo-Israeliism.
[2] Andy Oakley, *88: An Undercover News Reporter's Expose of America's Nazis and the Ku Klux Klan* (Skokie, Ill.: P.O. Publishing, 1987), 10.
[3] Ibid., 8.
[4] Ibid., 10.
[5] Ibid., 153–61
[6] Dennis Tourish D. and Tim Wolforth, *On the Edge: Political Cults Right and Left* (New York: Sharpe, 2000).
[7] Statement made by Matthias Koehl, leader of the National Socialist White People's Party, Arlington, Virginia, as quoted in an article by Paul Henderson, *Pacific* (Sunday Magazine of *Seattle Times*) (April 17, 1983), 7.
[8] Ibid., 10.
[9] Vada Lovell, "What We Believe," *Kingdom Digest* 27/10 (October 1977).
[10] William P. Gale, *Identity* (Glendale, CA.: Ministry of Christ Church, n.d.), 8–9.
[11] Jack Mohr, *The Christian Patriot Crusader* 1/1 (November 1982), 3.
[12] Verne Becker, "The Counterfeit Christianity of the Ku Klux Klan," *Christianity Today* (April 20, 1984), 32–33.
[13] Henderson, *Pacific*, 10–12.
[14] John Snell, "The Order Seen as Representative of White Supremacist's Terrorism," *Oregonian* (December 15, 1985), B4.
[15] Oakley, *88*, 152.
[16] Mohr, *Christian Patriot Crusader*, 7–8.
[17] *www.evnetwork.org/fallkreis.html*, p. 2.
[18] Henderson, *Pacific*, 15.

INTERNATIONAL CHURCHES OF CHRIST (ICOC); BOSTON CHURCH OF CHRIST (BCC); THE BOSTON MOVEMENT; CAMPUS ADVANCE; CROSSROADS MINISTRIES

One of the most active and popular cults on college campuses, the International Churches of Christ (hereafter referred to as the ICOC) has had a significant impact and rapid growth particularly resulting from its recruiting techniques and discipleship practices.

HISTORY

The ICOC has a relatively short history. It grew out of the mainline denomination Churches of Christ (which is now completely disassociated with the ICOC). In 1967, Chuck Lucas, a campus minister at the University of Florida, was gaining converts and began employing ʼdiscipleship techniques. Lucas was a part of the Crossroads Church of Christ in Gainseville, Florida. One of his converts was Kip ʼMcKean, whom Lucas baptized and trained.[1]

After graduating, McKean left Florida to begin campus ministry work at Northeastern Christian Junior College outside of Philadelphia. His tour of duty was only ten months, after which time he moved to Charleston, Illinois, to do campus ministry at Eastern Illinois University. He and another individual named Roger Lamb were both fired from their posts by their sponsoring church, the Memorial Church of Christ in Houston, Texas, because of their excessive discipling techniques.[2] More and more articles were appearing in newspapers throughout the country, citing instances of abusive recruiting techniques (see below).

In June 1979, McKean, now twenty-five years old, and his wife, Elena, moved to the Lexington Church of Christ in Lexington, Massachusetts, where he began practicing the same discipleship techniques. The church had thirty members when McKean arrived. By 1983, the congregation had grown so large that the building was no longer large enough to hold worship services in. The group moved into and began to rent the Boston Opera House. The name "Boston Churches of Christ" was first used here.[3]

It was in Boston that the movement began to define itself exclusively as the one true church of the modern era. Its ambitions were captured in the words of one member: "Whether we are a teen, college student, single adult, single parent, married adult, or senior adult, we must realize that we can effect 'great numbers' for the cause of Christ."[4] Also in 1983, a New York City church was planted and a ministry called "Daytime" was begun for artists and entertainers. Two years later, an ICOC church was planted in Toronto, Canada. In 1986, missions abroad were begun with church plantings in South Africa, India, France, and Sweden. By 1987, the church in Boston was attracting over three thousand attendees each week.

At a congregational meeting in Gainesville in 1988, the Crossroads Church, recognizing that the new movement in Boston was going in a different direction from their own, officially voted to disassociate itself. The reasons cited at the meeting were "usurping congregational autonomy, reconstructing churches, taking control of congregations, granting too much authority to leaders, and requiring that members obey their ʼdiscipler in all matters (even in areas of opinion)."[5] The "congregational autonomy" issue was important in terms of polity. Each congregation in Congregationalism is independent of other congregations with regards to government. But in the case of the ICOC, the organizational structure is strictly hierarchical.

In June 1988, McKean announced that he was no longer the leading evangelist of the movement but was now assuming the title of Missions Evangelist. He surrounded himself with a cabinet of sorts, called his "Focused Few" (later renamed the World Sector Leaders). Church planting became the chief goal of the leadership of the now blossoming movement. The ambitious goal of the group was to "evangelize the world within one generation."

Since then, growth of the ICOC has been rapid. The World Missions Seminar held in the Boston Gardens in 1989 had 12,000 in attendance. McKean shortly thereafter left Massachusetts, taking on a new congregation in Los Angeles. By 1991, the hundredth church was planted (in Moscow), and within a year, 850 people were baptized there. In 1994, the ICOC set a goal to evangelize all countries with a population of 100,000 or more by 2000. That same year, the movement boasted a regular overall Sunday attendance of almost 75,000 worldwide. In 1995, the ICOC planted its two hundredth church worldwide in Pakistan. Only two years later, the ICOC announced its three hundredth overall planting in Armenia and held a World Missions Leadership Conference in Jerusalem. By 1999, there were 372 churches in 158 nations. Sunday worship attendance was tallied at around 186,000. By the year 2000, the movement claimed that its 1994 Evangelism Proclamation goal had been fulfilled, with 171 nations having churches planted.[6]

But serious problems were also developing in the ICOC. There were, and are, many defections. Newspapers abound with stories of ex-members who have told of being manipulated and controlled by their disciplers. Those who leave report that their disengagement from the group was the result of such things as being told how much money to give, how to spend their time during the week, how many times to be in church, which service projects to engage in, which classes to take in college, and in some instances even to leave college. Others spoke of having to confess their sins to their disciplers and of their disciplers threatening and even using confidential confessions as blackmail in order to manipulate and control the person. In 1993, ABC's *20/20* reported that lists of privately confessed sins are sent on to the hierarchy, are computerized and are made available on request of leaders. The Los Angeles church is the Super Church, and it is here where the highest ranked leaders receive their training.

Following the terrorist attacks on the United States on September 11, 2001, Kip McKean announced that he was taking a "sabbatical" with Elena, his wife, in order to address issues relative to their marriage. The McKeans decided to delegate leadership of the ICOC to several World Sector Leaders. In the posted letter, Kip McKean explained how the leadership of the Los Angeles church and the international movement would be divided up. In November, McKean's sabbatical became an official stepping down from the ICOC. The leadership of the movement issued a response to the announcement by stating that McKean would be missed. But the letter admonished that there were "sins" that necessitated his stepping down. The entire ICOC leadership was urged to pray for him and his family.

ORGANIZATION

Until recently, Kip McKean was the World Sector Leader. The ICOC divides their territories of ministry into nine world sectors. World Sector Leaders lead the World Missions Conferences; on the local level, congregations are led by leaders, who appoint disciplers assigned to each new convert.

BELIEFS AND PRACTICES

The actual doctrines of the ICOC are not significantly different from other denominations within broad-based evangelicalism. Important doctrines, for example, are as follows.

God

The ICOC teaches that there is only one true God and that he is revealed as Father, Son, and Holy Spirit in the traditional orthodox sense.

Jesus Christ

Jesus is the Son of God and the Savior of the world. He was crucified and raised from the dead on the third day.

Bible

The Bible is the only inspired and inerrant source and norm of authority. However, McKean reserves for himself the final authority on what the interpretation of Scripture is. Members consult with their disciplers when a question arises as to the meaning of a passage of Scripture.

Salvation

Salvation is by grace through faith. A person must decide to receive God's free gift of salvation. But obe-

dience to Christ's command to baptize is integral to being saved (see below). Note too that the very structure of the church bespeaks a system of legalism and works righteousness. The polity of the church is set up so that one works his or her way to upper leadership positions through good performance and obedience to leaders. The church leaders set goals for evangelism and obligate members (even if only psychologically) to recruit new members; they are made to feel guilty and less secure in their salvation if they do not.

Baptism

Water baptism is an absolute requirement for all members. Apart from this there is no forgiveness. All previous baptisms, regardless of whether one was baptized as a Roman Catholic or any other Protestant church, infant or adult, are invalid. Members are rebaptized by the one true church on earth, the ICOC. The ICOC follows a similar pattern as those denominations that deny the validity of infant baptism. One must make a profession of faith and repent, receiving Christ as Savior. Faith is necessary but not sufficient. It must also be accompanied by baptism because Christ commanded it. Baptism is called "Lordship Baptism."

Personal Confession

Each new member of the movement is assigned a discipler. This is a member who has been trained and is deemed fit to disciple others. Disciplers form a close relationship to the persons they are assigned to. They meet with them for prayer, phone them on a steady basis, teach, council, prompt, urge, and ultimately control the new convert. As alluded to above, private confessions are made to the discipler on the basis of James 5:16. Once a sin or a secret is confessed, it is readily available to any leader in the hierarchy.

Exclusivity

The movement regards itself as the one true church on earth and all others are corrupt. In the words of McKean:

> As for those who continue to oppose us, they are lost, not because their baptism became invalid, but the Scriptures are clear that those who oppose and grumble against God's leadership, and divide God's church, are, in fact, opposing God (Exodus 16:8; Numbers 16). Thus the rebellious become lost because they do not have a true God.[7]

Almost all cults or sects make claims of exclusivity. Without such a claim, they would have no reason to stress that potential converts leave their own churches.

Obedience

The ICOC is perhaps one of the strictest groups in terms of a disciplined procedure of enforcing obedience. Members are taught that leaders should be obeyed even in matters where Scripture is silent. This is justified because leaders, according to Hebrews 13:17, are the caretakers of the souls of each of the members. Traditional orthodox Christianity, however, holds to a more balanced view that demands accountability of its ministers and teachers, as, for example, in the account of the believers in Berea (Acts 17:11).

Discipleship

The model for discipleship adopted by the group is the Matthew 28:18–20 model. Jesus chose twelve disciples and out of the twelve had an inner circle . Hence the ICOC term: "Focus on a few!" Then according to Luke 6:40, a disciple is fully trained to then go and make more disciples. Evangelists in turn continue to make more disciples, and the cycle is repeated. In the case of traditional Christianity, there is no one prescribed New Testament model for discipleship that defines methods and rules for holding converts accountable. Membership in an external organization can never save a person. Only faith in Jesus Christ can (Acts 4:12).

Discipline

When a member fails to submit to the admonishment and fails to confess his or her sins, the senior prayer partner begins a process of withdrawal and inaccessibility, and ultimately, the member is cut off from the group.

Church

McKean considers himself God's anointed for this age. Just as God had raised up reformers throughout the history of the Church, McKean is God's chosen restorer for the modern era.

The ICOC does not conform to biblical and historical Christianity. McKean and leaders of the movement have sought to "restore" the church to its original purity. But the very attempt to "restore" the New Testament church is in itself problematic. Note that Luther, Calvin, and other great figures of the Christian past were "reformers," *not* "restorers." The assumption of the "restorationist" movements is that the church today is no longer a viable or legitimate form of Christianity. Jesus, however, said that "the gates of Hades will not overcome [my church]" (Matt. 16:18). In other words, the church *has always been* in every age. The ICOC contends that they are alone called by God to restore what has been lost and that the church of the New Testament was pure.

Any cursory reading of the Bible, both Old Testament and New, however, finds that the church is comprised of sinners saved by grace. If the ICOC contends that the New Testament church was in some sort of a pristine state, they must explain all of the problems that Paul attempted to correct when he wrote his two letters to the Corinthians (pride, cliques, incest, idolatry, etc.) as problems existing *within the church*. Paul speaks in Romans 7:14–8:1 about the sin nature that remains with the Christian while in this life. That is, Christians are citizens of two kingdoms, earth and heaven. They are simultaneously sinners, yet saved.

A third problem with 'restorationism is the presumption that the church is a human work. Jesus said, "On this rock *I will build* my church (Matt. 16:18). A careful reading of Paul's letter to the Ephesians reveals that the church is the bride of Christ. God alone builds the church, and the church is not of human origin (Eph. 1:4,10; 2:20–22; 4:11–12). Restorationism has always been the inspiration of sectarianism and ultimately exclusivistic cults.

CONCLUSION

The ICOC continues to proliferate on college campuses and continues to be a prominent part of the discipleship movement. Some college campuses have succeeded in having the ICOC banned from being a recognized organization on their campuses. Other campuses have allowed the ICOC to exist and recognize them as a legitimate organization.

ADDITIONAL INFORMATION

Headquarters
Los Angeles continues to serve as the headquarters for the movement that was born in Boston. Each ICOC church maintains a local identity with the particular city that they are in.

Website
www.icoc.org

Sacred Text
The Bible

Publications
Revolution through Restoration; Revolution through Restoration II; Evangelization Proclamation; First Principles; A New Look at Authority; Revolution through Restoration: An Update

Membership
As reported above, by 2000 there were some 186,000 people worldwide attending churches in 171 countries. The movement continues to grow.

Notes

[1] Carol Giambalvo and Herbert Rosedale, *The Boston Movement* (Bonita Springs, FL: American Family Foundation, 1996), 1.

[2] Ibid., 3.

[3] Stephen Cannon, "The Boston Church of Christ: Has Mind Control Come to Beantown?" *The Quarterly Journal* 9 (April–June, 1992): 5–6.

[4] Daniel Terris, "Come All Ye Faithful," *Globe Magazine* (June 7, 1986).

[5] Giambalvo and Rosedale, *The Boston Movement*, 5.

[6] Ibid., 6.

[7] William Bevier, "The Boston Church of Christ," *The Discerner* 14 (October-December, 1994): 16.

INTERNATIONAL COMMUNITY OF CHRIST; CHURCH OF THE SECOND ADVENT (CSA); JAMILIANS

This is one of the numerous personality ♦cults that grew out of CHRISTIANITY. Formerly called the Jamilians, the group is now called the Church of the Second Advent. The CSA's teachings approximate the NEW AGE MOVEMENT and the ♦occult.

HISTORY

The CSA was founded by Eugene Douglas ♦Savoy (b. 1927). Savoy was born and raised in Bellingham, Washington, the grandson of a Baptist minister. He proved to be a rather precocious youngster. At six years old he claimed the uncanny ability to receive ♦revelations and spiritual visions and to manifest panpsychic experiences. Later he developed an interest in exploring world religions. This led him to an investigation of JUDAISM, particularly the doctrines of the ♦Essene community at Qumran. As he studied this and other religions, Savoy became convinced that Jesus was "inspired of God." The New Testament contains some of Jesus' teachings, but the most crucial of these had remained undisclosed to a waiting world and to mainstream Christianity. Savoy concluded that now was the time to bring forth the precious truths that he had received by careful scrutiny of the Gospels and other Essene literature.

Savoy claimed his teachings were substantiated by the fact that his only son, Jamil Sean ♦Savoy (1959–1962), was a reincarnate Christ, based on the passage of Scripture in Isaiah, "A little child shall lead them" (Isa. 11:6). According to Savoy, Jamil is the one to whom this passage refers. Savoy made the claim that three-year-old Jamil's prophecies concerning the restoration of truth to the church were inspired by God, who had sent him.

In 1962, at the age of three, Jamil died. Savoy insisted that this was in keeping with what was supposed to transpire and that the child had not really died but was translated into the "world of light." Savoy then decided it was time to propagate his teachings in a more organized fashion. In 1972 he set up headquarters in Reno, Nevada, and founded the Jamilians. Three years later the community was publicizing its doctrines.

ORGANIZATION

The Jamilians are now referred to as the First Order of the Community. The highest office of the church is called the head bishop. Savoy holds this office. There are other administrative offices, including an office of public information, office of sacramental and liturgical rites, music, charisticary (the handling of donations), a speaker's bureau, a university chapel, and apostolic chancellery. The community offers services that are open to the public. Those who wish to join the community and learn the secret truths of Jesus are invited to enroll in the Academy and Sacred College and take their Spiritual Awareness Aptitude Test.

TEACHINGS

The theology of the Jamilians centers around the revelation of the cryptic teachings of Jesus. Savoy contends that humankind is in reality a race of "light-beings." The ancient sun worshipers of Egypt and Peru had discovered this long ago. Christ's work was essentially not to redeem humanity from sin but to convey this and other truths.

The cosmos derives its sustenance from the sun, which is the source of all energy. Jamilian devotees are taught that they can experience the redeeming power of the sun. By learning how to absorb solar energy properly, they can increase their life spans by as much as 20 percent. The power in Jesus' miracles came from the sun. Christ will return to earth someday, not as a triumphant Savior but as a new and radiant sun, "unlike any sun that ever shone."

Christianity teaches far different doctrines than those taught by the Jamilians. There are several obvious points of divergence. First, Savoy places far greater emphasis on the importance of visions and revelations than on the 'Bible or the apostolic canons of faith. The Scriptures in Christian tradition make a sharp distinction between God and his creation. HINDUISM and other religions of 'pantheism, by contrast, reject the concept of God's 'transcendence (i.e., his separateness from the cosmos), with no real differentiation between the two.

Savoy introduces an interesting twist to these two classic positions. By insisting that Jesus received his supernatural power from "solar energy," that is, the sun, he actually arrives at the reverse of the Creator/creation distinction of Christianity. Rather than God being the sustenance of creation, as the church teaches, and rather than God and creation collapsing into an undifferentiated 'monism, as Hinduism teaches, the Jamilians arrive at the third position of the creation (the sun) providing sustenance to God (Jesus as incarnate deity). Realistically, however, the only real divergence is with Christianity. A pantheist would not argue the point as to which governs which (creation or Creator), because in the end they are indistinguishable.

Second, for the Jamilians, Christ is essentially a way-demonstrator, or messenger, pointing to the eternal sun. The Christian church teaches that Jesus was indeed a messenger, sent to proclaim the kingdom of God. Jesus, however, made it possible for fallen humankind to enter the kingdom through his death and resurrection. Therefore, the person and work of Christ constitute the critical essence of the Christian faith. The ecumenical creeds (*see* Appendix 1) recognize the teachings of Scripture regarding Christ by carefully recounting the details of his birth, death, descent into 'hell, resurrection, ascension, and the future promise of his return.

Third, Savoy distances himself sharply from Christianity with his bold assertion that his son Jamil was a reincarnate Christ. Rather, the church awaits the return of the historical Jesus Christ to judge and reign supreme. Nowhere does the Bible hint that Jesus will return as a child. Isaiah 11:6 refers prophetically to Jesus' first coming.

CONCLUSION

Many eclectic religious ideas abound in the CSA. It maintains an active website and organization. Despite the Christian influences of its founder, there is little if any resemblance to traditional Christianity in the organization today.

ADDITIONAL INFORMATION_____

World Center
Located in Apostolicv Chancellery, Office of Public Information, 643 Ralston Street, Reno, NV 89503.

Website
www.communityofChrist.org

Sacred Texts
The Decoded New Testament, *The Essae Document*, *The Lost Gospel of Jesus*, and *The Jamilians*

Publication
Community Communique

Membership
No accurate figures available.

ISKCON; INTERNATIONAL SOCIETY FOR KRISHNA CONSCIOUSNESS

The latter half of the twentieth century witnessed a significant growth in interest and involvement in Eastern 'sects derived from HINDUISM. The International Society for Krishna Consciousness (ISKCON) is one such group. Like many of the others, ISKCON's particular identity and teachings are shaped by the views and contributions of its founder.

HISTORY

The International Society for Krishna Consciousness, also known as 'Hare Krishna, arrived in the United States in 1965 when 'A. C. Bhakdivedanta Swami Prabhupada (1896–1977) arrived in New York. Prabhupada received his education at both the Vaisnava school and Scottish Church College. He studied philosophy, English, economics, and business. He also studied Hinduism under 'Guru Srila Bhaktisiddhanta Saraswati Goswami Maharaja, one in a line of gurus dating back to the sixteenth-century guru 'Chaitanya, who had taught that Krishna (also spelled Krsna) was the supreme Lord over all other deities, including 'Vishnu. Chaitanya also became critical of the prevailing academic and philosophical tendencies of Hinduism in his day and led the way back to a more religious and devotional emphasis. Soon Chaitanya amassed a following, and from that point on, Krishna consciousness was born, laying the groundwork for ISKCON. Chanting in the name of Krishna became common. A succession of gurus dedicated to Chaitanya's teachings evolved through the centuries, and it was this chain to which Swami Prabhupada was eventually linked.

In 1922 Prabhupada was initiated by his mentor Goswami into ▸bhakti ▸yoga. The next several decades found him spreading his doctrines and studying the ▸*Bhagavad Gita*. In 1944 he published a magazine titled *Back to Godhead*. Fifteen years later Prabhupada decided that in order to serve Lord Krishna fully, he would have to renounce all family ties, and in 1959 he took the vows called ▸*samyasin*.

America was Prabhupada's next focus. After he arrived in 1965 (he is alleged to have arrived with eight dollars in his possession), he immediately began to spread the teachings of Krishna consciousness to many of the countercultural groups and soon gained a following. Centers were established in many major cities, including Los Angeles, Berkeley, and Boston. The humble following steadily grew during the turbulent late 1960s and early 1970s. George Harrison, one of the Beatles, became a follower and dedicated his top-selling song, "My Sweet Lord," to Krishna.

Trouble broke out in the early 1980s. At a Minnesota state fair, a ruling had been passed down that no religions could distribute their literature without a license and that they had to do so from a designated location. ISKCON leaders protested, arguing that this was a violation of their First Amendment rights. The Supreme Court ruled against ISKCON. Another case involved a former member charging the group with "brainwashing." In June, 1992, ISKCON sued the port authorities of both New York and New Jersey for restricting their movements and proselytizing efforts. Again, the ruling by the courts went against ISKCON, based on the conclusion that businesses could be negatively affected by such groups.

Another significant issue arose in the late 1980s and into the 1990s when a series of complaints about child abuse were substantiated at various ISKCON schools worldwide. The problems stemmed from the fact that

The Hindu deity Krsna.

Courtesy George A. Mather

parents had formerly been discouraged from being involved in the boarding schools. These schools are no longer in operation and the child abuse issues have disappeared with the exclusive day schools that are now in operation. However, on June 12, 2000, a lawsuit was filed in Dallas, Texas, against the emotional, physical, and sexual abuse of forty-four ISKCON children. Included are the charges that Prabhupada himself knew about the abuse since 1972, but did nothing to halt it. The plaintiffs are seeking damages of 400 million dollars. The case has not yet been settled at the time of this writing.[1]

Many modifications have been made in recent years. Gone for the most part are the long robes and shaved heads (many still shave their heads but wear wigs). Members no longer are required to live in temples as long as worship is carried on before altars erected in homes. The focus of members is service to others and meditation.

ORGANIZATION

A body called the Governing Body Commission (GBC) elects an executive each year. There are currently thirty members serving on the GBC, which meets annually in

Mayapur, India. Each GBC member is responsible for a given zone and the temples within that zone. National councils are appointed in each country. Each temple is its own unit and is responsible to run its affairs unsubsidized. Each temple appoints a president who, along with department heads, comprise a temple board. Smaller than temples are preaching centers. Finally there are what are called *nama-hatta* centers, where non-devotees may gather to hear a traveling teacher.

TEACHINGS

The most distinguishing feature of ISKCON thought is the belief that ▸*sankirtana* is the all-sufficient means of attaining salvation, or freedom from ▸*samsara*. Devotees often gathered on city streets, airports, or other public places. They were distinguished by long robes and shaved heads (with all but a patch of hair called a ▸*sikha* remaining). The chant, called ▸*kirtanya*, is a sixteen-word ▸mantra: *Hare Krishna, Hare Krishna, Krishna, Krishna, Hare, Hare, Hare Rama, Hare Rama, Rama, Rama, Hare, Hare.*

The underlying religious philosophy of ISKCON is essentially identical to its parent religion—Hinduism. A ▸dualism between body, or material, and spirit is taught. Because the flesh is material, it is continually at war with the spirit. Hence, all desires of the body are essentially evil and should be suppressed. In fact, the mere existence of the human body is evidence that ▸karma had produced different, if not better, results in a previous existence.

God

ISKCON, like its parent religion, is essentially ▸pantheistic. Krishna is all, and all is Krishna. He alone is the personality of the godhead.[2]

Jesus Christ

Jesus is the son of Krishna or an ▸incarnation thereof.[3]

Hell

▸Hell is a state of punishment, but it is not a state of eternal damnation as taught by traditional CHRISTIANITY. "Those who are very sinful in their earthly life have to undergo different kinds of punishment on different planets. This punishment, however, is not eternal."[4]

Salvation

Salvation is achieved through complete devotion to Krishna.[5] Like its parent religion (Hinduism), the category of salvation is not sin for which forgiveness is given, but ignorance through which knowledge and ▸enlightenment are bestowed.

Authority

The authoritative texts of ISKCON include the sacred Hindu writings as well as those of Prabhupada.

PRACTICES

When ISKCON started to become popular and centers and temples were established, some students, called ▸*brahmacharin*, undertook vows of abstinence from eating meat, drinking intoxicating liquors, sex, gambling, and so on. They lived in the established temples. Each day at 3:00 A.M., they arose for ▸*puja*. This consisted chiefly of chanting sixteen rounds of the Krishna mantra. An important part of the student's training was to submit to the discipline of a legitimately recognized guru (one trained by Prabhupada, who was himself linked to Chaitanya through evolutionary succession). In addition to training, the devotee spent the remainder of the day on the streets and in airports engaged in chanting the Kirtanya, soliciting, and proselytizing. On June 26, 1992, the United States Supreme Court ruled that "solicitors seeking donations can be banned from airport terminals." A spokesman for the Hare Krishna ▸cult declared this "a serious blow."[6]

A second group of devotees, called ▸*grihastha*, are distinguished from the *brahmacharin* in that they live outside the temple. Their submission to a guru and their love and devotion to Krishna, however, remain uncompromised.

CONCLUSION

ISKCON has not remained unscathed by criticism in America. Improved marketing techniques have not significantly dampened the unfavorable image of yesteryear, but numbers have remained stable in the United States during the 1980s. Currently there are hundreds of ISKCON temples all over the world. A Food for Life Program has been organized since 1973 in order to combat the dreadful hunger conditions, particularly in India, but it extends itself to other areas of need as well.

ADDITIONAL INFORMATION_____

Headquarters
ISKCON, 3764 Watseka Avenue, Los Angeles, CA 90034.

Websites
www.iskcon.com (American); *www.iskcon.org* (international)

Sacred Texts
Back to Godhead; *Bhagavad Gita*, renamed *Bhagavad Gita As It Is, Srimad-Bhagavatam, Caitanya-caritamrta, Krsna*

Publication

ISKCON Communications Journal(ICJ)

Membership

In 1977, membership included six thousand devotees in the Bombay temple alone, to say nothing of the many followers in temples established worldwide. Total membership includes approximately 2,500 monks, 250,000 lay priests, and 1,000,000 worshiping members. ISKCON never grew as rapidly in the United States as it did elsewhere. Eleven gurus have succeeded Prabhupada since his death.

Notes

[1] *http://religiousmovements.lib.virginia.edu/nrms/iskcon. html*, 2.
[2] Comparisons and contrasts with Christianity are made in HINDUISM.
[3] See Hinduism.
[4] A. C. Bhaktivedanta Swami Prabhupada, *Bhagavad Gita As It Is* (Los Angeles: The Bhaktivedanta Book Trust, 1968, 1972), 172.
[5] The same as in Hinduism (see n. 1).
[6] "In Brief," *Christian Research Journal* (Summer 1992), 34.

ISLAM

"There is no God but *Allah, and *Muhammad is his prophet." This often-repeated phrase within *Muslim or *Moslem circles, called the *shahada*, is the theological matrix of the youngest world religion and yet the world's second largest, next to CHRISTIANITY. Since the Persian Gulf War in the last decade of the twentieth century and the events of September 11, 2001 at the beginning of the twenty-first, interest, awareness, and the sheer amount of literature written about Islam, its theology, and its thought are unprecedented since its emergence from the desert regions of Saudi Arabia sixteen centuries ago.

HISTORY

The founder of Islam was the prophet Muhammad, born approximately A.D. 570 in *Mecca. Accounts of Muhammad's childhood are sketchy. His parents died while he was very young. Brought up by his uncle and grandfather as a shepherd, young Muhammad later became a camel driver along the trade route between Syria and Arabia. At the age of twenty-five, he married a wealthy widow, Khadija. Before his marriage, he had been employed by Khadija, who was fifteen years his senior. His relationship with her resulted in his elevation to a position of prominence and status in wealthy Meccan social circles.

Muhammad had encountered JUDAISM and Christianity on the trade routes and for the next fifteen years observed the degenerate state of religion and morals among his own countrymen. He often retreated to a cave on Mount Hira outside of Mecca, where he spent periods of time meditating and even contemplating suicide. These visits were possible, of course, since he was less obligated to work with the camel caravan because of his wife's great wealth. During one of these

visits to the cave in the year 610, Muhammad, now forty years old, reported that he was visited by the angel Gabriel, who commanded him "to recite in the name of the Lord who had created man out of a clot of blood." The message he received later became the essence of the *Koran (also spelled *Qu'ran). With the approval of his wife and friends, Muhammad arrived at the belief that he had been ordained a prophet, called to bring his people out of moral decadence, superstition, and *polytheism.

Muhammad began preaching that there was but one God and his name was Allah. Allah was the supreme deity already familiar to the Bedouin tribes of northern Arabia. As he moved throughout Mecca proclaiming that Allah alone was God to the exclusion of all other deities, he met with extreme opposition. Some of his countrymen believed he was possessed by a *jinn. Muhammad himself believed this at first, but he became even more convinced that he was truly a chosen prophet of Allah, concluding that the opposition he experienced was not unlike what Moses and Jesus faced.

Shortly after the first reported vision, Gabriel reappeared to Muhammad adding further disclosures. Opposition to him and his preaching continued, but at a much more dangerous level. His message was in contradistinction to the polytheism of his countrymen. Even more significantly, it ran counter to the hedonism and general belief of the time that the acquisition of wealth was the highest priority in life. Muhammad did not meet with total failure, however, having gained for his cause approximately seventy followers.

It is interesting to note that the Arabian people, especially the Bedouin tribes, maintained a strict provincialism. They were not answerable to, obligated by, or interested in anyone outside their own tribal circles. Muhammad's initial followers were labeled as being "weak," meaning that they were outside the particular tribe of Quraysh. Muhammad provided a meaningful identity for these social misfits.

Historians offer different reasons for the opposition Muhammad experienced. Some argue that his sharp criticism of ▸polytheism threatened the merchant trade. The more commonly held view is that because many Meccans were beginning to at least listen to him, deeply respecting his character and wisdom, it was feared that the prophet would one day rise to political prominence, threatening the existing establishment.

Khadija died in A.D. 619. A sudden withdrawal of support from the clan that had been backing Muhammad put the prophet in certain danger and forced him to flee from Mecca to the neighboring town of at-Taif. Not finding an adequate following there, he secured the protection of another clan and returned to Mecca, where he met and married a widow named Sauda. Almost immediately following that marriage, Muhammad entered into a polygamous marriage to yet another wife named Aisha, the six-year-old daughter of Abu ▸Bakr, who would one day succeed the prophet as the chief ▸caliph of Islam. Muhammad subsequently married more wives, having a total of at least nine. Some sources argue that he had as many as twenty wives and some concubines.[1]

In 620, Muhammad entered into a relationship and negotiations with clans from the city of Medina, three hundred miles north of Mecca. Two years later, in what is known among Muslims as the ▸hegira, Muhammad left Mecca because of mounting persecution against his cause and took up residency in Medina with new clans whom he had gained to his side.

The prophet's experience in Medina began a new period in Muslim history. After settling into Medina, Muhammad organized raids, or *razzias*, on innocent caravans traveling to Mecca. The first razzias were unsuccessful, but he did eventually succeed with additional attacks. Having gained strength as a result of his conquering caravans, Muhammad now presented a significant threat to the city of Mecca. Jews living in Medina raised a cry of opposition against Muhammad, especially because the prophet had made the audacious claim to be Allah's true prophet. Disappointed that the Jews rejected him, Muhammad instructed his followers to face Mecca when praying rather than Jerusalem, which had been the traditional practice. He believed that facing Jerusalem would have attracted Jews to his cause. To this day, Muslims face Mecca in prayer, the act itself remaining a long-standing symbol of the hostility between Jews and Arabs.

Eight years in Medina proved to be sufficient time for Muhammad to rally substantial forces to promote his cause. From 624–630, his followers attacked and conquered villages in the regions surrounding Medina. In 628 he attempted to make a pilgrimage to Mecca with sixteen hundred followers. The clans of Mecca were determined to check Muhammad and keep him from entering the city. He and his men were halted at al-Hudaybiyah. After a few critical days, the tensions ceased and a treaty was signed between the Meccans and Muhammad. Part of the agreement was that the Muslims would be allowed to make the pilgrimage the following year in 629. Muhammad's power grew steadily, and the social, economic, and moral state of affairs in Mecca was in sharp decline. In 629, the Treaty of al-Hudaybiyah was broken through additional clan wars. Finally in January 630, Muhammad, accompanied by ten thousand men, marched into Mecca. He was met by some of the Meccan leaders, who surrendered to him with little resistance. Because he issued a general amnesty and later a generous pardon to his former enemies, many Meccans were won over to his cause, and many followed him into future campaigns.

Although all of Mecca did not convert to Islam, Muhammad purged Mecca of hundreds of its pagan gods and deities, thus establishing a monotheistic religion. His further *razzias* eventually led to his becoming the most powerful religious and political figure in Arabia. He was successful in uniting a federation of Arab tribes that eventually conquered the Byzantine and Persian empires, extending itself throughout northern Africa and Byzantium.

Muhammad died in 632, just two years after his conquest of Mecca. His death immediately raised the issue of who would succeed him as the chief caliph. Abu Bakr, the prophet's father-in-law, assumed the position for two years until his death in 634. Omar, another father-in-law, became the next caliph. Uthman became the third caliph (644–656). These first caliphs set the stage for the long succession of caliphs throughout much of Muslim history.

By the year 750, Islam had spread to China, the Indian Ocean, and as far west as Morocco, and from there it invaded the Iberian Peninsula in 710. For the next eight hundred years, Islam occupied most of Spain and Portugal. In 732 Muslims marched into Gaul (France), seeking to conquer more of Western Europe, but this time their war-mongering acts failed. Charles Martel halted their onslaught at the Battle of Tours. Failing to conquer more of Europe from the West, they remained in the Iberian Peninsula, and by the time of the Reformation in Europe, the Muslim Ottoman Turks, led by the famous ᵇsultan Suleiman the Magnificent, were at the very gates of the Holy Roman Empire, besieging Vienna in 1529. Christians looked on the expansion of Islam with great fear. One person observed the phenomenon as "a daily increasing flame, catching hold of whatsoever comes next, still to proceed further."[2]

Emperor Charles V of the Holy Roman Empire pleaded with the Lutheran foes to unite with Roman Catholics against their common enemy, the Turks. In 1492, Queen Isabella and King Ferdinand had succeeded in expelling Islam from the Iberian Peninsula, establishing Roman Catholicism as the supreme religion. In an age of religious fanaticism, it is a well-known yet regrettable fact that both Christians and Muslims spilled much blood between them, and both also conducted continuous pogroms against the Jews.

During and after the sixteenth century, Islam suffered a decline in its influence and ethical character. This was due partly to the rise of corrupt sultans, given not to the propagation of Muslim theology and leadership but to hedonism and self-interest. Another reason for decline was the steady refusal of Muslims to learn from the West. With an air of arrogance and superiority, Muslims turned away from Christian Europe, ignoring both the great wealth that Europeans were acquiring through establishing trade routes and the great scientific and cultural advances made during the Renaissance. Concerning the trade routes, the Muslim empires were all chiefly "land empires." Europeans, particularly the Portuguese and the Spanish, used sea routes to bridge commercial and cultural gaps that eventually hastened the discovery and settlement of the Americas.

The expansion of Islam during its first thousand years saw a division into three separate empires. The first was the Ottoman Empire, comprised chiefly of Turks. As noted above, it was the Turks who pressed westward into Europe in the sixteenth century. The second was the Mogul Empire, which established itself in India and consisted chiefly of Arab Muslims who came into India under the leadership of Akbar in 1500. Akbar was intensely interested in religion. After building the famous Hall of Worship, he tried eclectically to blend facets of Hindu thought with Islam. Akbar's interests proved, however, to be too intellectual for the people of India, and his "divine faith," as it was called, never gained a serious foothold. The third distinct Muslim empire was the Safavid Empire of Persia, or modern-day Iraq and Iran. The Safavid dynasty, like the Mogul, was also established in 1500. Under Abbas I, who reigned from 1587–1629, the Persian Empire grew in power and prominence.

Shiᵇite Muslims

Shiᵇites are one of two major ᵇsects of Islam. A dispute arose after Muhammad's death as to who would be the rightful successor (caliph) to the prophet. The Shiᵇites, or "partisans," believed that Muhammad's cousin and son-in-law, Ali, was the rightful heir. This sect was extremely small until popularized by Safavid in Persia. Today, Shiᵇites constitute approximately 10 percent of the Muslim world. Although small in number, they are highly visible and the most vocal of the sects. Shiᵇite leaders are referred to by the title ᵇimam. The imams wield extreme spiritual authority over their subjects, seeking to uphold a strictly fundamentalist and fiercely authoritarian interpretation of the Koran.

The obvious example of this in modern times was the leadership provided in the 1980s by the late ᵇAyatollah ᵇKhomeini (1900?–1989). He came to power in 1979 by overthrowing the late Mohammad Reza Shah Pahlavi. In a manner not unlike what happened in medieval Europe's Holy Roman Empire, where the Roman popes exercised complete political and ecclesiastical control over much of Europe, Khomeini became the sovereign spiritual and political leader of Iran, rallying Shiᵇites together around strict enforcement of the Shariah law. The beginning of his decade-long tenure in office was featured by the holding of a number of American hostages for 444 days, and shortly before his death, he regained additional international attention by issuing a death threat against Salman Rushdie, author of *The Satanic Verses*, which Khomeini and Shiᵇites regarded as being blasphemous to the Koran.

Sunni Muslims

The majority (90 percent) of all Muslims are Sunnites. In contrast to the Shiᵇites, Sunnites are considered to be the mainstream traditionalists within the corpus of the Muslim world. They accept the first four caliphs—Abu Bakr, Omar, Othman, and Ali—as the legitimate successors to Muhammad.[3] Sunnites are radically different from Shiᵇites from a political standpoint. While the Shiᵇites view government as being a divine institution of Allah, thereby attempting to establish a theonomy on earth, Sunnites believe Muslim doctrines must be lived out within the context of existing earthly governments. On the whole, Sunnites are more tolerant of diversity and therefore more able to adapt to divergent cultures throughout the world.

Sunnite and Shiʾite Muslims have persecuted each other bitterly throughout the centuries. The hatred is not unlike the bitter religious wars that have plagued Christendom, particularly after the Reformation when Roman Catholics and Protestants chose to settle many of their differences with the sword.

The traditional clash between Islamic religion and culture has resurfaced in the modern world. In the past thirty years the politics and economics of oil have redefined life globally. The early 1970s marked the beginning of a new era. Billions of dollars poured into OPEC nations, particularly Saudi Arabia and Kuwait. The result was an unprecedented prosperity and wealth. The huge dependence of the United States on Mid-Eastern oil made for an economic relationship between the United States and the oil-producing nations. This has complicated world politics because the United States is a supporter of Israel, which traditionally all of the Mid-Eastern countries, in varying degrees, have opposed. Further, when Iraq invaded Kuwait under the leadership of Saddam Hussein in 1991, the United States, with its huge oil interests at stake, swiftly pushed back the invasion in the Gulf War. This muddied the waters even more because some of the Islamic countries, because of business and economic interests, found themselves pitted against other Islamic countries. Islam opposes these broken ties both ideologically and religiously. The United States came to be viewed as the evil empire (the Great Satan) that brought about this divided house. This division, among other factors, helped set up the conditions that resulted in the growth of terrorist organizations and the eventual rise to power of Osama bin Laden and his ʾAl-Qaeda network, which has declared war (a ʾjihad) on the United States (see Conclusion below).

TEACHINGS, BELIEFS, PRACTICES

Despite the wide ethnic and cultural diversities among Muslims, basic theological tenets are shared by both sects, serving to bind them together.

All of Muslim thought is summarized in the *shahada*: "There is no God but Allah, and Muhammad is his prophet." This motto is used in all facets of Muslim life.

The sacred book of Islam is the Koran. Muslims believe the Koran to be the ʾrevelation that Allah imparted to Muhammad, who transferred this divine knowledge into writing. Although there are no extant writings of Muhammad himself, early followers of the prophet gathered his sayings together through oral tra-

dition. The Koran is comprised of 114 chapters called ʾsuras. Each sura is subdivided into four sections: (1) the title; (2) the *basmalah*, or the prayer, "In the name of God, the merciful and compassionate"; (3) a mention of the location of where the sura was revealed, either in Mecca or Medina; and (4) *fawatih* letters believed to have some hidden meaning. Muslims look to the Koran as being one of their principal authorities in matters of belief. The Hadith and Shariah are two additional authorities, carrying almost the same weight. Where the Koran is silent, *sunna* ("tradition") commonly accepted is authoritative. When widely accepted customs are silent, the individual customs, or ʾadet, take precedence.

Five basic demands, known as the ʾfive pillars, are required of every adherent to Islam:

1. The daily recitation of the *shahada*. This is the Muslim creed. Every Muslim must memorize it in Arabic and recite it daily. Many Muslims say it many times daily.

2. The prescribed prayers, called ʾsalat (meaning "prayer") must be said five times daily while facing Mecca: in the morning, at noon, mid-afternoon, after sunset, and before sleep. These prayers serve the believer as an ever-present reminder that the *shahada* is true. Each of these prayer times is announced in Arabic publicly over loud speakers.

3. The giving of alms, called *sakat* (meaning "alms"). The Old Testament required the Jews to give a tithe, or 10 percent, of all goods accumulated, the Muslim gives one-fortieth of his income, or approximately 2.5 percent annually. Alms are given exclusively to poor Muslims or wherever Muslim need is deemed greatest.

4. A period of fasting, known as *sawm*. This is observed during ʾRamadan, which falls on the ninth month in the Muslim calendar that is based on the lunar year. Therefore the actual month that it falls varies from year to year. The ninth month is believed to be the time when Muhammad received the revelation of the Koran. Muhammad fasted during this period of sacred dispensation, so his followers must do so as well. During Ramadan, the faithful fast from sunup to sundown and attempt to hear the reading of the entire Koran.

5. The ʾhajj or pilgrimage to Mecca that is required of every Muslim at least once in a lifetime. The *hajj* greatly enhances the chances for salvation and reminds a Muslim of the great devotion owed to Allah.

In addition to the five pillars, other important facets of Muslim life include the ›*shariah* laws (holy laws). Included in these important laws or codes of ethics are total abstinence from alcoholic beverages and all forms of gambling. Males must be circumcised and are regarded as being superior to females. *Shariah* laws also require young girls to undergo clitoridectomy, also known as female genital mutilation. According to a well-known verse in the Koran, "Men have authority over women because Allah has made the one superior to the others." (Sura 4:34). This verse also gives a husband the right to beat his wife physically. Muslim women are required to be veiled (Sura 24:31; 33:59) Some women wear the ›*purdah*, which covers the entire body, with opening only for the eyes. Although the practice of wearing the *purdah* has been abandoned in many parts of the Muslim world, it was reinstated in Iran when Ayatollah Khomeini came to power in 1979. In recent years, the Taliban in Afghanistan also required all women to wear the *purdah*, also called a *burqa*. The Koran permits ›polygamy, allowing a Muslim man to have up to four wives (Sura 4:3). However, for economic reasons, most Muslim men have monogamous relationships in modern times, though the patriarchal structure remains intact.

Muslims often say Islam is an egalitarian, nonracist religion. This claim has been uncritically accepted in the West, forgetting that Muslim women have far fewer rights than men; for example, a woman's testimony in court is worth only half of a man's; she may not marry a non-Muslim man, but a man may marry a non-Muslim woman; only a Muslim man may have up to four wives, but a woman may have only one husband, etc. Regarding racism, it needs to be known that modern Sudan, predominantly governed by Arabic Muslims, has enslaved and killed thousands of black Christians and animists; the Koran commands Muslims "do not take the Jews and Christians for friends" (Sura 5:51).

God

Many religious groups are less than clear about their understanding of the doctrine of God. Not so with Islam, which upholds a strict monotheism. Muslims attack the Christian doctrine of the ›Trinity with a fierce intensity, accusing Christendom of worshiping three gods. The Koran states, "So believe in Allah and His apostles and do not say, Three. Forbear and it shall be better for you. Allah is but one God" (Sura 4:171). The Koran goes on to state that Jesus himself regards it blasphemous that he is raised to the level of deity.[4] Chris-

tians experience difficulty in articulating clearly the doctrine of the Trinity to Muslims because the Koran states that Christianity is polytheistic (see ›polytheism); no amount of evidence to the contrary can convince them otherwise. For a Muslim to even consider the mysteries of the Christian doctrine of God is to show disregard for the holy Koran. Josef van Ess assesses the matter:

> Compared with the triune God of the Christians, the God of the Muslims is indeed a God without mystery; or, rather, his mystery lies not in his nature, but in his actions, in the unfathomable way by which he directs humanity or has made certain things obligatory through his law.[5]

Traditional Christianity also embraces an uncompromising monotheism. The Hebrew *shema*—"Hear O Israel, the LORD our God, the LORD is one" (Deut. 6:4)—is an often-quoted verse in Christian pulpits. The Nicene Creed states clearly, "I believe in one God, the Father Almighty" (*see* Appendix 1). The Athanasian Creed further says:

> And the catholic faith is this, that we worship one God in three persons and three persons in one God, neither confusing the persons nor dividing the substance.... But the Godhead of the Father, of the Son, and of the Holy Spirit is all one. (Appendix 1)

The great mystery of the Christian faith, which the creedal formulations make an attempt to capture, lies in the essential unity of God within the divine economy of three separate persons, Father, Son, and Holy Spirit. For Islam, God does not share in any divine associations. Yet the New Testament, although not containing the word "Trinity," has consciously and strongly implied such a doctrine in many passages (e.g., Matt. 28:18–20; Mark 1:9–11; John 1:1; 2 Cor. 13:14).[6]

Muslims rejoice in such passages from the Koran as: "Praise be to God, Lord of all the worlds, The Compassionate, the Merciful, King on the Day of reckoning! Thee only do we worship, and to Thee do we cry for help" (Sura 1). But as much as this passage speaks of God as being merciful, the Koran does not refer to Allah in such personal terms. Where John 3:16 speaks of God as being one who "so loved the world ... that whoever believes in him shall not perish but have eternal life" (John 3:16), the Koran alludes to Allah as being capricious at times. Some Christian apologists have noted that Allah appears to be dispassionate and arbitrary and even one who misleads for the sake of populating ›hell: "If the Lord pleased, He had made all men of one religion;. . . but unto this has He created them; for the Word of the Lord shall be fulfilled: Verily I will fill hell altogether with genii and men" (Sura 11:119).[7]

Traditional Islam has viewed Allah as being completely sovereign over the lives of his people, who must respond by bowing in passive resignation to his will. Many Muslims in modern times are beginning to rethink the issue of determinism and its relationship to human responsibility before Allah.[8] Christianity has struggled with this issue for centuries, particularly in the theologies of such leading thinkers as Augustine, Thomas Aquinas, Martin Luther, and John Calvin.

Jesus Christ

Muslims to some degree have a high regard for Jesus Christ as a prophet. In the Koran, Jesus is made to herald the coming of Muhammad with the words, "An apostle will come after me" (Sura 61:6). Muslims regard Moses and Jesus as being true prophets of Allah, but Muhammad is the greatest of all the prophets.

For traditional Christians, this Islamic idea is unacceptable because, again, Muhammad is the greatest of all prophets. The center of the Christian faith is the person and work of Jesus Christ as attested to throughout the writings of the New Testament and summarized in the second articles of both the Nicene and Apostles' Creeds (Appendix 1). For Christianity, Jesus is the Son of God who became incarnate; he was born of a virgin and fulfilled the will of God by dying on the cross and rising from the dead in order to atone for the sins of the world. Muslims in turn flatly reject these ideas as superstitious, blasphemous, and pagan. For Islam, Jesus was completely and totally human. The Koran states that all (meaning Christians) who regard Jesus as being divine are "infidels," for whom is reserved a special hell (*laza*). Interestingly enough, Jesus' miracles and even his sinlessness are recognized in the Koran, however, not by virtue of his deity. Jesus exercised such powers and abilities through Allah to be a servant and forerunner.

Somewhat surprisingly, Muslims reject the fact that Jesus was crucified: "They did not really slay him, neither crucified him; only a likeness of that was shown unto them" (Sura 4:157). The Bible, however, teaches that Jesus was undeniably crucified. The early Christian sermons in Acts (e.g., 2:14–40; 3:12–26) are all predicated not only on the death of Christ and his subsequent resurrection, but on the necessity of his death. Paul is adamant about the importance of the crucifixion (1 Cor. 2:2). To deny it, as Islam does, is to deny the very means of atonement for which Christ came into the world.

Holy Spirit

The Holy Spirit is spoken of in the Koran and in the New Testament as being the Paraclete (Counselor). While Christianity teaches that the Holy Spirit is the third person of the divine Trinity, Islam regards the Spirit as being a divine instrument of Allah.

Humanity

The Koran to some degree teaches that the human race was created as described in the Genesis account of Adam and Eve. Human beings are superior to the angels because they are endowed with a higher intellect. Furthermore, they have earned the place of highest respect and dignity in all of creation. The chief purpose of humankind is to obey and serve Allah. But juxtaposed aside humanity's nobility lies its frail and sinful nature. The chief sin of humankind is pride. Pride, defined as self-love, leads to a desire to share God's nature. It has already been noted that Muslims reject the doctrine of the Trinity because it implies the association of the human Jesus with God. Any confusion of Creator and creature is sin (*shirk*). Humanity's chief end is to worship the one true God and recite the *shahada* to remind one of one's own creatureliness.

Christianity agrees with Islam on some of these points. The chief purpose of humankind is indeed to serve God and obey his will as expressed in the divinely revealed law. The human fall from grace was the result of pride. The eating of the forbidden fruit in the garden (Gen. 3) was precipitated by humanity's desire to be like God. Christianity rejects the confusion of Creator/creature.[9]

These two world religions differ with respect to this doctrine on the point of how humankind obtains, or is restored to, a right relationship to God/Allah after the Fall. For Christianity, this amounts to repentance from sin and accepting by faith the atonement made by Jesus Christ (see sections on sin and salvation, below). For Islam, it is strict adherence to the Koran and the five pillars.

Sin

Islam teaches that Satan, or *Shaytan/Iblis*, fell from heaven when he did not conform to the divine will by refusing to acknowledge Adam's place of honor. Satan's chief activity, corroborated in both the Koran and the Bible, is to torment and beguile human beings away from God. The chief sin for both religions is pride, which results in unbelief (*irtidād*).

Salvation

According to the Koran (Sura 10:109), a Muslim who hopes to escape the wrath of Allah and the tormenting fires of hell must diligently strive to fulfill the requirements set forth in the five pillars. God has raised up prophets throughout history in order to call people to repentance.

The central focus of *soteriology for Christianity lies in the person and work of Jesus Christ. The salient feature of Christian salvation lies in the fact that the work of Christ dying on the cross is deemed the all-sufficient atonement for sin, apart from any human works of righteousness. This Pauline emphasis on "justification by grace through faith" apart from the works of the law (Eph. 2:8–9) has been revived repeatedly throughout the history of the Christian church. Augustine, Luther, Calvin, Karl Barth, and the more popular forms of *evangelicalism and *fundamentalism have persistently raised the banner of "grace alone" with respect to salvation. Traditionally, the Christian church as a whole has denounced Islam as being another religion of legalistic works-righteousness. The Koran states clearly that salvation is focused on strivings and works: "In the day of judgment, they whose balances shall be heavy with good works, shall be happy; but they, whose balances shall be light, are those who shall lose their souls, and shall remain in hell forever" (Sura 23:104–5).

For Christianity, salvation is dependent solely on the work of the second person of the Trinity. The heart of the matter is made clear in the book of Hebrews, which argues that blood atonement for sin must be made and has been made in the Old Testament by the *high priest, who offered up the blood of sacrificial animals on the altar and before the *mercy seat of God (Heb. 9:7). But this sacrifice was insufficient because it was made by a priest who himself needed to atone for his own sins as well as those of the people; second, this human high priest had to offer such atonement yearly. But God brought an end to this imperfection by offering up his own Son, Jesus Christ, as a once-for-all perfect sacrifice (9:24–28). When this sacrificial work was completed, this great high priest sat down in the very presence of God (10:12), sealing his work for all time.

This is why traditional Christianity has rejected the claims of Muhammad to be a true prophet of God, much less the greatest of all of God's prophets. By trusting in the works of Christ, the great high priest, the Christian can enjoy a certainty of salvation that a Muslim can never have. "Allah will lead into error whom he pleaseth, and whom he pleaseth he will put in the right way" (Sura 6:39). "None can guide those whom Allah has led astray" (Sura 13:33). The Muslim is all too aware of these references from the Koran to ever rest in the certainty of eternal salvation or to be assured by such comforting words as, "There is now no condemnation for those who are in Christ Jesus" (Rom. 8:1).

Modern Christianity, particularly Roman Catholicism, has recently undergone a sharp change of attitude with respect to Islam. The traditional Roman Catholic *dictum extra ecclesiam non salus* ("there is no salvation outside of the church") is no longer the official position of Rome since Vatican II. Article 16 of the Dogmatic Constitution of the church states unequivocally:

> Finally, those who have not yet received the gospel are related in various ways to the People of God. In the first place there is the people to whom the covenants and the promises were given and from whom Christ was born according to the flesh (cf. Rom. 9:4–5). On account of their fathers, this people remains most dear to God, for God does not repent of the gifts He makes nor of the calls He issues (cf. Rom. 11:28–29).

> But the plan of salvation also includes those who acknowledge the Creator. In the first place among these there are the Moslems, who, professing to hold the faith of Abraham, along with us adore the one and merciful God, who on the last day will judge mankind. Nor is God Himself far distant from those who in shadows and images seek the unknown God, for it is He who gives to all men life and breath and every other gift (cf. Acts 17:25–28), and who as Savior wills that all men be saved (cf. 1 Tim. 2:4).

> Those also can attain to everlasting salvation who through no fault of their own do not know the gospel of Christ or His Church, yet sincerely seek God and, moved by grace, strive by their deeds to do His will as it is known to them through the dictates of conscience. Nor does divine Providence deny the help necessary for salvation to those who, without blame on their part, have not yet arrived at an explicit knowledge of God, but who strive to live a good life, thanks to His grace. Whatever goodness or truth is found among them is looked on by the Church as a preparation for the gospel. She regards such qualities as given by Him who enlightens all men so that they may finally have life.

The mention of Muslims in this statement evidences the remarkably tolerant and open posture that the Roman Catholic church has assumed. The World Council of Churches has also adopted an extremely open and liberal, though somewhat more ambiguous, attitude toward Islam and non-Christian religions with respect to salvation.[10] Traditional orthodoxy, however, has not yielded to such modern trends. Any reformulations are basically repristinations along the guidelines set forth in the ecumenical creeds (*see* Appendix 1).

CONCLUSION

Spread of Islam

Like any of the world religions, Islam is plagued with factions, divisions, and plurality. The differences between the strict fundamentalism of Shiʾites and the looser, more tolerant Sunnites have already been discussed. The strictest and most conservative of all Moslem sects is the Saudi Arabian Wahhabi, founded in the eighteenth century. SUFISM represents another significant movement within the Muslim world and is discussed separately, as is the Nation of Islam (the World Community of Ali Islam in the West). Cultural differences vary from country to country. The lack of a centralized authority structure is part of the explanation for such a phenomenon.

Islam has appealed to approximately 3.5 million Americans as of 2000. The Koran is growing in popularity and has been translated into modern English. Well-known musician Cat Stevens converted to Islam in 1977 and now goes by the name Yusuf Islam. Basketball great Kareem Abdul-Jabbar is another popular convert. Large Muslim communities have formed in major metropolitan areas of the country. Orange County, California, for example, has well over twenty thousand Muslims. Reportedly, part of its appeal has been its simplicity. It is said to be much easier to embrace the concept of a religion whose monotheism is not couched in mystery but in simplicity. Yet this simplicity becomes somewhat paradoxical when placed side by side with its doctrine of a completely transcendent deity.

Islam is also growing in other parts of the world as well. Europe and America have seen the erection of mosques. Asia has the highest population of Muslims. After Muslim terrorists struck on September 11, 2001, much attention was focused on the Muslim world. Educational television and extensive media coverage devoted hours to exploring the contrasts of Islam with the West, and indeed, the contrasts are significant. The collapse of the Soviet Union has also drawn the world's attention to Islam. Especially following Iraq's defeat in the Gulf War (1991), tensions between Sunni and Shiʾite Muslims have exacerbated.

In 1989 Salmon Rushdie published a novel, *The Satanic Verses*. This book brought down the wrath of Ayatollah Kohmeini in Iran as he issued a *fatwa* calling for the assassination of Rushdie. Although Kohmeini is now deceased, the *fatwa* still stands. This incident reflects the high degree of intolerance present in Islam.

Women in Islam

An important ideological phenomenon in today's world is the role of women in traditional Islamic countries. During the Gulf War of 1991, the world became far more aware of Islam's view of women. Muslim fundamentalists have argued that the female is responsible for the Fall. They are forced to wear the *hajib*, or the veil. The harsh treatment of women became particularly and painfully obvious on a global level when the war in Afghanistan revealed the degree to which the Taliban completely controlled the lives of women. One explanation for this has been that women should be regarded for their cognitive abilities and not for their beauty or lack thereof.[11] Western feminism has countered sharply by contending that the role of women should not be defined by patriarchal ideology. Women should possess the freedom to define themselves. This will no doubt continue to be a huge challenge to Islam as it continues to grow, especially in the West.

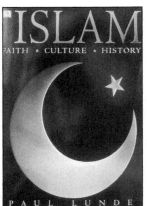

Islam has been making a significant impact in the English-speaking world, as these writings indicate. Be sure also to read the article on THE NATION OF ISLAM.

Courtesy George A. Mather

Terrorism

A new reality and a new way of waging war has come onto the world scene known as terrorism (see also Islamic terrorist cults). A large number of terrorist organizations have come to be associated with Islam, but certainly not exclusively. One example of terrorism using weapons of mass destruction came in the use of the poisonous gas sarin by the Japanese group AUM SHINRIKYA. Nevertheless, Islamic extremists comprise many organizations, networks, and terrorist cells. ▸Al Qaeda, Hezbollah, and the Islamic ▸*jihad* have been known for the use of car bombs driven by suicidal extremists in an ongoing assault against Israel. The bombing of the World Trade Center in 1993, the bombings of two American embassies in Kenya and Tanzania in October 2000, the bombing of the USS Cole where seventeen crew members lost their lives, and the unprecedented September 11, 2001, attacks on the World Trade Center and the Pentagon have brought this extreme faction of Islam to the forefront. Islam has become the focus of an unprecedented media blitz as a result of September 11.

To what degree does Islam itself support or oppose such attacks has been the key discussion in various public forums, talk shows, college campuses, books, and so on. Some in the Islamic world have denounced the attacks and renounced the extremists. By ignoring what the Koran and Hadith teach, some have argued that religion plays little or no role in the overall terrorist campaigns. This argument, however, is not plausible, given the simple fact that terrorists commit suicide in the name of Allah and cite the Koran in support of their acts. The Islamic terrorists say that death in the name of Allah glorifies his name and gives the promise of an endless eternity of bliss.

This is dramatically different from what Christ taught, namely, that Christians are to turn the other cheek when confronted by personal violence. Moreover, Christianity teaches that eternal bliss is attained by faith in Christ's redemptive work, not by taking up the sword in the name of God. Christ has said that those who take the sword will perish by the sword (Matt. 26:52).

However, killing in the name of religion is not an exclusively Islamic trait. Japanese kamikaze pilots were motivated by religious principles. Christian IDENTITY MOVEMENTS have interpreted passages from the Bible to justify hatred and the killing of minorities and Jews. Ideologues and scholars desperately struggle to understand human behavior and particularly extremist behavior. Sociological and psychological profiles and models as well as political and economic descriptions and analyses can only serve to aid in a limited understanding of the harsh realities of terrorism. ▸Orthodox Christianity asserts that there can be no peace and liberation of the soul without the gospel of Christ.

ADDITIONAL INFORMATION

Websites
*www.islam.about.com; www.islam101.com;
http://islamicity.org*

Sacred Text
The Koran; *Hadith* (collected sayings of Muhammad)

Membership
Sunni–940 million; Shi⁾ite–120 million; Ahmadiyya–10 million; Druze–450,000.

Notes
[1] Al Dashti, *Twenty Three Years: A Study of the Prophet Career of Muhammad*, trans. F. R. C. Bagley (London: Allen & sons, 1985), 129.

[2] L. S. Stavrianos, *The World Since 1500—A Global History* (Englewood Cliffs, NJ: Prentice-Hall, 1975), 513.

[3] See the article on the COMMUNITY OF CHRIST: REORGANIZED CHURCH OF JESUS CHRIST OF LATTER-DAY SAINTS for a comparison of how this Mormon sect considers itself to be the true succession of Mormonism after Joseph ▸Smith, rejecting as apostate the much larger Utah Mormons led by Brigham ▸Young. The similar motifs between Shi⁾ites and the RCJCLDS are remarkable.

[4] See the Koran, particularly Sura 5:116.

[5] Hans Küng, Josef van Ess, Heinrich von Stietencron, and Heinz Bechert, *Christianity and the World Religions; Paths to Dialogue with Islam, Hinduism, and Buddhism* (New York: Doubleday, 1986), 70.

[6] See also CHRISTADELPHIANISM, JEHOVAH'S WITNESSES, THE WAY INTERNATIONAL, WORLDWIDE CHURCH OF GOD, UNIFICATION CHURCH, etc., for further discussions on the doctrine of the Trinity.

[7] See S. H. Kellogg, *A Handbook of Comparative Religions* (Philadelphia: Westminster, 1925), 21. This work is somewhat dated but is an excellent summary of traditional Christian responses to the world religions.

[8] See Küng et al., *Christianity and the World Religions*, 85–93.

[9] See the doctrine of God in UNITY SCHOOL OF CHRISTIANITY, THEOSOPHY, TRANSCENDENTAL MEDITATION, WORLDWIDE CHURCH OF GOD, etc., for a further discussion of the Creator/creature distinction.

[10] See particularly the WCC statement, "Guidelines for Dialogue for Men and Women of Different Religions and Ideologies" (1977/79).

[11] *http://www.islam101.com/women/hijbene.html*

JAINISM

This is a religion of ancient origins that has elements of both HINDUISM and BUDDHISM.

HISTORY

From the *Sanskrit word *jina, meaning "he who conquers," Jainism has a relatively long history. The founder was Vardhamana Mahavira (599–527 B.C.) in Kundalapur, India. In a life similar to that of *Gautama Buddha, he renounced the ways of the world and set out to discover true *enlightenment. Unlike the Buddha, however, Mahavira limited himself to a life of *asceticism. In Buddhist tradition, suffering must be conquered by eliminating it. In Jainist thought, Mahavira was one of twenty-four *jinas*, or *tirthankara*—that is to say, those who have gained perfect knowledge and have overcome all suffering. The Hindu aspect to Jainism lies in its more religious dimension, namely, that all knowledge leads to the elimination of all *karma.

After the death of Mahavira, a following developed around his teachings. In the third century, also similar to Buddhism, the group split into two distinct sects—the Stanakvasis and the Terapanthis. While the former is more a movement of the priestly caste, the latter is the relatively modern movement and is more liberal in that it is open to the laity. Jainism in general as well as both major sects exist largely in India today. In the early twentieth century there was a reformer of the movement whose name was Kanji Svami Panth.

ORGANIZATION

Most Jain centers and temples are in India, though there are centers throughout the world. World gatherings are held for participants worldwide. Each center is independently run and operated. The websites list the various events and their locations.

TEACHINGS

Jainism follows the pattern of the Eastern religions and teaches a cyclical view of history. The soul is eternal and is on a wheel of rebirth, the goal of which is to obtain *moksha* (liberation through knowledge or enlightenment). The liberation process comes through the concept of *ahimsa (absence of harm to living creatures).

Karma

Like Hinduism, Jainism teaches that karma is the universal law of retributive justice. There is a twist, however. The soul collects karma tangibly. The amass-ing of good karma results in the ability of souls (plural) to attain enlightenment.

Asikayas

In Jainist thought, five *asikayas* summarize all that there is in the known universe: *jiva (soul), *dharma (motion), *adharma* (rest), *pugdala* (atoms), and *akasha* (space).[1]

Cosmology

The Jainist conception of the world is tripartite, namely, heaven, earth, and *hell. As in the case of Hinduism, the highest levels are occupied by the most enlightened, the *tirthankaras*. The level to which a soul is assigned depends on the amount of enlightenment attained.

Sin

Sin is ignorance and the lack of an ascetic life.

Salvation

Salvation, called *moksha* or "liberation," depends on the willingness to live an ascetic life. The complete ascetic achieves complete knowledge (salvation).

Time

There are six ascending and six descending periods of time. The six ascending eras are characterized by complete happiness and bliss; the six descending periods are periods of suffering, misery, and unhappiness. Jainists believe that the earth is currently in the fifth of the descending eras.[2] But these eras can overlap each other and exist at one and the same time as an admixture to life and a balance. Too much bliss and happiness will result in complacency and the postponing of *moksha*; a life filled with too much misery will result in a despairing attitude.

Much of the response of traditional Christianity to Jainism can be read in the book's evaluations of Hinduism and Buddhism. Most important to reiterate here is that the soul, for Christianity, does indeed have a beginning, originating at birth. Jainism, like Hinduism, understands that salvation lies in a gnostic (see *gnosticism) quest for inner enlightenment and self-knowledge. For Christianity, salvation is based on faith and trust, and if there is any knowledge at issue, it is the knowledge of sin, for which Jesus Christ atoned in his death on the cross (Rom. 3:21–24; 1 Cor. 2:2).

CONCLUSION

Jainists are among the wealthiest of India's citizenry, largely because they tend to pursue business careers and shy away from agricultural and vocational professions. But since they believe in an ascetic lifestyle, there is a strong tendency away from crass materialism. The Jainist websites listed below contain a wealth of information on Jainist activity in the world today.

ADDITIONAL INFORMATION_____

Sacred Texts

The fourteen *Purvas* and the teachings of the twenty-four *tirthankaras*

Websites

www.jainworld.com; www.atmadharma.com

Periodicals

Anuvibha Reporter; Ahimsa Voice; Gommatvani; Jain Gazette

Membership

There are estimated to be four to six million adherents to Jainism worldwide, with the majority living in India. There are, however, at least 75,000 practicing Jainists in America and adherents in Europe, particularly England. In Canada and the United States there are fifty-five Jainist centers.

Notes

[1] *www.religiousmovements.lib.virginia.edu/nrms/jainism .html*, p. 4.
[2] Ibid.

JEHOVAH'S WITNESSES; THE WATCHTOWER BIBLE AND TRACT SOCIETY; JW'S

One of the most familiar of the *cults that developed and emerged from the American religious experience of the nineteenth century and enjoyed its greatest popularity and growth in the last half of the twentieth century and on into the twenty-first century, the Watchtower Bible and Tract Society has become a worldwide movement.

HISTORY

The late church historian Sydney Ahlstrom made the deft observation that the theological climate in America in the mid-nineteenth century bred five distinctive movements, all of which were reactions against and dissatisfactions with mainstream *Protestantism:

> Most obvious were those like Robert Ingersoll, Henry George, Edward Bellamy, Francis E. Abbot, and Clarence Darrow, who left the church despite their sometimes strong religious interests, becoming outspoken advocates of agnosticism, socialism, free religion, or at least total disestablishment. More moderate but similarly perturbed were the liberals and social gospelers, who sought to adapt Christian faith and practice to more urgent modern needs. A third group included those whose ethnic background or particular claims (or both) were not part of the old Protestant mainstream. Mormons, Christian Scientists, Mennonites, Unitarians, and other divergent movements belong in this category. . . . The fourth group was a vast interdenominational movement of those who protested innovation in reli-

gion. Most of its adherents were troubled by the decline of the old-time religion with its accent on conversion. . . . Whether rich or poor, educated or illiterate, rural or urban, Baptist or Presbyterian, they were troubled by the advance of theological liberalism and the passing of Puritan moralism. Fundamentalism is a name for the movement that its own leaders adopted and used. The fifth and final group effected a more distinct separation from mainstream Protestantism than most fundamentalists sought.[1]

Ahlstrom considers the Holiness Movement with its emphasis on sanctification and its revolt against birthright church membership to comprise this fifth group. A second element that the Holiness Movement readily incorporated into its theology was radical *millennialism, which itself was enjoying a revival in England and America. Out of this veritable melting pot of ideas emerged a movement that would rival MORMONISM in terms of growth and success in the twentieth century in America. This movement has become known as the Watchtower Bible and Tract Society, better known as Jehovah's Witnesses.

The story of the Watchtower begins with the story of its founder, Charles Taze *Russell (1852–1916). Russell was born in Allegheny (now a section of Pittsburgh), Pennsylvania, on February 16, 1852. Raised Presbyterian, Russell showed a keen interest in religion in his teens and began to examine the doctrines of his faith. When he was fifteen he worked as a partner in his father's haberdashery (men's clothing store). At this time he decided that Congregationalism was far more suitable to his theological tastes. It was not long, however, before Russell concluded that Congregationalism, like Presbyterianism, did not agree with him. He was particularly disturbed by the Calvinist doctrine of predestination and eternal damnation. At age seventeen, Russell distanced himself from CHRISTIANITY, declaring himself a skeptic. Like Joseph ⁾Smith a half century earlier, Russell concluded that his confidence

Charles Russell, founder of the Jehovah's Witnesses.
Courtesy George A. Mather

in human creeds and churches was wrecked. Unlike Smith, however, Russell did not then claim to have been visited by a celestial angel anxious to impart new ⁾revelation against corrupt, apostate churches.

Russell remained skeptical of religion until 1870 when he chanced on the meeting of a group who called themselves "Second Adventists," led by Jonas Wendell. Russell later recalled, "Though his Scripture exposition was not entirely clear, and though it was very far from what we now rejoice in, it was sufficient, under God, to re-establish my wavering faith in the divine inspiration of the Bible."[2] This Second Advent group was a remnant of the disbanded ⁾Millerite Movement. The ⁾Great Disappointment of 1844 had caused many millennialists to abandon the Millerite or Adventist cause. But a rem-

nant went back to the drawing board and, based on recalculations, predicted that Christ would return sometime between 1873 and 1874. These were part of the remnant that Russell encountered in 1870.

For the next five years (1870–1875), Russell assembled a small group of students for a Bible study that met on a regular basis. At first, Russell found himself in agreement with the Adventists and was convinced that the Lord would in fact return in the 1873–1874 period. But again, the Adventists were proven wrong when 1874 came and went with no visible return of Christ. In 1876 Russell met N. H. Barbour, who led a group of Adventists in Rochester, New York. Barbour had broken away from the mainstream Adventists because he, like Russell, had become convinced that Christ had in fact returned in 1874, not visibly but invisibly and spiritually. Barbour and Russell joined forces and began to publish the magazine *The Herald of the Morning.* In 1877 they published *Three Worlds or Plan of Redemption,* in which they more fully expounded their view that the Millennium had begun in 1874.

Predictably, Russell and Barbour parted company in 1879 over a theological dispute concerning the atonement of Christ. Proceeding at his own rapid pace, impelled by a zeal rarely matched by other religious leaders, Russell immediately began publishing a new magazine titled *Zion's Watch Tower and Herald of Christ's Presence.* Russell's ideas began to spread. "By 1880, some thirty congregations had come into existence in seven states."[3] Another significant event in Russell's life took place in 1879. He met and married one of his Bible students, Maria F. Ackley. For the next eighteen years she diligently and enthusiastically supported her husband's work until their separation in 1897.

In 1881 Russell formed the unincorporated Zion's Watch Tower Tract Society. His wife became the first treasurer-secretary. Much of the financing, however, came from Russell's own income from the haberdashery that he had kept up all of this time. On December 13, 1884, the rapidly growing society became chartered and incorporated, signaling the official beginning of Zion's Watchtower Bible and Tract Society. Twelve years later, it dropped "Zion" from the name, leaving what is presently the official title of the movement.

Russell began, in 1886, to publish the *Millennial Dawn,* later renamed *Studies in the Scriptures,* which became a seven-volume series. The first volume, *The Divine Plan of the Ages,* continued Russell's millennial ideas, which had become more sophisticated through his study of Greek and Hebrew. Russell never mastered the original languages of the ⁾Bible but was able to make use of lexicons and dictionaries. The last volume of the series was published in 1917, one year after Russell's death, and comprised a collection of Russell's writings.

The Allegheny-based society found itself growing rapidly, with its first branch office established in London in 1900. The success made it possible to begin publishing its various books and pamphlets in several foreign languages. Subsequent societies were soon opened in Europe and one in Australia in 1904. In 1908 Russell moved the headquarters of the society to Brooklyn, New York. It continued to acquire property in Columbia Heights, where it houses its central headquarters to this day.

In the midst of success, trouble erupted for Russell on many fronts. One instance is the embarrassment resulting from Russell's so-called Miracle Wheat. Russell had published in his periodical that he was selling wheat for one dollar per pound that had the capability of growing five times more quickly than any conventional wheat sold on the market. The proceeds were to go to the Watchtower Society and for the financing of the ongoing publication of Russell's sermons and teachings. On January 1, 1913, *The Brooklyn Daily Eagle* published an article sharply criticizing and poking fun at Russell's wheat. Russell immediately sued for libel, claiming that he had been falsely slandered. The U.S. government investigated the wheat and discovered that it was not miraculous in any way; it was, in fact, an inferior brand. Government testimony in the trial resulted in Russell's defeat.

This was not the first time Russell had sued for libel, nor was it the first time he suffered an embarrassing defeat for fraudulent claims. One-half year before the wheat scandal, the Rev. J. J. Ross from Hamilton, Ontario, Canada, a Baptist minister, published an apologetic pamphlet titled *Some Facts about the Self-styled "Pastor," Charles T. Russell.* The pamphlet was a fierce denunciation of Russell, accusing him of being a self-appointed pastor with no ministerial credentials, not ordained by any recognized church body. Ross also attacked Russell's morals and personal life. Russell immediately sued for libel. By denying Ross's accusations, the burden of proof rested on Russell's shoulders to prove that they were not true. The heart of his defense was in his insistence that he was a scholar, familiar with biblical languages, and that he was legitimately ordained into the public ministry. Walter Martin's *Kingdom of the Cults* records the transcript of the portions of the trial centering around these two key issues. Martin notes:

The following reproduction of the Russell v. Ross transcript relative to the perjury charge made against Russell is taken from a copy on file in the headquarters in Brooklyn and is presented in the interests of thorough investigation.

Question: *(Attorney Staunton)* "Do you know the Greek alphabet?"
Answer: *(Russell)* "Oh yes."
Question: (Staunton) "Can you tell me the correct letters if you see them?"
Answer: *(Russell)* "Some of them, I might make a mistake on some of them."
Question: *(Staunton)* "Would you tell me the names of those on top of the page, page 447 I have got here?"
Answer: *(Russell)* "Well, I don't know that I would be able to."
Question: *(Staunton)* "You can't tell what those letters are, look at them and see if you know?"
Answer: *(Russell)* "My way . . ." (he was interrupted at this point and not allowed to explain).
Question: *(Staunton)* "Are you familiar with the Greek language?"
Answer: *(Russell)* "No."[4]

Further questioning resulted in Russell's admission that he had never been ordained by any "bishop, clergyman, presbytery, council, or any body of men living."[5]

Russell's public perjury proved to be another key factor in his demise. While he continued as the leader of the movement, his respectability among the learned ceased. Russell died on October 31, 1916, while aboard a train in Pampa, Texas. But the Watchtower Bible and Tract Society did not die. In fact, under Russell's leadership, it was only in its infant stage. The mantle of leadership was passed on to Judge Joseph Franklin Rutherford (1869–1942), none other than the society's lawyer who had defended Russell in the suit against Ross.

Rutherford became the society's new president on January 6, 1917. Because he had briefly served as a special judge in Missouri, he was popularly called Judge Rutherford. Under Rutherford's leadership, a new era in the Watchtower Society began. The judge introduced some major changes and innovations not taught by Russell. First, he taught that the special message of the Bible was the vindication of God's name—Jehovah. All who worship in the name of Jehovah are true worshipers. Rutherford also introduced a program of vigorous renewal in witnessing and proselytizing efforts. He reproduced many of his sermons on phonograph machines that were played for prospective converts all over the country. The themes of such sermons were the fierce denunciation of denominational churches, particularly Roman Catholicism, and the impending doom on those who did not embrace the teachings of Jehovah God and the Watchtower. After 1944 the phonograph approach was abandoned and replaced by personal and confrontational proselytism, which had previously been introduced by Rutherford.

The most significant change in the society during Rutherford's tenure was the movement from a democratic to a more centrally controlled, or as Rutherford referred to it, "theocratically" controlled, approach. The Brooklyn office became the Watchtower version of the Vatican.

As in Russell's case, trouble erupted for Rutherford almost immediately on his accession to the presidency. Because of the strict stand the Watchtower took in refusing to serve in the military, in May 1918 a U.S. district court issued warrants for the arrests of Rutherford and seven other members on charges of conspiracy to cause insubordination. The eight were convicted of these charges and sentenced to twenty years in prison. This forced the Brooklyn headquarters to close. The society ran its affairs from Pittsburgh for the time being. After the war was over in November 1918, the charges were dropped, however, and all eight were released. Rutherford immediately reopened the Brooklyn headquarters and resumed control of his "theocracy."

The resolution of the external struggle with the government soon gave way to an internal controversy. Because of Rutherford's domineering approach to leadership, some members of the society became resentful. Rutherford exacerbated this tension by introducing some innovative interpretations to Russell's prophetic scheme. He argued, for example, that the battle of Armageddon did not begin in 1914 as Russell had taught. Rutherford also argued that "[9]Satan was cast out of heaven and confined to this earth."[6] The result was that the loyal followers of Russell, intent on retaining the pure teachings of their mentor, broke away into several schismatic movements. Milton Backman summarizes these divergent groups as follows:

> One group who claimed to preserve the basic theology of Pastor Russell formed the Dawn Bible Student's Association. Other offshoots of this movement are known as the Standfast Movement, Paul Johnson Movement (later renamed the Layman's Home Missionary Movement), Elijah Voice Movement, Eagle Society, and Pastoral Bible Institute of Brooklyn.[7]

In order to differentiate between the schismatics and the followers of Rutherford, the society adopted the name Jehovah's Witnesses in 1931 at a convention in Columbus, Ohio. The new appellation was based on Isaiah 43:10, "Ye are my witnesses, saith [Jehovah], and my servant whom I have chosen" (KJV).

The outbreak of the Second World War in 1939 caused the society to reaffirm its pacifistic stand against serving in the military. Several thousand were arrested, while many others claimed the title of [9]minister, thereby exempting them from enlistment. Hoekema writes, "It is significant to note that the number of Jehovah's Witness 'ministers' doubled between the years 1939 and 1945. . . ."[8] In addition to the draft issue, Jehovah's Witnesses were imprisoned throughout the country on various other charges, including illegal solicitation and sales without licenses, distribution of literature, and proselytizing on private property without permission.

The Rutherford era came to an end on January 13, 1942, when he died. Rutherford was most noted for his administrative and organizational skills, his ambitious propagandizing, and his voluminous writings, which far outdistanced those of his predecessor.

The third president of the Jehovah's Witnesses, Nathan Homer [9]Knorr (1905–1977), elected just five days after Rutherford's death, brought a new and entirely different approach to leadership. Recognizing that public hostility was at an all-time high, Knorr did his best to alter the negative image of

The Watchtower building in Brooklyn, New York, headquarters for the Jehovah's Witnesses. Courtesy George A. Mather

the society in the public eye. He did not compromise the doctrines of the society or the convictions concerning the evils of government, schools, and churches. But he did alter Rutherford's *blitzkrieg* approach to recruitment by toning down the aggression and insisting on more diplomatic and educational methods. He founded the Gilead Watchtower Bible School in 1943 in South Lansing, New York, in order to help educate Jehovah's Witness disciples.

Other important changes came to the society during Knorr's tenure. First was the huge increase in printed literature containing doctrinal and devotional helps. The most significant literary production was the translation of the Bible into modern English. The *New World Translation* appeared in 1950 in successive volumes, with the entire Bible produced in a single volume in 1961. Knorr also introduced a new doctrinal accent referred to as the "New World Society," which embellished Russell's eschatology and posited that following Armageddon all of Jehovah's people would reinhabit the nations of the earth.

Guided by Knorr's able leadership, the society experienced its greatest growth. With 129,000 members in 1942, the movement reported well over 410,000 members in the United States alone by 1971. Knorr died in 1977 and was succeeded by the fourth president of the Watchtower—Frederick W. *Franz, who died at the age of ninety-eight on December 22, 1992. Under Franz's leadership, missionary activity has continued to increase, along with literary output. Millions of copies of two of its official publications, *Awake* and *The Watchtower*, are printed and distributed annually.

In February 1982, Franz's fifty-nine-year-old nephew, Raymond Franz, a member of the organization's top governing body, defected and was *disfellowshiped. In an interview with *Time* (February 1982), Franz reported that discipline in the Watchtower Society was "too harsh." The younger Franz believes that his being disfellowshiped from the organization was due, among other things, to his insistence on relying on the "Bible alone" rather than on all of the aids and helps that Witnesses are required to read in conjunction with the Bible. He reported that strict monitoring and control of Witnesses' lives is strongest right at the *Bethel headquarters.[9]

ORGANIZATION

In October 2000 some important changes were introduced that sent shockwaves throughout the organization. A major reorganization took place whereby the president is, in effect, no longer the leader of the church body. The new leadership centers on the Governing Body, which is completely separated from the office of the president and the Board of Directors. Previously, the Governing Body and the Board of Directors had overlapped in membership. This is no longer the case. The result was the resignation of president who succeeded Franz, Milton Henschel (1920–2003). The eighty-year-old Henschel was replaced by Don Adams. The significant factor surrounding this move is that the Watchtower formed three new corporations to shield members of the Governing Board. If, for example, a member dies as a result of failure to receive a blood transfusion, formerly, the president and members of the Governing Body could be held responsible as spiritual leaders, and because they were also members of the organization's Board of Directors, the assets of the Society could be attached in a legal suit. Now, because no member of the Governing Body is a member of the Board of Directors, they are protected.

Another important result of this change was theological in nature. All members of the Governing Body were previously members of the Anointed Class. This prevented younger members from being a part of the Governing Body. In the 1990s, this became increasingly difficult and exceptions had to be made as the Anointed Class grew older, making it difficult to govern the church. But this had the effect of bringing into question the doctrine of the Anointed Class. The brilliant move of separating of the Governing Body and the Board of Directors now enables an entire cast of younger men to run the affairs of the church without changing this important doctrine. One does wonder, however, what the Watchtower will do once the Anointed Class, now numbering about 8,000, have all died. The few who are left are in their eighties and nineties.

TEACHINGS

The theology of the Jehovah's Witnesses has been introduced in the above historical analysis. What follows is a brief elaboration on specific doctrines with comparisons to *orthodox Christian doctrines.

The essential ingredient to Witness theology is the doctrine of the eschatological renewal of society. Jesus preached the message of "the kingdom of God." This future kingdom will be established as a theocracy wherein Jehovah brings peace, restoration, and utopia to the world. Such peace will come only after the battle of Armageddon has been fought, bringing destruction to the present order.

Prophecy/fulfillment motifs, particularly in the books of Daniel and Revelation, have been characteristic of Jehovah's Witnesses since the days of Russell. The groundwork for Witness theology was laid in the nineteenth century. It was largely through the influence of three Christian proponents of ▸dispensationalism—Edward Irving (1792–1834), John Nelson Darby (1800–1882), and William Miller (1782–1849; see ▸Millerite Movement)—who first expounded the millennialism so zealously taught by Russell. Irving's eschatological speculations, Darby's doctrine of the pretribulation rapture, and Scofield's supportive reference Bible and interpretive keys each contributed to the millenarian movements of the nineteenth century, chiefly within Protestant Christendom. Out of this ethos grew the ▸Millerites (later Seventh-Day Adventists) and the followers of Charles Taze Russell. It is precisely this eschatological hope that continues to inspire Jehovah's Witnesses to eagerly search for the signs of the end of this present evil order.

Rejection by traditional Christianity has only bolstered their belief that all of the denominations of "Christendom" (the word is used pejoratively by Witnesses to describe corrupted Christianity) are utterly false and apostate. The Watchtower Bible and Tract Society is God's only true organization on earth, being used as a witness to prepare for the end and the coming of God's kingdom. Along with the various churches of Christendom, the evils and corruption of government and the economic enslavement wrought on humanity by business enterprises are also regarded as being objects of Jehovah's wrath and are fiercely denounced by the society. Consequently, Jehovah's Witnesses take a strong stand against culture and the world.

Jehovah's Witnesses do not observe Christmas, Good Friday, Easter, and family birthdays because they regard them as pagan. Members use extreme discretion in their selection of leisure activities such as dancing, movie-going, and television viewing. Watchtower members do not salute the flag of any nation and refuse to participate in war and military activity.[10] Rather, they feel that Jehovah alone will bring vengeance and justice and will fight all battles.

Jehovah's Witnesses also observe the strict prohibition of the consumption of blood and unbled meats. They base this conviction on the Old Testament dietary laws as contained in Leviticus 17:10–14. Witnesses also prohibit members from receiving blood transfusions, based on Acts 15:20, "but we write to them to abstain from . . . blood." Traditional Christianity argues that this is a faulty interpretation of the text. James Sire points out that the blood-infusion issue is based on an analogy. To Witnesses, this text instructs us not to eat blood. "But," argues Sire,

> a blood transfusion is not eating. A transfusion replenishes the supply of essential, life sustaining fluid that has otherwise drained away or become incapable of performing its vital tasks in the body. A blood transfusion is not even equivalent to intravenous feeding because the blood so given does not function as food. The Jehovah's Witnesses argument is based on a false analogy.[11]

Witnesses have recently been ordered by the Watchtower Society to resist all attempts to receive blood transfusions.

Specific doctrines that have caused traditional Protestant denominations to label the Watchtower as being heterodox include the rejection of the ▸Trinity and the accompanying denial of the deity and eternality of Jesus Christ, to which all orthodox Christian churches ascribe. A brief treatment of these and other doctrines of Jehovah's Witnesses now follows.

God

Jehovah's Witnesses are unitarian with respect to their doctrine of God.[12] In their most popular publication, *Let God Be True*, the society vehemently opposes the traditional Christian doctrine of the Trinity, concluding "that Satan is the originator of the trinity doctrine."[13] In a pamphlet titled *"The Word": Who Is He According to John?* the Watchtower attempts to interpret the classic Christological text from John's prologue, "In the beginning was the Word, and the Word was with God, and the Word was God" (John 1:1). The traditional interpretation of this text is that it is clearly an attestation to the deity of the second member of the triune Godhead—Jesus Christ. The *New World Translation* renders the last phrase of the passage "the Word was [a] god." The Jehovah's Witnesses argue that the rules of Greek grammar mandate the insertion of the indefinite article "a," thereby nullifying the use of this text to defend the doctrine of the deity of Christ as being the unique Word that is God. They then ridicule the Christian doctrine of the Trinity in statements such as the following:

> And yet the trinitarians teach that the God of John 1:1, 2 is only one God, not three Gods! So is the Word only one-third of God? Since we cannot scientifically calculate that 1 God (the Father) + 1 God (the Son) + 1 God (the Holy Ghost) = 1 God, then we must calculate that 1/3 God (the Father) + 1/3

God (the Son) + 1/3 God (the Holy Ghost) = 3/3 God or 1 God. Furthermore, we would have to conclude that the term "God" in John 1:1,2 changes its personality, or that "God" changes his personality in one sentence. Does he?... Any trying to reason out the Trinity teaching leads to confusion of mind. So the Trinity teaching confuses the meaning of John 1:1,2; it does not simplify it or make it clear or easily understandable.[14]

Classical Christian apologetics responds first by asserting a belief not in three gods but one God (Deut. 6:4). But God manifests himself in three distinct persons who are coequal and cosubstantial with each other within the economy of the divine being. Second, while Jehovah's Witnesses argue that the word "trinity" does not appear in the Bible, traditional Christianity responds by pointing out that while the *word* does not exist, the basis of this *concept* does.[15] They use many passages to prove this (Matt. 28:19; Mark 1:9–11; John 1:1–18; 2 Cor. 13:14; et al.). The Witnesses themselves contradict this line of argument when they use, for example, the term "theocracy," a word that is also not in the Bible though the concept is.

The ecumenical creeds base their understanding of the nature of the Godhead on Scripture. The Apostles' Creed, for example, asserts belief in "God the Father Almighty, maker of heaven and earth"; belief in the Son, as "conceived," "born," "suffered," "died," "was buried," "rose," "ascended," "sits at the right hand of God," and "will come to judge"; and belief in the "Holy Spirit" (Appendix 1). The creeds were used for apologetic reasons against the various heresies that sprang up to challenge the canon or rule of faith of the church. They were especially useful for catechesis before the church had in her possession the entire New Testament.[16] The creeds facilitate a simple confession of the nature of the Godhead, based on the collective texts of the apostolic writings. The greatest defense of the Trinity and the deity and eternality of Christ is put forth by the Athanasian Creed (Appendix 1).

The Watchtower puts a great deal of time into John 1:1, defending their insertion of the indefinite article "a" and arguing against the doctrine of the Trinity. Much traditional Christian literature has been written in response, so much so that it would be impossible to recall it all within the confines of this article.[17] One excellent publication is a pamphlet by Michael Van Buskirk, *The Scholastic Dishonesty of the Watchtower* (1975), in which he points out that the Jehovah's Witnesses have wrongly quoted the famous Christian Greek scholars H. E. Dana and J. R. Mantey in their

classic *A Manual Grammar of the Greek New Testament*. Van Buskirk includes an interview with Professor Mantey, who insists that indeed the Watchtower has falsely quoted his work in order to force using the indefinite article "a" in the *New World Translation* of John 1:1. Mantey relates that the context, the grammar, and the usage demand the subject "God" (as a definite noun) and the predicate "Word" be connected by the verb "was." Mantey states the following concerning the Watchtower:

> When they do meet certain passages of Scripture that seem to be against their viewpoint, to my great disappointment, they mistranslate them deliberately and deceptively—deliberate deception—in some cases and, to me, that is unpardonable. It's dishonest and, to a certain extent, it's diabolical.[18]

Authority

Professor Mantey's comments point to an important distinction in the notion of authority in Jehovah's Witness circles. The Watchtower's *New World Translation* did indeed introduce significant changes from conventional English translations of the Bible in a number of passages that support their own theology. For example, traditional Christianity has always understood Philippians 2:6 to be one of the great Christological passages referring to the deity of Christ. The KJV of Philippians 2:6 reads as follows with reference to Jesus Christ: "Who, being in the form of God, thought it not robbery to be equal with God." Other English translations have altered the text to read somewhat differently. The RSV reads, "who, though he was in the form of God, did not count equality with God a thing to be grasped." The NIV reads similarly, "Who, being in very nature God, did not consider equality with God something to be grasped." In each instance the deity of Christ is affirmed (most clearly in the KJV). The *New World Translation*, however, reads, "who, although he was existing in God's form, gave no consideration to a seizure, namely, that he should be equal with God." In addition to being convoluted, this rendering inverts the meaning derived from traditional translations. According to J. R. Mantey and another highly respected scholar, Bruce Metzger, this rendering is made to fit the Watchtower's theology of the subordinationism of Christ (see below).[19]

Another obvious example is the insertion of the word "other" in brackets in Colossians 1:16. The *New World Translation* reads, "because by means of him all [other] things were created in the heavens and upon the earth, the things visible and the things invisible.... All

Materials printed by the Watchtower Bible and Tract Society are one of the chief means by which Jehovah's Witnesses train their own members as well as promote their teachings in door-to-door witnessing.

[other] things have been created through him and for him." Once again, to support the doctrine that Christ was not coeternal with the Father but had a created beginning, the Watchtower felt compelled to bolster this idea by inserting the word "other," even though neither the Greek nor any other English translations contain or warrant it.

According to the Watchtower, "The Holy Scriptures of the Bible are the standard by which to judge all religions."[20] It is true that the Jehovah's Witnesses cling to the Protestant tenet that the Bible alone is their final authority. Unlike, for example, the Church of Jesus Christ of Latter-Day Saints (*see* Mormonism), which supplements the Bible with other sources of authority (i.e., the ▶Book of Mormon), the Jehovah's Witnesses argue that the Bible is the Word of Jehovah God. What appears to be a traditional Protestant principle of authority is rapidly eroded, however, when their translation is made to fit their theology rather than the opposite. This is what Professor Mantey meant when he labeled this methodology "diabolical."

Another major difference between the Watchtower and traditional Christianity with respect to the authority of the Bible is that, realistically and pragmatically, the society ultimately appeals to its own helps and tools in order to ensure that the Bible is interpreted and understood "correctly." Walter Martin points out that Russell, from the very beginning, believed that the Bible need not even be read apart from his own (Russell's) notes and books. Martin quotes Russell's *Studies in the Scriptures*:

> Furthermore, not only do we find that people cannot see the divine plan in studying the Bible by itself, but we see, also, that if anyone lays the *Scrip-*

ture Studies aside, even after he has used them . . . after he has read them for ten years—if he then lays them aside and ignores them and goes to the Bible alone, though he has understood his Bible for ten years, our experience shows that within two years he goes into darkness. On the other hand, if he had merely read the *Scripture Studies* with their references, and had not read a page of the Bible, as such, he would be in the light at the end of two years, because he would have the light of the Scriptures.[21]

Although many Jehovah's Witnesses may disregard these statements or may even be embarrassed by them, nevertheless the organization still attempts to promulgate its doctrines through the various publications issued from its press.

Jehovah's Witnesses are taught that all other versions of the Bible besides the *New World Translation* are unsuitable and tainted. Furthermore, interpretations of the Bible that differ from the Watchtower's are invariably false. It is difficult to conduct a two-way dialogue with those convinced from the outset that only a Jehovah's Witness can understand Scripture. This is true with respect to any verses of Scripture a Trinitarian Christian uses to attempt to defend the doctrine of the Trinity, the deity of Jesus Christ, or any other orthodox doctrine.

Jesus Christ

As noted to above, the Watchtower teaches a subordinationist ▶Christology that parallels the teaching of Arius (A.D. 250–336). ▶Arianism was opposed by Athanasius (296–373), who understood that the denial of the eternality of Christ was tantamount to the denial of the deity of Christ. According to Russell, "Jesus never spoke of himself as God or called himself God. He always put himself below God rather than on an equality with God. . . . Jesus was not God whose will was to be done, but was lower than God, doing God's will.[22]

The traditional Christian response to this polemic is that while it is true that Jesus preached the gospel of the kingdom of God, he pointed to his own person and work as being the focus of that kingdom (Matt. 24:30; Rev. 1:7–8).

> Jehovah's Witnesses distinguish between three states of Christ's person: a pre-human, human, and post-human state. Before Jesus was born of Mary, he existed as the living Word of God. He was created by or born of God, but he was not God, who by definition had no beginning. In this position, he en-

joyed a superiority to all other creatures. As a point of fact, Jesus existed in this pre-human state as Michael the Archangel.[23]

In Jesus' human state, Witnesses agree with orthodox Christianity that Jesus was born of the virgin Mary. But because he was not God, his birth cannot be spoken of as an ʼincarnation. He was born a man. Jesus simply laid aside his prehuman spirit state and took on a human nature. The Witnesses forthrightly deny, therefore, that Jesus Christ had two natures, human and divine, as traditional Christianity professes. It was at Jesus' baptism that Jehovah poured out on him his spirit to empower him to fulfill his mission. Jesus, in his humanity, was born sinless and remained so.

The heart of the contrast between traditional Christianity and Witness theology lies in the fundamental Christological differences. According to orthodoxy, the early church condemned Arianism at the Council of Nicaea (A.D. 325) because by conceding to a subordinationist view of Christ the church would have failed to recognize the validity of ample scriptural references attesting to Christ's deity (Isa. 7:14; 9:6; Mic. 5:2; John 1:1; 5:18, 21–24; 8:58; 10:30; 17:5; Phil. 2:11; Col. 2:9; 1 Tim. 3:16; Heb. 1:3; 1 John 5:20; et al.).[24] This led to the formulation of the Chalcedonian or two-natures Christology that the church recognized as being most harmonious to the Bible and the apostolic rule of faith. Christ was born the incarnate God (Isa. 7:14; Matt. 1:23) and for this reason was born fully human and fully divine.

How are these two natures related to one another? The church answered at Chalcedon (A.D. 451) that by nature of the *communicatio idiomaticum* ("communication of attributes"), the divine and the human each share in the properties of the other. For example, when the Bible declares that Jesus' blood cleanses from sin (1 John 1:7), it means that human blood is salvific because of its personal union with the divine nature. Chalcedon reached the conclusion that the two natures of Christ are so related to each other that they are "indivisible," "inseparable," "unchangeable," and "unconfused."[25] The Watchtower, in addition to advancing Arianism in its denial of the eternal preexistence of Christ, also becomes a proponent of the Ebionite heresy in teaching that Jesus was merely human.

In the posthuman state, Witnesses teach that Jesus' resurrection body was not physical. In place of his body, Jehovah raised up Jesus with a "spirit body." Jehovah disposed of Jesus' body in a mysterious and unknown way. The Watchtower has proposed two theories: (1) the body dissipated into gases (vaporized); (2) angels took the body to a place where it will be revived as a memorial in the future. Orthodox Christianity, on the other hand, teaches that by virtue of the personal union (above), the human and divine natures of Christ remained as inseparable after the resurrection as before. Therefore Jesus showed Thomas the print of the nails in his hands (John 20:24–27) and ate breakfast with the disciples (John 21:12–13; cf. Luke 24:30–34), offering clear attestation to his retaining a physical body.

Salvation

It is clear that the Watchtower teaches that Christ passed through three different states of existence. For Orthodox Christianity, this is not warranted or supported by Scripture and has far-reaching consequences with respect to the work of Christ and salvation.

Concerning the atoning work of Christ, the Watchtower teaches that Jesus' death on the cross and shed blood reversed and removed the effects of Adam's sin and the sins of Adam's offspring. Jesus' sacrifice is a ransom that reversed the order of death set in motion by Adam's sin. The *human* Jesus came as the Second Adam and with the help of the "holy spirit" remained sinless, unlike the first Adam. Not tainted by sin, Jesus was free from the guilt of sin and the wrath of Jehovah. Therefore, Jesus was able to become a ransom or substitute for the sins of the world. There are both similarities and differences here between traditional Christianity and the Watchtower. While it is true that Jesus was sinless and became a ransom for many, orthodoxy affirms that Christ's sinlessness was not due to the Holy Spirit's aid, but because Jesus in himself remained sinless by virtue of the personal union of the divine and human natures.

For Witnesses, Christ's ransom and Jehovah's offer of salvation is extended to two sets of people. First is the ʼAnointed Class, that is, the exclusive or heavenly congregation comprised of 144,000 (see Rev. 14:3–4).[26] These were members who had become Witnesses before 1935. Second, the ransom of Jesus "must embrace more than those of his bride."[27] These are the Earthly Class, who are saved and are destined to dwell on earth. Only those who meet specific requirements, who undergo sacrifices and sufferings modeled after Christ, will make up this exclusive class, also known as "the little flock."[28]

Traditional Christian ʼsoteriology knows no distinction between an earthly and heavenly class. All Christians receive the forgiveness won for them through

Christ's ransom (John 3:16). Moreover, the Christian does not earn a higher status before God through merit and works. This status is freely given by virtue of Christ's merits and righteousness (Rom. 3:24; Eph. 2:8–9). All believers will one day stand before God in heaven (Phil. 2:9–11).

Christians and Jehovah's Witnesses also greatly differ in their beliefs regarding the extent of the atonement. Most denominations of Christendom teach that Christ died for the entire human race. Witnesses, by contrast, teach that Christ died both for the Earthly Class and the Anointed Class. Neither of these, however, include Adam, who died in sin.

Orthodox Christians may see a degree of ambiguity in Witness soteriology in that the latter teach that one must believe and then be baptized, yet the state of being saved does not come until *after* one has proven oneself worthy through keeping the laws of God throughout life. For Christianity, the gift of eternal life is bestowed on the believer immediately and is brought to completion at death.

Holy Spirit

The Watchtower teaches that the Holy Spirit is not a divine person within the triune Godhead, as traditional orthodox Christianity asserts (Mark 1:9–12; John 14:16; Acts 13:2, 4). The Spirit for Witnesses is "God's *active force* by which he accomplishes his purpose and executes his will."[29] The *New World Translation* therefore supplies the words "active force" in place of "spirit" in Genesis 1:2. Traditional Christianity assiduously maintains the personhood of the Spirit (John 14:16–18; 16:7–14; Acts 5:3–4). The Nicene Creed (Appendix 1) understands the Holy Spirit to be "the Lord and giver of life . . . who with the Father and the Son together is worshiped and glorified."

Hell

An important departure from Christian tradition occurs in the Watchtower doctrine of hell and eternal damnation. The society holds that there is no eternal hell or state of everlasting condemnation. While believers become members of either the heavenly bride or the earthly kingdom dwellers (see above), unbelievers who do not repent will suffer eternal death. Like the WORLDWIDE CHURCH OF GOD, the Witnesses subscribe wholeheartedly to ʼannihilationism. They arrive at this position for several reasons. They argue that the Hebrew word *sheol*, translated "hell," means literally "the grave," a point that has gained wide acceptance among Hebrew scholars. Second, the Watchtower

argues that the Greek word for "hell" (*gehenna*) means "everlasting destruction," not everlasting torment in such New Testament passages as Matthew 5:22; 16:18; 18:9; Mark 9:45. Third, the New Testament Greek word *hades* (Matt. 11:23; 16:18; Luke 10:15; Acts 2:27; et al.), like *sheol*, means "the grave." Finally, for the Witnesses, the idea of "destruction" means annihilation.

Traditional Christianity does not teach annihilationism. The Christian understanding is that while the words *sheol* and *hades* may refer to "grave" and *gehenna* may mean "final destruction," the context in which these words appear demands that "death" be understood not as being mere extinction, but as complete and total separation from God forever (Rev. 14:10–11). Second, many passages from the Bible demonstrate that eternal death means eternal torment (e.g., Matt. 8:11–12; Mark 9:42–48; Luke 13:24–28; 2 Pet. 2:17; Jude 13; Rev. 19:20; 20:10).

Satan

Like traditional Christianity, the Watchtower holds to the existence of the ʼdevil or Satan. His evil purpose is to keep people from the kingdom of God, which he does with false teaching, lies, and deception. The important contrast between orthodoxy and the Watchtower is that Witnesses teach that Satan, too, will be annihilated. The context of Revelation 20:10, however, declares that the devil will suffer eternal torment.

Humanity

The Watchtower teaches that human beings are comprised of both "body" and "breath" (soul) but that the soul is not eternal or immortal. This is a natural conclusion, given the doctrine of annihilationism. In *Let God be True*, the Watchtower argues that the source of the deception and error that the soul is immortal emerged in the deceptions of Satan in the Garden of Eden when he said to Eve, "You will not surely die" (Gen. 3:4).[30]

Christianity disagrees with the Watchtower on this doctrine. According to Genesis 1:26, humankind was created in the image and likeness of God and therefore has a beginning. This beginning, however, does not mean that the eternal nature of the soul is abrogated or is a contradiction. It means that the eternal nature of the soul is a future blessing not yet attained (1 Cor. 15:53–54; 1 Pet. 1:4). "When we use the term 'eternal' in association with the soul of man, we mean that the human soul *after* its creating by God will (future) exist somewhere into the eternal, into the everlasting."[31] Ample biblical evidence attests to the existence of eternal or spiritual consciousness immediately following death and the separation of the soul from the body (1 Cor. 15:35–57; 2 Cor. 5:1–9; Phil. 1:21–26). Furthermore, for the Christian, immortality is far more a process of transformation than it is a state of mere existence (1 Thess. 4:14–17).

For Witnesses salvation consists of believing in Jesus' message and being obedient to the laws of Jehovah. Only 144,000 may be "born again," however; only they will reign eternally. The rest of the believers are Jehovah's "other sheep." This latter group cannot be born again. The souls of both the celestial 144,000 and the "other sheep" live on, the former without a body, the latter with a corporeal existence. The Watchtower's denial of the immortality of the soul is directly concerned, however, not so much with the believer as with the unbeliever. Because the punishment meted out by Jehovah for sin is final death and not eternal torment, the soul itself must perish.

Church

Like so many religious movements, the Watchtower believes itself to be the only true church on earth. All organized religion is apostate, and all of the denominational churches of Christendom are false and will constitute the enemy of God in the battle of Armageddon. The false churches have their source in Satan and

Kingdom halls are found in virtually every metropolitan area throughout the world.

teach false doctrine, such as the various doctrines discussed above. The true church is God's one true organization on earth, namely, the Watchtower Bible and Tract Society. Witnesses believe that ▸apostasy entered the church shortly after Jesus' resurrection and was ensured a long reign throughout the Middle Ages,

beginning when the Council of Nicea (A.D. 325) vindicated the doctrine of the Trinity. Although the ▸Reformation did bring about some changes, too much of the old leaven was retained, especially when the doctrine of the Trinity was not only affirmed by Luther, Calvin, and other Reformers, but was more emphatically supported.

The Watchtower does not like the term *church*. The *New World Translation* translates the Greek word *ekklesia* as "congregation." However, when the word "congregation" is used in the Bible, Witnesses believe it to refer more often to the anointed class of 144,000 than to the whole corpus of Jehovah's people.[32]

Traditional Christianity maintains that the church is the assembly of believers who gather around the doctrines and teachings of the apostles (Acts 2:41–47). The congregation is a visible local assembly where a body of believers assemble to worship and to hear God's Word. There is no anointed class of believers distinguished from other believers. All Christians are a part of the "holy catholic church, the communion of saints" (Apostles' Creed). Furthermore, this visibly local assembly will one day be a heavenly gathering. Witnesses are guilty of an inconsistency in their distinction between the "congregation" as being the anointed class (144,000) and the "other sheep" as not being part of this congregation. Anthony Hoekema points out this inconsistency:

> Whereas the Scriptures say, in Rev. 21:2, that the holy city comes down out of heaven from God, prepared as a bride adorned for her husband (implying that this bride will be on the new earth thereafter, so that heaven and earth are now become one), Jehovah's Witnesses, in defiance of Scripture, wish to keep the bride of Christ in heaven throughout eternity and to leave the lower class of adherents on earth.[33]

In the Bible, the church is a unifying institution, never one for advocating divisions (1 Cor. 1:10; Gal. 3:28). The only proper hierarchical distinction that orthodox Christianity insists on is the distinction between Christ the bridegroom and the church the bride (Eph. 5:21–33), or between Christ the head (Eph. 1:22–23) and the church the body (1 Cor. 12:12–31).

The Watchtower teaches that within the "congregation" Jehovah has ordained particular ministries. Older members are appointed to serve as ▸overseers within the local gatherings called ▸kingdom halls. A distinction is also made between overseers (*episkopos*) and ▸ministerial servants (*diakonos*).[34] Several congregations are organized into circuits with a traveling minister visiting each for a short period of time (usually a week). Each member is considered a missionary. Pioneers are those who devote one hundred hours per month to conducting the work of the society at the local congregational level.

All denominations within Christendom conform to one of three church polities. The episcopal polity is the hierarchical or pyramidical polity that characterizes the Roman Catholic, Eastern Orthodox, and Episcopal churches. Many Protestant denominations reject this polity on the grounds that Jesus never advocated a monarchial episcopacy (Matt. 23:2–12). The congregational polity, which advocates the autonomy of each congregation, represents the opposite extreme and is advocated by independent and congregational churches. The Watchtower does not embrace this polity on the grounds that each local congregation should be part of a whole society. The third polity is called presbyterian. The presbyterian approach recognizes the autonomy of each local assembly while at the same time has a central control or headquarters that exists to serve the local congregations.

There is some ambivalence concerning which polity best describes the Watchtower. At different times in its short history, particularly under the leadership of Judge Rutherford, the society exhibited episcopal tendencies, controlled closely from the central headquarters of its theocracy. The presbyterian polity most accurately fits the way that the organization is presently run. The Brooklyn headquarters serves as the general administrative nerve center. The publishing houses and Bible schools all comprise an important part of the network.

Sacraments

The Watchtower Society administers two ᵇsacraments, baptism and holy communion. Regarding baptism, the Watchtower teaches that baptism, by immersion only, is to be administered following conversion. According to Matthew 28:19, believers are baptized "in the name of the Father, and of the Son, and of the holy spirit" (NWT). Some Witness groups, because of their theology of the Holy Spirit, use an alternate formula: "in the name of the Father, and of the Son, and of the Spirit-filled organization." Jesus commanded baptism in this passage as a sign of obedience. It signifies death to the previous sinful life and resurrection to faith and obedience. Infant baptism is therefore rejected on the grounds that infants cannot believe or cannot repent and so should not be baptized.

The anointed class of 144,000 undergoes a second baptism called a "baptism in the holy spirit." Based on Revelation 14, the Watchtower concludes that the anointed class are "sealed" and that the seal is the holy spirit.[35] After this elect group, God turns to his "other sheep" (John 10:16), which Revelation calls the "great crowd" (cf. Rev. 7:4 with 7:9). Because of faith sealed by the obedience of water baptism, the "other sheep" will be kept by God through the perils of the great tribulation.

Within the confines of traditional Christianity, there is a degree of pluralism regarding baptism. The Roman Catholic, Eastern Orthodox, Lutheran, Episcopal, and most Reformed churches all practice infant baptism, based on a variety of arguments from the Bible and the history of the church. Quickly summarized, these arguments include the following:

Infants are part of God's creation; and because the Bible states that all humanity sins (Ps. 51:5; Rom. 3:23), all humanity, including children, are in need of God's saving grace.

God's Old Testament covenant with Abraham—that Abraham would be the father of many nations—was sealed by an outward mark—circumcision of the male child at eight days old (Gen. 17). This covenant was fulfilled on the Day of Pentecost when the Holy Spirit was poured out and Gentiles were brought to faith in Christ's redeeming sacrifice. Acts 2:38–39 states that the promise (God's promise to Abraham) was to children as well as adults (2:39). The visible sign of the old covenant was circumcision. The visible sign of the new covenant is baptism (Acts 2:38; Col. 2:11–12).

Baptism is a sacrament because it conveys the forgiveness of sins (Acts 22:16), and children are in need of such forgiveness.

Many adults were converted *with* their households (Acts 10:48; 11:14; 16:15, 32–34; 18:8; 1 Cor. 1:16), which certainly can imply the inclusion of children.

Luther advanced the argument that Jesus held up children as being capable of possessing faith (Matt. 19:13–15; Luke 1:41) and that it is the reasoning of an adult that works against faith.[36]

Other arguments are often used in a more detailed discussion, but these five are the most common. It was the Anabaptist tradition within the Radical Reformation that rejected infant baptism for some of the same reasons that Witnesses also rejected the practice centuries later. The Anabaptist tradition set the standard for many denominations, particularly those within the ᵇfundamentalist framework. However, all Christian denominations reject the Watchtower's baptismal formula, "in the name of the Father, and of the Son, and of the holy spirit," chiefly because the denial of the Trinity nullifies Matthew 28:19.

Concerning the Lord's Supper, Witnesses believe it to have been instituted by Jesus Christ as a memorial meal to be celebrated once annually. They base this on the idea that Jesus celebrated the supper during the Passover, which was an annual holy day. Like many Protestant denominations, Witnesses reject the doctrine of the real presence and also dismiss as being unbiblical the Roman Catholic doctrine of transubstantiation, which asserts that the bread and wine become the body and blood of Christ during the celebration of the mass. Also in agreement with most Protestant denominations, Witnesses believe that the elements of bread and wine symbolize the body and blood of Christ.

Only the 144,000 are allowed to participate in the Lord's Supper on the grounds that Jesus celebrated the meal with his chosen apostles only and that the meal was intended only for those who would partake of it forever in heaven (Luke 22:28–30). Though the "other sheep" are denied the meal, they must attend and observe while the anointed class (however few or many are in the assembly) partake of the sacrament.

Many denominations (Baptist, Pentecostal, Methodist, etc.) celebrate the Lord's Supper as being a memorial meal and believe that the elements are symbols. All Christians, however, disagree that the sacrament is only for an anointed class of 144,000. Some denominations practice supervised or "close" communion, meaning that only members of a particular denomination may participate. But this is based not on one's status as a select heaven-bound saint, but on Paul's instructions that participants must be able to rightly discern the Lord's body and blood (1 Cor. 11:27–29).

End Times

As we have observed, Watchtower eschatology grew out of the milieu of nineteenth-century dispensational millennialism. Moreover, the heart of Witness theology lies in its doctrine of the coming kingdom of God, namely, that this kingdom was to arrive with the overthrow of earth's present rulership in A.D. 1914 (though this prophecy, like so many others, failed to happen). The Witnesses call the period from 607 B.C., when Nebuchadnezzar conquered Jerusalem, to 1914 "the times of the Gentiles." In 1914 a heavenly war took place between Christ (also called Michael the Archangel) and Satan. After the devil's defeat, Jesus took up rulership in heaven as King of kings. The second coming of 1914 was therefore not a physical return of Christ to earth but the coronation of Christ as King in heaven, from where he now rules. Satan was thrown out of heaven—to earth—after being defeated in the celestial war and immediately vented his rage by pouring out his vengeance and wrath on the human race, as is evidenced by the start of World War I (1914–18).

The period following 1914 is described as the "time of the end."[37] Rutherford often preached that "millions now living will never die." The urgency of witnessing for Jehovah lay in the impulse to warn all people of the imminence of coming judgment and to present them with the opportunity to become a part of Jehovah's kingdom.

Another important prophecy took place in 1918, namely, the coming of Christ to God's temple in order to cleanse it. This is based on the words of Malachi 3:1. Traditional interpretations of this text point to Jesus' cleansing of the temple in Matthew 21:12–13. Witnesses argue that this was only a partial fulfillment. The prophecy was completed in 1918.[38]

As per Revelation 20:6, the "first resurrection" of God's Anointed Class has taken place, also in 1918. This first resurrection was spiritual and not physical in nature. All future resurrections of the anointed will be physical.[30] This spiritual resurrection was, of course, not visible to people on earth. Those of the 144,000 remaining on earth are called "the remnant." They will, upon death, rise to join the remainder of the Anointed Class already ruling with Jesus from his throne since the time of the first resurrection in 1918. Witnesses teach that the War of Armageddon and the dawning of the Millennium must occur before the last of the 144,000 die. In 1961, during a worldwide memorial meal, 13,284 partook of the sacrament, meaning, of course, that there were presumed to be at least this many of the Anointed Class yet remaining at that time. Presently, it is estimated that there are at least 10,000 of the Anointed Class remaining.[40]

Additional details concerning the time of the end in Watchtower eschatology include the belief that during the Millennium not all will be raised up. Those who were not believers, those who fought against Jehovah at Armageddon, or those who are not redeemable by God's grace must suffer the annihilation of their souls (see above). The resurrection itself is reserved for two groups, the righteous and the redeemable. The former will face the "resurrection of life," while the latter group must undergo the "resurrection of judgment." These include those who died unrighteously but will, through judgment, be given a chance to repent. The period of judgment is a testing and preparation time. Those who do in fact repent will be saved. Those who do not will be annihilated at the Great White Throne Judgment, also called the "second death" (Rev. 20:14). Along with the unrighteous, Satan will be cast into the "lake of burning sulfur" (Rev. 20:10). This is the final state of the wicked. Witnesses speak of it as being eternal, only insofar as it is a death that will no more be quickened and it is an eternal death or annihilation within the memory of God. At this time, a new heaven and a new earth will be established, and perfect peace and righteousness will prevail forever under the lordship and dominion of Jehovah.

The Watchtower is not the only organization that has pieced together an elaborate scheme of events for the end times based on Scripture. Many movements within the Christian church have been influenced by millennialism. Adventist groups, evangelicals, fundamentalists, and Pentecostals have brought forth an abundance of futuristic/prophetic literature that attempts to explain the biblical texts that speak about the last days.[41]

Traditional orthodoxy has by and large avoided what it perceives to be the pitfalls of premillennial dispensationalism. For centuries the church has been content to rest its hope on the certainty of the second advent of Jesus Christ to earth. Jesus' words "Be on guard! Be alert! You do not know when that time will come" (Mark 13:33) have meant that God has hidden this time from all but himself. This divine appointment is future but not to be determined by the elaborately worked-out details of prophetic time charts. The church embodies its eschatological hope in the words of the Apostles' Creed, "From thence he will come to judge the living and the dead."

The Watchtower has undergone much criticism throughout the twentieth century for its continuing efforts to affix specific dates for end-time events. Originally early Watchtower members believed that 1914 would not only signal the time of the spiritual return of Christ (see above), but the actual time of the end of all earthly kingdoms. "We consider it an established truth that the final end of the kingdoms of this world, and the full establishment of the Kingdom of God will be accomplished at the end of A.D. 1914."[42]

When the end did not come as expected, the Watchtower then published the statement, "We did not positively say that this [1914] would be the year."[43] The year 1915 was then suggested by the organization to be the possible time of Armageddon. Russell himself

was convinced of this. When this date failed to yield results, 1918 was then determined to be the time when all-out tribulation and war would break out. Ironically, World War I came to an end in 1918. Undaunted, the Watchtower then set 1925 as being the year that would fulfill the end-times prophecies. When 1925 passed without interruption, the Watchtower stated that "some anticipated that the work of the Lord would end in 1925, but the Lord did not state so."[44]

After the 1925 failure, however, many Witnesses were extremely discouraged. But the society continued to persist in its efforts to decipher the cryptic riddles of biblical prophecy and arrive at a date for the beginning of the end. The Watchtower next set 1975 to be the year of destiny. Once again the events prophesied failed to come to pass. One wonders how many more dates the Watchtower, and other millennial movements within Christendom, will set before they collectively realize that God has purposely kept his future appointment with his church and the world for a time unknown to all but himself (Matt. 24:36).

From the standpoint of orthodox Christianity, the Watchtower Bible and Tract Society, far from being "God's true organization on earth," is a heretical movement guilty of false prophecy. Indeed, they seem to condemn themselves from the pages of their own literature. *Aid to Bible Understanding* (1971) states the criteria for a true prophet:

> The three essentials for establishing the credentials of the true prophet, as given through Moses, were: the true prophet would speak in Jehovah's name; the things foretold *would come to pass* (Deut. 18:20–22); and his prophesying must promote true worship, being in harmony with God's revealed word and commandments.[45] (emphasis added)

CONCLUSION

The Watchtower Bible and Tract Society continues to grow in the twenty-first century, although the growth has been much more slowly than in the past, despite the fact that its predictions concerning end-time events have failed to come to pass. There are various reasons for this.

Many new converts simply are not aware of or told the history of the organization.

Many converts join from mainline Christian denominations who do not know their own denomination's history or reasons why they are members of the multifarious churches within the pale of Christendom. Consequently, when a Jehovah's

Witness knocks on a door, he or she encounters many who are members of churches in name only. A Witness has undergone training in teaching the society's doctrines from the Bible. Most who consider themselves Christians are ignorant and helpless to defend traditional Christian doctrines such as the Trinity, the deity of Christ, or issues relevant to end-time events.

The proselytizing efforts of the Watchtower are ambitious and extensive. The printed literature that issues forth from their press is voluminous. *The Watchtower*, published bimonthly, has a circulation of well over twenty-five million per issue. More than one billion Bibles, books, and booklets have been distributed since 1920.[46] *Awake* magazine is also published bimonthly and has a circulation of over twenty-two million per issue. Every member is a missionary and is active in door-to-door witnessing. They devote anywhere from fifteen to fifty hours per week to personal evangelism and missions work. This factor by itself explains the remarkable growth the organization has experienced.

Kingdom Halls are organized into circuits consisting of from twenty to twenty-two congregations each. Circuits in turn are organized into twenty-two districts in the United States. Districts are then further formed into branches.

Discipline can be very strict in Witness circles. Members who grow morally lax or break the laws of Jehovah are subject to discipline. Failure to repent may result in being disfellowshiped. Shunning is also practiced, and many have been known to shun members of their own family for disciplinary reasons.

Frederick W. Franz, who led the Watchtower into the 1990s until his death, reported that

over a thousand "Godly Devotion" conventions held by the Witnesses in 107 countries were highlights of 1989.... The book *The Bible—God's Word or Man's?* was released at the conventions. A new 320-page book, *Questions that Young People Ask—Answers that Work* was designed to provide practical, Bible-based answers to young people's questions about morals and drugs and to help them get along with their parents and cope with depression, loneliness, and problems at school. In less than a year, nearly nine million copies of this book were produced in fourteen languages.[47]

Franz also reports that in March 1991, the Watchtower became legally recognized in the Soviet Union.[48]

Blood transfusions continue to remain an important issue in Witness circles at the beginning of the twenty-first century. The Supreme Court in 1958 ruled that the constitutional rights of a Witness are abridged when the court orders a blood transfusion.[49] Other continuing issues include the role of the organization with respect to its prophecies, and the involvement of the membership in military duties and the refusal of Witnesses to take oaths of allegiance to their respective countries. Another important issue is the manner in which the leadership has handled crises that have arisen in the organization. As a predominantly closed community, cases, for example of child molestation, have not been reported or even addressed in a straightforward way by the leadership, as some ex-members have charged. This has caused numerous resignations in the organization.[50] There is perhaps no other religious organization that has been involved in as many lawsuits as have the Jehovah's Witnesses.

ADDITIONAL INFORMATION

Headquarters
Watchtower Bible and Tract Society, 25 Columbia Heights, Brooklyn, NY 11201.

Websites
www.watchtower.org; www.jw-media.org

Sacred Text
The New World Translation of the Bible; Studies in the Scriptures

Publications
Awake; The Watchtower (137 languages and an aggregate circulation of 47 million); many booklets and pamphlets.

Membership
In the United States there are presently over 1,029,652 members in 11,930 congregations, up from 730,000 in 1993. World membership is presently estimated at 6.4 million.

Notes
[1] Sydney Ahlstrom, *A Religious History of the American People*, 2 vols. (Garden City, NY: Image Books, 1975), 274–75.
[2] *Jehovah's Witnesses and the Divine Purpose* (Brooklyn, 1959), as recorded in Anthony Hoekema, *The Four Major Cults* (Grand Rapids: Eerdmans, 1963), 224.
[3] Hoekema, *Four Major Cults*, 225.
[4] Walter Martin, *The Kingdom of the Cults* (Minneapolis: Bethany, 1985), 43–44.
[5] Ibid., 45.
[6] Milton V. Backman, *Christian Churches of America* (Provo, Utah: Brigham Young Univ. Press, 1976), 178.
[7] Ibid., 179.
[8] Hoekema, *Four Major Cults*, 231.

[9] Richard N. Ostling, "Witness Under Prosecution," *Time* (February 22, 1982), 66.

[10] *A Handbook for Chaplains* (Washington, D.C.: Headquarters, Department of the Army, 1978), 1–71.

[11] James Sire, *Scripture Twisting: 20 Ways the Cults Misread the Bible* (Downers Grove, Ill.: InterVarsity Press, 1980), 86.

[12] See UNITARIAN-UNIVERSALIST ASSOCIATION; WORLDWIDE CHURCH OF GOD.

[13] *Let God Be True,* 2d ed. (Brooklyn: Watchtower Bible and Tract Society, 1946), 100.

[14] *The Word, Who is He? According to John* (Brooklyn: Watchtower Bible and Tract Society, 1962), 7.

[15] See CHRISTADELPHIANISM, especially the discussion on how the Campbellites also rejected the use of the *word* "Trinity" but not the *concept*. This, however, led to a rejection of the concept also by John Thomas, founder of Christadelphianism.

[16] See J. N. D. Kelly, *The Creeds of Christendom*, 3rd ed. (New York: Longman, 1960).

[17] See the recommended readings for follow-up study.

[18] Michael Van Buskirk, *The Scholastic Dishonesty of the Watchtower* (Santa Ana, Calif.: CARIS, 1975), 13.

[19] See Bruce M. Metzger, "The Jehovah's Witnesses and Jesus Christ," *Theology Today* 10 (April 1953): 65–85.

[20] *What Has Religion Done for Mankind?* (Brooklyn: Watchtower Bible and Tract Society, 1946), 32.

[21] Charles Taze Russell, *Studies in the Scriptures*, 7 vols., as quoted by Martin, *Kingdom of the Cults*, 46.

[22] *The Word, Who is He?* 40–41.

[23] See *New Heavens and a New Earth* (Brooklyn: Watchtower Bible and Tract Society, 1953), 28–30.

[24] The 1 Timothy 3:16 passage, "God was manifested in the flesh" (KJV) has caused a good deal of controversy among evangelicals concerning whether it could or even should be used as a proof text for the deity of Christ, because of the variant reading that replaces the noun *theos* ("God") with the relative pronoun *hos* ("who"). For further discussion of this issue, see Larry Nichols, "Text Criticism and the Cultic Milieu," *The Bulletin of the Institute for Reformation Biblical Studies* 1/1 (1989): 8.

[25] See CHRISTADELPHIANISM and ROSICRUCIANISM for further discussion of the Christological issue.

[26] *Aid to Bible Understanding* (Brooklyn: Watchtower Bible and Tract Society, 1971), 1373.

[27] Ibid.

[28] *The Kingdom Is at Hand* (Brooklyn: Watchtower Bible and Tract Society, 1944), 291–92.

[29] *Aid to Bible Understanding*, 1543.

[30] *Let God Be True,* 74–75.

[31] Martin, *Kingdom of the Cults*, 107.

[32] *Aid to Bible Understanding*, 371.

[33] Hoekema, *Four Major Cults*, 290.

[34] *Aid to Bible Understanding*, 1260.

[35] Ibid., 189.

[36] Paul Althaus, *The Theology of Martin Luther*, trans. Robert C. Schultz (Philadelphia: Fortress, 1966), 362–63.

[37] Backman, *Christian Churches of America*, 183.

[38] See *You May Survive Armageddon into God's New World* (Brooklyn: Watchtower Bible and Tract, 1955), 90–97.

[39] Hoekema, *Four Major Cults*, 302.

[40] Bob Larson, *Larson's Book of Cults* (Wheaton: Tyndale, 1986), 150.

[41] For example, see Hal Lindsey, *The Late Great Planet Earth* (Grand Rapids: Zondervan, 1970).

[42] Studies in the Scriptures, Vol. 2, *The Time Is at Hand* (1908), 99.

[43] *Watchtower* (November 11, 1914), 325.

[44] *Watchtower* (October 15, 1926), 232.

[45] *Aid to Bible Understanding*, 1348.

[46] Frank Mead, *Handbook of Denominations in the United States*, 6th ed. (Nashville: Abingdon, 1975), 155.

[47] *1990 Britannica Book of the Year* (Chicago: Encyclopedia Britannica Inc., 1990), 311.

[48] *1992 Britannica Book of the Year* (Chicago: Encyclopedia Britannica Inc., 1992), 264.

[49] Charles H. Lippy and Peter W. Williams, eds., *Encyclopedia of the American Religious Experience* (New York: Scribners, 1988), 838.

[50] Kimberly Hefling, Associated Press Report, "Elder Resigns, Protests Faith's Policy on Abuse Charges" (Feb. 11, 2001). See also, *Christianity Today* 45/4 (March 5, 2001): 23.

JUDAISM

The parent religion of CHRISTIANITY, Judaism stands in its own right as the world's oldest ᵇmonotheism. Its history stretches from the time when God brought Abraham into a covenant relationship.

Judaism proffers claims of particularity and universality. In a world of paganism, heathenism, and ᵇpolytheism, God revealed himself as the one true God over against the plethora of competing deities; in this ᵇrev-elation, he called a particular man, Abram, to father a particular nation (Israel), which in turn would be given a particular geographical arena (Palestine), which itself would constitute the "promised land." From this particularity, God revealed a message in history that was destined to become universally applicable to all nations and all peoples. God's covenant with Abram (Gen. 12:1–3) was established and renewed. Israel was selected to be the standard-bearer of this great revelation, both by example to the heathen nations and by obedience to the precepts of God's divine covenant made known in the sacred ᵇTorah (the law).

HISTORY

The story of Judaism is a story derived chiefly from the Old Testament portion of the ᵇBible. The text as we have it today comes from three main sources: the Masoretic text (assembled in the tenth century A.D.), the ᵇSeptuagint (Greek translation), and the Dead Sea Scrolls (discovered in 1947 at Qumran). Before the formation of the actual text, however, the oral tradition (songs, stories, poems) rehearsed and preserved the deeds of God (Yahweh) and his covenant people, Israel. Many of these facets of the oral tradition were eventually incorporated into the collections of books that now comprise the threefold division of the Hebrew canon: the Law (*Torah*), the Prophets (*Nevi'im*), and the Writings (*Kethuvim*).

Archaeological discoveries have shed much light on the world in which the Jewish nation was born and developed.

1. The *Code of Hammurabi* in Babylon, dated about 1700 B.C., outlines laws similar to those of the Torah.
2. *Enuma Elish*, dating to 2000 B.C., records a creation account in which a cosmic battle between Marduk and Tiamet takes place. It erupts in chaos. The Genesis account is orderly and clearly testifies to the fact that God is in control.
3. The *Epic of Gilgamesh* (seventh century B.C.) is a flood story, telling of an ark that was built to preserve life. A dove was sent out and returned. The Genesis account of the Noahic flood no doubt exerted great influence on other cultures that borrowed from much of the oral tradition.
4. The *Ebla Tablets*, discovered in 1974, date back to the kingdom of Ebla (2300 B.C.). The tablets are bilingual and are written in the known language of Sumerian and that of Ebla. These tablets mention Sodom, Gomorrah, Abraham, Saul, and numerous other biblical names.
5. Canaanite literature, particularly that written in Ugaritic, date to the fourteenth century B.C. and refer to pagan mythology and Baal worship, clearly alluded to in the Old Testament.
6. The *Nuzi Tablets* are Assyrian tablets dating to 1500 B.C.; they elucidate many of the customs of the Old Testament. For example, in Genesis 16 Sarai asks Abram to produce a child through her servant Hagar; the Nuzi tablets explain that it was an obligation for a wife to bring forth a child. If she failed, she had to provide another woman for her husband. The difference between this custom and the covenant of Yahweh and Israel was that Yahweh transcended that custom by bringing forth a child of promise (Isaac) in spite of Abram and Sarai's old age and the impossibility of pregnancy ensuing.
7. The *Mari Letters* make it clear that travel was common between Palestine and the Near East.
8. The *Tell el-Amarna Letters* date back to the eighteenth century B.C. These letters were correspondence between an Egyptian king and his son ruling in Palestine. Mention is made of a people called the *Habiru*, who were causing trouble in the land. This is possibly an allusion to the *Hebrews* at the time when Joshua invaded the land.

Old Testament Times

Judaism really begins with God's call to Abram around 2000 B.C. Genesis records his journey into Canaan, the establishment of Yahweh's divine covenant to make him the father of many nations (12:1–9), his parting with his nephew Lot (ch. 13), the renewal of the covenant (ch. 17), and the destruction of Sodom and Gomorrah (ch. 19).

Yahweh promised Abram that he would make him the father of a great nation and give him the land of Canaan for his home and that through this nation the whole world would be blessed. As God repeated these promises, he also subjected Abraham (his new name) to three major tests. First was a famine that forced him and his family to flee into Egypt; second, Abraham was asked to believe that God would provide a son through Sarah; third, after his son Isaac was born, God told Abraham to sacrifice Isaac.

> The story of the four patriarchs, Abraham, Isaac, Jacob, and Joseph, unfolds in the rest of Genesis. The travels of these four, along with the growing size of the infant nation as a tribe, had exposed it to a variety of religions and religious influences from Egypt to Mesopotamia. One must be cautioned, therefore, against oversimplification when it comes to accounting for the origins of Israel. It is not simply the matter of a genealogical process. The Bible makes it quite clear that Israel was born out of a social, political, and religious amalgamation.[1]

Following the era of the four patriarchs, the covenant was passed on to Moses, who led Israel out of slavery in Egypt during the new kingdom era (1540–1150 B.C.). It was through Moses that God established the first pillar of later Judaism—the law, or Torah.

Two dates have been surmised for the Exodus from Egypt. Some scholars place it during the eighteenth dynasty under Amenhotep III (1400–1360 B.C.). This date is supported by 1 Kings 6:1, which refers to Solomon's temple being built 480 years after the Exodus. This earlier date is also favored because of the reference to the *Habiru* in the Tell el-Amarna tablets. A later date for the Exodus occurring during the nineteenth dynasty of Ramses II is based on Exodus 1:11. The ten plagues of judgment, the Passover, and the crossing of the Red Sea were mighty deeds Yahweh performed to assure his people that he would protect and guide them.

Mount Sinai marks the place where Israel was assembled in order to receive the sacred Torah. Initially, Moses filled the role of both prophet and priest. The giving of the law during his leadership marks a transition in Israel's history from a patriarchal family priesthood to a tribal priesthood, with Aaron becoming the Levitical high priest.

The differences between the Torah and Hammurabi's law code are significant enough to guard against the notion that Moses may have simply borrowed from Hammurabi. Moreover, Hammurabi's laws were civil in nature, intended for urban life in ancient Mesopotamia. The laws given to Moses dealt not only with civil codes but also with a host of social practices and religious observances; they also contained instructions for how to build the tabernacle.

After the Israelites wandered for forty years in the desert, God called them to enter the Promised Land and conduct a series of conquests to secure it for habitation. Canaan, meaning "low country," was the land lying between the Mediterranean and the Jordan River. It was essentially a land bridge bordering Egypt to the south, Babylon and Mesopotamia to the east, Syria to the north, and Anatolia (present-day Turkey) to the northwest.

The Canaanites were a mixed people who practiced a variety of religions, centered primarily around the Canaanite goddess Asherah ("the lady of the sea"), her offspring Baal, and his sister-spouse Anat. The religion was characterized by fertility and vicious sex rituals. The instructions of Yahweh for Israel to enter and destroy the Canaanites rested on the judgment of God on the utter depravity of sexual cult activity over against the morality and uprightness of the covenant people of God.

The conquest took place in three stages. First came the occupation of eastern Palestine, before the conquest of Jericho. Second was the fall and capture of Jericho and its surrounding territory. Third came the conquest of Galilee and northern Palestine. The end of the conquests resulted in the possession of the land through the establishment of a tribal league. Each of the twelve tribes settled in a designated part of the land.

The period of the judges (from approximately 1200–1050 B.C.), was marked by adaptation and adjustment. Not all of the Canaanites had been destroyed and not all of the land occupied. Because the tribes were spread throughout the land, disunity resulted. Acculturation and syncretization between Israel and the Canaanite nations set in motion a series of six major cycles in which Israel experienced the wrath and judgment of Yahweh at the hands of a pagan nation on the one hand, and his mercy and forgiveness through a judge raised up by him to deliver them on the other. Each cycle contained four recognizable steps:

1. Sin and apostasy (rebellion against God)
2. Servitude and bondage (God's judgment for sin)
3. Supplication and prayer (repentance and a cry for mercy)
4. Salvation and deliverance (at the hands of God's chosen judge)

The following chart depicts the cycles and the accompanying judges:

NATION	JUDGE	REFERENCE (Judges)
1. Mesopotamia	Othniel	3:7–11
2. Moab	Ehud	3:12–30
3. Canaan	Deborah	4–5
4. Midian	Gideon	6–8
5. Ammon	Jephthah	10–12
6. Philistia	Samson	13:1–16:31

The period of the judges was also marked by a steady movement away from a notion of a theocracy as Israel continued to rebel against Yahweh and carry on its affairs apart from him. During the time of the prophet Samuel, the nation requested to be governed by an earthly king. Samuel was displeased with this request and warned the nation of what to expect (1 Sam. 8). The grim words of God to Samuel, "Listen to all that

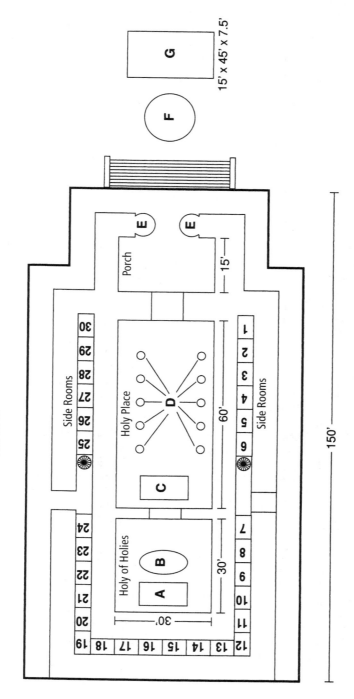

NORTH

15' x 45' x 7.5'

PLAN OF SOLOMON'S TEMPLE

A. Ark of the Covenant (with mercy seat)
B. Cherubim
C. Altar of Incense
D. 10 Lampstands
E. 2 Brass Pillars
F. Molten Sea
G. Great Brass Altar

the people are saying to you; it is not you they have rejected, but they have rejected me as their king" (8:7), echo a theme that would be repeated time and again in the history of the nation.

Saul was selected as Israel's first reigning monarch. A series of military victories over the Philistines and the Ammonites was overshadowed by Saul's personal failure to remain obedient to God. His sparing the Amalekite king Agag, keeping the plunder of war, and making his own sacrifices to God without the mediation of Samuel and the prescribed priesthood brought an end to his reign. A tension between king and priest (i.e., state and religion), which would plague Israel from this time forward, began at this time. Note the strong distinction between the two in the climactic statement of Samuel, "Does the LORD delight in burnt offerings and sacrifices as much as in obeying the voice of the LORD?" (1 Sam. 15:22).

David (b. 1085 B.C.), the son of Jesse, was chosen as the second king; the Old Testament devotes a sizable portion of narrative to his life. For the purposes of this essay, David's reign was significant for three reasons. First, the unity of the nation reached its zenith at the height of his power. He reigned from approximately 1000–961 B.C. Second, he relocated the capital of Israel from Hebron to Jerusalem and brought the ark of the covenant from Kiriath Jearim to the capital, placing it in a new tabernacle. When he desired to build a temple in which to house the ark, he was told by a prophetic oracle that this would be the task of his son. David's act of bringing the ark to Jerusalem was significant in that it made that city both the religious and political capital of the nation. Third, David's repentance before God in the wake of his serious sin with Bathsheba resulted in the continuance of the promise to Abraham through his lineage.

Solomon, David's son and successor, continued the united monarchy; he reigned from 961–922 B.C. He wasted no time in firmly establishing and solidifying his father's throne by executing all those who threatened it. He also fortified key cities and territories throughout the land, including Hazor, Megiddo, Gezer, Beth Horon, and Tamar. These were all strategically located for future military campaigns and defense. Solomon is significant because he was the one whom God selected to build the temple. The climate of political stability paralleled the need to secure a place of permanence for the holy place. God also gave Solomon the gift of wisdom, so that his fame spread abroad. In addition, he became the wealthiest monarch of his day. His financial support came from the following sources:

1. Taxation—twelve districts created with an officer in charge of each for collecting taxes
2. Labor conscriptions—While David limited forced labor to foreigners, Solomon drafted thirty thousand Israelites.
3. Gifts from foreign sources (1 Kings 10:24–25)
4. Trade and commerce—Solomon's use of the sea (Red Sea and Mediterranean) for trade with Phoenicia, Southern Arabia, etc.
5. Copper mines developed

Solomon began the temple in his fourth year (1 Kings 6:1; 2 Chron. 3:2) in 967–966 B.C. Its design, taken from his father, was modeled after the tabernacle. See the diagram in this article for the design of the temple. Solomon's life can best be described in three stages:

1. Consolidation of power—building, organization, trade
2. Height of his reign—temple complete, his fame, the visit of the Queen of Sheba
3. Decline and division of Israel—Solomon's blessings overshadowed by personal character flaws. Clearly against the Mosaic precepts, Solomon built up a harem consisting of seven hundred wives and three hundred concubines. Moreover, his heart was turned toward idolatry, and he built "high places" of idol worship to the gods of his many wives. This resulted in national tragedy as the unified kingdom fell.

The period of the divided kingdom began after Solomon's death. His unified kingdom was split into northern and southern sections (called, in the Old Testament, Israel and Judah). This came as the result of many factors. In addition to the sins of Solomon that brought on the Lord's judgment, tribal quarrels of a long-standing nature, especially between Ephraim and Judah, broke out. Geographically, Judah was isolated from the northern tribes. Furthermore, pagan religions infiltrated the kingdom in Solomon's reign, dissipating any sense of national religious unity. And Solomon's extravagance had served only to isolate him from his countrymen. His son Rehoboam's unwise political policies ensured the division (1 Kings 12). Invasion of Judah by Egypt gave Jeroboam more freedom and time to gather strength in the north.

In the period of the divided kingdom, the kings of both north and south reigned. The accompanying chart represents the parallel reigns of the monarchs, together with accompanying prophets and foreign kings raised up in judgment against Israel and Judah.

CHRONOLOGY OF THE DIVIDED KINGDOM

DATE	NORTHERN K	PROPHETS	SOUTHERN K	ASSYRIA	SYRIA
931	Jerobam Nadab	Ahijah Shemaiah Iddo Asa	Rehoboam Abijah	Rezon	
909	Baasha Elah (Zimri)	Azariah Hanani Jehu			
885	Omri (Tibni) Ahab Ahaziah Joram	Elijah Micaiah Eliezer Elisha Jehoiada	Jehoshaphat Jehoram Ahaziah	Ashurnasirpal Shalmaneser III	Benhadad
841	Jehu Jehoahaz Jehoash Jeroboam II Zechariah	Zechariah Jonah Hosea Amos	Athaliah Joash Amaziah Azariah		Hazael Benhadad
752	Shallum Menahem Pekahiah Pekah Hoshea	Isaiah Oded	Jotham Ahaz	Tiglath-pileser III Shalmaneser V Sargon II	Rezin
722	*Fall of Samaria*	Micah	Hezekiah Manasseh Amon	Sennacherib Esarhaddon Ashurbanipal	
640		Jeremiah Huldah (Ezekiel) (Daniel)	Josiah Johoahaz Jehoiakim Zedekiah	*Babylon* Nabopolassar Nebuchadnezzar	
586			*Fall of Jerusalem*		

The date of the division of the kingdom is variously placed between 983 B.C. and 931 B.C. There are difficulties in the chronology of the period, and apparent discrepancies, which may, in part, be accounted for by "overlapping reigns," "associated sovereignty," "intervals of anarchy," and "parts of years as years." These dates are only approximate.[2]

The northern kingdom fell to the Assyrians in 722 B.C. The southern kingdom fell to the Babylonians during the reign of Nebuchadnezzar. Most scholars assign 586 B.C. as the time of the destruction of Jerusalem and the exile of the people of God to Babylon.

At the beginning of the monarchy, Samuel had offered a prophetic voice to the ambitious and disobedient Saul. Throughout the time of the kings, God continually raised up prophets to speak the "word of the LORD," to rebuke the rebellious people, to exhort and instruct them, and to foretell coming judgment and blessings. The thunderings of Elijah, the courage of Amos, the pleas of Isaiah, the weeping of Jeremiah, the visions of Joel, and so on provided an assurance to divided Israel that God was still active in history and that despite her continuous disobedience, idolatry, and ignorance, he would be merciful to the repentant and optimistic toward the future when a deliverer (ᵖMessiah) would be sent. The golden age of prophecy, as it is often called, lasted throughout the centuries of the kings.

The Exile refers to Judah's seventy-year captivity in the land of Babylon. The prophecies of Jeremiah and Ezekiel during this time contained the themes of a triumphant future and a new covenant that God promised one day to bring to pass. During the Exile, many of Israel's institutions (especially the elders, the prophets, and the law) were maintained. But some important changes now took place. No longer were they living in the land God had promised, nor did they possess a temple. The ritual sacrifices therefore came to a halt. From this time on, the Israelites turned more strongly to the law. They became known as "the people of the book." It was also at this time that the synagogue appeared as a new institution that would remain a permanent structure to a people disenfranchised from both temple and the land.

The conquest of Babylon by the Persians marked the end of Judah's captivity and the beginning of her restoration. Cyrus the Great of Persia reigned from 540–530 B.C. He issued an edict granting all foreigners permission to return to their homelands. However, the restoration was not as simple, for the scattered remnants did not return to Palestine in a single concerted effort. The process was slow and stilted. Some Jews returned in 536 with permission to rebuild the temple and the walls of Jerusalem, but the people began concentrating on their own houses instead. God raised up the prophets Haggai and Zechariah to exhort the people to continue building the temple first.

A second return began in 458, led by Ezra during the reign of Artaxerxes. During his era, many of the people began intermingling with the heathen and even intermarrying with them. At this time, a new group emerged, the Hasidim (or "separated ones"), who accompanied Ezra in his mission. A third return was begun in 444 B.C., led by Nehemiah, who unlike Ezra, was a layman. Under his leadership, the walls of the city were restored. It is significant that in that same year (444), Artaxerxes recognized the Torah as the law of the land and had it published and distributed throughout the empire. The great attention paid to God's law by the Jewish leaders in the ensuing centuries after the restoration to the time of Jesus led to the development of the tradition known as the "oral law."

Between the Testaments

The next period was Hellenization, perhaps the greatest change wrought on Palestine as a result of its conquest by Alexander the Great in 332 B.C. The Greek Empire eventually stretched itself eastward all the way to India. Along with conquest came the spread of Greek language, social patterns, and culture. Greek became the *lingua franca* of commerce and trade. By the time of Jesus, a large portion of the Jewish population had become Hellenized. Hellenistic Judaism predominated from the time of Alexander through the second century A.D.

The history during this period is complicated and fraught with intrigue. After the death of Alexander in 323 B.C. the kingdom was divided between three of Alexander's generals. Two of these divisions, the Ptolemaic and Seleucid kingdoms, are relevant to the history of Judaism. The former reigned in Egypt while the latter maintained control over Syria, Mesopotamia, and eastward. The Jews were under Ptolemaic reign from 320–198 and enjoyed relative peace and prosperity. Under Ptolemy Philadelphus (285–246 B.C.), seventy-two Greek-speaking Jewish scholars began translating the Hebrew Scriptures into the Greek Septuagint.

In 198 B.C., Ptolemaic reign came to an end through Antiochus III's triumph in war. Two rival factions developed within Judaism, one loyal to the Egyptian Ptolemies (the house of Onias) and the other loyal to the Syrian Antiochus (the house of Tobias). Unlike rule under the Ptolemies, the Seleucid domination proved repressive and cruel. Antiochus IV Epiphanes (175–163 B.C.) issued decrees against Judaism and its religious practices. In 168, his armies ransacked Jerusalem, slaughtered many Jews, enslaved many women and children, and made Sabbath worship and possessing copies of the Jewish Scriptures illegal and punishable by death. The Seleucids committed ultimate blasphemy by erecting an altar to Zeus within the temple. Prostitution and the sacrifice of unclean animals also occurred within the temple precincts.

These abominable practices soon led to the Jewish uprising known as the Maccabean revolt. By guerrilla warfare inspired by Judas Maccabeus (d. 160 B.C.), the son of the Hasmonean Mattathias, the Jews eventually defeated Syrian forces. When Judas was killed in a battle, his brothers Simon and Jonathan continued the campaign, establishing the Hasmonean dynasty (142–137 B.C.). Continual rivalries and ambitious quests for power characterized the Hasmonean period. It was at this juncture in Israel's history that the rival Jewish factions familiar to readers of the New Testament arose, namely the 'Sadducees, the 'Pharisees, and the 'Essenes.

Hasmonean rule gave way to the Roman Empire when Pompey marched into Palestine in 63 B.C. and brought the Jewish world under the dominion of Rome. The Romans set up a puppet government, allowing vassal kings to rule in Palestine. The most famous (or infamous) of these was Herod the Great, who ruled Palestine from 37–4 B.C. Extremely cruel but able to maintain order, Herod was hated yet respected. His contribution included restoration of the temple. Following Herod, each of his sons ruled various segments of Palestine. Herod Archelaus became tetrarch of Judea, Samaria, and Idumea (4 B.C.–A.D. 6); Herod Antipas ruled over Perea and Galilee from 4 B.C.–A.D. 39; Herod Philip presided over Iturea Trachonitis, Gaulanitis, Auranitis, and Batanea from 4 B.C.–A.D. 3. It was before Herod Antipas that Jesus stood trial (A.D. 33?). Herod Archelaus was removed from office and banished in A.D. 6 because of mismanagement and incompetence; he was replaced by a series of Roman governors or procurators, such as Pontius Pilate, the governor famous for his judgment over Jesus.

New Testament Times and Rabbinic Judaism

During this time Jewish worship continued with its temple sacrifices and its gatherings in the local synagogues. In A.D. 70, however, during the First Jewish War (A.D. 66–73), Jerusalem was destroyed by Titus in a war provoked by a growing series of edicts from Rome that became intolerable to many Jews. Zealots and Herodians stirred the people to rise up and fight for an independent Jewish state.

After the destruction of Jerusalem, when Domitian was emperor (A.D. 81–96), Judaism underwent a major reconstitution at Jamnia. Much like the time of the Exile, emphasis was again placed on the Torah. Also at Jamnia Christianity was denounced, largely because of the refusal of the Christians (largely Jewish in number) to help in the fight against Rome. Though some Jews continued to embrace Christianity after Jamnia, they were small in number. After A.D. 70, Christianity's growth came primarily from non-Jewish sources.

The Second Jewish War (A.D. 132–35) was precipitated by Emperor Hadrian (117–38). He forbade the rite of circumcision and erected a temple to Jupiter in Jerusalem. Leading the Jews was Bar Cochba, who was widely hailed as the new Messiah. The Jews, however, could not prevail against the mighty Roman forces, and they were crushed in 135. Jerusalem was rebuilt after this but as a Roman city. Jews were forbidden even to enter that new city.

The second destruction of the temple (one of the two great pillars of Judaism) and the extinction of the Jewish state led to the formation of rabbinic Judaism, a period that stretched on into the eighteenth century. The Jews of the 'Diaspora moved to many places throughout the empire and beyond its borders. The "people of the land" would possess no land again until 1948.

The rabbinic period is marked by a great development of the 'Mishnah and the production of the two 'Talmuds (Palestinian and Babylonian). It was the age of the *tannaim* (or "teachers") and the *amoraim* (or "interpreters" of the Torah). The Talmuds elucidated a code for Jewish daily life. The death of Gamaliel IV in 425 marked a period of fragmentation, but Judaism was held together as a concept and as a people by the teachings of the rabbis and the strong maintenance of the 'Jewish calendar.

During the Middle Ages, two main branches of Judaism evolved. The 'Sephardic Jews traced their roots to Babylon. They were situated largely in Spain, and their culture is derived mainly from Arabic and Muslim sources because of the seventh and eighth-century expansions of ISLAM. The second branch, called 'Ashkenazic, was rooted in Europe, particularly France and Germany, and traces its heritage back to Palestine.

Two 'mystical traditions sprang up in the late Middle Ages within the ranks of Judaism. One was called

Hasidism, which was influenced largely by Ashkenazic culture; the second was the Kabbala or Kabbalistic mystical tradition, rising out of the Talmudic academies and the Sephardic communities of Spain. These two cultures clashed from time to time, though far more serious was the direct clash between the Christian church and Judaism. In 1306 Jews were expelled from France. The next five centuries were earmarked by a continuous series of persecutions of Jews throughout Europe.

Modern Jewish History, Including Zionism

During the Haskala-Jewish enlightenment period, the same things began influencing Judaism as were influencing Christianity in France and elsewhere. The hegemony of reason began to affect the religious traditions of earlier centuries. For Judaism, this meant the turning away from a belief in the miracles of the Old Testament and the longing for a Messiah. Many began concentrating on a this-worldly philosophy of life, leading to a rekindling of the nationalistic spirit that had been endemic to Judaism centuries before. The new nationalism, however, was characterized by a much more rationalistic spirit. In the spirit of Hegel, Moses Mendelssohn (1729–86) attempted to articulate a religion built on universal reason. One of Mendelssohn's many accomplishments was to interpret Judaism within the context of the German culture of the eighteenth century.

Jews settling in Russia were also influenced by the Haskala. Acculturation to European and Russian cultures and languages sublimated the romantic longing for a homeland with the reality of alienation and with coping in the here and now. Many Jews began to distinguish between nationality and religion, claiming to be Russian, German, (later) American, and so on by nationality, but Jewish by religion. Persecutions or "pogroms" broke out in Russia in 1881. After this time, the quest for a national identity within the context of Russia and later Eastern Germany for the most part came to a halt.

The Haskala gave rise to Reform Judaism early in the nineteenth century. Reform Judaism had its roots in France during the Napoleonic era. Napoleon appointed a new Jewish Sanhedrin, whose charge it was to furnish a new definition of Judaism that was to be much more spiritual and much less nationalistic. The Reform movement spread to other parts of Europe but was less doctrinal and more aesthetic in its development than in France. In general, Reform Judaism represented an attempt to assimilate, accommodate, and compromise

strict Jewish ways with the Christianized cultures of Europe. Most orthodox Jews rejected Reform measures. However, Jews in the United States embraced them warmly. Jews in Germany in the 1840s institutionalized the Reform movement, attempting to create a theological rationale for such sweeping changes. Circumcision was halted, only a limited amount of Hebrew was spoken, and dietary laws were eliminated.

Reaction to Reform Judaism soon came from Germany. In 1845 Zacharias Frankel and a group of followers broke away from a reforming Synod in Frankfurt, largely over the issue of the growing disuse of Hebrew. Frankel argued that the Hebrew language was one of the few sources of identity and links with the past that the Jews had left. While even conservative Jews readily acknowledged that Judaism was unavoidably "developmental" in nature, religious observances should retain their strict orthodox character.

A word must be said about Jewish-Christian relations. Since the first century, the relationship between Judaism and Christianity has been strained at best. In France, during and after the French Revolution, the Roman Catholic church was openly hostile. In Russia, the Russian Orthodox Church viewed Judaism as a threat to Christianity and to the peace of the nation. Many accounts document a tragic history of persecution of Jews in Russia in the late nineteenth and early twentieth centuries.

In America, a more tolerant attitude toward Jews was maintained. Anti-Semitism was often denounced in the liberal Protestant churches as it is today in the World Council and National Council of Churches. The National Conference of Christians and Jews was founded in 1928, in response to Henry Ford's anti-Semitism propagated in his *Dearborn Independent*.[3]

The most devastating tragedy in all of Jewish history was the Nazi Holocaust, wherein nearly six million European Jews were exterminated in Germany between 1937 and 1945. Hitler's *Mein Kampf* portrayed Jews as "culture destroyers" and "Christ-killers." He even invoked the name of Martin Luther as "a most excellent German," citing out-of-context quotes from the German reformer to support the notion that the Lutheran cause advocated anti-Semitism. While Luther did utter pejorative comments about the Jews toward the end of his life, the context for such statements was not the same as that which motivated Hitler. While the latter was provoked by an intense albeit mythical notion of nationalism, blended with pseudoscientific racial theories prevalent at the close of the nineteenth century, Luther's motives were strictly religious in nature.

Blatant nationalism was an anachronism in sixteenth-century Germany. Luther's comments about the Jews must be understood in the context of the Jews rejecting the gospel. Nevertheless, his comments do not rank among his most noble. Most Lutherans today repudiate the Reformer's unfortunate words.

One of the aspects of the Holocaust is that Jews largely viewed the actions of Naziism as Christian in nature. Nothing could be further from the truth. It is true, of course, that many who called themselves Christians gave the distinct impression that the Holocaust was justifiable from a Christian perspective. But equally important is the fact that many Christians in Germany opposed Naziism and harbored and protected Jews from Hitler's forces.[4]

The most recent phase of Jewish history is that of Zionism, a movement that began in Germany in the 1890s. As a reaction against anti-Semitism in the nineteenth century, many Jews concluded that the only solution to their desperate plight was to rekindle a national spirit by setting their sights toward the Promised Land. Resettlement of Palestine became the preoccupation of the Zionists. Between 1922 and 1939 the Jewish population in Israel rose from 83,790 to 445,457. Naziism drove the number of immigrants to Palestine up by the hundreds of thousands more. In 1942, at the Biltmore Hotel in New York City, it was decided that Jews be allowed to return to Palestine unrestricted and that a new Jewish commonwealth be established.

The Biltmore Resolution was presented to the British, who were the rulers of Palestine at this time. Britain, unable to deal with growing tension between Arab and Zionist factions, welcomed American involvement and the presence of the United Nations. On May 15, 1947, the United Nations General Assembly voted to create a Special Committee on Palestine (UNSCOP). The solution to the Jewish problem was to partition Palestine into Jewish and Arab settlements. UNSCOP resolutions were approved in November 1947 but met with bitter opposition by the Arabs in Palestine—largely because the partitioning process left a disproportionate amount of land to the Zionists. Arabs gathered forces to resist the United Nations proposal. Zionist forces overwhelmed the Arab resistance in 1948 and captured the portions of land allotted to Israel by the United Nations. Portions of Arab territories were also secured by force.

On May 18, 1948, Israel as a nation was once again in existence; after centuries the Star of David again flew over the land once given to Abraham's seed. The British announced the end of their mandate in Palestine and immediately withdrew. Arab forces from Egypt, Syria, Lebanon, and Iraq came into Palestine and attempted to offer continued resistance with a blockade of Jewish Jerusalem. On May 20, the United Nations sent Count Folke Bernadotte to serve as mediator between Jewish and Arab forces. He succeeded in securing a temporary truce but was assassinated by Zionist terrorists on September 17, 1948. By July, 1949, Israel was granted all of the territories it had won by conquest. These included all of Galilee, a section of the Gaza strip, and the Mediterranean coast. Remaining territories of the Transjordan became part of the kingdom of Jordan to the east. Palestine as a strictly Arab land was no more. The struggle between Israelis and Arabs continues to this day.

BELIEFS AND PRACTICES

Much of what constitutes Jewish beliefs and practices has already been elucidated in the brief history. What follows are some expanded observations, coupled with comparisons/contrasts with Christianity.

Torah

The law served a crucial religious function in delineating the relationship between Yahweh and Israel, and between each Israelite and his or her neighbor. As such, it knows no precedent and serves as one of the foundations of Judaism to this day.

For Christianity the Torah played an important role as well. Jesus himself said, "Do not think that I have come to abolish the Law or the Prophets; I have not come to abolish them but to fulfill them" (Matt. 5:17). As indicated here, however, Jesus radically reinterpreted the law as being fulfilled in his own person. A further reinterpretation was his teaching that mere outward observance was not in keeping with the real intent of the law. God had intended his law to be kept within the heart of his people. Jesus regarded anger and hatred to be as culpable as murder (Matt. 5:21) or lust as condemnatory as the external act of adultery (Matt. 5:27). Jesus dismissed the oral law as the "traditions of men" (Mark 7:8–9, 13). The religious professionals, such as the scribes and Pharisees, had erected a fence around the Torah, rendering it inaccessible to the common people.

The Tabernacle/Temple

Yahweh had provided careful instruction for the building of the tabernacle or "tent of the LORD" (later the temple). Here, at a specific time and place in history, God's people focalized the daily ritual sacrifices and the yearly sacrifice on the Day of Atonement for sin by the ᵖhigh priest in the ᵖholy of holies.

Christianity has also radically reinterpreted the significance of the temple in Jewish life. Throughout the Old Testament, the shedding of blood for the remission of sin was a religious rite believed crucial for acceptance with God and appeasement of divine wrath (Lev. 17:11). Leviticus 16 contains a detailed account of how the high priest was to enter the holy of holies once a year and offer up a bullock (ox) for a sin offering for himself. Two goats would then be selected. Lots were cast, and one goat became a sin offering and the other a scapegoat. The goat used for the sin offering was killed before the ᵖmercy seat of God in the holy of holies by the high priest, thereby making atonement for the sins of the people. The scapegoat was presented alive before Yahweh and then released into the desert, bearing the sins of the people.

For Christianity the significance of the tabernacle/temple continues—but with one important difference. The activity of the temple became embodied in the person of Jesus Christ himself (John 2:18–21). The book of Hebrews presents an extended argument for Jews to recognize Jesus as the great high priest. (1) The high priest in the Old Testament had to offer up a sacrifice often; Jesus' sacrifice was once for all (Heb. 9:25). (2) The high priest offered up the blood of animals; Jesus offers up himself (9:12–14). (3) The high priest offered up an atonement for his own sins; Jesus was sinless and therefore able to offer up himself as an atonement for all (Heb. 4:15). (4) The high priests of the Old Testament each grew old and died and, on the basis of ancestry, were replaced. Jesus' priesthood was based not on ancestry but on "the power of an indestructible life" (Heb. 7:16).

At the death of Jesus, the curtain separating the holy of holies was torn down the middle (Matt. 27:51). Christians understand this to mean that in the person of Jesus, the holy of holies, accessible only to the high priest once annually, is now no more. Jesus himself became the holy of holies, and access is not for Jews only in an earthly temple. God's promise that in Abraham's seed, all the nations of the earth would be blessed was now coming to fulfillment.

WORSHIP

Jewish worship originally focused around the Torah and the temple. Temple rituals remained possible only as long as the Jews remained the "people of the land." After the destruction of the temple in A.D. 70 and the expulsion of the Jews from Jerusalem, such rituals ceased altogether. In its place the Torah and the interpretive traditions of the Mishnah, the Talmuds, and the Midrash became increasingly more important (see above).

Jewish worship was grounded in beliefs about God and creation. God as wholly other is accessible only through mediation of the priesthood and the prophets. Yet God's whole revelation is grounded in a spacio-temporal frame of reference. That is to say, God chose a people, a time, and a place to manifest his presence and will. And because people are subject to space and time, God conformed to these human limitations. Jewish worship was prescribed in such a way that careful instructions were given to Israel to celebrate and remember God's creation and salvation events through the observance of annual feasts, fasts, holy days, and the Sabbath. The Jewish calendar delineates each of these events.

Three great annual festivals that are celebrated in Jewish worship are: (1) the festivals connected with the Sabbath; (2) the Passover or Great Festival; and (3) the Day of Atonement (for this last one, see above).

Sabbath

The Jewish Sabbath (meaning "rest") is observed on Saturday, the seventh day of the week. According to the creation account in Genesis 1, God created the earth in six days and on the seventh day, rested. Therefore, the Sabbath day coming at the end of six days of labor was understood to be: (1) a time of *rest* for the people of God—for, as God rested from his creative labors, so God's people may rest from their labors within creation; (2) a time to *remember* God and his creative works. Jewish worship in space and time became an ongoing story told and retold. The *leitmotif* of the divine story of creation for Israel was the perpetual weekly celebration of the Sabbath. Therefore the resonating themes of rest and worship constitute the heart of Sabbath observance.

Christianity introduced radical changes in the understanding of the Sabbath. By the time of Christ, Sabbath worship had become a matter of observing multitudinous external prohibitions that Jesus denounced as the "traditions of men." In order to fulfill the law, Jesus kept the Sabbath (Mark 1:27), but he had no regard for the traditions of the Pharisees. The occasion of the disciples eating grain on the Sabbath serves as one example. On that occasion Jesus made the bold assertion, "The Sabbath was made for man, not man for the Sabbath" (Mark 2:23–27). In the passage immediately following (3:1–5), Jesus healed a man on the Sabbath day and asked the pointed question to the outraged Pharisees, "Which is lawful on the Sabbath: to do good or to do evil, to save life or to kill?" (3:4).

Jesus' teachings offended the Pharisees, to the point that they began to plot his death (Mark 3:6), but the most radical reversal to Jewish worship was yet to come. The early (Jewish) Christians began worshiping on the *first day* of the week (Sunday), in celebration of the resurrection. Several church fathers taught that Sunday worship was a celebration of *re-creation*. That is, Jesus' resurrection on the first day made salvation a new creation, righting the wrongs of the old creation. A further step in the development of a distinctly Christian theology of the Sabbath in contrast to Judaism is the understanding of Jesus as the actual embodiment and fulfillment of the Sabbath. All those who believe in Christ as the Messiah enter into the Sabbath rest of God (Heb. 4:1–11). For the Christian, in other words, the worship of God need no longer be tied to the Sabbath.

The scandal of Jesus' teaching, therefore, is that he reinterpreted the basic pillars of Judaism. He became the fulfillment of the law for all lawbreakers. He became the very mercy seat of God, replacing the temple and holy of holies. He became the Sabbath rest of God in place of traditional Sabbath observances. None of these things were intended to be novel; rather, they were in fulfillment of the "Law of Moses, the Prophets and the Psalms" (Luke 24:44).

The Passover

Central to Jewish worship and religion is the Passover festival, one of the great pilgrimage feasts. The Passover is celebrated in the spring, in the month of Nisan (March–April). The first Passover dates back to Israel's final deliverance from slavery in Egypt. Moses instructed the people of Israel to smear the doors and lintels of their homes with blood (Ex. 12:1–51), and the angel of destruction "passed over" the firstborn of Israel in order to slay the firstborn of the Egyptians. This event represented the dawn of a new era in Israel's history. Not only was there now a story of creation to recall but also a supreme instance of salvation and deliverance. As the Sabbath was an enactment of God's work of creation, the Passover was an enactment of God's work of salvation. And just as the Sabbath was to be repeated weekly, the "perpetual Passover" was initiated to celebrate and remember the Egyptian Passover once a year (see ▸Passover meal; ▸Seder).

The Christian tradition has been greatly influenced by the Jewish Passover tradition. Jesus chose the evening before the Passover, and before his crucifixion, to initiate the Lord's Supper (Matt. 27:62; Mark 15:42; Luke 23:54; John 19:31). While Joachim Jeremias raises the question as to whether this was a Passover meal or not,[5] the passion and resurrection of Christ lie at the heart of Christianity; because they occurred during the Passover, the Lord's Supper later came to be called the "paschal mystery." The early Jewish Christians readily connected Jesus' death and resurrection as God's new Passover. Instead of bringing death to all sinners, for the sake of Christ, God passes over the sins of all who are covered with Jesus' blood as that of the new Passover Lamb. In other words, as was the case with the Sabbath and the temple, the Jewish Passover is also reinterpreted in Christianity. Christians regard the Passover as a foreshadowing of God's full disclosure of events, culminating in the new covenant (Jer. 31:31–34).

Messianic Hope and Prophecy

The prophetic literature of the Old Testament is filled with declarations of the coming of a *messiah* (lit., "anointed one") to bring God's deliverance and salvation through a kingly figure in the likeness of David (Pss. 2; 18; 20; 21; 45). The Messiah is called by various names—e.g., "Wonderful, Counselor, Mighty God, Everlasting Father, Prince of Peace" (Isa. 9:6).

The Jews believed that the Messiah would arise out of one of several traditions within Judaism. By the time of Jesus, the messianic hope of many of the Jews was that the Anointed One would be a powerful political-military king who would vanquish the Romans. Others looked at the coming Messiah as one who would bring a new beginning (a new heaven and a new earth), with Israel at the center ruling the nations of the world. Not in the list of expected roles, however, was the category of a messianic king who would suffer and die. Christianity champions this interpretation of the messianic hope and sees it fulfilled in Jesus of Nazareth. The "suffering servant" text of Isaiah 53 became the *locus classicus* for the description of Jesus as the Christ who suffered and died to deliver his people from sin. The Jews found this notion to be scandalous. Little wonder that Paul said that the cross of Christ was a stumbling block to the Jews (1 Cor. 1:23). The eschatological hope of Israel is still linked today among orthodox Jews with its messianic hope.

The Elect of God

The phrases "chosen people," "children of Abraham," "elect of God," and so on are commonly linked to Israel. Through the promise God made to Abraham (above), Israel was selected by God to be a standard-bearer of the one true God and the example for the nations. After the Diaspora, the nation of God's elect moved from a spiritual concept to a strongly national-istic one. Being the "children of Abraham" bred a spirit of sectarianism and pride. Jesus challenged this with strong language (John 8:39–44). The early church adopted the language of election from Judaism (Acts 2:47; Rom. 8:28–31; Eph. 1:5; 1 Pet. 2:9)—but with one important difference. Rather than an elect people called from a specific nation, Israel, the people of God are now the elect from every nation (Acts 3:25). The covenant God made with Abraham comes to fruition in the birth of the Christian church on the Day of Pente-cost (Acts 2). The church, the new Israel of God, is now comprised of all people in Christ (Gal. 3:28; 6:16).

MODERN JUDAISM

The following is a brief summary of the different forms of Judaism existing today. Just as Christianity is a vast pluralism of denominations in the modern world, Judaism has undergone a similar phenomenon.[6]

1. *Conservative Judaism.* This movement began in the mid-nineteenth century as a reaction against the Reform rabbis. Conservative Judaism in America is called the United Synagogue of America.

2. *Orthodox Judaism.* This is the oldest form of Judaism. Orthodox Judaism came to America in 1625, and all the synagogues organized from 1730–1801 followed the Sephardic rite. In 1831 in Philadelphia, the Ashkenazic rite began. Orthodox institutions include Yeshivos Seminar-ies of Torah Study; Hebrew Theological College in Chicago; Yeshiva University; New Israel Rab-binical College in Baltimore; and the Rabbini-cal Council of America.

3. *Reform Judaism.* As noted above, this movement began in Germany in the 1800s. The creation of the Reformed Society of Israelites in Charleston, South Carolina, brought the Reform movement to America. Reform Judaism introduced changes and updating in the rituals and the use of English in worship services. Reform organizations include the National Federation of Temple Broth-erhoods; NFT Sisterhoods; NFT Youth; Ameri-can Conference of Cantors; National Association of Temple Educators; NAT Administrators; and World Union for Progressive Judaism. Educa-tional institutions include Hebrew Union Col-lege of Cincinnati.

4. *Reconstructionist Judaism.* Mordecai Kaplan (1881–1983), a professor at Conservative Jewish Theological Seminary in New York, "recon-structed" Judaism by altering some fundamental tenets of orthodox Judaism. Reconstructionists deny original sin and, in keeping with modern tenor, uphold the basic goodness of humankind. The Jewish Reconstructionist Foundation was formed in 1940. Reconstructionist organizations include Reconstructionist Federation of Congre-gations and Fellowships (1951) and Reconstruc-tionist Rabbinical College (1968) in Philadelphia.

5. *Humanistic Judaism.* Comprised mainly of agnostics and atheists, humanistic Judaism rejects the notion of a God who is "out there." Theism is replaced with a thoroughly humanis-tic approach. That is, morality lies within each person. Right and wrong acts are not done in response to God but to self. Humanistic Judaism was supported by an organization known as the Ethical Cultural Movement, founded in New York in 1876. Sherwin T. Wine founded the Society for Humanistic Judaism in 1969. Some human-istic Jews are also members of the UNITARIAN-UNIVERSALIST ASSOCIATION.

CONCLUSION

Modern Judaism has undergone significant changes in the latter half of the twentieth century.[7] Radical secu-lar ideologies have resulted in a religionless or secular nationalism, countered by conservative and moderately religious factions. Intermarriage between Jews and non-Jews, especially in the United States, has risen rap-idly. Attendance at synagogues is marginal at best. The secularism currently being experienced is countered by a growing interest in orthodoxy as more Jews in the 1980s and 1990s have turned to their historical roots than in previous decades. Anti-Semitism has under-gone a resurgence in the IDENTITY movements in Amer-ica. Most recent is a growing anti-Semitism in the new German nation. The problem is not limited to Germany, however. It is a worldwide phenomenon.

ADDITIONAL INFORMATION_____

Headquarters

Orthodox Judaism: Union of Orthodox Congregations of Amer-ica, 45 W. 36th Street, New York, NY 10018.

Reform: Union of American Hebrew Congregations in the US and Canada, 790 Madison Avenue, New York, NY 10021.

Reconstructionist: Jewish Reconstructionist Foundation, 432 Park Avenue S., New York, NY 10016.

Conservative: United Synagogue of America, 155 5th Avenue, New York, NY 10010.

Humanistic: Society for Humanistic Judaism, 28611 W. 12 Mile Road; Farmington Hills, MI 48334.

Websites

Orthodox: *www.ou.org*
Reform: *www.rj.org*
Reconstructionist: *www.jrf.com*
Conservative: *www.uscj.org*
Humanistic: *www.shj.org*

Primary Documents and Authoritative Sources

Orthodox Judaism: The Hebrew Bible; The Torah; Joseph Caro, *Sulhan Arukh*

Reformed Judaism: Hebrew Bible

Reconstructionist: Mordecai M. Kaplan, *Judaism As a Civilization: Toward a Reconstruction of American-Jewish Life;* _____, *Dynamic Judaism: Essential Writings of M.M. Kaplan; Reconstructionist Magazine*

Conservative: Hebrew Bible; Talmud; *Responsa Literature; The Codes;* Joseph Caro, *Sulhan Arukh*

Humanistic: Sherwin T. Wine, *Judaism Beyond God: A Radical New Way to be Jewish; Humanistic Judaism* (journal)

Statistics

According to 2000 figures, there are approximately fourteen million Jews in the world with 5,600,000 in America. The approximate breakdown of the Jewish population in the United States is:

Orthodox: 1,000,000 in approximately 1,000 congregations
Reform: 1,300,000 in app. 850 congregations
Reconstructionist: 50,000
Conservative: 2,000,000
Humanistic: 2,200

Notes

[1] John Bright, *A History of Israel* (Philadelphia: Westminster, 1981), 133.

[2] Chart taken from *Zondervan Pictorial Encyclopedia of the Bible* (Grand Rapids: Zondervan, 1975–76), s.v. "Kings, Books of," 3:817.

[3] *Encyclopedia Britannica,* 15th ed. (1988), s.v. "Judaism," 22:425.

[4] See IDENTITY MOVEMENTS.

[5] Joachim Jeremias, *The Eucharistic Words of Jesus* (London: SCM, 1966).

[6] Information compiled by The Institute for World Religions, P.O. Box CC, Irvine, CA 92716–6003.

[7] A helpful book for modern-day Judaism in America is written by Howard M. Sachar, *A History of the Jews in America* (New York: Knopf, 1992). See also the bibliography.

LIFESPRING; LIFE SPRING

A self-help organization that provides an eclectic blend of NEW AGE ideology with psychology, mind dynamics, and religious ideas.

HISTORY

"To our knowledge the research on Lifespring constitutes the most extensive body of scientific inquiry on any experiential program available today."[1] Lifespring was founded in 1974 by John Hanley, who had formerly been a member of Mind Dynamics. He developed his ideas with the help of John Enright of the Gestalt Institute and several other entrepreneurs of the human potential movement. Since 1974 Lifespring (also spelled Life Spring) has shown impressive growth statistics. By 1977 over twenty thousand people had enrolled in the training seminars. In 1980 the numbers exceeded one hundred thousand. By the end of the 1980s, officials claimed that three hundred thousand had enrolled in Lifespring seminars. The movement quickly became a multimillion dollar enterprise with Hanley earning a six-figure salary. The cost to enroll in the seminar was originally $200, but that fee rose to $350 in 1980 and to $450 by 1984. A high percentage of those who enroll are businessmen seeking ways of improving performance in the workplace.

Lifespring has not gone unnoticed in the media. ABC's *20/20* focused on the movement on October 30 and November 6, 1980, and drew several conclusions. Lifespring teachers and trainers were practicing psychology, not as professionals but as mere amateurs. Moreover, the techniques used in the training were extremely manipulative psychologically. Many of the students have sought the help of professionals as a result of "the damage" suffered by undergoing Lifespring's training. There have even been rumors and reports of deaths and suicides of several trainees occurring as a result of the influences of the group's teachings.

Lifespring faced a host of legal suits in the late 1980s. As of 2005, there are no more courses being advertised, and the official website, in place up to 2004, has been removed.

ORGANIZATION

Before 2005, Lifespring underwent a complete makeover. It was organized around its seminars and courses at various levels. The courses and seminars were offered regularly and Hanley's son, John Hanley Jr., served as a trainer in the organization. Until the early 1990s, initiates, after payment of the required fee, underwent fifty hours of training over a five-day period. If one chose, he or she could then elect to go beyond the basic training and enroll in the advanced course (called "Interpersonal Experience" [IPE]). Approximately 50 percent of the students went on to the advanced course, which consists of five more days of intensified training. The senior course, titled Training Coordinator Program [TC], includes another seventy days of training. At this stage, trainees are ready to serve Lifespring in varying roles as instructors, recruiters, and so on.

Courses were offered under such names as The Lifespring Basic/Adventure, The Lifespring Advanced/Challenge, and The Lifespring Quest. These courses were held over a three- or four-day period and are comprised of approximately thirty-five hours of instruction. Lesser involved courses are offered in public speaking, intimacy, sexuality, and so on. To become a trainer, a person could elect to take the "Trainer in Training" program. The training was held over a period of six months.

TEACHINGS

Lifespring emphasized the idea that truth is a subjective enterprise whose source lies within the "core" of the human soul. Within the core lies all truth, love, and identity. The goal is to tap the core, that is, to discover the potential that lies within and to actualize that potential. Part of the training was to have the trainees pair off in groups of two (called "dyads") or three (called "triads"), for the purpose of sharing and confrontation.[2] They attempt to discover the "space" inside the mind of the other, thereby discovering the potential that is latent within. Actualizing one's potential then becomes possible with further training.

All problems and difficulties in life arise from the fundamental errors of one's thought process. The solution, therefore, is to undergo a radical change in the way one thinks or conceptualizes reality. Even sickness, disease, and all forms of physiological malady were attributed to problems within the mind.[3]

Traditional CHRISTIANITY differs radically in orientation from Lifespring. Illness, disease, problems, and difficulties are not the result of wrong thinking. Rather, wrong thinking itself, as well as sicknesses and diseases, is symptomatic of and has its source in the much deeper spiritual malady of separation from God through sin (Gen. 3). For Lifespring, the concept of sin is the result of a diseased philosophy or outlook on life.

Because truth, love, and self-identity have their source in humankind, the logical conclusion is that humanity is its own god. It is this concept that locates Lifespring within the philosophical foundations of Eastern religion and, more recently, within the complex meta-network of organizations that constitute the New Age Movement. The ▸occult is also a vital part of Lifespring's agenda, as "psychic" powers are thought to be the source of human powers, developed and made stronger through exercise and training.

Second, the Christian focuses attention on a transcendent God (see ▸transcendence), who lies outside of and apart from creation. Christian worship is a movement outward and upward. The ▸existentialist orientation of Lifespring militates against this notion. Because latent deity resides in each person, worship is curved inward and directed toward the self.

CONCLUSION

Lifespring has catered to a diversified group of people. Special programs were designed for prisoners, teens, children, families, students, businessmen, and so on. Many programs that were broadcast on cable networks across the United States and that emphasized New Age themes of health, personal prosperity, overcoming fear, self-actualization, sexuality, and the like reflected the goals and teachings of Lifespring. Lectures and training sessions focused on the needs of the particular group in question.

ADDITIONAL INFORMATION_____

Headquarters
Dallas, TX.

Website
www.lifespring.com. This website was the official site up to 2004. In 2005, however, the site has been removed.

Statistics
Over 500,000 people have enrolled and taken various Lifespring courses.

Notes
[1] From Lifespring's official website (see note above).
[2] See CHRISTIAN SCIENCE.
[3] James Evans, "Shrinking Without a License," *California* (March 1989), 15.

MACUMBA

The various Macumba (meaning "sanctuary") ᐅcults that exist in Brazil are divided according to the African cultures that were transported to the New World through the slave trade from the sixteenth through the nineteenth centuries.

HISTORY

Failure to enslave successfully native Americans forced the Portuguese to seek the profitable alternative of importing African slave labor to work the plantations and mines. When slavery was finally abandoned in Brazil in 1888, over three million blacks had been uprooted from their homelands and brought to this tropical country. Most of these people came from the ᐅDahomean and ᐅYoruba cultures of West Africa. The ᐅBantu people of the Congo also constituted a sizable contribution to the population. The cultural and ethnic diversity was an important factor in the religious developments of Brazil, as it was in the West Indies in general.

Native Indians mixed with the diverse African cultures and the Portuguese Europeans. Through the influence of the Portuguese language and Portuguese Roman Catholic missionary efforts, the religion of a majority of Brazil is Roman Catholic. Up until 1889 it was the official religion. The various cults, however, have preserved their own religious traditions and have eclectically blended them with Roman Catholicism, as was also the case in the West Indies. The Yorubic cults have been successful in preserving their unique religious heritage despite attempts by Jesuit missionaries to proselytize them to the fullest.

BELIEFS

In most of the Yorubic cults, the priests are called ᐅbabalao. Together with their assistants (called ᐅachogun), they care for and prepare the animals used in the sacrifices to the ᐅorisha. Initiation into the Yorubic cults involves certain rigid requirements, such as intense study of the ritualistic dances and chants, abstinence from certain foods and sex, and a period of religious contemplation, after which time the initiate is inducted into the cult.

The various magical rites that the subject participates in are called ᐅebo.

In their book *Healing States* (1986), Alberto Villoldo and Stanley Krippner found that the CANDOMBLE and ᐅUmbanda faiths have three common traits:

- Humans have both a physical and spiritual body.
- Discarnate entities constantly contact the physical world.
- Humans can learn to contact and incorporate the spirits for the purposes of healing and spiritual evolution.[1]

The chief Dahomean influence on the Macumba has been the cult of VOODOO. The practice of voodoo or vodun (as it is also called) is similar to the voodoo practiced in Haiti. The chief difference between the two lies in the Brazilian belief that a ᐅtokhueni opens the door to other deities, enabling possession by more than one spirit. In Haitian voodoo, a person becomes possessed by a single spirit. The concept of dual possession also differentiates the Dahomeans from the Yorubic cults, which teach that only one *orisha* may inhabit the human subject at a time. The creator-god in Dahomean cults is ᐅMawu Lisa. Other deities include ᐅ*Hevioso*, ᐅ*Legba*, and ᐅ*Loko*.

The Bantu people have also contributed a host of deities to Brazilian cultic traditions. ᐅ*Nzambi* is the supreme deity. "He" is attended to by the priest or ᐅ*quimbanda*. ᐅZombiism also has its roots in the Bantu religious heritage. As in the Yorubic and Dahomean cults, the deities of the Bantu cults are numerous, such as ᐅ*Cariapemba*, ᐅ*Calunga*, and ᐅ*Orodere*.

It is not feasible within the scope of this volume to treat the tremendous variety of the Macumba cults.

CONCLUSION

Today there has been an assimilation of religion and culture among the diverse people of Brazil. Many of the cults carry on their ceremonies in the thousands of villages scattered throughout the Brazilian countryside. In the cities, where education and religious pluralism are more concentrated, the cultic traditions are not as prevalent or influential as they once were. Umbanda sects are found in the urban areas, while the largest of the rural sects is Candomble.

ADDITIONAL INFORMATION_____

Sacred Texts
Largely oral tradition

Websites
www.aumbhandan.org.br (in Portuguese);
www.stirlinglaw.com/ea/macumba.htm

Statistics
Millions of people practice Macumba, but do so in secret while practicing Roman Catholicism openly. In Rio de Janeiro there are 65,000 temples with 40 million Brazilians estimated practicing Macumba.

Note
[1] Cited on *http://religiousmovements.lib.virginia.edu/nrms/macu.html*.

MAHAYANA BUDDHISM

BUDDHISM is not a monolithic world religion. Like all other major faiths, its history unfolds into ▶sects and sundry schools of thought. Mahayana is one of the two great schools of the Buddhist world.

HISTORY

Mahayana Buddhism arose ca. 185 B.C., following the death of the great "missionary general" ▶Asoka. Mahayana is alternately known as the "Greater School" or "Greater Vehicle" (lit., the "great ox cart" or the "way of the many"), in contrast to THERAVADA BUD-DHISM, the other main school of Buddhist thought. Mahayana is the more liberal of the two schools. Geographically, it is practiced in the northern Buddhist countries—Korea, Japan, China, Tibet, Nepal, Indonesia, and Vietnam. The more conservative Theravada school became centered in southern Asia. The Mahayana School was a reform movement that made it possible for the masses to find access to the Buddhist way of life.

TEACHINGS

There were at least three significant contributions noteworthy to the development of Mahayana Buddhist theology. (1) First is the emergence of the ▶*bodhisattva*. The *bodhisattvas* are the series of emanations or prestages to the life of ▶Siddharta Gautama. In these previous lives, the Buddha performed acts of love, generosity, and kindness, important themes in the emergence of Mahayana.

(2) Next is accessibility. Therevada Buddhism taught a form of Buddhism that was much too esoteric and therefore virtually unattainable for the masses. While the attainment of complete and total enlightenment is indeed the ultimate goal, Mahayana saw the development of two lesser forms of enlightenment that greatly facilitated participation of the masses. One could become a *pratyeka-buddha*, that is, one who achieves a certain degree of enlightenment but keeps it a secret. The other is the *arhant*, that is, one who learns the truth from others, applies it to himself, and then achieves nirvana.

(3) Mahayana Buddhist theology teaches that Gautama was not human but divine. But instead of entering nirvana he chose to remain behind in order to assist others who are on the path of suffering. Mahayana Buddhists, therefore, regard compassion and love as the highest virtues and regard those who seek salvation and ▶enlightenment exclusively for themselves as being selfish.

Several Mahayana themes prompt noteworthy comparisons and contrasts with CHRISTIANITY. Love and compassion are also major motifs of Christian thought. God's love was extended toward humanity when Jesus Christ died on the cross. That sacrifice was the supreme act of love because it was offered in order to atone for the sins of the world. For Christianity, however, Jesus' death was necessary in order to bring humanity into a right relationship with God. For the Buddhist, salvation is not a matter of the forgiveness of sins as much as it is release from suffering within the cycle of rebirth. As Jesus' merit and righteousness is transferred to a penitent sinner, the merits of the *bodhisattva* are conferred on those seeking nirvana.

Mahayana's accentuation of the divine nature of the Buddha led to the need for expressing the modes in which he manifested himself. This is the *trikaya* ("three-bodies") doctrine. The three bodies are the "physical," the "mental," and the non-manifest body of the "law." Similarly, for Christianity, Jesus Christ was "born of the virgin Mary" (Apostles' Creed). Traditional Chalcedonian ▶Christology confesses Christ to be divine and, therefore, the ▶incarnation is the "physical body" of the divine Son of God. Christ is also the fulfillment of the "law" (Luke 24:44).

CONCLUSION

The Mahayana school has always been the larger of the two movements. This is attributed to its rejection of rigorous ▶asceticism and its emphasis on compassion and the orientation toward the everyday affairs of life. Mahayana also exhibited an ability to adjust itself to the indigenous gods in each of the countries to which it spread rather than conducting a campaign of exclusivity. This alone explains its rapid growth.

ADDITIONAL INFORMATION_____

Website

http://www.buddhanet.net/l_maha.htm (This site lists many of the existing Mahayana organizations, websites, and links to the greater Buddhist world.)

Statistics

Mahayana Buddhists are the largest group of Buddhists, comprising 56 percent of the Buddhist population in the world with 185 million members.

MEHER BABA

"I have come not to teach but to awaken. Therefore I lay down no precepts." These are the words of Meher Baba (1894–1969), the founder of a ▸sect named after himself.

HISTORY

Baba grew up as Merwan Sheriar ▸Irani in Poona, India, the son of ▸Zoroastrian parents. When he attended college, Irani met an old ▸Muslim lady with whom he developed a close relationship. She was regarded as being one of the world's ▸perfect masters. Quite unexpectedly one day, the lady kissed him on the forehead. Like magic, this event transported him into instant ▸enlightenment and God-consciousness.

Irani proceeded to study under the perfect masters. This led to a second momentous event. One of the perfect masters threw a stone at Irani, and it allegedly struck him on the forehead in the very spot where the kiss had been planted. Things would never be the same again. He was renamed Meher Baba ("compassionate father") and believed himself to be the new ▸avatar of the twentieth century, as were ▸Buddha, ▸Muhammad, and Jesus Christ for their respective eras. For the next several years, Baba busied himself with teaching and also founded a small community complete with a hospital and a school.

In 1925 Baba decided that he had said all that there was to say. What he and the other avatars had taught constituted the accumulated divine wisdom of the ages. Believing that it was now time to live out the truth, Baba took a vow of silence, which he honored, so it is believed, for the rest of his life (nearly forty-five years). He did communicate, however, with the use of hand signals, bodily gestures, and an alphabet board.

Baba seemed to have no doubt about his own importance. He claimed that he was "the ancient one" and the very "highest of the high." Where the preceding avatars had left off, he alone was the fulfillment of divine power in the modern world.

For almost three decades (1931–1958) Meher Baba made continued trips to the United States, Europe, and other parts of the world.

ORGANIZATION

Several centers for the study of his teachings were established, such as the Meher Spiritual Center in Myrtle Beach, South Carolina, and the Avatar's Abode in Australia. Today there are many such centers. They all focus on the teachings and the writings of Meher Baba. There are centers in nineteen states in the United States and ten centers in seven other countries.

TEACHINGS

Meher Baba's message appeared to be ecumenical in scope. He organized no formal religious institution, nor did he formulate a creed or dogma. Those who heard his teachings and read his books came from many different faiths.

Meher Baba's theology eclectically combines the ideas of several of the Oriental religions—BUDDHISM, HINDUISM, Zoroastrianism, and SUFISM. The central feature of his thought lies in the contention that God is monistic and that the goal of all creation is to realize the absolute oneness of the deity. A ▸dualism between matter and spirit exists along with the Neoplatonic and Hindu ideas that all of life is arranged in an ontological hierarchy.

The soul journeys to earth from two planets and becomes incarnate in the base forms of matter (stones, earth, plants, and on upward to human beings). Baba taught that once the human stage is attained, a human being could then achieve ▸nirvana. Baba believed that every soul must pass through this hierarchy and enter into each of the life forms in order to achieve perfect enlightenment.

The fundamental ideas endemic to Meher Baba's thought contrast greatly with CHRISTIANITY. While Baba held that all reality moves upward from lower life forms to higher, Christianity teaches that God is the "maker of heaven and earth" (Apostles' Creed, Appendix 1) and that, as Creator, God made each aspect of the creation with its own unique ontological dignity and order. In other words, a stone was created to be a stone and remains so. A plant was created to be a plant and remains so, sprouting new seeds and reproducing additional plants after its own kind. The same is true for the other forms of creation.

Human beings were created in the image of God and are comprised of soul and body. At death the soul separates from the body. The former rises to heaven or descends into ‣hell, while the body goes to the ground from which it came. There is no concept of ‣reincarnation into higher life forms in Christian ‣orthodoxy. Each created being is unique. While it is true that ‣gnosticism did influence the Christian church in the first five centuries, orthodoxy opposed the Greek dualism between flesh and spirit. Oneness and wholeness more accurately describe the biblical Hebrew view of life. The flesh in and of itself is not evil. Sin, which has entered in as a foreign entity, is the nature of evil, as Paul argues in Romans 7:14–25.

Concerning the doctrine of salvation, Christianity and Meher Baba are in contrast as well. Christianity maintains that salvation is based on repentance from sin and faith in the person and work of Jesus Christ as described in Scripture and summarized in the Apostles' and Nicene creeds. Meher Baba taught that salvation was the attainment of total awareness and absolute enlightenment. For Christianity, the Holy Spirit brings grace and light to believers from without. For Meher Baba the source of goodness, truth, and salvation lies *within*.

Eschatologically, for Christianity all of history is consummated in Jesus Christ, who will "come to judge the living and the dead" (Apostles' Creed). Meher Baba's view of history is at once progressive and cyclical: progressive in that all life is yearning for oneness with God and moving toward that end; cyclical in the sense that all of life is embarked on the wheel of reincarnation, marking progress only when one of the ‣seven stages is surmounted.

Yet there are several notable similarities between Jesus and Meher Baba. Both taught that love is the highest virtue and the highest ideal of law. Baba, like Christ, renounced the uncertainty and corruptibility of riches. Both spent a great deal of time ministering to the poor and the sick. Meher Baba, however, considered himself to be the supreme avatar of our age. In this role, he declared that he would one day break his vow of silence, speaking words that would change the course of history. January 31, 1969, was the last day he would have that chance. He died at the age of seventy-five. Jesus Christ declared himself to be the only true way to God for every person of every age in history (John 10:1–18; 14:1–6). As the living, ‣incarnate Word of God, he continued to speak throughout his earthly life. He never took a vow of silence, and his last three words before his death—"it is finished"—echo throughout the corridors of history.

Meher Baba is to be admired for his stand against the use of nonprescriptive drugs in the turbulent 1960s. In a decade where substance abuse was openly advocated by the rock-and-roll subculture, Meher Baba warned that "drugs are harmful mentally, physically, and spiritually."

CONCLUSION

Meher Baba's teachings continue to attract those interested in Eastern religious ideas. Though the personality cults have tended to wane since the 1980s, the NEW AGE MOVEMENT continues to be an umbrella to house the syncretistic blend of ideas characteristic of Meher Baba and other ‣gurus of the Far East. Followers of Meher Baba carry on a rich dialogue and tradition via the internet, where many of Baba's writings and teachings are preserved and accessible.

Meher Baba groups exist in India, Europe, Australia, and the United States. Followers gather to hear and read the messages and writings of Baba, and some centers continue to celebrate his birthday each year. Organizations centered around Baba'a life and teachings include a retreat center called Meherana in Mariposa, California; the Abode in Queensland, Australia; a Sheriar Foundation; and Meher Mount, located on Sulphur Mountain in Ojai, California.

ADDITIONAL INFORMATION

Centers
These are located throughout the United States and the world.

Websites
www.avatarmeherbaba.org; www.avatarsabode.com.au; (numerous other links)

Sacred Texts
Some of Baba's works include his five-volume *Discourses*; *God Speaks: The Theme of Creation and Its Purposes* (1955); *The Everything and the Nothing* (1963); and *Listen Humanity*. He also read the Hindu scriptures and urged his students to do the same.

MORMONISM; THE CHURCH OF JESUS CHRIST OF LATTER-DAY SAINTS; CJCLDS

Founded by Joseph ⁰Smith Jr. (1805–1844) in 1830, Mormonism's unique development together with its growth worldwide constitutes an important narrative in the survey of religious groups found in this volume. Rising above all of the other competing ⁰cults and ⁰sects that flourished in the nineteenth and twentieth centuries, Mormonism is the most successful and distinctive religion born on American soil. If Puritanism shaped a way of life in New England, Mormonism influenced and shaped a way of life in a different region of the country, far removed from New England (where its founder was born).

HISTORY

On December 23, 1805, in Sharon, Vermont, Joseph and Lucy Smith gave birth to their fourth child, Joseph Jr. His was not a pleasant childhood. The elder Joseph found it very difficult to make ends meet as a farmer in Vermont, meeting with repeated failure. In his spare time, he sublimated these frustrations by spending hours reliving a boyhood fantasy, hunting for buried treasure. It is even alleged that he once attempted to mint his own money. With no hope in sight for a farming boom in Vermont, the Smith family moved further west to Palmyra, New York. Here they met with no greater success than in Vermont. Young Joseph proved to be a bright young boy, but he never received much of a formal education. His father continued to hunt for treasure in Palmyra, and young Joseph also gained an interest in his father's pastime. Friends and neighbors later testified that the Smith family indeed had a reputation for treasure hunting.

Young Joseph's mother was also given to excesses. She was an impressionable woman, paying credence to the most extreme and superstitious of religious ideas. During his boyhood and teen years, Joseph Smith Jr. was exposed to several different sects within the Christian religion. ⁰Revivalism was prevalent at the time and was particularly so in Ontario (now Wayne) County in New York.

Young Joseph encountered Methodism and later reported that he had been attracted to it. But when he was fifteen, his mother, his two brothers Hyrum and Samuel, and his sister Sophronia all converted to Presbyterianism. Joseph gave himself to a serious reflection of religion. But the existence of many religions, albeit sects, confused him. A question that incessantly plagued his mind was, Which of all the sects was right? While reading James in his King James ⁰Bible, he came on these words: "If any of you lack wisdom, let him ask of God, that giveth to all men liberally, and upbraideth not; and it shall be given him" (James 1:5). This passage seemed to leap from the page, and he later wrote these words:

> I reflected on it again and again, knowing that if any person needed wisdom from God, I did; for how to act I did not know, and unless I could get more wisdom than I then had, I would never know; for the teachers of religion of the different sects understood the same passage of scripture so differently as to destroy all confidence in settling the question by an appeal to the Bible.[1]

Joseph Smith, founder of the Mormons.

Smith had the choice either to ignore James's instructions or to follow them; so he opted for the latter course, fearing that otherwise he would forever remain in utter confusion. In 1820 he retreated into the woods to be alone and began to pray. Here is Smith's own testimony, as he reported it in ›*The Pearl of Great Price*, of what happened to him on that day:

> After I had retired to the place where I had previously designed to go, having looked around me, and finding myself alone, I kneeled down and began to offer up the desires of my heart to God. I had scarcely done so, when immediately I was seized upon by some power which entirely overcame me, and had such an astonishing influence over me as to bind my tongue so that I could not speak. Thick darkness gathered around me, and it seemed to me for a time as if I were doomed to sudden destruction.
>
> But, exerting all my powers to call upon God to deliver me out of the power of this enemy which had seized on me, and at the very moment when I was ready to sink into despair and abandon myself to destruction—not to an imaginary ruin, but to the power of some actual being from the unseen world, who had such marvelous power as I had never before felt in any being—just at this moment of great alarm, I saw a pillar of light exactly over my head, above the brightness of the sun, which descended gradually until it fell on me.
>
> It no sooner appeared than I found myself delivered from the enemy which held me bound. When the light rested on me I saw two Personages, whose brightness and glory defy all description, standing above me in the air. One of them spake unto me, calling me by name, and said—pointing to the other—This is My Beloved Son. Hear Him!
>
> My object in going to inquire of the Lord was to know which of all the sects was right, that I might know which to join. No sooner, therefore, did I get possession of myself, so as to be able to speak, than I asked the Personages who stood above me in the light, which of all the sects was right—and which I should join?
>
> I was answered that I must join none of them, for they were all wrong, and the Personage who addressed me said that all their creeds were an abomination in His sight; that those professors were all corrupt; that "they draw near to me with their lips, but their hearts are far from me; they teach for doctrines the commandments of men: having a form of godliness, but they deny the power thereof."
>
> He again forbade me to join with any of them; and many other things did he say unto me, which I cannot write at this time. When I came to myself again, I found myself lying on my back, looking up into heaven.[2]

Mormons refer to this account as Smith's ›first vision. Problems arise with this testimony, however. Smith did not write down this account until years later. In the earlier edition of *The Pearl of Great Price*, Smith identified one of the personages as Nephi. But in a later edition of the same book, Smith identifies the celestial visitor as being ›Moroni. Nephi and Moroni are two distinct characters in Mormon literature. Moreover, in the first edition of *The Pearl of Great Price*, Smith had mentioned having been visited by "one personage," while later editions speak of "two personages," constituting a serious discrepancy, especially because the truth of Mormon revelation rests on the prophetic authority of its books.

Immediately after Smith received his first vision, he reported this experience to a Methodist minister. Smith wrote that the minister reacted contemptuously, telling him that visions and voices were of the ›devil. Smith also noted that as divided as the sects were against each other, they "all united to persecute me." Despite the persecution, however, Smith stood firmly by the vision and insisted it was authentic. He then made up his mind that he would not join any of the sects, but rather would wait and receive divine direction as to which course he should follow.

The answer soon came. On the evening of September 21, 1823, while retiring to bed, Smith began to pray. As he was calling on God, a bright light filled the room and a brilliantly illumined figure appeared beside the bed. The personage identified himself to Smith as Moroni, a messenger sent from God to commission Joseph with a task. Moroni told him that there was a book written on golden plates. Inscribed on the plates was a history of the former inhabitants of America and how they arrived here. Moroni went on to explain that the plates contained the fullness of the gospel. Along with the plates, Smith was promised two "stones in silver bows" called ›Urim and Thummim. God has prepared these two devices to enable Smith to translate the plates into English.

Smith was not told at that time where the plates were located. But he was given a vision of the place where they were and later would be able to recall clearly that precise location.

Moroni then left the room. While Smith was lying in bed reflecting on all that had just taken place, Moroni suddenly appeared beside his bed again. The same message was given along with several additional instructions, and then Moroni again disappeared. This incident happened a third time.

The next day, while working with his father in the field, young Joseph was so overwhelmed and exhausted by the experience that his father told him to go home. On his way back to the house, he collapsed in fatigue. As he was lying there, Joseph was again visited by Moroni, who told him the same message a fourth time. Moroni then instructed Joseph to go to his father and tell him what had happened. Unlike many others, Smith's father believed Joseph's words and told him that God had indeed spoken to him. Joseph Jr. then went to the place where his vision had directed him, and when he arrived there, he knew right away that it was the precise spot that had been shown him. While attempting to dig up the plates, he was interrupted by Moroni, who told him that it would be four years before he would be allowed to take the plates from the ground. Rather, he was to return to this same spot each year to receive new instructions, a task to which Smith faithfully attended.

At last the time arrived. On September 22, 1827, the plates were given to Smith with the instructions to guard them carefully until such time as they would be required of him again.

In January of the same year, Smith had married Emma Hale from Harmony, Pennsylvania. They eloped because her father had refused to give his consent to the marriage. Smith attributed this refusal to the intense persecution that had surrounded his life. One historian, Fawn Brodie (herself a former Mormon), reports, however, that the real reason for it was because Smith's one occupation in life was hunting for buried treasure with the aid of a "peepstone."[3] According to the Rev. Wesley Walters, a noted authority on Mormonism, Joseph Smith was indeed a "money diviner" who used a "peepstone to find buried treasure." Walters made a startling discovery in 1971 when he announced that a 140-year-old court document had been found in Norwich, New York. Jerald and Sandra Tanner report, "This document proves that Joseph Smith was a 'glass looker' and that he was arrested, tried, and found guilty by a justice of the peace in Bainbridge, New York in 1826."[4]

The term *glass looker* appeared on the court bill of Justice Albert Neely of Bainbridge. If it is indeed true that Smith had been tried for such a matter, his reputation as one given to superstition and his later claims to have been divinely assisted in his discoveries and revelations are brought into strong disrepute.

Undergoing intense persecution, Smith then moved to Harmony, into the home of his father-in-law. Here he began to translate the plates with the aid of the Urim and Thummim. Meanwhile, a friend named Martin Harris, who had previously given Joseph and Emma fifty dollars to finance their trip to Harmony, arrived there himself. He took the characters that Smith had drawn from the plates to Columbia University to Professor Charles Anthon, a linguistics scholar. Evidently, Harris had planned to finance the publication of the book and was taking the precautionary step of testing whether the plates were authentic and whether Smith's translation was correct. Smith reports the results of Harris's expedition in Harris's own words:

> I went to the city of New York, and presented the characters which had been translated, with the translation thereof, to Professor Charles Anthon, a gentleman celebrated for his literary attainments. Professor Anthon stated that the translation was correct, more so than any he had before seen translated from Egyptian. I then showed him those which were not yet translated, and he said that they were Egyptian, Chaldaic, Assyriac, and Arabic; and he said they were true characters. He gave me a certificate, certifying to the people of Palmyra that they were true characters, and that the translation of such of them as had been translated was also correct. I took the certificate and put it into my pocket, and was just leaving the house, when Mr. Anthon called me back, and asked me how the young man found out that there were gold plates in the place where he found them. I answered that an angel of God had revealed it unto him.
>
> He then said to me, "Let me see that certificate." I accordingly took it out of my pocket and gave it to him, when he took it and tore it to pieces, saying that there was no such thing now as ministering of angels, and that if I would bring the plates to him he would translate them. I informed him that part of the plates were sealed, and that I was forbidden to bring them. He replied, "I cannot read a sealed book." I left him and went to Dr. Mitchell, who sanctioned what Professor Anthon had said respecting both the characters and the translation.[5]

Later, when Professor Anthon heard about Harris's claim from a Mr. E. D. Howe, who had been investigating Smith, he wrote a letter to Howe vehemently denying that he had stated that the plates were written in "reformed Egyptian hieroglyphics" (a nonexistent language).

On April 5, 1829, a third key figure in Mormon history entered the picture, a schoolteacher named Oliver Cowdery from the area near Palmyra. Joseph Sr. had related to Cowdery all that had transpired with his son concerning the visions and the plates, and Cowdery immediately took an interest in the affair. The schoolmaster took a trip to Smith's home, bent on satiating his curiosity. Within two days of his arrival, Cowdery was writing into English what Smith was translating from the plates. The resulting document was the ᵇBook of Mormon.

On May 15, 1829, Smith and Cowdery allegedly went out into the woods to pray. While doing so, suddenly they were surrounded with light and John the Baptist appeared to them. Laying his hands on the two men, he ordained them, and spoke the following words:

> On you my fellow servants, in the name of the Messiah, I confer the Priesthood of Aaron, which holds the keys of the ministering of angels, and the gospel of repentance, and of baptism by immersion for the remission of sins; and this shall never be taken again from the earth until the sons of Levi do offer again an offering unto the Lord in righteousness.[6]

This incident is known in Mormon history as being the restoration of the ᵇAaronic priesthood. This commissioning had certain limitations to it. For instance, they could not themselves lay hands on others to impart the gift of the Holy Spirit. Nevertheless, it was at this point that both Cowdery and Smith were given the gift of prophecy and new spiritual understanding. John the Baptist also commissioned Smith to be ordained the first elder of the church and Cowdery the second. They then proceeded, on instruction from the divine messenger, to baptize each other.

During the translation of the plates into the Book of Mormon, it was determined that three witnesses should be granted the privilege of seeing them; the three chosen were Oliver Cowdery, David Whitmer, and Martin Harris. While engaged once again in prayer, Whitmer, Cowdery, and a little later, Harris, all saw the plates and were able to testify as to their authenticity.

Following the witness of the three was the witness of eight additional men: Christian Whitmer, Jacob Whitmer, Peter Whitmer, John Whitmer, Hiram Page, Joseph Smith Sr., Hyrum Smith, and Samuel H. Smith. Thereupon, Jesus' disciples Peter, James, and John conferred the ᵇMelchizedek priesthood on Smith and Cowdery along the banks of the Susquehanna River. This gave the two leaders the power of laying on of hands for the gift of the Holy Spirit.

On April 6, 1830, Smith and Cowdery laid hands on each other and thereby ordained each another as "elders of the Church of Christ" (later "Jesus" and "Latter Day Saints" were added) This is the date on which the Mormon church was born in Fayette, New York. Smith and Cowdery proceeded to lay hands on the other members of the group that were present, and they too received the gift of the Holy Spirit. The Mormon church began to grow rapidly. Beginning with six members, within one month the number rose to approximately forty.

Sensing a mission to the American Indians, the small group of Mormons moved to Kirtland, Ohio, near present-day Cleveland. A prominent Campbellite preacher, Sidney Rigdon, here converted to Mormonism along with many of his own flock. In Kirtland, the first Mormon temple was erected.

Not all was a story of success, however. Severe persecutions broke out as the group experienced opposition from non-Mormon neighbors. Many of Smith's followers left Kirtland and plodded farther west to Jackson County, Missouri, where many settled in the city of Independence. Here Smith received another of his many revelations. He declared Jackson County as being the promised land or the new ᵇZion. Just as in the promised land of the Israelites, however, the new promised land also contained inhabitants hostile to the new settlers. Persecutions became harsh, but the Mormon church grew steadily. By 1839 there were several thousand members living in and around Independence, Missouri.

The non-Mormon neighbors grew hostile toward the new community for several reasons. (1) They were indignant that Smith had claimed their homeland as being his new Zion. (2) The rugged individualism of the frontier was a philosophy of life that militated against an organization ruled by an ecclesiastical aristocracy. (3) The violence was in some sense retaliatory. When the persecutions proved to be too much in Independence, many moved north to Far West, Missouri. (4) Mormons were accused of practicing polygamy. The resistance continued to the point where the Mormons fought back, and the state militia was forced to intervene. Smith and several of the Mormon leaders were imprisoned but soon escaped, and Smith led his faithful followers east over the Mississippi into Commerce, Illinois, which Smith renamed Nauvoo.

In Nauvoo Smith continued to rule theocratically by announcing revelations as they occurred. The population of Nauvoo grew tremendously, and within the next four years it became one of the largest cities in Illinois, with a population of over twenty thousand. Interesting developments took place politically in that the two major parties, the Whigs and the Democrats, competed for the Mormon vote. Nauvoo was granted a charter by Illinois, and Smith became its first mayor. He also commanded the Nauvoo Legion, which was one part of the state's militia, gaining for himself a respectable reputation. Non-Mormons, nevertheless, continued their hostility toward Smith's church.

In February 1844 Smith decided that his political ambitions needed expression on a national level and announced his candidacy for the presidency of the United States. Some of his own Mormon dissenters quickly criticized him, and the *Nauvoo Expositor* published material sharply denouncing Smith and Mormonism. On June 10, 1844, Smith ordered his men to destroy the newspaper's press, which they did with sledgehammers. The building was also set on fire, though it did not burn down. When the owners complained, accusing Smith of reckless vandalism, he was imprisoned. Released, he was arrested again on charges of treason, along with his brother Hyrum. The two were jailed in Carthage, Illinois, for violating freedom of the press. On June 27, 1844, a mob of armed men angrily stormed the prison house and ruthlessly murdered the two brothers. Some of these were ex-Mormons.

Later the specific reasons for Smith's murder came to light. First, it had been declared by the Mormon "Council of Fifty" that Joseph Smith had been ordained "King over the Immediate House of Israel." "Gentiles" (a term for non-Mormons) interpreted this as being Smith's attempt to overthrow the United States government and establish a theocracy. The action against Smith's destruction of the *Nauvoo Expositor* became an excuse on the part of Gentiles to halt his political ambitions. Second, many were incensed by the *Nauvoo Expositor*'s declaration that Smith had been advocating the practice of polygamy. Eight years after Smith's death, the Mormon church declared that polygamy was indeed a practice revealed and ordained by God, thereby confirming the *Nauvoo Expositor*'s original reports.

Smith's followers immediately proclaimed him to be a martyr, and his death proved to be a watershed event in the history of the Mormon church. Who would be the new leader? The two most likely candidates were Sidney Rigdon, who claimed the right to lead because he had been selected by Smith as being his "First Counselor," and Brigham Young (1801–77), Rigdon's rival, who claimed that the rulership of the church had passed on to the "twelve apostles," of whom he was the president. A majority of Mormons opted for Young's leadership, and he thus became the second president of the church, though not officially until 1847.

Receiving an ultimatum from the state of Illinois that the Mormons had to leave, Young immediately gathered a group of followers and headed west on a long, hard trek through the Rocky Mountains. The journey began in February of 1846. In June of 1847 the company of wagons arrived at the Salt Lake Valley, and it was here that Young declared, "This is the place!" Here the Mormon church would finally establish itself. Salt Lake City, located ten miles east of the Great Salt Lake, became the headquarters of the church. Over the next several decades, thousands of Mormon converts migrated to Salt Lake City from points east. Young proved to be an ambitious leader as he sent missionaries abroad, chiefly to England and Scandinavia. Many of these converts also came to the Salt Lake Valley, financed through a fund set up by the church.

Young proved to be more administrator than theologian. Unlike Smith, he added very little in the way of dogmatic contributions to the church. It was under his administration, however, that polygamy was formally instituted. Young himself had twenty wives and fathered a total of forty-seven children.

As is the case in all religious movements, however, splinter groups developed. Salt Lake City is today the headquarters of the largest fragment of the Mormon church. A significant minority of Mormons did not acknowledge Young's leadership. They remained behind in Missouri and Illinois under the leadership of Smith's wife Emma and son Joseph III and formed the REORGANIZED CHURCH OF JESUS CHRIST OF LATTER-DAY SAINTS (now called the Community of Christ), with present-day headquarters in Independence, Missouri.

Sidney Rigdon led another splinter group of the Mormon church; he denounced Young's doctrine of polygamy. This group is known as the Bickertonites, named after William Bickerton, a former elder of Sidney Rigdon.

Lyman Wight, an apostle under Joseph Smith, led a third group to Texas. Martin Harris and David Whitmer remained in Kirtland and founded a church. Another movement was led by James Strang, a more recent convert. Strang established a polygamous community of Mormons in Burlington, Wisconsin, in 1844. Declared the "King of Zion" on Beaver Island in Lake Michigan in 1850, Strang was murdered in 1856 by anti-Mormon protestors. This movement became known as Strangites. A final group within Mormonism is the Church of Christ (Temple Lot).

Those Mormons who had left Missouri and Illinois had become embittered by the persecution they were receiving from non-Mormon Gentiles. They were also angry at the U.S. government. They brought their hatreds with them to the Salt Lake basin. It had been Brigham Young's intention all along to lead the Mormons outside the territory of the United States by migrating south into Mexico. The Mexican War (1846–1848) prevented this, however. This anger and bitterness came to a climax in September 1857 when some Arkansas emigrants, passing through Utah on their way to California, were attacked by some Mormons, led by John Doyle Lee, and a band of Paiute Indians at an encampment forty miles from Cedar City. The attackers promised the emigrants safe conduct in exchange for laying down their weapons. As the party of 137 marched south, they were suddenly ambushed, and all but small children were brutally murdered. This became known as the Mountain Meadows Massacre.

Lee was later arrested and executed by the authorities. Juanita Brooks, in her monograph *The Mountain Meadows Massacre* (1950), relates that the Mormon church was in the end forced to excommunicate Lee only after it realized that any attempt to acquit him would bring incrimination on the church and its leadership. That Brigham Young had known about the incident is well documented.[7] The significance of the massacre lay in the fact that the United States immediately stepped up government and troop activity in Utah, bringing an end to Mormon political hegemony. This in turn paved the way for the eventual acceptance of Utah into statehood, once the polygamy problem was removed.

The United States government conducted an intense campaign against the Mormon doctrine of polygamy in the years following the Civil War. The Edmunds Act (1882) required substantial penalties of those caught practicing it. In 1887 the church lost its corporation privileges. The Mormons applied for statehood six times between 1849 and 1887, and each time they were refused. Finally, with pressure rising to insurmountable proportions, President Wilford ▶Woodruff officially abolished polygamy in 1890, clearing the way for Utah to become the forty-fifth state in 1896. It goes without saying, however, that the practice of polygamy did not come to a halt because of religion but because of political and economic survival.

Mormonism has continued to play a prominent role in the expansion of cults and sects throughout the world. After the former Soviet Union relaxed its antireligious laws, Mormons came in droves in an attempt to make Mormons out of formerly atheist Russians. The Mormons maintain a presence in many countries throughout the world. In May 1989, Brigham Young University opened a Jerusalem Center for Near Eastern Studies.

The authors of this volume are presently working on a book that discusses modern-day issues relative to the claims of Mormonism at the onset of the twenty-first century. A reconsideration of the Spaulding Theory (see below), the claim that the American Indian was of European descent, the relationship between Mormonism and the Masonic Lodge, and Mormonism being influenced by ISLAM are all focuses of the most recent concerns of current scholarship.

ORGANIZATION

The hierarchy of the Mormon church became well rooted and was based on the two priesthoods: the Aaronic priesthood and the Melchizedek priesthood. The latter order includes the power of the presidency and governance of the church; officers include apostles, patriarchs, high priests, and elders, the last mentioned being responsible for the spiritual affairs in the church. The temporal affairs are governed by the Aaronic priesthood through the offices of bishop, priest, deacon, and teacher. Three high priests—the president and two counselors—constitute the ▶First Presidency. This body exercises supreme and final authority in all matters of faith, life, and doctrine. The president enjoys the highest power in the church and, according to the church's teachings, passes down the decrees as they are given him by God through the process of continued revelation.

Below the president stands the ▶Council of the Twelve Apostles. The function of this body is to supervise and govern the work of the ▶stakes or geographical regions. The stakes are further broken down into territorial divisions called ▶wards. Another smaller territorial division is called a ▶branch. Currently there are 12,000 wards, 6,000 branches, 1,800 stakes, and 500 larger districts in the United States.

The First ▶Quorum of the Seventy is a group of seventy whose primary responsibility is to direct the evangelistic activities of the church. This body presides over other quorums of seventy, each of which is governed by a president.

Every male Mormon has the privilege of belonging to one of the two priesthoods, provided he is in good standing with the church. One must be twelve years of age to qualify for the Aaronic priesthood and nineteen to be accepted into the Melchizedek priesthood.

Mormons are expected to dedicate two years of their lives to missionary service. Women also participate in this activity, but they are fewer in number. Mormon missionaries raise the support they need from sources outside the church, either from family members or elsewhere.

TEACHINGS

Articles of Faith

"The Articles of Faith of the Church of Jesus Christ of Latter-Day Saints "are set forth as follows:

1. We believe in God, the Eternal Father, and in His Son, Jesus Christ, and in the Holy Ghost.
2. We believe that men will be punished for their own sins, and not for Adam's transgression.
3. We believe that through the Atonement of Christ, all mankind may be saved, by obedience to the laws and ordinances of the Gospel.
4. We believe that the first principles and ordinances of the Gospel are: first, Faith in the Lord Jesus Christ; second, Repentance; third, Baptism by immersion for the remission of sins; fourth, Laying on of hands for the gift of the Holy Ghost.
5. We believe that a man must be called of God, by prophecy, and by the laying on of hands by those who are in authority, to preach the Gospel and administer in the ordinances thereof.
6. We believe in the same organization that existed in the Primitive Church, namely, apostles, prophets, pastors, teachers, evangelists, and so forth.
7. We believe in the gift of tongues, prophecy, revelation, visions, healing, interpretation of tongues, and so forth.
8. We believe the Bible to be the word of God as far as it is translated correctly; we also believe the *Book of Mormon* to be the word of God.
9. We believe all that God has revealed, all that He does now reveal, and we believe that He will yet reveal many great and important things pertaining to the Kingdom of God.
10. We believe in the literal gathering of Israel and in the restoration of the Ten Tribes; that Zion (the New Jerusalem) will be built on the American continent; that Christ will reign personally on the earth; and, that the earth will be renewed and receive its paradisaical glory.
11. We claim the privilege of worshipping Almighty God according to the dictates of our own conscience, and allow all men the same privilege, let them worship how, where, or what they may.
12. We believe in being subject to kings, presidents, rulers and magistrates, in obeying, honoring, and sustaining the law.
13. We believe in being honest, true, chaste, benevolent, virtuous, and in doing good to all men; indeed, we may say that we follow the admonition of Paul—We believe all things, we hope all

things, we have endured many things, and hope to be able to endure all things. If there is anything virtuous, lovely, or of good report or praiseworthy, we seek after these things.

Joseph Smith[8]

Basic to the theology of the Mormon church are the two priesthoods—the lower Aaronic priesthood and the higher Melchizedek priesthood. Authority within the church is conferred through these two priesthoods to each of the officers, from the president on down. Every male member twelve years old and older may participate in the infrastructure of the church. However, before June 1978 the church held that blacks were not eligible to join the priesthood. Mormonism had held throughout its short history that Africans were under a divine curse because of certain failures of this race in premortal existence. This ordinance was revoked in 1978 because of a growing concern that the church was being labeled a racist organization.

Another key foundation of Mormon theology is the doctrine of continued ▸revelation as described in Article 9 in the Articles of Faith (see above). This article is pivotal in Mormon thought, as Mormonism teaches that God continually brings new information to his church. Unlike much of CHRISTIANITY, which holds to a closed canon of Scripture and revelation, the Mormons believe that God continues to reveal new truth as is necessary and on a continual basis. This presupposition allowed for the elevation of the *Book of Mormon* to the level of Word of God alongside the Bible (Art. 8). The King James Version of the Bible is the translation the Mormon church endorses. The Reorganized Church has adopted the ▸Inspired Version as its official translation. This version, written by Smith, was published in 1867, some twenty years after his death. The Utah Mormons have not adopted Smith's translation on the grounds that it was never completed. Some scholars contend, however, that the real reason is that it varies significantly from the KJV and is thus a hindrance to proselytizing efforts.

The Spaulding Theory

In a publication appearing in 1834 titled *Mormonism Unveiled*, it was claimed that before 1821, a Congregational minister named Solomon Spaulding, who lived in Pittsburgh at the time, had published a story called *Manuscript Found*. According to the traditional theory, Sidney Rigdon, Smith's close friend and his "First Counselor" (see above), obtained Spaulding's manuscript and turned it over to Smith, and Smith then

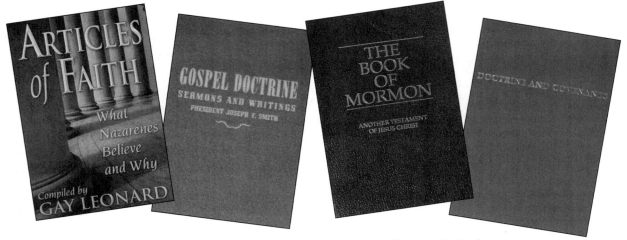

Mormon writings have been placed alongside the Bible as authoritative texts for Mormons.

simply plagiarized large portions of it and produced the Book of Mormon. This, of course, calls a lie to the whole testimony of Moroni, the golden plates, and the inspired nature of the Book of Mormon. Mormon apologists responded to the theory by insisting that there was no proof that Rigdon could have taken the manuscript because he was simply not in Pittsburgh until after 1821. Until recently, there indeed had, in fact, been no proof linking Spaulding to Rigdon.

New evidence, however, has surfaced. Authors Wayne Cowdery, Howard A. Davis, Hugh Lee O'Neal, and Arthur Varnick have conducted extensive research and have produced *The Spaulding Enigma: Who Really Wrote the Book of Mormon?* They note that an eyewitness named Mrs. Rebecca Eichbaum (a postal worker) wrote that she had seen Spaulding and Rigdon together. In the Pittsburgh newspaper called *Commonwealth* a list of names under the heading "List of Letters" included the names of Rigdon and Spaulding. The date of this edition of the newspaper was June 30, 1816. If the authors of *The Spaulding Enigma* are correct, then new ground has been broken that validates the original thesis that the Spaulding Theory was correct.[9]

Another source of authority in the Mormon church is *The Pearl of Great Price*, written by Smith and containing the Articles of Faith. The important doctrines that apply to present-day Mormonism are found in yet another authoritative text called *Doctrine and Covenants*. First published in 1876, it contains 136 sections, 135 of which are said to be revelations by Smith. The last section is a revelation given by Brigham Young. Added to these sections, the current version of *Doctrine and Covenants* contains the famous manifesto of 1890, in which President Woodruff received a revelation that prohibited the continuation of polygamy.

Perhaps the most famous example of the doctrine of continued revelation is the so-called "Word of Wisdom" (*Doctrine and Covenants*, sec. 89). In 1833 Joseph Smith revealed that the Lord had spoken to him, indicating that Mormons are to abstain from wine, strong drink, tobacco, and hot drinks. Moderate consumption of meats is enjoined, and wholesome herbs are recommended for eating. Like the 1890 revelation given to Woodruff, it is more than likely that the times dictated the necessity for the Word of Wisdom. Continued practice of polygamy would have prevented the Mormons from receiving a charter for statehood. The occasion for the Word of Wisdom was the onset of the temperance movement of the early nineteenth century.

In addition to the Bible and the above-named books, the Mormon church also reserves for itself the option of ever-unfolding additional revelations. For the leadership of the church, the president is considered the "seer, revelator, a translator, and a prophet, having all the gifts of God which he bestows on the head of the church" (*Doctrine and Covenants* 107:92). Other members of the priesthood may also receive revelations, but these concern only the sphere of their own ministries. The president is the "revelator" in the matters of faith and doctrine in the church.

What follows is a systematic analysis of the major theological tenets of the Church of Jesus Christ of Latter-Day Saints.

God

In Mormonism God is expressed as Father, as Jesus Christ his Son, and as the Holy Spirit. The Book of Mormon describes God as being one, revealed in the Father, the Son, and the Spirit as being perfect unity (Alma 11:44). But some of Smith's early statements cast a degree of ambivalence on clearer passages like the one just referred to. For example, Smith preached a sermon in 1844 titled "The Christian Godhead—Plurality Godheads," in which he said:

> I will preach the plurality of Gods, . . . I have always declared God to be a distinct personage, Jesus Christ a separate and distinct personage from God the Father, and that the Holy Ghost was a distinct personage and a Spirit. . . . Many men say there is one God; the Father, the Son, and the Holy Ghost are only one God. I say that is a strange God anyhow—three in one and one in three![10]

The Father and the Son both possess bodies. Not only does Jesus have a body of flesh and blood, but so does the Father. This begs the question of gender. In the sermon quoted above, Smith makes the following statement: "Paul says that there are Gods and Lords many." As it turns out, Mormons contend that the Father God of the Bible is a particular god of earth. There are multiple numbers of gods scattered throughout the universe, assigned to various realms. Many Mormon sources make it clear that this is an accepted doctrine of the Latter-Day Saints. This point becomes clearer in the Mormon doctrine of man (see below).

Mormonism departs from historic Christian ▸orthodoxy in its teachings about God. The Christian church has always taught and maintained that God exists in himself apart from creation and that he is one. The Hebrew *Shema*, "Hear, O Israel: the LORD our God, the LORD is one" (Deut. 6:4), is enjoined by the first commandment of the Decalogue (Ex. 20:3–5). God does not share his sovereignty or his divinity with any aspect of the cosmos.

Against Smith's contention that the triune God is "a strange God," the church teaches that the ▸Trinity is indeed a scriptural doctrine. Summarizing such passages as Matthew 28:19; Mark 1:10–11; 2 Corinthians 13:14; and the like, the Athanasian Creed (Appendix 1) states clearly the historic doctrine of the Trinity:

> And the catholic faith is this, that we worship one God in three persons and three persons in one God, neither confusing the persons nor dividing the substance. For there is one person of the Father, another of the Son, and another of the Holy Spirit. But the Godhead of the Father, of the Son, and of the Holy Spirit is all one.[11]

The doctrine of the Trinity is a mystery that is incomprehensible to human reason but has never been regarded as being "strange" or foreign to the teachings of the church.

Dissent has arisen in the Mormon church with respect to what is known as the ▸Adam-God doctrine. In addition to a theology of the Trinity, Mormonism teaches that there is a plurality of gods. Smith continues in the above-quoted sermon: "The doctrine of the plurality of gods is as prominent in the Bible as any other doctrine. It is all over the face of the Bible. It stands beyond the power of controversy. A wayfaring man, though a fool, need not err therein."[12]

Smith goes on to explain that when the Bible speaks of one God, it is one God "pertaining to us." But that does not mean that there are not a plurality of gods throughout the universe. Furthermore, Mormonism teaches that each god is begotten of other gods in succession. God the Father is a superior god because of his particular line of progression in the process.

Perhaps the most widely divergent teaching from that of orthodox Christianity is the Mormon belief that God and the plurality of gods were men before they were gods. One of the often-quoted statements to this effect (resonating the orthodox doctrine of the deity of Christ) was made by Joseph Smith: "God himself was once as we are now, and is an exalted man, and sits enthroned in yonder heavens! . . . He was once a man like us . . . God himself, the Father of us all, dwelt on an earth."[13]

Contrariwise, orthodoxy firmly stands on the doctrine of the eternality and sovereignty of God. For Mormonism, the eternality of God means a prehuman spiritual existence followed by a period of probation in a physical body, and then evolution to a status of godhood once again. The thrust of this idea is that humankind itself is destined to become a god. The widely quoted epigram articulated by Lorenzo Snow, the fifth president of the church, captures this curious and paradoxical equation: "As man is, God once was; as God is, man may become." Numerous other statements by Mormon theologians confirm this teaching.

Jesus Christ

Mormons acknowledge that for Christians, Jesus Christ is certainly the founder of their faith. But they then assert that the great error of Christianity is the lack of unity concerning the person and work of Christ.

Violent variance of opinion is found concerning every part of his ministry and mission, and concerning every essential part of the faith he founded. Salvation itself is at stake in the acceptance or rejection of the various basic doctrines about Christ and his mission, doctrines that often are espoused openly by one body of religionists but shunned and rejected by another.[14]

While it is true that throughout Christian history different thinkers have advanced numerous teachings concerning the person and work of Jesus Christ, the fact of the matter is that by the fourth century, orthodoxy recognized a catholic ᵖChristology embodied in the ecumenical creeds. For both catechetical and apologetical reasons, the church summarized the Bible's teachings of the two natures of Christ at the Council of Chalcedon (A.D. 451), which recognized and refined the church's accepted Christology. There is one Christ, Jesus; yet he possesses two natures, human and divine, which are "inseparable," "indivisible," "unconfused," and "unchanging." Variant Christologies arising within many sects merely repeat many of the motifs of ancient heresies that the church rejected at Chalcedon.

While Mormons argue vehemently for the truth that Jesus was the "son of God," they reject forthrightly the idea that Jesus' divinity implies that he is God, the Son, exclusive of all others. For Mormons, Jesus was God's firstborn, while all others were born at a later time. This is not to imply that before the earthly Jesus was born, no others were yet born. Mormons distinguish Jesus' birth into mortality from his premortal existence. Here, Christ is referred to as being the "firstborn spirit child," based on such passages as Colossians 1:15. Just as Jesus was the firstborn on earth, it is conceivable that other planets have been incarnated by other gods.

Concerning Christ's birth, Christian orthodoxy maintains that Jesus was born of a virgin (Isa. 7:14; Matt. 1:23) and that he was conceived by the Holy Spirit (Matt. 1:18). Brigham Young declared on the one hand that Jesus was born when "the Father came Himself and favoured that spirit with a tabernacle instead of letting any other man do it."[15] In another place, Young states that "Jesus, our elder brother, was begotten in the flesh by the same character that was in the garden of Eden, and who is our Father in heaven"[16] (*see* ᵖAdam-God Doctrine). This latter statement has proved embarrassing to Mormon apologists, and some make bold attempts to deny that Young taught it. In the midst of these ideas, popular Mormon literature states that the Latter-Day Saints do in fact teach the virgin birth, but Young makes no reference to this in the *Journal of Discourses*.

As to the work of Christ, Mormons teach that Jesus is the Savior and Redeemer (see above, Articles of Faith 3 and 4). Numerous passages of Mormon literature confirm this.

> And he also said unto him: If thou wilt turn unto me, and hearken unto my voice, and believe, and repent of all thy transgressions, and be baptized, even in water, in the name of my Only Begotten Son, who is full of grace and truth, which is Jesus Christ, the only name which shall be given under heaven, whereby salvation shall come unto the children of men, ye shall receive the gift of the Holy Ghost, asking all things in his name.[17]

The atonement of Christ affects two different kinds of salvation, *general* and *individual*. General salvation is the salvation granted to all people by virtue of Christ's resurrection from the dead. It simply means that all creatures have been given the gift of immortality. Individual salvation is conditional on adhering to Articles 3 and 4 in the Articles of Faith (see above).

Salvation

"The resurrection of Christ brings to pass the resurrection of all men."[18] This is simply another way of speaking about the general salvation mentioned above. All human beings are resurrected from temporal or physical death. But only those who are obedient to the "laws and ordinances of the gospel" (Art. 3) are resurrected to spiritual life. Mormonism insists, along with traditional Christianity, that the atonement of Christ is necessary for salvation. The Mormon idea of grace lends itself to the idea that God is loving and merciful and that "it is by grace that we are saved" (Eph. 2:8; 2 Nephi 25:23). But Mormonism departs from the Pauline and Protestant concept of grace alone apart from works.

> In addition to this redemption from death, all men, by the grace of God, have the power to gain eternal life. This is called salvation by grace coupled with obedience to the laws and ordinances of the gospel. Hence Nephi was led to write: "We labor diligently to write, to persuade our children, and also our brethren, to believe in Christ, and to be reconciled to God; for we know that it is by grace that we are saved, after all we can do." (2 Nephi 25:23) . . . Salvation in the kingdom of God is available because of the atoning blood of Christ. But it is received only on condition of faith, repentance, baptism, and enduring to the end by keeping the commandments of God.[19]

Evangelical Christians protest vehemently the idea that works or the law play any part in salvation (Eph. 2:8–9). To insist that they do is to nullify the grace of God and render ineffective the atonement of Christ (Gal. 2:21).

The plan of salvation for Mormons has a series of stages. All human beings had a pre-earth life in the spirit, as spirit children of God the Father. They passed through the veil and entered into earthly life, gaining a physical yet mortal body, and during life on earth prove their worthiness to be saved by keeping the commandments and ordinances of the Gospel and God's law. At the time of death, the spirit awaits the general resurrection (2 Nephi 9:12–13; Alma 11:43; Alma 21:9).[20]

Blood Atonement

A discussion of Mormon ▸soteriology cannot omit brief mention of the doctrine of blood atonement from a historical perspective. In 1845 William Smith (Joseph's brother) gave testimony in court that he had to leave Nauvoo because he was fearful for his life. Joseph Smith had been voicing strong objections to the fact that Brigham Young had been teaching a doctrine of blood atonement whereby a "man might be killed to save his soul."[21] In Utah the doctrine of blood atonement was taught openly and regularly. Brigham Young's sermons contained ample references to the doctrine. Jerald and Sandra Tanner recorded them. One reference is as follows:

> There are sins that men commit for which they cannot receive forgiveness in this world, or in that which is to come, and if they had their eyes open to see their true condition, they would be perfectly willing to HAVE THEIR BLOOD SPILT on the ground, that the smoke thereof might arise to heaven as an OFFERING FOR THEIR SINS; and the smoking incense would ATONE for their sins.[22] (emphasis in original)

Numerous sins qualified as being worthy of death (i.e., capital punishment by shedding blood), according to Mormon leaders in the nineteenth century. They included murder, adultery and immorality, stealing, using God's name in vain, resisting the Gospel, marrying a black person, covenant breaking, ▸apostasy, and lying.[23] Mormons deny that this doctrine was ever actually practiced. There is every indication, however, that it was indeed put into practice in the 1850s, but had to be stopped because of the large influx of non-Mormons into Utah. Mormon leaders, however, have continued to insist that the most "humane" form of execution is through the "shedding of blood," that is, firing squad or beheading.

Orthodox Christianity maintains that Christ's blood *alone* was shed for the remission of sins. While it is true that in the Middle Ages, during the Inquisition, many were executed in order to atone for unorthodox convictions, all of Christendom realizes and readily acknowledges that this practice was aberrant and grotesquely out of line with the teachings of Christianity.

Celestial Marriage

For a man and a woman to receive the fullest blessings in the ▸celestial kingdom, they must be married in a Mormon temple. Failure to do so results in a dissolution of the marriage at death, a single life in eternity, and consignment to the lower estate of an angel rather than a god (*Doctrine and Covenants* 132:15–16). Furthermore, all Mormons who have had their marriages signed and sealed in a temple ceremony will be "blessed with an innumerable posterity." Therefore, the most important thing a Mormon can do in this world is "to marry the right person by the right authority in the right place."[24]

For the Christian, marriage is an important part of the order of creation (Gen. 2:23–24; Heb. 13:4). But marriage is not the primal focus or obligation of the Christian with respect to the order of salvation. Jesus Christ becomes the center of faith (1 Cor. 2:2; Apostles' and Nicene creeds, Art. 2, Appendix 1). Marriage is an honorable estate in this life but has no consequence for the life to come (Matt. 22:29–30). The spiritual marriage on which the New Testament places a great deal of emphasis is the spiritual marriage of Christ as the Bridegroom and his church as the bride (Eph. 5:21–33).

Church

As noted above, Joseph Smith believed the church to be in a state of utter corruption before 1830. He was singled out by Moroni to restore purity and truth through the extensive series of new revelations embodied in Mormon sacred literature. Consequently, the Church of Jesus Christ of Latter-Day Saints is the true church of God on earth. All other churches on earth are apostate, and seekers of the truth are commanded to come out from among them.

Christianity makes no such audacious claim. God's true church is not embodied in any one specific organization or denomination. The true (catholic) church consists of the "communion of saints" (Apostles' and Nicene Creeds), who have been "born again" through baptism and who have faith in Jesus Christ. Such are scattered throughout all Christian denominations of the world.

Sacraments

Mormonism teaches that baptism is absolutely necessary for salvation. *Doctrine and Covenants* 84:74 reads as follows:

> Verily, verily, I say unto you, they who believe not on your words, and are not baptized in water in my name, for the remission of their sins, that they may receive the Holy Ghost, shall be damned, and shall not come into my Father's kingdom where my Father and I am.

Mormons consider only baptism by immersion as legitimate. They reject baptism of infants because repentance must precede the rite and because children do not sin.

Baptismal practices vary among Christian denominations, and the doctrines of some parallel Mormonism. For example, Baptists also immerse and baptize only adults. But the Mormon teaching that children do not commit sin is in sharp contrast to the traditional orthodox view. According to Psalm 51:5; Romans 3:23; and ample other passages of Scripture, since Adam (Gen. 2–3), the entire human race has been conceived and born in sin.

Baptism for the Dead

This doctrine, peculiar to Mormons, is described in *Doctrine and Covenants* as being necessary for the salvation of the souls of all who died before the restoration of the true church in 1830 (128:5). Paul alludes to baptism for the dead in 1 Corinthians 15:29, but most Bible scholars believe he was referring to an erroneous practice in the Corinthian church. Interestingly, the Reorganized Church does not practice baptism for the dead, another reason for the Salt Lake Mormons to denounce their Missouri counterparts as damned and corrupt along with the rest of the world's false churches. A baptism in behalf of one who has died must take place in a temple and be witnessed by at least three individuals (*Doctrine and Covenants* 128:3). Because meticulous records are kept of such baptisms, and because the Mormon church is compelled to conduct these baptisms on into the future, the church has accumulated the most complete records of ancestry in the world. Persons researching their family history usually succeed in the Mormon Library and branch libraries scattered throughout the country and world.

The Lord's Supper

The Lord's Supper is a ᵖsacrament. Mormons partake of communion after the age of eight, immediately following baptism, and subsequently celebrate it weekly. Water is used rather than wine, based on a revelation that Smith received stating that the element used is of little consequence. As with baptism, Christian churches vary in their practices of the Lord's Supper. But all traditional churches use either grape juice or wine (fruit of the vine), following the pattern of the Bible (Matt. 26:26–28; Mark 14:25; Luke 22:20; 1 Cor. 10:16; 11:23–24).

Temple Rituals

Detailed rituals surround the various practices conducted in a Mormon temple. Baptism for the dead contains a prescribed ceremony, as does confirmation for the dead, ordination, washing, marriage, the ceremony at the veil, and so on. The various ceremonies are called ᵖendowments. A Mormon who wishes to enter the temple must obtain a "temple recommend" signed by a branch president. Various rules govern the behavior of temple workers and people who enter the temple. Temple garments are worn, certain symbolic gestures are made, and liturgical rites are cited. Members take oaths not to betray the secrets of the temple.

Various reforms have been introduced as dissenting Mormons have protested that the endowment contains inconsistencies.[25] Oaths swearing that betrayal of Mormon secrets is punishable by having throats slashed from ear to ear, tongues torn out, or breasts cut open were modified in the 1990s, and the graphic descriptions of the manners of punishment

The Mormon view of baptism for the dead has produced the most complete genealogical archive in the world (located near Salt Lake City). Courtesy George A. Mather

were removed. Other more recent changes include no longer obligating women to swear an oath of obedience to their husbands and no longer requiring them to veil their faces in the temple. Women, however, are still barred from serving in the priesthood. Non-Mormon priests are no longer regarded as being agents of ▶Satan.[26]

There is little doubt among scholars that Smith's temple rites were borrowed from FREEMASONRY. The endowment ceremonies and the practices of the Masonic lodge are remarkably similar. Smith himself became a Mason in 1842 along with at least twelve hundred Mormons. They quickly adopted many of the Masonic rituals, incorporating them into their own temple rites. For example, in their temple ritual Mormons have adopted the Masonic "five points of fellowship." They are as follows:

> FOR MASONS: He (the candidate) is raised on what is called the five points of fellowship. . . . This is done by putting the inside of your right foot to the inside of the right foot of the person to whom you are going to give the word, the inside of your knee to his, laying your right breast against his, your left hands on the back of each other, and your mouths to each other's right ear (in which position alone you are permitted to give the word), and whisper the word Mahhah-bone. . . . He is also told that Mahhah-bone signifies marrow in the bone.
>
> FOR MORMONS: The five points of fellowship are given by putting the inside of the right foot to the inside of the Lord's, the inside of your knee to his, laying your breast close to his, your left hands on each other's backs, and each one putting his mouth to the other's ear, in which position the Lord whispers: "Lord—'This is the sign of the token: Health to the navel, marrow in the bones.'"[27]

It should be noted that in the above ritual a Mormon role-plays God.

End Times

Mormons believe in the concept of the gatherings (Art. 10 of "The Articles of Faith") of the lost ten tribes and that the new Jerusalem will be built on earth, where Christ will return to reign. Most Mormons believe themselves to be the gathering of Ephraimites, taking place at the present. Mormons also will witness the gathering of the Jews from both Judah and Israel.

During the ▶millennium, two resurrections will take place. As Christ descends to the earth, the righteous will be resurrected to meet the Lord and descend with him.[28] At the beginning of the millennium, the wicked will be destroyed by fire. The spirits of the dead reside in a ▶purgatory or prison house, where they may atone for themselves through suffering. During the peaceful millennium, the central activity will be continued baptism for the dead, led by Jesus Christ himself. When the millennium draws to a close, there will be a second resurrection in which the wicked will be raised. Satan will be released from prison, and the forces of evil will unite in a war against Jesus Christ, who will defeat them, making way for the final judgment. That judgment will see the dissolution of the earth in preparation for eternity. It will be resurrected as a celestial body much like the sun and stars of the universe.

Concerning the final state of humanity, *Doctrine and Covenants* distinguishes four different classes of people. The "sons of perdition" are those who have "suffered themselves through the power of the devil to be overcome, and to deny the truth and defy my power" (76:31). The sons of perdition consist of the devil and his fallen army of demons, and human beings who have committed the unpardonable sin. Only the sons of perdition will be consumed at the second judgment, being destroyed in the lake of fire and overpowered by the "second death" (76:36–38).

Those who are saved will spend eternity in one of three kingdoms. The highest of these is the celestial kingdom, reserved for the righteous and faithful. They will live forever as gods with the spouses they married in a Mormon temple on earth, and they will continue to procreate spirit children throughout eternity.

The second kingdom is called the ▶terrestrial kingdom, located on some specific planet in the universe. To this kingdom will go the less faithful, the lukewarm, and even those who rejected the gospel but again embraced it in the afterlife. This idea parallels the Roman Catholic concept of purgatory. Protestant Christians protest this on several grounds. First, the Bible does not allude to a purgatory in the afterlife where humans have a "second chance." More important, if salvation may be accomplished through self-help in the terrestrial kingdom, then one is no longer saved by the atonement and merits of Jesus Christ but by works.

The third and final kingdom is the ▶telestial kingdom. This kingdom, located on still another planet, is the depository for the remaining souls not inhabiting the celestial or terrestrial kingdoms. These include the lawless and wicked who, after much punishment and suffering at the hands of Satan, will be offered salvation. This last kingdom will be the most heavily populated.

Only Mormons in good standing can enter the magnificent Mormon Temple in Salt Lake City, the headquarters for the Church of Jesus Christ of Latter Day Saints. © Mark E. Gibson/CORBIS

CONCLUSION

The Church of Jesus Christ of Latter-Day Saints is active and growing throughout the world. Factors largely responsible for this include the widespread appeal to traditional morality, a high birthrate, and an emphasis on a return to family values. The popular image of the church is positively portrayed in advertising. Commercials featuring celebrities and campaigns against drugs, smoking, and alcohol are commonly seen on television. The Mormon missionary campaign "dwarfs that of other U.S. churches."[29] It is estimated that over thirty thousand missionaries are sent out around the world. The closest correspondent to that among Christian denominations is the Southern

Baptists, who field almost four thousand missionaries (only 10 percent of Mormon missionary efforts).[30] In 1962 the total reported number of Mormons was 1,965,786. Most lived in the United States. In 1987 the church boasted 6.5 million members, with congregations in nearly one hundred countries. The present world membership is over eight million.

Visitors and tourists are always made to feel welcome at the beautiful temple site in the Salt Lake basin. Mormon tour guides gladly recount the Mormon legacy and hand out ample amounts of free literature. The Mormon Tabernacle Choir performs worldwide.

The Mormon church is an extremely wealthy organization and is growing wealthier. The *U.S. Catholic* reported in 1989 that the annual income of the church is about two billion dollars. Seventy-five percent of this income is generated by tithes from church members. The remaining support comes from church-owned business enterprises, which include the following:

> *Deseret News*, a daily newspaper in Salt Lake City; the Beneficial Life Insurance Co.; two TV stations; six radio stations; hotels; about one million acres of ranch land and farmland around the country; department stores and shopping malls; office buildings; bookstores and publishing firms; factories; and holdings in utilities and major corporations, such as IBM, Exxon, and AT&T. It is no exaggeration to state that the Mormon church is the dominant financial institution in the Rocky Mountain area and ranks as the wealthiest church per capita in the U.S.[31]

Mormonism has become one of the significant cultural and intellectual facets of American religious life. An important historian of American religious history, the late Sydney Ahlstrom, concluded:

> With attractive edifices on Brattle Street in Cambridge, Massachusetts, and in many other cities and suburbs, and with a reputation for conservatism in both personal ethics and social policy, Mormons sometimes appear to have become another white middle-class denomination with obvious Yankee origins. Yet they remain a people apart, bound to a very distinctive tradition that was brought into the world by a most unusual man. Their inner intellectual and spiritual problems cannot easily be shared with others. The problem of history—in the Book of Mormon itself and as it pertains to the people of that book since 1830—has been especially acute; and the fact of contradictory interpretations is inescapably felt by every historian. In retrospect, nevertheless, the Mormons can be likened to a fast-

growing hardwood towering above the sectarian underbrush of the burnt-over district: a witness to the possible social potency of prophetic religious ideas. Interpreted in detail, the movement yields innumerable clues to the religious and social consciousness of the American people.[32]

ADDITIONAL INFORMATION

Headquarters
Temple Square, Salt Lake City, Utah.

Websites
www.mormon.org; www.utlm.org

Sacred Texts
The Book of Mormon; *Doctrine and Covenants*; *The Pearl of Great Price*; The Bible. Other study aids include a Bible dictionary and other writings that Mormons refer to.

Periodicals
Liahona; Ensign; New Era; Friend; Deseret News

Membership Statistics
Total Church membership (A.D. 2000) is 11,068,861. Full-time missionaries are 60,784; 34 new temples were dedicated in 2000. Converts baptized in 2000: 273,973. Increase in the Children of Record over the same period: 81,450. The number of stakes: 2,581; districts: 621; missions: 334; wards and branches: 25,915.

Notes
[1] Joseph Smith, *The Pearl of Great Price* (Salt Lake City: Church of Jesus Christ of Latter-Day Saints, 1951), 47.

[2] Ibid., 48.

[3] Fawn Brodie, *No Man Knows My History* (New York: Knopf, 1957), 29–33.

[4] Jerald and Sandra Tanner, *Mormonism, Shadow or Reality*, 5th ed. (Salt Lake City: Utah Lighthouse Ministry, 1987), 32.

[5] Smith, *The Pearl of Great Price*, 55–56.

[6] Ibid., 56.

[7] Tanner, *Mormonism*, 493–515. The documentation the Tanners offer is detailed and well researched.

[8] James E. Talmage, *The Articles of Faith* (Salt Lake City: The Church of Jesus Christ of Latter-Day Saints, 1974).

[9] See Wayne Cowdrey, Howard Davis, Hugh Leo O'Neal, and Arthur Vanick, *The Spaulding Enigma: Who Really Wrote the Book of Mormon?* (Manhattan Beach, Calif.: Digital Voice), 2000 (CD-ROM ed.).

[10] "The Christian Godhead—Plurality of Gods," a sermon preached on June 16, 1844; quoted in Anthony Hoekema, *The Four Major Cults* (Grand Rapids: Eerdmans, 1963), 35.

[11] See also ISLAM, CHRISTADELPHIANISM, UNIFICATION CHURCH and HINDUISM for further discussions of the doctrine of the ▸Trinity.

[12] Quoted in Hoekema, *Four Major Cults*, 37.

[13] "King Follet Discourse" (1844). Reproduced in the *Teachings of the Prophet Joseph Smith*, ed. Joseph Fielding Smith (Salt Lake City: Deseret, 1958), 345–46.

[14] *What Mormons Think of Jesus Christ* (Salt Lake City: Church of Jesus Christ of Latter-Day Saints, 1982), 2.

[15] John A. Widstoe, ed., *Discourses of Brigham Young* (Salt Lake City: Deseret, 1954); from Young's *Journal of Discourses* (1901), 4:218.

[16] Ibid., vol. 1, pp. 50–51.

[17] Smith, *The Pearl of Great Price*, 18.

[18] *What Mormons Think of Jesus Christ*, 17.

[19] Ibid., 18–19.

[20] The Book of Mormon, trans. by Joseph Smith (Salt Lake City, 1986).

[21] Tanner, *Mormonism*, 398.

[22] Ibid.

[23] Ibid., 402–3.

[24] Bruce McConkie, *Mormon Doctrine* (Salt Lake City: Bookcraft, 1958), 111.

[25] See, e.g., the pamphlet *A Mormon Temple Worker Asks Some Questions*, written by an ex-Mormon temple worker named Charles Sackett. The pamphlet is available by request from "Saints Alive in Jesus," P.O. Box 1076, Issaquah, WA 98027.

[26] "The Mormon Gender Gap," *U.S. News and World Report* (May 14, 1990), 14.

[27] Tanner, *Mormonism*, 486.

[28] Hoekema, *Four Major Cults*, 69.

[29] William J. Whalen, "Why Mormonism Is the Fastest Growing Region in the West," *U.S. Catholic* (June 1989), 33.

[30] Ibid.

[31] Ibid.

[32] Sydney Ahlstrom, *A Religious History of the American People*, 2 vols. (Garden City, NY: Image, 1975), 1:613–14.

MYAL

Myal is an Afro-Jamaican ▸cult whose beginning is uncertain. It was originally composed exclusively of males. The Myal cult imported its religious traditions from West Africa, most likely from the Ashanti people of Togo and the Ivory Coast. The British and the Dutch carried the blacks from this region to the West Indies during the slave trade. Whatever the origin of Myal, there are vital links between Myal ritual and ▸obeah, that is, groups practicing VOODOO who worship supernatural spirits and forces. The Ashanti people to this day conceive of the world as being a place inhabited by a pantheon of gods, spirits, and spirits of ancestors who can be contacted through dance ritual.

Like the many other movements imported from West Africa, the Myal cult contains a syncretistic blend of a variety of native religious practices and African rituals. The pantheistic (see ▸pantheism) orientation of these people has made it difficult for Christian missionaries to impact them with the message of a monotheistic God who has revealed himself in the person of Jesus Christ.

Where CHRISTIANITY has gained acceptance, it has been commonplace to find the God of Christianity sharing dominion with a host of other deities.[1]

ADDITIONAL INFORMATION

Note

[1] For additional comparisons/contrasts between SOUTH AMERICAN, CENTRAL AMERICAN, AND CARIBBEAN CULTS, see VOODOO and SANTERIA.

NATION OF ISLAM; NOI

Also called the World Community of Ali Islam in the West, the Black Muslim Movement [BMM], and the Nation of Peace. The Nation of Islam movement was born with an objective to urge and encourage black Americans, who were socially and economically deprived in urban ghettos, to overcome their plight by instilling in them a strong sense of black pride. The parent religion of the NOI is ISLAM. This article specifically treats the NOI, but there are several other prominent black Muslim movements in America and abroad, such as the Islamic Society of North America and the Muslim American Society.

HISTORY

Two prominent black leaders arose in the early 1900s before the organization of the Nation of Islam. The most vocally aggressive of these two was Timothy Drew. He founded the Moorish Science Temple of America in 1913 in Newark, New Jersey, resulting in his followers calling him Noble Drew Ali. He taught that the black race was of Moorish origin, so that black people in America should identify with the cultural and religious beliefs of Islam. Drew's organization was a major forerunner to the activism of the later Black Muslim Movement. The other noteworthy leader was Marcus Garvey (1887–1940). In 1914 he found the Universal Negro Improvement Association; it too gave a major impetus to ensuing NOI.[1]

The NOI began with the efforts of Wallace ▸Fard (1877–1934). Fard was born in Mecca and raised as a Muslim. He migrated to the United States in 1930 and founded the Temple of Islam in Detroit in 1931. Immediately, Fard began to propagate the teachings of Islam, but with a new twist. Blacks, he said, were eventually to confront whites in race war; that would result in the restoration of the black race to dominion and supremacy. CHRISTIANITY was a white religion and used by whites to oppress blacks. Fard gave his followers Arabic names to replace their present "white" names. In 1934 Fard mysteriously disappeared and was not heard from again. The followers of Fard believed he was the incarnation of ▸Allah, and members of the NOI celebrate his birthday (February 26) as "Saviour's Day."

Elijah ▸Poole (1897–1975) succeeded Fard and was renamed Elijah ▸Muhammad. He founded the Nation of Islam in 1934 and established the second temple, this one in Chicago. As the movement grew over the next decade, ▸mosques and Islamic centers were built in every major city where large numbers of blacks resided.

Muhammad, in the mold of Fard, continued to argue that blacks were racially superior to whites, the latter of whom he referred to as "devils" who resulted from a black scientist's mad genetic experiment. Eventually, blacks would overthrow the inferior white race.

The most articulate spokesman for the NOI at the time was ▸Malcolm X (1925–1965), one of Elijah Muhammad's devoted followers. He did much to stir the passions of the black youth with his charisma. Because of factionalism, Malcolm split from the main group and founded the Muslim Mosque, Inc. Disagreement between the two groups grew violent, and Malcolm took a sabbatical leave abroad. Witnessing an entirely different culture where whites and blacks lived in relative harmony resulted in a complete attitude change in the forceful leader, who previously had denounced racial integration, nonviolence, and the existence of black Christian churches. After returning to the United States, he began espousing a much more ameliorated approach. This ignited the anger of his former followers, and he was assassinated by gunmen in 1965.

Next in the succession of leaders was Elijah Muhammad's son, Wallace Deen Muhammad. Following his father's death in 1975, he broke away from the NOI and formed the Muslim American Society. Under his leadership the MAS made radical changes, more in line with the direction Malcolm X desired following his return to the United States. Wallace Deen Muhammad denounced the racism of the movement and rejected the tendency to worship Fard as the incarnation of Allah. Islam, as it was practiced by the orthodox followers of 'Muhammad (the originator of Islam), was introduced.

Another radical black group is the Hanafi Madh-Hab Center, founded by Hammas Abdul 'Khaalis in 1968. Khaalis rose to the rank of national secretary of the Nation of Islam in 1956, but a study of the doctrines of Islam convinced him that orthodox Islam was the correct expression of the Koran and that Muhammad was Allah's true prophet, not the American Elijah Muhammad.[2]

In 1972 Khaalis moved the headquarters from New York City to Washington, D.C., into facilities provided by basketball star Kareem Abdul-Jabbar.[3] Tragedy struck one year later when seven Hanafi members were slain. Five members of the Nation of Islam were accused of the murders, and were convicted in court. Further trouble came in 1977 when Khaalis and eleven associates took control of three buildings in Washington and held a number of people as hostages for thirty hours. One of the Hanafi Muslims, Abdul Musikir, murdered a reporter, Maurice Williams. All twelve were arrested. Khaalis issued a warning that if a film titled *Muhammad, the Messenger of God* was shown, more violence would erupt. Khaalis was convicted for his involvement in the murder of the reporter and sentenced to serve from 41 to 120 years in prison. This murderous event of 1977 greatly minimized the future influence of Hanafi Muslims.

The NOI since 1978 has been headed by Louis 'Farrakhan (b. 1933), who before he changed his name was Louis Eugene Walcott. He once was an understudy of Malcolm X in the 1960s. He has been trying to maintain the original doctrines of the movement. His organization rejects saluting the American flag, voting, and registering for the selective service, and it advocates a separate nation in the United States for blacks. Given the introduction of Farrakhan's "power" concept in 1985, it rejects the policy of peaceful nonresistance in achieving civil rights progress that Martin Luther King Jr. so successfully advocated.

In 1995, Farrakhan was instrumental in organizing what was called the "Million Man March" in Washington, D.C., which was an effort to convey a message to males that they should repent of their sins and consider their responsibility to God, wives, family, and workplace. As positive an effort as the march was, there were problems posed by the sheer fact that it was Farrakhan who was leading it. Some black religious leaders refused to endorse the effort because Farrakhan had just issued a statement containing negative sentiments about Jews, Koreans, and Vietnamese as being "bloodsuckers." Also, because women were not invited to the march, many considered it to be sexist. Nevertheless, it was indeed a successful effort in terms of some changes it made in some lives, and a greater black participation in voting also resulted.

On February 25, 2000, a date marking the twenty-fifth anniversary of the death of Elijah Muhammad, Farrakhan met with Wallace Deen Muhammad, resulting in the reconciliation between the Nation of Islam and the Muslim American Society. On September 16, 2001, Farrakhan issued a strong address condemning the terrorist attacks on the World Trade Center on September 11. In April 2003, Farrakhan celebrated his seventieth birthday by launching a prostate cancer foundation. He had himself been battling with prostate cancer for several years. Most recently he suggested that a levee protecting New Orleans was purposely blown up to flood a black neighborhood during Hurricane Katrina in 2005.

ORGANIZATION

In the United States, the NOI is divided geographically into seven regions. The many mosques are called "Muhammad Mosques" and are accompanied by a number. For example, the Central Regional Headquarters is located in Chicago and is called Muhammad Mosque No. 2. The spiritual leader of a mosque center is called a minister. Chicago is also home to the National Center and the NOI's national headquarters. The NOI maintains an active presence on both radio and television, has a student association called the Nation of Islam Student Association (NOISA), and owns Muhammad Farms, where food is grown and distributed to the needy.

TEACHINGS

The basic religious teachings of the NOI stem from Islam. Changes and/or contributions to the religion of Muhammad have been introduced by each of the personalities who came to the forefront of leadership in the movement. The obvious mark of distinction has been the racial concerns that gave the NOI its initial impetus. Historically, this racial emphasis can best be understood within the context of the socio-economic-cultural status of blacks in the United States, especially before the 1960s, when black Americans were largely second-class citizens. It was within this context, not from any influences of the Christian religion but contrary to its teachings, that NOI assumed its racist posture in reaction to racism in America. The NOI is also anti-Semitic.

There are several important differences between NOI teachings and that of its parent religion, Islam. For example, on the Koran, there are varying interpretations. *Orthodox Muslims hold that the Koran is the final revelation of Allah. Members of the NOI believe this to varying degrees but then add to it the belief that the NOI predates the time of Muhammad and the *Bible.

Muslims believe that Allah is wholly other and transcends space and time; NOI adherents believe that Wallace Fard was an incarnation of Allah. While orthodox Islam upholds the belief that the Koran is Allah's final revelation to the human race and to Muslims in particular, NOI adherents believe in the possibility of continued revelation in the person of Elijah Muhammad.

While it is true that many adherents of the NOI have moved beyond the narrow boundaries of racial identity, the fact remains that the NOI developed historically as a movement that believes in the superiority of the black race. Islam, by contrast, upholds the belief that its mission is to all people of every nation.

Traditional Christianity teaches that the one true God has revealed himself in the divine context of the *Trinity, and that Jesus Christ is the second person of the Godhead. The reader should consult Islam for additional comparisons/contrasts.

CONCLUSION

Farrakhan maintains an active speaking schedule, and one can access many of his statements and sermons on the Nation of Islam website. Recent years have seen attempts to build bridges between Black Muslims, who had previously been divided. Farrakhan has been active and vocal in a number of important issues, including the need to end the ever-escalating violence and war in the Middle East.

The problem of racism is an issue that the NOI must continue to face within its ranks. In traditional Christianity, God is not a respecter of persons. All people are created by God, and salvation is available for all people on the basis of Christ's death (John 3:16).

ADDITIONAL INFORMATION

Headquarters
National Center of the NOI—Mosque Maryam, 7351 Stony Island Ave., Chicago, IL 60649.

Website
www.noi.org

Sacred Text
The Koran

Publication
The Final Call (available online)

Statistics
As of 2005, it has been estimated that there are about 200,000 members.

Notes
[1] See RASTAFARIANISM.
[2] J. Gordon Melton, *The Encyclopedia of American Religion*, 2 vols. (Wilmington, NC: McGrath, 1978), 2:342.
[3] Ibid.

NATION OF YAHWEH; CHURCH OF LOVE; BLACK HEBREW ISRAELITES

The Nation of Yahweh is a controversial religious group that developed in the United States in the last several decades.

HISTORY

This movement was founded in 1979 by Yahweh Ben *Yahweh, originally named Hulon Mitchell Jr. He believed and taught that blacks are the true Jews and it was his calling to lead blacks out of oppression experienced in America and elsewhere back to the "Promised Land," meaning Israel. All of his followers were expected to relinquish their "slave" names and were given Hebrew names, all ending in the word "Israel." His following and financial base grew, and in 1980 he built his "Temple of Love" in Miami, Florida. Members were required to work full time and give their possessions and money to the temple.

Businesses were started inside the temple, including

a bakery, print shop, grocery store, and beauty salon. In 1982, changes came rapidly. Mitchell announced to the group that he was the son of God. Members were required to wear robes and turbans and to renounce their biological families. Members moved into the temple and tight security was kept. Mitchell appointed a "Circle of Ten" bodyguards to be posted around him for security. Any intruders into the temple were threatened with death. Mitchell appointed a female member of the group, Linda Gaines, to be his personal aid. She had a bodyguard and much control over the financial affairs of the temple. By 1985 several more temples were established in other cities.

Mitchell, typical of an extremist ᵇcult leader, demanded complete and total loyalty of the members of the group. Dissenters to his doctrines and laws received ridicule and beatings. Terrified members followed his bidding, even swearing their willingness to die for him and to kill at his command. As his power and influence continued to grow throughout the decade of the 1980s, his vicious racism and hatred for the white race became a constant theme of his emotional tirades. He called America a haven for the enemies of the God Yahweh. Not only was it his mission to lead blacks back to Israel, but this now grew into a mission to chase all white people from the face of the earth by killing them. This was Yahweh's will.

A group within the group, known as the Brotherhood, became the inner sanctum. It was within this group that orders to murder were issued and carried out in the Miami area. In order to become a member of the Brotherhood, one had to kill a white person and bring proof of the kill to Mitchell. Members who carried out a murder were called "Death Angels." The Death Angels also murdered blacks who interfered in any way with the work of the "Church of Love." In 1990 Mitchell and sixteen of his followers were arrested in Miami under charges known as "Racketeering Influenced Corrupt Organization" (RICO). In January, 1996, Mitchell and seven members of the group were convicted of eighteen charges of racketeering, including murders and attempted murders. Mitchell was sentenced to eighteen years in prison.

In July, 2001, it was reported the Mitchell would probably be released because of liberal federal regulations and technicalities with respect to his parole. This happened on September 25, 2001, two weeks following the September 11 terrorist attack on the World Trade Center. Interestingly enough, in the two weeks before his release, he was placed in solitary confinement because he was considered to be a terrorist. After his release, ben Yahweh's followers were able to secure a home for him, where he began to live by himself. His daughter, Venita Mitchell, issued a statement that it is no longer true that members of the group hate whites, but that all human beings are children of God.

BELIEFS

The members of the group believe the following:

- Yahweh ben Yahweh is the Son of God. He is now referred to as the "Grand Master of the Celestial Lodge," "Architect of the Universe," and the "Blessed and Only Potentate."
- The black race is the true Israel of God (also now repudiated by the group).
- Yahweh himself is black and so was Jesus Christ.
- Total obedience to Yahweh and his appointed son, Yahweh ben Yahweh.
- The ᵇBible is the exclusive Word of God.
- The inculcation of morality and the "love of moral men."
- The love for learning.
- Respect for the government.

The group refers to the "crucifixion" as the arrests and imprisonment of Yahweh ben Yahweh and the other seven members of the group along with the lying, the injustice, and the mistreatment throughout the prison ordeal.

Traditional CHRISTIANITY teaches that Jesus Christ alone is the true and incarnate Son of God (John 1). God promised Abraham that in his seed, all the nations of the earth would be blessed (Gen. 13–17). On the Day of Pentecost (Acts 2), Peter stood up and announced that "this promise" (Acts 2:39) was fulfilled. The occasion for this fulfillment was the coming of the Holy Spirit to pilgrims from many nations, who were present at that time. Yahweh, Jesus teaches, is a "spirit, and those who worship him must worship in spirit and in truth" (John 4:24).

Christianity teaches that God loves the world (John 3:16), not just "moral men." Sin has rendered all of humanity as guilty and accountable to God. It was the atonement of Jesus Christ that makes it possible for a person to place all trust on Christ.

CONCLUSION

Ever since ben Yahweh's release from prison, the group has been attempting to expose the perceived injustice on the part of the US government, particularly the FBI.

ADDITIONAL INFORMATION_____
Official Website
www.yahwehbenyahweh.com/

Sacred Text
The Bible.

Total Membership
Undetermined.

Note
[1] See *http://yahwehbenyahweh.com/index02.htm*

NATIVE AMERICAN RELIGION

Given the recent American accent on multiculturalism, college textbooks on world religions now commonly feature a chapter on the religion of Native Americans. The following discussion briefly highlights some of the more prominent elements of Native American religious beliefs and practices.

HISTORY

One of the first things one notices in studying the religious beliefs and practices of Native Americans (especially before the Europeans arrived on the continent) is that they were an amorphous and varied people, consisting of more than three hundred tribes in North and Central America alone. Thus, they have many different religious beliefs and practices, so that there never has been, nor is there now, one common Native American religion.

Since the first European contact in the 1490s, some Native Americans have adopted some Christian beliefs and practices, most often those of Roman Catholicism. The few Christian beliefs that were adopted were often syncretized and adapted to pagan beliefs or practices of given tribes. The present discussion, however, focuses on religious beliefs and rituals that are non-Christian (pagan) in nature and thus in most instances hark back to the time before the arrival of the Europeans in America.

ORGANIZATION

The great variations in Native American religious beliefs and practices, along with the nomadic nature of the one-time Native American culture, have resulted in virtually no formal religious organizations. Native American religion has been, and still is, mostly an amorphous phenomenon. One prominent exception is the Native American Church of North America, organized in Oklahoma City in 1918. This organization has no professional clergy. The NACNA has some eighty chapters and represents some seventy Native American nations. Its current membership (2003) stands at about 250,000. Its president resides in Osseo, Wisconsin, which evidently is its headquarters.

TEACHINGS/BELIEFS

▶Animism

Since there were so many Native American tribes, certain religious beliefs and customs present in some tribes were not found in other tribes. Some religious elements or beliefs, however, were common and widespread. The belief in animism was one such belief. Animism is the belief in a spiritual force that some people believe manifests itself in all natural phenomena and potentially is present at all times. Different Native American tribes often gave animism different names. For instance, the Aleuts called it *agudar*, the Lakotas (Sioux) named it *wakan*, the Iroquois saw it as *orenda*, the Kwakiutl said *nauala*, and the Algonquins labeled it as *manitou*.

For example, when an Iroquois hunter was successful in slaying a deer, it was because he had more *orenda* in his favor. If he failed, it was result of the deer having had more *orenda* in its favor. Some tribes (e.g,. the Lakotas) envisioned a type of supreme being by the name of *Wakan Tanka* (Great Spirit), but in other tribes (e.g., the Algonquins), this concept was not present.

In contrast to biblical CHRISTIANITY, animism, although seen as a spiritual force, is unlike the force and influence of the Holy Spirit, who in the ▶Bible is revealed as one of the three persons in the ▶Trinity. Biblically speaking, the Holy Spirit does not reside in natural phenomena as the believers in animism hold. Unlike biblical Christianity, animism also does not teach that the spirit is able to convert, guide, comfort, and lead people to seek and follow God's truth, as Christ said: "When the Counselor comes, whom I will send from the Father, the Spirit of truth who goes out from the Father, he will testify about me" (John 15:26).

Sun Dance

The Plains Indians (Blackfeet, Lakotas, Pawnee, Crows, Kiowas, Poncas, Cheyenne, and others) had the social institution of the sun dance, which usually took place in early summer. Each dancer (a young man) had his flesh on each side of his chest skewered. Then from each of the two skewers (wooden pegs), punctured through the muscular part of his chest, a long, raw leather rope was tied near the top of a tall wooden pole, especially erected for this ritual. Tribal members, who came from various directions, surrounded the pole and the dancer, enjoying every moment of this ceremonial event. Leaning backward so that the ropes were taut, the young man would dance three to four days as he looked up in the direction of the sun to a sacred bundle perched on top of the pole. The pole, pointing to the sky, symbolized the supreme deity; it was also seen as the axis of the earth. During the dance, the young man did not receive rest, food, or water in the scorching heat, all of which eventually produced hallucinations before the two pegs tore through the flesh and brought the torturous ordeal to an end. Among the Blackfoot Indians, for example, sun dance hallucinations were seen as sacred manifestations, and the mutilated chest wounds with their ragged pieces of flesh were trimmed and laid at the base of the pole for an offering to the sun. Presiding at these torturous ceremonies was a shaman' (medicine man), a sacred leader.

In 1884, the United States officially condemned and banned all sun dances. In the 1930s some of these dances reportedly came back into being, and in recent years, with the promotion of multiculturalism in the United States, sun dances are taking place once again among some of the Indians on the Plains. Reportedly, these revived dances now are performed in a more civilized manner, that is, without piercing the dancer's chest.[1]

The perceived sacred manifestations, produced by the lack of water, food, and hot sun, are a noteworthy contrast to the Christian understanding of God's sacred manifestations, which he has given in his inspired Word (the Bible) and most significantly in his Son Jesus Christ. As Paul wrote: "Great is the mystery of godliness; God was manifest in the flesh" (1 Tim. 3:16). In short, God's sacred manifestations are given to his people not through their mutilating their bodies but

Kachina doll (coyote—American Indian devil)   Jack M. Roper/CARIS

through faith in the gracious acts of his saving revelation in the life, death, and resurrection of his Son Jesus Christ.

Shaman (Medicine Man)

Although the roles of the shaman, commonly known as the medicine man, varied from tribe to tribe, all Native Americans had these functionaries, who essentially combined religious and medicinal practices. Typically, a medicine man wore a grotesque mask, used rattles and bells, and carried sticks on which he had carved spirit images. He was powerful, respected, and also feared. Some of his practices were repulsive and abhorrent—for instance, his displaying a shriveled hand of a dead person in some of his incantations. Accompanied by drums and monotonic singing, the shaman led dances, most of which were complicated and highly esoteric. He also smoked tobacco from a sacred calumet (peace pipe). His incantations were directed to the spirit world, seeking to fend off ills or to bring about some good omen.

Although from the biblical and Christian perspective the medicine man's acts can only be called pagan hocus-pocus, they were often received with considerable credulity by the Native American populace, especially when some of his prescribed herbs and diets at times produced some beneficial effects.[2] Here Christians need to remember that the devil, as the Bible shows, can sometimes appear as the angel of light, even performing signs and wonders (Matt. 24:24). But Christ warns his followers not to be deceived by such false manifestations. Instead, he tells Christians to abide by his Word: "If you hold to my teaching, you are really my disciples. Then you will know the truth, and the truth will set you free" (John 8:31–32).

Totemism

Another religious belief among Native Americans is the concept of totem worship (totemism). The word "totem" comes from the word *ototeman* of the Ojibwa tribe, who, like other Native Americans, believed there was a spiritual bond between human beings and animals, as well as birds. The animal or bird was the totem, which had animistic religious significance. One tribe or clan would adopt the fox as its totem, another took the bear, others identified with the eagle, and still others saw the buffalo as their totem. The totem also represented the tribe vis-à-vis other tribes. Each tribe's totem was honored by specialized religious rituals, and the totem was sacred and revered. Thus, a totemic animal or bird was not to be killed, except in self-defense, and only then could it be eaten and only in special sacred ceremonies in which the eating of its flesh enhanced the bonds between the totem and its clan members. In some clans or tribes (e.g., the Omahas), the totem animal or bird could not even be touched by its members.

The well-known French sociologist Emile Durkheim (d. 1917) argued that each Indian clan worshiped its totem, and since the totem represented the clan, the clan (society) was unwittingly worshiping itself. Thus, the totem was in essence God.[3] In other words, the social force of the clan (society) treated its own representation as God. This radical conclusion has been called turning Moses on his head, because it states that society (the clan) created God, rather than God having created society. Expressed in another way, Durkheim's thesis says religion is not a social phenomenon; rather, society is a religious phenomenon, meaning that in religion society worships itself.

Regardless of the conception of totemism that may exist, it is at odds with the biblical doctrine of orthodox Christianity, for Christians are commanded to worship God, not man-made objects or symbols representing themselves. The Scriptures say: "Do not worship any other god, for the LORD . . . is a jealous God" (Ex. 34:14).

Peyote Worship

A number of Indian tribes (Oto, Navajo, Apache, Comanche, Cheyenne, Arapaho, and some others), largely in the southwestern United States, have, especially since the 1890s, sought euphoric religious experiences by eating the dried "buttons" taken from the top of a small cactus plant known as peyote. Sometimes the peyote "buttons" are made into tea to drink. Whether chewed, eaten, or drunk, the peyote ingredients may induce hypnotic behavior as well as "visions," which now are reportedly rare, given that peyote ceremonies are more structured as a result of their being under the direction of the NACNA. According to Jay Fikes, members of this organization see peyote as a gift from God.[4]

In some instances, peyote worshipers have syncretistically incorporated a certain amount of Christian symbolism in their religious gatherings. Some tribes use the Bible and the name of Jesus in an eclectic manner, and sometimes even the crucifix is displayed. This is particularly true with regard to Indians who are part of the NACNA. Its leaders say that their church is "a new patch in the American quilt of Christianity [and] peyote [is] their 'sacrament,' just as wine or grape juice [is] the sacrament for white Christian brothers."[5] The NACNA has become the mother church of the peyote cultists, who contend that the use of peyote enables them to communicate with God whose spirit they say is infused in the world of nature. This latter belief is consistent with the belief in animism (similar to pantheism) that is so common among most Native Americans. Any Christian symbolism that the peyotists use is contaminated by the pagan belief in animism, along with other non-Christian elements and practices found in the NACNA.

Peyote meetings do not occur on any regular schedule, and when they take place, many peyotists assemble in tepees and some in churches (often in polygonal houses), wherein they sit cross-legged with no back rest, commonly for twelve hours or more. Unlike so many Native Americans, who have abused and misused alcohol, peyotists spurn the use of all alcohol. No one can become and remain a peyote worshiper unless he is teetotaler.

To orthodox Christianity, the pursuit of the peyotists is contrary to God's will, for he does not approve of his people seeking spiritual enlightenment in induced substances, even when such substances are linked with the Lord's Supper. When Christ instituted the Lord's Supper, he told the disciples "Do this in remembrance of me" (Luke 22:19). By "this" he did not leave room for new additions or innovations to his sacred supper.

Kiva Activities

In the southwestern United States, the Pueblo Indians (primarily the Hopi and Zuni), since about A.D. 750 used underground chambers called *kivas*. While these subterranean chambers largely served as sacred places for religious gatherings, occasionally they also were used for council meetings. *Kivas* were, and to some extent still are, seen as sacred houses by the Zuni and Hopi Indians. Some *kivas* are above ground; some circular and some rectangular. In the center of the *kiva's* earthen floor is a hole called *sipapu;* it is the reputed opening to the underworld, which religiously symbolizes the womb of Mother Earth from which humanity emerged. The *sipapu*, covered by a stone, is in certain Hopi ceremonies danced and stomped on vigorously so that the dead will be aroused. After a certain amount of stomping, the stone is removed so that the dead can ascend to participate in initiation rituals for young males. The Hopi also use the *kiva* for certain fertility rites, such as blessing ears of seed corn that are laid on an altar.

Virtually all *kiva* ceremonies, especially those of a religious nature, are conducted in secret by men, and hence they are often referred to as men's houses. Among the Hopi, women and children are allowed only to enter the *kiva* on solstice days.

Kiva activities are far removed from the biblical teachings of Christianity. They bear no acceptable resemblances to anything that God wants his people to practice or follow. God does not approve of people using sacred facilities, such as places of worship, to attempt to arouse the dead or to practice pagan fertility rites. When speaking about his presence in a place of worship, God had Habakkuk declare to his people: "The LORD is in his holy temple, let all the earth be silent before him" (Hab. 2:20).

ADDITIONAL INFORMATION

Website
http://www.well.com/user/dpd/nachurch.html

Notes
[1] Some of the sun dance information is from Jeffrey Brodd, "Sun Dance," *World Religions: A Voyage of Discovery* (Winona, MN: St. Mary's, 1998), 32–33.
[2] Some of the information is taken from Monroe Heath, "Religion," in his *Our Native Americans* (Pacific Coast Publishers, 1961), 11.
[3] Emile Durkheim, *The Elementary Forms of the Religious Life* (New York: Free Press, 1965).
[4] "A Brief History of the Native American Church"; see (*www.Csp.org/communities/docs/fikes-nac_history.html*).
[5] Garrett Epps, *To An Unknown God* (New York: St. Martin's, 2001), 63.

NEW AGE MOVEMENT

This volume is almost entirely devoted to specific organized religions of the world. The New Age Movement stands out as an exception in that it is not represented by any one particular organization, institution, ᐟsect, or cult. This is not to say, of course, that there are not particular religious organizations that may properly be called New Age for reasons delineated below. This volume does include several of these specific organizations.[1] But as a movement, and a popular one at that, it is only possible, within the confines of this volume, to attempt to define it, outline its basic parameters, and make some basic comparisons between its ideology and that of traditional CHRISTIANITY.

HISTORY

The amount of literature classified as being new age is voluminous.[2] The 1970s through 1990s saw a phenomenal growth in advocates, literature, and interest in New Age Movement ideology. Many have attempted to define it and, indeed, have offered a variety of definitions and/or models.

During the heyday of the countercultural revolution in the 1970s, a new social order began to emerge. A basic redefinition of morality and a genuine "transvaluation of values" was underway. This was, for such countercultural ideologies, the beginning of the "age of ᐟAquarius."

The "God is dead" movement of the 1960s had descended from the ivory towers of theological reflection within the university divinity schools, religion departments, and seminaries onto the streets. It was not so much a theology as it was a general attitude that was ripe for the shaping by such other intellectual movements as ᐟexistentialism, Marxism, evolution, the theology of hope, and process theology. On the one hand, by the 1960s many felt the Judeo-Christian heritage had lost its ability to continue to furnish a viable model to shape Western civilization as it had done so successfully for centuries. But on the other hand, the dispassionate "science" of secular humanism, which had replaced it decades prior, was equally distasteful and unacceptable to a society in desperate quest for a spiritual dimension to life that science failed to provide. Since Christianity was no longer an option with its "prescientific" cosmology, and because secular humanism had virtually robbed Western civilization of the divine dimension to life, the time was ripe for the discovery of a new approach. The gaze turned eastward.

Eastern religion, embodied for the most part within HINDUISM, had already been introduced to the West in the previous century. The VEDANTA SOCIETY was among the first to establish itself in the United States in the 1890s. Other influential movements, Eastern in orientation, were being cultivated even before the advent of ⏺Swami ⏺Vivekananda; ⏺transcendentalism, spearheaded by Thoreau; the Theosophical Society (*see* THEOSOPHY), cofounded by Helen ⏺Blavatsky and Henry Steel ⏺Olcott; and SPIRITUALISM all constituted a new order of thinking in the Christianized Western world. These became the seedbed for the New Age "explosion" that took place in the 1970s. According to J. Gordon Melton,

> By that year [1971], Eastern teachers had opened ⏺ashrams and centers and books had been published representing the various strains of new age concern.... *East-West Journal*, possibly the first national periodical to focus the issues of the New Age Movement, was begun by a Boston macrobiotic community, and the first popular book representative of the movement appeared: *Be Here Now* by ⏺Baba Ram Dass.[3]

BASIC BELIEFS

This section is titled as such because there are no doctrinal formulations that are drawn up as constituting official New Age dogma. An understanding of what qualifies as being New Age thinking is essential. What follows are general themes and overarching beliefs.

The most helpful way of defining the New Age Movement, and perhaps the most accurate, is to see it as being a "network" of organizations or, to coin the phrase of New Agers Jessica Lipnack and Jeffrey Stamps, a *metanetwork* of organizations that are autonomous, yet bound together. "Networks are composed of self-reliant and autonomous participants—people and organizations who simultaneously function as independent 'wholes' and as interdependent 'parts.'"[4]

What basic factor or factors tie such individuals and organizations together under the New Age umbrella? Put differently, what are the basic components that, when brought together, formulate the "network" or "metanetwork"? Despite the many factors that distinguish groups within the network, these are several common themes that bind them together.

1. Monism

The New Ager believes that the plurality in the cosmos is derived from an ultimate and single source. All diversity flows out from a uniform and divine energy. In *The Turning Point* (1982), New Age author and physicist Fritjof Capra attempts to point out that the basic malady of the human race is that it has been unable to discern the basic unity of all reality.

2. Pantheism

Monism quite naturally leads to pantheism. For New Agers, "God" is an ultimate principle that is identified with the universe. God is all and all is God. The only quest, then, is for humanity to discover and tap the knowledge of the divine that resides within each person. Separation from God is separation from a conscious or psychological cognition of divinity that resides within the entirety of nature. As Capra hinted at above, the movement of history therefore must be a movement or motion toward cognition of the divine. Therefore, every person must choose a ⏺*sadhana*, or path, through which he or she will undergo a transformation that will eventually yield such knowledge of the divine.

3. Reincarnation and Karma

For many, this *sadhana* may require more than one lifetime to fulfill. Therefore, the New Ager believes in concepts of reincarnation and karma, derived directly from Hinduism. Virtually all New Agers embrace the notion that good and bad karma will result in retributive justice (punishment or reward) as persons are cast on the wheel of rebirth. Belief in reincarnation furnishes an alternate explanation of the problem of evil to that of Christianity with its concept of ⏺hell and everlasting damnation for the unrighteous.

4. Universal Religion

Since discovery of the inner divinity is the ultimate goal of the New Ager, and because monism is the basic theological framework on which the New Age is based, there is really only one religion. All diverse religions of the world are simply alternate paths to the same goal. The New Ager believes that he or she is able to transcend the limited scope of the particular world religions. This is because too many religions are based on propositional truths expressed in creedal formulations and are therefore limited to language and cognition. J. Gordon Melton points out that Truth (the trueness of life expressed by the true religion) is "non-cognitive for New Agers, inexpressible in mere language. It is experienced but can only be partially expressed in words. There are, they believe, numerous means for arriving at Truth, distinguished for their efficiency more than their rightness."[5]

This is not to say, however, that a New Ager is not open to formulating his or her basic beliefs as being a set of systematic propositions. Indeed, one may believe one's beliefs are a "better way." But what is the "better way" to one may be a prohibitive way to another. As there are many trails that lead up a mountain toward the peak (some difficult, others easier), each trail in the end yields the same result, the reaching of the summit. The universal religion is a mountain with many paths, or *sadhanas*. No one path is the only correct path.

5. Personal Transformation

Whichever path an individual chooses, several goals loom on the horizon. The first is "personal transformation." This entails undergoing a personal mystical or psychic experience that will usually result in a paradigm shift from an "old world" belief system to a realization of "New Age" or "Aquarian" beliefs. The first step in this transformational process is to embrace a monistic worldview. Again, this does not come through cognition of propositional truths or creedal formulations, but rather through mystical experience.

Several important movements come into view that, in finding their places on the "network," contribute greatly to the transformation process within individuals. These are the holistic health movement, the consciousness movement, and the human potential movement.

a. Holistic health movement. Transformation involves healing. New Agers, however, are generally not avid fans of the medical industry. Traditional medical practices advocated by the American Medical Association are deemed "unnatural." In their place, new models for healing have been explored. The basic premise of the holistic health movement is that human beings deserve to be treated as real persons, not merely physical bodies having diseases of various sorts. Elisabeth Kübler-Ross, the pioneer of the hospice movement, is an outstanding example of medical treatment that attempts to afford the greatest dignity to human beings with terminal illnesses. To this effect, there is no incompatibility between orthodox Christianity and certain aspects of holistic health.

Coupled with this is the overriding principle consistent with New Age philosophy that the human being, and all other living things, are part of the natural order. Therefore, natural healing involving such practices as acupuncture, biofeedback, chiropractic, exercise, massage techniques, diet (many holistic-health advocates are vegetarians), natural medicines derived from plants (Bach Flower Remedies, etc.), and numerous other therapies are used. What is avoided is any treatment involving artificial drugs, surgery, or psychological manipulation. Natural healing will enable the universal life energy or force (see above) to take its course. According to the *International Journal of Holistic Health and Medicine*:

> The Eastern philosophy/spiritualism movement has also contributed to holistic health by its appreciation of a unifying invisible dynamic force within and around the human body that is called ▸ch-i by the Chinese, "ki" by the Japanese, ▸prana by the ▸yogis and numerous other names by various cultures throughout the world. Unlike the word "spirit" in the West, the words for this energetic force in the East generally have a very practical meaning and have direct and specific influences on health.[6]

b. The consciousness movement. Strictly speaking, there is no organized "consciousness movement." The phrase is used to more accurately describe the collective efforts of organizations and people within the "network" to bring about a greater realization of New Age ideals. This takes place across the spectrum within business, art, philosophy, culture, training seminars, and so on. The consciousness movement includes those who advocate the inducement of ▸altered states of consciousness. That is, the basic premise is that experiencing spiritual awareness outside of conventional norms will enable the participant to bridge the gap between matter and spirit, which in reality are one (monism). Important advocates of this enterprise included Timothy ▸Leary and Richard ▸Alpert. The use of hallucinogenic drugs, ▸hypnosis, and the like are important elements in achieving altered states of consciousness.

c. Human potential movement. A third important aspect of the "transformation" process is the so-called human potential movement. Perhaps more than any other single contributing factor, the human potential movement has made the greatest inroads in the spread of New Age ideals throughout Western culture. Douglas Groothuis observes, "Ranging from the low key pop-psychology of transactional analysis ('I'm OK, You're OK') to the myriad of encounter groups begun by Carl Rogers, the movement stressed human goodness and potential."[7] Associated with the human potential movement is the concept of ▸visualization. Thoughts and consciousness are considered superior to the material world. Therefore a person can think into reality things that they would like to have, such as a new car or a prosperous life.

Organizations and seminars classified as being part of the human potential movement include the Esalen Institute, FORUM, LIFESPRING, ARICA, Summit Workshops,

SCIENTOLOGY, the Movement of Spiritual Inner Awareness (MSIA), and numerous other groups. Businesses and corporations throughout the West have been involved in human-potential techniques. The workplace is the ideal place to capitalize on the increase of productivity made possible through sponsorship of training seminars. Major corporations, including RCA, IBM, Boeing, Ford Motor Co., and General Dynamics, have sponsored employee training sessions designed to realize greater productivity and potential. Psychological techniques used in such training, however, are New Age and humanistic in orientation.

6. Planetary vision

Coupled with, yet beyond the goal of, personal transformation is the New Age goal of planetary transformation. Because nature is viewed as being an aspect of the One, the earth is the single most important entity on which life is sustained. The ᴾGaia hypothesis basically asserts that the earth is itself a living organism. Consequently, the New Age vision is a collective assimilation of ideas gathered around a religio-socio-political consciousness.

New Agers favor a political platform in which issues concerning the environment are hegemonic. Pollution coming from the discharge of industrial waste, nuclear radiation, carbon monoxide from automobile exhaust, acid rain, chemical insecticides, destruction of wetlands, and so on are of paramount concern to those caught up in the all-important New Age ideal of a paradigm shift toward planetary consciousness. The hope of such leaders as Donald Keys and his organization known as Planetary Citizens is that even though the present political situation does not provide for the realization of planetary goals, a shift in political power will result in a shift toward such goals. Planetary Citizens is but one of many activist groups worldwide. These include the Green Movement and Global Education Associates (GEA).

7. New Age Eschatology

Early forerunners to the New Age Movement had envisioned the coming of a world leader or great ᴾavatar who would herald the dawning of the New Age. In the early 1980s New Age spokesman Benjamin ᴾCreme attracted much attention in the media by announcing that the Christ would appear in the person of Lord Maitreya. When Maitreya failed to appear, Creme's popularity quickly died. Nevertheless, the vision of a one-world leader remains the hope of New Agers dedicated to the cause of a world religio-political order.

Those who have abandoned this ideal have turned their attention away from a personal avatar to the personification of the cosmos itself. In August 1987, thousands of New Agers and New Age recruits gathered for the highly touted "Harmonic Convergence"—the time in which the New Age would begin.

8. Personalities

One must distinguish carefully between New Age popularizers and intellectuals. The latter are those whose abstract writings and technical conceptualizations have been translated into pragmatic and popular marching orders for the prevailing (predominantly Western) culture.

The major architects of New Age thought include a voluminous number of authors and thinkers. These cover the spectrum of philosophy, religion, physics, the ᴾoccult, psychology, mythology, holistic health, education, politics, economics, and sociology. Within this broad spectrum appear such names as Alice Bailey, Ian Barbour, Annie ᴾBesant, Helen Blavatsky, Richard Bucke, Joseph Campbell, Fritz Capra, Carlos ᴾCastáneda, Pierre Teilhard de Chardin, Norman Cousins, Benjamin Creme, Baba Ram Dass, Buckminster Fuller, Jean Houston, Barbara Marx Hubbard, Aldous Huxley, Carl Jung, Ken Keyes, Jiddu Krishnamurti, Thomas Kuhn, John Lilly, Jessica Lipnack, Shirley Maclaine, Abraham Maslow, P.D. ᴾOuspensky, Ramtha, Carl Rogers, Theodore Roszak, Mark Satin, David Spangler, Jeffrey Stamps, Rudolf ᴾSteiner, Ken Wilber, Paramahansa ᴾYogananda, and ᴾMaharishi Mahesh Yogi.

Because the expressed goal of the New Age Movement is to realize the ultimate oneness of reality, it is not surprising that the whole spectrum of knowledge is being retooled and rethought in terms of a major paradigm shift. Instead of viewing knowledge as being diverse and multivaried, the New Age Movement seeks to bring all the fields of knowledge under a single monistic canopy, fully united and integrated. This is the thrust of seminal works such as Fritjof Capra's *The Tao of Physics: An Exploration of the Parallels Between Modern Physics and Eastern Mysticism* (1975), and *The Turning Point: Science, Society, and the Rising Culture* (1982); as well as Ken Wilber's *The Spectrum of Consciousness* (1977) and *Eye to Eye* (1983). In this latter work Wilber is frank about his ideal.

We hear a lot today about "paradigms," and especially about "new and higher" paradigms—"supertheories" that would include, beyond the physical sciences, the higher knowledge claims of philosophy-psychology and of transcendental-mystical religion—a type of truly unified world view. The vision itself is fascinating: finally, an overall paradigm or theory that would unite science, philosophy-psychology, and religion-mysticism; finally, a truly "unified field theory"; finally, a comprehensive overview. Some very skilled, very sober, very gifted scholars, from all sorts of different fields, are today taking exactly that.[8]

Along with the philosophers and theorists of the New Age, there are a host of popularizers. One of these has been Shirley MacLaine, whose autobiography, *Out on a Limb*, became an instant bestseller. ABC aired a five-hour program on MacLaine's newfound spirituality. Her writings have won thousands of converts to her cause.

Despite all of her success, MacLaine herself seems disillusioned by her role as a popular New Age leader. In several interviews with popular magazines, she has expressed regret that her interest in the New Age Movement has won her the status of ‣guru. She disavows such a role or status and longs for her older role as simply an actress or stage performer. Her books, however, are still being read by countless devotees.[9]

In addition to MacLaine, we can cite other celebrities and prominent people especially in the arts and entertainment industries, such as singers John Denver, Tina Turner, Willie Nelson; movie producers Steven Spielberg, George Lucas, "Star Trek's" Gene Rodenberry; actors Levar Burton ("Roots"; "Star Trek—The Next Generation"), David Carradine ("Kung Fu"), Dennis Weaver; actresses Sharon Gless, Linda Evans, and Sally Kirkland.

Followers of the New Age Movement wearing pyramid hats at a New Age fair.
Courtesy Spiritual Counterfeit Project

9. New Age Communities

This volume makes reference to numerous groups that may properly be classified as either New Age in and of themselves or as ascribing to ideals that are New Age in content. Prominent New Age communities and organized groups include New Group of World Servers, Pacific Institute, People for the American Way, Planetary Initiative for the World We Choose, URANTIA, Tara Center, Zero Population Growth, Third Force, Third Wave, Sirius Community, Findhorn (Scotland), Chinook Learning Center, Science of Happiness, Lama Foundation (New Mexico), Renaissance Community (Massachusetts), Twin Oaks (Virginia), Stelle Community (Illinois), Perelandra (Washington, D.C.), Esalen, FORUM, The Farm, Planetary Citizens, and the numerous Eastern groups throughout the world (Vedanta Society, SATCHIDANANDA ASHRAM INTEGRAL YOGA INSTITUTE, THE BAHAI FAITH, CHURCH UNIVERSAL AND TRIUMPHANT, ELAN VITAL, MEHER BABA, TRANSCENDENTAL MEDITATION, ANANDA MARGA YOGA SOCIETY, SELF REALIZATION FELLOWSHIP, SIKH DHARMA, SRI CHINMOY CENTER, ISKCON [INTERNATIONAL SOCIETY OF KRISHNA CONSCIOUSNESS]).

THEOLOGICAL THEMES

Some of the major New Age themes have been noted above. What follows is a brief examination of some of the major points and how they differ from a traditional Christian world and life view.

God

As already discussed, the New Age Movement embraces the concept of monism, which leads quite readily into pantheism. Therefore, the New Ager does not conceptualize God in the same way that a Christian does. The former seeks God within the self and in the universe. Because all is God, one need not trouble to search for a metaphysical being existing beyond creation. One need only look within.

The Christian outlook is significantly different. The Christian concept of theology/anthropology, Creator/creation, grace/nature, and so on is held in a "together yet distinct" mode of thought. That is to say, while God is ‣immanent, God is also ‣transcendent. While God has created the world and cares for the creation, God is above and beyond the creation. Christianity holds that the scientific and humanistic communities have dismissed the very concept of God. Therefore, religious thought is relegated to the noumenal world of non-intelligibility. For science, only matter is real. For the numerous religions comprising New Age thought, only the spiritual is real. Christianity discriminates between two realities. God is an integral part of both realms. "God is spirit" (John 4:24), yet God also became "flesh and made his dwelling among us" (John 1:14), as the Christian doctrine of the ▸incarnation ascribes.

Christ and Salvation

For the New Ager, therefore, conversations about God are in reality anthropocentric (human-centered). That is to say, conversation about God must begin and end with a human point of reference. The New Ager believes that even though he or she evolved from physical things, there is at the same time a spiritual nature that is called the "higher self." The New Ager often refers to this higher self as being the "Christ" within. While Jesus was a historical figure, the Christ that propelled and inspired him was a divine energy that may be harnessed by anyone. Therefore, "Christ" is not only within a person in the Christian sense of Christ coming to dwell *with* the believer, but in the final analysis Christ is all people and all people are potential Christs.

For Christianity, Jesus Christ is the second person of the divine ▸Trinity. The creeds describe both his person and work (*see* Appendix 1). While the Christ "in us" is certainly a Christian teaching taken from such biblical passages as Colossians 1:27 ("Christ in you, the hope of glory") and Revelation 3:20 ("Here I am! I stand at the door and knock. If any one hears my voice and opens the door, I will come in and eat with him"), nevertheless, far more dominant to Christendom is the concept of Christ "for us." In this designation, Jesus Christ acted on behalf of the church by offering himself as an atoning sacrifice for sin (Rom. 3:21–25; 2 Cor. 5:15–21). This notion is foreign to New Age thought because it blurs the clear distinction between Jesus Christ and other human beings. It was Jesus' activity of dying on a cross, shedding blood, being buried, and being resurrected *for the sins of the world* that constitutes the Christian doctrine of salvation. Furthermore, this activity took place in history in a specific setting (Palestine), a specific time (Gal. 4:4), and among a specific people (Israel). Consequently, Jesus' historical death and resurrection resulted in salvation for all time and among all people.

Sin

Because in the New Age Movement there is no transcendent God separate from creation, it follows that there is no conception of sin as being rebellion against such a transcendent being. Sin is simply "ignorance" of one's own inner potential. For Christianity sin is certainly ignorance, but ignorance of an opposite sort. One who worships the creation and calls it "god" is guilty of "ignorance" of the worst kind (Rom. 1:18–24). Regarding one's "inner potential," there is no human capacity that enables a person to find God. It is God who finds the person (Eph. 2:8–9). Jesus Christ's death on the cross is a necessary atonement for sin. The ▸Bible is clear in its delineation of all human beings as sinners (Rom. 3:23).

Death

Virtually every religion in human history advances notions concerning death. In the modern world, among "a-religious" secular humanists, death is the end or cessation of life. There is no "life beyond life" or no transcendent Creator who will be met on "the other side." The New Age Movement has not been content with this nonspiritual and rather dismal rendition, however. As already noted, for the New Age Movement, death is illusory, as the biological cessation of this present life is merely the stepping-stone to entrance into the next life in the cycle of rebirth, or reincarnation. Contrary to both of these views is the Christian doctrine concerning death. The Christian church teaches that on death the soul separates from the body and goes to an eternal state of glory in heaven with God or to eternal punishment in hell without God. Which of the two destinies the soul will go to is dependent on the person's having been regenerated (born again) through baptism and faith in Christ's redeeming work on the cross (John 3:1–18).

End Times

The imminence of utopia is a common theme for those who announce that the age of ▸Aquarius is now here. The time will soon arrive when global famine, the threat of nuclear warfare, the destruction of the environment, drugs, AIDS, crime, and so on will end and the "New Age" will fully realize itself.

Christianity shares the common hope of a future utopia. The Bible speaks of a "new heaven and a new earth" (Rev. 21:1). A time will come that through faith in Christ, "gladness and joy will overtake [Christians], and sorrow and sighing will flee away" (Isa. 35:10). The New Testament promises: "God himself will be with them and be their God. He will wipe every tear from their eyes. There will be no more death or mourning or crying or pain, for the old order of things has passed away" (Rev. 21:3–4).

There is one crucial difference, however, between the New Age Movement and Christianity regarding the future. For the former, achievement of utopia is the result of human effort. For the latter, the ushering in of lasting utopia will only come when it is brought to pass by God. The time of peace will begin only when it is hailed by the "Prince of Peace" (Isa. 9:6). Human initiative further exacerbates the problems and can result only in continued failure.

This does not mean, however, that Christianity advocates a philosophy of passivity and acquiescence to critical issues that plague the world. Certainly there have been isolated groups within the church throughout the centuries that have adopted an escapist mentality. The monastic orders may be regarded in this way. By retreating within the walls of the monastery, one could escape the evils of the world and remain relatively uninvolved. Some Protestant sects tend toward a theology of noninvolvement with the world and its ᵇapostasy. And some consider that the eschatology of many conservative Christians is a form of escapism from the problems of the world—the doctrine of a premillennial, pretribulation "rapture" of the church. This particular theology, popularized by Hal Lindsey's *The Late Great Planet Earth* (1970), the *Left Behind* novels of Tim LaHaye and Jerry Jenkins, and many other authors, teaches that a thousand-year utopia on earth will be preceded by a terrible and cataclysmic tribulation period culminated by the battle of Armageddon. Christians will not have to face this crisis, because before it takes place and before the Antichrist will rise up to rule, Jesus will appear in the heavens to rapture his church out of the world. Many in this theological camp are eager to save as many people as they can before the rapture occurs.

We cannot discuss this particular eschatology in detail here. Christ does expect us is to go to all nations, bringing the message of the salvation (Matt. 28:18–19). Jesus walked among the common people and the "undesirables" of society. When he prayed for his disciples, he did not pray that they escape from the world, but rather that they be protected from evil while in the world (John 17:15). The apostle Paul launched a missionary effort that changed the globe for the cause of Christ.

Therefore, far from advocating a philosophy of passivity, Christianity teaches that the world must be spiritually cultivated. Unlike the New Age Movement, however, the church does not believe that change is effected through autonomous self-effort or human potential. The church, as the bride of Christ, does not exist independently from her Bridegroom. The individual Christian's battle cry is that Christ is the enabler for all of his or her activities (Phil. 4:13). The church is a prophetic and alien institution in a world filled with sin and rebellion against God. It is the distinct mission of the church to make a difference in the world and to strive to effect change. Indeed, the Christian should take more seriously than anyone else the importance of taking care of the environment, seeking peace, playing an active role in government, and the like, because the Christian knows that this world was created by God.

NEW AGE CHRISTIANITY (LIBERAL)

Mainline liberal Christians have attempted to merge Christianity with their positive perception of New Age teachings. New Age influence now infiltrates many Christian branches. In Catholicism, however, Pope John Paul II brought a universal halt to New Age infiltration in an address on May 28, 1993, by renouncing New Age teachings as "incompatible" with Christ's message. In contrast, liberal European Protestants, lacking a uniform warning, found many clergy and church members already embracing New Age teachings by the 1980s. This caused the Dutch Protestant churches to hold three inquiry conferences in 2000 and 2001. These fell short of official renunciation, but turned instead toward tolerance of New Agers within the church's framework by citing parallels between Christian mysticism and New Age meditation.

Blurred terminology and loose definitions cultivate this sentiment, as is seen in British churches that more openly allow New Age practices by clergy and members with little or no restraint. From this came such British conclaves as the ᵇChristaquarians, a confederacy of Christian church members, mostly Anglican, who fearlessly merge New Age principles with Christianity. The New Age program *A Course in Miracles* blazed virtually unabated through liberal Protestant churches in America and Europe, which only confused members as to truth claims. In the end, the New Age has penetrated Christianity in untold measures, which is warning enough for conservative and orthodox believers to mount a defense.

CONCLUSION

In the beginning of the twenty-first century, much of what has been "new" about the New Age has now become dated. Newer nomenclature has become more fashionable. The name "New Age" itself is no longer used by ardent devotees. More in vogue is the term "spirituality," or "new spirituality." It is a "do-it-yourself" form of religion well adapted to the postmodern world, where an inquiry into truth is utterly abandoned

New Age writing.
Courtesy George A. Mather

along with all forms of organized religion. The New Age spirituality, rather, aims at what suits the immediate situation, moment, or feeling, rather than any form or notion of absolute truth.

As can be expected, the movement continues to take on numerous forms and emphases. Neo-paganism continues to press in the direction of ecology and a spirituality to surround it. Interests in astrology abound in such New Age persona as Solara and her insights into the significance and meaning of the number "11." James 'Redfield's '*The Celestine Prophecy* well represents the recent conglomerate of New Age books. Pop cultural spirituality continues to reflect the New Age in such personalities as Louise Hay and Deepak 'Chopra—perhaps the most popular current representative of the movement. Self-help programs and seminars featuring New Age ideologues continue to abound.

Much more could be said about the New Age Movement. Virtually nothing has been discussed concerning the 'occult, 'channeling, 'crystals, New Age music,

art, cultural influences, and so on. The reader is asked to refer to the extensive bibliography in the back of this volume for excellent sources concerning any special areas of interest. Also, a cursory search on the internet will yield literally millions of New age websites. More and more scholarly analyses of the movement are being published as well.[10]

ADDITIONAL INFORMATION

Notes

[1] See LIFESPRING, THE FORUM, ARICA, RAJNEESHSIM, TRANSCENDENTAL MEDITATION, HANUMAN FOUNDATION, SELF REALIZATION FELLOWSHIP, VEDANTA SOCIETY, ZEN BUDDHISM, SIKH DHARMA, ELAN VITAL, SUFISM, CHURCH UNIVERSAL AND TRIUMPHANT, URANTIA, HEAVEN'S GATE, UNITY SCHOOL OF CHRISTIANITY, RELIGIOUS SCIENCE. These groups best represent specific religious organizations dedicated to New Age ideology.

[2] See list of readings in bibliography.

[3] J. Gordon Melton, *Encyclopedic Handbook of Cults in America* (New York and London: Garland, 1986), 108.

[4] Jessica Lipnack and Jeffrey Stamps, *Networking* (Garden City, NY: Doubleday, 1982), 7.

[5] J. Gordon Melton, *New Age Encyclopedia* (Detroit: Gale Research, 1990), xv–xvi.

[6] Dana Ullman, "Holistic Health: Friend and Foe of Progressive Health Care," *International Journal of Holistic Health and Medicine* 2 (Winter 1984): 22.

[7] Douglas R. Groothuis, *Unmasking the New Age* (Downers Grove, Ill.: InterVarsity Press, 1986), 79.

[8] Ken Wilber, *Eye to Eye: The Quest For the New Paradigm* (Garden City, NY: Anchor Books, 1983), 1.

[9] See Patricia Nolan, "Is Hollywood Being Brainwashed?" *Woman's World* (April 30, 1991), 35.

[10] See, e.g., Paul Heelas, *The New Age Movement: The Celebration of the Self and the Sacralization of Modernity* (Malden, MA: Blackwell, 1996); Eugene Taylor, *Shadow Culture: Psychology and Spirituality in America* (New York: Counterpoint, 2000).

NEW THOUGHT

Phineas Parkhurst 'Quimby (1802–1866), born in Lebanon, New Hampshire, takes his rightful place as 'guru of the 'mind sciences. His influence on Mary Baker 'Eddy and CHRISTIAN SCIENCE has been noted elsewhere in this volume. Quimby practiced 'mesmerism and advanced the notion that sin, sickness, and disease exist solely in the mind.

HISTORY

Resisting the exclusive authoritarianism and dogmatism of Eddy, many Quimbyites challenged and broke away from Christian Science.[1] Out of this reaction grew such movements as UNITY SCHOOL OF CHRISTIANITY, DIVINE SCIENCE, RELIGIOUS SCIENCE, and New Thought. This last group received its initial impetus in the writings and leadership of Warren Felt 'Evans (1817–1889), Julius 'Dresser (1838–1893), and Dresser's son, Horatio 'Dresser (1866–1954).

Evans, a Methodist minister, first experienced healing at the hands of Quimby in 1863. Soon afterward, he began to espouse the ideas of 'Swedenborg and his CHURCH OF THE NEW JERUSALEM in a book titled *The New Age and Its Messenger* (1863). Other books, *The Mental Cure* (1869), *Mental Medicine* (1872), and *Soul and Body* (1876), followed, each articulating ideas learned from both Swedenborg and Quimby. Evans showed great interest in the 'occult and its use in healing. His great contribution to the field of New Thought, however, lies in his articulation of such ideas in published essays and monographs.

On many occasions the popularization of a movement is not accomplished by the writers and thinkers as much as through the communicators. Such was the case with New Thought. The most articulate spokesman for the movement was Julius Dresser. Also a student of Quimby, Dresser, his wife, Annetta, and subsequently his son Horatio did much to promote the ideas of Quimby. Dresser boldly challenged Mary Baker Eddy's authority and denied her an exclusive monopoly on Quimbyism in Boston when he and his own followers established the Church of the Higher Life. After 1890 the term *New Thought* came into vogue when a periodical by the same name began. In 1895, 1899, and 1915 organized movements were founded under the umbrella of New Thought.

New Thought celebrated the bicentennial celebration Quimby's birthday in 2002.

ORGANIZATION

New Thought Centers are located in fifteen states. Each center is independently run. However, there is an Affiliated New Thought Network (ANTN) that has a board of directors comprised of a president, vice-president, secretary/treasurer, director/educational liaison, and a member. Those who join a New Thought community are given a right to vote and are asked to uphold the teachings of New Thought, participate in activities, exchange ideas, and serve on various committees.

TEACHINGS

In 1915 the International New Thought Alliance was established. Its constitution summarizes the basic ideas endemic to the growing movement.

> To teach the Infinitude of the Supreme One, the Divinity of Man and his Infinite possibilities through the creative power of constructive thinking and obedience to the voice of the Indwelling Presence, which is our source of Inspiration, Power, Health, and Prosperity.[2]

As is the case generally with the mind sciences, New Thought finds Platonic 'dualism as the underlying basis for its ideas. Believing that the realm of "spirit" is superior to matter, Plato introduced a concept of reality that held sway in Western thought for centuries. Platonic dualism underwent a revival in the nineteenth century, and indeed, the romantic era furnished the backdrop for the mind sciences. Quimby's conviction that sickness and disease were components of the mind could only be accepted during an era in which the very notion of a bifurcation between spirit and matter was strongly in vogue, as it is today yet. Swedenborgianism, German idealism, and American 'transcendentalism became obvious testimonies to the fact that the spirit of the age was indeed the age of the spirit. In the case of the Quimbyites, matter had but an insignificant role to play. New Thought Movement's proponents were many and their beliefs were so divergent that it is difficult to assess them precisely or systematically.

Truth

One belief on which New Thought advocates generally agree is that the search for truth is an ongoing process. In this regard, New Thought more closely resembles the thinking of the UNITARIAN-UNIVERSALIST ASSOCIATION than it does Christian Science. Many followers of Mary Baker Eddy believed that her revelations were absolute and unalterable truths.

Traditional CHRISTIANITY parts company with all of the above-named groups in that its basic premise is that God is the author of all truth. Revealed truth is conveyed in the propositional statements of the 'Bible, which embodies the history of Israel and the proclamation of the gospel of Jesus Christ, who himself claimed to be the sum and substance of truth personified: "I am the way and the truth and the life. No one comes to the Father, except through me" (John 14:6). All theological truth has been made known and is finalized in Scripture.

God

God is immanent with respect to the world. One may find aspects of divinity in all things. Unlike Christianity, which holds to a balance between the immanence and transcendence of God, New Thought does not distinguish between the Creator and the creation.[3]

Humanity

As can be deduced from the above premise, humankind possesses a divine nature. To seek God is to peer into the inner self.

Once again, in contradistinction to this, the Christian church has traditionally taught that the locus of the divine nature is God. God and humanity are separate and distinct from each other. Because of rebellion and sin, humans are not only distinct from God in an ontological sense, but also spiritually. Modern trends in Christian theology have found more in common with some of the premises of the mind sciences than with traditional ᐧorthodoxy. Quimby's ideas paralleled those of Friedrich Schleiermacher (1768–1834), who laid the groundwork for a liberal Protestant anthropology that still dominates mainline Christianity. Schleiermacher, the architect of romantic Christianity, reflected this in his well-known words:

> The immediate feeling of absolute dependence is presupposed and actually contained in every religious and Christian self-consciousness as the only way in which, in general, our own being and the infinite being of God can be one in self-consciousness.[4]

Sin

For New Thought, sin is succumbing to and therefore being the victim of the illusory world of matter. Sin in the sense of rebellion against God does not exist. All sin, sickness, and diseases are illusions and phantasms of the mind. Right thinking may cure one of all such illnesses.[5]

Jesus Christ and Salvation

New Thought advocates maintain that Jesus was a teacher and that he consistently taught that "the kingdom of God is within you." They flatly reject that Jesus is "the Christ, the Son of the living God" (Matt. 16:16) or the only way to salvation (John 3:16, 18; 14:6). Sal- vation is not a matter of contrition and repentance before God in order to receive the forgiveness of sins and the promise of eternal life, but rather, the discovery of the divinity that lies within. As in Christianity, salvation is offered to all. But only those initiated into the movement are able to receive the ᐧgnostic knowledge of the distinction between spirit and matter.

CONCLUSION

As in Christian Science, those attracted to New Thought are predisposed to an intellectual and philosophical approach to religion. New Thought continues to be one of the active mind science religions.

ADDITIONAL INFORMATION

Websites

www.newthought.org; www.new-thought.org; http://neweverymoment.com/nthp.html; Also see websites listed under UNITY SCHOOL OF CHRISTIANITY; DIVINE SCIENCE; CHRISTIAN SCIENCE, and RELIGIOUS SCIENCE.

Sacred Texts

The Bible

Periodical

The Phoenix; Bright Ideas; Daily Word; Dialogue and Distinction; New Thought

Membership

Currently, there are eight listed practitioners; total membership unknown.

Notes

[1] Sydney Ahlstrom, *A Religious History of the American People*, 2 vols. (Garden City, N.Y.: Image Books, 1975), 2:536.

[2] Ibid., 2:537.

[3] See HINDUISM, UNITY SCHOOL OF CHRISTIANITY, WORLDWIDE CHURCH OF GOD, THEOSOPHY, TRANSCENDENTAL MEDITATION, etc. for a further treatment of the Creator/creature distinction.

[4] Friedrich Schleiermacher, *The Christian Faith* (Edinburgh: T. & T. Clark, 1928), 131.

[5] For a Christian evaluation, see CHRISTIAN SCIENCE.

NICHIREN SHOSHU BUDDHISM; NICHIREN SHOSHU OF AMERICA (NSA)

Before the thirteenth century, BUDDHISM had misinterpreted the teachings of ᐧGautama. Such was the conviction of a Japanese monk ᐧNichiren Daishonin (1222–1282). He believed that he alone, through the teachings of the ᐧLotus Sutra, had discovered the nature of true Buddhism. Along with denunciation of the exist- ing religion(s) came Nichiren's sharp criticism of the Japanese government that had sprung out of such religious errors. Japanese history at the time of Nichiren was characterized by social upheaval and discontent with prevailing affairs. Consequently, his ideas were well received by the populace.

HISTORY

Two ‖sects grew out of Nichiren's teachings after his death in 1282. The first, called the Nichiren sect, predominated until the mid-twentieth century, when it was surpassed in size and importance by the Nichiren Shoshu sect. This latter sect experienced rapid growth under the leadership of its lay organization called SOKA-GAKKAI (Value Creation Society), founded by Tsonesaburo ‖Makiguchi in 1930. Today, Nichiren Shoshu Buddhism comprises the largest group of Buddhists, with numbers in excess of seventeen million and ten million in Japan alone. This is due to the leadership of the third president of Soka-Gakkai, Daisaku ‖Ikeda, elected in 1960. Ikeda insisted that power was the key to the realization of goals. Consequently, a political party called ‖Komei was formed. From a political vantage point, the success and growth of the Nichiren Shoshu sect were phenomenal.

Despite NSA's efforts to follow suit with its Japanese counterpart in the pursuance of "clean government," the American organization has not been without its problems, particularly in the 1980s. In 1984–1986, the NSA broke the IRS Revenue Code by contributing $13,700 to Tom Bradley's California mayoral and gubernatorial campaigns. Bradley returned the money after the discrepancy was made public.[1] Despite this and other related political problems, NSA is prospering in the United States. In 1987 it established a headquarters building for $14.5 million in San Francisco.

Tensions came to a head when, in November 1991, Nichiren Shoshu high priest Nikken Abe issued an order for Soka-Gakkai to disband. The president, Einosuke ‖Akiya, promptly refused to comply.[2]

In 1992, Soka-Gakkai was excommunicated from the Nichiren Shoshu organization. The cause was a tremendous power struggle between the lay organization and the priesthood. The specific charge was that Ikeda, as far back as 1977, had seriously strayed from the pure doctrines of the faith. Even though he asked for forgiveness at the time, this set the process in motion that would culminate in the 1991 split as a result of growing frustrations. In 1990, Soka Gakkai International charged the priesthood of Nicherin Shosu with corruption, and abuse of power.

The recoil was the removal of Ikeda as the representative of the priesthood's lay groups. Soka Gakkai then accused Nichiren Shoshu of inappropriate spending. Further accusations from both groups were exchanged, and the culminating result was the excommunication of Soka Gakkai from Nichiren Shoshu. In 1997, members of Soka Gakkai were informed by letter that they could no longer be members of both groups.[3]

ORGANIZATION

Nichiren Shoshu has experienced rapid growth in the United States, where it is called Nichiren Shoshu of America (NSA). The movement is organized into districts comprised of fifteen to thirty people. Districts then are combined together to form chapters, regions, and zones. Centers are located throughout the world, but the main headquarters is still in Japan at the site of the temple.

TEACHINGS

The success and growth of the sect are attributed to its doctrines. A conversion method known as ‖shakubuku, or "browbeating," has proven extremely effective.

The Nichiren Shoshu sect ascribes to its founder, Nichiren Daishonin, a higher place than the ‖Buddha himself. Nichiren had identified himself as being the

Two books on Nichiren Shoshu Buddhism published by the Seikyo Press in Tokyo. Most of the writing is in Japanese. Courtesy Jack M. Roper/CARIS

‖bodhisattva, one who would arise to teach the truth in an era eclipsed by total darkness. Such truth centered around three basic principles or laws. The first deals with the ‖gohonzon, the chief object of its worship life. The gohonzon is a sacred scroll that contains a drawing of the Lotus Sutra and various divine names. It is kept in a black box called the ‖butsodun and is located in the original temple of Nichiren Shoshu called ‖Daisekiji, at the base of Mount Fuji. Millions of pilgrims travel annually to the temple to worship.

The second great principle is ‖daimoku, wherein the worshiper chants the words nam-myoho-renge-kyo, translated "glory to the *Lotus Sutra*," sometimes for many hours.

The third principle is *kaidan*, or the sacred place of ordination.

The goal of the pilgrimages and the chanting of the *daimoku* is to merge the worshiper with the Buddha himself. Repeating the chant brings one to *enlighten-ment and harmony with the universe. The theory is that if the masses can be brought to such enlightenment, the world will be a much better place in which to live.

The success of Nichiren Buddhism is a result of the sect's emphasis on the practical elements of life as well as the ambitious recruitment program carried out in society. To suggest that changes can be made in the world by involvement in politics has triggered a posi-tive appeal to the masses.

Both Nichiren Shoshu and CHRISTIANITY are similar in that they are missionary religions, dedicated to the advancement of the kingdom of God, though they have different deities. The important distinction, however, is that Christianity does not advocate the need for acquisition of political power to bring about such advancement. This is accomplished through procla-mation of the gospel of Jesus Christ and effected through the Holy Spirit.

Nichiren Buddhism, like its parent, Buddhism, is this-worldly in its orientation. However, Gautama emphasized the importance of pursuing the *middle path. In Buddhist thought, materialism on the one hand and austerity on the other both fail to eliminate desire, and thus suffering remains. Gautama would certainly not advocate ambitious political involvement. Such endeavors are laden with suffering.

Christianity has taught a message that is other-worldly in its *soteriology and worldview (Col. 3:1). Nevertheless, there has always been a rich variety of traditions within the church concerning the degree to which it should be involved in social, political, and eco-nomic affairs. A political voice has been a strong legacy in the Roman Catholic Church. Recently, mainline Protestant churches in America have involved them-selves rather extensively in political affairs. Unlike Nichiren Shoshu, however, some believe that this has led to their demise in the past several decades.[4] Con-servative *evangelicals have also played an important role in American politics, particularly since the 1980s.

CONCLUSION

One must fulfill no requirements to join NSA other than paying a nominal fee for a copy of the *gohonzon*.[5] NSA maintains an active calendar. Conferences, exhibits, and educational seminars are among the orga-nization's featured activities. It continues to remain a significant movement in the United States.

ADDITIONAL INFORMATION_____

Headquarters
The address is Soka-Gakkai International Office, 32 Shinano-machi, Shinjuku-ku, Tokyo 160, Japan; Soka-Gakkai Inter-national–USA; 606 Wilshire Blvd. Santa Monica, CA, 90401

Websites
www.sgi-usa.org; www.sokagakkai.or.jp

Sacred Texts
The Lotus Sutra

Periodicals
Periodicals include *World Tribune; World Tribune Express* (email news); *Living Buddhism* (monthly magazine).

Membership
Growth of Nichiren Shoshu Buddhism has been rapid. In 1980 well over thirty million people considered themselves mem-bers of its various sects. Today, however, there are probably around eight million members worldwide. Some have esti-mated at least 500,000 people associated with the move-ment in the United States, but in reality, there are probably about 200,000 with a smaller active membership of about 20,000.

Notes
[1] Shannon Hickey, "Chanting for Clout," *California* (Febru-ary 1990), 14.
[2] See William Alnor, "Infighting, Division, and Scandal Afflicting Nichiren Shoshu Buddhists," *Christian Research Journal* (Winter, 1992), 5–6.
[3] Trevor Astley, "A Note on the Recent Conflict between Nichiren Shshu and Soka Gakkai, " *Japanese Religions* 17 (1992), 167–75.
[4] Encyclopaedia Britannica, *15th ed., s.v. "Nichiren Shoshu."*
[5] Hickey, "Chanting for Clout," 14.

ONENESS PENTECOSTALISM; UNITED PENTECOSTAL CHURCH INTERNATIONAL; UPCI

Pentecostalism has been an increasingly popular form of CHRISTIANITY. As a movement, it was born in the twentieth century. Oneness Pentecostalism is a unique development within the greater Pentecostal movement and was a heretical outgrowth of the Assemblies of God. There have been various anti-Trinitarian (see ▶Trinity) movements within ▶orthodox Christianity throughout its history; the United Pentecostal Church International (UPCI) is the largest anti-Trinitarian Pentecostal movement.

HISTORY

Oneness Pentecostalism grew out of the Assemblies of God (AG), a Pentecostal movement that began in 1906 on Azusa Street in Los Angeles. The impulse that caused the outburst of what quickly came to be called Oneness was a Pentecostal camp meeting held in April 1913 at Arroyo Seco, outside of Los Angeles. William Menzies writes:

> The main speaker at the camp meeting was Mrs. Mary Woodworth-Etter, but the speaker who unwittingly triggered the eruption was R. E. McAlister. At a baptismal service held near the main camp meeting tent, Brother McAlister casually observed that the apostles invariably baptized their converts once in the name of Jesus Christ, and that the words Father, Son, and Holy Ghost were never used in Christian baptism. When they heard this, a shudder swept the preachers on the platform.[1]

The shudder has had many aftershocks. When McAlister was informed that his statement had some heretical overtones, he tried to clarify what he meant, but his words had their effect. John Sheppe was inspired to a night of prayer and reflection, considering the preacher's words. David Reed relates that "in the early hours of the morning, he [John Sheppe] ran through the camp, shouting that the Lord had shown him the truth on baptism in the name of Jesus Christ. Many listened, and not long hence, many believed."[2]

A second individual to hear McAlister's preaching was an Australian-born preacher, Frank J. Ewart. After spending much time with McAlister after the revival and in studying the Scriptures, Ewart began to teach his new insights to a waiting world. On April 15, 1914, Ewart erected a tent in Belvedere, outside of Los Angeles, and preached a sermon on the baptismal formula of

Acts 2:38, comparing it with Matthew 28:19. Ewart concluded that the ▶Bible taught that baptism in the name of Jesus only was the only true and doctrinally correct formula for Christian baptism. Reed correctly notes that "the oneness revelation was initially and primarily a discovery of the name of God as used in Christian baptism."[3]

Baptism in the name of Jesus was not uncommon. Some Pentecostal ministers (Howard Goss and Andrew Urshan) had initiated this practice in previous years. What was different, if anything, about Ewart's emphasis? "As the First Theologian of the New Issue, Ewart's particular contribution was a modalistic view of God and a theology of the name of Jesus."[4]

In other words, before this time the baptismal formulas in Matthew 28:19 and Acts 2:38 were used interchangeably. Through the influence of Ewart and others, however, an entirely innovative way of understanding developed, namely, that Christians should conduct baptism exclusively "in the name of Jesus only." On April 15, 1914, Ewart and one of his first converts, Glenn A. Cook, rebaptized each other using the new baptismal formula. The new movement was referred to by a variety of names: the "New Issue," "Jesus Only" movement, "Jesus Name," "Apostolic," or "Oneness Pentecostalism."[5]

By 1915 Oneness had spread from southern states up through Canada. Two prominent Assemblies of God ministers, J. Roswell Flower and E. N. Bell, each opposed the New Issue. The former denounced it as being heretical mainly because of the denial of the Trinity; the latter was more conciliatory, allowing for baptism in the name of Jesus but disavowing rebaptism. Bell shockingly capitulated to Oneness in the summer of 1915. The mantle of leadership fell exclusively on Flower, who continued to publish against the movement, chiefly through the *Weekly Evangel* and the *Word and Witness*. A prominent black Pentecostal minister, Garfield Haywood, also became a strong advocate for Oneness, leading many blacks into the new theology.

The defections into Oneness of significant numbers of Assemblies of God ministers and members succeeded in polarizing two opposing forces within Pentecostal ranks. The Trinitarians (almost exclusively Flower) offered vehement apologetics in defense of the position that Matthew 28:19 and many other passages of Scripture offer clear proof that God is one in being, yet comprised of three distinct persons, Father, Son, and Holy Spirit, and that baptism should therefore be conducted in the name of the triune God. Oneness converts, on the other hand, argued that baptism is ineffective unless it is conducted in Jesus' name alone.

Threatened by a dangerous schism, the Assemblies decided to convene the Third General Council in October 1915. The general tone of the council was conciliatory. Neither side succeeded in convincing the other of its respective position. The lack of decisive action, however, weighed in on the side of the Trinitarians. The controversy seemed to have awakened the "silent majority" of Pentecostals around the country. More and more came forward in support of orthodoxy, upholding the Trinitarian baptismal formula. Bell was eventually won back to the Assemblies, supporting Flower's campaign once again.

The peaceful note on which the third council had concluded did not last, however. Several months after the final session had closed, the controversy welled up once again. Flower was told that spiritual disaster would befall him if he opposed the movement. But the closing of the Trinitarian ranks proved a decisive defense against the advocates of Oneness, who were progressively being viewed as schismatics. The general assembly of 1916, held in St. Louis, again had to face the New Issue and respond to it with a doctrinal formulation. A statement of fundamental truths that clearly articulated an anti-Oneness theology came to the floor for approval. This was a daring move in itself because the first council, held in 1914, had decided against creating any formulas, creeds, or statements as being counterproductive to the work of the Holy Spirit. The council's decision to uphold the traditional doctrine of the Trinity resulted in the immediate withdrawal of 156 ministers and accompanying congregations. As is so often the case, however, schisms generate new movements, and Oneness was no exception.

Several prominent Oneness leaders met in December 1916 in Eureka Springs, Arkansas, and formed the General Assembly of Apostolic Assemblies (GAAA). Nearly all the ministers who had resigned from the Assemblies of God joined ranks with the GAAA. Immediate complications arose because of the timing of the formulation of the new organization. World War I had erupted, and the GAAA was unable to furnish credentials to ministers who needed them.

The assembly solved this problem, however, when they found another Pentecostal organization with an active legal charter. The Pentecostal Assemblies of the World (PAW) originated as a loose fellowship in 1907 in the Los Angeles area.[6] The PAW proved most willing to embrace the new theology of Oneness. Thus, in 1918 the PAW and the GAAA merged to form the first significant Oneness group, retaining the name Pentecostal Assemblies of the World. Haywood's dream and philosophy of leadership for the PAW was to see the organization racially integrated. This ideal met with raw failure, however, because of bitter race relations, particularly in the South. The PAW experienced fragmentation in the years following 1924. Many regional groups formed during this era. The theologies of each of these small ▶sects varied significantly.

In 1931 a conference held in Columbus, Ohio, attempted to bring the sundry Oneness sects together and made progress to that end. In November 1931 a merger between the racially segregated sects took effect in the formation of the Pentecostal Assemblies of Jesus Christ (PAJC). This, however, did not prevent some of the black leaders from remaining suspicious of the motives behind the new merger. This latter group decided to remain within the PAW.

The two primarily white organizations, the Pentecostal Church, Inc. (PCI) and the PAJC, continually attempted to merge in the 1930s and 1940s. The efforts proved successful in 1945 with the formation of the largest of the Pentecostal Oneness groups, the United Pentecostal Church International (UPCI). The UPCI grew quickly and soon contained about 50 percent of all Oneness advocates. Today the UPCI has nine Bible colleges with headquarters in St. Louis. Many of its doctrines are parallel to its forebear, the Assemblies of God. The major difference is its anti-Trinitarianism. The UPCI has a much more rigorous pietism than the AG. Strict holiness codes regarding dress and behavior are key characteristics of the UPCI.

A third major Oneness group emerged in 1971. This group, called the Apostolic World Christian Fellowship (AWCF), took its place next to the UPCI and the PAW as one of the three major Oneness groups. The Rev. Worthy Rowe provided the impetus for the formation of the AWCF. Rowe's father, G. B. Rowe, had been disfellowshiped from the UPCI for what was considered to be an erroneous ▶Christology. Because his son did not rescind the teachings of his father, he too was excluded from fellowship in the UPCI. Not recognized as being a legitimate expression of Oneness theology by the UPCI, the AWCF has nevertheless received the recognition and respect of many other Oneness sects throughout the country and the world.

D. A. Reed well summarizes the present-day situation that Oneness Pentecostals find themselves in in relationship to the greater Pentecostal world:

> As the Oneness movement matures, it will need to address the theological and spiritual virtues that bind it to its evangelical-pentecostal roots. Trinitarian Christians likewise will be increasingly challenged to listen with patience to a growing presence among them that has not followed the way of the cult but whose commitments at present are not readily accommodated within the historic Christian tradition.[7]

ORGANIZATION

The UPCI is governed by a congregational structure in that all its churches are autonomous. A loosely structured presbyterian polity is also in place by mutual consent of the member churches. The church has local sections, broader districts, and a national general conference that meets to elect church leaders, including a general superintendent. A central headquarters in Hazelwood, Missouri, serves the denomination's organizational, publishing, and missions outreach arm. Area churches are located throughout the United States, Canada, and numerous other countries (below). The UPCI places great emphasis on foreign missions work. A program called Harvest is organized to address worldwide evangelism. The website provides links to all of the various suborganizations within the movement, along with a link containing current news and information about the general conference.

TEACHINGS

The essence of Oneness Pentecostalism is a rigorously applied theology centering around the "name" of God. McAlister (see above) seems to have been the first to point out that in the New Testament the words "Father, Son, and Holy Ghost" were simply not used in Christian baptisms. The norm for baptism was rather to use the "name of Jesus" (as in Acts 2:38). The task for McAlister, Sheppe, Ewart, and other early advocates of a doctrine of baptism in the name of "Jesus only" was to reconcile Acts 2:38 with Matthew 28:19, where the names Father, Son, and Holy Ghost are referred to in connection with baptism. Oneness thinkers resolved the discrepancy when they understood the word "name" used in Matthew 28:19 to mean that Father, Son, and Holy Spirit were simply singular names for Jesus. Therefore, the baptismal formula in Acts serves as the norm for all baptisms.

The next step was the denial of the Trinity itself.

This "Pentecostal Unitarianism," as it is called by some, was forged out of modalistic monarchianism based on the Old Testament theology of the unity and oneness of God. The Jewish Shema, "Hear, O Israel: The LORD our God, the LORD is one" (Deut. 6:4), led to the conviction that God's presence is manifested singularly. Any reference to a Trinitarian or "binitarian" expression of the deity must be understood in terms of various manifestations of God occurring at different times within the locus of revealed history.

It is not entirely accurate, however, to label Oneness Pentecostals as "unitarian" in at least one sense. The UNITARIAN-UNIVERSALIST ASSOCATION denies the Trinity essentially because it denies the deity of Jesus Christ. Oneness, however, while it denies the Trinity, does affirm the deity of Christ, because Christ represents the fullest manifestation of God: "In Christ all the fullness of the Deity lives in bodily form" (Col. 2:9). To them, the doctrine of the Trinity seemed to deny and/or weaken this full revelation of deity in Christ by admitting to the additional revelations of God in other persons. In other words, how could the revelation of God in Christ truly be a "full" revelation if God was simultaneously revealed or manifested in other competing persons?

Reed points out that Oneness theology is distinctively Jewish in flavor.

> The truth about God and Christ for oneness Pentecostals is rooted in the Old Testament doctrine of God and the oft-ignored doctrine of the name of God. Any plurality in the nature of God is straightway rejected on the grounds of the radical monotheism of the Old Testament (e.g., Deut. 6:4, Isa. 43:10). And the two concepts of nature and name are linked together by the ancient notion that a person and his name are inseparable. The name serves to reveal the person. Indeed, all the power that a person possesses can be taken up and demonstrated through His name.[8]

Reed's latter point is crucial to understanding the theology of Oneness. The name of God in the Old Testament, Yahweh (or YHWH, without the vowels—also translated "Jehovah") was as sacred and holy as God himself. In the New Testament dispensation, the sacred name of God becomes Jesus. Just as YHWH meant that God is absolutely holy according to his divine essence, the New Testament ascribes to Jesus a name that corresponds to his own nature. Jesus, or *Yeshua*, means "Jehovah saves." According to Matthew 1:21, the name Jesus was given to the divine Son born of Mary because he would "save his people from their sins." Name and nature go hand in hand. In the Old Testament, God's name was Yahweh. Now God's essential name is Jesus. Therefore, baptism, prayer, or any other sacred act must be conducted in the name of God as he is presently being manifested, that is, in the name of Jesus only. An important distinction between the modalistic monarchianism of Oneness and that of classical ᵇmonarchianism is that while the latter taught that God manifested himself in three different modes (Father, Son, and Spirit) at distinctive times chronologically, Oneness theologians teach that all three manifestations are present at one and the same time.

So strong was the conviction that the only correct baptism was "baptism in the name of Jesus" that Oneness advocates were rebaptized according to the new formula, denying the legitimacy of their former Trinitarian baptisms. This invited scorn from Trinitarian Pentecostals and was perhaps one of the most significant reasons for the latter's strong reactions against their Oneness counterparts.

According to Dr. Menzies, leaders within the Assemblies of God "concluded that the 'new revelation' was nothing more than the resurrection of ancient heresy."[9] The heresy that Oneness most closely approximates according to traditional Christianity is ᵇNestorianism, at least with respect to Christology. Nestorius had taught that the two natures of Christ, his human and divine, while related to one another, can be distinguished clearly like two boards that are glued together. The church's condemnation of Nestorianism as heretical at the Council of Ephesus in A.D. 431 was based on a number of problems, one of which was that by separating the two natures Nestorianism offered no way to understand how the ᵇincarnation could describe the communication of divine and human attributes to one another in a meaningful fashion.

The Council of Chalcedon (A.D. 451) advanced the traditional Christology accepted by all orthodox churches, stating: "We confess one and the same Jesus Christ, the Son and Lord only-begotten in two natures without mixture, without change, without division, and without separation." Such a formulation enabled the church to understand how the human aspects of Jesus' nature related to the divine. For example, how could human blood possibly cleanse from sin (1 John 1:7)? By confessing that the human and divine attributes are communicated to one another in such a way that each shares in the properties of the other, the church was able to recognize how human blood could be salvific.

The Nestorianizing tendency has always been influential in some Protestant Christologies, and this is true of Oneness Pentecostalism as well. Oneness Pentecostalism uniquely forges the necessary link between the human and divine natures of Christ through the concept of the "theology of the name." In other words, the name of God, "Jesus," is accompanied by all of the attributes that proved the needed bond between the otherwise separate and distinct natures of Christ. Nestorian Christology continues to dominate in Oneness thought.

Many sects tend not to develop or adhere to creeds. The basic conviction of Oneness Pentecostals, however, with respect to Christology is that the sonship of Jesus is temporary. God will one day abandon the name "Jesus" and will assume a new name that will in turn convey new characteristics and attributes. This idea, wherever stated or believed, is derived from the modalistic monarchianism deemed heretical by the orthodox church in the third and fourth centuries. All churches that hold to the Apostles', Nicene, and Athanasian creeds confess that the distinctive nature of the three persons in one God and one God in three persons is an accurate articulation of orthodox theology (*see* Appendix 1).

The theology of the name also spells out important implications for each individual Christian in Oneness Pentecostalism. Since the name Jesus conveys the various aspects and characteristics of God's nature, to know God is to know the name. Or rather, in order to know God, one must know his name. Indeed the name of Jesus is of utmost importance in all areas and dimensions of the Christian life. This is true of baptism where the "name" and the new birth are conjoined. Because of this, baptism takes on a significance unlike water baptism within Trinitarian Pentecostal groups. For the latter, ᵇsoteriology has two stages: (1) repentance and faith, accompanied by baptism as obedience to Jesus' command (Matt. 28:19; Mark 16:16); and (2) the infilling of the Holy Spirit as a subsequent grace (Acts 2:4–13). In general for Oneness, salvation has a three-step process. The added dimension simply lies in the emphasis on baptism as being an outward sign through which the name of God (Jesus) is appropriated. For Oneness, baptism in the name of Jesus is a necessity. Thus, the stages of soteriology are: (1) repentance and faith, (2) baptism in the name of Jesus, (3) the gift of the infilling of the Holy Spirit.

CONCLUSION

Numerous books, pamphlets, and essays that tell the story of Pentecostalism in America summarize quite well the particular and peculiar story of Oneness. Though the "New Issue" of the early 1900s has become a rather old issue, long since dismissed as being heretical within Assembly of God ranks, it is still an extant movement in the rich variety of American religious experience. The largest and most influential Oneness group continues to be the UPCI.

Because Oneness rejects the traditional Christian doctrine of the Trinity and invests the ᵇsacrament of baptism with a theology unlike any believed, taught, or confessed within the ranks of orthodoxy throughout the centuries, it must in the last instance be regarded as being a heretical sect by those Christian churches that uphold the ecumenical creeds. As has already been shown, however, its anti-Trinitarianism is not an expression of bias against the deity of Christ. Ironically, the opposite is true. For this reason, some Oneness advocates are more willing to acknowledge Trinitarians as being true Christians than are most Trinitarians willing to return the favor.

ADDITIONAL INFORMATION

Headquarters
The United Pentecostal Church International, 8855 Dunn Road, Hazelwood, MO 63042.

Website
www.upci.org

Sacred Text
The Bible

Publication
Pentecostal Herald

Membership Statistics
The UPCI in the United States has 600,000 plus members. There are groups in 170 other nations with 22,881 licensed ministers and 28,351 churches and meeting places; the estimated total membership worldwide is 4 million. The Oneness movement in general is estimated to have a worldwide following of fourteen million.

Notes
[1] William W. Menzies, *Anointed to Serve* (Springfield, Mo.: Gospel, 1971), 111.
[2] David Reed, "Aspects of the Origins of Oneness Pentecostalism," in *Aspects of Pentecostal-Charismatic Origins*, ed. Vinson Synon (Plainfield, NJ: Logos International, 1975), 145–46.
[3] Ibid., 146.
[4] David Reed, "Oneness Pentecostalism" in *The New International Dictionary of Pentecostal and Charismatic Movements*, ed. Stanley M. Burgess and Eduard M. van der Maas, rev. ed. (Grand Rapids: Zondervan, 2002), 937.
[5] Ibid.
[6] Ibid., 938.
[7] Ibid., 944.
[8] Reed, "Origins of Oneness Pentecostalism," 148.
[9] Menzies, *Anointed to Serve*, 114.

ORDER OF THE SOLAR TEMPLE; OST

Small religious ᵇsects generally do not come to the attention of the public until a tragedy or something sensational strikes, inviting the attention of the media, at which point the group receives instant notoriety in the public square. Such is the case with several groups covered in this volume, such as the BRANCH DAVIDIANS or HEAVEN'S GATE. The Order of the Solar Temple (OST) is another group in this category.

HISTORY

Also called the International Chivalric Organization of the Solar Tradition, the Order was founded by Luc ᵇJouret (1947–1994) and Joseph ᵇDiMambro (1924–1994). DiMambro joined the ROSICRUCIAN order in 1956, where he remained active for thirteen years. In 1970, DiMambro was accused of swindling and fled from France to a place near the Swiss border.

The 1970s marked the beginning of THE NEW AGE MOVEMENT, and DiMambro was caught up in this new ideology. In 1973 he founded the Center for Preparing the New Age and became a "spiritual master" three years later. The group was centered in France. On July 12, 1978, DiMambro organized the sect of the Golden Way Foundation in Geneva. In 1982 he was introduced to Luc Jouret. Jouret was a member of another organization called the Renewed Order of the Temple, founded by a former German Gestapo agent named Julian Origas.

Trouble erupted in 1983, and Jouret was forced out of the Renewed Order, but not before taking a large number of members with him. Jouret with his following, and DiMambro with his own, combined to form the Order of the Solar Temple. Jouret proved to be the far more charismatic leader and DiMambro largely supported him in this role. Jouret was a gifted speaker and traveled between France, Switzerland, and across the Atlantic to Canada. In the years that followed, the organization, largely under Jouret's leadership, was divided into three areas. The first was called *Amanta.* This was the lecturing arm, headed by Jouret. The second and more exclusive group was called the *Archedia Clubs.* This involved more in-depth study and commitment. The third level was the *International Chivalric Organization of the Solar Tradition.*

More problems arose in the years before the tragedy of 1994. DiMambro's son, Elie, became a sharp critic of his father, accusing him of being a fake. He openly doubted the existence of the "masters," and this eventually led to his and fourteen other members leaving the group. Further, both DiMambro and Jouret came into conflict with each other. Members of the group attended meetings less frequently and began to donate less of their time and money. The divisiveness growing between Jouret and DiMambro contributed to the growing volatility of the members. Confusion, anger, disarray, and other factors contributed to the horror that lay ahead.

Like other recent cults, the Solar Temple started to move toward a "final solution." On October 5–6, 1994, fifty-three members of the group in both Switzerland and Quebec, Canada, committed suicide, including DiMambro and Jouret. In December, 1995, sixteen additional members of the Solar Temple also committed suicide. Five additional members died in Quebec in 1997, leaving three teens behind to explain what happened.[1] They insisted that the members of the Solar Temple had all died willingly.

ORGANIZATION

With the deaths of most of its members and leaders, the Solar Temple no longer exists. Various Templar organizations, from which many of the group's ideas were formulated, do however, have active chapters.

BELIEFS

New Age, environmental, and various strands of esoteric beliefs of the Knights Templar characterized the loosely structured beliefs held to by members of the Solar Temple. The beliefs parallel those of another group called the Sovereign Order of the Solar Temple (OSTS), which are listed as follows:

- reestablishing the correct notions of authority and power in the world
- affirming the primacy of the spiritual over the temporal
- giving back to man the conscience of his dignity
- helping humanity through its transition
- participating in the Assumption of the Earth in its three frameworks: body, soul, and spirit

- contributing to the union of the churches and working toward the meeting of Christianity and Islam
- preparing for the return of Christ in solar glory[2]

The mass suicides are not easily explainable. Beliefs, however, are powerful agents for action. Jouret had taught that civilization was being prepared for an "apocalyptic disaster," which, by interpretation, culminated in the subsequent suicides. And/or it was perhaps the belief that members of the group had concerning their role and responsibility to the world. It is true that they held to the conviction that they were not citizens of planet earth but were "noble travelers." They were simply passing through on a journey homeward.[3] Another suggestion has been that the burnings were "purification" rituals, death being the final process of purgation. Did this belief system combine with a growing awareness that there were insurmountable problems relative to the environment (pollution etc.)?

Jean-Francois Mayer believes that the situation is far more complicated. Rather than a manufactured cosmological myth about other worlds, Mayer believes that it was DiMambro's complete control over the members of the group that affords the more plausible explanation. As alluded to above, when DiMambro's son Elie started to call his father into question and doubting the existence of the so-called "master" in Switzerland, defections started to take place. As it turns out, DiMambro had fabricated a story about his son's birth as a "child of destiny." DiMambro had lied about the year of his son's birth, claiming that it was in Israel in 1969 and that he was destined to be the first "Grand Master of the Temple of the New Age of the Era of the Virgin." In fact, Elie was born in 1983 and was raised by his mother under normal circumstances.[4]

There are virtually no similarities in the teachings of OST and traditional CHRISTIANITY. There is no place where Christians are called to commit suicide. No amount of ritual effort is efficacious for the cleansing from sin. Christ alone has died to atone for the sins of a world that God so loved. Jouret and DiMambro are modern examples of leaders who, unlike the founder of Christianity, led their followers to mass destruction rather than to the gates of the kingdom of God.

CONCLUSION

The Solar Temple in some ways prefigured and paralleled the Heaven's Gate cult, led by Marshall Applewhite. Still, it may be difficult to finally and fully understand the dynamics that caused the suicides. Much remained secretive and perished in the ashes of those who died.

ADDITIONAL INFORMATION_____

Website
www.religioustolerance.org/dc_solar.htm

Sacred Texts
The Bible, the Koran, a book by Jouret titled *Medicine and Conscience,* and a tape called "Fundamental Time of Life" on audiocassette.

Membership Statistics
In 1989 there were 442 members (Switzerland, 90; France, 187; Canada, 86; Martinique, 53; United States, 16; Spain,

10). The group was in decline at the time of the mass suicide in 1994.[5]

Notes
[1] *http://religiousmovements.lib.virginia.edu/profiles/listalpha.html*, 3.

[2] Ibid., 5, quoted from Peronnik (pseudonym of Robert Chabrier), *Porquoi la resurgence de l'ordre du temple? Tome premier: Le corps* (Why a Templar Revival? Vol. One: The Body) 1975, 147–49.

[3] Jean-Francois Mayer, "Myths of the Solar Temple," paper presented to the ISAR/CESNUR Symposium on Violence and the New Religions (Nashville, 1996), 11–12.

[4] *http://religiousmovements.lib.virginia.edu/profiles/listalpha.html*, 6.

OUSPENSKY-GURDJIEFF

A number of societies have formed around the thought of the Russian philosopher/mystic George Ivanovitch ▸Gurdjieff (1872–1949). He would have remained a relatively obscure figure if it had not been for the popularization of his ideas through Peter Demianovich ▸Ouspensky. Gurdjieff's ideas, characterized as esoteric, NEW AGE, ▸occult-like, psychological, and certainly spiritual did, in fact, become relatively well known in the mid-twentieth century.

HISTORY

Gurdjieff was born in Alexandropol, Armenia, in 1872. His childhood years are difficult to recount. His father introduced the world of the occult to him early on, and he retained a profound interest in the subject for the rest of his life. He traveled a great deal in his formative years throughout northeast Africa, Europe, the Middle East, and Asia. He settled in Russia in 1913, where he remained until the outbreak of the Revolution in 1917. Returning to the Caucasus region, Gurdjieff founded the Institute for the Development of Man in 1919. Three years later he migrated to France, where he lived for the remainder of his life. He reopened the institute in Fontainebleau, France, and it remained open until 1933. He spent his final sixteen years teaching in Paris and died on October 29, 1949.

Gurdjieff's ideas did not die, however. One of his disciples, Peter Demianovich Ouspensky, popularized Gurdjieff's teachings to the point where followers met in groups called "G-O" (G for Gurdjieff and O for Ouspensky).

Shortly after Gurdjieff's death, the Gurdjieff Foundation of New York was established. Other centers were set up in San Francisco, Los Angeles, and Washington, D.C. In 1978, Jeanne de Salzmann produced a film based on Gurdjieff's life and teachings and named it after Gurdjieff's autobiography—*Meetings with Remarkable Men!* In the 1990s there were still some disciples who had known Gurdjieff personally. Those who became followers after his death have formed societies and developed websites that distribute Gurdjieff's books, tapes, and videos.

ORGANIZATION

There are various independent foundations located around the world that meet to study and promote the writings of Gurdjieff. Some of the names are listed below (see Conclusion). Many can also be found on the various websites listed below.

TEACHINGS

Gurdjieff tried to harness what he called the "wisdom of the East and the energy of the West." His philosophy has been alternately labeled "esoteric CHRISTIANITY." It is much more "esoteric" than it is "Christian" (if the latter refers to traditional Christian ▸orthodoxy). One quickly discovers the orphic nature of Gurdjieff's thought in his writings, which combine elements of the occult, ▸mysticism, ▸existentialism, and psychology.

Basic to Gurdjieff was the contention that the human quest is the existential search for "self." Before discovering self, all human beings live in a state of sleep consciousness. The goal is to awaken the conscience. This is done by being transported to higher levels of self-awareness. Ascending to these heightened levels of awareness is no easy task, however, but with ample effort the goal can indeed be realized.

Borrowing from Freud's paradigm, Gurdjieff contended that the self is composed of multilayered egos. The task comes in sifting through all of these different egos and pinpointing what is authentic. Gurdjieff describes this process in his book *The Fourth Way*. This "fourth way" is that human beings can cultivate an active center of the self that transcends yet remains with three other dimensions to the human person. These are the body, mind, and emotions. The "fourth way" remains in the midst of these three centers.

Devotees who seek to mount from sleep consciousness to discover their authentic self do so through studying Gurdjieff's books, practicing a series of mental exercises that enable them to experience awareness in each part of their bodies. Disciples also engage in dance rituals accompanied by music composed by Gurdjieff himself.

In addition to *The Fourth Way*, Gurdjieff's philosophy is found in the following works: *Meetings with Remarkable Men*, *Life Is Only Real When I Am*, and *Beelzebub's Tales to His Grandson*.

Traditional Christianity bears little resemblance to Gurdjieff's thought. Because of the eclectic combination of various religions, philosophy, and psychology, it is difficult to note any degree of concomitance between the church and the Russian philosopher. Comparisons can be more readily made between Gurdjieff and the Christianity that emerged in the nineteenth century, which was heavily influenced by speculative idealism and existentialism. Russia was indeed experiencing a new renaissance of existentialist thought in Christian circles, particularly in the writings of Nicolas Berdyaev and Fyodor Dostoevsky.[1]

For Berdyaev, the objective world is a world where human freedom is forfeited and alienation is heightened. True freedom lies in the spiritual realm, where one discovers "his existential depth."[2] Similarly, Gurdjieff contends that freedom lies where the authentic self is discovered. Berdyaev argued that evil and suffering were the necessary results of freedom.[3] Gurdjieff, however, saw evil as being the way of life for those having not yet discovered true freedom.

Traditional Christianity differs sharply from existentialism. The former holds that truth, particularly the truths of the faith as recorded in the ▶Bible, are cognitive, propositional, and objective statements of and about reality. The existentialists deny the relevance of objectivity by insisting that truth is apprehended *before* or a priori to outer reality. Truth must be experienced before it is recognized as being true. Jean-Paul Sartre, the French existentialist, advanced this principle in his famous statement, "Existence precedes essence." This is true also for Gurdjieff. The material world of objective reality is an illusion and a mirage, overcome only through emerging from sleep consciousness.

Gurdjieff's "theology" leaves no place for the notion of the existence of an objective God who is other than the self. That the human race is in a state of sin and active rebellion against God, or that God has provided means of atonement for sin in the person and work of Jesus Christ as reported in the Bible (Rom. 3:21–26) and in the ecumenical confessions of the church (*see* Appendix 1), is inimical to Gurdjieff's thought. By building on the foundation of speculative philosophy, Ouspensky-Gurdjieff emerged as a system of thought far different from that of the Christian church. Like THEOSOPHY, CHURCH OF THE NEW JERUSALEM (SWEDENBORGIANISM), THE NEW AGE MOVEMENT, CHRISTIAN SCIENCE, and so on, Ouspensky-Gurdjieff continues to appeal to an educated constituency, many of whom have dismissed traditional Christianity as being an outmoded vestige of the past.

CONCLUSION

There are collective groups that meet to study the writings of Gurdjieff. One such group, the Aretetelos Society, meets in California and conducts four seminars each year—two on the east coast and two on the west coast. Members gather to study and hear papers on Gurdjieff's writings, life, and thought. There are approximately five thousand followers scattered throughout the major cities of the United States. The influence of Gurdjieff extends far beyond its own ranks, however. For example, Gurdjieff prophesied the coming of a great prophet in his book *Beelzebub's Tales to His Grandson*. Many members believed that Muhammed ▶Subud fulfilled the prophecy when in 1925 he claimed that a ball of light descended on him. Subud subsequently founded a movement that he called Subud. Another significant movement that emerged out of Ouspensky-Gurdjieff is the Fellowship of Friends, also called Renaissance.

Ouspensky-Gurdjieff has also influenced the New Age Movement. Consciousness-raising techniques, used to heighten planetary awareness and personal transformation, are the common parlance of the last decades of the twentieth century. "Organizational Development" (OD) programs, developed by Charles

Krone and used in many Fortune 500 companies in the 1980s, were indirectly influenced by Gurdjieff.[4]

ADDITIONAL INFORMATION_____

Headquarters
Aretetelos Society for Ouspensky-Gurdjieff is located in New York City.

Websites
www.gurdjieff.org/; www.gurdjieff-legacy.org; www.bmrc .berkeley.edu/people/misc/G.html

Sacred Texts
Followers read the writings of Gurdjieff.

Publications
The Gurdjieff Journal (formerly called *Telos*).

Membership
Roughly estimated to be around 5000 loosely associated followers.

Notes
[1] See Berdyaev's *The Destiny of Man*, 1959, and *The Beginning and the End*, 1952; Matthew Spinka, *Nicolas Berdyaev, Captive of Freedom* (Philadelphia: Westminster, 1950); for Dostoevsky see his novels *The Idiot*, 1869; *Crime and Punishment*, 1866; and *The Brothers Karamazov*, 1880.

[2] Nicolas Berdyaev, *The Beginning and the End* (New York: Harper, 1952), 60.

[3] Berdyaev, *Spirit and Reality* (New York: Scribners, 1939), 115.

[4] Elliot Miller, *A Crash Course on the New Age Movement* (Grand Rapids: Baker, 1989), 100. See bibliography and the above-listed websites for more recent writings.

PENITENTES; BROTHERS OF OUR FATHER JESUS

"It's always been hard to be a penitente. We've endured a lot of persecution, not just from Anglos, but from Hispanics who think we're different and strange."[1]

HISTORY

The Penitentes or the Brothers of Our Father Jesus is a ▸sect that grew out of CHRISTIANITY, specifically, Roman Catholic Christianity. In Spanish, the name is *Los Hermanōs Penitentes del Tercer Orden de Franciscanos.* Some sources trace its beginnings to the fifth century of the Christian era when monasticism began to flourish in the church. The sect was transported to the United States in the early eighteenth century when the Spanish settled in western portions of the United States, planting both settlements and missions.

The Penitentes arose largely when, as a result of a shortage of priests, religious brotherhoods were formed by laypeople. In the mountain area of Sangre de Cristos, adherents began to practice the ceremonies of self-flagellation and mock crucifixions, particularly during the Lenten season. A nineteenth-century archbishop attempted to halt the practice but to no avail. Currently, the Catholic church tolerates the sect as long as those practices of the early years, such as inflicting pain and injury and conducting actual crucifixions, do not now occur. This group has never been large and is today settled in southern Colorado and northern New Mexico.

TEACHINGS

Aside from the common influence of Roman Catholic theology in the thought of the Penitentes, what is peculiar is its belief that atonement for sin comes not exclusively through Christ's sacrifice, suffering, bloodshed, and death on the cross, as Christianity maintains, but rather through the dramatic reenactment of the crucifixion each year at Easter. Witnesses at one time claimed to have seen the Penitentes actually perform literal crucifixions complete with nails and accompanying death, though members of the sect have vehemently denied this. What is certain, however, is that they maintain that true atonement for sin is only accomplished through self-inflicted pain and personal suffering.

According to ▸orthodox Christianity, Jesus' crucifixion was the all-sufficient sacrifice for the sins of the world (Rom. 3:21–26; Heb. 9:28). To teach that the atonement of Christ was not in itself vicarious and all-sufficient is a marked contrast to both the ▸Bible and Christian doctrine. Christian suffering and self-denial is a form of servanthood and discipleship; it is not ▸soteriological (Rom. 5:12ff.). To suggest otherwise is to deny the basic foundation on which the church is built: "On this rock I will build my church, and the gates of Hades will not overcome it" (Matt. 16:18).

CONCLUSION

There are other groups that practice self-flagellation. There have been reports that the Penitentes still undergo their ritualistic practices secretly. Outside the reports of several eyewitnesses, there is little evidence extant to verify the actual practices taking place within the sect. It continues, however, to attract attention among the curious.

ADDITIONAL INFORMATION_____

Note

[1] Quotation from Bill Roybal on *http://www.csindy.com/csindy/2000–04–20/cover.html*, which contains a recent account of a visit and interview by Conger Beasley to a Penitentes family.

PEOPLE'S TEMPLE

This ʼcult is now defunct through literal attrition when its leader, Jim ʼJones (1931–1978), and his flock migrated to the northwest district of Guyana in South America to the place the group called ʼJonestown. It was there that the group shocked the world in 1978 by committing mass suicide. What follows is a brief account of the tragedy.

HISTORY

The People's Temple was founded in 1953 by James Warren ("Jim") Jones. The blossoming movement was then known as the Community Unity Church. Largely because of Jones's charisma and initial concern for the urban poor, his congregation, comprised of mostly black followers, grew substantially. In 1965 the group moved to Ukiah, California, and then to San Francisco in 1971.

However humble Jones may have been in the early years of his ministry, he became obsessed with power and control in the latter years. He began to use amphetamines on a regular basis and conducted fake faith healings. Both defectors and journalists began to accuse Jones of diverting group funds for private use. In the face of these mounting accusations, Jones decided to move the People's Temple to Guyana in 1977. There he established an agricultural community called Jonestown. Jones's power knew no bounds. Passports were confiscated, members were forced to work long hours, certain women were selected by Jones to sleep with him, and rebellious members were punished under threat of blackmail, beatings, and death.

On November 14, 1978, Congressman Leo Ryan, a state representative from California, arrived in Jonestown with journalists and relatives of cult members to conduct an investigation. Offering to take home any who wished to accompany him, Ryan planned on leaving on November 18 with fourteen defectors. Fearing public exposure, Jones ordered Ryan and all who accompanied him assassinated. Ryan, three reporters, and one defector were gunned down just before boarding their plane. Realizing that those who had escaped would certainly bring in authorities, Jones initiated his well-rehearsed mass suicide called "white night," commanding his devotees to drink cyanide-laced punch. The next day Guyanese troops arrived, and soon after the world was rocked by the news of the deaths. The final death toll reached 913. Jones himself was found dead of a gunshot wound to the head.

On the twentieth anniversary of the tragedy, there was an attempt by the Congressional House Committee on International Relations to declassify much of the government documentation so as to learn more about what actually happened at Jonestown.

TEACHINGS

Jones's early theological influence was CHRISTIANITY. He attended a Pentecostal Bible College in Springfield, Missouri. As he became more and more enamored by his own sense of self-importance within his religious community, he forsook any sense of traditional ʼorthodoxy that he may have possessed. He openly denied the deity of Christ and the authority of the ʼBible, setting himself up as the final authority for the community. Jones also taught the doctrine of ʼreincarnation and was influenced by the "prosperity gospel" of Father Divine and the principles of Marxist socialism, which he initiated at Jonestown. Jones appointed a private army, called Angels, who were in charge of maintaining strict discipline and control. Rule breakers were regularly punished through beatings and catharsis sessions.[1]

Today, the building in Ukiah, California, that played home to the movement before it migrated to South America has been turned into an Assemblies of God church. On November 8, 1997, four hundred people attended a "Raise the Cross Sunday," and the building was "reclaimed" for Christianity, as some residents refer to the event.

We must remember that many of the documents relative to the People's Temple are still under lock and key. This has led to conspiracy theories, one of which claims that Jones was really employed by the CIA and that he led his followers to Guyana to participate in a project known as MK ULTRA. This was a CIA effort to experiment with and duplicate techniques used in Soviet and Chinese brainwashing. The MK ULTRA project ended in 1973, and there has never been any proof that there is any substance to these claims.[2] But at the same time there are 5,000 plus documents that Congress has not yet declassified.

CONCLUSION

The fact that Jones ordered his followers to drink the poison that killed most of them is not as inexplicable as the fact of his followers' compliance. Such obedience is only explainable when one fully realizes the dynamics of cult mind control.[3] These dynamics are well rehearsed in many cults worldwide. Had the mass suicide not occurred, People's Temple may well have remained an obscure cult amidst many others. The event in November 1978, however, became instant shock therapy, waking up a public that had seemingly come to accept the cults, ever so popular and numerous in the 1970s, as a part of everyday life.

The significance of Peoples' Temple is that the Jonestown massacre served as a watershed, marking the beginning of mass public awareness of the dynamics of personality and mind control cults and of their potential threat. Perhaps for a while it did just that. But then came the news of the BRANCH DAVIDIAN tragedy, HEAVEN'S GATE, the SOLAR TEMPLE, AUM SUPREME TRUTH,

and the ʾAl Quaeda terrorist organization and the tragedy on September 11, 2001. These events, and their relative close proximity to one another, have quickly erased the notion that we can lightly dismiss the power and effectiveness of cults.

A book written by Laurie Efrein Kahalas, a survivor of Jonestown, is titled *Snake Dance: Unraveling the Mysteries of Jonestown*.[4] Surprisingly, Kahalas attempts to tell the story from a sympathetic perspective and is highly critical of those outsiders—the government, media, scholars, and so on—who have been exclusively critical and have not brought out key factors from the People's Temple's own perspective on what happened. In counter measure, Deborah Layton, described as a high level surviving member of the People's Temple, published *Seductive Poison: A Jonestown Survivor's Story of Life and Death in the People's Temple* in 1998,[5] describing the evil that permeated this cult and its leadership.

ADDITIONAL INFORMATION

Websites

www.jones-town.org

Notes

[1] William Watson, *A Concise Dictionary of Cults and Religions* (Chicago, Moody Press, 1991), 179.

[2] Michael Taylor and Donald Lattin, "Most People's Temple Documents Still Sealed," *San Francisco Chronicle* (Nov. 13, 1998).

[3] See Steve Hassan's *Combatting Cult Mind Control*, (Rochester, VT.: Park Street, 1990).

[4] Laurie Efrein Kahalas, *Snakedance: Unraveling the Mysteries of Jonestown* (New York: Red Robin, 1998).

[5] Deborah Layton, *Seductive Poison: A Jonestown Survivor's Story of Life and Death in the People's Temple* (New York: Doubleday Anchor, 1998).

PROCESS CHURCH OF THE FINAL JUDGMENT; THE PROCESS

Labeled one of the most controversial cults of the 1960s, the Process Church of the Final Judgment was a unique group in that it changed in four separate stages. It sprang up as a result of a leader influenced heavily by interests and ideas not necessarily tied to religion, but more to psychology, SCIENTOLOGY, and other sundry sources. However, through a gradual transformation process, a religious cult emerged. Following that, the organization then renounced its reli-

gious underpinnings to become largely secular once again.

HISTORY

The Process Church of the Final Judgment was founded in 1963 by Robert de Grimston (b. 1935) along with his wife, Mary Anne MacLean. De Grimston's birth name was Robert Moore, but he and his wife changed their names to de Grimston following their marriage. The couple met in the early 1960s while both were involved in Scientology. Their mutual interest in psychology and common assessments of Scientology formed a bond of love between them.

Psychologist Alfred Adler became the focus of de Grimston's interests, particularly Adler's emphasis upon what underlying or unconscious forces exist that drive a person toward certain behaviors, impulses, or goals. Scientology attempted to penetrate the unconscious to remove negative past experiences through a process called "auditing" (see ▸auditor). De Grimston and his wife began to disagree with the techniques and emphasis of Scientology and its founder and focused more attention on Adler's work. In 1963, they broke ties with Scientology and formed Compulsions Analysis in London. They began to attract a clientele who came to them seeking fulfillment in life. Sessions were conducted both in one-on-one between clients and Robert and Mary Anne, and in group therapy. Consequently, a close-knit bond was formed between members of the group, who began to isolate themselves more and more from friends and family outside the group.

On June 23, 1966, the group left London for Nassau in the Bahamas. They did not remain there for long, however. The group became aware of the existence of some old buildings in ruins in Xtul on Mexico's Yucatan Peninsula, and they moved there, repairing the buildings and growing food through gardening. There the members starting shifting more toward religion and away from psychology. They began to pray and practice fasting.

In September 1968, Hurricane Inez passed through Xtul and lingered for two days. This had some important theological significance in that members believed their survival of this storm was the result of divine favor. Also, they interpreted it as nature manifesting itself in the gods, of which there is both a bad and a good side. One of the members stated that it was at Xtul that "we met God face to face."[1] The religious orientation of the group evolved rapidly as a result of the hurricane.

Shortly thereafter, however, trouble erupted when the parents of three of the members of the Process attempted to intervene. The Process abandoned Mexico and returned to England, no longer as a self-help therapy group but as a full-fledged religion. Soon there were chapters in numerous large cities throughout the world, including New York, San Francisco, New Orleans, Boston, Chicago, Paris, Munich, Hamburg, Amsterdam, and Rome. Members successfully solicited monies for the group, and Robert and Mary Anne

began to live quite well. Like numerous other cults, the couple began to isolate themselves from the rest of the group and traveled and lived more private lives. They called themselves *The Omega* while followers, who were now going out two by two recruiting and raising money, were called "The Processeans."

Also like numerous other groups in the 1970s, trouble began and a number of members exited. Questions arose about finance and de Grimstone developed a growing interest in ▸Satan. He implemented the New Game, a euphemism for sexual liberation between members of the group. However, on March 23, 1974, the ruling body of the Process, called the Council of Masters, removed de Grimston as "chief theologian" from the organization. He and Mary Anne separated, and de Grimston never regained power. Mary Anne and remaining leaders refocused the organization and called it the Foundation Faith of the New Millennium, known today as the Foundation Faith of God.

De Grimston attempted to reorganize and begin anew in 1979. It met with some success. The focus became assistance to the poor and homeless. In 1987, the organization expanded and private chapters were established. In 1988, the new name for the organization became The ▸Society of the Processeans. Members renounced the religious teachings of the past as "obsolete," destroyed their existing records and archives, and disbanded in 1993. The members who remain have continued to define themselves as a self-help organization.

ORGANIZATION

During its religious phase, Processeans were organized in a strict hierarchy, not of rank but of function: acolyte, initiate, outside messenger (OP), inside messenger (IP), prophets, priests, masters, and the Omega. In order to move from one status to another a person underwent a baptism.[2] When a member reached the third level of OP, he or she received an initiatory or sacred name and moved into a community home for one year. Specific chants accompanied the various rites. Sabbath assemblies were held on Saturday nights.

TEACHINGS

Because of the changes in the organization since the 1960s the beliefs and practices have varied widely. We can separate them into four main phases:

1. The first was the psychology phase. This early period was the time in which de Grimston focused on the writings and teachings of Alfred Adler.

2. The second was the movement toward religious beliefs when they arrived in Mexico. Here the focus was belief in God as the one supreme and holy one. The end of the world would be that time when God brings judgment to those who refuse to leave the realm and status of Satan.

3. In the third phase de Grimston started to speak of God as a trinity of Jehovah, Lucifer, and Satan—the three "great gods of the universe." Another claim is that there were actually "four" deities—this version including Jesus with the above three. Members were urged to discover which deity they felt most closely aligned toward and focus energy on serving that particular one.

4. The fourth phase, of course, is the present one, in which members participate in social and humanitarian activities.

During the religious phase of the group, the basic teachings were as follows:

God

The perfect and infinite one. God is perfectly free and limitless.

Humanity

Regarded as opposite God in every way and ensnared by limitations.

Sin

Sin was essentially bondage to limitation.

Christ

Christ fulfilled the role of bringing unity between God and that aspect of humanity that is separated from God. Christ was the great communicator between the gods and humanity. Christ also came to bring reconciliation between God, Lucifer, and Satan. Not unlike the Taoist (see TAOISM) doctrine of yin and yang, de Grimston taught that the entire universe is comprised of bipolar opposites (*The Two Pole Universe*) that are to be brought together in Christ. Therefore, Satan and God, as opposites, are reconciled in Christ.

Satan

Satan was believed at one time in the group to possess equal powers with Christ. He does not hurt the world as Christianity teaches, but fulfills the role of carrying out the acts of judgment meted out by Christ. Satan is as important to the world as is Christ in the final outcome of all things.

Processes

The name "The Process" was a series of actions or rituals that were believed to aid in escaping the fate of fallen humanity.

ANALYSIS

Traditional Christianity differs with Process theology and practice on most every point of doctrine. The heart of the matter is the dualism between Satan and Jesus Christ. Christianity teaches that Jesus Christ is God incarnate and that Satan's powers are limited to this world (2 Cor. 4:4).

CONCLUSION

The Processeans still participate in social and humanitarian activities. The future of the group, however, remains uncertain.

ADDITIONAL INFORMATION

Headquarters and Address
Not available

Official Websites
www.process.org; www.forteantimes.com/134_process.shtml (informative website, particularly in the account of the Process's early beginnings). See also: *www.disinfo.com/pages/dossier/id275/pg1/*

Sacred Texts
During the religious phase, the Bible (particularly the book of Matthew); several of the writings of de Grimston, including *Xtul Dialogs*: *As It Is! For Christ Has Come*, and *The Tide of the End*. Some selections are also found on the website and accompanying links.

Periodicals
"Process" and *"The Processeans"* (monthly newsletter).

Membership Statistics
At the peak of membership, the group probably had a following of 100,000 with a present actual membership of much less.

Notes
[1] William Bainbridge, *Satan's Power* (Berkeley: Univ. of California Press, 1978), 68.
[2] *http://religiousmovements.lib.virginia.edu/nrms/Process.html*

RAJNEESHISM; OSHU

Deriving its original name, Rajneesh Foundation International, from its founder, Bhagwan Shree ᐳRajneesh (1931–90), Rajneeshism became one of the numerous Eastern ᐳcults that found a home in the United States during the 1970s and 1980s. Since his death, the leadership has changed hands in the midst of severe legal battles and has changed its name to OSHO. It derived much of its religious content from HINDUISM.

HISTORY

The Bhagwan Shree Rajneesh (roughly translated "God Sir Rajneesh" or "Sir God Rajneesh") was born as Rajneesh Chandra Mohan in 1931 in Kuchwara, a small village in India. He was the oldest of twelve children with five sisters and six brothers. His parents, Swami Devateerth Bharti and Ma Amrit Saraswati, raised the family in JAINISM (a derivative of BUDDHISM that emphasizes ᐳasceticism and reverence for all living things).

Rajneesh did not understand his mission in life to be that of a ᐳguru until his college years. Before that, he was described as being "a radical critic of his own culture."[1] Even as a child he manifested a keen interest in religion. The death of his grandfather, to whom he was very close, resulted in a preoccupation with death. Rajneesh attended Jabalrur University where he majored in philosophy. Upon receiving a master's degree, he taught for several years at Madhya State University. In 1966, however, Rajneesh left his teaching post to become a guru after his receiving an experience of ᐳenlightenment.

Rajneesh traveled throughout his native land proclaiming his teachings. He never gained as large a following in India as he did in the United States and in other parts of the world. He did, however, acquire the reputation as being India's "sex guru." From 1969–1974 Rajneesh taught from Mount Abu in Rajasthan. In 1974 he opened the "lushly gardened Bhagwan Shree Rajneesh ᐳashram in the sedate city of Poona."[2] The ashram operated for seven years at Poona, during which time fifty thousand Americans made the pilgrimage. Another noted convert to Rajneesh was Shannon Jo Ryan, the daughter of Congressman Leo Ryan. The latter was killed while investigating the Jonestown PEOPLE'S TEMPLE in 1978.[3]

In 1981 Rajneesh suddenly fled Poona because of charges of income tax evasion.[4] On July 10, 1981, he purchased a ranch covering about thirty-nine square miles in Oregon, at a price of six million dollars. The new site was named Rajneeshpuram (expression of Rajneesh). It is also called the Big Muddy Ranch.

Trouble broke out almost immediately when Oregon residents began a petition drive to oust Rajneesh from the state. Pressure from the attorney general resulted in the eventual abandonment of the ashram, but not before one of Rajneesh's followers named Sheela was charged with poisoning drinking water with salmonella,[5] along with being charged with murder. She served 2.5 years in prison and was released. Rajneesh fled and turned up in Charlotte, North Carolina, where he sought sanctuary, attempting to avoid arrest for "overstaying his visa and arranging sham marriages so that selected followers could become permanent U.S. residents."[6] While boarding a plane bound for Bermuda, Rajneesh was captured by federal agents. *Newsweek* reports that Rajneesh pleaded guilty on two counts (violating U.S. immigration law and lying on his visa application four years ago, and conspiring to arrange one of the many sham marriages that allowed his Indian disciples to settle in the United States).[7] By October 20, 1986, with Rajneeshpuram abandoned to its rural setting, the last Rajneesh commune in the United States was closed in Laguna Beach.[8]

Rajneesh did not reestablish any formal ashrams after his arrival back in India. He died in January 1990 in Poona. Scandals and crimes involving the top leaders caused a number of investigations into the Rajneesh community that resulted in prison terms for them.

Today, the name of Rajneesh lives on in his followers. His books, writings, and tapes are published under the name of Osho. There is a ten-acre luxury spa in Pune, India, where followers continue to gather. Books and audio tapes surpass one million dollars in annual sales. In May, 2000, a book entitled *The Autobiography of the Spiritually Incorrect Mystic* was published.

TEACHINGS

Rajneesh's thought was derived basically from Hinduism. As a philosopher, he was a monist (*see* ᐳmonism). All reality is one in essence. The quest in the cycle of ᐳreincarnations is to attain enlightenment, ultimately reached through love/sex meditation. Death results in one's being cast back into the universe to emerge once again at some point along the cycle.

Rajneesh espoused open sex and complete freedom from inhibitions. The permissiveness of the 1960s and 1970s brought many 'sannyasi to the feet of the radical guru from Poona. In America, followers became known as neosannyas because Rajneesh, adapting to the result-oriented pragmatism of the West in general and Americans in particular, changed the concept of *sannyasi* (where a disciple meditates for years before attaining enlightenment) to the possibility of immediate attainment. Rajneesh stated his reason succinctly; "Westerners want things quickly, so we give it to them right away."[9]

In addition to free sex, Rajneesh's most radical teaching was that the family unit should be completely dismantled. He saw the family as "the biggest threat to human progress." While many Christian writers see this as being one of the earmarks of a cult, Rajneesh returned the charge, denouncing the pope and Mother Teresa and accusing CHRISTIANITY itself of being a cult.

"I don't profess anything," Rajneesh said.[10] While it is true that he did not espouse any system of thought, basic motifs do outline his religious conceptualizations. "To be free to contradict is a great phenomenon because then I am not worried at all about what I say. I don't keep any accounts, I need not be worried about what I said yesterday. I cannot contradict: this is a great freedom."[11]

Other basic doctrines espoused by Rajneesh are as follows:

God

Rajneesh was not a systematic thinker. Therefore it is more difficult to gather his thoughts on any religious subject as they are spread throughout his voluminous writings and tapes. As can be expected, Rajneesh taught a view of God and the universe that was essentially Hindu. "God is not a person somewhere waiting for you."[12] God is you.

> God is the ultimate synthesis; the atom, the ultimate analysis. Science reaches to the atom: it goes on analyzing, dividing, until it comes to the minutest part which cannot be added to it. It is already the whole. Nothing exists beyond it. Science is atomic; religion is "wholly." Use both.[13]

Because God is all things, all things, including human beings, are gods. This 'pantheism is diametrically opposed to the Christian conception of God. Christianity makes a radical distinction between the Creator and the creation (Rom. 1:18ff.), whereas in Rajneesh's thought, as in all Hindu thought, this distinction collapses into a monism.[14]

Jesus Christ

For Rajneesh, Jesus "became Christ on the cross when he said, 'Thy will be done, not mine.'"[15] Christhood is the state of enlightenment, 'nirvana, or 'moksha (as it is variously called). Anyone who seeks enlightenment can become Christ. Jesus the man was not born of a virgin as Christianity upholds but was human in the same sense that all are human. When Jesus spoke of fulfilling the Scriptures (Matt. 26:54; Mark 14:49), Rajneesh believed it was the Hindu scriptures to which Jesus referred, not the Hebrew Old Testament. He also believed that Jesus lived after he was crucified. Jesus died at the age of 112 in Kashmir, India.

Humanity

Central to Rajneesh's philosophy was the concept of "the new man" or "Zorba the Buddha." The new man is spiritual, materialistic, hedonistic, and preoccupied with the present. Experiences, love, sex, and meditation are the combined preoccupations of the 'sannyasi. The difference between Zorba and the old human nature is that the latter is owned by his or her wealth while the former is master of it and all things, as gods are apt to be.

Christianity certainly teaches that experience, love, and sex are important aspects of life. But Christian love is a selfless love for God and neighbor, as Christ demonstrated in his own person and work. Sexual intercourse is prohibited outside of marriage (Gen. 2:23–24; 4:1; 1 Cor. 6:16–20). Marriage is consummated in all of its richness and beauty between a husband and a wife (1 Cor. 7:2–3). Hedonism and worldliness are forbidden to the Christian. The prime focus of life is eternal life (Col. 3:1) where, immediately on death, the believer is ushered into the presence of God, not onto the wheel of reincarnation.

Sin

Sin for Rajneesh was essentially to be or possess the quality of unconsciousness. "Your being a sinner is not the result of the sins you have committed. Your being a sinner is a state of unconsciousness."[16] Sex, even outside marriage, is not sinful because it helps usher one to higher levels of consciousness. "Morality is a game; it changes. From society to society, age to age, period to period, it goes on changing. It depends, it has nothing ultimate about it."[17]

For Christianity, sin does possess reality (Rom. 3:23; 6:23), and it is only the believer in Jesus who will escape its ultimate consequences (John 3:18; Apostles' Creed, Articles 2 and 3, Appendix 1).

Salvation

To Rajneesh salvation occurs when a person becomes Christ or is enlightened. Christianity teaches that a person through faith *in Christ* obtains salvation.

Other Teachings

History is cyclical in Hindu thought. Because all is one, all lies on a continuous plane. Rajneesh believed that he was once John the Baptist but was reincarnated to function as Christ.

One of the most controversial aspects of Rajneesh's teaching is his anti-Semitism. In *The Mustard Seed*, Rajneesh states, "Jews are always in search of their Adolph Hitlers, somebody who can kill them—then they feel at ease."[18]

One of the more notable converts to Rajneesh was Richard Price, one of the gurus of the human potential movement and cofounder/director of the Esalen Institute. Many who attended EST (FORUM) seminars or considered themselves to be dabblers in the NEW AGE MOVEMENT found a home at the feet of the "sex guru" from Poona. *Time* describes the initiation process that a new convert underwent:

> [Converts] must undergo the elaborate ceremony led by Rajneesh himself. They buy orange robes at the ashram's boutique, then wash thoroughly. No one may approach the asthmatic guru with any trace of dust, perfume, or hair oil. Two tall blonde vestals at the gate carefully sniff at all who seek entrance. A single cough during the rite can be cause for ejection.

Then, reports *Time*'s New Delhi bureau chief, Lawrence Malkin,

> the screened initiates are placed in the lotus position on the hard terrazzo veranda. Rajneesh enters in a floor length white robe. One by one, the candidates for instant sanyas prostrate themselves before him and receive a 108 bead mala (necklace) with the guru's plastic covered picture dangling like a locket, and a personalized tidbit of wisdom from the guru's lips. . . . Each apostle also receives a new name.[19]

CONCLUSION

The influence of Rajneesh has continued well after his death. His followers now refer to him as Osho. Many New Agers look to the writings of Rajneesh, and numerous followers since his death have embraced the New Age Movement. James S. Gordon, in his book *The Golden Guru*, made some targeted remarks that proved somewhat prophetic, having been written two years before the guru's death:

In the end, Rajneesh became the kind of man, the kind of religious leader, he had always derided. If indeed his ego had once dissolved and melted like a drop into the ocean, it seemed over the years to have renewed and enlarged, and in his isolation it grew gross with his attachment to power and luxury and position. He became more power-hungry and more deceitful than any of the politicians he attacked, more papal than "the Polack," more sanctimonious than the saints he derided. On his ranch, surrounded by armed guards, dressed up and doped up, imperious and imperial, he resembled Jim Jones far more than Buddha or Krishna or Jesus. He was unwilling to learn or change, or to admit that there was anything to be learned or to change.[20]

According to one source, many people who purchase his various tapes, books, and lectures are perhaps unaware that these materials are simply the "rehashed ramblings of the late Rajneesh."[21]

ADDITIONAL INFORMATION

Websites
www.sannyas.net/index.shtml
www.otoons.com/oshu.html

Sacred Writings
Hindu sacred writings; books, tapes, lectures of Rajneesh

Membership
At the height of popularity, Rajneesh attracted over two hundred thousand followers in well over five hundred centers throughout the world.

Notes
[1] "Asiatic Religions in Europe," *Update* (a quarterly journal on new religious movements) 7/2 (June 1983): 5.
[2] "'God Sir' at Esalen East," *Time* (January 16, 1978), 59.
[3] See feature article on Shannon Ryan in *People* (February 16, 1981), 36–38.
[4] "Sins of Bhagwan," *India Today* (June 15, 1982), 135.
[5] "Busting the Bhagwan," *Newsweek* (Nov. 11, 1985), 32.
[6] Ibid., 26.
[7] "Goodbye Guru," *Newsweek* (Nov. 25, 1985), 50.
[8] "Last Rajneesh Commune Closed," *Blade Tribune* (Oct. 20, 1986), 8.
[9] "'God Sir,'" 59.
[10] Ibid.
[11] Bhagwan Shree Rajneesh, *Words Like Fire* (San Francisco: Harper & Row, 1976), 37.
[12] Bhagwan Shree Rajneesh, *The Mustard Seed* (San Francisco: Harper & Row, 1975), 110.
[13] Rajneesh, *Words Like Fire*, 202.
[14] See HINDUISM and ANANDA MARGA YOGA SOCIETY for a further discussion of the Creator/creation distinction in Christianity.

[15] Rajneesh, *Words Like Fire*, 271.
[16] Ibid., 191.
[17] Ibid., 176.
[18] Rajneesh, *Mustard Seed*, 32.
[19] "'God Sir,'" 59.

[20] James S. Gordon, *The Golden Guru* (Lexington, Mass.: Stephen Green, 1987), 245.
[21] Dennis McCafferty, "Old Bhagwan, New Bottles," *Salon* (Oct. 20, 1999).

RASTAFARIANISM

Rastafarianism is a movement defined by black nationalism combined with a distinctive theology that advances the idea of the superiority of the African peoples and the black race. Rastafarianism joins the ranks of other groups that are informed by race and ethnicity.

HISTORY

The story of the Rastafarians is the story of the black nationalist movement that began in the 1920s and 1930s. Marcus 'Garvey (1887–1940), a prominent leader of this movement, was born in Jamaica and in 1914 founded the Universal Negro Improvement Association and the African Communities League. Garvey's mission was to bring blacks to a consciousness of their own sense of history, self-esteem, and destiny. He was able to garner much support for his cause in America, particularly among the black urban masses. In 1927 he prophesied, "Look to Africa, where a black king shall be crowned, for the day of deliverance is here."

Three years later, in 1930, Ras Tafari 'Makonnen (1893–1975) was crowned Emperor 'Selassie of Ethiopia. Makonnen immediately was recognized by the ostentatious title "King of Kings, Lord of Lords, His Imperial Majesty of the Conquering Lion of the Tribe of Judah, Elect of God." This event was hailed as being the fulfillment of Garvey's prophecy.

As a result of Garvey's leadership many smaller movements arose, rallying around the tremendous revival of black consciousness that he was able to awaken. One of these movements, small as it was, took Garvey's prophecy seriously and hailed Emperor Selassie as being the great liberator of blacks.

His most eminent follower was L. P. Howell, a charismatic preacher and leader. In 1940 Howell established a settlement in Kingston, Jamaica, called Pinnacle. The settlement lasted for fourteen years, disbanding in 1954.

The followers of Selassie, adopting the emperor's name, called themselves Rastafarians. After Pinnacle had disbanded, the Rastafarians scattered throughout Jamaica. Many migrated to the United States during the 1960s and 1970s. Selassie was peacefully deposed in 1974 and died the following year. Selassie's death was accompanied by a great deal of controversy. Followers were disillusioned and some even uncertain as to whether or not Selassie's death had been fabricated by the media and enemies of their faith in order to discredit it.

ORGANIZATION

Several movements spawned as a result of Rastafarianism include Bobos and the Twelve Tribes. While these latter groups are structured and organized, traditional Rastafarianism remains without a high degree of structure. However, two "houses," as they are called, did arise—the House of 'Dreadlocks and the House of Combsomes. These two groups were distinguished by whether they combed their hair or opted for the more radical dreadlocks. The latter house has long since disbanded while the latter continued with its signature hair style that readily identified Rastafarians. The House is run by an assembly of elders as its governing body.

Marcus Garvey and the Rastafarians have made a significant impact on the black nationalist movement in America. *Courtesy Jack M. Roper/CARIS*

TEACHINGS

Some Rastafarians believe that Selassie is still alive, while most maintain that it is his memory and spirit that live on. An important tenet of Rastafarian teaching is the notion of a ▸black Judaism—that is, the idea that the Hebrews of the Old Testament were black. The black race is the living ▸reincarnation of the Israel of the ▸Bible. Whites are responsible for bringing blacks to the West, especially to the West Indies and Jamaica.

Though whites are not necessarily inferior to blacks, Rastafarians believe that the white race emerged from an ancient wicked civilization devoid of a spiritual dimension to life and that the very existence of the white race is "unnatural." This notion was advanced in an extreme form by the World Community of Ali Islam in the West; this group insisted that the black race was indeed a superior race and was destined to conquer and rule over all other races, especially whites (see NATION OF ISLAM).[1]

The basic beliefs of the Rastafarians were summarized by Howell as follows.

- hatred of the white race
- superiority of the black race
- revenge on the white race for its wickedness
- negation, persecution, and humiliation of the Jamaican government and all legal bodies of Jamaica
- preparation for a return to Africa
- acknowledgment of Selassie as the supreme being.[2]

The eschatological vision of Rastafarian thought lies in the belief that blacks will one day return to their true spiritual home—Ethiopia. When the black race returns to Europe, the white-ruled West will experience a total collapse, paving the way for the rightful rule of the black race.

Three important terms in the teaching of Rastafarianism are as follows:

1. *Babylon*: the white political power structure that Rastafarians must war against and eventually destroy.
2. *I and I*: the concept that all of what constitutes god resides within and that there is a oneness that unites all. This oneness does not exempt one, however, from the need to worship Selassie as the supreme being.
3. *Jah*: the Rastafarian word for "God." *Jah* will rule over his people and one day lead them back to Ethiopia, the equivalent of heaven on earth.[3]

Selassie wore a ring with the lion of Judah inscribed on it. This has come to be the symbol of Selassie.

There is no literal hell or belief in an afterlife, but the devil is the god of the white race.

Rastafarian colors were traditionally red, green, gold, and black. Red represents the blood of Rastafarian martyrs; green stands for the rich fauna of the Ethiopian homeland; gold reminds Rastafarians to observe a strict moral code:

- objection to any and all desecration of the body (such activities as shaving, tattooing, cutting the flesh, etc.)
- discouraging the eating of meat, with pork and shellfish strictly forbidden.
- belief in Jah as the one supreme god
- encouragement of love for humanity
- rejection of the sundry vices—jealousy, hate, gossip, envy, treachery, etc.
- desire to unite the entire world under the rulership of Selassie, with followers constituting a united brotherhood
- rejection of all worldliness and hedonism
- Rastafarians in need of help taking the highest priority; then any other human, animal, or plant
- obedience to the "ancient laws" of Ethiopia
- no respect of persons because of wealth, title, or any other; a Rastafarian is motivated in all things because of love for the truth

This last point strikes a similar chord with the teachings of Jesus Christ. Jesus declared that truth is the key to freedom (John 8:32). But the sharp contrast between Rastafarianism and Christianity lies in what each contends the truth to be. For Rastafarians, truth is embodied in the person of Ras Tafari Makonnen. It is he who, even in death, is looked on as being the savior of the black race (see also ▸twenty-one points).

Contrariwise, truth in the Christian religion is embodied in the person of Jesus Christ (John 14:6). It is the work of Jesus to offer the forgiveness of sins to *all* who repent and believe, regardless of race. The gospel of forgiveness is for the world (John 3:16), and the "communion of saints" (Apostles' Creed, Appendix 1) is not limited to a superior people. Christian missionaries are sent to preach Jesus Christ to every nation (Matt. 28:19).

The book of Acts alone abounds in testimonies of the conversions of people from all walks of life and from every conceivable social and economic background:

- Gentiles—Acts 2:39
- the sick—3:1–8
- those of mixed blood—8:4–25
- a Roman soldier—10:1–45
- a Roman governor—13:6–12
- a wealthy Gentile woman—16:11–15
- an Ethiopian [black]—8:26–40
- the intellectually elite—17:16–34
- the Jews—21:20
- pagans—1 Thess. 1:7–10

In another place, Paul declared that all are one through faith in Christ, with no distinctions made with respect to race, sex, or status: "There is neither Jew nor Greek, slave nor free, male nor female, for you are all one in Christ Jesus" (Gal. 3:27–28).

CONCLUSION

Many Rastafarians grow dreadlocks and smoke 'ganja. However, in the last decade, much of what was a strictly religious impulse has now become secularized. The dreadlocks are now much more a popular and trendy fashion than they are a religious symbol. Their music, called reggae, originated in Jamaica but has gained wide acceptance in the United States. In the United States, the feminist movement has radically changed the way that women's roles were traditionally defined in this traditionally patriarchal society.

ADDITIONAL INFORMATION

Headquarters
Kingston, Jamaica

Websites
There are a host of informational websites available on the Rastafarian movement. One good one that will lead to other good links is *www.aspects.net/~nick/religion.htm*.

Sacred Texts
Parts of the Christian Bible; *Holy Piby* (black man's Bible); *Kebra Negast*

Publication
A major Rastafarian periodical is titled *ARISE*, published by Creative Publishers, Ltd., 8 Waterloo Ave., Kingston, Jamaica.

Membership
It is estimated that at least five thousand Rastafarians are now living in the United States. It is extremely difficult, however, to determine the accuracy of this figure because many who do not embrace Rastafarian teaching are Rastafarian in appearance. Worldwide, there are estimated to be as many as one million Rastafarians.

Notes
[1] Note that the white race has also developed religious movements for its own superiority; see IDENTITY MOVEMENTS.
[2] *http://religiousmovements.lib.virginia.edu/nrms/rast.html.*
[3] Ibid.

RELIGIOUS SCIENCE; THE UNITED CHURCH OF RELIGIOUS SCIENCE; RELIGIOUS SCIENCE INTERNATIONAL

Religious Science is classified as one of the 'mind science religions that has gained prominence in America and abroad. Healing is the main focus of the mind sciences in general. It presents, along with DIVINE SCIENCE and CHRISTIAN SCIENCE, an approach that is quite different from traditional Christianity.

HISTORY

The movement known as Religious Science had its beginning with Ernest 'Holmes (1887–1960). Emma Curtis 'Hopkins had a great influence on Ernest and his brother, Fenwicke, and drew them into more intense study of the power of the mind for healing and happiness in life. In 1917 the two brothers founded the Metaphysical Institute in Los Angeles and began a periodical called *Uplift*.[1] In 1919 Holmes, a self-taught philosopher, published his first book, entitled *Creative Mind*. Moving to Los Angeles, he published *The Science of Mind* in 1927, which contains many ideas and teachings that parallel those of Hopkins, Emmanuel 'Swedenborg, Mary Baker 'Eddy, Phineas Parkhurst 'Quimby, and Helen 'Blavatsky.

In 1927 Holmes founded the Institute of Religious Science in Los Angeles, where students studied the principles that he and Fenwicke taught and enumerated in their various writings and lectures. Graduates of the institute went on to establish their own churches, and in 1949 the International Association of Religious Science Churches was formed. During the 1950s the movement rapidly moved toward a national organization structure.

This met with opposition from those who favored the looser, decentralized structure characteristic of the organization at its founding. Nineteen churches rejected the new constitution while forty-six moved toward adoption. Out of this, two main branches or churches stemming from the original Religious Science Movement were formed, with several independent bodies. The United Church of Religious Science is the larger group; Religious Science International, the smaller. The doctrines and teachings within each are similar, although the latter does not have a central governing body.

ORGANIZATION

The several independent bodies remain somewhat conversant with each other, and there is little acrimony, despite the polity differences. In the United Church of Religious Science, there are biennial district conventions from which a board of trustees are chosen. This board elects a president, who then serves a two-year term. The national board supervises education, Ernest Holmes College, Ministry of Prayer (a twenty-four-hour prayer and counseling hotline), and publication of its various forms of literature.

TEACHINGS

Religious Science follows essentially ▸monism. God is the impersonal self that becomes personalized in humanity. Individual minds are like rivers flowing from a central source, God.

Like Christian Science and Divine Science, Religious Science teaches that evil is the direct result of ignorance. Eliminating the latter will cure the former. The absence of evil will inevitably result in the omnipresence of good. People by nature have this good latent within themselves. This contention is, of course, a recurring theme within the Mind Sciences but is also a basic premise in Eastern religions, particularly HINDUISM.

Traditional Christianity militates against this idea by asserting the antithesis. Good does not stem from humankind but from God alone, who is the source of all good. Humanity is now evil and godless from conception (Ps. 51:5). It is the goodness of God coming from without that makes good possible. Different strands within the broad structures of Christendom offer a variety of interpretations to this concept of the study of man. Eastern Orthodoxy speaks of the "deification" of humanity, Roman Catholicism of the idea of "cooperative grace," the mystical tradition of the scintilla or "divine spark" within, the Reformation of "total depravity" that needs to be redirected through salvation by grace through faith. But all these tradi-

tions agree that the *source* of all good is God. The distinction between God and humankind is firmly maintained, whereas in Religious Science, this distinction becomes obliterated.

"Positive thinking" plays an important role in Religious Science. ▸Affirmative prayer—that is, the stress on the positive aspects of the mind's union with the infinite—is practiced. Any such prayer that leads to the healing of mind or body is referred to as being ▸spiritual mind treatment. The results of such prayer is called ▸demonstration.

God

God is all-pervasive and universal, an impersonal mind. For traditional ▸orthodoxy, God is certainly all-pervasive and universal, yet at the same time he is personal. God is at once ▸transcendent and ▸immanent, revealing himself to the nation of Israel through the voice of the ▸prophets in the Old Testament and through the apostles of Jesus Christ in the New Testament. Religious Science also has a pantheistic concept of God in that it believes that "all is God."[2]

Jesus Christ

Jesus was extremely advanced in his mastery of mind science techniques. "Jesus" is distinguished from "Christ."[3] Jesus was a man, but he was Christ in his "universal divine son-ship." That is, Jesus the man had an unusual grasp of the infinite and the laws of the universe. He was therefore able to perform miracles and healings. This Christ-realization is open to all who follow Jesus' example. When a person comes into a realization of a oneness with the divine, that person becomes Christ.

Holy Spirit

The Holy Spirit is a force within humanity; it is humanity's self-conscious powers or abilities to comprehend the infinite.

Humanity

Humanity is "the image and the likeness of the Universal Father." Similar to the nineteenth-century German theologian Ludwig Feuerbach, Holmes taught that humanity was god and god is what humankind is. Monistically, a human being is a microcosm of god. It is the ultimatum of humanity to know freedom from poverty, weakness, and fear.

Sin

Ignorance is the whole of sin. People are punished by their sins, not for them.

Salvation

There is no separation from God, hence no need for salvation in the traditional sense. The only breach between God and humanity is that the latter fails to realize its infinite oneness with God and the universe.

ᴾHell

Like sin, hell is nothing but ignorance. There can be no hell in a universe that is fully inhabited by God. Hell is merely seen as a state of mind.

Devil

The concept of the devil is seen as avoiding responsibility; thus there is no devil.

ᴾTrinity

Spirit, Soul, and Body make up the Trinity. The Spirit is the latent force enabling one to realize God within. The Soul obeys the will of the Spirit, and Body is the form Spirit assumes in each individual.

The doctrine of the Trinity marks perhaps the sharpest contrast between Religious Science and traditional Christian thought. The Trinity for orthodoxy is a clear reference to God; both in himself and in the divine economy God is revealed to humanity through Israel, the church, and Scripture. For Religious Science the Trinity represents a reductionism of God to the different aspects of a trichotomized self.

Church

Worship services are held regularly and closely resemble those of conventional mainline Protestant churches, with an emphasis on the inherent goodness of humanity. Holmes was self-taught in the doctrines of Religious Science. Most of the movement's ministers and ᴾpractitioners were also self-taught up until the early 1970s, after which time more of the constituency have been educated in colleges and the Science of Mind Institute.[4]

Holmes was a prolific writer. Religious Science looks to his collective works as being its source of authority. Such titles include: *The Science of Mind, What Religious Science Teaches, Practical Applications of Science of Mind, The Basic Ideas of Science of Mind, The Spiritual Universe and You, Know Yourself, Keys to Wisdom,* and *The Voice Celestial.*

CONCLUSION

Religious Science, like the other mind sciences, appeals to people who are looking for cures to illness and suffering that conventional medicine or traditional Christianity does not offer. This includes those with a philosophical disposition as well as those who have suffered from illnesses. Some prominent followers have included Robert Young (*Father Knows Best*), Norman Cousins (*Saturday Review*), and Robert Stack.[5] Leaders within the movement have held powerful positions with the International New Thought Alliance since Holmes's death in 1960.

ADDITIONAL INFORMATION_____

Headquarters

The United Church of Religious Science, 3251 West Sixth Street, Los Angeles, California 90020; Religious Science International, 901 East Second Avenue, Suite 301, Spokane, WA 99202.

Websites

www.religiousscience.org; www.rsintl.org

Sacred Texts

Holmes's *Science of Mind* and the sacred texts of the Bible and the Koran are also read and highly regarded.

Publications

Science of Mind (The United Church of Religious Science); *Creative Thought Magazine* (Religious Science International)

Membership

The United Church of Religious Science—40,000 members worldwide; 160 churches and 106 study groups

Notes

[1] J. Gordon Melton, *The Encyclopedia of American Religions,* 2 vols. (Wilmington, N.C.: McGrath, 1978), 2:61.

[2] "Frequently Asked Questions about Religious Science," *www.ccrs.org/FAQs.ntm (2001),* 5.

[3] See CHRISTIAN SCIENCE.

[4] Melton, *Encyclopedia,* 2:61.

[5] Charles L. Manske, *World Religions: Major World Religions in Comparative Outline Form* (Irvine, Calif.: The Institute for World Religions, 1988), 7:31.02.

ROSICRUCIANISM

A religion formed as a blending of ⸰gnosticism, CHRIS-TIANITY, the ⸰occult, continental rationalist philosophy, and various other traditions and ideas. The traditional form of Rosicrucianism has today become the impetus for separate and distinct orders.

HISTORY

The story of Rosicrucianism is largely the story of its alleged founder, Christian ⸰Rosenkreutz. (1378–1484). However, in an effort to establish a much earlier founding of the order, some Rosicrucians maintain that the name Rosenkreutz is merely symbolic. Alvin Schmidt points out that some trace the beginnings of Rosicrucian thought back to antiquity.

> In terms of legend the AMORC [Ancient Mystical Order of the Rose Cross—see below] traces its roots back to the mystery schools of learning that existed as far back as 115 B.C. in Egypt. Chronologically, however, the order is first mentioned in Germany in A.D. 1115.[1]

Whether historical fact or literary fiction, the story begins with the personality of Rosenkreutz, who, like some other founders of new movements, set out on a pilgrimage in search of truth and wisdom. He journeyed through many countries, including Palestine, Arabia, Egypt, Spain, and Morocco. In 1408 Rosenkreutz founded the Fraternity of the Rose Cross, taken from his own surname. At the age of 106, he died in Morocco. Before his death, however, he managed to amass a following, to whom he conveyed his mystical and esoteric teachings. These teachings included an eclectic blend of many religions and philosophies, including HINDUISM, JUDAISM (particularly the mystical elements), ⸰alchemy, ⸰hermeticism, the occult, and Paracelsian medicine. Some, without convincing evidence, have argued that Rosicrucian philosophy influenced Freemasonry through Elias ⸰Ashmole (1617–1692), who became a Freemason in 1642.

Despite the many legends that attend the founding of the Rosicrucian Order, Schmidt notes that

> more accurately . . . the origins of the order go back to the early seventeenth century, following the appearance of the publication *Fama Fraternitatis Bendicti Ordinis Rosae-Crucis* (1614), commonly abbreviated as *Fama*. Some evidence exists, however, that the *Fama* was already in circulation as early as 1610.[2]

For the longest time it was commonly accepted that a Lutheran theologian named Johann Valentin ⸰Andrae (1586–1654) was the author of the *Fama*. However, John Warwick Montgomery, in his excellent study *Cross and Crucible* (1973), provides convincing evidence that Andrae was not in fact the author. Many Rosicrucians credit Sir Francis Bacon (1561–1626) as having written the *Fama*.[3] The *Fama* is the definitive source of Rosicrucian philosophy. Several other publications are considered important sources in Rosicrucian thought, such as the *Confessio Fraternitatis* (1615) and *Chymische Hochzeit Christiani Rosenkreutz* (1616). Given the clandestine nature of Rosicrucian practice, much of what is known about the origins of the order comes from the above sources.

Rosenkreutz had opposed the teachings of the Roman Catholic church. This later became significant in light of the instructions he left to his followers. Rosenkreutz died in 1484, and his future disciples were to open his tomb 120 years later, an event they came to believe would signal the beginning of a new epoch in the history of Europe. The year 1604 marked the 120th anniversary of Rosenkreutz's death. When the tomb was opened, his body was reported to be undecayed. Accompanying the body were manuscripts that contained his teachings.

The timing was right. Rosenkreutz had died one year after the birth of the great German Reformer, Martin Luther (1483–1546). The tomb was opened in 1604 at a time when the ⸰Reformation had been in full force for well over seventy-five years. Anti-Catholic sentiment then was perhaps at its height in Europe. This was, of course, the time when the *Fama* appeared.

If Andrae had indeed not authored the *Fama*, he nevertheless believed that the writings were a satire. He believed that the teachings of Rosicrucianism were false and that the history of the movement was dotted with legends and fabrications. However, in an age given over to ⸰mysticism, the doctrines of Rosicrucianism were received wholeheartedly, particularly in Bohemia where popular superstition flourished.

It is also significant that it was in Bohemia where Frederick V and Princess Elizabeth had reigned until 1620. Andrae's *Chymische Hochzeit* (*Chemical Wedding*) turned out to be an alchemistic description of Rosenkreutz's teachings concerning initiation into the order of secret knowledge, which Andrae based partly on the wedding between Frederick and Elizabeth.

Rosicrucianism came to America in 1694 through the teachings of Johann ▶Kelpius (1673–1708), a student of the hermetic tradition. Kelpius and his pietistic followers settled near Philadelphia. Though Rosicrucian teachings had aroused much interest at the close of the seventeenth century, the fires of enthusiasm were doused as the eighteenth century got underway. It was not until the late nineteenth century that sparks were again ignited, reviving a new interest in the order, particularly among Freemasons and the CHURCH OF THE NEW JERUSALEM.

The twentieth century has witnessed continued interest in Rosicrucianism and the founding of numerous orders. In 1902 R. Swiburne Clymer founded a Fraternitatis Rosae Crucis in Quakertown, Pennsylvania, and in 1915 H. Spencer Lewis founded the Ancient Mystical Order Rosae Crucis (AMORC), headquartered first in San Francisco (1918), then in Tampa, Florida (1925), and finally in San Jose, California (1927). During the 1930s a planetarium, a student research center, the Rose Croix University of America, and a library were established.

Spencer Lewis died in 1939. His son, Ralph M. Lewis, served as Grand Imperator until 1987. There has been much infighting and scandal in the California-based AMORC. Gary Stewart, who became Grand Imperator in 1987, was "ousted by an apparent coup from within the AMORC,"[4] under claims that he had embezzled funds received from members of the order. Christian Bernard, age thirty-nine, was elected the new leader of the group. Stewart challenged the order with a $31.5 million countersuit.[5] The charges and countercharges were the focus of much media attention in the San Jose area at the time. The monies were eventually returned to the Order. Stewart in turn founded his own order in the 1990s called Order Militia Crucifera Evangelica.

A third order includes the Rosicrucian Fellowship, founded by Louis von ▶Grasshof, alias Max ▶Heindel (1865–1919). This particular branch of Rosicrucianism has direct links with both the Anthroposophical Society and THEOSOPHY. Heindel had met Rudolf ▶Steiner and also had become a member of the Theosophical Society in Los Angeles in 1903. Heindel reported that he was visited by a presence known as an elder brother of the Rosicrucian Order. The being revealed to him that he would help him and led him to the Temple of the Rosy Cross in Bohemia. Here Heindel received the information that would become his first book, *The Rosicrucian Cosmo-Conception*, which that particular order regards as authoritative.

ORGANIZATION

The leader of the AMORC is called the Grand Imperator (international leader). Its headquarters are now in San Jose. Local groups are called affiliated bodies. Then come what are called a lodge, chapter, pronaos, or atrium group. There are regions throughout North America. They sponsor regional events and hold conventions. One may join the order simply by downloading an application online and keeping current on dues.

TEACHINGS

The basic themes of Rosicrucian thought have parallels with NEW THOUGHT and the NEW AGE MOVEMENT. Ideas gathered from Rosenkreutz's mythical travels and writings constitute the theology of Rosicrucianism. Basic is the idea that all knowledge of humankind has been made available. Even forgotten or unrecorded civilizations, including ▶Atlantis and Lemuria, have been unearthed in the knowledge banks of those who have sought to know.

Humankind is able to discover truth, and to do so the "cosmic blueprint" must be followed. The cosmos is broken down into three spheres. One attains each of these spheres through suffering, through contemplation, and through various ascents via ▶reincarnation.

Basic also is the idea that the heavenly sphere(s) is sharply differentiated from the physical or material.

The AMORC headquarters includes this museum, located in San Jose, California. This religious order is rooted in ancient Egyptian mysticism.
Courtesy Jack M. Roper/CARIS

But in this separation also lies their analogous oneness. "As above, so below" reads the oft-quoted ⟩hermetic axiom. The parallels with Platonism are also apparent, and indeed, Rosicrucian writings have sought to maintain that Plato was an incipient Rosicrucianist because he was able to grasp the essence of universal truth as expounded in the doctrines of the order.

Two systems of mathematics were expounded, one for the noumenal world, the other for the earthly or phenomenal world. The initiate learns those principles and realizes that perfect knowledge of all things is available and the essence of reality is able to be penetrated. Seven is the perfect number. At birth a human being possesses a ⟩dense body. At age seven he or she attains a "vital body," at fourteen, the "desire body," and at twenty-one, "mind" is formed.

The medieval science of alchemy also plays a role in Rosicrucian literature, particularly in *Chymische Hochzeit*. Marriage as the union of male and female was regarded as a metaphor of the alchemic elemental fusion that the soul undergoes in its ascent to spiritual illumination. Alchemy is thereby directly linked to reincarnation. It may even be that the symbol of the rose cross is tied to alchemy. "Ros," or dew, is the solvent of gold, while the "crux," or cross, represents light. The fundamental elements of the two spheres, earthly and heavenly, are not only visible but are thereby fused in the symbols of the rose superimposed on the cross.

Like Hinduism, Rosicrucianism seeks eclectically to blend all other existing religions into itself. CHRISTIANITY, by contrast, maintains that all other religions and philosophies are false (John 3:3–18).

Some have connected the symbol of the "rose cross" with the Christian cross. As already observed, the rose cross most likely derived its symbolic significance from alchemy. There is no hint or allusion in Rosicrucianism to the Christian concept of the cross as being the means for Christ's death for the sins of the world. The following represents Rosicrucian thought on various Christian doctrines.

God

"The seven spirits before the throne . . . collectively, they are God, and make up the triune godhead . . . the Father is the highest initiate among the humanity of the Saturn. . . . The Son is the highest initiate of the Sun . . . the Holy Spirit (Jehovah) is the highest initiate of the Moon. . . ."[6] The God of Rosicrucian thought is a detached and impersonal entity. Rosicrucians believe that God is comprised of seven spirits that are presented as being different aspects of the Christian ⟩Trinity—Father, Son, and Holy Spirit. On second glance, however, there is no real concomitance with the biblical Trinity.

For Christianity, the divine Trinity is not "initiated" by various aspects of the cosmos. In the divine economy, God is one (Deut. 6:4) and is only distinguished with regard to creation. Rosicrucianism, like all of the pantheistic religions, does not ultimately distinguish between God and creation. As noted numerous times in this volume, inevitable implications result with respect to anthropology (see below).[7]

Jesus Christ

"The Son [Christ] is the highest initiate of the sun period. The ordinary humanity of that period are now the archangels."[8] The denial of the Trinity leads to the denial of the Christian doctrine of the deity of Jesus Christ. As in CHRISTIAN SCIENCE and a number of other religions, "Jesus" is distinguished from "the Christ." Rosicrucians speak of the Christ-spirit as being an aspect of the universal Christ, while Jesus was merely human. Traditional Christianity does not allow for such a distinction in its ⟩Christology.[9] By virtue of the personal union, the divine aspects of Christ are not to be Nestorianized (see ⟩Nestorianism) or separated from the human aspects. The early church recognized this from such passages of Scripture as Romans 1:3–4 and John 1:1–18. In Nestorianism Jesus Christ is the highest ranking among the world's spiritual teachers, but he differs from humanity only in degree, not in substance or kind.

Holy Spirit

"While retaining the individuality hard won through its incalculable journey through incarnation after incarnation, the Holy Ghost aspect of the triune Unity after the occupancy of the Jesus vehicle . . . 'diffused' itself throughout and about the planet."[10]

Humanity

We showed above that the Rosicrucian movement holds to a pantheistic worldview. The Creator/creation distinction collapses, thereby rendering deity and humanity synonymous. The saga of human history is marked by progress and evolution. Eventually all will come to realize salvation. Humanity has also developed in different epochs throughout history. For example, blacks were believed to have emerged from the ancient Lemurian race. The lost civilization of Atlantis was populated by the ancestors of the Aryan race.

Biblical anthropology yields a considerably different account. "In the beginning God created the heavens and the earth" (Gen. 1:1). While God lived with the first man and woman in the Garden of Eden (Gen. 2:15ff.), he remained wholly distinct from his creation. The Christian tradition, as well as the biblical narrative, does not carefully chronicle the composite histories of lost civilizations, or for that matter, all known civilizations. It does, however, carefully trace the history of God's ▶revelation and covenant with Adam after the Fall (Gen. 3), Noah (Gen. 6–9), and Abraham (Gen. 12; 15). The sin and disobedience of Adam resulted in the corporate guilt of the human race (Rom. 5).

The subsequent history of sin and rebellion, along with the deposit of faith and the establishing and maintaining of the sacred covenant, are of prime importance in the biblical narratives. It was sin and rebellion that resulted in the alienation between God and humankind. God's ultimate revelation to the human race was in the ▶incarnation of Jesus Christ (Luke 2:1–20; John 1:1; Gal. 4:4; Heb. 1:1–13). Jesus is reported as being that "second Adam" who overcame the destruction and harm of the first Adam (Rom. 5:12–21). But this does not imply universalism.[11] Salvation is given to those who trust in the work of Christ (*see* Apostles' and Nicene Creeds, Article 2, Appendix 1) to atone for sin, not on a rosy cross but rather one stained with Jesus' blood.

CONCLUSION

Rosicrucians claim that many prominent figures in history were members of the order. Such include Francis Bacon (some have pointed to him as having founded the order), René Descartes (1596–1650), Isaac Newton (1642–1727), Gottfried Leibniz (1646–1716), Benjamin Franklin (1706–90), and Claude Debussy (1862–1918).

Rosicrucianism is the product of an eclectic combination of varying traditions. The names above testify to the intellectual appeal of the movement. But this also makes it an exclusive group. One writer believes Rosicrucianism to be the movement that ushered in the beginning of modern occultism.[12] The New Age Movement and New Thought resemble Rosicrucianism in some ways. It also joins some "theosophical organizations ... in sustaining throughout America a vast amorphous constituency that overlaps other denominations and faiths."[13] Its influence extends far beyond the scope of its own membership and organizations.

ADDITIONAL INFORMATION

Headquarters

Ancient and Mystical Order of Rosae Crucis (AMORC), Rosicrucian Park, San Jose, CA 95191. Periodical: *Rosicrucian Digest.*

Other Rosicrucian societies with their respective periodicals include: Societas Rosicruciana in America, 321 W. 101st St., New York, NY 10025. Quarterly magazine: *Mercury*; also *The Rosicrucian Digest, The Rosicrucian Forum,* and *The English Grand Lodge Bulletin.*

Rosicrucian Fellowship (1907), 2222 Mission Ave., Box 713, Oceanside, CA 92054. Periodical: *Rays from the Rose Cross.*

Lectorium Rosicrucianum (1971), Box 9246, Bakersfield, CA 93309.

Rosicrucian Anthroposophical League (1932). No address available.

Websites

www.rosecross.org (Rosicrucian Fraternity); *www.rosicrucian.org* (AMORC)

Sacred Texts

There are no official sacred texts. The writings of Spencer Lewis, however, are considered extremely important.

Membership

There are estimates of approximately 250,000 Rosicrucians in the various orders.

Notes

[1] Alvin J. Schmidt, "Fraternal Organizations," in *The Greenwood Encyclopedia of American Institutions* (Westport, CT: Greenwood, 1980), 290.

[2] Ibid., 291.

[3] H. Spencer Lewis, ed., *Rosicrucian Manual* (San Jose, CA: Supreme Grand Lodge of AMOC, 1978), 123..

[4] William M. Alner, "Infighting and Lawsuits Affecting AMORC Rosicrucians," *Christian Research Journal* (Fall 1990), 6.

[5] Sydney Ahlstrom, *A Religious History of the American People,* 2 vols. (Garden City, NY: Image Books, 1975), 559.

[6] Max Heindel, *The Rosicrucian Cosmo-Conception* (San Jose, Calif.: AMORC, n.d.), 376, 252, as quoted in Walter Martin, *The Kingdom of the Cults* (Minneapolis: Bethany, 1985), 510.

[7] See also HINDUISM, THEOSOPHY, UNITARIAN-UNIVERSALIST ASSOCIATION, CHRISTIAN SCIENCE, NEW THOUGHT, ISKCON, and the NEW AGE MOVEMENT.

[8] Heindel, *Rosicrucian Cosmo-Conception,* 376.

[9] For an analysis of the Chalcedonian Christology of the ancient church, see THE WAY INTERNATIONAL, UNITY SCHOOL OF CHRISTIANITY, UNIFICATION CHURCH, and CHRISTADELPHIANISM.

[10] *Occult Science,* Liber VI, 12.

[11] See Unitarian-Universalist Association.

[12] Sydney Ahlstrom, 557.

[13] Ibid., 559.

SANTERIA; CHURCH OF THE LUKUMI BABALAO AYE; CLBA

INTRODUCTION

[Case 1] A farmer had an altercation with a Cuban tenant concerning the upkeep of the property and the lack of care rendered the tenant's animals (goats, pigs, and chickens). The next morning, the farmer found on his front porch a decapitated chicken (the head was shoved into the cloaca), a split coconut, and fourteen pennies, all wrapped in white cloth. The farmer immediately went to the tenant's shack where he saw a bizarre ▸altar. In the center was an iron ▸cauldron filled with dirt. On top of that was a goat skull that supported a blood-drenched human skull, which in turn supported a chicken head. A chain was draped across the front of the skull. To the left of the skull was a small doll with an appropriately sized sword piercing its chest. Behind the skull were deer antlers (draped with a red ribbon), an antique-appearing sword, and a machete. Two knives were also thrust into the dirt of the cauldron.

Candles were burning in and around the cauldron, and some (on the floor) had the depiction of Saint Barbara. In front was plywood board with a glyph drawn in chalk, a decapitated chicken, and a section of railroad track. Above this, hanging from the ceiling, were multiple strands of colored beads, with most strands having only two alternating colors. At the foot of the cauldron was a pan of water containing two split coconuts, a turtle shell, and an intact coconut. To the right was a smaller black cauldron filled with dirt, numerous railroad spikes, a knife, deer antlers, and a strand of yellow beads. A chain with ▸amulets of agricultural tools was wound around the outside of the cauldron. Nearby was a box filled with dirt (about 30 cm square and 10 cm deep) with a small plastic skeleton on top. Another glyph was chalked on a nearby wall. Behind the door in a paper bag was a 30-cm-high figurine of the trickster god, Eleggua.[1]

[Case 2] A cemetery work crew was to complete a grave site that had been dug the previous day in preparation for a burial. They discovered human bones in two plastic garbage bags at the site and called the police. One bag contained a skull with mandible and a few vertebrae. The other contained a nearly complete skeleton. The overall morphologic features were those of a black male. One skull was covered with chicken feathers and blood. The other skull was covered with dirt and apparent rust. The distal ends of some of the long bones had been sawed off.[2]

[Case 3] Cemetery workers, picking up debris along a low cemetery wall, discovered a plastic bag buried just beneath the surface of the ground. It contained two human skulls and fifteen pennies. One skull had a 2.5-cm-diameter area of bright copper oxide staining. Both had adherent dirt and dried grass. The skulls were small but from adults. One had a broken spring attached to the mandible by a screw, and another screw was in the maxilla.[3]

HISTORY

These cases, and many more like them, have been linked to the ▸cult popularly known today as Santeria. It is a syncretistic religious movement blending elements of Roman Catholicism and African religions. Santeria is located in Cuba, and the Afro-Cubans, or Lucumi, who make up the cult were formerly from southern Nigeria. The divinities that were transported from Africa were brought by black slaves. Spaniards captured and carted off massive numbers of these slaves to work the sugar plantations in the eighteenth century. These people came from Nigeria, Senegal, and the Guinea coast and were chiefly of ▸Yoruba and ▸Bantu tribal backgrounds. The efforts of Spanish missionaries introduced the slaves to Roman Catholicism. They did not, however, entirely abandon their own religious traditions. Instead, they acculturated them with the newfound faith imparted to them by their Spanish overlords.

In 1974 the Church of the Lukumo Babalu Aye (CLBA) was formed in southern Florida. Other churches started cropping up in Spanish and Cuban neighborhoods in the United States. In the 1980s, the Church of Seven African Powers was formed, also in Florida.

In April 1989 the dismembered bodies of thirteen men were exhumed from shallow graves near Matamoros, Mexico. One of the victims was a twenty-one-year-old college student studying at the University of Texas. Four suspects confessed to the killings, claiming that the victims were used as a "magical shield" to protect them from their enemies. The officials dealing with the case linked the crime to VOODOO and Santeria.[4] The four suspects were also marijuana traffickers.

In the early 1990s the CLBA attracted national attention as it was caught up in a legal battle concerning the use of chickens for blood sacrifices. The year 2001 marked the beginning of important changes in the church's policies and administrative structures.

ORGANIZATION

The following represents the organizational structure of the CLBA. Previously, the Santeria gatherings were ruled by "clan monopolies," which tended to centralize power and alienated others not in the inner circle. Priests that enjoyed high ranks were engaging in administrative functions that were not their competence. Now responsibilities are meted out according to gifts and abilities rather than rank.

Two administrative structures are in place, which separate the religious from the administrative. The administrative is run by a founder and board of directors. The religious is run by a series of councils, committees, and an assembly. There are several different designations for members of the CLBA. An annual fee of $10.00 makes one an associate member. A sponsor member contributes $20.00 monthly. The ordained clergy are called "certified clergy." All ministers of mainstream denominations may become "certified clergy," based on the training already received by any particular denomination that led to ordination. A one-time contribution of $250 is required, along with a

sponsorship contribution of $60.00. There are also clergy family memberships, and honorary clergy certifications for clergy forty-two years old and older.

BELIEFS AND PRACTICES

The supreme deity of the Afro-Cubans, or Lucumi, is ᵇOlurun. There are hundreds of lesser ᵇorisha under Olurun. Much like Roman Catholicism's and Eastern Orthodoxy's multitude of patron saints, so too Santeria has its plethora of deities assigned to every area of life. Despite this veritable pantheon, the Lucumi do believe in the concept of a "supreme" deity. Reasons for this are twofold. First, it is endemic to the cult itself. As noted, Olurun is the chief deity to whom all others are lesser in rank. Second, the Roman Catholic church, which has certainly played a vital role in most of the Afro-Cuban and SOUTH AMERICAN, CENTRAL AMERICAN AND CARIBEAN CULTS, has itself been influential in the proliferation of ᵇpolytheism, particularly in Santeria.

It is somewhat paradoxical that missionaries have attempted to introduce a ᵇmonotheistic religion, yet at the same time offer a host of patron saints and accompanying statues believed to be intermediaries between God and humankind. This has reinforced a mass syncretism of Yorubic deities and Christian saints. The table below contains a list of the important deities of Santeria known as the Seven African Powers. Alongside each deity is a brief description and the corresponding Christian adaptation.[5]

DEITY		CHRISTIAN SYNCRETISM
Olurun, Elegua, Eshu	Controls roads, gates, doors; allows communication between santero and orisha	Holy Guardian Angel; Saint Anthony of Padua; Christ child
Obatalla	Father of all the creation; patron of hysterics and melancholiacs; source of energy, wisdom, purity	Our Lady of Las Mercedes; Holy Eucharist; Christ resurrected
Chango	Controls thunder, lightning, fire; sometimes invoked in malevolent sorcery	Saint Barbara
Oshun	Controls gold, money, sensual love; makes marriages; protects genitals and lower abdomen	Our Lady of Charity
Yemaya	Primordial mother of the santos; protects motherhood, womanhood; controls fertility and intestinal function; owns the seas	Our Lady of Regla
Babalu-Aye	Patron of the sick, especially skin diseases	Saint Lazarus
Oggun	Warrior deity; owns all metals and weapons; invoked in malevolent sorcery	Saint Peter

A Santeria cultic ceremony usually begins by invoking *Olurun*. As the god of fate, he is considered to be the principal mediator between the gods and humanity. During this invocation, drums are playing a certain well-rehearsed cadence. After *Olurun* has been ceremoniously invoked, the drummers alter the rhythm, or *oru*, in order to usher in another deity. Which particular one or ones vary according to the occasion and the need.

The priests of Lucumi, or Santeria, are called ▸*babalao* or ▸*santeros*. They guard the secrets of the cult, possess the necessary knowledge of the cultic practices, and serve as the oracle of *Ifa*. The *babalao* is initiated after a long period of study under older priests and stands before his tribe, quite able to reply to hundreds of questions put to him with carefully memorized answers.

Animals are frequently killed by *santeros* in order to offer up blood ▸sacrifices believed to be pleasing to the gods. It is not uncommon for one to find the headless carcass of a chicken left behind after such a rite.

Many Cubans have migrated to the United States and brought Santeria with them into larger Spanish communities, particularly in Miami and New York. Animal sacrifices have become a significant problem. According to one source,

> "It's frighteningly popular," says Thomas Langdon, an officer of the American Society for the Prevention of Cruelty to Animals [ASPCA]. "I think it is a lot more widespread than anyone would like to admit."[6]

Sacrifices are believed to bring good fortune. They are also performed during the initiation of a new priest into the cult. One American initiate from Brooklyn named Gene Bailly said his induction process lasted a week and was accompanied by drums, incense, and the sacrifice of thirty goats, lambs, and fowl.[7]

The sacrifices often take place within the homes of the *santeros*. ASPCA raiders have found many animals caged in houses awaiting ritualistic sacrifice.[8] Regarding animal sacrifices themselves,

> the discoveries can be gruesome: a goat's head nailed to a tree, bags of entrails on a path. Though beheaded chickens turn up most often, Langdon says the ASPCA has gotten "reports of animal carcasses, in numbers, flopping out of 30-gallon garbage bags—in a vacant lot, along a highway, near a cemetery.[9]

Members of the cult argue that such sacrifices are necessary and are conducted in a humane manner.

Without them, a vital dimension of the cult's belief system is undermined. Members also argue that a denial of their rights to sacrifice animals is a direct violation of their First Amendment rights (i.e., their freedom of religion).

This issue surfaced in Hialeah, Florida, a suburb of Miami. City ordinances passed in 1987 forbade animal sacrifices for "unnecessary" reasons.[10] Members of the CLBA, along with the church's president, Ernesto Pichardo, decided to take on the city's ordinance on the basis of the First Amendment. In addition to the religious reasons for the sacrifice, the group claimed that the chickens are killed and then eaten. City officials countered that the animal carcasses are left strewn about the city streets, endangering public health.[11] Jorge Duarte, an attorney for the Santeria congregation, argued, "You can buy Chicken McNuggets in Hialeah . . . but you can't kill a chicken for religious reasons."[12] In 1993, in a landmark decision, the Supreme Court overruled the city's ordinance and allowed for the group to exercise its beliefs. The city also paid $500,000 to cover the church's legal fees. Interestingly, mainstream Christian denominations backed the cause of the Hialeah church for the very same reason that conservative Christian leaders chimed in with Sun Myung ▸Moon (*see* UNIFICATION CHURCH), so that precedents would not be set that further and further erode religious freedom.

The issue of blood sacrifice has been a problem that Christian missionaries have attempted to address. CHRISTIANITY believes in the necessity of blood sacrifice, a doctrine that has its roots in the Old Testament. The Hebrew practice is described in detail in the book of Leviticus, where the high priest was instructed to offer up the blood of various acceptable animals (bulls, goats, turtledoves, etc.) as a sacrifice for the sins of the people. Christianity made a break with JUDAISM, however, not by doing away with the idea of blood sacrifice, but by advancing the doctrine of the exclusivity of Jesus Christ as the only high priest who offered *himself* as the ultimate sacrifice for sin by the shedding of his own blood (Heb 9:12). Furthermore, this sacrifice was offered once and is sufficient for all time (9:25–7). Therefore, tension between Christianity and Santeria (as well as with the other transplanted African cults) is an inevitable consequence. The need for atonement in Santeria is one of the focal points of the worship. The ▸*omo* hopes that through sacrifice that the deity will absolve and purify him.

In addition to the sacrifices, the cultic ceremonies include ritualistic dances. Many ▸fetishes and instru-

Mount Nebo Cemetery in Miami contains the graves of many followers of Santeria. The six-inch coffin, as object of sorcery or ▸black magic, was found resting by a grave site. Such items are often found in the cemetery.

Courtesy Jack M. Roper/CARIS

ments are used, such as drums of various sizes, bells, ▸maracas, sticks, and metals. The rhythm and dance come directly from the African traditions.

Stores carrying the supplies used by the cult are known as ▸botanicas. They are located in many Spanish communities in the United States and Canada, as well as in Cuba, and contain thousands of fetishes, ▸charms, herbs, potions, and other objects used by the cult.

Not only does the devotee to Santeria invoke the deity to acquire atonement, but another chief objective is to become possessed by the *orisha*. The intensity of such an intimate relationship with the deities attracts many people to the cult. It is in this area that Santeria most closely approximates voodoo.

CONCLUSION

Santeria, like Catholicism, has been suppressed by Fidel Castro on Cuban soil.[13] Because of this, the cult's membership has declined in recent years, but only in Cuba. In the United States the growth in practitioners has increased at a surprising rate and is expected to continue to grow, particularly in the Spanish communities of major metropolitan areas. In addition to Cuban exiles, both blacks and whites are attracted to this ancient African religion. There are an estimated three hundred thousand practitioners of Santeria in New York City alone.

Many of the specific rituals remain guarded. It is difficult to obtain information because the movement lacks an official publication. Newspapers across the country frequently report stories about the remains of the cult's animal sacrifices. Some practitioners openly discuss their involvement in Santeria.

Santeria has preserved its African idioms much more strongly than have the other cults of the Caribbean and South America. One reason for this is that African slaves were shipped to Cuba as late as the twentieth century.[14] The cultural traditions and rituals have been steadily reinforced. In America, Santeria has become more sophisticated and organized.[15]

ADDITIONAL INFORMATION

Headquarters

The first Santeria church in America: Church of the Lucumi Babalu Aye, P.O. Box 22627, Hialeah, FL 33002.

Website

www.church-of-the-lukumi.org (there are numerous other Santeria sites)

Sacred Texts

None; a heavy emphasis on oral tradition.

Publication

CLBA Journal

Membership

It is estimated that there are over five million practitioners of Santeria worldwide. In the United States, there are 70,000 in Miami, 300,000 in New York City, and 1,000 in Boston, as well as many others throughout the country.

Notes

[1] C. D. Wetli and R. Martinez, "Forensic Sciences Aspects of Santeria, a Religious Cult of African Origin," *Journal of Forensic Sciences* 26/3 (July 1981): 507.

[2] Ibid., 509–10.

[3] Ibid., 510–11.

4 "Voodoo in Mexico," *U.S. News and World Report* (April 24, 1989), 16.

5 Ibid., 508.

6 Gary Langer, "Cult Attracting a Surprising Mix of Followers," *Las Vegas Review Journal* (May 13, 1984), 14J.

7 Ibid.

8 Ibid.

9 Ibid.

10 "Necessary Sacrifice?" *The Economist* (Nov. 14–20, 1992), 28.

11 Ibid.

12 Richard N. Ostling, "Shedding Blood in Sacred Bowls," *Time* (Oct. 19, 1992), 60.

13 George Eaton Simpson, *Black Religions in the New World* (New York: Columbia Univ. Press, 1978), 94.

14 Miriam Joel, *African Traditions in Latin America* (Cidoc Cuadermo 73; Cuernavaca, Mexico: Centro Intercultural de Cocumentacion, 1972), 39.

15 See also ABAKUA and VOODOO.

SATANISM; THE CHURCH OF SATAN

Commonly referred to as ᴾdevil worship, Satanism is the general term for worship of the biblical fallen angel ᴾLucifer, or ᴾSatan (Gen. 3:1–15; Isa. 14:12). The history of the worship of Satan is a difficult story to recount. Evidence and sources before the seventeenth century are scanty. Even with post-seventeenth-century data, it is difficult to report an accurate history because many of the extant documents have been handed down by Christians during the time when ᴾwitch hunting was in its heyday. Therefore, as can be expected, the amount of actual satanic activity or devil ᴾcults in existence have been greatly exaggerated.

Satanism should not be confused with WITCHCRAFT, though both are part of the ᴾoccult. There is evidence that links the two in some instances. Witchcraft, however, can only be classed as Satanism insofar as the former understands itself as practicing its craft over and against the Judeo-Christian God. Many witchcraft groups are aligned with non-Christian, pre-Christian, or pagan deities. Satanism is distinguished from witchcraft in that it is dedicated to the antithesis of the God of the Christian ᴾBible.

HISTORY

Satanism, therefore, grew as a reaction against CHRISTIANITY. It has a long and checkered history, and much of what took place in its past remains unrecorded. Documented accounts of satanist groups date back to the seventeenth century in Europe and America.

Satanism has been attributed to heretical groups throughout history. The Roman Catholic Church charged the heretical Bogomils, Cathari, and Albigensis with practicing satanic rituals. The Dominicans gave Cathari meetings the title *synagoga satanae* during the Inquisition.[1] The charges, however, in most cases were unfounded and appear to be an attempt on the part of the medieval Roman church to maintain control and gain lands and wealth belonging to the accused. Charges of Satanism and witchcraft became the order of the day, and it was especially easy to accuse all who transgressed the boundaries of ᴾorthodoxy and conformity.

Protestants have also tended to suspect people of being witches, ᴾdemons, or devil worshipers. After the Reformation of the sixteenth century had established a firm foothold in northern Europe, it was easy enough on the part of loyal Lutherans and committed Calvinists to view everything that was Roman Catholic to be of the devil. Martin Luther (1483–1546) eventually concluded that the papacy was the very seat of the Antichrist and that Rome was the harlot spoken of in Revelation 17.

Fear of the devil reached its climax in America in Puritan New England. Though popularly known as the Salem Witch Trials of 1692, in reality devil possession was the charge initially leveled against the accused. Several girls, including the daughters of the minister Samuel Parris, claimed to have been influenced by VOODOO ᴾmagic through Parris's slave-girl, Tituba, from Barbados. Tituba indeed confessed to being a witch and said that she and seven others had made a pact with the devil. Soon more accusations followed, resulting in a hysteria that led to the hangings of nineteen persons accused of witchcraft and devil worship.[2]

MODERN SATANISM

In a society historically impatient with long-term solutions and advocating drugs as a standard way of dealing with anxiety, it is not surprising that psychedelics should become a shortcut to ᴾ*samadhi*, the state in Eastern religious disciplines in which man achieves union with the Infinite. But eastern mystics have always professed that shortcuts to ᴗnirvana can be dangerous. Once the doors of consciousness are thrown open, those without the proper discipline cannot control what gets in. Along with the ᴗ*Bhagavad Gita*, kids discovered the works of Aleister ᴗCrowley.[3]

The story of modern Satanism begins with the life of Aleister Crowley (1875–1947). Crowley never considered himself a satanist, but his writings and teachings on ᴗmagick (Crowley's chosen spelling of the word *magic*) did much to influence the Satanism of the twentieth-century counterculture in America.

Crowley exhibited a potent personality from his earliest childhood. Reared in a Plymouth Brethren church, Crowley resisted the teachings of Christianity almost from the start. Richard Cavendish candidly observes that Crowley "preferred the evil characters in the Bible to the good ones, and when his mother told him he was the Great Beast 666 of Revelation, he gladly accepted the identification."[4]

In 1898 Crowley joined the ᴗHermetic Order of the Golden Dawn, where he made the acquaintance of his temporary mentor, MacGregor Mathers, leader of the occult group. Cavendish points out that Crowley joined the order fresh out of Cambridge,

The two standard works of Satanism are *The Satanic Bible* and *The Satanic Rituals*, both by Anton LaVey. This picture also shows a copy of the "Nine Satanic Statements" of LaVey.

Courtesy Jack M. Roper/CARIS

taking on the magical name of Brother Perdurabo ("I will endure") and beginning his experiments with drugs. His voracious bisexuality and his interests in the darker forces in the human animal gave him a sinister reputation. Crowley was very much a figure of the "decadence" of the *fin de siècle*, with its hymning of scarlet sins and purple passions, its loathing of Christianity and its Romantic admiration for evil and Satan.[5]

The Golden Dawn taught a form of magic derived from the ᴗKaballah and ROSICRUCIANISM. There are some similarities to FREEMASONRY and THEOSOPHY. That magic soon proved to be insufficient for Crowley, who was convinced that more potent magic could be harnessed through sex and drugs. A violent eruption between Mathers and Crowley followed. In the end, Crowley claimed that Mathers was killed in a magical duel by a vampire that Crowley had conjured up.[6]

Crowley proved to be too perverted and bizarre for the order and was cast out. Not put off for a moment, he began to formulate his own magical ideas, seeking the aid of the Secret Chiefs of the Hermetic Order (divine beings with supernatural intellects). ᴗRevelation came to Crowley in Cairo, Egypt, while he was visited by a guardian angel named ᴗAiwaz. Crowley began to write down the revelations he claimed he received from Aiwaz. Later those dictations became the basis for Crowley's ᴗ*The Book of the Law*. The major axioms of Satanism as it would later develop in the 1960s were formulated in *The Book of the Law*. The credo of the book, called the *Law of Thelema*, is summed up in the now-famous phrase, "Do what thou wilt shall be the whole of the Law." Crowley's next important literary contribution was *The Equinox* (1909–1913). Many of the ideas contained in this latter work became the basis for modern Satanism.

In 1912 Crowley joined a German secret society founded by Freemason/occultist Karl Kellner and called the Ordo Templi Orientis (ᴗOTO). The OTO emphasis on sexual magic was precisely what Crowley had been searching for. After Kellner's death in 1905, the OTO's new leader became Theodor Reuss. Reuss was a member of the German Secret Service. Because Crowley was privy to many of the secrets of the OTO, Reuss, so it seems, in an effort to remove Crowley from the German operation, offered him the leadership post in the English chapter of the OTO. Crowley gladly accepted the post.

Crowley also spent time in the United States between 1914 and 1919. In 1916, while living in New Hampshire, he raised himself to the rank of ▸magus. During his ceremony of induction, he baptized a frog that he called "Jesus Christ" and then crucified it.

The remainder of Crowley's life is a long legacy of perversion and evil. In 1920 he founded an "Abbey of Thelema" in Cefalu, Sicily. When it was discovered that the abbey was the scene of perverse sexual orgies, Mussolini expelled Crowley in 1923. In the next two decades before his death, Crowley continued to teach, write, and practice his perverted sexual magic. Examples of some of the classifications of his sex magic included the "VIIIth Degree Masturbatory or Auto Sexual degree," the "IXth Degree Heterosexual magick," "XIth Degree Homosexual magick," and "Anal intercourse."

Crowley believed that perverse sexual practice and drug use destroyed the consciousness of any sense of morality. This in turn enabled the conscience, deprived of a sense of "ought" or "law," to come under the influence of powerful supernatural beings.

Jack Parsons (John Whiteside Parsons [1914–1952]), a rocket scientist, started a chapter called the Church of Thelema based in Pasadena, California. Arthur Lyons notes a fascinating connection between Parsons and L. Ron ▸Hubbard, founder of SCIENTOLOGY. In March 1946 Parsons held a masturbation ritual based on Aleister Crowley's VIIIth Degree, in which Parson's goal was to conjure a ▸"familiar." During this ritual, Hubbard acted as scribe.[7] Subsequently, this ritual was known as the "Babalon Working." Over the three days of the Working, Parsons produced the *Fourth Chapter of the Book of the Law*. This work was also known as the *Book of Babalon*, since it was channeled from the goddess Babalon. Crowley, on hearing of the incident, and of Parson's "incantations" during the ceremony, wrote to the leadership of the OTO. His reaction is interesting, if not ironic: "Apparently Parsons or Hubbard or somebody is producing a Moonchild. I get fairly frantic when I contemplate the idiocy of these louts."[8] Hubbard later ran off with Parson's girlfriend and a great deal of his money.

Crowley died peacefully on returning to Hastings in 1947. Parsons, on the other hand, blew himself up while experimenting with chemicals on June 17, 1952.

There are two ways that satanists view Satan. (1) Some groups and individuals believe that Satan exists and that he is a powerful force who, if worshiped, will mete out rewards to devotees aligned with his cause. Much of the activity of such groups is clandestine because of the criminal nature of their evil rites. Satanists of this ilk feel compelled to offer blood sacrifices to the devil. Children have sometimes been sacrificed on satanic ▸altars during a ▸black mass, the focal point of satanist worship. More common is the use of animals. Investigations and studies have linked missing children to areas where satanists are believed to be practicing. The increased findings of the scattered remains of the bloodied carcasses of animals have also been attributed to satanists. (2) Then there are those satanists who generally do not believe in the existence of the devil but practice their craft for a variety of other reasons (see below).

Before discussing the modern satanic groups and their teachings, it is necessary at this point to attempt to classify the different kinds of satanists and satanist groups as they exist today.

There are a variety of ways of classifying Satanists. Christian Research Institute (CRI) provides a helpful classification by distinguishing "group satanists" from "individual satanists." Each of these categories is broken down further.[9] Generally speaking, however, sociologists of religion break satanists into three broad categories that overlap with those of CRI. Arthur Lyons summarizes these as follows: "As it emerged in the mid–1960s, a contemporary Satanism can be divided into three distinct realities: (1) solitary Satanists, (2) 'outlaw' cults, and (3) neo-Satanic churches."[10]

The chart in this article uses two proposed models to classify satanist groups.

The Church of Satan

There are those satanists (individuals or groups), as observed above, who do not necessarily believe that Satan is a real metaphysical being, but merely the symbol or personification of fleshly human desires and appetites. They react against the Christian teaching that the desires of the flesh should be suppressed in the interest of pursuing spiritual values.

Anton Szandor ▸LaVey (1930–1997, born as Howard Staton Levey) founded the Church of Satan in 1966 in San Francisco, California, on Walpurgisnacht (April 30). This was the night that, in Germany, witches were said to fly about and celebrate. Of the kinds of Satanism described above, LaVey's "church" falls into the category of public Satanism.

LaVey describes his particular form of Satanism in his book *The Satanic Bible*, published in 1969.

CATEGORIES OF SATANISTS

MODEL 1	MODEL 2

I. Group Satanists

   A. Traditional

      1. Secretive

      2. Hatred for Christianity

      3. Black Mass celebrated (communion cup sometimes filled with blood from a sacrificial victim, either human or animal)

      4. Belief that Satan exists

   B. Nontraditional

      1. Secretive

      2. Also exhibit hatred toward Christianity, but unlike *A*, the non-traditionalists formulate beliefs derived from non-Christian sources, such as Neo-Platonic philosophy or Eastern mysticism

      3. The drinking of blood during a rite is not necessarily meant to parody the Roman Catholic Mass, but rather, to partake of the "life energy" that blood provides.

      4. Believe that Satan exists

   C. Public Satanists

      1. Non-secretive

      2. Hold worship services open to the public

      3. Based largely on the writings of Anton LaVey's *Satanic Bible*

      4. Believe Satan is a force or symbol of evil

   D. Youth Gang Satanists

      1. "Dabblers," young people who are not avowed satanists but merely entertain interests in the occult and Satanism through the influence of drugs, and rock-and-roll/ heavy-metal music

      2. Those who see Satanism as a symbol of rebellion against authority

      3. For most, interest in Satanism is a passing fad

      4. Generally speaking, little or no knowledge of what traditional Satanism is all about

      5. May or may not believe Satan exists

II. Individual Satanists

   A. Not members of any group

   B. Highly individualized and eclectic belief systems

   C. Includes highly disturbed individuals— neurotic/psychotic

---

MODEL 2

"Outlaw Cults"

Secretive, illegal, involving violence and criminal actions far beyond the freedoms allowed by the First Amendment. Drug use and illicit sex.

Neo-satanic Churches

Modern movements that operate within the confines of the law.

Solitary Satanists

Individuals who operate without a group and who practice self-styled forms of Satanism.
Youth Gang Satanists are also highly independent.

Satan represents indulgence instead of abstinence. Satan represents vital existence instead of spiritual pipe dreams. Satan represents vengeance instead of turning the other cheek. Satan represents all the so-called sins, as they all lead to physical, mental, or emotional gratification.[11]

LaVey's themes found their way into rock-drug sub-cultures, but his influence on mainstream middle-class values should not be underestimated. LaVey espoused materialism and hedonism. Though rejecting the blatant references to Satan, many are attracted by the stress on one's rights to satisfy one's natural desires. The Marquis de Sade (1740–1814) had formulated this philosophy several centuries earlier, namely, that natural urges should not be suppressed. Rejecting God, de Sade taught that the only crimes or the only sins of humanity are those that prevent one from obeying the voice of nature. He faulted Christianity for this first and foremost. LaVey represented a modern and popularized form of Sadism and its accompanying motifs. Additional books by LaVey include *The Satanic Rituals* (1972) and *The Compleat Witch* (1970). He was writing *Satan Speaks* at the time of his death and it was published posthumously in 1998 with an introduction by Marilyn Manson.[12]

LaVey resided in a San Francisco house known simply as "the Black House," because of its black and purple colors. He began experimenting with the occult and started gaining a following. People came to the Black House and paid $2.50 for admission to his Magic Circle. In addition to his writings, LaVey also had a hand in composing music. In the 1990s he produced several albums, including the title "Satan Takes a Holiday."

Conflict came LaVey's way when his youngest daughter, Zeena Schreck, publicly denounced her father and joined the Temple of Set. Schreck accused her father of being a liar and a phony. Lawrence Wright from *Rolling Stone* magazine wrote an article titled "It's Not Easy Being Evil in a World That's Gone to Hell." In this article, Wright disclosed numerous factual inconsistencies in LaVey's account of his life.[13] Following LaVey's death in 1997, Blanche Barton took over the running of the Church of Satan.

The Church of Satan celebrates two major holidays, Halloween and Walpurgisnacht. Members also see birthdays as noteworthy of celebration. The Black Mass is celebrated only symbolically.

Temple of Set

As is the case with most religions, derivative groups soon sprang forth. The Temple of Set was founded in 1975 by Michael Aquino. Aquino first joined the Church of Satan under LaVey in 1969. He rose to the rank of Magister IV, just under the ranking of the High Priest LaVey. Aquino claims to have had a revelation from Satan informing him to begin afresh with an organization that would worship the true powers of darkness. What really happened, however, was that LaVey was selling priesthoods in the church for money. This disillusioned many members, and Aquino came to believe that LaVey was making a mockery of the true ideals of Satanism. He and twenty-eight of LaVey's followers broke away and formed the Temple of Set that same year.

Though founded in 1975, the organization claims roots that date back to prehistory and traces its history through the schools of abstract philosophy and mystery religions particularly endemic to ancient Egyptian and Greek cultures. Aquino resisted strongly the idea that Satan is a mere symbol of power. Instead, he believed that Satan was indeed a real supernatural reality who derived his name from the Egyptian deity Set, which Aquino claims was the model for the Christian Satan.

Another distinction between the Church of Satan and the Temple of Set lies in the latter's emphasis on the military. Aquino maintains an avid interest in Nazi culture, and Nazi insignia are occasionally worn by members of the group. In 1986, Aquino was investigated in connection with allegations of child molestatioin but was never charged.

These books contain the secret rituals of the OTO. Tarot cards are also used.

Courtesy Jack M. Roper/CARIS

Aquino's tenure as high priest came to an end in 1996. He was succeeded by Don Webb. Much of the activities of the organization are secretive, unlike the Church of Satan.

Ordo Templi Orientis

As mentioned above in reference to Aleister Crowley, OTO is not specifically a satanic movement. Crowley understood himself to be a worker of "magick," not a satanist. Yet Crowley and his followers have had a profound impact on satanic groups in America. Many derivative groups have come forth from OTO. These groups include: OTO (Fort Myers, Florida); OTO (Roanoke, Virginia); OTO (Dublin, California); Ordo Templi Astarte (O.T.A.), also called the Church of Hermetic Science, begun in 1970; and Bennu Phoenix Temple of the Hermetic Order of the Golden Dawn. This latter group rejected both Aleister Crowley as being "impervious to discipline" and MacGregor Mathers as being unworthy of the title "leader" of the OTO.[14]

Appeal

People who become involved with modern forms of Satanism have often been heavily influenced by drugs, illicit sex, and heavy-metal rock music. Some see it as a way of venting hostilities, while others seek out Satanism as a means of overtly rebelling against authority.

"When you kill someone, it's irreversible," relates one Satanist. "It comes out of insecurity."[15] Satanists seek freedom from traditional customs, moral and ethical values, and institutionalism. Many report having had a natural attraction for the devil and the religiously forbidden (*see* ▶diabolism).

The imagery and lyrics created by heavy-metal rock music have contributed greatly to the occult renaissance of the twentieth century. According to the Associated Press, Richard Ramirez, the California "night stalker," was obsessed with the Australian band AC-DC. Ray Garcia, a one-time friend of Ramirez, claimed that AC-DC's 1979 album *Highway to Hell* played a special role in influencing Ramirez. He was captivated by the song "Night Prowler," the lyrics of which describe an intruder who enters homes while the residents sleep.

The lyrics of many heavy-metal songs have the common themes of rebellion against authority, pre- and extramarital sex, drug use, and occult practice. The title track of the album *Show No Mercy* by the Slayer contains the following lines: "Through the night we ride in

This wooden coffin was made by a Milwaukee, Wisconsin, teenager in his basement with the intent to use it as his bed. He was into death metal music and had made death masks for his bedroom wall. He also had a goat's head in his room and a live tarantula.
Courtesy Jack M. Roper/CARIS

pairs . . . / From the depths of hell's domain . . . / Worried from the gates of hell / In Lord Satan we trust."[16]

The author of these lyrics, Kerr King, claims that he is not really a satanist but is merely using satanist symbols to bolster the band's image. This may be true for many heavy-metal bands. But this has not prevented those fans who hear such lyrics from being drawn into authentic and dangerous forms of Satanism.[17] The group Black Sabbath produced an album titled *Sabbath Bloody Sabbath*, which is accompanied by the numerals 666 (*see* ▶six-six-six). The group has sold T-shirts and caps with the satanist symbol—a goat's head superimposed inside an inverted ▶pentagram. Motley Crüe, another heavy-metal band, produced an album titled *Shout at the Devil*, where the satanist symbol also

This teenager's T-shirt and the grafitti painted on this concrete column express the sentiments of death culture.

Courtesy Jack M. Roper/CARIS

appears. The group Guns N' Roses displays a cross inundated with skulls. Heavy-metal stars such as Ozzy Osbourne and the groups Judas Priest, KISS, and Iron Maiden have all used satanic symbols on album jackets, in lyrics, and on their clothes. This phenomena continues in modern metal bands and in other musical genres.

Music is but one of many vehicles for the satanist, however. There are numerous causes for the appeal and interest in the occult. Some are attracted to charismatic authority figures who successfully draw others to themselves.

An interest in the future, a common theme of the NEW AGE MOVEMENT, presents still another vehicle. Many ᵇfundamentalist Christians hold to an ᵇeschatology known as ᵇmillennialism (the view that a future thousand-year utopian peace will be brought to earth). LaVey's *Satanic Bible* opens with a parallel theme for Satanists. The followers of the devil will inherit a place of prominence in the coming new order. However disillusioned one is with the past and the present, the satanist places hope in the future.

Some have been introduced to Satanism through the use of the ᵇouija board manufactured by Parker Brothers. In a pamphlet titled "The Weird and Wonderful Ouija Talking Board Set," Parker Brothers makes clear the company's perspective on the game. "Where does the Ouija Talking Board come from?" the pamphlet asks. Parker Brothers admits that they do not know.

But they do know that many people who use it and have fun with it are people who are "interested in the occult." At least one ex-satanist admitted that his involvement in the occult started with a ouija board.

Sensationalism

Of all of the religious movements included in this volume, groups related to Satanism receive perhaps the most attention within the media, on talk shows, and in popular literature. For example, public interest was heightened greatly when members of several satanic churches were featured on *Geraldo* in 1988. In March 1991, *20/20* featured a Roman Catholic rite of ᵇexorcism.

The attendant danger to such popularization is a tendency toward sensationalism. Because Satanism is a subject with which the average American is unfamiliar, curiosity is naturally aroused when satanic groups practicing the Black Mass or digging up graves to extract bones or body parts are reported in the media. Additional problems surface when self-styled "experts" on cults and the occult arise within Christian evangelical and fundamentalist circles. Through lectures, seminars, tapes, and books, the "experts," taking advantage of an unlearned constituency all too willing to afford them a hearing, greatly exaggerate the reality of the problem, and in many instances, present false information.[18] For example, it has been claimed that upwards of fifty thousand to two million children per year are kidnapped and sacrificed to the devil. David Alexander, a writer for the magazine *The Humanist*, points to the obvious absurdity of such claims:

Think about the logistics required to kill two million people a year. A recent example will provide us with some perspective. During World War II, millions of Jews, Gypsies, Slavs, Poles, and others considered "subhuman" by the Nazis were rounded up and systematically exterminated. . . . The Nazis ran six major killing centers and sixteen hundred smaller camps. Researchers estimate that there were over one hundred fifty thousand people involved in running and servicing the death camps, from railroad clerks to the guards who ran the gas chambers. It was a large operation which ran at its peak from 1941–1944. It takes a large and efficient organization to exterminate two million people a year. . . . *Could an organization of crazed baby killers—an organization a hundred times larger than organized crime—exist without any of us catching on?* Where is the evidence for such an operation in this country?[19] (emphasis added)

Alexander drives his point home:

Even the low estimate of fifty thousand ritual victims a year is a little less than the total number of Americans killed in Vietnam *during the entire war.* Virtually everyone in the United States over the age of thirty knows someone who was killed in Vietnam or knows someone who knew someone who was killed. How many people do you know who have been ritually sacrificed? Moreover, the Federal Bureau of Investigation compiles statistics about crime in the United States. If, as some "experts" claim, there are fifty thousand *unreported* ritual sacrifice murders being committed, then we must have a nation of very inefficient police and sheriffs' departments, as that figure is *two and one-half times* the twenty thousand murders annually recorded by the FBI.[20]

Alexander goes on to point out correctly that the vast majority of children abducted each year are in reality the victims of kidnapping arising from domestic disputes. In other words, the evidence simply has not been presented to substantiate the claims that child kidnapping is positively correlated to satanic activity in most instances.

A popular satanist-turned-Christian and author of *The Satan Seller* is Mike Warnke. Concerning the book and its author, Father Richard Woods of Loyola University wrote the following in his book *The Devil*:

Purporting to be a veridical account of a young man's meteoric rise to power in a vast Satanic conspiracy and his abrupt fall from "grace," *The Satan Seller* would be an incredibly bad novel. But although he was a drug-drenched and paranoid speed-freak with delusions of grandeur during the events narrated, Warnke (and his ghostwriters) assure us that the incidents occurred "absolutely as described." Truth is indeed stranger than fiction.[21]

Inverted cross and "Hate God" graffiti.
Courtesy Jack M. Roper/CARIS

The Satan Seller is precisely the kind of literature emerging from Christian circles that capitalizes on the ignorance of the masses. Warnke tells of having led his own ▸coven of satanists during his college days. In his popular audio-cassette *Mike Warnke Alive*, he reports to have had "cars, liquor, dope, chicks [girls]" and to have been involved in other criminal activities. *The Satan Seller* claims that rape, drugs, animal mutilations, and other such things are regularly practiced by satanists whom Warnke himself knew. Once again, Alexander points out the startling inconsistency in these claims: "Yet, despite his newfound born-again beliefs, Warnke has yet to supply law enforcement agencies with names, dates, or any other evidence necessary to assist them in investigating his claims."[22]

Harboring the names of known criminals is not only contrary to the teachings of Christianity, it may also be illegal. Some have suggested that ex-satanists cannot go public with the details of their involvement in satanic groups without fear of recrimination. The obvious question in Warnke's case then becomes why he says as much as he does in his book about satanist groups involved in criminal activity. If he had a good reason to be afraid for his life or the life of his family, perhaps he should not be speaking of such matters or amusing his audiences with stories about his Satan-filled past.[23]

An article calling for caution to sensationalism is Bob and Gretchen Passantino's "Hard Facts about Satanic Ritual Abuse." The Passantinos point out in a well-researched essay that satanic ritual abuse as a conspiratorial movement involving thousands of cases simply does not accord with the facts, nor is there evidence in most of these cases to substantiate the claims made.[24]

Recently, however, there have been counterclaims. In 1994, anthropologist Jean La Fontaine submitted a report to the Department of Health in England that of eighty-four cases that she investigated, none of them contained any evidence of satanic ritual abuse (SRA). The Health Secretary at the time concluded that SRA was indeed a myth. Two psychiatrists, Dr. Valerie Sinason and Dr. Rob Hale, countered the secretary's conclusion by documenting evidence of such abuse. It should also be noted that Sinason and Hale were paid 22,000 British pounds for researching numerous cases where patients claimed to have undergone SRA. Sinason claimed that as many as forty-six of her patients claimed to have witnessed murder during a satanic ritual. The controversy rages on.[25]

CONTRASTS TO CHRISTIANITY

The Christian church has always abhorred Satanism and its various practices. The biblical warnings against the occult are abundantly clear (Lev. 19:26–31; 20:6, 27; Deut. 13:1–5; 18:9–14; Isa. 8:19–22; Jer. 29:8–9; et al.). Additionally, the Bible speaks of Satan as being the "god of this age" (2 Cor. 4:4), who is the deceiver of the human race (Gen. 3:4–13) and the archenemy of God (Matt. 4:6; John 8:44; 2 Cor. 2:11). He is permitted to afflict the righteous (Job), reigns in dominion over sinners (Acts 26:18), attempts to reclaim Christians for himself (Eph. 6:12), and inspires deceptive and lying wonders (2 Thess. 2:9).

The ecumenical creeds (Appendix 1) do not make a direct allusion to Satan. However, the second article in the Apostles' and Nicene creeds is consumed with the person and work of Jesus Christ. In his person, Jesus defeated Satan first by being born (Gen. 3:15). In his person, he defeated Satan by overcoming all of the latter's temptations (Matt. 4:1–11), chief of which was the temptation to avoid the cross (Matt. 16:21–23). According to the Bible and the Christian faith, Jesus' death and resurrection signaled the end of the reign of Satan on the earth, with his impending doom a fixed certainty in the future (Rev. 20:7–10). Until that time, God has permitted Satan to exert an evil influence on the world (Job 1; 2 Cor. 4:4).

Like Satanism, Christianity is split in their belief over whether Satan is real, though the Bible teaches that he is a real, literal angelic being. Theologians have wrestled deeply with the "why" questions raised by the "problem of evil," especially in the twentieth century, influenced as it is by modernizing tendencies. Theologian Rudolf Bultmann, for example, dismissed the existence of a literal devil as being the product of "mythical" and prescientific thinking. There are many within the churches today who agree with him. Many, however, still attribute evil to the devil. Traditional orthodoxy has steadily continued to defend the classical biblical paradigms. Increasingly, there is evidence that the belief in the existence of the devil and in a literal hell is rising among Americans.[26]

The Black Mass

A discussion of the contrasts between Christianity and Satanism cannot exclude a treatment of the Black Mass. It is here that one may readily observe the contrast between the two. As was stated at the beginning of this article, Satanism, unlike witchcraft, defines itself as the very antithesis of Christianity. Classical satanic lore is dedicated to vituperative hatred toward all that Christianity stands for.

The Black Mass specifically focuses on the Lord's Supper, particularly the Roman Catholic church's theology of the Eucharist. With the exception of Lutheranism and high Anglicanism, the remainder of Protestantism does not embrace the doctrine of the real

A ritual robe that would be worn by a satanist priest during the Black Mass (the color is red). Note the dagger in the hand of the priest, to be used in sacrifice.
Courtesy Jack Roper/CARIS

presence of Christ in the bread and wine. The Black Mass is not directed, therefore, as an antithesis to the Protestant "Eucharist."

Richard Cavendish's *The Black Arts* (1968) contains an extensive treatment of the mass from a historical perspective. It must be remembered, however, that not all satanists use the Black Mass to vent hatred toward Christianity. Cavendish points out that

> the implication of practices like these was that the Mass contained inherent force which could be put to many uses. This implication was strengthened by Catholic insistence that a priest could say Mass effectively even if he was in a state of sin (because he did not say it in his own person but in the person of Christ). The ceremony and the objects connected with it seemed to have a magical power of their own, regardless of the spiritual condition of those who used them or the purposes for which they were used. From the use of the Mass in ▸white magic came its use in ▸black magic.[27]

Exorcism

Exorcism has played an important role in the church's response toward the demon-possessed. Both Jews and the ▸apostles cast out or exorcised demons. The practice of exorcism has continued throughout the centuries and is still practiced under carefully prescribed conditions, chiefly within the Roman Catholic church. Until the 1960s, the Roman church contained the rite of exorcism in the *Ritual Romanum*. The Lutheran church had the rite in its liturgical books until the nineteenth century.

Traditional Christianity still regards the existence of the devil as being a metaphysical reality. In modern times, however, many within Christendom and without, as noted to above, dismiss the existence of the devil as being a myth, looking to psychology to account for the existence of evil. Miscreants who in former ages were treated by the church authorities as being possessed by the devil are today regarded as being in need of various levels of psychiatric care. As was brought out in a live Roman Catholic exorcism aired for television on *20/20* (March 1991), before the Roman Catholic Church will conduct an exorcism, various psychological evaluations are first exercised, and only as a last resort is an exorcism then performed. The issue is still debated among divines in various Christian denominations.

Exorcism is also still practiced in a Roman Catholic baptismal rite. But this particular exorcism is not intended to cast demons out of a *possessed* non-Christian. Rather, it is a rite that prepares the candidate for baptism by renouncing the devil and all that held sway in the convert's life before baptism. This practice emerges from third- and fourth-century sources in the East. St. Cyril (A.D. 315–386) describes how baptismal candidates, during their baptisms, turned to the west and in four separate acts renounced Satan, his works, his pomp, and his worship.[28]

CONCLUSION

Satanism is a complex phenomenon in the world of the occult. The subject must be treated at many levels in order to render a fair and well-rounded presentation. There are ample scholarly sources listed as suggested reading in the bibliography.

Satanism continues to attract interest and involvement among people at each of the various levels. There are those who merely "dabble," those mercenaries who use it for commercial interests, those who use it for hedonistic purposes (LaVey), and finally those who immerse themselves with the utmost seriousness in ritualistic worship of Satan and commit violent crimes in their zealous quest to carry out their master's bidding.

Exact numbers of authentic satanists cannot be reported for reasons already stated. What interest future generations will have in Satanism and in the occult remains to be seen. New outbursts of interest in satanic activity are taking place in numerous places worldwide at the beginning of the twenty-first century.

ADDITIONAL INFORMATION

The Church of Satan
Headquarters: PO Box 210666, San Francisco, CA 94121.
Website: *www.thechurchofsatan.com/home*
Sacred Texts: LaVey's *The Satanic Bible, The Satanic Witch, The Satanic Rituals*
Publication: *The Black Star Chronicles*
Membership: about 10,000

The Temple of Set
Headquarters: PO Box 470307, San Francisco, CA 94147.
Website: *www.xeper.org*
Sacred Texts: Michael Aquino. *The Book of Coming Forth By Night*; Don Webb, *Xeper, The Eternal Word of Set,* (plus numerous other of his writings)
Membership: 500 estimated. However the Temple of Set does not publish membership statistics.

Notes
[1] Arthur Lyons, *Satan Wants You: The Cult of Devil Worship in America* (New York: Mysterious Press, 1988), 30.
[2] See WITCHCRAFT.
[3] Lyons, *Satan Wants You*, 86.

[4] Richard Cavendish, *A History of Magic* (London: Weidenfeld and Nicholson, n.d.), 148. See also Rosemary Guiley, *The Encyclopedia of Witches and Witchcraft* (New York: Facts on File, Inc., 1984), 75.

[5] Ibid.

[6] Wade Baskin, *Dictionary of Satanism* (New York: Philosophical Library, Inc., 1972), 147.

[7] Lyons, *Satan Wants You*, 82.

[8] Ibid.

[9] Craig S. Hawkins, "The Many Faces of Satanism," *Forward* (Fall 1986), 17–22.

[10] Lyons, *Satan Wants You*, 9.

[11] Anton Szandor LaVey, *The Satanic Bible* (New York: Avon Books, 1969), 25

[12] *http://religiousmovements.lib.virginia.edu/nrms/Satanism/pop.html*

[13] Ibid., 5

[14] See J. Gordon Melton, *The Encyclopedia of American Religions*, 2 vols. (Wilmington, NC: McGrath, 1978).

[15] This statement and those that follow are taken from Larry Nichols and George Mather, "Doorways to the Demonic," *Lutheran Witness* (October 1987), 3–5.

[16] As quoted in "Doorways to the Demonic," 4.

[17] Child kidnapping, pornography, and the ritualistic sacrifices of children are all characteristics of the danger of authentic Satanism.

[18] See Shawn Carlson,et al., *Satanism in America* (El Cerrito, CA: Gaia Press, 1989), a study conducted by Carlson, a Berkeley physicist and a team of researchers called the Committee for the Scientific Examination of Religions (CSER).

[19] David Alexander, "Giving the Devil More Than His Due," *The Humanist* (March/April 1990), 6.

[20] Ibid.

[21] Ibid., 10.

[22] Ibid.

[23] For an excellent article on Mike Warnke, see Jon Trott and Mike Hertenstein, "Selling Satan," *Cornerstone*, 21/98 (1992), 7; idem, *Selling Satan* (Chicago: Cornerstone, 1993).

[24] Bob and Gretchen Passantino, "The Hard Facts About Satanic Ritual Abuse," *Christian Research Journal* (Winter, 1992), 21.

[25] David Brindle, "Satanic Ritual Abuse Erupts," *The Guardian*–UK (Feb. 10, 2000).

[26] See "Hell's Sober Comeback," *U.S. News and World Report* (March 25, 1991), 56–57.

[27] Richard Cavendish, *The Black Arts* (New York: Capricorn, 1968), 356.

[28] J. N. D. Kelly, *Early Christian Creeds*, 3d ed. (New York: Longman, 1972), 33.

SCIENTOLOGY

"Writing for a penny a word is ridiculous. If a man really wanted to make a million dollars, the best way would be to start his own religion." These words, quoted in *Time* magazine (April 5, 1976, p. 57), were spoken by L. (Lafayette) Ron ⁍Hubbard (1911–1986). Hubbard had actually made this statement proleptically in 1949, not in 1976. In 1950 he published his bestseller, *Dianetics: The Modern Science of Mental Health*, which became the textbook for a religion that he founded in 1954, popularly known as The Church of Scientology.

HISTORY

Born in Tilden, Nebraska, Hubbard spent much of his childhood in Helena, Montana. He attended George Washington University and, according to his publications, graduated with a major in civil engineering. However, campus records indicate that Hubbard had attended the college for only two years and that during his second year he failed physics and was placed on academic probation.

Hubbard did meet with success as a science fiction writer in the 1930s before the publication of *Dianetics*. At age twenty-nine, in 1940, he organized the Hubbard Association of Scientologists International. Ten years later in 1950 he became famous through the publication of *Dianetics*, which by the year 2000 reportedly had sold eighteen million copies.

On February 18, 1954, Hubbard incorporated the Church of Scientology of California. In 1955 he established the Founding Church of Scientology in Washington, D.C., and New York. The international headquarters for Scientology was originally located at Saint Hill in East Grinstead, England, but is now located in Los Angeles, California. From 1965–1975, Hubbard divided his time and residence between Sussex, England, and a three-hundred-foot ship, Apollo, along with a flotilla called The Sea Org.

Trouble with the law broke out in 1963 when the Food and Drug Administration raided the Washington, D.C., church on the grounds that Hubbard's ⁍E-meter device, which the church utilized, should be banned,

L. Ron Hubbard and two of the bestselling books of Scientology that he has written.

Courtesy Jack M. Roper/CARIS

because it was seen as an unlawful device. The organization in 1971 appealed its case on the freedom of religion clause in the First Amendment of the United States Constitution and won the rights to use the E-meter as a religious instrument.

In 1980 Hubbard disappeared from the public and from his family as he withdrew into seclusion. That same year, Hubbard's wife and eight members of the organization were sent to prison for infiltrating several branches of the U.S. government to steal investigative files on Scientology and Hubbard. Eleven top Scientologists were convicted of criminal activity, out of which nine went to prison. This event marred Scientology's ethics, which was based on a moral code written by Hubbard.

In 1982 Hubbard's son, Ronald DeWolf (Hubbard Jr.), petitioned a California court to name him trustee of his father's estate on the grounds that he believed his father had died. The court ruled, however, that Hubbard was still very much alive. DeWolf was one of five children and had changed his name to renounce his father, claiming that he was "one of the biggest con men of the century." Death came to L. Ron Hubbard in 1986. During his last years, in a manner not unlike the late Howard Hughes, Hubbard had become a veritable hermit. He left a movement behind, however, which as of 2001 reportedly had about three million members, although former staffers say that the number of members is somewhere between 200,000 and two million.

In 1991 the organization filed a $416 million libel suit against *Time* magazine, Time-Warner, and reporter Richard Behar for his article that appeared in *Time,* May 6, 1991, titled, "The Thriving Cult of Greed and Power."

Several sources that Behar quoted were also sued in answer to mounting criticism. In early 1992, David Miscavige, the head of Scientology, appeared on ABC's *Nightline* in an exclusive interview with Ted Koppel. Miscavige gave Scientology a polished image for a new generation of converts. The suit against *Time* was later dismissed.

In a botched deprogramming of a UNITED PENTECOSTALISM church member, the Church of Scientology, a longtime foe of deprogrammers, funded the "Jason-Scott" case, to break one of the largest secular organizations on cults, the Cult Awareness Network (CAN). CAN lost the suit and the appeal, and their assets were ordered sold through liquidation. On October 23, 1996, Scientology purchased several CAN assets, including the name Cult Awareness Network. CAN became staffed by Scientology members as well as others. It is being run under the name Foundation for Religious Freedom (FRF).

Continued media exposure has been the result of ongoing legal battles and lawsuits. In March 1999, a major lawsuit was filed concerning copyright infringement between FACTNet Inc. and the Church of Scientology. The latter claimed that the former was using Hubbard's materials on the internet. The case resulted in millions of dollars in legal fees incurred by both sides and Hubbard's materials were removed from FACTNet's website. In 2002, Scientology sent the Google search engine a list of 126 web pages that it claimed infringed its copyright. Google promptly removed these pages because of the Digital Millennium Copyright Act (DMCA). One anti-Scientology website (xenu.net), after being removed, was promptly restored.[1]

Another large controversy was the issue surrounding the 1995 death of Lisa McPherson. According to the *St. Petersburg Times*, "She was kept in a room at Scientology's Fort Harrison Hotel as fellow Scientologists tried to nurse her through a psychotic episode, in part by force-feeding her food, liquids, medicines and herbal remedies, according to an affidavit filed with the charges."[2] McPherson died, which death was blamed on the church by some, but the church consistently maintained it was innocent. In February of 2000, McPherson's death was ruled "accidental" and charges against the church were dropped.

The largest controversy that Scientology has faced abroad in the 1990s was in Germany. The German government under Chancellor Helmut Kohl has attempted to ban Scientology from being practiced. Members of the United States Congress as well as numerous others, including celebrities, issued letters of protest centering around the Kohl government's posturing toward Scientologists.

Recently, Scientology suffered its largest defeat in the ongoing legal battles that it has faced in the last decade. In Wollersheim vs. Church of Scientology (May 9, 2002), the church was ordered to pay $8.6 million to ex-member Lawrence Wollersheim and his legal team. This was a legal battle that had been drawn out over twenty-two years, the claim being that the church practiced counseling methods that were considered dangerous enough to drive Wollersheim to the point of insanity. Wollersheim, in an interview with FACTNet, said: "It is my opinion that there are hundreds of thousands of people all over the US, Europe, and South America who have been destroyed by this cult and then intimidated into silence. But I do not think that these people will remain silent any longer."[3] It was changed to $2.5 million.

Like the UNIFICATION CHURCH and TRANSCENDENTAL MEDITATION, Scientology has managed to regroup and reorganize itself in order to promulgate successfully its religio/psychological presuppositions in secular guise. In addition to education, other areas in which the organization has involved itself include health care, business, entertainment, and book publishing. Scientology has numerous organizations. IHELP is an organizational structure designed to assist field auditors in their work outside of the organization. SMI or Scientology Mission International is an organization that promotes the literature and the church throughout the world. The churches themselves are referred to as Class V organizations. It is at this local level that courses are offered and services rendered. There are celebrity centers that do the same work as the churches except gear themselves toward artists and performers. The auditing courses are provided at Saint Hill Organizations. The premium level courses are offered at the Flag Service Organization.

The watchdog part of the church is the Religious Technology Center. Here the teachings of Hubbard are closely monitored. Narconon is the movement's drug abuse treatment program. Criminon is a ministry set up for the rehabilitation of criminals. WISE, or the World Institute of Scientology Enterprise, promotes Scientology in the business world. The Citizen's Commission on Human Rights (CCHR) devotes itself to the ardent battle against psychiatry, the organization's greatest enemy.

ORGANIZATION

The headquarters for Scientology is in Los Angeles. The church there, The Church of Scientology International, is also called The Mother Church. The organization is run by a board of directors. Heber C. Jentzsch has served as president since 1982. There are churches in over 133 countries. Staff members perform Scientology techniques and serve for periods of $2^1/_2$ and/or 5 years; they receive training at the headquarters. The organization celebrates its own holidays, such as Hubbard's birthday on March 13; the second Sunday in September is Auditor's Day; May 9 commemorates the publishing date of *Dianetics*; and October 7 is celebrated because that is the founding date of the International Association of Scientologists.[4]

TEACHINGS

Hubbard combined Freudian psychoanalysis with Eastern thought and ideas from his science fiction writings and produced a religion that has gained a wide appeal with those seeking improved mental health. The basic beliefs of Scientology, that members adhere to are as follows:

There is to be no discrimination between human beings with regards to race or creed.

Everyone possesses inalienable rights, such as to practice one's religion, congregate, think speak, defend one's self, procreate, and live a healthy life.

The souls of man have the same rights as man.

The discipline of Psychology should not be studied or practiced outside of the aid of spiritual principles as taught by religion.

God alone make all these rights unalienable.

Human beings are basically good and are seeking to survive, which depends upon brotherhood with the universe.

God expressly forbids certain things: murder, destroying the sanity or harming the soul of another,

Several prominent actors and actresses, such as Tom Cruise, are adherents of Scientology.
Courtesy Getty Images/Kevin Winter

and destroying the right of another or a group to survive.

Lastly, Scientology believes that the spirit is what is saved and the spirit is the source of healing for mind and body.

The complete creed is posted by the church of Scientology on its website as *www.scientology.org.*

Fundamental to Scientology is the concept that the mind is divided into two basic parts: the *analytical and *reactive mind. The analytical mind perceives, remembers, and conducts the reasoning processes. The reactive mind records *engrams. The mind is vulnerable to engrams during traumatic moments, particularly during prenatal stages and at birth. The analytical mind does not remember these experiences, which are often extremely painful, and they are therefore not at the level of consciousness. The key to achieving mental health is to subject oneself to the examination and treatment of an *auditor, who has the status of an ordained clergy. The goal is to expose the engrams hidden by the reactive mind within the *preclear person and remove them. One who has had all engrams removed is called a *clear. Being a clear means one is free from the "reactive mind." Auditors use a device called an E-meter (short for electro-psychometer), which purports to measure the mental state of a preclear person's resistance to engrams.

The above describes the psychological orientation of Scientology. The religious foundation on which it is built stems from the notion that human beings were once immortal spiritual beings called *thetans. Thetans relinquished their godlike powers to enter MEST (matter, energy, space, time), that is, earth. On earth, a process of evolution took place, and human beings, who could no longer remember their preexistent state as thetans, emerged onto the stages of history. Similar to MORMONISM, Eastern religions, and the NEW AGE MOVEMENT, Scientology teaches that within a human being is a latent preexistent entity that can evolve into a "god-like" being called Homo Novus.

A frequent recruiting technique in Scientology is to ask an individual on the street if he or she would like to take a free personality test. The test answers are graphed, and the individual is then shown his or her results. Most often the results indicate the presence of personality flaws that may later be linked to engrams within the person's reactive mind. But the personality test is the only part of the process that is free. According to the latest figures, the cost of becoming a clear is a minimum of about $3,000 (but often tens of thousands more).

Having achieved the state of clear, the initiate then takes courses with such titles as "Clear Certainty Rundown." This five-hour course is taken for about another $3,000. At this stage, the clear is able to move on to the advanced courses in order to become an OT (operating thetan). There are fifteen OT stages, attainment of which may cost the participant in excess of about $90,000.

Paul *Twitchell joined the Church of Scientology before he founded ECKANKAR. He is allegedly one of the first to ever achieve the status of a clear.

The basic doctrines of Scientology, along with some comparisons to CHRISTIANITY, are listed below:

God

The universe contains many gods, and there are gods beyond even these gods. Christianity, by contrast, is strictly *monotheistic (Ex. 20:3; Deut. 6:4; Isa. 44:6). The church has always confessed "one God, the Father Almighty" (Nicene Creed, Appendix 1), who is manifested in three persons—Father, Son, and Holy Spirit.

Jesus Christ

"Neither Lord Buddha nor Jesus Christ were OTs (Operating Thetans, the highest Scientology level) according to evidence. They were just a shade above clear."[5]

Scientology falls into a predictable pattern here with other Eastern groups, who have high regard for Jesus as an *avatar, yet deny his exclusive place as King of kings and Lord of lords, as "very God of very God, begotten, not made, being of one substance with the Father, by whom all things were made" (Nicene Creed). Numerous Scripture passages reflect the church's *Christology (e.g., John 1:1–18; Col. 1:15–17; 1 Tim.3:16; Heb. 1:13).

Scientology denigrates the cross as an ancient symbol introduced by "preclears a million years ago."[6] Yet the cross is a pivotal symbol for the church that cannot be dismissed in the biblical tradition (Acts 2:14–36; 3:11–26; 1 Cor. 2:2).[7]

Humanity

As stated above, Scientology sees the human being as a fallen thetan. Human beings have the potential to be coached (audited) to an awareness of their preMEST condition. Like so many Eastern religious groups, Scientology teaches that the spirit can have power over matter and does not distinguish between the Creator and the creation.[8] Inevitably this entails important considerations. Christianity strongly maintains the distinction between God and creation. Human beings are made in God's image, not in the likeness of a three-trillion-year-old thetan. The human race is in a state of fallen, active rebellion against God (Gen. 3). The essential message of the Christian church is that God has made it possible through the person and work of Jesus Christ to motivate people to bring an end to sin and rebellion, by his promise of eternal life through Jesus Christ (John 3:16).

Sin and Hell

All human beings are seen as good in their basic nature. Sin and bad deeds are linked to engrams, but once engrams are erased, one progresses toward survival, which means one is ultimately released from ᵖreincarnation. ᵖHell is a myth and an invention; it is a cruel hoax perpetrated by the miserable in order that others might be miserable as well.

For Christianity, sin is not linked to engrams but to sin, for which the consequences are dire indeed (Gen. 3:1–17; Rom. 3:23; 6:23). Hell or a state of everlasting torment is no myth. Jesus spoke candidly on the subject (Matt. 25:41–46). John refers to a "lake of fire" (Rev 20:15) into which the wicked will be cast on the Day of Judgment. Admittedly, the belief in a literal hell is not in vogue in modern liberal expressions of Christian thought, yet traditional Christianity, in its various denominational settings, has consistently maintained that the hell that the Bible speaks of is certainly a reality in the afterlife of the impenitent.

Salvation and Heaven

Freedom from rebirth; here it can readily be seen how Scientology embraces Buddhist and Hindu concepts concerning reincarnation. All religions are paths that lead to salvation, but none is as short or effective as Scientology. There is no heaven in the sense that the ᵖBible defines it. But heaven does exist in that it is the embodiment of a deified state to which humanity may return.

Here Hubbard proposes nothing that is not already endemic to an Eastern conceptualization of ᵖsoteriology. Without a doctrine of original sin or eternal damnation and coupled with a pantheistic view of life and God, Scientology leaves one to seek out a salvation that is latent within the human soul and grounded in the past and in past lives in the cycle of reincarnation. Christianity, by contrast, grounds salvation not in latent ability residing in a human being but rather in the person and work of Jesus Christ. The Scientologist searches for the answers to life in the deep recesses of the psychology of one's past

and past lives. Christianity, too, is dependent on the past, but a past that historically occurred in the crucifixion and resurrection of Jesus of Nazareth, not a past grounded in psychological ruminations.

CONCLUSION

Scientology continues to remain a controversial organization within the media. However, Hubbard's books remain popular and are offered on the organization's official website. One can now take the free personality test online as well. After the devastating terrorist attacks of September 11, 2001, Scientologists were well represented among the many religious organizations that provided help and assistance at Ground Zero.

As a word of qualification, Scientology claims harmony with Christianity and often produces letters by liberal ministers who support them. The biblical message of salvation though Jesus Christ as "the way and the truth and the life" (John 14:6) opposes the message of Scientology.

ADDITIONAL INFORMATION

Headquarters
Church of Scientology, L. Ron Hubbard Way, Los Angeles, CA 90027.

Website
www.scientology.org

Sacred Texts
The numerous writings of Hubbard. A source published by the Church of Scientology is the book *Theology and Practice of a Contemporary Religion: A Reference Work by the Church of Scientology International* (Los Angeles: Bridge Publications, 1998).

Periodicals
Major publications of Scientology include *SOURCE*, published by Scientology's Flag Organization Service; *The Auditor*, published by the Church of Scientology in California—the Saint Hill Organization; and *Advance*, published by the Church of Scientology in California.

Membership
Very difficult to calculate because of the levels of members. In some instances simply buying a copy of Hubbard's *Dianetics* qualified one to be counted into the statistics. This puts the number as high as eight million. Realistically, the number of actual members is between two hundred thousand and two million. There are 2,600 churches around the world with 17,000 staff members.

Notes
[1] See Danny Sullivan, ed., "Google Embroiled in Scientology Debate" (*http://searchenginewatch.com/sereport/article.php/2164661*).

[2] Thomas C. Tobin, "Church Pleads Innocent to Criminal Charges," *St. Petersburg Times* (December 1, 1998).

[3] *www.factnet.org/letters/FACTNewsMay2002Wollersheim.html*, 3.

[4] Information concerning the group's organizational structure was taken from *http://religiousmovements.lib.virginia.edu/nrms/scientology.html*.

[5] L. Ron Hubbard, *Certainty Magazine* 5/10 (n.d.): 73, as quoted by Martin, *Kingdom of the Cults*, 348.

[6] L. Ron Hubbard, *Professional Auditor's Bulletin #31*, as quoted by Martin, *Kingdom of the Cults*, 348.

[7] See the UNIFICATION CHURCH, wherein Sun Myung ▸Moon taught that the cross was an unfortunate circumstance in the life of Jesus. Moon, however, does not deny the historicity of the crucifixion.

[8] See HINDUISM, CHURCH OF THE SECOND ADVENT, NEW AGE MOVEMENT, and numerous Eastern groups appearing in this volume for a further reference to the Creator/creation distinction.

SELF REALIZATION FELLOWSHIP (SRF)

One of the numerous movements that proliferated in America in the twentieth century derived from HINDUISM. Self Realization Fellowship has proved to be among the most influential of the Eastern religions, pioneering the way for many other groups that would arrive in the United States some decades later.

HISTORY

Paramahansa ▸Yogananda (1893–1952) was one of the earliest teachers of ▸yoga to come to the West, preceded only by ▸Swami ▸Vivekananda, who introduced Hinduism to the West in 1893 at the Parliament of World Religions in Chicago. Paramahansa Yogananda organized Self Realization Fellowship in 1914, which became chartered in 1935 with headquarters in Los Angeles. In 1920 Yogananda addressed the International Congress of Religious Liberals and also lectured widely on college campuses and churches throughout America. He represents an early precedent to the rising interest in the United States in the teachings of ▸gurus from the Far East during the 1960s and 1970s. His *Autobiography of a Yogi* (1946) brought him fame and popularity.

Sri Daya Mata, known as the "Mother of the Society," was one of Yogananda's early disciples from his lecture tours. She was raised a Mormon in Salt Lake City, Utah, but converted to SFR in 1933 after hearing Yogananda's lecture in that city. She served as the president of SFR beginning in 1955.

Yogananda died in 1952. By the 1960s, SRF claimed two hundred thousand members. A millionaire from Kansas who had converted to SRF, Sri Daya Mata, became Yogananda's successor. At the time of Yogananda's death, his disciples alleged that there was no apparent decay of his body because of yogic techniques that oxygenated the blood. The society remains active at the start of the twenty-first century. The website lists all of the lecture tours that are regularly conducted.

ORGANIZATION

The SRF is comprised of monks and nuns; this is called the monastic order. They teach in the ashram centers and travel throughout the world to conduct lectures and teaching seminars. Temples and meditation centers are located throughout the world. The society holds an annual convocation in Los Angeles and members come from all the other societies, temples, and meditation centers to hear and learn the teachings of Yogananda. Paramahansa Yogananda served as the president of the society up to the time of his death.

TEACHINGS

Yogananda taught a method of ▸enlightenment called ▸*kriya yoga*. He had formerly believed and taught the Hindu concept of enlightenment as being attainable only after many ▸reincarnations over successive lifetimes. Yogananda introduced a significant and practical variation of this, however. Utilization of his techniques promised to reduce the amount of time needed to achieve enlightenment to just three years. *Kriya yoga* was a technique that, when practiced, enabled the devotee to direct the motions of outer-life energy toward the inner self.

Like its parent, Hinduism, SRF attempts to emphasize the elements common to all religions.[1] Yogananda lectured and taught in Christian churches that were favorably disposed toward interfaith ecumenical dialog.

Lay members are distinguished from those who have taken monastic vows. The latter frequently assume clerical and other leadership positions in the movement.

Like BUDDHISM, SRF follows an eightfold path utilizing preliminary and advanced forms of yoga: (1) moral conduct (*yoga yama*); (2) religious practice (*yoga niyama*); (3) correct posture (*yoga asana*); (4) control of life energy (*yoga pranayama*); (5) withdrawal of sense objects (*yoga pratyahara*); (6) concentration (*yoga dharana*); (7) meditation (*yoga dhyana*); and (8) superconscious experience (*yoga *samadhi*).

CONCLUSION

SRF has had a significant influence on other movements. Recently the society re-released Yogananda's two-volume interpretation of Jesus Christ to capitalize on the popularity of Jesus in the media from Mel Gibson's movie, *The Passion of the Christ*. The two-volume set, *The Second Coming of Christ* (SRF, 2004), echoes the New Age/Hindu reinterpretation that Christ is "a Christ consciousness" that indwells all living beings and needs to be awakened for "self realization." Through esoteric interpretation, the biblical passages cited take on an allegorical, nonliteral, nonhistorical, nongrammatical meaning.

The Self Realization Church of Absolute Monism, also founded by Yogananda in 1927, grew directly out of SRF. It became independent from its parent organization under the leadership of Swami Premananda in 1928. This group's teachings are parallel to SRF with additional emphasis on the teachings of *Gandhi. It is a very small movement with one congregation in Washington, D.C., and a missionary outreach in West Bengal.[2]

Other students of Yogananda included Swami Kriyananda, founder of the Temple of Kriya Yoga in Chicago; Vasudevadas and Devaki, founders of Prema Dharmasala; Beth Hand, founder of the International Church of Ageless Wisdom; Anita Afton, founder of New Age Teachings; and Paul *Twitchell, founder of ECKANKAR. Twitchell was also a former member of Premananda's church.

SRF centers are located throughout the United States and are part of a worldwide network with 150 centers. Each has a small following.[3] Lectures, tapes, books, regular meetings, and an annual convocation constitute regular activities of the organization.

ADDITIONAL INFORMATION

Headquarters
Self-Realization Fellowship, The Mother Center, 3880 San Rafael Avenue, Los Angeles, California, 90065–3298.

Website
www.yogananda-srf.org

Sacred Texts
There are no particular texts defined as such. However, parts of the autobiography of Yogananda's life, *Autobiography of a Yogi*, and the New Testament of the Bible and *Bhagavad Gita* are read.

Publication
Self Realization (magazine)

Statistics
There are nearly five hundred meditation centers located in fifty-four countries.

Notes
[1] See HINDUISM, ECKANKAR, and VEDANTA SOCIETY for an analysis and comparison between the teachings of these respective groups and CHRISTIANITY, as they relate directly to SRF.
[2] J. Gordon Melton, *The Encyclopedia of American Religions*, 2 vols. (Wilmington, NC: McGrath, 1978), 2:362.
[3] Growth statistics, provided by the Institute for World Religions, P.O. Box CC, Irvine, CA 92716–6003, were made available in 1988.

SEVENTH-DAY ADVENTISM; SDA

Seventh-day Adventism is one of the important developments in America during the nineteenth century. In the previous edition of this dictionary, the authors limited Seventh-day Adventism to an article titled the *Millerite Movement. SDA, however, is a significant movement in the marketplace of religious ideas that developed in the American religious experience.

HISTORY

The story of the development of Seventh-day Adventism belongs in several stages with key personalities plotting the course along the way. The first is William Miller (*see *Millerite Movement and the *Great Disappointment). After the Great Disappointment, the fledgling movement almost came to nothing and was thrown into disarray.

After Miller's demise began the second phase in the development of Adventist theology. A follower of Miller named Hiram Edson was determined to explore further the idea of Christ's return. Miller had assumed that the seventy weeks of Daniel 9:24–27 were seventy weeks of years (490 years), which he dated from the beginning of the reign of King Artaxerxes (Ezra 7:11–26). Miller had calculated this 490 period to have begun in 457 B.C. This would have taken history to the point of Christ's crucifixion in A.D. 33. Miller had then calculated, based on Daniel 8:14, that a period of 2,300 days (which he also interpreted as years) would elapse before the "cleansing of the temple." For Miller, this "cleansing" was the literal return of Christ to the earth. He dated this time also from 457 B.C., thereby arriving at the year 1843 for the Second Coming.

Edson, puzzled by the failure of Christ to return that year or the following October (1844), claimed to have been given a vision in which he was told that there were two sanctuaries, an earthly as well as a heavenly. For Edson, Miller's calculations had been correct. His big mistake, however, was figuring that the Lord was cleansing the earthly sanctuary. Further, Edson surmised that there were two returns of Christ, the heavenly and then the earthly. He derived this from a study of Hebrews in the New Testament. Edson came to believe that the ministry of the Old Testament priesthood was itself twofold. He and several companions, including O. R. L. Crosier, made the claim that when the priests daily sprinkled the horns of the altar with blood, the sins of the people were not absolved but transferred. Sin moved from the people to the altar. The cleansing of the altar took place once yearly on the Day of Atonement when the high priest entered the Holy of Holies and sprinkled the blood of a slain sacrificial goat on the atonement cover. The sins of the people were then placed on another goat, called a "scapegoat," which was then set free into the wilderness. This action brought about the cleansing of the people from their sin. Thus, the idea of two priestly ministries was born.

This scenario made possible a way of keeping Miller's theology alive. The date of October 22, 1844, was assigned to be the time of Christ's cleansing of the heavenly sanctuary. But this action is not complete in a literal day, as was the case in the Old Testament Day of Atonement. This began a process that remains incomplete until the sins have been placed on the scapegoat, which Crosier taught was not Christ but the devil.

Another important figure in the development of Adventist doctrine was Joseph Bates. His contribution was in laying the groundwork for the later incorporation of the phrase "Seventh-day" into the movement's current name. Through a series of studies and associations with some Seventh-day Baptists, Bates came to believe that God had commanded that the day of worship was the Jewish Sabbath or seventh day (Saturday). The legacy that would become a characteristic feature of the modern Seventh-day Adventist movement was born through a lengthy tract that Bates titled *The Seventh-day Sabbath, a Perpetual Sign*. A second work called *A Seal of the Living God* (1849), a study of Revelation 7, brought Bates to the conclusion that 144,000 would obediently keep the Sabbath and other commandments of God. Those who observe the Saturday Sabbath were, and are today, those who are sealed by God.

The name Ellen G. White is the most prominent in the formulation of Seventh-day Adventism into what it is today. As a young girl, Ellen G. Harmon's (her maiden name) family attended a Methodist church but were drawn to the teachings of William Miller in Portland, Maine. Following the Great Disappointment, Harmon experienced two visions. In the first, she was leading a group of followers to the city of God; in the second, she was told that she would encounter hardship and rejection but despite this, she must reveal to others the revelations she had received.

Her encounters with God through visions increased. The most important one came in February 1845, when she reported that Jesus had entered the Holy of Holies in the heavenly sanctuary, "confirming Hiram Edson's vision received in October of the preceding year."[1] White herself claimed to have been transported to this heavenly sanctuary. Here she saw the ark of the covenant and the Ten Commandments. A halo encircled the fourth (Sabbath) commandment. This in effect confirmed Bates's vision as well.[2] White came to be recognized as the true prophetess of God, who had been chosen to reveal the new work that God was doing. In effect, she became the glue that fused together Miller, Edson, and Bates each in their respective visions.

James White, who married Harmon in 1846, also became an important figure. In 1849 he published a paper called *Present Truth*, which was renamed the following year, *The Advent Review and Sabbath Herald*. The earliest name for the followers of the new teaching was "Sabbath-keepers." In 1855, the group moved from Rochester, New York, and relocated its headquarters in Battle Creek, Michigan. It was in 1860 in Battle Creek that the group adopted the name Seventh-day Adventists. A famous name that crops up in Adventist history is John Kellogg, a follower of the Whites and founder of the Kellogg's Cereal Company. In 1903, the Adventist headquarters moved to Takoma Park near Washington, D.C., and called this location its home. In 1989, the headquarters were moved to Silver Spring, Maryland, where they remain to this day. Other Adventist groups include Adventist Christian Church, now merged with Life and Advent Union, and the Church of God General Conference.

The Seventh-day Adventist movement remained largely isolated from other religious bodies until well on into the twentieth century, when it became more acculturated into the American landscape and was regarded as another fundamentalist (see ▸fundamentalism) denomination. The prominent American church historian Sydney Ahlstrom points out, however, that "any significant cooperation with these groups was prevented by the Adventists' extreme legalism, Sabbatarianism, and unusual doctrines on the Atonement, Satan, and the damned, as well as their strongly held views on health, medicine, and diet."[3]

Seventh-day Adventism underwent significant changes in the last half of the twentieth century. Tensions arose from within the ranks and went in several directions. The rise of higher criticism caused some within Adventist ranks to press toward a more liberal treatment of Scripture. The more influential controversies, however, centered around a more conservative, ▸Protestant, and Reformation theological orientation. In 1970s a group known as the "new theologians" arose within the ranks. One such was Robert Brinsmead, a Reformation scholar who had studied for some years in Europe. Brinsmead advocated that Adventism was not a true heir of Reformation theology as traditional Seventh-day teachings had in fact maintained. This had the effect of introducing polarizations in Adventist universities, some pushing toward the "new theology" while many resisted. The conservative resistance became reactionary and in some instances inquisitional in nature.

Another "new theologian" who invited further controversy was Desmond ▸Ford. Ford went to the heart of Seventh-day Adventism. As a movement, a large portion of Adventist thought had historically come to be defined around the issue of the end times. Ford maintained that there were other ways of understanding the role of prophecy in the Bible than the traditional "historicist" method. He was promptly dismissed from his teaching post, and his ministerial credentials were removed. Ford also rejected the observance of the Sabbath, as had Brinsmead before him.

The movement had a ripple effect. By the 1980s the new spirit spread to the churches and to the rank-and-file membership. A book by Walter Rea entitled *The White Lie* even went so far as to suggest that Ellen G. White was guilty of plagiarism. He contends that she copied significant portions of her book *The Great Controversy* from other sources. More and more professors were turning to the higher critical methods of interpreting the Bible, thereby inviting still further reaction from traditional ranks. "Our Firm Foundation" arose as a movement to bring the church back to its traditional theology. Books such as *Keepers of the Faith* called for a return to original Adventist teachings. It is interesting to note that the "new theologians" have raised many of the same issues that were raised recently by those who led the reform movement within the WORLDWIDE CHURCH OF GOD.[4] Note too that the BRANCH DAVIDIANS were an offshoot of Seventh-day Adventism.

ORGANIZATION

The local church comprises the basic unit of Adventism. A local conference is made up of a number of local churches (also called local field or mission). A union conference is comprised of several local conferences. The largest organizational body in the movement is called the general conference, which oversees the administration of Seventh-day Adventism worldwide. Officers at each level are elected. The general conference elects a president, secretary, and treasurer. An executive committee is appointed to serve between the various sessions of the church. On a world scale, there are twelve divisions over which the general conference administrates. Education, mission, and evangelism are important themes in SDA ministry. The denomination has the second-largest Protestant parochial school system.

TEACHINGS

It is Harold Bloom's scholarly opinion that "no American faith, not even Jehovah's Witnesses, has a theology so convoluted as that of Seventh Day Adventism."[5] This may or may not be true, but what is certain is that Seventh-day Adventism is clear and well published and systematic with regards to their doctrines. A book called *Seventh-day Adventists Believe. . . A Biblical Exposition of 27 Fundamental Doctrines*, which has undergone numerous editions, is readily available. The SDA website lists in summary fashion the most important doctrines. The formal statement of beliefs is titled "Fundamental Beliefs of Seventh-day Adventists." The basics are as follows:

The Bible

The Bible is the revealed, inspired, and infallible Word of God. It represents "the essential truth about God." A criticism of Seventh-day Adventism has been that it also regards the writings of Ellen G. White as authoritative and normative. SDA apologists deny this charge and quote White herself when she stated that followers should regard the Bible as the Word of God. They also claim that they judge the writings of Ellen G. White by the Bible. Anthony Hoekema challenges this view by arguing that Adventists have stated that the writings of White are in harmony with the Bible. If this is true, then Hoekema wonders by what standard then do they judge the "harmonious" writings of White, especially when they regard her writings as "inspired councils from the Lord." "If this is so, however, who may criticize her writings? If they are inspired, they must be true."[6]

White told her followers in 1909, in her last address to the general session of the church body: "I commend to you this book [the Bible]!" But she then went on to comment: "I took the precious Bible and surrounded it with the several Testimonies for the Church, given for the people of God. You are not familiar with the Scriptures. If you had made God's Word your study, with a desire to reach the Bible standard and attain to Christian perfection, you would not have needed the Testimonies."[7] The question that must be raised, then, is in what sense is Seventh-day Adventism any different from the Jehovah's Witnesses? Founder Charles Taze *Russell claimed that in order to understand the Bible, a Jehovah's Witness must have as his or her guide his own *Truth That Leads to Eternal Life*. Adventists today sometimes do in fact regard the writings of White as authoritative, but at the same time, many adherents of Adventism no longer read her writings, at least on the same level as Scripture.

God

Adventists teach that God is revealed in the three persons of the Holy Trinity as taught in historical and *orthodox Christianity.

Creation

Seventh-day Adventism holds to a literal seven-day creation and to the Genesis account of the Garden of Eden.

Jesus Christ

Earlier Adventist theology had held to Jesus' full deity with respect to his divine nature, but some had insisted that there was some confusion with respect to whether Christ's human nature was sinless. Adventist doctrine no longer invites such ambiguity as they do teach that even though Jesus was made "in the likeness of sinful flesh," there is no way that he can be regarded as sinful.

Also controversial is Ellen G. White's naming Jesus as Michael the archangel in his preexistence. Many Adventist theologians are quick to clarify that their position still holds that he is God, the Creator, and is not a created being. This unclear mixture remains controversial within and outside Adventism.

Investigative Judgment

This peculiar doctrine dates back to Adventist beginnings where it was believed that on October 22, 1844, Jesus Christ entered the Holy of Holies in the heavenly sanctuary and began the process of blotting out sins. From the time of the ascension of Christ to 1844, Jesus was to have been "forgiving sins" in the manner of the Old Testament priests. The latter date began a new and second process for the actual "blotting out" of sins. This was tantamount to the work of the high priest on the Day of Atonement. The reason for the phrase "investigative judgment" is that after 1844, each person who has ever lived is brought to judgment. Jesus acts as advocate, and careful determination is made as to whether true believers have had all of their sins confessed and forgiven.

The key to understanding this doctrine is to note the distinction that Adventists make between sins being "forgiven" and being "blotted out." Confessed sins of believers are forgiven but not blotted out until an investigative judgment is made and the ruling is favorable. All investigative judgments must take place before the Second Coming. The conclusive part of the blotting out process is the placing of all of the sins on the scapegoat, who is set free. This scapegoat is Satan, as we saw above.

Concerning the investigative judgment, some important departures from traditional Christian orthodoxy are readily apparent. Since a person's sins are not blotted out at the time that they are forgiven, the blotting out of sins will not take place, for many, for a considerable amount of time after a person dies. Also, because the blotting out process involves the necessity of laying the sins on Satan as the scapegoat, the rather surprising conclusion here is that Satan is involved in the final work of atonement and that the final blotting out cannot take place without Satan. The Adventist response is to deny that Satan atones for sin, but he must bear the ultimate and final responsibility for it. Seventh-day Adventism teachings do in fact deny that Satan atones for sin in any way. But at the very least, the clear reference to the all-sufficiency of Christ is compromised whenever any other contribution to the atonement is introduced.

Anthony Hoekema has presented a clear and concise exposition of the problems with the doctrine of the investigative judgment. To briefly summarize, Hoekema points out that (1) "the doctrine of the investigative judgment is based upon a faulty interpretation Daniel 8:14"; (2) ". . . a mistaken understanding of the Old Testament sacrificial system"; (3) the role of Christ in the Old Testament sacrificial system; (4) the distinction between the forgiveness of sins and the blotting out of sins as being "foreign to Scripture," thus "robbing believers of all assurance of salvation"; (5) a violation of the "Sovereignty of God."[8]

To this, we add that the doctrine of investigative judgment also confuses the law and the gospel, the fundamental problem that Seventh-day Adventism falls into in its doctrine of the Sabbath as well. The gospel's power lies in its ability to "impute" (Rom. 3–4; Gal. 2–3) the righteousness of Christ to the believer. If this righteousness is not given to the Christian and they are not freely justified by grace through faith at the time that it takes place but only later, this renders most of the New Testament's descriptions of justification and imputation invalid.

A final note: If the investigative judgment is a doctrine that is clear in the Word of God, then why is it that none of the early church fathers encountered, believed, or embraced it? Why did it take 1,800 plus years for it to surface as a doctrine considered clear only to the Adventists and not to those faithful luminaries who have studied the Bible over the centuries?

The Holy Spirit

The Holy Spirit is the third person of the Holy Trinity as understood traditionally by historical Christianity.

The Sabbath

As explained above, the fourth commandment is of particular importance to Seventh-day Adventism, which is understood as an ultimatum that God has ordained the Jewish ▸Sabbath as the correct day of the week to be worshiping. Jesus, they argue, worshiped on the Sabbath, and it is a sin for his followers to do otherwise.

But this Sabbath-day teaching concerning worship is contrary to the teachings of traditional Christianity. The early church, even as early as the New Testament church, quickly switched from Saturday worship to Sunday in honor of the resurrection.

(1) Jesus rose on the first day of the week (John 20:19–20).

(2) The Holy Spirit came on the first day of the week (Acts 2:1–4).

(3) The first Christian sermon occurred on the first day of the week (Acts 2:14–36 by Peter), and conversions followed. Adventists must surely note that these are worship activities.

(4) The "Lord's Day" was early associated with Sunday by the early church fathers and in classical Christian literature.

(5) Liturgically, the early church saw Sunday as the day that could also be thought of as the eighth day or the beginning of the new week. This came to be strongly associated with a "new beginning." The resurrection of Christ on Sunday began a new creation. The old Sabbath week now gives way to the new week, new creation, new birth, and the newness of life in Christ.

(6) Scripture itself makes it clear (Heb. 4:4–8) that Christ himself is the Sabbath rest that the Christian is called to.

(7) Jesus said, in response to the legalism of the Pharisees, that "the Sabbath was made for man and not man for the Sabbath" (Matt. 12:1–8). Paul teaches clearly that the Christian is free to worship on any day of the week and that there are no days holier than others (Col. 2:16–17).

The Second Advent

Adventists today still affirm the true and literal return of Christ to earth and understand that this will take place soon. But the modern-day movement does not make attempts to set dates for this, as did Miller and others in the early history of the movement. The general eschatological position held to by Seventh-day Adventism is ▸dispensational and millennial.

Humanity

Seventh-day Adventism teaches that human beings are created by God and made in the image of God according to the Genesis account. But human beings are not completely immortal. That is to say, upon death, the person goes into a state of unconscious sleep. At the time of the resurrection, he or she will be raised. If a person is deemed to be lost, that person will ultimately be annihilated (see ▸annihilationism).

Faith

To be saved, a person must have a personal relationship with and knowledge of Christ. This comes through the life of faith, that is, completely trusting God's Word.

The Gospel

The gospel is the good news that Jesus Christ died for the sins of the world.

The Church

The church as understood by Adventists is that they are "the remnant" spoken of in Revelation 12:17. But does the Bible teach that the Seventh-day Adventist movement is the one true church on earth? The Adventist answer is not unlike the answer rendered by many other denominations, namely, that even though a clearer expression of the truth is taught in Adventist ranks, Christians do exist in every other denomination, including Roman Catholicism, where faith in Christ exists. Further, the movement is even willing to grant that the Saturday Sabbath is no longer constitutive of true worshipers, but it should be observed to be in true obedience to God. In order to join the church, prospective members are also told to abstain from alcoholic beverages, tobacco, and certain foods forbidden in the dietary laws of the Old Testament.

The Sacraments

There are two sacraments in the church—baptism and the Lord's Supper. Infant baptism is rejected on the grounds that one must come to repentance and faith in Christ as Savior. The Lord's Supper is a memorial feast.

CONCLUSION

Different theologians have found it difficult to assess Seventh-day Adventists today. We ourselves would by no means conclude that the movement is a 'cult in the way that we have defined it in this volume, especially given some of the changes that have taken place among the "evangelical Adventists." There is a tendency toward legalism that has informed the development of some of its key doctrines. Its growth has been significant and its contributions to education and hospital ministry have been significant in the Protestant world.

The late Walter Martin is credited with forging groundbreaking work among SDA scholars both in academic dialogue and in restating their theology in Protestant terms. The culmination of his work is found in a rather lengthy chapter of *Kingdom of the Cults* (2003), where SDA is found in an appendix.

ADDITIONAL INFORMATION

Headquarters
General Council of Seventh-day Adventists 12501 Old Columbia Pike, Silver Spring, MD 20904–6600.

Website
www.adventist.org

Sacred Texts
The Bible; to a lesser extent, the writings of Ellen G. White.

Publications
Collegiate Quarterly; Celebrations; Adventist Review; Christian Record; Cornerstone Connection; Guide; Insight; Journal of Adventist Education; Liberty; Listen; Message; Ministry; Our Life and Times; Our Little Friend; Primary Treasure; Signs of the Times; Vibrant Life; Youth Ministry Accent.

Membership Statistics
Total membership is 12,894,005 members throughout the world (2005 figure). Ordained ministers: 14,804; churches: 53,502 throughout the world; 5,605 schools, colleges, and universities; 166 hospitals and sanitariums; 56 publishing houses.

Notes
[1] Anthony A. Hoekema, *The Four Major Cults* (Grand Rapids: Eerdmans, 1963), 97.
[2] Ibid., 98.
[3] Sydney Ahlstrom, *A Religious History of the American People*, 2 vols. (Garden City, NY: Image Books, 1975), 1:582.
[4] See Larry Nichols and George Mather, *Discovering the Plain Truth* (Downers Grove, Ill.: InterVarsity Press, 1997).
[5] Harold Bloom, *The American Religion: The Emergence of the Post-Christian Nation* (New York: Simon & Schuster, 1992), 150.
[6] Hoekema, *The Four Major Cults*, 103.
[7] *What Seventh Day Adventists Believe* (Hagerstown, MD: Review and Herald, 1988), 227.
[8] Hoekema, *The Four Major Cults*, 144–60.

SHINTOISM

Shinto is a traditional religion of Japan that developed as a result of the influences of BUDDHISM and CONFUCIANISM. Shinto comes from the Chinese word "*shin tao*," which means "way of the gods." It is the ancient religion of Japan that is as much about Japanese culture as it is about religion. Having no real founder, Shinto claims no sacred texts in the sense of holding their writings to be inspired or revered. They are regarded more as useful. One in particular, called *Kojiki*, is widely read. It otherwise possesses no body of written laws or no liturgy. The priesthood is not well organized.

HISTORY

Shinto emerged in fifth century B.C. when several ♦sects developed in a reaction against Buddhism. One of these was called Ise Shinto. It was not until the nineteenth century under Emperor Meiji (1868–1912) that Shinto became adopted as the official religion of Japan. This was at the time when the emperor was considered divine. Meiji traced his line back in succession to the first mythical emperor Jimmu (660 B.C.). Before and beyond Jimmu, succession stretched to the sun goddess, Amaterasu Omikami. Shintoism was Japan's national religion before World War II, out of which the successive divine emperors led to the belief that one is granted life for giving his life to the emperor. This formed the basis for kamikaze suicide pilots during the War. After Japan surrendered to America in World War II, the American army forced the Japanese emperor to renounce his divinity. Since then, religion and politics have been separated.

BELIEFS AND PRACTICES

Shinto is an eclectic blend of nature worship, fertility cults, ♦divination, emperor worship, and ♦shamanism. Worship focuses on gratitude to the *kami*, who are people or natural entities that have for centuries evoked the wonder of the Japanese. *Kami* may be hills, mountains, or animals. Often the *kami* are deities and special human individuals, the latter commonly being emperors. This accounts for Japan's longstanding worship of its emperors.

Shinto worship also occurs in homes, where a small altar (called a *kami dana* or *kami* shelf) may contain a number of items that are worshiped and revered, such as the names of the departed ancestors or statues of deities. In Shinto, ancestors are greatly revered and worshiped.

One of the popular *kamis* has a divine couple, Izanagi-no-mikoto and Izanami-no-mikoto giving birth to the Japanese islands. One of their daughters, Amaterasu Omikami, became the sun goddess. She has a shrine in her honor at Ise, a tribute to the fact that she is believed to have brought unity to the country.

Since there are no prescribed liturgies or specific sacred writings that guide the practitioner of Shinto, the canons of Confucianism are followed.

There are four affirmations in Shinto. They are:

1. Tradition and family. The family preserves the ancient memory and identity of each member of the family.
2. Love for nature. Nature is a vehicle for bringing one closer to the gods. It is considered sacred.
3. Physical cleanliness. Practitioners of Shinto constantly bathe themselves and are greatly concerned about hygiene. The ideal place for bathing is at a river near the shrines, where the *kami* are worshiped.
4. *Matsuri*. This is the worship of the *kami*.

Shrines are built to specific *kami*. Upon entering a shrine, a *tori*, or gateway, is passed through. When passing through the *tori* one leaves the world behind and transcends to the infinite realm, where the deity dwells. Shrine ceremonies include cleansings, prayers, and offerings. Worshipful dances, called *kagura*, are performed by both men and virgin women.

Celebrations of the seasons are held in the fall and the spring. National Founding Day takes place on February 11; this day is believed to be the birthday of Japan. A number of other festivals and rites of passage are observed.

Origami ("paper of the spirits") is the art of folding paper into various shapes. The folded paper is placed in shrines. This paper is never cut because it is believed that the trees from which they came are sacred.

There are four major traditions in Shinto. These include:

1. *Koshitsu Shinto*. This pertains to the emperor himself and the rituals specifically performed by him.
2. *Jinja Shinto*. As the largest and oldest form of Shinto ritual, *Jinja* ritual focuses on prayers directed to the emperor, thanksgiving for the *kami*, and obedience to the emperor.
3. *Kyoha Shinto*. There are thirteen sects formed in the modern world (from the nineteenth century on), each following its own particular rituals.
4. *Minzoku Shinto*. These are privatized and local rituals.

CONCLUSION

Traditional CHRISTIANITY bears little resemblance theologically to Shinto. In reality, the worshiping of the *kami* is a form of ♦polytheism, whereas Christianity adheres to monotheism.

Some Protestant and Catholic Christians in Japan do use the word *kami* to denote God. They blend the word *kami* with the word *sama* to make *kamisama*, a title of respect for God. But as is the case with Buddhism and Confucianism, Shinto's predilection for understanding divinity as immanent separates it from a traditional understanding of Christianity that understands God in transcendent categories, made immanent through special ▸revelation and ▸incarnation.

Christianity believes in the worship of the triune God. The royal ancestral line in Christianity is carefully recorded in the genealogies of both the Old and New Testaments. But they point to the birth of the one who was the Son of God, come in the flesh. The worship of human emperors or ancestors is not a Christian practice. Jesus' followers must regard each other as equals (Matt. 23:8–10; Gal. 3:28).

Christianity is a missionary religion that points to the need for salvation from sin and that God has rescued the world from sin through Jesus Christ (John 3:16). Shinto is by no means a sectarian religion. It openly advocates the legitimacy of all other religions and their respective claims.

ADDITIONAL INFORMATION

Website
www.shinto.org

Sacred Texts
The Kojiki; The Rokkokushi; The Shoku Nihonji; The Jinno Shotoki. The latter three are not sacred in the sense of being inspired or revered.

Statistics
In Japan, 85 percent of its people are practitioners of Shinto and Buddhism. Worldwide population of Shinto worshipers are: Asia: 2,727,000; Latin America: 7,000; North America: 55,000; Africa: 1,200; Europe: 2,500; World: 2,790,000.

SIKH DHARMA; INTERNATIONAL KUNDALINI YOGA TEACHERS ASSOCIATION; IKYTA; HEALTHY, HAPPY, HOLY ORGANIZATION (₃HO)

Numerous small ▸sects and ▸cults sprang up in America in the latter half of the twentieth century. Many of these have emerged from HINDUISM. Sikh Dharma is one example of this phenomenon.

HISTORY

Sikh Dharma had its roots in the fifteenth and sixteenth centuries with the teachings of ▸Guru ▸Nanak (1469–1538). His reform movement within the broad structures of Hinduism became known as SIKHISM. Four centuries later, in 1971, ▸Sri Singh Sahib Harbhajan Khalsa ▸Yogi, popularly known as ▸Yogi Bhajan (b. 1930), was ordained as the chief spiritual leader for the sect of Sikh Dharma in all parts of the world outside of India.

Yogi ▸Bhajan came to the United States, by way of Canada, in 1968 and founded the Healthy, Happy, Holy Organization (₃HO), beginning his first ▸ashram in a Los Angeles garage. Previously an unknown Delhi airport customs official, Bhajan saw his popularity rise quickly in America because many young Americans in the 1960s and 1970s were turning to countercultural movements, the widespread appeal of Eastern religion, and the incipient NEW AGE MOVEMENT. Bhajan claims to use a counseling technique he calls the "science of humanology."

In 1977 *Time* magazine reported that Bhajan's teachings had spread to 110 ashrams in the United States, Canada, and abroad.[1] From Los Angeles, Bhajan emigrated to a forty-acre ranch in New Mexico. Bhajan claimed to have amassed 250,000 followers by 1978, but more realistic estimates would cite no more than several thousand at that time.[2]

₃HO is the educational wing of Sikh Dharma. Bhajan has incurred the criticism of Sikh leaders, particularly for his acquisition of great wealth while teaching, lecturing, and founding ashrams throughout the United States. He began the expansion of ₃HO through teaching ▸yoga classes. Bhajan's followers supported themselves through small businesses. "We earn our living by the sweat of the brow," related one of Bhajan's faithful followers in 1980.[3] But there was dissent, and many left the ashrams.

Philip Hoskins, a Los Angeles attorney and former ₃HO member, assesses the matter from a critical point of view in an article appearing in the *Houston Chronicle* in 1980. Reflecting Hoskins' sentiments, the *Chronicle* writes:

Some say he's [Bhajan] the right hand of God. . . . Others believe he is the right hand of the ▸devil. . . . It started out as sort of a club. . . . There was no

Guru Yogi Bhajan, who founded the 3HO
in the United States.
Courtesy Spiritual Counterfeit Project

organization at all. You did your own thing, there
was no money to pay, that was the whole appeal.
But as the members became more dedicated, Yogi
Bhajan became more domineering. He'd tell you
when to eat, what to eat, when to blink. There is no
question that he is the dominant person of the group
who has directed, controlled, or influenced the
minds of group members.[4]

The *Houston Chronicle* continues:

Equally harsh criticism comes from the families of
members. A California member said her "brainwashed" daughter turned over a $1.3 million inher-
itance to the yogi's group after a group-arranged
marriage to another member. A mid-western couple
said two of their children joined the group and
became human robots programmed by Yogi Bhajan. And Texas United for Freedom, a group dedicated to disseminating information about cults, has
placed 3HO on its "destructive cult" list.[5]

ORGANIZATION

In 1994, Bhajan founded the International Kundalini
Yoga Teachers Association (IKYTA). It is organized
around teachers and membership at the various
ashrams. Bhajan travels frequently between them and
offers talks and seminars. Membership information is
available on the websites (below).

The Khalsa Council heads up the 3HO organization.
It is governed by administrative and regional ministers,
the latter being responsible to carry out local training
and ministry.

TEACHINGS

Bhajan denies all allegations of being the leader of a
cult. He claims there is "freedom," "divinity," "dignity,"
and "grace" in his organization. "And the difference
between other religions and this religion is in other religions people can promise you that. We can deliver."[6]

The fundamental aim of 3HO is to teach and instruct its
adherents in methods for awakening the ▸*kundalini*. Students stare into the eyes of fellow practitioners, or, in many
cases, at a picture of Yogi Bhajan, and utter a ▸mantra
spelled out as follows: *Ik Ony Kar Sat Nam Siri Wha
Guru*. This is the name of God in the sacred language.

Bhajan teaches a strenuous form of yoga called
▸taantrism, of which he claims to be the only living
master. "Ashram members rise at 3:30 a.m. to practice
yoga and meditate."[7] Converts dress in white, wear turbans ("The man who ties a turban on his head must
live up to the purity of the whiteness and radiance of his
soul"[8]), and follow the ▸Five K's.[9] Bhajan counsels
members to live a strict disciplinary life with respect to
diet (strict vegetarian) and work ethic. Alcohol, drugs,
or any other intoxicants are strictly forbidden.

Baptized members of the group are called ▸*amritdhari* Sikhs. Others are referred to as ▸*sahajdhari*.
Women are called ▸*shakti*, and the group maintains a
policy of egalitarianism, affording the women a chance
to enter leadership roles at every level.

CHRISTIANITY differs with 3HO on the same score as
it does with all of the personality cults. For the Christian faith, the second article of the Apostles' Creed
places Jesus Christ at the center of the church's faith
and practice. For 3HO, the focus becomes Yogi Bhajan.

The potential for salvation lies essentially within
the 3HO devotee. One learns to "awaken" the *kundalini*
in order to achieve ▸enlightenment. For Christianity,
salvation is accomplished when the believer realizes
that he or she has, in fact, no abilities to become
enlightened from within. Rather, salvation comes to
the Christian when he or she repents of sin and places
faith in the redemptive work of Christ. This is a divine
activity through which the Holy Spirit moves the person to accept that work. 3HO emphasizes that the sub-

jective latent energies within human beings are important for salvation.

Despite this, ₃HO members are taught that Christianity and all religions are compatible. A Sikh dictum is "My God plus your God is our God." This concept arises out of Hinduism.

A traditional holiday in Sikh Dharma is Baisakhi Day (April 13), commemorating the birthday of the Khalsa. The Martyrdom Days of Guru Tegh Behadur and Guru Arjun Mal are also observed along with the birthdays of all of the ten gurus.

CONCLUSION

The impact of Sikh Dharma and Yogi Bhajan was felt chiefly in the 1970s. Bhajan's success as a leader was shaped by the era in which he lived. For many Americans, that time has come and gone. But the motifs inherent in ₃HO are paralleled within the New Age Movement, which is enjoying growing popularity in the West.

ADDITIONAL INFORMATION_____

Headquarters
Sikh Dharma, 1620 Pruess Road, Los Angeles, CA 90035.

Website
www.kundaliniyoga.com, www.yogibhajan.com

Sacred Text
Sikh Holy Book

Publications
Aquarian Times; Journal of Sikh Thought; Beads of Truth

Membership
250,000 Sikhs in North America; 10,000 ₃HO members; 140 ashrams, and 27 countries.

Notes
[1] "Yogi Bhajan's Synthetic Sikhism," *Time* (Sept. 5, 1977), 70.
[2] Ibid.
[3] Jon Verboon, "Bhajan, 'Great Respected Sir': Is He Cult Leader or Guru?" *Houston Chronicle* (Sept. 24, 1980), sec. 3.
[4] Ibid.
[5] Ibid.
[6] Ibid.
[7] "Yogi Bhajan's Synthetic Sikhism."
[8] Ibid.
[9] Ibid.

SIKHISM

Sikhism was an outgrowth of both HINDUISM and ISLAM, which found themselves in sharp conflict in India from the eleventh through the fifteenth centuries. Hindu *bhakti* and Islamic SUFISM found compatibility in certain elements from each tradition. The word "Sikh" is derived from the Sanskrit word for "learner" or "disciple."

HISTORY

The formal beginnings of Sikhism are marked by the era of the ten gurus, beginning with Guru Nanak (1469–1538). Nanak was born in the village of Rai Bhoi di Talvandi in the Punjab region of present-day Pakistan. His education included instruction in both Hinduism and Islam. In his formative years, Nanak met and befriended a Muslim named Mardana, with whom he composed hymns. Both Hindus and Muslims met together to sing these hymns at a place called Sultanpur. It was here that Nanak had a vision in which he perceived his calling to preach and teach the way to enlightenment and God. According to the story, Nanak disappeared while bathing in a stream and emerged

from seclusion three days later to proclaim "there is no Hindu, there is no Muslim." This dictum became one of the pillars of Sikhism.

Nanak taught for the rest of his life and founded the first Sikh temple in Katarpur. Before his death in 1538, he appointed his successor, Angad, who became the second of the ten gurus. The ten are listed as follows, along with their respective tenures:

1. Nanak (1469–1538)
2. Angad (1538–1552)
3. Amar Das (1552–1574)
4. Ram Das Sodhi (1574–1581)
5. Arjun Mal (1581–1606) (executed)
6. Hargobind (1606–1644)
7. Har Raj (1644–1661)
8. Hari Krishen (1661–1664)
9. Tegh Bahadur (1664–1675) (executed)
10. Gobind Rai (1675–1708)

Although Sikhism was originally pacifist in philosophy and theology, the execution of two of the gurus precipitated more militant Sikhs in generations to follow. The tenth guru, Gobind Rai, founded the *Khalsa* Order, the chief order of Sikhism. Because Rai had lost all of his sons during the course of his life, he had no compulsion to appoint a successor. Consequently, he declared that the reign of the gurus had come to an end.

Gobind Rai did, however, have successors, but many of them met with bitter persecution in the Punjab region, governed by Muslims. Toleration gradually developed as both Afghans and Persians invaded and eventually came to power. In the early nineteenth century, a Sikh state was formed under Ranjat Singh (1780–1839); it lasted until the British moved forces into the land. This led to the Sikh Wars (1845–1846 and 1848–1849), which culminated in the defeat of the Sikhs and takeover by Great Britain.

Several factions developed in Sikhism in the nineteenth century. Relations with the British were considerably better than under Muslim domination, but the British slaughter of civilians in Amritsar in 1919 resulted in ensuing Sikh bitterness toward their "imperialist overlords." Many Sikhs joined *Mahatma *Gandhi's movement against British domination.

Great changes came demographically and culturally in 1947 when India received independence. The land was partitioned into what is now Pakistan to the north and west and India to the east and south. Because of rioting between Sikh and Muslim factions, 2.5 million Sikhs were forced to leave Pakistan and move to India. This resulted in further violence, as Muslims in turn moved into Pakistan. As the Sikh population grew, they sought an independent Sikh nation called Khalistan; this movement resulted in continued outbreaks of violence with the government that culminated in the June 1984 attack of the Indian army on *Harimandir, the holiest of all Sikh shrines. The following October Prime Minister Indira Gandhi was assassinated by two of her Sikh bodyguards. This exacerbated tensions between Sikhs and Hindus, precipitating more violence. These tensions were eased in 1989 when Prime Minister Rajiv Gandhi announced that all of the Sikh militants imprisoned after the 1984 attack would be released.

In 1994, new wave of violence erupted, resulting in mob violence and killings by fundamentalist Hindu nationalists. As many as 5,000 Muslims were killed. To this day, Sikhs are calling for an independent nation called Khalistan, decrying the injustice of having been denied such. This quest has indeed been at the root of the problems that is so frequently reported in world news, especially in the area known as Kashmir.

ORGANIZATION

There are a number of service organizations in Sikhism, such as the Nishkam Sikh Welfare Council, a Sikh Missionary Council, a central Gurdwara Resource Center, Dal Khalsa International, the Institute of Sikh Studies, a Sikh Youth Federation, a Khalistan Affairs Center, and other organizations loosely linked to Sikhism.

TEACHINGS

The mission of Nanak had been to draw together the common elements of both Hinduism and Islam. Sikhs were considered later, therefore, to be dissenters from *Brahmanism*. Nanak rejected the ceremonial and ritualistic tenets of Hinduism in the interest of compatibility.

Guru Arjun, the fifth of the ten gurus, gathered together the many writings and hymns that up to that point had remained separated and independent from each other. This collecting process continued until it was completed by the tenth guru, Gobind Rai. The volume that resulted, containing the doctrines of Sikhism, is called *Siri Guru Granth Sahib* (also called the *Adi Granth*), an anthology of the writings of the ten gurus, considered to be the Sikh bible.

God, as confessed in Islam, is one. He has created all things. The experience of coming to know God can be had through the practice of *meditation. Sikhs embrace the Hindu concept of *samsara, *karma, and *reincarnation. By being born human, one possesses the ultimate opportunity to escape *samsara*.[1]

Stricter Sikhs, called Khalsa saints, adhere to what is known as the *Five K's, which are as follows: (1) *kesa*—"long hair," which the Khalsa retains uncut; (2) *kangha*—"comb"; (3) *kacha*—"short pants"; (4) *kachu*—"metal bracelet"; and (5) *kirpan*—"weapon" or "sword."

The Sikh temples, numbering more than two hundred in India, are called *gurdwaras*. The chief temple is the above-mentioned Harimandir at Amritsar. The second holiest shrine is Nankana, the birthplace of Nanak. Although Sikhs, like Muslims, are strictly forbidden to worship icons and idols, the *Adi Granth* does indeed become an object of devotion. As is the case in Islam, sacred times, usually in the morning, are reserved for prayer.

CONCLUSION

Sikhs and Hindus have become increasingly separated from one another, both politically and theologically, despite Nanak's conviction that "there is no Hindu, there is no Muslim." In Sikhism, all are entitled to read the sacred writings; they are not for the privileged classes only. Hinduism, on the other hand, allows only the spiritually elite under the caste system to have access to the scriptures.

This idea parallels in a remarkable way the doctrine of the priesthood of all believers, championed by the Protestant Reformers within CHRISTIANITY (William Tyndale, Martin Luther, John Calvin, etc.). This doctrine implies that all Christians may read the ▸Bible, which up until the sixteenth century had been reserved for the educated and elite priestly caste within the Roman Catholic Church. This concept resulted in a cultural explosion in Europe that went hand in hand with the Renaissance, bringing an end to the feudal state and eventually giving rise to a more privileged and educated "middle class." Sikhs rejected the narrow social structures of the Hindu caste system, but ethnic divisions still persist, chiefly among the less educated in rural villages.

Sikhism has had considerable influence in the West, chiefly through the teachings of Yogi ▸Bhajan and his particular form of Sikhism known as SIKH DHARMA. With the terrorist attacks on September 11, 2001, many Sikhs in the United States have been subject to harsh treatment. Cases have appeared throughout the United States where Sikhs were attacked or their property was vandalized.[2]

ADDITIONAL INFORMATION_____

Headquarters
Guru Ram Das Ashram, 1620 Preus Road, Los Angeles, CA 90035.

Website
www.sikhs.org; www.internationalgatka.org

Sacred Text
Sri Guru Granth Sahib; Adi Granth

Periodicals
See SIKH DHARMA

Membership
There are estimated to be 20 million Sikhs worldwide.

Notes
[1] Comparisons and contrasts between Sikhism and Christianity are parallel to observations made in the articles on ISLAM and HINDUISM. See also SIKH DHARMA.
[2] See, e.g., the *Denver Post,* in an article by Jeff Hughes, titled "Sikhs Face Misplaced Anger" (Nov. 18, 2001).

SILVA MIND CONTROL (SMC); PSYCHORIENTOLOGY

Silva Mind Control (SMC) is one of the many different movements begun in the last half of the twentieth century that focus on therapeutic self-help techniques in a context divorced from traditional religious moorings. Insights from psychotherapy combined with NEW AGE MOVEMENT categories constitute the large volume of what comprises SMC and other groups like it, such as LIFESPRING and the FORUM.

HISTORY

Silva Mind Control began with the research of Jose ▸Silva (1914–1999), a hypnotist from Laredo, Texas. Silva began investigating "alphagenics" (the science of brain-wave analysis) in 1944 in Laredo. Originally, he intended to use his techniques to enable participants to increase their intelligence quotients (IQ). The idea is essentially that the mind is able to generate far more energy at lower states of brain-wave frequency than at average frequency levels.

Silva worked with the concept for several decades. In 1967 he began to travel from city to city in Texas to field-test his techniques. He intended to determine whether the public would be willing to try his methods. He ambitiously taught and lectured wherever he went. Silva died on February 7, 1999.

ORGANIZATION

SMC did gain a following, which began to grow beyond the borders of Texas. Presently, SMC seminars are being offered in every state in the United States and in Mexico, Canada, Spain, South America, Central America, and countries throughout Europe. What was originally a method taught by a single individual rapidly became an organization complete with regional directors throughout the country. Certified instructors teach the courses. Those enrolled may become members and are issued a Silva ID card. The website contains a directory for the locations of the instructors worldwide.

TEACHINGS

The basic goal of SMC is to help enable participants to better use their minds in order to become more successful. Silva taught that there are four levels of consciousness: the *beta*, *alpha*, *delta*, and *theta* levels. The beta level is the normal level of wake consciousness. The alpha, along with delta and theta levels, are the subconscious levels that Silva purports to be able to unlock with his training techniques. At the alpha level, the mind is able to relax and can begin to meditate. Silva claimed that to

> start learning to use the Alpha dimension with controlled awareness is like being born again. Humanity using two dimensions and two sets of senses can project the mind to function from a superior perspective; from that superior perspective we can use a larger store of knowledge, develop greater wisdom, and conceive a more realistic and truer sense of values.[1]

Silva's techniques are alleged to enable one to awaken the genius within. Instructors teach participants to detect and diagnose diseases and literally "think" the disease away. By thinking they are cured, they are in fact cured. Only positive thoughts are allowed, which lead to positive perceptions.

SMC uses ›hypnosis to bring the trainee into an imaginary world where the trainee meets his or her ›counselors. Counselors are always two beings, known or unknown, from the trainee's past. A counselor may be a famous celebrity whom the subject respects or admires. The character of the counselors varies from virtuousness to capriciousness, prankishness, or unpredictability. They guide the participant into making right choices in particular situations and problems. They are the guardian angels or ›mediums that the student is taught to conjure up within the mind.

Basic also to SMC is the use of "memory pegs." These are words that, when used, focus the mind onto a mental screen. This is the area the mind perceives when the eyes are closed.

The initial program of SMC consists of four classes lasting twelve hours each. Mind controllers teach clients to induce a state of mental relaxation (alpha stage). The program then teaches meditation techniques, self-hypnosis, and guided expansion of consciousness. Clients discover that through positive thinking they can begin to affect their own immediate environment. By thinking positively, negative habits such as smoking and other forms of substance abuse may be eliminated. They learn how to "visualize"

solutions to problems. This is called "mental imaging techniques."

More recently, SMC offers two-day seminars. These forty-eight hours are filled with lectures and meditations based on Silva's teachings. These Silva Basic Lecture Techniques, as he called them, are geared toward business people, artists, professionals, and the public. Silva finally introduced the Silva "UltraMind ESP System," designed to provide the most intense training available utilizing Silva's methods.

All religions are of the same spiritual substance for Silva. As participants desire to help humanity, they help themselves. Their talents increase, and they become more accurate in predictions and healings.[2]

SMC is not an organized religion, but rather a form of psychological self-help therapy. However, elements of Eastern religion, the ›occult, and ›spiritism are eclectically utilized in the training seminars. Belief in the spirit realm is a basic presupposition. God is essentially an "energy" within you; God is not a being wholly outside of the world, as theism and CHRISTIANITY traditionally have taught. Following cues from HINDUISM, SMC believes in a ›pantheistic conception of God. Transcending one's limited surface ego (beta level), one is able to control the nature of reality itself. New Age motifs are readily apparent as well.[3]

›Soteriology for SMC is basically coming to the higher levels of consciousness as described above. One achieves salvation by escaping "problems" that prevent one from realizing one's full potential. There is no concept of sin and subsequent atonement.

CONCLUSION

As many as two million people have paid the fee of $200 in order to enroll in the entry-level course. Like Arica, the Forum, and other self-help therapies, SMC has had a wide appeal in a culture that is preoccupied with what Peter Marin has called "The New Narcissism," and the "deification of the isolated self."[4] The group continues to offer courses and maintains an active website (below), along with a radio broadcast known as "Wisdom."

ADDITIONAL INFORMATION_____

Headquarters
Silva International, Inc., Laredo, TX, 78040.

Website
www.silvamethod.com

Sacred Text
The Silva Mind Control Method

Periodical
WISDOMNews

Statistics

Silva's materials are distributed in 107 countries and 29 languages. Millions of people internationally have studied Silva's techniques.

Notes

[1] Jose Silva, *Silva Mind Control—Alpha Theta Brain Waves* (Laredo: Jose Silva, 1973), 3.

[2] Jose Silva, *MC404-ESP(2)* (Laredo: Jose Silva, 1969), 2.

[3] See also THE FORUM, LIFESPRING, ARICA, and the NEW AGE MOVEMENT. The New Age quest for planetary unity in the "age of Aquarius" is compatible to the goals of SMC.

[4] Peter Marin, "The New Narcissism," *Harper's* (October 1975), 45.

SOKA-GAKKAI

Soka-Gakkai is one of the more significant religious movements that originated in Japan. The reader should also refer to NICHIREN SHOSHU and BUDDHISM when reading Soka-Gakkai.

HISTORY

Also called the Value Creation Society from its translation, Soka-Gakkai is the lay organization of NICHIREN SHOSHU BUDDHISM. The movement was founded by Tsonesaburo *Makiguchi in 1930, though it was originally called Soka Kyocku Gakkai. Because the movement derives its basic philosophy from the thirteenth-century teacher Nichiren, its twentieth-century beginning should not be misleading.

During World War II the Japanese government banned Soka-Gakkai, and Makiguchi was arrested and died in prison. Josei *Toda, one of Makiguchi's closest disciples, rejuvenated the movement in 1946, at which time the organization adopted the name Soka-Gakkai. Subsequent leaders were Daisaku *Ikeda, who governed from 1960–1979; Hojo *Hiroshi (1979–1981); and Einasuke *Akiya, who began leading the organization in 1981. Ikeda would continue to hold the honorary title *sakoto* (head of all Nichiren lay believers).

ORGANIZATION

The basic organizational unit of Soka-Gakkai in the United States is called a district. Districts meet regularly, usually in gatherings of fifteen to thirty people. Groups are part of the district, and larger groups, called chapters, areas, regions, and zones, comprise the regional and national organizational structure; they are responsible for planning and conducting larger scale activities.[1]

TEACHINGS

Since 1965 the organization has operated its own political party called *Komei. It is indeed a force to be reckoned with. Through a high-pressured and coercive conversion method known as *shakabuku*, the organization has gone from three thousand families in the 1950s to well over sixteen million by the 1980s. The organization believes that being active in politics is a way of bringing about a happier world.[2]

Makiguchi stressed three important principles: *bi* (beauty), *ri* (gain), and *zen* (goodness). Like Nichiren, Soka-Gakkai teaches the importance of the chant *nam-Myoho-renge-kyo*, translated "glory to the *Lotus Sutra*."

CONCLUSION

Soka-Gakkai continues to be an expanding *sect of Buddhism. Much literature disseminates from its presses. The base of the movement is in Japan, but its influence is worldwide. While there are over seventeen million devotees of Nichiren Shoshu in Japan, there are estimated to be twenty million devotees of Soka-Gakkai worldwide and at least half a million in the United States. Many American advocates are not of Japanese lineage.

In December 1990, tension between Soka-Gakkai and the Nichiren Shoshu organization became apparent when Daisaku Ikeda was stripped of his title as *sokoto*.[3] More recently, on November 8, 1991, the Nichiren high priest ordered the Soka-Gakkai movement to disband. Three days later, Einasoke Akiya made it known that Soka-Gakkai would refuse to comply. The movement suffered from severe financial pressures. In May 1991, they were forced to pay $4.5 million in back taxes. The motto "clean government" was further soiled when a stock market scandal brought $3.3 million into its treasuries while other investors in Japan who had lost millions did not receive any monies at all. Media wars and lawsuits that contain accusations of violence have soiled the reputations of the two groups in recent years, especially in America.

For an update on the recent developments of the last ten years in Soka-Gakkai, please refer to the article on Nichiren Shoshu.

ADDITIONAL INFORMATION

Headquarters
International: Soka-Gakkai International Office, 32 Shinanomachi, Shinjuku-ku, Tokyo 160, Japan. U.S. headquarters: Soka Gakkai International (SGI-USA), 606 Wilshire Blvd., Santa Monica, CA, 90401.

Websites
International–*www.sokagakkai.or.jp*; USA–*www.sgi-usa.org*

Sacred Text
The Lotus Sutra

Periodicals
Living Buddhism (formerly *Seikyo Times*); *World Tribune*

Membership
Estimated at twenty million (at the time of its excommunication from Nichiren Shoshu–1992).

Notes
[1] *www.sgi-usa.org/thesgiusa/aboutsgi/organization.html.*
[2] See NICHIREN SHOSHU BUDDHISM for a more complete evaluation of the doctrinal elements of Soka-Gakkai. Further insights can be had from the article on BUDDHISM.
[3] William M. Alner, "Infighting, Division, and Scandal Afflicting Nichiren Shoshu Buddhists," *Christian Research Journal* (Winter 1992), 5.
[4] Ibid., 6.

SOUTH AMERICAN, CENTRAL AMERICAN, AND CARIBBEAN CULTS

Appearing in alphabetical order throughout this encyclopedia are some of the more prominent *cults in Latin America, particularly in Brazil, Central America, and the Caribbean, including Cuba, Jamaica, and Haiti. Numerous factors differentiate these groups from one another, but there are also basic components that make them similar.

Common to all of the significant cultic traditions in this region of the world is the influence of West African religion. During the days of the slave trade, thousands of natives from the *Yoruba and *Bantu tribes were transported to the West Indies and to Brazil to work the plantations and the farms. They brought their cultures and religions with them. As they mingled with the natives in the New World, they syncretized their religious practices with those indigenous to the various areas in which they settled. This resulted in a curious and fascinating religious eclecticism that was further influenced by CHRISTIANITY, particularly Roman Catholicism as it was imported by Spanish and Portuguese missionaries. Although there was much diversity among the many cults that sprang up, the West African influence provided for a basic homogeneity, evidenced by a number of factors.

First, most of the cults of this region teach that there is a superior or supreme being. This does not necessarily mean that these cults are monotheistic. A problem that arose and continues to arise from the perspective of Christian missionaries is the syncretism of religious *monotheism with the thousands of lesser deities that the cults embrace. These deities come in the form of ancestral spirits and gods who control the cosmos. The cults also follow the principles of *animism.

Second, the multitudes of deities are shared by the various cults. The Yorubic deities *Eshu, *Ifa, *Elegba, and *Shango are but a few examples.

Third, though names may vary, many practices and rituals are common to all of the cults. For instance, the priests in the Yorubic cults of Brazil are called *babalao. In Haiti they are called *paploi. Yet their duties are similar. They tend to the preparations for sacrifices and serve as intermediaries in the summoning of the spirits. The initiation practices are also similar.

Finally, another phenomenon common to the South American cults is the belief that devotees can be possessed by the *orisha. Some groups believe that a subject can be possessed by only one spirit. Others claim that any number of spirits can inhabit the body of a willing recipient.

Given each of these factors, it is not altogether surprising that Christianity, despite its two-thousand-year-old claim to be the only true religion, has not had the exclusive impact that missionaries have hoped. There have been some reports of complete conversions to Christianity, but generally this is not the case. One of the problems has been with the missionaries themselves. Rather than importing a transcultural gospel, all too often the mission workers have been unwittingly more interested in spreading Western culture, lifestyles, and language.

Although many of the Caribbean, Central American, and South American countries are nominally Roman Catholic, the reality is, as pointed out, that there are hundreds of provincial and obscure ▸sects and cults existing in this area of the world. While Roman Catholic missionaries have attempted to introduce Catholicism to the various South American and Caribbean religions, for the most part, the native religions have simply incorporated and blended Catholicism into the pantheon of deities endemic to the respective religions of this area of the world.

That has, more recently, not been the case for Pentecostal churches. While other Protestant churches have sent missionaries to these regions with some pos-

itive results, Pentecostal groups have remarkably succeeded in seeing conversions to Christianity exclusively. The focus of Pentecostals on the power of the Holy Spirit, miracles, and the casting out of demons has seemingly provided a more effective Christian response to the same phenomena defined by the native religions of these South American and Caribbean regions.

Our purpose here has been primarily to make some general observations of principles common to these groups. Some of the more significant and influential groups treated in this volume are ABAKUA, CABILDO, CANDOMBLE, CONVINCE, MACUMBA, MYAL, SANTERIA, and VOODOO.

SPIRITUALISM; UNIVERSAL CHURCH OF THE MASTER (UCM)

Spiritualism[1] began as a movement in the nineteenth century. The age of romanticism, characterized by pathos, feeling, and existential longing, provided the cultural milieu for many ▸cults and ▸sects and a revival of interest in the ▸occult.

HISTORY

The Universal Church of the Master was founded in 1908 in Los Angeles. The spiritualism from which it derived its essence is centuries old. New interest in spiritualism began in 1843 when a cobbler from New York named Andrew Jackson ▸Davis claimed that he possessed the ability to communicate as a ▸medium with the spirit world. Davis claimed that he was able to successfully channel the spirit of Emmanuel ▸Swedenborg in 1844. Through Davis, Swedenborg could live on and continue his teachings. Davis went on to author many books on his studies and experiences, such as *Principles of Nature* (1847).

Five years later, in 1848, Kate ▸Fox and her sisters, Margaret and Leah, claimed to have heard spiritual rapping noises in their home in Hydesville, New York. The house they were living in had a reputation of being haunted. The noises varied from raps to the sound of moving furniture. The Fox sisters soon discovered that they could communicate with the unseen presence. They claimed that the spirit identified himself as being Mr. Splitfoot and that he had been murdered in their home. Later a skeleton was dug up in the basement.

An interesting development took place in 1855 when

both Kate and Margaret Fox publicly admitted that they themselves had caused the rapping noises by the "cracking" of their toes. Later they retracted this confession, claiming to have been bribed into making it.

The tale of the Fox sisters spurred immediate interest, and the rapid spread of spiritualism was underway. In 1852, four years after the reported rappings, a convention was held in Cleveland for all who considered themselves to be spiritualists. With the help of Horace Greeley, the editor of the *New York Tribune*, the movement received additional impetus and began to flourish. Imported from the United States, spiritualism soon gained many avid practitioners throughout Europe. The writings of Allan Kardec in France, along with many others, reflect the interest and fascination that spiritualism held during the romantic era.

The most popular of all the mediums were Daniel Douglas Home and Eusapia Palladino. Home is alleged to have experienced ▸levitation near ceilings, floated out windows, and stretched his body twelve inches longer than usual. Eusapia Palladino was a young girl of peasant extraction who is reported to have been able to make objects move with a mere glance or blink of the eye. By the end of the century, many spiritualist movements and organized churches began to blossom. The oldest of these was the Universal Church of the Master (UCM), formed in 1908 and incorporated in 1918. The UCM soon spread its influence from California to across the continental United States. Today, the movement continues to thrive.

In 1893, the National Spiritualist Association of Churches was formed. As an organization, it provides a liaison to many of the different spiritualist churches around the world.

Douglas Hill and Pat Williams, in their informative work *The Supernatural*, claim that there are certainly more skeptics than advocates of spiritualism. Quoting D. J. West, Hill and Williams encapsulate this prevailing cynicism:

> Spiritualism thrives on simple souls. The average small Spiritualist service has all the crudity of meetings of any °fundamentalist sect. Middle-aged women make up the bulk of the audience. After the set number of hymns, they settle down to the address of °clairvoyance given by the visiting medium, who pours out a stream of verbiage about vibrations and harmony, astral bodies, attuning with the Godhead, or whatever else may be the patter of the moment. She begs her hearers to make themselves receptive to the loved ones on the other side, who are waiting to communicate.... Nothing could be more pathetic or boring.[2]

Social reformer Robert Dale Owen (1801–1877) became an ardent spiritualist. His book *Footfalls on the Boundary of Another World* won him fame and popularity as a spokesman for the movement. Owen was invited to the White House to read an essay on his spiritualist convictions. On hearing the paper, President Lincoln made the famous, yet skeptical, remark: "Well, for those who like that sort of thing, I should think it is just about the sort of thing they would like."[3]

One of the most outspoken critics of spiritualism was the famous magician Harry Houdini. Hill and Williams report:

> Houdini had a curiously ambivalent attitude to spiritualism: always anxious to establish that spirit communication was in fact possible, each successful exposure seemed to sadden him. His close friendship with Sir Arthur Conan Doyle was broken when Lady Conan Doyle (an automatic writer) produced a message from Houdini's dead mother. Though at first much moved by the message, Houdini later rejected it as being false on the grounds that it was the sort of message that any mother might have sent and that it showed a greater command of English than his mother possessed.
>
> Houdini also figured in an investigation conducted by the magazine *Scientific American*, which in 1923, offered $5000 to any medium who could satisfy a committee of scientists that he was genuine. Houdini was a member of the committee that tested several mediums. One, claiming to produce "independent voice" phenomena, was shown by a galvanometer (an instrument that detects any unseen movements) to have been walking around the room producing the manifestations himself. Another slipped his bonds and produced phenomena with his free hand—except when Houdini took 45 minutes to tie him up. Then nothing happened.[4]

In short, many who have claimed to be legitimate mediums have been found to be frauds. But apparently not all! Some spiritualist manifestations have remained a puzzle and still continue to divide the scientific community.

Many instances could be reported of mediums and spiritualist phenomena that have indeed been thought to be authentic. One such medium was Mrs. Leonora E. Piper. The wife of a Boston merchant, Piper began her career as a medium in 1885, and for forty years the scientific community never succeeded in refuting her claims or her feats.

According to one source,

> Mrs. Piper gave some 88 sittings, for example, carefully observed at all times by members of the British Society for Psychical Research. Professor Oliver Lodge, later Sir Oliver Lodge, one of England's most brilliant scientists and a careful psychic investigator, compiled a checklist of some 41 specific incidents wherein Mrs. Piper stated facts and general information concerning those who attended her seances, facts that were unknown to those persons at the very time the séances were in session! This is carefully verified and is beyond refutation.... Mrs. Piper convinced Sir Oliver Lodge, Sir William Crooks, Dr. William James, Dr. Hodgson and Dr. Hyslop ... that she was indeed possessed of supernatural capacities.[5]

A continuing voice of opposition to spiritualism has been the Christian church. Based on many passages in the °Bible (e.g., Ex. 22:18; Lev. 19:31; 1 Sam. 28:7–19; Acts 13:1–11), the church is warned by God not to dabble in the hidden things. The church, far from denying the reality of phenomena of the spirit world, has concluded that although fraud is more common than the authentic manifestations of spiritualists, the authentic phenomena are attributed to the demonic world and the °devil himself (John 8:44; 2 Cor. 4:4). Spiritualism, as an occult phenomenon, is as old as any of the ancient religions, yet it continues to spark interest for those who find a fascination in the secret arts.

The recent new wave of spiritualism has been manifested in the NEW AGE MOVEMENT, starting in the early 1970s. According to a mid-1980s opinion poll conducted by "Andrew Greeley and the University of Chicago's National Opinion Research Council, 42 percent of American adults believe that they have had some type of direct contact with a person who has died."[6] The New Age nomenclature for contact with the unseen spirit world is call ʼchanneling.[7]

Spiritualism encompasses a wide range of ideas within the sphere of metaphysical thought. It possesses its own unique vocabulary. Such terms as clairvoyance, medium, clairaudience, ʼtelepathy, ʼcontrol, ʼseance, and a host of others have emerged from spiritualism. On a popular level, spiritualism has been touted by the ʼOuija board manufactured and sold by Parker Brothers.[8]

Spiritualism in general is more popular in such countries as Brazil, France, and England than it is in the United States. The National Spiritualist Association, founded in 1893, is headquartered in Washington, D.C.

Spiritualism is so wide-ranging and all encompassing that many religious movements have been influenced by its teachings. In turn, spiritualism itself has its roots in ʼmysticism and the religions of the Far East, particularly HINDUISM. Though much of what constitutes spiritualism has been discovered to be fraudulent, there are several cases, like that of Mrs. Piper, that have remained, and will perhaps continue to remain, unexplained.

This essay now turns its attention to the teachings of spiritualism in general and the UCM in particular.

ORGANIZATION

The UCM is governed by a board of trustees that exercises full and total administrative control. Yearly elections are held. The board, in turn, elects the president, who appoints the various members of the organization's council.

Ministers are licensed by the organization and are divided into three groups. (1) Licentiates are ministers in training. (2) Healing ministers are practitioners and also are enabled to administer healings. (3) Ordained ministers are full-fledged mediums. To be ordained, one must be a licentiate or a healing minister for one year.[9] Ministers are trained at the Morris Pratt Institute in Whitewater, Wisconsin.

Most of the meetings, and interest from outsiders who attend such gatherings, are centered on contacting the spirits of departed loved ones. The medium becomes the central focus of gatherings, and members of any religious organization are welcome to participate.

TEACHINGS

The basic teachings of spiritualism, outlined in *The Seven Principles of Spiritualism* published by the National Spiritualist Association, are as follows:

1. The Fatherhood of God
2. The brotherhood of man
3. Continuous existence
4. Communion of spirits and ministry of angels
5. Personal responsibility
6. Compensation and retribution hereafter for good and evil done on earth
7. A path of endless progression

Authoritative texts for spiritualism and the UCM include *The Aquarian Gospel of Jesus Christ* and *A New Text of Spiritual Philosophy and Religion.* According to these writings, the general principles of the UCM presented as being an expanded version of *The Seven Principles,* are as follows:

1. "We" believe in the fatherhood of God and the brotherhood of man.
2. "We" believe that all phenomena that occur within the realms of nature, both physical and spiritual, are manifestations of infinite intelligence.
3. "We" believe that true religion is discovered by understanding the laws of nature and of God, and by living in harmony therein.
4. "We" believe that individual existence, personal identity, and memory continue after the transitional period called death.
5. "We" believe that communication with those in the unseen or etheric world is a scientific fact, fully proven under test conditions by the phenomena of psychical research.
6. "We" believe that the Golden Rule, "Whatsoever ye would that others should do unto you, do ye also unto them," is the essence of morality.
7. "We" believe that every individual is morally self-responsible. Happiness flows from obedience of the laws of nature and of God and unhappiness and misery follow their disobedience.
8. "We" believe that genuine improvement and reformation of the human soul are always possible in this world and the next.
9. "We" believe that prophecy exists in our times as in biblical days.
10. "We" believe that the universe, as a spiritual system expressing divine wisdom, makes possible the eternal progress of the soul who loves truth and goodness.[10]

Aside from the Christian taboo on dabbling in the hidden and secret things (Deut. 29:29), the church also finds itself at odds with the spiritualist denial of the deity of Jesus Christ. Various spiritualists have dismissed the ▸incarnation, deity, and atoning work of Christ on the cross as being "unrighteous," "immoral," and "deranged."[11] Along with the rejection of the deity of Christ, prominent spiritualists also deny the ▸Trinity and, in keeping with teachings common to many selected religious sects within the scope of this volume, assert the deity of humankind.

The church has consistently maintained that God has revealed himself in history through the voice of the ▸prophets and ▸apostles, and more completely through Jesus Christ (Gal. 4:4; Heb. 1:1–2). The apostolic rule of faith, the tradition of the church, and the sacred canons of Scripture are the sole deposits of ▸revelation. The church has always forbidden its adherents from seeking additional revelations from any other source of extraneous authority. To do so is to grapple with unseen powers of darkness (Eph. 6:12).

Spiritualists deny the existence of the ▸devil and ▸demons.[12] They hold that communication with the spirit world leads to enlightenment, higher awareness, and the tapping into the "creative intelligence" of the universe (Principle 2 above). Ethically, the Golden Rule (Principle 6) presents the highest ideal in spiritualist thought.

CONCLUSION

The spiritualist movement continues to exert an influence on those seeking alternate forms of "spirituality" outside the spheres of ▸orthodoxy.[13] Often, those most attracted to the UCM and spiritualism are grieving over the death of loved ones and are in hopes of maintaining contact with them. Spiritualism presents a major challenge to traditional CHRISTIANITY as it continues through New Age paradigms to present a "spiritual" alternative to the church.[14] Readers may wish to consult two highly critical books on the occult by James Randi. They are: *An Encyclopedia of Claims, Frauds, and Hoaxes of the Occult and Supernatural* (New York: St. Martin's, 1997), and *Flim-Flam: Psychics, ESP, Unicorns, and Other Delusions* (Buffalo: Prometheus, 1995).

ADDITIONAL INFORMATION

Headquarters

Universal Church of the Master, 100 West Rincon, Suite 222, Campbell, CA, 95008; there are many other spiritualist locations. The second website listed below is the National Spiritualist Association of Churches, which provides links to other spiritualist centers and locations.

Websites

www.u-c-m.org; www.nsac.org

Sacred Texts

Spiritualist sacred texts include: *The Heavenly Arcana; Apocalypse Revealed; Principles of Nature; The Aquarian Gospel of Jesus Christ, A New Text of Spiritual Philosophy and Religion*

Statistics

The number of people who actively participate in spiritualist concepts far exceeds the actual number of organizations like the Universal Church of the Master, the CHURCH OF THE NEW JERUSALEM, or the New Age Movement. Presently, there are approximately three hundred UCM congregations in the United States, with over thirteen hundred ministers and ten thousand members.

Notes

[1] The British term is *spiritism*.

[2] Douglas Hill and Pat Williams, *The Supernatural* (New York: Hawthorne, 1965), 115–16.

[3] Sydney E. Ahlstrom, *A Religious History of the American People*, 2 vols. (New York: Image Books, 1975), 2:592.

[4] Hill and Williams, *The Supernatural*, 128.

[5] Walter Martin, *The Kingdom of the Cults* (Minneapolis: Bethany, 1985), 231–32.

[6] *Religious Requirements and Practices of Certain Select Groups*, "A Handbook Supplement for Chaplains" (U.S. Dept. of Defense, n.d.), 2.

[7] *Religious Requirements and Practices*, 2.

[8] William Edward Biederwolf, *Spiritualism* (Grand Rapids: Eerdmans, 1952), 241.

[9] See SATANISM.

[10] Elliot Miller, *A Crash Course on the New Age Movement* (Grand Rapids: Baker, 1977), 141.

[11] See NEW AGE MOVEMENT for a more detailed analysis of ▸channeling.

[12] The article on Satanism gives a more detailed analysis of the ouija board phenomenon.

[13] See also ASSOCIATION FOR RESEARCH AND ENLIGHTENMENT, VOODOO, SANTERIA, THEOSOPHY, CHURCH OF THE NEW JERUSALEM (SWEDENBORGIANISM), HINDUISM, URANTIA, etc. for additional insights into groups influenced by the ideas of spiritualism.

[14] In addition to the Universal Church of the Master, other prominent spiritualist movements in America include the International General Assembly of Spiritualists (1936) with 164,072 members in 209 churches; the National Spiritual Alliance of the U.S.A. (1913) with over 3,000 members in 34 churches; the National Spiritualist Association of Churches (1893) with over 5,000 in 164 churches; and the Progressive Spiritual Church (1907) with 11,000 members in 21 churches (statistics provided by Frank S. Mead, *Handbook of Denominations in the United States*, 8th ed. [Nashville: Abingdon, 1988], 235–36).

SRI CHINMOY CENTER

The popularity of multiculturalism, the NEW AGE MOVE-MENT, and the continued interest and fascination with Eastern and particularly Hindu (*see* HINDUISM) thought has produced a most receptive climate for religious leaders like Sri Chinmoy.

HISTORY

Sri Chinmoy was born in 1931 in Bengal, India. His father, a railroad inspector, did not see his son follow in his footsteps. Motivated by the Hindu teachings with which he was raised, Chinmoy achieved the highest state of *samadhi* at age twelve or thirteen. Shortly after this great spiritual accomplishment, Chinmoy entered an *ashram, where he began a twenty-year period of inner contemplation and meditation. Obeying what he claimed was an inner voice, he came to the United States in 1964. He soon amassed a small following of several hundred, but centers were rapidly established in major cities throughout the United States, Canada, and Europe. Chinmoy enjoyed an audience with the pope as well as other prominent leaders. He has also lectured at major universities and colleges and even supervises bimonthly meditation meetings at the United Nations.

ORGANIZATION

There are Sri Chinmoy centers around the world. Each center serves as a spiritual home for its members as well as a meeting place for prayer and meditation, study, and the enjoyment of spiritual music. The center also represents Sri Chinmoy's teachings in action, through classes and other public programs.[1]

TEACHINGS

Chinmoy's followers number under five thousand. Chinmoy, however, stresses that it is the *quality* of a devotee's development, not the *quantity* of devotees, that counts. Central to his teaching is the importance of a disciple's close relationship with his *guru. By yielding the mind to the guru (Chinmoy), *enlightenment becomes possible. So important and basic is this idea that followers construct an altar in their homes and hang a photo of Chinmoy above it or rest one on it, before which they meditate daily.

Traditional CHRISTIANITY also places special emphasis on the centrality of a person, Jesus Christ. He is the center of the Christian faith, however, not as a mere influential person like Chinmoy, but because by his exemplary teachings, flawless life, death, and resurrection from the dead, he empirically demonstrated his deity. Thus to Christians he is, as the disciple Thomas confessed, "Lord and God" (John 20:28).

The *Bhagavad Gita* and the *Upanishads* constitute the sacred writings for Chinmoy. He has adapted these writings, however, to accommodate Western thought, culture, and lifestyles. That is to say, Chinmoy is more pragmatic than other gurus. One does not achieve enlightenment, for example, by meditating in a remote cave. It must happen amid the realities of life on a day-to-day basis.

God is not realized exclusively through the cultivation of the mind. It is with the heart that one grasps the inner light, source, and fountain of all truth. This is achieved through devotion and submission to the divine will, made possible through the mediation of the guru, who has gone before and already tasted of the divine fruit himself. It may take the student a lengthy period of time, even years, before achieving enlightenment.

Within most, if not all, religious movements, a familiar pattern takes place. Over time, a religious expression tends to become intellectualized and systematized. Inevitably, this process results in a dialectic wherein the emphasis becomes the experiential or feeling dimension. Thus we have, for example, SUFISM arising as a mystical expression of ISLAM. Within Christianity, this dialectic is an oft-repeated scenario in the history of the church. The various monastic orders arose in reaction to a former order's lack of spirituality. Or Pietism arose in the seventeenth century as a reaction against the cold, sterile, and often dispassionate *Protestant *orthodoxy.

All of this is not to say that Chinmoy is consciously rebelling against any other religious expression within his own Hindu tradition. Hinduism is so all-encompassing that nearly all varying motifs are conformable to the essence of Hindu thought—namely, achievement of total enlightenment—by overcoming *karma and thereby escaping from the cycle of *reincarnation. Chinmoy purposes one of many paths toward that end.[2]

The uniqueness of Sri Chinmoy, like that of any other guru or religious leader, depends necessarily on the uniqueness of demeanor and originality. Chinmoy's distinctiveness lies in his emphasis on each individual student's devotion to the guru. But even this is not absolutely essential. It is simply a quicker way to achieve salvation or enlightenment than if one does not follow the guru's path. The process of yielding one's life to a teacher is known as ‣*siksha*.

The aim of Chinmoy is to achieve world peace. While this is certainly a noble goal, Christianity firmly holds to the belief that peace is only made possible through Jesus Christ. The apostle Paul writes, "For God was pleased to have all his fullness dwell in him, and through him to reconcile to himself all things, whether things on earth or things in heaven, *by making peace through his blood, shed on the cross*" (Col. 1:19–20, emphasis added).

Another unique teaching of Chinmoy is that disciples can benefit spiritually through extreme physical activity. His followers go to great lengths to apply this principle. One such disciple, Ashrita Furman, has received notice in the *Guinness Book of World Records* for such things as walking twenty-four miles with a milk bottle on his head, clapping his hands together at the rate of 140 claps per minute for fifty hours and seventeen seconds, somersaulting for ten miles around Central Park in New York City, a failed attempt at pogo-sticking to the summit of Mount Fuji, and rolling in the reverse route of Paul Revere's historic twelve-mile ride.[3]

Chinmoy himself combines artistic and literary talents with sheer volume of output. According to one source, Chinmoy claims to have completed over sixteen thousand paintings in a single day, though this would mean two paintings per second.[4] One of the most remarkable achievements of Chinmoy is his Sri Chinmoy Marathon Team, which organizes five hundred peace runs per year around the world.

CONCLUSION

Many pamphlets, poems, and books have flowed from Chinmoy's pen. As stated above, Chinmoy never amassed a substantial following, but his influence extends far beyond his immediate students. Chinmoy's website contains current entries on Shinmoy's spiritual teachings and devotional thoughts. Sri Chinmoy continues to write, teach, and exert his influence at the start of the twenty-first century.

ADDITIONAL INFORMATION

Headquarters
The Sri Chinmoy Center, Jamaica Plains, New York. There are also centers in Chicago, Seattle, and Washington, D.C., as well as in numerous countries abroad.

Website
www.srichinmoy.org

Sacred Texts
The *Bhagavad Gita*; the *Upanishads*

Periodicals
Aum; Chinmoy Family.

Membership
5,000 worldwide; 1,500 in the United States and 1,000 in Canada.

Notes
[1] *www.srichinmoy.org/html/sri_chinmoy/centre.html*, 2003.
[2] For a further evaluation and comparison of the teachings of Sri Chinmoy with traditional Christianity, see HINDUISM.
[3] "To Revere His Guru, Ashrita Furman Goes on a Roll," *People* (May 19, 1986), 65.
[4] Bob Larson, *Larson's Book of Cults* (Wheaton: Tyndale, 1986), 240.

SUFISM; THE SUFI ORDER; SUFI ISLAMIC RUHANIAT SOCIETY

The quest for "deeper spirituality" is a common characteristic of certain adherents to most religions of the world. Splits or divisions often occur within a religious movement as a result of one group or faction rising up to protest the formality, worldliness, or externality of the rest of them. In place of a merely intellectual or ceremonial approach to religion, these people pursue a more spiritual, inward, and mystical alternative. This has certainly been true of CHRISTIANITY. The numerous monastic orders, particularly in medieval Roman Catholicism, grew out of a desire by ‣ascetic monks and nuns to seek holy lives apart from the world in order to better serve God. They were protesting the materialism and politics of many of the Catholic clergy. The rise of the various denominations within Protestant Christendom evidences the quest for the deeper life. The Holiness Movement, which grew out of Methodism in England, is an obvious example.

This phenomenon is also true of ISLAM. Early in its development arose a faction that reacted against the formalism and external laws of the ‣Koran and maintained that truth and knowledge are to be sought through personal experience. This faction is called Sufism.

HISTORY

The word *sufi* means "mystic" and is a derivative of *suf*, or "wool." Early Muslim ascetics were accustomed to wearing woolen garments. The mystical tradition of Sufism dates back almost to the beginning of Islam in the seventh century A.D. The earliest supporter was *Al-Hassan of Basra (A.D. 643–728). In an effort to purify Islam and attain a more spiritual knowledge of *Allah, the early Sufists practiced long vigils, intense meditation, and celibacy. For the next five centuries, Sufism began to develop, but it operated in small and rather exclusive circles. The Sufi leaders, called *shaykhs*, were forced to write basic statements concerning the creeds of Sufism in order to placate growing concern in orthodox Islamic circles that the mystical order was teaching heresies. For the most part, it managed to stay within the confines of traditional Islam.

The thirteenth century marked the "golden age of Sufism." By the twelfth century, monastic orders had been firmly established. Many writers came to the forefront to espouse Sufist *mysticism. The greatest of these during this period was Meluana Celadin *Rumi (1207–73). His great work, *Masnavi*, is considered second only to the *Koran in religious importance. It was Rumi who advocated and influenced the development of *whirling dervishes—twirl dancing as being a means of achieving oneness with God.

Over the centuries, Sufism began to wane in both influence and importance. It never entirely died out, however, as the monastic orders continued to espouse its teachings. In 1925 Kemal Atatürk outlawed the dervishes and existing orders on the grounds that they were too primitive and that they were counterproductive to the advance of civilization and modernity.

The ban was recently lifted in Turkey, and Sufism has been enjoying a resurgence. While Islam has always been extremely conservative, Sufism, with its mystical, antiformal orientation, has won many adherents in the United States. Sufism entered into the United States in 1910 through the efforts of Haerat Pir-O-Murshid Inayat *Kahn (1881–1927). His mission and goal were to westernize Sufism. He lived a relatively short life; at his death, his son, Pir Vilayat Inayat *Kahn, became the leader. In the decades following, Sufism grew rapidly in the United States. Centers have been established in most major cities, with camps in New York and Arizona.

Problems broke out in the early 1970s when the San Francisco order, formerly led by *Murshi Samuel L. Lewis (d. 1971), began to clash with Kahn, particularly over Kahn's refusal to allow homosexuals into the order. Kahn's policies against drugs such as marijuana, cocaine, heroin, and LSD proved to be too great a constraint, and in 1977 the San Francisco group broke off from the main order and formed the Sufi Islamic Ruhaniat Society. The doctrines, programs, and policies of the new order are similar to the parent group, with the exception of the more liberal guidelines for membership and substance intake.

ORGANIZATION

The International Association of Sufism (IAS) has set up various departments in order to facilitate its ongoing ministry worldwide. A Sufi Women's Organization (SWO) was established in 1993. There is also a Sufi Youth International (SYI), established as a support network for Sufi youth. A Sufism and Psychology Forum (SPF) was founded in order to discover the relationship between Sufism and psychology. Several healing centers provide counseling and support. A children's organization exists for the younger generation of members of the IAS. Anyone can become a member of IAS by filling out an application and paying an annual membership fee.

TEACHINGS

The basic thrust of Sufism is an emphasis on the "spirit and not the letter." Sufists seek a basic union with God through mystical means achieved through meditation and ritual rather than through strict observance of the Koran. Mere outward observance is hardly an adequate or correct approach to religious truth. One must be able to experience for oneself a direct contact and oneness with Allah.

In order to achieve this oneness, adherents follow a *tariqah (path) and a *haquigah (reality). The *tariqah* begins with repentance. The disciple then undergoes rigorous asceticism and training by a master in order to fight the authentic "holy war" within. The various stages in the training eventually give way to an inner *enlightenment or knowledge, called *marifah. *Marifah* then leads to *mahabbah (love), which is the love between God and his beloved. The goal of tariqah is *fana (annihilation), the point at which the personality is extinguished in an absorbing illumination and all-consuming love for God. There are three stages in the annihilation process, which are achieved through obedience to the *shariah (law): annihilation in the master, annihilation in the prophet, and annihilation in God.

Orthodox Islam has reacted strongly against the concept of *fana*, contending that the relationship between God and humankind is essentially one of subject to object. Nevertheless, the retention of the law by Sufi mystics has been an important factor in keeping the movement within the bounds of traditional Islam throughout the centuries.

We can detect a similar pattern in the relationship between mysticism and ▸orthodoxy in Christendom. Christian mystics have also attempted to bridge the gap between God and humanity, or between subject and object. Both Sufism and Christianity posit that the essence of the mystical union is "love" for the divine. However, in the Christian tradition, the Creator/creature distinction is never "annihilated" but always maintained.

Another important difference between Sufism and the mystical tradition in Christendom is a matter of theological center. For Sufism, the essence of the religious life is achieving oneness with the divine. In Christendom the focus certainly varies in the differing traditions, and it is perhaps inaccurate to speak of an exclusive "theological center." However, most would agree that the essence of the Christian message is God's free offer of salvation made possible through the person and work of Jesus Christ. This is certainly the central focus of the Apostles' and Nicene creeds (Appendix 1).

A concern for the degree to which Sufism is orthodox with respect to Islam is roughly analogous to the concern that traditional Christendom has exhibited toward mysticism in its own ranks throughout the centuries. The difference, however, for the latter is that so many of the church's thinkers have had traces of mysticism. John has been thought of as being a mystic, along with Paul. The long train of theologians in the postapostolic period (Clement of Alexandria, Augustine, Gregory of Nyssa, Francis of Assisi, Tauler) are but a few names drawn from a considerable list.[1]

One of the methods for achieving the desired oneness with God for a Sufi is the "twirl dancing" introduced by Rumi (see above). His disciples were known as whirling dervishes—the dervish was a style of dance requiring 1,001 hours of training to master. Once the dance has been mastered, the disciple is able to work himself into a spiritual awakening through the twirling dance motions. The dervish was performed secretly in the past but is now performed openly.

CONCLUSION

The impact of Sufism on the art, literature, and culture of Islamic peoples has been tremendous. It was Sufi missionaries who brought the Islamic faith into Africa, Asia, and India. Though not enjoying a large following, the Sufi orders in the United States have attracted approximately five to six thousand adherents in recent decades, a small figure when compared to the over two million Muslims in North America; nevertheless, the Sufi orders' influence extends far beyond its own membership ranks. There are now many Sufi orders throughout the United States and the world. We list a few websites for the main orders below.

ADDITIONAL INFORMATION_____

Headquarters
The Sufi Order, PO Box 396, New Lebanon, NY 12125; International Association of Sufism, 14 Commercial Blvd., Suite 101, Novato, California 94949 USA; Sufi Islamic Ruhaniat Society, PO Box 51118, Eugene, OR 97405.

Websites
www.ias.org; www.ruhaniat.org

Sacred Text
The Koran

Periodicals
Sufism: An Inquiry; Insight (newsletter) (both of these publications are put out by the International Association of Sufism)*; Bismillah; Inshallah* (The Sufi Order); *Hearts and Wing*

Membership
There are 5,000 to 6,000 Sufis in the United States. Current worldwide figures are difficult to determine, but the published figure of 9,000,000 worldwide was a mid-twentieth century figure.

Note
[1] For a more detailed comparison between Sufism and Christianity, see ISLAM.

TAOISM

Taoism, founded by ▸Lao-tse (604–531 B.C.), is one of the three great religions of China, along with BUDDHISM and CONFUCIANISM. Though classified as a religion, initially Taoism was a philosophy and did not become organized into a religion until A.D. 440 when it was adopted as a state ▸cult.

The word ▸*tao* has no direct English equivalent but roughly corresponds to such terms as *way, truth,* or *path*. Its philosophy underlies many of the currents of modern cultic movements and has itself undergone many changes since the time of Lao-tse.

HISTORY

Much of the life of Lao-tse is unknown. What is known is that he was an archivist for the state but dropped out of public service and went into seclusion, living like a hermit in a small hut on the side of a mountain.

Chuang-tzu (third century B.C.), author of the work that carries his name, the ᵇ*Chuang-tzu*, is the first to mention Lao-tse, describing the latter as being one of his great teachers. The *Chuang-tzu* contains much of Lao-tse's teachings and also describes a meeting between him and ᵇConfucius. Lao-tse was originally regarded as being a great teacher and philosopher. Centuries after his death, however, he was deified by those who developed his philosophy into a ritualistic religion. Lao-tse is also credited with writing the classic Taoist text, ᵇ*Tao-te-Ching* (*The Way of Power*), in which he describes the basic principles a ruler should be guided by.

During the period of Chuang-tzu, an era known in Chinese history as the period of "Warring States" (475–221 B.C.), Taoism began to imbibe elements not original to its teachings, chiefly from Buddhist thought. A modern rendition of Taoism is said to have been founded by Chuang Tao-ling in the first century A.D. Here, syncretism with the ᵇoccult, superstition, and the elevation of the ᵇThree Pure Ones (Lao-tse being one) to a position of deity comes to the forefront. A plethora of deities for everything imaginable was adopted with accompanying priests, sacrifices, and temples. Many of these practices remain intact today. Taoism has influenced Chinese thought and culture tremendously.

ORGANIZATION

There are many Taoist communities throughout the world, but because of its antiquity in multicultural settings, there is no single world headquarters. In the contemporary world, Taoism is advocated in self-help and New Age books, with millions of followers. One revivalist community is the Taoist Restoration Society (TRS), with headquarters in Honolulu, Hawaii. This organization is run by a board of directors, which elects an executive director. The society conducts projects around the world of various sorts. They are rebuilding a T'ang Dynasty monastery in China to house Taoist nuns. Also in China, a Dongba Training Center is being built as a place to study Buddhism and Taoism. All Taoist communities offer classes and courses on a regular basis.

TEACHINGS

Taoism was born in China at a time of great intellectual activity. Confucius (551–479 B.C.) also lived at this time and developed his great system of thought. Lao-tse regarded the Tao as the first cause of all reality. The total quest of the human race is to become one with the Tao. The Tao transcends all matter in the universe. It lies beyond it, yet embodies the forms for the phenomena that are perceived. This idea is somewhat similar to Plato's notion of the world of the forms that are the archetypes of lesser realities in the universe.

Reality, as represented in the macrocosmic universe, finds a correspondence in the specific life forms, particularly human. For example, human beings behave and function, act and react, in much the same way as nature does. To understand humankind is to understand the structure of the universe (microcosm-macrocosm). Blood, which is the fount of life, circulates throughout the body as the waters of a river flow out from its source.

Lao-tse had a cyclical view of history. He saw that all that flows out returns to its starting point. Life comes from nonlife and returns to nonlife again. Therefore, true wisdom becomes a matter of attuning oneself to the rhythm of the universe, which corresponds strictly to the rhythm of life. Five main orifices and organs of the body mirror the "five directions," or as they are alternately called, the "five parts of the sky" or the "five holy mountains." They are water, fire, wood, metal, and earth.

These correspondences and rhythmic movements became characterized by the concepts of ᵇyin and yang (dark side–sunny side). Yang is the breath that transcends the world and formed the heavens. Yin is breath that formed the earth. All of reality operates according to the principle of yin and yang. The two bipolar forces—good/evil, light/darkness, male/female, and so on (all paired opposites in the universe)—constantly react to and with one another. Human intervention in these forces displaces universal rhythm and results in an improper balance between them. Civilization is therefore not a positive factor, but one that has upset the balance of yin and yang. Thus, an agrarian society is seen as being one most in harmony with nature and the universe.

Lao-tse stressed the character of the individual and his ethical conduct and development. The cultivation of virtue is the chief end of humankind. The "three jewels" of life are compassion, moderation, and humility. Yet to actively seek virtue is to display a lack of virtue; "the man of superior virtue never acts [ᵇ*wu-wei*], and yet there is nothing he leaves undone." The deposit of human intervention is always upsetting to the natural course of events. The Taoist would relate that a tree does not interfere in the process of growing or shedding its leaves. There is no trace of its own activity left visibly behind. "The man of superior virtue is not virtuous, and that is why he has virtue."

The concept of *ch'i* (air, breath) is related to yin and yang. *Ch'i* is the cosmic energy or breath that is given proportionately to every man. The lifelong task is to nurture this energy and to strengthen it. The martial arts have been greatly influenced by the Taoist concept of *ch'i*. The expert in the martial arts is able to harness the cosmic energy of *ch'i* and deprive or empty his or her opponent of the same.

The deities of Taoism include *Sanching* ("the three pure ones"), *San-kuan* ("the three officials," rulers over the heavens, earth, and subterranean waters), *San-yuan* ("the three primordials," creator deities), and *Pa-hsien* ("the eight immortals," eight historical figures who are famous in Taoism—Chung-li Ch'uan, Ho Hsien-ku, Chang Kou-lao, Lu Tung-pin, Han Hsiang-tzu, Ts'ao Kuo-chiu, Li T'ieh-kuai, and Lan Ts'ai-ho.[1]

The harsh criticism leveled against Taoism by its opponents has long been that it is a religion that rejects human activity at every level, whether it be political, social, familial, or the like. At the same time it venerates weakness, passivity, receptivity, uselessness, emptiness, and so on. Taoism rejects all forms of government, elevating as its hegemonic concern the nurturing of a life of bliss and ease. These criticisms are not unjustified. For human beings to intervene in any way with the laws of the universe is to upset the intricate balance of yin and yang. Therefore, it is not surprising that the Chinese government in the twentieth century tried to stamp out Taoism because it reinforced laziness, non-involvement, and apathy—problems that a communist regime is faced with anyway, without having a religion to reinforce such ideals.

In many ways, the inactivity and passivity of Taoist thought is comparable to the ideals of the Buddhist quest for nirvana through the cultivation of the middle path, and indeed "Buddhism found no difficulty in adapting it to its own way of life and thought."[2] Both religions have been labeled as atheistic in that in their original forms they were philosophies that proffered no particular deities. Taoism became a religion rapidly during the Han dynasty, however, when Lao-tse himself became venerated as a deity.

The basic worldview of Taoism stands in contrast with the worldview of traditional CHRISTIANITY. The latter makes bold claim to the fact that God is "Father Almighty, maker of heaven and earth" (Apostles' Creed, Appendix 1). Moreover, Christianity maintains that far from being an impersonal force, God is personal in Jesus Christ. In addition, Jesus did not merely philosophize about virtuous living; he claimed to be the "only-begotten Son of God" (Nicene Creed, Appendix 1). In that all of the human race has fallen into sin and active rebellion against the living God, Christianity places central focus on the person and work of Jesus Christ to atone for such sin by dying on a cross, shedding his blood, and subsequently being raised up by God, thereby assuring the forgiveness of sins and eternal life to all who are penitent.

While it is true that both Christianity and Taoism reject such vices as hedonism and materialism, the latter seeks to overcome them through inactivity (*wu-wei*), while the former insists on the necessity of activity—God's activity to forgive for the sake of Jesus Christ, and our activity as sinners (e.g., hedonism and materialism) to repent of sin and receive the forgiveness offered through Christ. The Christian must then become active in fulfilling whatever vocation he or she is called to do within the body of Christ, which is the church.

CONCLUSION

In A.D. 440, Taoism became an official cult of the state. It is interesting to note that only one century earlier Christianity was recognized as the "official" religion of the Roman Empire. The basic motifs of Taoist philosophy are found in the many Eastern cults that have migrated to the West. Taoism itself, however, is practiced chiefly on the island of Taiwan, where its greatest concentration of devotees reside.

ADDITIONAL INFORMATION

Headquarters
Taoist Restoration Society; PO Box 29516, Honolulu, HI, 96820.

Websites
www.clas.ufl.edu/users/gthursby/taoism;
www.taoresource.com; www.tao.org

Sacred Texts
Tao Te Ching; Chuang-tzu

Publications
Many publications issue forth from the Sacred Mountain Press.

Statistics
Currently there are approximately 20 million Taoists, 30,000 of whom are in the United States.

Notes
[1] *http://religiousmovements.lib.virginia.edu/nrms/taoism.html*
[2] Edwin Oliver James, *History of Religions* (New York: Harper & Brothers, 1957), 104–5.

THEOSOPHY

The word "theosophy" comes from the Greek words *theos* (God) and *sophia* (wisdom). It describes the quest of Theosophy, namely, the application of wisdom to the quest for knowledge of divine matters. Theosophy takes its place as one of the ▸mind sciences.

HISTORY

Theosophy as a movement was founded by Madame Helena Petrovna ▸Blavatsky (1831–91), Colonel Henry Steel ▸Olcott (1832–1907), and William Q. ▸Judge (1851–96). Blavatsky was born in the Ukraine in 1831 as Helen Petrovna. She married czarist General Nikifor V. Blavatsky at age seventeen, but the union between them was an unhappy one and ended after only three months. Blavatsky had a keen interest in the ▸occult and traveled extensively, and she is alleged to have studied for some time in India. She came to the United States in 1872. After arriving in America, she met Olcott and Judge. Together they founded the Theosophical Society in New York in 1875.

Blavatsky's first monograph, *Isis Unveiled*, was published in 1877. The book, although read in some circles, did little to attract attention to the society itself, whose numbers declined in the ensuing years. Blavatsky and Olcott left the United States in 1879 and went to India, where in 1882 they established an international headquarters in Adyar, where it remains to this day. The society met with more success in India, and Blavatsky began to attract a following.

Trouble broke out when she was investigated by the press in India and was accused of being a fraud, though her popularity did not wane. In 1885, however, the London Society for Psychical Research declared publicly that Blavatsky was indeed a fraud. She left India and moved to Germany, Belgium, and then London, where she remained writing extensively until the end of her life. Her major work was *The Secret Doctrine* (1888) followed by *The Voice of Silence* (1889). She died on May 8, 1891, in London. Olcott continued to lead the movement from India.

After Olcott's death in 1907, one of Blavatsky's ardent disciples, Annie W. ▸Besant (1847–1933), became the president of the international movement, a post she retained until her death. Besant's writings are considered the best extant expressions of theosophical ideas. Controversy continued to be a factor in America during her tenure, but she provided stable leadership for the movement as a whole.

One failed aspect that caught international attention was Mrs. Basant's adopted Indian-born son, Jiddu Krishnamunti (1895–1986), who she claimed in 1911 was the long-awaited ▸Maitreya or "Jesus Christ reincarnated," the twenty-seventh "world teacher" incarnation. All joy was suddenly dashed when Krishnamurti officially resigned as the Messiah (*New York Times*, Aug. 11, 1929) and dissolved his 100,000 member organization, Order of the Star of the East. He continued publishing mystical philosophy but never regained any status within Theosophy.

During this time, Theosophy in America was under the leadership of William Judge. The American movement underwent a tremendous revival under his leadership. Prominent individuals who were instrumental in Theosophy's early and formative years included General Abner Doubleday, the inventor of baseball, and Thomas Alva Edison. Eventually a power struggle broke out between Besant and Judge, resulting in a split between the American and international movements in 1895. Judge's death the following year brought Katherine A. ▸Tingley (1847–1929) to the helm. Her accomplishments included the relocation of the American headquarters to Point Loma, California.

Currently there are schools, camps, seminars, and ongoing instructions in many countries around the world. Members of the society travel to oppressed regions of the world and engage in issues of social justice and the reconciliation of the world's religions.

ORGANIZATION

The Theosophy Company, the publishing arm of the movement located in Los Angeles, was formed in 1925 and disseminated theosophical literature. Today, the headquarters for the Theosophical Society in America is in Wheaton, Illinois, and the international headquarters continues to be in Adyar, India. Centers are located in seventy countries around the world. They are independent, yet work closely with one another.

There are two kinds of members: those actually attached to a "lodge" or a "study center," and those who are unaffiliated, called members-at-large. A lodge is comprised of at least seven members who meet to discuss and study Theosophy and present programs and educational forums. A study center is less formal and can be comprised of three members. There is a $36.00 annual membership fee, which is reduced for students.

In America, there are six districts, each of which elects a member to sit on the National Board of Directors. Names and photos of the directors are posted and kept up to date on the website.

TEACHINGS

Theosophy teaches that a red thread runs throughout all religions of the world and binds them together. In other words, there is a universal philosophy to which all religions adhere or strive toward. Second, it distinguishes between exoteric and esoteric knowledge. Like the neo-Platonic and ›gnostic traditions of the first three centuries A.D., Theosophy teaches that all of the major texts of religion possess an outer (exoteric) meaning and an inner (esoteric) secret meaning. The task is to discover the hidden meanings of sacred texts. The ability to grasp the esoteric is the ability to identify the "red thread." Theosophy is monistic in that it believes that the many are an expression of the one.

In *The Secret Doctrine*, Blavatsky articulates three basic tenets of Theosophy.

> (1) An Omnipresent, Eternal, Boundless and Immutable PRINCIPLE, on which all speculation is impossible, since it transcends the power of human conception.... (2) The Eternity of the Universe in toto as a boundless plane; periodically the playground of numberless Universes incessantly manifesting and disappearing, called the Manifesting Stars and the "Sparks of Eternity." ... The absolute universality of that law of periodicity, of flux and reflux, ebb and flow, which physical science has observed and recorded in all departments of nature. (3) The fundamental identity of all Souls with the Universal Over-Soul, the latter being itself an aspect of the Unknown Root; and the obligatory pilgrimage for every Soul.... The Pivotal doctrine of the Esoteric Philosophy admits no privileges or special gifts in man, save those won by his own Ego through personal effort and merit throughout a long series of metempsychoses and reincarnations.[1]

The basic motifs of Theosophy have their source in ancient philosophical and theological foundations. Some authorities have traced the beginnings of Theosophy to the ancient ›vedas, which posit the ›immanence of God and the immediacy of divine knowledge and revelation. Others suggest that the principle source from which Theosophy derives its substance is the writings of ›*Hermes Trismegistus* (Hermes the Thrice Greatest), a later name of the ancient Egyptian god ›Thoth, the guardian of all knowledge. These Latin and Greek writings are a syncretistic blend of Platonic philosophy and Eastern religions brought together in summary fashion within the Platonic dialogues. The primary focus of the ›Hermetic corpus was the elevation of humankind to the position of deity through initiation into secret *gnosis* (knowledge). Theosophy has simply restated this focus. Humanity is able to achieve perfection through a mystical experience of the imminent deity of which it is but an extension.

In her *Key to Theosophy* (1889), Blavatsky restates the threefold purpose of the Theosophical Society, which Ahlstrom sums up as follows: "to establish a nucleus of the universal brotherhood of humanity, to promote the study of comparative religion and philosophy, and to make a systematic investigation of the mystic potencies of man and nature."[2] Modern-day Theosophy has not altered these principles.

The basic doctrines of Theosophy are outlined as follows:

God

God is the impersonal divine source from which all else extends and in which all is reflected. Essentially, Theosophy holds to a form of ›pantheism derived from its roots in HINDUISM and/or ancient Egyptian religion.

Contrariwise, CHRISTIANITY vigorously maintains that God is indeed personal. Not only is he "maker of heaven and earth," but also "Father" (Apostles' Creed, Appendix 1). Second, pantheism dictates a view of God that does not make a clear delineation between God and creation. The biblical doctrine of creation, by contrast, makes a definitive distinction between God and humanity (Gen. 1:27). The Creator/creation distinction is a doctrine that ›orthodox Christianity has always maintained.

Jesus Christ

In Theosophy, Jesus was divine in the same sense in which all people are divine. According to Annie Besant, "all men become Christs."[3] This is a common assessment of Jesus' deity among many religious groups.[4]

This conception of Jesus' divinity differs from the church's confessions. As incarnate deity (1 Tim. 3:16), Jesus Christ is uniquely divine. As confessed by the church, he is "God of God, Light of Light, very God of very God" (Nicene Creed, Appendix 1). Second, by virtue of his deity, Jesus is the second person of the divine ›Trinity consisting of Father, Son, and Holy Spirit. Third, Christianity confesses that Christ offered himself as a sacrifice for the sins of the world (1 John 2:2). There are a diverse number of theories of the atonement in Christian tradition, but vicarious satisfaction (that Christ satisfied the Father's wrath against sin by Jesus' death on the cross) is the one most widely considered biblical in orthodox circles. Theosophy opposes this theory. One popular theosophical writer, L. W. Rogers, sums it up as follows:

> Back of the ancient doctrine of the vicarious atonement is a profound and beautiful truth, but it has been degraded into a teaching that is as selfish as it is false. That natural truth is the sacrifice of the Solar Logos, the Deity of our system. Sacrifice consists of limiting himself in the manner of manifested worlds, and it is reflected in the sacrifice of the Christ and other great teachers. Not the sacrifice of life, but a voluntary returning to live in the confinement of material body.... It is the pernicious doctrine that wrongdoing by one can be set right by the sacrifice of another. It is simply astounding that such a belief could have survived the middle ages and should continue to find millions who accept it in these days of clearer thinking.
>
> The man who is willing to purchase bliss by the agony of another is unfit for heaven, and could not recognize it if he were there.
>
> A heaven that is populated with those who see in the vicarious atonement the happy arrangement letting them in pleasantly and easily, would not be worth having.[5]

For Theosophy, Jesus' deity therefore consists in the fact that he became part of our "manifest world," and he shares this distinction with all other great religious teachers who have done the same. In contrast, the Apostles' Creed sets forth the church's understanding of the person and work of Christ. Each of its elements is deeply rooted in Christian tradition and the Bible. Jesus was "conceived by the Holy Spirit" (Matt. 1:20–23), "born of the virgin Mary" (Luke 2:7), "suffered under Pontius Pilate" (John 19:1–3), "was crucified, died and was buried" (Matt. 27:57–60; John 19:30). "He descended into hell" (1 Peter 3:18–19). "The third day he rose again from the dead" (John 20:1–12). "He ascended into heaven" (Acts 1:9–11), and "sits at the right hand of God the Father Almighty" (Eph. 1:20–23). "From thence he will come to judge the living and the dead" (Acts 10:42). By opposing this central focus of the Christian faith on the person and work of Jesus Christ, Theosophy is incompatible with Christianity. It is more closely aligned to Eastern thought. This becomes more obvious when we observe Theosophy's doctrine of ▸soteriology (salvation; see below).

Humanity

Human beings consist of seven parts: body, vitality, astral body, animal soul, human soul, spiritual soul, and spirit. Humans are evolving individually and corporately and are an extension of God. God is latent within all of humanity. As already observed, this is basically a Hindu concept that finds its way into many other religious groups. Because Christianity makes the sharp distinction between Creator/creation, there is no concomitance between Theosophy and the church.

Sin and Hell

For Theosophy, sin is irresponsibility. One can determine for oneself one's eternal destiny. The law of ▸karma is a deciding factor as to whether one advances or regresses on the wheel of ▸reincarnation through the material realm. ▸Hell as a place of eternal punishment, as taught by traditional Christianity, is mythical. According to Blavatsky, "The idea of a hot hell is an afterthought, the distortion of an astronomical allegory."[6]

Salvation

In Theosophy, people are saved if they seek to become conscious of the deep and hidden knowledge within themselves and the universe. Reincarnation is the process through which the ▸adept ascends the celestial ladder of knowledge to occupy an ▸astral body. Through self-effort and prayer (concentrated thought) an individual weans his or her way into a salvific state called ▸nirvana, in which the individual is absorbed by the impersonal world and loses all personal cognizance. Reincarnation is the "method by which the latent becomes actual."[7] Theosophy's tie to the occult as well as Eastern mysticism has resulted in the accumulation of an elaborate theological vocabulary utilized to advance its teachings.[8]

Obviously, Christian soteriology is widely divergent from that of Theosophy. Because of the separation of God from creation and because of the sin of the human race, it became necessary for God to make atonement between himself and humanity. This Jesus, the second person of the Trinity, accomplished through his person and work.

CONCLUSION

Theosophy, like other mind sciences, never gained a large following. There are reported to be approximately forty thousand members in the various societies that together comprise Theosophy, and there are only six thousand members in the United States.[9] But as a religious philosophy, its ideas and influences far transcend the boundaries of its own ranks, affecting many other groups, including the CHURCH UNIVERSAL AND TRIUMPHANT, NEW THOUGHT, ROSICRUCIANISM, NEW AGE

MOVEMENT, and many other SPIRITUALIST movements. Present-day headquarters in the United States are in several locations.

ADDITIONAL INFORMATION_____

Societies

The Theosophical Society of America is located in Wheaton, Illinois; the United Lodge of Theosophists in Los Angeles, California; the Theosophical Society in Covina, California; and the International Group of Theosophists in southern California. The international headquarters for the Theosophical Society is in Adyar, India.

Websites

www.thesociety.org; www.kfa.org

Sacred Text

The Secret Doctrine

Periodical

The Theosophist; Adyar Newsletter (International headquarters); *The Quest, The Messenger* (Newsletter) *(*Theosophical Society in America).

Statistics

40,000 worldwide and under 5,000 in the United States.

Notes

[1] Helen Blavatsky, "Proem," in *The Secret Doctrine*, as quoted by Sydney Ahlstrom, *A Religious History of the American People*, 2 vols. (New York: Image Books, 1975), 2:551.

[2] Ibid., 2:553.

[3] Annie Besant, *Is Theosophy Anti-Christian?* (London: Theosophical Publishing Society, 1901), 16.

[4] See MORMONISM, JEHOVAH'S WITNESSES, and the HINDUISM family of religions for similar concepts of the deity of Jesus Christ.

[5] L. W. Rogers, *Elementary Theosophy* (Wheaton: Theosophical Press, 1956), 201–6, as quoted by Walter Martin, *The Kingdom of the Cults* (Minneapolis: Bethany, 1985), 255.

[6] Helen Blavatsky, *Theosophical Glossary* (Los Angeles: Theosophy Company, 1892, 1973), 139.

[7] Rogers, *Elementary Theosophy*, 206.

[8] See ▶occult.

[9] These figures are not totally reliable because different sources vary in their statistics.

THERAVADA BUDDHISM

One of the two great divisions or systems of Buddhist thought, Theravada Buddhism prevails in the southern regions of Asia, chiefly in such countries as Sri Lanka, Burma, Thailand, Laos, and Kampuchea. More conservative than its northern counterpart, MAHAYANA BUDDHISM, Theravada preserved the ancient Pali canon. In the third century B.C., after the reign of ▶Asoka, Theravada began to spread as far as Sri Lanka, where it further divided into subgroups.

HISTORY

(See buddhism.)

TEACHINGS

The doctrines of Theravada are extremely complex, and the language technical and involved. The basic philosophy is that the ▶*arhat* attains ▶enlightenment through exerting himself toward that end. One must become a monk to attain enlightenment, unlike the more relaxed doctrine of Mahayana, where laypersons can achieve enlightenment in this life. Theravada Buddhists pay homage to the Buddha alone, while Mahayana Buddhists worship a plurality of ▶*bodhisattvas*.

To be born human is considered a gift because the ▶Buddha himself was born human. Free choice determines one's good or bad ▶karma. To pursue the good eventually leads to the attainment of Buddha-hood.

There are four stages in Theravada Buddhism. (1) The first is the beginning of the process, at which time the devotee is faced with pursuing one of two paths—devotion or intellectual discipline. Rebirth becomes less a possibility once this first step has been taken; (2) The second is being reborn only one more time. (3) Next is freedom from rebirth. (4) Finally, one becomes an arhat and achieves total enlightenment.

Religious movements throughout history have tended to become fragmented in time. This is equally true of Theravada and Mahayana Buddhism. But the essence of Buddhism is not lost in its schools and hundreds of sects. Both Theravadins and Mahayanins revere the Buddha immensely and seek to follow his teachings. The former, however, bring a more conservative understanding to the matter. It is frequently referred to as the "lesser vehicle" because of its restrictions on the laity and its more narrow focus on the Buddha rather than on other deities.

The official texts of Theravada Buddhism are the ▸*Tripitaka* and numerous commentaries on the same. Independent writers have also sprung up, invaluable in their contributions to philosophy and literature in India.

CONCLUSION

The Therevada tradition is the only surviving school from what is called the Hinayana tradition in Buddhism. The reader should consult the articles on Buddhism and Mahayana Buddhism in this volume for a fuller comparison and information.

ADDITIONAL INFORMATION_____

Organizations

The International Meditation Centers work as loci to unite Therevada Buddhists.

Websites

www.webcom.com/~incuk/welcome.html;
  www.buddhanet.net/1–thera.htm

Sacred Texts

The Sutra Pitake; The Vinaya Pitaka, Abhidharma Pitaka.

Statistics

123,600,000 worldwide, approximately 38 percent of all Buddhists.

TRANSCENDENTAL MEDITATION (TM)

Transcendental Meditation is an offshoot of HINDUISM, the great parent of Eastern religions. Much of its philosophy and many of its concepts come from its progenitor. TM has been especially tailored by its founder, Maharishi Mahesh ▸Yogi, to fit into the American lifestyle. Maharishi has replaced much of its religious terminology with psychological nomenclature and emphasized the pragmatic concern for immediate results. TM is also part of the human potential movement (see NEW AGE MOVEMENT).

HISTORY

Maharishi Yogi was born in 1911 in Jabalpur in northern India, with the name of Mahesh Brasad ▸Warma. He attended Allahabad University and successfully completed a degree in physics, graduating in 1942. Shortly after graduation, he met Swami Brahmananda Saraswati, Jagadguru, Bhagovan Shankaracharya, otherwise known as ▸Guru ▸Dev. Guru Dev had become an ▸avatar under the teachings of Swami Krishanand Saraswati. For the next decade Maharishi attached himself to the sage and soon became his mentor's most prized pupil. In 1953 Guru Dev died, however, and Maharishi retreated to a cave in the Himalayan mountains for two years. During this time he assimilated the knowledge that Guru Dev had imparted to him. These teachings became the fundamentals of TM.

Maharishi brought his philosophy to America in 1958 and began teaching in Los Angeles. The movement made little progress during the next decade and operated under the name of the Spiritual Regeneration Movement. In the late 1960s, however, things changed drastically. Great rips in the fabric of American society occurred during this turbulent decade. The younger generation cried out against all forms of institutional authority and organizational structure. The moment was ripe for Maharishi, who stepped in at an opportune time bearing a message of peace, love, and serenity without all the trappings of "the establishment."

The growth of Maharishi's following was rapid. Even the Beatles followed him for a period of time until they arrived at the conclusion that the guru was a fraud. John Lennon called him "a lecherous womanizer." After the Beatles lost faith in Maharishi, many followers dropped away as well in the early 1970s.

Maharishi returned to India, acknowledging defeat. But eventually he decided to make another attempt. He changed his strategy, omitting from the movement's vocabulary all religious terminology and replacing it with the language of psychology. A new name was adopted for his teachings—the ▸Science of Creative Intelligence.

The change of strategy immediately proved successful. Great numbers of people signed up for sessions in TM, and Maharishi was reportedly taking in over twenty million dollars yearly during the mid–1970s, with over one thousand people per month joining, chiefly college students who received discount rates.

Maharishi proclaimed 1975 as the year that began the age of "enlightenment." The goal was that if just one percent of the population of each city in the world would practice TM, the world's major problems—hunger, crime, drugs, and so on—would begin to disappear.

In 1977 trouble arose again for Maharishi, for the New Jersey Federal Court ruled that SCI/TM was a religion and was therefore banned from being taught in New Jersey public schools. Other states followed suit, and TM was once again generally regarded as being a religion, despite the movement's fervent and oft-repeated claim that it is not.

In 1984 thousands of practitioners gathered at Maharishi International University in Fairfield, Iowa, for a conference titled "Taste of Utopia." The goal was to enact a global meditational effort in order to solve some of the world's major problems through a practice

Maharishi Yogi, the founder of TM.
© Bettmann/CORBIS

called "positivity." Some seven thousand ▸*siddhas* attended the conference, sitting in lotus-like positions, engaging in intense meditation, and hopping. In 1988 Maharishi launched his "Master Plan to Create Heaven on Earth." His ambition was to bring world peace through a proposal for total reconstruction of the world.

In 1991 Yogi acquired forty-four million acres of land in Zambia. President Kenneth Kaunda invited opposition from his political opponents as a result. in the early 1990s the Holland office of TM launched a campaign called "American City Project," which was a

plea to mayors and citizens to participate in a program to clean up the cities of crime and disease. The program was based on the Unified Field of Natural Law as expounded by Dr. John Hagelin. The Maharishi used the term "natural law" as an identification word for TM's newly proposed program.

Because of continued attacks from a hostile media and a growing skepticism expressed by the scientific community, Maharishi has continually made alterations to shield the movement. However, though the late 1970s saw a rapid decline in interest in TM, particularly in America, Maharishi continues his mission and the optimistic vision that peace and harmony will prevail on the earth someday.

ORGANIZATION

Many organizations have grown out of TM. Maharishi founded a "university," formerly called Maharishi International University (MIU) but now Maharishi University of Management (MUM), located in Fairfield, Iowa. He is also opening up what are called Maharishi Vedic universities and Maharishi Ayur-Veda universities. The American Meditation Society, the American Foundation for Creative Intelligence, the Student International Meditation Society, Maharishi European Research University, an Institute for Fitness and Athletic Excellence, and several other newer organizations exist. In addition, Maharishi has founded meditation centers in cities around the world. He himself controls all of the organizational arms from his headquarters in Seelisberg, Switzerland.

TM is practiced in instruction centers. In 2000 there were reported to be 1,200 instruction centers in 137 countries, with 135 centers in the United States. Classes can be taken at the Maharishi Open University and can be registered for online.

TEACHINGS

There is no doubt that regardless of any declarations of immunity from religion, Hinduism provides the foundation on which TM has erected itself. The categories and thought patterns are expressly derived from its parent.

Maharishi had originally taught TM in religious categories and language. What follows here is a brief review of those teachings. Following this is a summary review of modern TM and its changes in articulation and language.

Original Transcendental Meditation

The Maharishi taught that the principles of TM were based on the Hindu concept of monistic ▸*pantheism.*

The goal for the initiate of TM was to achieve a oneness with ♦Brahman, the impersonal creative principle in the Hindu literature.

The initiate was (and still is) given a personal ♦mantra, which the initiate repeats over and over again while meditating. To reach the goal of oneness, the individual sought to transcend the first three "stages of consciousness," as Maharishi called them. They were the stages of (1) dreamless sleep consciousness, (2) dream consciousness, and (3) wake consciousness. All people live through these three stages in their lives. But TM promises that the practitioner will transcend these initial planes of existence. Four remaining stages of consciousness are available and must be surmounted to attain oneness with Brahman: (4) transcendental or "bliss" consciousness, (5) cosmic consciousness, (6) God-consciousness, and finally (7) unity consciousness. When one achieves unity consciousness, one has achieved total oneness with God, is at peace with oneself, and has been freed from the laws of ♦karma.

In terms of technique, Maharishi taught that the initiate to TM was to sit in a prescribed position. The key is the personal mantra that each individual is given on payment of the required fee. The mantra will become the sole vehicle by which he or she will be transported into the deeper levels of cosmic consciousness. No other cognitive process was required. One need only reflect on one's mantra while sitting for a period of twenty minutes, twice daily, once in the morning and once at night, but before eating and sleeping.

Reorganized Teachings of TM—the Science of Creative Intelligence

The goal of TM is "to create a perfect world as soon as possible problem-free, perfect life for every individual and every nation."[2] This can be done through learning to transcend one's physical boundaries to become one with "creative force." This creative force is universal as well as personal.

Learning proper meditation techniques can result in stress reduction, lower blood pressure, a lower recidivism rate among criminals released back to society, and the like. Its meditation techniques are described as "natural" and "effortless."

The process of learning meditation comes from following several relatively easy steps. Two free lectures are offered as the first step in getting involved in the process. The "client" is then given a mantra, just as in the older form of TM. One is then free to practice the techniques and is under no obligation to return for further instruction unless desired. On one of the websites, the steps, the subject matter, and the time required are listed. We list them here so that the reader can see the obvious changes in nomenclature in the modern version of TM.[3]

CHRISTIANITY and TM contrast significantly with each other. Many of the differences between them are parallel to the contrasts between Hinduism and Christianity, as can be expected. A Christian response to the original teachings of TM are here offered, followed by a response to the modern changes.

1. Introductory lecture	A vision of all possibilities through the TM program	1 hour and 30 minutes
2. Preparatory lecture	The mechanics and origin of the TM technique	1 hour and 30 minutes
3. Personal interview	Interview with a qualified teacher of the TM program	10 minutes
4. Personal instruction	Learning the TM technique	2 hours
5. Verification and validation of experiences	Verifying the correctness of the practice and further instruction	2 hours
6. Verification and validation of experiences	Understanding the mechanics of the TM technique from personal experiences	2 hours
7. Verification and validation of experiences	Understanding the mechanics of the development of higher states of consciousness	2 hours[4]

God

TM is essentially pantheistic, as is Hinduism. God is one with the universe. TM also embraces the Hindu trinity. God is manifested as ▸*Brahman,* ▸*Vishnu, and* ▸*Shiva.*[5] Christianity, while embracing the concept that God is immanent in creation, also teaches that God is transcendent. Christianity confesses that God is manifested in three persons: Father, Son, and Holy Spirit. Both ▸immanence and ▸transcendence are included in each of the divine persons. According to the Apostles' Creed, God is "Father," yet he is also "Almighty, maker of heaven and earth" (Appendix 1). Creator and creation are sharply distinguished from each other. The second person of the ▸Trinity, Jesus Christ, became incarnate (immanence) in human form. Yet "he ascended into heaven" (transcendence). Similarly, the Holy Spirit is poured out on the church (immanence), yet "proceeds from the Father and the Son" (transcendence) (Nicene Creed, Appendix 1).

Salvation

Salvation in TM is escape from rebirth. One achieves salvation when one is released from the law of karma and thus is able to enter into union with creative intelligence. This is achieved through meditation and repeated recitation of one's personal mantra.

According to Christianity, salvation is based on the person and work of Jesus Christ, who was "crucified, died and was buried.... The third day he rose again from the dead" (Apostles' Creed). In this way one is released from the grip of sin and active rebellion against God. For TM, the human predicament is not so much one of sin for which forgiveness need be provided, as it is one of ignorance for which knowledge need be provided. This divine knowledge (salvation) comes through meditation, observing the teachings of Maharishi, faithful recitation of one's personal mantra, and passing through the seven stages.

Authority

Devotees of TM observe the teachings of Maharishi and also read the ▸Vedic scriptures and the ▸*Bhagavad Gita.* Maharishi has himself authored a number of books and pamphlets.[6]

Concerning the changes made in TM in recent years, Maharishi has insisted that his teachings are based on scientific principles and therefore are not religious in nature. This has been difficult to validate since challenges to the scientific nature of his claims have been offered from the scientific community itself. Moreover, even in recasting the religion with scientific language,

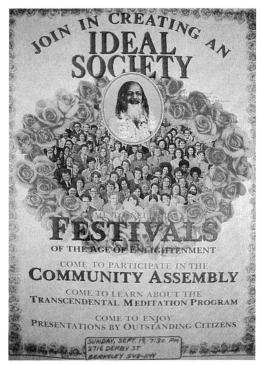

A poster announcing a festival to help create an ideal society through TM.
Courtesy Spiritual Counterfeit Project

Hindu references are still utilized. For example, at the two free lectures, inquirers listen to a Hindu prayer, are given mantras, and learn to meditate.

CONCLUSION

The official website offers the seven-step guide to learning to meditate, and Maharishi continues to lecture and tour throughout the world. His critics abound, particularly those who have left the movement and who have set up numerous websites in order to expose what they claim are the fraudulent foundations on which TM is based.

An important and scholarly assessment of TM comes from sociologist William S. Bainbridge, who concludes that TM presents a way to introduce a simplified (and therefore accessible) form of Hinduism to the West. In order to market itself to the nonreligious, it has simply taken on language that sounds more scientific.[7] In the twenty-first century the leaders in the movement continue to insist that TM is not a religion and that TM is based on scientific principles validated by scientific studies. But TM's foundations are clearly that of Hinduism.

ADDITIONAL INFORMATION_____

Headquarters

World Plan Executive Council, 1015 Gayley Ave., Los Angeles, CA 90024.

Websites

www.tm.org; www.mum.edu/tm_research/tm_charts/welcome.html

http://www.tm.org/main_pages/maharishi.html

Sacred Text

The Hindu sacred texts: *Rig Veda* and the *Bhagavad Gita* are referred to but are not regarded as "sacred" to TM.

Statistics

Five million people practice TM worldwide according to the official website, with 1.5 million Americans having taken Maharishi's courses.

Notes

[1] John W. Kennedy, "Field of TM Dreams," *Christianity Today* (Jan. 8, 2001), 74.

[2] *http://www.mou.org/mou/overview/index.html*

[3] *http://www.maharishi.org/tm/learn_tm.html*

[4] From the webpage *www.religiousmovements.lib.virginia.edu/nrms/tm.html.*

[5] See HINDUISM.

[6] See especially Yogi's books titled *The Science of Being and Art of Living* (1968) and *Maharishi Mahesh Yogi on the "Bhagavad Gita"* (1967).

[7] William Sims Bainbridge, *The Sociology of Religious Movements* (New York and London: Routledge, 1997), 187–88.

TWELVE TRIBES

The countercultural movement of the 1960s saw the advent of numerous autonomous ▸sects and ▸cults. The Twelve Tribes are one such group that arose out of the ranks of CHRISTIANITY. Relatively small sects and cults achieve some degree of notoriety and media attention when controversial issues arise. Such is the case with the Twelve Tribes (see also BRANCH DAVIDIANS and HEAVEN'S GATE).

HISTORY

The Twelve Tribes was founded by Elbert Eugene Spriggs (b. 1937). Spriggs came from a troubled background and was in many ways affected by the turbulence of the 1960s and 1970s. In his twenties he became part of the Jesus People movement in California and in 1970 became a "born again" Christian. He started working with homeless people and traveled extensively, witnessing to his faith. In 1972, he married Marsha Ann Duvall. The couple moved to Tennessee and began ministry in Chattanooga. Spriggs became a member of a local Presbyterian church, where he began a teen ministry called the "Light Brigade."

Because the mainline churches of the area did not look favorably on his ministry to disenfranchised youth, he became disillusioned and came to the conclusion that Christianity was not being lived authentically in organized denominations. He broke away and formed a home-based church called the Vine Community Church. Spriggs was attempting to capture the idea of the church as a community of believers who live and work together. Consequently, the group started business enterprises that served as means of support for the Vine community. They started a chain of restaurants in several southern states called "Yellow Deli's."

The group began to experience persecution from the media, universities, and cult awareness groups. Spriggs then moved the community to Island Pond, Vermont, in 1977, where they adopted the name "Northeast Kingdom Community Church." Here this group embraced the notion that they were the true restoration of the New Testament church.[1] They resumed their practice of engaging in business for means of support, beginning a candle business, a futon store, and a food store called Common Sense Wholesome Food Store and Restaurant. But all was not well in Vermont either. Local residents, pastors, and churches protested the arrival of the group as disturbing to the serenity of the area. They accused the group of teaching false doctrine.

The Vermont group did, however, settle in and adopted a common way of life, simple clothing styles, and communal living and eating. In the last decade, the community spread to other areas in New England, New York, Colorado, Missouri, as well as north to Canada and abroad to Spain, France, Germany, England, and several South American countries and Australia. The group(s) adopted the name Twelve Tribes with the specific purpose of emulating the Old Testament model of the twelve tribes of Israel.

In the 1980s controversy broke out when charges of extreme child abuse were leveled. In one instance, a mother was charged with beating a thirteen-year-old child with a wooden paddle for seven hours. Charges in that case were dropped. Several other cases were made public. On June 22, 1984, ninety state troopers and fifty social workers invaded the Island Pond community. A total of 112 children were removed.[2] Later, a judge found no evidence that the children were being abused.

Spokespersons for the Twelve Tribes claimed that the charges were based on false accusations by enemies of the group and by a secular society that had grown intolerant of biblical injunctions that call for disciplining children. In the 1990s these charges continued to surface. One anticult organization in particular, The New England Institute for Religious Research, led by Robert Pardon, has actively sought to expose and provide information regarding the group's teachings and practices around the issue of child abuse.

One of the sadder stories that surfaced involved one ex-member, Juan Mattatall. Mattatall was awarded custody of his five children after charges that his wife had beaten them. He then moved to Florida and never allowed the children to have contact with their mother. But while they were living in orphanages and under foster care, Mattatall was charged with pedophilia. In April 1990, Mattatall's mother shot and killed her son and then committed suicide. This is an extreme case that caused much grief and perhaps was instrumental in bringing unwarranted accusations against the group.

One apologist for the group, Jean Swatko, has been a prominent apologist for the Twelve Tribes, defending them against various attacks. Swatko stated at one point: "Religious freedom is jeopardized when governments rely upon the mere subjective opinions of anti-religious zealots as true, and act upon them."[3] In April, 2001, allegations were made that at their Common Sense Farm in Cambridge, New York, and in other locations in the state the Twelve Tribes were violating child labor laws and were using children to work in the businesses run by the group. An article published in the *New York Post* claimed that Spriggs was a racist as well as being abusive to children.[4] The state made plans to send officials to visit five sites run by the group. The group strongly protested that it was practicing unlawful child labor. Members claimed that the children were simply assisting their parents, were not working under filthy or adverse conditions, and were not denying their children an education, and they insisted it is not wrong for a child to spend time with their parents.[5] A fine of one thousand dollars was levied and the case (at the time of this writing) is under appeal.

ORGANIZATION

The various Twelve Tribes communities practice communal living. Worship and service are one and the same. They divide themselves into households, clans, and tribes, but share all possessions. They describe themselves as a culture unto themselves apart from the world.

TEACHINGS

The central focus of the Twelve Tribes' doctrine is the hope for the return of Jesus, whom they refer to by the Hebrew name Yashua. The purpose for Yashua's return is to rescue his true people, the Twelve Tribes communities, and bring vengeance on all who disobey God's commands. The communities practice Old Testament dietary laws and observe the Saturday Sabbath. Other beliefs include those commonly held by Protestant evangelicals, such as the Trinity, the inspiration and authority of the Bible, and the need to live a holy life through the power of the Holy Spirit. The Twelve Tribes also emphasize the importance of community. While critics conclude that this is a hangover from the subculture of the 1960s, no one can deny that building a close-knit community around the teachings of Christ describes the church in New Testament times (Acts 2:41–42).

A response from traditional orthodox Christianity is that the Twelve Tribes is a restorationist group that attempts to reconstruct the New Testament church rather than reform it.

Second, the Twelve Tribes community is a millennial group, believing in the literal thousand-year reign of Yashua on earth. The traditional understanding of the end of the world before the nineteenth century was amillennialism, meaning that Christ will return at the end of time and bring all things to completion.

Third, the name "Yashua" is used to the exclusion of the traditional English rendering—"Jesus." The transliteration from the Hebrew is certainly permissible. Orthodoxy would not place a legal insistence on one usage over another, but the common name in English is the one used most frequently.

CONCLUSION

The Twelve Tribes has continued into the twenty-first century as a holdover from the countercultural movement of the 1960s. The attack by the media, public, and conventional religious groups has presented yet another instance of the reality of the hostility that exists when a group operates outside the parameters of societal norms. The government attack on the Branch Davidians in 1993 is perhaps the most well-known example. Questions are raised, however, regarding legality, government involvement in the freedom of religion, and the fairness of objective investigation by the media.

ADDITIONAL INFORMATION

Headquarters
Each community serves as its own headquarters.

Website
www.twelvetribes.com

Sacred Text
The Bible

Publications
Common Sense Sentry; Common Sense Chronicle (both monthly).

Membership
Approximately 2,500 in 17 communities in North America; 8 communities in Europe; 3 in South America; 1 in Australia

Notes
[1] For an assessment of ʼrestorationism, the reader should consult the article on the INTERNATIONAL CHURCHES OF CHRIST.
[2] *http://religiousmovements.lib.virginia.edu/nrms/tribes/html*
[3] Ibid.
[4] Kenneth Lovett, "State Takes Close Look at Cult Kids in Factories," *New York Post* (April 12, 2001).
[5] Associated Press article, "Twelve Tribes Sect Denies Charges of Child Labor Abuse" (April 13, 2001).

UNIFICATION CHURCH; THE HOLY SPIRIT ASSOCIATION FOR THE UNIFICATION OF WORLD CHRISTIANITY

Followers of this religious group are commonly called "Moonies." The development of this twentieth-century movement was rapid and most popular in the 1970s and 1980s. Like many other ʼcults and ʼsects in this volume, the Unification Church grew out of CHRISTIANITY.

HISTORY

The Unification Church was founded by Sun Myung ʼMoon, who was born in 1920 in Pyungan Buk-do, a province in what has since become North Korea. His name at birth was Yong Myung Moon, or literally "Shining Dragon Moon." He was raised in a Presbyterian family and exhibited ʼclairvoyant tendencies during his formative years. In 1936, at age sixteen, Moon claimed to have received a vision in which Jesus Christ appeared to him, instructing him to complete the task that Jesus had left undone. That is to say, Jesus had "spiritually" redeemed humankind, but his work was cut short when he was arrested and crucified. The task of "physical" redemption remained unfulfilled.

In 1944 Moon married the first of several wives. At this time he changed his first name, "Yong," to "Sun," his whole name now literally rendered as being "Sun Shining Moon." Presbyterianism did not appeal to him. Though he did not leave the church (he was excommunicated in the 1950s), he dabbled with an eccentric Pentecostal group that taught him that Korea was the new promised land of the ʼBible and that the future ʼMessiah would be Korean-born. Moon probably believed himself to be that Messiah, based on his vision a decade earlier coupled with the teachings of the group.

One year after his first marriage, Moon began what would become the Unification Church. He was soon imprisoned but claimed that it was due to his stand against communism. Other sources indicate, however, that he was accused of charges of immorality (bigamy) and the practice of capitalism in

Rev. Sun Myung Moon, the self-proclaimed leader of the Unification church, whose devotees are commonly known as "Moonies."
Courtesy George A. Mather

Unification Church publications.
Courtesy George A. Mather

Marxist North Korea. After his release he moved to South Korea, where he resumed his teaching. In 1954 Moon founded the Holy Spirit Association for the Unification of World Christianity in Seoul. That same year he was also divorced from his first wife, and in 1955 he was again arrested on charges of immorality and draft evasion. The charges were not upheld, however, and he was again released after three months.

At this time, Moon began to write the work that would become the chief text of the Unification Church, his ▶*Divine Principle*. Actually written by a follower of Moon, it reinterprets the Bible through Taoist (see TAO-ISM) philosophy. Everything is interpreted in dualistic terms, including God, humanity's fall, mission, and salvation. It proclaims a new messiah (dualism, two messiahs); the future one is to complete Jesus' unfinished work. Moon's followers have always read him into this messianic role, but he waited until March 23, 2004, to make this proclamation concerning himself.

Business success and a strong stand against communism brought Moon fame and fortune, particularly in the West. In 1972 he announced that America was chosen as the next area of his concentrated mission activity. He purchased an estate in upstate New York, valued at $850,000. The church spent much money revitalizing failing capitalist ventures; this, of course, received favorable publicity.

Another event that brought publicity to Moon and the Unification Church was a single wedding service he performed in 1982 at Madison Square Garden, where over two thousand couples were united at once. The couples had been matched by Moon just one month before the wedding. Many group marriages have taken place in the church since that time. In 1988 Moon performed a mass wedding ceremony that broke his 1982 record. The *Toronto Star* (Oct. 31, 1988) reported that Moon officiated at the wedding of 6,500 couples.

Moon's greatest evangelistic success has been with young people who, leaving home and going off to college, often face loneliness and insecurity. They are approached by friendly proselytizers who offer them the needed security during this vulnerable time. The prospective convert is invited to an initial visit in a home where other followers are present to offer love and compassion. After this follows a weekend retreat where the candidate is showered with more special attention, lectures, singing, and prayer. The initiate's resistance is steadily broken down. The showering of Unification teachings, coupled with the emotional attachments acquired over the many hours of training, are effective in winning the individual over as a full-fledged convert.

In the early 1980s Moon found himself plagued by charges of tax evasion. Specifically, the leader of the Unification Church was accused of failing to include approximately $112,000 in his income tax return. Additionally, Moon was found guilty of "diverting" these funds. Moon's conviction and thirteen-month imprisonment beginning in July of 1984 brought a storm of protest from religious communities and leaders around the nation, centered around the issue of government imposition on religious freedom. Critics countered that the protesting churches had nothing to fear, since his trial was base entirely on the question of tax evasion. After his release from the federal prison in Danbury, Connecticut, in August 1985, a religious-freedom press conference was held in Washington, D.C. In attendance were many prominent religious leaders, who expressed concern over the precedent set by Moon's imprisonment.

Growth in the Unification Church has subsided in recent years, perhaps a result of unfavorable publicity from the media. The U.S. membership in 2002 is estimated to be at about 200,000. The U.S. Immigration and Naturalization Service has attempted to have Moon deported, based on charges of fraud regarding his wife's application for permanent resident-alien status.

Although the Unification Church is not growing with the fury it did in the 1970s, Moon's influence has continued to be effective on the political scene, particularly with the conservative right. One of the new political organizations that has been exerting powerful influence is the American Freedom Coalition (AFC), headed by Moon's chief lieutenant Col. Bo Hi Pak. The agenda of the AFC is to unite conservative groups in order to control and influence a conservative party platform. On January 1, 1987, Moon made the rather extravagant, if not frightening, boast that he wished to expand the church's political influence, his aim being "the natural subjugation of the American government and population."[1]

During the 1990s and into the twenty-first century, Moon has vigorously spent money in order to gain support, particularly from the conservative right, both politically and religiously. Some conservative evangelicals have received monies and support from the Unification Church. The interesting irony lies in the fact that they receive such support from an organization that teaches doctrines completely contrary to those of ᵇevangelicalism and ᵇfundamentalism.

ORGANIZATION

The Unification Church continues to maintain a massive array of organizations in the United States. Some of the prominent organizations include:

A. Religious Organizations
  1. Holy Spirit Association for the Unification of World Christianity (HSA-UWC).
  2. Washington Institute for Values in Public Policy
  3. International Religious Foundation
  4. International Clergy and Laity in Shared Action
  5. International Cultural Foundation
B. Political Groups
  1. International Federation for Victory Over Communism
  2. CAUSA—USA
  3. CAUSA—International
  4. American Constitution Committee
C. Businesses
  1. One Up Enterprises
  2. International Oceanic Enterprises
  3. News World Communications
  4. World Media Association
  5. Washington Times Co.
  6. Free Press International

These are the more significant organizations tied to the Unification Church. For a complete listing plus a description of each, see the Unification publication titled *People Serving People*, HSA-UWC, or the organization's official website (below).

TEACHINGS

Moon claims that the goal of the Unification Church was, and still is, to unite all of Christendom as well as all the people of the world under God. The International One World Crusade, or IOWC, sponsors rallies throughout the world in an effort to unite churches.

Moon has compiled a nine-hundred-page volume in which he shows the points of harmony and convergence between the religions of the world.

Moon divides history into three theological dispensations: the Old Testament age, the New Testament age, and the "Completed Age." The last mentioned is the time when humanity will become fully redeemed. The *Divine Principle* provides the revelatory information of this period.

The fundamental theology of the Unification Church centers around the doctrine of physical redemption. As stated above, Moon teaches that Jesus Christ finished only half of his mission and was cut short by an unfortunate crucifixion. Jesus failed to marry and therefore did not establish the "perfect marriage" intended to supplant the imperfect marriage between the first Adam and Eve. Since this work was left incomplete by the second Adam, Jesus Christ, a ᵇthird Adam is needed to complete this mission.

The Unification Church is reluctant to declare publicly that Sun Myung Moon is the third Adam. There are members, however, who do so quite openly. Moon's fourth wife, Hak Ja Kan, was declared to be the "perfect mother" after the first three Eves proved to be failures.

The doctrines of the Unification Church are as follows:

God

"There is one living, eternal, and true God, a person beyond space and time, who possesses perfect intellect, emotion, and will, whose deepest nature is heart and love . . . the source of truth, beauty, and goodness." The doctrine of God is interpreted through the lens of Taoism and therefore is composed of "positivity" and "negativity," or masculinity and femininity, respectively.[2] God is known through general revelation of himself in nature as well as in the life of Jesus Christ.

The Unification Church teaches, however, that God is not Trinitarian: Father, Son, and Holy Spirit. "Many Christians seem to worship three Gods: Father, Son, and Holy Spirit. . . . Christians are not ᵇmonotheists in faith and practice."[3]

The Christian church has often been accused of worshiping more than one God by ISLAM, JUDAISM, JEHOVAH'S WITNESSES, and a host of cults and sects. The early church, accused of this by the Arians, responded definitively in the Athanasian Creed:

> And the catholic faith is this, that we worship one God in three persons and three persons in one God, neither confusing the persons nor dividing the substance. For there is one person of the Father, another

of the Son, and another of the Holy Spirit. But the Godhead of the Father, of the Son, and of the Holy Spirit is all one: the glory equal, the majesty coeternal. . . . So the Father is God, the Son is God, and the Holy Spirit is God. And yet they are not three Gods but one God. (Appendix 1)

God, in Moon's theology, is a "perpetual, self-generating energy," the uncaused first cause of all that exists, but also the inner character of all that exists. God has both masculine and feminine characteristics that are completely in harmony with one another and with the universe. After all, human beings as well as all living things within creation exist in a bipolar coexistence and mutual sharing relationship.

The creation reflects the physical aspect of God's nature and creative energy. More will be discussed on this below with respect to the ▸incarnation.

Jesus Christ

Moon taught that Jesus Christ was not God incarnate, and he blames Christianity for making Jesus into God after his crucifixion. Moon sees all men with equal divine qualities. But Jesus differed from all other human beings in that he was without original sin. He was raised spiritually in his resurrection, but his body remained in the grave.

> The chosen nation rejected him and he went to the cross without having built the kingdom of God on earth. Yet Jesus was victorious over ▸Satan through his crucifixion and resurrection and thus made possible spiritual salvation for those who are reborn through him and the Holy Spirit.[4]

Jesus, in other words, accomplished spiritual redemption for the world, but physical redemption was cut short by an untimely crucifixion. Furthermore, Jesus failed to marry during his earthly ministry and therefore failed to right the wrongs of the first Adam and Eve. Only the third Adam together with the new Eve will bring about physical redemption.

This physical redemption plays a key role in the Unification Church's concept of the incarnation. Young Oon Kim expresses the idea as follows:

> Why did God seek to be incarnate? He wanted to participate fully in human life, to feel the full range of our experiences. God sought for Himself what it means to live at a physical level. Thus we could say that God created man to be his body.[5]

The emphasis that ▸orthodox Christianity places on the incarnation is strictly ▸soteriological in contrast to Moon's more psycho-spiritual orientation. The basic difference lies in a fundamental distinction that Moon makes between the physical and spiritual dimensions of life, a distinction that in the end Christianity does not make. The concept that Jesus' body remained in the grave while his spirit arose to heaven was taught in the second and third centuries by gnostic (*see* ▸gnosticism) dualists (*see* ▸dualism). The Council of Chalcedon in A.D. 451 reaffirmed that Christ's two natures are united "unconfusedly, unchangeably, indivisibly, and inseparably." It is the personal union of the two natures of Christ that the incarnation expresses. Jesus rose bodily and spiritually to redeem the human race both bodily and spiritually. The need for a third Adam simply does not exist, at least within the pale of orthodoxy.

Another point should be raised here concerning ▸Christology. Because Moon teaches that the physical or temporal kingdom was not realized by Christ, there arose a need in the apostolic age to "explain" why Jesus died prematurely. For Moon, it was the creative genius of Paul that "transformed his master's shameful death into a glorious one and his failed mission into a victory."[6] According to the Unification Church, Paul preached the person of Jesus, while Jesus preached, not himself, but the kingdom of God.

This is the same view held by Jehovah's Witnesses and many non-Trinitarian groups. The basic question that arises, therefore, is whether there is a diversity between the message of Jesus and the church, or between the Gospels and the New Testament letters. We cannot delve into all the literature devoted to this subject. James Dunn's *Unity and Diversity in the New Testament* (1977) is representative of the general position some scholars take in seeing varying strands of theology in the New Testament. But Brevard Childs points out what he believes are the problems with such an approach in his *New Testament as Canon—An Introduction* (1984). He argues that modern scholarship has failed to place the theology of the early church within its canonical context. In other words, the issue of diversity was not an issue for the church of the first four centuries. It is a modern problem superimposed on the church, forcing it to ask questions of itself that were never asked at the time.

Suffice it to say that regardless of where the battle lines are drawn on this issue, it is certain that the writers of the New Testament were not aware of any diversities that would lead to contradictions in theological perspective. Luke, for example, vindicates Paul's "divergent" mission to the Gentiles at the church's first council (Acts 15). Jewish Christianity was not perceived as being contradictory to the ministry to Gentiles, but merely different. The Gospel writers certainly perceived Jesus to be pointing to himself as the focus of the kingdom of God (John 2:19; 4:14).

Traditional Christianity never taught that Jesus failed in his mission. His suffering, death, and resurrection were crowning acts of God (Mark 8–10). The first Christian sermons recorded in Acts also defended the absolute necessity of Christ's suffering (Acts 3:18; 4:10ff.). The middle section of the Apostles' Creed summarizes the canonical impact of Jesus' life and mission on the church.

> [I believe] in Jesus Christ, his only Son, our Lord, who was conceived by the Holy Spirit, born of the virgin Mary, suffered under Pontius Pilate, was crucified, died and was buried. He descended into hell. The third day he rose again from the dead. He ascended into heaven and sits at the right hand of God the Father Almighty. From thence he will come to judge the living and the dead. (Appendix 1)

The central point of contrast between traditional Christianity and the Unification Church is Christological in nature. The third Adam concept is found nowhere within the Bible or in the confessional writings of the church. However, given Moon's insights, it is not difficult to perceive the origin of such a doctrine. Once the separation between spirit and flesh was made, it could flow logically from a creative mind.

Holy Spirit

For Moon, the Holy Spirit is the feminine aspect of God's dual nature and is the counterpart to the Father. For a family of children to exist, there must be a "true Father" and a "true Mother." The true Mother is the Holy Spirit, coming as the second Eve. She is the mother of the fallen children who are reborn. Because the Holy Spirit is essentially a female spirit, we cannot become the bride of Jesus unless we receive the Holy Spirit.[7]

The Holy Spirit is not, therefore, a person in the sense of being a distinct personality within the ʾTrinity. It is described as being an energy derived from God and pervading the soul. Other groups define the Holy Spirit in similar fashion. For example, Jehovah's Witnesses understand the Holy Spirit to be God's "active-force." Like God, the Holy Spirit is incorporeal and flows out from God like light rays from its source.

Like UNITARIANISM, Unification theologians insist that the Holy Spirit did not enjoy the privileged status of being the third member of a tripartite God in the primitive Christian communities. Some scholars are quick to agree.[8] J. N. D. Kelly argues contrariwise: "The juxtaposition of the Father and the Lord Jesus Christ as parallel realities and the collocation of the Father, the Son, and the Holy Spirit had become categories of Christian thinking long before the New Testament documents were written down."[9] The Christian church has always recognized the Holy Spirit as possessing all the qualities of personality that are ascribed both to God the Father and to God the Son, Jesus Christ. Jesus himself used the Trinitarian formulation "Father, Son, and Holy Spirit" (Matt. 28:19), as did the earliest Christian communities (Acts 5:3–4; 2 Cor. 13:14; Titus 2:13; 2 Peter 1:17).

Humanity

Humankind has a

> responsibility to fulfill three potential blessings: first, to grow to perfection so as to be one in heart, will, and action with God, having body and mind united together in perfect harmony; second, to be united to God as husband and wife and giving birth to sinless children ... establishing a sinless family and ultimately a sinless world; and third, to become benevolent masters of the created world.[10]

Moon also teaches that a human being is an "incarnate God." By contrast, Christianity teaches that a person is not only not God, but that, as a human, is neither perfect nor capable of attaining perfection in this life, whether married or unmarried.

According to Hebrews 2:6–8, humanity was created "lower than the angels." First, by being "created," the existence of the human race is ascribed to God alone: "I believe in God the Father Almighty, *maker* of heaven and earth ..." (Apostles' Creed, emphasis added). Second, the Christian doctrine of original sin as reflected in such passages as Psalm 51:5 and Romans 3:23, leaves no room for a notion of latent incarnate deity. The Christian is one who grows in grace and knowledge of the Lord Jesus Christ and through the Holy Spirit becomes more like Christ (the Christian doctrine of ʾsanctification). One does not achieve perfection in this life. This is reserved for eternity, where Christians put on immortality and live everlastingly with God with a body incorruptible.

Sin

In Moon's theology, Adam and Eve fell into an illicit and forbidden love. Their offspring were the product, therefore, of lustful fornication. By being born of the first Adam, humanity is born sinful. ♦Lucifer now took over the governing of earth, a role formerly held by humankind's true Parent, God the Father. Therefore, people oppose God and serve Lucifer, the usurper. God has been struggling to regain his world and his children.

There are similarities and noted differences between Unification teaching and orthodoxy on the doctrine of sin. Both concur in the point that Adam and Eve fell from grace. In the early church, particularly in the writings of second- and third-century church fathers Justin, Tatian, Irenaeus, Tertullian, and even Athanasius, sin was universally taught as active disobedience against the holy will of God. However, it was Augustine's concept of concupiscence—the doctrine that the propagation of a sinful human nature is passed on from the first couple to the whole of the human race from generation to generation—that became the doctrine of the orthodox tradition in the West. Moon teaches that the sin of Adam and Eve was eating from the forbidden fruit of the garden. But here Moon asserts that Adam and Eve were the first of a threefold series of blessings. This first blessing was called "Becoming Perfect"; the second, "Ideal Marriage"; and the third man's "Dominion over All of Creation."

While Christianity teaches that the Fall was the act of disobedience in eating of the forbidden fruit, Moon asserts that during the first stage of development, Eve was sexually seduced by Lucifer. This caused the "spiritual Fall," bringing Eve great shame, to which Adam then married Eve. Because this union was not supposed to happen until the Second Blessing, this resulted in their physical fall. This further resulted in failed blessings for them and the rest of the human race thereafter.[11]

Christianity teaches clearly that original sin is linked directly to the disobedience of Adam and Eve in eating the forbidden fruit. The first couple was given freedom of choice and chose to do that which God had forbidden. Like Unification teaching, Christianity maintains that the cause of sin is Lucifer, who is the "god of this age" (2 Cor. 4:4). But God is not locked in a cosmic dualistic struggle with Satan. God is not "struggling to regain his world." He already has by the vindication of Jesus Christ. It was God's will that Jesus be crucified in order that sin might be atoned for. The Almighty God does not share power with any other; therefore, all other forces are powerless against him. Lucifer's control of this world is permitted by the Almighty; eschatologically God has set a Day of Judgment when the devil's defeat will be accomplished once for all.

Hell

To Moon, because God is not the center of humanity's thought, ♦hell exists on earth. This "hell on earth will one day be transformed to the kingdom of heaven on earth."[12]

The Bible alludes to hell as being a place of eternal torment in the afterlife for the devil and his fallen angels (Rev. 20:13–15). The Apostles' Creed speaks of Jesus *descending* into hell, and the Athanasian Creed, again reflecting on the teachings of the Bible, says that all who do not "hold the catholic faith . . . will without doubt . . . perish eternally." More specifically, the conclusion of the Athanasian Creed tells us that "they that have done evil [will go] into everlasting fire." The Christian church has traditionally upheld the belief of this doctrine of hell; it will not undergo a genesis of transformation into the "kingdom of heaven on earth" as the *Divine Principle* states. Hell and heaven are separate entities and will remain so for eternity.

Salvation

In Moon's theology, salvation consists of two parts, spiritual and physical. Jesus accomplished the former, but the cross prevented the latter. If Jesus' life had not been cut short, he would have accomplished complete salvation. That was not the case, and therefore it remains the task of the third Adam.

The center of Moon's soteriology is the concept of the third Adam. Christianity knows of no such concept. All of salvation centers around the person and work of Jesus Christ as articulated ever so clearly in many verses of the New Testament and in the Christian creeds. Various forms of SPIRITISM enter Unification theology here, which not only fits with Moon's continued dabbling in the ♦occult, but is also borrowed from ancestral veneration popularized in his native Korea. Moon taught that the spirits of the deceased climb to higher levels by helping the living. This is why it is uncommon for members of the Unification Church to claim sightings of the deceased. In the end, Moon teaches a modified form of ♦Universalism, that is to say, that all will eventually climb out of the lower levels of departed spirits to become a comprising spirit within the form of God.

Bible

According to the Unification Church,

the Old and New Testament scriptures are a record of God's progressive revelation to humankind. The Bible is not the truth itself, but a textbook teaching truth, and its purpose is to bring us to Christ, who is himself the living truth. . . . Truth is unique, eternal, and unchanging, so any new message from God will be in conformity with the Bible and will only illuminate it more deeply. In these last days, God will speak anew in order that humanity may accomplish what is yet undone.[13]

The last statement is particularly at odds with the orthodox position on biblical ʼrevelation. It is not necessary for God to speak anew in the sense of bringing forth "new" or more relevant information for today. God has spoken definitively through the Holy Scriptures, the church, and the sacred "canon of faith." The Unification Church must, of necessity, deny this. Otherwise there would be no basis for introducing new concepts such as the third Adam doctrine or the *Divine Principle*.

End Times

To Moon, Jesus' second coming will occur as did the first: "A perfect man and woman will become the true spiritual parents of humankind."[14] Those who accept the perfect parents, obey them, and follow their example will be heirs to the kingdom of God. The day is now at hand.

The spiritual hope of the Christian church is different: "He will come again with glory to judge both the living and the dead" (Nicene Creed, Appendix 1). Jesus will return as Ruler, Judge, and Prince of Peace. Nowhere is there any reference to Jesus' return with a "perfect woman" to become, with her, true "spiritual parents." There is no example, no model, and certainly no obedience ascribed to any other than he whose kingdom shall have no end.

CONCLUSION

The Reverend Moon continues to perform mass weddings, and these remain at the center of much controversy, particularly in the West. Many of the couples that Moon pairs up have never previously met. In a culture where most people select their own mates, this is a foreign concept. It meets, however, with less resistance in those parts of the world where couples continue to be paired by families.

Publications of the Unification Church are voluminous. In the early 1990s the controversial cult leader has invested close to one billion dollars in the *Washington Times* in order to make the newspaper "an instrument to save America and the world."[15]

At the beginning of the twenty-first century the Unification Church is still actively involved in societal and world affairs. In June 2004, for example, Moon, at eighty-five years of age, was honored at a reception where he declared himself to be the messiah, was crowned, and delivered a lengthy speech in which he stated that he was "sent to earth to save the world's six billion people." Several legislators attending the gathering said that they were duped by the organizers of the event.[16]

ADDITIONAL INFORMATION

Headquarters
The Holy Spirit Association for the Unification of World Christianity, 4 W. 43rd St., New York, NY 10036.

Websites
www.unification.net; www.unification.org

Sacred Text
The Divine Principle

Publications
Family Federation News (online news via email); *Unification News; Washington Times; Insight on the News* (magazine); *New York City Tribune*; many writings of Moon and the organization itself

Statistics
200,000 members in the United States and 3 million worldwide.

Notes
[1] John Judis, "Rev. Moon's Rising Political Influence," *U.S. News and World Report* (March 27, 1989).
[2] Sun Myung Moon, *Divine Principle* (New York: Holy Spirit Association for the Unification of World Christianity, 1976), 24.
[3] Young Oon Kim, *Speeches on Unification Teaching* (Barrytown, NY, 1986), 4.
[4] Unification publication, *People Serving People*, 13.
[5] Young Oon Kim, *Speeches on Unification Teaching*, 9.
[6] Ibid., 3.
[7] Moon, *Divine Principle*, 78–80.
[8] Oscar Cullman, *The Earliest Christian Confessions* (London, 1949).
[9] J. N. D. Kelly, *Early Christian Creeds*, 3rd ed. (New York: Longman, 1972), 26.
[10] *People Serving People, 12.*
[11] *http://religiousmovements.lib.virginia.edu/nrms/unification2.html*
[12] Moon, *Divine Principle*, 111–12.
[13] *People Serving People, 13.*
[14] Ibid.
[15] "In Brief," *Christian Research Journal* (Summer, 1992), 34.
[16] "Lawmakers 'Duped' into Honoring Moon," *The Washington Post* (June 23, 2004).

UNITARIAN-UNIVERSALIST ASSOCIATION (UUA)

The Unitarian-Universalist Association developed out of two separate histories and is an important development within the intellectual and religious history of American CHRISTIANITY. In 1961 at what was known as the Boston Joint Assembly, ʼuniversalism and ʼunitarianism merged into a single movement. Though the ideas prevalent in each are similar, each developed somewhat independently of the other, and each has its own unique story. We relate these two stories separately and then bring them together.

HISTORY

Unitarianism as a theology had its roots in the anti-Trinitarian controversies of the first four centuries of the Christian church. It was called by various titles—ʼmonarchianism, ʼSabellianism, and ʼpartripassianism. In the sixteenth century it took on the name ʼSocinianism, after its leading proponent, F. P. Socinus, (1539–1604). With the onset of the ʼenlightenment in the eighteenth century, unitarianism attracted attention among certain of the rational supernaturalists and deists in England and on the Continent.

It was not until the close of the eighteenth century that unitarianism grew rapidly, not in Europe or England but in America, and specifically New England. Its leading exponents were James Freeman ʼClarke, William Ellery ʼChanning, and Ralph Waldo ʼEmerson. King's Chapel (Episcopalian) in Boston became the spawning ground for unitarian thought in 1785. The lectures of Emerson and the sermons of Channing, particularly his 1819 sermon "Unitarian Christianity," served as catalysts for this important intellectual movement in America. Unitarianism flourished for the most part in Boston. It was largely a reaction to the hardcore ʼCalvinism of Puritan New England. Later, unitarianism reacted against the revivalist theology of the Second Great Awakening.

Universalism, like unitarianism, enjoyed an early beginning in the history of ideas. It can be traced back to ʼZoroastrianism and the Eastern religions. It too has had various proponents through the centuries. Like unitarianism, universalism did not become popular in New England until the close of the eighteenth century. Again, Calvinism has often been seen as having, by way of reaction, prompted its development. However, while unitarianism appealed to the "genteel" intellectual community of Boston, universalism grew among the less urbane, more rural country dwellers. It was

especially the Calvinistic ideas of predestination, total depravity, and eternal damnation against which many reacted. In a land where one could exercise the Yankee spirit of "rugged individualism" and could experience the "bootstrap" success of Horatio Alger, an opportunistic and optimistic spirit clashed violently against the stern austerity of Puritan Calvinism. It received its main impetus from John ʼMurray in 1785 in Oxford, Massachusetts, where the theology of universalism developed into a denomination.

Both movements were largely restricted to New England. In a derisive way, the critics summed up unitarianism as constituting "the fatherhood of God, the brotherhood of man, and the neighborhood of Boston." To a large extent, this was true geographically. But it was only partially true with respect to theology. Unitarianism went through three distinct phases in its historical development. From 1800–1835, the leading thinkers still embraced a belief in the supernatural elements of the Christian religion. Andrews ʼNorton, referred to as being the "Pope of Unitarianism," vehemently defended Christianity against the attacks of its critics, particularly in the area of biblical studies.

The second period (roughly 1835–1885) demonstrated a much less conservative spirit. German idealistic philosophy had a great influence on the academic institutions of the eastern United States, chiefly Harvard. Ralph Waldo Emerson, in his famous *Divinity School Address* (1838), expounded the ideas of unitarianism prevalent during this second phase of development, namely, the freedom of the human soul, particularly the American soul, and the predominance of reason and its close relationship to the ʼoversoul of nature.

Hosea ʼBallou (1771–1852) is considered to be the "Father of American Universalism." He differed from Murray in his complete departure from Calvinism. It was Ballou who did much in a preliminary way to lay the groundwork on which both unitarianism and universalism were eventually united. The third period (1885 to the present) is marked by a thoroughgoing secularism within both movements, and it was in this final phase that they merged in 1961.

Involvement in various social causes, feminism, and lay leadership have characterized the frontal activities of the UUA during the past forty years. In 1987, at the convention held in Little Rock, Arkansas, support for AIDS sufferers was a large item on the agenda. Often their building is draped with a rainbow flag or a banner proclaiming it to be a "hate-free zone," particularly for gays. Other issues have included euthanasia and human rights to "shelter, personal dignity, and self-determination." The 2000 convention centered around racism and poverty and a call to eliminate both. A complete listing of the issues and conventions can be accessed online at the church's website (below). The UUA is typically nonevangelistic, but the diminishing number of young people in their churches caused a unified pro-evangelism effort in the year 2000 by the UUA executive board.

ORGANIZATION

The headquarters for the UUA is in Boston. A general assembly elects the officers, and the church is governed by a board of trustees. The various districts appoint district trustees; the general assembly elects at-large trustees. The general assembly meets annually at various locations throughout North America. The chief administrator is called the CEO or president. An executive vice-president is responsible for the daily operations of the UUA.

At the start of the twenty-first century, the UUA has initiated changes in its organizational structure to make the organization more community-oriented and interactive. The restructuring centers around being missions-driven. The mission itself is to strive toward social justice and the elimination of racism. A ministry and professional leadership department is responsible for the ordination of ministers of the UUA. The restructuring calls for the addition of many new departments as well. Their place in the UUA is clearly delineated on the UUA website.

TEACHINGS

In 1825 the American Unitarian Association was formed. Its emphasis on freedom naturally dictated against any creedal formulations. The same was true of universalism, although four declarations of faith were drawn up as summaries of the basic principles of the movement. In 1790, in Philadelphia, the first statement was drawn up basically retaining most of Calvinist 'orthodoxy. The Winchester Profession of 1803 declared that the Holy Spirit will "finally restore the whole family of mankind to holiness and happiness." Another statement issued in 1935 represents the last phase of development before the merger with unitarianism:

> The bond of fellowship in this Convention shall be a common purpose to do the will of God as Jesus revealed it and to cooperate in establishing the kingdom for which He lived and died.

To that end we avow our faith in God as Eternal and All-Conquering Love, in the spiritual leadership of Jesus, in the supreme worth of every human personality, in the authority of truth known or to be known, and in the power of men of good will and sacrificial spirit to overcome all evil and progressively establish the kingdom of God. Neither this nor any other statement shall be imposed as a creedal test, provided that the faith thus indicated be professed.[1]

In a finalized summary, the Universalist Church in America declared its express purpose to be "to promote harmony among adherents of all religious faiths, whether Christian or otherwise."

In 1961 the two movements united to form the Unitarian-Universalist Association (UUA). The newly formed association set forth its purpose in the following statement:

> The members of the Unitarian-Universalist Association, dedicated to the principles of a free faith, unite in seeking:
>
> 1. To strengthen one another in a free and disciplined search for truth as the foundation of our religious fellowship;
> 2. To cherish and spread the universal truth taught by the great prophets and teachers of humanity in every age and tradition, immemorially summarized in their essence as love to God and love to man;
> 3. To affirm, defend and promote the supreme worth of every human personality, the dignity of man, and the use of the democratic method in human relationships;
> 4. To implement our vision of one world by striving for a world community founded on ideals of brotherhood, justice and peace;
> 5. To serve the needs of member churches and fellowships, to organize new churches and fellowships, and to extend and strengthen liberal religion;
> 6. To encourage cooperation with men of good will of all faiths in every land.[2]

In 1985, the association again revised its statement of purpose, summarizing its ideals in the most liberal and open expression yet cited.

> The living tradition which we share draws from many sources:
>
> • Direct experience of that transcending mystery and wonder, affirmed in all cultures, which moves us to the renewal of the spirit and an openness to the forces which create and uphold life;

- Words and deeds of prophetic women and men which challenge us to confront powers and structures of evil with justice, compassion and transforming power of love;
- Wisdom from the world's religions which inspires us in our ethical and spiritual life;
- Jewish and Christian teachings which call us to respond to God's love by loving our neighbors as ourselves;
- Humanist teachings which counsel us to heed the guidance of reason and the results of science, and warn us against idolatries of the mind and spirit.

We, the member congregations of the Unitarian-Universalist Association, covenant to affirm and promote:

- The inherent worth and dignity of every person;
- Justice, equity and compassion in human relations;
- Acceptance of one another and encouragement to spiritual growth in our congregations;
- A free and responsible search for truth and meaning;
- The right of conscience and the use of the democratic process within our congregations and in society at large;
- The goal of world community with peace, liberty and justice for all;
- Respect for the interdependent web of all existence of which we are a part.[3]

The sharpest divergence between the UUA and traditional Christianity is in the former's reaction against the doctrine of the ▸Trinity. The traditional Trinitarian creeds are denounced and rejected. The unitarian attitude toward Jesus Christ was expressed matter-of-factly by Carl M. Chorowsky, minister of the First Unitarian Church of Fairfield, Connecticut, in a 1955 interview with *Look* magazine:

In general, a Unitarian is a religious person whose ethic derives primarily from that of Jesus, who believed in One God, not the Trinity. . . . Unitarians hold that the orthodox Christian world has forsaken the real, human Jesus of the Gospel, and has substituted a Christ of dogmatism, metaphysics and pagan philosophy. . . .

Unitarians repudiate the doctrine and dogma of the Virgin Birth. . . . Unitarians do not believe that Jesus is the Messiah, either of Jewish hope or of Christian fantasy. They do not believe He is "God Incarnate," or the Second Person of the Trinity, as the final arbitrator at the end of time, who shall come to judge the quick and the dead.[4]

Because of its anti-Trinitarian bias, unitarianism is non-Christian. There are some in the UUA, however, who are more influenced by the "universalist" emphasis rather than the "unitarian" and who accept Trinitarian dogma. Against unitarian polemic, Christian theologians argue that the ecumenical creeds, far from being rooted in "pagan philosophy" or "metaphysics," are biblical.[5] That God is one yet three is firmly supported by biblical references quoted within the Christian tradition (Gen. 1:26; Deut. 6:4; Matt. 3:13–17; 28:19; 2 Cor. 13:14). But this does little to satisfy the modern-day unitarians. They do not regard the ▸Bible as a definitive source of authority. Reason takes precedence over the Bible, creeds, or dogmatic formulations of any kind.

Salvation (*see* ▸soteriology) is a matter not of rescue from sin and redemption through the blood of Jesus, as Christian orthodoxy asserts, but rather the cultivation of character and the nurture of the human spirit (see 1961 statement above). The traditional expression "God helps those who help themselves" is well acclimated to UUA thought.[6]

CONCLUSION

The UUA maintains a large publishing house, Beacon Press. Also, the Unitarian-Universalist Service Committee is an extension of the UUA's social ministry program. Unitarianism and Universalism both continue to be important parts of American intellectual life. Their leaders are among the most highly educated in all denominational groups.

ADDITIONAL INFORMATION

Headquarters
UUA, 25 Beacon St. Boston, MA 02108.

Website
www.uua.org

Sacred Text
There is no one sacred text or creed. UUA is open to all texts and do not tolerate the concept of a sacred confession of faith or a creed.

Publications
UUWorld (magazine); *Synapse* (youth publication); *Ferment* (young adult); online newsletters are available at the official website.

Statistics
At the time of the 1959 merger, there were close to 70,000 UUA members and 334 churches. Because of a looser, more broad-based appeal, the numbers more than doubled to approximately 175,000 members and 1,005 congregations

in 1983. In 2001, the organization reported having 218,404 members in 1054 congregations and 1,584 ministers. Worldwide there are over 600,000 members.

Notes

[1] The Bond of Fellowship of the Universalist Church, adopted in Washington, D.C., in 1935; see Russell E. Miller, *The Larger Hope* (Boston: Unitarian-Universalist Association, 1978), 2:114.

[2] Article 2, section 2, of the Constitution of the Unitarian-Universalist Association.

[3] Article 2, section C2.1, of the Bylaws of the Unitarian-Universalist Association.

[4] Carl M. Chorowsky, "What is a Unitarian?" *Look* (March 8, 1955), as quoted by Walter Martin, *The Kingdom of the Cults* (Minneapolis: Bethany, 1985), 503.

[5] See THEOSOPHY for an analysis of the second article of the Apostles' and Nicene creeds with respect to the scriptural basis for each of the articles that the creeds contain. Also refer to Appendix 1.

[6] Within some universalist circles, salvation is indeed a matter of biblical warrant. Jesus' work of justification and redemption are applied to all humanity, much the same way that the sin of Adam was itself universal in its effects on the human community (Rom. 5:12ff.).

UNITY

Formerly Unity School of Christianity, now simply called Unity, is one of the religious groups classed commonly as one of the ▶mind sciences. Chiefly through advertising and dissemination of literature, it reaches an audience disproportionately large compared to it actual membership and is therefore a considerably influential group.

HISTORY

Unity School of Christianity was founded in 1889 by Charles ▶Fillmore (1854–1948) and his wife, Myrtle ▶Fillmore (1845–1931). A failed real estate agent, Charles was also a cripple and nearly bankrupt; Myrtle was stricken with tuberculosis. In 1884 she moved from New England to Kansas City, Missouri, and shortly thereafter became a convert to CHRISTIAN SCIENCE. Convinced that all sickness and disease was an illusion, she claimed to have been healed of her lung malady. As she said, "I am a child of God and therefore I do not inherit sickness." Charles maintained an interest in the ▶occult and SPIRITUALISM. Eastern religion, particularly HINDUISM with its concept of ▶reincarnation, also influenced him. When he became converted to Christian Science through his wife, the blend of their diverse ideas resulted in a unique form of harmonious religion known as Unity.

Emma Curtis ▶Hopkins, one of Mary Baker ▶Eddy's chief disciples, was perhaps the most important influence on the Fillmores. But Unity eventually took on an identity much closer to NEW THOUGHT than it did to Christian Science, the basic difference being that the latter treated sin, sickness, and disease as illusory maladies of the mind. In New Thought, the material world, sin, and sickness are considered real.

The Fillmores published *Modern Thought*, the first periodical of Unity, in 1887. One year later they renamed it *Christian Science Thought*. Eddy protested the name change, accusing the Fillmores of capitalizing on the popularity and success of her movement. The Fillmores yielded to Eddy's pressures and renamed the magazine *Thought*.

The growth of Unity (so named in 1891) was phenomenal. By 1922 it had far exceeded its rivals New Thought and Christian Science in membership. After World War I the Fillmores built a headquarters known today as Unity Village, just outside Kansas City. By 1950 the entire machinery of the movement was operating from Unity Village. From its press a variety of publications issue forth: *Daily Word*, *Wee Wisdom* (a children's publication), *Unity*, *Progress Weekly Unity*, and *Good Business*.

For decades, Unity School of Christianity has promoted itself through widespread distribution of printed material.

The core membership of Unity became known as Silent Unity. This group was originally called the Society of Silent Help and was the factor most responsible for the rapid growth of the movement. The idea was to offer twenty-four-hour ministry, which is conducted today through a large staff at Unity Village. Prayer, counseling, and correspondence is obtainable through Silent Unity. The volume of mail flowing into and out of Unity Village was so great that the United States government established a separate post office in Lees Summit, Missouri, to handle it. Unity fields an average of fifteen thousand phone calls weekly and reportedly receives well over two million letters annually. Other areas of public exposure include widespread use of radio and television and a tape ministry.

Although Unity prefers not to call itself a religion, it has become its own denomination. As early as 1903, the Fillmores established an ordination policy. They did not request people to leave their own particular denominational affiliations. They believed that they had succeeded in producing a religion that eclectically extracted the best elements from each existing religion. One may therefore retain one's own particular belief system or denominational affiliation and still be a part of Unity.

Although Unity has no strict creedal statements, in 1921 the Unity Statement of Faith was formulated. The church holds no annual conferences, but its ministers belong to the Unity Ministers Association, which does in fact meet annually. Ministers, or candidates seeking placement within the denomination, must complete a prescribed course that the church reviews and subsequently approves or rejects. If approved, the candidate is ordained.

After Myrtle Fillmore died in 1931, Charles continued to run the organization alone. Eventually he married his secretary, Cora Derick, and the two managed the movement until their own deaths. After Charles died in 1948, his sons assumed control. The Fillmore family still leads the organization.

ORGANIZATION

As an organization, Unity is centered around its headquarters at Unity Village in Missouri. There are 915 affiliated Unity churches, called The Association of Unity Churches. There is a two-year training program for those who wish to become ministers. Unity holds regular spiritual retreats. It employs 650 staff members. There is no statement of faith, though it does have a mission statement. A constant prayer vigil is conducted at the Silent Unity chapel. According to Frank S. Mead,

A large staff of workers is available for consultation day and night, answering telephone calls, telegrams, letters. . . . All calls and requests are answered. There is no charge for this service, but love offerings are accepted. Unity answers seven hundred fifty thousand such calls yearly, most of them coming from members of various Christian churches. . . . Some two hundred million books, booklets, tracts, and magazines are published and undoubtedly used by many who never contact headquarters at all. . . . About fifteen new cassettes are produced annually, and more than one thousand radio and television stations broadcast two hundred fifty Unity programs a week.[1]

TEACHINGS

Rather than offering itself as being a religion or belief system, Unity portrays itself as an educational system open to the public. However, the most liberal definition of religion must include Unity. The ministry of counseling and prayer offered by Silent Unity, the publications, the ordination of ministers, and its basic doctrines combine to classify Unity as being a religious denomination.

Unity is philosophically monistic (see ▸monism) because it teaches that all that is emanates from a single source—God. The group's main focus is on spiritual healing and personal health and prosperity. Though sin and illness are real, sickness is an unnatural state of existence. Spiritual means of healing are diligently sought after. They also advise seeking medical help.

Truth is found in every aspect of life, including all religions. It is up to each individual to achieve an understanding of truth in whichever way he or she discovers to be both practical and successful. Devotees seek to exercise, develop, and harness the power of the mind as being a means of meeting the multiplicities of human needs both physically and spiritually. Harmful emotions such as anger or hatred, therefore, are discouraged, and much of the literature concentrates on developing emotional and spiritual well-being.

Unity's influence reaches far beyond its own membership. Its vocabulary is well adapted to other religions, particularly CHRISTIANITY. But because of its wide acceptance of Eastern, ▸occult, and metaphysical doctrines, ▸orthodox Christianity does not extend mutual recognition to Unity. Since the vocabulary of Unity is taken chiefly from the ▸Bible, it is particularly helpful to note the organization's teachings and compare them to traditional Christian doctrines.

God

God is "Principle, Law, Being, Mind, Spirit, All Good, omnipotent, omniscient, unchangeable, Creator,

Father, Cause and Source of all that is."[2] As a principle, Unity teaches that God is not a unique and separate being from self. God is therefore an emanation of the soul of the self-conscious subject.

This motif repeats itself often in the history of religions. It is basically Eastern, stemming from HINDUISM, but where Hinduism is pantheistic (see ▸pantheism), Unity taught a modified form called ▸panentheism, that is, God is found in all living things. Neither view fits traditional Christian thought, which has always maintained a clear distinction between God and creation. God, while ▸immanent and intricately involved in creation, is also distinctly ▸transcendent above and beyond the universe. However, the vocabulary used to describe the attributes of God in their *Metaphysical Bible Dictionary* are concomitant with the attributes of God as described in the Bible. The difference is one of reference.

Jesus Christ

The Son is a "Principle revealed in the creative plan." Like other groups, Unity draws a wedge between the name "Jesus" and the title "Christ." Jesus was the name of a particular person; Christ was a spiritual aspect of him. It is the spirit that enabled Jesus to be a Christ. It is the title Christ that enabled Jesus to be a son of God. There is no qualitative difference between other human beings and Jesus. "Jesus was potentially perfect and He expressed that perfection; we are potentially perfect and we have not expressed it."[3]

This is a sharp departure from traditional Christian ▸Christology.[4] For the Christian faith, Jesus Christ is "God of God, Light of Light, very God of very God . . . being of one substance with the Father" (Nicene Creed, Appendix 1). By virtue of the personal union between the two natures, both human and divine, there is no place in which to separate the "spiritual aspects" of Jesus from the human. They are inseparably conjoined. The separation between the two natures of Christ was early taught by Nestorius (*see* ▸Nestorianism) and was condemned as heretical in A.D. 430.

Holy Spirit

The Holy Spirit is the "executive power of both Father and Son carrying out the plan." The Holy Spirit is that desire within each individual soul that prompts the mind toward holiness and oneness with the divine mind.

For orthodox Christianity, the Holy Spirit, like the Father and the Son, is a distinct member of the Trinity and is an essential personality within the Godhead. It is the Holy Spirit who "proceeds from the Father and the Son . . . is worshiped and glorified . . . who spoke by the prophets" and is "Lord and giver of life" (Nicene Creed). According to Unity, there can be no distinct separation between God and creation (see above). Therefore, the Holy Spirit cannot be distinguished from the created order either, and it would be inconsistent to maintain otherwise. Christianity can do so because of the fundamental distinction between Creator and creation.

Humanity

There is no qualitative distinction between God and humankind. As in the case of Jesus, there is a "Christ" who lies innate within each person. The goal is to pass from the personal consciousness to the Christ consciousness, or from the natural to the spiritual consciousness. Again, this is a logical conclusion from what has already been stated about God, Jesus, and the Holy Spirit (see above). If God is one with humanity, then humanity is one with God.

Salvation

Unity teaches that through a series of reincarnations, a person achieves salvation when the physical human body is replaced by the true spiritual body. Each stage he or she passes through is a higher plane than the previous one. Eventually, everyone will become Christ.

This is, of course, similar to Christian Science, Hinduism, and ancient ▸gnosticism, but it is sharply contrasted with Christian ▸soteriology. We receive salvation through the free grace of God in Jesus Christ, whose work offers us the forgiveness of sins by virtue of his shed blood on the cross and his resurrection from the dead. The Christian, on death, is translated to heaven, and the sinner to everlasting condemnation. Neither saint nor sinner will ever be reincarnated. The Christian never "becomes Christ," but rather will someday become *like* Christ (1 John 3:2).

Sin

There is a degree of ambiguity in Unity's theology of sin. On the one hand, sin is, along with all sickness, disease, pain, poverty, and death, not real. On the other hand, in contrast to Christian Science, which teaches that sin, sickness, and disease are illusions, Unity insists that they are real. Unity resolves this ambiguity by saying that ontologically it is real, but its reality is unnatural *within the mind*; that is, it is not real to the person who denies its existence.[5]

Church

Unity is the collective composite of all existing religions. Truth is contained in all religions and churches.

People may simultaneously join a church and join Unity.

The "communion of saints" comprises the church for Christendom. The saints are those who have placed trust in the finished work of redemption accomplished in Jesus Christ. While Unity includes all adherents to different faiths, Christianity, by definition, is exclusive vis-à-vis all other religions. Jesus Christ asserted himself to be the "way and the truth and the life" (John 14:6). For the Christian there is no access to God or heaven except through Christ. Expressed in nuptial imagery, Christ is the bridegroom of his church, which is the bride. The bride remains faithful to her groom.

Authority

There are no formal creeds in Unity. Members are encouraged to read the literature published by Unity Village. The Bible is widely quoted, but it is not an exclusive authority of the organization.

CONCLUSION

The Unity School of Christianity has a broad-ranging influence. It is difficult to cite statistics because of its influence outside its own membership ranks. Unity has reached as many as six million people, most of whom are not members. Though stemming from Christian Science, it has reportedly a much higher success rate because of its emphasis on the practical issues of life

(e.g., acknowledging sickness as being real), while its more esoteric parent attracts the more intellectual and philosophically minded.

ADDITIONAL INFORMATION_____

Headquarters
Unity School of Christianity, 1901 NW Blue Parkway, Unity Village, MO, 64065.

Websites
www.unityworldhq.org; www.unity.org (official website for the Association of Unity Churches)

Sacred Text
The Bible is highly regarded and openly quoted.

Publications
Daily Word (1.5 million circulation monthly); *Unity Magazine*

Statistics
Almost 1000 congregations worldwide.

Notes
[1] Frank S. Mead, *Handbook of Denominations in the United States*, rev. Samuel S. Hill, 8th ed. (Nashville: Abingdon, 1985), 257.
[2] *Metaphysical Bible Dictionary* (Lees Summit, Mo.: Unity School of Christianity, 1962).
[3] *What Unity Teaches* (Lees Summit, Mo.: Unity School of Christianity, 1952), 3.
[4] See CHRISTADELPHIANISM on Jesus Christ.
[5] Charles Fillmore, *Christian Healing* (Lees Summit, Mo.: Unity School of Christianity, 1942), 68.

UNIVERSAL FELLOWSHIP OF METROPOLITAN COMMUNITY CHURCHES (MCC); DIGNITY; GAY THEOLOGY

It's not the genitals God is concerned with—it's the quality of the relationship. And there can be just as loving a relationship, I know, within a gay or lesbian couple as a heterosexual couple. . . . Churches treat sex like it's eating spinach or something. We know better.[1]

These somewhat startling words were first uttered in June 1986 over the telephone in an Associated Press interview conducted by Joseph Garcia with Troy ▸Perry (b. 1941), founder of the Metropolitan Community Church (MCC).

Perry, a one-time Baptist minister and father of two children, formed the MCC in 1968, largely in reaction against the lack of acceptance of homosexuals in the

Christian churches that he and other homosexuals experienced on "coming out of the closet." The MCC claims today to be the largest Christian denomination that has a ministry geared specifically to gays, lesbians, bisexuals, and transgendered persons.

HISTORY

Beginning in Los Angeles with a membership of twelve, the MCC grew rapidly. Perry attributes the growth to the fact that the MCC provides a church home where homosexuals can be loved and accepted for who they are instead of trying to live as Christians within the hostile rank and file of status quo mainline churches.

The MCC applied for membership as a denomination in the mostly Protestant National Council of Churches (NCC) in 1981. Although two member churches, the United Church of Christ and the Episcopal Church, formally approved the ordination of homosexuals and lesbians into the ministry, the NCC itself was reticent and turned down the application. The MCC does, however, have official observer status with the NCC.

The MCC has experienced a wide range of reactions from the churches and culture. Anita Bryant's "Save Our Children" campaign of the 1970s came into sharp media focus in Florida in June 1977: "Florida voters repealed by a two-to-one margin an ordinance that protected homosexuals from discrimination in housing, employment, and public accommodations."[2] Although Bryant's battles were more specifically geared to the national political scene and the National Gay Task Force, members of the MCC rallied against Bryant's cause, and many new members were attracted to its ranks, which grew to more than twenty thousand by 1978.

The MCC is not the only community in which homosexuals and lesbians can find a safe haven to protect their sexual orientations and worship God simultaneously. A movement called Dignity rose up from within the ranks of the Roman Catholic church. The movement's newsletter, named *Dignity*, tells of its agenda: "The primary purpose of *Dignity* is to help the gay Catholic realize that to be Christian he need not deny his homosexuality, but rather he should be fully himself in order to be fully Christian."[3] Pope John Paul II responded in an address to the bishops of the United States in Chicago on October 5, 1979, that "homosexual activity . . . as distinguished from homosexual orientation, is morally wrong."[4] The Catholic-based National Parents League united with a univocal voice upholding the church's position.

'Evangelical and 'fundamentalist Christians responded with as much vigor as did Roman Catholics to the issue of homosexuality in the churches. Like the Roman Catholics, a vocal minority of evangelicals defended the notion that Scripture does not condemn one's sexual preference. Most, however, take up the position that the 'Bible clearly does condemn homosexual activity as being immoral and sinful. Tracts witnessing to conversions from homosexual orientation to CHRISTIANITY, with a resolve toward celibacy or heterosexual marriage, abound. Tapes, lectures, workshops, special ministries, and counseling services are offered in almost every Protestant denomination and are geared toward helping homosexuals/lesbians cope with their sexuality on a spiritual level.

Anita Bryant had rather adamantly insisted that her motivations were inspired by the Bible and a Christian love for homosexuals. On June 8, 1977, Bryant appeared as the guest speaker at a religious crusade in Norfolk, Virginia. About 125 homosexuals came to the service but promptly got up and walked out after she read a passage from the Bible naming gays as being among those who would not "inherit the kingdom of God" (1 Cor. 6:9–10). A newspaper account recorded Bryant's reaction:

> "I saw the long lines of them outside when we came," she said at a news conference later. She added tearfully, "It breaks my heart that after I said the word homosexual, they didn't hear the rest."[5] [The rest of the passage reads, "But ye were washed, ye were sanctified . . . in the name of the Lord Jesus Christ"(1 Cor. 6:11).]

Bryant's attitude and posture appears to reflect the popular cliché, "God hates the sin but loves the sinner."

In 1976 an international coalition called Exodus was organized for the sole purpose of providing ministry and counseling to homosexuals in the hopes that they could make the "exodus" to a morally responsible and Christian lifestyle. The host agency of the coalition was EXIT (EX-gay Intervention Team). Agencies listed in the Exodus directory include the Hotline Center, Come Out, Greatest is Love, Shiloh Temple, Liberation, Christian Encounters, Jesus Outreach, Eagle, His Place, Good News, and a number of others.

Rev. Perry has visited the White House on four different occasions. In 1979 he met President Jimmy Carter to discuss gay rights. He met with President Clinton three times during his two terms. In 1993 he was at the White House's first conference on AIDS. In 1997 he traveled to participate in the White House Conference on Hate Crimes. That same year, he participated in a White House conference honoring one hundred spiritual leaders throughout the country.

On July 11, 1999, over three thousand people gathered in Santa Monica, California, to dedicate the MCC's new headquarters and worship center of the organization's mother church.

A Founders' Circle was established in 2002 to honor the thirty-four-year ministry of Troy Perry. Any proceeds from interested members go toward funding areas of ministry that honor Perry's vision for ministry. In a letter dated Oct. 6, 2002, Perry, addressing the church body, announced his plans to retire as moderator of the MCC in 2005.

ORGANIZATION

The leader of the MCC is called a moderator. Perry has been the only moderator since the church's founding in 1968. The denomination also has a board of administration. Members are appointed by the MCC board of elders and serve one to two years without remuneration. The board of administration presents a report at the annual general conference. Member churches are in most states in the United States and in twenty-two countries abroad.

TEACHINGS

Troy Perry summarizes the theology of the MCC in creedal fashion in this way:

> I believe in the personal commitment to Christ, as Savior, Lord, and Master. I believe that Jesus died upon Calvary for all the people of the world and that he was the one supreme sacrifice for all sins. I believe in the fundamentalist doctrine of being "born again" of the Spirit and the water. I know that I am a "born again" child of God. I also know that I am a homosexual. Can this change my relationship with my Lord? No, never! Jesus said: "Come unto me, all ye that labor and are heavy laden, and I will give you rest. Take my yoke upon you, and learn of me; for I am meek and lowly in heart; and ye shall find rest unto your souls." And again, "For God so loved the world, that he gave his only begotten Son, that whosoever believeth in him should not perish, but have everlasting life." Not once do I read Jesus saying in the Gospels, "Come unto me, all you heterosexuals who, if you have sex or intercourse, must have it in the missionary position with another heterosexual, and I will accept you as the only true believers." No, Jesus, my Lord, sent the invitation to all, whosoever will.[6]

The modern mission statement, appearing on the MCC website, reads:

> "The Universal Fellowship of Metropolitan Community Churches is a Christian Church founded in and reaching beyond the Gay and Lesbian communities. We embody and proclaim Christian salvation and liberation, Christian inclusivity and community, and Christian social action and justice. We serve among those seeking and celebrating the integration of their spirituality and sexuality."[7]

Apart from the emphasis on a ministry to gays, the MCC appears as a traditional Christian church in every sense of the word. Visitors encounter worship services complete with conventional liturgies, the ⸰sacraments, preaching, and hymn singing.

The basic contention of Perry and other leaders within the movement is that God and the Bible do not condemn the homosexual/lesbian lifestyle. Biblical texts such as Leviticus 18:22; 20:13; Isaiah 42:16; Ezekiel 36:26; Romans 1:26–27; 1 Corinthians 6:9–11; and 1 Timothy 1:8–11 present the traditional Christian attitude toward homosexuality. Theologians who advocate that homosexual/lesbian lifestyles are not condemned by these passages radically reinterpret them, claiming that they do not apply to modern times and modern culture. William Countryman, a New Testament professor at the Church Divinity School of the Pacific in Berkeley, California, argues that

> biblical references to homosexuality pertain to ancient Jewish purity rites, which included rules forbidding Jews from eating unclean food, handling corpses or having sex with a menstruating woman. Paul never says homosexuals are sinful but that they are unclean. . . . And Paul does not regard ritual uncleanness as a barrier between gentiles and God.[8]

A small number of evangelicals join ranks with feminist and radical revisionists in insisting that the moral issues that homosexuality raises are not real issues at all. Dr. Ralph Blair, the director of the Homosexual Community Counseling Center in New York City, is one such example. In an essay titled "An Evangelical Look at Homosexuality," Blair argues that traditional texts such as Leviticus 18:22 are misinterpreted and misunderstood by most evangelicals (see below). Others claim that in order to be consistent with such passages as Leviticus 18:22 ("Do not lie with a man as one lies with a woman; that is detestable"), one should observe all other aspects of the Old Testament laws, such as not engaging in sexual intercourse with a woman during her menstrual cycle (15:19), abstaining from certain foods (Lev. 11), or executing those who commit adultery (20:10).

The majority of nonrevisionist Christian theologians respond that this is a faulty understanding of such passages. Traditionally, a distinction is made between the moral and ceremonial laws of the Old Testament. The ceremonial laws, such as the dietary laws, are aspects of the Levitical code and pertain to Israelites. The moral law, spelled out in, for example, "You shall not murder" (Ex. 20:13) or "You shall not commit adultery" (v. 14), is universally applicable to Jew and Gentile alike.

Pro-homosexual advocates interpret the Leviticus passage as being one of the ceremonial laws because it is given within the context of purification rites. Ralph Blair writes:

That the very pronounced Old Testament judgment against a man's having sexual relations with another man is included in the priestly Holiness Code of Leviticus (18:22 and 20:13) is significant because the concern of the priests was one of ritual purity. It was not the moral preaching of the prophets. From this priestly point of view, it is clear that above all else, Israel was to be uncontaminated by her pagan neighbors. In all things, she was to remain a separate "pure vessel unto the Lord." At this time, male prostitutes in the temples of the Canaanites, Babylonians, and other neighboring peoples, were common features of the pagan rites. There, it is understandable that this "homosexuality" connected with the worship of false gods would certainly color Israel's perspective on any and all homosexual activity.[9]

P. Michael Ukleja responds that such an observation

begs the question on several counts. The first major fault is in assuming that ritual purity and moral purity are always distinct. Those who make this dichotomy argue that Leviticus 18 and 20 cannot be of an ethical or moral nature. Blair states this when he divides the priests with their ritual purity and the prophets with their moral teaching into two groups that were not to transgress each other's territory. But the prophets preached to the needs of their day. Anything not included in their teaching is more logically explained by that particular sin's absence among the sins of that generation rather than by a rigid distinction between ceremonial and moral purity. To hold to such a distinction one would have to conclude that adultery was not morally wrong (18:20), child sacrifice had no moral implications (18:21), and that nothing is inherently evil with bestiality (18:23). The point is that ceremonial purity and moral purity often coincide.[10]

Because the prohibition against homosexuality occurs three times in the New Testament (Rom. 1:26–27; 1 Cor. 6:9; 1 Tim. 1:10), it is evident to most Bible scholars that its prohibition extends beyond the specific rites pertaining to Israel. Rather, homosexuality is a moral issue that is transcultural; it is not a subject addressed exclusively to Jews but extends itself to Gentile Christians as well.

Another Old Testament text, Genesis 19:4–11, contains the classic story of Lot and the sins of Sodom. The King James Bible translates verse 5 as "Bring them out unto us, that we may know them." The standard interpretation has been that the word "know" means to "know sexually." Revisionists respond that the word

"know" occurs over nine hundred times in the Old Testament, and in only twelve instances does it have a sexual connotation. D. Sherwin Bailey, an Anglican scholar and author of a standard work, *Homosexuality and the Western Christian Tradition*, argues that in the Sodom passage, the word "know" means "to get acquainted with." Bailey argues that the strangers were foreigners and therefore the men of the city merely wished to grow acquainted with them.

This, however, is problematic because of the internal inconsistency it creates. In verse 8, Lot responds to the men by insisting that they take his daughters because they "have not known a man" (KJV). The same word for "know" occurs in verses 5 and 8. It is unlikely that Lot thought the men's request to merely get acquainted was "wicked" (see v. 7) and then insisted that they instead become acquainted with his daughters. Second, the sexual interpretation of "know" was ascribed to within the New Testament centuries later. Jude 7 refers to the great sin of Sodom and Gomorrah as their "sexual immorality" and the going after "strange flesh" (KJV).

Concerning the New Testament passages (Rom. 1:26–27; 1 Cor. 6:9; 1 Tim. 1:10), the key words that are usually translated as "homosexual" are *malakos* and *arsenokoites*. Bauer's standard *Greek-English Lexicon of the New Testament* defines *arsenokoites* as "a male who practices homosexuality, pederast, sodomite."[11] *Malakos* is defined as one who wears soft clothing so as to appear effeminate. The word was used commonly in noncanonical literature for "men and boys who allow themselves to be misused homosexually."[12] Revisionists argue that the standard lexicons are wrong because the sin of Sodom was not homosexuality.[13]

Ukleja warns, however:

First, one should be cautious when going against the tide of scholarly opinion. . . . Second, it is an assumption based on erroneous exegesis to see the Sodomites not being punished for homosexuality. Third, even if *arsenokoites* had only a tangential relationship to homosexuality, it could have easily become a euphemism for homosexuality.[14]

Ukleja notes that pro-homosexual revisionists suggest that the Pauline passages noted above do not condemn homosexuality but rather the overindulgence or abuse of homosexuality. Often it is maintained that God opposes homosexual *lust* but not homosexual *love*. Paul advocates temperance (1 Cor. 9:25 KJV), not abstinence on the one hand, or overindulgence on the other, with respect to eating and drinking. Ukleja indicates that these appear as strong arguments on the surface, except that they fail the test of consistency.

> But to use the abuse argument, one must be consistent. In each instance the Bible clearly states the responsible norm as opposed to irresponsible or abusive behavior. A specific and consistent approach of this nature leads to a clear answer as to what is the responsible norm opposed to homosexuality. The responsible norm clearly taught in Scripture is heterosexuality in marriage. Gay theologians say that "Homosexual love is not mentioned or condemned in Scripture." They are exactly right. Homosexual love is nowhere mentioned in Scripture. The Bible refers only to lust and degrading passions, as in Romans 1.[15]

Radical feminism has contributed much to the revisionist approach to biblical hermeneutics. Mary Daly posits the following:

> The categories of heterosexuality and homosexuality are patriarchal classifications.... Male fear and hostility regarding "homosexuality" reflects anxiety over losing power which is based upon sex-role stereotyping.... By its sex role stereotyping, phallic morality has created the "problem" of homosexuality, which prevents us from seeing that two people of the same sex may relate authentically to one another.[16]

Such an approach becomes what Daly (borrowing from Nietzsche) calls a "transvaluation of values." The difficulty that traditional Christians have in remaining conversant any longer on the issue of homosexuality lies in the fact that now a newer and more important issue replaces it, namely: Is Scripture any longer an authoritative text since it is laden with the ancient encumbrances of Jewish patriarchy?[17] How can effective dialogue continue when one party adheres to the canon of the believing community and another wishes to move "beyond God the Father?"

CONCLUSION

The MCC, Dignity, and other homosexual churches do wish to remain conversant with the Bible. As indicated above, how one views and interprets a text is largely determined by one's preconceived philosophy of life and overarching worldview. For traditional Christians it seems to be the case in many instances that Christian homosexuals are not as interested in rigorous exegesis of Scripture as they are in being loved and accepted. Christian homosexuals regard traditional Christians as being prejudiced, bigoted, and misinformed and in turn

bring a jaundiced approach to the Bible. It is then easy to extract "proof texts" to support such a view.

The challenge on the part of Christian traditionalists remains in showing the love and acceptance that the founder of Christendom had for humankind when he said, "For God so loved the world that he gave his only Son, that whoever believes in him shall not perish but have eternal life" (John 3:16). It remains for advocates of a "Christian homosexuality" to not be so suspicious of mendacious motives on the part of traditionalists and to consider the possibility that timeworn interpretations of the sacred text are not necessarily antiquated and may in fact be correct.

Gay theology in general has become an issue that has moved into center stage in many church bodies and into the public square at the beginning of the twenty-first century. In the fall of 2003, the Protestant Episcopal Church ordained its first openly gay bishop, sparking a negative reaction from the more conservative members of the Anglican communion worldwide. Other Protestant denominations have visited the issue of gay ordinations and the marriage of gay people within its ranks and will continue to do so.

The issue of legally recognized gay marriages moved from church to state in February, 2004, when Massachusetts took the lead in passing legislation allowing same sex unions. Other states will follow suit and may consider passing the same law (or banning the practice of gay marriage). The justification for such, however, is not religion or theology. Here the reasoning process relies on the First Amendment's separation of church and state, the argument being that while many churches may wish to deny marriages to gay couples on religious grounds, there is no reason to deny the same on the basis of civil law. Opponents continue to maintain that failure to recognize such civil unions does not deny basic human rights to anyone, but that it is ultimately not in the best interests of a state to recognize same sex marriages on the grounds that this does not ultimately ensure the proliferation of the life of its citizenry and the preservation of the family as an institution established by God.

ADDITIONAL INFORMATION_____

Headquarters
MCC World Center, 8704 Santa Monica Blvd., 2nd floor, West Hollywood, CA, 90069.

Website
www.ufmcc.com

Sacred Text
The Bible

Publications

Email news, called *LeaderLink* is available on the website; *Vocation* (occasional newsletter for preparing for ministry); Perry has authored a book, *The Lord Is My Shepherd and He Knows I'm Gay* (1972), which is widely read in MCC circles.

Statistics

There are 44,000 members in 300 congregations in 22 countries. The MCC has an 80 percent gay membership. Clergy are of both sexes and 85 percent of them openly acknowledge being gay. Marriages between same-sex partners are performed at the discretion of MCC clergy. Troy Perry maintains the official title of moderator of the board of elders of the MCC.

Notes

[1] Troy Perry in a telephone interview with Joseph Garcia of the Associated Press, printed in the *Denver Herald* (June 28, 1986).

[2] "Miami Vote: Tide Turning Against Homosexuals?" *U.S. News and World Report* (June 20, 1977), 46.

[3] "Don't Be Misled," *Seattle Times* (Sept. 3, 1983), D7. This article was an advertisement paid for by the National Parents League, rebutting this statement, which was quoted from *Dignity: A Monthly Newsletter for Catholic Homophiles and Concerned Heterophiles* 3/4 (May 5, 1972).

[4] Pope John Paul II, addressing the bishops of the United States in Chicago (Oct. 5, 1979), as quoted in "Don't Be Misled," D7.

[5] "Gays Walk Out on Anita's Church Speech," *Los Angeles Herald Examiner* (June 9, 1977), A2.

[6] Statement of belief written by Troy Perry and recorded in Ralph Blair's, *An Evangelical Look at Homosexuality* (Chicago: Moody Press, 1963), 11.

[7] http://www.ufmcc.com/index2.htm, 2003.

[8] Jeffery L. Sheler, "Homosexuality Doctrines," *U.S. News and World Report* (July 16, 1990), 55. See also William Countryman and M. R. Ritley, *Gifted by Otherness: Gay and Lesbian Christians in the Church* (Harrisburg, PA: Morehouse, 2001),

[9] Blair, *An Evangelical Look*, 3.

[10] P. Michael Ukleja, "Homosexuality and the Old Testament," *Bibliotheca Sacra* (July–September 1983), 263.

[11] William F. Arndt and F. Wilbur Gingrich, *A Greek-English Lexicon of the New Testament and Other Early Christian Literature*, 2d ed. (Chicago and London: Univ. of Chicago Press, 1957), 109.

[12] Ibid., 488.

[13] See John Boswell, *Christianity, Social Tolerance, and Homosexuality* (Chicago: Univ. of Chicago Press, 1980).

[14] Ukleja, "Homosexuality in the New Testament," *Bibliotheca Sacra* (October–December 1983), 352.

[15] Ibid., 353.

[16] Mary Daly, *Beyond God the Father: Toward a Philosophy of Women's Liberation* (Boston: Beacon, 1973), 125–26.

[17] See *Interpretation* (January 1988) for a well-rounded assessment of feminist hermeneutics.

URANTIA; THE URANTIA SOCIETY

The quest for life on other planets or somewhere in the universe has always been a subject of intrigue and speculation. It was the question that inspired scientist Carl Sagan to wonder about in his book *Contact*, produced through the SETI (Search for Extra-Terrestrial Intelligence) project. Many others have simply assumed that extraterrestrial life is a given. Out of this belief has come religions, organizations, and societies built on the assumption and worldview that life in other parts of the universe is a reality that affects life on Planet Earth in some spiritual or religious way. The Urantia Society is one such organization. The cult HEAVEN'S GATE is another, more recent example.

HISTORY

In 1903, a house was built on Diversey Parkway in Chicago dedicated to housing peculiar readings that were said to have come from above. It was not, however, until 1934 that *The Urantia Book* was delivered to Bill Sadler "from seven spirit beings" from another world. The book is an exposition of the "finest major divine revelation since the coming of Christ to our planet," so the Urantia Society claims. The book, not published until 1955, is an exhaustive (2,097 pages) revelation of the cosmos told from the perspective of highly intelligent space beings and communicated to the inhabitants of Urantia ("Earth").

Between 1934 and 1956, a group of Urantia devotees gathered on a regular basis to study the Urantia manuscripts. Known as the Forum, the group, consisting of thirty-six members, incorporated in 1950 as the Urantia Foundation. The group filed for tax-exempt status in Cook County, Illinois, as an educational society. The sole purpose of the organization is to disseminate the teachings of *The Urantia Book*.

In 1969, the house and properties on Diversey Parkway were transferred to the Urantia Society, which is its headquarters to the present day. In recent years, the foundation has been publishing the book in many other languages.

ORGANIZATION

The society is run and guided by a declaration of trust. Urantia is organized around its various ᵇsocieties. When ten or more gather together, the Urantia Brotherhood charters a society. A general council, consisting of thirty-six members, supervises the organization. Also, there is a board of trustees consisting of five members appointed for life to manage the society. A president is also appointed as the chief executive.

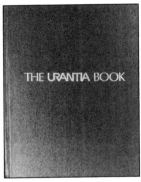

The Urantia Book by Bill Sadler can be obtained at many secular and occult bookstores.
Courtesy Jack M. Roper/CARIS

TEACHINGS

Basic to the teachings of the society is the rejection of the doctrines of other "outdated" religions. Paradoxically, however, one may become a member of the society and still retain membership in one's own respective denomination, as is also the case in SCIEN-TOLOGY and UNITY SCHOOL OF CHRISTIANITY.

The parents of the human race, according to *The Urantia Book*, were named ᵇAndon and ᵇFonta, who gave birth to the first human born on earth, whose name was ᵇSontad. Spiritual locations are described, such as the Isle of Paradise, where the ᵇTrinity of Trinities resides.

Much of *The Urantia Book* grows out of a reaction to biblical literature. A considerable amount of space, for example, is devoted to explaining what Jesus did during the so-called silent years (between the ages of twelve and around thirty), about which the Gospels are silent. Other reactions to CHRISTIANITY as elucidated in *The Urantia Book* are as follows:

God

There are three trinities in Urantia thought: the ᵇParadise Trinity, the ᵇUltimate Trinity, and the ᵇAbsolute Trinity. Within the Paradise Trinity is the Universal Father.

Traditional Christianity confesses a singular Trinity. The ᵇBible refers to God as manifest in three persons—Father, Son, and Holy Spirit—and the ecumenical creeds testify to the Trinity (*see* Appendix 1). Much of the apologetic activity of the Christian church has centered around defending the doctrine of the Trinity against the accusation that Christians worship three gods instead of one.[1] Urantia presents a unique alternative. Rather than one Trinity, there are three.

Jesus Christ

Jesus is one of the many sons of God. He became perfect deity in a culmination of seven ᵇincarnations. The Urantia Society also holds that Christ's death by crucifixion was not necessary to atone for sin, as traditional Christianity teaches, but was an unfortunate accident brought about by humankind. Jesus took on the title "Son of Man" when he was fifteen years old after reading the book of *Enoch*. He roamed throughout the Roman Empire during the silent years with two Far Eastern (Indian) companions. Jesus' seventh incarnation resulted in his manifestation as "Michael of Nebadon." It was then that he revealed to us that divinity does not abide outside of us but dwells richly within.

For the Christian church, these assertions are pure speculation. While Jesus is a Son of God, according to the Nicene Creed he is also the "only-begotten Son of God," who is also "God of God, Light of Light, very God of very God." The same creed speaks of Jesus as "incarnate by the Holy Spirit of the virgin Mary." Jesus was and is God's unique incarnation, not one of seven.

The UNIFICATION CHURCH also teaches that Jesus' death was an unfortunate accident. The apostles themselves were aware of this charge and responded to it by proclaiming that it was indeed in keeping with God's will that Jesus was crucified (Acts 2:23). The absence of the crucifixion of Jesus would mean that there is no atonement for sin (cf. 3:11–4:12; 5:21–31).[2]

There is much speculation about what Jesus did during his silent years. The ᵇgnostic literature discovered at Nag Hammadi demonstrates that interest in Jesus' activity between ages twelve and thirty dates back very early. Urantia joins ranks with these speculators. In the Christian tradition, it is believed generally that Jesus worked as a "carpenter" with his earthly father, Joseph, and spent most of his formative years in Nazareth of Galilee.

The most serious departure of Urantia from ᵇorthodox ᵇChristology lies in its belief that Jesus' divinity is not objectively true but becomes a reality within the individual. According to the Christian faith, Jesus is both God and man. He did not achieve this status because his followers believed his gospel; rather, his status existed *before* humans believed. Indeed, it is his status that creates faith. Nowhere, for example, in the Apostles' and Nicene creeds is there made mention of Jesus' person and work being dependent on human beings or faith. The confession "I believe . . ." is a possibility only because of what follows the assertion, namely, "in Jesus Christ, his only Son, our Lord" (*see* Apostles' Creed).

Holy Spirit

Urantia distinguishes between the Holy Spirit and the Infinite Spirit. The Holy Spirit is described as an "influence" or a "supermind" that resides within a human being as an active energy. The Infinite Spirit is part of the Trinity of Trinities.

Like the novelty of introducing two additional trinities to the one Trinity of the church, Urantia adds a second Spirit. The church has always confessed a singular Holy Spirit who is a distinct personality of the Godhead, not merely an active energy. The Spirit is "Lord and giver of life, who proceeds from the Father and the Son, who with the Father and the Son together is worshiped and glorified" (Nicene Creed).

Humanity

Human beings are reincarnated beings evolving through the stages of life. They have ascended from the animal kingdom, achieving the level of human, and will eventually ascend onward to the angelic spirit world, where they will become gods.

This idea is as ancient as it is modern. According to the Bible, ¹Satan likened himself unto God and succeeded in convincing the first man and woman, Adam and Eve, that they too could become like God (Gen. 3:1ff.). The concept of deity residing within humanity is a fundamental principle of HINDUISM and finds modern expression in many religions.³

Salvation

For Urantia, the goal of all life is to reach the spiritual Isle of Paradise. The means of achieving this goal is through self-effort. Members rely heavily on study, training, and divine guidance and, in turn, devote their lives to divine service, thereby accomplishing salvation. The Christian idea of salvation is discussed in *The Urantia Book* at some length. It dismisses the notion of blood atonement as being primitive and rejects divine wrath against sin and the shedding of innocent blood on behalf of the sinner as fictitious. The basic thrust of Urantia's assessment of Christianity can be summarized in a single sentence: "The cardinal religious idea of inspiration, revelation, propitiation, repentance,

atonement, intercession, sacrifice, prayer, confession, worship, survival after death, sacrament, ritual, ransom, salvation, covenant, uncleanness, purification, prophecy, original sin—they all go back to the early times of primordial ghost fear."⁴ Additional excerpts from *The Urantia Book* include the following:

Nineteen hundred years ago, unlearned Galileans surveyed Jesus giving his life as a spiritual contribution to man's inner experience and then went out and turned the whole Roman Empire upside down.⁵

IN SCIENCE, GOD IS the First Cause; in religion, the universal and loving Father; in philosophy, the one being who exists by himself, not dependent on any other being for existence but beneficently conferring reality of existence on all things and upon all other beings. But it requires revelation to show that the First Cause of science and the self-existent Unity of philosophy are the God of religion, full of mercy and goodness and pledged to effect the eternal survival of his children on earth.⁶

JESUS TAUGHT: You shall not portray your teacher as a man of sorrows. Future generations shall know also the radiance of our joy, the buoyancy of our good will, and the inspiration of our good humor. We proclaim a message of good news that is infectious in its transforming power. Our religion is throbbing with new life and new meanings. Those who accept this teaching are filled with joy and in their hearts are constrained to rejoice evermore. Increasing happiness is always the experience of all who are certain about God.⁷

A NEW AND FULLER revelation of the religion of Jesus is destined to conquer an empire of materialistic secularism and to overthrow a world sway of mechanistic naturalism. Urantia is now quivering on the very brink of one of its most amazing and enthralling epochs of social readjustment, moral quickening, and spiritual enlightenment.⁸

A THOROUGHLY SELFISH soul cannot pray in the true sense of the word. But real prayer does attain reality. Even when the air currents are ascending, no bird can soar except by outstretched wings. Prayer elevates man because it is a technique of progressing by the utilization of the ascending spiritual currents of the universe. . . . Words are irrelevant to prayer . . . God answers the soul's attitude, not the words.⁹

THE FATHER in heaven has forgiven you even before you have thought to ask him, but such forgiveness is not available in your personal religious experience until such a time as you forgive your fellow men. God's forgiveness in fact is not conditioned upon your forgiving your fellows, but in *experience* it is exactly so conditioned.[10]

CONCLUSION

While Urantia presents some original ideas and is the product of the ingenuity of Bill Sadler, it is evident that many of its doctrines arise from a reaction to the Bible and Christian tradition. The Urantia Society takes its place as part of a network of the NEW AGE MOVEMENT and SPIRITUALIST groups, whose basic agenda is to harmonize humanity and deity with the cosmos. *The Urantia Book* can now be read online (see websites below).

ADDITIONAL INFORMATION

Headquarters
Urantia Foundation, 533 Diversey Parkway, Chicago, IL 60614.

Websites
www.ubook.org; www.urantia.com

Sacred Text
The Urantia Book

Publication
URANTIAN News (available on the website); *International Urantia Association Journal*

Statistics
Exact numbers are not available. Anyone can order and read excerpts from *The Urantia Book*; 250,000 copies of it have been sold as of this writing.

Notes
[1] For a more detailed analysis of the Christian doctrine of the Trinity, see JEHOVAH'S WITNESSES and CHRISTADELPHIANISM.
[2] See UNIFICATION CHURCH.
[3] See HINDUISM and MORMONISM.
[4] *The Urantia Book* (Urantia Society, 1955), 1005.
[5] Ibid., 2077.
[6] Ibid., 59.
[7] Ibid., 1766.
[8] Ibid., 2082.
[9] Ibid., 1002.
[10] Ibid., 1638.

VEDANTA SOCIETY

Vedanta arrived in the United States in 1895, the first Hindu ᐅsect to come here, transported by the eloquent and charming lecturer and teacher ᐅSwami ᐅVivekananda (1863–1902). Born Narendranath Datta in 1863 in a middle-upper-class Hindu family, his education included the study of Western culture, philosophy, and religion. The name Vivekananda means "bliss of discrimination," which describes well the basic posture of his life's work, namely, to discriminate between the spirituality of HINDUISM and the material philosophy of the West so as to combine them.

HISTORY

Vivekananda studied under and became an ardent disciple of ᐅSri ᐅRamakrishna (1836–1886), a priest in the Kali Temple in Calcutta and one of the most famous of the Hindu ᐅgurus of India in the nineteenth century.

In 1893 Vivekananda came to America and addressed the Parliament of World Religions held in Chicago. The 1880s and 1890s were considered to be the years of the "liberal ascendancy" in American CHRISTIANITY. The world parliament, held in conjunction with the Columbian Exposition (1892–1893), was attended by 150,000 people. The motto of the parliament, using the words of Malachi from the Old Testament, was "Have we not all one Father? Hath not one God created us?" Although the parliament was dominated by Roman Catholics and Protestants, the motto provided an opportunity for representatives of Eastern religions to gain a hearing.[1] Some sources claim that Annie ᐅBesant (1897–1933), leader of the THEOSOPHICAL SOCIETY, was the highlight of the parliament. Others, however, assert that Swami Vivekananda dominated it with his charm, eloquence, and wit. Whichever the case may be, the parliament provided the platform for Vivekananda to present Hinduism to the American public at a time when its arms were open more widely than ever before.

The Vedanta Society was subsequently formed in 1895 in New York City. Vivekananda worked in the U.S. center for one year but returned to Calcutta in 1897 to open the Ramakrishna mission in India. There he remained until his death in 1902. Vivekananda had bridged both East and West with the teachings of Hinduism. He planted a seed in America that would sprout in the twentieth century, first with SELF REALIZATION FELLOWSHIP (1914) and then with many other Hindu movements and sects that came into being in the 1960s and 1970s.

The Vedanta Society of Southern California was founded in 1934 in Hollywood. Many more followed. In 1938, the Ramakrishna Institute was founded in Calcutta, India.

ORGANIZATION

Today the Vedanta Society has centers in over one hundred countries around the world. Activities in these centers include lectures, debates, worship, cultural events, and so on. The Ramakrishna Institute has study circles, including children, and also promotes the study of foreign languages.

TEACHINGS

Vivekananda's great teacher, Sri Ramakrishna, taught that all the world's religions lead to the same goal, namely, the realization of God. This concept is summarized in the following utterance by Ramakrishna:

> There are in a tank or pool, various *ghats*. The Hindus draw out the liquid and call it *jal*. The Muslims draw out the liquid and call it *pani*. The Christians draw out the liquid and call it water, but it is all the same substance, no essential difference.[2]

Ramakrishna's basic philosophy of unity among all religions became the essential thrust of Vivekananda and the Vedanta Society. Vivekananda believed that every nation has its own unique contribution to bring to the world. When such is offered up, that nation goes into decline. It remains for India to bring forth its unique contribution, that is, the gift of understanding the true nature of religion. Hinduism provides the basic foundation on which such a truth will be propagated to the world.

> Therein lies the strength that has made India invincible through hundreds of years of oppression and foreign invasions and foreign tyranny. The nation lives today, and in that nation, even in the days of the direst disaster, spiritual giants have never failed to arise. Asia produces giants in spirituality, just as the Occident produces giants in politics, giants in science.[3]

All religion leads to the same end, just as all spokes on a wheel lead to the hub or all rivers flow into a single lake. Each river has a lake as its final goal. Speaking of his master, Ramakrishna, Vivekananda says:

> The next desire that seized upon the soul of this man was to know the truth about the various reli-

gions. . . . So he sought teachers of different religions. By a teacher, you must always remember what we mean in India; not a bookworm, but a man of realization, one who knows truth at first hand and not through an intermediary. He found a Mohammedan saint and underwent the disciplines prescribed by him. To his astonishment he found that, when faithfully carried out, these devotional methods led to the same goal he had already attained. He gathered a similar experience from following the religion of Jesus Christ. He went to all the sects he could find, and whatever he took up he went into with his whole heart. He did exactly as he was told, and in every instance, arrived at the same result. . . . At the core, all sects and all religions have the same aim; they only quarrel for their own selfish purposes.[4]

The essence and goal of life is to become God-conscious. Such knowledge is not empirical, nor does it take on merely cognitive aspects. Rather, it is intuitive or inspired by a direct illumination. *Avidya* ("ignorance") is the chief reason human beings do not achieve such God-consciousness. Its removal is made possible by supplying in its place its opposite, *vidya* ("knowledge"). According to another prominent Vedanta teacher, Swami Prabhavananda, this true knowledge comes in a sevenfold manner or in seven steps:

1. The convincing realization that all knowledge lies within
2. Illumination that marks the absence of suffering[5]
3. Attainment of full illumination
4. Establishment of the Self, when the Self is no longer identified with the non-Self, the seer with the seen

After this fourth stage, all duty and desire disappears. This is referred to as *karma-vimukti*, or the attainment of liberation through one's own individual effort. Then follow the last three stages, in that the Self is ultimately released from the non-Self.

5. The release of the mind from Self
6. The release of the impressions of the mind and the mind itself, never to return to the Self
7. The establishment of the glory of our own Self, wherein lies perfect peace and bliss[6]

It is obvious from these seven principles that Vedanta shares most of the ideology of its parent religion, Hinduism. While Vivekananda hoped to achieve a synthesis with the religions of the world, his hopes were idealistic at best and farfetched and superficial at worst. To assert that "the goal of all religions is the same" is to display a surprising ignorance of religions. It is not, for example, the goal of traditional Christianity to achieve oneness with the higher Self or to realize the divinity within. Rather, the Christian does not search for deity within oneself at all. The Christian centers his or her faith around the person and work of Jesus Christ. The eschatological hope for the Christian is to worship the triune God throughout all eternity. Other comparisons and contrasts with Christianity follow in the discussion below on God, Jesus Christ, humanity, salvation, and authority.

God

The frequently used term for God is OM. By it is meant the idea of Absolute Reality. Vivekananda, following the principles of Hindu thought, taught that God is both ʼtranscendent and ʼimmanent. He calls the transcendent God ʼ*Brahman* and the revealed or immanent God ʼ*Atman*. Atman and Brahman are one in essence. This idea is similar to the Christian idea of transcendence/immanence. In the medieval church, the distinction was made between God, *coram Deo* and *coram homnibus*—"God in the face of God and God in the face of man." For Christianity, the ʼincarnation of Jesus Christ constitutes the revealed God. However, both the hidden God and the revealed God are absolute deity and are distinct and separate in essence from the created order. In Hinduism, as in Vedanta, the distinction between the Creator and the creation is removed. The only reality is spiritual reality, and because God is pure spirit, material things are an encumbrance to the spirit, or God.

Another important aspect of Vedanta's doctrine of God is the concept of the Divine Mother. This describes God as an infinite expression of love and the very nature of God. The Divine Mother comprises the triune concept of God, the human soul, and nature. Again, traditional Christianity differs because of the transcendence of God as clearly distinct from his immanence.

Jesus Christ

Vivekananda makes much of the idea of incarnation. The classic prologue of John's Gospel becomes a central motif in his thought.

> "In the beginning was the Word, and the Word was with God, and the Word was God." The Hindu calls this ʼ*Maya*, the manifestation of God, because it is the power of God. . . . The Word has two manifestations: the general one of nature, and the special one of the great Incarnations of God—ʼKrishna, ʼBuddha, Jesus, and Ramakrishna. Christ, the special manifestation of the Absolute, is known and knowable. The Absolute cannot be known. We cannot know the Father. We can only know the Son. We can only see the Absolute through the "tint of humanity," through Christ.
>
> In the first five verses of John is the whole essence of Christianity; each verse is full of the profoundest philosophy.[7]

For Vedanta, Jesus is the "special manifestation of the Absolute." But he is still one of many. Orthodox Christianity maintains, however, the exclusive claims that Jesus Christ alone is God revealed in the flesh. He shares his deity with no other human being (Phil. 2:5–11; 1 Tim. 3:16; Heb. 1:1–13). Vivekananda did not recognize the uniqueness of Jesus as being the real and absolute incarnation of God apart from all other human beings. Ultimately Christ and creation are collapsed into one entity; "God became Christ to show man his true nature—that we too are God. We are human coverings over the Divine; but as the Divine Man, Christ and we are one."[8]

In Vedanta, the significance of Jesus does not lie in his own person and work or in his distinction as the incarnation of the triune God. Rather, Jesus is the Christ idea. Jesus represents the true God-consciousness present in every human soul. Who the Christian church and the Vedanta Society each understand Jesus Christ to be is a difficult point to dialogue over, largely because of semantics. When similar language has different reference points or different definitions, the first task at hand in dialogue is to understand what the terms mean. Otherwise, one is unable to communicate successfully. This remains the difficulty in all religious dialogue.

For Vivekananda, Jesus "was the Soul." There was no significance in his humanity other than to point the way of all humanity toward the Soul. The ʼChristology of the church does not understand Jesus' incarnation in this way. Both Jesus' humanity and divinity are of utmost importance and are not distinguished or divided from one another, as ʼSabellianism held in the first centuries of Christian history, nor are they confused as being only one divine nature, as ʼEutychianism held. Both of these positions were rejected at the Council of Chalcedon in A.D. 451. For Christianity, the human body of Jesus is as crucial as the divine Spirit. To speak of Jesus' blood as being salvific (Rom. 3:25) would be of no importance in the case of a Christ whose only mission was to show forth the deity inherent in all of humanity.

Humanity

For Hinduism, Vedanta, and Eastern thought in general, the material world is an encumbrance to reality. *Monism collapses all differences into one. Man is part of that oneness. The physical body is not essential to humankind's true nature and ultimately must be put aside. The goal of humanity is to achieve total God-consciousness through the seven stages described above. The body inhibits progress through these stages because its desires lead to suffering. *Avidya* is a further obstacle that prevents its *vidya*. The goal of humanity is to achieve God-consciousness.

For traditional Christianity, the flesh or body is not an encumbrance to the nature of humankind. The distinction between the body and the spirit is an idea endemic to Greek philosophy, specifically Platonism, neo-Platonism, and *gnosticism. The *Bible does not make such a distinction. Paul does not consider the flesh to be evil. Rather, it is sin that has corrupted the flesh (Rom. 7:17, 23). In classic Christian thought, humankind's goal is not to achieve God-consciousness (although this is certainly an idea close to the nineteenth-century Christian theologian Friedrich Schleiermacher), but rather to receive atonement for sin, become spiritually reborn through faith in Christ, and at death, remain forever alive to worship and serve the triune God who has created, redeemed, and sanctified him. Human beings do not ultimately become God, but by virtue of the divine image (Gen. 1:26) are destined to become *like* God (1 John 3:2).

Salvation

The *soteriology of Vedanta is the same as that of Hinduism. The escape from the cycle of reincarnation, freedom from *karma, attainment of knowledge of the Absolute, and the path of the *margas are all components of Vivekananda's idea of salvation.

Christianity does not share these ideas. Salvation is centered around the person and work of Jesus Christ as confessed by the church in its Apostles' and Nicene creeds (Appendix 1). Salvation is not escape from ignorance. It is release from the bondage of sin (Rom. 8:1ff.). Further, it is not the loss of an earthly body that is important, but the acquiring of a heavenly and incorruptible body, once possessed by Adam and Eve before the Fall (Gen. 1–2; 1 Cor. 15:52–54).

Authority

The authority of the Vedanta Society is contained in its name—the *Vedas. Members of the society read all Hindu literature and also the sacred writings of the great religions of the world, including the *Koran, the Bible, and works of great religious thinkers. The complete works of Swami Vivekananda are published in eight volumes.

Much of Christianity is divided on the issue of authority. The final source of authority is the Bible for Protestant Christians. For Roman Catholics, the Bible, as interpreted by the church and the apostolic rule of faith, constitutes final authority. In both instances, however, the Christian church is not bound by writings in nonecclesiastical sources.

Other

Vedanta itself is one of the six schools of Hinduism. The modern Vedanta Society is a development within the long Vedanta tradition, within which there are three distinct schools of thought: (1) The dualistic school, called *dvaita*, was propounded by Madhva in the thirteenth century. In this school, the spirit and material world are completely separated from each other. The common people of India accept this basic distinction. (2) An earlier school, founded in the eleventh century by Ramanuja and called *visishtadvaita,* propounded qualified nondualism. Here the distinction between material and spiritual collapsed into a monism. (3) The third school represents the system of Vedanta taught by Vivekananda and the view popular in the West. This school is called *advaita,* or school of absolute nondualism. As already observed, the final step or goal of life is the release or transmigration of the self (*samsara*) into the Absolute.

*Yoga is an essential vehicle through which the self (*atman*) achieves union with Brahman. The Vedanta Society published a book titled *Karma Yoga and Bhakti-Yoga* (1970), containing the teachings of Vivekananda, taken from his lectures and a previous work titled *Vivekananda: The Yogas and Other Works*, published by the Ramakrishna-Vivekananda Center in New York in 1953. Yoga is an integral part of the seven points of worship described above.[9]

CONCLUSION

Vivekananda has been dead for over a century, but his influence lives on in both the East and the West. Among the prominent individuals influenced by Vivekananda were Aldous Huxley, Gertrude Stein, and Gerald Heard. The society sponsors lectures, trains disciples in the disciplines of yoga, propagates the writings of Vivekananda and Hinduism, and is involved directly in public relations and social work, particularly among the poor in India.

ADDITIONAL INFORMATION_____

Headquarters
The Vedanta Society of Southern California, 1946 Vedanta Place, Hollywood, CA 90068.

Website
www.vedanta.org

Sacred Texts
Bhagavad Gita; Upanishads; The Bible; *How to Know God: The Yoga Aphorisms of Patanjali; Shankara's Crest Jewel of Discrimination; Self-Knowledge*

Periodical
Vedanta Kesari

Statistics
Presently there are approximately 150 Vedanta centers through-out the world, 124 of which are in India alone. The United States has 11, with a total membership of about 1,500. There are 125 centers of the Ramakrishna Order.

Notes
[1] Winthrop Hudson, *Religion in America*, 3rd ed. (New York: Scribner, 1981), 288.

[2] *Encyclopaedia Britannica,* 15th ed., s.v. "Ramakrishna."

[3] Swami Vivekananda, *Inspired Talks* (New York: Ramakrishna-Vivekananda Center, 1958), 153.

[4] Ibid., 168.

[5] See BUDDHISM, particularly the eightfold path.

[6] Swami Prabhavananda, "The Goal of Yoga," in *Vedanta for the Western World*, ed. Christopher Isherwood (New York: Viking, 1945), 49–50.

[7] Vivekananda, *Inspired Talks*, 19–20.

[8] Ibid., 20.

[9] See Swami Prabhavananda, "What Yoga Is," in *Vedanta for the Western World*, 41–46.

VOODOO; VODUN

The term *vodun*, or as it is popularly known, voodoo, is the generic name for the religious *cults of the West African kingdom of *Dahomey that flourished in the eighteenth and nineteenth centuries. Since independence in 1960, Dahomey is now the country of Benin. Natives of Dahomey were captured during the centuries of slave trade and transported, mainly by Spanish merchants, to the New World. Slaves from Dahomey settled in many parts of the West Indies. However, the most concentrated number made their new home in Haiti.

HISTORY

Today, a majority of the people of Haiti profess to be Roman Catholic. Spanish missionaries established Catholicism early in the settlement of the island. Unlike most of the other islands of the West Indies, however, the Christian church was not maintained by missionaries. For a long period of time the country did not even have clergy to minister to the people. It was not until 1860 that the pope signed a concordat granting Haiti an all-French clergy (French culture and language was present during the eighteenth and nineteenth centuries).

The extended absence of clergy in Haiti resulted in an interesting development in the religious history there. Uninhibited, the slaves eclectically combined their native religion of voodoo with Roman Catholicism. Instead of a strict *monotheism, the new religion became a syncretistic *polytheism. The triune God of CHRISTIANITY became the supreme deity (*loa) in a pantheon of African deities, These deities extended beyond the gods of the Dahomey kingdom and included many others from areas in West Africa that had contributed to the slave trade.

Tales and legends rapidly spread throughout the West concerning the mysteries and magic of voodoo. In 1884 a British consul in Haiti, Spencer St. John, provided an impetus for fear and fascination with his book *Haiti or the Black Republic*. He reported stories of cannibalism, child sacrifice, and evil cultic rituals. Not until 1959 was a more objective and scholarly study of voodoo written by the French anthropologist Alfred Metraux in his classic study *Voodoo in Haiti*. Metraux analyzed in detail voodoo and its major paradigms, its African origins, and its relationship to and influence by Roman Catholicism. He concluded that voodoo served as an important identity factor and linked the black slaves with their homeland against the horrors, cruelty, and uprootedness in the New World. Douglas Hill and Pat Williams have also attempted to put Haitian voodoo in perspective:

A further reason for the preservation of the slaves' religion can be found in Haiti's social and economic background. In the centuries that followed their arrival, generation after generation of Haitians continued to live the same harsh and comfortless existence as their slave forefathers. The population of Haiti today is one of the densest in the world; and so the struggle to earn his living from his meager and infertile plot condemns the Haitian peasant to a lifetime of backbreaking labor. Add to these ills of poverty and hard work the dread disease (malaria, tuberculosis, and hookworm are rife in Haiti) and it is easy to understand the powerful appeal of a religion such as voodoo.[1]

Voodoo was practiced by the dictator of Haiti, Jean-Claude "Baby Doc" Duvalier (b. 1951). Many Haitians accused Duvalier and his father, Francois Duvalier (1907–1971), of using voodoo to control and suppress Haitian citizens. Since Duvalier's ouster in 1986, however, voodoo proliferates as strongly as ever.

BELIEFS AND PRACTICES

There has been much misunderstanding concerning voodoo's religious aspects. The many cults in Haiti, Cuba, and Brazil are influenced by voodoo, and there does not seem to be a consensus on just how to define precisely what it is. Different cults follow different traditions that they all understand as derived from the essence of voodoo. How to distinguish between its mystical, magical, and religious aspects is an ongoing problem. We will attempt to unravel some of the mystery, where possible, and describe the voodoo rituals and ceremonies, deities, *divination, initiation into the cult, and ideas of death and magical powers, both good and evil.

Voodoo worship centers around a temple. Located in the center of the temple is a sacred pillar called a *poteau-mitan, lavishly decorated with icons and artwork. The *poteau-mitan* is the focal point of the ceremony, the place where communication between God (or gods) and human beings initially takes place. Dances, rituals, and sacrifices are conducted in the areas surrounding it. On the floor surrounding the *poteau-mitan* are decorative drawings called *vevers, on which sacrifices are performed. Each *loa* has its own *vever*.

Voodoo worships numerous deities. All attempts to classify them have shortcomings. The number of deities in any one region is constantly changing. In different areas, the same deity may have varying names. Most of them have traditionally come from the West African pantheon, but new ones native to Haiti and other areas where voodoo is practiced are frequently introduced. Often the new deities are the spirits of prominent persons who have died—warriors, priests, or princes. The following is a list of some of the *loa* that are common to the numerous voodoo cults.

- Agwe—god of the sea, ships, marine life
- Zaka—the god of agriculture
- Ezili—female goddess of love and erotic passion
- Aida Wedo—rainbow deity
- Ayza—protector deity
- Damballah-wedo—serpent deity of the waters
- *Mawu Lisa—creator god
- Ogu Bodagris—warrior deity
- *Baron Samedi—the feared guardian of cemeteries and the god of the grave

The many *loa* are classed into two groups. *Rada* deities are those transported from Dahomey, while *petro* deities come mostly from the West Indies. The system of deities is immensely complex. *Rada* and *petro* attributes are both manifested within the same deities, and they often have personalities and sensitivities that must be attended to by human subjects. Many deities are personal to given families and individuals, while others are in the public domain.

A male priest in voodoo is called a *hungan, a female priestess *mambo. Hungans and *mambos* lead their own particular cults, and each is autonomous. The *hungan* presides over the religious sanctuary known as a *humfort* (*humfo*) and is usually the wealthiest and most important figure within a community. According to Metraux, the *hungan* is "at one and the same time priest, healer, soothsayer, exorciser, organizer of public entertainments, and choirmaster."[2] The *hungan* possesses powers to predict the future, called *obtenir les yeux*. The *hungan* passes his knowledge of the magical rites down to the *bokor. The latter often purchases this divine knowledge, and he too is then able to predict the future. In the case of the *bokor*, this prophetic power is called *prendre les yeux*.

One of the important features of voodoo is the concept of divination. With the use of *wangas, the *hungan* conjures up benevolent spirits or good luck. The *hungan* conversely uses a *paquet for bad luck, a curse, or even retribution resulting in death. Evil or erring spirits are called *bakas and *azetos.

Candidates for initiation into voodoo receive instruction from the *hungan* or the *mambo. The initiate undergoes several stages. There is the cleansing process known as *laver-tete; following this are the fire ritual or *kanzo; the study of the peculiar language, deities, and *loas* of the cult; and miscellaneous aspects of the ceremony such as dance, rhythms, and symbols. It usually takes six months to three years to complete the initiation process.

Stemming from Dahomean beliefs, Haitian voodooists believe that one possesses two souls: the *gros *bon ange* and the ᵇ*petit bon ange*. When a person is asleep, the *gros bon ange* is free to leave the body. If it does not return, death has occurred. The *gros bon ange* then lingers around the corpse's home until such time as a certain ceremony is held that ushers it off. Such a ceremony is usually held on the ninth day after burial.

The function of the *petit bon ange* is to guide and protect the individual. Like the *gros bon ange*, the *petit bon ange* may also leave the body. It sometimes travels to far-off lands to receive messages from the ancestors, which it brings back to the person. After the departure of the *gros bon ange* from the body at death, the *petit bon ange* may remain behind for several days. It is also believed that after death, the *petit bon ange* may undergo a metamorphosis; that is, it may transform itself into an object such as a stone or stick, or it may even turn into an animal (most commonly a snake). If the *petit bon ange* hides in a jar or container, the jar must be covered to prevent the spirit from escaping to vex or harm members of the family. The *petit bon ange* may also mete out retribution on members of the family if they have neglected their ceremonial responsibilities and sacrifices. The *gros bon ange* may also be captured, in which case it is kept in a clay jar known as a *govi*.

Voodoo ceremonies are usually held at night. An altar inside the *humfort* is decked with bottles of rum, fruits, and *govis*. Hill and Williams describe a typical ceremony as follows:

> The drinks are lifted as an offering to the *loa*. Food and drink are used to summon and placate the *loa*. Food offerings include birds, various animals (pigs, chickens, goats, etc.). When the food offering is complete, followed sometimes by ritual dance and bodily gesticulations, the *loa* begin to possess their human subjects.
>
> The length of time in which a subject remains possessed varies from a few seconds to a more extended period of time. Sometimes the *hungan* must intervene to assist the worshiper in returning to full consciousness and awareness.[3]

An important aspect of the voodoo ceremony is the rhythmic dancing. The movements are directed toward a deity and center around the *poteau-mitan*, though not all dancing is conducted inside a temple. The dance leads the worshiper to a heightened state of spiritual awareness, and he or she eventually reaches the state where possession by a *loa* may take place. Drums beat out specific rhythms for specific deities. This practice goes back to Dahomey. The ceremonial drums and other instruments must be cleansed and purified in order for them to be used in the sacred ceremony. Some of the instruments used in voodoo cults include the ᵇ*assoto*, the ᵇ*acon*, the ᵇ*maracas*, and the ᵇ*ogan*. Music is an intrinsic part of Afro-Haitian life.

Voodoo distinguishes between good and evil ᵇmagic. *Hungan*s or *mambos* generally do not practice evil magic. Their spiritism and magical incantations are directed toward good, as in treating the sick or warding off evil spirits. To do so the *hungan* makes a *wanga*. The practice of evil magic is linked to the *bokor* or the ᵇ*caplata*. Instead of a *wanga*, a *bokor* makes a *paquet* to produce evil.

ᵇ*Zombi* is a term more familiar to outsiders. The *zombi* is popularly thought to be the body of a dead person that has been inhabited by a deity and is directed by that deity to some ulterior purpose. However, the Hollywood version does not accord with the voodoo facts. A *zombi* is a living person whose mind has been altered by drugs or poison, and in a state beyond personal control is directed toward the purposes and aims of the *bakas*.

The evil magic of Haitian voodoo has been a source of intrigue and superstition. Using dolls in order to harm an intended victim is still practiced, but there are other, less familiar workings. Participants use various potions and incantations to bring harm or death to a person. The most feared and dreaded working of black magic is known as the "sending of the dead."

> In this spell, the *boko* is possessed by Baron Samedi who, speaking through his mouth, orders the client to go to a cemetery at midnight, with special offerings of food. There he must gather a handful of earth for each person whom he wishes to kill, which he later spreads on some path frequently taken by his victim. Alternatively a client takes a stone from the graveyard, which will transform itself into a being ready to carry out his evil designs as soon as he throws it against the door of his victim's house. Metraux comments: "Whoever has become the prey of one or more dead people sent against him begins to grow thin, spit blood, and is soon dead. The laying on of this spell is always attended by fatal results unless it is diagnosed in time and a capable *hungan* succeeds in making the dead let go."[4]

In voodoo—as in SANTERIA and most of the SOUTH AMERICAN, CENTRAL AMERICAN, AND CARIBBEAN CULTS—CHRISTIANITY, specifically Roman Catholic Christianity, has made a profound impact on the cultures, but certainly not in a way that was expected or desired by the Catholic church. The syncretistic blending of the sundry deities with the triune God of Christianity made for a unique religion.

Roman Catholic (and Protestant) missionaries have met this phenomenon with mixed emotions. Some priests have learned to tolerate it in order to retain the respect and attention of the people. While some missionaries do lend a sympathetic ear, the church in general does not allow syncretism of this nature to proliferate because it endangers the fundamental nature of its mission and message.

Christianity and voodoo subscribe to two entirely different worldviews. The former is strictly a monotheistic religion while the latter is polytheistic and/or *animistic. Most voodoo cults profess belief in a supreme deity, but this deity must share a place with a multitude of subservient *loas* within the pantheon. Where Christianity has had an impact, missionaries have encountered difficulty in conveying that the God of the *Bible is sovereign Lord of the universe and shares his deity and attributes with no other. Syncretistic in orientation, voodoo readily absorbs Christianity into itself. Roman Catholic saints are incorporated as well, and each is assigned a respective role in the pantheon.[5]

While Christianity teaches that God is one (Deut. 6:4), it also teaches the doctrine of the *Trinity. God is one, yet is comprised of three persons, the Father, the Son, and the Holy Spirit. Each person proceeds out of one essence (Athanasian Creed, Appendix 1). According to the Apostles' Creed (Appendix 1), the Father is "maker of heaven and earth," the Son "suffered . . . was crucified, died and was buried. . . . He rose again from the dead. . . . [and] will come to judge the living and the dead." The Holy Spirit sanctifies, teaches, comforts, and draws sinners to repentance and faith (John 16:5–15). The concepts of sin, the Fall, and the possibility of grace and redemption are foreign to the animistic religions of West Africa, where the emphasis lies more in appeasing the various *loas* through dance, ritual, magic, and ceremony, with the hopes that protection and help might be afforded against *bakas*. The *loas* function in a way not dissimilar to guardian angels in the Christian tradition (Heb. 1:14).

Along with the sharp contrast between monotheism and polytheism, Christianity reacts against the widespread use in voodoo of *sorcery, the *occult, magic, and WITCHCRAFT. The Bible contains numerous injunctions against such practices (e.g., Deut. 18:10–13; 1 Sam. 28:3–25; Mic. 5:12–13; 1 John 4:1–3). These passages alone testify to the seriousness of the church's task in extirpating all of the residual heathenism from those whom it attempts to reach with the gospel.[6]

Voodoo's popularity has spread far and wide beyond Haiti, including the United States. Newspaper articles include cases of voodoo practice. The *Toronto Star* on April 6, 1983, reported that "an estimated three per cent of Hispanic Roman Catholics surveyed in a two year study by the Archdiocese of New York practice voodoo or spiritism." The December 1981 issue of *Newsweek* included the following story:

"You are leaving the U.S.," reads the sign marking the entrance to Oyo Tunji. An African "enclave" in Beaufort County, S.C., founded by eighteen disaffected American blacks in 1970, the village now boasts a population of 172. One resident calls it "the only place in America where a black person can truly discover his identity." But Oyo Tunji has drawn criticism from both state authorities and native Africans.

The village founders wanted to return to the tribal lifestyle of the ancient *Yorubas of Nigeria; they adopted the Yoruba language and dress and built huts with no electricity or running water. Villagers also practice the Yoruba religion—voodoo—complete with oracles, ancestor worship and animal sacrifice. An early-morning visitor may find the remains of a chicken or goat still impaled on an altar. Most of the residents subsist on food stamps and tourist dollars. Their leader, Detroit-born King Oba Seijeman Adefumni I (a.k.a. Walter King), recently started a school to initiate people into one of twelve African priesthoods for a fee of $1,250.[7]

Dr. James Gardner, a Newport Beach, California, psychologist, spent some years teaching in South Africa where he was exposed to the powers of *black magic, eventually becoming convinced that the supernatural forces of voodoo were real. An interview with Gardner appearing in the *Anaheim Register* in 1983 reports:

"The world is a world of spirits. Our lives, our bodies, are insignificant; we are a moment in time and space. We're here to honor the traditions of the past and lay the groundwork for the future," he said.

People become ill when they fail to honor their ancestors, Gardner said. The witch doctors help eliminate the pain by putting their patients back in contact with the spiritual world, he said.

Gardner said he became convinced in South Africa the witch doctors were right.

"There were a number of incidents where the receiving of messages (from my ancestors) made profound and significant differences in my life."

Gardner told of a time when he was driving at night in the South African desert. He said he had 10 minutes worth of gas left in his car but the nearest city was two hours away.

An impulse told him to turn off onto a side road that seemed to lead nowhere, Gardner said. It turned out a gas station was several hundred yards down the side road.

"The station should have been closed and the place should have been deserted. But there just happened to be a night watchman there, and he agreed to sell me some gas."

Gardner said he has other examples too personal to reveal.

He said messages from his ancestors help him trade on the stock market.

"I trade thousands of shares every year, and I've never lost money on a stock deal."

Gardner said the stock market messages are spiritual signs of approval for his living a good life. He knows when he goes astray, Gardner said, because he becomes ill or suffers injury.

It was also in South Africa that Gardner began undergoing a mid-life crisis of sorts, he said, and decided to ease out of his psychology career.[8]

Voodoo has been practiced in New Orleans for over one hundred years. Marie Laveau, the nineteenth-century voodoo queen, led ritualistic ceremonies in Congo Square (now Louis Armstrong Park). Voodoo devotees still visit Laveau's tomb in order to receive good fortune, blessings, and luck. The New Orleans version of voodoo contains the same music, dance, and orgiastic rituals of its Haitian counterpart.

In Mississippi, drugstore pharmacist Joseph A. Gerache reportedly sells his wares not only to those "looking for drugs to alleviate their aches and pains; some are there for potions to drive away evil spirits, win a law suit, control another person, hold onto money, have peace in the home, or catch a lover."[9] Gerache says requests for drugs and pharmaceuticals of this nature are common and are in fact becoming more and more so.

CONCLUSION

There are a large number of cults within voodoo in Haiti today. It is futile to attempt to name or classify them. The general religious motifs of each have been treated in the corpus of this essay. In the religious and sociological matrix of this unique area of the world, the religious syncretism has even become a chief tourist attraction. Popular forms of voodoo are exploited in such main tourist cities as Port-au-Prince. Religious wares and artifacts have proved to be a substantial source of revenue. But far removed from the tourist and cash registers, deep within the heart of the Haitian countryside, in the towns and villages scattered throughout this beautiful yet poverty-stricken tropical island, voodoo magic, ceremonies, and rituals flourish as popularly now as they did in Dahomey centuries ago.[10] Numerous voodoo groups proliferate on the worldwide web. An extensive listing is provided on *www.religious tolerance.org/voodoo.htm*.

Such innocent-looking things as comic books attempt to popularize voodoo for children and young people.
Courtesy Jack M. Roper/CARIS

ADDITIONAL INFORMATION_____

Notes

[1] Douglas Hill and Pat Williams, *The Supernatural* (New York: Hawthorne, 1965), 246.

[2] Ibid., 255.

[3] For a good description of what takes place during possession, see ibid., 277–78.

[4] Ibid., 261.

[5] See SANTERIA for an example of how the Christian saints were renamed for the pantheon of deities within the South American and Caribbean cults.

[6] See also ABAKUA, CABILDO, CANDOMBLE, CONVINCE, MACUMBA, MYAL, SANTERIA, and SOUTH AMERICAN, CENTRAL AMERICAN, AND CARIBBEAN CULTS.

[7] "Old Yoruba Customs Draw New Criticism," *Newsweek* (Dec. 17, 1981), 17.

[8] Dolores Brooks Irwin, "Witch Doctors More Than Comic Relief to Psychologist," *Register* (Aug. 29, 1983), B4.

[9] "Faces in Pharmacy—Witches' Brew," *Drug Topics* (May 3, 1982), 56.

[10] Consult the bibliography for the most recent monographs and periodicals on voodoo.

WAY INTERNATIONAL, THE

By the middle of the 1970s thousands of families and college students had taken the *Power for Abundant Living* (PFAL) course, which first appeared in 1953. To the outsider, the phrase sounds like one of the numerous typical self-help titles sold in many bookstores. Not so! The PFAL course was a series of indoctrinations of a ›cult known as The Way International (TWI). Its founder and leading authority figure was Victor Paul ›Wierwille (1916–1985).

HISTORY

Wierwille was born in 1916 in New Knoxville, Ohio. He was reared in the Evangelical and Reformed Church, which in 1963 was absorbed into the United Church of Christ. Wierwille recalled having been desirous of entering the ministry when he was only eight years old. After graduating from high school, he attended Mission House College and Seminary in Plymouth, Wisconsin, and received a bachelor of divinity degree in 1940. From there he entered the University of Chicago, where he took courses during the summer quarters of 1938–1940. In 1941 he attended and graduated from Princeton Theological Seminary. In 1948 he reportedly received a doctor of theology (Th.D.) degree from Pike's Peak Bible Seminary in Manitou Springs, Colorado. However, in an article titled "A Degree from Pike's Peak," appearing in *Christianity Today*, Wierwille's educational credentials are challenged.

> In a letter from the Colorado Commission on Higher Education, a state official says that Pike's Peak seminary had no resident instruction, no published list of faculty, and no accreditation, and no agency of government supervised it. It offered its degree programs by "extramural" methods, involving the sending of book reviews and papers by mail. The degrees, the official says, have no status except with the institution that conferred them.[1]

Additional education that Wierwille claimed to have acquired included "everything I could take at the Moody Bible Institute, too, through their correspondence courses." No records extant at Moody, however, can confirm this claim.

Wierwille was ordained in 1941 in the Evangelical and Reformed Church. His first assignment was to a church in Payne, Ohio. During this time he began to wrestle with what he believed and started to doubt the theology of ›orthodox CHRISTIANITY. Like so many cult leaders, Wierwille claimed that God spoke to him directly: "He spoke to me audibly, just like I am talking to you now. He said he would teach me the Word as it had not been known since the first century, if I would teach it to others."[2]

In order to assert the uniqueness of their privileged understanding of newfound doctrines, most cult leaders not only claim to have heard divine and audible voices, but also insist that their particular insights are unique and that all others have apostatized. Wierwille is no exception to this general rule: He claimed that all other denominations, both Catholic and Protestant, were wrong. He alone had been gifted to bring God's truth to the world. Wierwille had accumulated up to this time a sizable personal library. Deciding that its pages were filled with waste and error, he threw away over three thousand volumes.

Wierwille began teaching the first series of studies in his PFAL in 1953. In these teachings and in his earlier writings, it was apparent that Wierwille had broken away from his orthodox roots. The PFAL course was an early version of what later evolved into a powerful and effective recruitment program for The Way in the 1970s and 1980s.

While still a clergyman in the Evangelical and Reformed Church, Wierwille took an unendorsed trip to India in 1955, traveling as a missionary. The event caused considerable concern and embarrassment for the Evangelical and Reformed Church. Other missionaries sent letters testifying to the harm Wierwille was causing on the field. The church called for his resignation in 1957, and Wierwille submitted it willingly.

Operating independently now, Wierwille began to develop his ideas, and in 1958 he formed the movement known as The Way International, although the origins of TWI go all the back to Wierwille's radio program, *Vesper Chimes*, that he first aired in Lima, Ohio, in 1942. The name of The Way comes from Acts in the ›Bible, where the Christians are referred to as followers of "the way" (Acts 9:2). Wierwille devised a "biblical research center" on the farm site where he grew up in New Knoxville, Ohio, which became the organization's headquarters.

Success and growth in numbers occurred in the wake of the countercultural Jesus movement of the late 1960s. Wierwille's *Power for Abundant Living* course (conducted over a twelve-week period) became a full-fledged film series in 1967 and brought thousands into its fold in the ensuing two decades. In the 1970s TWI purchased major sites. In 1974 it acquired a former college campus in Emporia, Kansas, which it called The Way College; in 1977 it acquired an existing health spa facility in Rome City, Indiana, calling it The Way College of Biblical Research. Soon it also acquired other assets such as land in New Mexico and Colorado, a prop jet, a Cessna plane, a motor coach, and outreach houses. It also established a publishing arm called the American Christian Press, also located in New Knoxville, Ohio.

Under Wierville's leadership individuals became members of the organization by taking his required course, *Power for Abundant Living*. In order to take this course, everyone had to make a donation. Originally, the "donation" fee was twenty dollars, but it kept rising to two hundred dollars. Advanced courses were also offered after graduating from the PFAL course. As of the year 2002, the PFAL course has been altered and renamed *The Way of Abundance and Power Class Series*.

What newly enlisted members are never told in any of Wierwille's courses was that his organization functions as a mind-controlling cult. According to Steven Hassan, The Way is one of many "destructive cults that combine the characteristics of small ▸fundamentalist Bible ▸sects with the sophisticated training techniques of groups such as the FORUM and the radical politics of purely political cults."[3] Hassan records the testimony of Wendy Ford, a defector from The Way, who related the daily regimen of the group and its "thought-stopping" techniques: "In my group we were taught how to speak in tongues, which was supposed to be a manifestation of the Holy Spirit. We were to do it whenever we started to think for ourselves or to question anything."[4] Ford goes on to disclose that members are told that disagreement or critical thinking was a sign of the ▸devil possessing or tempting one toward unbelief. Thus, fear became a useful tool Wierwille used to keep his disciples subdued. Ronald Enroth's *Youth, Brainwashing, and the Extremist Cults* (Zondervan, 1977) devotes an important chapter to the control techniques employed in this organization.

The various books written by Wierwille include such titles as *Power for Abundant Living*; *Receiving the Holy Spirit Today*; *The Bible Tells Me So*; *The New Dynamic Church*; *The Word's Way*; *God's Magnified Word*; *Jesus Christ Is Not God*; and *Are the Dead Alive Now?* Many pamphlets, tracts, and tapes are available as well.[5] And in 1996, L. Craig Martindale, whom Wierwille appointed as his successor three years before he died in

1985, wrote *The Rise and Expansion of the Church*. This became a required course for The Way members. Martindale, who once was president of the Fellowship of Christian Athletes at the University of Kansas, also replaced Wierwille's *Power for Abundant Living*.

In recent years, TWI has experienced some traumatic changes. In September 2000, Martindale resigned after two former members filed a lawsuit against him. One, a married female member, said he had sexual relations with her, an accusation he admitted. The organization has also suffered financial setbacks and ran afoul of the Internal Revenue Service on several occasions, even once having their tax-exempt status revoked. In 1991, it had to divest itself of its campus in Emporia, Kansas. The site in Rome City, Indiana, on which it had spent hundreds of thousands of dollars in remodeling costs, also had to be sold in 1999, at a substantial loss.

After Martindale resigned, Rosalie Rivenbank became president of TWI (October 2000). She directs the organization out of its New Knoxville, Ohio, headquarters. Under her leadership the organization continues to present itself as a biblically based religious group. For instance, its website currently cites such passages as John 14:6, 1 Thessalonians 5:21, and 2 Timothy 3:16–17 in support of its activities, and the heretically unchristian teachings, introduced by Wierwille, are still in vogue. It still also publishes *The Way Magazine*, a bimonthly periodical that promotes TWI's heretical teachings.

Given TWI's recent intra-organizational turmoil and financial losses, together with the many deceptions it perpetrated on its members for years, its membership has dropped dramatically from its touted number of 100,000 members in the mid 1980s. But this figure, says Sue Pierce, an ex-leader of the TWI who once had access to the group's records, was highly exaggerated. She argues there were never more than 35,000 members. In 2003, it is estimated that there are only about 5,000 members.

Obviously, TWI's success was largely the result of Wierville's personality and his psychologically appealing methods, promoted chiefly through his *Power for Abundant Living* course. Yet, many of its members join because of disenchantment with religious experiences, or lack thereof, in mainline churches, and because individuals have received little or no solid biblical instruction in the churches in which they grew up. It is these unfortunate phenomena that have often helped produce followers of clever charismatic cult leaders, of which Victor Paul Wierwille was a prime example. Since his death in 1985, the intense appeal that TWI had in the

1970s waned. The infighting over leadership after Wierwille's death caused a number of long-time leaders to break away into several factions, causing financial turmoil at the headquarters. But the organization is by no means dead; it still masquerades as a biblically based Christian group.

ORGANIZATION

The Way is organized around the symbol of a tree. Each part of a tree represents the structural components of the organization. The breakdown is as follows: the "Root"—Victor Paul Wierwille; the "Trunk"—various national organizations; the "Branches"—various statewide units; the "Limbs"—city units. Each limb is divided into "Twigs," which are the individual home Bible study groups.[6]

TEACHINGS

The basic doctrines of The Way International are outlined as follows.

God

God is not a triune being. Jesus is not God the Son, and the Holy Spirit is certainly not God. In a discussion of God's attributes, Wierwille contends that "God's ability always equals God's willingness." Along with this comes the assessment: "What God is able to do, He is willing to do, and what He is willing to do, He is able to do."[7]

Wierwille's basic contention is that there has never been a theological concept of God as being a ▸Trinity in the context of the Old or New Testaments. Rather, he attributes the triuneness of God to a pagan origin. Like ISLAM, JUDAISM, the UNITARIAN-UNIVERSALIST ASSOCIATION, and many modern religious sects, Wierwille accuses Christianity of teaching a plurality of gods.

Against this polemic, traditional Christianity responds by reaffirming the belief in one God. The Athanasian Creed summarizes the whole of Christian doctrine in this matter: "And the catholic faith is this, that we worship one God in three persons and three persons in one God, neither confusing the persons nor dividing the substance" (Appendix 1).[8] This formula is not the product of pagan thought. Athanasius and the orthodox church fathers reached this conclusion against ▸Arianism on the basis of such Bible passages as Matthew 28:19; Luke 3:21–22; 2 Corinthians 13:14; and others. The heart of Wierwille's opposition to the Trinity lies in his opposition to the deity of Christ (see below). This is, of course, the same point on which Athanasius opposed Arius in the fourth century, and

this scenario has repeated itself on several occasions in the ensuing centuries.

Jesus Christ

Wierwille contends that Jesus Christ is the Son of God but not God the Son, and that we may know this based on the sheer weight of the witness of Scripture. Wierwille writes:

> We note that Jesus Christ is directly referred to as the "Son of God" in more than 50 verses in the New Testament; he is called "God" in four. (Never is he called "God the Son.") By sheer weight of this evidence alone, 50 to 4, the truth should be evident.[9]

Jesus was born of Mary and Joseph but was not God. He was sinless because God created a sperm that was endowed with sinless ▸soul life. Therefore Jesus was born sinless. The essential relationship, then, between God and Jesus is Father to Son, because God provided Joseph with the sperm necessary to impregnate Mary with a sinless child. Jesus therefore was certainly not coeternal with the Father. The Son was only in existence when he was born of the virgin. Before this, Jesus existed in God's foreknowledge only.

Concerning Christ's crucifixion, Jesus could not have been God and at the same time have been able to atone for the sins of the world. Jesus, rather, had to be a man. Only men die, not God.

The Way's understanding of Christ is more heterodox than ancient Arianism in that the latter, while denying Jesus' coeternality with the Father, did not deny that Jesus existed before his human birth. Moreover, Arius did not deny the virgin birth of Christ as did Wierwille.

By asserting that Jesus could not have been God because God cannot die, Wierwille ignores or fails to comprehend the historic Chalcedonian ▸Christology, which held to the personal union between the human and divine natures of Christ (Rom. 1:3–4). Jesus' humanity and deity are united in such a way that they are "inseparable," "unconfused," "unchanged," and "indivisible." In the Christian tradition, therefore, when the Bible speaks of the human qualities of Jesus as being salvific—"The blood of Jesus, his Son, purifies us from all sin" (1 John 1:7)—it is understood that human blood saves insofar as it is *Jesus'* human blood. The human qualities of Christ are inseparably linked to the divine. Therefore, when the church contends that God indeed died on the cross, it is by virtue of the personal union between the humanity and deity of Christ that one can speak of God dying.

Holy Spirit

To Wierwille, the Holy Spirit is not a third person of the Christian Trinity. God is Spirit and God is holy, he therefore must be the "holy spirit."

There is a second reference to the Holy Spirit. When reading Wierwille, one must distinguish between the capitalized "Holy Spirit" and the lowercase "holy spirit." In the first instance, as we have seen, the reference is to the Father. In the second use, "holy spirit" speaks of a unique gift of grace that God has bestowed on humanity—a power or gift placed within the believer. God does not dwell within the believer, but this "inherent power," or holy spirit, does. Wierwille's *Receiving the Holy Spirit Today* describes also how one may receive the holy spirit. He argues that the sound of the "rushing mighty wind" of Acts 2 was in reality the sound of the breathing of the apostles in the Upper Room. The seeker of the holy spirit is taught to breathe in a prescribed manner as one means of receiving the gift.

Against these ideas, orthodox Christianity firmly upholds the doctrine of the Holy Spirit as being the third person of the Trinity. Nowhere in the Bible or in Christian tradition is the Holy Spirit portrayed as consisting of two separate entities. The Holy Spirit is clearly distinguished from the Father in many passages of Scripture (e.g., Matt. 28:19; Luke 3:21–22; John 7:39; 14:16–17; 15:26; 16:13; Acts 2:17; 2 Cor. 13:14). For this reason, the ecumenical creeds (Nicene and Apostles' creeds, Appendix I) recognize that the Holy Spirit is the third person of the Trinity, who is the Sanctifier, Teacher, and Comforter of believers. Second, one searches in vain in Scripture for the existence of a lowercase holy spirit who replaces the fallen spirit of humankind. For example, Romans 8:16 clearly distinguishes between the Holy Spirit and the human spirit (sometimes called the soul). The Holy Spirit comes to and dwells in and with the believer. Never has the human spirit been eradicated and replaced by a nonhuman holy spirit.

Humanity

Before the Fall, human beings possessed body, soul, and spirit. As a result of the fall into sin, Wierwille teaches that the spirit, or that aspect of human nature that was able to know God, was forfeited. A human being is, like the animals, a physical body endowed with soul, or "breath." As observed above, the human race was deprived of spirit until such time as God poured it out, and this took place on the Day of Pentecost in Acts 2 when the believers were gathered together in the Upper Room. At this time the spirit-less were given the holy spirit once again. This, of course, spells

out important implications about The Way's understanding of salvation (see below).

Sin

Wierwille draws up a dichotomy between the "spirit" and the flesh/soul. He defines sin as the breaking of God's laws and concludes that believers continue to sin throughout their lives in their body/soul, but in their "spirit" they cannot sin.

This dichotomy once again stands in contrast to the Bible and Christian tradition. While different Christian traditions have argued that a person is a trichotomy (body, soul, and spirit) or a dichotomy (body, soul/spirit), it has never been the case that the "body" and human "soul" remain sinful while the "spirit" is sinless. The Hebraic and biblical view of the human being is that all of life is a composite whole. The separation between "soul and body," or "flesh and spirit," arose out of Greek dualism, which, as some believe, Paul contended against as he brought Christianity into the Greek world. Sin is what separates the human race from God (Rom. 3:23). Sin is not part of the substance of humankind; rather, it is a foreign entity introduced at the Fall (Rom. 7:17).

Salvation

The quest of salvation is to regain the lost aspect of human nature, the "spirit." Salvation must be accompanied by an oral confession of faith. Evidence to indicate that one has been saved is that the "speaking in other tongues" or languages must be present. At death, the believer remains in the grave until the final resurrection from the dead.

There is no convergence in the doctrine of salvation between The Way and Christianity. There is no biblical warrant for the necessity of the presence of tongues to prove one's salvation. Many conversions in the New Testament take place with no mention of tongues (e.g., Acts 16:15; 30–32; 18:24–28; 28:24).

Salvation is the direct result of being "justified by faith" (Rom. 3:28), with no human works included in the process (Eph. 2:8–9). Moreover, the early church evidenced a clear understanding of salvation as the direct result of the person and work of the Lord Jesus Christ as articulated in the Nicene and Apostles' creeds (Appendix 1) and in many biblical passages.

Church

The one true church is The Way International. God has spoken to and called Victor Paul Wierwille as his one instrument for establishing his true church on earth. If members of The Way are serious in upholding this position, they must realize that a multitude of other religious leaders have made claims similar to those of Wierwille.[10]

Christianity teaches that the one true church is the "holy catholic (universal) church," comprised of the "communion of saints" (Apostles' Creed). It is the church as the bride of Christ that has existed since the Day of Pentecost (Acts 2) and has triumphantly marched through history. It has existed throughout history and is worldwide.

Eschatology

The Way maintains a strong belief in ᐧdispensationalism. Various traditions within the pale of Christianity have also embraced some form of dispensationalism.

Additional Teachings

Wierwille's teachings also included the startling claim, contrary to the consensus of scholarship, that the New Testament was originally written in Aramaic. He also taught that Christ was raised from the dead on the Jewish Sabbath, or Saturday, instead of Sunday; and that water baptism is to be replaced by a baptism in the "holy spirit."

CONCLUSION

The Way International was most influential in the 1970s, particularly among college students. Its numbers went into sharp decline in the decades following. The Way members continue to reside in New Knoxville, a rural part of Ohio, and they continue to meet in supervised home fellowships.

ADDITIONAL INFORMATION_____

Headquarters
The Way International, P.O. Box 328, New Knoxville, OH 45871.

Website
www.theway.com

Sacred Text
The Bible (Aramaic version). Numerous writings of Wierwille, such as *Jesus Christ Is Not God*. George Lamsa's *The Holy Bible from Ancient Eastern Manuscripts*. Indian bishop K. C. Pilla: *The Orientalisms of the Bible* and *Light Through an Eastern Window* (Melton, 1986).

Publication
The Way Magazine

Statistics
The largest membership is estimated to have been 35,000 in the 1970s. The numbers declined after that. In 1995 the group had declined to 20,000, and it is estimated that it got as low as 10,000 by the end of the century and 5,000 in 2003.[11]

Notes
[1] Herbert Diamond, "A Degree From Pike's Peak," *Christianity Today* (Nov. 21, 1975).
[2] Elena S. Whiteside, *The Way—Living in Love*, 2nd ed. (New Knoxville, Ohio: American Christian Press, 1972), 178.
[3] Steven Hassan, *Combatting Cult Mind Control* (Rochester, Vt.: Park Street Press, 1990), 91.
[4] Ibid., 91–92.
[5] See the bibliography for additional recommended readings.
[6] Walter Martin, *The New Cults* (Ventura, Calif.: Regal, 1980), 43.
[7] Victor Paul Wierwille, *Power for Abundant Living* (New Knoxville, Ohio: American Christian Press, 1971), 21–22.
[8] See also the article on CHRISTADELPHIANISM for further observations on the Trinity.
[9] Victor Paul Wierwille, *Jesus Christ Is Not God* (1975), as quoted by Martin, *The New Cults*, 55.
[10] See Joseph ᐧSmith, Moses ᐧDavid, Herbert W. ᐧArmstrong, Charles Taze ᐧRussell, John Robert ᐧStevens, ᐧBubba Free John, to name just a few.
[11] Cited by John C. Juedes, "The Incredible Shrinking Way," furnished by email (January, 2002).

WITCHCRAFT

Witchcraft as a term is difficult to assign any single definition. In some cases, it is closely associated with the harnessing of supernatural powers, in which case its definition is strongly synonymous with ᐧmagic. When such magic is used for the malevolent purposes, it is called ᐧblack magic; when used for benevolent reasons, it is commonly referred to as ᐧwhite magic. Also, we must make a classic distinction between witchcraft as it developed in the Middle Ages and modern witchcraft. The former is called ᐧGothic witch-craft, more commonly associated with traditional SATANISM. Modern witchcraft, sometimes termed ᐧwicca, has undergone a separate historical development. Aspects of each of these developments are treated in this essay.

HISTORY

Gothic Witchcraft

The medieval Catholic Church saw devils and witches as being virtually identical and, for this reason,

Even today the city of Salem, Massachusetts, is known for the seventeenth-century witch trials, as evidenced by the insignia on their police patrol vehicles.
Courtesy George A. Mather

launched an all-out crusade to stamp them out. Feminist scholar Mary Daly notes:

A most striking example of the selective total destruction of a large number of women was the torturing and burning of women condemned by the church as witches. The most important medieval work on the subject, *Malleus Maleficarum*, written by two Dominican priests (>Sprenger and >Kraemer) in the fifteenth century, proclaims that "it is women who are chiefly addicted to evil superstitions." This is, after all, only to be expected, for "all witchcraft comes from carnal lust, which is in women, insatiable." According to the authors, men are protected from such a crime because Jesus was a man. Unlike the mythical Eve, the witches were real living persons condemned by the church's hierarchy, which was threatened by their power.[1]

>*Malleus Maleficarum* (*The Witches' Hammer*) was commissioned by Pope Innocent VIII and was published in 1486. It set forth rules for identifying, prosecuting, and punishing witches. Paul Jewett, commenting on the manuscript of Sprenger and Kraemer, observes:

Of all the parts of the *Witches' Hammer*, none is so infamous as the author's vile estimate of woman. The very title, *Malleus Maleficarum*, is in the feminine because, as the authors inform their readers, the overwhelming majority of those involved in this hellish conspiracy are women. . . . Helen, Jezebel, and Cleopatra are cited as exemplifying that pernicious agency which has wrought the destruction of whole kingdoms.[2]

In the Middle Ages, many believed that witches were the devil's handmaids and that they were numerous. Many accused of witchcraft were rounded up and executed during the Inquisition. Protestants were also vehement in their zeal to eradicate witches. This came to a climax in America in the infamous Salem witch trials of 1692.

Popular myth has it that witchcraft was rampant in early colonial America. But this is not supported by the facts. While it is perhaps true that hundreds of thousands of those accused of witchcraft were tried and condemned in Europe during the 1600s, only twelve were executed in the Massachusetts Bay Colony before 1692.

Trouble broke out in Salem, Massachusetts, however, when two daughters of a minister, Samuel Parris, had undergone a series of convulsions. They had participated in a session of >divination with Parris's slave girl, Tituba. Tituba was from the East Indies and had allegedly been asked to help the girls see into the future. The girls explained that they had been bewitched by Tituba along with other "witches," whom the girls started to name. The accusations continued until more than fifty women had been named, including the governor's wife. In May 1692 the executions of the accused began. By July the jails were full of those suspected of witchcraft. About fifty repented and were subsequently released, but by September, twenty-two "witches" had been hanged.

The clergy had continually cried out for mercy to be extended to the many who were being accused. In 1697 the mood changed dramatically when it was learned through recantations that much innocent blood had been spilled. A day for fasting was proclaimed throughout Massachusetts (Jan. 14, 1697, called the Official Day of Humiliation), and the magistrates issued a public apology. This set in motion an incipient anger that would redefine the attitude of New Englanders for centuries to come, shaping a peculiar spirituality endemic to the Northeast. Traditional witchcraft would dissipate at the close of the 1600s, not to emerge again until the twentieth century.

Modern Witchcraft

Anthropologist and supposed >witch Margaret >Murray (1863–1963) argued that witchcraft predates CHRIS-

TIANITY. She believed witches existed in ancient pagan cultures before the time of the ᵇBible's development. While it is true that ancient pagans practiced various rituals that can indeed be construed as being the activity of witches, it is difficult to substantiate Murray's thesis in lieu of the scattered history of preindustrial societies. It is simply too difficult to piece together so many eclectic fragments of various beliefs and practices endemic to cultures unrelated to each other. Moreover, scholars cannot trace a single organized matriarchal or witchcraft religion in ancient times.

Nevertheless, it is important to point out that modern witches do disavow ties to Christianity. There are several reasons for this. First, it is in fact true that ancient pagans practiced sorcery and magic that could easily be construed as being the "craft" of the witch. ᵇDruid priests, Mesopotamians, Egyptians, Greeks, and Romans used magic for such various purposes as healing, harnessing nature's powers, seeking military victories, political offices, and the like. There is indeed evidence that the ancient Mesopotamians practiced black magic. That the Bible mentions the witch of Endor (1 Sam. 28:7), to whom Saul went for spiritual guidance, shows that sorcery was an established institution contemporaneous with, if not before, the arrival of the Hebrews in Palestine. Witches, therefore, following Murray's cues, point to this history as being evidence that witchcraft has been an ancient and well-established institution throughout the centuries, not a hybrid offshoot of Christianity.

Second and more important, many modern witches distance themselves from Christianity because of what they claim is the latter's proliferation of a patriarchal, male-dominated religion that has historically ignored the role of women in the church and society. For example, Janet and Stewart Ferrar, in comparing ISLAM with Christianity, make the following observation:

> Islam's heaven is much more interesting, if only because ᵇMohammed was sexually healthy and bequeathed to his followers none of the inhibitions and neuroses which woman-hating Paul of Tarsus imposed on Christianity.... To the ᵇMoslem, woman is inferior but intended by ᵇAllah to be the giver and receiver of delight. To Pauline Christianity, woman is not only inferior, she is a temptation to sin, and herself morally weak if not actually wicked (a view of which the church has never entirely rid itself—though we can find no authority for it in the words and deeds of Jesus).[3]

Earlier in their volume titled *A Witches Bible Compleat*, the Ferrars note:

One might also point out that ... Catholicism, JUDAISM, Islam, and much of Protestantism still stubbornly cling to the male monopoly of priesthood as "divinely ordained;" the Priestess is still banned, to the great spiritual impoverishment of mankind.[4]

This of course implies that witchcraft is a religion for women only. This, too, is untrue. Witches portrayed popularly as being old female hags with black pointed hats riding on broomsticks and casting ᵇspells brewed from a ᵇcauldron are as much a part of folklore and myth as is the idea of the ᵇdevil being a red-suited, horned-headed creature bearing a pitchfork. Witchcraft is, more correctly, a religion that focuses on nature worship and fertility rituals. For this reason, the feminine aspect of witchcraft plays a prominent role. There have traditionally been as many, if not more, male witches/sorcerers than female in some pagan circles in the past (e.g., the Druids). Nevertheless, witchcraft/sorcery has

Many people today perpetuate the myth of the devil being a red-suited, horned-headed creature. The costume is especially popular at Mardi Gras and on Halloween.

Courtesy Jack M. Roper/CARIS

been dominated by women. Douglas Hill and Pat Williams ponder why this is so:

> Women have always predominated in the history of witches, and a host of more or less unsatisfactory explanations of this fact could be cited. For instance, sixteenth century writers felt women were more credulous and impressionable than men, and so more easily tempted by ᵇSatan. Others felt that Satan, being a male personification of evil, preferred women assistants. Later authorities like the nineteenth century pathologist J. M. Chariot saw that demonic possession was in fact a form of hysteria (from *hystera*, the Greek word for uterus), and considered it primarily a female sexual disorder. Anthropologists, recalling the female ᵇshamans of many primitive tribes, suggested that the supposedly "irrational" tendencies of the female left an opening for ᵇoccult and quasi-religious belief. Probably the real explanation (if there is one) will somehow be connected with the fact that women were for so long thought to be inferior beings and thus were considered more susceptible to foolishness and sin; also they were less able to protect themselves against accusations leveled at them by the entirely male and officially celibate Church and Inquisition.[5]

The story of modern witchcraft is another chapter in the book on traditional witchcraft, however. The modern craft goes by the name *witchcraft* or *wicca*. We have already observed Margaret Murray's contribution to the modern cause. Her article in the 1922 edition of *Encyclopaedia Britannica* and her books, *The Witch-cult in Western Europe* (1921) and *The God of the Witches* (1933), were responsible for keeping both memory and interest alive.

The definitive start of the modern witchcraft era began with Gerald ᵇGardner (1884–1964). Gardner had accumulated an extensive occult background. As an archaeologist, he had spent considerable time in his formative years in Southeast Asia, where he learned the secrets of the Malaysian magical knife (*kris*—a dagger with a wavy blade) and became a Mason (in Ceylon) and a nudist. In 1939 Gardner returned to England as an avid occultist. He immediately became a member of the Crotona Fellowship of ROSICRUCIANS. Through these associations, Gardner met Dorothy Clutterbuck, whom he called "Old Dorothy" in his writings.

It was Dorothy Clutterbuck who is believed to have initiated Gardner into witchcraft. Under the name of "Scire," Gardner authored the book *High Magic's Aid* (1949) and published another work titled *Witchcraft*

Today (1954). Of this latter monograph, J. Gordon Melton states, "*Witchcraft Today* maintained that Witchcraft was a dying religion and that Gardner wanted to record what witches actually did for posterity."[6] Confirming the weakness of the Murray thesis (above), Melton continues:

> Research suggests that Gardner did not discover a pre-existing Witchcraft group. A paper by Gardner published by *Ripley's Believe It or Not* disclosed that Gardner took the magical resources he acquired in Asia and a selection of Western magical texts and created a new religion centered upon the worship of the Mother-Goddess.[7]

This latter point is crucial, for it is precisely ᵇMother Goddess worship that has become the focus of modern witches. Gardner simply reaffirmed Murray's thesis that a preexistent Mother Goddess religion had been extant through many centuries before the arrival of Christianity. *Witchcraft Today* was also a deposit of ideas gathered from numerous occult sources.

In addition to Murray, the influence of Aleister ᵇCrowley, THEOSOPHY, FREEMASONRY, ritual/sex magic, and so on all blended together eclectically in the writings of Gerald Gardner. Out of the cauldron of his mind emerged modern witchcraft. From this, a new generation of advocates for a new feminist spirituality has emerged. Among these are Alexander ᵇSanders (d. 1988), Sybil ᵇLeek (d. 1983), Raymond and Rosemary Buckland (the first American witches), Starhawk, Margot Adler, Jim Alan, Jessie Wicker Bell, Gavin and Yvonne Frost, Doreen Valiente, Zsuzanna Budapest, Donna Cole, Ed Fitch, Janet and Stewart Ferrar, and many others.

BELIEFS AND PRACTICES

The sheer number of modern-day witches suggests a wide variety of beliefs and practices. However, despite the pluralism and diversity, distinct principles derived from Gardnerian wicca are common to most modern witches.

First and foremost is the belief in the Great Mother Goddess. Throughout history, she has been manifested in numerous forms: for example, Artemis, Astarte, Aphrodite, Diana, Kore, Hecate. The consort Pan (the Horned God) is the male principal of wicca. He too possesses a varied nomenclature, including such names as Adonis, Apollo, Baphomet, Cernunnos, Dionysius, Lucifer, Osiris, and Thor. The symbolism is rich. The Mother Goddess is represented by the moon and the Horned God by the sun. Each year, Pan dies and is brought back to life in a ceremony called ᵇ"drawing down the sun." The ceremony associated with the Mother Goddess is called ▸"drawing down the moon." Each coven varies in the ceremonial details.

Second, wiccans practice certain rites that are believed to harmonize with the rhythm of nature. The witches calendar includes high festival days that pinpoint key phases in the seasonal progress of Mother Earth. The eight seasonal festivals, known as ▸sabbats, are as follows (in chronological order):

1. ▸Imbolg—February 2 (also called Imbolc or Oimelc)
2. ▸Spring Equinox—March 21 (also called Ostara.)
3. ▸Beltane—April 30
4. ▸Midsummer Solstice—June 22 (usually called Summer Solstice.)
5. ▸Lughnasadh—July 31 (also called Lammas.)
6. ▸Autumn Equinox—September 21
7. ▸Samhain—October 31 (▸Halloween)
8. ▸Winter Solstice—December 22 (▸Yule)[8]

Imbolg, Beltane, Lughnasadh, and Samhain are known as the major sabbats. The two equinoxes and two solstices are the minor sabbats. Their exact dates vary from year to year and can occur on the 20th, 21st, or 22nd of the month. Additional meeting times for covens are called ▸esbats and often occur on the full and/or new moon.

Third, witches and pagans practice various forms of magic. This includes ▸clairvoyance, ▸divination, ▸astral projection, and ▸spells. High magic includes the art of healing. Witches are drawn to the principle that healing is a natural process of Mother Earth. Nature provides medicines in the form of herbs. Knowing which ones to apply to which ailments of the body is an area of expertise in which many witches specialize. Spells are also employed to effect healing.

Fourth, witches follow a principle of ethics known as the ▸Wiccan Rede: "That ye harm none, do what ye will." Implied within this principle is the notion held among witches that to be a witch means to seek to effect harmony with the world, nature, and other human beings. This principle dispels the notion that witches perceive their work as effecting evil. According to

The rituals of witchcraft are found in *A Witches Bible Compleat.*
Courtesy Jack M. Roper/CARIS

Melton, witches believe that "the effects of magic will be returned threefold upon the person working it, a belief that severely limits the pronouncing of curses."[9]

Fifth, religion is generally viewed as being synonymous with the practice of magic. Magic is able to develop and nurture the inner planes of the mind, the "collective unconscious," the spirit world, and so on. Carl Jung used the term *collective unconsciousness*, that individuals draw on a deep memory pool from the past. This pool holds experiences common to each race or to humanity in general. Modern witches, according to one theory, believe that the gods and goddesses are simply these Jungian archetypes symbolizing the capabilities and potentialities that are part of every human being. The most commonly held view among witches and pagans, however, is that the gods and goddesses are "personifications of the ▸monistic, genderless, universal, and eternal Life Force—the divine primal energy or principle."[10]

Sixth, the belief in gods (plural) and goddesses (plural), whether symbolic or not, advances the point that wiccan groups embrace a ▸polytheistic conceptualization of the universe. For modern witches, this does not mean so much that they believe in a pantheon of male and female deities, but that reality itself is understood in many different ways. Truth is not a matter of correspondence between language, the world, or any one conceptual model. Put differently, there is no singular expression of truth. Truths that are contradictory are held to simultaneously.

Seventh, witches in many covens pass through three distinct stages or "degrees" of initiation. After passing through the first degree, the neophyte becomes a member of a coven. But at the same time, some are already witches from birth, because of ▸reincarnation from a past life. Initiation into a coven may be conducted by a high priest or high priestess. As a member of the coven, the new priest/priestess begins to work toward passing through the second degree. The witch who does the training and subsequent initiating of another into the second degree does so with caution. Janet and Stewart Ferrar note:

Initiation can have deep psychic and karmic repercussions, and if it is irresponsibly given, the result may become part of the initiator's own *karma. Coven leaders should remember this when they are deciding whether somebody is ready for his or her second degree, and ask themselves in particular whether the candidate is mature enough to be entrusted with the right to initiate others; if not, his or her mistakes may well rebound on *their* karma.[11]

Third-degree initiation is the highest attainment. In this stage the witch becomes a high priest/priestess, who is then able to begin and govern a new coven, exercising complete authority over the other lower-ranking witches. As long as the third-degree witch remains in the parent coven, however, he or she must submit to the authority of the high priest/priestess of that coven.

To attain the third degree, a candidate must participate in the Great Rite. This involves a ceremony in which the initiate participates "symbolically" or "actually" in sexual intercourse with the high priest/priestess (of the opposite sex). Practices vary greatly among covens. In the Gardnerian and *Alexandrian traditions, many covens only perform this part of the Great Rite after all other witches leave the room. In some, the "actual rite" is performed only when it involves a husband and wife. If the Great Rite is conducted symbolically, the *athame* (for the male witch) and the cup (for the female) are joined together. At a point during the ceremony, the *athame* is plunged into the cup or chalice filled with wine.

Some witches practice their craft *skyclad (in the nude). Others dress in ceremonial robes and still others simply wear street clothes. The most ideal environment is outdoors, where the ceremony is closest to nature.

Finally, many symbols accompany wiccan lore. Most of them have a standing tradition within the history of the occult. The *amulet, *talisman, *ankh, *athame*, circle, pentagram, cup or chalice, *pentacle, *rune, *sigil, *tarot, *wand, cauldron, altar, and *witches ladder all play a role in wicca.[12]

CONTRASTS WITH CHRISTIANITY

At the outset, it is apparent that the religion espoused by witchcraft is sharply at odds with traditional Christianity. Divination, SPIRITUALISM, magic, sorcery, witchcraft, and the occult in general are condemned in the Bible (e.g., Ex. 22:18; Lev. 19:26, 31; 20:6; Deut. 18:10–12; 2 Kings 17:10–20; 21:1–6; 23:4–7, 24–25; 2 Chron. 33:6; Acts 13:6–12; 16:16–18; Gal. 5:19–20).

The polytheism in witchcraft is also a gross contradiction to the strict *monotheism of the Judeo-Christian heritage. Like most non-Christian religions of the world, witchcraft obliterates the distinction between the Creator and creation. Wiccans deify nature in such a way that both God and nature are synonymous. Further, since divinity lies in nature and in the cosmos, it also resides within each person. Here we can observe that wiccan thought closely parallels HINDUISM and other Eastern paradigms.

Chalices are a common utensil used in ceremonial rituals.
Courtesy Jack M. Roper

Traditional Christian thought holds that witchcraft, like all other contrasting religions, has its source in Satan, the "god of this age" (2 Cor. 4:4). To teach that God resides outside of the *revelation of himself in history and in the Bible is to deny the most fundamental principle on which the Christian faith is grounded. God has created and revealed himself to the world in the person of the Son of God, Jesus Christ. Jesus' purpose for coming into the world was to win salvation for the human race by offering himself as an atonement for sin (Rom. 3:21–26). For wiccan groups, the concept of sin and the subsequent need for salvation are archaic notions at best. If sin is anything at all, it is alienation from one's own divine potential.

Wiccan thought offers a variety of views concerning the existence of evil. In the most common view, evil is not a separate reality apart from good, as *Manichaeans, satanists, and other groups hold, but rather is a necessary aspect of good. However any witch understands the relationship of evil to good, he or she is still left with an enormous problem that is not explained by the wiccan worldview. Is the evil that human beings encounter in the world and in history an acceptable and healthy aspect of a reality that, according to wiccan thought, has no flaws to begin with? How can such a view of evil be reconciled to the Wiccan Rede, "That ye harm none, do what ye will"? Is not evil harmful? To the victims and families of a murderer it certainly is.

Moreover, the question that remains unanswered is: If there is no one absolute standard or set of truths exclusive of all falsities, how can even the Wiccan Rede be regarded as true? To grant that it is, is to grant that there is at least one absolute truth. Many witches are willing to live with this blatant contradiction because of either naïveté, intellectual dishonesty, or convenience.

For Christianity, God is the source of all truth, and the Bible is God's revelation of such truth, deemed necessary for the world.

There are many other points of discussion concerning the contrasts between Christianity and wicca. But to elucidate them here would serve no purpose simply because these two systems of thought differ on nearly every count.

CONCLUSION

According to J. Gordon Melton, there were an estimated thirty thousand witches and neopagans in North America (as of 1986).[13] Many belong to local covens, of which there are hundreds around the United States. The average size of a coven is thirteen members.

As with Satanism, the reader should be cautioned concerning the sensationalism so prevalent in the media, which caters willingly to the public. Many people simply do not know much about the occult, and unfortunately are all too willing to believe what they hear or read. One should also beware of the Christian "experts," who are usually those who have been converted to Christianity and are instantly ready to conduct seminars and lectures, informing and educating the ignorant.[14]

ADDITIONAL INFORMATION

Major Witchcraft Groups

See the table below for the five major witchcraft groups in the United States.

Some covens attach themselves to these major organizations and become integral parts of their infrastructures. The majority of witchcraft covens, like those in Satanism, operate covertly and independently. A number of covens in the United States have fought for and have won the status of legitimate religions protected by the First Amendment, thereby achieving tax-exempt status. For example, the Rosegate Coven located in Providence, Rhode Island, achieved tax-exempt status in 1989.[15] Other covens around the country are following suit.

Witchcraft and Wiccan Covens and Traditions

In addition to the chart below, there are many covens and traditions. These include Algard, Alexandrian, American Celtic Wicca, The American Order for the Brotherhood of Wicca, Church and School of Wicca, Church of Circle Wicca, Cymmry Wicca, Dianic (feminist) Wicca, Georgian Wicca, Maidenhill Wicca, Nova Wicca, Pecti-Wicca, Reformed Congregation of the Goddess, Seax Wicca, Temple of Wicca.

Associations and Organizations

Association of Cymmry Wicca, the Athanor Fellowship, Branches, Center of the Divine Ishtar, Circle, the Council of Isis Community, the Covenant of the Goddess, Goddess Rising, the New Wiccan Church, Our Lady of Enchantment, Our Lady of the Woods, the Pagan Federation, Women in Constant Creative Action (W.I.C.C.A.).

NAME	LOCATION	FOUNDERS	PUBLICATIONS
Circle Sanctuary	Mount Horeb, Wisconsin	Selena Fox, Jim Alan	*Circle Network News; Circle Guide to Wicca and Pagan Resources*
Covenant of the Goddess	Berkeley, California	No one person	*Covenant of the Goddess Newsletter*
Feminist Wicca	Nationwide	Numerous personalities	*The Wise Woman*
Gardnerian Wicca (Usually called Gardnerian Tradition)	Long Island, New York	Gerald Gardner; Rosemary and Raymond Buckland	*The Hidden Wicca Path*
Saxon Witchcraft	Charlottesville, Virgina	Raymond Bucklin	*The Tree* (1974) (book)

Fesivals and Gatherings

There are many. A few are the Ancient Ways Festival, Australian Wiccan Conference, Celebration of Womanhood, Covenant of the Goddess Grand Council, Festival of Women's Spirituality, Goddess Gathering, Harvest Survival and Healing Gathering, Pacific Circle Gathering, Pagan Spirit Gathering, Samhain Festival, Samhain Seminar, Samhain Witches' Ball, The Solitary Convention, The Spiral Dance.[16]

Websites

Many of the individual covens and wiccan groups have websites. Interested persons can search for them via internet search engines.

Statistics

Estimates of witches range from 50,000 to 200,000, with 300,000 to 400,000 neopagans in total around the world.[17]

Notes

[1] Mary Daly, *Beyond God the Father: Toward a Philosophy of Women's Liberation* (Boston: Beacon Press, 1973), 63.

[2] Paul K. Jewett, *Man as Male and Female* (Grand Rapids: Eerdmans, 1975), 157–58.

[3] Janet and Stewart Ferrar, *A Witches Bible Compleat*, 2 vols. (New York: Magickal Childe, 1984), 2:111–12.

[4] Ibid., 1:20–21.

[5] Douglas Hill and Pat Williams, *The Supernatural* (New York: Hawthorn, 1965), 174.

[6] J. Gordon Melton, *Encyclopedic Handbook of Cults in America* (New York: Garland, 1986), 212.

[7] Ibid.

[8] See the dictionary portion of this volume for a more detailed treatment of each of the eight sabbats.

[9] Melton, *Handbook of Cults*, 213.

[10] Craig S. Hawkins, "The Modern World of Witchcraft," *Christian Research Journal* (Winter/Spring, 1990), 13. There are other commonly held views that we have excluded here.

[11] Ferrar, *A Witches Bible Compleat*, 2:22.

[12] For an outstanding treatment of symbols employed in witchcraft and feminist wicca, see Barbara G. Walker, *The Women's Dictionary of Symbols and Sacred Objects* (San Francisco: Harper & Row, 1988).

[13] Melton, *Handbook of Cults*, 214.

[14] For a more detailed word about sensationalism, see SATANISM.

[15] See Mario Mira Johnson, "Witches in Search of Respect," *Providence Journal Bulletin* (Aug. 10, 1989), 1–2.

[16] The names and groups from Craig Hawkins, *Goddess Worship, Witchcraft and Neo-Paganism* (Grand Rapids: Zondervan, 1998), 28.

[17] Ibid., 26.

WORLD CHURCH OF THE CREATOR (WCOTC)

This organization, although it calls itself a church, openly admits being a prowhite supremacy group as well as being anti-Christian and anti-Semitic. It is currently headed by Matt Hale, who has the Latin title of "Pontifex Maximus." On its website the question is asked: "Who is the 'Creator?'" It answers: "The White Race [*sic*]. White people are the creators of all worthwhile culture and civilization." All of its members are called "creators." It further states: "Our race is our religion." Citing Islam's *jihad* (holy war) as a precedent, the organization touts a similar concept that it calls RAHOWA, derived from the first two letters of the three words "Racial Holy War."

One of the logos of WCOTC has within a circle the letter W (symbol for "white"), superimposed by a crown and a halo above the crown. Another symbol has to the left of the W a circle with the Star of David in flames, along with a circle on the right showing the Christian cross, also in flames. For an extensive treatment of race theology as a movement, see IDENTITY MOVEMENTS.

This organization began in 1973. On its website it lists "churches" (local units) within virtually every state within the United States. One of its rallying cries says: "In Klassen We Trust."

ADDITIONAL INFORMATION

Headquarters

World Church of the Creator, PO Box 2002, East Peoria, IL 61611.

Website

www.wcotc.com

Important books

Ben Klassen, *Nature's Eternal Religion* (1973); *White Man's Bible* (1981); *Salubrious Living* (1982).

Statistics

Their size is not revealed, and membership roles are secret.

WORLDWIDE CHURCH OF GOD (WCG)

The Worldwide Church of God was formerly a 'cult whose founder, Herbert W. 'Armstrong (1892–1986), was influenced greatly by SEVENTH-DAY ADVENTISM in his early years. But Armstrong went far beyond Adventist theology when he developed his own theology in the organization that would come to be known as the Worldwide Church of God. Then, after Armstrong's death, the WCG with new leadership underwent dramatic changes in its theology. This transformation, in the view of some religion historians, is unprecedented in church history. For example, Ruth A. Tucker wrote, "Never before in the history of Christianity has there been such a complete move to orthodox Christianity by an unorthodox fringe church."[1]

HISTORY

Herbert W. Armstrong was born in Des Moines, Iowa, to Quaker parents. As a young adult, he worked as an advertising agent who wrote copy for the *Merchants Trade Journal* in Des Moines. In 1920 his own advertising firm folded, and four years later he moved to Oregon, where he witnessed two more business failures.

According to Armstrong, his religious training in his formative years did not teach him that Christianity is a way of life. In 1926 he tried to disprove his wife's beliefs, which were derived from Seventh-day Adventist influence. Notably, his wife Loma insisted that to be saved people must obey the laws of God as they are found in the Ten Commandments and especially the 'Sabbath Day injunction. But after a year of study, Armstrong embraced Loma's doctrines and was baptized into the Oregon Conference of the Church of God. He was ordained as a pastor in this church body in 1931.

In 1933, in Eugene, Oregon, he began broadcasting his preaching under the title of *The Radio Church of God*, and early in 1934 he began his weekly prophecy program *The World Tomorrow*. That same year he launched the *Plain Truth*, a mimeographed magazine, with a meager circulation of 106. The next few years, his radio broadcast, his magazine, and his organization grew to unmatched proportions. After World War II he moved his headquarters to Pasadena, California, and in 1947 he founded and built Ambassador College there also. The college's auditorium alone cost eleven million dollars, a sensational amount of money at the time. Pictures of this campus often dotted the pages of the *Plain Truth* and of Armstrong's second publication, *The World Tomorrow*.

In 1960 the second Ambassador College was opened in Bricket Wood, England, and in 1964 a third Ambassador College came into being in Big Sandy, Texas. In 1953 Armstrong began broadcasting in Europe via Radio Luxembourg. This gave him and his preaching worldwide popularity. Often Armstrong was pictured on the pages of the *Plain Truth* interacting with heads of states of various countries.

The year 1975 marked a crucial time for the WCG. That was to be the year, Armstrong had dogmatically predicted, when the one true church, the Worldwide Church of God, would be raptured and removed to Petra, Jordan. The prophecy failed—which is understandable in view of Christ's words that clearly state the end of the world and the second coming will not be known even to the angels or to the Son of God (Mark 13:32). That failed prophecy, together with the ousting of Herbert's son Garner Ted 'Armstrong (1930–2003) in 1978, resulted in a loss of over five thousand members over five years. Garner had been involved in a sex scandal, which prompted his father to say that the son had been "in the bonds of Satan." The father 'disfellowshiped his son, who responded by opening the Church of God International (COGI) in Tyler, Texas, that same year. The COGI grew rapidly as more people left the WCG. Even some of the top leaders resigned their posts.

Loma Armstrong died in 1967. Ten years later, at age eighty-five, Herbert married divorcee Ramona Martin, age thirty-nine. Even at that age he continued

Herbert W. Armstrong, holding up a copy of his *Plain Truth* magazine.　　Courtesy George A. Mather

on the airwaves and also made frequent TV appearances, all with the goal of promulgating the doctrines of the WCG.

In 1979 the state of California charged Herbert and a financial advisor, Stanley Rader, with diverting millions of dollars for personal use. The investigation ended two years later, in large part because Rader had marshaled various religious organizations to bring about passage of a state law that prevented the state attorney general from investigating religious organizations over allegations of fraud. Rader received a court settlement of $750,000 and also resigned his position in the WCG.

Also at about that time, Rader and Armstrong's wife, Ramona, conspired to have Armstrong removed from the WCG by declaring him to be mentally incompetent. Armstrong responded by announcing plans to divorce Ramona and taking steps to ensure a favorable successor should he die or become incapacitated to lead. Then the shocking news hit the media that Jack Kessler, an attorney and former member of the WCG who had been disfellowshiped, publicly declared Herbert financially corrupt and morally bankrupt in that he had lived in incest with his own daughter for more than a decade in the early days of the church's ministry.

The controversies were taking their toll. The WCG lost many members and experienced declining income. Its broadcast outlets dropped from 457 in 1972 to 133 in 1979. By contrast, Garner Ted's COGI prospered; in 1979 it was on forty radio and TV stations and had an income approaching a million dollars.

But then the tide turned again for the seemingly ever-resurgent WCG, largely the result of good marketing methods. WCG membership grew to more than 70,000, and both income and literature output increased. Some 8.2 million copies of *Plain Truth* were distributed in 1985. And Herbert continued to appear on radio and TV until his death in 1986.

Meanwhile, Garner Ted's church began to decline. Accused of sexual assault, the younger Armstrong was removed from the presidency of the COGI in 1995 and from the organization altogether in 1997. In 1998 he formed the Intercontinental Church of God and remained its president until his death in September 2003.

Just before Herbert died in 1986, he appointed Joseph Tkach Sr. (1927–1995) to succeed him as pastor general. Within weeks after Armstrong's death came the first challenge to Armstrong's dogmatic teachings—from an Ambassador professor who found in them a minute contradiction of the Bible in regard to Arm-

strong's interpretation of the original Passover event in Egypt. This tiny "crack in the dam,"[2] as one administrator put it, led to Tkach and the Council of Elders' initiating a complete review of Armstrong's writings. At the same time, Tkach took some cautious first steps toward tapering the authoritarian approach to church government.

The doctrinal shift evolved over several years and became irreversible in 1995 when Tkach issued a "new covenant" that showed the WCG was in the process of adopting a more ▶orthodox theology. Under his leadership, the church became a Christian organization discovering and teaching doctrines that were more in line with ▶Evangelicalism. For example, Armstrong's anti-trinitarianism was renounced and the message that salvation comes only through the grace of God in Jesus Christ became the focal point of some of the prominent WCG pastors and leaders.

Both processes—the doctrinal and the institutional change—continued after Tkach's death to cancer in September 1995, when his designated successor—his son, Joseph Tkach Jr. (b. 1951)—became the pastor general.

In March 1996, Tkach wrote an article for the *Plain Truth*, apologizing to members and former members for the church's erroneous teachings and for practices that led to great confusion. In July 1996, *Christianity Today* presented the WCG to the evangelical world in a favorable light. The following year, the WCG was accepted into the National Association of Evangelicals (NAE)—a noteworthy affirmation of the extent of the church's doctrinal transformation.

During these years of change, a significant number of members remained loyal to Armstrong's teaching, resulting in splinter groups breaking away from the WCG and thereby greatly reducing its membership. For instance, in 1986 the WCG had about 150,000 members worldwide, of which 89,000 members resided in the United States. By 1996 the American membership had dropped to 49,000. (About 40,000 of the members who left never joined the splinter groups.) The various splinter groups continued to promote Armstrong's theology. Some of the more prominent breakaway groups include Triumph Prophetic Ministries (founded in 1987), the Philadelphia Church of God (1989), the Twentieth Century Church of God (1990), the Global Church of God (1990), the Church of the Great God (1992), the United Biblical Church of God (1992), and the United Church of God (1995). This last group had reached 17,000 members by 1996, thus becoming "the greatest threat to the WCG."

Amid all the changes of the 1990s and beyond, the WCG has endured much turmoil. The church has struggled with doctrinal formulations that are looked on favorably by many evangelicals even as they have failed to assuage the many dissenters who have left. Others would argue quite forcefully that the WCG's march toward evangelical orthodoxy has been derailed. (See "Teachings" below). Also, the critics have charged that the new WCG has not renounced Armstrong in any clear way, but rather has made every attempt to exercise caution so as to not alienate members who still have close affinities to the founder.

ORGANIZATION

The WCG has consistently maintained a polity of centralized control. From the beginning, the structure of the WCG has had the pastor general as the head of the church. Joseph Tkach Jr., however, adopted a consensual style of leadership that gives some accountability and responsibility to a board of directors.

The international headquarters in Pasadena currently views its mission as serving to encourage member congregations to uphold the Statement of Beliefs, to provide literature and biblical instruction materials for the congregations and teachers, to keep members abreast of news and information as it unfolds, to provide education for its pastors, to promote foreign missions, and to interact with other denominations.

The new WCG still publishes the *Plain Truth* magazine and now regularly invites a number of evangelical writers to contribute, which adds credibility and diversity to the publication. This periodical once had a circulation rate of several million, but most of them were not paid subscriptions. Armstrong had millions of copies printed and then widely distributed them in mass quantities, free for the taking. It was one method of advertising the WCG. The magazine's present readership is about 50,000, most of whom are paid subscribers. The WCG also conducts a radio program, known as *Plain Truth Ministries*, carried by about forty stations.

The loss of members and revenue during its transformation prompted the WCG to sell its Ambassador College campus in Big Sandy, Texas, in 1997 and Ambassador's main campus in Pasadena in 2001. Except for its headquarters and a few local church buildings in different parts of the country, the WCG has divested itself of all its properties.

TEACHINGS

In this section, we have a threefold task. The traditional teachings of Armstrong are presented, followed by the new doctrines, and then a comparison/contrast with traditional ▸orthodoxy will follow.

God

Armstrong denied the ▸Trinity, which he said was a pagan doctrine. In denying the Trinity, the WCG had much in common with other anti-Trinitarian cults, such as JEHOVAH'S WITNESSES, CHRISTADELPHIANISM, and MORMONISM, who argue that God not only has to be one essence but also one person. Armstrong, however, denied the Trinity because he said it limited God only to three persons. Similar to Mormonism, he taught that in the believer "God is really re-creating his *own kind*— reproducing himself after his *own kind*."[4] Thus, Armstrong did not really distinguish between God and humankind; expressed differently, he taught that all believers became little gods after their resurrection.

The WCG now accepts the orthodox doctrine of the Trinity. In February 1996, Tkach wrote: "Gone is our long-held view that God is a 'family' of multiple 'spirit beings' into which humans may be born, replaced by a biblically accurate view of one God who exists eternally in three Persons, the Father, the Son, and the Holy Spirit."[5]

Orthodox Christianity believes, teaches, and confesses the doctrine of the Trinity as formulated in the Athanasian Creed: "The catholic faith is this, that we worship one God in three persons and three persons in one God." (Appendix 1).

Jesus Christ

Although Armstrong accepted the virgin birth of Christ, he presented a heretical picture of Christ's crucifixion and resurrection. When Christ was crucified, the body that died on the cross was not the body with which he was raised. This conclusion led him to distinguish between "revived" and "made alive." Said he:

> It was *Christ Himself* who was *dead*. He was *revived*. Nowhere does the Scripture say He was alive and active, or that God had Him get back into the human *body*, that had died and was now resurrected . . . Jesus was *dead*—but was *revived*.[6]

Armstrong's view of Christ had been reminiscent of the ▸Monophysites (a fifth-century heretical group) that taught that Jesus had but one nature—the divine only. Similarly, Armstrong argued that Jesus, after his death, did not retain his human nature but was completely and solely a spiritual entity after his resurrection. This belief conflicts with ancient Christianity, which at the Council of Chalcedon (A.D. 451) maintained that according to

Scripture, Christ continued to possess two natures, human and divine. These two natures are united in one person in such a way that they are "unconfused, unchanged, unseparated, and undivided."

In Christian theology this is known as the ▸hypostatic union, meaning that both natures of Christ, by virtue of the ▸incarnation, share the properties of the other. Thus, when Jesus in John 2:19–21 spoke of the temple, referring metaphorically to himself, he was speaking of his physical body, which would be raised in communication with the divine nature. Or in John 20:27, when the resurrected Christ asked Thomas to touch the nail prints in his hands, he showed him the physical wounds in his resurrected and physical, yet incorruptible and glorified, body. Today the WCG teaches that Jesus Christ is "God manifested in the flesh for our salvation. He was begotten of the Holy Spirit and born of the virgin Mary, fully God and fully human, two natures in one Person."[7] The WCG has now clearly rejected the teachings of Armstrong, although the degree to which they understand how Christology profoundly impacts other doctrines remains to be seen.

Holy Spirit

Armstrong's doctrine of the Holy Spirit closely resembled that of the Jehovah's Witnesses. He argued that "the Holy Spirit functions as a divine force." To insist that the Holy Spirit is a person is to limit God, and to limit God is to deny the whole process of salvation. "That heresy," he said, "denies the true born-again experience!"[8]

Armstrong had been in clear conflict with historic Christianity on this doctrine as well. The Nicene Creed, for instance, in recognizing the Bible's position regarding the Holy Spirit, states: "I believe in the Holy Spirit, the Lord and giver of life, who proceeds from the Father and the Son, who with the Father and the Son together is worshiped and glorified."

The new WCG teaching affirms the traditional orthodox doctrine of the Holy Spirit as the third person of the Trinity.

Born Again

Armstrong's WCG denied that Christians could be born again before the resurrection of the just, at the time of Christ's second coming. In other words, the new birth is a future event unattainable in this present life. He even claimed that the traditional understanding of being born again held to by ▸Protestants was heretical.

In January, 1991, the WCG changed their teaching on this and now understand the new birth to be a this-worldly occurrence and their understanding of the doctrine falls in line with evangelicalism. People are born again when they confess that they are sinners saved by the grace of God in Christ Jesus.

The phrase "born again" has enjoyed various interpretations and understanding under the pale of orthodoxy. In Roman Catholic, Eastern Orthodox, and some historic Protestant denominations such as Lutheranism and Anglicanism, the new birth is connected to the doctrine of baptism. Other Protestant traditions have defined "born again" as a conversion *experience* preceding baptism that involves a person's decision to receive Jesus Christ as Lord and Savior. In both instances, the new birth is attainable in this life. No orthodox traditions teach as Armstrong did, that the new birth is not attainable in this life.

Salvation

For Armstrong, salvation was a process. One had to become obedient to the ordinances of the God's law, meaning that whatever laws bound the ancient Israelites also bound Christians today. Jesus obeyed the law to show humanity that they could indeed be kept. This includes keeping the Sabbath, the food laws, festivals, new moons, and holy days. Only those who obey the laws of God will achieve salvation.

Armstrong's understanding of salvation was certainly in direct conflict with what Jesus taught, for he said: "God so loved the world that he gave his only begotten Son that whoever believes in him shall not perish but have eternal life" (John 3:16). It is also opposed to what Paul told the Ephesian Christians, when he wrote: "For it is by grace that you have been saved, through faith—and this not from yourselves, it is the gift of God—not of works, so that no one can boast" (Ephesians 2:8–9). These references underlie what orthodox Christians for centuries have confessed regarding their salvation. Note the Apostles' Creed, which says: "I believe in ... the forgiveness of sins"; similarly, the Nicene Creed of the fourth century states: "I acknowledge one baptism for the remission of sins." Therefore, the Christian church has said from its beginning: "Where there is forgiveness of sins, there is life and salvation." If Christ's finished work of salvation for the world was intended to be understood as automatic, the nature of grace, faith, and the ministry of the church would be compromised and in need of redefinition.

The Worldwide Church of God now teaches that salvation comes by God's grace through faith and that human works cannot save a person. There has been some concern, however, with what appears to be a hint of ‎universalism in present WCG teaching concerning the doctrine of salvation. The WCG states clearly that they are not universalists in the sense that salvation can come without Jesus. The presentation on the WCG's official website contains an essay that suggests that by virtue of Jesus' death and resurrection, all people are drawn to Christ. "In short, Jesus Christ is the only path to salvation, and he draws absolutely everybody to himself—in his way, in his time."9

Hell

Armstrong denied the existence and reality of ‎hell. Instead it taught the doctrine of ‎annihilationism, namely, that when unbelievers die, they remain dead eternally. The movement published a brief pamphlet (*Is There a Real Hell Fire?*) in which the ancient Christian teaching of hell is spurned.

The new WCG has not divested itself totally from Armstrong on this doctrine. Hell is defined as the separation between God and incorrigible sinners. The term "lake of fire," synonymous with the Greek word *Gehenna*, is distinguished from *Sheol* and *Hades* (the grave), but "[the Bible] does not make absolutely clear whether this means annihilation or conscious spiritual alienation from God."10

Orthodox Christianity, on the contrary, has never accepted the doctrine of annihilation for unbelievers; rather, all who do not believe in Jesus Christ will suffer eternal damnation, where, as Jesus said, "there will be weeping and gnashing of teeth" (Matt. 8:12). Hell is a literal place of eternal torment. Jesus also said, "Do not be afraid of those who kill the body but cannot kill the soul. Rather be afraid of the one who can destroy both body and soul in hell" (Matt. 10:28). Destroying the body and the soul in hell cannot be understood to mean the cessation of torment.

The Sabbath

Under Armstrong's direction, the WCG taught that the Old Testament Sabbath (Saturday) had to be strictly kept. In fact, keeping the Sabbath was God's sign as to who really are the people of God. Keeping the dietary laws of Leviticus was also mandatory for every Christian.

In January 1995, the new WCG issued a statement known as the "new covenant" doctrine. The statement made it clear that there is no obligation for Christians to observe the Sabbath. The Old Testament Sabbath is understood to be a shadow of things to come and was a precursor to Christ, who is the Sabbath rest of the Christian. Many of the present WCG churches still wor-

ship on the Saturday Sabbath. The leaders claim that this is simply from force of habit over the years, but it is no longer binding, and there is certainly now no condemnation directed against church bodies that worship on Sunday or any other day.

Traditional Christianity departed from worship on the Sabbath in honor of the resurrection of Christ on the first day of the week. But Paul also made it clear that the Christian church is not bound by the observance of the Sabbath or other holy days. "Therefore do not let anyone judge you by what you eat or drink or with regard to a religious festival, a New Moon celebration or a Sabbath day. These are a shadow of the things to come; the reality, however, is found in Christ" (Col. 2:16–17).

Other Holy Days

WCG members were prohibited from celebrating Christmas and Easter. Armstrong declared these as pagan holidays. In their place, his members were enjoined to observe seven holy days, namely: Passover, the Festival of Unleavened Bread, Pentecost, the Festival of Trumpets, the Festival of Tabernacles, the Day of Atonement, and the Last Great Day. These mandates were consistent with Armstrong's insistence that the Old Testament laws were to be strictly observed.

Current WCG teaching regarding the observance of the Old Testament holy days is that they are no longer considered binding or necessary. Many congregations still observe them, however, but they are now regarded as "memorials" and "celebrations" of God's great acts in redemptive history.

The Roman Catholic Church observes what are known as Holy Days of Obligation. According to the 1917 Code of Canon Law, there are ten holy days of obligation. Protestant Christianity, as noted above, does not mandate the observance of special holy days. The liturgical year, observed by many traditional denominations, presents important festival Sundays and seasons throughout the year (Advent, Christmas, Epiphany, Lent, Easter, Pentecost), and these are observed not to merit righteousness but to celebrate the ongoing narrative of the life of Christ and his church.

Tithing

Members of the WCG were required to tithe. Strictly observant members were expected to give thirty percent, that is, ten percent for a regular tithe, ten percent to support the annual Feast of the Tabernacles, and another ten percent to support widows and orphans within the WCG.

Armstrong ignored the fact that the Christians in the New Testament were no longer commanded to give a specific percentage of income (1 Cor. 16:2). They were to give generously out of thankfulness for their gift of salvation in Christ.

In the new WCG era, the triple tithe has been abandoned. Members are still taught to give ten percent of their income. According to the Statement of Faith, tithing was an Old Testament commandment and is carried over in the New Testament as a voluntary expression of worship.

Physical Illness

WCG members who became physically ill were forbidden to see physicians. This issue was one of the first to change in the new administration. In 1987, only one year following Armstrong's death, members were taught that they can and should seek a physician's care when needed.

Armstrong's restrictions about not visiting doctors and taking medicine cannot be found in Scripture. Christ and the apostles never told individuals they were not to see a physician when sick. In Colossians 4:14 Paul mentions his coworker Luke, whom he affectionately calls "our dear friend Luke, the doctor." Barring members from physicians was another man-made law that grew out of Armstrong's legalistic theology that ignored the New Testament: "It is for the freedom that Christ has set us free. Stand firm, then, and do not let yourselves be burdened again with the yoke of slavery" (Gal. 5:1).

Anglo-Israelism

This concept refers to Armstrong's belief that the British people are the literal descendants of the ten "lost" tribes of Israel, the tribes that disappeared when the Assyrians conquered them in 722 B.C. This theory suggested that after the ten tribes were subjugated, they migrated to Western Europe, Scandinavia, and the British Isles, and that the members of the WCG were the "faithful remnant of the people of God . . . the true Israel."[11] The fact that the WCG members observed the Sabbath Day and the Old Testament feasts was additional evidence that they were Israelites. Armstrong argued that since Israel was God's chosen people with whom he had made his covenant, the Hebrew word for covenant (*berith*) becomes significant in the English language when combined with the Hebrew word for man (*ish*). Since vowels do not appear in the original spelling of Hebrew words, the *e* drops off from *berith* to form the word *brith*. Moreover, the Hebrews did not

pronounce *h*, so the original *berith* becomes *brit*. Combined with *ish* for God's covenant with man, the Hebrew *berith–ish* becomes the English "Brit–ish," or "British."

Armstrong was equally creative in the etymology of the word *Saxon* for Anglo-Saxons. Since it was Isaac's seed that God had promised to bless (Gen. 21:12), and if the *i* is dropped, we are left with "saac," and it is "Saac's sons" or "Saxons" with whom God has established his covenant.

Furthermore, Armstrong insisted that the English throne is the modern-day extension of the throne of David, contending that the Stone of Scone, on which Queen Elizabeth II was crowned, was the very stone that Jacob used for a pillow. Later it was transported by the prophet Jeremiah to the British Isles. Geologists investigating the stone conclude, however, that it is calcareous, a type of reddish stone common to Scotland.

While provocative to the imagination, these ideas are not in conformity with traditional Christianity or historical scholarship. Nevertheless, Anglo-Israelism has been embraced by MORMONISM and IDENTITY MOVEMENTS.

Changes in this doctrine came in 1992–1994. Lengthy study papers were conducted during this time, and the doctrine faded into oblivion. Joseph Tkach Jr. wrote in 1992: "All of our traditional proofs are based upon folklore, legend, myth, and superstition."[12]

Church

Armstrong taught: "There is only one true church. All others are counterfeits produced by Satan, especially the Roman Catholic Church that is 'The Great Whore of Babylon.' The true church has to bear the name 'church of God.'" And this church, of course, was the Worldwide Church of God that Armstrong fashioned.

Historically, the Christian church has from its beginning said that there is only "one holy catholic and apostolic church" (Nicene Creed). What makes a church or denomination orthodox is whether it embraces the tenets of the three ecumenical creeds. Groups that deny the Trinity and the deity of Christ and deny that the Christian is justified by faith in Christ are heretical and schismatic, not part of the one true church. Because the WCG formerly denied these Christian doctrines it was at that time not part of the "holy catholic and apostolic church."

The new WCG has come to understand the church as the "body of Christ," comprising all those who believe in Jesus for salvation. The church's mission and ministry are to preach, baptize, and nurture the flock of God.

End Times

Armstrong had made predictions about Armageddon taking place twice before he made his third one in 1972. Although this one and the previous ones failed, that did not deter him from making yet another in which he prophesied that the WCG would be raptured and taken to Petra, Jordan, in 1975. After this prophecy too failed, Armstrong became reticent about making future predictions of the end times.

But his failed prophecies did not hinder him from making other false theological statements. For one, he argued that there would be three resurrections of the dead: (1) The true church and departed saints would return with Herbert W. Armstrong in the "world tomorrow." This was to occur in the future 'millennium. (2) There would also be a "resurrection of the ignorant" that would happen after the millennium, and the enlightened saints would teach the ignorant the ways of God. It they refused this second chance, which some would, then there would be (3) a final resurrection of sinners, after which they would be cast into the lake of fire. There they would perish and all memory of them would be erased.

Here Armstrong contradicts traditional Christian teaching, which understands the Apostles' and Nicene creeds to confess only one resurrection, at which time God will judge the "living and the dead." Moreover, the church in its history, whether assembled in synods or councils, has never set a date for Christ's second coming. The millennial posture of Armstrong colored all of his preaching and teaching. As Mike Feazell, the former WCG director of church administration, has said: "For Herbert W. Armstrong, the gospel was the gospel about the arrival of Jesus on earth at his Second Coming to establish the kingdom of God on earth."[13]

Current teachings on the subject of the end times place the WCG within the spectrum of evangelical churches that teach that the end will come either before or after the thousand-year reign period known as the millennium.

CONCLUSION

Evangelicals have raised many questions about certain areas in which the WCG has remained reticent to introduce changes. For example, the leadership of the organization has taken great care not to denounce Armstrong outright. The question of accountability has also been raised. In an interview with the authors, Tkach explained that the accountability issue is being remedied in three ways. While the organization under Armstrong was characterized by the appointment of "dummy boards," the new approach is to have boards appointed independently. Second, a statement of ethics and accountability is forthcoming. Finally, greater emphasis is being made to ensure that the WCG is a movement controlled by the members as much as it is by the headquarters and that the present membership will never allow the church to go back to the old days.[14]

ADDITIONAL INFORMATION

Headquarters
Worldwide Church of God, Pasadena, CA 91123.

Website
www.wcg.org

Sacred Text
The Bible (presently); formerly the writings of Armstrong were regarded with the Bible as authoritative teaching guides.

Publications
Plain Truth; The Worldwide News; The Statement of Beliefs, Good Shepherding

Statistics
58,000 members. About 25,000 of these are in 90 countries and the remaining in the United States. There are 870 congregations.

Notes
[1] Ruth A. Tucker, "From the Fringe to the Fold," *Christianity Today* (July 15, 1996).
[2] J. Michael Feazell, *The Liberation of the Worldwide Church of God* (Grand Rapids: Zondervan, 2001), 22.
[3] The statistical information is derived from Joseph M. Hopkins, professor of religion, Westminster College, New Wilmington, Pa. (n.d.).
[4] Herbert W. Armstrong, *Why Were You Born?* (Pasadena, Calif.: Ambassador College Press, n.d.), 21–22.
[5] Joseph Tkach Jr., "Personal," *Plain Truth* (February 1996), 1.
[6] Herbert W. Armstrong, *Plain Truth* (April, 1963).
[7] Statement of Beliefs of the Worldwide Church of God *(Pasadena, Calif.: Worldwide Church of God, 1993, 1995), 2.*
[8] See Herbert W. Armstrong, *Just What Do You Mean—Born Again?* (Pasadena, Calif..: Ambassador College Press, 1962).
[9] See *www.wcg.org/lit/gospel/bestnews.htm.*
[10] *www.wcg.org/lit/aboutus/beliefs/default/htm#hell.*
[11] Joseph Tkach, *Transformed by Truth* (Sisters, Ore.: Multnomah Books, 1997), 119.
[12] Cited by Larry Nichols and George Mather, *Discovering the Plain Truth: How the Worldwide Church Encountered the Gospel of Grace* (Downers Grove, Ill.: InterVarsity Press, 1998), 93
[13] Ibid., 104.
[14] Ibid., 85.

ZEN BUDDHISM; ROCHESTER ZEN CENTER

The word *zen*, derived from the Chinese word *ch'an* and from the still older Sanskrit word *dhyana*, means meditation. Zen developed mainly in BUDDHISM.

HISTORY

The founder of Zen was ˢTao-Sheng (A.D. 360–434). But the popularly recognized founder was ˢBodhidharma (d. A.D. 534). He was a Persian who, as legend has it, journeyed to South India, where he adopted the form of MAHAYANA BUDDHISM prevalent to that area. He then allegedly carried these teachings to China during the Wu dynasty. The teachings and philosophy of Zen were then taken to Japan where they greatly influenced, and were in turn influenced by, Japanese culture.

Zen Buddhism centers have been established in the United States and in other parts of the West. For instance, the Rochester Zen Center was founded in 1966 by Philip ˢKapleau. Kapleau was a war crimes reporter in Japan. After attending Columbia University, he met D. T. ˢSuzuki and soon attended his lectures. Returning to Japan, Kapleau continued his studies in Zen under Soen Nakagawa Roshi. Five years later he reportedly experienced ˢenlightenment and then spent eight more years in training. In 1966 he became a teacher (ˢroshi) himself and founded the Rochester Zen Center that same year. Other centers, considered affiliates of the Rochester group, are located in Colorado, California, New Mexico, North Carolina, Wisconsin, and Vermont. Foreign centers also exist in Canada, Mexico, Sweden, Germany, and New Zealand.

The writings of Alan Watts promoted Zen on a popular level, made it palatable for the average reader, and moved it into mainstream acceptance on college and university campuses in the 1950s, 1960s, and 1970s.

ORGANIZATION

The Rochester Zen Center is a training center where adherents gather to practice daily meditation, attend workshops, and receive training on the principles of Zen. Newcomers may attend the center for a trial period of three months. The only requirements are to attend an orientation meeting and to make a minimum donation of $3.00 each time one attends. Membership is based after filling out an application, making a pledge, and submitting a photo. Those who live within fifty miles of the Zen Center are considered "local members," while those living beyond the fifty mile radius are "out-of-town" members. Membership grants voting privi-

leges at the center. Friends of the center make annual contributions of $50.00 as of this writing. The leader who instructs members is called the Head of Zendo.

TEACHINGS

Zen philosophy is an eclectic blend of various impulses. The Mahayana emphasis on the ability to become a ˢBuddha and the importance of individuality and independence in meditation are coupled with the TAOIST idea of oneness between humanity and nature.

Reason and rationality are denigrated in Zen philosophy. This is because of its stress on ˢmysticism and subjective experience in the religious life of the devotee. Both subject and object coexist. Nature is completely identified in the experience of the contemplative life.

Zen teaches that enlightenment, or ˢsatori, is achievable with effort and training in contemplation. *Bodhi,* or the awakening of the self to truth, is possible in a single life. This is a significant variation from BUDDHISM and HINDUISM, both of which teach that the awakening is only possible after several reincarnated lives. Two ˢsects, the Rinzai (founded by ˢEisai in 1191) and the Soto (founded by ˢDogen in 1225), sprang up in Zen during the Middle Ages. It is the writings and teachings of the Rinzai sect that were introduced to the West by Suzuki (1870–1966). These teachings and writings stressed the idea of sudden illumination, where all diversity is blurred unto unity. One does not, and cannot, gain enlightenment through striving. It just comes—thus the paradox that effort must be expended so that the devotee may reach the point of effortlessness.[1]

The yogic master (*roshi*) instructs the subject by giving him or her an object to meditate on. This can be a table, a wall, or anything. The *roshi* then gives the subject a ˢkoan to guide his or her meditation (ˢzazen). For instance, the *roshi* asks: "What is the sound of hand clapping?" "These koans are designed to break down the conceptualization superimposed on the flow of experience and to bring about intuitive insight."[2] They do not make sense. The pupil moves beyond reason.

In Soto, the devotee is not guided by *koans*. The pupils of Dogen were taught to meditate in silence. In *zazen*, they must not think of a future state or about being other than what they are presently. Each moment defines itself. "Firewood has no intention of becoming ash," said Dogen. "By the time it has become ash, it is no longer firewood." Wishing to "become" is a fruitless endeavor.

The relationship between the *roshi* and the pupil is integral and important. Enlightenment comes through Dharma transmission, which means that the teacher's role is to see that the student's understanding is the same.

Zen does not encourage a detached life divorced from the happenings of day-to-day events. It is a programmatic religion in this regard. This is true even after *satori* is experienced. Nature, as stated above, becomes an integral part of the self.

God

There are notable contrasts between Zen and CHRIS-TIANITY. To begin, Zen, like Buddhism as a whole, denies the existence of a transcendent God. This statement, however, can be misleading. To say that Zen "denies" means that by not affirming or denying God, God is denied. Denial and affirmation are logical assertions made with reason, language, and words. Zen attempts to use no logic or reason. Interestingly, however, it uses language in order to render language useless. The ▸pantheistic nature of Zen's concept of God makes such a conundrum possible. By contrast, in Christianity ▸transcendence and ▸immanence both comprise the Triune God, who is Father, Son, and Holy Spirit. Such a notion of a personal, providential, and redemptive God is inimical to the mind of the Zen Buddhist.

Revelation

Related to the concept of God is that of ▸revelation. For Zen, truth and knowledge come from "radical intuition." This is to say, truth emerges from within the self-conscious subject. For Christianity it is much the opposite. Truth is a matter of revelation from without. God confronts humankind with his Word spoken to the children of Israel through the mouths and writings of the prophets in the Old Testament and the gospel in the New Testament. Jesus Christ is the ▸incarnation of God, and the ▸Bible is the written Word of God.

Sin/Evil

Evil or the dark side of life is, like God, neither affirmed nor denied. It is simply recognized as being necessary. Without evil, good remains meaningless. Without darkness, what is light? (See ▸yin and yang). Since there is no transcendent God as in Christianity, then there is no possibility of offense or active rebellion to the deity. Sin and offense remain within the self. It is the quest of the self to move from darkness to light. This is very different from Christianity, which teaches that all humans "have sinned and fall short of the glory of God" (Rom. 3:23).

Salvation

Enlightenment or *satori* is achieved through training and meditation. Similar to Christianity, Zen insists that we can attain truth in the present life without an endless cycle of ▸reincarnations. Unlike Christianity, however, Zen teaches that if one does not achieve salvation in one's lifetime, one then may succeed by being subsumed in the process of reincarnation. In Christian thought and doctrine, salvation is made possible through the person and work of Jesus Christ as articulated in the Nicene and Apostles' creeds (see Appendix 1). The story of Christ is, for the Christian, the story of God, who intervenes in and for humanity. Because Zen denies a transcendent God, it must of necessity also deny the intervention of that God in human form. "There is no supernatural intervention, ways or refuges. We bear the whole responsibility for our actions."[3]

Authority

The essential authority for Zen Buddhism is the person's self. This is true by definition. There are no creeds, no doctrines, no dogmas, no writings to which one can look to for guidance. The only sure guide for truth is within oneself. Contrary to this kind of subjectivism, Christianity acknowledges the lordship of Jesus Christ, who will "come to judge the living and the dead." The earliest Christians yielded to the authority of the ▸apostles (Acts 2:41–44).

The issue of authority does indeed have varying interpretations within Christendom. For instance, the Roman Catholics see the authority of the pope and tradition of the church as the prominent authorities. The Protestant Reformation, by contrast, established the Bible (▸*sola scriptura*) as the final and only authority for doctrine, faith, and practice. A third variation obtains in the tradition of the Eastern church, which broke from Rome, acknowledging the authority of its patriarchs and rejecting the exclusivity of the pope of Rome.

Amid this diversity, however, emerges one similarity that is the antithesis to Zen. Authority in orthodox Christendom does not lie within the intuitions of the subject. This was true historically until the Enlightenment (mid-1700s), when theology became less and less a matter of supernatural revelation and more and more a matter of pronounced rationalism. A much closer comparison between Zen and Christianity developed in the romantic era. Rejecting the notion of supernatural revelation, Friedrich Schleiermacher, a prominently liberal theologian of the nineteenth century, insisted that religious authority emerged not from the Bible but from self-conscious intuitions of the theologically searching subject. This position was virtually identical to that of Zen Buddhism.

CONCLUSION

It is estimated that over eight million people in the world today see themselves following Zen Buddhism. It is by far the most popular form of Buddhism in the United States. In the past, Zen has appealed to Americans who sought an alternate system of values. Many of those who have become disillusioned by the materialism of the West have sought meaning in the seemingly higher spiritual values of the religions of the Orient.

Some good background sources for Zen philosophy have been published by D. T. Suzuki: *Studies in the "Lankavatara Sutra"* (London, 1930); *Essays in Zen Buddhism* (London, 1927–34); *The Lankavatara Sutra* (London, 1932). To this we can add Kapleau's *Three Pillars of Zen* and writings by Alan Watts, *The Way of Zen* (New York, 1957), and Christmas Humphreys, *Zen: A Way of Life* (London, 1962).

ADDITIONAL INFORMATION_____

Headquarters
Rochester Zen Center, 7 Arnold Park, Rochester, NY 14607–2082

Website
www.rzc.org
http://irizhanazono.ac.jp/zen_centers/country_list_e.html

Sacred Text
There are no official texts, but see Kapleau's *The Three Pillars of Zen*

Publications
Zen Bow; Zen Arrow

Statistics
There are over 3,000,000 followers of Zen worldwide. The Rochester Zen Center has a relatively small membership with approximately 500 members and less than 200 in the rest of the world. Concerning Zen Buddhism itself, there are over eight million adherents in Japan, and much smaller scattered numbers throughout Asia and Europe.

Notes
[1] Ninian Smart, "Zen" in *Encyclopedia of Philosophy* (New York: Macmillan and the Freee Press, 1967), 7:367.
[2] Ibid.
[2] The sayings of Linchi, as recorded in Lit-sen Chang, *Zen Existentialism: The Spiritual Decline of the West* (Nutley, N.J.: Presbyterian and Reformed, 1969).

Dictionary
Entries

A.. A.. (⟡occult). Abbreviation for Argentium Astrum, which was an order formed by Aleister ⟡Crowley in 1904.

Aaronic Priesthood (MORMONISM). Mormons distinguish between the Aaronic priesthood and the ⟡Melchizedek priesthood. Of the two, the Aaronic priesthood is considered to be inferior in power and authority. It began with Aaron and continued until the time of John the Baptist, who was himself a priest in the Aaronic order (*Doctrine and Covenants* 84:26–27). By virtue of this authority, he was able to baptize and prepare the way for Jesus. Approximately 1,900 years later, the allegedly resurrected John was sent from heaven to bestow the Aaronic priesthood on Joseph ⟡Smith and Oliver ⟡Cowdery (*Doctrine and Covenants* 13). This occurred on May 15, 1829, near Harmony, Pennsylvania, on the banks of the Susquehanna River. The Aaronic priesthood remains to this day under the direction of the priesthood of Melchizedek.

Abaddon (⟡occult; SATANISM). In Satanism, the chief of the demons of the seventh hierarchy—the Destroyer. In the Old Testament, Abaddon refers to the underworld (Job 26:2) and in the New Testament, the name refers to the angel of the bottomless pit and lord of the plague of locusts (Rev. 9:7–11).

Abdul Khaalis, Hamaas (ISLAM; NATION OF ISLAM; n.d.). Founder of the Hanafi Madh-hab Center in 1968. In 1973, five members of his family were brutally murdered by members of the Nation of Islam. In 1977, Abdul Khaalis with other Hanafis seized three Washington, D.C., buildings (city hall, the B'nai B'rith Center, and the Islamic Center) in protest to the filming of a movie entitled *Muhammed Messenger of God*. Several hostages were abducted and injured, and one was killed. Khallis was sentenced to 21–120 years for his participation in the storming of the buildings, kidnappings, and murder.

Aberdeen Witches (⟡occult; WITCHCRAFT). In 1597 in Aberdeen, Scotland, a group of twenty-four individuals (twenty-three women and one man) were accused of practicing witchcraft. They were tried, found guilty, and executed.

Abhiyoga (JAINISM). A general title or name for servant deities in Jainism. They herald and serve the great gods called ⟡Indra.

Abracadabra (⟡occult; ⟡mysticism). A medieval incantation used to cure diseases or ward off impending troubles. The word was believed to be especially effective when inscribed on an ⟡amulet.

Abrahadabra (⟡occult). A term similar to the ⟡occult word ⟡abracadabra. Aleister ⟡Crowley made use of it as a magical designation for the aeon of Horus.

Abraham the Jew (⟡occult; 1362–1416). Medieval alchemist (*see* ⟡alchemy) and occult ⟡magician. He wrote his famous work, *The Sacred Magic of Abramelin*, when he was ninety-six years old. He greatly influenced Aleister ⟡Crowley.

Abraxas (⟡occult). A gnostic deity who had historic links with the Iranian/Persian god of time.

Absent Healing (⟡occult). A form of occult faith healing wherein a practitioner is able to pray and/or project positive thought toward an afflicted person who is not present.

Absolute Trinity (URANTIA). One of the principal trinities of Urantia. Like the ⟡ultimate trinity and unlike the ⟡paradise trinity, the absolute trinity is finite because it consists of "derived deities" that emerged from the paradise trinity. It is comprised of three persons in one deity—"God the supreme," "God the ultimate," and the revealed "consummator of universal destiny." The absolute trinity exists on a personal and "super-personal" level.

Abulafla, Abraham ben Samuel (⟡kabbala; 1240–1291). A kabbalistic mystic, Abulafla placed emphasis on cognition in the place of soul travel.

Abyss (⟡occult). A place at the end of the evolutionary cycle ruled by demons into which certain individuals or groups will be cast. It is the realm of higher spiritual consciousness.

Acarya (ISKCON; HINDUISM). A spiritual master or leader who teaches by example. The word also signifies the act of purifying oneself.

A. C. Bhaktivedanta Swami Prabhupada (HINDUISM; 1896–1977). Born as Abhay Charan De on September 1,

1896, in Calcutta, India, his early years were relatively insignificant. Attending the University of Calcutta, he studied English, economics, and philosophy, but never graduated. During his university days, however, he met Bhaktisiddhanta Saraswati, who became his spiritual master. In 1933 Bhaktisiddhanta gave his promising student the command to go forth and proclaim ʼKrishna consciousness. In 1947 a society called the ʼVaishnavites formally recognized Abhay Charan De as "Bhaktivedanta." He forsook his wife and family in 1959 to study under another *acarya*, a guru named ʼGosvami. In 1965 Bhaktivedanta visited the United States, sent by Gosvami to proclaim the message of Krishna. He founded the International Society for Krishna Consciousness in 1966. Bhaktivedanta died on November 4, 1977. His followers and eleven disciples, whom he appointed just before his death, continue to look on him as an ʼincarnation of their god Krishna.

Achad Foster (ʼoccult; 1886–1950). The occult pseudonym for Charles Stanley Jones. Foster was "spiritually adopted" by Aleister ʼCrowley.

Ache (SANTERIA; VOODOO). The power that pervades the universe.

Achogun (ʼoccult; CANDOMBLE; MACUMBA; SOUTH AMERICAN, CENTRAL AMERICAN, AND CARIBBEAN CULTS). An Afro-Brazilian priest.

Acolyte (ʼoccult; SATANISM). A person initiated into certain occult societies, including some Satanic groups.

Acon (ʼoccult; VOODOO). Sacred ceremonial drum used in voodoo.

Acronymics (General reference). The practice of forming a word from the initial letters of a phrase or grouping of words. Acronyms are used frequently in religious writings or in the naming of groups. For example, ISKCON is formed from the words International Society of Krishna Consciousness.

Acupuncture (ʼoccult). A medical practice that originated in China in the second century B.C. Acupuncture is the technique of inserting needles into key areas along the twelve ʼmeridians (apexes in the pathways) on the human body. Though a medical practice both then and now, acupuncture had religious connotations in that the meridians divided into two groups of six lines. One group was ʼyin and the other yang. Along the meridians flow the life force, called ʼCh'i.

Acuto-Manzia (ʼoccult). A form of ʼdivination in which the practitioner drops thirteen pins on a table previously dusted with talcum powder. Like other forms of divination, the pattern formed by the pins is studied in order to determine certain future outcomes.

Adad (ʼoccult). The Babylonian god of rain and weather. Adad was believed to have been the son of the supreme god "An."

Adam-God Doctrine (MORMONISM). This teaching of the Mormon church was first articulated by Brigham ʼYoung in the following often-quoted passage:

> When our Father Adam came into the garden of Eden he came into it with a celestial body, and brought Eve, one of his wives, with him. He helped to make and organize this world. He is Michael, the Archangel, the Ancient of Days, about whom holy men have written and spoken—He is our Father and our God, and the only God with whom we have to do. (*Journal of Discourses* 1:50)

Mormons have had a great deal of difficulty with this doctrine, as it certainly implies that Adam and God the Father are identical. When it comes to the ʼincarnation of Jesus, though presently denied, the Mormon church once taught that Jesus was not conceived by the Holy Spirit but by Adam. Thus Mary had intercourse with her own father, implying that Jesus was the product of an incestuous relationship. Joseph Fielding ʼSmith, nephew of Joseph ʼSmith Sr., attempted to counter the confusion and misunderstanding by insisting that Brigham Young only meant that Adam in his preexistent spirit was known as Michael. Adam became the father of all physical/fleshly bodies. Only in this context was Young saying that Adam was "the only God with whom we have to do." Brigham Young stated that unbelief existed in the minds of Latter-Day Saints even though God revealed Adam to be "our Father and our God" (*Present News* [June 18, 1873], 308).

Adept (SATANISM; THEOSOPHY). One who has undergone the initiation process and is well on the way to receiving an ʼastral body. Adepts are members of what is known in Theosophy as the Great White Lodge. There are four grades of adepts described in the ʼHermetic Order of the Golden Dawn, a society founded in England in 1888 that propagated many of the beliefs revived in Theosophy. The four grades or ranks of an adept are: Zelator Adeptus Minor; Theoricus Adeptus Minor; Adeptus Major; and the highest grade, the Adeptus Exemptus. In Satanism, an adept is simply an initiate; he is also called a ʼneophyte.

Adet (ISLAM). Individual Muslim customs that may take priority over common customs (see ʼ*sunna*) when the latter remain silent. In order of importance, the ʼKoran is the chief authority, the *sunni* or sacred traditions are second, and the *adet* come into play when the first two do not apply.

Adjanikon (ᵛoccult; VOODOO). A male initiate to voodoo.

Adjikone (ᵛoccult; CANDOMBLE; MACUMBA; SOUTH AMERICAN, CENTRAL AMERICAN, AND CARIBBEAN CULTS). Small rock used in religious ceremonies in South America.

Adjuration (ᵛoccult). The command that an ᵛexorcist directs toward an evil spirit.

Adoptionism See ᵛdynamic monarchianism.

Adramᵛmelech The Mesopotamian god also known as ᵛAdad.

Adventism/Adventist See SEVENTH-DAY ADVENTISM.

Aeon (ᵛoccult; VOODOO). A ceremonial gourd or rattle used by priests in voodoo ceremonies. Also, a prolonged period of time, used in many ᵛcult and ᵛoccult groups.

Aeromancy (ᵛoccult). Divining the future by analyzing various signs in both the day and night skies.

Affirmative Prayer (RELIGIOUS SCIENCE). Prayer or meditation that is positive in nature so as to direct one toward unity with the infinite. Negative thoughts serve only to create negative attitudes, which in turn prevents one from tapping into the powers of God and being healed (see ᵛspiritual mind treatment).

Agape (ᵛoccult; CHRISTIANITY). One of several Greek words for "love." In Christianity it means "selfless love." In the occult world, it is a symbolic word for the number "93." This means that it is connected to the ᵛaeon of Horus (see ᵛAiwaz).

Agave (VOODOO). An ocean deity.

Agent (ᵛoccult). An individual used in experiments involving ᵛtelepathy.

Agrippa (ᵛoccult). An occult book containing various and sundry ᵛspells and ᵛincantations. The book is shaped like a human being and the text appears on purple and black pages.

Agrippa, Von Nettesheim, Heinrich Cornelius (ᵛoccult; 1486–1535). An occult scholar and astrologer.

Ahad (ISLAM). An Islamic name for ᵛAllah that means "oneness," further exemplifying the strict ᵛmonotheism that characterizes Islam.

Ahimsa (HINDUISM; JAINISM). The belief that ultimately all living things intend no harm toward any other living thing.

Ahura Mazdah (ᵛZoroastrianism). Sacred deity of Zoroastrianism.

Aidia-Wedo (VOODOO). The deity of the rainbow.

Air (ᵛoccult). One of the four basic elements in the world, the other three being earth, wind, and fire.

Aiwaz (ᵛoccult; SATANISM). Also spelled "Aiwass." This is the name of the spirit whom Aleister ᵛCrowley credits for giving him the words for his ᵛ*Book of the Dead* (1906). The book was dictated by Aiwaz through Crowley's wife while he was in Cairo in 1904.

Ajna Chakra (ᵛoccult). Also called "the ᵛthird eye," located in the lower forehead between the two eyes. Occultists consider it the locus of occult power.

Akasha Principle (ᵛoccult). A spiritual presence, seen and described as a purple aura that encompasses and surrounds all life.

Akashic Records (ᵛoccult; THEOSOPHY). The belief that a vast storehouse or library exists in the ᵛastral plane containing all human events, thoughts, and emotions since the beginning of life. Mystical contemplation of the Akashic records can lead to ᵛenlightenment.

Akiya, Einasuke (SOKA-GAKKAI; n.d.). Became the leader of the Soka-Gakkai organization in 1981.

Akoveo (ᵛoccult; CANDOMBLE; MACUMBA; SOUTH AMERICAN, CENTRAL AMERICAN, AND CARIBBEAN CULTS). Rhythmic instrument constructed from two nuts that are fastened together. The *akoveo* is used in ᵛcult dance ceremonies.

Alamo, Susan (ALAMO CHRISTIAN MINISTRIES; 1926–1982). Her real name was Edith Opal ᵛHorn; she established the Alamo Christian Foundation.

Alamo, Tony (ALAMO CHRISTIAN MINISTRIES; 1934–). Had been the leader of the Alamo Christian Foundation with the help of his wife, Susan ᵛAlamo. Tony Alamo's real name is Bernard Lazar ᵛHoffman.

Alastor (SATANISM). The chief demon of Hades or hell, known particularly for cruelty.

Albahaca (ᵛoccult; ABAKUA). "Plants" that are sprinkled on the initiate in the Abakua ritual.

Albigenses (CHRISTIANITY). A heretical ᵛsect that rose up in Albi, France. The Albigensians, as they were called, revived portions of the ancient ᵛManichaeism. They taught that the flesh was evil, that sex was a wicked instrument of the devil, and that Jesus' death on the cross was an illusion (see ᵛdocetism). The Albigensian heresy spread throughout southern France until a crusade resulted in their total annihilation some time after 1330.

Alchemy (ᵖoccult; NEW AGE MOVEMENT; ROSICRU-CIANISM). An ancient science believed to have arisen in Egypt. It was believed that metals possessed magical powers when in their alloy forms. Alchemists sought to make gold from lesser base metals; a second goal was to discover the "elixir" or the mythical "fountain of life," from which liquid would yield immortality. The term *alchemy* has also been used as a metaphor to describe the spiritual perfection one achieves when expunging the various maladies that keep the soul in darkness. Alchemy is also used as a metaphor by New Agers to describe the old world order, which manipulated the environment with fire. The New Age is one in which a major paradigm shift from pyrotechnics to biotechnology occurs. Some describe this new paradigm as being a movement from alchemy to ᵖalgeny.

Aldinach (ᵖoccult). An Egyptain ᵖdemon who sometimes appears as a woman and brings about storms and earthquakes.

Alectorius (ᵖoccult). A magical stone believed to possess occult power and to cause both love and pain.

Alectromancy (ᵖoccult). A form of ᵖdivination where several answers to questions are written on paper and baked into dough. One of the strips of paper is chosen, read, and believed to be a source of insight and guidance. Alectromancy is the forerunner to the so-called "fortune cookie."

Alectryomancy (ᵖoccult). A form of ᵖdivination involving a ᵖseer, who makes a circle out of the letters of the alphabet. The circle is then covered by grains of corn. A hen is released in the circle to eat the grain. The letters that get exposed as a result are then noted and interpreted by the seer.

Alexandrian (WITCHCRAFT). The form of contemporary witchcraft that takes its name from Alexander ᵖSanders.

Algeny (NEW AGE MOVEMENT). Algeny is the New Age term for the major paradigm shift from old world industrial technology to the new order's emphasis on biotechnology. The word was first coined by Dr. Joshua Lederberg, nobel laureate from Rockefeller University. Algeny means to change or alter the essence of a material substance through transformation. In the old world technology, this was done through pyrotechnology, or the use of fire (i.e., industry) to alter or manipulate the environment. The New Age will alter or transform, not the outer world of a substance but its inner composition. In living organisms, this is accomplished through genetics, microbiology, etc.

Algoi or Algol (ᵖoccult). An Arabic name for "head of the ᵖdemons." A bright star in the Perseus constellation is said to be the most evil star. Hebrew astrologers called it the head of ᵖSatan.

Al-Hassan (SUFISM; 643–728). A Muslim leader from Basra, who strongly supported the Sufi Order, a ᵖsect concerned about the purification of ISLAM in order to gain more spiritual knowledge of ᵖAllah.

Ali (ISLAM; 600–661). ᵖMuhammad's son-in-law, who became the fourth ᵖcaliph, following the death of ᵖUthman. Ali is most noted for his being the first to arrange the ᵖKoran chronologically.

Ali, Mirza Husayn (BAHA'I FAITH; 1817–1892). Also called the ᵖBaha'U'llah, considered to be the great prophet of ᵖAllah.

Allah (ISLAM). The divine name for God in Islam.

All Hallows' Eve (ᵖoccult). A pagan festival celebrated on October 31, the evening preceding All Saints' Day. The ancient ᵖdruids believed this occasion merited celebration because Saman, the lord of death, brought back the souls of the wicked who had been condemned to inhabit the bodies of animals. Children celebrate this festival today by donning masks and dressing up as ᵖghosts, animals, and so on. The beginning of the new year for the ancient Celtic tribes was signaled by All Hallows' Eve. See also ᵖwitches' calendar and ᵖHalloween.

Alma (SANTERIA; VOODOO). The name for a person's soul.

Almodel (ᵖoccult). A book containing basic instructions on how to make wax ᵖtalismans used to summon ᵖangels or spiritual beings.

Alomancy (ᵖoccult). A form of divination in which salt is sprinkled on a surface and its patterns are analyzed to foretell future events.

Alpert, Richard (HANUMAN FOUNDATION; 1933–). Son of a wealthy lawyer who was the founder of Brandeis University, Alpert attended Harvard University from 1958 through 1963. It was here that he met Timothy ᵖLeary. Together with Leary, Aldous Huxley, and Allen Ginsberg, they experimented with LSD and other drugs, claiming to be exploring the depths of human consciousness. Alpert and Leary were dismissed from their teaching posts at Harvard in 1963. Alpert changed his name to Baba Ram ᵖDass while studying in India under guru ᵖMaharaj Ji. Baba Ram Dass founded the Hanuman Foundation along with the Hanuman Temple.

Al-Qaeda (ISLAM). Terrorist organization founded by Osama bin Laden. See ᵖIslamic terrorist cults.

Altar (ᵇoccult; SATANISM; WITCHCRAFT). The table around which satanists celebrate the ᵇblack mass. It can be made from any variety of materials. The altar has no ritualistic significance in and of itself. It is simply a surface used to hold the ritual tools—chalice, incense, ᵇathame, and so on. It is usually located at the center of the ᵇcircle or inside the circle at the north candle. The Great Rite is performed at the altar. There are also altars in ᵇwicca, SANTERIA, VOODOO, and the like.

(ᵇoccult). An awareness that transcends the normal states of everyday consciousness. Altered states are induced in a variety of ways: meditation techniques, psychedelic drugs, and influences such as ᵇguided imagery, ᵇastral projection, ᵇhypnotism, dreams, and ᵇtrance.

Amachitis (ᵇoccult). A ceremonial stone used to summon water spirits.

Amaterasu (SHINTO). A Japanese sun goddess.

Ambassador College Press (WORLDWIDE CHURCH OF GOD). The now defunct publishing division of the Worldwide Church of God, located in Pasadena, California, and linked with Ambassador College.

American Christian Press (THE WAY INTERNATIONAL). Publishing arm of The Way International, located in New Knoxville, Ohio.

American Study Group (MORMONISM). A now defunct branch of Mormonism that specialized in end-times speculations.

Amduscias (ᵇSATANISM). A grand duke of Hades who sometimes transforms himself into human form when appearing to magicians.

Amnesia (ᵇoccult). Loss of memory experienced usually by a ᵇmedium during a ᵇséance or ᵇpossession. The medium often experiences amnesia while in a trance-like state.

AMORC (ROSICRUCIANISM). Acronym for Ancient Mystical Order of the Rosy Cross.

Amoymon (SATANISM). A king of Hades.

Amritdhari (SIKH DHARMA). Baptized members of the Healthy, Happy, Holy Organization (₃HO).

Amulet (ᵇoccult). An object worn to ward off evil spirits or ᵇspells. The proverbial rabbit's foot is a popular amulet. The Egyptians had many amulets.

Anacithidus (ᵇoccult). A stone used to summon a ᵇdemon.

Analects (CONFUCIANISM). A collection of the sayings of ᵇConfucius.

Analytical Mind (SCIENTOLOGY). One of the two basic divisions of the human mind. The analytical mind carries out rational and reasoning functions. See also ᵇreactive mind.

Anami Lok (ECKANKAR). The ultimate heaven or the highest ᵇastral plane. ᵇSugmad dwells in this celestial place.

Ananda (HINDUISM). The delight and joy that lies within; the divine bliss of the spirit; ᵇtranscendental happiness.

Anandamurti, Shrii Shrii. (ANANDA MARGA YOGA SOCIETY; 1921–1990). Born Prabhat Ranjan Sarkar and founder of the Ananda Marga Yoga Society.

Ananse (ᵇoccult). Name of the spider believed to have supplied the material that the sky god needed to create humanity.

Anatta (BUDDHISM). The Buddhist doctrine that the process of ᵇreincarnation involves experiences and events specific to each individual soul. There is no permanent soul that survives death to undergo further reincarnation.

Ancestor Worship (SHINTO; NATIVE AMERICAN RELIGIONS). The belief that the departed ancestors in a family line are consciously watching over the affairs of the living. By directing prayer to them, one hopes to avoid evil and secure good fortune.

Ancient One (ᵇoccult; SATANISM). The priestess who officiates at the ᵇblack mass.

Andon (URANTIA). Name of one of the human race's first parents (see ᵇFonta).

Andrae, Johann Valentin (ROSICRUCIANISM; 1586–1654). Lutheran theologian, whom some falsely accuse as the author of the *Fama Fraternitatis Bendicti Ordinis Rosae-Crucis*.

Androgyne (ᵇoccult). Commonly, the characteristic of having the traits of both sexes; hermaphroditic; in ᵇmysticism and in occult circles, androgyne symbolizes complete oneness and unity, as opposed to duality.

Angas (JAINISM). Word designating the twelve sacred texts of Jainism.

Angels (CHRISTIANITY; ISLAM; MORMONISM). Those spirit beings depicted in the ᵇBible and created by God to serve as guardians, protectors, mediators, and messengers. The Nicene Creed confesses belief in all things "visible and invisible." For Christianity, part of the invisible realm is comprised of good angels, such as cherubim and seraphim. Two angels, Michael the archangel and Gabriel, are named in the Bible. These celestial servants of the living God carry out the divine will and purpose of God in Christ. The other part of the invisible realm is comprised of evil angels or *demons. *Lucifer is a "fallen angel" who rules over a vast host of demons from *hell. In this present work, the authors' particular interest lies in the prominent role angels have played in the current popular culture and its interest in "spirituality" prominent in many NEW AGE groups. Angels have become the subject of numerous Hollywood films.

Also, angels are invoked in numerous religions as the bearers of new revelation. In the case of Islam, for example, it was the angel Gabriel who reportedly appeared to *Muhammad and revealed to him the *Koran. For Mormonism, an angel named *Moroni visited Joseph *Smith and gave knowledge to him that would eventually direct him toward translating the Book of Mormon.

Anglo-Israeliism (CHURCH UNIVERSAL AND TRIUMPHANT; WORLDWIDE CHURCH OF GOD). The belief that the Anglo-Saxons of Great Britain are the descendants of the lost ten tribes of Israel. Some religious groups in America believe they are the extension of this principle because of the migration of the English to America. The theory was first proposed by John Sadler in 1649 and later developed by Richard Brothers (1757–1824). Different forms of Anglo-Israeliism are held by different groups, such as Church Universal and Triumphant and the Worldwide Church of God. The Worldwide Church of God no longer accepts or teaches the doctrine of Anglo-Israeliism, with the exception of those groups who have broken away and continue to proliferate the teachings of Herbert W. *Armstrong. This doctrine is alternately known as British Israeliism.

Angra Mainyu (*Zoroastrianism). The evil god or spirit.

Anima (HINDUISM). The ability of a yogic (see *yogi) practitioner to modify the mass and density of matter.

Animal Magnetism (*occult; *parapsychology). Theory advanced by Friedrich Anton Mesmer (1733–1815) that suggested that an unseen magnetic energy field surrounds a person and, when transferred properly, can be used as a healing force for others. Mesmer experimented with animal magnetism by placing a person in a tub filled with water and randomly placed iron filings. The person's "magnetism" could then arrange the filings in the magnetic field and be harnessed in order to transfer healing energies to a sick person.

Animism (*occult). The idea that all things in the universe are invested with a life force, soul, or mind. Animism is also commonly referred to as *panpsychism and *hylozoism. Philosophically, animism is opposed to materialism. A philosophical animist would argue, for example, that a stone or a tree is not simply a conglomeration of atoms and molecules (materialism), but rather possesses an "awareness" of forces or other bodies surrounding it. Although encountered more frequently in philosophical circles, animism is nevertheless an important constituent of the religious lives of primitive people.

Ankh (*occult; WITCHCRAFT). The ancient Egyptian symbol made up of a cross with a loop replacing the top portion. Egyptian deities were often portrayed carrying an ankh, and it is still used in many occult circles. The ankh symbolizes life. It is also called the *crux ansata*. In Christian symbolism, the *tau*, or T-shaped, cross most closely recalls the shape of the staff on which Moses lifted the bronze serpent in the wilderness as a life-giving sign to those who looked upon it. Most likely, the connection can be made between the ankh and the *tau* cross because the Israelites were familiar with the Egyptian ankh while held in captivity. Christian groups such as the Coptics use the ankh cross with no connection to the occult.

Annihilationism (JEHOVAH'S WITNESSES; SEVENTH-DAY ADVENTISM; WORLDWIDE CHURCH OF GOD). The doctrine that after death, the souls of the wicked will not be punished eternally in a literal hell but will simply cease to exist. Annihilationism constitutes a middle ground between wholesale *universalism and the traditional Christian doctrine of eternal damnation.

Anointed Class (JEHOVAH'S WITNESSES). See *little flock.

Antaskarana (*occult; THEOSOPHY). A compound word in Sanskrit that means, literally, "the sensory organ within." In Theosophy the *antaskarana* is the liaison between the spiritual and the personal dimensions of life.

Anthropomancy (*occult). The ritual practice of eating human flesh.

Anthropomorphism (CHRISTIANITY). The attribution of human characteristics, personality, volitions, and emotions to God. For example, God walks "in the cool of the day" (Gen. 3:8).

Anthropopathism (CHRISTIANITY). Those numerous occasions when God manifests human emotions such as pity or anger (e.g., Hos. 1:6–7; 8:5).

Apana (HINDUISM). One of the five forms of *prana, *apana* is said to control the excretory functions of the body.

Apocalypse, Apocalyptic (CHRISTIANITY). Unveiling or a revealing of future events. As a literary genre, apocalyptic literature abounds. The last book of the ᵇBible is called Revelation, or alternately the Apocalypse of Saint John. Other works classified in this manner include the *Apocalypse of Adam*, the *First and Second Apocalypses of James*, the *Apocalypse of Peter*, etc. Characteristic of apocalyptic literature is deep symbolism alluding to impending doom and judgment on the wicked, and deliverance and reward for the righteous. Only the righteous are able to interpret the symbols, while their meanings remain hidden to the wicked. Most apocalyptic literature was written between 200 B.C. and A.D. 200, and many of the works of ᵇgnosticism uncovered at Nag-Hammadi are apocalyptic.

Apocrypha (CHRISTIANITY). A compound word from the Greek meaning "hidden from." The apocryphal writings are regarded as esoteric in nature. Fourteen books, called the Apocrypha, are included in the Old Testament Latin Vulgate ᵇBible.

Apollinarianism (CHRISTIANITY). A ᵇChristology espoused by Apollinarius (c. A.D. 310–c. 390), who vigorously opposed ᵇArianism. Apollinarius taught that Christ was divine and that no human nature existed in him. He believed that for Christ to possess a human nature would imply that as a man, Jesus would have to undergo suffering, moral development, and so on. For Apollinarius, this was inconceivable. In place of Jesus' human nature was the divine ᵇLogos. Apollinarianism was condemned at the Council of Constantinople in A.D. 381 on the grounds that this Christology did not recognize the human nature of Christ, of which the ᵇBible so clearly speaks. To reject the human nature of Christ is to reject the very point of the ᵇIncarnation, namely, that God clothed himself in human flesh to redeem humanity. (See Appendix 2).

Apophis (ᵇoccult). A giant serpent that lived in the Nile and tried to prevent the Egyptian sun god Ra from traveling.

Apostasy (CHRISTIANITY; MORMONISM; JEHOVAH'S WITNESSES; etc.). To renounce, abandon, or fall away from. Every exclusivistic religion—that is, those that believe their articles of faith are the truth to the exclusion of all others—inevitably concludes that people who hold to a doctrine, creed, or belief at variance with theirs are in a state of apostasy. The concept of apostasy receives more attention in some ᵇcults, ᵇsects, and religions than in others. Mormonism holds that almost immediately after the apostolic days of Christianity, there was a great "apostatizing" wherein the gospel was corrupted and lost. Only after eighteen centuries was the "truth" restored when it was revealed to Joseph ᵇSmith. Since his time, the Mormons have reportedly upheld the "truth" to the exclusion of all other groups. In similar fashion, Jehovah's Witnesses fervently maintain that any member who holds to a doctrine other than what they teach and confess is to be regarded as being in a state of apostasy.

Apostle (CHRISTIANITY). From the Greek *apostolos*, meaning "messenger," used in the ᵇBible to designate those chief disciples chosen by Jesus in Matthew 10:2–4; Mark 1:16–20; Luke 22:14; and Acts 1:2. The criteria recognized by the early church for the apostolic office were those who were (1) chosen by Christ and were (2) eyewitnesses of Christ, beginning from his baptism through his ascension (Acts 1:22). Apostolic authorship later became a crucial criterion for the recognition of the authenticity of the New Testament canon. See also ᵇCouncil of the Twelve Apostles for a use of this term in MORMONISM.

Apostolic Brotherhood (CHRIST THE SAVIOR BROTHERHOOD). Name given to the governing board of the Christ the Savior Brotherhood, formerly called the Holy Order of Mans.

Apostolic Succession (CHRISTIANITY). The term has several meanings within the pale of Christian history. For Roman Catholicism and Eastern Orthodoxy, apostolic succession means that all of the bishops, priests, and deacons of the church receive their ordination into the office of the holy ministry by virtue of a long line of succession from Jesus through St. Peter (Matt. 16:18), on to the other apostles, and then to the future generations of clergy throughout history. For numerous ᵇProtestant churches, apostolic succession is understood as a succession of confession. That is, the clergy of the church have succeeded the apostles not by virtue of Peter as a man, but by virtue of his confession of faith that Jesus is the Christ (Matt. 16:18). To still other Protestants, the notion of succession lies in the continued work of the Holy Spirit to intervene directly in the lives of the clergy and the church.

Apotheosis See ᵇdeification.

Apparition (ᵇoccult; SPIRITUALISM). Term often used synonymously with ᵇghost. An apparition is a spirit that, though invisible, appears or manifests itself so as to be seen. There have been many reported sightings of apparitions with no logical or physical cause to account for their effects.

Applewhite, Marshall Herff (HEAVEN'S GATE; 1931–1997). The leader of the now-defunct ♭cult known as Heaven's Gate.

Apport (♭occult; SPIRITUALISM). The appearance of a physical object during a ♭seance. The object appears mysteriously in full view of the participants.

Aqamas (HINDUISM). A collection of manuals on ritual and worship.

Aquarian Age (♭astrology; ♭occult; NEW AGE MOVEMENT). According to astrological belief, the earth must pass through each of the signs of the ♭zodiac in the course of its thousands of years of history. Each epoch lasts for approximately two thousand years. The dawning of the age of ♭Aquarius was to have begun in the nineteenth century, heralding the start of a new and cosmic worldview. The previous age was Pisces, which represented the Christian era (Jesus as the "fisher of man"). The New Age Movement embraces a spirituality that it attempts to wed with modern science and technology. Such spirituality leaves behind the conceptual schema of the Judeo-Christian heritage characteristic of the last two thousand years of human history.

Aquarian Gospel, The (NEW AGE MOVEMENT). This book, authored by Levi Dowling in 1997, claims to be an account of the life of Jesus as he grew up in Nazareth. Dowling purportedly received the information conveyed or "channeled" from ♭Akashic records. Based on these records and on the fact that John's Gospel admits that there were other things that Jesus did that are not written in his Gospel (John 20:30), Dowling claims that Jesus traveled far and wide in the ancient world, including such places as India, Tibet, Persia, Assyria, Greece, and Egypt.

There is, however, no credible historical evidence to support these amazing claims. No historians of the ancient world or any responsible scholarship today has been able to provide any conclusive insights about the "silent years" of the life of Christ. There were, of course, numerous apocryphal accounts of the life of Jesus in the ancient world. Dowling's book is simply one more apocryphal extrapolation based not on sound scholarship, but on a fertile imagination.

Aquarius (♭astrology; ♭occult). Latin for water-bearer. The eleventh ♭sign of the ♭zodiac covering the period between January 21 and February 18. The popular depiction shows Aquarius emptying water into a stream from a jug. This tradition probably emerged from the association of Aquarius with times of flooding in the Middle East. The character of a person born under the sign of Aquarius is described as being shy, quiet, introspective, cautious, and persistent.

Aquino, Michael (SATANISM; n.d.). A one-time member of the Church of Satan and head of the Lilith Grotto in Spotswood, New Jersey. Aquino left the Church of Satan and formed the Temple of Set in 1975.

Arabs (ISLAM). The descendants of Ishmael and Keturah according to Hebrew history (Gen. 16:11ff. and 25:1–4). The significance of Arabs with respect to Islam is that they are considered to be the first ethnic group to embrace the message of ♭Muhammad. They are regarded as the elite class of the Islamic faith. The ♭Koran is written in the language of the Arabs (Arabic).

Arbatel of Magic (♭occult). A medieval ♭magic book that contains various ceremonies and descriptions of spirits that exist in the universe.

Archon (♭gnosticism). A world-governing deity created by a subordinate god (demiurge), who also created the worlds to which the archons were assigned. Because matter was regarded as evil in gnostic cosmology, the archons were viewed as evil as well. The souls of those who died ascended to the realm of light, but before they reached it they had to pass by the archons, who would not allow them to continue their journey until the rehearsed magical incantations and password slogan. Those who mastered the secret knowledge while still alive would be able to bypass the archons and ascend directly to the kingdom of light.

A.R.E. (association for research and enlightenment). ♭Acronym for this group.

Arguelles, Jose See ♭harmonic convergence.

Arhat (BUDDHISM). One who has attained ♭nirvana.

Arianism (CHRISTIANITY). A teaching that ancient Christianity regarded as heretical. Named after its founder, Arius (A.D. 250–336), Arianism is, in essence, the denial of the eternality of Jesus Christ. Christianity teaches that Jesus, the Son of God, was coeternal with the Father. Arius maintained that Jesus was "begotten" or created by the Father out of nothing. Arianism was vehemently opposed by Athanasius (A.D. 296–373) and was condemned at the Council of Nicea (A.D. 325). The council utilized the term *homoousios* to describe the consubstantiality ("the same substance") of the Son with the Father. Eusebius, sometimes recognized as the first church historian, was an Arian. Arianism also became the predominant persuasion of the Teutonic tribes to the north of the Roman Empire, which were evangelized by Ulphilas (311–383). Arianism lives on as a Christology predominantly with the JEHOVAH'S WITNESSES and certain other ▸cults.

Aries (▸astrology). Latin for "ram." The first ▸sign of the ▸zodiac, covering the period between March 21 and April 20. Aries is depicted as a ram. According to Greek mythology, Phrixus sacrificed the ram with a golden fleece to Zeus, the main Greek god. Zeus then placed the ram in the heavens, where it became a constellation. An Arien is described as being aggressive, self-centered, assertive, intractable, loyal, ambitious, and self-actuating.

Arijja (BUDDHISM). Ignorance, a lacking in knowledge. This deprivation of knowledge is, for Buddhism, the fundamental cause of evil.

Arimanius Aharman Dahak (SATANISM). Associated with the symbol of a black serpent and regarded as the ruler of ▸black magic.

Ariolist (▸occult; SATANISM). Satanist priests or ▸magicians who communicate with or summon ▸demons through the use of an ▸altar.

Aristha (HINDUISM). Signs a ▸yogi uses to pinpoint the time he will die.

Arithmancy (▸occult). A form of ▸divination whereby certain numbers, such as the date of one's birthday or the number association of the letter's in one's name, are used to calculate significant events in a person's life.

Arius of Alexandria (CHRISTIANITY). Arius (A.D. 250–336), an early church theologian who challenged the deity of Christ by teaching that Jesus was not God in the same sense as the Father was God. Arius taught that there was a time when the Son was not. His teaching sparked the fourth-century Trinitarian controversies that culminated in his condemnation at the Council of Nicea (325). The Nicene Creed (see Appendix 1) confessed against ▸Arianism that Jesus was "very God of very God" and that Jesus was "begotten, not made."

Arjuna (HINDUISM). Son of Pandu, Arjuna appears with ▸Hare Krishna to do battle with their opponents. Arjuna sees many of his own relatives among the ranks of the enemy and refuses to fight. He then engages in dialogue with Krishna, who in the end convinces him that he must indeed fight. Their conversation has been written in what Hindus consider to be one of their most prized classics, the ▸*Bhagavad Gita*.

Ark of the Covenant (JUDAISM). The sacred piece that God instructed the Hebrews to build in Exodus 25:10–22 and to place in the Most Holy Place in the tabernacle. The Hebrew word for "ark" can also mean "coffin" (Gen. 50:26) or "chest" (2 Kings 12:9–10). The original ark was constructed by Bezalel and was approximately 45 x 27 x 27 inches. It was made of acacia wood and lined with gold.

Two sets of rings were fastened to its sides to make it portable. The lid of the ark was called the ▸"mercy seat" (KJV) or "atonement cover" (NIV). The ark was transported by the Kohalites (Num. 7:9; 10:21). When in transit, it was covered by the veil of the dismantled tabernacle (Num. 4:5, 20). Once in Canaan, the ark had several resting places, especially before the time of David, but eventually resided within the first temple of Solomon.

There are several plausible theories concerning what became of the ark after the destruction of Jerusalem and the temple. According to one theory, Nebuchadnezzar seized or destroyed the ark (2 Esdras 10:22). During the rebuilding of the temple (see Ezra 3–6), there is no record of the ark being found or restored. Some modern-day scholars and archaeologists speculate that the ark may still remain buried in Solomon's vault in old Jerusalem.

Armageddon (CHRISTIANITY; JEHOVAH'S WITNESSES). The future war waged by all of God's enemies on earth against his heavenly and invisible armies. The outcome will result in the destruction of all but Jehovah's faithful. Many groups in Christianity have developed a theology centered around the cosmic battle between the antichrist, ▸Satan, and God at the end of the world.

Armstrong, Garner Ted (WORLDWIDE CHURCH OF GOD; 1930–2003). Son of the late Herbert W. ▸Armstrong. Garner Ted established the Church of God International after he was excommunicated by his father over a doctrinal disagreement. During the 1980s the COGI grew to about 5,000 members. Accused of sexual assault, Armstrong stepped down from the presidency of the organization in 1995. He continued to preach and conduct television ministry but was removed from the organization altogether in 1997. In 1998, he founded the Intercontinental Church of God, where he remained president until his death.

Armstrong, Herbert W. (WORLDWIDE CHURCH OF GOD; 1892–1986). Founder of the Worldwide Church of God. Armstrong was ordained as a clergyman of the Oregon Conference of the Church of God in June 1931 after much struggle and wrestling with the Scriptures and his conscience. He concluded, through the influence of his wife's convictions, that "obedience to God's spiritual laws summed up in the Ten Commandments is necessary for salvation." He also founded Ambassador College and broadcast a popular television program called *The World Tomorrow*. Following Armstrong's death in 1986, the WCG altered significant aspects of Armstrong's theology.

Aromatherapy   (NEW AGE MOVEMENT). The belief that certain illnesses can be treated through the inhalation of scented steam.

Ascended Masters   See church universal and triumphant.

Ascendant   (ᴵastrology; ᴵoccult). The ᴵsign that is rising on the horizon of the earth from the location where one is born.

Ascending Arc   (ᴵoccult; THEOSOPHY). The upward progress toward increasing spiritual and mystical existence. In Theosophy this is known as the "life stream." The opposite is the ᴵdescending arc.

Asceticism   (ᴵgnosticism; CHRISTIANITY; JUDAISM). Self-denial, usually connected with the view that matter and spirit are in opposition to each other. The physical body with its accompanying needs and desires is incompatible with the spirit and its divine nature. Asceticism champions the idea that by renouncing the flesh and the world one can achieve a higher spiritual status.

Asceticism was widely embraced in the religions of the past and is also a prevailing philosophy now. Plato idealized it, Jewish ᴵsects such as the Essenes practiced it fervently, and Christianity institutionalized it with the development of the various monastic orders. Early in the history of the Christian church, a system of thought known as gnosticism arose that clearly spelled out a doctrine of asceticism. The worldview of the gnostics was essentially dualistic. Matter was regarded as being inferior to spirit, and the physical body was a hindrance to holy living. Gnostic thought was challenged by early Christian apologists, but its influence on the church cannot be overlooked. Church history records some incredible instances of asceticism. Simeon Stylites (A.D. 390–459), for example, spent the majority of his life (almost thirty years) on the top of a pillar. He had his food raised up in a basket by some faithful followers. In his efforts to escape the evils of the world, he became a symbol that attracted streams of pilgrims for many years.

Asceticism is practiced within the ranks of virtually every religion. It is a dominant motif among many ᴵcults and Eastern religions.

Asheshe   (MACUMBA; SOUTH AMERICAN, CENTRAL AMERICAN, AND CARIBBEAN CULTS). Term used for a funeral rite in the Macumba ᴵcults of Brazil.

Ashkenazi   (JUDAISM). Name given to Jews who lived in France or in the Rhineland before their migration elsewhere, particularly to the Slavic lands after the ᴵCrusades. It refers to all Jews who came to adopt the "German rite" synagogue ritual, which was marked with an emphasis on ᴵasceticism, ᴵmysticism, and the chanting of the liturgy in Yiddish (until the twentieth century). The Ashkenazi are distinguished from the ᴵShephardic Jews. Ashkenazis comprise over 80 percent of the Jewish population worldwide. Most live in the United States and the former Soviet Union.

Ashmole, Elias   (ROSICRUCIANISM; 1617–1692). Believed to be responsible for introducing the beliefs of Rosicrucianism to Freemasonry.

Ashram   (HINDUISM). The worship and meditation place for an adherent to Hinduism, along with the place where people gather to hear sacred texts and teachings.

Ashrama   (HINDUISM). The stages of the devotional life in Hinduism. They include: (1) ᴵ*brachmacharin*, the learning stage; (2) ᴵ*grihastha*, the marriage stage; (3) ᴵ*vanaprastha* ("the forest life"), stage entered on becoming a grandparent; (4) ᴵ*sannyasin*, the wandering ascetic stage (optimal).

Ashteroth   (SATANISM). The "grand duke of hell." When this ᴵdemon is summoned, a ceremony occurs wherein a gold ring is placed on or near the front of the mouth or tongue in order to ward off the foul odors emitted by his breath.

Asmodeus   (SATANISM). The ruler over all ᴵdemons in ᴵhell. Asmodeus is also the demon of lust and rage.

Asoka   (272–232 B.C.; BUDDHISM; HINDUISM). King of India; he is considered to be one of the greatest of all kings not only because he conquered most of the Indian peninsula, but also because after converting to Buddhism he transformed it from a conglomerate of small ᴵsects into one of the chief religions of India. Only after Asoka sent missionaries throughout his empire did the movement flourish and become unified.

Aspect   (ᴵastrology; ᴵoccult). The angular relationship between earth and two other celestial bodies (stars, planets). In ᴵastrology the various angles between such bodies are measured for either positive or negative positions and are in turn believed to determine good or bad outcomes of daily and future events.

Assoto (ᵖoccult; VOODOO). Sacred ceremonial drum used in voodoo.

Astral Body (ᵖoccult; THEOSOPHY). The life-giving force of the human body. It is comprised of a universal substance that is a vital part of the body but may be separated out from it and survives after death. Theosophists and occultists believe the astral body first rises to the ᵖastral plane immediately following death.

Astral Plane (ᵖoccult; THEOSOPHY). A dimension or level of being lying just beyond the physical world. During ᵖastral projection, occultists believe the human soul is able to travel to this dimension. When death has occurred, the soul journeys to different planes, the first of which is the astral plane.

Astral Projection (ᵖoccult; THEOSOPHY). Occult belief whereby the human soul projects out from or leaves the physical body and journeys to other places, later to return unless death occurs. This phenomenon is also called an "out of body experience" (OBE) and "astral travel."

Astrogyromancy (ᵖoccult). The practice of using dice that contain letters and numbers in ᵖfortune-telling.

Astrology (ᵖoccult). The popularly held belief that the stars and other celestial bodies scattered throughout the skies are instrumental in arranging and influencing the lives of human beings on earth. An astrologer believes that the arrangement of the stars, planets, and constellations at the time of one's birth sets a determined pattern in the life of that person. The ᵖhoroscope outlines the twelve ᵖsigns of the ᵖzodiac and categorizes people by the particular signs under which they have been born: ᵖAries, ᵖTaurus, ᵖGemini, ᵖCancer, ᵖLeo, ᵖVirgo, ᵖLibra, ᵖScorpio, ᵖSagittarius, ᵖCapricorn, ᵖAquarius, and ᵖPisces.

Astrology probably originated in ancient Mesopotamia. The Babylonians were famous in the ancient world for their knowledge of the heavens. In all likelihood, the Magi or wise men mentioned in Matthew 2:1–12 were astrologers, following the new star they had seen in the East in order to find the baby Jesus.

Astrology was considered a science until the sixteenth century, when the Copernican Revolution challenged the geocentric view popularly held throughout the Middle Ages. Astrology continues, however, to attract widespread attention in occult circles as well as in popular periodicals, almanacs, and newspapers, commanding millions of readers.

Atchere (SANTERIA; VOODOO). A ceremonial rattle.

Athame (WITCHCRAFT). A ritual knife used in ceremony. It has a black handle and is not used for any purpose (cutting, etc.) apart from the ᵖcoven's ritual ceremonies, particularly the Great Rite.

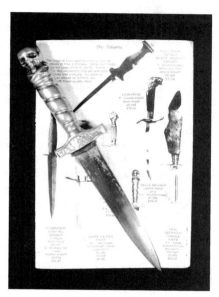

A variety of athames offered for sale through occult outlets.
Courtesy Jack M. Roper/CARIS

Atlantis (ᵖoccult). The legendary lost continent that is believed to have sunk as the result of natural disaster. Plato and Pliny both mention Atlantis in their writings. Musings about the lost civilization appear in various occult writings. Rudolf ᵖSteiner, for example, wrote what he believed to be an accurate account of the history of Atlantis. Some speculate that this lost culture was an other-worldly visitation by celestial beings. Archaeologists and historians hypothesize that the legends of Atlantis possibly arose through the destruction by volcanic eruption of the island of Thera, north of Crete in the Mediterranean Sea around 1475 B.C.

Atman (HINDUISM). The self. Atman refers to both body and soul, the senses and the whole being and constitution of the individual. It is sometimes referred to as the "universal life principle."

Auditor (SCIENTOLOGY). One trained in administering therapy to patients/students of Scientology. The auditor's goal is to eliminate ᵖengrams from the ᵖreactive mind so that the ᵖanalytical mind may function without hindrance. When this stage is reached, the auditor has enabled the patient to become a ▸clear. The auditor uses an ▸e-meter in the therapy process.

Augury (▸occult). A form of ▸divination that studies the flight patterns of birds.

Augustinian Order (CHRISTIANITY). Also called the Augustinian hermits or friars, this religious order was founded in 1256, receiving full sanction from Pope Alexander IV. The order was first comprised of hermits coming together from several congregations in Italy, but it soon spread to cities and towns throughout Western Europe. Their "rule" was taken from the Rule of St. Augustine, which, dating back to the time of Augustine, outlined the way of Augustine himself—the common life of shared poverty, celibacy, and obedience. He probably did not author the rule, but in all likelihood, one of his followers did, perhaps while Augustine was still living. Augustinians today live mostly in Western Europe and in South America and are involved in education and pastoral ministry.

Aura (▸occult). Some occult practitioners believe that people possess an energy field that emits light that emanates from the body. The particular color of the light reveals such things as temperaments, moods, and intellectual predispositions.

Automatic Writing (▸occult; NEW AGE MOVEMENT; SPIRITUALISM). A phenomenon whereby a ▸medium begins to write without apparent awareness. The source of such writing is believed to be from a dead person's spirit conjured up by the medium. The same phenomenon occurs in automatic drawing, painting, and speaking.

Autumn Equinox (▸occult; WITCHCRAFT). One of the eight ▸sabbats celebrated by ▸witches and others in the occult world. It is one of the lesser sabbats and usually occurs on September 21, but can also take place on the 20th or 22nd. Like the ▸spring equinox, it is a time of balance. The length of both day and night are equalized by the sun crossing the equator. This is a time of equilibrium and stability, a time of rest from labor, after the harvest has been gathered in (see ▸witches' holidays). The autumn equinox is also celebrated by many aboriginal religions.

Avatar (HINDUISM; NEW AGE MOVEMENT; THEOSOPHY). An ▸incarnation of the deity; one who never undergoes the cycle of ▸reincarnation. In New Age thought an avatar is a spiritual teacher appointed to a given era.

Avatara (HINDUISM). In the avatara doctrine, ▸Vishnu takes on an earthly form to rescue the world, which is threatened with imminent danger. There are at least ten ▸avatars or ▸incarnations in the literature.

Avidya (HINDUISM). Ignorance, the chief reason why human beings do not receive consciousness of God.

Awake (JEHOVAH'S WITNESSES). An official periodic publication of the Watchtower Bible and Tract Society.

Ayatollah (ISLAM). Iranian spiritual leader of the Shi²ite ▸sect of Islam.

Ayurvedic Medicine (HINDUISM). Medicines that combine herbal dieting, exercise, and hygiene. Ayurvedic medicine is currently promoted by Deepak ▸Chopra and several other prominent advocates of ▸holistic health.

Azetos (▸occult; VOODOO). Name given for vampires in Haiti.

B

Baal (▸occult). The Semitic god of fertility emphasizing sacred prostitution and animal sacrifices. Baal is depicted as a warrior god with a spear and horned helmet.

Baal-berith (▸occult). Semitic weather god sometimes referred to as "the lord of the covenant."

Baal-hadad (▸occult). An ancient Syrian god who controls the weather. His name means "the lord of thunder."

Baalim (▸occult). "The great lord," the Phoenician lord of heaven.

Baal-zebub (▸occult). Name for the ▸devil, meaning "the lord of the flies."

Baba, Meher (MEHER BABA; 1894–1969). Man who founded the Eastern ▸cult that bears his name. His birth name was Merwan Sheriar Irani.

Babalao (▸occult; CANDOMBLE; MACUMBA; SANTERIA; SOUTH AMERICAN, CENTRAL AMERICAN, AND CARIBBEAN CULTS). The head priest or diviner in Afro-Brazilian ▸cults. In Santeria the *babalao* possesses and carefully guards the secrets of the cult. Also called ▸*santero*. The *babalao* is extremely well respected and exercises powerful control over cult members.

Babaloa (SANTERIA; VOODOO). Cuban priest charged with the specific function of guardian over the oracle of ▸*Ifa*.

Babalorisha (▸occult; CANDOMBLE; MACUMBA; SANTERIA; SOUTH AMERICAN, CENTRAL AMERICAN, AND CARIBBEAN CULTS). The chief or head priest of the Candomble ▸cult. In Santeria, the *babalorisha* is an initiate into the priesthood.

Babalosaim (▸occult; ABAKUA; CANDOMBLE; MACUMBA; SOUTH AMERICAN, CENTRAL AMERICAN, AND CARIBBEAN CULTS). One of the hierarchy of priests in the Macumba ▸cults. The babalosaim presides specifically over the Ossaim cult (the deity of herbs).

Babaoge (▸occult; ABAKUA; CANDOMBLE; MACUMBA; SOUTH AMERICAN, CENTRAL AMERICAN, AND CARIBBEAN CULTS). One of the hierarchy of male priests in the Macumba ▸cults. In Abakua the *babaoge* is a priest presiding over the ceremonies of the ▸Egun cult.

Babe Christians (THE FAMILY). Also simply called "Babes," an alternate name for a new convert. The newcomer studies the ▸Bible together with the teachings of Children of God founder and leader, Moses ▸David.

Babes See ▸Babe Christians.

Babists (THE BAHA'I FAITH). Followers of Mirzi Husayn ▸Ali.

Back To Godhead (ISKCON). Periodical published by International Society for Krishna Consciousness.

Baculum (WITCHCRAFT). Alternate name for the instrument used by a ▸witch in ▸divination. Common baculums are broomsticks or staffs.

Baha, Abdu'l (THE BAHA'I FAITH; 1844–1921). Son of Baha'u'llah (Mirza Husayn Ali) and the head of the Baha'i Faith until 1921. During Abdu'l's reign, this religion was brought to the United States.

Baha'u'llah (THE BAHA'I FAITH; 1817–1892). Also known as Mirza Hussein ▸Ali, this man announced in 1863 that he was the long-awaited *Mahdi* ("him whom God should manifest").

Bakas (▸occult; VOODOO). Name for evil spirits that take on the form of animals or human beings.

Bakr, Abu (ISLAM; 573–634). When ▸Muhammad died in A.D. 632 in ▸Mecca, the spiritual capital of Islam, Abu Bakr became the first ▸caliph in Medina. Bakr, who had been a leading and influential businessman in Mecca, became an early convert to Islam. When Muhammad took flight, Bakr chose to accompany him. The two men were drawn close together by the fact that Bakr's daughter Aisha was Muhammad's favorite wife. When Muhammad was not present, Bakr provided leadership. He was therefore the natural successor when Muhammad died. Bakr held that post for just two years. He died in A.D. 634 and was succeeded by the great Omar I.

Balaam (SATANISM). The ▸demon of greed.

Ballard, Edna (CHURCH UNIVERSAL AND TRIUMPHANT; 1886–1971). Cofounder of the movement of the "I AM" Ascended Masters, along with her husband, Guy ▸Ballard.

Ballard, Guy (CHURCH UNIVERSAL AND TRIUMPHANT; 1878–1939). Founder of the "I AM" Ascended Masters, along with his wife, Edna. The largest and most significant offshoot of this movement is the Church Universal and Triumphant (CUT).

Ballou, Hosea (UNITARIAN-UNIVERSALIST ASSOCIATION; 1771–1852). Considered the father of ▸universalism. He was responsible for laying the groundwork that eventually united unitarians and universalists.

Bamboche (VOODOO). A ceremonial, yet extremely profane dance in Haitian voodoo.

Ban (▸occult). A curse, sometimes called a spell or a hex.

Bane (▸occult). A poison used with the combination of herbs.

Banishing (▸occult; ▸paganism; WITCHCRAFT). The term used in various occult groups for excommunication of a member.

Banishing Ritual (▸occult; WITCHCRAFT). The ceremony performed in witchcraft and various ▸pagan groups whereby a ▸pentagram is inscribed in the air with a sword while standing inside a ▸magic circle. This is believed to ward off evil spirits.

Banshee (▸occult). The nature spirit of Ireland who appears as an old woman. The spirit is said to visit and weep at the home of a person who is about to die.

Bantu (CABILDO; CANDOMBLE; SANTERIA; SOUTH AMERICAN, CENTRAL AMERICAN, AND CARIBBEAN CULTS). These African people are spread over much of middle and southern Africa. They seem to have originated in present-day Cameroon and along the Nigerian border. The Spanish captured and brought Bantu slaves to Cuba. These slaves influenced the development of

Cabildo as they combined the religions of their homelands with those in the New World.

Baphomet   (*occult; SATANISM). A *demon having the head of a man or goat, usually pictured with a lighted fire or torch between the horns. The history of this name is somewhat difficult to trace. Some have suggested that its roots lie in a corruption of the name of *Muhammad. Others claim that its history lies behind legends concerning the preserved head of John the Baptist.

Baptism   (CHRISTIANITY; *cults of Christianity). Within *orthodox Christianity, various denominations understand baptism differently. Some baptize infants, others adhere to believer baptism. For some, baptism is a sign of God's covenant, for others it is a sign of one's commitment of faith. Baptism is a *sacrament and a means of grace whereby the forgiveness of sins is received and/or certified. Various cults and sects that have sprouted out of Christianity have changed the meaning of baptism. Some groups dismiss its relevance altogether. Others have made it a necessary ordinance, a required work in order to be saved. This volume discusses baptism in the context of the various groups to which it pertains.

Baptism for the Dead   (MORMONISM). The Mormon practice of baptizing by proxy, of having a Mormon baptized in the place of a person who is deceased. Such a practice enables the departed to achieve salvation when they otherwise would be lost. The practice was introduced when Joseph *Smith said, "The greatest responsibility in this world that God has laid on us is to seek after our dead" (*Journal of Discourses*, 6:7). Mormons base the practice on the words of Paul in 1 Corinthians 15:29, "What will those do who are baptized for the dead?" This text has presented difficulties for theologians and scholars throughout the history of the church, and various interpretations have been offered. One view holds that since Christians expected to die soon, Paul is referring to the Christians themselves as they are baptized, dying to self (Rom. 6:1ff.) and contemplating their future death. Another view holds that as Christians were dying, through martyrdom or old age, new Christians were baptized to take their place. Several other interpretations, including the Mormon practice, have been suggested, but from Paul's use of the pronoun "they," we can conclude that this was a practice foreign to him and to the church. Otherwise, Paul would have written "us, we, I." Nothing in the text or the grammar suggests that Paul endorsed the practice or encouraged Christians to practice it. He only used it as an example to say that others believed in the practice.

Barret, Sir William F.   (SPIRITUALISM; 1844–1925). Born in Jamaica, Barret became a well-known pioneer in psychical research. A professor of physics at Dublin University, Barret practiced Spiritualism and studied *divination and other paranormal phenomena. He later helped found the Society for Psychical Research and eventually became its president.

Baron Samedi   (VOODOO): The guardian of cemeteries in Haitian voodoo. His symbol is a cross and skull.

Bast   (*occult). The Egyptian three-headed cat goddess of fertility, who is the daughter of Isis. This may have a connection to the lilith *cult.

Bat   (*occult; WITCHCRAFT). The symbol of darkness once believed associated with *Gothic witchcraft, specifically the *witches' sabbats. More commonly, bats are associated with occult beliefs surrounding vampires.

Bata   (SANTERIA). The drums used during a Santeria ceremony.

Beatific Vision   (CHRISTIANITY). The actual vision of the divine Being (God) in heaven. Some theologians within the church have maintained that certain privileged souls have been granted a vision of the divine in this life (e.g., Moses, Ex. 34:28–35; Paul, 2 Cor. 12:2–4). In the futuristic sense, the term describes what theologians believe is the vision of God beheld by the redeemed of heaven.

Beelzebub   (*occult; SATANISM). In the *Bible, and specifically within the New Testament, Beelzebub is identified with *Satan. In classic Satanism, he is also one of the highest ranking demons, sometimes referred to as "lord of the flies." See also *Baal-zebub.

Bel   (*occult; *paganism). The chief and patron god of Babylon, also called Merodach, the sun god. Bel is also the Celtic god of fertility.

Behemoth   (*occult). The personification of *Satan, often in the form of an elephant.

Belphegor   (*occult). A *demon who appears as a woman. The name comes from *Baal, an idol worshiped by the Moabites.

Beltane   (*occult; WITCHCRAFT). Also called May Eve, Beltane is one of the eight seasonal festivals or *sabbats celebrated by *witches and other occult groups on April 30. It takes its name from the Celtic god *Bel. It was a midsummer fertility festival that in Celtic paganism involved human sacrifice coupled with the cutting of mistletoe.

Bennet, Alan (ⁱoccult; HINDUISM; 1872–1923). English occultist who had a variety of religious experiences. He was a leader in the ⁱHermetic Order of the Golden Dawn, practiced Hinduism, and in 1900 left England to become a Buddhist monk. Bennet was Aleister ⁱCrowley's teacher.

Benson, Ezra Taft (MORMONISM). Once President of the ⁱCouncil of the Twelve Apostles in Mormonism.

Berg, David Brandt (THE FAMILY; 1919–1994). A man who changed his name to Moses David and established a group called the Children of God, now called The Family. His members referred to him as "Father David." David's doctrines were ⁱfundamentalist in nature, yet he openly advocated free sex outside of marriage, the chief reason being, as he put it in his writings (called ⁱMo Letters), for the salvation of souls.

Berith (ⁱoccult). An evil duke who rides a red horse and wears a red cloth and a golden crown. He is supposed to be able to turn metal into gold.

Besant, Annie (THEOSOPHY; 1847–1933). Prominent leader in the Theosophy movement. It was Besant's leadership that provided stability during some difficult days.

Bethel (JEHOVAH'S WITNESSES). Alternate name for the headquarters of the Watchtower Bible and Tract Society in Brooklyn, New York.

Bewitchment (ⁱoccult; ⁱpaganism; WITCHCRAFT). An attempt to gain control over someone by using various types of ⁱmagic or ⁱsorcery.

Bhagavad Gita (HINDUISM). "The Divine Song of the Lord." Perhaps the crowning jewel of Hindu and Indian literature, it contains all of the important motifs of Hindu thought. What the ⁱBible is for Christians, the *Bhagavad Gita* is to Hindus, with certain ramifications.

Bhagavad Gita As It Is (ISKCON). "The Divine Song of the Lord." An authoritative commentary on the ⁱBhagavad Gita, written by Abhay Charan De, also known as ⁱA. C. Bhaktivedanta Swami Prabhupada, who spearheaded the movement known as ISKCON. Extolling wisdom as the highest virtue, Prabhupada portrays the truly wise as being those who remain indifferent and callous to the calamities of the world, because it is unwise to lament for any worldly condition.

Bhajan, Yogi (SIKH DHARMA; 1930–). Founded the Healthy, Happy, Holy Organization (₃HO), the educational wing of Sikh Dharma.

Bhakta (HINDUISM). Possessing a deep love for the divine, also called ⁱbhakti; one who is devoted to God; a faithful follower of ⁱHare Krishna.

Bhakti (HINDUISM). One of the three paths of Hinduism. The word *bhakti* itself means "devotion." Bhakti ⁱyoga is, then, a yoga dedicated to "the way of devotion." It consists of meditation, recitation of ⁱmantras, and closely following the teachings of a ⁱguru. *Bhakti* is the most popular form of Hinduism.

Bhaktivedanta Book Trust (ISKCON). The publishing arm of ISKCON.

Bhastrika Bhumbaka (HINDUISM). Putting yogic techniques into practice; the training of oneself for ⁱyoga.

Bhikkhu (BUDDHISM). A wandering or mendicant monk who travels about teaching the principles of Buddhism. His food and lodging come from the various communities and individuals who host him.

Bible (CHRISTIANITY; JUDAISM). The sacred book of Christianity when speaking of both the Old and New Testaments, and the sacred writings of Judaism when speaking just of the Hebrew Scriptures. The Bible is also called the Holy Scriptures and the Word of God.

Bible Students (JEHOVAH'S WITNESSES). Various Bible study groups that splintered off from the Watchtower Bible and Tract Society. They go by various names based on the location of the group, such as Chicago Bible Students.

Bilocation (ⁱoccult; ECKANKAR). One of several methods through which a devotee of Eckankar may encounter ⁱSugmad. Bilocation is little more than ⁱastral projection.

Bilongo (SANTERIA). Also called ⁱbrujeria, a work that involves the use of ⁱsorcery and/or ⁱmagic.

Binding (ⁱoccult; ⁱpaganism; SATANISM; WITCHCRAFT). The casting of a ⁱspell on a person with the intent of having either a positive or a negative outcome.

Biofeedback BUDDHISM; HINDUISM; NEW AGE MOVEMENT). Physical therapists and medical doctors apply biofeedback in the common or medical sense in a variety of ways. Taking one's temperature and stepping on a scale are methods whereby a person receives biological information about oneself (hence, bio feedback). Medical biofeedback can be used to help patients cope with stress, anxiety, and pain. It can also denote the practice of using electroencephalographic (EEG) feedback to monitor brain waves in order that heart rates can be controlled and the subject relaxed enough to achieve a meditative state of mind. But the term is also applied to specifically New Age, Hindu, or Buddhist practices, where it represents shortcuts to spiritual meditation based on technological means called "electric meditation"; it became the craze of the 1970s. See also ▸altered states.

Bishop (CHRISTIANITY; MORMONISM). Leader of Mormonism, Roman Catholicism, or Eastern Orthodox churches, whose chief duty is to supervise the work of the priests within the various dioceses, parishes, ▸wards and ▸stakes. Mormon bishops are chosen from the unpaid laity of the ▸Melchizedek priesthood. They officiate at marriages and funerals in the Mormon church and essentially hold the same functions as pastors in ▸Protestant churches.

Black Arts (▸occult). Alternate name for ▸magic, ▸sorcery, and general practices normally associated with the occult.

Black Judaism (RASTAFARIANISM). The Rastafarian belief that the nation of Israel in Old Testament times was a black race. Therefore, adherents today believe that they are the living successors of biblical Israel.

Black Magic (▸occult; SATANISM; WITCHCRAFT). ▸Magic used in the occult to bring evil, cursings, or negative effects on the person(s) to whom it is directed. It applies to Satanism, some witchcraft groups, ▸sorcerers, or ▸magicians. The goal is to conjure up evil spirits and invoke them to carry out the intended harm. However, according to the ▸wiccan Rede and the threefold law, practitioners are warned against harming others with the fear that a curse may revisit the one using it sevenfold.

Black Mass (▸occult; SATANISM). A satanic parody of the sacramental ritual of the Roman Catholic Eucharist, in which the host is desecrated. Other practices may include a recital of the Lord's Prayer backwards or the sacrifice of animals and humans on the altar. In some cases, a nude woman is used as an altar, the celebrants also being nude. In other instances, blood from the sacrificial victim is mingled with wine and then drunk as an offering to the ▸devil. In the Middle Ages, a defrocked priest would often consecrate the desecrated host.

Blackball (FREEMASONRY). A negative vote cast by Freemasons in the process of considering whether or not a candidate is worthy to begin earning the initiatory degrees in the various rites.

Blackwood, Algernon (▸occult; 1869–1951). British occult novelist who was a member of the ▸Hermetic Order of the Golden Dawn. He was most noted for his stories surrounding the supernatural and was a journalist for *The New York Times*.

Blake, William (▸occult; SPIRITUALISM; 1757–1827). British poet and artist who cultivated a deep interest in the occult. He read and studied the writings of Emmanuel ▸Swedenborg and claimed that as a child he had made contact with spirit beings, including the spirit of his deceased mother. In a real sense, Blake was experimenting with ideas that would come to fruition in spiritualism, a movement that sprang up some twenty years after his death.

Blavatsky, Madame Helen Petrovna (THEOSOPHY; 1831–1891). Formerly named Helen Hahn, cofounder of Theosophy.

Blessed Be! (WITCHCRAFT). An utterance used in some witchcraft groups as a form of greeting or a farewell.

Blighton, Father Earl Paul (CHRIST THE SAVIOR BROTHERHOOD; 1900–1974). Founder of the Holy Order of Mans (currently named Christ the Savior Brotherhood).

Blissed Out (ELAN VITAL). Phrase used by Divine Light Mission devotees to describe a heightened sense of awareness of the Infinite, obtained after an excruciating exercise of rhythmic breathing.

Blood (▸occult; CHRISTIANITY; SATANISM). For Christianity, blood is the heart and soul of the faith. It is blood that is the issue of life (Lev. 17:11). The shedding of blood was the basic activity of the priests and temple in the Hebrew religion of the Old Testament. In the New Testament, Jesus is the great high priest who shed his blood for the remission of sins (Rom. 3:21–24),

In the occult, blood is said to be the life force, sometimes called ▸mana. It is occasionally used to inscribe magical names or to confirm pacts. It is consumed by or smeared on the bodies of some ▸satanists as an act of receiving supernatural/spiritual, sacramental power. The vitalizing or life-giving agent used in the sacrament of the ▸black mass. Blood is believed to provide power and life and therefore plays a central part in ritualistic sacrifices.

Blood Pact (▸occult; SATANISM). A ritual contract made through the act of cutting a finger to sign one's name under a covenant act to serve ▸Satan.

Blood Transfusion (JEHOVAH'S WITNESSES). Members of the Watchtower Bible and Tract Society refuse to receive blood transfusions on the grounds that the ▸Bible prohibits them from doing so. Quoting texts such as Genesis 9:3–4 or Leviticus 17:10–15, Jehovah's Witnesses claim that receiving blood by transfusion or through any other means is the equivalent of eating it—a practice forbidden by God in the above texts.

Blue Lodge (FREEMASONRY). The original and most authentic form of Freemasonry. It is the lodge of initiation through which every Mason must pass. Its original name was The Order of Ancient, Free, and Accepted Masons. It is also called Craft Masonry. The Blue Lodge is comprised of three degrees called ᵖEntered Apprentice, ᵖFellow Craft, and ᵖMaster Mason. As the candidate is about to reach the level of the Master Mason, he swears an oath, on pain of death, promising never to betray the secrets of the craft.

Board of Directors (CHRISTIAN SCIENCE). The people whose task it is to appoint the chief officers of the ᵖMother Church in the Christian Science movement.

Bodha (BUDDHISM). ᵖEnlightenment; intelligence.

Bodhi (ZEN BUDDHISM). The moment when one comes into complete harmony with the Absolute, perceiving the "all" to be but the "one."

Bodhidharma (ZEN BUDDHISM; d. A.D. 534). The popularly recognized founder of Zen Buddhism (see ᵖTao-Sheng).

Bodhisattva (MAHAYANA BUDDHISM). One who has reached the level where ᵖnirvana is achievable and where one is ready to become a ᵖbuddha. Yet *bodhisattvas* (Buddha-in-waiting) withhold themselves from this crossing over to nirvana in the hope that they may reach, through working diligently, the state of deification in this life. The term arose as a development and contribution of Mahayana Buddhism in order to enable Buddhist doctrine to be made available to the masses.

Bogeyman (ᵖoccult; VOODOO). An evil spirit.

Bokor (ᵖoccult; VOODOO). One who practices the ᵖsorcery and ᵖmagic of a ᵖwitch doctor.

Bolline (ᵖoccult). A ritual dagger shaped like a sickle.

Bongo Man (CONVINCE). Name given to a member of the Afro-Jamaican ᵖcult Convince.

Book of Changes (ᵖoccult). See ᵖ*I Ching.*

Book of Abraham (MORMONISM). Part of Mormon sacred writings now known as ᵖ*The Pearl of Great Price.* The central idea of these writings is to convey that God revealed to Abraham that there were certain intelligences or spirits that preexisted creation. "Now the Lord showed unto me, Abraham, the intelligences that were organized before the world was; and among these were many of the noble and great ones" (*The Pearl of Great Price,* Abraham 3:22). Recent evaluations critical of Mormonism, however, have attempted to show that this writing was derived mainly from the Egyptian ᵖ*Book of the Dead* and therefore had nothing to say of Abraham and the Hebrew people.

Book of Mormon, The (MORMONISM). Published in 1830 by Joseph ᵖSmith. The Church Of Jesus Christ of Latter-Day Saints considers the Book of Mormon, along with ᵖ*The Pearl of Great Price* and ᵖ*Doctrine and Covenants,* to be their major doctrinal supplements to the ᵖBible. They acknowledge all of these writings to be the Word of God.

On September 21, 1823, Smith reported that he had been visited by the angel ᵖMoroni, who told him the plates containing the records of the ancient inhabitants of the Americas were buried in a hill called Cumorah, near the western New York town of Rochester. Four years later Smith was allowed to go to the hill and dig up the plates, which were approximately six inches by seven inches and made of gold. Smith claimed the strange language written on the plates was called Reformed Egyptian. Aided by the ᵖUrim and Thummim that accompanied the plates, he was able to translate the writings, and in 1830 he presented the Book of Mormon for publication.

Three other men, Oliver ᵖCowdery, a frontier schoolteacher, David Whitmer, a young farmer, and Martin ᵖHarris, a wealthy landowner from Palmyra, New York, were reportedly allowed to see the plates as well. Mormons consider this eyewitness testimony to be strong evidence of the credibility of the Book of Mormon.

The document contains the history of three migrations of God's people to the Americas. The Jaredites were commanded over four thousand years ago to leave the Eastern Hemisphere and travel to the New World. Under the leadership of Jared, they sailed in barges and successfully reached land and founded what came to be a great civilization. Lasting for nearly two thousand years, the Jaredites were finally destroyed, largely because of internal conflicts.

The second migration took place during the reign of King Zedekiah in 600 B.C. Lehi and Ishmael, following God's instructions, left Jerusalem and set sail for the American continent, to be joined by the third migratory group shortly afterward. Zedekiah's son Mulek left Jerusalem after his father's reign had been brought to a devastating end. Mulek's people joined Lehi, and together the two groups merged to form a great nation. These people, Mormons believe, are ancestors of the Native American Indians. Most of the Book of Mormon is a running account of these three peoples, their movements, conflicts, kings, political and social developments, and the like.

Recent research has unearthed some interesting and telling information that challenges the Mormon explanation for the origins of its sacred text. Recent scientific study on tracing DNA in American aborigines show no consistency with The Book of Mormon's supposed Semitic origin. See Mormonism for more detail.

Modern translations of the *Book of the Dead* are available today and are used by occult groups.

Courtesy Jack M. Roper/CARIS

Book of the Dead (ᵇoccult). An ancient guide book written in Egypt containing instructions for leading the departed to the final resting place in the afterlife. This book is a collection of texts containing ᵇspells, incantations, and formulas designed to protect the dead in the afterlife. Scholars estimate that the texts were probably compiled in the sixteenth century B.C., some of the sections dating as far back as 2400 B.C. There are approximately two hundred chapters in the compiled texts, but no archaeological finds have unearthed a completed copy in the ancient burial sites.

Book of the Law (ᵇoccult). Book translated by Aleister ᵇCrowley's wife, Rose, while in Egypt on one of their travels there. The basic premise of the book is the adoption of Rabelais' Law, "Do what Thou wilt shall be the whole of the Law." Crowley used the phrase as a license for self-indulgence, particularly sexual in nature.

Book of Moses (ᵇoccult; NEW AGE MOVEMENT). An occult handbook that was written in the Middle Ages. It contains various rituals and instructions for initiates into ᵇmagic practices of that time. Some occultists continue to use the book today, but there are a multiple number of other sources that are now available. A modern work titled *The Sealed Magical Book of Moses* (1991) by William Oribello contends that in addition to the five traditional books of Moses known as the Pentateuch (first five books of the ᵇBible), Moses wrote five additional books containing various New Age and occult secrets hidden through the ages.

Book of Shadows (ᵇoccult; SATANISM; WITCHCRAFT). An occult book of ritual instructions that new initiates copy by hand from the copy owned by the particular ᵇcoven he or she is joining. There are several modern renditions of the book with titles such as *The Craft: A Witch's Book of Shadows* (2001), written by Dorothy

Morrison and Raymond Buckland, and *Your Book of Shadows: How to Write Your Own Magical Spells*, by Patricia Talesco. In modern practice, ᵇwiccans and other occultists fill in their own entries onto the blank pages of their own personal *Book of Shadows*.

Book of Thoth (ᵇoccult). Occult book authored by Aleister ᵇCrowley and recently (1986) reprinted. The term ᵇ*thoth* has its origins in ancient Egyptian religion, and the book contains much of Crowley's thought on the wisdom of the gods of ancient Egypt.

Borley Rectory (ᵇoccult; SPIRITUALISM). Allegedly the most haunted house in all of England. The house was the rectory for the Borley Church in Essex until 1939, when it burned down. Sightings of a phantom nun and a phantom coach-and-horses were reported by the family of Reverend Bull, rector of Borley Church from 1862–1892. Lights, footsteps, ringing bells, and other mysterious phenomena have reportedly emerged from the site of the rectory. The British philosopher and parapsychologist Henry Habberly Price (1899–1985) investigated the site but reached no certain conclusions. Mystery surrounds Borley Rectory to this day.

Born Again (ᵇoccult; CHRISTIANITY; HINDUISM; NEW AGE MOVEMENT; WORLDWIDE CHURCH OF GOD). A term used by many religious traditions. Within the context of Christianity, the traditional historical understanding of John 3:3–7 was that it is a baptismal text (associated with "baptismal regeneration"). The noun form of the Greek word used in John 3 is translated as "regeneration" in Titus 3:5. In Protestant Christianity and in ᵇevangelical and ᵇfundamentalist circles, the word has come to be associated with a conversion experience, a "personal decision" to embrace and believe the saving message of Christ. Where the traditional understanding was to view the new birth in the context of the sacrament of baptism, the latter has disconnected it from baptism.

According to MORMONISM, to be born again is to acquire salvation. This occurs for Mormons at baptism (see Article 4 of the "Articles of Faith").

For Hinduism and in occult and New Age circles, the new birth has come to mean ᵇreincarnation. Another term that is frequently used in this context is "rebirthing."

Herbert W. ᵇArmstrong, the former leader of the Worldwide Church of God, had a different understanding. He taught that being born again meant an experience one attains, not in this life, but in heaven. The present-day Worldwide Church of God has renounced Armstrong's teachings on this subject.

Botanica (ᵇoccult; SANTERIA; VOODOO). A herbal store that sells the necessary items to carry out the rituals performed in Santeria and voodoo rites. Botanicas are located in the United States, particularly in urban areas populated by Spanish-Americans.

This Botanica is found in Miami, Florida.
Courtesy Jack M. Roper/CARIS

Boucan (VOODOO). A bonfire lit by voodoo devotees to recharge the powers of the sun. This ritual is performed before each new year.

Brahma (HINDUISM). The member of the Hindu Trinity (ᵇBrahma, ᵇVishnu, and ᵇShiva), who is the creating deity.

Brahmacharin (HINDUISM; ISKCON). A celibate student who devotes his life to a ᵇguru. He practices celibacy outwardly and has disciplined his inner thoughts to the same effect. By doing so, he submits himself to rigorous study and discipline. When the student is ready, he enters into a second stage, known as ᵇ*grihastha*.

Brahmajnan (HINDUISM). Wisdom, the source of which stems from ᵇBrahma.

Brahman (HINDUISM). The creative principle of all life in the universe. It is the "One." Also, term for the Hindu priestly caste.

Brahmanism (HINDUISM). See ᵇBrahman.

Brahma-Sutra-Bhashya (HINDUISM; VEDANTA SOCIETY). A running commentary on the writings of the Vedanta Society.

Brahmin (HINDUISM). The English spelling for ᵇBrahman.

Branch (MORMONISM). Small congregation in Mormonism not yet fully organized. Branches are mission churches, which when sufficiently advanced in size (over two hundred) are then classified as ᵇwards.

Branham, William Marion (BRANHAMISM; 1909–1965). Branham received his first vision in 1916 at the age of seven. His most important revelation came on May 7, 1946, when an angel appeared to him, related to him his past, and gave him a vision for the future. The angel told him that he would become a healing evangelist. He declared himself the angel of Revelation 3:14 and 10:7. He was the founder of Branhamism.

Breeder (SATANISM). The female who allegedly becomes pregnant with the intention of offering the child/infant to be sacrificed on a satanic ᵇaltar. Though believed by some, there is no evidence for this practice occurring.

British Israeliism (WORLDWIDE CHURCH OF GOD; CHURCH UNIVERSAL AND TRIUMPHANT). See ᵇAnglo-Israeliism.

Brooks, Nona (DIVINE SCIENCE; 1861–1945). Co-founder of and considered one of the important figures in the New Thought movement.

Broomstick (WITCHCRAFT). The broomstick is perhaps the most common symbol associated with witchcraft itself. It is the ever-familiar mode of transportation in literature, folklore, and television. The broomstick is used in genuine witchcraft in wedding rituals and in the sweeping of the ᵇcircle in order to purify it from evil during ᵇcoven ceremonies.

Brother (JEHOVAH'S WITNESSES). A technical term for a member of the Watchtower Bible and Tract Society; a brother is a baptized male who often exercises leadership in the local congregations, usually as an elder.

Brother of Christ See CHRISTADELPHIANISM.

Brothers of the Shadow (THEOSOPHY). Term used to designate those who are studying ᵇblack magic.

Brown Brothers (CHRIST THE SAVIOR BROTHERHOOD). The male members of the Christ the Savior Brotherhood, formerly known as the Holy Order of Mans, who have entered their first year of training.

Brujeria (SANTERIA). See ᵇ*bilongo*.

Brujo (ᵇoccult). Hispanic term for a ᵇwitch or ᵇshaman.

Bubba Free John (HINDUISM; VEDANTA SOCIETY; 1939–) Born as Franklin Jones, Bubba Free John enjoys the marked distinction of being the first American-born ᵇ*siddha*. Early in life he experienced a "blissful self-awareness." This ᵇenlightenment did not last, however, and he entered his college years seeking the ecstatic experience once again. He experimented with LSD and practiced meditation. Teachers included both ᵇSwami ᵇMuktananda and Rudranand (Albert Rudolph). In addition, he made pilgrimages to India and even studied at a Lutheran school, where he claims to have undergone a "transient death experience."

Bubba Free John unabashedly claims to be ♦*Brahman*. At the Hollywood Vedanta Society, he experienced once again the long-sought illumination of his early years. This time it was for keeps, and he entered what he described as being total enlightenment. He claimed, "I am Reality, the Self, and Nature and Support of all things and all beings. I am the One Being known as God, Brahman, ♦Atman, the One Mind, the Self" (*The Knee of Listening* [Los Angeles: Dawn Horse, 1972], 135).

Bubba Free John's teachings are based essentially on Hindu thought, particularly the doctrines of Advaita Vedanta. The material universe is an illusion. The divine being, God, is the only true reality. Human beings, to achieve salvation, must put the material world behind and devote themselves totally to God. This comes through total devotion to the ♦guru.

Buddha (BUDDHISM). A buddha is a practitioner of Buddhism who has achieved the state of divine ♦enlightenment, after having followed the teachings of Sridhar ♦Gautama, the first buddha.

Butsodun (BUDDHISM; NICHIREN SHOSHU BUDDHISM; SOKA-GAKKAI). A black box that houses the ♦*gohonzon*. The *butsodun* is kept on the sacred altar in the original Nichiren Shoshu temple at the base of Mount Fuji.

C

Cacodemon (♦occult). An evil spirit who has the ability to rapidly change its appearance.

Caille Loa (VOODOO). A room dedicated to the pantheon of deities or ♦*loa*.

Caliph (ISLAM). Viceroy, representative, or successor. After the death of ♦Muhammad, the caliph became ♦Allah's representative spokesman and leader. The first four caliphs—Abu ♦Bakr, ♦Umar, ♦Uthman, and ♦Ali—are designated the "rightly guided caliphs," because there is no dispute concerning their respective claims to being Muhammad's successors.

Calunga (♦occult; MACUMBA). The deity of death as well as the deity of the ocean in the South American Macumba ♦cults.

Cancer (♦astrology; ♦occult). Also called the crab, Cancer is the fourth ♦sign in the ♦zodiac in astrology, falling between June 22 and July 23. According to Greek mythology, the crab bit Heracles while he was fighting the Lernaean hydra and was then crushed by Heracles. As a reward, Heracles's enemy, Hera, placed the crab in the heavens. Persons born under the sign of Cancer are characterized as being sensitive, maternal, impressionable, and unprincipled.

Candlemas (♦occult; WITCHCRAFT). See ♦witches' calendar.

Cantrip (♦occult; WITCHCRAFT). A ♦witch's ♦spell.

Capitular Degrees (FREEMASONRY). The alternate name for ♦chapter degrees in Freemasonry.

Caplata (♦occult; VOODOO). A practitioner of ♦sorcery.

Capnomancy (♦occult). A particular kind of ♦fortune telling that divines the future through the use of ♦tarot cards or even regular playing cards.

Capricorn (♦astrology; ♦occult). Also called the goat in astrology, Capricorn is the tenth ♦sign in the ♦zodiac, falling between December 22 and January 19. Capricorn is pictured as a goat with a fish tail. People born under Capricorn are characterized as sure-footed and confident, maintaining high personal standards.

Cariapemba (♦occult; MACUMBA). An evil deity of the Macumba ♦cults. See also ♦*Orodere*.

CARP (UNIFICATION CHURCH). An acronym for the Unification Church's "Collegiate Association for the Research of Principles."

Case, Paul Foster (♦occult; 1884–1954) An American occultist who founded an occult center known as The Builders of the "Adytum" (Bota) in Los Angeles. He established the American branch of the ♦Hermetic Order of the Golden Dawn."

Casican (♦occult; ABAKUA; SOUTH AMERICAN, CENTRAL AMERICAN, AND CARIBBEAN CULTS). The term for "priestess" in Abakua; a female priest.

Castaneda, Carlos (ᴾoccult; NEW AGE MOVEMENT; 1925–1988). Peruvian-born anthropologist whose real name is Carlos Arana. He studied at the University of California, Los Angeles. Castaneda claims to have come into communication with an elderly Yaqui Indian named Don Juan Matus, who became Castaneda's mentor. He taught Castaneda ᴾsorcery and ᴾmagic. Castaneda, though deceased, remains a popular New Age author of "The Teachings of Don Juan" series. He is especially noted for popularizing Native American ᴾshamanism, New Age occultism, and the hallucinogenic plant, peyote. Toward the end of his life, academic investigation found his theory to be wanting. It was later discovered that the entire Don Juan shaman anthropological study was fraudulent. Don Juan simply never existed (see K. Lindskoog, *Fakes, Frauds, and Other Malarkey* [Grand Rapids: Zondervan, 1992]).

Caste System (HINDUISM). The system of cultural ranking and structuring of Hindu society (*see* Hinduism for a description of each of the five castes into which Hindus are grouped). Although many Western religious movements have been greatly influenced by Hinduism, the caste system is not recognized outside of Hindu culture.

Cauldron (ᴾoccult; VOODOO; WITCHCRAFT). A magical symbol conveying change and birth. Also, the container which ᴾGothic witches used to stir their magical brews.

Cavendish, Richard (ᴾoccult; 1930–). An Oxford University graduate and one of the foremost contemporary authorities in the field of the occult, particularly ᴾmagick theory. His noted works, *The Black Arts* and *Encyclopedia of the Unexplained*, are major resources in their field.

Cayce, Edgar (ASSOCIATION FOR RESEARCH AND ENLIGHTENMENT; 1877–1945). Born in Kentucky in 1877, Cayce exhibited remarkable abilities as a ᴾclairvoyant as early as age seven. He was raised in a Christian home, became a Sunday school teacher, and claimed to have read the ᴾBible through once each year, from approximately age twenty-two till he died in 1945. At age thirteen a woman appeared to him and offered him the fulfillment of any request he desired. He responded that he wanted to possess the abilities to heal. As soon as he had asked for this power, the woman vanished.

Cayce taught ᴾreincarnation and claimed to have been, in a previous existence, the nephew of Luke, author of the third gospel in the New Testament. Known as the "sleeping prophet," Cayce claimed the uncanny ability to transfer healing energies to patients in need. In 1931 he founded the Association for Research and Enlightenment to preserve, study, and apply his readings. Other basic teachings include: Jesus Christ was a reincarnation of four prominent figures, three of whom appear in the Bible—Adam, Melchizedek, and Joshua; the fourth was Zen—leader of ᴾZoroastrianism. Also, God comprises both male and female and is not omniscient. Reincarnation, if understood correctly, is able to account for most events and people in history.

Cayce, Hugh Lynn (ASSOCIATION FOR RESEARCH AND ENLIGHTENMENT; 1907–82). Son of Edgar ᴾCayce, who succeeded his father as leader of the Association for Research and Enlightenment.

Celestial Kingdom (MORMONISM). One of the three heavens in Mormon theology. The celestial kingdom is the most blessed of the three because it is the only one "prepared for the righteous, those who have been faithful in keeping the commandments of the Lord, and have been cleansed of all their sins" (Joseph ᴾSmith, *Answers to Gospel Questions*, 2:208). The inhabitants of this kingdom dwell in the very presence of God. They make up the "Church of the Firstborn" (ᴾ*Doctrine And Covenants* 76:54). In this heaven exclusively, Mormons are able to live with their spouses and children and possess the ability of continual procreation.

Celestial Marriage (MORMONISM). One of the central doctrines of Mormonism. According to Mormon apologist Bruce McConkie, "the most important single thing that any member of the Church of Jesus Christ of Latter Day Saints can ever do in this world is to marry the right person by the right authority, in the right place" (*Mormon Doctrine* [Salt Lake City: Bookcraft, 1958], 111).

Mormons distinguish between celestial marriage (eternal) and marriage in time (temporal). Temporal marriage is one that has not been performed in a temple. Such a marriage will be dissolved at death and such people will be unable to attain the status of godhood. Rather, they will become angels, who will serve the more worthy married believers.

Celestial marriage, by contrast, is performed in a temple and is sealed for time and eternity, a marriage never to be dissolved. A temple marriage is also in obedience to the covenant God made with humanity in the "holy and perfect order of matrimony," which then assures the obedient couple of an inheritance of exaltation in the ᴾcelestial kingdom (ibid., 118).

Celestine Prophecy, The (ᵇoccult; NEW AGE MOVE-MENT). A bestselling New Age book written by James Redfield. It teaches ᵇenlightenment through the "nine insights" contained in esoteric manuscripts written by natives in the Peruvian jungles.

Chador (ISLAM). "The tent." A large fabric wrapped around the body. A chador is worn by ᵇShiᵖite women.

Chaitanya, Guru (ISCKON; 1485–1533). ᵇGuru who taught that ᵇHare Krishna was the supreme Lord over all other deities, including ᵇVishnu.

Chaitanyana (HINDUISM). Consciousness.

Chakras (ᵇoccult; NEW AGE MOVEMENT; TAOISM). Believed to be centers for cosmic energy that are in alignment; they adjust the ᵇkundalini energy as it proceeds from the base of the spine to the forehead.

Chamador (SANTERIA; VOODOO). Small drums used in Santeria and voodoo ceremonies.

Changeling (ᵇoccult). A deformed child who supposedly is left by ᵇfairies in place of a healthy child. Sometimes believed to be senile fairies disguised as children.

Channeling (ᵇoccult; ASSOCIATION FOR RESEARCH AND ENLIGHTENMENT; NEW AGE MOVEMENT; SPIRITUALISM). It is sometimes called ᵇtrance channeling. It is a practice similar to that in spiritualism, where a ᵇmedium invokes the spirit of the departed for the purpose of communication. There is one important difference between the New Age practice of channeling and what a medium does in spiritualism. In spiritualism, the medium conjures up the spirit of a departed relative specifically to communicate a message that is usually personal in nature. In New Age thought, the spirit conjured up is an unrelated spirit being who communicates a message or teaching of guidance, knowledge, or direction to the New Ager. With channeling, the teachers/spirit beings may be ᵇascended masters, deceased humans, or animal spirits supposedly communicating meaningful messages by entering the body and using the voice of the channeler or medium.

Channing, William Ellery (UNITARIAN-UNIVERSALIST ASSOCIATION; 1780–1842. A leading voice of unitarianism in the eighteenth century.

Chapter (FREEMASONRY). A lodge in both ᵇYork and ᵇScottish Rite Freemasonry.

Chapter Degrees (FREEMASONRY). The fourth through the seventh degrees in the ᵇYork Rite of Freemasonry: ᵇMark Master, ᵇPast Master, ᵇMost Excellent Master,

and ᵇRoyal Arch Mason. These are also known as ᵇcapitular degrees. These four degrees recall the exile of the people of Israel and their return from exile into captivity by Nebuchadnezzar.

Charm (ᵇoccult). An object or incantation in the occult world, such as a ᵇtalisman, which is believed to contain supernatural powers.

Charvaka (HINDUISM). One who has not achieved ᵇenlightenment and is still in the grips of the illusory world of matter.

Chemosh (ᵇoccult). Deity of the Moabites. Children were sacrificed by fire to him.

Cheng-Ming (CONFUCIANISM). Term used to describe the responsibility of each person to live responsible lives in whatever capacity or vocation they find themselves. A ruler is responsible to rule well. A laborer is responsible to work diligently.

Cherubim (*See* ᵇangels).

Cheval (ᵇoccult; VOODOO). Symbolizing spirit possession, a person is mounted like a horse by deified spirits in order to take a journey into a trancelike state.

Chᵖi (TAOISM). The Taoist concept of "the breath of life." *Chᵖi* is the life force or invisible energy that makes up the universe and flows through channels in the body known as "meridians" or ᵇ*chakras*. Any imbalance in the *chᵖi* leads to negativity in the body, which usually manifests itself through sickness, disease, and ultimately death. ᵇAcupuncture is believed to aid in rectifying the imbalance of the *chᵖi*.

Chidakasa (HINDUISM). Attainment of true ᵇenlightenment through knowledge.

Child Guides (ᵇoccult; SPIRITUALISM). Children who serve as a personality for a ᵇmedium in spiritualism.

Chinmoy, Sri (SRI CHINMOY CENTER; 1931–). Born in Bengal, India, Sri came to the United States and instituted the Sri Chinmoy Center.

Chiromancy (*See* ᵇpalm reading).

Chiu King (CONFUCIANISM). The name of ᵇConfucius.

Chopra, Deepak (NEW AGE MOVEMENT; 1947–). Born in New Delhi, India, Chopra was heavily influenced by HINDUISM and its sacred texts, chiefly the ᵇ*Vedanta* and the ᵇ*Bhagavad Gita*. A trained medical physician, Chopra received his education at the All India Institute of Medical Sciences in New Delhi, graduating in 1968. He then came to America, where he furthered his medical studies with an internship at a hospital in New Jersey and then at the Lahey Clinic in Burlington, Massachusetts, and the University of Virginia Hospital. He studied TRANSCENDENTAL MEDITATION for a short time but then moved on to establish his own understanding of spiritual matters, to which he directs much of his writing and lectures.

Chopra has become a popular figure amongst New Age writers in the United States. He has invited both followers and critics. Critics focus on Chopra's frequent references to a positive correlation between quantum physics and a spiritual healing method known as ayurvedic medicine.

Choronzon (*occult). According to Western *magic, the *demon of chaos. He is believed to be the deadliest of all the powers of evil.

Christ (CHRISTIANITY; CHRISTIAN SCIENCE; MIND SCIENCES; NEW AGE MOVEMENT; UNIFICATION CHURCH). This word means "anointed one" (Heb. "Messiah"). Jesus fulfilled the mission of the Messiah perfectly. Its usage in *cults most commonly lies in the separation of the title "Christ" from the person "Jesus." For example, the New Age Movement advances the idea that "Christ" is a principle of deity that resides within, called "Christ-consciousness." Sun Myung *Moon declared himself to be the new Christ. The Mind Sciences generally separate a "Christ principle" from the physical or material. The former is considered "spiritual" and the latter illusory. Mary Baker *Eddy, the founder of Christian Science, regarded Jesus as a mere human within whom lived or resided the Christ, which lives on after Jesus' death.

Christaquarians (NEW AGE MOVEMENT). The development in the last twenty years of eclectically blending liberal CHRISTIANITY with New Age principles and ideology.

Christ-Consciousness (MIND SCIENCE; NEW AGE MOVEMENT). The New Age belief that we can all become enlightened to the fact that the *Christ, or deity, resides in all of humanity. In the Mind Sciences, it is the attainment of oneness or unity with the divine mind.

Christed (CHRIST THE SAVIOR BROTHERHOOD). One who, through the training, discipline, and guidance of a *class master, receives *Christ-consciousness, which promises him or her a future reign with the cosmic *Christ.

Christian, Paul (*astrology; *magic; *occult; SPIRITUALISM; 1811–1877). The pen name of J. B. Pitois, a well-known French occultist who wrote a considerable number of books on astrology, kabbalah, magic, and spiritualism.

Christology (CHRISTIANITY). That element in Christian doctrine that treats the person and work of Jesus Christ, particularly how Jesus' human and divine natures are related. The Christian church has undergone various Christological controversies throughout history (*see* Appendix 2).

Chuang-tzu (TAOISM). Writings that bear the same name as their author and contain the teachings and experiences of *Lao-Tse.

Cingulum (*paganism; WITCHCRAFT). A cincture or chord of rope that is tied around the waist in the ritual garb of *witches.

Circle (*occult; SATANISM; WITCHCRAFT). Ancient symbol of wholeness, infinity, and eternality. The circle, or *magic circle, is used by *sorcerers, *magicians, *satanists, and *witches. Around a magic circle appear the names of gods and other occult symbols. Inside the circle a *pentagram is often drawn. Standing within the magic circle provides blessings and protection from evil forces. In witchcraft, the circle is intended to keep the positive forces generated by the witches within.

Circuit (JEHOVAH'S WITNESSES). A group of congregations among the Jehovah's Witnesses numbering approximately twenty-one. Collectively, all the circuits within a given area constitute a *district. There are thirty-eight districts in the United States.

Circuit Overseer (JEHOVAH'S WITNESSES). See *overseer.

Cit (HINDUISM). The manifest universe that transcends the human intelligence; also pure consciousness, the authentic self.

Clairvoyance (*occult; ASSOCIATION FOR RESEARCH AND ENLIGHTENMENT). The term used to designate the uncanny psychic ability to perceive things beyond physical reality, the transcending of the empirical realm into the supernatural (*see* *extrasensory perception (ESP) and *divination). Also, clairvoyance describes the psychic ability to see and describe future events. Edgar *Cayce was a noted clairvoyant.

Clarke, James Freeman (UNITARIAN-UNIVERSALIST ASSOCIATION; 1810–1888). A leading proponent of Unitarian-Universalist Association thought at the close of the eighteenth century.

Class Master (CHRIST THE SAVIOR BROTHERHOOD). The leader and instructor of a group of the Holy Order of Mans devotees to whom is sworn absolute allegiance. Initiates must swear loyalty and obedience to their class master, who, in turn, must provide the necessary training to lead them toward "Christ-consciousness."

Clear (SCIENTOLOGY). Technical concept in Scientology referring to a person who has transcended the release grades. Such an individual has undergone a clearing course at an "advanced organization." The idea is that the subconscious is like a blackboard full of erroneous facts, equations, data, and the like (called ▶engrams). Each phase of training is analogous to an eraser wiping away error after error until the subject reaches the point where his or her blackboard, or mind, has been "cleared" of all erroneous thoughts or painful or damaging patterns acquired in the past.

Cloven Hooves (SATANISM). Worn during a ▶sabbat by Satanists. Cloven hooves are one of the numerous symbols of the ▶devil.

Colors (▶occult; SATANISM). Colors play an important role in the symbolism within Satanism.

- Black—the ▶devil, evil, darkness
- Blue—despair, sexuality
- Green—life, vegetation, peace
- Orange—beauty
- Pink—success
- Red—blood, life, physical energy
- White—goodness; purity
- Yellow—success, power, wealth.

Commandery Degrees (FREEMASONRY). The degrees in the ▶York Rite of Freemasonry that are subdegrees of the ninth degree or ▶Select Master. The Commandery degrees are ▶Order of the Red Cross, ▶Order of the Knights of Malta, and the ▶Order of the Knights Templar.

Communal House (CHURCH OF BIBLE UNDERSTANDING). A local meeting house for the COBU.

Communicants (CHURCH UNIVERSAL AND TRIUMPHANT). The most zealously committed members of the Church Universal and Triumphant.

Company (JEHOVAH'S WITNESSES). A local assembly of Jehovah's Witnesses that meets in a ▶kingdom hall. The total membership of a company (also called a congregation) ideally should not exceed two hundred.

Company Servant (JEHOVAH'S WITNESSES). Individual who is placed in a position of leadership over a ▶company of Witnesses.

Cone of Power (▶paganism; WITCHCRAFT). The "cone" is a field of energy or focus of concentration engaged in to accomplish a given or desired task.

Conference (MORMONISM). Gathering of members of the Church of Jesus Christ of Latter Day Saints who come together intermittently to hear the leaders expound ▶revelation from God.

Confession of the Order (ROSICRUCIANISM). A writing outlining various practices of Rosicrucianism.

Confucius (CONFUCIANISM; 551–479 B.C.). Original named as ▶K'ung Fu Tzu, Confucius was born in approximately 551 B.C. in Lu, the modern-day Shantung Province of China. He died ca. 479 B.C. He was deeply concerned about the corruptions of society in his day, particularly among rulers. He searched earnestly for the means for living in a just society. He stressed loyalty to the state, honor to the family, the elevation of virtue and ethics, the moral life, and honor of the individual.

Confucius is a legendary figure in Chinese and world history. He is said to have authored the classic *Ch'un Ch'iu* (*The Annals of Spring and Autumn*), along with four volumes containing a collection of his famous sayings. Confucius also edited and wrote commentaries on the ▶*I Ching*. Among his most well-known teachings are ▶ancestor worship, devotion to the elder of the family, and the inherent moral goodness of humankind.

Congregation of God Seventh Day (WORLDWIDE CHURCH OF GOD). A splinter group of the Worldwide Church of God led by John Pinkston. Loyal to the teachings of Herbert W. ▶Armstrong, the church publishes *The Herald* magazine.

Conjuration (▶occult; SATANISM; WITCHCRAFT). Ritual and ceremonial incantations used by occultists to call up the ▶devil or other spirits. Conjuration almost always is performed with accompanying ceremonies. An example of a conjuration from the *Great Key of Solomon* is as follows: "Emperor Lucifer, Master of all the rebellious spirits, I beg you to be favorable in the invocation that I make to your great Minister Lucifuge Rofocale, as I wish to make a pact with him."

Contract (SATANISM). The time when a person renounces Christian baptism/faith and makes an agreement/pact with ▶Satan in order to acquire power over others or to manipulate certain situations through ▶magick.

Control (▶occult; NEW AGE MOVEMENT; SPIRITUALISM). A disembodied spirit who manifests itself through a ▶medium during a ▶séance.

Cosmic Christ (▶occult; NEW AGE MOVEMENT). The spiritual entity or being that is believed by the New Age practitioner to have indwelt Jesus from his baptism through his crucifixion. The New Ager often speaks of Jesus as being "divine," but it is the cosmic Christ, not Jesus of Nazareth, who is being referred to.

Council Degrees (FREEMASONRY). The eighth and ninth degrees in the ›York Rite of Freemasonry: ›Royal Master and the ›Select Master. These council degrees contain rituals and teachings surrounding the construction of Solomon's temple.

Council of Imams (ISLAM). Religious scholars regarded as the most sacrosanct and authoritative spokesmen of Islamic theology and canon law. This holy council has the responsibility of preaching, leading in prayer, officiating in conversions and marriages, offering counsel, and other related matters.

Council of the Twelve Apostles (MORMONISM). The authoritative governing body within the Mormon church, just under the ›First Presidency, whose decisions are considered as binding as those of the ›president (especially in his absence). When a president dies, the council rules the church while nominating a new candidate.

Counselors (SILVA MIND CONTROL). Known or unknown spirit beings (sometimes called "laboratory technicians") who are conjured up to provide divine assistance in day-to-day situations.

Course in Miracles, A (NEW AGE MOVEMENT). A book authored by Ellen Schucman (1909)1981), a professor of medical psychology at Columbia University. In 1965 Schucman claimed to have heard an inner voice that identified itself as Jesus. Following the directions of the voice, Schucman recorded through dictation what would be her book, *A Course in Miracles.* The publication of the book resulted in the birth of hundreds of study groups worldwide. The basic teachings of the book are centered around a message of love and forgiveness. The world, sin, and sickness are illusions. The real world is heaven and that is where human beings are.

These teachings run contrary to the traditional doctrines of CHRISTIANITY. The world is not an illusion and sin is the transgressions of the laws of God. Heaven is the goal and destiny of every Christian, but one arrives there following death. "To be absent from the body is to be present with the Lord" (2 Cor. 5:8).

Coven (›paganism; WITCHCRAFT). A localized assembly of ›witches, constituting the most elemental organization in witchcraft. A coven may consist of as few as five or as many as fifty members. Twelve to fifteen is the norm, however. The coven is under the leadership of either a ›high priest or ›high priestess. Many covens are united by fraternal bonds, while others remain autonomous.

Covensted (›paganism; WITCHCRAFT). The actual place where a ›coven gathers.

Coverdom (›paganism; WITCHCRAFT). The general area in which a ›coven is located. A coverdom is usually a three-mile radius surrounding the location of the coven.

Cowdery, Oliver (MORMONISM; 1806–1850). A former schoolteacher who was ordained the second elder, Joseph ›Smith Jr. being the first, of the Church of Jesus Christ of Latter Day Saints.

Craft (›paganism; WITCHCRAFT). A shortened form of the term "witchcraft," used to describe the actual practices of followers.

Cramer, Melinda (DIVINE SCIENCE; ??–1907). Together with Nona ›Brooks, she formed a divine science college.

Crème, Benjamin (NEW AGE MOVEMENT; 1922–). Born in Glasgow, Scotland, Crème was a student of art and an accomplished artist. He also studied THEOSOPHY and numerous other New Age writers. In 1959, he came to believe that the world has been governed throughout history by the "Great Masters." Crème claims to have been contacted by one of the Masters, who told him to expect, in about twenty years, the return of the greatest of all the Masters, ›Maitreya. He was also told that he himself would play a major role in Maitreya's return.

Crème lectured throughout the world and first came to the United States in 1980. He gained worldwide notoriety for his New Age Tara Center, where he placed advertisements in seventeen of the world's largest newspapers for a simultaneous announcement on April 23, 1982, that "the Christ is now here." He believed that his mission was to reveal the Christ/›Maitreya to the world, whom he declared was alive and living in the Pakistani community of London. He began a monthly magazine called ›*Share International*, which is read in over seventy countries worldwide. The topics of his writings and lectures include poverty, crime, world peace, world hunger, a vision for religious harmony, an end to war, a vision for peace, and so on. Crème does not profit financially from his efforts and has been well received by the media and the public through the years. He continues to travel and lecture.

Crescent (›occult). The crescent-shaped moon represents fertility.

Cross (›occult; CHRISTIANITY). The cross has been adopted as a universal symbol of the church and Christianity itself. The cross is the means whereby Jesus

Christ was executed. Some religious groups maintain that traditional Christianity borrowed this symbol from pagan sources. There is no evidence, however, to link the two other than the fact that crucifixion itself was a form of execution common in the Roman Empire before the rise of Christianity.

There are four main forms or shapes of the cross that come down to us from various traditions. The *Greek cross* has four equal arms (+). In the *Latin cross*, the base is longer than the other three arms (traditionally the one that Jesus Christ was thought to be executed upon [†]). *St. Anthony's or tau cross* is shaped like the letter "T." *St. Andrew's cross* is X-shaped. Many other derivative cross shapes have abounded through history.

In the world of the occult, the cross is sometimes used to symbolize the unity of the sexual organs of the male and female. The horizontal bar represents the female and the vertical bar the male.

Crossroads (ᐧpaganism; SATANISM). During the Middle Ages, crossroads were places of burial. In more ancient times, it was a place where human sacrifices were performed by pagan tribes throughout Europe. In contemporary Satanism, crossroads are places that symbolize the "crossing over" from the physical world to the spirit realm. For example, a graveyard is a crossroad because it lies between heaven and earth.

Crowley, Aleister (ᐧoccult; SATANISM; WITCHCRAFT; 1875–1947). The most famous ᐧoccult figure of the twentieth century, noted for his profound influence on modern Satanism and his study and practice of ᐧmagick. The spelling of "magick with the "k" is Crowley's own contribution as he was attempting to make a clear distinction between magic as "slight of hand" and magick as the practice of the supernatural and the harnessing of the powers of the occult.

Crowley was raised in a strict ᐧfundamentalist Plymouth Brethren church, but he forsook his faith after studying the occult. Eventually his mother called him "the great beast" (ᐧsix-six-six) of Revelation. In 1898, Crowley became a member of the ᐧHermetic Order of the Golden Dawn. He worked his way through the various ranks of the order and desired to be the order's leader, competing against the poet William Butler Yeats. Quarrels between Crowley and other members of the order, particularly Samuel Liddell Mathers, led to Crowley's breaking away and forming his own group, which he called Order of the Silver Star.

Crowley traveled extensively in his life—such as to India, Egypt, and Italy. Many of the magick rituals he practiced involved aberrant sexual deviancy, including homosexuality, group sex, bestiality, and ritual sex. While in Italy, Crowley was expelled by Benito Mussolini when the Italian dictator found out what Crowley was advocating. In Egypt, Crowley and his wife, Rose, encountered an exhibit of the god Horus, which happened to be numbered "666." He came to the conclusion that the god was the antichrist because of the correspondence of this display with the biblical number 666.

His wife began to dictate, while in a trance state, the *Liber Legis* (*The ᐧBook of the Law*). Crowley went on to found another order called Argentium Astrum (*see* ᐧA..A..). He has greatly influenced the modern world of the occult, ᐧpaganism, Satanism, ᐧwicca, and other such groups. More on Crowley's life is covered in the article on Satanism.

Crystal balls are commonly used in fortune telling. This photo was taken at a Renaissance/occult fair in Bristol, Wisconsin.

Courtesy Jack M. Roper/CARIS

Crystal Ball (▸occult). A glass or crystal ball-shaped object used by fortune-tellers (*see* ▸fortune-telling), ▸clairvoyants, and diviners (*see* ▸divination) in the technique known as ▸skrying. Gazing into the glass, the clairvoyant enters into a ▸trance-like state and is supposedly able to view future events. This is also known as "crystal gazing," and the practice of using a crystal ball is called ▸crystalomancy.

Crystalomancy (▸occult). The practice and use of a ▸crystal ball in ▸divination.

Crystals used in fortune-telling or psychic healing.
Courtesy Jack M. Roper/CARIS

Crystals (▸occult; NEW AGE MOVEMENT). Solid objects (stones) that are either clear or colored yet transparent. It is believed that the crystal is able to transmit cosmic energy in much the same way they do when used in a radio. The New Age Movement involves those who use crystals for a variety of reasons, particularly to bring spiritual power, health, fortune, and the like. A woman, for example, may use them to induce pregnancy. Or one may seek direction for a future event, or most often, for psychic healing.

Cult There is an inherent difficulty in defining the word "cult." Sociologists offer varying definitions based on anthropological and sociological considerations. Under such definitions, cults are relatively small, often transitory religious groups that commonly follow a radical or highly charismatic leader. A cult, unlike a ▸sect, espouses radically new religious beliefs and practices that frequently threaten the basic values and cultural norms of society at large. Therefore, people who are involved in cults frequently exhibit antisocial and neurotic behavior.

The sociological model hardly seems adequate, however. These factors are relativistic and subjective. What constitutes "transitory?" How "highly charis-

matic" does a leader have to be? Under this definition, CHRISTIANITY was a cult in the first few centuries of its existence because it introduced "radical" changes and "threatened" basic societal norms. How antisocial or neurotic must one be to be classed as cultlike?

The authors of this book therefore offer a model that is theological and doctrinal in nature. We accept the definition developed by Alan Gomes in his *Unmasking the Cults*. Gomes makes a distinction between cults of Christianity, cults of ISLAM, cults of BUDDHISM, and so on. With respect to Christianity, Enroth's definition is as follows:

> A cult of Christianity is a group of people, which claiming to be Christian, embraces a particular doctrinal system taught by an individual leader, group of leaders, or organization, which (system) denies (either explicitly or implicitly) one or more of the central doctrines of the Christian faith as taught in the sixty-six books of the Bible.[1]

Therefore for ▸orthodox Christianity, cults of Christianity are groups that, while claiming to be Christian, deny central doctrinal tenets such as the ▸Trinity and the deity of Jesus Christ. They deviate from the doctrinal norms set forth in the ▸Bible and the historical creeds of Christendom.

Note

[1] Alan Gomes, *Unmasking the Cults* (Grand Rapids: Zondervan, 1995), 7.

Cummins, Geraldine (▸occult; 1890–1969). An Irish ▸medium who was known as the "medium with integrity" and claimed to have successfully contacted the biblical evangelist Philip.

Cumorah (MORMONISM). A hill near Rochester, New York, where Joseph ▸Smith claimed to have been visited by ▸Moroni, who instructed him to dig and locate the golden plates, which, when eventually translated, became the ▸Book of Mormon.

Cups (▸occult). One of the four ▸elemental tools. To various occult groups, chiefly those who use ▸tarot cards, cups are symbolic of water.

Curse (▸occult; SATANISM). An oath or pronouncement directing evil toward another individual or party. In ▸black magic the oath is almost always intended to bring harm. Cursing has the effect of negating the forces of good within a religion.

Cursing Finger (▸occult). See ▸finger.

Cusp (▸occult; ▸astrology). The imaginary dividing line between the various ▸signs of the ▸zodiac.

D

Daba (SANTERIA). Large drums used in Santeria ceremonies.

Daemon (ᵇoccult; SATANISM). An evil demonic being. The word has also come to be associated with genius-like intelligence because, ontologically, daemons in gnostic thought were intermediary beings—higher than humanity but somewhat lower than God. See also ᵇgnosticism.

Dagoba (BUDDHISM). A Buddhist holy place or shrine where the various relics of the Buddha are preserved. Dagobas are scattered throughout Buddhist lands.

Dagyde (ᵇpaganism; WITCHCRAFT). A ᵇwitch's pin.

Dahomey; Dahomean (CANDOMBLE; SOUTH AMERICAN, CENTRAL AMERICAN, AND CARIBBEAN CULTS). The people originating in the West African area now known as southern Benin. Dahomey became a powerful kingdom in the early nineteenth century. Slaves were sold to Europeans, often in exchange for weapons and food. They were then brought to the West Indies and South America, where they were used as laborers on the plantations and farms.

Dai Gohonzon (NICHIREN SHOSHU BUDDHISM). The largest shrine of Nichiren Shoshu Buddhism, located at the base of Mount Fuji in Japan.

Daimoku (BUDDHISM; NICHIREN SHOSHU BUDDHISM; SOKA-GAKKAI). The chanted and oft-repeated words *nam-Myoho-renge-kyo*, translated "glory to the ᵇ*Lotus Sutra*." The worshiper chants this ᵇmantra before the ᵇaltar, on which sits the ᵇ*butsodun*. Daimoku is the second great principle of Nichiren Shoshu (*see* ᵇgohonzon and ᵇkaidan).

Daisekiji (BUDDHISM; NICHIREN SHOSHU BUDDHISM; SOKA-GAKKAI). The name of the original and chief temple of Nichiren Shoshu Buddhism located at the base of Mount Fuji. The Daisekiji contains the ᵇ*butsodun*, which in turn contains the sacred ᵇ*gohonzon*.

Daishonen, Nichiren (BUDDHISM; NICHIREN SHOSHU BUDDHISM; 1222–1282). Claimed to be the only one who understood the nature of true Buddhism. He was the founder of Nichiren Shoshu Buddhism.

Dakini (ᵇoccult; WITCHCRAFT). Tibetan term for ᵇwitch or demonic being, not however, to be associated with a witch of the ᵇwiccan tradition.

Dalai Lama (BUDDHISM). The leader of Tibetan Buddhism (from *dalai*, "ocean," and *lama*, "spiritual leader," hence the Tibetan translation, "Ocean of Wisdom") The current (fourteenth) Dalai Lama was born to a farmer as Lhamo Thondup in Taktser, Amdo, Tibet, on July 6, 1935. The thirteenth Dalai Lama died in 1933, so the Tibetans anticipated his incarnation soon thereafter. The Tibetan Regent had a vision that the incarnation would occur in Amdo, so a search party was sent to find the child. Once the party encountered Lhamo, he supposedly called one of the members of the party by name. They returned with several items belonging to the thirteenth Dalai Lama and several unrelated items. The story goes that Lhamo, in each case, said, "It's mine," in reference to the thirteenth Dalai Lama's possessions, but not with the unrelated items. He was briefly trained at a monastery and then traveled to the capital where governmental officials confirmed him as their spiritual leader, the fourteenth Dalai Lama. His succession in this rank of thirteen previous incarnations stretches to 1351 AD.

The Dalai Lama continued his education and training until he was enthroned at the outbreak of the Chinese invasion of Tibet in 1950, when the Dalai Lama was age 15. In his bid to prevent all out war, his delegation to Bejing "agreed" to a "local government of Tibet" under Chinese authority on May 23, 1951. In 1959 the Dalai Lama escaped into India as the exiled leader of Tibet while Chinese authorities installed their puppet powers. He has since traveled the world, speaking boldly on behalf of his country and religion and winning the Nobel Peace Prize in 1989.

Tibetan Buddhism is an integration of old Tibetan Bon religion with MAHAYANA BUDDHISM in the traditions of Madyamika (only the Void exists and ᵇNirvana already exists, but is unrealized), Yogacara (reality is in the mind and the Void is external), and Tantric (see ᵇTantraism, reliance on sacred texts). It is much more mystical than traditional Buddhism since it relies on ritual postures, secret initiation rituals, and mantras. Tibetan Buddhism has several sects, some noted by their red hats and yellow hats.

Tibetan Buddhism is separate from CHRISTIANITY in its worldview. They teach that the natural world evolved, hence denying the Creator God of Christianity (Gen. 1:1; John 1:3). The law of *karma and *reincarnation governs all life in Buddhism, but Christianity teaches that man is born once (Heb. 9:27), with a sinful nature (Ps. 51:5). Sin separates him from God and results in death (Rom. 6:23). God's remedy for sin and eternal death is the blood of Jesus Christ, who provides an atonement (covering) to appease God's wrath against our sins (Heb. 2:17; 1 John 2:2). While Buddhism teaches that nirvana comes through human effort and work, the Bible teaches that there is nothing we can do to save ourselves except to rely on the mercy, love, and grace of God (Eph. 2:8–10).

Dan (VOODOO). The deity of the air, or the "wind deity."

Daphnomancy (*occult). *Divination by means of a laurel plant. A laurel branch is cast into fire. If it crackles and flares up, the signs are favorable. If it fails to crackle but merely burns noiselessly, then the future is dim.

Dass, Baba Ram See Richard *Alpert.

Dasya (HINDUISM). The state of complete discipline and devotion to God.

Daughters of the Eastern Star (FREEMASONRY). Order for the daughters of Masons.

David, Moses. See David Brand *Berg.

Davis, Andrew Jackson (*occult; SPIRITUALISM; 1826–1910). A cobbler from New York who claimed to have the ability to communicate as a *medium with the spirit world.

Dawn Bible Students' Association (JEHOVAH'S WITNESSES). One of the largest and most successful splinter groups of the Watchtower Bible and Tract Society that parted company with Judge *Rutherford, the movement's second president, following Charles *Russell's death in 1916. Several Russellite groups formed in order to safeguard Pastor Charles Taze *Russell's teaching that they felt were compromised by the current Watchtower leader, namely Judge *Rutherford. In 1931, the Watchtower had a radio program called *Frank and Ernest*, created by Norman Woodworth. When the Watchtower eliminated the program, Mr. Woodworth left the organization and began a radio program by the same name, which gained an audience of former *Frank and Ernest* listeners. The program is still broadcast around the world on various radio stations.

Shortly afterward (1932) C. Russell began a bimonthly publication of the radio messages, *The Dawn and Herald of Christ Presence*, which is still today's official magazine of the Dawn Bible Students Association. Many independent, small, and fledging Bible Students studies that left the Watchtower to continue studying Russell joined with the Dawn Bible Students, giving it immense growth that challenged the Watchtower Society in New York. Holding true to Russell, they republished the *Studies in the Scriptures* and continue as the main disseminators of Russell's teachings. They have a television program *The Bible Answers*, which is seen mostly by cable outlets and a few California UFH broadcasters. The Dawn magazine publishes 250,000 annual copies and their study booklets number about 150,000 annual copies. The Dawn Bible Students hold conventions around the world and their core doctrines are much like those of the Jehovah's Witnesses.

Deacon (MORMONISM; CHRISTIANITY). The deacon is the office of the lower priesthood or *Aaronic priesthood, which according to Mormonism, is the assistant to the teachers and to the congregations. Young Mormons are called to this office beginning at age twelve. Mormons also follow the *Bible's description of the office of a deacon (Phil. 1:1; 1 Tim. 3:8–13). Deacons may not baptize, administer the *sacrament, or lay on hands.

In Christianity, deacons comprise one of the three historic offices of bishop/elder, priest, and deacon. It comes from the Greek word *diakonos*, which means "to serve." As an office in the historic churches, it has enjoyed a long history. It has come into disuse and/or abandonment in many Protestant churches.

Death Angel See NATION OF YAHWEH.

Death Magic (*occult; VOODOO; SATANISM). Evil *magic used to bring death to an intended victim, either an animal or a person. This practice is most closely associated with Haitian voodoo but is practiced by a variety of occult groups.

Debility (*astrology; *occult). Astrological concept in which the position of a planet in the *horoscope negatively affects life and living conditions (*see* dignity).

Deggial (ISLAM). Antichrist, or one who will one day rise to power with an army of seventy thousand Jews to make war on Islamic nations.

Degree (*occult). The ranking system within occult organizations.

Deification (CHRISTIANITY; HINDUISM, MORMONISM; NEW AGE MOVEMENT). Eastern Orthodox doctrine that speaks of humanity becoming deified in the sense of sharing in and partaking of the communicable aspects of the divine nature. Humankind becomes "by grace what God is by nature." Athanasius summed up the doctrine of deification by stating, "God became man that we might be made god" (*On the Incarnation*, 54). This is in no wise to be interpreted, however, in the way that modern ᐟcults, Hinduism, Mormonism, or the New Age Movement thinkers do. For these, humankind is deified in that it possesses latent deity within, or, in some cases, the potential of becoming a future god. What modern cults forget is that the early church fathers never stated or implied that God's unique or incommunicable attributes could be shared by any created being.

Deism (CHRISTIANITY; UNITARIAN-UNIVERSALISM). A theology that grew largely out of the Enlightenment, especially in France and England, that adhered to the general idea that religious truths can be arrived at completely through reason and apart from ᐟrevelation. Deists up till the end of the end of the eighteenth century appealed to cosmological (God can be proven from the existence of the world) and teleological (God can be proven from the existence of design and order) arguments. Neither of these classical arguments appealed to revelation and therefore they were considered accommodating to the modern mind. Unitarians and universalists appeal to deistic and various other modern and postmodern paradigms.

Dematerialization (ᐟoccult). The literal disappearance of matter. Dematerialization has been reported in ᐟséances, where parts of the human body, particularly the body of the ᐟmedium, were said to have vanished for a short time, along with other numerous objects in the immediate vicinity.

Demon (CHRISTIANITY; SATANISM; VOODOO). An evil spirit or, as it is sometimes translated, a ᐟdevil. In Christianity, demons are agents of ᐟSatan to carry out the mission of perpetrating evil in the world and preventing the faithful from ascending to heaven after death. C. S. Lewis's classic *The Screwtape Letters* represents the best in classical Christian literature in describing a Christian understanding of demons.

In Haitian voodoo, a demon was the male counterpart of the *loup-garou* (a Haitian werewolf, who is a red-eyed female). Protection against this demon comes through possessing and carrying the correct ᐟcharms.

Demonology (ᐟoccult; SATANISM). The study of ᐟdemons, ᐟdemon possession, and the various accompanying rites.

Demonomancy (ᐟoccult). In the occult practice of ᐟdivination, the belief that ᐟdemons can be called upon or conjured up.

Demonization (ᐟoccult). See ᐟdemon possession.

Demon Possession (ᐟoccult; SATANISM). The phenomenon in which a ᐟdemon overcomes the mind and/or body of an animal or a human being in order to exercise control in part or in full. Demon possession is described in the ᐟBible, and cases have been reported throughout the centuries. In modern times most cases of demon possession are diagnosed as psychological disorders and are treated as such. The Christian church, especially the Roman Catholic church, still practices the rite of ᐟexorcism in cases where clinical therapy has proven to be ineffective.

Demonstration (RELIGIOUS SCIENCE). Achieving healing of either body or mind or both through the power of positive thinking.

Denomination (CHRISTIANITY). A common term for ᐟsects within Christianity.

Dense Body (THEOSOPHY). The teaching that matter is the densest of all the emanations from the realm of spirit. Having density is to be the furthest removed from the realm of pure spirit.

Deosil (ᐟoccult; WITCHCRAFT). This is direction of movement opposite of ᐟwiddershins. It is the movement of ᐟwitches in a clockwise direction in a ᐟcircle for the build up of power.

Deprogramming A method used by psychologists and other trained persons to discourage and/or dissolve the relationship a person has with a religious or cultic group. A deprogrammer attempts to create cognitive dissonance in the devotee. Various methods are used and are largely at the discretion of each individual deprogrammer. Most commonly, a question/answer approach is utilized. The ultimate aim in deprogramming is to enable the "client" to achieve "re-personalization," wherein the subject is brought to a position of being capable of making rational judgments. Deprogramming is usually employed as a last resort and is used particularly with adherents and devotees to ᐟcults that display bizarre psychotic behavior and/or are suicidal.

Dermatoglyphics (ᐟoccult). The study of the inferior surfaces of the skin. Palmistry advocates often appeal to the science of dermatoglyphics to substantiate their less-than-scientific practices.

Dermography (ᐟoccult). The sudden appearance of writing on the surface of the skin. ᐟMediums have allegedly used dermography as a means of communication.

Dervish Orders (SUFISM). A ▸sect deriving from Sufism.

Descending Arc (▸gnosticism; THEOSOPHY). The ontological schema within the Theosophy worldview that presents spirit beings as gradually losing their spiritual composition as they move closer to the physical world. Contrariwise, the further from the physical realm, the more spiritual in essence (*see* ▸ascending arc).

Deseret News Press (MORMONISM). One of the publishing arms of the Church of Jesus Christ of Latter Day Saints. "Deseret" means "honey bee," from the ▸Book of Mormon.

Despojo (SANTERIA; VOODOO): A rite performed for the purpose of thwarting off evil.

Dev (▸occult). The name for ▸Satan in Persian.

Dev, Guru (TRANCENDENTAL MEDITATION; 1869–1953). Also known as Swami Brahmananda Saraswati, Jagadgury, Bhagovan Shankaracharya. Guru Dev was the teacher of Maharishi Mahesh ▸Yogi, founder of Trancendental Meditation. It is believed that after Guru Dev died, he imparted the knowledge to the Maharishi, which then became the fundamentals of the movement.

Deva (▸Zoroastrianism; HINDUISM; THEOSOPHY). In Zoroastrianism, devas are evil spirits who are enemies of humankind. For Hinduism, deva is the general word for God. In Theosophy, it refers to a person who has escaped the material (bodily) world and has ascended to a purely spiritual plane of existence.

Devachan (THEOSOPHY). The Persian word for heaven. A stage of transition in the soul's gradual emanations toward the spirit realm.

Devi (HINDUISM). The proper title for a goddess (*see also* ▸Kundalini).

Devil (▸occult; CHRISTIANITY; SATANISM; WITCHCRAFT). Derived from the Greek *diabolos*, which is translated "accuser" or "slanderer." The devil is the personification of evil in the Christian ▸Bible and is the enemy of God. His name is ▸Lucifer ("son of the morning") or ▸Satan. The Bible describes Satan as being the "tempter" (Matt. 4:3), the great "liar" (John 8:44), or the "god of this age" (2 Cor. 4:4). In Satanism, the devil is the master or absolute within the realm of evil. He is the object of worship and sacrifice. He is the embodiment of evil to whom allegiance is sworn and service rendered.

In ▸Gothic witchcraft, particularly in ▸black magic, the devil is a principle of evil. Some Gothic witchcraft groups, both past and present, make pacts with the devil and understand their roles as servants consecrated to carrying out his evil purposes. Newly initiated ▸witches are presented to the devil during a ▸sabbat. In traditional Christianity, the devil is permitted to reign until the Final Judgment (Rev. 20:7ff.), at which time he will be cast into the lake of fire.

Devil's Garter (▸occult; SATANISM). An incomplete or imperfect rainbow.

Devil's Mark (▸occult; SATANISM; WITCHCRAFT). A mark of identification in ▸Gothic witchcraft allegedly planted on the body of a ▸witch in an initiation rite or in order to seal a compact. There is no one particular mark but they were usually moles or birthmarks. In some instances, the marks vary in the shape of insects, animals, or other telltale signs and are implanted in discreet areas of the body. In the case of a male, underneath the eyelid was common. During the Inquisition, persons accused of witchcraft were examined in order to find the mark and so ascertain their guilt.

Devil's Pillar (▸occult; SATANISM). A site in Prague, Czechoslovakia, made up of three large stones that are supposedly the remains of a site where an apostate Roman Catholic priest recanted and abandoned his practice of Satanism. ▸Satan in his anger broke the pillars.

DFing (THE FAMILY). A term used by The Family (formerly Children of God) that stood for "daily food," which was the implementation of devotional booklets used to gain converts. Earlier, leader David Brandt ▸Berg had additionally advocated the practice of "Flirty Fishing" or ▸*Ffing* in order to gain converts.

Dhamma (BUDDHISM). The wisdom of the ▸Buddha.

Dhammapada (BUDDHISM). The most popular and most quoted book in Buddhist literature. Its literary style is versicle, and it contains twenty-six chapters with a total of 423 stanzas. The *Dhammapada* is an anthology of the most treasured teachings of ▸Gautama, including allusions to the ▸Four Noble Truths, the ▸Eightfold Path, and other great teachings and writings.

Dharana (HINDUISM). The concentration of the mind on a single thought.

Dharana Yoga (HINDUISM). That aspect of ▸yoga pertaining to ▸*dharana*.

Dharma (HINDUISM). The natural laws embedded in a living soul that function as guidelines to ethical behavior.

Dharsana (HINDUISM). Of or pertaining to the six schools of Hindu thought and religion.

Dhimmis (ISLAM). Non-Muslims conquered in the years of ʾMuslim expansion. Whether Christians or Jews, they were allowed to practice their respective religions, but higher taxes were usually exacted from them. Despite the fact that *dhimmis* were tolerated, they were considered inferior to the true worshipers of ʾAllah.

Diablito (ʾoccult; ABAKUA). The spirit called on by members of the Abakua ʾcult. The center of all cultic worship is directed toward conjuring up the *diablitos*. See also ʾireme.

Diabolism (ʾoccult; SATANISM). All acts associated with the worship of the ʾdevil.

Dianetics (SCIENTOLOGY). The title of the introductory book for the Church of Scientololgy, *Dianetics: The Modern Science of Mental Health* (Hubbard, 1950). Scientology's founder, L. Ron ʾHubbard, coined the word Dianetics from *dia* (Greek, "through") and *nous* (Greek, "soul"), to suggest that physical trauma results from latent picture images left on the soul from past experience. These images, called ʾengrams by Scientology, must be erased for optimum mental and physical health.

Diaspora (JUDAISM). Term used to describe all Jews who live outside of the promised land of Palestine, beginning with the Babylonian Captivity and on into today.

Digambaras (JAINISM). A religious order within Jainism that believes nudity is integral to the spiritual life.

Dignity (ʾastrology; ʾoccult). Astrological concept in which the position of a planet positively influences the ʾhoroscope (*see* ʾdebility).

Dimambro, Joseph (ORDER OF THE SOLAR TEMPLE). One of the founders of this order.

Directions (ʾoccult). Representation of the four elements: earth, fire, water, and air by the four directions.

Director General (CHRIST THE SAVIOR BROTHERHOOD). The highest ranking leader of the Holy Order of Mans organization. Father Earl Paul ʾBlighton served as the first director general.

Disassociate (JEHOVAH'S WITNESSES). A member who separates and/or leaves the Watchtower Bible and Tract Society. Such an individual is ʾshunned by other members in the same manner as a person who has been ʾdisfellowshiped.

Discipler (INTERNATIONAL CHURCHES OF CHRIST). A person deemed spiritually mature enough to take on the assignment of a new convert to the ICOC. The various duties and responsibilities of a discipler include praying for new coverts, encouraging them to attend all church meetings and activities, hearing their personal confessions, and giving account to the leadership as to their progress.

Discipleship (INTERNATIONAL CHURCHES OF CHRIST). A term used in the ICOC to designate how initiates into the group are accounted for and tended to. A new convert is assigned a ʾdiscipler, who then reports to leaders above him. The idea is taken from the Bible and Jesus' calling of his disciples.

Disfellowship (JEHOVAH'S WITNESSES). Occurs when a member of the Watchtower Bible and Tract Society has been accused and found guilty of violating the teachings and practices of the group and refuses to repent. Such a person is marked and summarily ʾshunned by other members of the group, even when those members are direct family. For a Jehovah's Witness, being disfellowshiped is among the worst things that can happen because it is tantamount to being judged unworthy of life and thus facing ʾannihilation upon death.

Dispensationalism (CHRISTIANITY). A dispensation was defined by the Scofield Reference Bible as "a period of time during which man is tested in respect of obedience to some specific revelation of the will of God." By this term Cyrus I. Scofield (1843–1921) meant that God has set aside certain ages or "dispensations" for specific activities that may differ from those before or after. There were seven ages or dispensations: (1) the age of innocence, before the Fall; (2) the period of time up to the Flood when the human race, governed by conscience, again failed; (3) the era of civil government, ending with moral collapse and the destruction of Sodom and Gomorrah; (4) the promise to the patriarchs, ending in the destruction of the Egyptians at the Red Sea; (5) the time of the Mosaic covenant up to and including the crucifixion of Jesus; (6) the age of grace (church age), in which we are currently; (7) the final dispensation or Millennium, which is yet to come.

Dispensationalism was popularized in the nineteenth century and has been adopted by many ʾfundamentalist and Holiness Pentecostal denominations. The most popular rendition is premillennialism, in which the future Millennium, beginning at the return of Jesus Christ, will bring an end to the present church age and usher in a thousand-year dispensation of peace.

Dispensationalism has been challenged by two other major ways of interpreting the doctrine of the end times. The postmillennial view sees conditions of the world as generally improving because of the presence of the kingdom of God in the world. The amillennial view asserts that the Bible does not teach a literal thousand-year millennium and that there are no special dispensations where God does different things in different epochs of history.

District   (JEHOVAH'S WITNESSES). Part of the organizational structure of the Watchtower Bible and Tract Society. There are thirty-eight districts in the United States. Each district is further divided into *circuits.

Divali   (HINDUISM). The philosophy of self-awareness and enlightenment.

Divination   (*occult). The attempt to foretell and/or explore the future. The most common means of divination are *astrology, *tarot cards, *crystal balls, *numerology, *palmistry, random symbols (*I Ching), and various *omens.

Divine Light Mission   (See ELAN VITAL).

Divine Nectar   (ELAN VITAL). Method through which the divine knowledge of *guru *Maharaj Ji is imparted. The divine nectar is believed by members to be a heavenly elixir extracted from the brain. The *initiator pushes the tongue back into the throat of a *premie until it is touching the uvula. The result is a mucous that is considered to be "sweet" to the taste. The premie is expected to receive divine knowledge through partaking of the divine nectar. See also *third eye, *third ear, *primordial vibration, and *Fourfold Path.

Divine Principle   (UNIFICATION CHURCH). The authoritative text of the Unification Church, written by one of Sun Myung *Moon's close followers and published in 1957. *The Divine Principle* contains the basic doctrines of Moon. Overall, it reinterprets the Bible under the guise of TAOISM (positive/negative, yang/yin, male/female). Everything in the Bible, then, is dualistic, including salvation. The book states that humankind was only saved halfway by Jesus, and a new *Messiah must arise to complete the second half (dual aspect) of salvation. The movement also teaches that the *Bible needs updating as God continues to grant *revelation to each and every generation. The book represents such an updating of divine information for the twentieth century.

Divine Soul   (THEOSOPHY). The deity or manifestation of divinity that lies within the soul. In the different world religions it is known by different expressions. For example, it is the "inner-Christ" (or "the Christ within") in some elements of CHRISTIANITY, or the "inner *buddha " in BUDDHISM.

Divining Rod   (*occult). Also called a dowser, a divining rod is used to locate underground water, minerals, metals, or in some cases, lost items or treasures. The divining rod is a Y-shaped device formed by metal or wooden sticks brought together. When the divining rod passes over the sought item, the sticks move, indicating the location of the item.

Dixon, Jean   (*astrology; *occult; 1918–1997). American psychic who used a *crystal ball, astrology, and *numerology as methods of *divination. Dixon's claim to fame was her apparent success in predicting the assassinations of President John F. Kennedy and Dr. Martin Luther King Jr. However, most of her predictions did not come to pass.

Docetism   From the Greek word *dokeo*, "to think, seem." Docetism was an early *Christological heresy that taught that Christ was not human and did not assume human form. Jesus merely "seemed" human. His appearance in the flesh was a phantasm. Docetic tendencies have cropped up time and again within the Christian church. It is based on the Greek notion of *dualism. See also *gnosticism.

Doctrine and Covenants   (MORMONISM). One of the sacred Mormon texts first published in 1835. In 1870 it was published in its present form, now containing 138 "sections" and two "official declarations," each of which is divided into two verses. The revelations are by Joseph *Smith, except section 136 (by Brigham *Young), section 138 (by Joseph Fielding *Smith), and the "official declarations" by Wilford *Woodruff and Spencer Kimball. The writings address the various loci of systematic theology, such as the doctrine of God, the church, humanity, the doctrine of salvation, etc. Along with the *Book of Mormon, *The Pearl of Great Price*, the King James *Bible, and continued direct revelations, *Doctrine and Covenants* stands as being one of the norms for faith and practice in the Mormon church (Utah) and the COMMUNITY OF CHRIST (formerly the Reorganized Church of Jesus Christ of Latter Day Saints). The Community of Christ has fewer revelations by Smith in the *Doctrine and Covenants*, and they have added a number of subsequent revelations by their succeeding prophets.

Dogen   (ZEN BUDDHISM; d. 1225). Founder of Soto, a *sect which has its roots in ZEN.

Dolman   (*paganism; WITCHCRAFT). Stone monuments that have been dedicated to the meeting place of a *coven.

Donatism   (CHRISTIANITY). The Donatists were a schismatic group in North Africa in the early fourth century who split with the Roman Catholic church. They refused to accept Caecilian as the rightful Bishop of Carthage because he had been consecrated by Felix of Aptunga, a traditur during the Diocletian persecution (a traditur was someone who had lapsed from faith or handed over copies of the Holy Scriptures to authorities during persecution, usually under threat of death). The Donatists believed that the church was comprised of only the saints who remained faithful to the end. To them, 'sacraments ministered by traditurs were invalid. Augustine opposed Donatism, teaching that the sacrament's validity was based not on the worthiness or holiness of the minister but on the worthiness of Christ, the true administrator.

Doyle, Sir Arthur Conan ('occult; SPIRITUALISM). Famous British author of the Sherlock Holmes series and a famous practitioner of spiritualism and the occult.

Dowsing ('occult). Also known as rhabdomancy and radiesthesia, it is the practice of seeking or discovering the location of hidden objects through the use of 'divining rods, pendulums, or in some instances, a hand. Though a method employed in 'divination, dowsing is also applied to other fields (mineral prospecting, healing, etc.).

Dracula ('occult). See Prince 'Vlad.

Drawing Down the Moon ('occult; WITCHCRAFT). A witchcraft ceremony where the 'high priest invokes the goddess aspect into the 'high priestess. See also 'drawing down the sun.

Drawing Down the Sun ('occult; WITCHCRAFT) The ceremony in witchcraft that invokes the god aspect into the 'high priest. This is done by the 'high priestess of a 'coven, through a prescribed ceremony. See also 'drawing down the moon.

Dreadlocks (RASTAFARIANISM). The long hair grown by a 'Rastafarian. The dreadlocks on a Rastafarian male symbolize a lion's mane and promote the image of strength.

Dream Body (THEOSOPHY). Synonym for 'astral body.

Dresser, Horatio (NEW THOUGHT; 1866–1954). Julius 'Dresser's son and former leader of New Thought.

Dresser, Julius (NEW THOUGHT; 1838–1893). One-time leader of New Thought.

Druids ('paganism). In Celtic, the word *druid* meant "finding or knowing the oak tree." The druids were the learned priestly caste among the ancient Celts in pre-Christian Britain and Gaul (France). Julius Caesar, the principal source of knowledge on the druids, relates that they were one of two respected classes of people, the other being the noblemen.

The druids held sacrificial rituals in the forests and worshiped the sun. They were also considered the intellectual leaders of the Celtic community, studying astronomy, medicine, and philosophy. They believed in immortality of the soul and 'reincarnation. With the conquest of England and Gaul by the armies of Caesar in the first century A.D., the Celtic religion disappeared. The priestly caste lost their religious functions but continued in their capacity as leaders and scholars.

Druj ('occult; HINDUISM). A class of 'demons dating back to the Vedic (*see 'Vedas*) times. In Iranian/Persian beliefs, Druj was the god of falsehood.

Dualism ('gnosticism; CHRISTIANITY). Term used to describe the neo-Platonic and gnostic bifurcation between spirit and matter. Rather than viewing the body, or flesh, and the spirit, or soul, as being harmoniously conjoined, dualists see the flesh and the spirit at war with each other. Furthermore, the flesh is viewed as being evil and counterproductive to the soul.

The 'Manichaeans were dualists. The ascetic traditions within the Christian church were influenced by dualistic tendencies. Many 'cults and religious movements today embrace dualism in one form or another. Traditional Christianity rejects it as being heretical to view the body, or the whole of creation, as being evil while the spirit is conceived of as being good. All of God's creation is believed to be good precisely because God created it (Gen. 1:1ff.). The 'Bible declares "sin" as evil (Rom. 7:17), not the body or the flesh.

Dumb Signs ('astrology; 'occult). In astrology, the "mute" 'signs are 'Cancer, 'Scorpio, and 'Pisces.

Dungeons and Dragons ('occult). Also called "D and D"; a game that involves role-playing. The player takes on any number of pseudonymous personalities—thief, monster, 'demon, 'witch, warrior, etc. The Dungeon Master draws up maps, determines the roles, positions, treasures to be found, etc. The characters and roles are comprised mainly of the world of the 'occult. Players who participate in "D and D" are usually teenagers. Because it is so involved and absorbing, it involves a great deal of time. Players have been known to fulfill roles that transport them great distances from home. Some psychologists believe "D and D" has the potential of distorting a person's ability to distinguish fantasy from reality. Reports of harm and even death attributed to "D and D" have appeared in newspapers across the United States.

Dynamic Monarchianism (CHRISTIANITY). Ancient Christological heresy that denied the deity of Jesus Christ by asserting that Jesus was God only in the sense that the power of God rested on him. Also called adoptionism, dynamic monarchianism was first taught by Artemon, Paul of Samosata, and Theodotus. Intended as a safeguard of the unity of God, it was one of two monarchian errors (see *monarchianism). The other was called *modalistic monarchianism.

E

Eadie, Betty (NEW AGE MOVEMENT). Author of the best-selling book *Embraced by the Light*. Eadie's book is perhaps the best example of books that address the modern fascination with the idea of *near-death experiences (NDE). The book was published in 1992 and almost immediately became a best seller. Eadie claims to have died in 1973 following surgery, whereupon she met Jesus. Jesus and a "council of men" told her to return to the earth. She claims to have bartered with them that if she would agree to return to earth, she "*made them* promise that the moment my mission was complete, they would take me back home."[1] Eadie contends that "they [meaning Jesus and the twelve disciples] agreed to my terms."

No tradition within Christianity supports the notion that one is in control of his or her own destiny. In the place of Christianity, *Embraced by the Light* is a mixture of MORMONISM and NEW AGE beliefs. Eadie is a Mormon. She frequently alludes to a belief in premortal existence, as does Mormonism. She strongly associates sin not with the transgression of God's law but with the notion of "forgetting." While she was undergoing her NDE, she claims to have been omniscient. During this moment of *enlightenment, Eadie reports that human beings are divine and that all people can eventually become deity. There is ultimately no punishment for sin and all will return to God.

The great interest in NDE lies in the fact that it greatly romanticizes death and reports to people what they want to hear—dying brings one to a world where God, light, peace, eternal bliss, and total joy are waiting. Despite the book's success, Eadie's claims about actually dying and returning remain unsubstantiated. She has not allowed her medical records to be released to confirm her actual death experience. There has been at least one documented case where Eadie's unbiblical teachings concerning death resulted in a suicide.[2]

Notes

[1] Betty J. Eadie with Curtis Taylor, *Embraced by the Light* (Placerville, Calif.: Gold Leaf Press, 1992), 40–42.
[2] See Douglas Groothuis, *Deceived by the Light: A Christian Response to "Embraced by the Light."* (CRI Statement DE305 found at *www.equip.org/free/DE305.htm/*.

Earth Plane (*occult). The physical plane of reality and existence, as distinguished from the *astral plane.

Earthbound (SPIRITUALISM). The spirits of the departed who remain in close proximity to the location where they lived during their earthly lives are said to be earthbound.

Eastern Star (FREEMASONRY). See *Order of the Eastern Star.

Ebionites (CHRISTIANITY; JUDAISM). From the Hebrew word for "poor," the term was first applied to all Christians, and shortly thereafter to a specific group of Jewish Christians. In the latter, the term describes an extremist Jewish *sect of the second century that practiced a rigorous *asceticism. The Ebionites were Jews who acknowledged that Jesus was the promised *Messiah, but they rejected the idea of his divinity or that he was born of the Virgin Mary. The Ebionites were among the first to reject the deity of Christ in the early Christological controversies.

Eblis (ISLAM). The Islamic term for the *devil.

Ebo (*occult; CANDOMBLE; MACUMBA; SOUTH AMERICAN, CENTRAL AMERICAN, AND CARIBBEAN CULTS). General name for Afro-Brazilian cultic instruments, or the magical rites in the Brazilian state of Bahia; also the name of food sacrificed to deities.

Ecclesia (CHRISTADELPHIANISM). Term used to designate a local assembly of Christadelphians. The word is derived from the Greek word *ekklesia*, the common New Testament word for "assembly, congregation, church."

Ecclesiology (CHRISTIANITY). The Christian doctrine of the church, from the Greek *ekklesia*, "assembly, church."

Ectenic Force (SPIRITUALISM). The word used to designate the peculiar force that causes objects to move without physical means.

Ectoplasm (ᵇoccult; SPIRITUALISM). Spiritualists believe ectoplasm is the substance that causes materialization of nonmatter and ᵇtelekinesis. Though invisible, ectoplasm is capable of assuming the three states of solid, liquid, or gas (vapor). It emerges primarily from the sundry orifices (including pores) of the body. As it is slightly luminous, it can be seen in the dark and has the effect of producing a chill, especially if one makes contact with it. Additionally, ectoplasm produces an odor.

Eddy, Mary Baker (CHRISTIAN SCIENCE; 1821–1910). Founder of Christian Science.

Effendi, Shoghi (BAHAʾI FAITH; ??–1953). Grandson of Abduʾl ᵇBaha. During Abduʾl's reign as leader of the Baha'i Faith until 1921, Baha'ism was brought to the United States.

Efi (ABAKUA). One of two large groups of adherents to the Abakua religion (the other being the ᵇ*Efo* group). The *Efi* are the more liberal in that they allow non-blacks to become members. When initiating a member to the group, the *Efi* advocate pouring water on the initiate or sprinkling him or her with ᵇ*albahaca*.

Efo (ABAKUA). One of two large groups of adherents to the Abakua religion (the other being the ᵇ*Efi* group). The *Efo* are the more traditional group, disallowing whites from membership. New members are initiated through a "baptism" of soil contained in a skull.

Egun (ᵇoccult; ABAKUA; CANDOMBLE; MACUMBA; SOUTH AMERICAN, CENTRAL AMERICAN, AND CARIBBEAN CULTS). A corpse or cadaver; also, the name of one of the ᵇYoruba ᵇorisha.

Eidolism (ᵇoccult; SPIRITUALISM). The belief in the existence of ᵇghosts, ᵇapparitions, and disincarnate spirits.

Eightfold Path (BUDDHISM). The steps proposed by ᵇGautama and designed to lead one to ᵇnirvana. The eight steps are as follows: (1) right belief, (2) right resolve, (3) right speech, (4) right conduct, (5) right livelihood, (6) right effort, (7) right thought, (8) right concentration.

Eighth Sphere (ᵇoccult; THEOSOPHY). The place where evil souls are sent for final destruction.

Einasuke, Akiya (SOKA-GAKKAI; n.d.). Became leader of the Soka-Gakkai organizaton in 1981.

Eisai (ZEN BUDDHISM; d. 1191). Founder of Rinzai, a ᵇsect that sprang from Zen during the Middle Ages.

Eisegesis (CHRISTIANITY). Term used in ᵇhermeneutics, the reverse of ᵇexegesis. Particularly prominent in ᵇcult leaders, who read "into" (*eis*) a biblical passage something outside of its immediate context. This process can give them unique doctrines, but doctrines that are not scriptural.

Ekon (ABAKUA). Name for the drums used in Abakua ceremonies and rituals. The drums are strictly African in origin.

Elca (SANTERIA; VOODOO). A ᵇfetish used in Santeria voodoo.

Elder (CHRISTIANITY; MORMONISM; WITCHCRAFT). In many Christian denominations, especially in ᵇProtestant Christianity, church leaders are often called "elders" (based on the Greek word *presbyteros* in such passages as 1 Tim. 5:17; Titus 1:5; 1 Peter 5:1, 5).

"Elder" is also an office within Mormonism that is derived from the ᵇMelchizedek priesthood. The functions of the elder are to baptize; to ordain priests, ᵇdeacons, and other elders; to administer the sacraments; to confirm by the laying on of hands; to teach; to conduct meetings; and to supervise the spiritual affairs of a congregation. The elder presides strictly within the local church. In witchcraft, members of a ᵇcoven that have reached the level of second and third degree.

Elder Brother (THEOSOPHY). Term for an initiate.

Elegba (ᵇoccult; SOUTH AMERICAN, CENTRAL AMERICAN, AND CARIBBEAN CULTS). See ᵇ*Eshu*.

Elementals (ᵇoccult). Four categories or classes of ᵇdemons or ᵇnature spirits: "undines" (inhabit water), "gnomes" (live on the earth), "salamanders" (present in fire), and "sylphs" (live in the air).

Elementary (ᵇoccult; SATANISM; THEOSOPHY). The disincarnate soul of a wicked individual. While the souls or ᵇastral bodies of the good progress toward a new phase of development, the elementary remains nearer the ᵇearth plane. In some forms of Satanism, they are "spirit beings."

Elements (ᵇoccult). The five basic elements of earth, air, fire, water, and spirit (excluded from some lists) that are named after gods and are assigned specific symbols. They are *Nanta*, associated with earth and with the symbol of a yellow square; *Exarp*, associated with air and with the symbol of a blue square; *Bitom*, associated with fire and with a red triangle for its symbol; *Heoma*, associated with water and symbolized by the silver crescent; *Akaha*, associated with spirit and represented by a black egg.

Elongation (ʼoccult; SPIRITUALISM). The expansion or elongation of the body by a ʼmedium.

Elves See ʼnature spirits.

Elvinfolk (ʼoccult). A descendent of a god or goddess.

Embraced by the Light (NEW AGE MOVEMENT). See Betty ʼEadie.

Emerson, Ralph Waldo (UNITARIAN-UNIVERSALIST ASSOCIATION; 1803–1882). The principal figure in propagating unitarianism in the eighteenth century. He abandoned his Unitarian ministry to write on rationalism and mysticism and gained a following in Transcendental philosophy, namely, that God is in every human being. Some thought he borrowed his ʼpantheism from HINDUISM or Eastern philosophy. His ʼTranscendentalism attracted a number of followers and became a springboard for incorporating these ideas in THEOSOPHY, metaphysical groups, NEW THOUGHT, and Mind Sciences.]

E-meter (SCIENTOLOGY). A device used by an ʼauditor or practitioner of Scientology to measure electrical impulses flowing from the body during a counseling session. Scientologists claim the E-meter helps in the diagnosis and removal of negative forces in a patient's life, thereby paving the way to becoming a ʼclear.

Endowments (MORMONISM). Term used to designate any and all ceremonies and rituals in the Latter-Day Saints temples, such as secret oaths and other forms of symbolic gesture.

Engrams (SCIENTOLOGY). Negative events that transpire in one's life are recorded on the ʼreactive mind in the form of engrams. These negative forces are not available to the ʼanalytical mind but affect it by blocking messages, thereby causing a reaction directly because of undetected previous experiences. Once detected through auditing (see ʼauditor), the engram can be erased and normal behavior follows.

Enkanika (ʼoccult; ABAKUA). Afro-Cuban bells (usually metal) used in Abakua cultic rituals.

Enlightenment (CHRISTIANITY; HINDUISM; NEW AGE MOVEMENT). In Christianity, the Enlightenment was the time in which reason enjoyed an hegemonic role in Christian culture. For Hinduism, enlightenment is the state reached when ʼatman (the inner soul) arrives at the end of its quest and realizes a sense of deity and personal oneness with the universe (*see* ʼnirvana). For the New Age Movement, enlightenment is a theme that repristinates back to the meaning generally accepted in Hindu thought, namely, that salvation is a matter of self-understanding and enlightenment.

Enlil (ʼoccult). The Sumerian god of the storms, wind, and air, who later became known as the god of the earth and was eventually adopted as the Babylonian god ʼBel.

Enneagram (ʼastrology; ʼoccult). A circle divided into nine equal points. The ennegram is rooted in the Kabbalist (see ʼKabbala) tradition, astrology, and ʼdivination. The numbers are linked to personality types. The enneagram has come into popular usage among many people today; there is a growing number of books written about how to understand and use it.

Entered Apprentice; First Degree (FREEMASONRY). The first degree awarded to a candidate for membership in the ʼBlue Lodge in Freemasonry. A member can only begin to earn this degree if recommended by a member and presented before the lodge.

Eon (ʼoccult; ABAKUA; SOUTH AMERICAN, CENTRAL AMERICAN, AND CARIBBEAN CULTS). Afro-Cuban rhythmic instrument or rattle used in Abakua rituals.

Ephemerus (ʼastrology; ʼoccult). Book used by practitioners of astrology to chart planets.

Equinox (ʼoccult; WITCHCRAFT). See ʼwitches' calendar.

Erhard Seminars Training, EST; Landmark Forum; Landmark Education (FORUM, LANDMARK FORUM). Erhard Seminars Training was founded by Werner Hans ʼErhard (aka, Jack ʼRosenberg) in 1971 as part of the "human potential movement," which eventually blended into the NEW AGE MOVEMENT. EST is its abbreviated form. After a series of legal battles, EST was repackaged as The Forum, which was the same basic training. Erhard quit his corporations in 1991 and left the United States, after training some 700,000 people in EST. In 1985, his brother, Harry Rosenberg, purchased Erhard's training and founded Landmark Forum. This was changed in 1991 to Landmark Education of San Francisco, California, which boasts 42 offices in 11 countries and an annual income that exceeds fifty million dollars. The new course has changed some 300,000 people thus far and is foundationally a Zen Buddhist (ZEN BUDDHISM) philosophy mixed with existential philosophy and motivational speaking to destroy old beliefs and build the new you.

Erhard, Werner Hans (FORUM, LANDMARK FORUM; NEW AGE MOVEMENT; 1935–). Werner Hans Erhard, born as John Paul (Jack) ʾRosenberg on September 5, 1935, was a former Scientologist (SCIENTOLOGY) and ʾMind Dynamics student, who founded ʾEST/Erhard Seminars Training.

Erikunde (ʾoccult; ABAKUA; SOUTH AMERICAN, CENTRAL AMERICAN, AND CARIBBEAN CULTS). Cuban drums or ʾmaracas; *erikunde* are also cowbells adorned in straw.

Erzulie (VOODOO). The Haitian voodoo goddess who represents both love and beauty.

Esbat (ʾoccult; SATANISM; WITCHCRAFT). The term designating the ʾwitches' Sabbath, occurring on the night of each full moon. In Satanism, esbats are weekly meetings.

Eschatology (CHRISTIANITY). From the Greek word *eschatos*, meaning "last things." Eschatology is the study of the doctrine of the end of time and how Christianity understands the consummation of history. Eschatology is a key theme in many ʾcults, especially in their views of ʾArmageddon, the ʾMillennium, ʾhell, and the like.

Eshu (CANDOMBLE; SOUTH AMERICAN, CENTRAL AMERICAN, AND CARIBBEAN CULTS; VOODOO). The mediator between the gods and humanity; Eshu is also the deity of fate and destiny. In Candomble, Eshu is usually the first deity to be invoked at a ceremony.

Esoteric (ʾgnosticism; ʾoccult). A general term that remains virtually unaltered from its conventional definition in English dictionaries. The basic thrust is that of possessing knowledge or truths that remain hidden, secret, or veiled to those who have not been designated or initiated to receive it. The ancient gnostics defined themselves as possessing esoteric knowledge.

Esoteric Council (CHRIST THE SAVIOR BROTHERHOOD). Name formerly given to priests who were directly under the ʾdirector general in the Holy Order of Mans, now called Christ the Savior Brotherhood. The new name for esoteric council is ʾapostolic council.

ESP (ʾoccult). ʾAcronym for ʾExtrasensory Perception.

Essenes (JUDAISM). An important Jewish ʾsect that lived on the western shore of the Dead Sea. The Essenes probably first banded together around the second century B.C. and lasted throughout the second century A.D., though they are not mentioned in the New Testament. Josephus, Philo of Alexandria, and Pliny the Elder all give varying accounts of how the Essenes lived. Despite differing accounts, we do know that the Essenes were rigorous ʾascetics, strictly adhering to the ʾTorah. They observed the ʾSabbath as a day of prayer and fasting. Proselytes underwent three years of training before they were allowed to be incorporated into the community and participate in its communal meals. Some scholars have surmised that John the Baptist and Jesus were Essenes, but these claims are not upheld by the evidence. Through the discovery of the Dead Sea Scrolls in the late 1940s in the vicinity of Qumran, a consensus among scholars have developed that that ancient community was Essene.

EST See the forum.

Eternal Life (CHRISTIANITY; MORMONISM). In Christianity, eternal life is that which Jesus promises to all those who believe in him (see John 3:16). They will escape the punishment of ʾhell.

In Mormonism, eternal life, also called ʾexaltation, is the highest degree of attainment for the Mormon. One who receives it is able to become a god. The teaching specifically states,

> Very gladly would the Lord give to everyone eternal life, but since that blessing can come only on merit—through the faithful performance of duty—only those who are worthy shall receive it. . . . To receive the exaltation of the righteous, in other words, eternal life, the commandments of the Lord must be kept in all things. (Smith, *Doctrines of Salvation*, 2:5–6).

An essential requirement of the law that must be kept is that one must have a ʾcelestial marriage. Such a marriage will allow those who receive eternal life to bear children in heaven. Eternal life transports one to the highest of the three Mormon heavens.

Eternal Retribution See ʾhell.

Ether (ʾoccult). The life fluid that pervades all matter.

Etheric Body (ʾoccult; SPIRITUALISM). Also called ʾspirit body. The prevailing idea is that a person possesses two bodies: the physical body, which is visible and dies; and the etheric body, which is nonmaterial and lives on after death.

Etheric Plane (ʾoccult). The spiritual dimension where the spirits of the departed pass through the gates of death. It lies near but outside the earth and is the plane that ʾmediums contact in an attempt to communicate with the spirit world.

Eutychianism (CHRISTIANITY). See ʾmonophysitism.

Evangelicalism; Evangelicals (CHRISTIANITY). General term used in a wide sense for all forms of Christianity that emphasize the importance of preaching the gospel. In the narrower sense, this term is applied to a trans-denominational movement of conservative Christians who shy away from the negative connotations of ʼfundamentalism, chief of which is its alleged anti-intellectual tendencies. Evangelicals strive to combine faith with reason and find compatibility and common ground with science and academia.

Evans, Warren Felt (NEW THOUGHT; 1817–1889). One of the founding leaders of New Thought.

Evil Eye (ʼoccult; SATANISM). The superstitious belief that certain individuals possess the power to cast a ʼspell on others by merely looking at them. ʼAmulets and ʼcharms are believed to be successful protection against, or antidotes to, the evil eye.

Evil Slave (JEHOVAH'S WITNESSES). Term used for those whom the Watchtower Bible and Tract Society has deemed ʼapostates or enemies of the organization.

Evocation (ʼoccult). The calling up of a ʼspirit in ceremonial ʼmagic. The contemporary ceremonies are generally done within the eternal ʼcircle in order to protect the practitioner from harm by any spirit that is successfully called up or evoked.

Exaltation (MORMONISM). Synonymous with "eternal life," exaltation is the highest degree of salvation. Only those who have been obedient to the "laws and ordinances of the gospel" are eligible for this estate. Those meriting exaltation actually become gods and procreate continuously throughout all eternity, according to Mormon theology.

Exegesis (CHRISTIANITY). Term used in ʼhermeneutics. The meaning of a passage is determined or taken "out of" (*ex*) Scripture, based on the context and intended meaning of the biblical author. The reverse of this process is called ʼeisegesis, that is, the reading "into" (*eis*) a text something outside of the immediate context of a given passage. It is important to note this distinction since many ʼcult leaders, when quoting the Bible, do not consider the context and intended meaning of a passage. Instead, they tend to read into the Bible an agenda foreign to the biblical context.

Existentialism (CHRISTIANITY). More of a philosophical term than a theological one, existentialism has played a significant role in the last two centuries of Christian history. Many consider the Danish philosopher Søren Kierkegaard (1813–1855) as the "father of existentialism." Kierkegaard contended that true Christianity involves experiencing it in one's present state of consciousness and being aware of one's existence in the way that was experienced by Jesus Christ himself. It is an awareness and state of the human subject and condition, not a phenomenon that can be merely reported as historical objectivity. Such authentic experience includes a life of self-denial, an emphasis on servanthood, renunciation of this-worldly ambition and prosperity, and a personal encounter with God.

Kierkegaard's writings greatly influenced Christianity in the latter half of the twentieth century. It gave birth to a significant part of the formulation of the theology of ʼevangelicalism, chiefly in the ʼborn again movement. Other Christian existentialists include prominent Russian thinkers and philosophers such as Fyodor Dostoevsky (1821–1881) and Nickolas Berdyev (1874–1948).

A non-Christian existentialism also developed in the nineteenth and twentieth centuries. When the emphasis of personal experience became a chief criteria for evaluating both epistemological and ontological truth claims with regard to Christianity, the stage was set for personal experience to eventually overrule Christian truth claims altogether and describe human existence *apart* from Christianity. The chief architect of a non-Christian existentialism was the French philosopher Jean Paul Sartre (1905–1980). Numerous others have followed in his steps, including such postmodernist thinkers as Michael Foucault (1926–1984) and Jacques Derrida (1930–2004).

Exorcism (ʼoccult; SATANISM). The practice of driving out an evil spirit (or spirits) through the aid of divine power. The Christian church practices exorcism to a lesser extent than in the past, but it still occurs. Generally, it is regarded as an occult phenomenon.

Extrasensory Perception (ESP) (ʼoccult). The ability to perceive an event or idea through a means beyond the five senses. ʼtelepathy, ʼdivination, and ʼclairvoyance are among the many ʼoccult practices that utilize ESP. Extrasensory perception can be practiced in various states of awareness, such as while being awake or by sleeping and dreaming. It is often called "the sixth sense."

Eye Biting (ʼoccult). To bring a curse by the mere glance of an eye (same as ʼevil eye).

F

Fairies   See ▸nature spirits.

Fakir   (ISLAM). A Muslim ▸ascetic, from the Arabic word meaning "a poor person." Fakirs were associated with the ▸whirling dervish and were often found to be beggars and alms-seekers.

Fall   (CHRISTIANITY; MORMONISM). The Mormon church teaches that the fall of Adam and Eve resulted in temporal death and mortality. But Mormons do not see the Fall as an unfortunate event. Rather, it was desirable and highly necessary. As it turns out, without the Fall no children would ever have been born (2 Nephi 2:22–25).

But here arises a theological problem of great import, as Christianity is quick to point out: What of God's commandment that Adam and Eve were not to partake of the forbidden fruit? Did not their disobedience constitute a sin in the eyes of the Lord? Mormons are not agreed on how to solve this dilemma. Some maintain that Adam had in fact sinned, but God used it for good (Brigham ▸Young), while others argue that the Fall did not constitute a real sin (Joseph ▸Smith Jr.). In either case, while mortality and physical death was brought on by the Fall, the virtue of its necessity prevents the Mormon church from maintaining that humankind inherited a fallen and sinful nature.

False Prophecy; False Prophet   (CHRISTIANITY). Any teaching by a ▸prophet that turns out to be false or a prediction that does not come to pass labels that so-called prophet as false. The ▸Bible clearly states this guideline in identifying and distinguishing false prophets from true (Deuteronomy 13:1–5; 18:20–22). Many ▸cult leaders make predictions that do not come to pass.

Fama Fraternitatis   (▸occult; ROSICRUCIANISM). Reference book explaining the teachings of practices of Rosicrucianism.

Famba   (▸occult; ABAKUA; SOUTH AMERICAN, CENTRAL AMERICAN, AND CARIBBEAN CULTS). Afro-Cuban temple; the temple used for Abakua worship.

Familiar   (▸occult; SATANISM; WITCHCRAFT). In older forms of ▸Gothic witchcraft, a familiar was a ▸demon who acted as a companion or attendant to ▸witches.

Sometimes human, familiars were believed to assume the shape of animals. Witches, according to these beliefs, frequently consulted their familiars for various purposes, such as ▸spell-casting and ▸omens. In the literature, familiars were addressed by name, such as Phrin, Josophat, Grimoald (the name of Oliver Cromwell's familiar), and Zewviel.

Fana   (ISLAM; SUFISM). "Consumed with God." The mystic Abu Hamid Ghazali wrote, "When the worshiper no longer thinks of his worship or himself but is altogether absorbed in Him whom he worships, that state is called *fana*." After the worshiper seeks forgiveness from ▸Allah, he or she then is absolved by ▸Muhammad and is then able to merge into oneness with the divine. The concept of *fana* finds greatest appeal in the ▸Sufist expression of Islam.

Fantasy Role Playing Games: (FRP)   (▸occult). Games such as ▸*Dungeons and Dragons*, where players assume roles of mythical or historical characters. These games have caused concern because of the addictive and time-consuming nature of the games, the emphasis on ▸spells, the occult, violence, rape, theft, and in some cases even suicide.

Farrakhan, Louis   (NATION OF ISLAM; b. 1933). Present leader of the Nation of Islam.

Fard, Wallace   (NATION OF ISLAM; 1877–1940). Born in ▸Mecca, founder of the Black Muslim Movement.

Fascination   (▸occult; SATANISM; WITCHCRAFT). Casting a ▸spell through the use of the ▸evil eye. In Satanism and some extreme witchcraft, fascination was used for evil purposes. Modern ▸witches, however, do not. They are forbidden by the ▸wiccan Rede from doing so.

Father David   (THE FAMILY; 1919–1994). An assumed name for David ▸Berg, the founder of the former Children of God, now called The Family.

Fatwa   (ISLAM). An Islamic religious ruling or an informed scholarly opinion. A *fatwa* is issued by an authority figure and is binding in most, but not all, cases.

Feast of Sacrifice   (ISLAM). The offering up and sacrifice of sheep. Half of the meat is to be allocated to the poor, according to Islam.

Fellow Craft; Second Degree (FREEMASONRY). The second degree one achieves as an initiate in the ᐧBlue Lodge of Freemasonry.

Feminine Signs (ᐧastrology; ᐧoccult). Those ᐧsigns of the ᐧzodiac whose sequence occurs in even numbers, namely, ᐧTaurus, ᐧCancer, ᐧVirgo, ᐧScorpio, ᐧCapricorn, and ᐧPisces.

Fertility Deities (ᐧoccult). Gods and goddesses who represent the cycles of rebirth that take place throughout the rhythm of the year and seasons. Fertility is that part of the cycle in which death is transformed into life.

This pentagram ring was worn by a former witch as a fetish or talisman in order protect her from evil spirits.
Courtesy Jack M. Roper/CARIS

Fetish (ᐧoccult; SANTERIA; SOUTH AMERICAN, CENTRAL AMERICAN, AND CARIBBEAN CULTS). Belief held particularly in West African religions that spirits are able to possess objects. Also the belief that certain objects or ᐧtalismans may ward off evil spirits.

FFing (THE FAMILY). Term meaning "flirty fishing." FFing is one of Moses ᐧDavid's "evangelism" techniques. Female members of the Children of God offer sexual intercourse (for money) as a means to induce males to join the movement or to raise money for the movement.

Fifth Root Race (ᐧoccult; THEOSOPHY). The present state of existence of the human race. In Theosophy thought there are but two more root races to follow, the sixth and seventh, completing the wheel of development.

Figure (ᐧoccult). Synonym for ᐧhoroscope.

Fillmore, Charles S. (UNITY SCHOOL OF CHRISTIANITY; 1854–1948). Cofounder with his wife, Myrtle ᐧFillmore, of the Unity School of Christianity.

Fillmore, Myrtle (UNITY SCHOOL OF CHRISTIANITY; 1845–1931). Cofounder with her husband, Charles ᐧFillmore, of the Unity School of Christianity.

Finger (ᐧoccult; WITCHCRAFT). Spiritual power, according to certain witchcraft and occult beliefs, emanates from the index finger. It is known as the "cursing finger" or the "witch finger."

Fire (ᐧoccult). Symbolizing ᐧSatan, fire is one of the four ᐧelementals.

Fire-walking (ᐧoccult). The uncanny ability to walk through fire without being burned or harmed in any way. The practice is widespread in occult circles throughout the world.

First Church of Christ Scientist See CHRISTIAN SCIENCE.

First Presidency (MORMONISM). The highest authority within the Mormon church; the First Presidency consists of the ᐧpresident and two counselors. These are charged with the chief administrative functions in the church, and although each Mormon may receive private ᐧrevelations from God, only the president may speak officially with authoritative revelation for the church.

First Vision (MORMONISM). First vision is a reference to the first time God appeared to Joseph ᐧSmith in the spring of 1820 when he was fourteen years old. Smith reports that he had been meditating on James 1:5: "If any of you lack wisdom, let him ask of God, that giveth to all men liberally, and upbraideth not; and it shall be given him" (KJV).

Smith goes on to say that while alone in the woods, "I kneeled down and began to offer up the desires of my heart to God. I had scarcely done so when I was seized on by some power which entirely overcame me. . . . I saw a pillar of light exactly over my head. . . . When the light rested on me, I saw two Personages whose brightness and glory defy all description, standing above me in the air. One of them spoke unto me, calling me by name, and said—pointing to the other—This is My Beloved Son. Hear Him!" (*The Prophet Joseph Smith's Testimony* [Salt Lake City: Church of Jesus Christ of Latter-Day Saints, 1984], 5). Smith inquired of God which of all the ᐧsects he should join. He was reportedly told in the vision to "join none of them, for they were all wrong." Other visions soon followed. There are five different accounts of this "first vision" that contradict each other.

Five Great Vows (JAINISM). According to Jainist beliefs, five laws must be strictly followed: (1) the denial of killing living things; (2) do not practice dishonesty; (3) avoid avarice; (4) sexual gratification; and (5) avoid all worldly attachments.

Five K's, The (SIKHISM). Five principles ascribed to by orthodox ᐧSikhs, all beginning with the letter "k." These include long hair (*kesa*), comb (*kangha*), short pants (*kacha*), a metal bracelet (*kachu*), and sword (*kirpan*).

Five Pillars, The (ISLAM). The five basic practices required of every follower of Islam: (1) daily recitation of the ᐧshahada; (2) the ᐧsalat, or prayers uttered five times daily while facing ᐧMecca; (3) ᐧsakat, the giving of alms; (4) ʼ*sawm*, a period of fasting during the month of ʼRamadan; and (5) the ʼ*hajj*, or a pilgrimage to Mecca expected of every ʼMuslim at least once in a lifetime, provided one can afford to make the journey.

Five Violations (BUDDHISM). Crimes that, when committed, disqualify a person from attaining ʼenlightenment. They are parricide, matricide, the murder of an ʼ*arhat*, disturbing a community of Buddhist monks, and hitting a ʼbuddha and drawing blood.

Fivefold Kiss (WITCHCRAFT). Five separate kisses characterize the fivefold kiss. The devotee kisses each foot, each knee, the lower abdomen, each breast, and the lips.

Flagae (ʼoccult; WITCHCRAFT). An imaginary belief of ʼGothic witchcraft of ʼfamiliars appearing to a ʼwitch or ʼmedium who gives secretive information while appearing in a mirror.

Fluid Body (ʼoccult; THEOSOPHY). Synonymous with ʼastral body.

Flying Ointment (ʼoccult; WITCHCRAFT). Ointment used by ʼwitches in the Middle Ages to enable them to fly to the witches' ʼSabbath. Studies have shown that several of the ingredients used are able to produce delusions. A typical recipe for flying ointment included aconite, belladonna, hellebore root, and the drug-inducing atropine that may have caused the illusion of flying.

Fo (BUDDHISM). The term for a ʼbuddha who has reached the point where he is ready to attain ʼnirvana.

Fonta (URANTIA). Name for one of the parents of the human race (see ʼ*Andon*).

Forbidden (ISLAM). Practices that are forbidden according to Islam include: eating pork and other forbidden foods, slander, usury, sodomy, homosexuality, adultery, and the consumption of alcohol and all intoxicating beverages.

Forau (ʼoccult). A brigadier of hell who can disappear at will and has great knowledge of the occult.

Ford, Desmond (SEVENTH-DAY ADVENTISM; 1938–). Controversial figure within Adventist circles. Ford, Australian by birth, came to the United States in 1977 to teach at Pacific Union College. He was asked to lecture on his views concerning the "investigative judgment" and other related themes. This immediately invited controversy and he was told to commit his specific views to writing. The Seventh-day Adventist leadership decided in 1980 that his views were in error, despite the fact that they agreed with seven out of ten of his points. His dismissal from his teaching and removal of his ministerial credentials invited further controversy and received national media attention. Ford continues to work independently through a nonprofit ministry called Good News Unlimited, where he serves as president. He travels, teaches, and lectures worldwide and continues to write. His special areas of interest have included Pauline studies, the Reformation, health, fitness and nutrition, and ʼeschatology.

Forrest, Nathan Bedford (IDENTITY MOVEMENTS; 1821–1877). The first ʼgrand wizard of the ʼKu-Klux-Klan.

Fort, Charles Hoy (ʼoccult; 1847–1932). A nineteenth-century American author who wrote much about psychic research and ʼghost(s). Some argue that Hoy was a modern-day precursor of the widespread interest in UFOs. Hoy authored such books as *The Book of the Damned* (1919) and *Wild Talents* (1932).

Fortified (ʼastrology; ʼoccult). A well-aspected (*see* ʼaspect) ʼsign in a ʼhoroscope.

Fortune-Telling (ʼoccult). One of the three branches of the occult. Fortune-telling involves ʼdivination and takes such forms as the reading of ʼtarot cards, ʼcrystal balls, ʼnumerology, and the like. The two other branches of the occult are ʼmagic and SPIRITUALISM.

A fortune teller at work at the Renaissance Fair, held in Bristol, Wisconsin.   Courtesy Jack M. Roper/CARIS

Fortune-Telling Forms (ʼoccult). ʼRod and pendulum, ʼhoroscope, ʼcrystal ball, ʼpalmistry, ʼtarot cards, and ʼpsychometry.

Forum (FORUM, EST; URANTIA). In Urantia foundation, The Forum is the founding members of the Urantia Society. It is made up of thirty-six devotees dedicated to the study of *The Urantia Book*. In ᴾErhardt Seminar Training (EST), the second group name was the Forum, whose founder, Werner ᴾErhardt abandoned EST.

Fourfold Path (SATCHIDANANDA ASHRAM INTEGRAL YOGA INSTITUTE). The four different ways advocated by the Divine Light Society leading to knowledge of divine things as taught by ᴾguru ᴾMaharaj Ji: the ᴾthird ear, the ᴾthird eye, ᴾdivine nectar, and primordial vibration.

Four-Footed Signs (ᴾastrology; ᴾoccult). The ᴾsigns of the ᴾzodiac that are represented by four-footed creatures. They are ᴾAries, ᴾCapricorn, ᴾLeo, ᴾSagittarius, and ᴾTaurus.

Four Great Vows (ZEN BUDDHISM). Four daily chants of a devout Zen Buddhist.

Four Noble Truths (BUDDHISM; ZEN BUDDHISM). The four fundamental principles on which Buddhism is based. (1) All suffering is universal. (2) Suffering has a cause grounded in ignorance. (3) It is possible that suffering may be eliminated. (4) There is a path that leads to that cessation of suffering (see ᴾEightfold Path).

Fourth Root Race (ᴾoccult; THEOSOPHY). The civilization and epoch just before the one in which the human race now lives. It came to an abrupt end when the civilization of ᴾAtlantis disappeared into the ocean.

Fourth Way (OUSPENSKY-GURDJIEFF). Name for a principle developed by George Ivanovitch ᴾGurdjieff that proposes that one can develop a fully harmonized self through transcending of body, mind, and emotional centers of the self. This "transcending" is the "fourth way" and is an energy that intersperses and develops the former three.

Fox Sisters (SPIRITUALISM). Kate Fox (1841–1892) and Margaretta Fox (1838–1893) are the original initiators of modern spiritualism (see article).

Franz, Frederick (JEHOVAH'S WITNESSES; 1894–1992). President of the Watchtower Bible and Tract Society. Franz succeeded Nathan H. ᴾKnorr after the latter died in 1977. Franz has been successful in maintaining high visibility for the organization. He died of cardiac arrest on December 22, 1992.

Frazer, Sir James George (ᴾoccult; 1854–1951). English scholar, anthropologist, and author of a famous work, *The Golden Bough: A Study in Magic and Religion*. Frazer attempted to develop an anthropological evolution of religion, ᴾmagic, and science. He understood magic as it is defined in this book—the ability to control and manipulate nature through supernatural means, and he believed that those who practice magic were using faulty and illogical reasoning. To him, religion was the appeal to the supernatural for divine aid and help. Science is the emergence of the ways of the modern mind, no longer needing to appeal to religion and magic. These ideas, although rejected by modern anthropologists, represented the first attempt to narrate a wide-ranging phenomenological account of the development of magic and religion. Other works by Frazer include *Totemism and Exogamy* (1910) and *Folk-lore in the Old Testament* (1918). Frazer was knighted in 1914.

Friends (JEHOVAH'S WITNESSES). Term that the members of the Watchtower Bible and Tract Society use to identify fellow members.

Frig (ᴾoccult). The Saxon goddess of fertility known for incorporating sensuality and accused of adultery. She protects life and shares wisdom with her husband and is the maternal principle. Her name may be translated either "spouse" or "she who is loved."

Frustration (ᴾastrology; ᴾoccult). A condition in astrology involving three planets in conflict. Frustration occurs when one of the three "frustrates" the ᴾaspects of the remaining two.

Full Moon (ᴾoccult). The belief among many practitioners of the occult that a full moon more powerfully effects ᴾmagic.

Fuller, Curtis (ᴾoccult; 1912–). American journalist who in 1948 founded *Fate* magazine, which became a popular occult periodical internationally.

Fuller, John Frederick Charles (ᴾoccult; 1878–1966). British soldier and historian whose association with the occult came with his relationship to Aleister ᴾCrowley. Fuller became one of Crowley's disciples. His tribute to his mentor came in the form of a book titled *The Star in the West* (1907). Fuller is probably the one who invented the term "Crowleyanity" to describe his teacher's thought.

Fundamentalism (CHRISTIANITY). A movement within Christendom that began during the late nineteenth century and was carried to fruition in the early twentieth. It was a conservative movement that raised a voice against liberalism. The 1909 publication *The Fundamentals* was a reiteration of an earlier formulation of the 1895 Niagara Bible Conference, which proposed five necessary standards of Christian belief: (1) the inerrancy of the ᴾBible; (2) the virgin birth of Jesus; (3) the substitutionary atonement; (4) the physical resurrection of Jesus; (5) Jesus' imminent return to earth. Fundamentalism was embraced chiefly by Presbyterian and Baptist churches wishing to raise a voice of protest against those who espoused nineteenth-century liberalism and Darwinism. It became popularized throughout the Christian world in 1925 when William Jennings Bryan (1860–1925) prosecuted John T. Scopes, a Dayton, Tennessee, school teacher, who taught evolution in the public school.

The term "fundamentalism" is now applied to various conservative denominations that continue to repudiate liberalism. The term generally connotes an image of anti-intellectualism and is often used pejoratively as such. Many conservative Christians prefer to call themselves ᐟevangelicals.

"Fundamentalism" or "fundamentalist" is also used to describe the tendency toward right wing extremism in the many religions throughout the world.

Furfur (ᐟoccult; SATANISM). A winged stag with human arms and flaming tale that in ᐟdemonology is the count of hell.

Fylfot Cross (ᐟoccult). A cross shaped like a swastika, used in occult circles. Many fylfot crosses are divided into four squares bearing the twelve ᐟsigns of the ᐟzodiac with the sun at the center.

G

Gaia Hypothesis (NEW AGE MOVEMENT). The theory held to by some New Age Movement practitioners that the earth is a living organism comprising many living systems and behaves much like the human body. The word *gaia* is the Greek word for "earth."

Gandhi, Mahatma (HINDUISM; 1869–1948). One of the most influential religious leaders of the twentieth century, Gandhi is most well known for his philosophy, teaching, and practice of peaceful resistance to the oppression of British imperialism. Gandhi was educated in England where he first started reading the ᐟBible and the ᐟ*Bhagavad Gita*, ᐟBlavatsky's *Key to Theosophy,* and Edwin Arnold's *The Light of Asia.* He also became a vegetarian at this time. Reading the great religious texts led him to embrace the principles of religious toleration, renunciation, and nonviolence, which he practiced in both South Africa against the white government who held the small Indian population in contempt, and in India against British oppression of his countrymen.

Gandhi led India in a long struggle for independence, which came in 1947. Continued violence within India among Islamic and Hindu countrymen caused him to fast almost to the point of death. In spite of this, he was greatly disappointed when India was partitioned off religiously into Hindu India and Muslim Pakistan. He was killed by an assassin at the age of 79 in January, 1948, in New Delhi.

Ganges (HINDUISM). Located in India, the most sacred of rivers of Hinduism, called the Ganga Mai (Mother Ganges). The river's source is in the Himalayas, and it flows eastward for one thousand miles to empty into the Bay of Bengal in Bangladesh. Hindus believe its source to have been from the lotus feet of ᐟVishnu and that the river has the power to cleanse and purify. By bathing in it, one's soul may be washed of all sins. Drinking the water allegedly cures illnesses and disease. At numerous junctures along the banks of the river are *ghats* (steps leading down to the water). Here Hindus bathe before offering up their prayers; cremation also takes place here, and the ashes of the departed are scattered into the sacred waters. Currently, it is estimated that close to three hundred million people live in the Ganges Valley.

Ganja (RASTAFARIANISM). Marijuana smoked by members of the Rastafarians.

Gardner, Gerald (ᐟoccult; WITCHCRAFT; 1884–1964). Noted occult practitioner who joined the ᐟOrdo Templi Orientis under the influence of Aleister ᐟCrowley. When laws prohibiting the practice of witchcraft were repealed in 1951, Gardner broke away from the ᐟOTO and formed his own ᐟcoven. He has been largely touted as responsible for the revival of witchcraft in the twentieth century. His writings included *High Magick's Aid* (1949), *Witchcraft Today* (1954), and *The Meaning of Witchcraft* (1959). Besides Crowley, Gardner was also influenced by Margaret ᐟMurray and numerous occult writings; his own writings remain the largest influence over modern pagan and witchcraft groups. His noted converts include Alexander ᐟSanders, Sybil ᐟLeek, and Raymond and Rosemary Buckland.

Gardnerians (WITCHCRAFT). *Witches who belong to or follow the teachings of Gerald *Gardner.

Garments (MORMONISM). Mormons who serve in the temple wear special vestments and underclothes that are marked and cut in several places to symbolize the oaths made in temple rituals. The reason given for wearing garments is because Adam and Eve were covered when their nakedness became shameful because of their sinful act of disobedience against God.

Garters (*occult; WITCHCRAFT). Tabs tied to the leg above the knee marking one's rank in some witchcraft *covens.

Garuda (HINDUISM). The bird on which *Vishnu rides.

Garuda Mantra (HINDUISM). A *mantra that, when chanted, is able to cure one bitten by a poisonous snake.

Garvey, Marcus (NATION OF ISLAM; RASTAFARIANISM; 1887–1940). The person who started the Universal Negro Improvement Association.

Gautama, Siddharta (BUDDHISM; 563–483 B.C.). After much soul-searching, at the age of thirty-five, Gautama determined to sit down under a tree until he had attained *enlightenment. This effort resulted in the liquidation of all of his ignorance and the acquisition of the knowledge that became the essence of Buddhist thought.

Gede (VOODOO). Deity of death and specifically for the dead.

Geller, Uri (*occult; 1946–). Born in Israel, Geller achieved fame through his alleged ability to use the power of his mind to bend steel objects. Geller is a controversial figure. While being examined by scientists and Stanford University Research Institute, he refused to submit himself to the examination of the Society for Psychical Research in England. Illusionist James "the Amazing" Randi exposed Uri Geller's tricks by duplicating the same feats on the Johnny Carson show in 1972.

Gelospy (*occult). The act of performing *divination based on listening to a person's laughter.

Gemini (*astrology; *occult). Taken from the Latin word meaning "twins," Gemini is the third *sign of the *zodiac, governing the period between May 21 and June 21. In astronomy, the two brightest stars in the constellation of Gemini are Castor and Pollux, which are the names of the mythical twins. Geminis are said to be materialistic, unstable, and hypocritical, but also expressive, overt, and outgoing toward other people. Geminis are believed to possess the right combination of characteristics for politics, histrionics, and other forms of public expression.

Genii (ISLAM). Labeled in Islam as *jinn*, a class of superior beings that predates Adam and Eve. According to the *Koran, these creatures were in a state of existence between angels and humans and were even employed by Solomon to build his wondrous temple.

Gentile (JUDAISM; MORMONISM). In Mormonism, a non-Mormon; even Jews are considered to be Gentiles. In Judaism, the term Gentile is an ethnic term that applies to all non-Jews.

Geomancy (*occult). A form of *divination that utilizes a globe or map.

Germain See CHURCH UNIVERSAL AND TRIUMPHANT.

Germer, Karl (*occult; 1885–1962), Noted German occultist who succeeded Aleister *Crowley in 1947 as head of *Ordo Templi Orientis. Germer did much to promote the publication of Crowley's works, particularly those previously unpublished.

Gestic Magic (*occult). Seeking the aid of evil spirits to practice *black magic.

Ghost (*occult). An *apparition; a manifestation or appearance of a spirit being, usually of one who has departed this life. According to traditional CHRISTIANITY, ghosts are really the manifestations of *demons or *angels insofar as the departed are not able to return to the world and manifest themselves in any way. The Nicene Creed states that God created "all things visible and invisible." Angels and demons/ghosts are classed as part of this invisible world. The term ghost also applies to numerous other occult manifestations.

Ghoul (*occult; SATANISM). An evil spirit or demonic presence who robs graves in order to feed on the corpses of the dead. A ghoul is among the most frightening and dangerous of all the *demons. In Arabia, legends have it that ghouls lurk in secret, dark places and not only feed on dead bodies but terrorize and kill the living.

Gilead Watchtower Bible School (JEHOVAH'S WITNESSES). A Bible college opened in 1943 and owned and operated by the Watchtower Bible and Tract Society for the express purpose of educating and training workers. Originally located in upstate New York, the school was relocated to Columbia Heights in Brooklyn in 1960, across from the Society's headquarters. The training period normally lasts for ten months. Workers unable to attend the Gilead school can attend shorter training periods at the Kingdom Ministry School.

Glossolalia (CHRISTIANITY). From the Greek for "tongue" and "speaking," that is, "speaking in tongues."

This is one of the several gifts of the Holy Spirit mentioned by Paul in 1 Corinthians 12:8–10, whereby the one possessing such a gift is able to speak the praises of God in a tongue unknown to him or her. It became a popular phenomenon in the history of the church, especially in the nineteenth century when it was brought back into usage by revivalist groups in England and by Pentecostalism in early twentieth-century America. "Speaking in tongues" is a normative practice among Pentecostal and charismatic Christians.

Glottologus (ᴵoccult). A ᴵmedium who possesses the ability to speak in unknown tongues.

Gnomes (ᴵoccult). Name for ᴵelemental(s) spirits, also for subterranean dwarfs. They are believed to be friendly and live much like human beings do.

Gnosticism (CHRISTIANITY). From the Greek word *gnosis* (knowledge), second-century gnostics formed a ᴵsect that championed a secret knowledge that they claimed rendered them superior to common Christians. The movement arose from pre-Christian pagan philosophies emanating from Babylon, Egypt, Syria, and Greece (Macedonia). Combining pagan philosophy, some ᴵastrology, and Greek mystery religions with the apostolic doctrines of Christianity, gnosticism became a strong influence in the ancient church.

Gnosticism's basic premise is a dualistic (*see* ᴵdualism) worldview. The Supreme Father God emanated from the "good" spirit world. From him proceeded successive finite beings (ᴵaeons), one of which (Sophia) gave birth to a demiurge (creator-God). The creator-God brought forth the material (and hence evil) world together with all of the various organic and inorganic things that constitute it.

Christian gnostics such as Marcion (d. ca. A.D. 160) and Valentinus taught that salvation comes through one of the aeons, Christ, who slipped by the evil powers of darkness to convey the secret knowledge (*gnosis*) and release the captive spirits of light from the material earthly world to the higher spiritual world. Christ, although appearing to be human, never assumed a human body and therefore was not subject to human emotions and weaknesses.

Some evidence suggests that an incipient form of gnosticism arose in the apostolic era and was the focus of several of the New Testament letters (Colossians; Pastoral Letters; 1 John). The greatest polemic against the gnostics appears, however, in the patristic period with the apologetic writings of Irenaeus (ca. 130–ca. 200), Tertullian (ca. 160–ca. 225), and Hippolytus (ca. 170–ca. 236). Gnostics were branded as heretics and have always been regarded as such by ᴵorthodox Christians. Gnosticism is currently undergoing much research as a result of the discoveries in 1945–1946 of the Nag Hammadi texts in Egypt. Many ᴵcults and ᴵoccult groups claim some influence from ancient gnosticism. See also ᴵarchon.

Goat (ᴵoccult; SATANISM; WITCHCRAFT). A ᴵbaphomet image, also represented by "Pan," a mythological figure with the head of a goat with cloved hooves and the body of a man with arms and hands. In ᴵGothic witchcraft, it is the form or shape that the ᴵdevil assumes when he presides over the ᴵwitch's Sabbath. In Christianity, Christ is the Lamb of God who sacrificed himself to atone for the sins of the world. The followers of Jesus are therefore regarded as sheep. In the end of the world, the ᴵBible speaks of the Day of Judgment in which the sheep (believers) will be separated from the rebellious goats (children of the devil).

Goat's Foot (SATANISM). Symbol for the ᴵdevil.

Goat's Head (ᴵoccult; SATANISM). The goat's head is the direct symbol for ᴵSatan and death (*see also* ᴵgoat, ᴵbaphomet).

Jay Solomon (Yaj Nomolos), the leader of "The Embassy of Satan" (a splinter group of Anton ᴵLaVey's Church of Satan; *see* SATANISM), holds up a goat's head for sale in his ᴵoccult Emporium in a town in Pennsylvania. *Courtesy George Mather*

Goety (*occult). One form of *black magic among others, providing guidelines on how to make contact with the spirit world.

Gohonzon (BUDDHISM; NICHIREN SHOSHU BUDDHISM; SOKA-GAKKAI). Sacred scroll containing various divine names along with a drawing of the *Lotus Sutra. Gohonzon is one of the three sacred principles of Nichiren Shoshu (*see also* *Daimoku, *Kaidan).

Golden Candlestick (JUDAISM). Described in Exodus 25:31–37; 37:17–24, the golden candlestick (or lamp-stand or menorah) was actually seven lamps made of beaten gold. It consisted of a central stem with three branches on either side. The golden candlestick stood on the south side of the first section of the *tabernacle. It was lit each evening and restored each morning for use the next evening. Cotton drenched in olive oil nurtured and fueled the flame. When Solomon's *temple replaced the tabernacle, ten golden candlesticks were used instead of the one (1 Kings 7:49; 2 Chron. 4:7). During the Babylonian Captivity, the candlesticks, along with much of the other furnishings of the temple, were carried into Babylon. The new temple of Zerubbabel reverted back to the one candlestick (1 Macc. 1:21; 4:49). When Titus conquered Jerusalem in A.D. 70, the golden candlestick was removed and carried to Rome, where it later adorned the famous Arch of Titus built in A.D. 91, a monument to Rome's triumph over Jerusalem and Judaism.

Golden Plates See MORMONISM; *Book of Mormon.

Gorgon (*occult). A three-winged monster or three sisters, named Stethno, Eurale, and Medusa, possessing serpent-like hair. Their frightful stare could turn an unfortunate victim to stone.

Gospel of St. Barnabus (ISLAM). An apocryphal writing considered by Islam to be in basic concord with the *Koran insofar as doctrine and faith are concerned.

Gosvami (HINDUISM). Possessing control over the mind and senses.

Gothic Witchcraft (*occult; WITCHCRAFT). Name given for the specific form of witchcraft that dates back to the Middle Ages and popularized by The *Malleus Malificarum (*The Witches' Hammer*). This form of witchcraft is to be distinguished from modern-day *wicca, which claims that Gothic witchcraft had its beginnings in CHRISTIANITY, especially during the time of the Inquisition and beyond, when many people were accused of being witches and were executed by hangings, burnings, and torture. Modern day wicca argues that true witchcraft does not begin in the Gothic period but had its beginnings in Celtic paganism, which predated Christianity.

Govi (*occult; VOODOO). A clay jar used to retain the *petit bon ange, once it has been captured.

Grand Wizard (IDENTITY MOVEMENTS). The supreme leader in the *Ku Klux Klan.

Grant, Kenneth (*occult; 1924–). English occultist who, like Karl *Germer, continued to promote the teachings of Aleister *Crowley. Grant insisted he was head of the Ordo Templi Orientis, although his claim was disputed by the Berkley, California branch of the *OTO. Grant has authored several books on *magic, including *The Magical Review*, *Cults of the Shadow*, and *Outside the Circle of Time*.

Granth Sahib (SIKHISM). The sacred scriptures of Sikhism.

Grasshof, Louis von See Max *Heindel.

Great Awakenings, The (CHRISTIANITY). Two revival movements in American church history are known as the First and Second Great Awakening. The First Great Awakening was largely *Calvinist in spirit and broke out among the Dutch Reformed churches in New Jersey in 1726. The movement spread to New England, where it came under the influence of perhaps America's top theologian, Jonathan Edwards (1703–58), and his counterpart, George Whitefield (1714–70). Both of these, while interested in seeing genuine conversions to Christianity come about as a result of their preaching, repudiated excess emotionalism. As a result of the First Great Awakening, a sharp division ensued between the "Old Lights" (those who appealed to rationalism) and "New Lights" (those who appealed to emotionalism and human decision in conversion). The Old Lights eventually drifted toward UNITARIANISM.

Another revival or Awakening began in New England at the close of the eighteenth and beginning of the nineteenth centuries. This awakening was highly Arminian in temperament was highly charged with emotionalism. Success was now measured, not by faithfulness to the gospel, but by numbers and the popularity of the preacher. The openness to untrained "ministers" who used gimmicks and manipulative techniques in religious revivalism is the same openness that has permitted America to become a breeding ground for many new *cults. At the same time, this movement did bring religious revival to the growing and expanding United States.

Great Disappointment (SEVENTH-DAY ADVENTISM). Phrase used to describe the disillusionment experienced by followers of William Miller (see ▶Millerite Movement), who in 1831 began issuing warnings that the return of Christ would take place on or before March 21, 1844. The failure of this prophecy resulted in a recalculation to the date October 22, 1844. The failure of this second date resulted in the Great Disappointment in the history of Seventh-day Adventism—the name Miller's faithful followers later called themselves under the leadership of Ellen G. ▶White (1827–1915).

Greater Brotherhood (CHRIST THE SAVIOR BROTHERHOOD). Members of the Holy Order of Mans who have merited the privilege of reigning with Jesus Christ forever.

Great Invocation (NEW AGE MOVEMENT). A prayer written by Alice Bailey in 1937. Many New Age devotees recite this prayer, believing that it will aid in initiating the coming of a new paradigm or New Age utopia.

Great Renunciation (BUDDHISM). The moment in Siddharta ▶Gautama's life when at the age of twenty-nine he renounced his rightful succession to royalty, left his wife and child, and became a mendicant in search of truth.

Great Rite (WITCHCRAFT). The most important rite practiced by major ▶wicca traditions. It is a ceremony that invokes the principle of female/male polarity. It symbolizes the harmonization of life with nature and the world. It is performed either symbolically within a ▶coven in the presence of all of the participants, or is performed as an actual sex act in private between a male and female ▶witch.

Great Schism (CHRISTIANITY). The term used primarily to describe two events in the history of the Christian church. The first was the breach between the church of the East (Eastern Orthodox) and the West (Roman Catholic), occurring in A.D. 1054.

Great White Brotherhood (CHURCH UNIVERSAL AND TRIUMPHANT). The chain of outstanding spiritual figures (Ascended Masters) from history who have handed down the teachings of "I AM" to successive generations. These include Jesus Christ, ▶Buddha, ▶Muhammad, Saint Francis, Saint Germain, Mark ▶Prophet, and others.

Griffin (▶occult). A creature that has the legs of a lion and the wings and head of an eagle. It is said to be the largest of birds.

Grihastha (HINDUISM). The head of a family or household.

Grimories (▶occult). Collections of ▶magic ▶spells and rituals dating back to medieval times. The *Grimories* are frequently claimed to have descended from ancient Hebrew and Egyptian sources. Some of them are: "Key of Solomon," "Lesser Key of Solomon," "The Sacred Magic of Abra-Merlin the Mage," and "The Sworn Book of Honorius."

Gris-Gris (▶occult; ▶Yoruba; VOODOO). ▶Amulets used by African tribesmen to ward off evil spirits. The term also refers to ▶witch doctors who cast evil ▶spells through magical ▶incantations.

Gros Bon Ange (▶occult; VOODOO). Translated "great good angel," the *gros bon ange* is one of two souls that each person possesses. It is capable of leaving the body and roaming. If it fails to return, death occurs. See also ▶*petit bon ange.*

Gross, Darwin (ECKANKAR; n.d.). Living Eck Master number 972, who succeeded Paul ▶Twitchell as head of Eckankar after the latter's death in 1971. Gross was given the ostentatious title of "God's ▶guru for our age"; "the most splendid specimen of manhood, the noblest of the noble."

Group Soul (▶occult; SPIRITUALISM; THEOSOPHY). The idea that a spirit becomes the overseer to a given number of souls that are on the road to ▶enlightenment through the process of ▶reincarnation.

Guardians (CHURCH OF BIBLE UNDERSTANDING). The leaders in the Forever Family who exercise authority over ▶sheep and ▶lambs.

Guide (▶occult; SPIRITUALISM). The spirit in a ▶séance who is present to offer assistance, advice, or guidance to the ▶medium attempting to contact the spirit world. Guides are usually ▶gurus, sages, Hindu ▶masters, priests, and other great spiritual leaders from centuries past.

Guided Imagery (NEW AGE MOVEMENT). An alternate name for ▶visualization.

Guira (SANTERIA; VOODOO). Set of sticks used musically as a rhythm instrument.

Gurdjieff, George Ivanovitch (OUSPENSKY-GURDJIEFF; 1872–1949). Russian philosopher who founded the Institute for the Development of Man in 1919. His philosophy has been influential in the thinking of the NEW AGE MOVEMENT.

Gurdwara (SIKHISM). Name for a temple, shrine, or holy place in the ▶Sikh religion.

Guru (HINDUISM). A divine guide; a spiritual teacher or ▶master.

Guru Arian (SIKHISM). The gatherer/editor of the ▸*Granth Sahib*.

Guru Dev See ▸transcendental meditation.

Gyromancy (▸divination; ▸occult). Form of divination in which an individual walks in a circle repetitiously until he or she collapses from exhaustion or dizziness. The person then proceeds to predict the future based on the position of the fall.

H

Haborym (▸occult; SATANISM). Alternate name for the ▸devil or the duke of hell. Usually this depiction of the devil is portrayed with the three heads (of a man, a snake, and a cat) and bearing a torch. Haborym is the ultimate ▸demon of human calamity and holocausts.

Hadith (ISLAM). The words, sayings, and practices of ▸Muhammad, collected and assembled after the prophet's death. The *hadith*, or "traditions," serve to elaborate on as well as interpret the ▸Koran. See also ▸*sunna*.

Hair (▸occult). ▸Sorcerer's ▸magic power believed to be in the hair. This is an old tradition and may even be reflected in the ▸Bible's depiction of Samson losing his strength when his hair was cut (Judg. 14–17).

Hajj (ISLAM). The sacred pilgrimage to ▸Mecca that ▸Muslims are to perform at least once in a lifetime. The pilgrim customarily walks seven times around the ▸Ka²aba, Islam's main shrine located in Mecca. This act commemorates how Hagar searched for water to sustain Ishmael, who was cast out by Abraham into the desert. A visit to Mount Arafat and to the tomb of ▸Muhammad at Medina are also duties performed by a pilgrim on a *hajj*.

Hakata (▸divination; ▸occult). An African form of ▸geomancy, in which the ▸witch doctor takes bone, ivory, or wood and casts the pieces on the ground. The resulting configuration is then studied and interpreted.

Hall (JEHOVAH'S WITNESSES). Hall is short for ▸kingdom hall, where members of the Watchtower Bible and Tract Society assemble locally for worship.

Halloween See ▸witch's calendar.

Halomancy (▸divination; ▸occult). Also spelled alomancy, it is a form of divination in which salt granules are dropped on a surface and the resulting patterns and configurations are then studied and interpreted.

Hamsa (HINDUISM). The soul in and of itself, and by itself.

Handfasting (▸occult; WITCHCRAFT). Wedding rites of the ▸wiccan tradition; witch's wedding performed within the ▸magic circle, which can include ring exchange, broom jumping, and the ▸great rite of sexual union, whether actual or symbolic.

Hand of Glory (▸occult; SATANISM). In Satanism the term applies to the practice of severing the hand of a person who was executed, usually by hanging. The hand is then wrapped in a cloth and pickled in a jar. Several weeks following, it is dried either by the sun or in an oven.

Hands of Spirits (▸divination; ▸occult). The situation in a ▸séance in which only the hands of a spirit appear instead of a full body.

Hanley, John (LIFESPRING; n.d.). Founder of Life Spring, which emphasizes New Age self-actualizing training.

Hanukkah (JUDAISM). Jewish holy day celebrating the victory of Judas Maccabeus, who in 167 B.C. led a rebellion against Syrian oppression.

Hanuman (HINDUISM). The intense lover of god (*see* ▸Bhakta) who looks after ▸Rama. Hanuman is also called the god of monkeys, and for this reason, monkeys, like cows, are considered to be sacred.

Haquigah (ISLAM; SUFISM). The mystical yet true reality that is sought by the spiritual wayfarer.

Hare Krishna (ISKCON). Name given to the deity of love and devotion in the Hare Krishna movement. Members of the movement attribute the founding of their faith to the sixteenth-century Indian saint, Sri Chaitanya Mahaprabhu. This man introduced an expressive and devotional worship of Krishna, using chanting, dance, etc. Modern Krishna worship was introduced to the United States by *A. C. Bhaktivedanta Swami *Prabhupada.

Harimandir (SIKHISM). Name given to the Golden Temple, the holiest of the *Sikh shrines located in India.

Harijan (HINDUISM). The untouchables or outcasts, a *caste in Hinduism. This and other castes are arranged within accepted religious, social, and economic orders.

Harmonic Convergence (NEW AGE MOVEMENT). A prophecy offered by New Age adherent Jose Arguelles. Arguelles believes that there was a Mayan prophet by the name of Quetzalcoatl, who lived at the turn of the first millennium. Quetzalcoatl prophesied the reality of thirteen heavens and nine hells. In 1953, after a Mayan tomb was opened the previous year, Arguelles began to study and seek out the meanings of the prophecies. Arguelles believed that the Mayan calendar was the true calendar in the measurement of time. "Normal society" is governed by what Arguelles calls "consensus reality driven by an unconscious, irregular, artificial timing frequency called the 12:60: twelve-month calendar, 60-minute hour" (see Arguelles' website at *www.indigosun.com/april98/harmony.htm*).

Arguelles called the Mayan calendar the Law of Time. Because the earth is living according to a wrong calendar and hence out of step with real time, we are heading for a "moral emergency." Arguelles proposes that a correction from the use of the Gregorian calendar to the Mayan 28-day 13-moon calendar will usher in harmony and peace.

Arguelles held a gathering of followers on August 16–17, 1987, at what he believed were the earth's vortexes. After chanting and meditations were offered up, it was revealed that there remained only 25 years to the time of the Mayan Great Cycle. Reckoning from 1987, this would mark the year 2012 as the year in which the prophecy of earth's cleansing will take place. A great deal of interest has arisen in Arguelles' work. He has written a considerable amount of material and there are many websites and links to sites related to harmonic convergence.

Harris, Martin (MORMONISM; 1783–1875). Friend of Joseph *Smith who financed the publication of the golden plates that were given to Smith by the angel *Moroni. He is also claimed as one of the three main witnesses of the *Book of Mormon.

Hasidism (JUDAISM). Ancient movement within Judaism, following the conquests of Alexander the Great (d. 323 B.C.), which stubbornly resisted the Hellenization of Palestine. Modern Hasidism began in the 1740s in Poland under the leadership of Israel ben Eliezer, renamed Baal Shem-Tob (Master of the Good Name). He began to teach the common people that true devotion to God cannot be obtained through *asceticism or rabbinic knowledge. He emphasized God is *immanent and he cannot therefore be contained in a mere *temple or synagogue. True worship must take place in everyday life and throughout all of God's creation.

Hasidic worship is characterized by zeal, emotion, prayer, and festivity. In the nineteenth century, Hasidism lost much of its original zeal and as a movement became highly reactionary, particularly to the cultural revolution of the Haskala. Many Hasidic Jews were murdered in the Holocaust of Nazi Germany. Today, the relatively few that remain live in Eastern Europe, Israel, the United States (especially New York City), and Canada.

Hatha Yoga (HINDUISM). A form of meditation in which the practitioner seeks to arouse the *kundalini by using *mudras. The physical aspect of *yoga, hatha yoga is the initial stage that leads the practitioner to eventually experience the religious and/or philosophical dimension (see also *prana, *apana).

Hauntings (*occult). The occurrence of supernatural visitations; the sources of hauntings are usually *ghosts, *apparitions, or other manifestations of spirits returning from the dead. The nature of a haunting is not always evil, although much of the time it is. Accompanying phenomena include noises, lights, objects being moved or transported by an invisible source, drops in temperature, and extremely unpleasant odors.

Heart (*occult). The heart is the center of life, emotions, and character of the individual. Historically, in many cultures it was believed that by eating the heart, one could acquire the victim's character and strength.

Hegira (ISLAM). Arabic word meaning "flight" that is ascribed to the historic journey of *Muhammad from *Mecca to Yathrib (later changed to Medina) in A.D. 622.

Heindel, Max (ROSICRUCIANISM; 1862–1919). Greatly influenced by Rudolf *Steiner, Heindel claimed to be an authentic Rosicrucian. He created the fellowship of Rosicrucianism in Oceanside, California. Max Heindel was formerly called Louis von *Grasshof.

Hell (*occult; CHRISTIANITY). The place or domain where evil reigns and where the wicked go after death. Certain occultists who reject the idea of a literal hell believe hell is a state of mind or state of negative mental imagery. Hell remains an important concept in traditional Christianity as the place where the wicked will spend all of eternity in torment.

Henbane (›occult; WITCHCRAFT). A poisonous herb used in ›Gothic witchcraft to create certain hallucinogenic effects, such as believing that one has been transformed into someone else or something else. Modern practitioners of witchcraft do not use henbane.

Heptad (›numerology; ›occult). The numeral seven.

Hereditaries (WITCHCRAFT). Those ›witches who are in a long line of succession in the practice witchcraft.

Hermeneutics (CHRISTIANITY). The theological discipline and study of how to rightly interpret the ›Bible.

Hermes Trismegistus (THEOSOPHY). Phrase meaning "thrice-greatest Hermes," who was a character in the ›*Hermetica*, a collection of ancient mythical Greek writings. Hermes Trismegistus is believed to have been comprised of the Egyptian deity of wisdom, ›Thoth, and the Greek god Hermes. He appears as a powerful deity who possesses the capability of halting the destructive forces of evil in the world. Theosophy derives much of its thought from the literature surrounding Hermes Trismegistus.

Hermetic Axiom (›occult). The famous thesis of ›*Hermes Trismegistus*, "As above—so below," which is an attempt to describe the relationship between the heavenly sphere and the earthly. The axiom is based on the Platonic notion that earthly objects have a corresponding reality in the spiritual realm of the forms.

Hermetic Chain (›occult; THEOSOPHY). In Theosophy, the idea that highly qualified, spiritual individuals have preserved and passed along the ›esoteric teachings to those qualified to receive them, who in turn pass them on to the next generation.

Hermetic Order of the Golden Dawn (›occult; SATANISM). A popular occult society formed in the late nineteenth century for the purpose of practicing ›magic. The teachings were derived from a blend of occult writings including the ›Kabbalah and Freemasonry. Members of the Order included Aleister ›Crowley.

Hermetic Teachings (›occult). The doctrines contained in the ›*Hermetica*.

Hermetica (›occult; ROSICRUCIANISM). Body of mystical alchemist (*see* ›alchemy) writings of Greek and Egyptian origin having to do with the Egyptian god ›Thoth and the Greek god Hermes. The writings date from the first through the third centuries A.D. and contain an eclectic blend of influences. Contributions come from Greek writers and even from some of the early church fathers. See also ›*Hermes Trismegistus*. The writings combine Greek philosophy, particularly Platonic thought, with Eastern religion.

Hevioso (›occult; VOODOO). The deity of turbulence and destruction.

Hex (›occult; SATANISM; WITCHCRAFT). From the German *Hexe*, or "wizard." In ›Gothic witchcraft to cast a hex is to cast a ›spell on an individual, the usual intention being to bring misfortune or evil on that person. Occult experts insist that the power to cast a spell or hex has its roots in pacts made between ›witches and the ›devil. Hex signs were commonly painted on barn doors in Pennsylvania Dutch country settled by immigrants who brought with them the superstitious belief that such a symbol would ward off evil spirits and protect the farm animals from the spells of witches. Modern witches do not practice hexing because they are forbidden by the ›wiccan Rede from doing so.

Hexagram (›occult; SATANISM; WITCHCRAFT). The hexagram consists of two triangles superimposed on one another, the point or apex of one pointing up, the other pointing down. It is used in a number of occult contexts such as ›mysticism, ›magic, Satanism, and ›Gothic witchcraft. In the mystic tradition, it is thought that the upper and lower apexes represent the ›hermetic axiom, "As above—so below." In Satanism, the sign is used as a powerful symbol that is able to harness and control the powers of ›demons.

High Magic (›occult). Also known as ›theurgy, high magic is the practices used in an attempt to attain the highest level of awareness of spiritual consciousness possible.

High Priest (›occult; JUDAISM; MORMONISM; SATANISM; WITCHCRAFT). In Mormonism, one of the offices in the ›Melchizedek priesthood; the high priest is ranked above the ›elders and the ›presidents in the Quorum of the Seventy. With respect to Judaism in biblical times, the high priest was the most important religious figure in the worship of the Lord; only he could enter the ›Holy of Holies in the temple on the Day of Atonement to offer the prescribed sacrifices (Lev. 16). Jesus Christ is the high priest in CHRISTIANITY, because he offered up himself as a sacrifice for sin.

In witchcraft and Satanism, the high priest is the highest ranking male leader in a witchcraft or a satanist ›coven.

High Priestess (›occult; SATANISM; WITCHCRAFT). The highest ranking female leader in witchcraft ›covens. The high priestess receives her authority by passing through several stages. First, she must become a member of the coven by becoming a skilled ᵇwitch. Second, she proves her leadership capabilities. Finally, she is admitted to the priesthood before being chosen as the high priestess.

Hippomancy (ᵇdivination; ᵇoccult). Form of divination, practiced particularly among the Celts, in which the gait of a white horse was analyzed and interpreted for purposes of prognostication.

Hiroshi, Hojo (SOKA-GAKKAI; n.d.). Reigned as leader of Soka-Gakkai from 1979–1981.

Hiving Off (ᵇoccult; WITCHCRAFT). The common practice of breaking away from a ᵇcoven in order to start another.

Hobgoblin (ᵇoccult). A goblin that vexes little children, causing fear.

Hocus-Pocus (ᵇoccult). An idiomatic expression used to refer to beliefs that are founded on superstition and nonsense. It is thought that the etymology of the phrase reverts back to the Latin language of the Christian Eucharist, *Hoc est corpus meum* ("This is my body").

Hoffman, Bernard Lazar See Tony ᵇAlamo.

Holistic Health See NEW AGE MOVEMENT.

Holly King (WITCHCRAFT). See ᵇsolstice.

Holmes, Ernest (RELIGIOUS SCIENCE; 1887–1960). Established the movement known as Religious Science, which is comprised of two churches: The United Church of Religious Science and Religious Science International. He wrote *Science of Mind* (1926), which is used by numerous ᵇmind science and NEW AGE teachers.

Holy of Holies (JUDAISM). The innermost and most sacred holy place of the ᵇtabernacle and the ᵇtemple. In it God himself lived and was accessible only to the ᵇhigh priest, once yearly. The Holy of Holies contained the ᵇark of the covenant and the ᵇmercy seat (or atonement cover), where the high priest made atonement for the sins of the people. CHRISTIANITY and the New Testament interpret Jesus' crucifixion and death on Good Friday as ending the sacrificial system of the Old Testament and the need for tabernacle/temple with its Holy of Holies (Matt. 27:51). Jesus became the "Lamb of God" (John 1:29), through whom full atonement for sin was made (Rom. 3:21–26). The Holy of Holies therefore foreshadowed God's true dwelling place among his people in the ᵇincarnation of his Son, Jesus Christ.

Holy Spirit Association for the Unification of World Christianity See UNIFICATION CHURCH.

Homeopathy (ᵇholistic health; NEW AGE MOVEMENT). The general belief that the intake of natural foods containing the basic elements are able to cure diseases. Homeopathy was developed by Samuel Hahneman.

Homonculus (ᵇmysticism; ᵇoccult). Medieval ᵇmagicians claimed power to create a small child by placing sperm in a sealed container and incubating it in horse manure for forty days. After the forty days, the embryo would begin to develop. The homonculus would grow to be only twelve inches in height, and it was usually kept in a glass jar.

Honddon (SHINTOISM). The innermost sanctuary of a Shinto holy place or shrine.

Hopkins, Emma Curtis (DIVINE SCIENCE; n.d.). A student of Mary Baker ᵇEddy and a Divine Science teacher, who began a school of metaphysics in Chicago.

Horn, Edith Opal See Susan ᵇAlamo.

Horned God (SATANISM; WITCHCRAFT). Male deity in witchcraft. The name of the horned god is usually designated as ᵇPan, the Greek god of nature and shepherding. In Satanism, he is a ᵇbaphomet.

Horoscope (ᵇastrology; ᵇoccult). In astrology, the heavens are arranged in 360 degrees, the purpose of which is to ascertain the precise positions of the planets at a moment in time and so to examine the ᵇsigns of the ᵇzodiac. Astrologers use the horoscope to counsel persons concerning the future. For example, whether conditions are deemed favorable for airplane travel, marriage, pursuit of a particular career, and so on are all determined in this manner. There are different kinds of horoscopes. A natal horoscope pinpoints the exact moment of birth. In a progressed horoscope, the astrologer assigns "one day to one year."

Horse Brasses (ᵇoccult). ᵇAmulets attached to a horse's harness used to ward off evil spirits. Today they are more decorative than religious.

Horseshoe (ᵇoccult). The horseshoe is believed to be able to ward off evil, especially when nailed above a door. The iron is believed to possess actual power.

House of Yahweh (WORLDWIDE CHURCH OF GOD). A splinter movement of the Worldwide Church of God. Its founder and leader, Yisrayl Hawkins (Buffalo Bill Hawkins), maintains that the House of Yahweh is the one and only true church. The group believes in the basic doctrines taught by Herbert W. ᵇArmstrong, including ᵇAnglo-Israelism and the belief in Saturday ᵇSabbath.

Houston, Jean (NEW AGE MOVEMENT; 1941–). An important voice in the New Age Movement, Houston has authored at least seventeen books. She became familiar to the public at large when she claimed to aid Hillary Rodham Clinton in conducting "imaginary conversations" with Eleanore Roosevelt. Houston is cofounder, along with her husband, Dr. Robert Masters, of the Foundation for Mind Research in New York City and Pomona, New York. She is a frequent guest speaker at colleges and universities and has received many awards and recognitions for her accomplishments, particularly in the fields of psychology and education.

Howell, Vernon (BRANCH DAVIDIANS). The birth name of David Koresh, who became the leader of the Branch Davidians at Mount Carmel in Waco, Texas.

Huldra (ᵇoccult). A wood fairy who appeared as a woman in Norse mythology.

Humfort (VOODOO). A voodoo temple.

Hungan (VOODOO). A voodoo male priest.

Hubbard, Lafayette Ronald (SCIENTOLOGY; 1911–1986). The founder of Scientology published the essence of his thought in *Dianetics: The Modern Science of Mental Health* (1950). The book combines Buddhist ideas with psychology and the creative imagination of a science fiction writer, which Hubbard also was.

Hungan (ᵇoccult; VOODOO). Name of the voodoo priest.

Hunsi (VOODOO). A female initiate to voodoo.

Hylozoism (ᵇoccult). The belief that all of the matter of the cosmos is animated or living (*see*ᵇ panpsychism).

Hypnotism (ᵇoccult). A word derived from the Greek god of sleep, Hypnos. Hypnotism is the practice of bringing a person into a trancelike state in order to probe the unconscious or to recall memories from the past and is popularly used in the occult. The hypnotist provides the client with certain cues that, when used, enable the patient to overcome initial fears and emotions. Memories are then free to surface without inhibition (*see also* ᵇtrancing; ᵇmesmerism; ᵇaltered states of consciousness). Note that hypnotism is also a legitimate medical practice used by physicians as an aid in psychotherapy.

Hypostatic Union; Hypostasis (CHRISTIANITY). From the Greek word *hypostasis*, which generally means "substance." Hypostasis has a variety of meanings, but its most significant impact on the history of the church was its usage in the Christological controversies. In the Council of Nicea, *hypostasis* was used in the sense of "person" to describe the substantial distinction between the "persons" of the Godhead. In Chalcedonian Christology, the term *hypostatic union* came to mean as it presently does in Christianity, that is, the union of the human and the divine natures of Jesus Christ, commonly referred to as the "personal union."

I

Iblis (ISLAM). An Arabic word for ᵇSatan. See also ᵇ*Shaytan*.

Ichazo, Oscar (ARICA; n.d.). Person who formed the Arica Institute, which is a mixture of Eastern religions and psychotherapy.

I Ching (ᵇoccult; TAOISM). Also called the ᵇ*Book of Changes*, it is a Chinese book of ᵇdivination that some date as late as 1000 B.C. The philosophy of I Ching, which is Taoist in essence, dates back to almost 3000 B.C. The *I Ching* gauges the flow of ᵇyin and yang, the positive and negative life forces that, when read properly, can determine the course of future actions. Most divination techniques utilize material objects as a channel for their operation; I Ching frequently uses yarrow

sticks. The user counts out fifty sticks, dividing them into two random piles. They are then counted in groups of threes and fives. The arrangements of the sticks when grouped in forty-six different mutations is believed to offer correspondence to psychic situations. Also, practitioners read and interpret the ᵇhexagram, formed from six lines in the yarrow sticks. Leading advocates of *I Ching* were psychologist Carl Jung and John Blofield, translator of Taoist and ᵇBuddhist texts.

Iconoclastic Controversy (CHRISTIANITY). From the Greek *iconoclastes*, meaning "image-breaker," a controversy in the Eastern Church broke out in the seventh and eighth centuries over the veneration of "icons" or images. The conflict was precipitated by ᵇMonophysitism, which held a low view of Jesus' human nature, and ‣Manichaeism, which maintained that matter was evil. Emperor Leo III (717–41) believed that icons were being venerated to an excess and that they were an obstacle to conversions of both Jews and ‣Muslims. His 726 edict against icons caused harsh controversy. Many monks who supported the use of icons were martyred. The Second Council of Nicea met in 787 and decided in favor of icons, but defined a stricter manner in which they were to be used.

The use of images, despite the mandate against them in God's law (Ex. 20:4), was the result of the recognition of the deep theological implications of the ‣incarnation and the two natures of Christ as expressed at the Council of Chalcedon (A.D. 451). While God himself cannot be depicted in art or image, he has sent his Son Jesus into the world, who has put on flesh and blood. It was not considered as inappropriate, therefore, to "picture" Jesus in art or in icon. This tradition has been carried on especially in the Eastern Church, but also among Roman Catholics and ‣Lutherans.

Id al-Adha   (ISLAM). See ‣Islamic holidays and ‣feast of sacrifice.

Id al-Fitr   (ISLAM). Breaking the fast of ‣Ramadan (see ‣Islamic holidays and ‣feast of sacrifice).

Id Al-Qurbani   (ISLAM). (See ‣Islamic holidays and ‣feast of sacrifice).

Ifa   (‣occult; SANTERIA; SOUTH AMERICAN, CENTRAL AMERICAN, AND CARIBBEAN CULTS; VOODOO). The deity of destiny. *Ifa* is a Yorubic (*see* ‣Yoruba) deity. Like many of the deities in the vast pantheon of gods emanating from the African tribal religions, *Ifa* is shared among them. *Ifa* is a "protector deity," particularly, the "protector of birth."

Ifan   (‣occult; ABAKUA). Sacred branch held in an Abakua ceremony directed toward conjuring up ‣Ireme.

Ifon   (‣occult; ABAKUA; SOUTH AMERICAN, CENTRAL AMERICAN, AND CARIBBEAN CULTS). Rhythmic instrument used in ‣cult rituals.

Ijma   (ISLAM). The common consent and agreement of the Islamic community.

Ijtihad   (ISLAM). The occasion when a ‣Muslim offers a personal opinion that is not an official teaching or belief of Islam.

Ikeda, Daisaku   (SOKA-GAKKAI; n.d.). Governed the Soka-Gakkai movement during 1960–1979. Most recently, the priesthood of Nichiren Shoshu Buddhism

took away Ikeda's title as *sokoto* (head of all Nichiren Shoshu devotees). Ikeda was a dynamic leader and has authored over two hundred books containing his teachings.

Image Magic   (‣occult). The practice of creating an image of a person out of any numbers of materials and then poking it with pins, breaking off a limb, burning it in effigy, and so on, in order to cause harm to the person that the image represents.

Imagery   (NEW AGE MOVEMENT). See ‣guided imagery; ‣visualization.

Imam Mahdi   (ISLAM). Name for the spiritual leader of the ‣Shiʾite ‣sect of Islam; also, one who leads the prayer in the ‣mosque.

Imbolg   (‣occult; WITCHCRAFT). Witchcraft ceremony celebrated on February 2, the Christian equivalent of which is Candlemas. Imbolg is believed to come from an archaic Gaelic expression "in the belly," which signaled the first stirrings of life within the womb of mother earth (*see* ‣Witches' Calendar).

Immaculate Sisterhood   (CHRIST THE SAVIOR BROTHERHOOD). The female members of the Christ the Savior Brotherhood, formerly known as the Holy Order of Mans, who have entered into their first year of training.

Immanence   (CHRISTIANITY). The term used by Christian theologians to designate the nearness of God to creation (contrasted with ‣transcendence). Traditional Christianity speaks of both immanence and transcendence to describe God's relationship to the creation. Many non-Christian religions and ‣cults assert the immanence of God at the loss of his transcendence, or the transcendence of God at the loss of his immanence.

Immortality   (MORMONISM). Term used to designate resurrected saints who live on the earth during the Millennium (*see* ‣millennialism) and those who have been gifted with resurrection solely on account of Christ's bodily resurrection. Mormons will acknowledge that they have received "salvation by grace." What they mean by this is that they have been given "immortality." Mormons distinguish this from the higher degree of ‣eternal life, earned by obeying "laws and ordinances of the Gospel."

Imp   (‣occult). A small ‣demon stored in a bottle and used for ‣magic and in occult practices.

Incantation   (‣occult). The hope of producing ‣magic by ritually reciting the prescribed words to ‣spells.

Incarnation   (CHRISTIANITY). The Christian teaching that the second person of the ‣Trinity was born of a virgin and took on human flesh. The incarnation embraces the fullness of Jesus' humanity and divinity in one person. The limits of the incarnation were drawn up at the Council of Chalcedon in 451 (see Appendix 1). Virtually all non-Trinitarian groups derived from Christianity oppose this doctrine as traditionally expressed.

Incense (᾽occult). Ingredients of various sorts that, when lighted, emit fragrances used as part of worship. In the world of the occult, its use is believed to attract ᾽demons and other beings of the underworld.

Incubus; Incubi (᾽occult; SATANISM). An evil ᾽demon or spirit that has sexual intercourse with a woman, believed to have existed during the time of the Inquisition in the Middle Ages. See also ᾽succubus.

Indra (HINDUISM). The Hindu god of weather and warfare. According to the ᾽*Rigveda*, Indra gave birth to the sun and the dawn. He was replaced by ᾽Vishnu and ᾽Shiva but is still worshiped as a god of the Hindu pantheon.

Indulgences (CHRISTIANITY). The Roman Catholic Church's practice, especially in the Middle Ages, of issuing pardons for sin based on the merits of Christ. It has its roots in the ancient practice of penitential discipline. During the time just before the ᾽Reformation, some priests took to hawking indulgences, which motivated Martin Luther to write his famous Ninety-Five Theses against them. As a result of the Reformation, the abuses associated with sale of indulgences as a scheme to raise money were halted by Pius VI in 1567.

Initiate (᾽occult). A participant in various occult groups who, after going through particular instructions or ceremonial stages, achieves a level of membership within the group.

Initiator (ELAN VITAL). The active disciples and leaders who follow ᾽Guru ᾽Maharaj Ji. Initiators were originally called ᾽mahatmas.

Inspired Version (MORMONISM; COMMUNITY OF CHRIST, REORGANIZED CHURCH OF JESUS CHRIST OF THE LATTER-DAY SAINTS). Joseph ᾽Smith's revision of the King James ᾽Bible, originally published in 1867 and adopted by the Reorganized Church of Jesus Christ of Latter-Day Saints, now called Community of Christ. Smith's version went far beyond the original text with its interpretations. For example, in Genesis 7:10 (Inspired Version), Smith wrote that the children of Canaan were made black as a result of their sins. Genesis 50 in the Inspired Version prophesies the coming of Joseph Smith as the prophet or seer whom God will bless. Because the Reorganized COC Church members

consider themselves to be the true followers of Joseph Smith, rejecting the Utah Mormons as being false, the Inspired Version has become the official Bible of the Missouri-based Reorganized COC Mormons. The Utah Mormons use the King James Version "insofar as it is correctly translated," but they have added a large number of Joseph Smith's translation to the footnotes of their church's edition since 1984.

International Bible Students (JEHOVAH'S WITNESSES). A former name for the Watchtower Bible and Tract Society.

Intuition (᾽occult; THEOSOPHY). The process of rationalization based not on empirical criteria (the five senses) but on an appeal to the inner feelings, emotions, and cognition. Intuition is an integral part of ᾽mysticism and is a crucial component of philosophy and Theosophy.

Ipsissimus (᾽occult; SATANISM). The highest ranking one can achieve in Satanism. Its recipients are rare. Aleister ᾽Crowley allegedly achieved this status before his death.

Iridology See ᾽iris diagnosis.

Irani, Merwan Sheriar See MEHER BABA.

Ireme (᾽occult; ABAKUA). Name of the ᾽*diablitos*. Ireme symbolizes both good and evil.

Iris Diagnosis (᾽occult). Also called iridology, the practice of diagnosing diseases by observation of the iris or, as it is otherwise called, the rainbow membrane of the eye. The iris is divided into a series of organic fields, each of which corresponds to a particular part of the body. For example, "sector six" represents the foot, knee, and leg. If a disease arises in a particular part of the body, a modification in the organic field will arise. There were originally five zones in the iris, but the popularity of ᾽astrology led to a later division into the twelve fields currently in effect.

Irvine, William (CHURCH WITH NO NAME; 1863–1947). The founder of the Church with No Name in 1897, William Irvine was born in Kilsyth, Scotland. He was a powerful and persuasive preacher.

Ishtapurta (HINDUISM). The good works and deeds that are performed in order to achieve the bliss of ᾽nirvana.

Ishtar (᾽occult). The supreme Babylonian and Assyrian goddess of war, love, and fertility.

Islamic Holidays or Holy Days (ISLAM). The Muslim calendar is dated from ᾽Muhammad's emigration from ᵇMecca to ᵇMedina in A.D. 622. There are two festival days in Islam. The ᵇ*Id al-Fitr* celebrates the end of ᵇRamadan. The ᵇ*Id al-Adha*, a feast of "sacrifice," is held at the end of the annual pilgrimage. The Muslim calendar is based on the lunar year, with each month consisting of twenty-nine and thirty days, alternately. The year begins in the month called Muharram (July 16). The ninth month, Ramadan, begins the holy time of fasting.

Iton   (ᵇoccult; ABAKUA). A staff or rhythmic instrument used in an Abakua ceremony.

Itotele   (SANTERIA). A medium-sized drum used in Santeria ceremonies.

Iya   (SANTERIA). The main chief priestess in Santeria; also a synonym for the title of mother.

Iyalorishas   (SANTERIA). A female initiate into the priesthood in Santeria.

J

Jack Mormons   (MORMONISM). A slang term used to refer to inactive baptized members of the Latter-Day Saints church (similar to the term "backsliding" for Christians). The number of Jack Mormons is surprisingly high. Some authorities claim that as many as sixty percent of all Mormons are on the inactive lists.

James, William   (RELIGIOUS SCIENCE; 1842–1910). William James is regarded foremost as a philosopher and psychologist of religion. He contributed much to the field of religious studies and to other areas of philosophical inquiry. His monumental work, *Varieties of Religious Experience* (1902), marked him as a groundbreaker in exploring religion strictly from a psychological perspective, a discipline that was still relatively young while James taught at Harvard. His writings today regularly appear in philosophical, psychological, and religious textbooks in universities and colleges throughout the world.

James regarded religion strictly from a phenomenological point of view. For him, religion was a projection of human consciousness. Therefore, it is at its best when it contributes to moral development and personal self-improvement. James had no regard for the historicity of CHRISTIANITY or the truths conveyed in the ᵇBible or the historic Christian creeds.

What is perhaps less known is that James also maintained an interest in the ᵇoccult. He experimented with nitrous oxide that convinced him that through its use, one could successfully induce a state of mystic self-awareness.

Jamilians   See church of the second advent.

Japa   (HINDUISM). To repeat a designated ᵇmantra over and over.

Japa Yoga   (SATCHIDANANDA ASHRAM INTEGRAL YOGA INSTITUTE). ᵇYoga technique in which a ᵇmantra-like phrase is repeatedly uttered.

Jaquin, Noel   (ᵇoccult; 1893–1974). Author of several books on ᵇpalmistry. His titles include *The Human Hand* and *The Hand Speaks*. Jaquin devoted his studies to attempting to bridge the gap between the modern scientific approach and the ᵇoccult beliefs that so often present problems to the modern mind.

Jen   (CONFUCIANISM). The Confucian motivation for "considering others." It is the motivation for action based on *li*, of which one reciprocity is the Silver Rule: "What you do not want done to yourself, do not do to others" (ᵇAnalects 15:23). The *li*, unlike the Golden Rule taught by Christ, is in a negative form, where Jesus initiated positive benevolence: "Do to others what you would have them do to you" (Matt. 7:12). When Confucius was asked about repaying evil with kindness, he answer that kindness should be repaid with kindness and evil with justice.

Jesus Only   (ONENESS PENTECOSTALISM). Phrase used in Oneness Pentecostalism as meaning that appropriate prayer and mode for baptism is exclusively in the name of Jesus, not in the Trinitarian name of God as Father, Son, and Holy Spirit. See also ᵇmodalistic monarchianism.

Jewish Calendar   (JUDAISM). Judaism follows a clear liturgical or religious year, based mostly on the religious festivals outlined in the Old Testament. The chart on the following page shows this calendar, along with the corresponding dates in the Western calendar.

Jigai   (SHINTO). The practice in Japanese ᵇShinto whereby a female commits ritual suicide by cutting the

WESTERN/GREGORIAN CALENDAR	JEWISH CALENDAR	
1. September	Rosh Hashana	New Year
2. September	Yom Kippur	Day of Atonement
3. September	Sukkot	Feast of Tabernacles
4. September	Simchat Torah	Feast of Joy
5. November–December	Hanukkah	Feast of Dedication
6. February–March	Purim	Feast of Lots
7. March–April	Pesah	Passover; Feast of Unleavened Bread
8. May–June	Shavvot	Feast of Weeks/Pentecost
9. July–August	Tisha be-Av	Fast of Av

jugular vein. This serves as an atonement for sin and the preservation of honor.

Jihad (ISLAM). A ⸙Muslim holy war. Some Muslims believe that the goal of Islam is to transform land that is not Islamic through *jihad*; others personalize this concept to the fight against sin within oneself.

Jina (JAINISM). An alternate name for ⸙Mahavira, the founder of Jainism.

Jinn (ISLAM). Term used for a ⸙demonic spirit that is able to assume various forms. This is the word from which the English word "genie" comes.

Jiva (HINDUISM). The soul, or the most basic constituent of life.

Jivanmukta (HINDUISM). A devotee of Hinduism who reaches ⸙*moksha* before death.

Jnana Marga (HINDUISM; SATCHIDANANDA ASHRAM INTEGRAL YOGA INSTITUTE). The path of wisdom, one of three routes for attaining ⸙moksha (release from rebirth) and ⸙nirvana (ultimate bliss).

Jnana Yoga (HINDUISM). See ⸙*jnana marga*.

Jnani (HINDUISM). One dedicated to the pursuit of, or increase in, knowledge.

Jones, James Warren (PEOPLE'S TEMPLE; 1931–1978). The leader of the People's Temple who in November 1978 ordered the members of his cult to drink cyanide-laced punch in his Jonestown, Guyana, commune. Nine hundred and thirteen people fell victim to this mass

suicide. Jim Jones himself was found dead of a gunshot wound to his head.

Jonestown See people's temple.

Josei, Toda (SOKA-GAKKAI; n.d.). A disciple of ⸙Makiguchi who rejuvenated the Soka-Kyocki-Gakkai movement in 1946. During this time the organization changed its name to Soka-Gakkai.

Jouret, Luc (ORDER OF THE SOLAR TEMPLE; 1947–1994). One of the founders of this organization.

Journal of Discourses (MORMONISM). A twenty-six volume collection of official sermons by Mormon General Authorities published in series from 1856 to 1884. It represents selections from ⸙prophets and ⸙apostles ranging from Joseph ⸙Smith to Wilford ⸙Woodruff.

Judge, William Q. (THEOSOPHY; 1851–1896). The leader responsible for the revival of Theosophy in America. During his reign the Theosophy movement split into an American and an international group.

Justification (CHRISTIANITY). The doctrine of the Christian church that speaks of God's act of grace in bringing a sinner into a right standing and into a right relationship with himself. Justification is based not on the merits or worthiness of the sinner, but on the merits and worthiness of Jesus Christ, who atoned for sin (see especially Romans and Galatians). Most Protestant churches embrace justification as a chief focus in their theologies.

K

Ka'aba (ISLAM). The holy shrine of Islam, located in ♦Mecca.

Kabbala (♦occult; JUDAISM). Also spelled Kaballa; Kabbalah; Cabala; Cabbalah. A Jewish ♦mystical tradition that arose in the twelfth century A.D. and attempted to interpret the ♦Torah according to secret or hidden knowledge. The earliest roots of Kabbalistic tradition date back to first-century Palestine, where mystical Jews contemplated the divine throne or "chariot" spoken of in Ezekiel 1. The Hebrew word QBLH (i.e., *kabbala*) originally meant "oral tradition." The unwritten secrets of the Torah were interpreted and passed on from teacher to student. The major text of the Kabbala, containing much of the tradition, is *Sefer-ha-Zohar* ("the book of splendor"), written around 1280.

The heart of the Kabbala lies in unlocking the secrets to the wonder and majesty of God and his divine creation. The tradition also takes into account reflections on evil, the soul, salvation, and the future. Aspects of God's divine nature are revealed in a series of ten emanations. Moving from God on down through his creation, these emanations are as follows; (1) crown; (2) wisdom; (3) understanding; (4) mercy; (5) power; (6) beauty; (7) victory; (8) splendor; (9) foundation; (10) the kingdom. Kabbalism flourished in the sixteenth to eighteenth centuries and had a great impact on the ♦occult (see ♦*Hermetica*) and ♦Hasidism. Noteworthy Kabbalists were Moses de Leon, Isaac ben Solomon Ashkenazi Luria (1534–1572), and H. Vital (1543–1620).

Kachera (SIKH DHARMA). A specially designed underwear worn by ♦Sikhs, enabling them the greatest freedom of movement in combat.

Kahn, Haerat Pir-O-Murshid Inayat (SUFISM; 1881–1927). This person was responsible for importing Sufism to the United States.

Kahn, Pir Vilayat Inayat (SUFISM; n.d.). He succeeded his father Haerat Pir-O-Murshid Inayat ♦Kahn in 1927 as the next leader of Sufism.

Kaidan (BUDDHISM; NICHIREN SHOSHU BUDDHISM; SOKA-GAKKAI). Kaidan is the sacred place where the rite of ordination takes place. Kaidan is the third of the three sacred truths or mysteries of Nichiren Shoshu. *See also* ♦Gohonzon and ♦Daimoku.

Kal Nirajan (ECKANKAR). The name for the ♦devil or the spirit of evil in Eckankar. Because evil is closely attached to matter, Kal Nirajan dwells in the lowest physical plane and is ever seeking to prevent the soul of the *chela* (student) from ascending the ♦astral planes in its goal of becoming one of the ♦silent ones. Paul ♦Twitchell believed the ♦devil was the father of the Christian faith.

Kali (HINDUISM). The dark side of the mother goddess ♦Parvati. Kali at one time demanded human sacrifice, but later animal sacrifice became the norm.

Kali Yuga (HINDUISM). The final age of evil and decay. According to Hindu teaching, the present age is the time of Kali Yuga.

Kalima See ♦*Shahada*.

Kama (HINDUISM). For Hinduism, *kama* is sexual and erotic love. *Kama* in ♦Sanskrit is interpreted as sexual gratification and is found in a number of ♦sutras most often practiced in tantric (see ♦tantras; ♦taantrism) ♦yoga.

Kami (SHINTO). Power that lies within all matter, both living and dead.

Kan, Hak Ja (UNIFICATION CHURCH; n.d.). The Rev. Sun Myung ♦Moon's fourth wife, who was declared to be the "perfect mother" after the first three Eves proved failures.

Kanzo (♦occult; VOODOO). One of the several stages of initiation in voodoo whereby the candidate undergoes an ordeal by fire.

Kapila (HINDUISM; ISCKON). Incarnation of ♦Krishna, who appears as the founder of the Sankhya philosophy.

Kapilavistu (HINDUISM; BUDDHISM). The Himalayan town where Siddharta ♦Gautama was born. It is located in present-day Nepal.

Kapleau, Philip (ZEN BUDDHISM; d. 2004). A former war crimes court reporter in Japan who studied Zen under Soen Nakagawa ♦Roshi. Kapleau founded the Zen Center of Rochester in 1966, with other centers opening around the world.

Karma (HINDUISM; BUDDHISM). The law of retributive justice. One's karma determines one's place in the successive stages of the cycles of ᵖreincarnation. Karma represents the moral law of the universe by which all must be judged.

Karmakanda (HINDUISM). Parts of the ᵖVedas that describe rite and ritual; another route to ᵖnirvana, the way of works and duties.

Karma Marga, Karma Yoga (HINDUISM; SATCHIDANANDA ASHRAM INTEGRAL YOGA INSTITUTE). Karma marga is one of the three paths to ᵖnirvana in Hinduism that emphasizes works. Karma yoga is yoga in action, or the applying of these theoretical principles—the carrying out of duties and the way of works.

Kath (ARICA). The most important of the three centers of the human body. Kath is described as being the "vital center," which controls the other two centers (see ᵖpath and ᵖoth).

Katha Upanishad (HINDUISM). Important and popular part of the ᵖUpanishads.

Kaulah (HINDUISM). A sacred cow that is able to grant the wishes of its owner.

Kechari Mudra (HINDUISM). ᵖYoga practice that awakens ᵖKundalini.

Kelpius, Johann (ROSICRUCIANISM; 1673–1708). Person who brought Rosicrucianism to America.

Kensho (BUDDHISM). A term meaning ᵖenlightenment.

Kesh (SIKH DHARMA). Uncut hair that is tied at the top of the head and covered by a turban.

Keys of the Kingdom (MORMONISM). Power given to the highest ranking officials in the Church of Jesus Christ of Latter-Day Saints to bind on earth that which is bound by God in heaven.

Khaalis, Hamaas Abdul (NATION OF ISLAM). Founded the Hanafi Madh-Hab Center, an offshoot of the Nation of Islam in 1968.

Khadijah (ISLAM; n.d.). ᵖMuhammad's wife.

Khalife (ISLAM). See ᵖcaliph.

Khalsa Order (SIKHISM). The main order in the Sikh religion. The Khalsa Order was founded by Gobind Rai, the tenth of the ᵖten gurus.

Khawarij (ISLAM). A group of ᵖMuslims who believe that any qualified disciple may become a ᵖcaliph, regardless of social status.

Khoumeni, The ᵖAyatollah (ISLAM; 1982–1989). Former leader of Iran and its Islamic ᵖShiʔite ᵖsect.

Kiirtan (ANANDA MARGA YOGA SOCIETY). Term used to describe a particular dance used in the training rituals of Ananda Marga.

King David (THE FAMILY). Alternate name for David ᵖBerg, the founder of The Family, originally called The Children of God.

King, George (NEW AGE MOVEMENT; n.d.). The New Age vision that King, founder of the Aetherius Society in London, England, received from the "cosmic brotherhood of space masters," that he had been chosen by this celestial council to be earth's primary ᵖmedium through which cosmic energy would be channeled to the rest of the human race. The society was formed in 1954. King claims that as "primary terrestrial channel," he has spoken with Jesus Christ and the apostle Paul and that he rode in a flying saucer with the Virgin Mary.

King James Version (MORMONISM). The only English translation of the ᵖBible considered to be authoritative for ᵖMormons, with the qualification that authority extends only to those parts that are "correctly translated." For centuries, of course, this translation was the standard English translation in CHRISTIANITY.

Kingdom Farms (JEHOVAH'S WITNESSES). Two farms located in New York state that provide food—mainly vegetables, fruits, and dairy—to the low-salaried workers at the ᵖBethel headquarters in Brooklyn.

Kingdom Hall (JEHOVAH'S WITNESSES). The name designated for local meeting halls where the ᵖcompanies of the Watchtower Bible and Tract Society congregate and conduct their worship meetings. This becomes an important designation because Jehovah's Witnesses reject the name "church" as being apostate.

Kingdom Ministry School (JEHOVAH'S WITNESSES). School that provides shorter periods of training for willing workers who cannot attend the ᵖGilead school.

Kingdom of God (MORMONISM). Those who have entered the ᵖcelestial kingdom. Only those entering the kingdom of God are in God's presence. Inhabitants of the remaining two kingdoms (ᵖterrestrial and ᵖtelestial) are separated from the immediate divine presence.

Kirlian Photography (ᵖoccult). A technique used in ᵖparapsychology for reproducing ᵖauras through the use of photography.

Kirtanya (ISKCON). The sixteen-word ᵖmantra that ᵖHare Krishna devotees regularly recite: "Hare Krishna, Hare Krishna, Krishna, Krishna, Hare, Hare, Hare Rama, Hare Rama Rama, Rama, Hare, Hare."

Klemp, Sri Harold (ECKANKAR; n.d.) In October, 1981, Harold Klemp became the 973rd living Eck Master in Eckankar. Klemp grew up on a farm in rural Wisconsin. He attended college in Milwaukee and Fort Wayne, Indiana, and then joined the U.S. Air Force. Klemp believes that his mission is to bring people to God. He travels widely and conducts seminars, writes books, and broadcasts messages. Humor and practicality highlight his teaching style. Klemp has succeeded in essentially westernizing the Eckankar movement. Klemp emphasizes the importance of people to be involved in community service.

Knight Commander (FREEMASONRY). The highest ranking (thirty-third) degree in Freemasonry, conferred by the ᛚScottish Rite. The degree is conferred on a thirty-second degree Mason by the Supreme Council.

Knorr, Nathan H. (JEHOVAH'S WITNESSES; 1905–1977). From 1942 to 1977 he was president of the Watchtower Bible and Tract Society, after Judge ᛚRutherford died. Knorr served as one of the translators of the ᛚNew World Translation of the ᛚBible.

Koan (ZEN BUDDHISM). A paradoxical riddle that is impossible to solve through reason alone. Because reason is seen to be a major obstacle in the path of one who seeks the truth, it must be avoided. A devotee must meditate on a *koan* in order to awaken intuitive truths within. "What is the sound of one hand clapping?" is an example of a popular *koan*.

Kojiki (SHINTO). Composed about A.D. 700, it is a sacred text of Shinto.

Komei (BUDDHISM; NICHIREN SHOSHU BUDDHISM; SOKA-GAKKAI). Word translated "clean government." The Komei is the political party of Soka-Gakkai. Established in 1965 in Japan, the Komei pursues an active political platform advocating world peace, nuclear disarmament, and the belief that enough active force in the political arena may indeed achieve such goals.

Koran; Quᛚran (ISLAM). The sacred book of Islam believed by ᛚMuslims to be the revelation of ᛚAllah to ᛚMuhammad. The collective text is comprised of 114 chapters or *suras* (Arab—"that which opens or begins"), which mix biblical literature with Arab culture. It was compiled only after Muhammad's death during the reign of the third ᛚcaliph. The Koran outlines the sacred duty of the faithful followers of Muhammad and is characterized by a strict ᛚmonotheism throughout. For a long period, translations of the Koran were strictly forbidden, and many Muslims recite lines and phrases in Arabic without knowing or under-

standing the language. Several good translations have been published, however. A. J. Arberry's *The Koran Interpreted* (1955) is generally recognized as being the most reliable, but to strict Muslims, all translations are merely paraphrases of the original Arabic.

Koresh, David (BRANCH DAVIDIANS; 1959–1993). Leader of the Branch Davidians, who attracted international attention when the compound occupied by the ᛚcult in Waco, Texas, was burned to the ground in a war with United States federal agents. Koresh's original name was Vernon Howell. He changed it to David Koresh based on Isaiah 45, where King Cyrus (*koresh*) is spoken of as "the anointed." Many of Koresh's followers hailed him as a modern day ᛚmessiah.

Kosen Rufu (BUDDHISM; NICHIREN SHOSHU BUDDHISM). For Nichiren Shoshu Buddhism, Kosen Rufu is the realization of world peace, attained only after the teachings of Buddhism are disseminated worldwide.

Kraft, Karl Ernst (ᛚoccult; 1900–1945). A Swiss occult practitioner and astrologer (see ᛚastrology), who was enlisted by Hitler in 1938 to come to the aid of the Third Reich. He interpreted quatrains of ᛚNostradamus to predict the success of the Reich. Joseph Goebbels immediately adopted Kraft's interpretations for propaganda purposes in order to further the myth of the reign of Aryan supremacy.

Kraemer, Heinrich (WITCHCRAFT; 1430–1505). One of the two authors of the famous *Malleus Maleficarum* (*Witches' Hammer*), a medieval work that greatly added to the exacerbation of witchcraft fervor.

Krishmaloka (HINDUISM). The heavenly residence of ᛚHare Krishna.

Krishna (HINDUISM). The most well-known of all the deities of Hinduism, Krishna is the eighth ᛚincarnation of ᛚVishnu. The principal sources where Krishna appears in Hindu literature are the ᛚMabhabharata and the ᛚPuranas. His mother's brother, Kamsa, was a wicked king who attempted to have Krishna destroyed. Krishna was spared death by being smuggled across a river. He grew up as a prankster, miracle worker, and romantic charmer. Later, Krishna returned to Mathura to kill Kamsa. He then married Rukmini and several other wives and settled in modern day Dwarka, Gujarat. According to the ᛚBhagavad Gita, Krishna is ᛚArjuna's charioteer in a war fought between the Kavravas and the Pandavas. He survived the war but was later killed when the arrow of a hunter struck his heel, the only vulnerable spot on his body.

Kriya (HINDUISM). See ᛚkarma.

Kriya Yoga (HINDUISM; SELF-REALIZATION FELLOW-SHIP). A yogic technique developed by Paramahansa ▶Yogananda that enables practicing devotees to achieve ▶enlightenment in three years' time rather than through successive ▶reincarnations throughout many lifetimes. Kriya yoga involves what Yogananda called "intelligent self effort." By directing outer energy to the inner life, the practitioner of Kriya yoga is able to achieve in just thirty seconds what would normally take a year to accomplish.

Krsna (HARE KRISHNA; ISKCON). Another spelling for ▶Krishna.

Kshatriya (HINDUISM). Warriors.

Ku Klux Klan (IDENTITY MOVEMENTS). The Ku Klux Klan is the first white supremacist movement in the United States,

Kundalini (▶occult; HINDUISM; NEW AGE MOVEMENT). A "coil" or "spiral" energy located at the base of the spine that can be aroused through ▶yoga. The goal of such an exercise is to enable the individual to achieve ▶samadhi, heightened psychic abilities, and deeper spiritual awareness. The *kundalini* is channeled through the ▶*chakras*, located from the base of the spine to the crown of the forehead.

K'ung Fu Tzu (CONFUCIANISM). The original name for ▶Confucius, the founder of Confucianism.

Kupayogini (HINDUISM). One with the ability to arouse the psychic or ▶yoga center of the human body.

Kwanzaa (MYAL, RASTAFARIANISM, SANTERIA). The present volume discusses a number of groups that, although not African, have borrowed concepts and beliefs from different African cultures—for instance, Rastafarianism, Myal, Santeria, and the NATION OF ISLAM. In a similar manner, Kwanzaa, a quasi-religious holiday, recently introduced in the United States, also reflects some African concepts and beliefs, though it is not indigenous to Africa.

In 1966, Maulana (Ron) Karenga, a professor of black studies at California State University at Long Beach, proposed a new quasi-religious holiday for Afrocentric black Americans. Karenga called it "Kwanzaa," a Swahili word meaning "first fruits." Throughout the 1970s and 1980s Karenga's proposal lay dormant, but in the early 1990s, with the promoting of multiculturalism in America by the mass media, the idea of Kwanzaa began to attract some black Americans. Kwanzaa has been dubbed the "black Christmas," in part because it takes place immediately following Christmas (from December 26 through January 1).

Although its promoters say Kwanzaa is not a moral or religious holiday, at least one of its seven *nguzo saba* (principles), *imani* (faith), celebrated on the seventh day, has religious connotations. Each of the other six principles—*umoja* (unity), *kujichagulia* (self-determination), *ujima* (collective work), *ujamaa* (cooperative economics), *nia* (purpose), and *kuumba* (creativity)—are honored on the remaining six days, respectively. While not specifically religious, they do intersect with the goals and processes in one's life.

During the last decade or so, many U.S. stores have commercialized Kwanzaa by offering merchandise that reflects an African aura. Critics of Kwanzaa argue it promotes an ideology of racial segregation, one that runs counter to America's long-standing melting-pot philosophy and especially to the country's efforts to promote a racially integrated society (cf. the goals of Martin Luther King Jr., a strong advocate of integration).

L

Lady (▶occult; WITCHCRAFT). A designation sometimes used for a female leader of a witchcraft ▶coven.

Laksmi (HINDUISM). Wife of ▶Vishnu and the goddess of wealth.

Lalita Sahsaranama (HINDUISM). Text that contains the many names of ▶*Kundalini.*

Lama (BUDDHISM). Tibetan Buddhist monk.

Lamanites (MORMONISM). The darker skinned race of people believed in Mormonism to be the scattered remnant of the lost tribes of Israel and the ancestors to the American Indians. Recent scientific research into the DNA of Native Americans has devastated the Mormon claim that they are of Semitic origin.

Lambs (CHURCH OF BIBLE UNDERSTANDING). New converts or recruits to the COBU.

Lammas   See ▶*lughnasadh*.

Lao-tse   (TAOISM; 604–531 B.C.). Founder of Taoism, one of the great religions of China.

Laver-tete   (▶occult; VOODOO). The ceremonial cleansing process that prepares a candidate for initiation into voodoo. The candidate may only enter the next stage of initiation when completely cleansed.

LaVey, Anton Szandor   (SATANISM; 1930–1998). Founder of the Church of Satan (1966) in San Francisco, California.

Leary, Timothy   (▶occult; 1920–1996). American psychologist who, along with his colleague Richard ▶Alpert, as dismissed from Harvard during the 1960s because of their experimental use of LSD and other psychedelic drugs. Leary's writings include *The Psychedelic Experience*, *Politics of Ecstasy* (1968), and numerous other books on ▶altered states of consciousness.

Leek, Sybil   (▶occult; WITCHCRAFT; 1923–1983). Famous English witch noted for her writings, including *The Diary of a Witch*, *The Sybil Leek Book of Fortunetelling*, and *Cast Your Own Spell*. Leek traced her pagan ancestry back to the twelfth century. She was extremely popular because of her radio programs and an occult restaurant she owned, called "Sybil Leek's Cauldron." She came to America in 1966 and established ▶covens in the Midwest.

Left Hand Path   (▶occult, SATANISM). Term used in occult circles synonymous with evil. In the ▶Bible, the ▶goats (wicked) go to the left hand of God to be separated for judgment, while the sheep (righteous) go to the right to be saved (*see* ▶right hand path).

Legba   (▶occult; VOODOO). Name of Haitian deity who serves as a messenger between the deities and humanity. For this reason, Legba stands along the roads of travel and doorways of homes. Legba is of ▶Dahomean origin.

Legerdemain   (▶occult). A transliteration from a French word that means "sleight of hand," used in conventional ▶magic.

Leo   (▶astrology; ▶occult). Latin for "lion," Leo is the fifth ▶sign in the ▶zodiac in astrology. Leo is linked with the Nemean lion that was killed by Hercules in Greek mythology and falls between July 22 and August 21. Persons born under the sign of Leo are characterized by astrologers as being proud, ambitious, pragmatic, amicable, boastful, and good administrators, leaders, and organizers.

Leo, Alan   (▶astrology; THEOSOPHY; 1860–1917). A British theosophist who is credited as being the architect of modern astrology. He began publishing two magazines, *The Astrologer's Magazine* and *Modern Astrology*. He also founded The Astrological Lodge of the Theosophical Society.

Levitation   (▶occult; VOODOO). The phenomenon of "free-floating," where the human body or any animate or inanimate object is suspended in the air with no apparent means of support. Documented cases of feats of levitation have left scientists bewildered and without satisfactory explanation.

Libra   (▶astrology; ▶occult). The seventh ▶sign of the zodiac in astrology for people born between September 22 and October 22. Libra is depicted as a pair of scales born by the goddess Astraea. Persons born under the sign of Libra are said to be competitive, intuitive, artistic, moody, whimsical, and histrionic.

Lila   (HINDUISM). The great play; the act of creation played out by God in a cosmic drama.

Linga; Lingam   (HINDUISM). Stone idols featuring the phallic region of the body used in the worship of ▶Siva.

Litnessing   (THE FAMILY). Term used for the form of fund raising and evangelism by the group formerly called Children of God. Members distributed literature passing along the message of the group and at the same time received funds solicited in the practice.

Little Flock   (JEHOVAH'S WITNESSES). Term used by the Watchtower Bible and Tract Society to refer to the ▶anointed class of 144,000. These will be the only Witnesses who will actually go to heaven, while the remainder of Jehovah's larger flock will enjoy a new paradise on earth.

Loa   (▶occult; VOODOO). A general term for all voodoo spirits or their supernatural force.

Lodge, Sir Oliver   (▶occult; SPIRITUALISM; 1851–1940). Lodge was a celebrated physicist whose interest was in combining the physical world and the transcendental. "He affirmed, with great conviction, that life is the supreme, enduring essence in the universe; that it fills the vast interstellar spaces; and the matter of which the physical world is composed is a particular condensation of ether for the purpose of manifesting life into a conscious, individual form" (from *http://www.fst.org/lodge.htm*). Although some claim that he is the originator of spiritualism in Britain, Lodge was not an active supporter of the movement that gained a large following in Britain and the United States in the nineteenth century.

Logos (CHRISTIANITY). From the Greek word *logos*, meaning "word" or "reason." It was used by the ancient Greeks to convey, in a way consistent with *pantheism, the notion that the world was governed by a universal intelligence. In the New Testament, John adopted this word and applied it to Jesus Christ, the second person of the *Trinity (John 1:1–18). Early church fathers, particularly Ignatius, saw that *logos* could be used to accommodate the Christian gospel to Greek philosophy. Jesus, as Logos of God, was the Creative Word of God incarnate (see *incarnation) in the flesh.

Loko (*occult; VOODOO). God of agriculture in voodoo *cults.

Lord of the Second Advent; the Third Adam (UNIFI-CATION CHURCH). The belief in the return of the Lord to earth two thousand years after his first advent. He will be a man, and unlike Jesus, will marry and establish a family. Together, the divine couple will become the "true parents" of the human race, a belief required of adherents in order to receive forgiveness for sin and to participate in the kingdom on earth and heaven.

The Rev. Sun Myung *Moon was reluctant to proclaim himself as Lord of the Second Advent until July 1992, although Unification literature did so earlier. Moon was crowned *Messiah in a surreptitious coronation ceremony on March 23, 2004, by a group of United States senators and other politicians, which proved embarrassing to Capitol Hill when the news was released. According to the *Divine Principle*, this Christ was to be born in the East (Rev. 7:2–4). The Moonies consider South Korea, Moon's birthplace, as the country spoken of by the prophecy.

Lost Word (FREEMASONRY). A word claimed to have been lost during the building of Solomon's temple. The attainment of the *Royal Arch degree involves the repossession of the Lost Word.

Lotus Position (HINDUISM). The familiar cross-legged posture used in Hinduism for *meditation.

Lotus Sutra (BUDDHISM; NICHIREN SHOSHU BUDDHISM; SOKA-GAKKAI). Body of writings claimed to have been written by Siddharta *Gautama, containing the true teachings of Buddhism.

Love (ISKCON). For ISKCON, the essence of love is *prema*, a divine spiritual love that the devotee exercises toward *Hare Krishna.

Low Magic (*occult). *Magic that is less sensational or more mundane in nature. For example, one can use magic to benefit oneself, such as bringing on good fortune, a new job, acceptance to a college, etc.

Lucifer (*occult; CHRISTIANITY; MORMONISM; SATANISM). In Mormonism, Lucifer is the brother of Jesus Christ, who offered himself as redeemer. When God refused this offer, he rebelled (Gen. 3:1–5, *Inspired Version*). In the *occult, Lucifer is the personification of independent self-conscious mind. In Satanism, some Satanists hold to the occult view, while others view Lucifer as a more powerful god than the God of Christianity. In Christian thinking, Lucifer (Isa. 14:12) is the name of an important *angel (lit., "light-bearer") before the *Fall. After the Fall, he is known as *Satan or the *devil.

Luciferians (*occult, SATANISM). A schismatic *sect of *devil worshipers whose history dates back to the thirteenth century. Luciferians believe that the devil is real and by worshiping him, they receive an enriched, rewarded, and abundant life. There are groups of Luciferians still in existence today.

Lucky Charm (*occult). The belief that possessing or wearing a certain object will result in bringing good luck.

Lucky Horseshoe (*occult; WITCHCRAFT). An iron crescent nailed above the doorways of superstitious individuals in order to ward off evil spirits. Its iron casting affords power against witchcraft.

Lucumi (SANTERIA). Afro-Cubans of *Yoruba origin. Many of the Lucumi people are practitioners of Santeria.

Lughnasadh (*occult; WITCHCRAFT). Also spelled *Lugnasadh, Lughnassadh*, and *Lughnassad* (pronounced *loo-nus-uh*). One of the eight *sabbats observed by *witches and other occult groups. Lughnasadh is also called the August Eve Great Sabbat and is celebrated on July 31, the eve of August 1. The Christian equivalent is *lammas, which is closely associated with the harvest. Lughnasadh takes its name from the god Lugh, or light-bringer. August is the month of harvest. Witches recall the ancient festival of celebrating the earth's rich yield to sustain life (*see* *witches' calendar).

Lunar Almanac (*occult; WITCHCRAFT). Names for thirteen moons used in witchcraft. They are listed as follows:

Moon of Core—the Daughter
Moon of Hilde—the Crone
Moon of Hecate—the Witch
Moon of Astarte—the Queen
Moon of Themis—the Judge
Moon of Minerva—the Amazon
Moon of Isis—the Priestess
Moon of Olwen—the Green Goddess

Moon of Freja—the Shamones
Moon of Diana—the Huntress
Moon of Morrigan—the Seeress
Moon of Bridget—the Sorceress
Moon of Ceridwen—the Mother

LXX (CHRISTIANITY). Roman numeral for 70 (*see* ᵖSeptuagint).

Lycanthropy (ᵖoccult). Belief held by some occult practitioners that one can be transformed into an animal through the practice of ᵖmagic, especially a werewolf.

Magic (ᵖoccult; SATANISM). The ability to control or manipulate nature and the environment in order to serve a particular end or purpose. Aleister ᵖCrowley's spelling of the term added a *k* (ᵖmagick), but his meaning was essentially the same. Magic is one of the three branches of the ᵖoccult (ᵖfortune-telling and ᵖspiritualism are the other two). Satanism as an occult phenomena is classified under magic chiefly because of the rites surrounding the ᵖblack mass. ᵖMagick (spelled with the inclusion of the letter "k") was intended to distinguish between sleight-of-hand tricks by magicians (e.g., pulling rabbits out of a hat) from actual tricks accomplished through supernatural powers.

Magic Circle (ᵖoccult; SATANISM; WITCHCRAFT). The worship area used in witchcraft and Satanism. It is a ᵖcircle drawn on the floor within which the various rituals occur. A magic circle may be located any place where privacy is assured, but sometimes they are drawn in public. It marks boundaries, opens doorways. It contains the tools used for worship, which includes an ᵖaltar and candles placed at the four corners, also known as cardinal points.

Magic, High See ᵖhigh magic.

Magic, Image See ᵖimage magic.

Magic, Low See ᵖlow magic.

Magic, Mortuary See ᵖmortuary magic.

Magic, Natural See ᵖnatural magic.

Magic, Protective See ᵖprotective magic.

Magic, Sexual See ᵖsexual magic.

Magic—The Gathering (ᵖoccult). Like ᵖ*Dungeons and Dragons*, a popular role-playing game involving cards that contain themes drawn from various areas of the occult, such as ᵖGothic witchcraft, WITCHCRAFT, and SATANISM.

Magic, White See ᵖwhite magic.

Magical Name (ᵖoccult). A Latin name adopted by occult practitioners to designate their membership as practitioners of ᵖmagic. For example, Aleister ᵖCrowley adopted the name Perdurabo.

Magician (ᵖoccult). One skilled in the practice of ᵖmagic in its many forms.

Magick (ᵖoccult). The alternate spelling for ᵖmagic used by Aleister ᵖCrowley. Since his time, other practitioners of the occult use this spelling in order to distinguish sleight of hand tricks from the possession and harnessing of supernatural power.

Magister (ᵖoccult; WITCHCRAFT). A male leader in a witchcraft ᵖcoven.

Magus (ᵖoccult). Alternate name for a ᵖwizard.

Maha Bandha (HINDUISM). One of the various ᵖyoga practices for awakening ᵖ*Kundalini*. Maha Bandha is regarded as being the "greatest" means for doing so by its practitioners.

Mahabbah (SUFISM). Love.

Mahabharata (HINDUISM). One of the epic poems of Hindu literature. *Mahabharata* is a lengthy poem composed of one hundred thousand couplets describing the rivalry between the ᵖ*Pandavas* and their brothers (*Kavravas*), who were rulers in the land of Delhi. *Mahabharata* was begun around 400 B.C. and was developed and expanded on for nearly eight hundred years thereafter.

Maha-Mantra (ISKCON). The chant uttered by devotees to ᵖHare Krishna: "*Hare Krishna, Hare Krishna, Krishna, Krishna, Hare, Hare, Hare Rama, Hare Rama Rama, Rama, Hare, Hare.*"

Mahanta (ECKANKAR). An Eck master who has achieved the status of the "living manifestation of God," thereby being all-knowing, all-powerful, and above moral restraint and human law.

Maharaj Ji, Guru (ELAN VITAL; 1957–). Spiritual leader and founder of Divine Light Mission (now known as Elan Vital).

Maharaj, Sri Swami Sivananda (HINDUISM; 1887–1963). Established the Divine Life Society, a reform movement of Hinduism.

Maharishi International University See TRANSCENDENTAL MEDITATION.

Maharishi Mahesh Yogi See TRANSCENDENTAL MEDITATION.

Mahatma (ᵖoccult; ELAN VITAL; ISKCON; HINDUISM; THEOSOPHY). A great disciple of Lord ᵖKrishna in Hindu literature. In Hinduism, a great disciple to whom respect is owed. Mahatma is a Sanskrit term meaning "great soul" and is used in Hinduism for one who has attained great knowledge and wisdom. Mahatmas are those followers of ᵖguru ᵖMaharaj Ji, who actively evangelize for the Elan Vital (Divine Light Mission) (*see* ᵖinitiator). In Theosophy, it is an ᵖadept that obtains hidden knowledge through a living person, as opposed to SPIRITUALISM, where such knowledge is sought from the spirits of the departed.

Mahavira, Vardhamana (JAINISM; 599–527 B.C.). Born in Kundalapur, India, he was the founder of Jainism.

Mahdi (ISLAM). In the Sunnite tradition of Islam, the hope is that a *mahdi* will one day come to bring righteousness. The term is the rough equivalent to the Jewish and Christian concept of ᵖMessiah.

Maiden (WITCHCRAFT). Name given to a female who leads a ᵖcoven. *See also* ᵖlady.

Maitreya (BUDDHISM; NEW AGE MOVEMENT; THEOSOPHY). The phrase means "the ultimate teacher." In Buddhism it means the "final" ᵖbuddha. In the New Age Movement, Maitreya is believed to be a world leader who will be returning to earth. According to this movement, Maitreya is Christ for CHRISTIANITY, Maitreya for Buddhism, ᵖKrishna in HINDUISM, Messiah for JUDAISM, etc. Maitreya will come to bring peace to the world, true ᵖenlightenment and self-realization, a stable and healthy environment, and harmony among all of the world's religions. Between 1987 and 1992 in London, Benjamin ᵖCrème claims that Maitreya telepathically communicated a message or series of messages about the disturbing conditions of the world in terms of poverty, declining morality, etc.

Major Arcana (ᵖoccult). Twenty-two ᵖtarot cards that symbolize the human psyche.

Makiguchi, Tsonesaburo (SOKA-GAKKAI; n.d.). Founded the Value Creation Society in 1930, also called Soka-Gakkai.

Makonnen, Ras Tafari (RASTAFARIANISM; 1893–1975). Was crowned in 1930 Emperor ᵖSelassie of Ethiopia. He was viewed as the great liberator of the blacks, and his followers called themselves Rastafarians.

Malcolm X (NATION OF ISLAM; 1925–1965). One of the most popular spokesman for the Black Muslim movement of the World Community of Ali Islam in the West. However, he broke from the more pacifist position in his theology. He was gunned down by a fanatic in 1965.

Malleus Maleficarum (ᵖoccult; CHRISTIANITY; WITCHCRAFT). Latin for the title of a book published in the high Middle Ages by two Roman Catholic monks, Heinrich ᵖKraemer and Johannes ᵖSprenger, titled in English *The Witches' Hammer*. It is a classic manual in Gothic witchcraft.

Mambo (ᵖoccult; VOODOO). A female priestess in voodoo.

Mana (ᵖoccult; SATANISM). The belief in the existence of a supernatural life-force dwelling within sacred objects or persons. In Satanism and other occult religions that practice ritual sacrifice, it is believed that the shedding of blood produces power. This is often referred to as *mana*.

Manichaeism (CHRISTIANITY). A philosophy stemming from Mani, a Persian of the third century A.D. He taught a strict dualism, whereby light and darkness, good and evil, God and the ᵖdevil, are caught in an eternal conflict. Augustine was a Manichaean in his early years; later, after his conversion to Christianity, he offered an able defense against it by showing from the ᵖBible that God is the omnipotent source of all good and that it would be impossible for evil to prevail, or else God would not be omnipotent. Evil, for Augustine, was the privation of good. Manichaeism was suppressed in the church in the seventh century, but it reappeared in the Bogomils, Cathari, and other heretical ᵖsects.

Manifesto (MORMONISM). The famous statement issued in 1890 by the Mormon president Wilford ᵖWoodruff , suspending the practice of polygamy: "I now publicly declare that my advice . . . is to refrain from contracting any marriage forbidden by the law of the land." The Manifesto appears at the end of ᵖ*Doctrine and Covenants*.

Manman (VOODOO). Large drum used in voodoo worship rites.

Mantra (HINDUISM; ISKCON; TRANSCENDENTAL MEDITATION). A word or phrase given in Sanskrit to a transcendental meditation devotee during his or her initiation ceremony. The devotee is to meditate on this mantra twice daily, even though he or she does not know its true meaning. The mantra serves as a vehicle through which the subject passes into the various levels of consciousness until reaching absolute bliss consciousness. In ISKCON, devotees speak a specific mantra chanted in the name of *Krishna. The term mantra is commonly used to refer to repetitive religious chants or prayers.

Maracas (*occult; ABAKUA; SOUTH AMERICAN, CENTRAL AMERICAN, AND CARIBBEAN CULTS; VOODOO). Rhythmic instruments used in many of the South and Central American and Caribbean Cults in dance ritual and ceremonial worship. Maracas are usually gourds filled with pebbles or dried seeds.

Marga (HINDUISM). The Hindu word for "way"; the way of salvation that is the way of escape from the cycle of rebirth (*see* *reincarnation).

Marifah (SUFISM). The inner knowledge or *enlightenment one experiences after rigorous training and *asceticism.

Mark Master; Fourth Degree (FREEMASONRY). The fourth degree in or the first within the *York Rite. The first three degrees are completed in the *Blue Lodge. The degree involves the myth about finding a missing keystone in a pile of rubble in ancient Tyre. The stone was engraved with symbols and proved to be the missing stone needed the complete the building of the temple of Solomon.

Martial Arts (BUDDHISM; TAOISM). The various fighting sports such as karate, kung fu, t'ai chi ch'uan, judo, jujitsu, and aikido, the beginnings of which date back to almost 3000 B.C. The varieties of fighting styles are united by a spiritual center rooted in Taoism and Buddhism. Buddhist monk *Bodhidharma is believed to be the originator of the martial arts.

The religious significance of the arts lies in the harmonizing of life forces (*yin and yang) and the ability to harness *ch'i. Masters in the martial arts accomplish tremendous physical feats. The ability to strike or kick with tremendous physical force or to smash a pile of bricks with a single blow is attributed to *ch'i*. Many who practice the martial arts do so without an awareness of the religious nature of the sport(s) but in the interest of physical fitness or self-defense.

Masjid (ISLAM). A *mosque or designated place for worship and prayer. A *masjid* must be free from all idols and memorials. It must have clean running water at all times. No idols, symbolic objects, mirrors, or memorials are allowed either inside or outside the *masjid*.

Mass Incarnation (*occult; NEW AGE MOVEMENT). The Christ principle, or principle of divinity, that sparked the *cosmic Christ in the body of Jesus two thousand years ago is now believed by New Age Movement practitioners to be moving on collective humanity.

Master (*occult; *parapsychology). Occult *adept whose spiritual level far surpasses most people. Masters, by their own choice, have chosen to remain on the earth to guide others in a quest for truth. They are even said to be able to control affairs in the world by means of deep meditation. In so doing, they exert influence over pupils scattered throughout the world.

Master Mason; Third Degree (FREEMASONRY). The third degree awarded to an initiate in the *Blue Lodge in Freemasonry. This third degree is the final initiatory degree. Before a candidate is awarded the degree, they make an oath promising never to divulge the secrets that are to be shown them as they progress as Masons.

Master Speaks (UNIFICATION CHURCH). A collection of edited statements, lectures, and teachings by Sun Myung *Moon, founder of the Unification Church.

Masters, Roy, *See* *Obermeister, Ruben.

Material (*occult). Matter as distinguished from spirit.

Materialization (SPIRITUALISM). Matter or a person that appears physically during a *séance.

Mawu Lisa (*occult; VOODOO). The deity to whom is ascribed the activity of creation among the Haitians. Mawu Lisa was imported to Haiti from *Dahomey.

Maya (HINDUISM). Illusion; straying from the path or losing sight of the basic tenet of existence, i.e., of one's relationship with *Hare *Krishna.

May Day (*occult). Time annually when various ancient cults celebrated the fertility of the earth through engaging in ritualistic sex. The "May Pole" is the phallic symbol that dance rituals are performed around during May Day celebrations.

May Eve See *Witches Calendar and *Beltane.

McKean, Kip See INTERNATIONAL CHURCHES OF CHRIST.

Mecca (ISLAM). The most holy city in Islam, located in Saudi Arabia, and the birthplace of *Muhammad. A devout ▸Muslim prays five times daily while facing Mecca and is also expected to undergo a pilgrimage (▸*hajj*) to the holy city at least once in a lifetime.

Medicine Man (▸occult; VOODOO). The man in primitive cultures and in voodoo who is regarded as being a priest or ▸shaman and is responsible for diagnosing illness and prescribing magical remedies.

Meditation (BUDDHISM; HINDUISM; TRANSCENDENTAL MEDITATION). Virtually all of the eastern religions derived from Hinduism and Buddhism practice meditation. Meditation, as distinguished from prayer or the act of praying as practiced in CHRISTIANITY, JUDAISM, and ISLAM (where the person directs devotions to God apart from and outside of the self), meditation is the reflective focus on the latent deity within the self. It can also mean self-awareness and reflective rumination.

Medium (▸occult; SILVA MIND CONTROL; SPIRITUALISM). The occult term for one who acts as an intermediary between the spirit world and the physical world. Mediums make use of various objects, such as ▸ouija boards, drawings, rapping noises, etc., to convey a message from the spirits to the living. Often the medium will serve as the spokesperson. In Silva Mind Control, the medium may be conjured up within the mind of an individual (see also ▸counselor).

Melchizedek Priesthood (MORMONISM). The highest possible order in the Mormon church; superior to the ▸Aaronic Priesthood in both power and authority. According to Mormons, the Melchizedek priesthood was conferred upon Joseph ▸Smith and Oliver ▸Cowdery through Peter, James, and John (three of Jesus' disciples) in May 1829. It is conferred only on male members of the church after they have reached their sixteenth birthday. ▸*Doctrine and Covenants* sums up the Melchizedek priesthood well.

> All other authorities or officers in the church are appendages to this Priesthood ... the Melchizedek Priesthood comprehends the Aaronic or Levitical Priesthood and is the grand head, and holds the highest authority that pertains to the Priesthood, and the keys to the kingdom of God in all ages of the world to the latest prosperity on the earth: and is the channel through which all knowledge, doctrine, the plan of salvation and every important matter is revealed from heaven. (*Doctrine and Covenants*, sec. 107: 5)

Mendez, Goat of (▸occult; SATANISM). Also called ▸baphomet, the goat of Mendez is often pictured simply as a goat's head. In its fullest form, however, it is a goat's head attached to a full male body with female breasts. An inverted ▸pentagram is usually inscribed on the forehead along with a lighted torch. (*See also* ▸goat, ▸goat's head).

Menorah (JUDAISM). An eight-branched candle used in Judaism as a celebration of the Feast of Hannukah, the celebration of the triumph of Judas Maccabeus (d. 160 B.C.) over the Seleucid generals who were desecrating the Jewish Temple.

Mental Telepathy (▸occult). An occult practitioner who is able to hear the thoughts of another person's mind.

Mentor (▸occult; WITCHCRAFT). Leaders or older experienced members of a ▸coven.

Mercy Seat (JUDAISM). The mercy seat was the lid of the ▸ark of the covenant (Ex. 25:17, called "the atonement cover" in the NIV). It was made of solid gold and was decorated on each side with cherubim. The ▸high priest sprinkled blood on the mercy seat once yearly in order to atone for the sins of God's people. Here God promised to hear and answer prayer and in mercy to grant forgiveness or render judgment on Israel. CHRISTIANITY borrows from the idea of the mercy seat by referring to Jesus Christ as God's "propitiation through faith" (Rom. 3:25; KJV) or as a "sacrifice of atonement" (NIV). The English words "propitiation" and "atonement" are translated from the Greek word "*hilasterion*," the same word used in Hebrews 9:5 that the KJV translates "mercy seat" and the NIV "atonement cover."

Meridians See ▸ch'i, ▸yin and yang, and ▸acupuncture.

Mesmerism (▸occult; ▸parapsychology). A term named after Freidrich Anton Mesmer (1733–1815), an Austrian doctor who experimented a great deal with ▸hypnotism. Mesmer believed waves of energy formed a magnetic field around a person in a hypnotic state. Mesmerism is synonymous with hypnotism. *See also* ▸mind science and SPIRITUALISM.

Messiah (CHRISTIANITY; JUDAISM; UNIFICATION CHURCH). Meaning "anointed one," the Messiah in Judaism was one who would be God's anointed one to bring salvation. His coming is spoken of amply in the prophets. He would be of the lineage and the house of David (Zech. 12:10–14). David himself wrote frequently about the coming Messiah (Ps. 2; 16; 21; 22; 40; 110). The Messiah would bring to Israel a spiritual blessing, would be a suffering servant (Ps. 22; Isa. 53), and would be hailed as a great Prince and Ruler (Isa. 9:6).

Christianity assigned Jesus to this role as the promised Messiah long awaited by Israel. The name "Christ" (a Greek word meaning "anointed one") is the designated title for God's "anointed one." The early believers recognized that Jesus was the one whom Israel had been awaiting, yet was the one whom Israel rejected. That rejection was prophesied clearly for the earliest Christians in Psalm 22 and Isaiah 53 (cf. John 1:10–11). The Messiah as a conquering king (Ps. 2) also was fulfilled in the person of Jesus, who was a conqueror—not of an earthly kingdom won through military might, but rather as a victor over sin—and a king whose kingdom is not of this world (John 18:36).

For the Unification Church, Sun Myung ⟩Moon was proclaimed to be the Messiah in a coronation ceremony on March 23, 2004, by a somewhat embarrassed group of U.S. senators and other politicians when the news was released.

MEST (SCIENTOLOGY). Acronym for "matter, energy, space, time." MEST is the Scientologist designation for earth and all of its attendant contingencies and limitations. The goal of all therapy is to ultimately enable one to gain complete power over MEST.

Metanetwork (NEW AGE MOVEMENT). Term coined by New-Agers Jessica Lipnack and Jeffrey Stamps in their book *Networking* (1982). The term is used to attempt to describe how so many different organizations and New Age groups are connected or interrelated to one another. The answer furnished by Stamps and Lipnack is that the movements are related unconsciously or consciously by virtue of common goals: "Networks are composed of self reliant and autonomous participants . . . who simultaneously function as independent 'wholes' and as interdependent 'parts.'" (p. 7). Each group acts independently of the others insofar as each carries out its own agenda. But they share common New Age values rooted in Eastern ⟩mysticism and the quest for planetary transformation.

Metaphysical Bible Dictionary (UNITY SCHOOL OF CHRISTIANITY). Reference book written by Unity founder Charles ⟩Fillmore. Fillmore redefines many terms in his work that part company with their traditional meanings as understood in the orthodox traditions of CHRISTIANITY.

Middle Path (BUDDHISM; NICHIREN SHOSHU BUDDHISM; SOKA-GAKKAI). The famous compromise formulated by ⟩Gautama Buddha. The "middle way" between the excesses of indulgence in materialism on the one hand, and the austerity of total self-abnegation and denial on the other. Gautama realized that these extremes failed to eliminate suffering simply because they failed to eliminate desire. Rather, they only served to augment desire, thereby increasing the potential for human suffering. What was needed, he reasoned, was a third way, namely, the middle path (*see* ⟩eightfold path).

Midsummer Solstice (⟩occult; WITCHCRAFT). One of the eight ⟩Sabbats observed by ⟩witches and other ⟩occult groups, celebrated on June 22. The midsummer solstice is the longest day of the year. On this day the sun god is at his highest and brightest point. With the invoking of the sun god on this day, darkness is out to flight and fertility is brought to the earth (*see* ⟩witches calendar).

Mikado (SHINTO). The term used for the belief in ⟩Shinto that the emperor of Japan rules by divine sanction and command.

Millennial Dawn (JEHOVAH'S WITNESSES). Original title of Charles Taze ⟩Russell's seven-volume work on Jehovah Witness theology. The name of the set was later changed to ⟩*Studies in the Scriptures.*

Millennialism A belief, held by many religious groups, in a future period of one thousand years in which the kingdom of God is established and flourishes on earth (cf. Rev. 20:1–6).

Millerite Movement (CHRISTIANITY; SEVENTH-DAY ADVENTISM). Named after William Miller (1782–1849), a farmer from New York, who predicted the second coming of Christ. Miller succeeded in gaining a significant following, especially after he became precise in his calculations. Basing his claims on ⟩Bible prophecy, Miller concluded that the end of the world and Jesus' second advent would take place between March 21, 1843, and March 21, 1844. Converts became numerous during this time of heightened fervency. When the end did not come, there was great disappointment.

Miller, however, turned his attention to a "tarrying time" of seven months and ten days, according to Habakkuk 2:3. He recalculated that October 22, 1844, would mark the end. The fervor was rekindled and more followers became part of the movement. When the second prediction failed, many left, greatly disappointed (*see* ⟩great disappointment). Miller's remaining followers were reorganized under the leadership of Ellen G. ⟩White (1872–1915) and became known as Seventh-day Adventism.

Mind Dynamics (FORUM; LIFESPRING). A now-defunct organization that taught that the mind is the source of infinite possibility. By tapping its latent powers, one can come to fully realize personal transformation, health, and wealth. Mind Dynamics closed its doors in 1975, but several of its members, including John ▸Hanley and Werner ▸Erhard, founders of Life Spring and The Forum (formerly EST) respectively, carried its principles to their own organizations.

Mind Science   (RELIGIOUS SCIENCE). Term used as a general classification for religious groups that relegate religious truths (love, self-worth, etc.) to aspects of the mind or toward the latent divinity that resides in every individual. Mind science groups received their initial thrust from the "harmonial" and NEW THOUGHT religions (*see* CHRISTIAN SCIENCE, UNITY SCHOOL OF CHRISTIANITY). The ideas prevalent in New Thought religion heavily inspired Ernest ▸Holmes, considered to be the father of the mind sciences.

Generally, mind sciences are religions that emphasize the use of metaphysical science in order to prescribe therapy necessary to the aid and betterment of an individual. Generally speaking, practitioners of mind science regard God as being a concept to describe the unity of substance of which the universe is composed (*see* ▸monism) and evil as being merely a state of mind that may be changed.

Minister   (JEHOVAH'S WITNESSES). The Watchtower Bible and Tract Society understands the concept of minister as being one who is "called to serve." This includes all members of the society. The *Aid to Bible Understanding* (1971) lists several classifications of ministers: Jehovah's angelic ministers; the tribe of Levi; prophets; Jesus Christ; ▸ministerial servants; and earthly rulers.

Ministerial Servants   (JEHOVAH'S WITNESSES). Members of the Watchtower Bible and Tract Society who attend to the administrative affairs within a congregation. Their differentiation from ▸overseers is based on the distinction the ▸Bible makes between *episkopoi*, "overseer" (1 Tim. 3:1), and *diakonos*, "servant" (Matt. 20:26). Ministerial servants' roles are regarded as being extremely important, but it is not their responsibility to teach or "shepherd" a congregation. This is the responsibility of the overseers. Ministers assist the overseers in these duties.

Minor Arcana   (▸occult). The fifty-six ▸tarot cards, distinguished from the ▸major arcana. They comprise four suits called ▸pentacles, ▸swords, ▸wands, and ▸cups.

Mirror Magic   (▸occult). See ▸mirror mantic.

Mirror Mantic   (▸occult). A form of ▸fortune-telling that uses a mirror or some other means of reflection

such as water. A ▸spell is cast on the object reflected in the mirror.

Mishnah   (JUDAISM). That body of literature in Judaism that arose after the destruction of Jerusalem in A.D. 70; it was intended to supplement the ▸Torah. The word *mishnah* is a Hebrew word meaning "repeat" and refers to a rabbinic commentary on the sacred law. The Mishnah contains a multitude of additional laws and traditions. Along with a more lengthy commentary called the Gemara, it is included in the ▸Talmuds.

Mission   (MORMONISM). Term used to designate a period of eighteen months that most Mormons dedicate to proselytizing for the Church of Jesus Christ of Latter-Day Saints.

Mo Letters   (THE FAMILY). Also called Mo missives, these were letters of communication and teachings by Moses ▸David, the founder of the The Family.

Modalistic Monarchianism   (CHRISTIANITY). A slight variation of ▸monarchianism that held that God manifested himself in three different modes throughout history. According to this view, since God is a single entity not three persons, as traditional Christianity teaches, he manifested himself first as being the Father, or Creator. At the ▸incarnation, he became the Son (*see* ▸patripassianism). And as the Holy Spirit, God is the sanctifier, teacher, and comforter of the church. Monarchianism was condemned as being heretical because it failed to distinguish between the single essence of the Godhead and the three persons of the ▸Trinity.

Modern Thought   (UNITY SCHOOL OF CHRISTIANITY). A former name for Unity School of Christianity.

Moksha   (HINDUISM). Escape from the illusory process of ▸*Maya*. It is also called *moksa*, meaning "liberation."

Monarchianism   (CHRISTIANITY). Anti-Trinitarian doctrine that developed in the second and third centuries and taught that God comprised a single being and that Christ was not divine but a pure man miraculously born of a virgin and then adopted by God. This idea was also known as adoptionism. See also ▸dynamic monarchianism.

Monism   (HINDUISM). A philosophy that views everything in the universe as being an extension of one reality. All differentiation is an illusion and is absorbed into the one source of all that exists.

Monk   (SATCHIDANANDA ASHRAM INTEGRAL YOGA INSTITUTE). An individual who is set apart from the rest to serve. A monk is assigned tasks suited to his ability and the need for such services.

Monophysitism; Monophysites (CHRISTIANITY). A
▸Christology controversy that taught that Jesus possessed only one nature, not two, and that that one nature
was essentially divine. It was not until the ecumenical
council of Chalcedon (A.D. 451) that monophysitism
was condemned.

Monotheism (CHRISTIANITY; ISLAM; JUDAISM). The
belief in only one God.

Monothelitism (CHRISTIANITY). ▸Christology that
taught that Jesus possessed only one single divine will
or energy. Similar to ▸monophysitism, the monothelit-
ist controversy was fought in the seventh century. Hon-
orarius I issued his *Ecthesis*, in which he sanctioned
the use of the term "one will." Sophronius, the patriarch
of Jerusalem, challenged this notion, insisting on
describing Christ as having "two wills," human and
divine, and that the human will was subordinate to the
divine. The Council of Constantinople of A.D. 680 settled the controversy, accepting that Christ had two wills.

Moon, Sun Myung (UNIFICATION CHURCH; 1920–).
Born in Pyungan Buk-do, North Korea. Rev. Moon
started the Unification Church, believing that he must
fulfill the work Jesus Christ failed to finish. Moon
received his vision of his divine mission in 1945. It is
reported as follows:

> After nine years of search and struggle, the truth of
> God was sealed into his hands (Moon's). At that
> moment, he became the absolute victor of heaven
> and earth. The whole spirit world bowed down to
> him on that day of victory, for not only had he freed
> himself completely from the accusation of Satan,
> but he was now able to accuse Satan before God.
> Satan totally surrendered to him on that day, for he
> had elevated himself to the position of God's true
> son. The weapon to subjugate Satan then became
> available to all mankind. (Sun Myung Moon, *Mes-
> sage to the World Unification Family* [Washington,
> D.C.: The Holy Spirit Association for the Unifica-
> tion of World Christianity, 1964]).

Moonies (UNIFICATION CHURCH). Pejorative (usually)
label for followers of Sun Myung ▸Moon.

Moroni (MORMONISM). The name of the celestial messenger whom Joseph ▸Smith claimed to have been first
visited by in 1823. In a series of visitations, Moroni
allegedly conveyed to Smith the instructions needed to
locate the sacred writings found on golden plates that,
when translated, became the *Book of Mormon*.

Mortuary Magic (▸occult). An occult ceremony performed in order for benefits to be visited on the dead.

These benefits are various in number, such as comfort,
a more favorable rebirth, etc.

Moslem (ISLAM). Also spelled Muslim, one who
adheres to the Islamic religion.

Mosque (ISLAM). From the Arabic *masjid* or "temple." The mosque is the Muslim sacred gathering place
for prayer.

Most Excellent Master; Sixth Degree (FREEMA-
SONRY). The sixth degree in Freemasonry achieved in
the ▸York Lodge. The ritual involves reviewing the steps
necessary in completing Solomon's temple.

Mother Church (CHRISTIAN SCIENCE). The First
Church of Christ, Scientist, located in Boston, Massachusetts. The Mother Church was incorporated and
received its charter on August 23, 1879. It is the headquarters for Christian Science, which was begun in
1892 when Mary Baker ▸Eddy reorganized the movement she had founded in 1879. The full name for the
Mother Church is The Mother Church, the First Church
of Christ, Scientist. The Mother Church is the nerve
center for branch churches around the world.

Mother God (MORMONISM). "Mother in heaven." The
idea that all people have been spiritually born to God's
wife. All are the offspring of the Eternal Mother God.

Mother Goddess (▸occult; WITCHCRAFT). Term used
to personify nature, fertility, the female principle, etc.
Because life emerges from the womb of a woman,
witches celebrate and worship the mother goddess as
the fount and source of life.

Mudras (HINDUISM). The various ▸yoga practices that
awaken the ▸*kundalini.*

Muhadjir (ISLAM). ▸Muhammad's inner circle or closest followers; those who had complete faith in the legitimacy of the prophet's call and message.

Muhammad (ISLAM). In A.D. 610, at forty years of
age, the soon-to-be founder of Islam entered a cave
where he was confronted by the angel Gabriel, who
called him to: "Proclaim in the name of the Lord. You
are God's messenger." Here began Muhammad's career
as a prophet of ▸Allah. His most famous work is the
▸Koran, compiled after his death.

Muhammad, Elijah (NATION OF ISLAM; 1897–1975).
Formerly named Elijah ▸Pool. Elijah Muhammad
replaced Wallace ▸Fard as the leader of the Nation of
Islam, the Black Muslim movement.

Muhammad, Mirza Ali (BAHA'I FAITH; 1819–1850).
Also called the "the Bab" or the one who will herald the
coming of the prophet. He founded the Baha'i Faith.

Mukti (HINDUISM). The liberation of the soul from the wheel or cycle of rebirth.

Mulla (ISLAM). A scholar or teacher of Islamic law.

Munafikun (ISLAM). Those in Medina who followed ⟩Muhammad, not because of loyalty to the prophet or because of religious convictions, but because it was politically expedient to do so. They were, therefore, unreliable and could be expected at any time to forsake Muhammad and his cause.

Muni (HINDUISM). A sage.

Murray, John (UNITARIAN-UNIVERSALIST ASSOCIATION; 1741–1815). A leading lecturer on ⟩universalism in the eighteenth century.

Murray, Margaret (⟩occult; WITCHCRAFT; 1863–1963). Anthropologist, Egyptologist, occult dabbler, and herself perhaps a practicing ⟩witch. She expounded in her books *The Witch-Cult in Western Europe* (1921), *The God of the Witches* (1933), and through articles and lectures, that witchcraft predated Christianity by centuries, having its precedent in ancient paganism.

Murshi (ISLAM; SUFISM). Common term used for the title of a religious leader in Islam.

Musalman (HINDUISM). An Indian (India) term for a ⟩Muslim.

Muslim (ISLAM). Adjective relating to a practitioner or certain aspect or concept in Islam.

Muslim Lunar Calendar (ISLAM). The calendar that Islam follows. The Muslim lunar calendar is eleven days shorter than the Gregorian calendar. Muslim holidays are not assigned fixed dates; rather, they vary from year to year (*see* ⟩Islamic holidays).

Mysticism (⟩occult; CHRISTIANITY). The belief in the attainment of a knowledge of God, not through indirect means (chiefly the Word of God and/or the ⟩sacraments), but through an immediate experience. Certain mystics have described experiences of complete absorption into the divine, precipitated by a divine spark, or *scintilla*, from within. The mystical tradition within Christianity has enjoyed a long but not uncontroversial history. Christian mystics have existed in every age, and likewise, mysticism has had outspoken opponents—mostly from Protestant circles, who maintain that it was a derivative of ancient paganism and ⟩gnosticism because it diverts attention away from the gospel. Many ⟩sects and ⟩cults are mystical in orientation.

Naamah (⟩occult). A female ⟩demon of lust. According to Jewish tradition, Naamah also suffocates and kills newborn children.

Nanak, Guru (SIKHISM; 1469–1538). Founder of the reform version of Hinduism known as Sikhism.

Narayana (HINDUISM). Term designates a particular identification for God.

Natural Magic (⟩occult). The belief that one can effectively change weather patterns through the use of ⟩magic.

Nature Spirits (⟩occult). During the Middle Ages, it was believed that all of nature was under the power of the ⟩devil and that ⟩Satan controlled it as his domain. As a result, many came to embrace nature spirits as personifications of life forces. They considered natural disasters, for example, as demonic forces stirred up to manifest destruction and death. Other nature spirits include ⟩elementals, fairies, elves, and pixies.

Nauvoo (MORMONISM). A town in Illinois founded by Joseph ⟩Smith, where he was eventually arrested and died in 1844.

Nauvoo Expositor (MORMONISM). Newspaper printed in ⟩Nauvoo, Illinois, that was highly critical of Joseph ⟩Smith. It was when Smith ordered the destruction of this "free press" that he was charged with treason and eventually killed while in jail in Carthage, Illinois.

Near Death Experience; NDE (NEW AGE MOVEMENT). Many people have reported experiencing a "near death experience," meaning that their bodies have medically died, but they report a consciousness of themselves outside their bodies (see Betty ⟩Eadie). The circumstances and actual experiences that people report are very different. However, certain central themes unite most of the reporting:

- the soul leaving the body; experiencing a vortex or tunnel accompanied by light, or sometimes darkness

- the experience of joy (most reports), or extreme agitation and distress
- an awareness that one is in a critical moment, that of passing over to death, or becoming aware that one's time is not yet
- meeting other people and experiencing actual communication
- validation—that is to say, one is to return to life and further the righteous cause of whatever belief one has held to
- a monistic feeling of total knowledge or vision
- a crisis experience where one is faced with a decision to return to the body or move on to death and not return

Necromancy (ᵇoccult). The rite of communication with the dead. Such a practice involves incantations accompanying the opening of the coffin of the deceased. The necromancer's purpose is to seek out information regarding the future.

Necrophlia (ᵇoccult). Term meaning "love for the dead," it is the practice of having sexual relations with dead persons.

Neopaganism (ᵇoccult; WITCHCRAFT). A term for describing ancient practitioners of pagan (meaning "village") religions. The ancient forms of paganism included the cultic mystery religions such as existed during the time of the Roman Empire, the ancient Celtic religions, the Germanic and Gothic religions, and the like. Neo-paganism is a revival of these ancient religions in modern times, the nature of which is chiefly revolving around the themes of earth worship—the essence of witchcraft.

Neophyte (ᵇoccult; SATANISM). A new initiate to a ᵇcoven or various other occult groups.

Nest (ᵇoccult; WITCHCRAFT). Term used to designate the various occult and witchcraft ᵇcovens.

Nestorianism (CHRISTIANITY). A doctrine named after its chief proponent, Nestorius (d. ca. A.D. 451), which held that the two natures of Christ, the human and the divine, were completely separated from each other. This led, in its extreme form, to the conclusion that Jesus Christ was two separate persons. Nestorianism was rejected at the Council of Ephesus (A.D. 431), but remained an influential Christological (see ᵇChristology) view embraced by religious groups throughout the centuries (*see* Appendix 2).

New Birth (WORLDWIDE CHURCH OF GOD). One of the most peculiar definitions of this well-known phrase comes from the former Worldwide Church of God, which, under the leadership of Herbert W. ᵇArmstrong, taught that the new birth takes place only at the resurrection from the dead. In other words, one cannot be born again during one's earthly life. Armstrong interpreted John 3:3ff. (unless one is born of the Spirit, one cannot enter the kingdom of God) to mean that human flesh must die in order to put on incorruption. This spiritual raising cannot take place until the body has died physically. See also ᵇborn again. The new Worldwide Church of God has rejected this teaching. It continues to reside, however, in the various splinter groups loyal to Armstrong.

New Hope Singers International (UNIFICATION CHURCH). A singing group whose members are from the Unification Church. The purpose for the group is not so much one of direct proselytizing as it is for creating good public relations.

New Nation News (THE FAMILY). An irregular publication issued forth from the Family.

New World Translation of the Holy Scriptures (JEHOVAH'S WITNESSES). Published in one volume in 1961 by the Watchtower Bible and Tract Society, this work brought together smaller portions of the Bible published separately in 1953, 1955, 1957, 1958, and 1960.

Special alterations are introduced into the translation to conform to Watchtower theology. For example, the Holy Spirit is not addressed as being a personal member of the ᵇTrinity, as he is in orthodox Christianity. Rather, the Watchtower translates Holy Spirit as being God's "active force" in Genesis 1:2 or as being "holy spirit" in 2 Corinthians 13:14. Another example, perhaps the most conspicuous of all, is the translation of John 1:1. The KJV renders the verse "In the beginning was the Word, and the Word was with God, and the *Word was God*" (emphasis added). The New World Translation inserts the indefinite article *a* in the last three words to read "the Word was a god." Alterations like these have made the New World Translation theologically unique.

Nganga (SANTERIA; VOODOO). A ᵇcauldron used in rituals and ceremonies that contains various items used in worship. In some cases this includes human remains.

Nichiren Daishonin (NICHIREN SHOSHU BUDDHISM). The founder of Nichiren Shoshu Buddhism.

Nirgun (HINDUISM). That which is without conditions or attributes (see ᵇsagun).

Nirvana (HINDUISM). The final outcome of the life process. The state of ultimate bliss reached when ᵇat-

man becomes one with ▪*Brahman* and the release from the phenomenal world of illusory sensory perceptions is attained.

Norton, Andrews   (UNITARIANISM; 1786–1853). He is known as the "pope of unitarianism."

Nostradamus   (▪astrology; ▪occult; 1503–1566). Nostradamus is popular for his "prophecies" that today are closely associated with astrology. He was born in St. Remy in France. His book *The Centuries* was well publicized throughout Europe and soon other parts of the world. The title suggests the style of writing that Nostradamus employed. He arranged the writings into four-line verses called quatrains, grouped together in hundreds. Those interested in prophecy and astrology took special note that Nostradamus was seemingly able to predict, in poetic form, the coming of the French Revolution, the rise of dictators Mussolini and Hitler, and the assassinations of the Kennedy brothers.

Today Nostradamus scholars study his prediction of the end of the world, which is to be preceded by a coming "king of terror." Nostradamus critics and skeptics alike argue that the prophecies are couched in flowery, poetic, and highly symbolic language, leaving room for a wide variety of interpretations. They are also quick to point out that different persons have indeed offered a varying and diverse range of interpretations of the various quatrains.

Nostradamus gained sudden attention once again after the terrorist attack on America on September 11, 2001, when one of his quatrains seemed to notably correspond to the events of that day. A short portion of the lines said to have been written are as follows: "In the year of the new century and nine months, from the sky will come a great King of Terror." However, there are no lines in Nostradamus's writings that read about "a new century and nine months." As we have already noted, "the King of Terror" was applied, before September 11, 2001, to the end of the world. Again this points to the problem with Nostradamus's prophecies as being couched in such vague language that they can be applied to just about any event, subject to the imagination of the interpreter.

November Eve   (▪occult). Alternate name for ▪All Hallows Eve or ▪Halloween.

Nudity   (▪occult; WITCHCRAFT). Numerous occult ceremonies are conducted in the nude. In witchcraft, the term for nudity is ▪skyclad. Nudity is closely associated with themes of fertility, equality, and the most natural way in which to harmonize with nature.

Numerology   (▪occult). Occult numbering system that assigns specific values and meanings to numbers. Specific letters of the alphabet are also assigned numbers. Analysts then determine any number of things, such as intellectual acumen, emotional stability, and physical characteristics of people being examined. Numerology has had a long history in both philosophy and in the occult. The philosopher Pythagoras greatly influenced Kabbalist Cornelius Agrippa (1486–1535), who drew up a numbering system as follows:

1 = origin; source; creation of all things
2 = marriage; communion; evil
3 = trinity; wisdom
4 = permanence; the elements earth, wind, fire, water
5 = justice
6 = the Genesis account of God creating the world
7 = life
8 = fullness
9 = cosmic spheres
10 = fruition; completeness

Nyabingi   (RASTAFARIANISM). A Rastafarian convention held in various locations.

Nyaya   (HINDUISM). One of the six schools of Hindu philosophy and religion; Nyaya is the school of Hindu logic and epistemology.

Nzambi   (▪occult; CANDOMBLE; MACUMBA; SOUTH AMERICAN, CENTRAL AMERICAN, AND CARIBBEAN CULTS). Supreme deity among the ▪Bantu people of Africa and South America.

O

Obatala (SANTERIA; VOODOO). A Yorubic deity of creation (see *Yoruba).

Obeah (*Yoruba; SOUTH AMERICAN, CENTRAL AMERICAN, AND CARIBBEAN CULTS). Term used to designate belief in the powers of the supernatural. *Obeah* is the Jamaican term for "*Obia*." In Jamaica, *Obeah* *cults were composed of slave groups formed in order to provide support and protection from the ruthlessness of brutal masters.

Obermeister, Ruben (FOUNDATION OF HUMAN UNDERSTANDING; 1928–). Known today as Roy *Masters and founder of the Foundation of Human Understanding (FHU).

Obtenir les Yeux (*occult; VOODOO). The prophetic power of the *hungan* to predict the future (*see *prendre les yeux*).

Occult Phenomenon, events, and religious practices engaging a practitioner in a realm of the supernatural that is rooted in things secret or hidden. It comes from the Latin word *occultus* which means "things hidden." The study of the occult is generally classified into three different areas: (1) SPIRITUALISM, (2) *fortune-telling, and (3) *magic. SATANISM, WITCHCRAFT, and *Gothic witchcraft are areas that fall under magic. Many other groups in this volume practice the occult or have influences and historical roots in the occult. See THEOSOPHY, URANTIA, SANTERIA, VOODOO, ECKANKAR, and the like. Because so many different religions have sprung from occult origins, the history of the occult itself is varied, depending on each group.

Popular games such as *Dungeons and Dragons, the *Ouija board, and *tarot cards have their origins in the occult. The reading of *horoscopes and the widespread interest in *divination, *palmistry, and the like are also rooted in the occult. There are references to occult practices already in Bible times (e.g., Deut. 18:10–11).

Ogan (*occult; VOODOO). A piece of iron used as an instrument in ceremonial ritual. Sound is produced when the *ogan* is struck with a spike.

Occult paraphernalia can be purchased at occult bookstores, located in most major cities. The store on the left is Crow Haven Occult shop, in Salem, Mass., run by Laurie Cabot, official witch of Salem. The skulls on the right are in an occult emporium in Burbank, California. Courtesy Jack M. Roper/CARIS and George Mather

O-Harai (SHINTO). A cleansing ceremony, in Shinto. The literal meaning of the term is "the Great Purification!"

Okobio (ᵇoccult; ABAKUA; SOUTH AMERICAN, CENTRAL AMERICAN, AND CARIBBEAN CULTS). The term for a "priest" in the Abakua ᵇcult. An *okobio* is often the assistant to the greater Afro-Cuban priests.

Olcott, Henry Steel (THEOSOPHY; 1832–1907). The husband of Madame Helen Petrovna ᵇBlavatsky and cofounder of Theosophy.

Old Religion (WITCHCRAFT). Term used to describe witchcraft. It is believed by practitioners of the craft that the foundations of paganism predate CHRISTIANITY (*see* Margaret ᵇMurray).

Olurun (ᵇoccult; SANTERIA; SOUTH AMERICAN, CENTRAL AMERICAN, AND CARIBBEAN CULTS). Supreme deity of the ᵇYorubic people.

OM (HINDUISM). The Vedantic word for ᵇ*Brahman* or God as the Absolute Reality. The word is used in the ᵇ*Upanishads* and derives from the idea that all possible spoken sounds result ultimately in no sound at all. OM is the spoken yet unspoken sound that most closely approximates *Brahman*.

Omega (PROCESS CHURCH OF THE FINAL JUDGMENT). The highest rank attainable in the Process Church.

Omen (ᵇoccult). An occult sign relating to the anticipation or expectancy of a future event. Omens are detected through ᵇdivination and can be viewed as being either good or bad.

Omo (ᵇoccult; ABAKUA; SOUTH AMERICAN, CENTRAL AMERICAN, AND CARIBBEAN CULTS). One who serves an ᵇ*orisha*.

Omo-orisha (ᵇoccult; ABAKUA; SOUTH AMERICAN, CENTRAL AMERICAN, AND CARIBBEAN CULTS). The servant of a particular ᵇ*orisha*.

Opele (occult; CANDOMBLE; MACUMBA; SOUTH AMERICAN, CENTRAL AMERICAN, AND CARIBBEAN CULTS). Deity of fate among the ᵇ*orisha*. Also, *opele* are beads used in ceremonies of Macumba ᵇcults.

Ophiolatry (ᵇoccult). The worship of serpents.

Order of Amaranth, The (FREEMASONRY). An order supposed to have been founded in 1653 by Christina, Queen of Sweden, who desired to found a social organization comprised of fifteen knights and fifteen ladies. It was later reinvented and incorporated as an allied organization of Freemasonry.

Order of DeMolay, The See FREEMASONRY.

Order of the Eastern Star, The (FREEMASONRY). The women's order in Freemasonry.

Order of the Knights Templar (FREEMASONRY). The highest degree in ᵇYork Rite Freemasonry. The Order of the Knights Templar is one of three degrees given after the ᵇSelect Master or ninth degree.

Order of the White Shrine of Jerusalem, The (FREEMASONRY). A women's order in Freemasonry.

Orisha (ᵇYoruba; SOUTH AMERICAN, CENTRAL AMERICAN, AND CARIBBEAN CULTS). A term used for ᵇYoruba deities. The *orisha* are lower in rank than ᵇ*olurun* but superior to humanity.

Orodere (ᵇoccult; MACUMBA). Like ᵇ*Cariapemba*, an evil deity of the ᵇBantu people who later became incorporated into the pantheon of deities among the Macumba ᵇcults.

Orthodox; Orthodoxy (CHRISTIANITY). In a broad sense, the term *orthodoxy* with respect to Christianity and the Christian tradition is used throughout this volume. It speaks of conformity to the agreed-upon apostolic standards recognized by the church as the faith "once for all entrusted to the saints" (Jude 3). The term today refers to those communions within Christendom that hold to the standards set forth in the ecumenical creeds (Apostles', Nicene, Athanasian, and Constantinopolitan creeds; *see* Appendix 1).

In a narrower sense, *orthodox* is applied to the churches of Eastern Christianity that separated from Western or Roman Catholic Christianity in 1054.

Oru (ᵇoccult; SANTERIA; SOUTH AMERICAN, CENTRAL AMERICAN, AND CARIBBEAN CULTS). The rhythm of the ᵇ*orisha* in Santeria ceremonies.

Osho (RAJNEESHISM). The name that followers of Bhagwan Shree ᵇRajneesh now use when they refer to him posthumously.

Otanses (SANTERIA; SOUTH AMERICAN, CENTRAL AMERICAN, AND CARIBBEAN CULTS; VOODOO; WITCHCRAFT). Sacred stones that are used in Santeria rituals that are used to bring about harm to others. In witchcraft, the correspondence to this is ᵇblack magic.

Oth (ARICA). One of the three centers of the human body. *Oth* is the emotional center (see ᵇ*path* and ᵇ*kath*).

OTO (SATANISM). These initials stand for Ordo Templi Orientis, which translates Order of the Eastern Temple.

Ouija Board (ᵇoccult; SPIRITUALISM). A small game board containing numbers and letters used in spiritualism to contact the souls of the departed during a ᵇséance. Participants sit at a table around the ouija board

A ⸰ouija board is a "game" that can have serious consequences if played seriously.

Courtesy Jack M. Roper/CARIS

and place hands on a "pointer." The pointer is then moved around the board to various letters by the visiting spirit(s). The resulting message is the communication desired from the supernatural spirit world.

Ouspensky, Peter Demianovich (OUSPENSKY-GURDJIEFF; 1878–1948). A disciple of George D. ⸰Gurdjieff, responsible for popularizing Gurdjieff's beliefs.

Out of Body Experience See ⸰astral projection.

Overseer (CHRISTIANITY; JEHOVAH'S WITNESSES). Term used for a member of the Watchtower Bible and Tract Society who fills the role of guardian or watchman within a given congregation of Jehovah's Witnesses. The word overseer comes from the Greek word *episkopos*, meaning "one who watches over, keeps guard, inspects."

This term for church leaders is also used in many Christian churches. Requirements to fill the office of overseer (bishop/elder) are given in 1 Timothy 3:1ff. One such requirement is that of possessing the ability to teach, which distinguishes overseers from ministerial ⸰servants. Overseers are generally the older members of a congregation. The Greek word for "elder" (*presbyteros*) is used interchangeably with overseer. Overseers do not enjoy hierarchical ranking but are regarded as equals of and servants to the congregation. Primacy and headship belong to God's Son (Eph. 1:22).

Oversoul (UNITARIAN-UNIVERSALIST ASSOCIATION). Spiritual being in Unitarianism in which the ideal of nature is perfectly realized and in which our imperfect existence is grounded.

P

Paganism (⸰occult; WITCHCRAFT). Paganism is word that has undergone considerable evolution. It was historically used to designate that all religions and peoples that were not Christian or Jewish. Currently the word is used by numerous witchcraft and other modern groups.

Palmistry (⸰occult). The psychic practice of reading the lines on the palm of the hand in order to determine a person's future. Palmistry is one of the oldest and most highly developed methods of ⸰divination.

Palo Mayombe (⸰occult; SANTERIA). The darker side of Santeria where the concept of ⸰black magic is used for evil purposes.

The horned god Pan (statue located at the British Museum).

Courtesy Dave Brown

Pan (WITCHCRAFT). The horned god, the male deity of ⸰wicca. He has gone by various names throughout history and is important in the witchcraft ceremony ⸰drawing down the sun.

Panentheism (HINDUISM; UNITY). A modified form of ⸰pantheism whereby God is to be found in all living things (trees, animals, plants, insects, humans) but not in inanimate objects (rocks, metal, etc.).

Panpsychism (⸰occult). Theory that propounds that all of nature possesses a consciousness and that there is a certain mental dimension to inanimate matter in the cosmos.

Pantheism (HINDUISM). From the Greek *pan* ("all") and *theos* ("god");

thus, literally, "all-god." Pantheism is the belief that God is all, and all is God. For pantheism, God and nature are identified with each other. Matter is but an extension of one single reality. Hinduism and its multifarious derivatives all embrace some form of pantheism.

Paploi (ᵇoccult; ᵇYoruba; SOUTH AMERICAN, CENTRAL AMERICAN, AND CARIBBEAN CULTS; VOODOO). The Haitian word for a voodoo priest, also spelled *papaloa* or *papaloi*.

Paquet (ᵇoccult; VOODOO). An abstract figure made up of rags used as a ᵇcharm to bring down a curse, bad luck, or ultimately death on another.

Paradise Trinity (URANTIA). One of the principal trinities of Urantia. It is described in ᵇ*The Urantia Book* as being the "full expression and perfect revelation of the eternal nature of Deity." It is "inescapable inexistability." The Paradise Trinity is comprised of three persons referred to as being the Universal Father, the Eternal Son, and the Infinite Spirit.

Paramatma (HINDUISM). Great soul; super soul; universal soul.

Parapsychology (ᵇoccult). The pseudoscientific study of phenomena of the human psyche that are not accounted for through normal empirical means. Such studies are directed toward ᵇmental telepathy, ᵇclairvoyance, ᵇESP, ᵇpsychokinesis, etc.

Parousia (CHRISTIANITY). The Greek word meaning "presence" or "arrival." This word is used in the New Testament mostly to speak of the second return of Jesus Christ to earth.

Parsees See ZOROASTRIANISM.

Parvati (HINDUISM). Hindu goddess; ᵇSiva's source of power and seduction.

Passing Over (ᵇoccult). The transition period marking the passage from life to death to the afterlife.

Passover Meal (JUDAISM). Also called a Passover Seder, this meal commemorates God's "passing over" the firstborn sons of Israel in Egypt when he destroyed the firstborn sons of the Egyptians. The Passover itself was one of Israel's great festivals, celebrated in the month of Nisan (*see* ᵇJewish calendar).

Past Life Regression (NEW AGE MOVEMENT). The use of ᵇhypnosis in New Age Movement practice that enables the participant to discover past lives.

Past Master; Fifth Degree (FREEMASONRY). The degree in Freemasonry earned in the ᵇYork Rite that involves specific training in leadership skills as a Mason moves onto "higher" degrees and achievements.

Path (ARICA). One of the three centers of the human body. *Path* is the intellectual center (see ᵇ*oth* and ᵇ*kath*).

Patriarch of the Church (CHRISTIANITY; JUDAISM; MORMONISM). The patriarchs of the Old Testament are Abraham, Isaac, Jacob, Joseph, etc.

The leader of the each of the individual Eastern Orthodox churches (e.g., Russian Orthodox, Greek Orthodox, Coptic Orthodox) is called a patriarch.

Patriarch also applies to the spiritual leader in the Mormon church who is called to the office of evangelism. Wherever a church is established, a patriarch should be present. The Mormons consider the patriarchs of the New Testament those called to establish churches through a preaching ministry. They quote 2 Timothy 4:5 as being a model text for evangelists.

Patripassianism (CHRISTIANITY). Also called ᵇSabellianism and ᵇmodalistic monarchianism, Patripassianism (lit., "Father-suffering") teaches that since God is a single being, he manifested himself in three different modes at three distinct junctures. The phase or period in which God manifested himself as Jesus was the time in which he suffered and died for the sins of the world. Patripassianism was condemned as heretical because it made no distinction between the Father and the Son, thereby denying the doctrine of the ᵇTrinity.

Peace Symbol (ᵇoccult; SATANISM). Inverted cross. Emperor Nero, who despised Christianity, crucified countless numbers of Christians. According to tradition, Peter was, at his own request, crucified upside down. The inverted cross came to be a symbol for radical hatred of Christianity. This symbol has appeared time and again throughout the centuries. The Saracens used it in 1099 when warring against Christians who fought in the Crusades. The peace symbol was used to symbolize the ᵇblack mass. Anton Szandor ᵇLaVey, founder and high priest of the Church of Satan (*see* Satanism), uses the peace symbol.

Pearl of Great Price, The (MORMONISM). One of the sacred texts of Mormonism, first published in 1851. It underwent revision in 1878 and was finally recognized by the Church of Jesus Christ of Latter-Day Saints church as sacred writ, free from all error, in 1880. The book is broken down into five sections as follows: (1) The Book of Moses, the parallel account of Genesis 1–6 in the ᵇBible. (2) The Book of Abraham, which is a development of Joseph ᵇSmith's ideas about ᵇpolytheism. This book contains many of the ideas prevalent in Mormonism concerning creation and the preexistence of souls before the creation of the cosmos. (3) A section that contains Joseph Smith's translation of Matthew 24. (4) An autobiographical section recording Smith's discovery and subsequent translation of the golden plates in New York. (5) The Mormon articles of faith.

The Pearl of Great Price stands alongside the ▸Book of Mormon and ▸Doctrine and Covenants as the three great standard-bearers of Mormon theology. The King James Bible and continued revelations are also sources of authority for Mormons.

Peditherapy (▸occult). The practice of healing parts of the body through the examination of the foot. Peditherapy, like ▸iris diagnosis, divides the foot into zones that correspond to respective parts of the body. Disease or sickness is diagnosed when pain results from touching the reflex zones. Where the pain lies in the foot determines which organ or part of the body is affected. In peditherapy there are thirty-eight zones.

Pelagianism (CHRISTIANITY). The name is derived from its chief proponent, Pelagius (ca. 354/60–ca. 418/20), who, in opposition to Augustine, argued that human nature is not utterly depraved after the Fall, but rather is in a state of moral neutrality. It is only through habit that one becomes sinful, and one may exercise human will to surmount sin. Pelagius further taught that one may take the first step toward salvation apart from divine grace. Pelagianism was condemned as heresy in the fourth century, and Augustine's doctrines of the Fall and original sin were embraced as the ▸orthodox teaching.

Pendulum (▸occult). A circular metal weight suspended from a string used in the occult practice of ▸divination.

Pentacle (▸occult; WITCHCRAFT). A pentacle is a disc or ▸circle bearing the five-pointed star or ▸pentagram, often used in ▸magic. In the medieval ▸grimoire The Key of Solomon, there are instructions on how to make a pentacle. A portion reads as follows: "The pentacles are to be made on the day of mercury, and in its hour. The Moon is to be the sign of air, earth, and waxing, and her days shall be the same as those of the Sun. . . ." A prayer for the use of the pentacles then follows: "We with humility beg and implore Thee, Majestic and Holiest One, to cause the consecration of these Pentacles, through thy power: that they may be made potent against all the Spirits, through thee Adonai, Most Holy, forever and ever." In modern-day practice, pentacles are used on an ▸altar in ▸wicca and is the most important symbol used in witchcraft. A pentacle is also one of the four suits in the ▸tarot cards.

Pentagram (▸occult; SATANISM; WITCHCRAFT). A five-pointed star used as an important ▸magic symbol. The pentagram faces either three points up or three points down. If up (generally in witchcraft), it symbolizes human spirituality. Often a human being is sketched into the pentagram with arms stretched upward. If a pentagram's point is downward (used most frequently in ▸black magic and Satanism), the meaning conveyed is that of darkness and bestiality.

A chalice used in witchcraft ceremonies, inscribed with a pentagram.
Courtesy Dave Brown

It creates a ▸baphomet image with the ▸goat's head. In witchcraft, four points of a pentagram symbolize the four elements, while the fifth represents the spirit that governs them. A downward or inverted pentagram is used for a second-degree initiate.

Pentateuch (CHRISTIANITY; JUDAISM). The first five books of the Old Testament.

Perfectionism (CHRISTIANITY). The belief held by some denominations in Christendom as well as numerous ▸cults that one may fully realize perfection, sinlessness, or total sanctification in the present life. The Protestant Reformers argued vehemently that perfect sanctification is not possible in this life because the "old Adam," or the old sin nature, is not fully eradicated until the future life. Methodism and its father, John Wesley, championed the doctrine of perfectionism, having a profound impact on the development of the later Holiness movement in America and the various denominations that grew out of it.

Perfect Master (HINDUISM; MEHER BABA). One sent by God as a great ▸avatar to a given era in history. The perfect masters are ▸incarnations of divinity. They include Zoroaster, ▸Hare Krishna, ▸Rama, ▸Buddha, Jesus, ▸Muhammad, and various other spiritual teachers in modern times who claim (or whose followers claim) to be the perfect master for their time. Thus, Meher Baba and his followers believed him to be the perfect master for the present age (he died in 1969).

Other lists include Siddharta ⸲Gautama, Paul ⸲Twitchell, Sri ⸲Ramakrishna, etc.

Permanent 24 (ARICA). The designation used by Oscar ⸲Ichazo to describe the ultimate state of the union of the inner self with absolute consciousness or awareness.

Perry, Troy (UNIVERSAL FELLOWSHIP OF METROPOLITAN COMMUNITY CHURCHES; 1941–). Founder of the Universal Fellowship of Metropolitan Community Churches (MCC), an organization known for its prohomosexual stance.

Pesah (JUDAISM). The Hebrew name for "Passover" (see ⸲Passover meal).

Petit Bon Ange (⸲occult; VOODOO). Translated "little good angel," the *petit bon ange* is one of two souls that every person possesses. It protects and guides an individual and, after death, may linger for several days around the body or change into another form either animate or inanimate. See also ⸲*gros bon ange*.

Peyote (NATIVE AMERICAN RELIGION; NEW AGE MOVEMENT). A Native American term for an hallucinogenic drug used to attain ⸲altered states of consciousnness.

PFAL (THE WAY INTERNATIONAL). Acronym for the name of the course used by the Way International. The title for the course is ⸲Power for Abundant Living.

Phallic Symbol (⸲occult). Term for the male sex organ that is used as a symbol for fertility in certain occult and ⸲pagan groups.

Pharisees (JUDAISM). Translated as "the separated ones," the Pharisees were one of the chief religious institutions of the Jews and had an important role in their history. They came into existence in the intertestamental period, chiefly as a religious protest movement against the Hellenization of Judaism. They considered themselves the interpreters of the law or ⸲Torah. In a desire to protect the law, they formulated an "oral law" (see ⸲*Mishna*), which served to supplement the Mosaic law. The Pharisees believed in an afterlife and in the resurrection of the dead.

Jesus leveled sharp criticism against this ⸲sect (Matt. 5:20; 16:6, 11–12; 23:5, 13–15, 23; et al.). (1) The Pharisees placed more weight and authority on the oral law than they did on the Mosaic law, the one that Jesus said was God's law. (2) The Pharisees themselves were not willing to comply with the laws that they demanded others to obey. (3) They seemed, as a religious class, to be far more concerned about outward appearance than about the inward matters of religious faith. (4) They looked down on non-Jews and the common people of their own nation.

Pike, James Albert (⸲occult; 1913–1969). A liberal ⸲Protestant theologian and Episcopal bishop who embraced a number of heretical views, but was most controversial for his dabbling in the occult and ⸲séances.

Pioneer Publisher (JEHOVAH'S WITNESSES). Term used to designate a person who dedicates full time to the ministry. This includes door-to-door witnessing and distributing the society's literature. Witnesses do not ordain clergy as most Christian churches do. A pioneer publisher functions like a clergyman, however, on most counts. There are approximately thirty thousand pioneer publishers in the Watchtower Bible and Tract Society.

Pisces (⸲astrology; ⸲occult). Latin for "fish," Pisces is the twelfth ⸲sign of the ⸲zodiac in ⸲astrology, falling between February 19 and March 20. In Greek mythology, Aphrodite and Eros leaped into the river to escape from the monster Typhon and were transformed into fish as a result. Persons born under the sign Pisces are said to be worrisome, artistic, and impractical.

Pit Bull (⸲occult; SATANISM). A symbol, mascot, or representative of ⸲Satan or the ⸲devil.

Pitaka (BUDDHISM). Term used for sacred writings of Buddhism. This is what is called a "discipline basket" that contains 227 obligatory rules for the monks representing THERAVADA BUDDHISM.

Pixies (⸲occult). See ⸲nature spirits.

Plain Truth , The (WORLDWIDE CHURCH OF GOD). The regular periodical magazine of the Worldwide Church of God.

Planchette See ⸲ouija board.

Plural Marriage (MORMONISM). Considered to be synonymous with ⸲celestial marriage before 1890, when polygamy was discouraged. In order to follow the creation order, it was considered to be a great blessing for a man to marry more than one wife so that he might be "fruitful and multiply." However, since plural marriages have been outlawed since 1890, Mormons have ceased from practicing them officially (see ⸲Manifesto). During the ⸲Millennium, however, plural marriages will resume.

Poltergeist (⸲occult). Alternate term for ⸲ghost. (*also see* ⸲demon, SPIRITUALISM, ⸲necromancy, and occult).

Polygamy (ISLAM; MORMONISM). The practice of having multiple wives simultaneously. Polygamy was practiced in ancient Judaism and is still practiced in Islam.

In Mormonism the practice was outlawed in the late nineteenth century but it is still practiced illegally.

Polytheism   Belief in the existence of more than one god (*see* monotheism).

Poole, Elijah   (NATION OF ISLAM; 1897–1975). *See* Elijah ▸Muhammed.

Positive Confession   (CHRISTIANITY; NEW AGE MOVEMENT). The belief held to by some Christians that believers possess the latent power within themselves to create a change, a new reality, a miracle etc., by possessing the proper faith and speaking the proper words, usually "in the name of Jesus." The teaching accompanies the belief that faith creates prosperity, cures illnesses, and affords power for abundant and prosperous living. This is also sometimes called the health-and-wealth gospel. Some extreme forms of this movement even move into the arena of suggesting that believers are "little gods."

This teaching is contrary to traditional Christian doctrine where faith is a gift of God by which the believer "trusts" in the gospel of Jesus Christ, not in the power to manipulate God toward self-serving human ends.

Positive Thinking   (CHRISTIANITY). A belief held by some Christians and most closely associated with Norman Vincent Peale and his 1952 book *The Power of Positive Thinking*. The basic idea is that positive thoughts create attitudes that strengthen, heal, and provide a different outlook on life. Some ministries have taken this a step further into a theology known as ▸positive confession.

Poteau-mitan   (▸occult; VOODOO). The central and sacred pillars in a voodoo temple around which the rituals are performed.

Power for Abundant Living   (WAY INTERNATIONAL). See ▸PFAL.

Practitioner   (CHRISTIAN SCIENCE; RELLIGIOUS SCIENCE). A layperson who serves as a full-time minister in Christian Science and Religious Science. A practitioner's main area of service and responsibility is to pray and minister healing to other members of the church.

Prana   (HINDUISM). The ▸Sanskrit word for vital life forces. There are five vital fluids, or *pranas*, that energize the body. *Prana* is also used to denote the general principle of life itself.

Prayer Rug   (ISLAM). The mat used during an Islamic worship service on which the worshiper either stands or kneels. Though desirable, a prayer rug is not absolutely essential.

Pre-clear   (SCIENTOLOGY). A new convert to Scientology. Scientologists seek to assist the pre-clear to undergo therapy administered by an ▸auditor so as to become a ▸clear.

Precognition   (▸occult). The occult belief that one can possess the power to peer into the future.

Preexistence   (CHRISTIANITY; MORMONISM). The belief in Christianity that Jesus the Son preexisted with Father before his becoming a human being in his incarnation. This is part and parcel of the doctrine of the ▸Trinity.

Also, the doctrine of the Church of Jesus Christ of Latter-Day Saints that all of humanity preexisted spiritually before being born physically as inhabitants of the earth.

Prema   (HINDUISM). The ultimate expression of the love of God.

Premie   (ELAN VITAL). A new convert.

Prendre les Yeux   (▸occult; VOODOO). The prophetic power to predict the future passed down from the ▸hungan to his ▸bokor.

President   (MORMONISM). The highest office in the Mormon church. The president, along with two lesser ▸counselors, comprise the ▸first presidency. The president possesses complete authority to declare new and continuous "revelation" in an official capacity; he is considered to be a "seer, a revelator, a translator, and a prophet" (▸*Doctrine and Covenants* 107:92).

Presiding Bishopric   (MORMONISM). Usually consisting of three members, the presiding bishopric is charged with responsibility to make sure that all of the specific duties of the ▸Aaronic priesthood are carried out to their fullest.

Priest   (MORMONISM). The highest office within the ▸Aaronic priesthood, above the office of ▸deacon and ▸teacher. One may become a priest through ordination rites as early as age sixteen.

Priesthood   (MORMONISM). A central concept of Mormon teaching. The priesthood is of two types, the ▸Aaronic priesthood and the ▸Melchiedek priesthood. Authority to perform baptisms, ordinations, and other vital ministries comes only through one of these two priesthoods and the power that accompanies them.

Priests   (NICHIREN SHOSHU BUDDHISM). Those called to perform the basic functions of ministry. The priest upholds the teachings of the faith, carries out official duties such as weddings and funerals, and delivers sermons and lectures.

Primordial Vibration (ELAN VITAL). One of the four methods for imparting divine knowledge. Rhythmic, ᵖmantra-like breathing causes the mind to lose its sense of present awareness and consciousness, thereby opening up the possibility for consciousness with the inner spirit world where oneness with the cosmos may be experienced. (See also ᵖthird eye, ᵖthird ear, ᵖdivine nectar, and ᵖfourfold path).

Prince Hall (FREEMASONRY). An organization formed specifically for blacks who have traditionally been barred from membership in the Lodge.

Prince of the Underworld (ᵖoccult; SATANISM). Another reference or phrase for ᵖSatan, the ᵖdevil, or ᵖLucifer.

Prophet (CHRISTIANITY; JUDAISM; MORMONISM). The Hebrew word for "prophet" (*nabi*) means one who "forth-tells, proclaims, announces" God's word; that is, one who brings forth a message from God. The prophets whom God raised up in the ᵖBible announced God's word to the people through divine inspiration. Not only did the prophets "forth-tell" the truth, but they were also given divine ability to "foretell" future events.

Israel was in dire need of the prophets as God's spokesmen. After the Fall (Gen. 3), God no longer spoke "immediately" as frequently with humankind, but "mediately." The prophetic voice became the main channel of communication between God and his people. The respect shown to the prophets was marginal at best, however. Many were rejected in spite of the fact that they were God's spokesmen.

A "prophetic pattern" is therefore discernible in both the Old and New Testaments. First, the prophets "forth-told" divine truth from God. Second, miracles (often, though not always) accompanied the prophets' message or ᵖrevelation from God. Then the prophet experienced rejection. Moses, the chief prophet of the Old Testament, fulfills the prophetic pattern perfectly. He "forth-told" divine truth to Pharaoh and to Israel. He then validated his proclamation with accompanying miracles (the ten plagues and miracles in the desert). Finally, Moses experienced rejection, not only from Pharaoh, but also from Israel as he led them to the Promised Land.

In the New Testament, Christianity assigns the role of prophet to Jesus Christ and to the apostles. Jesus came preaching the "good news" (gospel) of the kingdom of God. This was the "forth-telling" aspect of Jesus' prophetic role. The greatest miracles of the Bible accompanied this role. Third, the greatest rejection took place when Jesus was crucified at Calvary. The apostles followed in similar fashion. They advanced revelation from God, performed miracles to substantiate this revelation, but also experienced great rejection.

Mormons have several meanings for the term *prophet*. Usually it refers to the first great prophet, Joseph ᵖSmith, but it can also refer to the ᵖpresident of the Latter-Day Saints church.

Prophet, Elizabeth Clare (CHURCH UNIVERSAL AND TRIUMPHANT; b. 1939) The past leader of the Church Universal and Triumphant. She was known to her followers as the "Mother of the Flame" and claimed to be a ᵖreincarnation of the biblical Martha. Prophet declares that Jesus spoke directly to her one day while she kneaded bread with Mary. The message was that she would continue to go through successive births until she reached the ᵖAquarian Age. Now that Aquarius has arrived, Prophet claims that she, too, has arrived to herald it. Though given by Jesus, this mission and message was endorsed by the long line of Ascended Masters. Prophet continued to receive revelations from the Ascended Masters, one of which is that the end of the world is near.

Prophet, Mark L. (CHURCH UNIVERSAL AND TRIUMPHANT; 1918–73). Founded the Summit Lighthouse, presently known as the Church Universal and Triumphant.

Prospective Elder (MORMONISM). Term used to designate an adult convert who aspires to an office within the ᵖAaronic priesthood, which is usually held by younger boys.

Protestant (CHRISTIANITY). This term arose when the Reformers "protested" at the Diet of Speyer in 1529 because it revoked the 1526 decision of the Diet of Speyer that permitted each prince to determine the religion in his territory. The "Protestant" churches during the Reformation were followers of Luther, Calvin, and Zwingli. Today, the term "Protestant" also includes Baptists, Mennonites, and Pentecostals.

Psychic (ᵖoccult). A practitioner of ᵖtelepathy or ᵖESP. This occult practice has been popularized on television and on the internet where viewers and users are invited to call in to a "psychic" in order to learn about the future. *Also see* ᵖdivination.

Psychic Surgery (ᵖoccult; NEW AGE MOVEMENT). The occult belief that one can successfully perform medical surgery without being trained as a medical doctor or without use of any of the conventional medical tools, instruments, or medicines. In New Age lore, this is in the general category of holistic health.

Psychokinesis (ᵖoccult; ᵖparapsychology). The ability to move material objects through the sheer power of mental energy.

Psychometry (ᵖoccult). Ability to foretell a person's future by possessing an object belonging to that person.

Publisher (JEHOVAH'S WITNESSES). Name given to a volunteer worker in the Watchtower Bible and Tract Society who distributes the literature of the society.

Puja (ISKCON). Morning devotion of ᵖHare Krishna devotees, which includes the chanting of the ᵖkirtanya.

Puranas (HINDUISM). Part of the collection of Hindu sacred literature. The *Puranas* contain narratives that relate the Hindu myths concerning the creation of the world, the epics concerning gods and saints, and the history of royal dynasties. In total, there are eighteen surviving *Purana* texts.

Purdah (ISLAM). Name for the veil worn by Islamic women.

Purgatory (CHRISTIANITY). A specifically Roman Catholic doctrine concerning the place where those Christians who die without having fully been absolved of all earthly sins are sent for a period of time before being allowed to enter heaven. The passage in the Old Testament Apocrypha (see ᵖBible) most frequently quoted to defend the doctrine of purgatory is 2 Maccabees 12:39–45. Paul's teaching concerning salvation "but only as one escaping through the flames" (1 Cor. 3:15) has been interpreted this way as well.

Gregory the Great was the first Roman pope to uphold the doctrine. The official doctrine of purgatory was articulated at the Council of Lyon in 1274 and was reaffirmed at the Council of Trent (1545–1563). Protestants, beginning with Luther, have always opposed the doctrine, insisting that it denies Jesus Christ and his finished work of redemption.

Purva Mimamsa (HINDUISM). One of the six schools of Hinduism. *Mimamsa* itself is perhaps the oldest school. Its train of thought is to furnish an interpretation of the ᵖVedas. *Purva mimamsa* ("prior study") is concerned with the interpretation of the earlier parts of the *Vedas* (called ᵖKarmakanda).

Pyramid Power (ᵖoccult). The belief that the ancient pyramids or objects shaped like the pyramids generate occult energy and power.

Pyramidology (ᵖoccult). The study of the ancient pyramids of Egypt as well as those of Mexico and Central America. Some occult practitioners believe that the pyramids contain certain hidden knowledge that is awaiting to be discovered and unlocked.

Pyromancy (ᵖoccult). The use of fire in ᵖdivination.

Q

Quimbanda (ᵖoccult; MACUMBA). Name for the high priest and chief magician in the Congo-Angola cults. The *quimbanda* are subpriests to ᵖnzambi in Macumba.

Quimby, Phineas Parkhurst (NEW THOUGHT; 1802–1866). Was known as the ᵖguru of the mind sciences and founder of New Thought. Mary Baker ᵖEddy depended heavily on the works and original thinking of ᵖQuimby (see Christian Science).

Quorum of the Seventy, The First (MORMONISM). High institution within the Mormon organizational infrastructure. The quorum is ranked below the ᵖFirst Presidency and the ᵖCouncil of the Twelve Apostles. It is comprised of at least seven ᵖpresidents. The primary function of the First Quorum of the Seventy is to oversee missions work. Members are voted into office at the semiannual general conferences.

Qur'an (ISLAM). An alternate English spelling for the Koran.

Q'tas (ISLAM). The use of reason in discourse and thought.

R

Ra (ˈoccult). An Egyptian goddess usually depicted with the head of lioness.

Rabbi (JUDAISM). Jewish clergy, religious leader, and teacher. The term does not appear in the Old Testament, but it does appear in the New Testament. For the most part, however, the Gospels use the Greek term *didaskalos* when they refer to a teacher. The title of rabbi apparently came into being during the time of Jesus in the early part of the first century. It was a title of respect and honor.

Radical Feminism Radical feminism, also known as gender feminism, is an outgrowth of the more moderate feminist ideology. Radical feminists seek to bring about changes in Western culture and society as it tries to free women from all male influences, what they commonly refer to as "male dominance" or "male oppression." Some radical feminists argue, for example, that all heterosexual sexual intercourse is rape, even when a married woman consents to it and enjoys it. This is the argument made by Andrea Dworkin in her book *Intercourse* (1987), in which the "f-word" appears on almost every page. Gloria Steinem and Catherine McKinnon are other well-known examples of radical feminist promoters. For the most part, the National Organization for Women (NOW) also advocates a radical feminist agenda.

In spite of scientific evidence to the contrary, radical feminists reject the premise that biological or genetic differences between men and women account for many of the different behaviors and dispositions that already manifest themselves early in the life of boys and girls. A book that combats the claims of radical feminism, showing the anti-male character of the radical feminists, is Christina Hoff Sommers' book, *Who Stole Feminism? How Women Have Betrayed Women* (New York: Simon & Shuster, 1994).

Rainbow (NEW AGE MOVEMENT). The rainbow, or color spectrum, that is refracted through a prism or a ˈcrystal demonstrates life's evolutionary progression throughout the epochs of history. It also has a symbolic significance for each individual and his or her own personal progress.

Raja (HINDUISM). The name given to a Hindu ruler.

Raja Yoga (HANUMAN FOUNDATION; HINDUISM; SATCHIDANANDA ASHRAM INTEGRAL YOGA INSTITUTE). A yogic technique that is divided into eight parts, each one referred to as being a limb. The eight limbs when brought into harmony lead the devotee to ˈ*Brahman*. The eight limbs are: (1) *yama* (ethics); (2) *niyama* (morality); (3) *asana* (meditation); (4) *pranayama* (breathing technique); (5) *pratyahara* (sensory coordination and restraint); (6) ˈ*dharana* (mental discipline); (7) *dhyana* (meditation); (8)ˈ*samadhi* (enlightenment).

Rajneesh, Bhagwan Shree (RAJNEESHISM; 1931–1990). He was born in Kuchwara, India, and became the leader of Rajneeshism. He was known as India's sex ˈguru.

Rama (HINDUISM). ˈIncarnation of ˈ*Vishnu*, who is the outstanding hero in the epic ˈ*Ramayana*. He kills a fierce ˈdemon named Ravana in present-day Sri Lanka. As a result, the ˈcult of Rama arose and is one of only a few that still survives in modern times.

Ramadan (ISLAM). The ninth lunar month in the Islamic calendar, which ˈMuslims designate as a sacred month (*see* ˈIslamic holidays). The observance of Ramadan occurs on different dates each year as a result of the Islamic calendar, which is based on the lunar month. Given that this calendar's year consists of only 354.3 days per year, the month of Ramadan goes through a complete cycle in 33.6 solar years. Thus if Ramadan occurs in mid-summer, it will in seventeen years occur in mid-winter, and in another seventeen years it will again take place in mid-summer. During this month, loyal Muslims are expected to read or memorize the entire ˈKoran. It is also this month during which Muslims are required to fast and abstain from sex from sunrise to sunset each day.

Ramakrishna, Sri (HINDUISM; 1836–1886). One of the most famous ˈgurus in Hinduism. He was a priest in the Kali Temple in Calcutta.

Ramayana (HINDUISM). One of the great epic poems of Indian literature describing the deeds of ˈRama.

Raphael (ˈoccult; SATANISM). Those who practice Western ˈmagic pray to Raphael as the archangel of the air, though his name does not appear in the Old Testament (as do Gabriel and Michael). The name does, however, appear in Tobit, one of the Old Testament 'Apocrypha.

Rasputin, Grigori Efemovich ('occult; 1882–1916). A Russian monk who was able to exercise unusual hypnotic abilities. He was invited to the royal court of Tsar Nicholas in 1907, where through his hypnotic methods he reportedly healed the bleeding leg of the tsar's infant son Alexis, who was a hemophiliac. His performance endeared him to the tsar's wife, Alexandra, who made Rasputin her advisor. This made him a powerful and influential individual in the court, virtually controlling many of the court's policies. This did not sit well with many noblemen and Prince Yusupov. Both plotted to kill him. They first tried to poison him, but he survived this attempt. The conspirators then shot him and tossed him into the Neva River.

Reactive Mind (SCIENTOLOGY). One of the two basic parts of the human mind. The reactive mind records 'engrams, which it accumulates and stores. Because the reactive mind does not rationalize, engrams are stored illogically and randomly. The degree and intensity of reactive experiences in a person's life, recorded by the engrams, are determinative of adverse behavior as well as mental and emotional instability.

Readers (CHRISTIAN SCIENCE). Persons elected by local congregations or members of branch churches to serve the church. A lay reader is charged with reading from the 'Bible and from selections in *Science and Health with Key to the Scriptures*, by Mary Baker 'Eddy. A reader usually serves for a three-year period.

Reading (ASSOCIATION FOR RESEARCH AND ENLIGHT-ENMENT). The term refers to the supernatural 'revelations conveyed to Edgar 'Cayce while in his 'trance-like sleeps during which he prescribed medical treatments for ailing individuals.

Redcap ('occult). An evil spirit, found in Scottish folklore, who is reputed to have long claws and the appearance of an old man. As with other forms of exorcism, he can be exorcised by making the sign of the Christian cross or by citing an appropriate 'Bible passage.

Redeemed (CHRISTIANITY; MORMONISM). A common term in Christian theology that denotes how God has "bought back" the sinners who believe in Jesus Christ (cf. 1 Cor. 6:20; Gal. 3:13). But 'Mormons use the term to say that humanity is redeemed only from physical death but not from spiritual death.

Reincarnation (HINDUISM; NEW AGE MOVEMENT; WITCHCRAFT). Literally translated "again in the flesh,"

reincarnation is the belief that after death, the soul does not enter an eternal state of existence but is "re-birthed" into another physical mode of existence. Virtually all religions deriving from Hinduism teach reincarnation. The New Age Movement, witchcraft, 'wicca, and many new 'cults and 'occult groups teach reincarnation.

CHRISTIANITY teaches the doctrine of the 'incarnation of Jesus Christ. That is, Jesus was God who took on himself human flesh. Human beings who experience salvation are "born-again," that is, born with a new and spiritual nature as they take Christ upon themselves, but at death, the body is separated from the soul. The body goes to the ground until the time of the resurrection while the soul immediately goes to heaven or to eternal judgment, not to a state ready for reincarnation.

Religion A socially organized pattern of beliefs, values, and practices that bind people together in their efforts to address the deity (or deities) to give them guidance, sustenance, and ultimate meaning in life and hereafter. Many religions have a body of written doctrines as well as established rituals and designated functionaries who act in behalf of the common, lay members.

Resguardo ('occult; SANTERIA; VOODOO). A bag worn around one's neck, similar to the 'nganga. It contains a number of 'occult items that Santeria members use in their voodoo rituals.

Restorationism Many 'cults, 'sects, and denominations are "restorationist" in nature, meaning that part of what defines and propels them is the need to reclaim or take back what was once a more pristine form of the particular religion that they deem has been corrupted or lost altogether. For example, Joseph 'Smith received a 'revelation that all the churches were corrupt. He therefore believed that God was using him to restore the truth.

In response to restorationism, traditional and 'orthodox Christianity believes that the church has always remained intact. It is not that the church should be restored to what it once was, because what it was, is, and always will be is a "communion of saints" who are at the same time sinners and in need of forgiveness. Therefore, what is needed in the church is not a restoration but a need for continued "reformation." The authors have included numerous restorationist movements in this volume. For a fuller explanation of restorationism itself, see INTERNATIONAL CHURCHES OF CHRIST.

Revelation (CHRISTIANITY; JUDAISM). The communication of divine knowledge and truth from God to human beings. According to Christian theology, revelation occurs in different forms. In the Old Testament, God revealed himself directly to Adam and Eve before the 'Fall. Immediately following, God revealed his message to Adam and Eve through an 'angel. To Moses God revealed himself in a burning bush. The most frequent revelation of God to the Israelites was through the voice of the 'prophets, who spoke messages from God to the people.

In the New Testament, the greatest revelation of all took place at the 'incarnation, when God took on himself human flesh. God also spoke through the 'apostles, who, inspired by the Holy Spirit, committed God's revelation to writing (later recognized as the New Testament canon; *see* 'Bible). In this regard, they fulfilled what Christ told his disciples, namely, "I have given them your word" (John 17:14). Some revelations also came through visions and dreams.

More recent ideas of divine revelation have been advanced by liberal scholars. Rather than seeing revelation consisting of statements of propositional truth, some argue that God reveals himself only through his divine acts, and the Bible is merely the record of such revelations. Theologians since Aquinas have distinguished between truths that may be apprehended by reason (scientific truths, etc.) and truths known only by faith. Traditional 'Protestantism has held that the Bible is God's final revelation of himself, while Roman Catholics gather around the Bible, tradition, and the pope.

Many 'cult leaders hold sway over their followers with their own personal claims to divine revelation. This view is diametrically at odds with the orthodox Christian understanding of revelation.

Revivalism (CHRISTIANITY). See 'Great Awakenings.

Right Hand Path ('occult). Term used in occult circles that designates "good," "light," "spiritual illumination," or "positivity." In the 'Bible, the sheep (the righteous) are separated from the 'goats (the wicked). The latter go to the left, and the former to the right. *See* 'left-hand path.

Rigveda (HINDUISM). The oldest of all Indian literature and one of the oldest pieces of religious literature in the world. The *Rigveda* is part of the collection of Hindu literature known as the 'Vedas. It contains over one thousand hymns composed between 1500 and 1200 B.C.

Rishis (HINDUISM) The Hindu name for a prophet, seer, or wise man.

Ritual Formal ceremonies or activities that are not only regularly performed but also institutionalized. Although many rituals are performed in the context of religion, many are also performed in nonreligious settings—for instance, patriotic rituals, such as singing the national anthem or, in America, saying the "Pledge of Allegiance." Rituals, whether religious or not, impart to its participants a sense of solidarity and social cohesion.

Rockwell, George Lincoln (IDENTITY MOVEMENTS; 1918–1967). Formed the American Nazi Party in 1958, which was renamed the National Socialist White People's Party.

Rod and Pendulum ('occult). Instruments used by a diviner for detecting "earth rays." A 'divining rod is usually a forked twig taken from a willow tree. Fish bone, metal, and other woods are used also, though less frequently. Others prefer the use of a pendulum, that is, a metal disk suspended by a thread enabling free-swinging motion. The so-called earth rays are not to be confused with the earth's magnetic field. The source of the magnetic field has at least been located near earth's North Pole. The earth rays, however, leave scientists puzzled. Though both the rod and pendulum do respond to this mysterious force, attempts to locate its point of origin have met with failure. The lack of understanding of this phenomenon has lent credence to superstitions prominent in occult practices.

Rowanwood ('occult). Handles or tools made from ash trees, commonly used to repel perceived evil spirits.

Rosenberg, John Paul See Werner 'Erhard.

Rosenkreutz, Christian (ROSICRUCIANISM; 1378–1484). The alleged founder of Rosicrucianism. He is believed to be the founder of the Fraternity of the "Rose Cross."

Rosh Hashanah (JUDAISM). The Jewish New Year, celebrated by 'orthodox Jews during the first two days of the Jewish month of Tishri, which usually occurs in September.

Roshi (ZEN BUDDHISM). A Zen master, one who has achieved 'satori and leads other disciples in 'zazen. A *roshi* sees himself as the link in a long chain of succession dating back to the 'Buddha, 'Tao-Sheng, and *Bodhidharma*.

Royal Arch Mason; Seventh Degree (FREEMASONRY). The seventh degree in Freemasonry that involves how the 'Three Most Excellent Masters are carried into captivity by King Nebuchadnezzar, later returning from exile to rebuild a second temple, the first being the temple of Solomon. The attainment of the Royal Arch degree involves the repossession of the 'Lost Word.

Royal Family (THE FAMILY). All who are hand-selected followers of Moses ᐟDavid. Most notably, they include members of his immediate family and close associates.

Royal Master; Eighth Degree (FREEMASONRY). The eighth degree in Freemasonry, which contains mythology besides that of the ᐟRoyal Arch Mason (seventh degree) surrounding the construction of Solomon's temple. Rituals in the initiation of Royal Arch Masons include the ceremonial reenactment of the Old Testament captivity of the Jews in Babylon. Royal Arch Masons participate in the struggle, captivity, and subsequent release by Cyrus the Persian monarch.

Rudra (HINDUISM). A ᐟVedic god who shoots disease-carrying arrows. Rudra also is able to reverse disease and effect healing through the use of herbs.

Rumi, Meluana Celadin (SUFISM; 1207–1273). One of the great leaders of the Sufi order during the thirteenth century, considered the golden age of Sufism.

Rune (ᐟoccult; WITCHCRAFT). From the German word *raunen*, meaning "secret, mystery, or whisper." The rune was a ᐟmagic letter in the early Teutonic alphabet. For witchcraft a rune is a magical chant. There are various rune alphabets used by occult groups.

Russell, Charles Taze (JEHOVAH'S WITNESSES; 1852–1916). Founder of the International Bible Students' Association of the Watchtower Bible and Tract Society. In 1876 Russell was elected, or called, to be the pastor of a small Bible class, organized in 1870, whose main functions were to denounce organized religions and to study eschatology. Russell did not report being visited by ᐟangels or celestial beings. Rather, he claimed that his revelations came from the ᐟBible alone and that they included disclosures of dates for key prophetic events. According to Russell, Christ was to have returned "invisibly" in 1874. The year 1914 was established as the "end of the time of the Gentiles." His major writing is a seven-volume work titled *Studies in the Scriptures.*

Rutherford, Judge Franklin (JEHOVAH'S WITNESSES; 1869–1942). The successor to Charles Taze ᐟRussell as leader of the Watchtower Bible And Tract Society, Rutherford continued to publish key dates that would mark the end of the world. These included 1920, 1925, and 1941. He is credited for the group's largest growth because of the door-to-door witnessing that he introduced, circulation of numerous writings, and his charismatic leadership.

S

Sabbat (ᐟoccult; WITCHCRAFT). The Latin/French spelling for ᐟSabbath most closely associated with witchcraft. The sabbats are periods of time when ᐟwitches gather for devotion to their goddess and god. For special sabbats, *see* ᐟwitches' holidays.

Sabbatarianism The belief that the last day of the week (Saturday), in accordance with the Old Testament, is the day for religious observance. Extreme Sabbatarianism holds that one's eternal salvation is dependent on whether the Sabbath laws are observed. Thus breaking the Sabbath, such as by observing Sunday (as most Christians do), results in people losing their salvation. Sabbatarians believe that all work, recreation, and travel must cease from sunset on Friday to sunset on Saturday.

Sabbath (CHRISTIANITY; JUDAISM; SEVENTH-DAY ADVENTISM; WORLDWIDE CHURCH OF GOD). The seventh day of the week, according to the Old Testament, was called the Sabbath. In the creation narrative of Genesis 1, God created the heavens and the earth in six days and rested on the seventh day. The Jews therefore set aside the seventh day as the Sabbath for rest and worship. In the early church, however, Christians began worshiping on the first day of the week (Sunday) in celebration of the resurrection of Christ. Sunday also symbolizes the dawning of a new week, or the eighth day. Christ's resurrection on Sunday, therefore, is symbolic of a "new covenant." Christ himself is regarded as the Sabbath rest in Hebrews 4:1–4.

In American church history, however, a movement known as Seventh-day Adventism sprung up, and Adventists returned to the practice of observing the Saturday Sabbath. This had a profound impact in the twentieth century on Herbert W. ᐟArmstrong, the leader of the Worldwide Church of God. In the most extreme form of these groups, there is no tolerance for those who worship on Sundays. Such people exhibit the "mark of the beast" and will be destroyed in the lake of fire.

Sabellianism   See ▸modalistic monarchianism.

Sabija Yoga   (HINDUISM). ▸*Yoga* meditation that is not free from the law of ▸karma.

Sacrament   (CHRISTIANITY). The English word "sacrament" is derived from the Latin word *sacramentum*, which in the Vulgate translated the Greek word *mysterion* ("mystery"). The word has been defined in different ways by various traditions within Christian history. St. Augustine's definition is perhaps most widely received: "a sign of that which is sacred" and a "visible form of invisible grace." The idea is that God has created the earth and since the Fall has remained hidden, appearing at times indirectly through things created. For example, God appeared to Moses in a burning bush (Ex. 3:3–4).

In the Roman Catholic tradition, Peter Lombard's *Sentences* enumerated what has become the traditional seven sacraments: baptism, confirmation, the Eucharist, penance, extreme unction, orders, and holy matrimony. Lutheranism reduced the number of sacraments to baptism and the Lord's Supper, because these were the only ones clearly mandated in the New Testament and the only two that offered remission for sin (Matt. 26:26–29; 28:19; Acts 2:38; 22:16). The Church of England placed special emphasis on these two chief sacraments but also recognized the validity of the remaining five.

The theological significance of the sacraments intersects both with ▸Christology and ▸ecclesiology. Christologically, the sacraments speak directly to the doctrine of the ▸Incarnation, whereby the second person of the divine ▸Trinity has become embodied as the God-Man. The sacraments are ecclesiological in that all of the "communion of saints" gathered around Christ are made a part of his "mystical body," which is the church.

Christian denominations remain divided today in their understanding of the sacraments. Protestant bodies (Lutheranism excepted) view the sacraments as signs, symbols, memorial acts, or acts of obedience to Christ's commands. The traditional ▸Orthodox, ▸Catholic, and Lutheran view holds to the sacraments as a means of grace, whereby through the symbol, a spiritual reality (the grace of God) is conveyed.

Sacred Mushroom and the Cross   (▸occult). A book published in 1970 by John Allegro, a Semitic language scholar. Allegro contended that JUDAISM and CHRISTIANITY grew out of a sex and mushroom ▸cult. The book claims that Christianity sprang up from a hoax whereby Jesus was invested with certain powers of the fly agaric. This became the true ▸sacrament of Christ's body and blood. Others who followed Allegro's general theory (see *www.bluehoney.org/mankind1.htm*) contend that the sacred mushroom, *Amanita muscasia*, served as the basis and origin of Christianity, Christmas, and the spiritualities of all ancient religion.

Sacrifice   (▸occult; CHRISTIANITY; JUDAISM; SATANISM). The practice of offering up an animal or a person to a deity in order to placate or appease. Sacrifice involves the shedding of blood. The concept of sacrifice is as old as religion itself and plays a central role in the ▸Bible. In Jewish and Christian circles, sacrifices were offered to atone for sin. According to Christianity, Jesus Christ became the one blood sacrifice for sin in the New Testament. In occult circles, especially in traditional Satanism, the rite of sacrifice is an integral part of the ▸black mass. A victim is laid on the ▸altar and is sacrificed by the ▸high priest (in the Middle Ages the high priest was sometimes a defrocked Roman Catholic priest). The shedding of blood or the life force releases vitality and energy (▸*mana*), which occultists believe then rejuvenates the deity and even themselves.

Sacrifist   (▸occult). A priest who, representing Jesus Christ, presides over a ▸black mass.

Sacrosanct   (▸occult). Something that is untouchable because of its being sacred.

Sadducees   (JUDAISM). A religious class among the Jews that arose in the intertestamental period. The Sadducees are mentioned in the New Testament on numerous occasions, chiefly in the Gospels (e.g., Matt. 3:7; 16:1, 11; 12:22–23, 34). The Sadducees, unlike the ▸Pharisees, did not embrace the oral law, but insisted on a more rigid adherence to the ▸Torah. The Sadducees also differed from the Pharisees in that they denied the resurrection of the dead, as well as any kind of spiritual life after death. Given that they were mostly priests, their life largely revolved around the ▸temple. When Titus, the Roman emperor, in A.D. 70 destroyed the temple in Jerusalem, they became extinct.

Sadhana   (SATCHIDANANDA ASHRAM INTEGRAL YOGA INSTITUTE). This word literally means the "road which leads to ▸enlightenment," that is, the path followed by the disciples of the Satchidananda Ashram Integral Yoga Institute.

Sadler, Bill   (URANTIA; n.d.). In 1934 Sadler claimed to have been visited by seven celestial spirit beings, who dictated to him the 2,097 ▸revelations that became known as *The Urantia Book*. Published in 1955, the book is believed by members of the Urantia Society to be the greatest revelation ever brought to the human race.

Sagittarius (❯astrology). Latin for "archer," Sagittarius is the ninth ❯sign of the ❯zodiac in astrology, falling between November 22 and December 21. It is commonly depicted as being a centaur drawing a bow. Persons born under the sign of Sagittarius are characterized by astrologers as being strong-willed, rebellious, honest, loyal, artistic, able organizers, and good managers.

Sagun (HINDUISM). That which is conditional, in contrast to ❯nirgun.

Sahajdhari (SIKHISM). Term used in Sikhism meaning "slow adopters." The *sahajdhari* are those who hesitate in joining the Sikh movement. They remain clean-shaven and do not take the required vows.

Saint Germain See church universal and triumphant.

Saints (CHRISTIANITY; MORMONISM). In Christianity there are varying understandings of what constitutes a saint. The New Testament letters are often addressed to the saints in the churches in various cities, suggesting that all Christians are saints. During the time of the Middle Ages, however, both Eastern and Western Churches began to canonize certain individuals as "saints." At the time of the ❯Protestant Reformation, Luther, Calvin, and other reformers returned to the New Testament usage, restoring the idea that the saints are believers. Luther called this doctrine the "priesthood of all believers." Both of these understandings prevail today in the various church bodies mentioned above.

For Mormonism, saints are considered to be all members of the Mormon church.

Sakat (ISLAM). One of the ❯five pillars of Islam. *Sakat* is the paying of alms (monies) by all who have a steady income, for such causes as the advancement of Islam, the needs of the poor, beggars, travelers, debtors, and the like. Adherents to Islam are expected to pay 2.5 percent of their annual income in order to fulfill this obligation.

Sakpata (VOODOO). The presiding deity who is above all earthly deities.

Sakya Muni (BUDDHISM). Another name for ❯Buddha.

Salamander (❯occult). A mythical lizard that supposedly lives in the flames of fire.

Salat (al-Salat) (ISLAM). This is one of the ❯five pillars of Islam. It refers to the saying of five prayers that every loyal Muslim is to utter every day. These prayers are to be said just before dawn, at noon, mid-afternoon, just before sunset, and in the evening. The latter may be said any time from one hour after sunset to midnight.

Salakhana (HINDUISM). The act of ceremonially starving oneself to death.

Samadhi (HINDUISM). The state of being in a yogic (*see* ❯yoga) ❯trance. The subject focuses his mind solely on what he considers to be the divine.

Samaeda (HINDUISM). Portion of the ❯*Vedas* that is chanted.

Samhain (❯occult; WITCHCRAFT). (Pronounced "sow-when") One of the eight ❯Sabbats celebrated by ❯witches and others involved in the occult. It is celebrated on the eve of November 1, that is, October 31. It is the counterbalance to ❯Beltane or ❯May Eve, which greets the summer. *Samhain* is the festival that ushers in the season of darkness, the last day for gathering in any remaining harvest. According to legend, spirits roamed the countryside on October 31, destroying all that was left unharvested. *Samhain* is also known as ❯Halloween. It was associated with the time for contacting the dead. The popular associations of Halloween are derived from ancient Celtic and ❯Druid pagan religious customs (*see* ❯*Witches Calendar*).

Samhitas (HINDUISM). The so-called wisdom books of the ❯*Vedas.*

Samkyha (HINDUISM). One of the six schools of Hinduism, Samkhya studies the evolution of both body and soul. One who pursues this system is said to be on the path that leads to a perfect ❯revelation of truth.

Sammael (❯occult). The so-called prince of darkness in some of the occult groups.

Samsara (HINDUISM). Endless wandering of the soul through various lower and higher life forms.

Samyasin (HINDUISM; ISKCON). See ❯*sannyasin.*

Sanctification (CHRISTIANITY). The doctrine espousing, in a wide sense, all of God's working within a Christian. In a narrow sense, sanctification describes the spiritual growth that a Christian undergoes following ❯justification. ❯Orthodox Christianity has held that full and complete sanctification takes place in heaven.

Many ❯cults that are offshoots of Christianity teach that it is possible to attain holiness or perfect sanctification in this life. The leader of the cult determines the criteria for perfection; the standards differ from group to group.

Sandalphon (❯occult). In Western ❯magic, an archangel who supposedly protects the earth.

Sanders, Alexander (WITCHCRAFT; 1916–1988). Leading figure in modern witchcraft along with Gerald

[*]Gardner. Sanders claimed that he was the product of a generation of [*]witches in his family, himself being initiated into the craft by his grandmother. His version of witchcraft is called [*]Alexandrian.

Sangha (BUDDHISM). Buddhism's oldest religious order.

Sankaracharya (HINDUISM). Incarnation of [*]*Siva* who expounded the Vedanta school of Hindu philosophy.

Sankhya (HINDUISM). One of the six schools of thought within Hinduism.

Sankirtana (HINDUISM). A chorus of praise sung or chanted by Hindu worshipers, a religious chant or [*]mantra repeated in order to draw practitioners into a closer state of god-consciousness.

Sannyas (HINDUISM). See [*]*sannyasin.*

Sannyasin (HINDUISML ISKCON). The stage in the progress wherein a devotee renounces all earthly treasures, all friends, and all family ties in order to become one with [*]Hare Krishna.

Sanskrit (HINDUISM). The standard dialect of the Hindu Scriptures.

Santana Dharma (HINDUISM). Term that means "true belief."

Santero (SANTERIA). A Santeria priest. See also [*]*babalao.*

Sarasvati (HINDUISM). Goddess of education and music; also a companion of [*]*Brahma.*

Sat (HINDUISM). Real existence; the opposite of illusory or apparent existence or *asat.*

Sat Nam (SIKH DHARMA). The "name" for God, which more literally means "God's name is truth." The [*]mantra that contains God's name is as follows: *Ek Ong Kar Sat Nam Siri Wha Gurv,* which is translated, "There is one Creation, Truth is His name. He is all Great, He is all Wisdom."

Satan (CHRISTIANITY; SATANISM). Biblical name for the [*]devil, Satan is the personification of all evil and the adversary of God. He has various other names, such as [*]Lucifer, Belial, and [*]Beelzebub. Jesus called him the "father of all lies" (John 8:44), and Paul called him the "god of this world" (2 Cor. 4:4).

Satanic Ritual Abuse (SRA) *See* SATANISM for a discussion of SRA.

Satanist ([*]occult; SATANISM). Those who practice Satanism of which there are different kinds and varieties.

Satori (ZEN BUDDHISM). The moment when one comes into complete harmony with the Absolute, perceiving the "all" to be but the "one."

Satsang (ECKANKAR; ELAN VITAL; HINDUISM). For Hinduism a satsang is intimate communion with God. Divine Light Mission devotees were required to attend [*]guru [*]Maharaj Ji's satsangs, or devotional talks. In Eckankar, it is a class where students study their monthly lesson.

Satyr ([*]occult). A Babylonian demonic creature known as the "he-goat."

Savoy, Douglas Eugene (CHURCH OF THE SECOND ADVENT; 1927–). Established the International Community Of Christ or the Jamilians. Savoy began to receive psychic visions at the age of six. At age twenty-eight, he discovered the teachings of the [*]Essenes, at which time he concluded that Jesus' most important teachings were not contained in the [*]Bible but were yet to be disclosed. Based on Isaiah 11:6 ("a little child shall lead them"), Savoy claimed that his only son, Jamil (see [*]Savoy, Jamil Sean), was the [*]incarnation of Christ. Savoy, through Jamil, claimed that the sun's energy was the key to all life. Increased solar energy increases life and leads to new birth.

Savoy, Jamil Sean (CHURCH OF THE SECOND ADVENT; 1959–1962). Son of Eugene Douglas [*]Savoy, who taught that Jamil was a reincarnate Christ. Although Jamil died at the age of three, Eugene insisted this was supposed to happen.

Sawm (ISLAM). One of the [*]five pillars of Islam. *Sawm* is divided into required fasts (*wajib sawms*), such as are celebrated in the annual observance of [*]Ramadan, and voluntary fasts (*nathr sawms*), after which, if [*]Allah grants such a prayer or wish, *nathr sawms* become *wajib sawms.*

Science and Health with Key to the Scriptures (CHRISTIAN SCIENCE). The official doctrinal statement of the Christian Science Church, written by Mary Baker [*]Eddy, which offers her interpretation of CHRISTIANITY and the Bible. Many believe it is a plagiarized work of P. P. [*]Quimby, Eddy's one-time mentor and teacher.

Science of Creative Intelligence (TRANSCENDENTAL MEDITATION). In an attempt to alter the negative image that Trancendental Meditation was having in the West, particularly in the United States, Maharishi Mahesh [*]Yogi abandoned religious nomenclature and replaced it with psychological concepts. His strategy proved to be successful on the whole, as membership began to grow rapidly within the movement, particularly through enrollment in the seminars.

Scorpio (▸astrology; ▸occult). Known in astrology as the scorpion, Scorpio is the eighth ▸sign of the ▸zodiac, falling between October 24 and November 21. According to Greek mythology, Scorpio is the serpent that stung Orion to death. Persons born under the sign of Scorpio are said to be cautious and have great strength of character and inner resolve, but passionate love affairs turned sour may be "stinging" to a Scorpio. Science, diplomacy, and medicine are careers most often associated with a Scorpio.

Scottish Rite (FREEMASONRY). Also known as the Ancient and Accepted Scottish Rite, it is one of two branches in Freemasonry where members join and work through a series of steps, taking oaths, participating in various rites and ceremonies, and eventually earning the award or degree. Scottish Rite, like ▸York Rite, are comprised of lodges and ▸chapters. There are two requirements for proceeding into the Scottish Rite. One must be a ▸Master Mason, and one must be a member in good standing in the ▸Blue Lodge. Scottish Rite Freemasonry is the more popular form and is found in every country where the Masonic Lodge has established itself. Twenty-nine additional degrees are conferred on a member in addition to the three degrees conferred on one by the Blue Lodge. The highest ranking degree is the thirty-third, an honary degree.

Séance (▸occult; SPIRITUALISM). The meeting of a group of people who, usually sitting in a circle in a dark room, attempt to communicate with the spirit world or souls of the dead through the use of a ▸medium. Mediums often use the assistance of a ▸guide, a ▸Ouija board, or ▸automatic writing. Critics say a dark room is used because it is easier in such a setting to deceive nonmembers.

Second Adventist Movement (SEVENTH-DAY ADVENTISM). A widespread trans-denominational movement that goes back to the 1830s when a group of people became followers of William Miller, who taught that Christ would return on March 21, 1844. When this prediction failed to occur, Miller recalculated the return of Christ to occur on October 22, 1844. Those who insisted that Miller's date was not wrong claim that Christ did appear but invisibly. These formed the Seventh-day Adventist church. In time, this church spawned some offshoots, one of them being the Worldwide Church of God. (*See also* ▸Millerite movement; ▸false prophecy).

Second Vision (MORMONISM). The alleged vision that enabled Joseph ▸Smith Jr. to locate what he called the ▸golden plates.

Sect A religious group that breaks away from an established, larger religious organization because the larger group is seen as having become too secular and worldly in its religious beliefs and practices. A sect, unlike the ▸cult (which introduces radically new doctrines and practices), seeks to restore traditional beliefs and practices.

Secret Tradition (▸occult). Secret knowledge passed on from generation to generation by those who function as masters, often known as ▸adepts.

Seder; Seder Meal (JUDAISM). The Jewish ceremony that is performed on the first night of ▸Passover, commemorating the experience the Israelites had before the Exodus from Egypt occurred. The meal associated with the celebration of the Passover is called a Seder meal.

Selassie, Haile (RASTAFARIANISM). In 1930, Ras Tafari ▸Makonnen (1893–1975) was crowned Emperor Selassie of Ethiopia. Makonnen immediately was recognized by the ostentatious title "King of Kings, Lord of Lords, His Imperial Majesty of the Conquering Lion of the Tribe of Judah, Elect of God." This was considered the fulfillment of a prophecy by Marcus ▸Garvey, a leader of the black nationalist movement. Followers of Selassie, adopting the emperor's name, called themselves Rastafarians.

Select Master; Ninth Degree (FREEMASONRY). The ninth degree in Freemasonry, which contains additional steps in addition to the ▸Royal Arch Mason (seventh degree) surrounding the construction of Solomon's temple. This ninth degree involves the candidate entering what is known as the ▸Commandery. This in itself comprises three orders: the Order of the Red Cross, the Order of the Knights of Malta, and the ▸Order of the Knights Templar. The latter is the highest award in York Rite Freemasonry.

Sephardim; Sephardic Rite (JUDAISM). Also spelled *sefarad* (plural *sefardim*), from the Hebrew *sepharad*. This name is given to the ▸Diaspora Jews who lived in Spain and Portugal until persecution drove them away in the last half of the fifteenth century. They migrated to France, North Africa, Holland, England, Italy, and Greece. The Sephardic Jews are distinguished from the ▸Ashkenazi, who resided in the Rhineland, France, and Germany until persecution exiled them to Poland, Russia, and other Eastern European countries.

Historically, Sephardic Jews differed from the Ashkenazi chiefly with regards to worship. The latter used a German rite that was Palestinian in origin while the former borrowed heavily from ancient Babylonian customs and used Ladino (a Spanish-Hebrew language). In addition, the Sephardic rite lacked a considerable number of poems, prayers, and liturgy that were endemic to the Ashkenazic rite. The Sephardim maintained a superior and therefore separatistic attitude over against their Ashkenazic counterparts, believing that they alone were the direct descendants of the tribe of Judah (see Albert Schulman, *Gateway to Judaism*, 2 vols. [London: Thomas Yoseloff, 1971], 639). The differences between these two groups have become minimized in the modern world. Only 15 percent of the world's Jewish population is Sephardic.

Septuagint (LXX) (▸Bible; CHRISTIANITY; JUDAISM). The Greek version of the Old Testament, translated approximately 285–132 B.C. It is called "Septuagint" (a Greek word meaning "seventy") because it was claimed that seventy-two individuals participated in the translation work. The Septuagint and the Hebrew Masoretic texts differ in a significant number of places and in the order and number of books. This translation was adopted and used widely among Greek-speaking Jews. Early Christians often quoted from the Septuagint, and New Testament writers used it frequently. The LXX was believed by many to be inspired despite the fact that Jerome translated his Latin Vulgate, not from the LXX as earlier Latin manuscripts, but from the Hebrew.

Serpent (SATANISM). The horned snake, a symbol of ▸demons.

Serpent Power (HINDUISM). See also ▸*kundalini*.

Serpent Seed (CHRISTIAN IDENTITY MOVEMENTS). Doctrine that alleges Eve's sin in the Garden of Eden (Gen. 3) was sexual and that Eve had sexual intercourse with the serpent and begot Cain. Thus, Cain's father was ▸Satan, not Adam. Cain's descendants were somehow perpetuated after the Flood through Noah's son Ham. Diverse groups teach variations of this doctrine; for example, the Identity Movement, a racist group, holds that the black race comes from Cain.

Serios, Ted (▸occult; 1918–). An American psychic who claims to possess the ability to transmit mental images onto film.

Servers (▸occult). Those who assist in conducting occult rituals.

Seven Stages (MEHER BABA). Also called the "seven realities." ▸Baba taught that the soul makes its journey to consciousness through a series of seven evolving forms: (1) stones and metal, (2) vegetable, (3) worm and insect, (4) fish, (5) bird, (6) animal, and (7) human. The last mentioned constitutes the highest form of consciousness.

Sexual Magic (▸occult). Performing or symbolically performing sexual acts to symbolize the bringing about of fertility and life and to symbolize unity with the earth and various deities.

Shabuot (JUDAISM). A Jewish feast that commemorates God's giving the Ten Commandments to Moses.

Shade (▸occult). A term that refers to the spirit of a dead person.

Shahada (ISLAM). The first of Islam's ▸five pillars. It says: "There is no God but the one God, and ▸Muhammad is his prophet." It is the declaration of all loyal ▸Muslims.

Sha'ir (ISLAM). One who is demonized in Arabic.

Shakti (HINDUISM). The great mother goddess, the wife of ▸Siva. Shakti is the underlying force of Siva, in whose absence the latter would be void of life. Shakti is also regarded as being the feminine principle of all deities.

Shakubuku (BUDDHISM; NICHIREN SHOSHU BUDDHISM; SOKA-GAKKAI). Literally "browbeating," *shakubuku* is a successful conversion technique that uses a high-pressured and emotionally charged reasoning that proves to be most persuasive with its recipients, though it has been labeled as being a coercive technique by antagonists.

Shaliach (CHRISTIANITY). The Aramaic word that is the equivalent of the Greek term for "apostle." It connotes one who has authority from those he represents.

Shaman (NATIVE AMERICAN RELIGION). A ▸sorcerer, ▸medicine man, and the like who becomes an intermediary between the spirit world and the material. Shamans experience ▸altered states of consciousness and soul travel, often using drums to "ride" into the ▸trance state.

Shamanism (NATIVE AMERICAN RELIGION). The spiritual practice of a sorcerer or medicine man, especially in Native American tribes of the past. The medicine man, also known as a ▸shaman, engages in various rituals and dances as he seeks to bring about healing of the sick, for example. Sometimes his soul is believed to leave his body as he in a trancelike manner dances and performs esoteric rituals. Frequently, a shaman is clothed in grotesque garb, including eerie masks. A shaman is sometimes also referred to as a ▶witch doctor.

Shambala (BUDDHISM). An imagined sacred kingdom believed to be located in the mountainous regions north of Tibet. Should unbelievers ever attempt to enter this kingdom, a savior will arise to wage war on the intruders, conquering them and then establishing a utopia on earth.

Shango (SOUTH AMERICAN, CENTRAL AMERICAN, AND CARIBBEAN CULTS). The name of one of the ▶orisha, who is believed to be the deity of thunder and war.

Shankara (HINDUISM; 700–750). Indian philosopher and theologian considered one of the great exponents of modern Hinduism. His numerous writings revolve around his chief conviction that direct knowledge of ▶Brahman is the only means of release from ▶karma.

Share International (NEW AGE MOVEMENT). Monthly magazine founded by Benjamin ▶Crème. It is published in England and is distributed in over seventy countries. It contains various New Age themes.

Shariah (ISLAM; SUFISM). A code of ethics or law that is consistent with and reinforces the doctrines and practices of the ▶Koran.

Shaykh (ISLAM; SUFISM). An alternate spelling for sheikh, a religious leader or teacher of Islam.

Shaytan (ISLAM). The Arabic word for ▶Satan. Sometimes it is also spelled Shaitan or Sheitan. See also ▶iblis.

Shemhaforash (JUDAISM). Talmudic word used for the incomprehensible name of God.

Shentao See ▶Shinto.

Shiʾite (ISLAM). Shiʾites constitute an important Islamic ▶sect. They are primarily found in Iran.

Shikishin Funi (BUDDHISM; NICHIREN SHOSHU BUDDHISM). A Nichiren Shoshu concept that holds that the universe and God are essentially one. From this ▶pantheistic expression follows the conclusion that there is no spiritual dimension to the cosmos, nor is there necessarily a God or spirit world.

Shinto (SHINTOISM). The Chinese word comes from "shin tao" or "way of the gods." The ancient religion of Japan that is as much cultural as it is religious. Shinto worship focuses on gratitude to the ▶kami, who are people or natural entities that have for centuries evoked the wonder of the Japanese. *Kami* may be hills, mountains, or animals. Often the *kami* are deities and

special human individuals, the latter commonly being emperors. This accounts for Japan's longstanding worship of its emperors. Shinto worship also occurs in the home, where a small altar called a *kamidana* or *kami* shelf may contain a number of items that are worshiped and revered, such as the names of the departed ancestors or statues of deities. In reality, the worshiping of the *kami* is a form of ▶polytheism. See also SPIRITUALISM.

Shirk (ISLAM). The Arabic word for the sin of associating any other person or thing with deity.

Shiva (HINDUISM). The destroyer and the third member of the triad of Hindu demigods.

Shofar (JUDAISM). The ram's horn used in Jewish ceremonies.

Showbread (JUDAISM). Translated literally as "bread of the presence," showbread was unleavened bread placed on a table made of acacia wood (Ex. 25:23) and overlaid with pure gold (v. 24). The ▶table of showbread was placed before God (v. 30) in the sanctuary of the ▶tabernacle along with the ▶golden candlestick and the altar of incense. On the ▶Sabbath, twelve loaves, representing the twelve tribes of Israel, were set on the table in two groups of six. The showbread was symbolic of the rich bounty of God's grace and his providence in sustaining Israel's journey through the desert as they left Egypt to enter the Promised Land.

Shriners (FREEMASONRY). Popular name for the Ancient Arabic Order of the Nobles of the Mystic Shrine, a Masonic-related fraternity.

Shruti (HINDUISM). Revealed knowledge.

Shunned; Shunning (JEHOVAH'S WITNESSES). If a Jehovah's Witness will not embrace the doctrines of the Watchtower Bible and Tract Society after continued attempts have been made to proselytize him or her, shunning or ▶disfellowshiping is practiced. That person is avoided, even by members or his or her own family.

Siddha (ELAN VITAL; HINDUISM). Divine masters or yogis who have acquired powers over the forces of nature. A form of ▶yoga.

Sigil (▶occult; WITCHCRAFT). Sigils are symbolic representations of ▶demons in the form of a seal or signature inscribed on a charm.

Sign (▶astrology; ▶occult). The term for the twelve divisions of the ▶zodiac. The twelve signs in order are ▶Aries, ▶Taurus, ▶Gemini, ▶Cancer, ▶Leo, ▶Virgo, ▶Libra, ▶Scorpio, ▶Sagittarius, ▶Capricorn, ▶Aquarius, ▶Pisces.

They are further grouped by the four elements and the classifications cardinal, fixed, mutable.

SIGN	CARDINAL	FIXED	MUTABLE
Fire	Aries	Leo	Sagittarius
Water	Cancer	Scorpio	Pisces
Air	Libra	Aquarius	Gemini
Earth	Capricorn	Taurus	Virgo

Sikha (ISKCON). The small patch of hair that remains on the shaven head of ISKCON devotees.

Siksha (SRI CHINMOY CENTER). The process whereby the devotee learns to yield his or her life to the teachings of the ▸guru.

Silent Ones (ECKANKAR). The eschatological hope of a ▸chela is to one day become one of the silent ones, or those who are forever in the service of ▸Sugmad, carrying out his divine will. One begins the journey by taking the necessary steps (training) toward the goal of undergoing release from the physical body.

Silva, Jose (SILVA MIND CONTROL; 1914–1999). Hypnotist who founded Silva Mind Control.

Sita (HINDUISM). The wife of ▸*Rama*, noted especially for her loyalty, truthfulness, and unswerving devotion to her husband.

Siva (HINDUISM). The god of destructive forces. Siva (also called Shiva) appears in many forms (e.g., *see* ▸Rudra), but essentially he is one of the gods of the Hindu trinity. ▸Brahman and ▸Vishnu—the gods of creation and preservation, respectively—are the remaining two. All that is undone in the material universe is attributed to Siva.

The number 666 scribbled on a stone monument.
Courtesy Bill Reisman

Six-Six-Six (666) (▸occult; CHRISTIANITY; SATANISM). A biblical reference in Revelation 13:18, which gives this number as a symbolic number to the dominion of evil in the world and the influence and reign of ▸Satan. Biblical commentators have suggested that in the numerological reckonings of the book of Revelation, "666" falls shy of the perfect number (seven), which is the number for God. In Satanism, the number 666 is a key symbol.

Sixteen Points (ANANDAN MARGA YOGA SOCIETY). A spiritual discipline for practitioners of the Ananda Marga Yoga Society, developed by P. R. Sarkar. They are intended to maximize one's spiritual and physical health. The sixteen points are as follows:

1. Water—To be used to cleanse the genital area in order to empty the bladder. Excessive urinary buildup in the bladder results in excessive sexual stimulation.
2. Skin—Circumcision should be performed on male children for cleanliness. If not the skin should be unfolded and cleaned regularly.
3. Joint Hair—Hair under armpits etc. should not be shaved. This is natural to the body, but these areas should be cleansed regularly.
4. Underwear—Should be worn to prevent bodily fluids (women should wear bras) from the sexual and urinary areas of the body.
5. Half Bath (*Vya'Paka Shaoca*)—For cleanliness and to prevent excessive build-up of bodily heat.
6. Bath—At least once daily while the desire is four times a day at morning, noon, evening, and midnight. Skin should be dried by sunlight or a light bulb.
7. Food—Sentient foods should be eaten rather than mutative or static. One should not eat more than four times per day.
8. *Upavasa*—One should fast the eleventh day after a full moon. This develops one's willpower and an awareness of and empathy for the poor.
9. *Sa'Dhana*—The achieving of ▸enlightenment.
10. *Is'ta*—"the chosen Ideal." One is to respect, honor, and obey a ▸guru and no negative words against him are to be tolerated.
11. *A'dharsa*—A practitioner of ▸yoga should follow their chosen path or "ideology."
12. Conduct Rules—Comprised of fifteen social conduct rules; The Supreme Command; forty social norms. When followed, complete mental equilibrium is maintained.

13. Supreme Command—The fundamental guidepost.
14. *Dharmacakra*—A weekly meditation session.
15. Oaths—Every effort to keep oaths that have been made should be meditated upon and followed.
16. C.S.D.K.—(*Conduct Rules, Seminar, Duty, Kiirtan*).

(Taken from *http://religiousmovements.lib.virginia .edu/nrms/amorc.html*)

Skrying (▸occult). Also spelled "scrying"; the occult practice of ▸divination through the use of various transparent, translucent, and reflective materials such as ▸crystal balls, water, mirrors, ▸crystals, etc.

Skull and Crossbones (▸occult; WITCHCRAFT). The symbol placed on a person or object signifying death, finality, or one who is marked for death. The skull is often used as a centerpiece on an occult group altar.

Skyclad (▸occult; WITCHCRAFT). The practice of some ▸witches celebrating and worshiping in the nude, or "clad" only by the sky. Its purpose is to portray equality. Many cover their bodies with only a robe. Most North American witches do not practice their craft skyclad.

Sleeping Prophet (▸occult). The nickname for Edgar ▸Cayce, a psychic who would close his eyes when he went into a trance to transfer energies to heal patients and also to make his predictions. Many of his predictions failed. For instance, he predicted that China would convert to Christianity in 1968. He had also predicted that 1933 would be a prosperous year, but it was one of the years of the Great Depression.

Smith, Joseph Sr. (MORMONISM; 1771–1840) The father of Joseph ▸Smith Jr. who founded Mormonism. The elder Smith was reported to have been intensely interested in treasure hunting, a fact not unrelated to the younger Smith's interest in digging in the place where he claimed to have found the translation tools for the ▸Book of Mormon.

Smith, Joseph Jr. (MORMONISM; 1805–1844). He was born in Sharon, Vermont, and was founder and "prophet" of The Church of Jesus Christ of Latter-Day Saints. Smith's first supposed vision came in the spring of 1820, wherein he inquired as to which of the sects (denominations) of CHRISTIANITY had the correct teachings. The angel who appeared answered that none were correct—"they were all wrong." Smith's second purported vision in 1823 included the message that a book,

preserved on golden plates, recorded a history of the American continent. The angel told Smith where the plates were but forbade him from translating them at that time. In 1827 the plates were given to Smith to be translated. The result was the ▸Book of Mormon, the most important document in Mormonism. Smith was killed by a mob while imprisoned in Carthage, Illinois, in 1844.

Smith, Joseph III (MORMONISM; 1838–1919). The son of Joseph ▸Smith Jr. and his wife Emma. She believed that after the death of her husband, her son should assume the leadership of the church, but Brigham ▸Young had other ideas. This resulted in a split that formed the Reorganized Church of Jesus Christ of The Latter-Day Saints (COMMUNITY OF CHRIST). Brigham Young led the much larger contingent of ▸Mormons to Salt Lake City, Utah.

Smith, Lucy (MORMONISM). The mother of Joseph ▸Smith Jr., the founder of Mormonism.

Smriti (HINDUISM). The secondary sacred Hindu writings that carry lesser authority than the ▸*Shruti*, which are proclaimed as revealed knowledge.

Snake (▸occult). A symbol of ▸Satan and demons when his worshipers wear horns.

Society of the Processians See PROCESS CHURCH OF THE FINAL JUDGMENT.

Societies (URANTIA). Groups dedicated to the study of ▸*The Urantia Book*. The societies are chartered by the brotherhood.

Socinianism (CHRISTIANITY). Anti-trinitarian movement of the sixteenth century that is believed to be the forerunner of ▸unitarianism. Led by F. P. Sozzini (1539–1604), Socinianism traces its roots back to the radical anti-trinitarian and ▸Anabaptist traditions and is characterized by a rationalism that denied the deity of Christ, original sin, the vicarious atonement, and the resurrection. In its more conservative expression, Socinianism rejected the deity of Christ in the interest of preserving the oneness of the Godhead over and against the plurality of the doctrine of the ▸Trinity.

Sola Fide (CHRISTIANITY). These two Latin words mean "by faith alone." This concept was first used by Martin Luther, and it became one of the basic principles of the ▸Protestant Reformation. This doctrine states that the repentant sinner by faith alone in Jesus Christ is justified before God without any merit or good works on his or her part. A Christian's good works are the fruits of his faith. Luther derived this theological concept from Romans 3:28; Galatians 2:16; Ephesians 2:8–9.

Sola Gratia (CHRISTIANITY). Literally, these two Latin words mean "by grace alone." This theological doctrine was loudly proclaimed by the reformers during the ▶Protestant Reformation. It asserts that Christians by their faith in Christ are saved by grace (undeserved unkindness). This grace is the consequence of God's gracious disposition and thus not something that is infused in the Christian. Similar to ▶*sola fidei*, this doctrine is derived from Ephesians 2:8–9.

Sola Scriptura (CHRISTIANITY). This third *sola* (alone) asserts that Scripture (the ▶Bible) is the only source of doctrine and authority for the Christian church and its members. Like ▶*sola fide* and ▶*sola gratia*, *sola scriptura* ("Scripture alone") became a hallmark of the ▶Protestant Reformation. As a doctrine it asserts that tradition and theologians of the church are all subordinate to Holy Scripture.

Solar Temple See ORDER OF THE SOLAR TEMPLE.

Solitary Practitioners (WITCHCRAFT). Those who engage in the practice of witchcraft outside of a ▶coven and by themselves.

Solstice (▶occult; WITCHCRAFT). See ▶*Witches Calendar*.

Solus Christus (CHRISTIANITY). Like ▶*Sola fide*,▶ *sola gratia*, and ▶*sola scriptura* (cited above), *solus Christus* says there is no salvation outside of Jesus Christ. It is a doctrine derived from John 3:36; 14:6; Acts 4:12. This doctrinal truth also states that Jesus Christ is the center of God's Word, the holy ▶Bible.

Soma (HINDUISM). A vine that has certain milkweed juices used in ritualistic sacrifices. The fluid is intoxicating but is consumed in the hopes of bestowing immortality to ▶Vedic worshipers.

Sons of God (MORMONISM). All human beings are "sons of God." That is, all enjoyed a spiritual existence as sons of God before obtaining earthly bodies. Therefore, being a son of God is in one way determinative of the final heavenly reward a Mormon will obtain.

Sontad (URANTIA). The name of the first human born on earth to the first parents, ▶Andon and ▶Fonta.

Soothsaying (▶fortune-telling; ▶occult). A term derived from the medieval English word that once meant telling the truth. Among fortune tellers the term now connotes making predictions relative a person's life in the future.

Sophia (▶occult; WITCHCRAFT). The Greek goddess of wisdom. In neo-pagan circles Sophia is personified in goddess worship. See ▶goddess; ▶neopaganism.

Sorcerer (▶occult). Someone who uses spells and ▶magic formulas to conjure up evil spirits. A sorcerer practices ▶sorcery. Sorcerers are referred to by different names, such as ▶wizard, ▶shaman, ▶magician, etc. See also ▶demons.

Sorcery (▶occult). The term used in the occult world that refers to the practice of manipulating or controlling supernatural spirits, often through the use of ▶black magic.

Soteriology (CHRISTIANITY). The study of the doctrine of salvation. This word derives from two Greek words: *soter* ("savior") and *logos* ("word, discourse"). For Christianity, soteriology is the doctrine concerning the person and work of Jesus Christ and how salvation is made possible through his finished work on the cross. Many religions and ▶cults have a doctrine of soteriology, and many are derivative of the Christian concept.

Soul-Life (THE WAY INTERNATIONAL). The Way International teaches that Jesus was sinless, not by virtue of his being the only begotten Son of God, but rather because of a sinless seed that impregnated Mary by the Holy Spirit. The Way uses the analogy of a "cow being covered by a bull" to express how God overshadowed Mary for Jesus' birth.

Soul Sleep (SEVENTH-DAY ADVENTSM). The belief that souls of dead human beings sleep or exist in an unconscious state until they are resurrected on Judgment Day.

Soul Travel (ECKANKAR). The ability of the soul to transcend the body and travel into the spiritual realm, where God dwells.

Sound and Light of Eck (ECKANKAR). Term roughly equivalent to the "Holy Spirit," through whom God appears in the lower worlds and people can discover, see, and hear within themselves.

Special Revelation (CHRISTIANITY). The process whereby God communicates knowledge about himself and regarding his will for humankind. In Christian theology, the ▶Bible is God's special revelation. God's special revelation is also particularly manifest in the incarnation of his only Son Jesus Christ. General or natural revelation reveals to all humankind that the world of nature obviously had to have a designer and maker, namely, God. But only special revelation reveals the saving works of Jesus.

Spell (ᵖoccult). A spoken word, ᵖcharm, or ᵖincantation that harnesses magical (*see* ᵖmagic) power. Spells may be cast on another person or may invoke power for selfish use on the part of a ᵖsorcerer.

A spell kit purchased in a hotel gift shop in Las Vegas. This hotel also provides fortune-telling services.
Courtesy Jack M. Roper/CARIS

Sphota (HINDUISM). The essence of everything in the universe.

Spirit Body (ᵖoccult). *See* ᵖetheric body.

Spirit Photography (ᵖoccult). The production of a photographic negative of a living or deceased person that supposedly results during a ᵖséance.

Spirit Raps (ᵖoccult). The alleged noises that are said to occur during a ᵖséance or ᵖpoltergeist occurrence.

Spirit Writing (ᵖoccult). The writing that is said to occur on a prepared piece of paper during the conduct of a ᵖséance.

Spiritual Abuse The physical or mental damage that can be done to someone who seeks spiritual aid and counsel from a religious figure and receives instead mind control, brainwashing, obsessive guilt, etc.

Spiritism (ᵖoccult; NEW AGE MOVEMENT; SPIRITUALISM). The esoteric belief that says the human personality exists after death and that it is able to communicate with the living through the ᵖmedium of psychics. Believers in this phenomenon say this communication comes from the spirit world and is commonly conveyed through ᵖapparitions, clairaudience, ᵖclairvoyance, the ᵖouija board, ᵖpoltergeist, ᵖséances, ᵖtelepathy, ᵖtelekinesis, etc.

Spiritual Mind Treatment (RELIGIOUS SCIENCE). The practice of positive thinking and ᵖaffirmative prayer in order to achieve healing of the body and mind.

Spiritual Regeneration Movement (HINDUISM). A movement founded by Maharishi Mahesh ᵖYogi in 1958. It was largely the forerunner or ancestor of transcendental meditation (TM).

Spirituality (HINDUISM). Spirituality in Hindu thought is ceremonial and external on the one hand, and mystical and subjective on the other. The devotee exhibits trust, love, loyalty, and a deep sense of reverence for the divine, channeling these virtues through ritual and ceremony.

Sprenger, Jacob (ᵖoccult; WITCHCRAFT; d. 1481). One of the two authors of the ᵖ*Malleus Malificarum* (*Witches' Hammer*, 1486), a work that greatly exacerbated the fervor over against ᵖwitches in this period of time (designated as the era of ᵖGothic witchcraft).

Spring Equinox (ᵖoccult; WITCHCRAFT). One of the eight seasonal festivals celebrated by ᵖwitches. Also many aboriginal religions give special attention to this day. The spring ᵖequinox occurs on March 21, when the length of both day and night are equalized by the sun crossing the equator. *See* ᵖ*Witches Calendar.*

Sri (HINDUISM; ECKANKAR). The Hindu term for "holy." It is also used to designate a spiritual leader who has attained ᵖenlightenment.

Sri Bhashya (HINDUISM). A running commentary on ᵖ*Vedanta*, authored by Ramanuja.

Sruti (HINDUISM). The ᵖ*Vedas*, or divine scriptures, that were conveyed orally by the father god to the son.

Stake (MORMONISM). A large grouping of Mormon churches within a given geographic area. There are approximately 390 stakes, and each stake is broken down into ᵖwards, local churches, and independent ᵖbranches. Though the numbers vary in each, a stake consists of an average of four thousand members.

Standard Works (MORMONISM). Four books qualify as "standard" resources in the Mormon church: ᵖBook of Mormon, ᵖ*The Pearl Of Great Price*, ᵖ*Doctrine And Covenants*, and the King James Bible, "insofar as it is translated correctly."

Star Time (ᵖastrology; ᵖoccult). Synonymous with sidereal time in astrology.

Steiner, Rudolf (ROSICRUCIANISM; 1861–1925). Founder of the Anthroposophical Society. He also started the Waldorf Schools and centers for the study of anthroposophical thought.

Sterling Management (SCIENTOLOGY). Promotes the philosophy of Scientology through various business management services. It is largely directed to attract dentists, chiropractors, doctors, and veterinarians.

Stevens, John Robert (CHURCH OF THE LIVING WORD; 1919–83). Started the Church of the Living Word; The Walk. In 1954 Stevens, leader of his group, claimed to have received a vision similar to that of Paul's on the road leading to Damascus. He taught that an individual can become a god. Central to Stevens's theology is the continuation of such 'revelations, which supplement the now-outdated 'Bible.

Stigmata (CHRISTIANITY). The term comes from the classical Greek meaning a visible prick mark on someone's body. Some Christians have reportedly had the wounds of Christ appear on their bodies. Such stigmata have supposedly appeared on the bodies of some Christians involved in 'mysticism. Sometimes these wounds were both visible and bloody; sometimes invisible and produced only pain to the individual. Most who have had stigmata have been women. Some notable examples are St. Catherine of Genoa (1447–1510) and Theresa Newmann (1898–1962); the best known example is St. Francis of Assisi (1181/2–1226).

Stonehenge ('occult). A man-made circular arrangement of large upright stones, located in Salisbury, England, about eighty miles west of London. A number of theories have been suggested for this construction. One says that the ancient 'Druids built this site as a temple. Another theory argues that it was built by extraterrestrials; still another maintains that the site was built to realize mystical powers of energy. Some recent research has suggested that the arrangement of the stones had sexual connotations, being used in ancient pagan fertility rites. Finally, some believe that it was constructed for astronomy purposes.

Studies in the Scriptures (JEHOVAH'S WITNESSES). A seven-volume teaching series written by Charles Taze 'Russell, the founder of The Watchtower Bible and Tract Society. It contains some of the group's early beliefs as well as prophecies that failed in 1914.

Study (JEHOVAH'S WITNESSES). The word *study* here takes on a twofold meaning. First, a Watchtower Bible and Tract Society member, visiting the home of an individual, is taught to refer to that person as being a "study." Second, the lessons presented at the doorstep or in a person's home are also called "studies." Consequently, a Witness conducts a study with a study, or a lesson with an individual.

Study Groups (ASSOCIATION FOR RESEARCH AND ENLIGHTENMENT). Groups that gather to study the writings of Edgar 'Cayce.

Stupas (BUDDHISM). The relic compartments found in many Buddhist burial mounds.

Subud (HINDUISM). A spiritual movement that stemmed from a Southeast Asian mystic, Muhammad 'Subuh. The movement spread to Europe through G. I. 'Gurdjeff. According to the beliefs, a "helper" prepares initiates to prepare for openness to new spiritual energy.

Subuh, Muhammad (HINDUISM; OUSPENSKY-GURDJIEFF; 1901–1987). Born in Java, Muhammed Subuh was the leader of a new spiritual movement. He underwent deep spiritual changes in his life where he experienced what he called the "Great Life Force," that is, the very "power of God." Those who wished to discover these powers became his disciples and so became known as the "Subud Brotherhood." The ideas spread in 1950 from Java through Husein Rolf, an English linguist, and subsequently through others.

Succubus ('occult; SATANISM; WITCHCRAFT). An evil 'demon or spirit who assumes the role of a female in order to have sexual intercourse with a man. This concept was widely believed during the Middle Ages. They were the figment of the fertile and driven imaginations of 'witch hunters.

Sudra/Sudhra (HINDUISM). One of the five major castes in India. It is the caste that exists to serve the upper three castes, namely, the 'Brahmin, 'Kshatriya, and the 'Vaishya castes and is a step above the 'Harijan ("untouchable") caste.

Sufi (ISLAM; SUFISM). The name of an Islamic monastic 'sect derived from Arabic word for "wool" (*suf*), a material worn by many of the sect's members. The devotees of Sufism view 'Allah mystically, meaning that he must be experienced inwardly.

Sugmad (ECKANKAR). The name for "God" in Eckankar. Paul 'Twitchell taught that *Sugmad* was the source of life that flows out in the form of a sound wave labeled "ECK." One may tap the powers of *Sugmad* through 'bilocation and various other methods.

Suhuf (ISLAM). The scripture books of Islam's prophets.

Sukkoth (JUDAISM). The commemoration of the Jewish Feast of the Tabernacles that celebrates the joy of harvest time.

Sultan (ISLAM). The name given to former 'Muslim rulers in Turkey, it also has been applied to any Muslim ruler.

Summerland (WITCHCRAFT). The place where the soul travels temporarily while awaiting ›reincarnation into another body. Not every neopagan believes in Summerland. Other names are Otherworld, Land of Faerie, and Tír na nÓg.

Summers, Montague (›occult; 1880–1948). The English scholar and author of numerous books, some of which were on ›magic, werewolves, etc.

Sunna (ISLAM). The sacred traditions of ›Muhammad's deeds ("way of life") and his reported sayings that are used as supplements to the ›Koran. The term is also spelled *sunni*. See also ›hadith.

Super Excellent Master; Unnumbered Degree (FREEMASONRY). An unnumbered degree in Freemasonry. This award is the third of three orders within the ›Commandery, part of the ›Select Master or ninth degree.

Sura/Surah (ISLAM). The name for chapter divisions in the ›Koran. There are 114 suras in the Koran; each one appears in a descending order of length, the longest first and the shortest last.

Sutta Pitaka (BUDDHISM). The sacred scriptures that Buddhism uses to teach its doctrines.

Sutras (BUDDHISM; HINDUISM). Translated as "thread." The *sutras* are collective series of aphorisms that furnish abbreviated commentary on the ›*Upanishads* and the ›*Vedas*. They are texts that summarize various discourses of the ›Buddha.

Suzuki, D. T. (ZEN BUDDHISM; 1870–1966). The person responsible for importing Zen to the West through the Rinzai ›sect.

Svami (HINDUISM). One who possesses the gift of self-discipline, control over the mind and body.

Swami (HINDUISM). A Hindu who renounces everything, including all efforts and labors, in order to reach the highest heaven. The founder of the eighth-century Swami Order was ›Shankara.

Swastika (›occult; HINDUISM). A type of Greek cross whose vertical and horizontal arms are of equal length, and each of its arms is bent clockwise at ninety-degree right angles. The name swastika is a ›Sanskrit word that means "good omen." The symbol has a long history of having been present among some of the ancient Greeks, Hindus, Celts, Indians of India, etc. It has also had an occult significance, symbolizing renewal and well-being.

In the 1920s the swastika became the official insignia of the National German Socialist Workers' Party (the Nazis) in Germany, and the Nazis imprinted it on Germany's flag. Since the Nazi use of the swastika, it has become a nefarious symbol, reminding people of the atrocities the Nazis committed.

Swedenborg, Emmanuel (CHURCH OF THE NEW JERUSALEM; 1688–1772). In April, 1744, Swedenborg, a brilliant scientist and philosopher, reported to have received a vision of Christ. In this vision Christ delivered Swedenborg from the guilt he felt because of his pride concerning his intellectual accomplishments. The following year, he abandoned all scientific pursuits and concentrated his efforts on theology alone. He is responsible for the beginning of the Church of the New Jerusalem, which also became a champion of Swedenborgianism.

Swedenborg did not start a church or movement, though his followers did. His voluminous theological writings are a collection of the visions and insights he claimed to have received through communication with the spirit world.

Sword (›occult). One of the four ›elemental tools. To some occult groups the sword symbolizes air and to others fire.

Sylph (›occult). An ›elemental evil spirit who lives in the air of the atmosphere.

Syncretism The blending of various and diverse religious beliefs in order to show religious unity and cooperation. It is a formal effort to agree to disagree. To ›orthodox CHRISTIANITY it is the mixing of God's revealed truth with pagan error, thus denying Christ as the only way of salvation (as spelled out in John 14:6 and Acts 4:12).

Systemites (THE FAMILY). Anyone not in agreement with the teachings of The Family (formerly called Children of God) was branded by Moses ›David as being in league with the this-worldly established order.

T

Tabernacle See JUDAISM.

Table of Showbread (JUDAISM). See *showbread.

Table Tilting (*occult). A phenomenon that is said to occur during a *séance and also with activities of a *poltergeist, the *ghost who tilts tables and makes rapping noises on tables.

Taj Mahal (ISLAM). A large seventeenth-century mausoleum built by an Indian ruler in memory of his favorite wife, Mumtaz-i-Mahal, whose name means "pride of the palace." Passages from the *Koran decorate much of the building's exterior. Some followers of the NEW AGE MOVEMENT see the building as a holy site.

Talismans (*occult). A *magic object, often engraved with a symbol or a picture of a character that is believed to harness special powers to protect or prosper the owner or possessor. Talismans are sometimes used to protect oneself against evil spirits or *demons. Sometimes they are also used attain love, health, success, and power. *See also* *amulet and *charm.

A talisman sold in a occult shop in Hollywood, California.
Courtesy Jack M. Roper/CARIS

Talmud (JUDAISM). The Talmud is a scholarly commentary on the *Mishna. It developed during the third to the sixth centuries A.D. in two distinct traditions, one with Palestinian influences, the other Babylonian. The Babylonian Talmud (*Talmud Bavli*) affords a more elaborate and lengthy commentary on the Mishna than the shorter Palestinian Talmud (*Talmud Yerushalmi*). Together with the Mishna, the Talmud supplemented the laws of the Pentateuch (see *Torah) for new situations. The Talmud was vital in keeping Israel's national identity and future vision intact after the destruction of the *temple and the dispersion of the Jews to foreign lands (*see* *Diaspora).

Tammuz (*occult). This is the name of the Babylonian god of plant life. It is also the name of the husband of *Ishtar, the pagan fertility goddess.

Tanha (BUDDHISM). Translated "lust," *tanha* constitutes the whole spectrum of desire, against which the Buddhist is called on to combat.

Tantras (HINDUISM). Writings regarded as being canonical according to *Vaishnava* devotees.

Tantrism (BUDDHISM; HINDUISM). A *sect arising within Mahayana Buddhism based on the teachings of the Hindu *tantras. Also a form of *kundalini *yoga, in which a sexual union takes place between the subject and *shakti (feminine energy). The orgasm is resisted, and the resultant energy arouses the kundalini.

Tao (TAOISM). A Chinese word roughly translated as "way, truth, or path." Discovering the Tao is the chief end of Taoist philosophy.

Tao-Sheng (ZEN BUDDHISM; A.D. 360–434). the actual founder of Zen (*see* *bodhidharma).

Tao-Te-Ching (TAOISM). Phrase meaning "the way of power." The *Tao-te-Ching* is one of the writings credited to *Lao-Tse. This classic text describes the basic guidelines that a ruler ought to live by. It also discusses the nature of life and the way to peace as contained in the Taoist concept of *wu-wei.

Tariqah (ISLAM; SUFISM). The spiritual path that leads to intimate oneness with God; *tariqah* involves *mystical contemplation and meditation.

Tarot Cards (*occult). The occult practice of using cards in *fortune-telling. There are seventy-eight cards in a tarot deck. The deck is divided into two types: major arcana and minor arcana. The former has twenty-two cards, with each one representing some aspect of a human being's psyche. The other fifty-six cards consist of four suits, called *wands, *cups, *pentacles, and *swords, symbolizing the various elements. Court cards

Sample of tarot cards used in fortune-telling.
Courtesy Jack M. Roper/CARIS

include the king, queen, knight, and page, symbolizing spirit, soul, vitality, and body, respectively. One card has a skeleton, symbolizing death. These are commonly spread out to form given patterns while some deity is invoked, who is expected to reveal the future of a given person's life.

Tat Tvam Asi   (HINDUISM). "That art thou" (*see* ▶*brahman*; ▶*atman*).

Tattvavit   (HINDUISM). One who has entered into the realm of absolute truth; one who has become a ▶*brahman*.

Tawhid   (ISLAM). The ▶Muslim doctrine of the unity of ▶Allah. It is sometimes presented to counter the Christian doctrine of the ▶Trinity.

Taurus   (▶astrology; ▶occult). Latin for "bull." Taurus is the second ▶sign of the ▶zodiac, falling between April 20 and May 20. Its precedent in Greek mythology comes from Zeus, who assumed the shape of a bull to abduct Europa. Astrologers depict persons born under the sign of Taurus as obstinate, lazy, unmotivated, appreciative of the arts, practical, and generous with money and material possessions.

Teacher   (MORMONISM). The second of the three offices in the ▶Aaronic priesthood. A boy may become a "teacher" as early as fourteen years of age, usually after serving as a ▶deacon.

Telekinesis   (▶occult; ▶parapsychology). The movement of physical or material objects without any observable or empirically verifiable cause.

Telepathy   (▶occult; ▶parapsychology). Communication from one mind to another without verbal exchange or other physical and empirical modes (also called mental telepathy).

Telestial Kingdom   (MORMONISM). The lowest, or third, of the heavens in the ▶eschatology of Mormonism, into which will enter all the evildoers of the earth who have completely and utterly rejected the gospel. The telestial kingdom is located on another earth. The vast majority of people consigned to this kingdom will have suffered the Great Tribulation and are granted this kingdom only after the ▶Millennium.

Temple, Jewish   See JUDAISM.

Temple, Mormon   (MORMONISM). One of several special temples that function only for the most worthy of Latter-Day Saints, who are only permitted to enter after examination by a ▶bishop, who then issues a "Temple Recommended Card." In these buildings Mormons conduct ▶baptism for the dead, weddings, and ▶endowments for eternal progression. Once completing their ceremonial rituals, "Temple Mormon" is a designation for a person who has been initiated through endowment ceremonies. Mormons in this latter category are few in number (as low as 20 percent, according to some estimates) compared to the LDS church as a whole.

Tempters   (ISLAM). When a person dies, two angels known as "tempters" are sent to the grave to test—through a series of questions—whether or not the dead person is worthy of going to heaven. If the answers are acceptable, then the deceased will rest in peace until the day he or she is resurrected for heavenly bliss.

Tendai   (BUDDHISM). A school of thought in Buddhism that received its name from a monastery in *Chekiang* province in China. Adherents are found in both China and Japan.

Ten Gurus   (SIKHISM). Ten men, living from approximately 1500–1700, considered to be the founding fathers of Sikhism.

Terreiro   (▶occult; CANDOMBLE; MACUMBA; SOUTH AMERICAN, CENTRAL AMERICAN, AND CARIBBEAN CULTS). Derived from the Portuguese language, a *terreiro* is a "temple" used for the cultic ceremonies of the Macumba and Candomble ▶cults.

Terrestrial Kingdom   (MORMONISM). The dominion or kingdom that pertains to what is earthly. One of the three heavens, the terrestrial kingdom will be located on a sphere or planet other than earth. The inhabitants of this kingdom will have rejected the gospel but will receive it in the future ("spirit world"). Compromising, or "lukewarm," ♦Mormons will also inhabit this kingdom. See also ♦telestial kingdom and ♦celestial kingdom.

Theocracy (ISLAM; JUDAISM). A form of government in which it is believed that God rules in the civil realm through the priests, clergy, or other religious figures. Thus God makes the laws in the civil, moral, and religious realms. Ancient Israel had a theocratic government before it was overthrown by the Babylonians. Since the founding of the Islamic religion in the seventh century, also many Islamic countries (e.g., Iran and Saudi Arabia) have theocratic governments. In theocratic governments there is no separation of church and state.

Theocratic (JEHOVAH'S WITNESSES). Apart from the conventional meaning of the term "theocratic" (see ♦theocracy), Jehovah's Witnesses use this term in their belief that they are governed by God alone, exclusive of secular authorities. That is why they do not participate in the armed services or salute the flag.

Therapeutic Touch (NEW AGE MOVEMENT; THEOSOPHY). Therapeutic Touch (TT) is an alternative healing method growing in popularity among nurses. Many professional nursing organizations promote the practice, colleges and universities teach it, and hospitals provide it. TT was developed in the 1970s by Dora Kunz, a self-proclaimed clairvoyant and then President of the Theosophical Society in America, and Dolores Krieger, RN, Ph.D. The Theosophical Society remains an active promoter of TT.

Physical touch is beneficial and comforting, especially when people are ill or anxious. Patients in today's high-tech hospitals often miss out on someone's reassuring touch. However, TT does *not* involve physical touch. Instead, proponents believe a human energy field, or aura, extends a few inches beyond people's skin. This energy is also known by the Hindu term ♦prana, or the Chinese term ♦chi. This energy is viewed as nonphysical, and therefore completely different from electricity or magnetism. Instruments can measure the latter, but even TT proponents admit there is no physical evidence to support the existence of their "energy fields."

Although a few clairvoyants (like Kunz) claim to see energy fields, they can be sensed with TT when people enter a state of meditation called centering. Active thinking is discouraged, and instead practitioners become aware of patients' energy fields and guidance from their own inner nature. In this state, practitioners pass their hands a few inches over patients' bodies. Although some practitioners touch patients, teachers emphasize that physical contact is not necessary.

Practitioners then assess if the energy fields are balanced, which is said to promote health. Problems are detected through "vague hunches, passing impressions, flights of fancy, or, in precious moments, true insights or intuitions."[1] Imbalances can be cleared, and the energy field smoothed, by passing the hands over the aura again, this time with strong intentions to help and heal. Balanced energy fields are said to reduce anxiety, relieve pain, and accelerate wound healing. However, many studies have found TT is no better than a placebo. Studies with positive results often have methodological problems.

Proponents also claim TT is a modern version of the biblical laying on of hands. However, the laying on of hands was never associated with healing in ancient Jewish writings, but was used to impart divine blessing or in commissioning ceremonies (Num. 28:18). In the New Testament, healing did sometimes involve laying on of hands (Mark 5:23). However, Jesus' healings were distinguished from TT by his incorporation of physical touch. Biblical laying on of hands is not an energy-manipulating healing technique, but a faith-based practice during which divine healing is asked (not demanded) of a personal God (James 5:15–16).[2]

The beliefs and practices promoted as TT are commonly found in Eastern religions, theosophy, and New Age writings. Krieger, a Buddhist, admits that TT is based on the same principles as Buddhism. Theosophical and occult writings have long described a practice called pranic (or auric) healing. This is identical to TT, including the lack of physical contact, emphasis on energy fields, importance of meditation, and even shaking one's hands to remove "negative energy."

While TT proponents deny its religious nature, the Equal Employment Opportunity Commission lists TT with other New Age religious practices that employers cannot require employees to learn or practice (EEOC Notice N–915.022). In spite of this, TT continues to infiltrate educational and health care institutions with its New Age beliefs.[3]

Notes

[1] Dolores Krieger, *Accepting Your Power to Heal: The Personal Practice of Therapeutic Touch* (Santa Fe, NM: Bear & Company, 1993), 29.

[2] Gerhard Friedrich (ed.), "Laying on of hands," in *The Theological Dictionary of the New Testament* (Grand Rapids: Eerdmans, 1974), 9:428–434.

[3] Article adapted from Dónal P. O'Mathúna, "The Subtle Allure of Therapeutic Touch," *Journal of Christian Nursing* 15 (Winter 1998): 4–13; used with permission.

Thetans (SCIENTOLOGY). The ancestors of the human race, who through ▸reincarnation evolved into human beings from a previous immortal spiritual state. Scientology attempts through what it calls psychological therapy to restore a person's mind back to its "thetan" state of existence.

Theurgy (▸occult). See ▸high magic.

Third Adam (UNIFICATION CHURCH). Concept within the Unification Church that holds that God has imparted his ▸revelation to the human race through three separate "Adams." The "first Adam" fell into sin, which lead to a fall from divine parenthood. Jesus Christ came as God's "second Adam" (Rom. 5). But Jesus' arrest, trial, and crucifixion were not a triumph, but an unfortunate tragedy. Jesus' mission was to bring full redemption to the human race. By failing to marry, Jesus accomplished only spiritual redemption. It therefore remains for a "third Adam" to complete the work of the second. Members of the Unification Church believe Sun Myung ▸Moon to be the third Adam.

Third Ear (ELAN VITAL). Method through which an initiate, or premie, in Divine Light Mission receives divine knowledge. The ▸initiator presses in with a finger on each ear. Eventually all external noise ceases and the subject hears only the sounds of his internal organs. See also ▸third eye; ▸divine nectar; ▸fourfold path, and ▸primordial vibration.

Third Eye (ELAN VITAL). The eye of spiritual vision located on the forehead between the two physical eyes. An ▸initiator places his or her thumb and third finger on the temples and with the index finger presses in on the forehead, thereby pinching the optic nerve and causing a light to flash for the initiate. Through this exercise, members receive divine knowledge. See also ▸third ear; ▸divine nectar; ▸primordial vibration; and ▸fourfold path.

Thomas, John (CHRISTADELPHIANISM; 1805–1871). Started the movement that is presently known as Christadelphianism. Thomas disagreed with the basic teachings of CHRISTIANITY, such as the doctrine of the ▸Trinity and the deity of Christ.

Thor (▸occult). Thor is the Scandinavian god of the sky and thunder; he is seen as the friend of farmers and sailors. Scandinavian mythology says he is the son of ▸*Odin*.

Thoth (THEOSOPHY). Ancient Egyptian god of wisdom and control, who was later combined with the Greek god Hermes to form the philosophy of ▸*Hermes Trismegistus*. Thoth was the scribal god who recorded the deeds of the dead to be used at the final judgment.

Three Degrees of Glory (MORMONISM). This doctrine concerns the final state of the saved. There are three "degrees of glory" to which the "saved" will ultimately journey: the ▸celestial, ▸terrestrial, and ▸telestial kingdoms. ▸Mormons do not teach ▸universalism per se because they hold that the "sons of perdition," though a minority, have in fact "denied the Holy Spirit after having received it" (▸*Doctrine and Covenants* 76:35) and will be annihilated along with Satan and his demons. Most, however, will ultimately end up in one of the three degrees.

Three Pure Ones (TAOISM). The deifying of three individuals by *Chuang Tao-ling*, the founder of modern Taoism. Included in the pantheon are ▸*Lao-Tse*, *San-Ching*, and the supreme deity, *Yu Hwang Shang-ti*.

Thunor (▸occult). The Saxon god of the weather.

Tiamet (▸occult). A Babylonian sea goddess, who is a dragon that personifies evil.

Tingley. Katherine (THEOSOPHY; 1847–1929). Succeeded William Q. ▸Judge as the head of the Theosophy movement.

Tithing (CHRISTIANITY; JUDAISM; MORMONISM). For Judaism, tithing was part of the expected practice of every faithful Jew. Mormons are expected to tithe, to give one-tenth of their income to the church. It is not optional. "Verily it is a day of sacrifice, and a day for the tithing of my people; for he that has tithed shall not be burned at his coming." (▸*Doctrine and Covenants* 64:23; see also 119, 120). In Christianity, many ▸Protestant denominations advocate that members practice tithing. In numerous ▸cults and ▸sects, members double and even in some instances triple-tithe their incomes.

Toad (▸occult; WITCHCRAFT). Reportedly, an amphibian used by some witches to bring evil into a person's life.

Toda, Josei (BUDDHISM; SOKA-GAKKAI). The co-founder of Soka-Gakkai, a Japanese religion.

Tokhueni (▸occult; VOODOO). Young voodoo spirits who "open the door" for other voodoo gods at a ceremony.

Torah (JUDAISM). The first of five books in the Old Testament. Sometimes they are also referred to as the Pentateuch.

Torat (ISLAM). The part of Scripture in Islam that is said to have contained the ▸Torah.

Totem(ism) (NATIVE AMERICAN RELIGION). The belief and religious veneration of an animal, bird, or plant (a totem) that is believed to be a given tribe's ancestor. Tribes distinguish themselves from other tribes by identifying themselves with a given totem. Thus one tribe or clan may identify with a bear, another with a wolf, and still another with an eagle. The totem of each tribe is sacred and may ordinarily not be killed or eaten.

Touch Therapy (TT) (THEOSOPHY; NEW AGE MOVEMENT). See ᵖtherapeutic touch.

Trabajo (SANTERIA). The Spanish word for "work" done to carry out given requirements of Santeria worship.

Traill, Stewart (CHURCH OF BIBLE UNDERSTANDING; 1936–). Started the Forever Family, which was later renamed The Church of Bible Understanding.

Trance (ᵖoccult). An ᵖaltered state of consciousness whereby a person becomes somnolent. As with ᵖhypnotism, the person in a trance experiences total relaxation of the body and motor skills. The powers of concentration are greatly augmented. The person who is trancing is able to reach into the deeper subconscious recesses of the mind, usually with the aid of a therapist. The therapist may also use what is known as guided imagery. The subject in a trance visualizes an image, with which he or she is then told to communicate. The purpose is to enable the subject to confront aspects of a disturbed psychological past.

Transformational Seminars (NEW AGE MOVEMENT). Sessions in which stress management is the objective, often directed toward business executives.

Transcendence (CHRISTIANITY). A traditional doctrine of Christianity wherein God is separate from and other than creation. This separation is not clearly made in pantheistic religions. See also ᵖimmanence.

Transcendentalism (CHRISTIANITY). A movement that evolved out of the "Transcendental Club," which arose in Massachusetts in the mid-nineteenth century. Three of its most well-known members were Theodore Parker (1810–1860), Ralph Waldo ᵖEmerson (1803–1882), and Henry David Thoreau (1817–1862). The movement rejected the dispassionate rationalism of the Enlightenment by combining ᵖmysticism with Romanticism. Its basic tenets were that God is ᵖimmanent, that truth is obtained by intuition rather than by rationalism, and that all dogmatically based religious teachings are to be rejected. The most outstanding advocate of transcendentalism was Thoreau. His book *Walden* (1854), which he wrote as a result of his having withdrawn from society and lived close to nature, is largely a treatise on transcendental thought.

Transference (ᵖoccult; CHURCH OF THE LIVING WORD). The doctrine advocated by the group alternately known as The Walk, which states that members of the group become Christ and thereby merge God with the believer. Such a concept of God and humanity obliterates the distinctiveness between the Creator and his creation.

There is also an occult belief of transference, which says that objects used in occult acts are capable of effecting negative change(s) on other objects with which they came in contact.

Translocation (ᵖoccult). A phenomenon prevalent in ancient folklore and myths as well as in modern occult circles where one possesses the ability to move rapidly to different locations. One need only recall the images conjured up in childhood literature about flying carpets, ᵖghosts moving effortlessly through matter, and ᵖwitches transported by broomsticks, etc. to capture the essence of translocation.

Transmigration of the Soul (ᵖoccult). An ancient belief among pagans that the human soul at death usually moves to a nonhuman being, such as a horse, cow, bird, mouse, or some insect.

Traveling Minister (JEHOVAH'S WITNESSES). A minister within the Watchtower Bible and Tract Society who travels between congregations within a ᵖcircuit (about twenty-one congregations), generally spending one week with each congregation.

Tree (THE WAY INTERNATIONAL). The Way International uses the symbol of a tree to describe its organizational structure. The pattern is as follows:

1. Root—the international headquarters, located in New Knoxville, Ohio; Victor Paul ᵖWierwille himself as president and founder, a vice president, and a secretary-treasurer
2. Trunk—the different regions into which the organization is divided considered together
3. Branches—state-wide divisions
4. Limbs—city units
5. Twigs—individual groups that meet for home Bible study
6. Leaves—individuals themselves

Triangle (ᵖoccult). The symbol used to summon supernatural forces. Generally, a magician stands inside a ᵖcircle as he invokes the power of darkness by use of a triangle.

Trinity (CHRISTIANITY). The Christian doctrine that teaches that the one true God is comprised of three coeternal and coequal persons, Father, Son, and Holy Spirit. Much concerning the Trinity is discussed throughout this volume, including the article on Christianity itself and will not be repeated here (*see also* Appendix 1).

Trinity of Trinities (URANTIA). The ultimate trinity in Urantia, which is contemplated in religious and philosophical circles worldwide and in different eras. For the Urantia Foundation, the closest proximity to a tangible expression of this trinity is the "Universal Father on the conceptual level of the I AM."

Tripitaka (BUDDHISM). From the Pali language, meaning "three baskets," the Tripitaka comprises the major historical sources of ancient Buddhism. The "three baskets" are the *Vinaya* ⁾*Pitaka*, *Sutta Pitaka*, and *Abidhamma Pitaka*.

Tritheism (MORMONISM). The belief in three separate gods, and hence the denial of the Christian ⁾Trinity. Tritheism is a form of polytheism.

True Father and True Mother (UNIFICATION CHURCH). These are the titles that the Reverend Sun Myung ⁾Moon and his wife of the Unification Church apply to themselves.

Trumpet Speaking (⁾occult; ⁾parapsychology). The musical note that is produced by a spirit during the conduct of a ⁾séance.

Truth That Leads to Eternal Life (JEHOVAH'S WITNESSES). This is an introductory book that the Watchtower Bible and Tract Society used to convert and instruct new members.

Tsunesaburo, Makiguchi (BUDDHISM; SOKA-GAKKAI). The founder of the Japanese religion known as Soka-Gakkai.

Tulasi (HINDUISM). A worshiper who has been transformed into a plant, the leaves of which are offered up to the lotus feet of Lord ⁾Vishnu.

Tundrida (⁾occult). An ancient Scandinavian female ⁾devil.

Tumba (SANTERIA). Ceremonial drums used in Santeria.

Tuza (ECKANKAR). The term for the "soul" in Eckankar. The tuza may separate from the physical body, resulting in ⁾bilocation. *See also* ⁾astral projection.

Twelve Tenets of Witchcraft (WITCHCRAFT). God is the being who created both the physical and spiritual world.

> The good in life is to enter the sphere of God.
> As it is above, so it is below.
> Hell is merely a mental concept.
> Good is outside of man.
> Personal evil can be progressively reduced by attaining higher levels.
> There is reincarnation.
> Be brought into harmony with nature.
> Development and care of the body is a sacred obligation.
> There is latent power with the human psyche.
> Good produces good.
> Evil produce evil

Twenty-One Points (RASTAFARIANISM). A series of statements issued by the Rastafarians that describe its relationship to the rest of society. This statement constitutes one of the foundations of the church's authority.

TWIG (WAY INTERNATIONAL). Acronym used by The Way International for "The Word in Government," a program designed to attract young people in order to train them for active political participation.

Twitchell, Paul (ECKANKAR; 1908?–1971). Founder of the religious ⁾cult called Eckankar. He has gained notoriety relative to his different ⁾occult experiences and ⁾astral travel.

U

UFOlogy (⁾occult). The study of the alleged sightings of unidentified flying objects (UFOs) and extraterrestrial encounters reported by various people around the world.

Ultimate Trinity (URANTIA). One of the trinities in Urantia. Unlike the infinite ⁾Paradise Trinity, the Ultimate ⁾Trinity is finite because it is composed of "derived deities" that were "created or eventuated" by the Paradise Trinity. The Ultimate Trinity, now evolving, will eventually consist of the "Supreme Being," the "Supreme Creator Personalities," and the "absolute Architects of the Master Universe."

Umar Ibn Al Khatab (ISLAM; 586–644). Second ▶caliph in Islam who succeeded Abu ▶Bakr in 634. Umar is noted for his success in getting the Medinian Moslems to accept Bakr. Under Umar, the Islamic religion expanded from a local to a world power.

Umayya (ISLAM). One of Islam's dynasties.

Umayyads (ISLAM). Armies of conquerors responsible for the greatest expansion of Islam. The *Umayyad* period lasted from A.D. 661 to 750 and stretched the empire as far as Spain.

Umbanda (▶occult; ▶Yoruba; CANDOMBLE; MACUMBA; SOUTH AMERICAN, CENTRAL AMERICAN, AND CARIBBEAN CULTS). The priest in certain of the Macumba ▶cults. The word originated among the ▶Bantu people of West Africa. In Brazil, the Umbanda is the equivalent of spiritualism in an African context.

Ummah (ISLAM). The community of the faithful in the ▶Muslim world.

Unitarianism (UNITARIAN-UNIVERSALIST ASSOCIATION). The doctrine that there is only one God, not a holy ▶Trinity of three persons, Father, Son, and Holy Spirit.

Universalism (UNITARIAN-UNIVERSALIST ASSOCIATION). Universalism holds that all living beings will attain complete salvation. Many religious groups outside the pale of traditional CHRISTIANITY hold to universalist views. It represents an undeniably important, albeit unorthodox, tradition within the history of Christianity. The doctrine is considered heretical in traditional Christian circles. In its place, ▶orthodox Christianity teaches that the saved are those who have been baptized into Christ and who exercise saving faith in his finished work of redemption. Early theologians such as Clement (ca. 150–ca. 215) and Origen (ca. 185–ca. 254) developed ideas of universalism, and it is carried on in full force by the Unitarian-Universalist Association in modern times. See also ▶Socinianism.

Untheocratic (JEHOVAH'S WITNESSES). This word is used to label the Watchtower Bible and Tract Society members who are out of step with the strict rule and guidelines of the organization. It is also used to designate "things." A person and the clothes that person is wearing may both be considered to be "untheocratic."

Upacaras (HINDUISM). Domestic rituals practiced by devotees of Hinduism.

Upanishads (HINDUISM). Secret doctrine; Sanskrit treatises that are a vital part of the ▶Vedas. They contain the collected wisdom and philosophy of the sages written between 800–600 B.C. There are 108 *Upanishads* in all. The basic concept of this literature is to teach that "all" can be drawn into the "one" and the "one" may become "all" (that is, a form of ▶pantheism).

Urantia Book, The (URANTIA). Definitive reference source for the beliefs of the Urantia Society. Members of the society believe that the 2,097 revelations published in 1955 were from superior beings of another world, channeled to Bill ▶Sadler by seven celestial spirits. The book spells out what members of the brotherhood believe as the essential truths given to Sadler, so that the human race might benefit and be illumined. Adherents consider the book is the "finest major divine revelation since the coming of Christ to our planet."

Included in *The Urantia Book* is the revelation of the trinities: the ▶Paradise Trinity, the ▶Ultimate Trinity, and the ▶Absolute Trinity. A section titled "The Life and Teachings of Jesus" retells the account given by the four Gospels. Jesus' unique deity, held to by traditional Christendom, and his work of atonement are categorically denied. Jesus' death on the cross is insignificant. The book contains highly esoteric language, rendering a cursory reading impossible.

Urim and Thummim (MORMONISM). The two discs that Joseph ▶Smith Jr. said he used in decoding the language inscribed on the golden plates. In ancient Israel, Urim and Thummim were attached to the breastplate of the high priest in the temple (see, e.g., Num. 27:21; 1 Sam. 28:6). Smith claimed his discs were attached to "silver bows," resembling a pair of eyeglasses, through which he looked to render intelligible the strange lettering on the plates.

Urshan, Andrew (ONENESS PENTECOSTALISM). An early writer and speaker of the ▶Jesus Only movement.

Uthman (ISLAM; d. A.D. 656). The third ▶caliph to head Islam after ▶Muhammad's death. Uthman, the son-in-law of Muhammad, was Muhammad's first convert from a high economic class. His caliphate is important because his death in 656, when he was murdered by a rival faction, marked the exacerbations of conflicts within Islam.

Uttara Mimamsa (HINDUISM). One of the six schools of Hindu religion and philosophy. *Uttara Mimamsa* is part of the Mimamsa school, which is itself perhaps the oldest school, and is concerned largely with study and interpretation of the ▶Vedas. *Uttara Mimamsa* ("posterior study") is concerned with the interpretation of the later *Vedas*, or ▶*Upanishads*.

V

Vaccine (VOODOO). A musical wind instrument made of a bamboo tube, used in voodoo rituals and ceremonies.

Vaisheshika (HINDUISM). One of the six schools of Hindu philosophy and religion. Vaisheshika emphasizes materialism and the classifications of matter. The Vaisheshika school teaches that the smallest and most indestructible part of the universe is the atom.

Vaishnavites (HINDUISM). One of the major Hindu ›sects whose devotees worship Lord ›Vishnu. Eighty percent of all Hindus are Vaishnavites.

Vaishya (HINDUISM). A ›caste of Hindus who practice farming and engage in business. This, and all castes, is arranged in accordance with the accepted religious and socioeconomic orders that are part of the Hindu religion.

Value Creation Society (SOKA-GAKKAI). The original name of the society founded by Tsonesaburo ›Makiguchi.

Vampire (›occult). According to legend, fiction, and occult beliefs, a vampire is a human corpse that has come back to life and lives off the blood it sucks from human beings. Vampires were popularized in American films with Bram Stoker's novel ›*Dracula* (1897). (*See also* Prince ›Vlad).

Vanaprastha (HINDUISM; TRANSCENDENTAL MEDITATION). One who leads a restive and contemplative life in the forest.

Varengan (›occult). A magical bird of Persian origin whose feathers are said to protect humans from sickness.

Varuna (HINDUISM). The ›*Rigveda* god of the arched sky. He is one of the most important deities and is seen as an omniscient guardian.

Vasudeva (HINDUISM). Father of ›Hare Krishna; an embodiment of the highest deity.

Vedanta (HINDUISM). One of the six ›*dharsanas*, or systems, of Hindu theology. It is the most important of the six, expressing the very core of Hindu philosophy. The chief spokesman for the thought underlying the Vedanta is ›Shankara (ca. 788–820). He is credited with

Ann Rice, the Vampire Queen's home. To the left is her office complex in New Orleans. She was the inspiration behind the movie *Interview with a Vampire*, starring Tom Cruise. Courtesy Jack M. Roper

articulating the idea, incipient within the ›*Upanishads*, that each soul is a distillation of ›Brahman. ›Maya prevents such a soul from achieving oneness with Brahman. Knowledge, or ›enlightenment, however, is able to bring the soul out from the illusory world and make possible such a oneness with Brahman. Herein lies the essence of Hindu thought, of which all else is derivative.

Vedas (HINDUISM). Essentially a collection of hymns sung to the Aryan gods. The term also applies to a large body of Hindu sacred literature compiled approximately between 1500 and 1200 B.C. The *Veda* collection consists of the three *vedas* (knowledge)—›*Rigveda*,

Samaveda, and *Yajurveda*. A fourth was later added, called *Atharvaveda*. There are three main sections of literary expositions in the *Vedas*: the *Brahmanas*, *Aranyakas*, and the *Upanishads*.

Venica (WITCHCRAFT). A witch who uses poison in her/his witchcraft activities.

Vedism (HINDUISM). An ancient form of Hinduism transported into India around 1500 B.C. by Indo-European and Iranian people. Knowledge of Vedism is contained in the *Rigveda*. Other writings that contain Vedic philosophy are *Yajurveda*, the *Samaveda*, the *Atharvaveda*, the *Brahmanas*, and the *Upanishads*. See also *Vedas*.

Vesak (ZEN BUDDHISM). A date in the latter part of May set aside for celebrating the birth of the Buddha.

Vevers (occult; VOODOO). Decorative floor drawings that surround the poteau-mitan in a voodoo temple. The sacred rites and sacrifices take place on the vevers.

Vidya (HINDUISM). Hindu word for enlightenment or knowledge.

Vimalananda, Acharya (ANANDA MARGA YOGA SOCIETY; n.d.). This is the person responsible for importing the teachings of Ananda Marga to the United States in 1969. He left Ananda Marga and founded the Yoga House Ashram.

Virgin Parchment (occult). A piece of skin from a young woman whereon an occult practitioner writes his desires in blood and then tosses this "parchment" into a ceremonial fire in order to have such desires come true.

Virgo (astrology; occult). The sixth sign of the zodiac in astrology, Virgo is pictured as being a young maiden holding a sheaf of wheat, symbolizing fertility. Virgo falls between August 22 and September 21. Persons born under the sixth sign are characterized by astrologers as being reserved, analytical, business-minded, loyal, nervous, self-centered, and judgmental.

Vishnu (HINDUISM). The second of the three gods of the Hindu triad. *Vishnu* is the supreme lord, the preserver deity, of the human race and is said to become occasionally incarnate to offer helpful divine intervention in the affairs of human beings.

Vishnuism (HINDUISM). A group within Hinduism that emphasizes Vishnu as the ultimate deity.

Vishtaspa (Zoroastrianism). A king who became the first prominent disciple of Zoroastrianism. Some believe he was the father of Cyrus the Great (ca. 585–529 B.C.).

Vision Quest (NATIVE AMERICAN RELIGION). A spiritual ceremony that is said to be accompanied by out-of-body experiences. See astral projection.

Visualization (occult; NEW AGE MOVEMENT). A New Age concept that embraces the idea that the material world can be brought under submission to the mental world or thought processes. New Agers teach that a person can "visualize" through the mind's eye a picture or a thought that can then be transposed into reality. Mental images, being more powerful than physical ones, therefore set up the conditions for the physical to become real. *New Age Magazine The Holy Encounter* in Jan./Feb. 1990 (p. 1) claimed that the fall of the Berlin Wall was the result of a "consciousness coup" on the part of New Agers who came together and visualized the Wall coming down. Louise Hay, renowned New Age leader, says in her book *You Can Heal Yourself* (p. 122), "Your prosperity consciousness is not dependant on money; your flow of money is dependent upon your prosperity consciousness. As you can conceive more, more will come into your life." An alternate name for visualization is guided imagery.

Traditional Christianity differs with visualization on the most basic level. Matter and mind are indeed two separate and distinct things. The universe and world existed before humanity (Gen. 1). Therefore it is readily apparent that the material world does not have any direct dependence on the conscious mind.

Vital Force (occult). Life energies in living things are released when their blood is shed. (See *mana*).

Vivekananda, Swami (HINDUISM; VEDANTA SOCIETY; 1863–1902). A disciple of Sri Ramakrishna and founder of the Vedanta Society. Vivekananda is responsible for bridging East and West with his teachings on Hinduism.

Vlad, Prince (occult). A fifteenth-century Romanian ruler who was famous for his conquest of the Turks. He was considered a great leader but was also greatly feared because of his extreme cruelty and methods of torture visited on both Turks and his own subjects. One of his methods of execution was impaling. In the late nineteenth century, Bram Stoker adopted Prince Vlad as a model for his dreaded character *Dracula* (1897), the famed blood-sucking vampire.

Vodun (VOODOO). Alternate or shortened term for voodoo.

Wah-Z (ECKANKAR). The spiritual name for Sri Harold ▶Klemp, it also means the "secret doctrine."

Waldorf Schools (▶occult). Offers mostly the esoteric teachings of Rudolf ▶Steiner.

Wand (▶occult; WITCHCRAFT). One of the four suits in ▶Tarot cards. In ceremonial ▶magic, the wand symbolizes the element "air." According to the *Key of Solomon*, the wand is made from the wood of either an ash or hazelnut tree. It is one of four basic instruments; inscribed on it are planetary symbols or names of deities. *See* ▶cup, ▶pentacle, ▶sword.

Wangas (▶occult; VOODOO). ▶Magic charms used in VOODOO to conjure up spirits or to bring good luck.

Ward (MORMONISM). A regional breakdown of each ▶stake in Mormonism. There are two to six wards per stake, which adds up to a total of around twenty-eight hundred wards altogether. Below the wards are the independent ▶branches. Ward membership varies, ranging from six hundred to as many as eleven or twelve hundred members.

Warlock (▶occult; WITCHCRAFT). A popular formerly used term to denote a male practitioner of witchcraft. However, in the technical sense, it is a term that is rarely used in modern witchcraft or ▶wicca. Both males and females are called ▶witches in the modern craft.

Warma, Mahesh Brasad (TRANSCENDENTAL MEDITATION). The original name of Maharishi Mahesh ▶Yogi.

Waxing Moon (WITCHCRAFT). A ritual performed after the first crescent of the moon becomes visible. It includes placing a bowl of seeds on an ▶altar, while a priestess reminds the attending ▶coven that the increasing of the moon is the sign of fertility and fruitfulness. Commonly one of the members of the coven serves as a seed priestess, who invokes a goddess as she takes the bowl of seed from the altar and hands it to each person standing around the ▶witch's ▶circle. Each person then visualizes what she wants to see grow, as seeds from the bowl are placed in the witch's cauldron. The ritual charges the seed and the earth to be fruitful. The ritual ends with cakes and wine.

Wemilere (▶Yoruba; CABILDO; SOUTH AMERICAN, CENTRAL AMERICAN, AND CARIBBEAN CULTS). The ritualistic dance of Cabildo. The term is also used for Afro-Cuban ▶cult dances in general.

Werewolf (▶occult). A man, according to the folklore, who has been changed into a wolf or someone who is capable of changing into a wolf.

Wheel Of 84 (ECKANKAR). Phrase used by Paul ▶Twitchell to describe the endless cycle of ▶reincarnation. To get off the Wheel of 84, one must rid oneself of all bad ▶karma by multiple out-of-body experiences (*see* ▶astral projection). This ageless process is greatly reduced by meeting and following the living Eck Master.

Whirling Dervish (ISLAM; SUFISM). One who practices a special dance ritual that includes the physical motion of twirling many times for an hour or more while reciting the name of ▶Allah in prayer. This leads to an unconscious, ecstatic ▶trance state, symbolizing the awakening from a state of indifference to a mystical experience of oneness with God.

White, Ellen G. (SEVENTH-DAY ADVENTISM; 1827–1915) Founder of Seventh-day Adventism. Facts about her life are covered in the SDA article.

White Magic (▶occult). ▶Magic in the occult that is used to effect good, blessings, favorable results, or a positive outcome.

Wicca (WITCHCRAFT). A common and much older name for the craft that ▶witches practice. The term comes from the old English meaning to practice witchcraft. It commonly refers to those witches who practice ▶white magic. Wicca is the term for the modern craft as distinguished from ▶Gothic witchcraft, the practice of witchcraft in the Middle Ages.

Wiccan Rede (▶occult; SATANISM; WITCHCRAFT). The ethical principle espoused by Aleister ▶Crowley and followed by witchcraft practitioners that says, "And it harm none, do what you will." It is important to point out that Satanism refers to this Rede as well but uses it the way that Crowley actually intended it to mean. The latter practice the principle by advocating self-fulfillment even at the expense of others. Witches, however, use the term to mean "do what you wish as long as it harms nobody, even yourself." This prohibits witches for cursing, hexing, or manipulating others.

Wiccaning (Witchcraft). Witches gathering to perform a ritual blessing on a newly born baby.

Widdershins (ʾoccult; WITCHCRAFT). The opposite of ʾdeosil. The direction of movement of ʾwitches in a ʾcircle in a counterclockwise direction, producing a reduction or winding down of power.

Wierwille, Victor Paul (THE WAY INTERNATIONAL; 1916–85). The founder and leader of The Way International. Similar to many ʾcult leaders, he said God spoke to him in an audible voice, telling him to teach God's word as it has not been taught since the first century of Christianity. His *Power for Abundant Living* course that he published in 1953, according to him, fulfilled that "divine" command.

Winning Formulas See the FORUM.

Winter Solstice (ʾoccult; WITCHCRAFT). One of the eight ʾSabbats celebrated by ʾwitches and other aboriginal religions around the world. The winter solstice or ʾyule (as it is called by CHRISTIANITY) is the shortest day of the year, occurring around December 22. In some groups it represents the death of the Holly King, or god of the waning year, and the birth of the Oak King, or god of the year about to be born.

Laurie Cabot has received the title "The Official Witch of Salem" (given to her by former Massachusetts governor Dukakis).
Courtesy Jack M. Roper/CARIS

Witch (WITCHCRAFT). A practitioner of witchcraft who has usually, but not always, been inducted into a ʾcoven. A number of witches practice their craft outside of a coven. These are ʾsolitary practitioners. The term *witch* generally applies to both males and females. Male witches are sometimes called ʾwarlocks by outsiders, but this term is rarely used inside the group.

Witch Balls (ʾoccult; WITCHCRAFT). Glass spheres hung in homes to ward off evil spirits.

Witch Doctor (ʾoccult; VOODOO). The chief practitioner of ʾmagic within primitive tribes. In voodoo, the witch doctor wards off evil spirits through ʾspells and ʾincantations. A witch doctor may also cast spells or invoke a curse on individuals.

Witch Queen (ʾoccult; WITCHCRAFT). A title given to a high priestess who has formed at least two ʾcovens.

Witches Calendar (WITCHCRAFT). Annually, there are four seasonal holidays; also called ʾSabbats.

1. ʾSpring equinox (March 21)
2. Summer solstice (June 22)
3. Fall equinox (September 21)
4. Winter solstice—ʾYule (December 22)

Additionally, four other Sabbats tied in with agricultural and herd farming are included in the calendar year:

1. ʾCandlemas (February 2)
2. ʾBeltane (April 30)
3. ʾLammas (July 31)
4. ʾHalloween (October 31)

Most ʾwiccan groups also meet both weekly or biweekly on the full and new moon. These regular meetings are called ʾesbats.

Witches Festival (ʾoccult; WITCHCRAFT). A gathering of ʾwitches in order to celebrate rites occurring on the various dates in the ʾ*Witches Calendar*.

Witches Finger See ʾfinger.

Witch's Cup (ʾoccult; WITCHCRAFT). A chalice used in some occult or witchcraft rituals. The chalice is commonly filled with wine and blood; sometimes urine is also added. The mixture is a drink offering to demons.

Witch's Ladder (ʾoccult; WITCHCRAFT). A string of forty beads, or a rope with forty knots in it, used for ceremonial worship.

Witch's Mask (ʾoccult; WITCHCRAFT). The supposed extra breast or nipple located on the body of a ʾwitch. In the Middle Ages its presence on a woman was a true sign that she was a witch. It was further believed that ▶familiar spirits (demons) sucked on this extra breast.

Wizard (▶occult; WITCHCRAFT). A male witch endowed with occult wisdom.

Woodruff, Wilford (MORMONISM; 1807–1898). Fourth president of the Church of Jesus Christ of Latter-Day Saints. In 1890 he issued the manifesto that relinquished the practice of polygamous marriages among Mormons.

Word of Wisdom (MORMONISM). Section 89 in ▶*Doctrine and Covenants* is called "the word of wisdom." It is here where ▶Mormons are instructed to refrain from coffee, tea, smoking, the consumption of alcohol, and other such substances.

WOW (THE WAY INTERNATIONAL). Acronym for "Word Over the World;" this is the recruitment conducted by missionaries of the Way International. The large growth that this group experienced in late 1970s and early 1980s was the result of the fervor, zeal, and intensity of Way International members.

Wu-Wei (TAOISM). The path of nonaction in Taoism. Human intervention serves only to upset the ebb and flow of ▶yin and yang.

Y

Yahweh Ben Yahweh (NATION OF YAHWEH; 1935–). Founder of the Nation of Yahweh in 1979, his birthname is Hulon Mitchell. He taught that the black race is superior and possessed a hatred for whites. He was incarcerated in 1996 along with seven other members of the movement on racketeering, murder, and attempted murder charges. He was sentenced to eighteen years in prison but was released on September 25, 2001. According to a statement issued by his daughter, ben Yahweh no longer believes that whites are "devils" but that God loves all people.

Yeshiva (JUDAISM). A Jewish school where students study the Hebrew ▶Bible and other sacred texts, especially the Talmud. Yeshivas are also elementary and/or secondary schools that include religious instruction as part of the curriculum.

Yin and Yang (TAOISM). The paired opposition or principles at work in Taoism. *Yin* is the feminine, passive, or negative force. It is also the breath that forms the earth. *Yang* is the masculine, active, positive force that radiates light and comprises the heavens. *Yin and yang* describe the bipolar forces of the universe (light/darkness; good/evil; male/female; outward/inward; sun/moon; fire/water, etc.) These forces continually react to one another, causing flux, balance, and imbalance in the universe.

Yoga (HINDUISM). One of the oldest words in the vocabulary of Hinduism. meaning "union." Yoga is the method, path, or course undertaken or followed in order to realize, experience, and become one with ▶Brah-

man—the god within oneself. This volume describes the many "yogas" of Hindu thought.

Yogananda, Pramahansa (SELF-REALIZATION FELLOWSHIP; 1893–1952). An early teacher and organizer of Self-Realization Fellowship founded in 1914.

Yogesvara (HINDUISM). An alternate name for ▶Hare Krishna Supreme or highest presence of supernatural powers.

Yogi (HINDUISM) A devotee and practitioner of ▶yoga.

Yogi, Maharishi Mahesh (TRANSCENDENTAL MEDITATION; 1911–). founder and leader of TM (Transcendental Meditation), which was renamed the Science of Creative Intelligence. His teachings are an offshoot of HINDUISM. Maharishi was formerly named Mahesh Brasad ▶Warma.

Yogi, Sirj Singh Sahir Harrhajan See Yogi ▶Bhajan.

York Rite (FREEMASONRY). A "higher" degree that a Mason may enter after completing the three degrees in the ▶Blue Lodge. The York Rite has also been called the "American Rite," but the appellation "York" remains the most common way to refer to it. It takes its name from York, England, and is considered the oldest rite in the history of Freemasonry. The York Rite is comprised of three distinct bodies called Grand Chapters.

Yoruba (SANTERIA; SOUTH AMERICAN, CENTRAL AMERICAN, AND CARIBBEAN CULTS; VOODOO). African people who originated in southern Nigeria. Brought to America by slave traders, the Yoruba slaves acculturated their own religious and cultural traditions with those endemic to their new homeland. The Santeria and voodoo ᐅcults are comprised largely of Yoruba people.

Young, Brigham (MORMONISM; 1801–1877). The second president of the Church of Jesus Christ of Latter-Day Saints. It was Young who led the larger group of Mormons to Utah. Upon setting eyes on the Great Salt Lake Valley, he is reputed to have said, "This is the place!" Like Joseph ᐅSmith Jr., Brigham Young endorsed and encouraged polygamy among Mormons.

Yule (CHRISTIANITY; WITCHCRAFT). This is the name that is sometimes given to the shortest day of the year, December 21. In the ᐅWitches Calendar, Yule is the celebration of the death of the old year and the birth of the new. In Christianity Yule was the time chosen as the birth of Jesus Christ as the ᐅincarnate Son of God, who is the "son of righteousness," as foretold by the prophet Malachi (Mal. 4:2).

Z

Zazen (ZEN BUDDHISM). An instruction period taking place in a *zendo* (meditation hall). During *zazen*, the disciple is under the tutelage of a ᐅroshi. The subject sits on a pillow in a carefully determined posture. The eyes are open and the mouth remains closed. A roshi attempts to help the disciple free his or her mind from all present reality. ᐅ*Koans* are frequently used in this process. Unanswerable riddles cause the subject to retreat to the inner recesses of his mind to seek solutions that are not accessible to the surface consciousness of humans.

Zion (MORMONISM). Although the word Zion is an Old Testament term, it has new and meanings among Mormons. They see all members of the Mormon church as Zion, and they also say, as did Brigham ᐅYoung, that Zion is wherever the true people of God (Mormons) reside. Another meaning of Zion refers to those who obey God's laws. Joseph Fielding ᐅSmith (sixth Mormon president) in his *Doctrine of Salvation* taught that Independence, Missouri, and Jerusalem in Israel will be the two Zion capitals for the kingdom of God during the coming Millennium.

Zodiac (ᐅastrology). In astrology, this refers to the twelvefold division of the sky into ᐅsigns. The word *zodiac* literally means the "circle of animals." The twelve signs of zodiac are: ᐅAries; ᐅTaurus; ᐅGemini; ᐅCancer; ᐅLeo; ᐅVirgo; ᐅLibra; ᐅScorpio; ᐅSagittarius; ᐅCapricorn; ᐅAquarius, and ᐅPisces. Astrologers believe that the sign one is born under largely determines the makeup of a person's character.

Zombi (ᐅoccult; VOODOO). This is the name of a snake deity in voodoo, as found in Haiti and in parts of Florida. The belief was imported from West African voodoo ᐅcults that worshiped the python. A zombi is also someone in voodoo circles who, as a result of having been put under a ᐅspell or having taken harmful potions or drugs, has had his or her mind come under the control of the substance and thus is easily manipulated to perform servile tasks mindlessly. The word "zombie" has been popularized in the American film industry to mean a dead corpse that is resuscitated to life to haunt, prey on, or feed on the living.

Zone Servants (JEHOVAH'S WITNESSES). These are members of the Watchtower Bible and Tract Society who function within the 153 smaller units (zones) that are part of the six regional divisions in the United States. Zone servants work directly with individual ᐅkingdom halls and the ᐅcompany servants appointed for each. See also ᐅregional servants.

Zoroastrianism The ancient religion of Persia, founded by Zororaster (b. ca. 660 B.C.). Zoroastrianism replaced ᐅpolytheism in Persia with ᐅmonotheism. The sacred text is called the *Avesta*. Zoroaster taught that the good god Ahura Mazdah enjoyed absolute supremacy over all other deities. The most noted feature of this religion is the idea of a cosmic ᐅdualism between Mazhad and the evil spirit, Angra Mainyu. All of humanity is caught up in this cosmic struggle, and each individual must choose between good and evil, with accompanying rewards or punishments depending on one's choice.

Zoroaster is the Greek name for Zarathustra. With the Islamic conquest of Persia in A.D. 650, a majority of the followers of Zoroastrianism fled to India. Today they number approximately one hundred thousand and are called ᐅParsees.

Zul Hijjah (ISLAM). See ᐅIslamic holidays.

Appendix 1:

The Ecumenical Creeds of Christendom

THE APOSTLES' CREED

I believe in God, the Father almighty, creator of heaven and earth.

And in Jesus Christ, his only Son, our Lord, who was conceived by the power of the Holy Spirit, born of the Virgin Mary, suffered under Pontius Pilate, was crucified, died, and was buried. He descended to the dead. The third day he rose again from the dead. He ascended into heaven, and sits at the right hand of the God, the Father almighty. From thence he will come to judge the living and the dead.

I believe in the Holy Spirit, the holy Christian Church, the communion of saints, the forgiveness of sins, the resurrection of the body, and the life everlasting. Amen.

THE NICENE CREED

I believe in one God, the Father Almighty, maker of heaven and earth, and of all things visible and invisible.

And in one Lord Jesus Christ, the only begotten Son of God, begotten of his Father before all worlds, God of God, Light of Light, very God of very God, begotten, not made, being of one substance with the Father; by whom all things were made; who for us men and for our salvation came down from heaven, and was incarnate by the Holy Spirit by the Virgin Mary, and was made man; and was crucified also for us under Pontius Pilate. He suffered and was buried. And the third day he rose again according to the Scriptures, and ascended into heaven, and sits at the right hand of the Father. And he will come again with glory to judge both the living and the dead; whose kingdom will have no end.

And I believe in the Holy Spirit, the Lord and giver of life, who proceeds from the Father and the Son, who with the Father and the Son together is worshiped and glorified; who spoke by the prophets.

And I believe one holy Christian and apostolic Church; I acknowledge one baptism for the remission of sins; and I look for the resurrection of the dead, and the life of the world to come. Amen.

ATHANASIAN CREED

Whosoever will be saved shall, above all else, hold the catholic faith.

Which faith except everyone keeps whole and undefiled, without doubt he will perish eternally.

And the catholic faith is this: that we worship one God in three persons and three persons in one God neither confounding the persons, nor dividing the substance.

For there is one Person of the Father, another of the Son, and another of the Holy Spirit.

But the Godhead of the Father, of the Son, and of the Holy Spirit, is all one, the glory equal, the majesty coeternal.

Such as the Father is, such is the Son, and such is the Holy Spirit.

The Father uncreated, the Son uncreated, and the Holy Spirit uncreated.

The Father incomprehensible, the Son incomprehensible, and the Holy Spirit incomprehensible.

The Father eternal, the Son eternal, and the Holy Spirit eternal.

And yet they are not three eternals, but one eternal.

As there are not three uncreated nor three incomprehensibles, but one uncreated and one incomprehensible.

So likewise the Father is almighty, the Son almighty, and the Holy Spirit almighty.

And yet they are not three almighties, but one almighty.

So the Father is God, the Son is God, and the Holy Spirit is God.

And yet they are not three Gods, but one God.

So likewise the Father is Lord, the Son Lord, and the Holy Spirit Lord.

And yet not three Lords, but one Lord.

For as we are compelled by the Christian truth to acknowledge every person by himself to be both God and Lord,

So we cannot by the catholic faith say that there are three Gods or three Lords.

The Father is made of none, neither created nor begotten.

The Son is of the Father alone, not made nor created but begotten.

The Holy Spirit is of the Father and of the Son, neither made nor created nor begotten but proceeding.

So there is one Father, not three Fathers; one Son, not three Sons; one Holy Spirit , not three Holy Spirits.

And in this Trinity none is before or after another; none is greater or less than another;

But the whole three persons are coeternal together and coequal, so that in all things, as is aforesaid, the Unity in Trinity and the Trinity in Unity is to be worshiped.

He therefore that will be saved is compelled thus to think of the Trinity.

Furthermore, it is necessary to everlasting salvation that he also believe faithfully the incarnation of our Lord Jesus Christ.

For the right faith is that we believe and confess, that our Lord Jesus Christ, the Son of God, is God and Man;

God of the substance of the Father, begotten before the worlds; and man of the substance of his mother, born in the world;

Perfect God and perfect man, of a reasonable soul and human flesh subsisting.

Equal to the Father, as touching his Godhead; and inferior to the Father, as touching his manhood;

Who, although he is God and man, yet he is not two but one Christ;

One, not by conversion of the Godhead into flesh but by taking of the manhood into God;

One altogether, not by confusion of substance but by unity of person.

For as the reasonable soul and flesh is one man, so God and man is one Christ;

Who suffered for our salvation, descended into hell, rose again the third day from the dead.

He ascended into heaven, he sits at the right hand of the Father, God Almighty, from whence he will come to judge the living and the dead.

At whose coming all men will rise again with their bodies and will give an account of their own works.

And they that have done good will go into life everlasting; and they that have done evil, into everlasting fire.

This is the catholic faith which, except a man believe faithfully and firmly, he cannot be saved.

THE CHALCEDONIAN DEFINITION

Therefore, following the holy Fathers, we all with one accord teach men to acknowledge one and the same Son, our Lord Jesus Christ, at once complete in Godhead and complete in manhood, truly God and truly man, consisting also of a reasonable soul and body, of one substance [*homoousios*] with the Father as regards his Godhead, and at the same time of one substance with us as reards his manhood; like us in all respects, apart from sin; as regards his Godhead begotten of the Father before the ages; but yet as regards his manhood begotten, for us men and for our salvation, of the Virgin Mary, the God-bearer [*theotokos*]; one and the same Christ, Son, Lord, Only-begotten, in two natures, without confusion, without change, without division, without separation; the distinction of natures being in no way annulled by the union, but rather the characteristics of each nature being preserved and coming together to form one person and subsistence [*hypostasis*], not as parted or separated into two persons, but one and the same Son and Only-begotten God the Word, Lord Jesus Christ; even as the prophets from earliest times spoke of him, and our Lord Jesus Christ himself taught us, and the creed of the Fathers has handed down to us.

Appendix 2:

Orthodox Christology and Heresy

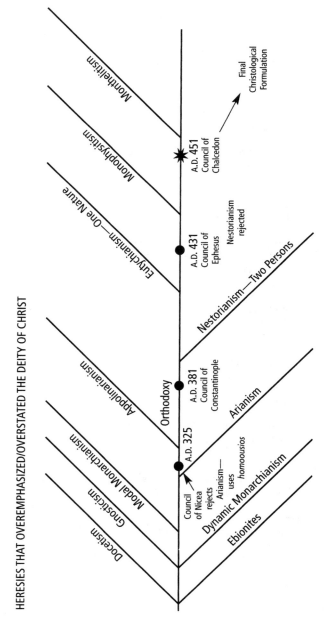

CHRISTOLOGICAL HERESIES OF THE EARLY CHURCH AND THE FOUR ECUMENICAL COUNCILS

HERESIES THAT OVEREMPHASIZED/OVERSTATED THE DEITY OF CHRIST

HERESIES THAT OVEREMPHASIZED/OVERSTATED THE HUMANITY OF CHRIST

Monotheletism

Monophysitism

Eutychianism—One Nature

Apollinarianism

Modal Monarchianism

Gnosticism

Docetism

A.D. 451
Council of
Chalcedon

Final
Christological
Formulation

A.D. 431
Council of
Ephesus

Nestorianism
rejected

Nestorianism—Two Persons

Orthodoxy

A.D. 381
Council of
Constantinople

Arianism

A.D. 325

Council
of Nicea
rejects
Arianism—
uses
homoousios

Dynamic Monarchianism

Ebionites

MODERN RELIGIOUS MOVEMENTS REFLECTING ANCIENT CHRISTOLOGICAL HERESIES

Many of the religious groups included in this volume have articulated a Christology that is in close proximity to the Christologies that were debated and weighed against the orthodox position as stated by the first four ecumenical councils of the church. Only those groups that have a clearly stated position with respect to the person of Christ and his human and divine natures have been included in the chart below. It should also be noted that the parallels drawn to the early Christological positions are only intended to be broad parallels that attempt to capture the main motifs of the group represented.

MODERN RELIGIOUS GROUP	CAPSULE SUMMARY	ANCIENT CHRISTOLOGY
1. Branch Davidians	Divine and human natures of Christ are totally separate with no communication between the two.	Nestorianism
2. Branhamism	Oneness theology—God is one person and one essence manifested in different modes.	Modal Monarchianism Sabellianism
3. Children of God	Confuses the two natures; Jesus had a beginning.	Nestorianism Arianism
4. Christadelphianism	Jesus atoned for his own sins and was perfected only with respect to his divine nature. They deny any unique divine nature of Christ	Nestorianism Arianism
5. Christian Science	Jesus possessed one nature only—a human nature. The Christ is a divine idea.	Ebionism Gnosticism
6. Church of Bible Understanding	Jesus is Savior, but not God the Savior.	Arianism
7. Church Universal and Triumphant	"Jesus" and "Christ" are two separate concepts. Jesus was a man who lived nearly 2,000 years ago.	Ebionism Nestorianism
8. Divine Science	Christ is an indwelling principle.	Gnosticism
9. International Church of Christ (a.k.a. The Boston Movement)	Divine and human natures of Christ are totally separate, with no communication between the two.	Nestorianism
10. International Church of Ageless Wisdom	God cannot be anthropomorphic; therefore, Jesus cannot be God.	Ebionism Nestorianism Arianism
11. Jehovah's Witnesses	Jesus had a beginning as the created Son of God	Arianism
12. Mormonism	Jesus' deity is no more unique than all of humankind	No real parallel—hints of Ebionism, Arianism, and Dynamic Monarchianism

MODERN RELIGIOUS GROUP	CAPSULE SUMMARY	ANCIENT CHRISTOLOGY
13. Oneness Pentecostalism	God is not a Trinity of three persons and one essence, but of one essence and person manifested in three different modes and in different dispensations.	Modal Monarchianism Sabellianism
14. Religious Science	"Jesus" is to be distinguished from "the Christ."	Ebionism Gnosticism
15. Rosicrucianism	Christology is identical with Religious Science and Mind Sciences.	Hints of Ebionism
16. Swedenborgianism	"Jesus" is to be distinguished from "the Christ." Jesus was merely human. The Trinity as "love, wisdom, and activity" are aspects of one person, not three.	Nestorianism Modal Monarchianism Sabellianism
17. Theosophy	Jesus is divine in the same sense as all people are divine. The historical Jesus was merely human	Hints of Arianism and Gnosticism
18. Unification Church	Jesus' body remained in the grave while his spirit rose to heaven. Jesus' death was an unfortunate accident.	Gnosticism Nestorianism
19. Unity School of Christianity	Jesus is the name of a particular person	Ebionism Gnosticism
20. Vedanta Society	Jesus' body died; this is insignificant; Jesus' divinity is solely important	Monophysitism
21. The Way International	Jesus is not God because God cannot die. Jesus was human.	Nestorianism Arianism
22. The Worldwide Church of God (Armstrong version)	The body that died on the cross was not the same body that was raised from the dead. After Jesus' resurrection, he possessed a single divine nature.	Monophysitism

Appendix 3:

Cults, Sects, and Religious Groups Stemming From World Religions

Many cults, sects, and religious groups have arisen from a variety of influences from major religious traditions. The accompanying charts attempt to diagram this process and to give a bird's-eye view of where many religious groups have derived their teachings.

1. SECTS OF CHRISTIANITY

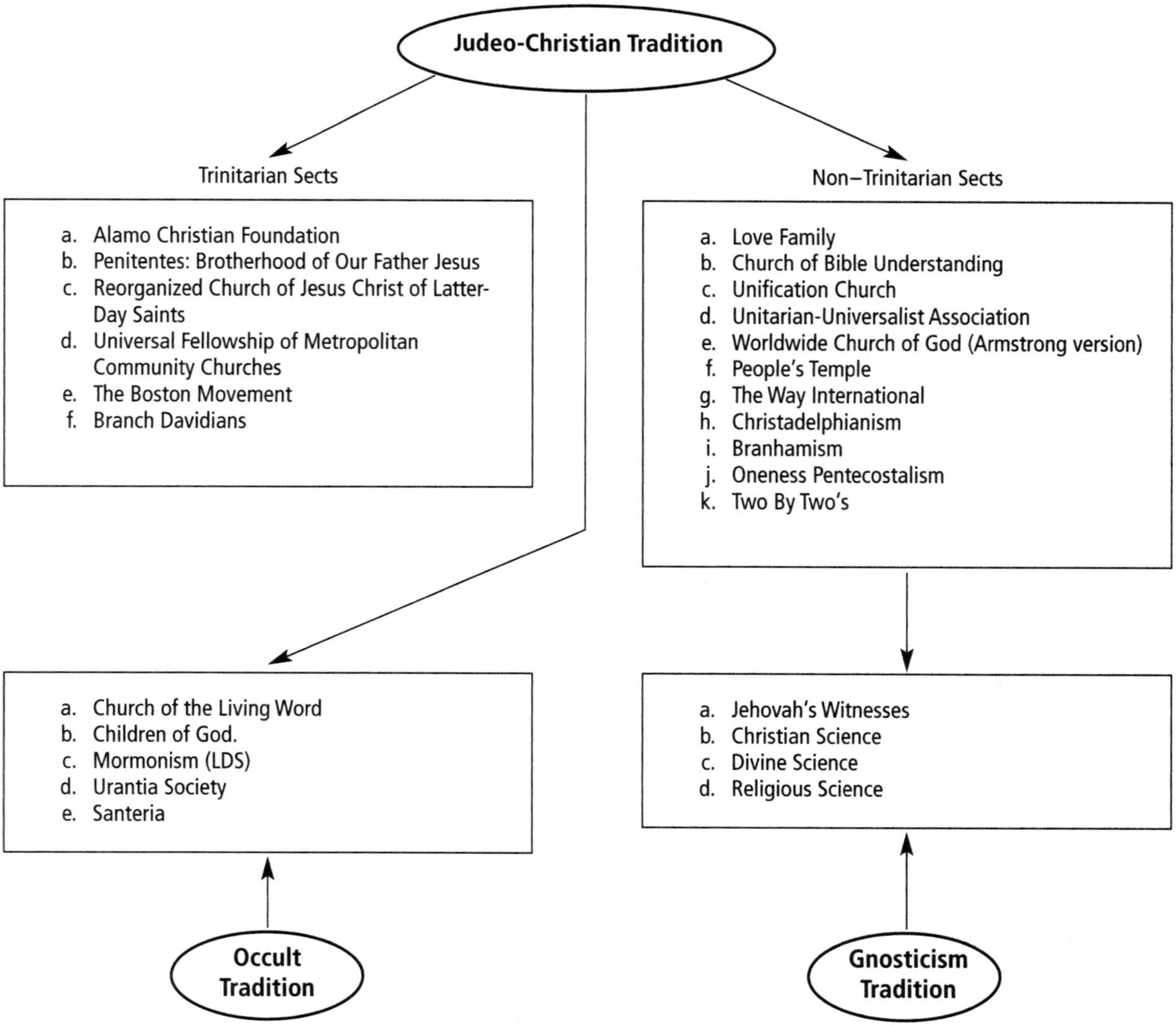

Judeo-Christian Tradition

Trinitarian Sects

a. Alamo Christian Foundation
b. Penitentes: Brotherhood of Our Father Jesus
c. Reorganized Church of Jesus Christ of Latter-Day Saints
d. Universal Fellowship of Metropolitan Community Churches
e. The Boston Movement
f. Branch Davidians

Non–Trinitarian Sects

a. Love Family
b. Church of Bible Understanding
c. Unification Church
d. Unitarian-Universalist Association
e. Worldwide Church of God (Armstrong version)
f. People's Temple
g. The Way International
h. Christadelphianism
i. Branhamism
j. Oneness Pentecostalism
k. Two By Two's

a. Church of the Living Word
b. Children of God.
c. Mormonism (LDS)
d. Urantia Society
e. Santeria

a. Jehovah's Witnesses
b. Christian Science
c. Divine Science
d. Religious Science

Occult Tradition

Gnosticism Tradition

2. SECTS OF OCCULTISM

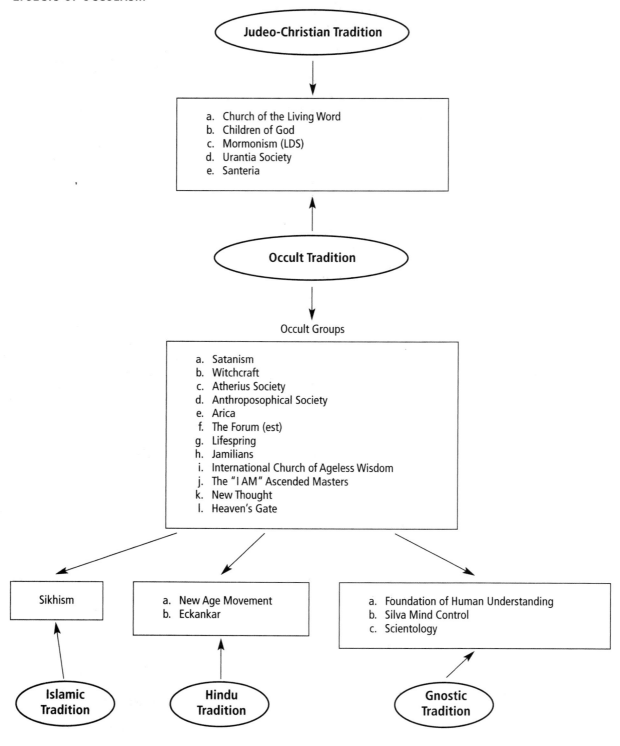

Judeo-Christian Tradition

a. Church of the Living Word
b. Children of God
c. Mormonism (LDS)
d. Urantia Society
e. Santeria

Occult Tradition

Occult Groups

a. Satanism
b. Witchcraft
c. Atherius Society
d. Anthroposophical Society
e. Arica
f. The Forum (est)
g. Lifespring
h. Jamilians
i. International Church of Ageless Wisdom
j. The "I AM" Ascended Masters
k. New Thought
l. Heaven's Gate

Sikhism

a. New Age Movement
b. Eckankar

a. Foundation of Human Understanding
b. Silva Mind Control
c. Scientology

Islamic Tradition

Hindu Tradition

Gnostic Tradition

3. SECTS OF ISLAM

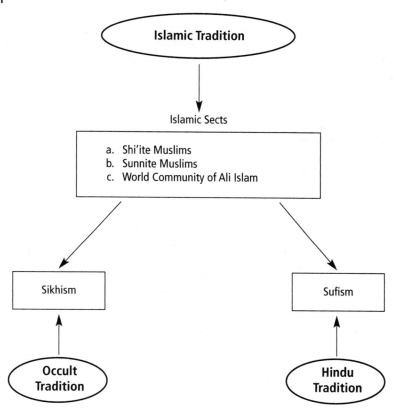

4. SECTS OF BUDDHISM

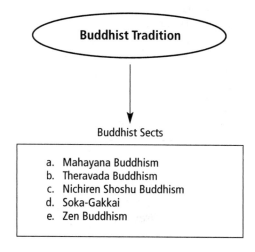

5. SECTS OF HINDUISM

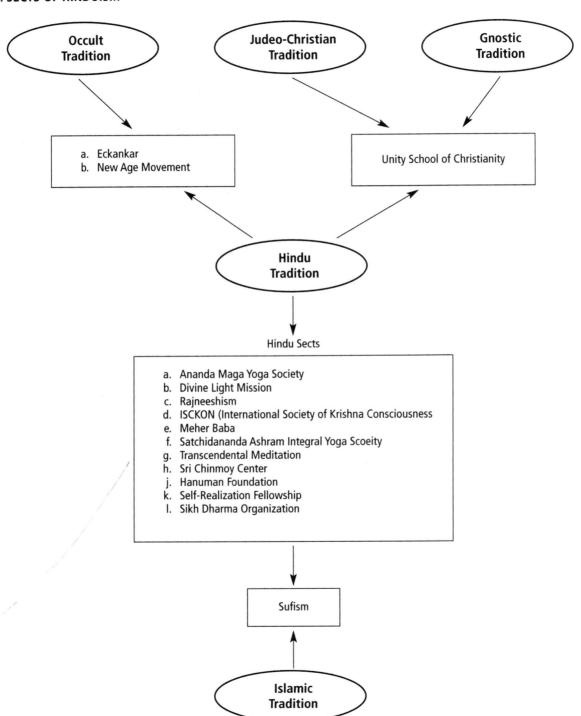

Bibliography

GENERAL BOOKS

Anderson, Sir Norman, ed. *The World's Religions.* Grand Rapids: Eerdmans, 1977.

Ankerberg, John and John. *Cult Watch: What You Need to Know about Spiritual Deception.* Weldon: Harvest House, 1999.

Antes, Peter, Armin W. Geetz, and Randi R. Warne, eds. *New Approaches to the Study of Religion.* Berlin/New York: Walter de Gruyter, 2004.

Anthony, Dick, and Thomas Robbins. "Brainwashing and Totalitarian Influence." Pages 457–71 in vol. 1, V. S. Ramachandran (ed.), *Encyclopedia of Human Behavior.* San Diego: Academic Press. 1994.

_____. (1995). "Negligence, Coercion, and the Protection of Religious Belief." *Journal of Church and State* 37 (1995): 509–36.

_____. (1995) "Religious Totalism, Violence and Exemplary Dualism: Beyond the Extrinsic Model." *Terrorism and Political Violence* 7 (1995): 10–50.

_____. "Pseudoscience and Minority Religions: An Evaluation of the Brainwashing Theories of Jean-Marie Abgrall." *Social Justice Research* 12 (1995): 421–56.

Appel, Willa. *Cults in America: Programmed for Paradise.* New York: Holt, Rinehart, & Winston, 1983.

Bainbridge, William S. *The Sociology of Religious Movements.* New York: Routledge, 1997.

Barrett, D. V. *The New Believers: A Survey of Sects, Cults, and Alternative Religions.* Delhi, Ind.: Sterling Publishers, 2001.

Beck, Hubert F. *How to Respond to the Cults.* Response Series. St. Louis: Concordia, 1977.

Beckford, James A. *Cult Controversies.* London and New York: Tavistock, 1985.

Bjornstadt, James *Counterfeits at Your Door.* Glendale, Calif.: Gospel Light, 1974.

Boa, Kenneth. *Cults, World Religions and the Occult.* Wheaton: Scripture Press, 1990.

Bromley, David, and J. Gordon Melton, eds. *Cults, Religion, and Violence.* Cambridge: Cambridge Univ. Press, 2002.

Cohen, Daniel. *The New Believers.* New York: Ballantine, 1975.

Collins, John J. *The Cult Experience: An Overview of Cults, Their Traditions, and Why People Join Them.* Springfield, Ill.: C. C. Thomas, 1991.

Cox, Harvey. *Turning East.* New York: Simon and Schuster, 1977.

Davis, Derek, ed. *New Religious Movements and Religious Freedom in America.* Waco: Baylor Univ. Press, 2002.

The Directory of Religious Organizations in the United States. 2d ed. Falls Church, Va.: McGrath, 1982.

Edwards, Christopher. *Crazy for God.* Englewood Cliffs, N.J.: Prentice-Hall, 1979.

Ellwood, Robert S. *Alternative Altars: Unconventional and Eastern Spirituality in America.* Chicago: Univ. of Chicago Press, 1979.

_____. *Religious and Spiritual Groups in Modern America.* Englewood Cliffs, N.J.: Prentice-Hall, 1973.

Enroth, Ronald. *Churches That Abuse.* Grand Rapids: Zondervan, 1992.

_____. *A Guide to Cults and New Religions.* Downers Grove, Ill.: InterVarsity Press, 1990.

_____. *Youth, Brainwashing, and the Extremist Cults.* Grand Rapids: Zondervan, 1977.

Evans, Christopher. *Cults of Unreason.* New York: Dell, 1973.

Galanter, Marc. *Cults: Faith, Healing, and Coercion.* New York: Oxford Univ. Press, 1989.

Geisler, Norman L. *Philosophy of Religion.* Grand Rapids: Zondervan, 1974.

Glock, Charles Y., and Robert N. Bellah, eds. *The New Religious Consciousness.* Berkeley: Univ. of California Press, 1976.

Gomes, Alan W. *Unmasking the Cults.* Grand Rapids: Zondervan, 1994.

_____. *Truth and Error*. Grand Rapids: Zondervan, 1998.

Guinness, Os. *The East: No Exit*. Downers Grove, Ill.: InterVarsity Press, 1974.

Hassan, Steven. *Combatting Cult Mind Control*. Rochester, Vt.: Park Street, 1990.

Hefley, James C. *The Youth Nappers*. Wheaton, Ill.: Victor, 1977.

Hexham, I., S. Rost, and J. Morehead II, eds. *Encountering New Religious Movements: A Holistic Evangelistic Approach*. Grand Rapids: Kregel, 2004.

Hoekema, Anthony A. *The Four Major Cults*. Grand Rapids: Eerdmans, 1963.

Hunt, Dave. *The Cult Explosion*. Eugene, Ore.: Harvest House, 1980.

Jenkins, P. *Mystics and Messiahs: Cults and New Religions in American History*. Oxford: Oxford Univ. Press, 2001.

Kaiser, Thomas, and Jacqueline Kaiser. *The Anatomy of Illusion: Religious Cults and Destructive Persuasion*. Springfield, Ill.: C. C. Thomas, 1987.

Lane, David C. *Understanding Cults and Spiritual Movements*. Albany, N.Y.: Del Mar, 1989.

Larson, Bob. *Larson's Book of Cults*. Wheaton, Ill.: Tyndale, 1982.

_____. *Larson's New Book of Cults*. 5th ed. Chicago: Moody Press, 1991.

Lewis, I. M. *Religion in Context: Cults and Charisma*. Cambridge: Cambridge Univ. Press, 1986.

Lewis, Gordon. *Confronting the Cults*. Grand Rapids: Baker, 1966.

Lewis, James. *Legitimating New Religions*. Piscataway, N.J.: Rutgers Univ. Press, 2003.

Lifton, Robert J. *Thought Reform and the Psychology of Totalism: A Study of Brainwashing in China*. Chapel Hill: Univ. of North Carolina Press, 1989.

Martin, Walter. *The Kingdom of the Cults*. Rev. ed. Minneapolis: Bethany, 2003.

_____. *Martin Speaks Out on the Cults*. Santa Ana, Calif.: Vision House, 1983.

_____. *The Rise of the Cults*. Santa Ana, Calif.: Vision House, 1980.

Martin, Walter, ed., with Robert and Gretchen Passantino. *The New Cults*. Santa Ana, Calif.: Vision House, 1980.

McBeth, Leon. *Strange New Religions*. Nashville: Broadman, 1977.

Mead, Frank S. *Handbook of Denominations*. 9th ed. Revised by Samuel S. Hill. Nashville: Abingdon, 1990.

Melton, J. Gordon. *Encyclopedia of American Religions*. 5th ed. Detroit: Gale Research, 2002.

_____. *Encyclopedic Handbook of Cults in America*. New York: Garland, 1986.

_____. *The Lure of the Cults*. Chappaqua, N.Y.: Christian Herald, 1979.

Melton, J. G., and R. L. Moore. *The Cult Experience: Responding to the New Religious Pluralism*. New York: Pilgrim, 1982.

Miller, Stephen, ed. *Misguiding Lights*. Kansas City, Mo.: Beacon Hill, 1991.

Miller, Timothy. *When Prophets Die: The Post-Charismatic Fate of New Religious Movements*. New York: State Univ. of New York Press, 1991.

Needleman, Jacob. *The New Religions*. New York: Dutton, 1976.

Needleman, Jacob, and George Baker, eds. *Understanding the New Religions*. New York: Seabury, 1979.

Parrinder, Jeffrey. *The Dictionary of Non-Christian Religions*. Philadelphia: Westminster, 1971.

Partridge, C., and Douglas Groothuis, eds. *Dictionary of Contemporary Religion in the Western World*. Downers Grove, Ill.: InterVarsity Press, 2002.

Passantino, Robert, and Gretchen Passantino. *Answers to the Cultists at Your Door*. Eugene, Ore.: Harvest House, 1981.

Patrick, Ted. *Let Our Children Go*. New York: Dutton, 1976.

Pavlos, Andrew J. *The Cult Experience*. Westport, Conn.: Greenwood, 1982.

Pement, Eric, and Keith Edward Tolbert. *The 1991 Directory of Cults*. Trenton, Mich.: American Religious Center, 1991.

Peterson, William J. *Those Curious New Cults*. New Canaan, Conn.: Keats, 1975.

Rhodes, Ronald. *The Challenge of the Cults and New Religions: The Essential Guide to Their History, Their Doctrine, and Our Response*. Grand Rapids: Zondervan, 2001.

Robbins, Thomas, and Dick Anthony, eds. *In Gods We Trust: New Patterns of Religious Pluralism in America*. New Brunswick, N.J.: Transaction, 1981.

Robertson, Irvine. *What the Cults Believe*. 2nd ed. Chicago: Moody Press, 1979.

Rudin, James, and Marcia Rudin. *Prison or Paradise? The New Religious Cults.* Philadelphia: Fortress, 1980.

Sargant, William. *Battle for the Mind: A Physiology of Conversion and Brainwashing.* Garden City, N.Y.: Doubleday, 1957.

Scheflin, Alan, and Edward Opton. *The Mind Manipulators.* New York: Paddington, 1978.

Schein, Edgar H. *Coercive Persuasion.* New York: Norton, 1961.

Shupe, Anson D., Jr. *Six Alternative Perspectives on New Religions: A Case Study Approach.* New York: Mellen, 1981.

_____, and David G. Bromley. *A Documentary History of the American Anti-Cult Movement.* New York: Mellen, 1981.

_____. *The New Vigilantes: Deprogrammers, Anti-Cultists, and the New Religions.* Beverly Hills, Calif.: Sage, 1980.

_____. *Strange Gods: The Great American Cult Scare.* Boston: Beacon, 1981.

Shupe, Anson D., Jr., Roger Spielmann, and Sam Stigall. "Deprogramming: The New Exorcism." *American Behavioral Scientist* 20 (1977): 941–56.

Sire, James W. *The Universe Next Door.* Downers Grove, Ill.: InterVarsity Press, 1970.

Smith, Huston. *The Religions of Men.* New York: Harper & Row, 1958.

Sparks, Jack. *The Mind Benders.* Nashville: Nelson, 1977.

Spittler, Russell. *Cults and Isms.* Grand Rapids: Baker, 1962.

Starkes, M. Thomas. *Confronting Popular Cults.* Nashville: Broadman, 1972.

Stoner, Carroll, and Joanne Parke. *All God's Children.* Radnor, Penn.: Chilton, 1977.

Streiker, L. D. *The Cults Are Coming.* Nashville: Abingdon, 1977.

Tanis, Edward J. *What the Sects Teach.* Grand Rapids: Baker, 1958.

Ungeleider, J. Thomas. *The New Religions: Insights into the Cult Phenomenon.* New York: Merck, Sharpe, & Dohme, 1979.

Van Baalen, Jan Karel. *Chaos of the Cults.* 4th ed. rev. Grand Rapids: Eerdmans, 1962.

Verdier, Paul A. *Brainwashing and the Cults.* Hollywood, Calif.: Institute for Behavioral Conditioning, 1977.

Washington, J. R. *Black Sects and Cults.* New York: Doubleday, 1972.

Watson, William. *A Concise Dictionary of Cults and Religions.* Chicago: Moody Press, 1991.

Wessinger, Catherine. *How the Millennium Comes Violently: From Jonestown to Heaven's Gate.* Washington, D.C. Chatham House, 2000.

Wilson, Bryan R. *The Social Dimensions of Sectarianism.* Oxford: Oxford Univ. Press, 1990.

_____, ed. *The Social Impact of New Religious Movements.* New York: Rose of Sharon, 1981.

Wilson, Herman O., and Morris M. Womack, eds. *Pillars of Faith.* Grand Rapids: Baker, 1973.

Yamauchi, Edwin M. *Jesus, Zoroaster, Buddha, Socrates, Muhammad.* Downers Grove, Ill.: InterVarsity Press, 1977.

Zaretsky, Irving, and Mark Leone. *Contemporary Religious Movements in America.* Princeton, N.J.: Princeton Univ. Press, 1974.

ABAKUA

Brown, David. *The Light Inside: Abakua Society Arts and Cuban Cultural History.* Washington, D.C.: Smithsonian, 2003.

Sloat, Susanna. *Caribbean Dance from Abakua to Zouk: How Movement Shapes Identity.* Hampshire. U.K.: Dance Books, 2002.

Maria Teresa Velez, *Drumming for the Gods: The Life and Times of Felips Garcia Villamil, Santero, Palero, and Abakua: Studies in Latin American and Caribbean Music.* Philadelphia, Pa.: Temple Univ. Press, 2000.

THE AETHERIUS SOCIETY

Elwood, Robert. "UFO Religious Movements." Pages 393–400 in *America's Alternative Religions.* Timothy Miller, ed. Albany: State Univ. of New York Press, 1995.

Keneipp, Brian C. *Operation EarthLight*, Los Angeles, Calif.: Aetherius, 2000.

Melton, J. Gordon. *Encyclopedia of American Religions.* 5th ed. Detroit: Gale Research, 2002.

_____. *New Age Encyclopedia.* Detroit: Gale Research, 1990.

ALAMO CHRISTIAN FOUNDATION

Alamo, Tony. *Tony Alamo's Answer to Rabbi Nur.* (Tract published by Alamo Church, n.d.).

_____. *The Pope's Secrets.* (Tract published by Alamo Church, n.d.).

"Alamo Calls Agency Poisonous to System." *Southwest Times Record* (Fort Smith, Ark.) (June 23, 1982).

"The Alamo Foundation." *US Magazine* (March 6, 1979), 18–20.

"Alamos Miss Psychiatric Test Deadline in Child Custody Suit." *Charleston Gazette* (August 1, 1986), 3A.

"Alamo Pressed to Take Psychiatric Exam." *Charleston Gazette* (July 24, 1986), 13A.

Alexander, David. "Remember the Alamos." *The Humanist* (January–February 1990): 43.

Cole-Bivine, Lois (Research Consultant for Christian Research Institute). Letter to the author (January 4, 1980).

"Cult Begins Local Recruiting Drive." *Citizens Freedom Foundation News*, 7 no. 12 and 8 no. 1 (1982 and 1983). Reprint from *Prospect Press* (Brooklyn, N.Y.) (Nov. 11, 1982).

Flippo, Chet. "Siege of the Alamos." *People's Weekly* (June 13, 1983), 29–34.

"Fugitive Cult Leader Is Arrested in Florida." *New York Times* (July 6, 1991), 9.

"Guilty by Association." *Register* (Anaheim, Calif.) (Feb. 6, 1983), C7.

Mather, George (Research Consultant for Christian Research Institute). Letter to the author. (Aug. 21, 1984).

Perrin, Gregory. "Cult Begins Local Recruiting Drive." *Prospect Press*, (November 1982), 11–24.

ANANDA MARGA YOGA SOCIETY

"A Catalogue of Cults: Where They Stand on the Deity of Christ." *Moody* (July-August 1979), 1.

"Ananda Marga Called Faith to Live By." *Los Angeles Times* (Feb. 7, 1976), part 1:21.

Andamurti, Shrii Shrii. *Baba's Grace: Discourses of Shrii Shrii Anadamurti*. Los Alto Hills, Calif.: Ananda Marga, 1973.

Ananda Marga: Elementary Philosophy. Ananda Marga Publications (Feb. 10, 2001).

"Ananda Spiritual-Family Letter." *Spiritual Family Letter*. Nevada City, Calif.: Yoga Fellowship.

Ananda Sutram. Ananda Marga Publications (Oct. 10, 2001).

Bowker, John. *Oxford Dictionary of World Religions*. Oxford: Oxford Univ. Press, 1997.

"FBI Investigating Reports Cult Runs Terrorist Camp." *Register* (Anaheim, Calif.) (Aug. 15, 1982), A26.

"India to Investigate Murders of Religious Sect Members." *New York Times* (May 5, 1982).

Lukas, Pam. "Ananda vs Jesus." (A personal testimony and refutation of Ananda by the author.)

Mather, Sharon (Research Consultant for Christian Research Institute). Letter to the author. (Sept. 19, 1983).

ANGLO-ISRAELISM, BRITISH-ISRAELISM

Allen, J. H. *Judah's Scepter and Joseph's Birthright*. 6th ed. Boston: Beauchamp, 1918.

Godbey, Allen H. *The Lost Tribes: A Myth—Suggestions Towards Rewriting Hebrew History*. Durham, N.C.: Duke Univ. Press, 1930.

Haggart, J. A. B. "Jack in the Beanstalk." *Kingdom Digest* 27/10 (Oct. 1977): 16–29.

Heydt, Henry J., "The Fallacy of British-Israelism." *The Chosen People* 68/8 (April, 1963): 14–16.

Martin, Walter R. *Kingdom of the Cults*. 2nd ed. Minneapolis: Bethany, 1977.

ANTHROPOSOPHICAL SOCIETY

"A Catalogue of Cults: Where They Stand on the Deity of Christ." *Moody* (July-August, 1979), 1.

Beredene, Jocelyn. *What Difference Did the Deed of Christ Make?* Hudson, N.Y.: Anthroposophic, 1979.

Bott, Victor. *Anthroposophical Medicine, Spiritual Science, and the Art of Healing*. Hudson, N.Y.: Anthroposophic, 1984.

Klocek, Dennis. *Knowledge, Teaching and the Death of the Mysterious*. Six lectures given at the West Coast Waldorf Teachers Conference, February 20–24, 2000. Fair Oaks, Calif.: Rudolf Steiner College Press, 2000.

Montgomery, John Warwick. *Principalities and Powers*. Minneapolis: Bethany, 1973.

Pailin, David A. *The Anthroposophical Character of Theology: Conditioning Theological Understanding*. Cambridge: Cambridge Univ. Press, 1990.

"Rudolf Steiner and the Anthroposophical Society." Reprint from *Spiritual Counterfeits Project Newsletter* (February 1977).

"Rudolf Steiner College: Anthroposophy, Theosophy and a Little Eurythmy, Too." *Sacramento Bee Community News North* (Feb. 18, 1981), G5.

Steiner, Rudolf. *Alchemy: The Evolution of the Mysteries. Selections from the Works of Rudolf Steiner*. Hudson, N.Y.: Anthroposophic Press, 2002.

_____. *Anthroposophy in Everyday Life*. Hudson, N.Y.: Anthroposophic Press, 1995.

_____. *The Christ Impulse and the Development of the Ego of Consciousness*. Spiritual Research Edition. Blauvelt, N.Y.: Garber Communications, 1991.

_____. *The Life between Death and Rebirth in Relation to Cosmic Facts*. Rev. ed. Spiritual Research Edition. Blauvelt, N.Y.: Garber Communications, 1991.

_____. *Man's Life on Earth and in the Spiritual Worlds*. Rev. ed. Spiritual Research Edition. Blauvelt, N.Y.: Garber Communications, 1991.

_____. *Supersensible Man*. Spiritual Research Edition. Blauvelt, N.Y.: Garber Communications, 1991.

_____. *From Jesus to Christ*. London: Rudolf Steiner Press, 1973.

ASSOCIATION FOR RESEARCH AND ENLIGHTENMENT—EDGAR CAYCE

"A Plodding Homage to Edgar Cayce." *Los Angeles Times* (March 5, 1984), part 6.

Bjornstadt, James. *Twentieth Century Prophecy—Jean Dixon; Edgar Cayce*. Minneapolis: Bethany, 1969.

Cayce, Edgar, et al. *A Search for God*. 2 vols. Virginia Beach, Va.: Association for Research and Enlightenment, 1968.

Cerminara, Gina. *Edgar Cayce Revisited*. Virginia Beach-Norfolk, Va.: Donning, 1983.

Drummond, Richard H. *Unto the Churches—Jesus Christ, Christianity, and the Edgar Cayce Readings*. Virginia Beach, Va.: Association for Research and Enlightenment, 1978.

Furst, Jeffrey. *Edgar Cayce's Story of Jesus*. New York: Coward-McCann, 1969.

"Interview: Lynn Sparrow." *Update, a Quarterly Journal on New Religious Movements* 7/1 (March 1983): 15–24.

Johnson, K. Paul. *Edgar Cayce in Context: The Readings*. Albany: State Univ. of New York Press. 1998.

Karp, Reba A. *Edgar Cayce Encyclopedia of Healing*. New York: Warner, 1988.

Kittler, Glen D. *Edgar Cayce on the Dead Sea Scrolls*. New York: Warner, 1988.

Langley, Noel. *Edgar Cayce on Reincarnation*. New York: Paperback Library, 1967.

Lucus, Phillip. 1995. "The Association for Research and Enlightenment: Saved by the New Age." Pages 353–61 in *America's Alternative Religions*. Ed. Timothy Miller. Albany: State Univ. of New York Press, 1995.

Melton, J. Gordon. "Edgar Cayce and Reincarnation: Past Life Readings as Religious Symbology." *Syzygy: Journal of Alternative Religion and Culture* 3 (1994). Reprinted online in *Journal of Cayce Studies*.

_____. "Edgar Cayce." *The Encyclopedia of American Religions*. 5th ed. (Detroit: Gale Research, 1996), 690–91.

Miller, Shane. *The Bible as a Handbook for Understanding Self*. Virginia Beach, Va.: A. R. E. Press, 1967.

Montgomery, John Warwick. *Principalities and Powers*. Minneapolis: Bethany, 1973.

Read, Anne. *Edgar Cayce on Jesus and His Church*. New York: Warner, 1988.

Reed, Henry. *Edgar Cayce on Channeling Your Higher Self*. New York: Warner, 1988.

"The Sleeping Prophet." *Update, a Quarterly Journal on New Religious Movements* 7/1 (March 1983): 12–14.

Smith, A. Robert. *Hugh Lynn Cayce: About My Father's Business: The Incredible Story of Edgar Cayce's Son*. Virginia Beach-Norfolk, Va.: Donning, 1988.

Stearn, Jess. *Edgar Cayce: The Sleeping Prophet*. New York: Doubleday, 1967.

Sugrue, Thomas. *There Is a River: The Story of Edgar Cayce*. Virginia Beach, Va.: A. R. E. Press, 1989.

Thurston, Mark. *Edgar Cayce's Millennium Prophecies: Predictions for the Coming Century from Edgar Cayce*. New York: Barnes & Noble, 1997.

Wilson, Colin. *The Occult: A History*. New York: Random House, 1971.

AUM SHINRIKYO

Bracket, David W. *Holy Terror: Armageddon in Tokyo*. Boston: Weatherhill, 1996.

Kaplan, David E., and Andrew Marshall. *The Cult at the End of the World: Aum Shinrikyo*. New York: Crown, 1996.

Leitenberg, Milton. "Aum Shinrikyo's Efforts to Produce Biological Weapons: A Case Study in the Serial Propagation of Misinformation." *Terrorism and Political Violence* 11 (Winter 1999): 149–58.

Lewis, James R., ed. *Syzygy: Journal of Alternative Religion and Culture*, 8 (January-February, 1999). 12 articles on AUM Shinrikyo.

Lifton, Robert J. *Destroying the World to Save It: Aum Shinrikyo, Apocalyptic Violence, and the New Global Terrorism*. New York: Metropolitan, 2000.

Metraux, Daniel A. *Aum Shinrikyo's Impact on Japanese Society*. Lewiston, N.Y.: Mellen, 2000.

Reader, Ian. *Religious Violence in Contemporary Japan: The Case of Aum Shinrikyo*. Richmond, U.K.: Curzon, 2000.

_____. *Scholarship, Aum Shinrikyo, and Academic Integrity*. Nova Religio, 2000.

Rosenau, Willem. "Aum Shinrikyo's Biological Weapons Program: Why Did it Fail?" *Studies in Conflict and Terrorism* 24 (July-August 2001), 289–93.

THE BAHA'I FAITH

Adamson, Hugh C. *Historical Dictionary of the Baha'i Faith*. Lanham, Md.: Scarecrow, 1998.

"A Catalogue of Cults: Where They Stand on the Deity of Christ." *Moody* (July-August 1979), 1.

Anonymous. *The Covenant and Administration*. Wilmette, Ill.: Baha'i Publishing Trust, 1971.

Anonymous. *Principles of the Baha'i Faith*. Wilmette, Ill.: Baha'i Publishing Trust, n.d.

Bahai Teachings: A Resurgent Model of the Universe. New York: Ronald, 1990.

Baha'u'llah. *Baha'i World Faith*. Wilmette, Ill: Baha'i Publishing Trust, 1971.

_____. *The Book of Certitude*. Wilmette, Ill.: Baha'i Publishing Trust, 1970.

_____. *The Proclamation of Baha'u'llah*. Haifa, Israel: Baha'i Publishing Trust, 1967.

_____. *The Seven Valleys*. Trans. Ali Kuli Khan, Chicago: Baha'i Publishing Trust, 1906.

_____. *The Seven Valleys and the Four Valleys*. Trans. Ali Kuli Kahn. New York: Baha'i Publishing Trust, 1936.

_____. *Three Tablets of Baha'u'llah*. Chicago: Baha'i Publishing Trust, 1918.

Baha'u'llah, and Abdul Baha. *Baha'i Scriptures*. New York: Baha'i Publishing Trust, 1928.

Balch, Robert W., et al. "Fifteen Years of Failed Prophecy: Coping with Cognitive Dissonance in a Baha'i Sect." Pages 73–90 in *Millennium, Messiahs, and Mayhem*. Ed. Thomas Robbins and Susan J. Palmer. New York: Routledge, 1997.

Bowers, Kenneth. *God Speaks Again: An Introduction to the Baha'i Faith*. Wilmette, Ill.: Baha'i Publishing Trust, 2004.

Cole, Juan, "The Baha Is of Iran." *History Today* (March 1990).

_____. *Modernity and the Millennium*. New York: Columbia Univ. Press. 1998.

Collins, William P. *Bibliography of English Language Works on the Babi and Baha'i Faiths 1844–1985*. New York: Ronald, 1991.

Effendi Shoghi. *The Advent of Divine Justice*. Wilmette, Ill.: Baha'i Publishing Trust, 1972.

_____. *Baha'i Administration*. Wilmette, Ill.: Baha'i Publishing Trust, 1968.

_____. *Citadel of Faith*. Wilmette, Ill: Baha'i Publishing Trust, 1970.

_____. *The Faith of Baha'u'llah*. Wilmette, Ill.: Baha'i Publishing Trust, 1971.

_____. *God Passes By*. Wilmette, Ill.: Baha'i Publishing Trust, 1970.

_____. *Messages to America*. Wilmette, Ill: Baha'i Publishing Trust, 1970.

_____. *Messages to the Baha'i World*. Wilmette, Ill.: Baha'i Publishing Trust, 1970.

_____. *The Promised Day is Come*. Wilmette, Ill.: Baha'i Publishing Trust, 1967.

_____. *The World Order of Baha'u'llah*. New York: Knopf, 1932.

Esslemont, J. E. *Baha'u'llah and the New Era*. 1923. Reprint. Wilmette, Ill.: Baha'i Publishing Trust, 1970.

Hatcher, William S. *Baha'i Faith, The Emerging Global Religion*. New York: HarperCollins, 1990.

_____. *The Baha'i Faith*. Wilmette, Ill.: Baha'i Distribution Service, 1998.

Maneck, Susan Stiles. "Women in the Baha'i Faith." *Religion and Women* (1994), 211–27.

McGlinn, Sen. "A Theology of the State from the Baha'i Teachings," *Journal of Church and State* 41 (Autumn 1999), 697–724.

Miller, William McElwee. *The Baha'i Faith: Its History and Teachings*. South Pasadena, Calif.: William Carey Library, 1974.

_____. *What Is the Baha'i Faith?* Grand Rapids: Eerdmans, 1978.

_____. *What Is the Baha'i World Faith?* (Booklet.) Santa Ana, Calif.: CARIS, 1976.

Sears, William. *Release the Sun: An Early History of the Baha'i Faith*. Reprint. Willmette, Ill.: Baha'i Publishing, 2003.

Sours, Michael. *A Study of Baha'u'llah's Tablet to the Christians*. Oxford, U.K.: Oneworld, 1990.

BHAGWAN SHREE RAJNEESH

Abbott, Carl. "Utopia and Bureaucracy: The Fall of Rajneeshpurum, Oregon." *Pacific Historical Review* (February 1990): 77.

"Asiatic Religions in Europe." *Update* 7, no. 2 (June 1983).

"Busting the Bhagwan." *Newsweek* (Nov. 11, 1985), 32.

"'God Sir' at Esalen East." *Time* (Jan. 16, 1978), 59.

"Goodbye Guru." *Newsweek* (Nov. 25, 1985), 50.

Gordon, James S. "The Cult Leaders: How Absolute Power Corrupts." *Utne Reader* (March-April 1989), 136.

_____. *The Golden Guru.* New York: Viking-Penguin, 1988.

"Last Rajneesh Commune Closed." *Blade Tribune* (Oct. 20, 1986), 8.

Mano, Keith D. "Dinner on Rajneesh." *National Review* (April 7, 1989).

Rajneesh, Bhagwan Shree. *The Mustard Seed.* San Francisco: Harper & Row, 1975.

_____. *Words Like Fire.* San Francisco: Harper & Row, 1976.

"Sins of Bhagwan." *India Today* (June 1982), 135.

BRANCH DAVIDIANS

Anthony, Dick, and Thomas Robbins. "Religious Totalism, Violence, and Exemplary Dualism." *Terrorism and Political Violence* 7 (1995): 10–50.

Houteff, Victor. *The Great Controversy over "The Shepherd's Rod."* Waco, Tex.: Universal Publishing, 1954.

Lewis, James R., ed. *From the Ashes: Making Sense of Waco.* Lanham, Md.: Rowman & Littlefield, 1994.

Moore, Carol. *The Davidian Massacre.* Franklin, Tenn.: Legacy Communications, 1995.

Reavis, Dick J. *The Ashes of Waco.* New York: Simon & Schuster, 1995.

Tabor, James D., and Eugene V. Gallagher. *Why Waco? Cults and the Battle for Religious Freedom in America.* Berkeley, Calif.: Univ. of California Press, 1995.

Thibodeau, David. *A Place Called Waco: A Survivor's Story.* New York: Public Affairs, 1999.

Wright, Stuart A., ed. *Armageddon in Waco: Critical Perspective on the Branch Davidian Conflict.* Chicago: Univ. of Chicago Press. 1995.

BRANHAMISM

Branham, William M. *Conduct, Order, Doctrine of the Church.* Jeffersonville, Ind.: Spoken Word, 1973.

_____. *Marriage and Divorce.* Vol. 3, No. 13 of The Spoken Word. Jeffersonville Jeffersonville, Ind.: Spoken Word, 1965.

_____. *Questions and Answers.* Jeffersonville, Ind.: Spoken Word, 1961.

_____. *Restoration of the Bride Tree.* Vol. 3, No. 15 of The Spoken Word. Jeffersonville Jeffersonville, Ind.: Spoken Word, 1982.

_____. *The Spoken Word.* Jeffersonville, Ind.: Spoken Word, 1972.

_____. *The Uniting Time and Sign.* Vol. 6, No. 10 of The Spoken Word. Jeffersonville, Ind.: Spoken Word, 1963.

Harrel, Ed, and C. Douglas Weaver. *The Healer-Prophet William Marion Branham: A Study of the Prophetic in American Pentecostalism.* Macon, Ga.: Mercer Univ. Press, 2000.

Jorgenson, Owen. *Supernatural: The Life of William Branham.* Tuscon, Ariz.: Tuscon Tabernacle, 1994.

The Lord God Hath Spoken. Sound recordings of the beliefs and prophecies of William Branham, Jeffersonville, Ind., n.d.

Stadsklev, Julius. *William Branham: A Prophet Visits South Africa.* Minneapolis, Minn.: n.p., 1952.

Wilson, D. J. "William Marion Branham." Pages 95–97 in *Dictionary of Pentecostal and Charismatic Movements.* Ed. Stanley M. Burgess and Gary B. McGee. Grand Rapids: Zondervan, 1988.

BUDDHISM: THERAVADA, ZEN, SOKA GAKKAI, MAHAYANA

Baker-Roshi, Richard. *Original Mind: The Practice of Zen in the West.* New York: Riverhead/Penguin, 2005.

Barrett, T. H. *Li Ao: Buddhist, Taoist, or Neo-Confucian.* New York: Oxford Univ. Press, 1991.

Bloteld, John. *Taoism: The Road to Immortality.* Boston: Shambhala, 1979.

Cadge, Wendy. *Heartwood: The 1st Generation of Therevada Buddhism in America.* Chicago: Univ. of Chicago Press, 2004.

Conze, Edward. *Buddhism: Its Essence and Development.* New York: Harper & Row, 1959.

Coonmarswamy, Ananda K. *Hinduism and Buddhism.* New York: Philosophical Library, n.d.

Delfs, Robert. "Priestly Putsch." *Far Eastern Economics Review* (July 1991), 16.

"Demons and Divinities." *Newsweek* (Sept. 20, 1982), 83–84.

Eliot, Charles. *Japanese Buddhism.* New York: Barnes & Noble, 1935.

Ellwood, Robert. *The Eagle and the Rising Sun.* Philadelphia: Westminster, 1974.

Flagler, J. M. "A Chanting in Japan." *New York Times* (Nov. 26, 1966), 152.

Gard, Charles Eliot. *Buddhism.* Englewood Cliffs, N.J.: Prentice-Hall, 1961.

"The God-Kings Visit." *Newsweek* (Sept. 17, 1979), 115.

Guruge, Ananda W. P. "A Golden Age." *UNESCO Courier* of Lanham, Md. (February 1991), 25.

Hawk, Patrick. "The Pathless Path." *Catholic World* (May-June 1990), 129.

Hickey, Shannon. "Chanting for Clout: The NSA Wants Inner Peace and Politicians." *Nichiren Shoshu Soka Gakkai, New West-San Francisco* (February 1990), 14.

"The Hidden Kingdom of Shambhala." *Natural History* (April 1983), 51–62.

"I Am a Human Being: A Monk." *Time* (Sept. 17, 1979), 96.

Ikeda, Daisaku. *Buddhism: The Living Philosophy.* Tokyo: East Publication, 1974.

Jackson, Peter A. *Buddhadasa: Theravada Buddhisim and Modernist Reform in Thailand.* Thailand: Silkworm Books, 2003.

Kotler, Arnold. ed. *Engaged Buddhist Reader.* Berkeley, Calif.: Parallax, 1996.

Küng, Hans, Josef van Ess, Heinrich von Steitencron, and Heinz Bechert. *Christianity and the World Religions: Paths to Dialogue with Islam, Hinduism, and Buddhism.* Translated by Peter Heinegg. Garden City, N.Y.: Doubleday, 1986.

Latourette, Kenneth Scott. *Introducing Buddhism.* New York: Friendship Press, 1963.

Masaharu, Anesaki. *History of Japanese Religion.* Rutland, Vt.: Tuttle, 1963.

Morgan, Kenneth W., ed. *The Path of Buddha.* New York: Ronald, 1956.

Murata, K. *Japan's New Buddhism.* New York: Weatherhill, 1969.

"Narita Stopover a Bonus in Japan." *Los Angeles Times* (Mar. 21, 1983), part 8.

"No. 15 Thailand Report: Christian Witness to Buddhist." *Let the Earth Hear His Voice: Lausanne Occasional Papers.* Lausanne: Lausanne Committee for World Evangelization, 1980.

Okamoto, Richard. "Japan." *Look Magazine* (Sept. 10, 1963), 16.

"The One Man Who Can Save a Nation." *Parade Magazine* (Mar. 4, 1984), 11.

Percheron, Maurice. *Buddha and Buddhism.* New York: Harper & Row, 1957.

Pratt, J. B. *The Pilgrimage of Buddhism.* New York: Macmillan, 1928.

Reishauer, A. K. *Studies in Japanese Buddhism.* New York: Macmillan, 1917.

Reuther, Rosemary Radford. "America Putting Own Brand on Buddhism." *National Catholic Reporter* (June 1989), 15.

Ringgren, Helmer, and Ake V. Strom. *Religions of Mankind.* Philadelphia: Fortress, 1967.

Seager, Richard Hughes. *Buddhism in America.* New York: Columbia Univ. Press, 1999.

Sedika, Katsuki. *Zen Training: Methods and Philosophy.* Boston: Shambhala, 2005.

Short, Stephen H. "Zen and the Act of Not Knowing God." *Christian Research Journal* (Winter-Spring 1990), 21–26.

Smith, Jean, ed. *Radiant Mind.* New York: Riverhead/Penguin, 1999.

Smith, Charles. "Throwing Dirt at Mr. Clean: Party Rebels Denounce Convert Control by Buddhist Sect." *Far Eastern Economic Review* (June 1988), 32.

Smith, Huston. *The Religions of Man.* New York: Harper & Row, 1958.

Snelling, John. *A Buddhist Handbook.* Rochester, Vt.: Inner Traditions International, 1991.

Suzuki, Daisetz T. *The Essence of Buddhism.* New York: International Publication Service, 1969.

_____. *Mahayana Buddhism.* San Francisco: Mandala, 1991.

Suzuki, Shunryo. *Zen Mind, Beginners Mind.* Boston: Shambhala, 2005.

Tambiah, S. J. *Buddhism and the Spirit Cults in Northern Thailand.* Cambridge: Cambridge Univ. Press, 1970.

Thomas, Edward J. *The Life of Buddha as Legend and History.* New York: Barnes & Noble, 1956.

Tibetan Cultural Resources in North America. 3d ed., updated and expanded. New York: Himalayas Council of the Asia Society, 1979.

Williams, Paul. *Mahayana Buddhism: The Doctrinal Foundations.* New York: Routledge, 1989.

"Zen Cultists Practice Their Discipline on Mt. Baldy." *Los Angeles Times* (July 25, 1982), part 8.

CABILDO

Daz, Arlene J. *Female Citizens, Patriarchs, and the Law in Venezuela, 1786–1904.* Lincoln: Univ. of Nebraska Press, 2004.

CANDOMBLE

Johnson, Paul Christopher. *Secrets, Gossip, and Gods.* New York: Oxford Univ. Press, 2002.

CHILDREN OF GOD, FAMILY OF LOVE

"A Catalogue of Cults: Where They Stand on the Deity of Christ." *Moody* (July-August 1979), 2.

Bainbridge, William S. *The Endtime Family: Children of God.* Albany: State Univ. of New York Press. 2002.

Berg, David Brant (Moses). *Alexander the Evil Magician.* Rome: Family of Love, 1978.

_____. *The Basic Mo Letters.* Hong Kong: Children of God, 1976.

_____. *Communicant.* Rome: Children of God, 1977.

_____. *The Crystal Pyramid.* Dallas: Children of God, 1973.

_____. *Death in Your Arms!* Rome: Family of Love, 1976.

_____. *Do You Want a Penis?—Or a Sword?* Rome: Children of God, 1976.

_____. *The Elixir of Love!* Rome: Family of Love, 1976.

_____. *The Fan.* Rome: Children of God, 1975.

_____. *The FF Revolution.* Rome: Children of God, 1976.

_____. *FF-ers Handbook!—Condensed Selected Quotes From More Than 50 FF Letters.* Ed. Justice Ashtree. Rome: Children of God, 1977.

_____. *Flying Saucers! UFO's! Spiritual Vehicles.* Rome: Children of God, 1973.

_____. *God's Whore.* Rome: Children of God, 1976.

_____. *Grace vs. Law.* Rome: Children of God, 1977.

_____. *He Stands in the Gap.* London: Children of God, 1971.

_____. *Married to Jesus.* London: Children of God, 1973.

_____. *More Truth.* Rome: Children of God, 1977.

_____. *"One Wife." Leaders Book.* London: Children of God, 1974.

_____. *The Shepherd's Rod.* Rome: Family of Love, 1978.

_____. *Snowman.* London: Children of God, 1972.

_____. *The Spirit World.* Rome: Children of God, 1977.

_____. *Teamwork!—The Gaffers!—Mo FF Tips!* Rome: Children of God, 1976.

_____. *Winning the System.* Rome: Children of God, 1976.

_____. *The Word—New and Old (Matt. 13:52).* London: Children of God, 1974.

_____. *The Wrath of God!* Rome: Children of God, 1977.

"Ex-Children of God 'Queen' Tells Story." *Eternity* (January 1983), 10.

Gibbons, Brian J. *Gender in Mystical and Occult Thought.* Cambridge: Cambridge Univ. Press, 2003.

Lynch, Dalva, and Paul Carden. "Inside the Heavenly Elite: The Children of God Today." *Christian Journal* (Summer 1990), 19.

Martin, Walter. *The New Cults.* Ventura, Calif.: Regal, 1980

Melton, J. Gordon. *The Children of God, "The Family."* Signature Books, 2004.

Moriconi, John. *Children of God, Family of Love.* Downer's Grove, Ill.: InterVarsity Press, 1980.

Van Zandt, David E. *Living in the Children of God.* Princeton, N.J.: Princeton Univ. Press, 1991.

CHRISTADELPHIANISM

An Appeal to Roman Catholics. Brighouse, Eng.: Kirklees, n.d.

Christadelphians Bible Study Circle. Letters 1–24. Birmingham, Eng.: Christadelphian, n.d.

Foster, Douglas A., Paul M. Blowers, Anthony L. Dunnavant, and D. Newell Williams, eds. *The Encyclopedia of the Stone-Campbell Movement.* Grand Rapids: Eerdmans, 2005.

Norris, Alfred. *Being Born Again.* Yorkshire, Eng.: Aletheia, 1967.

_____. *Believing the Bible.* Yorkshire, Eng.: Aletheia, 1967.

_____. *The Gospel of the Kingdom of God.* Yorkshire, Eng.: Aletheia, 1967.

_____. *On Reading the Bible.* Yorkshire, Eng.: Aletheia, 1967.

_____. *The Resurrection of Christ.* Brighouse, Eng.: Kirklees, n.d.

_____. *The Things We Stand For.* Yorkshire, Eng.: Aletheia, 1967.

_____. *Understanding the Bible.* Yorkshire, Eng.: Aletheia, 1967.

_____. *The Virgin Birth of the Son of God.* Brighouse, Eng.: Kirklees, n.d.

Williams, D. Newell. *Barton Stone: A Spiritual Biography.* Atlanta: Chalice, 2000.

Wilson, Bryan R. *Sects and Society.* Berkeley and Los Angeles: Univ. of California Press, 1961.

CHRISTIAN IDENTITY MOVEMENTS

Aho, James A. *The Politics of Righteousness: Idaho Christian Patriotism*. Seattle: Univ. of Washington Press, 1990.

"A Light for the White Race." *Times News* (Twin Falls Idaho) (Jan. 3, 1983), A1.

America's Promise Newsletter. Lord's Covenant Church. Various issues.

"The Angel of Auschwitz." *Time* (Oct. 25, 1982), 57.

Appiah, Kwame Anthony. *The Ethics of Identity*. Princeton, N.J.: Princeton Univ. Press, 2005.

Ballot-Box Bigotry: David Duke and the Populist Party. Atlanta: Center for Democratic Renewal, 1989.

Barkun, Michael. *Religion and the Racist Right: The Origins of the Christian Identity Movement*. Chapel Hill: Univ. of North Carolina Press, 1996.

Becker, Verne. "The Counterfeit Christianity of the Ku Klux Klan." *Christianity Today* (Apr. 20, 1985), 30–35.

Blee, Kathleen M. *Women of the Klan: Racism and Gender in the 1920s*. Berkeley: Univ. of California Press, 1991.

Brandon, Lewis (Director of Institute for Historical Review). Letter to the author, n.d.

Bushart, Howard L., John R. Craig, and Myra Edwards Barnes. *Soldiers of God: White Supremacists and Their Holy War for America*. New York: Kensington, 2000.

Cassutto, Ernest H. *A Protest against Anti-Semitism*. New York: Reformed Church in America (Board of Domestic Missions), n.d.

"CBS Looks at Black Americans." *Newsweek* (July 30, 1979), 77.

Cell, John W. *The Highest Stage of White Supremacy: The Origins of Segregation in South Africa and the American South*. Cambridge: Cambridge Univ. Press, 1982.

"Crews Look for Clues to Idaho Bombings." *San Jose Mercury News* (San Jose, Calif.) (Oct. 1, 1986), 6A.

Eaton, Richard (Research Department, Simon Wiesenthal Center). Letter to the author (March 12, 1987).

Emry, Sheldon. "Lord's Covenant Church: Preaching the Kingdom-Identity Message." Various newsletters.

Ewing, Curtis Clair. *A Study into the Meaning of the Word "Gentile" as Used in the Bible*. Reprint. America's Promise, n.d.

"FBI's Spy in Klan Linked to Violence." *Los Angeles Times* (Oct. 31, 1982), part 1.

"Five White Supremacists Get Long Prison Terms." *Los Angeles Times* (Feb. 7, 1986), part 1.

Flynn, Kevin. *The Silent Brotherhood: Inside America's Racist Underground*. New York: Free Press, 1989.

Frederickson, George M. *White Supremacy: A Comparative Study in American and South African History*. New York: Oxford Univ. Press, 1981.

Gaebelein, Frank E., ed. *A Christianity Today Reader*. New York: Meredith Press, n.d.

"Home Brew (White Supremacists: Terrorism)." *The Nation* (July 16, 1990), 75.

George, John, and Laird Wilcox. *American Extremists: Militias, Supremacists, Klansmen, Communists and Others*. New York: Prometheus Books, 1996.

Goldberg, Robert Alan. *Enemies Within: The Culture of Conspiracy in Modern America*. New Haven, Conn.: Yale Univ. Press, 2001.

"Identity Exposed." *Cult Awareness Network News* (April 1986), 4.

Jenkins, William D. *Steel Valley Klan: Ku Klux Klan in Ohio's Mahoning Valley*. Kent, Ohio: Kent State Univ. Press, 1990.

The Jews and Their Lies. Los Angeles: Christian National Crusade, 1948.

Kaplan, Jeffrey. *Encyclopedia of White Power: A Sourcebook on the Radical Racist Right*. Lanhan, Md.: Altamira Press, 2000.

Kennedy, Stetson. *The Klan Unmasked*. Boca Raton, Fl.: Florida Atlantic Univ. Press, 1990.

"Kill to Get In, Die to Get Out." *Register* (Anaheim, Calif.) (Nov. 18, 1981), F4.

"KKK Group, Anti-Klan Demonstrators Face Off." *Los Angeles Times* (June 30, 1986), part 1.

"The KKK Tries To Rise Again." *Newsweek* (June 18, 1979), 31.

"Klansmen Guarded." *Detroit Free Press* (Sept. 27, 1982), 8D.

Langer, Elinor, "The American Neo-Nazi Movement Today." *The Nation* (July 1990), 82.

Lay, Shawn, ed. *The Invisible Empire in the West: Toward a New Appraisal of the Ku Klux Klan of the 1920s*. Urbana: Univ. of Illinois Press, 1992.

Levitas, Daniel, *The Terrorist Next Door*. New York: St. Martins, 2002.

Lovell, Vada. "What We Believe." *Kingdom Digest* 27/10 (October 1977).

Lutholtz, M. William. *Grand Dragon: D. C. Stephenson and the Ku Klux Klan in Indiana.* West Lafayette, Ind.: Purdue Univ. Press, 1991.

"Lexis Nexis." *Seattle Times* (Apr. 17, 1983), 6–15.

"Lynching or Suicide? A City Is Gripped By Tension." *Los Angeles Times* (Feb. 11, 1986), part 2.

Marshall, Marilyn. "Beulah Mae Donald: The Black Woman Who Beat the Ku Klux Klan." *Ebony* (March 1988), 148.

Mohr, Jack. "Are You a Brainwashed Christian?" *America's Trojan Horse*, n.d.

_____. *The Christian Patriot Crusader.* Various issues.

_____. *Naked Aggression: The Next Government Victim Could Be You.* Published at 113 Ballentine St., St. Louis, MO 39520.

Moore, Leonard J. *Citizen Klansmen: The Ku Klux Klan in Indiana, 1921–28.* Chapel Hill: Univ. of North Carolina Press, 1991.

"New Furor over an Old Informant." *Time* (July 24, 1978), 17.

Newton, Michael. *The Ku Klux Klan: An Encyclopedia.* New York: Garland, 1991.

Oakley, Andy. *"88": An Undercover News Reporter's Expose of America's Nazis and the Ku Klux Klan.* Skokie, Ill.: P.O. Publishing, 1987.

"Posse: Ultraright Group Sees Self as 'True Hebrews.'" *Los Angeles Times* (Aug. 17, 1983), part 1.

Ridgeway, James. *Blood in the Face: The Ku Klux Klan, Aryan Nations, Nazi Skinheads, and the Rise of a New White Culture.* New York: Thunder Mountain, 1990.

Roberts, Charles H. *Race over Grace: The Racialist Religion of the Christian Identity Movement.* Lincoln, Neb.: iUniverse, 2003.

Robin, Martin. *Shades of Night: Nativist and Fascist Politics in Canada, 1920–40.* Toronto: Univ. of Toronto Press, 1992.

Rose, Douglas D., ed. *The Emergence of David Duke and the Politics of Race.* Chapel Hill: Univ. of North Carolina Press, 1992.

Rosen, Rebecca. "Redwoods and the Right." *The Progressive* (September 1990), 33.

"The Silence of the Jews." *Harper's Magazine* (November 1988), 20–23.

The Spotlight (Liberty Lobby Weekly Newspaper). Various issues.

Stanton, Bill. *Klanwatch: Bringing the Ku Klux Klan to Justice.* New York: Weidenfeld, 1991.

Stern, Kenneth S. *A Force upon the Plain: The American Militia Movement and the Politics of Hate.* New York: Simon and Schuster, 1996.

Swall, Irwin. *The KKK Today: A 1991 Status Report.* New York: Anti-Defamation League of the B'nai Brith, 1991.

"Stop Being Part of the Problem, Become Part of the Solution." Information about beliefs, taken from an application for membership to join the "Knights of the Ku Klux Klan" (Box 1, Metairie, LA 70004).

Tucker, Richard K. *The Dragon and the Cross: The Rise and Fall of the Ku Klux Klan in Middle America.* Hamden, Conn.: Archon, 1991.

WAR '84, White American Resistance. Various issues.

Watts, Tim J. *Politics of Hate: White Extremist Groups in the 1980s: A Bibliography.* Monticello, Ill.: Vance Bibliographies, 1989.

"When the Cross: Recent Violence against Jews Emphasize that Anti-Semitism Is Not Limited to Ridicule." *Moody* (February 1984), 70–72.

Williamson, Clark M. *Has God Rejected His People? Anti-Judaism in the Christian Church.* Nashville: Abingdon, 1982.

Wise, James E. *The Seed and the Serpent.* Harrison, Ark.: Message of Old Publications, n.d.

Zatarin, Michael. *David Duke: Evolution of a Klansman.* Gretna, La.: Pelican, 1990.

Zia, Helen. "Women in Hate Groups." *Ms. Magazine* (March–April 1991), 20.

CHRIST THE SAVIOR BROTHERHOOD

Gerjevic, Sandi. "A Saint's Subjects." *Anchorage Daily News* (Feb. 1, 1999).

Lucas, Phillip. *The Odyssey of a New Religion.* Indianapolis: Indiana Univ. Press, 1995.

CHRISTIANITY

Althaus, Paul. *The Theology of Martin Luther.* Translated by Robert C. Schultz. Philadelphia: Fortress, 1966.

Bainton, Roland. *Here I Stand: A Life of Martin Luther.* Nashville: Abingdon, 1950.

Barr, James. *Fundamentalism.* Philadelphia: Westminster, 1977.

Barraclough, Geoffrey. *The Medieval Papacy.* New York: Norton, 1968.

Brown, Peter. *Augustine of Hippo.* Berkeley: Univ. of California Press, 1967.

Burgess, Stanley M., and Eduard M. van der Maas, eds. *The New International Dictionary of Pentecostal and Charismatic Movements.* Revised and expanded ed. Grand Rapids: Zondervan, 2002.

Cantor, Norman F. *Medieval History: The Life and Death of a Civilization.* 2d. ed. London and New York: Macmillan, 1969.

Chadwick, Henry. *The Early Church.* New York: Penguin, 1967.

Cross, F. L., and E. A. Livingstone, eds. *The Oxford Dictionary of the Christian Church.* 3rd ed. London: Oxford Univ. Press, 1997.

Deanesly, Margaret. *A History of the Medieval Church.* Reprint. London: Methuen, 1978 (orig. 1925).

Dowley, Tim, J. H. Y. Briggs, Robert Dean Linder, and David F. Wright, eds. *Introduction to the History of Christianity.* Minneapolis: Augsburg Fortress, 2002.

Eadie, John, ed. *The Conversion of Constantine.* Huntington, N.Y.: Kroeger, 1977.

Fox, Robin Lane. *Pagans and Christians.* New York: Knopf, 1987.

Kelly, J. N. D. *Early Christian Creeds.* New York: Longman, 1960.

_____. *Early Christian Doctrines.* San Francisco: Harper & Row, 1960.

Kenyon, Sir Frederic. *Our Bible and the Ancient Manuscripts.* New York: Harper & Row, 1958.

Kittelson, James. *Luther the Reformer: The Study of the Man and His Career.* Minneapolis: Augsburg, 1986.

Latourette, Kenneth Scott. *A History of the Expansion of Christianity.* 7 vols. New York: Harper Brothers, 1937–45.

Letis, Theodore C., ed. *The Majority Text: Essays and Reviews in the Continuing Debate.* Fort Wayne, Ind.: Institute for Reformation Biblical Studies, 1987.

Livingstone, James C. *Modern Christian Thought: From the Enlightenment to Vatican II.* New York: Macmillan, 1971.

McNeill, John T. *The History and Character of Calvinism.* London: Oxford Univ. Press, 1954.

Melton, J. Gordon. *Encyclopedia of American Religions.* 5th ed. Detroit: Gale Research, 2002.

Neuhaus, Richard John. *The Catholic Moment.* San Francisco: Harper & Row, 1987.

Niesel, Wilhelm. *The Theology of Calvin.* Translated Harold Knight. Grand Rapids: Baker, 1980.

Nystrom, Bradley M., and David P. Nystrom. *The History of Christianity: An Introduction.* New York: McGraw-Hill, 2003.

Oberman, Heiko. *Forerunners of the Reformation: The Shape of Late Medieval Thought.* Philadelphia: Fortress, 1966.

_____. *The Harvest of Late Medieval Theology.* Durham, N.C.: Labyrinth, 1983.

Ozment, Steven. *The Age of Reform 1250–1550.* New Haven, Conn.: Yale Univ. Press, 1980.

Packer, J. I. *Fundamentalism and the Word of God.* Grand Rapids: Eerdmans, 1977.

Pelikan, Jaroslav. *The Christian Tradition: A History of the Development of Doctrine.* 5 vols. Chicago: Univ. of Chicago Press, 1975–89.

_____. *Jesus through the Centuries: His Place in the History of Culture.* New Haven, Conn.: Yale Univ. Press, 1987.

Piepkorn, Arthur C. *Profiles in Belief: The Religious Bodies of the United States and Canada.* New York: Harper & Row, 1977.

Schmidt, Alvin J. *How Christianity Changed the World.* Grand Rapids: Zondervan, 2004.

Seeberg, Reinhold. *The History of Doctrines.* 2 vols. Trans. Charles E. Hay. Grand Rapids: Baker, 1983.

Van Til, Cornelius. *Christianity and Barthianism.* Nutley, N.J.: Presbyterian & Reformed, 1977.

CHRISTIAN SCIENCE

Ahlstrom, Sydney. *A Religious History of the American People.* 2 vols. New York: Image, 1975.

"Attack on Mother Church." *Time* (Mar. 15, 1976), 44.

Bancroft, Samuel Putnam. *Mrs. Eddy as I Knew Her in 1870.* Boston: Geo. H. Ellis, 1923.

Bates, Ernest Sutherland, and John V. Dittemore. *Mary Baker Eddy: The Truth and the Tradition.* New York: Knopf, 1932.

Beasley, Norman. *The Cross and the Crown: The History of Christian Science.* New York: Duell, Sloan, & Pearce, 1952, 1963.

"Christian Science Church: Keeping a Low Profile." *Medical World News* (January 1984), 23.

"Christian Science Dispute." *Los Angeles Times* (Oct. 31, 1976), parts 2, 5.

"Christian Science Lecture on Family Set." *Ft. Wayne Sentinel* (Ft. Wayne, Ind.) (Mar. 27, 1987), 7D.

"Christian Science May Face Charges in Son's Meningitis Death." *Los Angeles Times* (Mar. 31, 1984), A9.

Christian Science Monitor (Daily Newspaper). 1908–present.

Christian Science Quarterly. 1884–present.

Christian Science Sentinel. 1908–present.

"Christian Science Sued over Boy's Body." *Detroit Free Press* (Feb. 6, 1980).

"Christian Scientist Charged in Death." *Sacramento Union* (Sacramento, Calif.) (Mar. 31, 1984).

"Christian Scientists Elect Paris as President." *Boston Globe* (Boston, Mass.) (June 9, 1981), 31.

"Christian Scientist's Strong Conviction." *Boston Globe* (Boston, Mass.) (June 14, 1981), 9.

A Complete Concordance to Science and Health with Key to the Scriptures. Boston: Christian Science, 1936.

A Complete Concordance to the Writings of Mary Baker Eddy Other Than Science and Health. Boston: Christian Science, 1936.

"Church Stands by Firing 2 Gays." *Boston Globe* (Boston, Mass.) (June 9, 1982), 45.

Dakin, Edwin Franden. *Mrs. Eddy*. New York: Scribner, 1929.

Dresser, Horatio W. *The Quimby Manuscripts*. 1st ed. New York: Crowell, 1921.

Eddy, Mary Baker. *Christ and Christmas*. Boston: Christian Science, 1907.

_____. *Christian Healing*. Boston: Christian Science, 1936.

_____. *Christian Science versus Pantheism*. Boston: New Trustees (under the will of Mary Baker Eddy), 1926.

_____. *Facts about Christian Science*. Boston: Christian Science, 1958.

_____. *The First Church of Christ Scientist and Miscellany*. Boston: Christian Science, 1941.

_____. *Manual of the Mother Church*. Boston: New Trustees (under the will of Mary Baker Eddy), 1904.

_____. *Miscellaneous Writings*. Boston: Christian Science, 1896.

_____. *No and Yes*. Boston: Christian Science, 1936.

_____. *The People's Idea of God*. Boston: New Trustees (under the will of Mary Baker Eddy), 1936.

_____. *Questions and Answers on Christian Science*. Boston: Christian Science, 1974.

_____. *Retrospection and Introspection*. Boston: Christian Science, 1935.

_____. *Rudimental Divine Science*. Boston: New Trustees (under the will of Mary Baker Eddy), 1936.

_____. *Science and Health with Key to the Scriptures*. Boston: Christian Science, 1875.

_____. *What Makes Christian Science Christian*. Boston: Christian Science, 1982.

Ehrenborg, Todd. *Mind Sciences: Christian Science, Religious Science, Unity School of Christianity*. Grand Rapids: Zondervan, 1995.

Eustace, Herbert W. *Christian Science: Its "Clear Correct Teaching" and Complete Writings*. Berkeley, Calif.: Eustace, 1985.

Fraser, Caroline. *God's Perfect Child: Living in and Dying in the Christian Science Church*. New York: Metropolitan Books/Henry Holt, 1999.

Haldeman, Isaac Massey. *Christian Science in the Light of Holy Scripture*. New York: Revell, 1909.

Haushalter, Walter M. *Mrs. Eddy Purloins from Hagel*. Boston: Beauchamp, 1936.

Hoekema, Anthony A. *Christian Science*. Grand Rapids: Eerdmans, 1974.

Johnson, Thomas C. "Historical Consensus and Christian Science: The Career of a Manuscript Controversy." *New England Quarterly* 53/1 (March 1980).

Johnston, Julia Michael. *Mary Baker Eddy: Her Mission and Triumph*. Boston: Christian Science, 1946.

Maclean, W. Gordon. "The Ministry of Healing." *Presbyterian Record* (December 1958), 10–11, 30.

Martin, Walter R. *Christian Science* (booklet). Minneapolis: Bethany, 1974.

"Medical Payments Cover Insured Christian Scientists." *The Forum* (September 1959), 14.

"Mixed Bill of Health in Centennial Checkup." *Christianity Today* (July 20, 1979), 36–37.

"Mom Charged in Daughter's Fatal Illness." *Sacramento Union* (Sacramento, Calif.) (Mar. 22, 1984), B1.

"Mother Church of Christian Science Facing Legal Challenge of Its Power." *New York Times* (Aug. 12, 1982).

"Mother of Dead Child Surrenders to Sheriffs." *Sacramento Union* (Sacramento, Calif.) (Mar. 23, 1984).

"The Myth of Mother Eddy." *Eternity* (January 1955), 14–15, 39–41.

"Neglect versus Creed." *The Economist* (July 1990), 31.

"Nursing the Faith." *Newsweek* (June 21, 1976), 87.

Ostling, Richard N. "Tumult in the Reading Rooms." *Time* (Oct. 14, 1991), 57.

Peabody, Frederick W. *The Religio-Medical Masquerade.* New York: Revell, 1910.

Peel, Robert, "Christian Science: What Is It?" *Christian Herald* (May 1960), 28–30, 79–80.

_____. "Christian Science: Cult for the Cultured." *Moody* (October 1981), 28–31.

Powell, Lyman P. *Christian Science: The Faith and Its Founder.* New York: Putnam, 1908.

Ramsey, E. Mary. *Christian Science and Its Discovery.* Boston: Christian Science, 1935.

Robins, Pam, and Whitson Robley. "Mary Baker Eddy's Christian Science." *Sign* (July-August 1980), 17–21.

Seal, Frances T. *How Christian Science Came to Germany.* Palm Springs, Calif.: Tree of Life, 1991.

Sheler, Jeffrey. "Healing an Ailing Church." *U.S. News and World Report* (Nov. 6, 1989), 75.

Simmons, Thomas. *The Unseen Shore: Memories of a Christian Science Childhood.* Boston: Beacon, 1991.

Skolnick, Andrew, "Christian Scientists Claim Healing Efficacy Equal If Not Superior to That of Medicine." *The Journal of the American Medical Association* (September 1990), 1379.

_____. "Religious Exemptions to Child Neglect Laws Still Being Passed Despite Convictions of Parents." *The Journal of the American Medical Association* (September 1990), 1226.

Smith, Clifford P. *Historical Sketches.* Boston: Christian Science, 1941.

Snowden, James H. *The Truth about Christian Science.* Philadelphia: Westminster, 1920.

Starr, Mark. "Prayer in the Courtroom: When Does Christian Science Become a Crime?" *Newsweek* (April 30, 1990), 64.

Stark, Rodney. "The Rise and Fall of Christian Science." *Journal of Contemporary Religion* 13 (1998): 189–214.

Wilbur, Sibyl. *The Life of Mary Baker Eddy.* Boston: Christian Science, 1923.

Wittmer, George W. *Christian Science in the Light of the Bible.* St. Louis: Concordia, 1949.

CHURCH OF ARMAGEDDON; LOVE FAMILY; LOVE ISRAEL

"An Ex-family Member Has No Love for Love." *Seattle Post-Intelligencer* (Sept. 25, 1986).

"Authority, Lifestyle Disputes Wrack 'Family.'" *The Seattle Times* (Oct. 3, 1983), C3.

"Family Fight Blows Apart Love Israel Commune." *The Seattle Times* (Oct. 3, 1983), C3.

"Love Family and Benefactor Settle." *Seattle Post-Intelligencer* (Jan. 27, 1984), sec. D.

"Love Family Slips toward Oblivion." *Seattle Post-Intelligencer* (Jan. 26, 1984), sec. D.

"Love Israel Lawsuit Settled out of Court." *The Seattle Times* (Jan. 27, 1984).

"Love Israel Postpones Move into Angered Idaho Community." *The Seattle Times* (Sept. 10, 1984).

"Love Was their Answer." *Seattle Post-Intelligencer* (Nov. 27, 1983), F7.

CHURCH OF BIBLE UNDERSTANDING—FOREVER FAMILY, COBU

"Forever Family: Leader Hostile to Those Outside His Cult." *Sandusky Register* (Mar. 27, 1976).

"Leader of Teen Cult Arrested." *New York Post* (Feb. 13, 1976).

"Other Gospels, New Religions: Church of Bible Understanding." *Spititual Counterfeits Project Newsletter* 6/2 (May-June 1980).

"Parents Lose Son to Forever Family." *Wyoming Observer* (Sept. 10, 1975).

"Scranton Man Wages Battle against Cults." *Catholic Light* (Scranton, Penn.) (Feb. 22, 1979).

"Sect Told to Vacate the Three Lofts." *New York Post* (Nov. 16, 1976).

Stevens, John Robert. *Plumb Perfect.* North Hollywood, Calif.: Living Word, 1977.

CHURCH OF THE LIVING WORD

"The Church of the Living Word." *Update* 7/1 (March 1983): 50–52.

Nichols, Woodrow. "The Occult Metaphysics of John Robert Stevens." *Update* 7/1 (March 1983).

Stevens, John Robert. *Apostolic Directives.* North Hollywood, Calif.: Living Word, 1976.

_____. *As Though Some Strange Things Were Happening.* North Hollywood, Calif.: Living Word, 1973.

_____. *Continuing in the Apostolic Teaching.* North Hollywood, Calif.: Living Word, 1976.

_____. *Dedicated to Total Loss.* North Hollywood, Calif.: Living Word, 1976.

_____. *Every Blow Has to Count.* North Hollywood, Calif.: Living Word, 1978.

_____. *First Principles.* North Hollywood, Calif.: Living Word, 1978.

CHURCH UNIVERSAL AND TRIUMPHANT—THE "I AM" ASCENDED MASTERS

Allman, William F. "Fatal Attraction: Why We Love Doomsday." *U.S. News and World Report* (Apr. 30, 1990), 12.

Anonymous. *Story of Atlantis*. London: Theosophical Publishing Society, 1902.

Ballard, Mrs. G. W., and Donald Ballard. *I AM Decrees for Ascended Masters Supply of All Good Things—Including Money*. Chicago: St. Germain, n.d.

_____. *Purpose of the Ascended Masters "I AM" Activity*. Chicago: St. Germain, 1942.

Creme, Benjamin. *The Reappearance of the Christ and the Masters of Wisdom*. Los Angeles: Tara, 1980.

"Finding Camelot in our Backyard." *Los Angeles Herald Examiner* (Jan. 27, 1985).

Harris, Michael. "Paradise under Siege: A New Age Guru Prepares for War in Montana." *Time* (Aug. 28, 1989), 61.

"Her Will Be Done." *Los Angeles Herald Examiner* (Jan. 28, 1985).

Jensen, Holger. "Trouble in Paradise: A Doomsday Prophet Wears Out." *Macleans* (May 1990), 33.

Jinarajadas. *The Early Teachings of the Masters*. 1881. Reprint. Chicago: Theosophical Press, 1923.

King, Godfrey Ray. *Unveiled Mysteries*. Chicago: St. Germain, 1939.

Kuthumi. *Studies of the Human Aura*. Colorado Springs, Colo.: Summit Univ. Press, 1971.

Lacayo, Richard. "Heading for the Hills: A New Age Guru Goes Underground." *Time* (Mar. 26, 1990), 20.

Martin, Walter R. *The New Cults*. Ventura, Calif.: Vision House, 1984.

McNeile, E. R. *From Theosophy to Christian Faith*. London: Longmans, 1919.

Morya, El. *The Chela and the Path*. Colorado Springs, Colo.: Summit Univ. Press, 1975.

Prophet, Elizabeth Clare. *Cosmic Consciousness: The Putting on of the Garment of the Lord*. Colorado Springs, Colo.: Summit Univ. Press, 1974.

_____. *St. Germain on Alchemy: For the Adept in the Aquarian Age*. Malibu, Calif.: Summit Univ. Press, 1975.

_____. *The Lost Years of Jesus: On the Discoveries of Notovitch, Abhedananda, Roerich, and Caspari*. Malibu, Calif.: Summit Univ. Press, 1984.

Prophet, Mark, and Elizabeth Prophet. *Climb the Highest Mountain*. Livingston, Mont.: Summit Univ. Press, 1975.

"Shelters of the Lord." *The Economist* (March 1990), 26.

CHURCH WITH NO NAME; 2 X 2'S

Cooper, L. *The Church With No Name: Known as Cooneyites, Two by Two*. Wellington, New Zealand: Wellington Mail Centre, 1996.

Fortt, Loyd. *A Search for "the Truth."* Chelsea, Mich.: Research and Information Services, 1994.

Johnson, Benton. "Christians in Hiding: The No Name Sect." Pages 37–55 in *Sex, Lies, and Sanctity: Religion and Deviance in Contemporary North America*. Ed. M. J. Neitz and M. S. Goldman. Greenwich, Conn.: JAJ Press, n.d.

Parker, Doug and Helen. *The Secret Sect*. Sydney, Australia: Macarthur, 1982.

Paul, W. E. *They Go About Two by Two: The History and Doctrines of a Little Known Cult*. Denver: Impact, 1977.

Wosters, C. *The No-Name Fellowship*, Bend, Ore.: Research and Information Services, 1988.

COMMUNITY OF CHRIST—(FORMERLY) THE REORGANIZED CHURCH OF JESUS CHRIST OF LATTER DAY SAINTS

Hansen, Carol. *Reorganized Latter Day Saint Church: Is it Christian?* Independence, Mo.: Refiner's Fire Ministries, 2000.

Launius, Roger D. "The RLDS Church and the Decade of Decision." *Sunstone* (September 1996), 45–55.

Stack, Peggy Fletcher. "RLDS Moving Further Away from Mormons." *The Salt Lake Tribune* (June 29, 1996).

CONFUCIANISM

Bell, Daniel, and Hahm Chaibong, eds. *Confucianism for the Modern World*. Cambridge: Cambridge Univ. Press, 2003.

Cleary, Thomas. *The Essential Confucius*. Edison, N.J.: Book Sales, 2000.

Confucius. *The Analects*. New York: Penguin, 1998.

Ivanhoe, P. J. *Confucian Moral Self Cultivation*. New York: Peter Lang, 1993.

Oldstone Moore, Jennifer. *Confucianism: Origins, Beliefs, Practices, Holy Texts, Sacred Places*. Oxford: Oxford Univ. Press, 2002.

DAFREE JOHN; BUBBA FREE JOHN

Bubba Free John. *Garbage and the Goddess*. Lower Lake, Calif.: Dawn Horse, 1974.

_____. *No Remedy*. Lower Lake, Calif.: Dawn Horse, 1976.

Jones, Franklin. *The Knee of Listening*. Los Angeles: Dawn Horse, 1972.

_____. *The Method of the Siddhas*. Los Angeles: Dawn Horse, 1978.

The Song of the Self Supreme: Astavakraita Gita. Translated by Radhakamal Mukerjee. Los Angeles: Dawn Horse, n.d.

"The Method of the Siddhas Home Study Course." The Johannine Daist Communion, 119 Paul Drive, San Rafael, Calif. 94903.

DIVINE SCIENCE

Braden, Charles S. *Spirits in Rebellion*. Dallas, Tex.: Southern Methodist Univ. Press, 1987.

Brooks, Louise McNamara. *Early History of Divine Science*. St. Louis: DSFI Publications, 1963.

Brooks, Nona L. *Short Lessons in Divine Science*, St. Louis: DSFI Publications, 1923.

Cramer, Malinda E. *Divine Science and Healing*, St. Louis: DSFI Publications. n.d.

_____, and Fannie B. James. *Divine Science, Its Principle and Practice*. St. Louis: DSFI Publications, 1957.

Deane, Hazel. *Powerful Is the Light*. St. Louis: First Divine Science Church, 1987.

Greg, Greg. *The Divine Science Way*. St. Louis: DSFI Publications, 1975.

ECKANKAR

"A Catalogue of Cults: Where They Stand on the Deity of Christ." *Moody* (July–August 1979), 3.

Cramer, Tod, and Doug Munson. *Eckankar: Ancient Wisdom for Today*. Minneapolis: Quality Books, 1998.

"ECK Explores New Realms." *Tigard Times* (Feb. 22, 1983), sect. C.

"Eckankar: A Hard Look at a New Religion." *Spiritual Counterfeits Project Journal* (September 1979).

"Eckankar Centers on Soul Travel." *El Paso Times* (June 24, 1978), sect. C.

"Eckankar: Freedom, Awareness, Responsibility." *Davis Enterprise* (Davis, Calif.) (Oct. 22, 1982), 11.

"Eckankar to Improve $3 Million Property." *Independent* (Cottonwood, Ariz.) (Feb. 23, 1977).

"Eckankar Spiritual Legacy of Atlantis?" *Point* (Univ. of Connecticut) (April 6, 1977).

Enroth, Ronald. *A Guide to Cults and New Religions*. Downers Grove, Ill.: InterVarsity Press, 1983.

Johnson, Ford. *Confessions of a God Seeker: A Journey to Higher Consciousness*. Silver Spring, Md.: "One" Publishing, 2003.

Klemp, Harold. *Autobiography of a Modern Prophet*. Minneapolis: Eckankar, 2000.

_____. *A Modern Prophet Answers Your Key Questions about Life*. Minneapolis: Eckankar, 1998.

Lane, David C., ed. "The Making of a Spiritual Movement: The Untold Story of Paul Twitchell and Eckankar." In *Understanding Cults and Spiritual Movements Series*, rev. ed. Del Mar, Calif.: Del Mar Press, 1989.

Nichols, Woodrow, and David Alexander. "Paul Twitchell and the Evolution of Eckankar." *Spiritual Counterfeits Project Journal* (September 1979).

"So You Want to Do an ECK Seminar!" *Seminar Directors Suggestions and Guidelines Manual*. Las Vegas, Nev.: Eckankar.

"Soul Travelers Say They Take Trips to Astral Planes." *The Seattle Times* (Jan. 27, 1983), E2.

"The Square Peg." *Seattle Post-Intelligencer* (July 9, 1963).

Steiger, Brad. *In My Soul I Am Free*. San Diego: Illuminated Way, n.d.

Twitchell, Paul. *Eckanker Dictionary*. 2nd ed. Golden Valley, Minn.: Illuminated Way, 1981.

_____. *Eckankar: The Key to Secret Worlds*. San Diego: Illuminated Way, 1969.

_____. *Eckankar: The Key to Secret Worlds*. 2nd ed. Minneapolis: Eckankar, 2001.

_____. *Eck-Vidya, Ancient Science of Prophecy*, Minneapolis: Eckankar, 2001.

_____. *The Shariyat-Ki-Sugmad*. San Diego: Illuminated Way, 1970.

_____. *The Wisdom of ECK*. San Diego: Illuminated Way, 1972.

ELAN VITAL [DIVINE LIGHT MISSION]

Barrett, David V. "Elan Vital." Pages 325–32 in *The New Believers*. London: Cassell, 2001.

_____. "Divine Light." Pages 134–36 in *Sects, "Cults" and Alternative Religions: A World Survey and Sourcebook*. Singapore: Blandford, 1998.

The Bhagavadgita or the Song Divine. Gorakhpur, India: Gita, 1971.

Cahill, Tim, "Perfect Master on the Ropes." *Rolling Stone Magazine* (Nov. 11, 1973).

Cameron, Charles, ed. *Who Is Guru Maharaj Ji?* New York: Bantam, 1973.

"Carroll Recalls Year with Divine Light." *Ohio Star* (Marion, Ohio) (Mar. 15, 1981).

"A Catalogue of Cults: Where They Stand on the Deity of Christ." *Moody* (July–August 1979), 3.

"The Cosmic Christ." *Signs of the Times* (May 1979), 8.

Downton, James V. Jr. *Sacred Journeys: The Conversion of Young Americans to Divine Light Mission.* New York: Columbia Univ. Press, 1979.

"For Parents: A Guide to Surviving a Child's Cultic Adventure." *Los Angeles Times* (Dec. 24, 1978), part 6.

"A Guide to Meditation Groups." *Los Angeles Times* (Feb. 13, 1977), G.

Kelsey, Morton. *Encounter with God.* Minneapolis: Bethany, 1972.

Melton, J. Gordon. "Divine Light Mission." Pages 890–91 in *Encyclopedia of American Religions.* 5th ed. Detroit: Gale, 1996.

_____. "Maharaj Ji, Guru." Page 803 in *Encyclopedia of Occultism and Parapsychology.* 4th ed. Detroit: Gale, 1996.

"Mother Ousts Guru, 17." *Los Angeles Times* (Apr. 25, 1975).

"Times Have Changed for Guru." *Herald Examiner* (Los Angeles, Calif.) (Dec. 4, 1976).

EST—THE FORUM

Bartley, W. W. *Werner Erhard: The Transformation of a Man, the Founding of EST.* New York: Charles N. Potter, 1978.

Bry, Adelaide. *EST: 60 Hours That Transform Your Life.* New York: Avon, 1976.

Burg, Bob. "EST: 60 Hours to Happiness." *Human Behavior* (November 1974), 16–23.

"Erhard Tries to Make It Happen." *The Sacramento Bee* (Dec. 15, 1984), A2.

"EST-Related Seminars Aid Clergy and Laity in Transformation." *The Voice* (Diocese of Newark) (April 1984).

"EST: There Is Nothing to Get." *Time* (June 7, 1976), 53–54.

"EST Puts Itself in Charge of Tomorrow." *Citizens Freedom Foundation News* 8/4 (April 1983).

"EST: The Philosophy of Self-Worship." *Spiritual Counterfeits Project Journal* (Winter 1981–82).

Frederick, Carl. *EST, Playing the Game the New Way.* New York: Delacourte, 2003.

Green, William. *EST: 4 Days to Make Your Life Work.* New York: Simon & Schuster, 1976.

Kettle, James. *The EST Experience.* Boulder, Colo.: Kensington, 1976.

Kirsch, M. A., and L. L. Glass. "Psychiatric Disturbances Associated with Erhard Seminars Training: II. Additional Cases and Theoretical Considerations." *American Journal of Psychiatry* 134 (1977): 1254–58.

"Lawsuit Reveals EST Secrets." *Council on Mind Abuse, Inc.* (News Release) (Nov. 11, 1983).

McNamara, Mark. "Guru II: The Return of Werner Erhard." *Los Angeles Magazine* (May 1988), 106.

Navarro, M. Robert, *The Est and Forum Phenomena in American Society*, Philadelphia: Xlibris, 2002.

"Nothin' This Good Ever Happened to Me Before!" *The EST Standard Training at San Quentin Prison*, 1981.

Rinehart, Luke. *The Book of EST.* New York: Holt, Rinehart & Winston, 1976.

Simon, J. "Observations on 67 Patients Who Took Erhard Seminars Training. *American Journal of Psychiatry* 135 (1978): 686–91.

"Werner Erhard: All I Can Do Is Lie." Reprint. *East West Journal* (September 1974).

THE FAMILY

Bainbridge, William Sims. *The Sociology of Religious Movements.* New York: Routledge, 1997.

Chancellor, James D. *Life in the Family: An Oral History of the Children of God.* Syracuse, N.Y.: Syracuse Univ. Press, 2000.

Lewis, James R., and J. Gordon Melton, eds. *Sex, Slander, and Salvation: Investigating The Family/Children of God.* Stanford, Calif.: Center for Academic Publication. 1994.

Palmer, Susan J., and Charlotte E. Hardman, eds. *Children in New Religions.* Piscataway, N.J.: Rutgers Univ. Press. 1999.

World Services. *The History of the Family.* Zurich, Switzerland, 1995.

FOUNDATION OF HUMAN UNDERSTANDING

"Blacklist: Townspeople Squabble over Business Boycotts." *Seattle Times* (Dec. 18, 1983), D6.

Masters, Roy. *The Adam and Eve Syndrome.* Athens, Ga.: Foundation of Human Understanding, 1985.

_____. *Be Still and Know.* Los Angeles: Foundation Press, 1976.

_____. *Beyond the Known*. Rev. ed. Edited Dorothy Baker. Athens, Ga.: Foundation of Human Understanding, 1989.

_____. *The God Game*. Los Angeles: Foundation Press, 1977.

_____. *How to Conquer Negative Emotion*. Edited Melrose H. Tappan. Athens, Ga.: Foundation for Human Understanding, 1988.

_____. *How Your Mind Can Keep You Well*. Los Angeles: Foundation Press, 1978.

_____. *The Hypnosis of Life*. Rev. ed. Athens, Ga.: Foundation for Human Understanding, 1988.

_____. *The Secret of Life and Death*. Los Angeles: Foundation Press, 1964.

_____. *Secret Power of Words*. Edited Dorothy Baker. Athens, Ga.: Foundation for Human Understanding, 1991.

_____. *Sex: The Substitute Love*. Los Angeles: Foundation Press, 1976.

_____. *Surviving the Comfort Zone*. Edited Dorothy Baker. Athens, Ga.: Foundation for Human Understanding, 1991.

_____. *Understanding Sexuality: The Mystery of Our Lost Identities*. Rev. ed. Athens, Ga.: Foundation for Human Understanding, 1988.

"Roy Masters: I Can Do No Wrong." *Northwest: The Sunday Oregonian Magazine* (Sept. 4, 1983).

"Your Time of Victory Is Coming, 'Billy Jack' Master." *Regional Daily Courier* (Grand Pass, Ore.) (Mar. 29, 1984).

GAY THEOLOGY

"Abandon Church." *Alberta Report* (Oct. 31, 1983), 24.

Alison, James. *Faith beyond Resentment*. Crossroad General Interest, 2001.

American Civil Liberties Union. *Sexual Child Abuse: A Contemporary Family Problem* (pamphlet). 1984.

Bailey, D. S. *Homosexuality and the Western Christian Tradition*. New York: Longmans, 1955.

Bell, A. P., M. Weinberg, S. Hammersmith, and S. K. Hammersmith. *Sexual Preference: Statistical Appendix*. Bloomington, Ind.: Indiana Univ. Press, 1981.

"BIAS: Case Pits Gay Student Groups against Jesuit Univ.'s Beliefs." *Los Angeles Times* (Nov. 19, 1984), part 1.

"Bible Analysis of Homosexuality." *Wave Newspapers* (May 16, 1984).

Blair, Ralph. *An Evangelical Look at Homosexuality*. Chicago: Moody Press, 1963.

Boswell, John. *Christianity, Social Tolerance, and Homosexuality*. Chicago: Univ. of Chicago Press, 1980.

Cameron, Paul. "Homosexual Molestation of Children—Sexual Interaction of Teacher and Pupil." *Psychological Reports* 57 (1985): 1227–36.

_____, and K. P. Ross, "Social, Psychological Aspects of the Judeo-Christian Stance Toward Homosexuality." *Journal of Psychology and Theology* (1981): 40–57.

"Church Will Not Try Bishop." *Los Angeles Times* (May 23, 1982), part 1.

"Church's Last Service Tomorrow before Move to Its New Home." *San Diego Union* (Sept. 18, 1982), B10.

Clark, J. Michael. *Defying the Darkness: Gay Theology in the Shadows*. Plymouth, Mass.: Pilgrim, 1997.

"Don't Be Misled." *The Seattle Times* (Sept. 3, 1983).

Exit Newsletter. Various issues.

Field, David. *The Homosexual Way—A Christian Option?* Downers Grove, Ill.: InterVarsity Press, 1979.

"Gay Churches Facing Rejection." *Los Angeles Times* (May 12, 1983), part 1.

"Gays under Fire." *Newsweek* (Sept. 14, 1992), 35–40.

"The Growing Issue: Saints in Sodom?" *Christianity Today* (May 5, 1978), 50–52.

Gudel, Joseph B. "Homosexuality: Fact and Fiction." *Christian Research Journal* (Summer 1972), 20.

"Homosexual Becomes Methodist Official in Texas." *Los Angeles Times* (June 2, 1982), part 2.

Homosexual Counseling Journal. Various issues.

"Homosexuality: Coming Out of the Closet." *Family Life Today* (February 1981).

Jay, K., and A. Young. *A Gay Report*. New York: Summit, 1979.

"Leader of Gay-Lesbian Church Pleased with Council's Compromise." *The Cincinnati Enquirer* (June 12, 1982), A8.

Lindsell, Harold, "Homosexuals and the Church." *Christianity Today* (Sept. 28, 1973), 8–12.

"Local Gay Community Finds Acceptance, Peace At Church." *Las Vegas Review-Journal* (March 18, 1984).

Marotta, T. *The Politics of Homosexuality*. Boston: Houghton Mifflin, 1981.

Melton, J. Gordon. *Encyclopedia of American Religions*. 5th ed. Detroit: Gale Research, 2002.

"Methodist Decision Encourages Bishop." *Los Angeles Times* (May 29, 1982), part 2.

"Methodist Ministers Protest Gay Cleric." *Toronto Star* (June 21, 1986).

"Metropolitan Community Churches Flourishing, Denomination Minister to Homosexuals." *The Herald* (June 28, 1986), 15.

Montagu, A. "A Kinsey Report on Homosexualities." *Psychology Today* 12 (March 1978): 62–91.

"National Church Council Debates Admission of MCC at S. F. Meeting." *For the Record, a Concise Review of Gay News* (June 1983).

Oberholtzer, W. D. *Is Gay Good?* Philadelphia: Westminster, 1971.

Ollendorff, R. H. *The Juvenile Homosexual Experience and Its Effects on Adult Sexuality*. New York: Julian, 1966.

"Panel OKs Church Bid by Gays." *Chicago Sun Times* (June 2, 1983), 28.

Record: Newsletter of Evangelicals Concerned. Various issues.

Scanzoni, Letha, and Virginia Ramey Mollenkott. *Is the Homosexual My Neighbor?* Revised and updated. San Francisco: HarperSanFrancisco, 1994.

Schofield, M. *The Sexual Behavior of Young People*. Boston: Little & Brown, 1965.

_____. *Sociological Aspects of Homosexuality*. Boston: Little & Brown, 1965.

"The Sex-Change Conspiracy." *Psychology Today* 13 (December 1979): 20–25.

Stablinshik, K. "Homosexuality: What the Bible Does and Does Not Say." *The Ladder* (June–July 1969).

Stott, John R. W. "Homosexual Marriage." *Christianity Today* (Nov. 22, 1985), 21–28.

Ukleja, P. Michael, "Homosexuality and the Old Testament." *Bibliotheca Sacra* (July–September 1983), 259–65.

"United Church Seriously Split on Homosexual Ministers." *Toronto Globe and Mail* (May 14, 1984).

Weinberg, G. *Society and the Healthy Homosexual*. New York: St. Martin's, 1972.

White, John. *Eros Defiled: The Christian and Sexual Sin*. Downers Grove, Ill.: InterVarsity Press, n.d.

Yancey, Philip. "We Have No Right to Scorn." *Christianity Today* (Jan. 14, 1988), 72.

G. I. GURDJIEFF AND P. D. OUSPENSKY

"The Fellowship of Friends." *Appeal-Democrat* (Marysville-Yuba City, Calif.) (Sept. 20, 1975).

"A Holy Teacher: Mystical Cult Prospers—and Stirs Some Fears." *San Francisco Chronicle* (Apr. 30, 1981).

Baker, George, and Walter Driscoll. *Gurdjieff in America: An Overview*. New York: State Univ. of New York Press. 1995.

Driscoll, J. Walter. 1985. *Gurdjieff: An Annotated Biography*. New York: Garland. 1985.

Gurdjieff, Georges I. *All and Everything: Beelzebub's Tales to His Grandson*. New York: Dutton. 1978.

_____. *Meetings with Remarkable Men*. New York: Dutton. 1973.

"Gurdjieff, a Sign of the Times: Occult Philosophy Comes to the Screen." *Spiritual Counterfeits Projects Newsletter* (June 4, 1979).

Henry, William. *The Keeper of Heaven's Gate*. Anchorage, Alaska: Earthpulse, 1997.

Moore, James. *Gurdjieff: A Biography*. Rockport, Mass.: Element. 1997.

Needleman, Jacob, and George Baker, eds. *Gurdjieff: Essays and Reflections on the Man*. New York: Continuum. 1998.

Pentland, John. *Exchanges Within: Questions from Everyday Life Selected from Gurdjieff Group Meetings with John Pentland in California*. New York: Continuum, 1997.

Rawlinson, Andrew. *The Book of Enlightened Masters: Western Teachers in Eastern Traditions*. Chicago: Open Court, 1997.

Webb, James. *The Harmonious Circle: The Lives and Works of Gurdjieff, P. D. Ouspensky, and Their Followers*. New York: Putnam, 1980.

HEAVEN'S GATE

Balch, Robert W., and David Taylor. "Making Sense of the Heaven's Gate Suicides." Pages 209–26 in *Cults, Religion, and Violence*. Ed. David Bromley and J. Gordon Melton (Cambridge: Cambridge Univ. Press, 2002).

_____. "Seekers and Saucers: The Role of the Cultic Milieu in Joining a UFO Cult." *American Behavioral Scientist* 20 (July/August 1977): 839–60.

_____. "The Metamorphosis of a UFO Cult: A Study of Organizational Change." (Unpublished paper presented at the annual meeting of the Pacific Sociological Association, San Diego, 1977).

Davis, Winston "Heaven's Gate: A Study of Religious Obedience." *Nova Religio* 3 (2000): 241–67

Gallagher, Eugene V. "Theology Is Life and Death: David Koresh on Violence, Persecution, and the Millennium." In *How the Millennium Comes Violently: From Jonestown to Heaven's Gate.* Ed. Catherine Wessinger. Washington, D.C.: Chatham House, 2000.

Henry, William, and Cary Anderson. *The Keepers of Heaven's Gate: The Millennial Madness: The Religion behind the Rancho Santa Fe Suicides.* Anchorage, Alaska: Earthpulse, 1997.

Hoffman, Bill, and Cathy Burke. *Heaven's Gate Cult Suicides in San Diego.* New York: Harper Paperbacks, 1997.

Perkins, Rodney, and Forrest Jackson. *Cosmic Suicide: The Tragedy and Transcendence of Heaven's Gate.* Dallas: Pentaradial, 1997.

Wessinger, Catherine. "Understanding the Branch Davidian Tragedy." *Nova Religio* 1/1 (1997): 122–38.

HINDUISM, GENERAL; HARE KRISHNA; TM

Bhaskarananda, Swami. *The Essentials of Hinduism: A Comprehensive Overview of the World's Earliest Religion.* Seattle: Viveka Press, 2002.

Benson, Herbert. *The Relaxation Response.* New York: William Morrow, 1975.

Clements, R. D. *God of the Gurus.* Downers Grove, Ill.: InterVarsity Press, 1975.

Cox, Harvey. *Turning East: The Promise and Peril of the New Orientalism.* New York: Simon & Schuster, 1977.

Dilley, John R. *Fundamentals of Progress.* Fairfield, Iowa: Maharishi International Univ. Press, 1975.

Doniger, Wendy. *The Rig Veda.* New York: Penguin Classics, 2005.

Embree, Ainslie T., ed. *The Hindu Tradition.* New York: Modern Library, 1966.

Forsthoefel, Thomas. *Gurus in America.* New York: State Univ. of New York Press, 2004.

Foulston, Lynn. *Hindu Goddesses: Beliefs and Practices.* Portland, Ore.: Sussex Academy, 2004.

Jones, Constance A., and James D. Ryan. *Encyclopedia of Hinduism.* New York: Facts on File, 2005.

Judah, Stillson, J. *Hare Krishna and the Counterculture.* New York: Wiley, 1974.

Krishna, Paul. *Journey from the East.* Downers Grove, Ill.: InterVarsity Press, 1977.

LaMore, George E. Jr. "The Secular Selling of a Religion." *The Christian Century* 92/41 (December 1975): 1133–37.

Levine, Faye. *The Strange World of the Hare Krishnas.* New York: Fawcett, 1974.

Mahesh Yogi, Maharishi. *Maharishi Mahesh Yogi on the Bhagavad-Gita.* New York: Viking-Penguin, 1990.

_____. *Meditations of Maharishi Mahesh Yogi.* New York: New American Library, 1968.

_____. *The Science of Being and Art of Living.* New York: New American Library, 1968.

Needleman, Jacob. *The New Religions: The Teachings of the East.* New York: Pocket Books, 1972.

O'Malley, L. S. S. *Popular Hinduism: The Religion of the Masses.* Cambridge: Cambridge Univ. Press, 1935.

Prabhavananda, Swami, and Frederick Manchest. *The Upanishads: Breath of the Eternal.* New York: New American Library, 1948.

Prabhupada, A. C., and Bhaktivedanta Swami. *Bhagavad-Gita As It Is.* New York: Bhaktivedanta Book Trust, 1968.

_____. *Krishna Consciousness: The Topmost Yoga System.* Los Angeles: Iskcon Books, 1970.

_____. *The Nectar of Devotion.* New York: Bhaktivedanta Book Trust, 1976.

_____. *On Chanting the Hare Krishna Mantra.* Boston: Iskcon Press, n.d.

_____. *Perfect Questions, Perfect Answers.* New York: Bhaktivedanta Book Trust, 1976.

Radhakrishnan. *Indian Philosopy.* London: Allen & Unwin, 1923

Ramacharaka, Yogi. *The Philosophies and Religions of India.* Homewood, Ill.: Yoga, n.d.

Rice, Mary Ann. *From Krishna to Christ.* Santa Ana, Calif.: CARIS, 1981.

Ringgren, Helmer, and Ake V. Strom. *Religions of Mankind.* Philadelphia: Fortress, 1967.

Smith, Huston. *The Religions of Man.* New York: Harper & Row, 1958.

Stoner, Carol, and Jo Anne Parke. *All God's Children.* Randor, Penn.: Chilton, 1977.

Wood, Ernest. *The Bhagavad Explained.* San Francisco: American Academy of Asian Studies Graduate School, 1961.

Younger, Paul. *Introduction to Indian Religious Thought.* Philadelphia: Westminster, 1972.

Yamamoto, J. Isamu. *Hare Krishna, Hare Krishna.* Downers Grove, Ill.: InterVarsity Press, 1978.

INTERNATIONAL CHURCHES OF CHRIST

Bjornstad, James. "At What Price Success? The Boston Church of Christ Movement." *Christian Research Journal (*Winter 1993), 24.

Cook, Gene. *The Baptism Cult: Exposing the International Church of Christ.* Santee, Calif.: Saint Aztec, 2002.

Enroth, Ronald M. *Churches That Abuse.* Grand Rapids: Zondervan, 1993.

Ferguson, Gordon. *Mine Eyes Have Seen the Glory: The Victory of the Lamb in the Book of Revelation,* Woburn, Mass.: Discipleship Publications International, 1993.

Gamill, Marion B. "Boston Church of Christ Recruiting on Campus." *The Harvard Crimson* (Jan. 13, 1994), 1, 5.

Giambalvo, Carol, and Herbert L. Rosedale, eds. *The Boston Movement: Critical Perspectives on the International Churches of Christ.* Bonita Springs, Fl.: American Family Foundation, 1996.

Horner, Kim. "International Church of Christ Celebrates Despite Criticism." *Dallas Morning News* (May 5, 2000).

Jones, Tom, and Roger Lamb. "You Might Be Fighting God." Pages 28–33 in *First Principles: The International Churches of Christ.* Ed. Kip McKean. Woburn, Mass.: Discipleship Publications International, 1993.

McKean, Kip. *First Principles: International Churches of Christ.* Woburn, Mass.: Discipleship Publications International, 1993.

Ostling, Richard N. "Keepers of the Flock." *Time* (May 18, 1992), 62.

Paden, Russell. "The Boston Church of Christ." Pages 133–40 in *America's Alternate Religions,* ed. Timothy Miller. Albany: State Univ. of New York Press, 1995.

Stockman, Farah. "A Christian Community Falters." *The Boston Globe* (May 17, 2003).

ISKCON

Bryant, Edwin F., and Maria L. Ekstrand, eds, *The Hare Krishna Movement: The Postcharismatic Fate of a Religious Transplant.* New York: Columbia Univ. Press, 2004.

Cooper, Kenneth J. "Lip-Syncing Robots Spread the Hare Krishna Word." *The Washington Post* (Apr. 13, 1998), A18.

Goswami, Mukunda. *Inside the Hare Krishna Movement: An Ancient Eastern Religious Tradition Comes of Age in the Western World.* Badger, Calif.: Torchlight, 2001.

Levine, F. *The Strange World of the Hare Krishnas.* New York: Fawcett, 1974.

Muster, Nori Jean. *Betrayal of the Spirit: My Life behind the Headlines of the Hare Krishna Movement.* Urbana: Univ. of Illinois Press. 1997.

Rochford, E. Burke Jr. "Reaction of Hare Krishna Devotees to Scandals of Leaders' Misconduct." Pages 101–70 in *Wolves within the Fold: Religious Leadership and Abuses of Power.* Ed. Anson Shupe. Piscataway, N.J.: Rutgers Univ. Press. 1998.

Prabhupada, A. C., and Bhaktivedanta Swami. *Bhagavad-Gita As It Is.* New York: Bhaktivedanta Book Trust, 1968.

_____. *The Nectar of Devotion.* New York: Bhaktivedanta Book Trust, 1970.

Williams, Rowan. *The Dwelling of the Light: Praying with Icons of Christ.* Grand Rapids: Eerdmans, 2004.

ISLAM, MUSLIM, MOHAMMEDANISM

Abdu 'L-Ahad Dawud. *Muhammed in the Bible.* Kuala Lumpur: Pustaka Antara, 1979.

Abdullah Yusuf Ali. *The Holy Qur-an: Text, Translation and Commentary.* Qatar: Qatar National Printing, 1946.

Ahmad A. Galwash. *The Religion of Islam.* Cambridge, Mass.: Murray, n.d.

Alhaj A. D. Ajijola. *The Myth of the Cross.* Lahore, Pakistan: Islamic Publications, 1977.

Andrae, Tor. *Mohammed: The Man and His Faith.* Trans. Theophil Menzel. New York: Harper & Row, 1960.

Arberry, Arthur J. *The Koran Interpreted.* New York: Macmillan, 1967.

Armstrong, Karen. *Islam: A Short History.* New York: Modern Library, 2002.

Azzam, Abd-al-Rahman. *The Eternal Message of Muhammed.* Trans. Caesar E. Farah. New York: American Library, 1965.

Barnett, Michael N. *Dialogues in Arab Politics.* New York: Columbia Univ. Press. 1998.

"Britain Bars Farrakhan." *Los Angeles Times* (Jan. 1, 1986), part 1.

Bucaille, Maurice. *The Bible, the Quran, and Science.* Trans. Alastair D. Pannell and Maurice Bucaille. Chicago: Kazi, 1978.

Bunt, Gary. *Virtually Islamic*. Cardiff: Univ. of Wales. 2000.

Encyclopedia of Islam. Leiden: Brill, 1960.

Caner, Ergun Mehet, and Emir Fethi Caner. *Unveiling Islam*. Grand Rapids: Kregel, 2002.

Esposito, John L. *Islam: The Straight Path*. Oxford: Oxford Univ. Press. 1998.

_____. *The Oxford History of Islam*. Oxford: Oxford Univ. Press, 1999.

"Farrakhan Speaks." *Voice* (May 1984), 15–20.

Fry, George C., and James R. King. *Islam: A Survey of the Muslim Faith*. Grand Rapids: Baker, 1980.

Gilchrist, John. *The Textual History of the Quran and the Bible*. Durban, South Africa: Jesus to the Muslims, 1981.

Haneef, Suzanne. *What Everyone Should Know About Islam and Muslims*. Chicago: Kazi, 1979.

Hazrat Mirza Bashir-Ud-Din Mahmud Ahmad. *Introduction to the Study of the Holy Quran*. London: London Mosque, 1949.

Holt, P. M. *A Seventeenth-Century Defender of Islam: Henry Stubb (1632–76) and his Book*. London: Friends of Dr. Williams Library, 1972.

Jones, L. Bevan. *Christianity Explained to Muslims*. Rev. ed. Calcutta, India: Baptist Mission Press, 1964.

_____. *The People of the Mosque*. London: SCM, 1931.

Kausar, Niazi. *Mirror of Trinity*. Lahore, Pakistan: Muhammad Ashraf, 1975.

Lewis, Bernard. *What Went Wrong? The Clash between Islam and Modernity in the Middle East*. New York: HarperTrade, 2003.

_____. *The Crisis of Islam: Holy War and Unholy Terror*. New York: Modern Library, 2003.

Marsh, C. R. *Share Your Faith with a Muslim*. Chicago: Moody Press, 1975.

Maudidi, A. A. *The Prophet of Islam as the Ideal Husband*. Chicago: Kazi, 1979.

Maulana Muhammad Ali. *The Religion of Islam*. Lahore, Pakistan: Ahmadiyyah Anjuman Isha'at Islam, 1950.

McCurry, Don M., and Carol A. Glasser. *Muslim Awareness Seminar*. Altadena, Calif.: Samuel Zwemer Institute, 1981.

Miller, William. *A Christian Response to Islam*. Nutley, N.J.: Presbyterian & Reformed, 1976.

Moaddel, Manssor, and Kamran Talattof, eds. *Contemporary Debates in Islam: An Anthology of Modernist and Fundamentalist Thought*. New York: St. Martin's, 2000.

"The Muslim Student's Association of the United States of America and Canada." *The Prophets of Allah*. Chicago: Madina Printers, 1976.

Nasr, Seyyed Hossein. *Islam: Religion, History, and Civilization*. San Francisco: HarperSanFrancisco, 2003.

Norcliffe, David. *Islam: Faith and Practice*. Portland, Ore.: Sussex Academic, 1999.

Parrinder, Geoffrey. *Jesus in the Qur'an*. New York: Oxford Univ. Press, 1977.

Pfander, C. G. *The Mizanu'l Haqq Balance of Truth*. Reprint. London: Religious Tract Society, 1910.

Pickthall, Mohammed Marmaduke. *The Meaning of the Glorious Koran*. New York: New American Library, 1963.

Pipes, Daniel. *Militant Islam Reaches America*. New York: Norton, 2002.

Ringgren, Helmer, and Ake V. Strom. *Religions of Mankind*. Philadelphia: Fortress, 1967.

Schmidt, Alvin. *The Great Divide: The Failure of Islam and the Triumph of the West*. Salisbury, Mass.: Regina Orthodox Press, 2004.

Smith, Huston. *The Religions of Man*. New York: Harper & Row, 1965.

Smith, Jane I. *Islam in America*. New York: Columbia Univ. Press. 1999.

Spencer, H. *Islam and the Gospel of God*. New Delhi, India: S.P.C.K., 1956.

Spencer, Robert. *Islam Unveiled: Disturbing Questions about the World's Fastest Growing Faith*. San Francisco: Encounter, 2002.

Stade, Robert Charles. *Ninety-Nine Names of God in Islam*. Ibadan, Nigeria: Daystar, 1974.

Trifkovic, Serge. *The Sword of the Prophet*. Salisbury, Mass.: Regina Orthodox Press, 2003.

Ulfat Aziz-Us-Samad. *Islam and Christianity*. Karachi, Pakistan: Begum Aisha Bawany Wakf, 1974.

Watt, W. Montgomery. *Muhammed: Prophet and Statesman*. London: Oxford Univ. Press, 1961.

Zwemer, Samuel M. *Islam: A Challenge to Faith*. New York: Layman's Missionary Movement, 1907.

JAINISM

Babb, L.A. *Absent Lord: Ascetics and Kings in a Jain Ritual Culture*. Berkeley: Univ. of California Press, 1995.

Banks, M. *Organizing Jainism in India and England*. Oxford: Clarendon, 1995.

Dundas, Paul. *The Jains*. Library of Religious Beliefs and Practices. New York: Routledge, 2002.

Chapple, Christopher Key. *Nonviolence to Animals, Earth, and Self in Asian Traditions*. Albany, N.Y.: State Univ. of New York Press, 1993.

Folkert, Kendall W., and John E. Court. "Jainism." Pages 340–68 in *A New Handbook of Living Religions*. Ed. John R. Hinnells. Oxford: Blackwell, 1998.

Padmanabh, S. *Gender and Salvation*. Delhi: Munshiram, 1991.

Shah, Natubhai. *Jainism: The World of Conquerors*. Portland, Ore.: Sussex Academic Press, 1998.

Tobias, Michael. *Life Force: The World of Jainism*. Fremont, Calif.: Jain Publishing, 2000.

Wiley, Kristi L. *Historic Dictionary of Jainism*. Lanham, Md.: Rowan & Littlefield, 2004.

JEHOVAH'S WITNESSES

Adair, James R., and Ted Miller. *We Found Our Way Out*. Grand Rapids: Baker, 1964.

Aid to Bible Understanding. Brooklyn: Watchtower Bible and Tract Society, 1971.

Alexander, David. "Fun with Missionaries." *The Humanist* (September–October 1990), 45.

All Scripture Is Inspired by God and Beneficial. Brooklyn: Watchtower Bible and Tract Society, 1963.

Babylon the Great Has Fallen! God's Kingdom Rules. Brooklyn: Watchtower Bible and Tract Society, 1963.

Blood, Medicine, and the Law of God. Brooklyn: Watchtower Bible and Tract Society, 1961.

Botting, Heather and Gary. *The Orwellian World of Jehovah's Witnesses*. Toronto: Univ. of Toronto Press, 1984.

Bowman, Robert M. *Understanding Jehovah's Witnesses.* Grand Rapids: Baker, 1991.

Braden, Charles S. *These Also Believe*. New York: Macmillan, 1949.

Cole, Marley. *Jehovah's Witnesses: The New World Society*. New York: Vantage, 1955.

_____. *Triumphant Kingdom*. New York: Criterion, 1957.

Conner, W. T. *The Teachings of "Pastor" Russell*. Nashville: Southern Baptist, 1926.

Crompton, Robert. *Counting the Days to Armageddon: The Jehovah's Witnesses and the Second Presence of Christ*. Cambridge: James Clarke, 1996.

Czatt, Milton Stacey. *The International Bible Students: Jehovah's Witnesses*. Scottdale, Penn.: Mennonite, 1933.

Dencher, Ted. *The Watchtower Heresy Verses and the Bible*. Chicago: Moody Press, 1961.

_____. *Why I Left Jehovah's Witnesses*. Toronto: Evangelical Publishers, 1966.

Franz, Raymond. *In Search of Christian Freedom*. Atlanta, Ga.: Commentary, 1991.

From Paradise Lost to Paradise Regained. Brooklyn: Watchtower Bible and Tract Society, 1958.

Fuller, Robert C. "Apocalypse Delayed: The Story of Jehovah's Witnesses." *The Journal of Religion* 70 (January 1990): 107.

Gardiner, Ron. *I Was a Jehovah's Witness*. Santa Ana, Calif.: CARIS, 1979.

Gruss, Edmond C. *Apostles of Denial*. 2nd ed. Nutley, N.J.: Presbyterian & Reformed, 1975.

_____. *Jehovah's Witnesses and Prophetic Speculation*. Nutley N.J.: Presbyterian & Reformed, 1972.

_____. *We Left Jehovah's Witnesses: A Non-Prophet Organization*. Nutley N.J.: Presbyterian & Reformed, 1974.

Harrison, Barbara. *Visions of Glory: A History and a Memory of Jehovah's Witnesses*. New York: Simon & Schuster, 1978.

Hefley, James. *The Youthsnappers*. Wheaton, Ill.: Victor, 1977.

Hewett, P. E. *Russellism Exposed*. 2nd ed. Grand Rapids: Zondervan, 1941.

Hoekema, Anthony. *Jehovah's Witnesses*. Grand Rapids: Eerdmans, 1963.

Hudson, John Allen. *Russell White Debate*. 2nd ed. Cincinnati: Rowe, 1912.

Jehovah's Witnesses. New York: Vantage, 1978.

Jehovah's Witnesses in the Divine Purpose. Brooklyn: Watchtower Bible and Tract Society, 1959.

The Kingdom Is at Hand. Brooklyn: Watchtower Bible and Tract Society, 1944.

Kneedler, William H. *Christian Answers to Jehovah's Witnesses*. Chicago: Moody Press, 1953.

Let God be True. Brooklyn: Watchtower Bible and Tract Society, 1952.

Let Your Name Be Sanctified. Brooklyn: Watchtower Bible and Tract Society, 1961.

MacMillan, A. H. *Faith on the March*. Englewood Cliffs, N.J.: Prentice-Hall, 1957.

Make Sure of All Things. Brooklyn: Watchtower Bible and Tract Society, 1965.

Manty, Julius R. *Is Death the Only Punishment for Believers?* Santa Ana, Calif.: CARIS, n.d.

Martin, Walter R. *Jehovah's Witnesses.* Minneapolis: Bethany, 1970.

_____. *The Kingdom of the Cults.* Minneapolis: Bethany, 1985.

Mayer, F. E. *Jehovah's Witnesses.* Rev. ed. St. Louis: Concordia, 1957.

McKinney, George D. *The Theology of the Jehovah's Witnesses.* Grand Rapids: Zondervan, 1962.

Metzger, Bruce. "The Jehovah's Witnesses and Jesus Christ." *Theology Today* (April 1953), 65–85.

Montague, Havor. *Jehovah's Witnesses and Blood Transfusions.* Santa Ana, Calif.: CARIS, 1978.

The New Earth. Brooklyn: Watchtower Bible and Tract Society, 1942.

New Heaven and a New Earth. Brooklyn: Watchtower Bible and Tract Society, 1953.

New World Translation of the Christian Greek Scriptures. Brooklyn: Watchtower Bible and Tract Society, 1951.

New World Translation of the Hebrew Scriptures. 5 vols. Brooklyn: Watchtower Bible and Tract Society, 1953–60.

Penton, James M. *Apocalypse Delayed: The Story of Jehovah's Witnesses.* Toronto: Univ. of Toronto Press, 1997.

Richardson, James T., and Pauline Cote. "Disciplined Litigation, Vigilante Litigation, and Deformation: Dramatic Organizational Change in Jehovah's Witnesses." *Journal for the Scientific Study of Religion* 40 (2001): 11–25.

Ross, J. J. *Some Facts about the Self-Styled "Pastor," Charles T. Russell.* New York: Charles C. Cook, n.d.

_____. *Some Facts and More Facts about the Self-Styled "Pastor" Charles T. Russell.* Philadelphia: Philadelphia School of the Bible, n.d.

Russell, Charles Taze. *Studies in the Scriptures.* 7 vols. Brooklyn: Watchtower Bible and Tract Society, 1886–1917.

Rutherford, Joseph Franklin. *Creation.* Brooklyn: Watchtower Bible and Tract Society, 1927.

_____. *Deliverance.* Brooklyn: Watchtower Bible and Tract Society, 1926.

_____. *The Harp of God.* Brooklyn: Watchtower Bible and Tract Society, 1921.

_____. *Jehovah.* Brooklyn: Watchtower Bible and Tract Society, 1934.

_____. *Life.* Brooklyn: Watchtower Bible and Tract Society, 1929.

_____. *Millions Now Living Will Never Die!* Brooklyn: International Bible Students Association, 1920.

_____. *Preparation.* Brooklyn: Watchtower Bible and Tract Society, 1933.

_____. *Prophecy.* Brooklyn: Watchtower Bible and Tract Society, 1929.

_____. *Religion.* Brooklyn: Watchtower Bible and Tract Society, 1940.

_____. *Salvation.* Brooklyn: Watchtower Bible and Tract Society, 1939.

_____. *Vindication.* Brooklyn: Watchtower Bible and Tract Society, 1931–32.

_____. *Where Are the Dead?* Brooklyn: Watchtower Bible and Tract Society, 1932.

Schnell, William J. *Christians: Awake!* Grand Rapids: Baker, 1959.

_____. *Into the Light of Christianity.* Grand Rapids: Baker, 1975.

_____. *Jehovah's Witnesses Errors Exposed.* Grand Rapids: Baker, 1977.

_____. *Thirty Years a Watchtower Slave.* Grand Rapids: Baker, 1956.

Stark, Rodney, and Laurence Iannaccone. "Why the Jehovah's Witnesses Grow So Rapidly: A Theoretical Application." *Journal of Contemporary Religion* 12 (1997): 133–56.

Sterling, Chandler W. *The Witnesses: One God, One Victory.* Chicago: Regency, 1975.

Stevenson, William C. *The Inside Story of Jehovah's Witnesses.* New York: Hart, 1967.

_____. *Year of Doom.* London: Hutchinson, 1967.

Stilson, Max. *How to Deal with Jehovah's Witnesses.* Grand Rapids: Zondervan, 1962.

Strauss, Lehman. *An Examination of the Doctrine of "Jehovah's Witnesses."* New York: Loizeaux Brothers, 1942.

Stroup, Herbert Hewitt. *The Jehovah's Witnesses.* New York: Columbia Univ. Press, 1945.

Theocratic Aid to Kingdom Publishers. Brooklyn: Watchtower Bible and Tract Society, 1945.

Things in Which it Is Impossible for God to Lie. Brooklyn: Watchtower Bible and Tract Society, 1965.

This Means Everlasting Life. Brooklyn: Watchtower Bible and Tract Society, 1950.

Thomas, F. W. *Masters of Deception.* Grand Rapids: Baker, 1972.

Thomas, Stan. *Jehovah's Witnesses and What They Believe.* Grand Rapids: Zondervan, 1967.

The Truth Shall Make You Free. Brooklyn: Watchtower Bible and Tract Society, 1968.

The Truth that Leads to Eternal Life. Brooklyn: Watchtower Bible and Tract Society, 1968.

Van Buskirk, Michael. *The Scholastic Dishonesty of the Watchtower.* Santa Ana, Calif.: CARIS, 1977.

Wah, Carolyn R. "Jehovah's Witnesses and the Responsibility of Religious Freedom: The European Experience." *Journal of Church and State* 43 (2001): 578–601.

The Watchtower. Brooklyn: Watchtower Bible and Tract Society. (Various issues).

Watchtower Reprints, 1879–1919. 7 vols. Brooklyn: Watchtower Bible and Tract Society, n.d.

You May Survive Armageddon. Brooklyn: Watchtower Bible and Tract Society, 1965.

Wilson, Diane. *Awakening of a Jehovah's Witness: Escape from the Watchtower Society.* Amherst, N.Y.: Prometheus, 2002.

Zellner, William, and William Kephart. *Extraordinary Groups: Jehovah's Witnesses.* New York; St. Martin's, 1993.

JUDAISM

Baron, Salo W. *A Social and Religious History of the Jews.* 2nd ed. 15 vols. New York: Columbia Univ. Press, 1952–73.

Breslauer, S. Daniel, *Understanding Judaism through History.* Belmont, Calif.: Wadsworth, 2002.

Bright, John, and William P. Brown. *A History of Israel.* 4th ed. Louisville: Westminster John Knox, 2000.

Childs, Brevard. *Introduction to the Old Testament as Scripture.* Philadelphia: Fortress, 1979.

Encyclopedia Judaica. New York: Macmillan, 1972.

Encyclopedia of Judaism. Ed. Geoffrey Wigoder. New York: Macmillan, 1989.

Mansoor, Menahem. *Jewish History and Thought: An Introduction.* Hoboken, N.J.: Ktav, 1991.

Neusner, Jacob. *American Judaism: Adventures in Modernity.* New York: Ktav, 1972.

_____. *Foundations of Judaism.* Minneapolis: Augsburg Fortress, 1988.

_____. *The Enchantments of Judaism.* Atlanta: Scholars Press, 1990.

Sachar, Howard M. *A History of the Jews in America.* New York: Knopf, 1992. (This work contains an exhaustive bibliography of contemporary Jewish sources.)

Schulman, Albert M. *Gateway to Judaism: Encyclopedia Home Reference.* 2 vols. New York: Yoseloff, 1971.

Schwarz, Leo W. *Great Ages and Ideas of the Jewish People.* New York: Random House, 1977.

von Rad, Gerhard. *Old Testament Theology.* 2 vols. Trans. D. M. G. Stalker. Louisville: Westminster John Knox, 2001.

Witty, Abraham B., and Rachel Witty. *Exploring Jewish Tradition.* New York: Doubleday, 2001.

Young, Edward J. *An Introduction to the Old Testament.* Grand Rapids: Eerdmans, 1964.

LIFESPRING

Haaken, Janice. "Pathology as 'Personal Growth': A Participant-Observation Study of Lifespring Training." *Psychiatry* 46 (1983): 270–80.

Masalkov, I. K. " *Lifespring* in Moscow: Impressions, Problems, Outlook." *Sotsiologicheskie-Issledovaniya* 17 (1990): 145–51.

Yalom, Irvin D. *The Theory and Practice of Group Psychotherapy.* 4th ed. New York: Basic Books, 1995.

MASONIC LODGE

Mather, George A, and Larry A. Nichols. *Masonic Lodge.* Grand Rapids: Zondervan, 1995. (An extensive bibliography of Freemasonry is contained in this volume).

MEHER BABA

Ball, Carolyn. *Meher Baba's Next Wave: Ordinary People's Encounters with God.* Asheville, N.C.: Arti, 2000.

Davy, Kitty. *Love Alone Prevails.* North Myrtle Beach, S.C.: Sheriar Foundation, 2001.

Lux, Kenneth. *Meher Baba: Avatar of the Tortoise.* Rockland, Md.: Seven Coin, 2001.

MORMONISM

Albanes, Richard. *One Nation under God: A History of the Mormon Church.* New York: Four Walls Eight Windows, 2002.

Allen, James B., and Glen M. Leonard. *The Secret of the Latter-day Saints.* Salt Lake City: Deseret, 1969.

_____. *The Story of the Latter-day Saints.* Salt Lake City: Deseret, 1992.

Anderson, Einar. *The Inside Story of Mormonism.* Grand Rapids: Kregel, 1973.

Ankerberg, John, and John Weldon. *What Do Mormons Really Believe?* Eugene, Ore.: Harvest House, 2002.

_____. *The Facts on the Mormon Church: A Handy Guide to Understanding the Claims of Mormonism.* Eugene, Ore.: Harvest House, 2003.

Baer, Hans A. *Recreating Utopia in the Deseret: A Sectarian Challenge to Modern Mormonism.* Albany, N.Y.: State Univ. of New York Press, 1988.

Barlow, Philip L. *Mormons and the Bible: The Place of the Latter-day Saints in America.* New York: Oxford Univ. Press, 1991.

Beckwith, Francis J., Carl Mosser, and Paul Owen. *The New Mormon Challenge: Responding to the Latest Defenses of a Fast-Growing Movement.* Grand Rapids: Zondervan, 2002.

Beecher, Maureen V., and Lavinia F. Anderson, eds. *Mormon Women in Historical and Cultural Perspective.* Urbana: Univ. of Illinois Press, 1987.

Bennett, Wallace Foster. *Why I Am a Mormon.* New York: Nelson, 1958.

Bitton, Davis, and Leonard J. Arrington. *Mormons and Their Historians.* Salt Lake City: Univ. of Utah Press, 1988.

Brodie, Fawn M. *No Man Knows My History.* New York: Knopf, 1971.

Brooks, John L. *The Refiner's Fire: The Making of Mormon Cosmology, 1644–1844.* New York: Cambridge Univ. Press, 1994.

Brooks, Juanita. *John D. Lee.* Glendale, Calif.: Arthur H. Clark, 1973.

Call, Lamoni. *2000 Changes in the Book of Mormon.* Salt Lake City: Modern Microfilm, n.d.

Carmer, Carl Lamson. *The Farm Boy and the Angel.* Garden City, N.Y.: Doubleday, 1970.

Carter, Kate B. *Our Pioneer Heritage.* Salt Lake City: Daughters of Utah Pioneers, 1962.

Coats, James. *In Mormon Circles, Gentiles, Jack Mormons, and Latter Day Saints.* Reading, Mass.: Addison-Wesley, 1991.

Cowan, Marvin. *Mormon Claims Answered.* Salt Lake City: Marvin W. Cowan, n.d.

Cowdery, Wayne, et al. *Who Really Wrote the Book of Mormon? The Spaulding Enigma.* Santa Ana, Calif.: Vision House, 1977.

Davies, Douglas. *An Introduction to Mormonism.* Cambridge: Cambridge Univ. Press, 2003.

Decker, Ed, and David Hunt. *The God Makers.* Eugene, Ore.: Harvest House, 1984.

Deming, A. B. *Naked Truths about Mormonism.* Oakland, Calif.: Deming, 1888.

Draper, Maurice I. *Christ's Church Restored.* Independence, Mo.: Herald House, 1948.

Edwards, Paul M. *Our Legacy of Faith: A Brief History of the RCJCLDS.* Independence, Mo.: Herald House, 1991.

Embry, Jessie L. *Mormon Polygamous Families.* Salt Lake City: Univ. of Utah Press, 1987.

The Encyclopedia of Mormonism. New York: Macmillan, 1991.

Evans, Arza. *The Keystone of Mormonism.* St. George, Ut.: Keystone, 2005.

Evans, R. H. *One Hundred Years of Mormonism.* Salt Lake City: Deseret, 1905.

Fales, Susan L., and Chad L. Flake, eds. *Mormons and Mormonism in the U.S. Government Documents: A Bibliography.* Salt Lake City: Univ. of Utah Press, 1989.

Firmage, Edwin B., and Richard C. Mangrum. *Zion in the Courts: A Legal History of the CJCLDS, 1830–1900.* Urbana: Univ. of Illinois Press, 1988.

Foster, Ralph Leonard. *The Book of Mormon on Trial.* Klamath Falls, Ore.: Foster, 1963.

Gibbs, Josiah F. *The Mountain Meadows Massacre.* Salt Lake City: Tribune, 1910.

Gottlieb, Robert, and Peter Wiley. *America's Saints: The Rise of Mormon Power.* New York: Putnam, 1984.

Hanson, Paul M. *Jesus Christ among the Early Americans.* Independence, Mo.: Herald House, 1959.

Hoekema, Anthony. *Mormonism.* Grand Rapids: Eerdmans, 1963.

Houghey, Hal. *Latter-day Saints, Where Do You Get Your Authority?* Concord, Calif.: Pacific, 1971.

Howe, Daniel Walker. "Mormonism and Music: A History." *Pacific Historical Review* 60 (May 1991): 257.

Howe, E. D. *History of Mormonism.* Painsville, Ohio: Howe, 1840.

Hughes, Dean. *The Mormon Church: A Basic History.* Salt Lake City: Deseret, 1990.

Johanson, W.F. Walker. *What Is Mormonism About? Answers to 150 Most Commonly Asked Questions about the Church of Latter-day Saints.* New York: St. Martin's, 2002.

Kaiser, Edgar I. *How to Respond to Latter-day Saints.* St. Louis: Concordia, 1977.

Launius, Roger D. *Joseph Smith III: Pragmatic Prophet*. Urbana: Univ. of Illinios Press, 1988.

Lee, John D. *Confessions of John D. Lee*. Salt Lake City: Modern Microfilm, n.d.

Lindsey, Robert. *A Gathering of Saints*. New York: Simon & Schuster, 1988.

Mallamo, Paul Douglas. "The Church of Modern Day Mormonism." *Whole Earth Review* (Fall 1988), 122–24.

Martin, Walter R. *Kingdom of the Cults*. 2nd ed. Minneapolis: Bethany, 1985.

_____. *The Maze of Mormonism*. Santa Ana, Calif.: Vision House, 1977.

McConkie, Bruce R. *Mormon Doctrine*. Salt Lake City: Bookcraft, 1958.

McConkie, Oscar W. *Aaronic Priesthood*. Salt Lake City: Deseret, 1977.

Millennial Star. 51 vols. Salt Lake City: Church of Jesus Christ of Latter-day Saints, 1957.

Naifeh, Steven W., and Gregory White Smith. *The Mormon Murders*. New York: Weidenfeld & Nicolson, 1988.

Nibley, Hugh. *The Message of the Joseph Smith Papyri: An Egyptian Endowment*. Salt Lake City: Deseret, 1975.

_____. *The Myth Makers*. Salt Lake City: Bookcraft, 1961.

O'Dea, Thomas F. *The Mormons*. Chicago: Univ. of Chicago Press, 1957.

Ostling, R., and J. Ostling, *The Power and the Promise: Mormon America*. San Fransico: Harper, 1999.

Peck, Reed. *Reed Peck Manuscripts*. Salt Lake City: Modern Microfilm, n.d.

Peterson, Mark E. *Adam: Who Is He?* Salt Lake City: Deseret, 1976.

Proctor, Scott. *Witness of the Light*. Salt Lake City: Deseret, 1991.

Reed, David A., and John R. Farakas. *Mormons: Answered Verse by Verse*. Grand Rapids: Baker, 1992.

Richards, LeGrand. *A Marvelous Work and a Wonder*. Salt Lake City: Deseret, 1950.

Rogers, Paul Brinkley. "Polygamy Thrives Among Maverick Mormons." *American Republic* (February 1992).

Ropp, Harry L. *The Mormon Papers*. Downers Grove, Ill.: InterVarsity Press, 1977.

Roston, Leo. *Religions in America*. New York: Simon & Schuster, 1963.

Sarna, Jonathan. *American Judaism*. New Haven, Conn.: Yale Univ. Press, 2004.

Schipps, Jan. *Mormonism: The Story of a New Religious Tradition*. Urbana: Univ. of Illinois Press, 1985.

Schook, Charles A. *The True Origin of the Book of Mormon*. Cincinnati: Standard, 1914.

Schupe, Anson. *The Darker Side of Virtue: Corruption, Scandal, and the Mormon Empire*. Buffalo, N.Y.: Prometheus, 1991.

Smith, Joseph Jr. *A Book of Commandments for the Government of the Church of Christ*. Zion, Mo.: Phelps, 1833.

_____. *The Book of Mormon*. Salt Lake City: Church of Jesus Christ of Latter-day Saints, 1974.

_____. *The Doctrine and Covenants of the Church of Latter-day Saints*. Salt Lake City: Church of Jesus Christ of Latter-day Saints, 1968.

_____. *History of the Church of Jesus Christ of Latter-day Saints*. 7 vols. Salt Lake City: Deseret, 1958.

_____. *Pearl of Great Price*. Salt Lake City: Church of Jesus Christ of Latter-day Saints, 1967.

Smith, Joseph Fielding. *Doctrines of Salvation*. 3 vols. Ed. Bruce R. McConkie. Salt Lake City: Bookcraft, 1972.

_____. *Gospel Doctrine*. Salt Lake City: Deseret, 1958.

_____. *The Way of Perfection*. Salt Lake City: Deseret, 1958.

Smith, Lucy. *Biographical Sketches of Joseph Smith the Prophet and His Progenitors of Many Generations*. Liverpool, Eng.: Richards, 1853.

Spalding, Solomon. *Manuscript Story*. Lamoni, Ia.: Reorganized Church of Christ Latter-day Saints, 1885.

Spencer, James R. "When Christians Meet Mormons. Mormons Aren't Protestants with Doctrinal Problems: They Worship a Different God." *Christian Herald* (February 1988), 45.

Starks, Arthur E. *A Complete Concordance to the Book of Mormon*. Independence, Mo.: Herald House, 1950.

Talmadge, James E. *The Articles of Faith*. Reprint. Salt Lake City: The Church of Jesus Christ of Latter-day Saints, 1974.

_____. *Jesus the Christ*. Salt Lake City: Deseret, 1916.

Tanner, Jerald, and Sandra Tanner. *The Changing World of Mormonism*. Chicago: Moody Press, 1979.

_____. *Changes in Joseph Smith's History*. Salt Lake City: Modern Microfilm, 1961.

_____. *Changes in the Key to Theology*. Salt Lake City: Modern Microfilm, n.d.

_____. *Changes in the Pearl of Great Price*. Salt Lake City: Modern Microfilm, n.d.

_____. *Mormonism: Shadow or Reality*. 5th ed. Salt Lake City: Utah Lighthouse, 1987.

Taves, Earnest H. *Trouble Enough: Joseph Smith and the Book of Mormon*. Buffalo, N.Y.: Prometheus, 1984.

Whalen, William J. "Why Mormonism Is the Fastest Growing Religion in the West." *U.S. Catholic* (June 1989), 28.

White, O Kendell. *Mormon Neo-Orthodoxy: A Crisis Theology*. Salt Lake City: Signature, 1987.

Widsoe, John A. *Discourses of Brigham Young*. Salt Lake City: Deseret, 1973.

Wise, William. *Massacre at Mountain Meadows*. New York: Crowell, 1976.

Wood, Wilford C. *Joseph Smith Begins His Work*. 2 vols. Salt Lake City: Deseret, 1962.

Young, Brigham. *Journal History*. Salt Lake City: Church of Jesus Christ of Latter-day Saints, 1846.

NATION OF YAHWEH

Boyd, Herb. "Leader of Black Hebrews Found Guilty of Conspiracy." *Amsterdam News* 4 (1992).

Freedberg, Sydney. *Brother Love: Murder, Money, and a Messiah*. New York: Pantheon, 1994.

_____, and Donna Gehrke. "Black Messiah Leads Followers into Legal Trouble." *Washington Post* 7/2 (1991).

Johnson, Terry E. "Yahweh Way." *Newsweek* 108/31 (1986).

Leerhsen, Charles. "Busting the Prince of Love." *Newsweek* 116/45 (1990).

Salaam, Yusef. "Murder Charges against Yahweh Dismissed." *Amsterdam News* 6/1 (1995).

NATIVE AMERICAN RELIGIONS

Hirschfelder, Arlene, and Paulette Moline. *Encyclopedia of Native American Religions*. New York: Facts on File, 2001.

Martin, Joel. *The Land Looks after Us: A History of Native American Religion*. Oxford: Oxford Univ. Press, 2001.

Stewart, Omer. *Peyote Religion: A History*. Oklahoma City: Univ. of Oklahoma Press, 1993.

Sullivan, Lawrence. *Native Religions and Cultures of North America: Anthropology of the Sacred*. New York: Continuum, 2003.

Vecsey, Christopher, ed. *Handbook of American Indian Religious Freedom*. New York: Crossroad, 1991.

Vine, Deloria, Jr. *God Is Red: A Nature View of Religion*, Golden, Colo.: Fulcrum, 1994.

NEW AGE MOVEMENT

Andrews, Lewis M. *To Thine Own Self Be True: The Rebirth of Values in the New Ethical Therapy*. Garden City, N.Y.: Doubleday, 1987.

Arnold, Ron. *Ecology Wars: Environmentalism as if People Mattered*. Bellevue, Wash.: Merril, 1987.

Baer, Randall N. *Inside the New Age Nightmare*. Lafayette, La.: Huntington, 1989.

Bahro, Rudolf. *Building the Green Movement*. London: GMP, 1986.

Barbour, Ian, G. *Issues in Science and Religion*. New York: Harper & Row, 1971.

_____. *Myths, Models, and Paradigms: A Comparative Study in Science and Religion*. San Francisco: Harper & Row, 1974.

Bateson, Gregory. "Faith in the Post-modern Millenium: God as the Pattern That Connects." *New Perspectives Quarterly* 8 (Spring 1991): 40–43.

Beckett, Samuel. *Lucis Trust-World Goodwill Newsletter* (Summer 1982).

Berry, Thomas, *The Dream of the Earth*. San Francisco: Sierra Club, 1990.

Brooke, Tal. *When the World Will Be as One*. Eugene Ore.: Harvest House, 1988.

Brow, Robert. "The Taming of a New Age Prophet: What Do Sweat Lodges and Mother Earth Have to Do with Christianity?" *Christianity Today* (June 16, 1989), 28–30.

Bryan, Gerald B., Talita Paolini, and Kenneth Paolini. *Psychic Dictatorship in America*. Paradise Valley, Mont.: Paolini International LLC, 2000.

Capra, Fritjof. *The Tao of Physics: An Exploration of the Parallels between Modern Physics and Eastern Mysticism*. Boston: Shambhala, 1990.

_____.*Turning Point: Science, Society, and Rising Culture*. New York: Simon & Schuster, 1982.

Carlson, Judith L., and Elizabeth R. Burchard. *19 Years in a New Age Group: Torn from the Arms of Satan*. Closter, N.J.: Ace Academics, 1999.

Chandler, Russell. *Racing Toward 2001: The Forces Shaping America's Religious Future*. Grand Rapids: Zondervan, 1992.

Cody, M. L., and J. M. Diamond. *Ecology and Evolution of Communities*. Cambridge, Mass.: Harvard Univ. Press, 1975.

Coffman, Michael S. *Environmentalism! The Dawn of Aquarius or the Twilight of a New Dark Age*. Bangor, Me.: Environmental Perspectives, 1992.

Creme, Benjamin. *The Reappearance of the Christ and the Masters of Wisdom*. Los Angeles: Tara, 1980.

Cumbey, Constance. *The Hidden Dangers of the Rainbow: The New Age Movement and Our Coming Age of Barbarism*. Shreveport, La.: Huntington House, 1983.

Dewitt, Calvin B. "The Religious Foundation of Ecology." In *The Mother Earth Handbook*. Ed. J. Scherff. New York: Continuum, 1991.

Diamond, Irene, and Gloria Feman Orenstein, eds. *Reweaving the World: The Emergence of Ecofeminism*. San Francisco: Sierra Club, 1990.

Dowd, Alice. "What's New in the New Age?" *Library Journal* 116 (March 1991): 58–61.

Ferguson, Marilyn. *The Aquarian Conspiracy: Personal and Social Transformation in the 1980s*. Los Angeles: Archer, 1980.

Fikes, Jay Courtney. *Carlos Castaneda, Academic Opportunism and the Psychedelic Sixties*. New York: Madison, 1993.

Fox, Warwick. *Toward a Transpersonal Ecology: Developing New Foundations for Environmentalism*. Boston: Shambhala, 1990.

Frankl, Viktor. *Man's Search for Meaning*. New York: Pocket Books, 1973.

_____. *The Unconscious God*. New York: Simon & Schuster, 1978.

_____. *The Unheard Cry for Meaning*. New York: Simon & Schuster, 1978.

Gobal, Frank. *The Third Force*. New York: Pocket Books, 1971.

Gordon, Suzanne. *Lonely in America*. New York: Simon & Schuster, 1976.

Gribbin, John. *Hothouse Earth: The Greenhouse Effect and Gaia*. New York: Grove Wiedenfield, 1990.

Groothuis, Douglas. "Confronting the New Age." *Christianity Today* (Jan. 13, 1989), 36–39.

_____. *Revealing the New Age*. Downers Grove, Ill.: InterVarsity Press, 1990.

_____. "The Shamanized Jesus: Simple Facts and Straightforward Arguments Can Refute New Agers Distortions of Jesus—and Draw Them to His Love." *Christianity Today* (Apr. 29, 1991), 20.

_____. *Unmasking the New Age*. Downers Grove, Ill.: InterVarsity Press, 1986.

Harman, Willis. *Global Mind Change: The Promise of the Last Years of the Twentieth Century*. Indianapolis: Knowledge Systems, 1988.

Heelas, Paul. *The New Age Movement: Celebrating the Self and the Sacralization of Modernity*. Oxford: Basil Blackwell, 1996.

Hexham, Irving, and Karla Poewe-Hexham. "The Soul of the New Age." *Christianity Today* (Sept. 2, 1988), 17–21.

Ingenito, Marcia Gervase, ed. *National New Age Yellow Pages*. Fullerton, Calif.: Highgate, 1988.

Kautz, William H., and Melanie Branon. *Channeling: The Intuitive Connection*. San Francisco: Harper & Row, 1987.

Keys, Donald. *Earth at Omega: Passage to Planetization*. Brookline Village, Mass.: Branden, 1982.

Kinney, Jay. "Déja Vu: The Hidden History of the New Age." *Utne Reader* (September–October 1989), 109.

Kjos, Beerit. *Under the Spell of Mother Earth*. Wheaton, Ill.: Victor, 1992.

Klimo, Jon. *Channeling: Investigations on Receiving Information from Paranormal Sources*. Los Angeles: Jeremy P. Tarcher, 1987.

Kuhn, Thomas. *The Structure of Scientific Revolutions*. Chicago: Univ. of Chicago Press, 1962.

Levi, H. Dowling. *The Aquarian Gospel of Jesus the Christ*. Santa Monica, Calif.: DeVorss, 1972.

Lipnack, Jessica, and Jeffrey Stamps. *Networking*. Garden City, N.Y.: Doubleday, 1982.

Lochhaas, Philip H. *How to Respond to the New Age Movement*. St. Louis: Concordia, 1973.

Lovelock, James E. *Healing Gaia: Practical Medicine for the Planet*. New York: Harmony, 1991.

_____. *The Ages of Gaia: A Biography of Our Living Earth*. New York: Bantam, 1988.

_____. *Gaia: A New Look at Life on Earth*. Oxford: Oxford Univ. Press, 1979.

Manes, Christopher. *Green Rage, Radical Environmentalism and the Unmaking of Civilization*. New York: Little & Brown, 1990.

Martin, Walter. *The New Age Cult*. Minneapolis: Bethany, 1989.

Melton, J. Gordon. *New Age Encyclopedia*. 1st ed. Detroit: Gale Research, 1990.

_____. *Finding Enlightenment: Ramtha's School of Ancient Wisdom*. Hillsboro, Ore.: Beyond Words, 1998.

Miller, Elliot. *A Crash Course in the New Age Movement*. Grand Rapids: Baker, 1989.

The New Age Catalog. Garden City, N.Y.: Doubleday, 1988.

"New Age No More." *U.S. News & World Report* (Dec. 17, 1990), 36.

Ostling, Richard N. "When God Was Woman." *Time* (May 6, 1991), 73.

Popenoe, Chris, and Oliver Popenoe. *Seeds of Tomorrow: New Age Communities That Work*. San Francisco: Harper & Row, 1984.

Porritt, Jonathan. *Seeing Green*. Oxford: Blackwell, 1986.

Ramtha, with Douglas James Mahr. *Voyage to the New World*. Friday Harbor, Wash.: Masterworks, 1985.

Ray, Dixie Lee. *Trashing the Planet*. Washington, D.C.: Regency Gateway, 1990.

Reisser, Paul C., Teri K. Reisser, and John Weldon. *The Holistic Healers*. Downers Grove, Ill.: InterVarsity Press, 1983.

Rhodes, Ronald. *New Age Movement*. Grand Rapids: Zondervan, 1995.

Rifkin, Jeremy. *Entropy: A New World*. New York: Viking, 1980.

Roberts, Jane. *The Seth Material*. Englewood Cliffs, N.J.: Prentice-Hall, 1970.

Roberts, Marjorie. "A Linguistic 'Nay' to Channeling." *Psychology Today* 23 (October 1989): 64.

Roszak, Theodore. *Seth Speaks: The Eternal Validity of the Soul*. Englewood Cliffs, N.J.: Prentice-Hall, 1972.

_____. *Unfinished Animal*. New York: Harper & Row, 1977.

_____. *Where the Wasteland Ends*. Garden City, N.Y.: Doubleday, 1972.

Russell, Peter. *The Global Brain*. Los Angeles: Tarcher, 1983.

Sagan, Carl. *Cosmos*. New York: Random House, 1980.

Saliba, John A. *Christian Responses to the New Age Movement: A Critical Assessment*. London: Geoffrey Chapman, 1999.

Satin, Mark. *New Age Politics: Healing Self and Society*. New York: Dell, 1978.

Scherf, Judith S., ed. *Mother Earth Handbook*. New York: Continuum, 1991.

Spangler, David. *Explorations: Emerging Aspects of the New Planetary Culture*. Morayshire, U.K.: Findhorn, 1980.

_____. *Reflections on the Christ*. 3rd ed. Morayshire, U.K.: Findhorn, 1977.

_____. *Relationship and Identity*. Morayshire, U.K.: Findhorn, 1978.

_____. *Revelation: The Birth of a New Age*. Middletown, Wis.: Lorian, 1976.

_____. *Towards a Planetary Vision*. 2nd ed. Morayshire, U.K.: Findhorn, 1977.

Stafford, Tim. "The Kingdom of Cult Watchers." *Christianity Today* (Oct. 7, 1991), 18–22.

Steiger, Brad. *Revelation: The Divine Fire*. Englewood Cliffs, N.J.: Prentice-Hall, 1973.

Talbot, Michael. *Mysticism and the New Physics*. New York: Bantam, 1981.

Taylor, Peggy. *New Age Sourcebook*. Brighton, Mass.: New Age Journal, 1992.

Tucker, Ruth A. *Another Gospel: Alternative Religons and the New Age Movement*. Grand Rapids: Zondervan, 2004.

Wallis, Claudia. "Why New Age Medicine Is Catching On." *Time* (Nov. 4, 1991), 68–75.

Wauk, John. "Paganism, American Style." *National Review* (March 1990), 43–44.

Weston, Robin. *Channels: A New Age Directory*. New York: Perigee, 1988.

Wilber, Ken. *Eye to Eye: The Quest of the New Paradigm*. Garden City, N.Y.: Anchor-Doubleday, 1983.

_____. *The Spectrum of Consciousness*. Wheaton, Ill.: Theosophical, 1977.

Winsor, James. *Self-Deception: The New Age Movement—A Scriptural Expose*. St Louis: Concordia, 1973.

OCCULT

Caldwell, Daniel H., ed. *The Occult World of Madame Blavatsky*. Tuscon, Ariz.: Impossible Dreams, 1991.

Furnham, Adrian. "Hooked on Horoscopes." *New Scientist* (January 1991), 33.

Montgomery, John Warwick. *Principalities and Powers: The World of the Occult*. Minneapolis: Bethany, 1973.

Vaughn, Richard. *Astrology in Modern Language*. Sebastopol, Calif.: CRCS Publications, 1992.

ONENESS PENTECOSTALS

Balmer, Randall. *Blessed Assurance: A History of Evangelicalism in America.* Boston: Beacon, 1999.

Bjornstad, James, and Walter Bjork. *Jesus Only: A Modalistic Interpretation.* Wayne, N.J.: Christian Research Institute, 1970.

Blumhofer, Edith L., Russell P. Spittler, and Grant A. Wacker, eds. *Pentecostal Currents in America.* Urbana and Chicago: Univ. of Illinois Press, 1999.

Bousset, Wilhelm. *Kyrios Christos: A History of the Belief in Christ from the Beginning of Christianity to Irenaeus.* 5th ed. Trans. John E. Steely. New York: Abingdon, 1970.

Brumbeck, Carl. *God in Three Persons.* Cleveland, Tenn.: Pathway, 1959.

Burgess, M. Stanley, and Eduard M. Van Der Maas, eds. Revised and expanded. *The New International Dictionary of Pentecostal and Charismatic Movements.* Grand Rapids: Zondervan, 2002.

Campbell, Alexander. *The Christian System in Reference to the Union of Christians, and a Restoration of Primitive Christianity, as Plead in the Current Reformation.* Nashville, Tenn.: Gospel Advocate, 1956.

Cagle, Odell. *Echoes of the Past.* Oneness Pentecostal Pioneer Series. Stockton, Calif.: Apostolic, 1972.

Clanton, Arthur L. *United We Stand: A History of Oneness Organizations.* Hazelwood, Mo.: Pentecostal, 1970.

Cox, Harvey. *Fire from Heaven: The Rise of Pentecostalism Spirituality and the Reshaping of Religion in the Twenty-first Century.* Reading, Mass.: Addison-Wesley. 1995.

Dugas, Paul D. *The Life and Writings of Elder G. T. Haywood.* Oneness Pentecostal Pioneer Series. Stockton, Calif.: Apostolic, 1968.

Ewart, Frank J. *Jesus: The Man and the Mystery.* Nashville: Baird-Ward, 1941.

_____. *The Phenomena of Pentecost: A History of the "Latter Rain."* St. Louis: Pentecostal, 1947.

Facts about the United Pentecostal Church International. Hazelwood, Mo.: Pentecostal, n.d.

Golder, Morris E. *The Principals of Our Doctrine.* Cincinnati, Ohio: Apostolic Light, n.d.

Hall, William Phillips. *Calling upon the Name of the Lord.* Cos Cob, Conn.: Christ Witness, 1920.

Hollenweger, Walter J. *Pentecostalism: Origins and Developments Worldwide.* Peabody, Mass.: Hendrickson, 1997.

Kenyon, Essex W. *The Father and His Family.* Spencer, Mass.: Reality, 1916.

Lampe, G. W. H. *The Seal of the Spirit.* New York: Longmans, 1951.

Menzies, William. *Anointed to Serve.* Springfield, Mo.: Gospel, 1971.

Miller, Luke. *A Review of the "Jesus Only" Doctrine.* Auston, Tex.: Firm Foundation, 1959.

Nichol, John T. *The Pentecostals: The Story of the Growth and Development of a Vital New Force in the Christian Church.* Rev. ed. Plainfield, N.J.: Logos International, 1971.

Norris, S. G. *The Mighty God in Christ.* St. Paul, Minn.: Apostolic Bible Institute, n.d.

Pugh, J. T. *For Preachers Only.* Hazelwood, Mo.: Pentecostal, 1971.

Reed, David. "Aspects of the Origins of Oneness Pentecostalism." In *Aspects of Pentecostal-Charismatic Origins.* Ed. Vinson Synan. Plainfield, N.J.: Logos International, 1975.

_____. "Oneness Pentecostalism." Pages 644–51 in *Dictionary of Pentecostal and Charismatic Movements.* Edited by Stanley M. Burgess and Gary B. McGee. Grand Rapids: Zondervan, 1988.

Reynolds, Ralph V. *Truth Shall Triumph: A Study of Pentecostal Doctrines.* St. Louis: Pentecostal, 1965.

Richardson, Cyril. *The Doctrine of the Trinity.* New York: Abingdon, 1958.

Sawyer, Thomas J. *Who Is Our God? The Son or the Father? A Review of Henry Ward Beecher.* New York: Thatcher & Hutchinson, 1859.

Smith, Timothy. *Revivalism and Social Reform in Mid-Nineteenth Century America.* New York: Abingdon, 1957.

Synan, Vinson. *The Century of the Holy Spirit: 100 Years of Pentecostal and Charismatic Renewal, 1901–2001.* Nashville: Nelson, 2001.

Urshan, Andrew D. *The Doctrine of the New Birth or the Perfect Way to Eternal Life.* Cochrane, Wis.: Witness of God, 1921.

Weeks, Robert D. *Jehovah-Jesus: The Oneness of God: The True Trinity.* New York: Dodd, Mead & Co., 1876.

What We Believe and Teach: Articles of Faith of the United Pentecostal Church. St. Louis: Pentecostal, n.d.

ORDER OF THE SOLAR TEMPLE

Hall, John, and Phillip Schuyler. "The Mystical Apocalypse of the Solar Temple." Pages 285–311 in *Millennium, Messiahs, and Mayhem*. Ed. Thomas Robbins and Susan J. Palmer. New York: Routledge. 1997.

Introvigne, Massimo. "Ordeal by Fire: The Tragedy of the Solar Temple," *Religion* 25 (July 1995): 267–83.

_____. "Armageddon in Switzerland: The Solar Temple Remembered." *Theosophical History* 5 (1995): 281–98.

Mayer, Jean-Francois. "Our Terrestrial Journey Is Coming to an End: The Last Voyage of the Solar Temple." *Nova Religio* 2 (April 1999).

_____. "Apocalyptic Millennialism in the West: The Case of the Solar Temple." Lecture at the Univ. of Virginia (Nov. 13, 1998).

_____. "Myths of the Solar Temple." Paper presented to the ISAR/CESNUR symposium on "Violence and the New Religions" (Nashville, Tenn., 1996).

Palmer, Susan J. "Purity and Danger in the Solar Temple." *Journal of Contemporary Religion* (1996), 303–18.

PENITENTES

Henderson, Alice Corban. *The Penitentes of the Southwest*. New York: Harcourt Brace Jovanovich, 1937.

PEOPLE'S TEMPLE

Axhelm, Peter, et al. "The Cult of Death" and "The Emperor Jones." *Newsweek* (Dec. 4, 1978).

Chidester, David. *Salvation and Suicide: Jim Jones, the People's Temple and Jonestown*. Rev. ed. Bloomington: Indiana Univ. Press, 2003.

De Angelis, Ginger. *Jonestown Massacre: Tragic End of a Cult*. Berkeley Heights, N.J.: Enslow, 2002.

Kahalas, Laurie Efrein. *Snake Dance: Unraveling the Mysteries of Jonestown*. New York: Red Robin, 1998.

Kilduff, Marshall, and Ron Jevers. *The Suicide Cult*. New York: Bantam, 1978.

Layton, Deborah. *Seductive Poison: A Jonestown Survivor's Story of Life and Death in the Peoples Temple*. New York: Anchor, 1998.

Maaga, Mary McCormick. *Hearing the Voices of Jonestown*. Syracuse: Syracuse Univ. Press, 1998.

Mills, Jeannie. *Six Years with God: Life Inside Reverend Jim Jones's People's Temple*. New York: A & W, 1979.

"Nightmare in Jonestown." *Time* (Dec. 4, 1978).

Weightsman, J. M. *Making Sense of the Jonestown Suicides*. Lewiston, N.Y.: Mellen, 1983.

Wessinger, Catherine. *How the Millennium Comes Violently*. New York: Chatham House, 2000.

Winfrey, C. "Why 900 Died in Guyana." *New York Times Magazine* (Feb. 26, 1979), 45.

PROCESS CHURCH OF THE FINAL JUDGMENT

Bainbridge, William Sims. "The Process Church of the Final Judgement." Pages 241–66 in *The Sociology of Religious Movements*. New York: Routledge, 1978.

_____. *Satan's Power*. Berkeley: Univ. of California Press, 1978.

_____. *Satan's Process: The Satanism Scare*. Ed. James T. Richardson and David Bromley. New York: de Gruyter. 1991.

Lachman, Gary. *A Secret History of Consciousness*. Great Barrington, Mass.: Lindisfarne, 2003.

Melton, J. Gordon. *Encyclopedia of American Religions*. 5th ed. Detroit: Gale Research, 2002.

Terry, Maury. *The Truth about the Cult Murders: Son of Sam and Beyond*. New York: Barnes & Noble, 2004.

RAJNEESHISM

Franklin, Satya Bharti. *The Promise of Paradise: A Woman's Intimate Story of the Perils of Life with Rajneesh*. Barrytown, N.Y.: Station Hill, 1992.

Hamilton, Rosemary. *Hellbent for Enlightenment: Unmasking Sex, Power, and Death with a Notorious Master*. Ashland, Ore.: White Cloud, 1998.

Osho. *Autobiography of a Spiritually Incorrect Mystic*. New York: St. Martin's Griffin, 2001.

Palmer, Susan J., and Charlotte E. Hardmann, eds. *Children in New Religions*. Piscataway, N.J.: Rutgers Univ. Press. 1999.

RASTAFARIAN—BLACK MUSLIM MOVEMENT

Barrett, Leonard E. *Rastafarians: Sounds of Cultural Dissonance*. Boston: Beacon. 1988.

_____. *The Rastafarians: A Study in Messianic Cultism in Jamaica*. Rio Peidras, P.R.: Institute of Caribbean Studies, Univ. of Puerto Rico, 1968.

Boot, Adrian, and Michael Thomas. *Jamaica: Babylon on a Thin Wire*. London: Thames & Hudson, 1976.

Chevannes, B. *Rastafari and Other African-Caribbean Worldviews*. Piscataway, N.J.: Rutgers Univ. Press, 1988.

_____. *Rastafari: Roots and Ideology.* Syracuse, N.Y.: Syracuse Univ. Press, 1994.

Clarke, John Henry, ed. *Marcus Garvey and the Vision of Africa.* New York: Random House, 1974.

Cronon, Edmund David. *Black Moses.* Madison: Univ. of Wisconsin Press, 1955.

Curtain, P. D. *Two Jamaicas.* Cambridge, Mass.: Harvard Univ. Press, 1955.

Fax, Elton. *Garvey: The Story of a Pioneer Black Nationalist.* New York: Dodd & Mead, 1972.

Hausman, G. *Black Paradise: The Rastafarian Movement.* San Bernadino, Calif.: Borgo, 1994.

_____. *The Kebra Negast: The Book of Rastafarian Wisdom and Faith from Ethiopia and Jamaica.* New York: St. Martin's, 1997.

Hoenisch, Michael. "Symbolic Politics: Perceptions of the Early Rastafari Movement." *Massachusetts Review* (Fall 1988), 432.

Junique, Kelleyana. *Rastafari? Rasta For You: Rastafarianism Explained.* San Diego: Athena Press Publishing, 2004.

Lake, Obiagele. "Religion, Patriarchy, and the Status of Rastfarian Women." Pages 141–58 in *New Trends and Developments in African Religions.* Ed. Peter B. Clarke. Westport, Conn.: Greenwood, 1998.

Lee, Helene, and Stephen Davis. *The First Rasta: Leonard Howell and the Rise of Rastafarianism.* Chicago: Lawrence Hill, 2003.

Lewis, W. *Soul Rebels: The Rastafari.* Prospect Heights, Ill.: Waveland, 1997.

Melton, J. Gordon. *Encyclopedia of American Religions.* 5th ed. Detroit: Gale Research, 2002.

Nettleford, Rex. *Mirror, Mirror: Identity, Race, and Protest in Jamaica.* Kingston, Jamaica: Collins & Sangster, 1970.

Norris, Katrin. *Jamaica: The Search for an Identity.* London: Oxford Univ. Press, 1962.

Owens, Joseph. *Dread: The Rastafarians of Jamaica.* Kingston, Jamaica: Collins & Sangster, 1976.

Simpson, George Eaton. "The Ras Tafi Movement in Jamaica: A Study in Race and Class Conflict." *Social Forces* 34 (December 1955).

_____. *Religious Cults of the Caribbean.* Rio Piedras, P.R.: Institute of Caribbean Studies, Univ. of Puerto Rico, 1970.

Smith, M. G. Augier, and Rex Nettleford. *The Rastafari Movement in Kingston, Jamaica.* Kingston, Jamaica: Univ. of the West Indies Press, 1960.

RELIGIOUS SCIENCE

Armor, Reginald. *Ernest Holmes the Man.* Los Angeles: Science of Mind, 1977.

Berrill, N. J. *You and the Universe.* Los Angeles: Science of Mind, 1973.

Brooks, Louise. *Early History of Divine Science.* Denver: Divine Science Federation, 1963.

Brooks, Nona L. *Mysteries.* Denver: Divine Science Federation, 1977.

Carter, Craig. *How to Use the Power of Mind in Everyday Life.* Los Angeles: Science of Mind, 1978.

Ehrenborg, Todd. *Mind Sciences: Christian Science, Religious Science, Unity School of Christianity.* Grand Rapids: Zondervan, 1995.

Holmes, Ernest. *The Basic Ideas of Science of Mind.* Los Angeles: Science of Mind, 1971.

_____. *The Ernest Holmes Dictionary of New Thought: Your Pocket Guidebook to Religious Science.* Marina del Rey, Calif.: DeVorss, 2003.

_____. *Gateway to Life.* Los Angeles: Science of Mind, 1977.

_____. *The Larger Life.* Los Angeles: Science of Mind, 1970.

_____. *New Horizons.* Los Angeles: Science of Mind, 1974.

_____. *Observations.* Los Angeles: Science of Mind, 1967.

_____. *The Philosophy of Jesus . . . for the World Today.* Ed. Willis Kinnear. Los Angeles: Science of Mind, 1971.

_____. *Science of Mind.* New York: Dodd & Mead, 1938.

_____. *Sermon by the Sea.* Los Angeles: Science of Mind, 1967.

_____. *Spiritual Awareness.* Los Angeles: Science of Mind, 1977.

_____. *The Spiritual Universe and You.* Ed. Willis Kinnear. Los Angeles: Science of Mind, 1971.

_____. *The Thing Called Life.* New York: Dodd & Mead, 1964.

_____. *What Religious Science Teaches.* Los Angeles: Science of Mind, 1970.

_____. *Your Invisible Power.* Los Angeles: Science of Mind, 1977.

Holmes, Ernest, and Willis Kinnear. *Practical Application of Science of Mind.* Los Angeles: Science of Mind, 1977.

Holmes, Ernest, and Fenwicke Holmes. *The Voice Celestial.* Los Angeles: Science of Mind, 1978.

Holmes, Fenwicke. *Ernest Holmes: His Life and Times*. New York: Dodd & Mead, 1953.

Irwin, Gregg. *The Divine Science Way*. Denver: Divine Science Federation, 1975.

James, Fannie B. *Divine Science: Its Principle and Practice*. Denver: Divine Science Federation, 1957.

Melton, J. Gordon. *Encyclopedia of American Religions*. 5th ed. Detroit: Gale Research, 2002.

Merritt Jones, Dennis. *How to Speak Religious Science*. Marina del Rey, Calif.: DeVorss, 2001.

Pool, Carolyn (Director of New Beginnings, Inc.) Letter to the author. n.d.

Stromberg, Gustaf. *A Scientist's View of Man, Mind, and the Universe*. Los Angeles: Science of Mind, 1977.

ROSICRUCIANISM

Ahlstrom, Sydney. *A Religious History of the American People*. 2 vols. Garden City, N.Y.: Image, 1975.

Lewis, Harvey Spencer. *Mansions of the Soul*. San Jose: AMORC, 1996

Lewis, James R. *The Encyclopedia of Cults, Sects, and New Religions*. Amherst, N.Y.: Prometheus, 1998.

Lewis, Ralph M. *Cosmic Mission Fulfilled*. San Jose: AMORC, 1994.

Melton, J. Gordon. *Encyclopedia of American Religions*. 5th ed. Detroit: Gale Research, 2002.

The Rosicrucian Cosmo-Conception. San Jose, Calif.: AMORC, n.d.

Schmidt, Alvin J. *Fraternal Organizations*. Westport, London: Greenwood, 1980.

Yates, Frances Amelia. *The Rosicrucian Enlightenment*. San Jose: AMORC. 1993.

SATANISM

Aiken, Steve. *Satanism: Sacrilege, Silly, or Serious*. Millburn, N.J.: American Focus, 1989.

Alexander, David. "Giving the Devil More Than His Due." *The Humanist* (March–April 1990).

Barton, Blanche. *The Secret Life of a Satanist: The Authorized Biography of Anton LaVey*. Los Angeles: Feral House, 1990.

_____. *The Church of Satan*. New York: Hell's Kitchen, 1990.

Baskin, Wade. *Satanism: A Guide to the Awesome Power of Satan*. Secaucus, N.J.: Citadel, 1972.

Biersach, William L. *The Endless Knot*. Arcadia, Calif.: Tumblar House, 2001.

Boulware, Jack. "Thirty-Two Years of Satan in Popular Culture." *The SF Weekly*. New York Times Inc. Features (June 17, 1998).

Bromley, David. "The Satanic Cult Scare." *Society* (May–June 1991), 55.

Bromley, David G., and Susan G. Ainsley. "Satanism and Satanic Churches: The Contemporary Incarnations." Pages 401–9 in *America's Alternative Religions*. Ed. Timothy Miller. Albany: State Univ. of New York Press, 1995.

Cavendish, Richard. *The Black Arts*. New York: Capricorn, 1968.

_____. *A History of Magic*. London: Wiedenfeld & Nicolson, n.d.

_____, ed. *Man, Myth and Magic: An Illustrated Encyclopedia of the Supernatural*. 18 vols. New York: Marshal Cavendish, n.d.

Garcia, Guy. "The Believers." *Rolling Stone* (June 29, 1989), 46.

Gettings, Fred. *Dictionary of Demons*. North Pomfret, Vt.: Trafalgar Square, 1988.

Givens, Ron. "California: Devilish Deeds?" *Newsweek* (Sept. 16, 1985), 43.

Hawkins, Craig S. "The Many Faces of Satan." *Forward* (Fall 1986), 17–22.

LaVey, Anton Szandor. *The Satanic Bible*. New York: Avon, 1969.

_____. *The Satanic Rituals*. New York: Avon, 1976.

Lewis, James R. *Satanism Today: An Encyclopedia of Religion, Folklore, and Popular Culture*. Santa Barbara, Calif.: ABC-Clio, 2001.

Lyons, Arthur. *Satan Wants You*. New York: Mysterious, 1988.

Martin, Walter R. (Founder and Director of the Christian Research Institute). Letter to the author. May 6, 1976.

Medway, Gareth J. *Lure of the Sinister: The Unnatural History of Satanism*. New York: Universe, 2001.

Melton, J. Gordon. *Encyclopedia of American Religions*. 5th ed. Detroit: Gale Research, 2002.

"Men Charged with 169 Sex Crimes." *Palm Beach Post* (Palm Beach, Fl.) (Jan. 13, 1985).

Michelet, Jules. *Satanism and Witchcraft*. Trans. A. R. Allinson. New York: Citadel, 1963.

"Molestation Probe Widens into Satanic Sex." *Modesto Bee* (Modesto, Calif.) (July 18, 1985).

"Muddled Son of Sam: Christian and Satanic." *San Francisco Examiner* (June 12, 1978), 20.

Nathan, Debbie, and Michael Snedeker. *Satan's Silence: Ritual Abuse and the Making of a Mod-

ern American Witch Hunt. New York: Basic Books, 1995.

Passantino, Bob and Gretchen. *Satanism*. Grand Rapids: Zondervan, 1995.

Raschke, Carl A. *Painted Black: From Drug Killings to Heavy Metal—The Epidemic of Satanic Crime Terrorizing Our Communities*. San Francisco: Harper, 1990.

Stratford, Lauren. *Satan's Underground*. Eugene Ore.: Harvest House, 1988.

Terry, Maury. *The Ultimate Evil*. Garden City, N.Y.: Doubleday, 1987.

Trott, Jon, and Mike Hertenstein. "Selling Satan: The Tragic History of Mike Warnke." *Cornerstone* 21 (1992).

Warnke, Mike. *The Satan Seller*. Plainfield, N.J.: Logos International, 1972.

Wheeler, Barbara R., Spence Wood, and Richard J. Hatch. "Assessment and Intervention with Adolescents Involved in Satanism." *Social Work* (November–December 1988).

Woodbury, Richard. "Cult of the Red Haired Devil: A Drug Bust Uncovers an Evil Brew of Satanism and Murder." *Time* (Apr. 24, 1989), 30.

Wright, Lawrence. "It's Not Easy Being Evil in a World That's Gone to Hell." *Rolling Stone* (Sept. 5, 1991), 63.

SCIENTOLOGY

Alexander, Brooks, and Dean Halverson. *Scientology: The Technology of Enlightenment*. Berkeley: Spiritual Counterfeits Project, 1982.

Bainbridge, William Sims, and Rodney Stark. "Scientology: To Be Perfectly Clear." *Sociological Analysis* 41 (Summer 1980): 128–36.

Behar, Richard. "The Thriving Cult of Greed and Power." *Time* (May 6, 1991).

"Church's Ads Assail Time." *The New York Times* (May 31, 1991), C5, D5.

Church of Scientology. *Theology & Practice of a Contemporary Religion: Scientology*. Los Angeles: Bridge, 1998.

Church of Scientology. *The Scientology Handbook*. Los Angeles: Bridge, 1994.

Cooper, Paulette. *The Scandal of Scientology*. New York: Tower, 1972.

Donaton, Scott. "Scientology Fires Ad Barrage at *Time*." *Advertising Age* 62 (June 1991): 50.

Gordon, Gregory. "Scientologists Plotted to Frame a Critic as a Criminal, Files Show." *The Boston Globe* (Nov. 24, 1979).

Hubbard, L. Ron. *Dianetics: The Modern Science of Mental Health*. Los Angeles: Bridge, 1972.

Kaufman, Robert. *Inside Scientology: Or How I Found Scientology and Became Super Human*. New York: Olympia, 1972.

Levin, Gary. "*Time* Squabble; Scientology Adds WPP Units to Attack." *Advertising Age* 62 (June 1991): 42.

Main, Jeremy. "Follow-ups: Shamed in Spain." *Fortune* (Jan. 16, 1989), 16.

Melton, J. Gordon. *The Church of Scientology*. Salt Lake City: Signature, 2000.

Methvin, Eugene H. "Scientology: Anatomy of a Frightening Cult." *Readers Digest* (May 1980), 86–91.

Miscavige, David (Scientology Leader). Interviewed on *NBC Nightline* (Feb. 14, 1982).

"Scientology." *Citizen's Freedom Foundation News* 8/10 (October 1983).

"Scientology: A Dangerous Cult Goes Mainstream." *Reader's Digest* (October 1991), 87–92.

Wallis, R. *The Road to Total Freedom: A Sociological Analysis of Scientology*. New York: Columbia Univ. Press, 1977.

SELF-REALIZATION FELLOWSHIP

Melton, J. Gordon. *Encyclopedia of American Religions*. 5th ed. Detroit: Gale Research, 2002.

Miller, Elliot. "Swami Yogananda and the Self-Realization Fellowship: A Successful Hindu Countermission to the West." *Christian Research Journal* 22/2 (1999): 33–41.

Walters, J. Donald. *A Place Called Ananda: The Trial by Fire That Forged One of the Most Successful Cooperative Communities in the World Today*. Nevada City, Calif.: Crystal Clarity, 1996.

Yogananda, Paramahansa. *The Divine Romance*. Los Angeles: Self-Realization Fellowship, 1986.

SEVENTH-DAY ADVENTISM

Cunningham, Louis F. "What Good is Hell Anyway?" *These Times* (November 1976).

Damsteegt, P Gerard. *Foundations of the SDA Message and Mission*. Grand Rapids: Eerdmanns, 1977.

Delafield, D. A. *Ellen G. White and the Seventh-day Adventist Church*. Omaha: Pacific, 1963.

Doan, Ruth A. *The Miller Heresy: Millennialism and American Culture*. Philadelphia: Temple Univ. Press, 1987.

General Conference of Seventh-day Adventists. *Seventh-day Adventists Believe*. Hagerstown, Md.: Review & Herald, 1988.

Hoekema, Anthony A. *Seventh-day Adventism*. Grand Rapids: Eerdmans, 1963.

Holt, Russell. "What Do You Know about Seventh-day Adventists?" *These Times* (June 1975).

Irvine, William C. *Heresies Exposed*. Neptune, N.J.: Loizeaux Brothers, 1976.

Knight, George R. *Joseph Bates: The Real Founder of Seventh-day Adventism*. Hagerstown, Md.: Review & Herald, 2004.

Lawson, Ronald. "American Seventh-day Adventism's Trajectory from Sect to Denomination." *Journal for the Scientific Study of Religion* 38 (1999): 83–102.

Lewis, Gordon R. *The Bible, the Christian and Seventh-day Adventists*. Nutley, N.J.: Presbyterian & Reformed, 1966.

Martin, Walter. *The Christian and the Cults*. Grand Rapids: Zondervan, 1956.

Maxwell, Arthur S. *Your Bible and You*. Washington, D.C.: Review & Herald, 1959.

Morgan, Douglas, and Martin Marty. *Adventism and the American Republic: The Public Involvement of a Major Apocalyptic Movement*. Knoxville: Univ. of Tennessee Press, 2001.

Rea, Walter. *The White Lie*. Durham, N.C.: Moore, 1983.

Samples, Kenneth. "From Crisis to Controversy: An Updated Assessment of Seventh-day Adventism." *Christian Research Journal* 11/1 (Summer, 1988): 9.

Slattery, William. *Seventh-day Adventists*; *False Prophets: A Former Insider Speaks Out*. Nutley, N.J.: Presbyterian & Reformed, 1990.

White, Ellen G. *The Great Controversy between Christ and Satan*. Hagerstown, Md.: Review & Herald, repr. 1974.

SIKH DHARMA

Barrier, N. Gerald, and Verne A. Dusenbery. *The Sikh Diaspora: Migration and the Experience Beyond Punjab*. Delhi: Chanakya, 1989

Dart, John. "Blessing the Quest for Success Seen as Boost to 2 Eastern Sects." *Los Angeles Times* (July 19, 1986), 4.

Melton, J. Gordon. *Encyclopedia of American Religions*. 5th ed. Detroit: Gale Research, 2002.

Singh, Khushwant. *The Sikhs Today*. New Delhi: Orient Longman, 1985.

_____. *A History of the Sikhs*. New Delhi: Oxford Univ. Press. 1977.

SILVA MIND CONTROL

Ankerberg, John, and John Weldon. "Silva Mind Control." Pages 553–72 in *Encyclopedia of New Age Beliefs*. Eugene, Ore.: Harvest House, 1996.

Casto, Karen C. "Mind Control! (Or How You Can Find a Parking Place in Tucson)." *Tucson Daily Citizen Magazine* (July 5, 1975).

Greil, Arthur L. "Explorations Along the Sacred Frontier: Notes on Para-Religions, Quasi-Religions, and Other Boundary Phenomena." Pages 153–72 in *Handbook on Cults and Sects in America*. Ed. David Bromley and Jeffrey K. Hadden. Religion and the Social Order 3A. Greenwich, Conn.: JAI, 1993.

McKnight, Harry. *Silva Mind Control: Key to Inner Kingdoms through Psychorientology*. Laredo, Tex.: Institute of Psychorientology, 1972.

Marin, Peter. "The New Narcissism." *Harper's Magazine* (October 1975).

Melton, J. Gordon. *Encyclopedia of Occultism and Parapsychology*. Detroit: Gale Research, 2002.

Mind Control "Silva Method." A Teacher's Manual. Laredo, Tex.: Institute of Psychorientology, 1969.

Powell, Tag, and Judy Powell. *The Silva Method of Mind Mastery*. Largo, Fla.: Top of the Mountain, 1969.

Silva, Jose. *Silva Mind Control: Alpha-Theta Brainwave Function*. Laredo, Tex.: Silva Mind Control, 1976.

Silva, Jose, and Philip Meile. *The Silva Mind Control Method*. New York: Simon & Schuster, 1977.

Silva, Jose, and Robert B. Stone. *You the Healer: The World-Famous Silva Method on How to Heal Yourself and Others*. Alexandria, Va.: Kramer, 1992.

Taylor, Robert. "The Descent into Alpha." *The Boston Globe* (Aug. 20, 1972).

SOKA GAKKAI

Astley, Trevor. "A Matter of Principles: A Note on the Recent Conflict Between Nichiren Shoshu and Soka Gakkai." *Japanese Religions* 17/2 (1992): 167–75.

Babbie, Earl T. "The Third Civilization: An Examination of Soka Gakkai." *Review of Religious Research* 7 (1966): 101–21.

Dawson, Lorne L. "The Cultural Significance of New Religious Movements: The Case of Soka

Gakkai." *Sociology of Religion* 62 (Fall 2001): 337.

Hammond, Phillip, and David Machecek. *Soka Gakkai in America: Accommodation and Conversion*. New York: Oxford Univ. Press, 1999.

Ikeda, Daisaku. *A New Humanism: The University Addresses of Daisaku Ikeda*. New York: Weatherhill, 1996.

Jordan, Mary. "A Major Eruption at the Foot of Fuji." *Washington Post* (June 14, 1998), A1.

Lewis, James R. "Sect-bashing in the Guise of Scholarship: A Critical Appraisal of Select Studies of Soka Gakkai." *Marburg Journal of Religion* 5/1 (2000).

Metraux, Daniel A. "The Dispute between the Soka Gakkai and the Nichiren Shoshu Priesthood: A Lay Revolution Against a Conservative Clergy." *Japanese Journal of Religious Studies* 19 (1992): 325–36.

Victoria, Brian. "The Putative Pacifism of Soka Gakkai Founder Makiguchi Tsunesabur?" *Japanese Studies* 21/3 (December 2001): 275.

White, James W. *The Sokagakkai and Mass Society*. Stanford, Calif.: Stanford Univ. Press. 1970.

SOUTH AMERICAN—CENTRAL AMERICAN—EAST INDIES—VOODOO—SANTERIA-MACUMBA-CANDOMBLE

Bramley, Serge. *Macumba: The Teachings of Marie-Josie, Mother of the Gods*. San Francisco: City Lights, 1994.

Brandon, G. *Santeria from Africa to the New World: The Dead Sell Memories*. Bloomington: Indiana Univ. Press. 1993.

Brown, Karen M. *Mama Lola: A Voodoo Priestess in Brooklyn*. Berkley, Calif.: Univ. of California Press, 1991.

Canizares, Raul. *Cuban Santeria*. Rochester, Vt.: Inner Traditions, 1999.

Cannon, W. B. "'Voodoo' Death." In *Reader in Comparative Religions: An Anthropological Approach*. Ed. W. A. Lessa and E. Z. Vogt. New York: Harper & Row, 1965.

Clark, Mary Ann. "!No Hay Nigun Santo Aqui! (There Are No Saints Here!): Symbolic Language within Santeria." *Journal of the American Academy of Religion* 68 (March 2001): 21–41.

Clark, Peter B. "Accounting for Recent Anti-Syncretist Trends in Candomble-Catholic Relations." Pages 17–35 in *New Trends and Developments in African Religions*. Ed. Peter B. Clarke. Westport, Conn.: Greenwood, 1998.

Cochran, Tracy. "Among the Believers: Converts to Santeria." *New Yorker* (Oct. 12, 1987), 33.

Courleander, H. *Haiti Singing*. Chapel Hill: Univ. of North Carolina Press, 1939.

Curry, Mary Cuthrell. *Making the Gods in New York: The Yoruba Religion in the African American Community*. New York: Garland, 1997.

De Marinis, Valerie. "With Dance and Drum: A Psycho-Cultural Investigation of the Meaning-Making System of an African-Brazilian, Macumba Community in Salvador, Brazil." Pages 59–73 in *New Trends and Developments in African Religions*. Ed. Peter B. Clarke. Westport, Conn.: Greenwood Press, 1998.

Doke, C. M. *Southern Bantu Languages*. Oxford: Oxford Univ. Press, 1954.

Dunham, Katherine. *Island Possessed*. Garden City, N.Y.: Doubleday, 1969.

Forde, Daryl. *African Worlds*. Oxford: Oxford Univ. Press, 1954.

Goldman, Irving, and Peter J. Wilson, eds. *Cubeo Hehenewa Religious Thought: Metaphysics of a Northwestern Amazonian People*. New York: Columbia Univ. Press, 2004.

Gonzales-Wippler, Migene, and Charles Wetli. *Santeria: The Religion: Faith, Rites, Magic (World Religion and Magic)*. 2nd ed. St. Paul, Minn. Llewellyn, 1994.

Gorov, Linda. "The War on Voodoo." *Mother Jones* (June 1990), 12.

Gravely, Wanda. "Haiti: Land of Deep Mysticism and Stark Reality." *Essence Magazine* (July 1981), 31.

Haskins, James. *Voodoo and Hoodoo*. Chelsea, Mich.: Scarborough House, 1990.

Herskovits, Melville J. *Dahomey: An Ancient West African Kingdom*. New York: Octagon, 1938.

_____. *Life in a Haitian Valley*. New York: Octagon, 1938.

_____. *Suriname Folklore*. New York: Octagon, 1938.

_____. *Trinidad Village*. New York: Octagon, 1947.

Herskovits, Melville, and Frances S. Herskovits. *Rebel Destiny among the Bush Negroes of Dutch Guiana*. New York: Octagon, 1934.

Hogg, Donald. "The Convince Cult in Jamaica." In *Papers in Caribbean Anthropology*, no. 58. Ed. Sidney Mintz. New Haven, Conn.: Yale Univ. Publications in Anthropology, 1960.

_____. *Haiti: Black Peasants and Voodoo*. Trans. P. Lengyel. New York: Universe Books, 1960.

Houk, James T. *Spirits, Blood, and Drums: The Orisha Religion in Trinidad*. Philadelphia: Temple Univ. Press, 1995.

Laguerre, Michel S. *Voodoo Heritage*. Beverly Hills, Calif.: Sage, 1980.

Langer, Gary. "Cult Attracting a Surprising Mix of Followers." *Las Vegas Review Journal* (May 13, 1984).

Loederer, Richard A. *Voodoo Fire in Haiti*. New York: Literary Guild, 1935.

Makin, William James. *Caribbean Night*. London: R. Hale, 1939.

McGregor, Pedro. *The Moon and Two Mountains: The Myths, Ritual and Magic of Brazilian Spiritism*. London: Souvenir, 1966.

Martin, Kevin. *The Complete Book of Voodoo*. New York: Putnam, 1972.

Metraux, Alfred. *Voodoo in Haiti*. Trans. H. Charteris. New York: Oxford Univ. Press, 1959.

Miriam, Joel. *African Traditions in Latin America*. Cuernavaca, Mexico: Centro Intercultural Documentation, 1972.

Motta, Roberto. "The Churchifying of Candomble: Priests, Anthropologists, and the Canonization of the African Religious Memory in Brazil." Pages 45–57 in *New Trends and Developments in African Religions*. Ed. Peter B. Clarke. Westport, Conn: Greenwood, 1998.

Murphy, Joseph. *Santeria: An African Religion in America*. Boston: Beacon, 1988.

_____. "Santeria: An African Religion in America." *Catholic World* (May–June 1989), 34.

Nunez, Luis M. *Santeria: A Practical Guide to Afro-Caribbean Magic*. Dallas, Tex.: Spring, 1991.

Ostling, Richard. "Shedding Blood in Sacred Bowls." *Time* (Oct. 19. 1992), 60.

Owen, Mary Alicia. *Voodoo Tales*. New York: Negro Univ. Press, 1960.

Parrinder, Geoffrey. *Religion in an African City*. London: Lutterworth, 1952.

_____. *West African Psychology*. London: Lutterworth, 1951.

_____. *Witchcraft*. London: Lutterworth, 1958.

Pelton, Robert W. *Voodoo Secrets from A to Z*. South Brunswick, N.J.: Barnes, 1973.

Pinn, Anthony B. *Varieties of African American Religious Experience*. Minneapolis: Fortress, 1998.

Puckett, Newbell Niles. *Folk Beliefs of the Southern Negro*. Montclair, N.J.: Patterson Smith, 1968.

Rattray, R. S. *Ashanti*. Oxford: Oxford Univ. Press, 1927.

_____. *Religion and Art in Ashanti*. Oxford: Oxford Univ. Press, 1927.

Rigaud, Milo. *Secrets of Voodoo*. New York: Arco, 1969.

Seabrook, William Buehler. *The Magic Island*. New York: Harcourt Brace, 1929.

Simpson, George Eaton. *Black Religions in the New World*. New York: Columbia Univ. Press, 1978.

Steedman, Mabel. *Unknown to the World*. London: Hurst and Blackett, 1939.

Thornton, John K. "On the Trail of Voodoo: African Christianity in Africa and the Americas." *The Americas* (January 1988), 261.

Wallsi, Claudia. "Zombies: Do They Exist? Yes, Says a Harvard Scientist Who Offers an Explanation." *Time* (Oct. 17, 1983), 60.

Wetli, C. D., and R. Martinez. "Forensic Sciences Aspects of Santeria, a Religious Cult of African Origin." *Journal of Forensic Sciences* 26/3 (July 1981).

Whippler, Migene-Gonzalez. *Santeria: The Religion—A Legacy of Faith, Rites, and Magic*. New York: Crown, 1989.

Williams, Joseph J. *Voodoos and Obeah: Phases of West Indian Witchcraft*. New York: MacVeagh, Dial Press, 1932.

Wirkus, Faustin, and Taney Dudley. *The White King of La Gonave*. Garden City, N.Y.: Doubleday, 1931.

SPIRITISM; SPIRITUALISM; UNIVERSAL CHURCH OF THE MASTER

Adler, Jerry. "Heaven's Gatekeepers: They Give the People What They Want: Talkative Spirits and a Laid-Back God." *Newsweek* (Mar. 16, 1998), 64.

Baer, Hans A. "The Limited Empowerment of Women in Black Spiritual Churches: An Alternative Vehicle to Religious Leadership." *Sociology of Religion* 65 (Spring 1993).

Biederwolf, William Edward. *Spiritualism*. Grand Rapids: Eerdmans, 1952.

Buescher, John B. *The Other Side of Salvation: Spiritualism and the Nineteenth-Century Religious Experience*. Boston: Skinner House, 2004.

Carroll, Bret E. *Spiritualism in Antebellum America*. Bloomington: Univ. of Indiana Press. 1997.

Cox, Robert. *Body and Soul: A Sympathetic History of Spiritualism*. Charlottesville: Univ. Press of Virginia, 2003.

Hill, Douglas, and Pat Williams. *The Supernatural.* New York: Hawthorne, 1965.

Weisberg, Barbara. *Talking to the Dead Kate and Maggie Fox and the Rise of Spiritualism.* San Francisco: HarperSanFrancisco, 2004.

SRI CHINMOY

Chinmoy, Sri. *The Garland of Nation-souls: Complete Talks at the United Nations.* Deerfield Beach, Fl.: Health Communications. 1995.

_____. *Heart Songs, Everyday Prayer & Meditations.* Minneapolis: Hazeldon, 1995.

_____. *Commentaries on The Vedas, The Upanishads, & The Bhagavad Gita.* New York: Aum, 1996.

Ellis, David. "Spiritual Aid Easier to Obtain." *Time* (July 29, 1991), 13.

Hersch, Hank. "An Uplifting Experience." *Sports Illustrated* (Sept. 18, 1989), 17.

Jackson, Devon. "Bless You Sir, May I Jog Another?" *Outside Magazine* (October 1996).

Melton, J. Gordon. *Encyclopedia of American Religions.* 5th ed. Detroit: Gale Research, 2002.

Union of International Associations. "The World Guide to Religious and Spiritual Organizations." New Providence, N.J.: Munchen, 1996.

SUFISM

Balbick, Julian. *Mystical Islam: An Introduction to Sufism.* New York: New Gods Univ. Press, 1989.

Barks, Coleman. *The Last Barrier: A Journey into the Essence of Sufi Teachings.* Great Barrington, Mass.: Lindisfarne, 2002.

Chittick, William C. *Sufism: A Short Introduction.* Oxford: Oneworld, 2000.

Fadiman, James, and Robert Frager. *Essential Sufism.* New York: HarperCollins, 1997.

SWEDENBORGIANISM

Bentley, G. E. Jr. *Blake Books Supplement.* Oxford: Clarendon, 1995.

Benz, Ernst. *Dreams, Hallucinations, and Visions.* New York: Swedenborg Foundation, 1982.

Bigalow, John. *The Bible That Was Lost and Is Found.* New York: Swedenborg Foundation, 1979.

Keller, Helen. *My Religion.* New York: Swedenborg Foundation, 1980.

King, Thomas. *Allegories of Genesis.* New York: Swedenborg Foundation, 1982.

Melton, J. Gordon. *Encyclopedia of American Religions.* 5th ed. Detroit: Gale Research, 2002.

Sechrist, Alice S. *Dictionary of Bible Imagery.* New York: Swedenborg Foundation, 1981.

Stanley, Michael. *Swedenborg: Essential Reading.* San Bernardino, Calif.: Borgo, 1990.

Swedenborg, Immanuel. *The Apocalypse Explained.* 6 vols. Trans. J. Whitehead. New York: Swedenborg Foundation, 1982.

_____. *The Apocalypse Revealed.* 2 vols. Trans. J. Whitehead. New York: Swedenborg Foundation, 1975.

_____. *Arcana Coelestia.* 12 vols. Trans. J. F. Potts. New York: Swedenborg Foundation, 1978.

_____. *Charity.* Trans. W. F. Wunsch. New York: Swedenborg Foundation, 1982.

_____. *Divine Love and Wisdom.* Trans. J. C. Ager. New York: Swedenborg Foundation, 1982.

_____. *Divine Providence.* Trans. J. C. Ager. New York: Swedenborg Foundation, 1982.

_____. *The Four Doctrines.* Trans. J. F. Potts. New York: Swedenborg Foundation, 1981.

_____. *Heaven and Hell.* Trans. G. F. Dole. New York: Swedenborg Foundation, 1979.

_____. *Miscellaneous Theological Works.* Trans. J. Whitehead. New York: Swedenborg Foundation, 1976.

_____. *Posthumous Theological Works.* 2 vols. Trans. J. Whitehead. New York: Swedenborg Foundation, 1978.

_____. *True Christian Religion.* 2 vols. Trans. J. C. Ager. New York: Swedenborg Foundation, 1980.

Synnestvedt, Sig, ed. *The Essential Swedenborg.* New York: Swedenborg Foundation, 1981.

Zacharias, Paul. *Celebrate Life.* Newton, Mass.: Swedenborg Press, 1981.

TAOISM

Clarke, J. J. *The Tao of the West.* New York: Routledge, 2000.

Kohn, Livia. *God of the Dao: Lord Lao in History and Myth.* Ann Arbor: Center for Chinese Studies, 1998.

Pas, Julian F. *Historical Dictionary of Taoism.* Lanham, Md.: Scarecrow, 1998.

Young, William A. *The World's Religions.* Englewood Cliffs, N.J.: Prentice Hall, 1995.

THEOSOPHY

Besant, Annie Wood. *Theosophist Magazine Oct 1911-Jan 1912.* Whitefish, Mont.: Kessinger, 2003.

Blavatsky, Helene Petrovna. *The Theosophical Glossary*. Los Angeles: Theosophy, 1966.

Ellwood, Robert. *Theosophy. A Modern Expression of the Wisdom of the Ages*. Wheaton, Ill.: Quest, 1994.

Faivre, Antoine. *Theosophy, Imagination, Tradition: Studies in Western Esotericism*. New York: State Univ. of New York Press, 2000.

Guenon, Rene. *Theosophy: History of a Pseudo-Religion*. Ghent, N.Y.: Sophia Perennis, 2004.

Johnson, Paul K. *Initiates of Theosophical Masters*. Albany: State Univ. of New York Press, 1995.

McNeile, E. R. *From Theosophy to Christian Faith: A Comparison of Theosophy with Christianity*. London: Longmans, 1919.

Melton, J. Gordon. *Encyclopedia of Occultism and Parapsychology*. Detroit: Gale Research, 2002.

_____. *Encyclopedia of American Religions*. 5th ed. Detroit: Gale Research, 2002.

Rogers, L. W. *Elementary Theosophy*. Wheaton, Ill.: Theosophical, 1956.

TRANSCENDENTAL MEDITATION (TM)

Alexander, Charles Nathaniel. *Transcendental Meditation in Criminal Rehabilitation and Crime Prevention*. New York: Hawthorne, 2003.

Bainbridge, William Sims. *Sociology of Religious Movements*. New York: Routledge, 1997.

Blackmore, Susan. "Is Meditation Good for You?" *New Scientist* (July 1991), 30.

Bloomfield, Harold H., et al. *TM: Discovering Inner Energy and Overcoming Stress*. New York: Dell, 1975.

Campbell, Colin, Gary E. Schwartz, and Leon S. Otis. "The Facts on Transcendental Meditation." *Psychology Today* 7 (April 1974): 37–46.

Campbell, Duncan. "Heaven on Earth." *New Statesman and Society* (September 1990), 10.

Corcoran, Elizabeth. "Entepreneurial Spirit: The Maharishi's University Is a High-Tech Magnet." *Scientific American* (August 1988), 99.

Dilley, John R. "T.M. Comes to the Heartland of the Midwest." *The Christian Century* 93/41 (December 1975): 1129–32.

Forem, Jack. *Transcendental Meditation, Maharishi Mahesh Yogi and the Science of Creative Intelligence*. New York: Dutton, 1974.

Garrett, Catherine. "Transcendental Meditation, Reiki and Yoga: Suffering, Ritual and Self-Transformation." *Journal of Contemporary Religion* 16/3 (2001): 329–42.

Gelderloos, Paul, et al. "Transcendence and Psychological Health: Studies with Long-Term Participants of the Transcendental Meditation and TM-Sidhi Program." *The Journal of Psychology* (March 1990), 177.

Haddon, David, and Vail Hamilton. *T.M. Wants You! A Christian Response to Transcendental Meditation*. Grand Rapids: Baker, 1976.

Kennedy, John W. "Field of TM Dreams." *Christianity Today* (Jan. 8, 2001), 74–79.

Melton, J. Gordon. *Encyclopedia of American Religions*. 5th ed. Detroit: Gale Research, 2002.

Lewis, Gordon, R. *What Everyone Should Know about Transcendental Meditation*. Glendale, Calif.: Regal, 1975.

Roth, Robert. *TM: Transcendental Meditation*. Rev. ed. New York: Penguin, 1994.

Russell, Peter. *The TM Technique*. Las Vegas: Elf Rock, 2002.

Starr, Douglas. "Levitation U.: Lofty Maharishi U. Raises Students Consciousness As Well As the Eyebrows of a Few Physicists." *Omni* (May 1989), 66.

Tierney, Patrick. "The Mechanics of Mysticism." *Omni* (November 1990), 84.

Underwood, Nora. "The Maharishi Effect." *Macleans* (October 1990), 64.

TWELVE TRIBES, THE

Bozeman, John M., and Susan J. Palmer. "The Northeast Kingdom Community Church of Island Pond, Vermont: Raising Up a People For Yahshua's Return." *The Journal of Contemporary Religion* 12/2 (1997): 181–90.

Palmer, Susan J. "Apostates and Their Role in the Construction of Grievance Claims against the Northeast Kingdom/Messianic Communities." Pages 181–90 in *The Politics of Religious Apostasy*. Ed. David Bromley. Westport, Conn.: Prager, 1998.

_____. "Frontiers and Families: The Children of Island Pond." Pages 153–71 in *Children in New Religions*. Ed. Susan J. Palmer and Charlotte E. Hardman. Piscataway, N.J.: Rutgers Univ. Press, 1999.

Swantko, Jean A. "A 25-Year Retrospective on the Impact of the Anti-Cult Movement on Children of the Twelve Tribes Communities." Paper presented at the 13th International Conference of CESNUR, Bryn Athyn College, Bryn Athyn, Pa. (June 2–5, 1999).

_____. "Messianic Communities, Sociologists, and the Law." *Communities Magazine* (Fall 1995).

_____. "Anti-Cultists, Social Policy, and the 1984 Island Pond Raid." Paper presented at the 14th International Conference of CESNUR, Riga, Latvia (Aug. 25–31, 2000).

_____. "The Twelve Tribes' Communities, the Anti-Cult Movements, and Government's Response." *Social Justice Research* 12/4 (2000): 341–64.

UFO CULTS

Balch, Robert, and David Taylor. "Salvation in a UFO." *Psychology Today* 9 (October 1976): 361–66.

_____. "Seekers and Saucers: The Role of the Cultic Milieu in Joining a UFO Cult." *American Behavioral Scientist* 20 (July–August 1977): 839–60.

UNIFICATION CHURCH

Barker, E. *The Making of a Moonie: Choice or Brainwashing*. Oxford, England: Basil Blackwell, 1984.

Boettcher, Robert, and Gordon L. Freedman. *Gifts of Deceit: Sun Myung Moon, Tongsun Park, and the Korean Scandal*. New York: Holt, Rinehart, & Winston, 1980.

Bjornstat, James. *The Moon Is Not the Son*. Minneapolis: Bethany, 1976.

Bromley, David G., and A. D. Shupe Jr. *"Moonies" in America: Cult, Church, and Crusade*. Beverly Hills, Calif.: Sage, 1979.

Bromley, David G., A. D. Shupe Jr., and J. C. Ventimiglia. "Atrocity Tales: The Unification Church and the Social Construction of Evil." *Journal of Communication* 29 (1979): 42–53.

Burtner, William Kent. "Don't Be So Sure You Could Say No to a Cult." *U.S. Catholic* (April 1990), 16.

Edwards, Christopher. *Crazy for God*. Englewood Cliffs, N.J.: Prentice-Hall, 1979.

English, Bella. "The New Moon Empire." *New York Daily News* (May 4, 1981).

Freed, Josh. *Moonwebs: Journey into the Mind of a Cult*. Toronto: Dorset, 1980.

Galanter, Marc. "Engaged Members of the Unification Church." *Archives of General Psychiatry* 40 (1983): 1197–202.

_____. "Moonies Get Married: A Psychiatric Follow-up Study of a Charismatic Religious Sect." *American Journal of Psychiatry* 143 (1986): 1245–49.

_____. "Unification Church ('Moonie') Dropouts: Psychological Readjustment after Leaving a Charismatic Religious Group." *American Journal of Psychiatry* 140 (1983): 984–88.

_____, Richard Rabkin, Judith Rabkin, and Alexander Deutsch. "The 'Moonies': A Psychological Study of Conversion and Membership in a Contemporary Religious Sect." *American Journal of Psychiatry* 136 (February 1979): 165–69.

Hong, Nansook. *In the Shadow of the Moons*. Boston: Little, Brown & Company, 1998.

Levitt, Zola. *The Spirit of Sun Myung Moon*. Irvine, Calif.: Harvest House, 1976.

Melton, J. Gordon. *The Unification Church*. New York: Garland, 1990.

_____. *Encyclopedia of American Religions*. 5th ed. Detroit: Gale Research, 1996.

"Moon and Son: Sun Myung Moon's Son Said to Be Reincarnated as Zimbabwean." *U.S. News and World Report* (Apr. 11, 1988), 13.

Neufeld, K. Gordon. *Heartbreak and Rage: Ten Years under Sun Myung Moon*. College Station, Tex.: Virtual Bookwork, 2002.

Pak, Bo Hi. *Messiah: My Testimony to Rev. Sun Myung Moon*. Vol. 1. Trans. Timothy Elder. Lanham, Md.: Univ. Press of America, 2000.

Parsons, A. S. "The Moonies: The Triumph of Family." *Smith Alumnae Quarterly* (Summer 1984), 8–13.

Ross, J. C. "Errors on 'Moonies.'" *American Journal of Psychiatry* 140 (1983): 643–44.

Rothmeyer, K. "Mapping out Moon's Media Empire." *Columbia Journalism Review* (November–December 1984), 23–31.

Sherwood, Carlton. *Inquisition: The Persecution and Prosecution of the Rev. Sun Myung Moon*. Washington, D.C.: Regnery Gateway, 1991.

Shupe, Anson. "Frame Alignment and Strategic Evolution in Social Movements: The Case of Sun Myung's Unification Church." Pages 197–215 in *Religion, Mobilization and Social Action*. Ed. Anson Shupe and Bronislaw Misztal. Westport, Conn.: Praeger, 1998.

Sontag, Frederick. *Sun Myung Moon and the Unification Church*. Nashville: Abingdon, 1977.

Wood, Allen T., and J. Vitek. *Moonstruck*. New York: Morrow, 1979.

Yamamoto, J. Isamu. *Unification Church*. Grand Rapids: Zondervan, 1995.

UNITARIAN UNIVERSALISM

Buehrens, John A., and F. Forrester Church. *Our Chosen Faith: An Introduction to Unitarian Universalism*. Boston: Beacon, 1989.

Booth, John Nicholls. *Introducing Unitarian Universalism*. Brochure. Boston: Unitarian Universalist Association, 1965.

Davies, A. Powell. *Unitarianism: Some Questions Answered*. Boston: Unitarian Publication, n.d.

"Easter Causes Little To-do for Unitarians." *Seattle Post-Intelligencer* (Mar. 29, 1986), A4.

Gomes, Alan. *Unitarian Universalism*. Grand Rapids: Zondervan, 1998.

Macaulay, John Allen. *Unitarianism in the Antebellum South: The Other Invisible Institution*. Tuscaloosa: Univ. of Alabama Press. 2001.

Marshall, George N. *Unitarian and Universalist Belief*. Boston: Unitarian Universalist Association, n.d.

Martin, Walter R. "Universal Salvation: Does the Bible Teach it?" *Eternity* (September 1956), 14.

"Neighbors, Church for All Reasons." *Miami Post* (Nov. 28, 1985).

Buehrens, John A., ed. *The Unitarian Universalist Pocket Guide*. Boston: Skinner House, 1999.

We Are People, Purposes, Programs. (Brochure.) Boston: Unitarian Universalist Association, n.d.

"What Is a Unitarian." *Look Magazine* (Mar. 8, 1955).

UNITY SCHOOL OF CHRISTIANITY

Butterworth, Eric. *Unity: A Quest for Truth*. Unity Village, Mo.: Unity School of Christianity, 1985.

Cady, H. Emilie. *Lessons in Truth*. Kansas City, Mo.: Unity School of Christianity, 1944.

Cameron, William Earle. "Unity: A Divine Idea." *Unity Magazine* (October 1979).

D'Andrade, Hugh. *Charles Fillmore: Herald of the New Age*. New York: Harper & Row, 1974.

Ehrenborg, Todd. *Mind Sciences: Christian Science, Religious Science, Unity School of Christianity*. Grand Rapids: Zondervan, 1995.

Freeman, James D. *Unity Leaves No One Out*. Kansas City, Mo.: Unity School of Christianity, 1954.

Lewis, James R. *The Encyclopedia of Cults and Sects and New Religions*. Amherst, N.Y.: Prometheus. 1998.

Martin, Walter R. "The Unity Cult." *Eternity* (February 1955), 8.

Melton, J. Gordon. *Encyclopedia of American Religions*. 5th ed. Detroit: Gale Research, 2002.

Simmons, John K. "The Forgotten Contribution of Annie Rix Miltiz to the Unity School of Christianity." *Novo Religio* 2/1 (1998).

Unity, a Magazine Devoted to Christian Healing (Various issues).

Wee Wisdom: A Children's Magazine from Unity (March 1984).

UNIVERSAL FELLOWSHIP OF METROPOLITAN COMMUNITY CHURCHES

Boswell, John. *Christianity, Social Tolerance, and Homosexuality*. Chicago: Univ. of Chicago Press, 1980.

Burns, Stephanie. *The Universal Fellowship of Metropolitan Community Churches (UFMCC): History and Governance*. Washington, D.C.: Wesley Theological Seminary, 2000.

Ukjela, P. Michael. "Homosexuality and the Old Testament." *Bibliotheca Sacra* (July–September, 1983).

_____. "Homosexuality and the New Testament." *Bibliotheca Sacra* (October–December, 1983).

URANTIA

Bradley, David. *An Introduction to the Urantia Revelation*. 2nd ed. Arcata, Calif.: White Egret, 2002.

Gardner, Martin. *Urantia: The Great Cult Mystery*. Amherst, N.Y.: Prometheus, 1995.

Mullins, Larry, and Meredith Justine Sprunger. *A History of the Urantia Papers*. Boulder, Colo.: Penumbra, 2000.

Sadler, William S., Jr. "A Brotherhood—Not a Church or a Sect." *Urantia: A Journal of Urantia Brotherhood* (March 1976).

Sprunger, Meredith J. "Leavening Our Religious Heritage." *Urantia: A Journal of Urantia Brotherhood* (1977).

The Urantia Book. Chicago: Urantia Foundation, 1955; indexed version, New York: Uversa, 2002.

VEDANTA

Adiswarananda, Swami. *Meditation and Practices: A Definitive Guide to Techniques and Traditions of Meditation in Yoga and Vedanta*. Woodstock, Vt.: Skylight Paths, 2003.

_____. *The Vedanta Way to Peace and Happiness*. Woodstock, Vt.: Skylight Paths, 2004.

Advent Media. *Vivekananda Foundation*. Seattle: Viveka, 1997.

Damrell, Joseph. *Seeking Spiritual Meaning: The World of Vedanta.* Beverly Hills, Calif.: Sage Publications, 1977.

"Hindu Influenced Southland." *Independent Press Telegram* (Long Beach, Calif.) (July 3, 1976).

Jackson, Carl T. *Vedanta for the West: The Ramakrishna Movement in the United States.* Bloomington: Indiana Univ. Press. 1994.

Kaushal, Radhey Shyam. *The Philosophy of the Vedanta: A Modern Perspective.* New Delhi: D.K. Printworld, 1994.

Mueller, F. M. *Vedanta Philosophy.* Philadelphia, Pa.: Coronet, 1984.

Prasad, Narayana. *Karma and Reincarnation: The Vedanta Perspective.* New Delhi: D.K. Printworld. 1994.

Sharma, Arvind. *Advaita Vedanta: An Introduction.* Motilal Banarsidass, 2004.

Tarabilda, Edward F. *Life Strategies for the Spiritual Quest.* Sandy, Ut.: Morson, 1990.

Vivekananda, Swami. *The Complete Works of Swami Vivekananda.* 8 vols. Hollywood: Vedanta, n.d.

Wolinsky, Stephen. *The Nirvana Sutras and Advaita-Vedanta: Beneath the Illusion of Being.* Aptos, Calif.: Quantum Institute, 2004.

THE WAY INTERNATIONAL

Tolbert, Keith. "Infighting Trims Branches of The Way International." *Christianity Today* (Feb. 19, 1988), 44.

The Way Magazine (1970–76).

Whiteside Elena. *The Way: Living in Love.* New Knoxville, Ohio: American Christian, 1970.

Wierwille, Victor Paul. *Jesus Christ Is Not God.* New Knoxville, Ohio: American Christian, 1975.

_____. *The New Dynamic Church.* New Knoxville, Ohio: American Christian, 1971.

_____. *Power for Abundant Living.* New Knoxville, Ohio: American Christian, 1971.

_____. *Receiving the Holy Spirit Today.* New Knoxville, Ohio: American Christian, n.d.

_____. *The Word's Way.* New Knoxville, Ohio: American Christian, n.d.

Williams, J. L. *Victor Paul Wierwille and the Way International.* Chicago: Moody Press, 1979.

WITCHCRAFT

Adler, Margot. *Drawing Down the Moon: Witches, Druids, Goddess-Worshippers, and Other Pagans in America.* Rev. ed. Boston: Beacon, 1986.

Buckland, Raymond. *Buckland's Complete Book of Witchcraft.* St. Paul, Minn.: Llewellyn, 1988.

Cunningham, Scott. *The Truth about Witchcraft Today.* St. Paul, Minn.: Llewellyn, 1988.

Daly, Mary. *Beyond God the Father: Toward a Philosophy of Women's Liberation.* Boston: Beacon, 1973.

De Angeles, Ly. *The Feast of Flesh and Spirit.* Australia: Wildwood Gate, 2002,

De Angeles, Ly. *Witchcraft: Theory and Practice.* Australia: Wildwood Gate, 2000.

Dullea, Georgia. "A Witch Speaks at the Smithsonian." *New York Times* (Oct. 31, 1991), B4.

Ferrar, Janet, and Stewart Ferrar. *A Witches Bible Compleat.* 2 vols. New York: Magickal Childe, 1984.

Farrar, Stewart. *What Witches Do: The Modern Coven Revealed.* London: Sphere, 1973.

Gardner, Gerald B. *Witchcraft Today.* New York: Magickal Childe, 1989.

Glass, Justine. *Witchcraft: The Sixth Sense.* North Hollywood, Calif.: Wilshire, 1974.

Griffin, Wendy. *Daughters of the Goddess: Studies of Healing, Identity and Empowerment.* Walnut Creek, Calif.: AltaMira, 2000.

Guiley, Rosemary Ellen. *The Encyclopedia of Witches and Witchcraft.* 2nd ed. New York: Facts on File, 1999.

Hawkins, Corinne Cullen. Review of E. Fuller Torrey, *Witchdoctors and Psychiatrists.* In *A Whole Earth Review* (Summer 1988), 115.

Hawkins, Craig S. "The Modern World of Witchcraft." *Christian Research Journal* (Winter/Spring 1990), 9–14.

_____. "The Modern World of Witchcraft." *Christian Research Journal* (Summer 1990), 22–27.

Hill, Douglas, and Pat Williams. *The Supernatural.* New York: Hawthorne, 1965.

Jewett, Paul K. *Man as Male and Female.* Grand Rapids: Eerdmans, 1986.

Johnson, Maria Miro. "Witches in Search of Respect." *The Providence Journal Bulletin* (August 1989), 1–2.

Karlsen, Carol F. *The Devil in the Shape of a Woman.* New York: Vintage, 1987.

Kelly, Aidan A. *Crafting the Art of Magick: A History of Modern Witchcraft 1939–64.* Modern Witchcraft Series. St. Paul, Minn.: Llewellyn, 1991.

LaVey, Anton Szandor. *The Complete Witch, or, What to Do When Virtue Fails.* New York: Dodd, Mead, 1971.

Leek, Sybil. *The Complete Art of Witchcraft.* New York: Signet, 1973.

_____. *Diary of a Witch.* New York: Signet, 1969.

Lehmann, Arthur, James Myers, and Pamela Moro. *Magic, Witchcraft, and Religion: An Anthropological Study of the Supernatural.* 5th ed. Burr Ridge, Ill.: McGraw-Hill Humanities, 2000.

Luhrmann, T. M. *Persuasion of the Witches Craft: Ritual Magic in Contemporary England.* Cambridge, Mass.: Harvard Univ. Press, 1989.

Michelet, Jules. *Satanism and Witchcraft.* Trans. A. R. Allinson. New York: Citadel, 1983.

Ostling, Richard N. "When God Was Woman." *Time* (May 6, 1991), 73.

Robbins, Russell Hope. *The Encyclopedia of Witchcraft and Demonology.* New York: Crown, 1959.

Robinson, Enders, A. *The Devil Discovered: Salem Witchcraft, 1692.* New York: Hippocrene, 1991.

Russell, Jeffrey B. *Witchcraft in the Middle Ages.* Ithaca, N.Y.: Cornell Univ. Press, 1985.

Starhawk. *Dreaming the Dark.* New ed. Boston: Beacon, 1988.

_____. *The Spiral Dance: A Rebirth of the Ancient Religion of the Great Goddess.* San Francisco: Harper & Row, 1979.

"The Ultimate Mother." *New York Times* (May 12, 1991), sec. 4, E16.

Unger, Rusty. "Oh, Goddess!" *New York Times* (June 4, 1990), 40–46.

Valiente, Doreen. *An ABC of Witchcraft: Past and Present.* New York: St. Martin's, 1973.

Walker, Barbara G. *The Woman's Dictionary of Symbols and Sacred Objects.* San Francisco: Harper & Row, 1988.

_____. *The Woman's Encyclopedia of Myths and Secrets.* San Francisco: Harper & Row, 1983.

WORLDWIDE CHURCH OF GOD

Ambassador Report (Various issues).

Armstrong, Herbert W. "Did God Create a Devil." *Tomorrow's World* (June 1977), 3–5.

_____. *Do You Have an Immortal Soul?* Pasadena, Calif.: Ambassador College Press, 1957.

_____. *Just What Do You Mean Born Again?* Pasadena, Calif.: Ambassador College Press, 1962.

_____. *Which Day Is the Sabbath of the New Testament?* Pasadena, Calif.: Ambassador College Press, 1971.

_____. *Why Were You Born?* Pasadena, Calif.: Ambassador College Press, 1972.

"Armstrong Reassuring Church Ties." *Los Angeles Herald Examiner* (Apr. 27, 1979).

"Armstrong Views Woes of Church." *Post Register* (Idaho Falls, Ida.) (Jan. 11, 1979).

"Church Loses $1.26 Million in Libel Suit." *Los Angeles Times* (Aug. 24, 1984), 6.

"Church of God Hints at Armstrong Reconciliation." *Register* (Anaheim, Calif.) (Feb. 28, 1981), D13.

"Exodus at Quest: Church vs. Schnayerson." *Time* (Jan. 12, 1981), 57.

Feazell, J. Michael. *The Liberation of the Worldwide Church of God.* Grand Rapids: Zondervan, 2001.

"Herbert W. Armstrong to Divorce Second Wife." *Los Angeles Times* (Apr. 22, 1982), 16.

Hill, David Jon. *Is There a Real Hellfire?* Pasadena, Calif.: Ambassador College Press, 1953.

Hopkins, Joseph. *The Armstrong Empire.* Grand Rapids: Eerdmans, 1974.

_____. "Armstrong's Church of God: Mellowed Aberrations?" *Christianity Today* (Apr. 15, 1977), 22–24.

_____. "Despite Scandals, Armstrong's Church Is Growing." *Christianity Today* (Aug. 6, 1982), 48–49.

_____. "Good Thinking! The Armstrong Family Business." *Eternity* (November 1977), 58–61.

_____. "Will Herbert W. Armstrong Rise Again?" *Christianity Today* (January 1988), 48.

Johnson, Maurice. *Herbert B. Armstrong and the Radio Church of God.* Minneapolis: Bethany, 1968.

Lapaka, J. Thomas. *Out of the Shadows.* St. Louis: Concordia, 2001.

Morrison, Michael. *Sabbath, Circumcision, and Tithing: Which Old Testament Laws Apply to Christians?* Lincoln, Neb.: Writers Club, 2002.

Nichols, Larry, and George Mather. *Discovering the Plain Truth: How the Worldwide Church of God Encountered the Gospel of Grace.* Downers Grove, Ill.: InterVarsity Press, 1998.

Pemente, Eric. "When Christians Meet the Worldwide Church of God." *Christian Herald* (October 1988), 40.

"Personal Letters to Robert Sumner, November 27, 1958." In *Kingdom of the Cults.* Ed. Walter Martin. Minneapolis: Bethany, 1985.

"Rader Receives $200,000 As Church of God Advisor." *Register* (Anaheim, Calif.) (Jan. 12, 1979), A3.

"Strong-Arming Garner Ted: The Ins and Outs of the Worldwide Church." *Time* (June 19, 1978).

"Successor Takes Over after Death of Herbert Armstrong." *Christianity Today* (Feb. 21, 1986), 48.

Tkach, Joseph. *Transformed by Truth.* Sisters, Ore.: Multnomah, 1997.

"Two Top Ministers Quit Armstrong Sect." *Los Angeles Times* (Jan. 13, 1976), 48.

"Worldwide Church: Is Tithe Shifting?" *St. Louis Post Dispatch* (Feb. 7, 1979).

"Worldwide Church of God Loses a Defamation Suit." *Christianity Today* (Oct. 19, 1984), 51.

Index

Note: Because the words cult, sect, occult, Christianity, Christendom, Jesus Christ (or Jesus), Trinity, or other common Christian nomenclature appear on numerous pages of the book, these words are referenced only where each appears as an article entry; otherwise *passim* appears behind each of these words.

A.A., 355
Aaronic Priesthood, 90, 190, 355
Abaddon, 355
Abakua, **17–18**, 281
Abdu'l Baha, 32
Abdul Khaalis, Hamaas, 355
Aberdeen Witches, 355
Abhidharma Pitaka, 44, 295
Abhiyoga, 355
Abracadabra, 355
Abrahadabra, 355
Abraham, the Jew, 355
Abraxas, 355
absent healing, 355
Absolute Trinity, 320, 355
Abulafla, Abraham ben Samuel, 355
abyss, 355
acacia, 117
acarya, 355
A.C. Bhaktivendanta Swami Prabhupada, 140, 355
Achad Foster, 356
ache, 356
achogun, 183, 356
acolyte, 356
acon, 328, 356
Acronymics, 356
acupuncture, 211, 356
acuto-manzia, 356
Adad, 356
Adam-God doctrine, 195, 356
Adams, Don, 157
adept, 356
adet, 356
adjanikon, 357
adjikone, 44, 357
adjuration, 357
Adler, Alfred, 232
Adler, Margot, 338

Adoptionism, 357
Adram'melech, 357
Adventism; Adventist, 357
aeon, 357
aeromancy, 357
Aetherius Society, **18–21**
Affirmative Power, 357
Affirmative Prayer, 240
agape, 357
Agave, 357
agent, 357
Age of Reason, *see* Enlightenment
Agrippa, von Nesttesheim, Heinrich Cornelius, 357
Ahad, 357
ahimsa, 152, 357
Ahura Mazdah, 357
Aidia-Wedo, 357
air, 357
Aiwaz 251, 357
ajna chakra, 357
akasha principle, 357
Akiya, Einasuke, 219, 279, 357
akoveo, 46, 357
Alamo Christian Ministries; Alamo Christian Foundation, **21–24**
Alamo, Tony and Susan, 21, 22, 23, 357
Alan, Jim, 338
Alastor, 357
albahaca, 357
Albingenses, 357
alchemy, 358
Aldinach, 358
alectorius, 358
alectromancy, 358
alectryomancy, 358
Alexandrian, 340, 358
algeny, 358
Algoi or Algol, 358

Al-Hassan, 287, 358
Ali, 358
Ali, Mirza Husayn, 32, 358
Allah, 32, 107, 143–52, 202, 204, 287, 337, 358
All Hallows' Eve, 358
All-Seeing Eye, 119, 358
alma, 358
alomancy, 358
Alpert, Richard, 121, 211, 358
alphagenics, 277
Al-Qaeda (Islam), 151, 358
altar, 246, 252, 340, 359
altered states of consciousness, 98, 211
Amachitis, 359
Amaranth, Order of, 117
Amaterasu, 359
Ambassador College Press, 359
Ambassador Colleges, 359
Ambrose, St., 62
Amducias, 359
American Christian Press, 359
American Freedom Coalition, AFC, 203
American Medical Association, 111
American Study Group, 359
Amman, Jacob, 67
amnesia, 359
AMORC, 359
Amoymon, 359
amritdhari, 359
Amritdhari Sikhs, 274
amulet, 246, 340, 359
Anabaptists, 67, 68
anacithidus, 359
Analects, 359
analytical mind, 263, 359
Anami Lok, 359
Ananda Marga Yoga Society, **24–25**, 213
Anandamurti, Shrii Shrii, 359
Ananse, 359
anatta, 359
ancestor worship, 359
Ancient One, 359
Anderson, James, 115
Andon, 359
Andrea, Johann Valentin, 242, 355
Andrew, J.J., 48
androgyne, 359
angas, 359
angels, 20, 359
Anglo-Israelism, 360
Angra Mainyu, 360
anima, 360
animal magnetism, 53, 360

animism, 46, 124, 206, 280, 329
ankh, 339, 360
annihilationism, 49, 162, 165, 360
Anointed Class, 161, 162, 164, 165, 270, 360
antaskarma, 360
Ante-Nicene era, 59
anthropomancy, 360
anthropomorphism, 360
anthropopathism, 360
anti-semitism, 31, 32, 106, 129, 131
Antony, St., 63
apana, 360
Apocalypse, 361
Apocrypha, 361
apologetics, 42, 59
Apophis, 360
apostasy, 163, 197, 360
apostle, 215, 259, 360
Apostles' Creed—*passim*
Apostolic Brotherhood, 47, 360
Apostolic fathers, 59
apostolic succession, 89, 360
apotheosis, 360
apparition, 360
Applewhite, Marshall Herff, 122, 226, 362
Appolinarianism, 61, 360
Apport, 362
Aqamas, 362
Aquarian Age, 209, 362
Aquarian Age Bible, 18, 19
Aquarian Gospel, The, 362
Aquarius, 214, 362
Aquino, Michael, 254, 255, 362
Arbatel of Magic, 362
Archon, 362
A.R.E., 362
Arguelles, Jose, 362
arhat, 42, 294, 362
Arianism, 49, 60, 61, 160, 333, 362
Arica, **25–26**, 211
Aries, 363
Arijia, 363
Arimanius Aharman Dahak, 363
Arius of Alexandria, 60, 363
Arjuna, 363
Arjun, Guru, 276
Ark of the Covenant, 172, 363
Armageddon, 87, 363
Arminius, Jacobus, 64
Armstrong, Garner Ted, 343, 344, 363
Armstrong, Herbert W., 132, 343–49, 363
aromatherapy, 364
Aryan Nations, 131, 132, 133, 135

aryas, 42
Ascendant, 364
Ascending Arc, 364
asceticism, 41, 42, 152, 184, 234, 286, 364
asheshe, 46, 364
Ashkenazi, 175, 364
Ashmole, Elias, 242, 364
ashram, 210, 234, 273, 274, 285, 364
ashrama, 128, 364
Ashram Integral Yoga Institute, **93–95**
Ashteroth, 364
Asoka, 41, 124, 184, 294
aspect, 364
Association for Research and Enlightenment (A.R.E),
    26–30, 284, 365
assoto, 328
astral plane, 19, 365
astral projection, 339, 365
astrogyromancy, 365
astrology, 365
Ataturk, Kemal, 287
atchere, 365
athame, 340, 365
Athanasian Creed, 50
Athanasius, 60, 61, 64
atheism, practical, 41
Atlantis, civilization of, 29, 243, 244
atman, 126, 127, 325, 365
Atmane, 365
auditing, 232
auditor, 263, 365
Augsburg Confession, 68
augury, 366
Augustine, St., 39, 55, 62, 63, 64, 66
Augustinian Order, 366
Aum Shinrikyo; Aum Supreme Truth, 12, **30–32**, 231,
    366
automatic writing, 36
Autumn Equinox, 339, 366
avatar, 28, 100, 128, 185, 263, 295, 366
Avatara, 366
avidya, 42, 323, 325, 366
ayatollah (Islam), 366
Ayatollah Khomeini, 145, 147
Ayurvedic medicine, 366
azetos, 327, 366

Baal, 366
Ba'al-berith, 366
Baal-hadad, 366
Ba'alim, 366
Ba'al-zebub, 366
Baba, Mehrer, 366

Babalao, 46, 183, 248, 280, 366
Babalorisha, 46, 367
Babalosaim, 367
Babaoge, 46, 367
Babe Christian, 367
babes, 104, 367
Babists, 367
Back to Godhead, 367
baculum, 367
Baha'i Faith, The, **32–34**, 213
Baha, Abdu'l, 32, 367
Baha'u'llah, Mirza Husayn Ali, 32
bakas, 327, 367
Bakr, Abu (Islam), 144, 367
Bainbridge, William S, 298
Baisakhi Day, 275
Balaam, 367
Ballard, Guy, 83, 367
Ballou, Hosea, 367
bamboche, 367
Ban, 367
bane, 367
banishing ritual, 367
Banshee, 367
Bantu, 17, 45, 246, 280, 367
Baphomet, 368
baptism, 368
baptism for the dead, 89, 198, 367
Barret, Sir William F., 368
Baron Samedhi, 368
Barth, Karl, 69, 70
Basil the Great, 61
Bast, 368
Bat, 368
bata, 368
Battle of Tours, 144
Bates, Joseph, 267
beatific vision, 368
Beelzebub, 368
Behar, Richard, 261
Behemoth, 368
Bel, 368
Belphegor, 368
Beltane, 339, 368
Benedict, St., 65
Benedictines, 65
Bennet, Alan, 369
Benson, Ezra Taft (Mormonism), 369
Berg, David Brandt, 103, 369
Berith, 369
Besant, Annie W., 212, 291, 369
Bethel, 157, 369

bewitchment, 369
Bhagavad Gita, 124, 126, 141, 251, 266, 285, 298, 369
Bhajan, Yogi, 369
Bhakstivedanta Book Trust, 369
bhakta, 369
bhakti, 275, 369
bhakti marga, 127
bhakti yoga, 94, 141
Bhasstrika Bhumbaka, 369
bhikkhu, 369
Bible, 264, 268, 269, 282, 300, 301, 369
bilocation, 98, 369
bilongo, 369
binding, 369
biofeedback, 211, 369
bishop, 90, 370
Black Arts, 370
blackball, 115
Black Hebrew Israelites, *see* Nation of Yahweh
Black Judaism, 238, 370
black magic, 46, 259, 370, 329, 335
black mass, 252, 256, 258, 259, 370
Black Muslim Movement, *see* Nation of Islam
Blackwood, Algernon, 370
Blake, William, 370
Blavatsky, Madame Helena Petrovna, 83, 210, 212, 239, 291, 370
blessed be! 370
Blighton, Father Earl Paul, 47, 370
blissed out, 370
blood pact, 370
blood transfusion, 167, 370
Blue Lodge (Freemasonry), 115, 116, 370
bodha, 371
bodhi, 371
Bodhi-dharma, 371
bodhisattva, 42, 43, 44, 184, 219, 294, 371
Bogeyman, 371
bokor, 327, 371
bolline, 371
Bonga Man, 371
Book of Abraham, 371
Book of Changes, 371
Book of the Dead, 372
Book of the Law, 251, 372
Book of Mormon, 90, 190, 193, 194, 195, 371
Book of Shadows, 372
Book of Thoth, 371
born again, 372
Boston Church of Christ, *see* International Churches of Christ
Boston Movement, The, *see* International Churches of Christ

botanica, 249, 373
boucan, 373
Boy Scouts, 119
Brahma, 125, 126, 373
brahmacharin, 128, 142, 373
brahmajnan, 373
Brahman, 126, 127, 297, 298, 324
brahmanas, 126
Brahma-Sutra-Bhashya, 373
Brahmanism, 124, 276
branch, 192
Branch Davidians, 12, **35–37**, 122, 225, 231, 268, 299, 301, 373
Branham, William Marion, 37–40
Branhamism, **37–40**, 373
breeder, 373
Bright, Bill, 71
Brinsmead, Robert, 268
British Israelism, 373
Brooks, Nona, 95, 373
broomstick, 373
Brother of Christ, 373
Brothers of Our Father Jesus, *see* Penitentes
Brothers of the Shadow, 373
Brown Brothers, 373
brujeria, 373
brujo, 373
Bubba Free John, 373
Buckland, Raymond and Rosemary, 338
Budapest, Zsuzanna, 338
Buddha, 19, 40–45, 85, 98, 127, 129, 185, 219, 294, 324, 374
Buddhism, 31, **40–45**, 91, 92, 125, 266, 271, 272, 273, 279, 288, 290, 294
Bultmann, Rudolph, 70
Butler, Richard, 130, 133
Butsodun, 219, 374

Cabildo, **45**, 281
Cacodemon, 374
Caille Loa, 374
caliph, 144, 374
Calunga, 183, 374
Calvary Chapel, 72
Calvin, 64, 67, 148, 163
Calvinists, 68, 154
Campbell, Alexander and Thomas, 48
Campus Advance, *see* International Churches of Christ
Campus Crusade for Christ, 71
Candlemas, 374
Candomble, **45–46**, 183, 281
canon (New Testament), 59
canonical hours, 65
cantrip, 374

Capitular Degrees (Freemasonry), 374
caplata, 328, 374
capnomancy, 374
Capricorn, 374
Cariapemba, 183, 374
CARP, 374
Cartesian dualism, 54
Case, Paul Foster, 374
Casican, 17, 374
Castaneda, Carlos, 212, 375
caste system (India), 42, 124, 375
categories of Satanists, 253
cauldron, 246, 337, 340, 375
Cavendish, Richard, 375
Cayce, Edgar, 26–30, 375
Cayse, Hugh Lynn, 375
celestial kingdom, 197, 375
celestial marriage (Mormonism), 375
Celestine Prophecy, The, 216, 376
chador (Islam), 376
Chaitanya, Guru, 376
Chaitanyana, 140, 141, 376
Chakras, 376
Chamador, 376
changeling, 376
channeling, 216, 283, 284, 376
Channing, William Ellery, 376
chapter degrees (Freemasonry), 376
charismatic movement, 70
Charles V, 68, 145
charm. 249, 376
charvaka, 376
chela, 98
Chemosh, 376
Cheng-Ming, 376
Cherubim, 376
cheval, 376
ch'i, 211, 290, 376
Children of God, The (COG)—*see* Family, The
Chinmoy, Sri, 285, 376
chiromancy, *see* palm reading
Chiu King, 376
Chopra, Deepak, 216, 376
Choronzon, 377
Christ, *see* Jesus Christ
Christadelphianism, **48–51**
Christaquarians, 215, 377
Christ-consciousness, 377
Christed, 377
Christian Fellowship Ministries; Potter's House; The
    Door; Victory Chapel, **51–52**
Christianity, **57–73** (all other references—*passim*)
Christian Identity, **129–35**

Christian Science, **53–57**, 228, 244
Christology, 49, 51, 61–62, 263, 377
Christ the Savior Brotherhood, **47–48**
Chrysostom, John, 61
Chuang-tzu, 289, 377
Church of Bible Understanding, The, **73–76**
Church of Jesus Christ of Latter-Day Saints (see,
    Mormonism)
Church of Love, *see* Nation of Yahweh
Church of Religious Science, CLBA, *see* Religious
    Science
Church of the Living Word; The Walk, **76–79**
Church of the Lukumi Babalao Aye, *see* Santeria
Church of the New Jerusalem, 28, **79–82**, **217**, 228,
    243, 284
Church of the Second Advent, *see* International
    Community of Christ
Church Universal and Triumphant, **83–87**, **213**, 293
Church Without a Name, **88–89**
cingulum, 377
circle, 340, 377
Circuit, 377
circuit overseer, 377
Cit, 377
City of God, The, 66
clairaudience, 283
clairvoyance, 26, 27, 282, 283, 301, 339, 377
clear, 97, 263, 378
Clement of Alexandria, 59
cloven hoofs, 378
Clovis, King (of Gaul), 66
colors, 378
Commandery degrees (Freemasonry), 378
communal house, 74, 378
communicants, 85, 378
communism, 68
Community of Christ (Reorganized Church of Latter-
    Day Saints), **89–91**, 190, 193
company servant, 378
cone of power, 378
conference, 378
confession of the order, 378
Confucianism, 33, **91–93**, 271, 272, 273, 288, 289, 378
conjuration, 378
Conservative Judaism, 180
Constantine (Roman emperor), 59, 60
contract, 378
control, 378
Convince, **92**, 281
Cooneyites, *see* Church Without a Name
Cosmic Christ, 378
Cosmic Master, 19, 20
Cosmic Voice, 19

Council degrees (Freemasonry), 379
Council of Chalcedon, 49, 62
Council of Constantinople, 60
Council of Ephesus, 60, 61, 62, 81
Council of Imams (Islam), 379
Council of Jerusalem (Acts 15), 58
Council of Nicea, 60
Council of Orange, 64
Council of Trent, 68
Council of Twelve Apostles, 90, 192, 379
counselors, 379
Counter Reformation, 68
Course in Miracles, A, 215, 379
coven, 257, 379
Covenant Sword and Arm of the Lord, 133
Covensted, 379
Coverdom, 379
Cowdery, Oliver, 189, 379
Craft (Freemasonry), 379
Cramer, Melinda, 95, 379
Cranmer, Thomas, 67
Crème, Benjamin, 212, 379
crescent, 379
Criminon, 262
Crosier, O. R. L., 267
cross (Christian), 379
crossroads, 380
Crossroads Church of Christ, 379
Crossroads Ministry, *see* International Churches of
    Christ
Crowley, Aleister, 251, 252, 255, 338, 380
crystal ball, 381
crystalomancy, 381
crystals, 216
cups, 381
cult, 381 (all other references—*passim*)
Cult Awareness Network, **261**
Cummins, Geraldine, 381
Cumorah Hill (Mormonism), 381
curse, 381
cursing finger, 381
cusp, 381
Cyril of Alexandria, 61

daba, 382
Dan, 383
daemon, 382
dagoba, 382
dagyde, 382
Dahomey, 17, 45, 326, 382
Dai Gohonzon, 382
daimoku, 219, 382
Daisekiji, 219, 382
Dalai Lama, 44, 382

daphnomancy, 383
Darby, John Nelson, 70, 158
Darbyites, 69
Darwinism, 68, 70
Dass, Baba Ram, 121, 383
dasya, 383
Daughters of Eastern Star, 117, 383
David, Moses, **103–7**, 383
Davidian Seventh-Day Adventist Association, **35**
Davis, Andrew Jackson, 281, 383
Dawn Bible Students' Association, 383
Day of Atonement, 267, 269
deacon, 90, 383
death angel, 205, 383
death dagic, 383
debility, 383
Decius (Roman emperor), 59, 63
Deggial, 383
degree, 383
De Grimston, Robert, 231–33
deification, 78, 86, 383
deism, 68, 119, 383
DeMolay, Order of, 117
demons, 19, 250, 284
demonology, 384
demonomancy, 384
demonization, 384
demon possession, 93, 384
demonstration, 384
demythologize, 70
denomination, 103, 118, 384
dense body, 88, 244, 384
deosil, 384
deprogramming, 261, 384
dermatoglyphics, 384
dermography, 384
Dervish Orders, 385
Desaguliers, Theophilus, 115
descending arc, 385
Deseret News Press (Mormonism), 385
despojo, 385
Dev, 385
Dev, Guru, 295, 385
deva, 385
devachan, 385
devaki, 266
devi, 385
devil, 23, 39, 50, 51, 106, 162, 250, 273, 282, 284, 337,
    385
devil's garter, 385
devil's mark, 385
devil's pillar, 385
DeWolf, Ronald, 261

DFing, 385
dhamma, 385
Dhammapada, 385
dharana, 385
dharma, 124, 127, 152, 385
Dharsana, 385
Dhimmi (Islam), 386
diablito, 17, 386
diabolism, 255, 386
Dianetics, 260, 262, 386
diaspora, 175, 386
dichotomy of man, 386
Digambaras, 386
Dignity, 386 (*see also* Universal Fellowship of
    Metropolitan Community Churches)
Dimambro, Joseph, 225, 226, 386
Dionysius of Alexandria, 39
Dionysus, 386
directions, 386
Director General, 386
disassociate, 386
discipler, 136, 386
discipleship, 386
Disciples of Christ, The, 48, 49
disfellowship, 343
dispensationalism, 50, 52, 70, 76, 77, 106, 158, 270,
    335, 386
district, 387
divali, 387
divination, 27, 272, 327, 336, 339, 340, 387
Divine Life Society, **93–95**
Divine Light Mission, The, *see* Elan Vital
Divine Nectar, 387
Divine Principle, 302, 387
Divine Science, **95–96**, 216
Divine Science Life International, 95
Divine Soul, 387
divining rod, 387
Dixon, Jean, 106, 387
Docetism, 54, 106, 387
Doctrine and Covenants, 90, 194, 197, 198, 387
Dogen, 387
Dolman, 387
Donatism; Donatist heresy, 63, 64, 387
Door, The, *see* Christian Fellowship Ministries
Doubleday, Abner, 291
dowsing, 27, 388
Doyle, Sir Arthur Conon, 288, 388
Dracula, 388
drawing down the moon, 339, 388
drawing down the sun, 338, 339, 388,
dreadlocks, 237, 388
dream body, 388

Dresser, Horatio, 388
Dresser, Julius, 217, 388
Drew, Timothy, 202
Druids, 337, 388
Druj, 388
dualism, 54, 63, 142, 185, 217, 334, 388
dumb signs, 388
Dungeons and Dragons, 388
Durkheim, Emile, 208
dynamic monarchianism, 49, 389

Eadie, Betty, 388
earthbound, 389
earth plane, 389
Eastern Orthodoxy, 47, 58, 62
Eastern Star, Order of the, 115–18, 389, 429
Ebionites, 389
eblis, 389
ebo, 183, 389
ecclesia, 48, 389
ecclesiology, 390
Eckankar, **96–100**, 263
Eck Master, 97, 98,
ectenic force, 390
ectoplasm, 390
ecumenical councils, 60
Eddy, Mary Baker, 53–55, 95, 216, 217, 239, 390
Edict of Milan, 60, 63
Edison, Thomas Alva, 291
Edson, Hiram, 266, 267
Edwards, Jonathon, 68
Effendi, Shoghi, 32, 390
efi group, 17, 390
efo, 17, 390
egun, 46, 390
eidolism, 390
eightfold path, 42, 44, 390
eighth sphere, 390
eight mortals, 290
Einasuke, Akiya, 390
Eisai, 390
eisegesis, 390
ekon, 17, 390
Elan Vital, **100–102**, 213
elca, 390
elder, 90, 390
elder brother, 390
Elegba, 45, 280, 390
elementals, 390
elementary, 390
elongation, 391
elves, 391
elvinfolk, 391

Embraced by the Light, 391
Emerson, Ralph Waldo, 391
e-meter, 260, 261, 262, 391
emperor worship, 272
endowments, 198, 391
energy planes, 20
engrams, 263, 391
enkanika, 391
enlightenment (also The Enlightenment), 54, 58, 68, 70,
   102, 111, 121, 124, 152, 184, 220, 234, 265, 274,
   275, 285, 287, 294, 295, 391
Enlil, 391
enneagram, 391
Entered Apprentice; First Degree, 115, 116, 391
eon, 391
Ephemerus, 391
equinox, 391
Erasmus, 63, 67
Erhard Seminars Training (EST), 108, 391
Erhard, Werner Hans, 108, 392
erikunde, 17, 392
Erzulie, 392
esbat, 339, 392
eschatology, 256, 392
Eshu, 46, 247, 280, 392
Esoteric Council, 47, 392
Essenes, 175, 392
EST, *see* Forum
eternal life, 392
eternal retribution, 392
ether, 392
etheric body, 392
etheric plane, 392
Eutyches, 62
Eutychianism, 62, 324, 392
evangelicalism; evangelicals, 70, 137, 149, 220, 303,
   344, 392
Evans, Warren Felt, 217, 393
evil eye, 393
evil slave, 393
evocation, 393
exaltation, 393
exegesis, 393
existentialism, 113, 227, 182, 209, 393
exorcism, 256, 393
exoteric, 293
extraordinary perception (ESP), 393
eye biting, 393

fairies, 394
faith, 270
fakir, 394
Fall, The, 394
false prophecy; false prophet(s), 394

Fama Fraternitatis, 394
famba, 17, 394
familiar, 252, 394
Family, The, **103–7**, 394
Family of Love; *see* Family, The
fana, 394
fantasy role playing games (FRP), 394
Fard, Wallace, 129, 202, 394
Farrakhan, Louis, 129, 203, 394
fascination, 394
Father David, 394
fatwah (Islam), 394
feast of sacrifice, 394
Fellow Craft Degree, 115, 116, 395
feminine signs, 395
Ferdinand, King, 145
Ferrar, Janet and Stewart, 338, 339, 340
fertility deities, 395
fetish, 248, 249, 395
FFing, 104, 106, 395
fifth root race, 395
figure, 395
Fillmore, Charles S., 395
Fillmore, Myrtle, 395
finger, 395
fire, 395
fire-walking, 395
first amendment (US Constitution), 11
First Church of Christ, Scientist, 53, 395
first presidency, 192, 395
first vision (Mormonism), 395
five great vows, 395
Five K's, The, 274, 276, 395
Five Percenters, **107**
five pillars (Islam), 146, 395
five violations, 396
fivefold kiss, 396
flagae, 396
fluid body, 396
flying ointment, 396
fo, 396
Fonta, 396
Forau, 396
forbidden, 396
Ford, Desmond, 268, 396
Forever Family, **73**
Forrest, Nathan, 130, 396
Fort, Charles Hoy, 396
fortified, 396
fortune telling, 396
fortune-telling forms, 396
Forum, **107–11**, 211, **236**, 277, 297, 319
Foundation for Religious Freedom, 261

Foundation of Human Understanding, **111–14**
fourfold path, 102, 397
four-footed Signs, 397
four great vows, 397
four noble truths, 42, 397
fourth root race, 397
fourth way, 397
Fox sisters, (Kate, Margaret, and Leah), 281, 397
Franz, Frederick, 157, 167, 397
Frazer, Sir James George (1854–1951), 397
Freemasonry, 12, **114–20**, 199, 251, 243, 338
Friends, 397
Frig, 397
Freud, Sigmund, 68
frustration, 397
full moon, 397
Full Gospel Temple, 76
Fuller, Curtis, 397
Fuller, John Frederick Charles, 397
fundamentalism, 52, 70, 88, 149, 164, 165, 256, 268,
    282, 303, 332, 397
Furfur, 398
Furman, Ashrita, 285
fylfot cross, 398

Gabriel, Angel, 143
Gaia Hypothesis, 212, 398
Gale, William P., 132
Gandhi, Mahatma, 24, 124, 128, 266, 276
Ganges, 128, 398
ganja, 239, 398
Gardner, Gerald, 338, 398
Gardnerians, 399
garments, 399
garters, 399
Garuda, 399
garuda mantra, 399
Garvey, Marcus, 129, 202, 237
Gautama, Siddharta, 40, 124, 184, 218, 399
gay theology, *see* Universal Fellowship of Metropolitan
    Community Churches
Gede, 399
Geller, Uri, 399
gelospy, 399
Gemini, 399
genni, 399
gentile, 399
geomancy, 399
Germain, 399
Germer, Karl, 399
gestic magic, 399
ghost, 399
ghoul, 399

Gilead Watchtower Bible School, 399
Glen, James, 82
glossolalia, 70, 399
glottologus, 400
gnomes, 400
Gnosticism, 47, 54, 59, 81, 99, 152, 186, 218, 242, 292,
    304, 320, 325, 400
Gnostic Order of Christ, 47
goat, 400
goat's foot, 400
goat's head, 400
Gods and Earths, *see* Five Percenters
goety, 401
gohonzon, 219, 220, 401
golden candlestick, 401
Golden Key, Order of the, 117
golden plates, 401
golden rule, 284
Google, 261
Go Preachers, *see* Church Without a Name, The
gosvami, 401
gorgon, 401
Gospel of St. Barnabas, 401
Gothic Constitutions, 115
Gothic Witchcraft, 335, 401
govi, 401
Graham, Billy, 71
grand wizard, 130, 401
Grant, Kenneth, 401
Granth Sahib, 401
Grasshof, Louis von, 243, 401
Great Awakenings, The, 68, 401
Great Disappointment, 154, 267, 401
Greater Brotherhood, 402
Great Invocation, 402
Great Renunciation, 402
Great Rite, 402
Great Schism, 62, 66, 402
Great Tribulation, The, 39
Great White Brotherhood, 84, 85, 402
Grebel, Conrad, 67
Gregory of Nyssa, 61
griffin, 402
grihastha, 142, 402
Grimories, 402
gris-gris, 402
gros bon ange, 327, 328, 402
Gross, Darwin, 97, 100, 402
group soul, 402
guardians, 74, 402
guide, 402
guided imagery, 402
Guideposts, 402

guira, 402
Gurdjieff, George Ivanovitch, 227–29, 402
gurdwaras, 276, 402
guru, 26, 94, 96, 100, 124, 186, 213, 234, 265, 285,
   286, 322, 402
Guru Arian, 403
Guru Dev, 403
Guru Maharaj Ji, 100, 121
Guru Nanak, 125, 129, 273, 275, 276
Guru Srila Bhaktisiddhanta Saraswati Goswami
   Maharaja, 140
Gustavus, Adolphus II, King, 68
gyromancy, 403

Haborym, 403
hadith (Islam), 146, 403
hair, 403
hajj, 146, 403
hakata, 403
hall, 403
Halloween, 254, 403
halomancy, 403
hamsa, 403
Hanafi Madh Hab Center, 203
Hand, Beth, 266
handfasting, 403
hand of glory, 403
hands of spirits, 403
Hanley, John, 181, 182, 403
Hanukkah, 403
Hanuman, 403
Hanuman Foundation, **121**
haquigah, 403
Hare Krishna, 98, 140, 403
harimandir, 276, 404
hariyan (Hindu caste), 404
harmonic convergence, 404
Harnack, Adolph von, 69
Harris, Martin, 404
Hasidism, 175, 404
hatha yoga, 94, 404
hauntings, 404
Healthy, Happy, Holy Organization (3HO), *see* Sikh
   Dharma
heart, 404
Heaven's Gate, 12, 103, **122–23**, 225, 226, 213, 299
Heaven's Magic, *see* Family, The
hegira, 144, 404
Heindel, Max, 243, 404
hell, 147, 185, 210, 264, 293, 404
Helvetic Confession, 68
henbane, 405
Henry VIII, King, 67

Henschel, Milton, 157
heptad, 405
hereditaries, 405
hermeneutics, 36, 318, 405
Hermes Trismegistus, 405
Hermes Trismegistus, 292
Hermetica, 405
hermetic axiom, 244, 405
hermetic chain, 405
hermeticism, 242
Hermetic Order of the Golden Dawn, 251, 405
hermetic teachings, 405
Hevioso, 183, 405
hex, 405
hexagram, 405
high magic, 405
high priest, 90, 178, 405
high priestess, 405
Hill, Douglas and Pat Williams, 282
Hinduism, 26, 31, 73, 85, 86, 121, **123–29**, 140, 234,
   242, 265, 266, 273, 275, 277, 278, 283, 284, 285,
   295, 298, 321, 340
Hindmarsh, Robert, 82
hippomancy, 406
Hiroshi, Hojo, 279, 406
Hitler, Adolph, 130, 132, 133
hiving off, 406
hobgoblin, 406
hocus-pocus, 406
Hodge, Charles, 70
Hoekema, Anthony, 269, 270, 271
Hoffman, Bernard Lazar, 406
Holistic Health, 211, 212, 406
Holly King, 406
Holmes, Ernest, 239–41, 406
holocaust, 177
holy laughter, 72, 406
Holy of Holies, 178, 406
Holy Order of MANS, 47–48
Holy Roman Empire, 65
Holy Spirit, 58, 270, 274
Holy Spirit Association for the Unification of World
   Christianity, The, *see* Unification Church
homeopathy, 406
homonculus, 406
homo novus, 263
honddon, 406
Hopkins, Emma Curtis, 95, 239, 406
Horn, Edith Opal, 406
horned god, 406
horoscope, 406
horse brasses, 406
horseshoe, 406

Hoskins, Philip, 273
Houdini, 282
House of Yahweh, 406
Houston Jean, 407
Houteff, Victor and Florence, 35
Howell, L.P., 237, 238
Howell, Vernon, 407
Hubbard, Lafayette Ronald, 97, 252, 260–65, 407
Huguenots, 68
huldra, 407
Humanistic Judaism, 180
humanity, 263, 270
Human Potential Movement, 211
humfort, 407
hungan, 327, 407
hunsi, 407
Hus, John, 66
hylozoism, 407
hypnosis, 98, 111, 211, 278, 407
hypostatic union, 62, 86, 407

"I AM" Ascended Masters, The, **83–87**
ibibio, 17
iblis, 407
Ichazo, Oscar, 25, 26, 407
I Ching, 407
iconolastic controversy, 66, 407
Id al-Adha, 408
Id al-Fitr, 408
Id Al-Qurbani, 408
Identity Movements, **129–35**
Ifa, 248, 280, 408
ifan, 408
ifon, 17, 408
IHELP, 262
Ijma, 408
Ijtihad, 408
Ikeda, Daisaku, 219, 279, 408
image magic, 408
imagery, 408
imam, 145
Imam Mahdi, 408
Imbolg, 339, 408
immaculate conception, 408
immaculate sisterhood, 408
immanence, 99, 126, 213, 240, 292, 298, 324, 408
immortality, 408
imp, 408
incantation, 408
incarnation, 34, 102, 126, 142, 161, 214, 224, 245, 273, 284, 408
incense, 409
incubus; *incubii*, 409
Indra, 409

indulgences, 67, 409
initiate, 409
initiator, 101, 409
Inspired Version, 90, 193, 409
International Bible Students, 409
International Church of Ageless Wisdom, **266**
International Churches of Christ, **135–39**
International Community of Christ, **139–40**
International Kundalini Yoga Teachers Association, *see* Sikh Dharma
International Order of Rainbow for Girls, 117
intuition, 409
investigative judgment, 269, 270
ipsissimus, 409
Irani, Merwan Sheriar, 185, 409
ireme, 17, 409
Irenaeus, St., 38, 59
iridology, 409
iris diagonsis, 409
Irvine, William, 88. 409
Irving, Edward, 69, 158
ishtapurta, 409
International Churches of Christ, **135–39**
International Community of Christ, **139–40**
International Kundalini Yoga Teachers Association, **273**
International Society for Krishna Consciousness, *see* ISKCON
Isabella, Queen, 145
Isis Unveiled, 291
ISKCON, 123, **140–43**, 213
Islam, 73, **143–52**, 275, 276, 285, 286, 288, 333
Islamic holidays or holy days, 409
iton, 410
itotele, 410
iya, 410
iyalorishas, 410

Jack Mormons, 410
Jainism, **152–53**, 234
James, William, 410
James, St., 58
Jamilians, *see* International Community of Christ
japa, 410
japa yoga, 94, 410
Jehovah's Witnesses, 50, 53, **153–67**, 268
jen, 410
Jentzsch, Herbert C, 262
Jerome, St., 62, 63
Jesus Christ—*passim*
Jesus Only, 221, 410
Jesus People, 21
Jewish calendar, 410
Ji, Maharaj, 100–102
jigai, 410

jihad, 151, 411
jina, 152, 411
jinn, 143, 411
jiva, 152, 411
jivanmukta, 411
jnana, 411
jnana marga, 127, 411
jnana yoga, 94, 411
jnani, 411
Job's Daughters, International Order of, 117
Jones, James Warren, 52, 230–31, 411
Jonestown, *see* People's Temple
Josei, Toda, 411
Jouret, Luc, 225, 226, 411
Journal of Discourses, 411
Judaism, 39, 57, 58, 143, **168–81**, 242, 333
Judge, William Q., 291, 411
Julian the Apostate (Roman emperor), 61
Jung, Karl, 411
justification, 411

Ka'aba, 412
Kabbalah, 175, 251, 412
kachera, 412
kafir, 148
kagura, 272
Kahn, Haerat Pir-O-Murshid Inayat, 287, 412
Kahn, Pir Vilayat Inayat, 287, 412
kaidan, 220, 412
Kali, 127
Kalima, 412
Kali Yuga, 412
Kal Nirajan, 99, 412
kami, 272
kamikaze pilots, 272
Kan, Hak Ja, 412
kanzo, 327, 412
Kapila, 412
Kapilasvistu, 412
Kapleau, Philip, 412
karma, 19, 27, 30, 42, 86, 87, 98, 99, 124, 127, 142,
    152, 210, 276, 285, 293, 294, 295, 297, 325, 413
karmakanda, 413
karma yoga, 94, 121, 127, 413
kath, 413
Katha Upanishad, 413
kaulah, 413
kechari mudra, 413
keepers of the flame, 85
Kellner, Karl, 251
Kellogg, John, 267
Kelpius, Johann, 243, 413
kensho, 413
kesh, 413

keys of the kingdom, 413
Khaalis, Hamas Abdul, 203, 413
Khadijah, 143, 413
khalife, 413
Khalsa Council, 274
Khalsa Order, 276, 413
khawarij, 413
Kheirall, Ibrahim George, 32
Khoumeni, Ayatollah, 145, 413
Kierkegaard, Søren, 69, 393
kiirtan, 24
King David (in the Bible), 58, 413
Kingdom Farms, 413
Kingdom Hall, 163, 167, 413
Kingdom Ministry School, 413
Kingdom of God, 413
King, George, 18–21, 413
King James Version (Bible), 413
kirlian photography, 413
kirtanya, 142, 413
kiva activities, 208, 209
Klemp. Sir Harold, 97, 99, 414
Koehl, Matthias, 132
Knight Commander, 414
Knights of the Red Cross, 117
Knights Templar, 116, 117
Knorr, Nathan H., 156, 157, 414
Knox, John, 67
koan, 414
Kojiki, 414
komei, 219, 279, 414
Koran, 143–52, 204, 286, 325, 414
Koresh, David, 12, 35–37
Kosen Rufu, 414
Krafft, Karl Ernst, 414
Kramer, Heinrich, 336, 414
Kreis, August B., 131, 134, 336
krishmaloka, 414
Krishna, 124, 127, 141, 324, 414, 415
Krishnamunti, Jiddu, 291
kriya, 414
kriya yoga, 265, 415
Kriyananda, Swami, 266
Krsna, see Krishna
kshatriya (Hindu caste), 414
Kubler-Ross, Elisabeth, 211
Ku Klux Klan, 130, 131, 133, 135, 415
kundalini, 24, 274, 415
K'ung Fu Tzu, 91, 415
kupayogini, 415
Kwanzaa, 415

Ladies Oriental Shrine of North America, 117

lady, 415
Laksmi, 415
Lalita Sahsaranama, 415
lama, 415
Lamanites, 415
lambs, 74, 415
lammas, 416
Landmark Education, *see* Forum
Landmark Forum, *see* Forum
Lao-tse, 288, 289, 416
laver-tete, 327, 416
LaVey, Anton Szandor, 252, 253, 254, 259, 416
laza, 148
Leary, Timothy, 121, 211, 416
Leek, Sybil, 338, 416
Left Hand Path, 416
Legba, 183, 416
Legerdemain, 416
Leo, 416
Leo, Alan, 416
levitation, 281, 416
Lewis, Samuel L., 287
libra, 416
Licinius, 60
Lifespring, **181–82**, 211
lila, 127, 416
Lincoln, Albert, 33
linga, 127, 416
literary criticism, 416
litnessing, 416
little flock, 416
loa, 326, 327, 328, 416
Lodge, Sir Oliver, 282, 416
Logos of God, Logos, 102, 61, 417
Loko, 183, 417
Lord Krishna, 124
Lord of the Second Advent; the third Adam, 417
lost word, 417
lotus position, 417
Lotus Sutra, 218, 417
love, 417
low magic, 417
Loyola, Ignatius, 67
Lucifer, 250, 417
Luciferians, 417
lucky charm, 417
lucky horseshoe, 417
Lucumi, 417
lughnasadh, 339, 417
Lunar Almanac, 417
Luther, Martin, 64, 67, 69, 81, 138, 148, 163, 164, 175, 175
Lutheranism, 81

LXX, 418
lycanthropy, 418

Mackey, Albert, 118, 119
Maclaine, Shirley, 213
Macumba, 45, 46, **183–84**, 281
magic, 250, 329, 335, 340, 418
magic circle, 418
magic, high, 418
magic, image, 418
magic, low, 418
magic, mortuary, 418
magic, natural, 418
magic, protective, 418
magic, sexual, 418
Magic—The Gathering, 418
magic, white, 418
magical name, 418
magician, 418
magick, 251, 255, 418
magister, 418
magus, 252, 418
maha bandha, 418
mahabbah, 286, 418
Mahabharata, 418
Mahayana Buddhism, 41, 43, 44
maha mantra, 418
mahanta, 98, 418
Maharaj, Ji. 100, 121, 419
Maharaj, Sri Swami Sivananda, 419
Maharishi International University, 419
Maharishi Mahesh Yogi, 212, 295, 419
mahatma, 101, 419
Mahavira, Vardhamana, 419
Mahayana Buddhism, **184–85**
mahdi, 419
maiden, 419
Maitreya, Lord, 212, 291, 419
Major Arcana, 419
Makiguchi, Tsonesaburo, 219, 279
Makonnen, Ras Tafari, 237, 419
Malcolm X, 129, 202, 419
Malleus Malificarum, 337, 419
mambo, 327, 419
mana, 419
Manichaeism, 63, 340, 419
manifesto, 419
manman, 420
Manoah, Vision of, 26
mantra, 20, 98, 142, 274, 295, 298, 420
Mantra Baba Nam Kevalam, 24
maracas, 17, 249, 328, 420
margas, 325, 420

marifah, 287, 420
Mark Master; Fourth Degree, 420
Martel, Charles, 144
martial arts, 290, 420
Marx, Karl; Marxism, 68
masjid, 420
masnavi, 287
Masonic Lodge, *see* Freemasonry
mass incarnation, 420
mass weddings, 302
master, 420
Master Mason, 115, 116, 420
Masters, Roy, 111–14, 420
Master Speaks, 420
Mata, Sri Daya, 265
material, 420
materialization, 420
matsuri, 272
Mawu Lisa, 183, 490
Maxentius, 59
maya, 127, 324, 420
May Day, 420
May Eve, 420
McKean, Kip, 133, 137, 138, 420
McPherson, Lisa, 261
McVeigh, Timothy, 37, 131
Mecca, 107, 143, 144, 420
medicine man, 421
Medina, 144
meditation, 276, 287, 298, 421
medium, 278, 281, 283, 421
Meher Baba, 185–86, 213
Melchizedek, Priesthood, 90, 190, 421
Mendez, Goat of, 421
menorah, 421
mental imaging techniques, 278
mental telepathy, 421
mentations, 25
mercy seat, 149, 178, 421
meridians, 421
mesmerism, 53, 216, 421
Messiah, 58, 60, 301, 421
MEST, 263, 422
metanetwork, 422
Metaphysical Bible Dictionary, 422
Methodism, 70
Michael the Archangel, 269
middle path, 290, 422
midsummer solstice, 339, 422
mikado, 422
millennial dawn, 422
millennialism, 50, 133, 153, 199, 256, 270, 300, 422
Miller, William, 158, 266, 267

Millerite Movement, 35, 158, 266, 422
Million Man March, 203
Mind Dynamics, 108, 181, 422
Mind Science, 85, 95, 216, 291, 423
minister, 156, 423
ministerial servants, 163, 423
minor arcana, 423
mirror magic, 423
Miscavige, David, 261
Mishna, 175, 178, 423
mission, 423
Mitchell, Hulon, 204, 205
Mitchell, Wayman, 51, 52
MK ULTRA, 231
Modalistic Monarchianism, 39, 80, 423
Modern Thought, 423
Mohammed, *see* Muhammad
Mohr, Brigadier General Gordon "Jack," 132, 133
moksha, 124, 127, 152, 235, 423
Mo Letters, 103, 423
monarchianism, 224, 423
monasticism, 65
monism, 99, 124, 140, 210, 234, 235, 240, 325, 339, 423
monk, 423
monophysitism, 61, 62, 424
monotheism, 54, 147, 168, 263, 272, 280, 326, 340, 424
monothelitism, 424
Montgomery, John Warwick, 29
Moon, Sun Myung, 23, 248, 265, 301–7, 424
moonies, 424
Morgan, William, 115
Mormonism, 53, 89–91, **187–201**, 263
Moroni, 188, 189, 424
Morris Pratt Institute, 283
mortuary magic, 424
moslem, *see* muslim
mosque, 129, 150, 424
Most Excellent Master; Sixth Degree, 424
mother church, 53, 54, 424
mother goddess, 238, 424
Mountain Meadows Massacre, 190
mudras, 424
muhajdir, 424
Muhammad (founder of Islam), 33, 43, 98, 143–52, 185, 203, 337, 424
Muhammad, Elijah, 129, 202, 424
Muhammad, Mirza Ali, 32, 424
Muhammad Mosques, 203
Muhammad, Wallace Dean, 203
mukti, 425
mulla, 425

multiculturalism, 11
munafikun, 425
muni, 425
Murray, John, 425
Murray, Margaret, 336, 337, 425
murshi, 287
muslim, 143–52, 275, 337, 425
muslim lunar calendar, 425
Myal, 93, **201–2**, 281
mysticism, 61, 96, 121, 227, 283, 287, 425

Naamah, 425
Nameless House Sect, The, *see* Church Without a Name
Nanak, Guru, 425
Naniguismo, 17
narayana, 425
narcanon, 262
narrative criticism, 425
national sojourners, 117
Nation of Islam, 129, 147, **202–4**, 238
Nation of Yahweh, **204–6**
National Founding Day, 272
National Socialist White People's Party, 132
Native American religion, 12, **206–9**
natural magic, 425
nature spirits, 425
Nauvoo, 425
Nauvoo Expositor, 425
near-death experience, 425
necromancy, 426
necrophilia, 426
neo-Nazis, 130, 131
neo-orthodoxy, 69
neo-paganism, 426
neophyte, 426
Nestorianism, 61, 81, 224, 244, 426
Nettles, Bonnie Lu, 122
New Age Movement, 91, 107, 121, 123, **209–16**, 227, 228, 236, 243, 245, 256, 263, 265, 273, 275, 277, 283, 285, 293, 295, 322
new birth, 426
New England Institute for Religious Research, 300
New Hope Singers International, 426
New Nation News, 426
New Thought, **216–18**, **243**, **245**, 293
New World Order, 33
New World Translaion, 157, 426
nganga, 426
Nicene Creed—*passim*
Nichiren, 279
Nichiren Daishonin, 218, 426
Nichiren Shoshu, 44, **218–20**, 279, 280
Nichiren Shoshu of America, *see* Nichiren Shoshu
Nile, Daughters of the, 117

Ninety-five Theses, 67
nirgun, 127, 426
nirvana, 26, 42, 128, 185, 235, 251, 290, 293, 426
No Name Church, *see* Church Without a Name
Nostradamus, 427
November Eve, 427
nudity, 427
numerology, 427
nyabingi, 427
nyaya, 427
Nzambi, 183, 427

oath, Masonic, 115, 428
obatala, 428
obeah, 201, 428
Obermeister, Ruben, 428
obtenir les yeux, 428
occult—*passim*
O-Harai, 429
ogan, 328
okobia, 17, 429
Olcott, Henry Steel, 210, 291, 429
old religion, 429
Olurun, 247, 429
OM, 429
omega, 429
omen, 429
omo, 248
omo-orisha, 17, 429
Oneness Pentecostalism, 28, **221–25**, 261
opele, 44, 429
operating thetan, 263
Operation Blue Water, 19
operation prayer power, 20, 21
ophiolatry, 429
Order of Amaranth, The, 429
Order of DeMolay, The, 429
Order of the Eastern Star, The, 429
Order of the Knights Templar, 429
Order of the Solar Temple; OST, **225–27**
Order of the White Shrine, 429
Order, The, 133
Ordo Templi Orientis, 251, 252, 255
origami, 272
Origen, 59
original sin, 39
orisha, 17, 183, 247, 280, 429
Orodere, 183, 429
orthodox; Orthodoxy, 429
Orthodox Judaism, 180
orthodoxy, 284, 285, 288
oru, 429
Osama bin Laden, 146
OSHO, *see* Rajneeshism

otanses, 429
oth, 429
OTO, 429
Ottoman Turks, 145
Ouija Board, 256, 283, 429
Ouspensky, P.D., 212, 227–29, 430
Ouspensky-Gurdjieff, 212, **227–29**
out-of-body experience, 430
overseers, 163, 430
oversoul, 430
Oxford Movement, 69, 430
Owen, Dale Robert, 282

paganism, 430
palmistry, 430
Palo Mayombe, 430
Pan, 430
panentheism, 430
panpsychism, 96, 430
pantheism, 28, 85, 99, 102, 126, 140, 142, 202, 210,
    235, 264, 278, 292, 296, 430
paploi, 280, 431
paquet, 327, 431
Paradise Trinity, 320, 431
Paramatma, 431
Parapsychology, 431
Parousia, 431
Parsees, 431
Parsons, Jack, 252
Parvati, 127, 431
passing over, 431
Passover, 179, 431
patriarch, 90, 431
patriarch of the church, 431
Patrick, St., 66
Patripassianism, 431
Patristic era, 59, 68
Paul, St., 58, 81
peace symbol, 431
Peace of Westphalia, 68
Pearl of Great Price, The, 187–201, 431
peditherapy, 432
Pelagius; Pelgianism, 62, 64, 432
pendulum, 432
Penitetes, **229–30**
pentacle, 340, 432
pentagram, 255, 340, 432
Pentateuch, 432
Pentecostalism, 70, 72, 106
People's Temple, 22, 47, 76, **230–31**, 234, 411
perfectionism, 78, 432
perfect masters, 185, 432
Permanent 24, 26, 433

permanent enlightenment, 108
Perry, Troy, 314–19, 433
personal transformation, 211
pessah, 433
Peter, St., 58
petit bon ange, 328, 433
Peyote Worship, 208, 433
PFAL, 433
phallic symbol, 433
Pharisees, 175, 433
Pietism, 69, 285, 433
Pike, James Albert, 433
Pioneer Publisher, 433
Piper, Lenora, 282
Pisces, 433
pit bull, 433
Pitaka, 433
Plain Truth, The, 433
planetary vision, 212
planchette, 433
plural marriages, 90, 433
Plymouth Brethren, 69
poltergeist, 433
Polycarp, 59
polygamy, 147, 433
polytheism, 55, 65, 124, 143, 168, 247, 272, 326, 339,
    340, 434
Poole, Elijah, 202, 434
Pope's Secrets, The, 23
positive confession, 434
positive thinking, 434
Post-Nicene era, 60
poteau-mitan, 328, 326, 434
Potter's House, *see* Christian Fellowship Ministries
Power for Abundant Living, 331, 332, 434
practitioners, 241, 434
prana, 211, 434
prayer rug, 434
pre-clear, 263, 434
precognition, 434
predestination, 154, 434
preexistence, 434
prema, 434
Prema Dharmasala, 266
premie, 100, 434
premillenialism, 70
prendre lex yeux, 327, 434
president, 434
presiding bishop, 434
priest, 90, 434
priesthood, 434
primordial vibration, 435

Prince Hall Masonry, 117, 118, 435
prince of the underworld, 435
Process Church of the Final Judgment, **231–33**
Process, The, *see* Process Church of the Final Judgment
Processions, The, 232
Promise Keepers, 71
Prophet, Elizabeth Claire, 84, 85, 435
Prophet, Mark L., 83, 84, 435
prophets, 240, 284, 435
prospective elder, 435
prosperity, 435
Protestantism, 106, 153, 268, 285, 435
psychic, 435
psychical research, 27
psychic surgery, 435
psychokinesis, 436
psychology, 113, 121
psychometry, 436
psychorientology, 277
publisher, 436
puja, 142, 436
Puranas, 125, 436
purdah, 147, 436
pure ones, 289, 290
purgatory, 199
Puritans, 68
pyramid power, 436
pyramidology, 436

quimbanda, 183, 436
Quimby, Phineas Parkhurst, 53, 54, 216, 239, 436
Quorum of the Seventy, 90, 192, 436
Qur'an, 436
q'tas, 436

Ra, 437
rabbi, 437
racism, 118
radical feminism, 437
Rai, Gobind, 276
Rainbow, 437
raja, 437
raja yoga, 94, 121, 437
Rajneesh, Bhagwan Shree, 123, 234–37, 437
Rajneeshism, **234–37**
Rama, 121, 437
Ramadan, 146, 437
Ramakrishna, Sri, 125, 127, 129, 322, 323, 437
Ramavana, 121, 437
Ramirez, Richard, 255
Raphael, 437
Rasputin, Grigori Efemovich, 438
Rastafarianism, 129, **237–39**
Rea, Walter, 268

reactive mind, 263, 438
readers, 438
readings, 27, 438
Reconstructionist Judaism, 180
redaction criticism, 438
Redcap, 438
redeemed, 438
Redfield, James, 216
Reformation, 58, 62, 64, 67, 68, 242
Reform Judaism, 180
reincarnation, 27–29, 42, 106, 186, 210, 234, 238, 243,
    264, 265, 276, 285, 292, 293, 339, 438
religion—*passim*
Religious Science, 216, **239–241**
Religious Science International, *see* Religious Science
Religious Technology Center, 262
Reorganized Church of Jesus Christ of Latter Day
    Saints, *see* Community of Christ
resguardo, 438
restorationism, 48, 138, 299, 300, 438
resurrection of the body, 43
revelation, divine, 69, 81, 100, 193, 245, 273, 284, 340,
    438
revivalism, 187, 439
Rigdon, Sydney, 190, 193
right hand path, 439
Rigveda, 124, 126, 439
rishis, 439
Ritschlian School, 69
ritual, 439
Roberts, Robert, 48
Rockwell, George Lincoln, 130, 439
rod and pendulum, 439
Roman Catholicism, 58, 66
Rosenberg, John Paul, 108, 439 (*see also* Werner,
    Erhard)
Rosenkreutz, Christian, 242, 439
Rosh Hashana, 439
Roshi, 439
Rosicrucianism, 28, 47, **242–45**, 251, 293
Rossi, Andrew, 47
rowanwood, 439
Royal Arch Mason, 439
royal family, 104, 440
Royal Master; Eighth Degree, 440
Rumi, Meluana Celadin, 287, 440
rune, 340, 440
Rushdie, Salman, 145, 150
Russell, Charles Taze, 153–67, 269, 440
Rutherford, Judge Franklin, 155, 156, 165, 440

Sabbatarianism, 440
sabbath, 270, 343, 440
sabbats, 339, 440

Sabellianism, 39, 80, 324, 441
Sabija Yoga, 441
sacraments, 56, 63, 82, 164, 198, 225, 271, 441
Sacred Mushroom and the Cross, 441
sacrifices, 248, 441
sacrifist, 441
sacrosanct, 441
Sadducees, 175, 441
sadhana, 210, 441
Sadler, Bill, 441
Saggitarius, 442
Sagun, 442
sahajdhari, 274, 442
saints, 442
Saint Germain, 442
Sakpata, 442
Sakya Muni, 442
salamander, 442
salakhana, 442
salat (Islam), 146, 442
salvation, *see* soteriology
samadhi, 94, 250, 266, 285, 442
Samaeda, 442
Samhain, 339, 442
Samhitas, 442
Samkyha, 442
Sammael, 442
samsara, 124, 127, 142, 276, 325, 442
samyasin, 442 (*see also sannyasin*)
sanctification, 305, 442
Sandalphon, 442
sangha, 443
Sankaracharya, 443
sankhya, 443
sankirtana, 142, 443
sannyasin, 128, 235, 443
Sanskrit, 152, 443
santana dharma, 443
Santeria, **236–40**, 281, 284
Santeros, 248, 443
Sarasvati, 443
Sarkar, Prabhat Ranjan (Shrii Shrii), 24
sat, 443
Satan, 50, 99, 132, 148, 162, 199, 250, 269, 286, 304, 338, 443
Satanic Ritual Abuse, SRA, 257, 258, 443
Satanic Verses, 145, 150
Satanism, 39, **250–60**, 284, 335, 443
Sat Nam, 443
Satchidananda Ashram Integral Yoga Institute, *see* Divine Life Society
satori, 443
satsang, 97, 100, 443

satyr, 443
Savanarola, 66
Savoy, Eugene Douglas, 139, 140, 443
Savoy, Jamil Sean, 139, 443
sawm (Islam), 146, 443
scapegoat, 267, 269
Scholasticism, 66
Schleiermacher, Friedrich, 50, 69
Schreck, Zeena, 254
Science and Health with Key to the Scriptures, 53, 83, 443
Science of Creative Intelligence, 295, 443
Scientology, Church of, 96, 108, 211, 231, 252, 260–65
Scientology Mission International (SMI), **262**
Scorpio, 444
Scottish Rite, 116, 444
séance, 444
Second Adventist Movement, 444
second vision, 444
Secret Doctrine, The, 291
secret tradition, 444
sect, 444
Seder meal, 179, 444
Selassie, Emperor, 237, 444
Select Master; Ninth Degree, 444
Self Realization Fellowship, 213, **265–66**
Separatists, 68
Sephardic, 175
Sephardim; Sephardic Rite, 444
Septuagint, 169, 444
Serios, Ted, 445
serpent, 445
serpent power, 445
serpent seed, 445
Serpent's Seed, 39
servers, 445
Seven Principles of Spiritualism, 283
seven stages, 186, 445
Seventh-day Adventism, 35, 36, 50, 120, **266–71**, 343
sexual magic, 445
shabuot, 445
shade, 445
shahada, 34, 143, 148, 445
sha'ir, 445
Shakti, 274, 445
shakubuku, 219, 279, 445
shaliach, 445
shamanism, shaman, 31, 207, 272, 338, 445
shambala, 446
Shango, 45, 280, 446
Shankara, 125, 128, 446
Share International, 446

shariah laws, 146, 147, 287, 446
shaykhs, 287, 446
Shaytan, 446
shema, 147
shemhaforash, 446
Shentao, 446
Sh'ites (Muslims), 145, 146, 446
shikishin funi, 446
Shinri Party, 30
Shintoism, **271–73**, 446
shirk, 148, 446
Shiva, 31, 125, 127, 298, 446
shofar, 446
Shoko, Asahara, 30
showbread, 446
Shriners, 446
shruti, 446
shunning, 167, 446
Shrine, Ancient Arabic Order of the Nobles of the
   Mystic, 116
siddhas, 100, 296, 446
sigil, 340, 446
Sigmad, 99
sign, 446
Sikh Dharma, 213, **273–75, 277**
sikha, 142, 447
Sikhism, **275–77**
siksha, 286, 447
silent ones, 98, 447
Silva, Jose, 277, 278, 279, 447
Silva Mind Control (SMC), **277–79**
Simons, Menno, 67
sin, 293
Singh, Kirpal, 97
Siri Guru Granth Sahib, 276
Sita, 447
Siva, see Shiva
Sivananda, Sri Swami, 93, 94
Sivananda Yoga Vedanta Center, 94
six-six-six, 255, 447
Sixteen Points, 25, 447
Skinheads of America, 133
Skrying, 448
Skull and Crossbones, 448
skyclad, 340, 448
sleeping prophet, 27, 448
Smith, Joseph Fielding, 89, 448
Smith, Joseph Jr., 89, 90, 151, 154, 187, 193, 197, 448
Smith, Joseph Sr., 448
Smith, Joseph III, 89, 448
Smith, Lucy, 448
Smriti, 448
snake, 448

Social Order of the Beauceant of the World, 117
societies, 320, 448
Society of the Processeans, 232, 448
Socinianism, 448
Soka-Gakkai, 31, 219, **279–80**
sola fidei, 448
sola gratia, 449
sola scriptura, 449
Solar Temple, The, 231, 449
solitary practitioners, 449
solstice, 449
Solus Christus, 449
soma, 449
sons of God, 449
Sontad, 449
soothsaying, 449
Sophia, 449
sorcerer, 449
sorcery, 329, 340, 449
soteriology, 75, 149, 161, 197, 220, 224, 229, 264, 274,
   278, 288, 293, 298, 449
soul life, 333, 449
soul sleep, 449
soul travel, 449
sound and light of Eck, 449
South American, Central American, and Caribbean
   Cults, 93, 247, 249, **280–81**, 328
Spalding, Baird T., 83
Spaulding Enigma, The, 194
Spaulding, Solomon, 193
Spaulding Theory, 193
special revelation, 449
spells, 337, 339, 450
spirit body, 450
Spiritism; Spiritualism, 258, **281–84**, 294, 322, 340,
   450
spirit photography, 450
spirit raps, 450
spiritual abuse, 450
Spiritual Regeneration Movement, 450
spirit writing, 450
Sprenger, Jacob, 336, 450
Spriggs, Elbert Eugene, 299, 300
Spring Equinox, 339, 450
sri, 450
Sri Bhashya, 450
Sri Chinmoy Center, 213, **285–86**
Sri Swami Sivananda Maharaj, 93–95
Sri Swami Viswanada Saraswati, 94
Sruti, 450
stake, 90, 192, 450
standard works, 450
star time, 450

Steiger, Brad, 96
Steiner, Rudolf, 212, 243, 450
Sterling Management, 451
Stevens, John Robert, 76–77, 451
stigmata, 451
Stonehenge, 451
Studies in the Scriptures, 451
study, 451
study groups, 451
stupas, 451
Subud, Muhammad, 228, 451
Succubus, 451
sudra/sudhra, 451
Sufi, 287, 451
Sufi Islamic Ruhaniat Society, *see* Sufism
Sufi Order, The, *see* Sufism
Sufism, 150, 285, **286–88**
Sugmad, 98, 451
Suhuf, 451
Sukkoth, 451
Sultan, 145, 452
Summerland, 452
Summers, Montague, 452
sunna, 452
Sunnis (Muslims), 145, 146
Super Excellent Master; Unnumbered Degree, 452
Sura/Surah, 452
Sutra Pitaka, 44, 295, 452
Sutras, 126, 452
swami, 93, 265, 452
Swami Vivekananda, 125, 127, 210, 265, 322–26
swastika, 452
Swedenborg, Emmanuel, 79–82, 217, 239, 452
Swedenborgiansim, *see* Church of the New Jerusalem
sword, 452
sylph, 452
syncretism, religious, 17
systemites, 106, 452

tabernacle, 453
Table of Showbread, 453
table tilting, 453
Taj Mahal, 453
talismans, 453
Talmud, 175, 178, 453
Tammuz, 453
tanha, 43, 453
Tantras, 24, 274, 453
Tantrism, 453
Taliban, 147
talisman, 340
Tall Cedars of Lebanon, 117
Tao, 453

Taoism, 26, 91, 233, **288–90**, 302
Tao-Sheng, 453
Tao-Te-Ching, 289
tariqah, 287, 453
tarot, 340
Tarot Cards, 453
tat tvam asi, 454
tattvavit, 454
tawhid, 454
Taurus, 454
teacher, 90, 454
telekinesis, 454
telepathy, 283, 454
Telestial Kingdom, 454
Temple, Jewish, *see* Judaism
temple (Mormon), 454
Temple of Set, 254
tempters, 454
tendai, 454
Ten Gurus, 275, 454
terreiro, 46, 454
Terrestrial Kingdom, 454
terrorism, 151
Tertullian, 59
theocracy, 455
theocratic, 455
Theodosius I, 61
Theodosius II, 61
Theosophy, 81, 123, 210, 228, 243, 251, 284, **291–94**, 338
theotokos, 61
The Pearl of Great Price, 188, 194
Therapeutic Touch, 455
Theravada Buddhism, 41, 43, 44, 184, **294–95**
thetans, 263, 456
Theurgy, see High Magic
third Adam, 456
third ear, third eye, 102
Thirty-Nine Articles, 68
Thirty Years War, 68
Thomas, John, 48, 456
Thomasites, 48
Thor, 456
Thoth, 292, 456
Three Degrees of Glory, 456
Three Pure Ones, 456
Thunor, 456
Tiamet, 456
Tillich, Paul, 70
Time (magazine), 261
Tingley, Katherine A., 291, 456
tithing, 456